Rick Steves®

CENTRAL EUROPE

THE CZECH REPUBLIC, POLAND, HUNGARY, SLOVENIA & MORE

Rick Steves & Cameron Hewitt

CONTENTS

▶ **Central Europe** 5
  Central Europe's
    Top Destinations 11
  Planning Your Trip 18
  Travel Smart 27

CZECH REPUBLIC 29

▶ **Prague**. 49

▶ **Near Prague** 161
  Kutná Hora 161
  Terezín Memorial 175
  Konopiště Castle 185

▶ **Český Krumlov** 190

POLAND 215

▶ **Kraków** 239

▶ **Auschwitz-Birkenau** 356

▶ **Warsaw**. 375

▶ **Gdańsk & the Tri-City** 443

▶ **Pomerania**. 512
  Malbork Castle 513
  Toruń. 526

HUNGARY 539

▶ **Budapest** 563

▶ **Eger** 685

SLOVENIA 709

▶ **Ljubljana**. 723

▶ **Lake Bled**. 777

▶ **The Julian Alps** 817
  Julian Alps Drive 818
  Bovec 832
  Kobarid 837

AUSTRIA 847

▶ **Vienna** 848

SLOVAKIA 947

▶ **Bratislava**. 948

MORE CENTRAL &
EASTERN EUROPE 981

▶ **Croatia**. 984

▶ **Bosnia-Herzegovina**. 998

▶ **Montenegro** 1007

▶ **Bulgaria** 1014

▶ **Romania** 1036

▶ **Understanding
  Yugoslavia**. 1066

▶ **Practicalities** 1072
  Travel Tips 1072
  Money. 1078
  Sightseeing 1085
  Sleeping. 1090
  Eating 1097
  Staying Connected 1102
  Transportation 1104
  Resources from
    Rick Steves. 1115

▶ **Appendix** 1119
  Holidays & Festivals 1119
  Books & Films. 1122
  Conversions & Climate 1127
  Packing Checklist 1130
  Pronouncing Central
    European Place Names. . . .1131

▶ **Index**. 1132

▶ **Map Index** 1158

Welcome to Rick Steves' Europe

Travel is intensified living—maximum thrills per minute and one of the last great sources of legal adventure. Travel is freedom. It's recess, and we need it.

I discovered a passion for European travel as a teen and have been sharing it ever since—through my bus tours, public television and radio shows, and travel guidebooks. Over the years, I've taught millions of travelers how to best enjoy Europe's blockbuster sights—and experience "Back Door" discoveries that most tourists miss.

Written with my talented co-author, Cameron Hewitt, this book offers a balanced mix of Central Europe's lively cities and cozy towns, from the Hungarian metropolis of Budapest to the quaint Czech village of Český Krumlov to the pristine Julian Alps of Slovenia. It's selective: Rather than listing dozens of Poland's medieval castles, we recommend only the best ones. And it's in-depth: Our self-guided museum tours and city walks provide insight into the region's vibrant history and today's living, breathing culture.

We advocate traveling simply and smartly. Take advantage of our money- and time-saving tips on sight-seeing, transportation, and more. Try local, characteristic alternatives to expensive hotels and restaurants. In many ways, spending more money only builds a thicker wall between you and what you traveled so far to see.

We visit Central Europe to experience it—to become temporary locals. Thoughtful travel engages us with the world, as we learn to appreciate other cultures and new ways to measure quality of life.

Judging by the positive feedback we receive from readers, this book will help you enjoy a fun, affordable, and rewarding vacation—whether it's your first trip or your tenth.

Šťastnou cestu! Jó utat kívánunk! Szczęśliwych podróży! Sretan put! Happy travels!

Rick Steves

CENTRAL EUROPE

Wander among Prague's fairy-tale spires, bask in the convivial bustle of Kraków's Main Market Square, and soak with chess players in a Budapest thermal bath. Ponder Europe's most moving Holocaust memorial at Auschwitz. Enjoy pristine nature as you glide across Lake Bled to a church-topped island in the shadow of the Julian Alps. Taste a proud Hungarian vintner's wine and say, *"Egészségedre!"* (or stick with "Cheers!").

From the Czech Republic and Poland to Hungary and Slovenia, Central Europe is a traveler's delight, with lively squares, fascinating history, reasonable prices, and friendly locals. This book covers a selective cross-section of this sprawling region's highlights, with enough in-depth coverage to fully appreciate each place. Most of this book is devoted to these four core countries:

The **Czech Republic** is home to Prague—the stunningly well-preserved showcase city of Central Europe—not to mention a countryside scattered with countless enchanting towns (Český Krumlov and Kutná Hora are tops).

Poland—bigger than the other three core countries combined—has an epic history, a noble spirit, and a variety of appealing cities, big and small: charming Kraków, bustling Warsaw, maritime Gdańsk, and red-brick Toruń.

Hungary is a delightfully enigmatic outlier—with a starkly different language, cuisine, and cultural heritage. Its huge capital city, Budapest, is the de facto capital of Central Europe.

Slovenia is a tiny, endearing alpine country tucked high in

Slovenia's Julian Alps are blanketed in lush forests; bask in Habsburg opulence at the lavish Hofburg in Vienna, Austria.

the mountains between Austria and Italy. It has an engaging cultural mix, wonderful locals, fabulous scenery, the adorable capital Ljubljana, the dreamy resort Lake Bled, and the cut-glass peaks of the Julian Alps.

I've also included in-depth coverage of two Danube capitals that link up well with the places mentioned above: The modern Austrian capital of **Vienna** was once the capital of everything else mentioned here and remains something of a Central European melting pot. Its grandiose landmarks, world-class museums, and refined ambience—from classical music to genteel coffeehouses—still evoke those glory days. And the Slovak capital of **Bratislava,** with its compact and historic core, is an easy stopover on the way between Vienna and Budapest.

Finally, the "More Central and Eastern Europe" section, near the back of this book, features abbreviated coverage of several neighboring countries likely to show up on your itinerary: **Croatia, Bosnia-Herzegovina, Montenegro, Bulgaria,** and **Romania.**

Wherever you go in Central Europe, you'll be impressed by each country's vibrant culture, proud traditions, and strong identity. The Czechs have a sarcastic sense of humor and a wickedly subversive attitude toward authority, while the Hungarians can be quite formal and have produced great analytical

What Is "Central Europe"?

If you had to sum up the wonderful lands of Central Europe in a single word, it might just be "underappreciated." The Czech Republic (except Prague), Poland, Hungary, Slovenia, and their neighbors get nowhere near the number of visitors that their ample charms merit. One reason: Many North American travelers still consider these countries to be part of "Eastern" Europe. But 35 years after the fall of the Iron Curtain, I'm here to set you straight: This is definitively Central Europe.

Germans call this region Mitteleuropa—"Middle Europe"—and looking at a map of Europe, it's easy to see why: These lands occupy the very heart of the Continent. In fact, Prague lies to the west of Vienna, Stockholm...and most of Italy.

The "Eastern" label dates from the age of Soviet influence (1945-1989). Back then, the Eastern Bloc was a foreboding, dark, and gloomy corner of the "Evil Empire." But that period represents just one brief chapter in the histories of these nations. (And today, "Eastern Europe" more properly refers to countries east of the ones in this book—Ukraine, Belarus, Russia, and so on—which have traditionally been more firmly in the Russian cultural orbit.)

While the countries of Central Europe are unique, strong cultural ties unite them. Except Hungary, all speak Slavic languages and were settled by the same ancestors. Historically, they were once part of a larger whole: the vast Habsburg (later Austro-Hungarian) Empire, which lasted for centuries and sprawled from Baltic beaches to Adriatic campaniles to Bosnian minarets. This realm included nearly every square inch covered by this guidebook, and much more.

The Habsburgs had a centralized government and brought standardized infrastructure and architecture to the ▶▶▶

Communist statue in Memento Park in Budapest, Hungary; Jamnik Church near Lake Bled in Slovenia; Poland's open-air folk museums bring traditions to life.

▶▶▶ far corners of their empire. At the same time, for the most part they respected their subjects' customs: German was the language of government, commerce, and urban life, but local languages and traditions lived on in the countryside. Later, revival movements swept across Europe starting in the mid-1800s, instilling pride in cultural differences.

Defeat in World War I spelled the end of Habsburg rule and ushered in an interwar scramble to establish modern, independent nation-states—in many cases (such as Czechoslovakia and Yugoslavia) for the first time. World War II saw most of this area quickly overrun by the Nazis. Then, by liberating this part of Europe (except Yugoslavia), the USSR won the right to draft the Czechs, Poles, Hungarians, and their neighbors into their Eastern Bloc of influence.

From 1945 to 1989, the USSR eroded cultural distinctions between each place, papering them over into a featureless block. It's no wonder that, to this day, locals prefer not to still be associated with this oppressive, "Eastern" chapter of their history. (Only Yugoslavia, liberated by its homegrown Partisan Army rather than the Red Army, set its own course—adopting a milder form of communism and refusing to join either the Warsaw Pact or NATO.)

A big milestone came in 2004, when all of this book's core countries joined the European Union. Two decades later, it's clearer than ever that the Czech Republic, Poland, Hungary, and Slovenia are "Eastern" no more. ◼

Habsburg royal regalia at the Hofburg Treasury in Vienna, Austria; picture-perfect Český Krumlov, Czech Republic; Váci Utca shopping street in Budapest, Hungary

minds. The Poles may be a bit brusque at first, then warm up beautifully; meanwhile, you'll hit it off immediately with the gregarious Slovenes.

Imagine a trip through this region as a scavenger hunt for cultural artifacts. Really try to understand why, unique among these lands, Poland's churches are packed with reverent worshippers. Check out a Black Light Theater performance in Prague and see whether you love it, like the Czechs...or leave perplexed, as many visitors do. Sipping a coffee with new Slovenian friends at a riverside café, ask them why the mountains are so close to their nation's heart and soul. Browse a bustling Hungarian market hall, savoring distinctive aromas and flavors. You'll leave inspired to sprinkle a little more paprika into your cooking back home.

Speaking of food, you'll find the cuisine in Central Europe hearty, delicious, affordable, and—like everything else—specific to each country. Dig into a gut-busting platter of Czech bread dumplings smothered in thick gravy, a steaming bowl of savory beetroot soup in a Polish milk bar, a Hungarian crêpe wrapped around meaty filling and blanketed in a spicy sauce, or a plate of handmade pasta at a trendy Slovenian sidewalk café.

And if you're on a tight budget, these destinations hit a sweet spot in terms of value for money: The prices are lower than what you'll pay in most of Europe, and standards are high enough that you won't feel you're compromising on quality.

Synagogue prayer platform from Gwoździec at the Museum of the History of Polish Jews in Warsaw, Poland; riverside café in Ljubljana, Slovenia

Historic brewery tour in Český Krumlov, Czech Republic; Budapest's grand Hungarian Parliament glows along the Danube

You can pay $3 for a mug of beer in a Prague pub, $6 for a basic but tasty meal in Poland, $10 for a seat in an opulent opera house in Budapest, or $15 for a riveting walking tour in Ljubljana. (Broadly speaking, Poland is on the lower end of the price spectrum, while Slovenia pushes the upper end, with Hungary and the Czech Republic somewhere in the middle.)

Wherever your travels take you in Central Europe, you'll appreciate the kind, unpretentious locals. The language barrier is easy enough to hurdle over (across this region, young people uniformly speak good English). And in most places—perhaps with the exception of Prague—people are refreshingly unjaded and enjoy getting to know visitors. Take advantage of the local hospitality.

With so much to experience in Central Europe, your visit may be just the first of many. Travelers can spend lifetimes exploring these beautiful and enticingly complex lands...and there's always more to discover.

Central Europe's Top Destinations

There's so much to see in Central Europe...and so little time. This overview breaks the region's top destinations into must-see places (to help first-time travelers plan their trip) and worth-it places (for those with extra time or special interests). I've also suggested a minimum number of days to allow per destination.

CZECH REPUBLIC

▲▲▲Prague (allow 2-3 days)

Prague, the Czech capital and one of Europe's most romantic cities, boasts a remarkably well-preserved Old Town, a bustling New Town packed with Art Nouveau, an evocative Jewish Quarter, the iconic Charles Bridge, a historic castle atop a hill, rollicking pubs, and intriguing 20th-century history.

▲Near Prague (1-2 days)

Worthwhile visits include Kutná Hora's offbeat bone church and grand cathedral, Terezín's Nazi concentration camp memorial, and Konopiště Castle—the onetime residence of Franz Ferdinand, whose assassination sparked World War I.

▲▲Český Krumlov (1 day)

The country's cutest and most touristic destination, this hill town huddles under a colorful castle (with a pristine Baroque theater) and hugs a river bend, fun for water sports such as canoeing.

POLAND

▲▲▲Kraków (2-3 days)

Poland's cultural, intellectual, and historical capital, this lovely city has a massive yet cozy-feeling main square, easy-to-enjoy Old Town, thought-provoking Jewish quarter, oodles of quality museums (art, history, and more), a robust food and nightlife scene, and the country's most important castle and cathedral.

▲▲▲Auschwitz-Birkenau Concentration Camp Memorial (1 day)

The largest and most notorious concentration camp in the Nazi system, this is now equal parts compelling museum and poignant memorial. Day-trip from Kraków and devote a day to the most powerful Holocaust site in Europe.

▲▲Warsaw (1-3 days)

Poland's underrated capital is a city of contrasts, from its towering communist landmarks to its glittering new skyscrapers to its pristinely reconstructed Old Town. Come here to tour world-class museums (art, history, science, Chopin, Jewish heritage, WWII uprisings, and more) and to get a taste of today's modern Poland, bustling with fashionable urbanites, hipster food halls, and artistic flair.

▲▲Gdańsk and the Tri-City (2 days)

This gorgeous Hanseatic trading city sits near Poland's Baltic seafront and features a cancan of marvelous facades, insightful museums, and the shipyard where Lech Wałęsa and the Solidarity trade union challenged the communists in 1980. The Tri-City gives more of a taste of the Baltic, from beach resort Sopot to industrial Gdynia, with Poland's top emigration museum.

▲Pomerania (1 day)

The Teutonic Knights' gigantic, Gothic Malbork Castle is one of Europe's most imposing fortresses; nearby, the red-brick, gingerbread-scented city of Toruń is a stroller's delight.

(Opposite) Old Town Square in Prague, Czech Republic; St. Mary's Church in Kraków, Poland; Auschwitz-Birkenau Concentration Camp Memorial

HUNGARY

▲▲▲Budapest (2-3 days)

This grand, Danube-spanning cityscape is slathered with opulent late 19th-century buildings (parliament, opera house, basilica, market halls, etc.), layers of epic history, a fantastic dining and nightlife scene, and uniquely exhilarating thermal baths.

▲Eger (1 day)

This small city is strollable and pleasant, with a gaggle of gorgeous Baroque buildings, fun thermal-bathing opportunities nearby, and locally produced wines.

SLOVENIA

▲▲Ljubljana (1-2 days)

Slovenia's capital is both vibrant and relaxing, simply a delightful place to hang out: Browse the riverside market, ogle the extravagant architecture, nurse a coffee along the willow-shaded promenade, savor one of the best food scenes in this part of Europe, and drop into a variety of quirky, artfully presented museums.

▲▲▲Lake Bled (1-2 days including side trips)

Slovenia's photogenic lake resort huddles in alpine foothills; it's famous for its church-topped island, cliff-hanging castle, lakefront path, and tasty desserts. And there are plenty of fun side trips: the less-developed Lake Bohinj, the spectacular Vintgar Gorge, and two towns with unaccountably intriguing museums: Radovljica (beekeeping) and Kropa (ironworking).

▲▲The Julian Alps (1 day)

Slovenia's peaks are easily conquered by a twisty, intensely scenic mountain road over the Vršič Pass, ending in the tranquil Soča River Valley—filled with gorgeous scenery, low-key mountain towns and tourist farms, whitewater rafting near Bovec, and the exceptional WWI museum in Kobarid. While it's doable as a long day trip from Lake Bled or Ljubljana, Alp-ophiles can spend a night (or several).

I

Central Europe's Top Destinations

(Clockwise from top) Széchenyi Baths in Budapest, Hungary; Slovenia's National and University Library in Ljubljana; Lake Bled, Slovenia; Soča River near Kobarid, Slovenia

(Clockwise from top) Hofburg Palace in Vienna, Austria; Old Town in Bratislava, Slovakia; café in Sarajevo, Bosnia; Rila Monastery in Bulgaria

GATEWAY CITIES

▲▲▲Vienna, Austria (2-3 days)

Austria's regal capital is rich with swirling architecture and world-class museums (including the art-packed Kunsthistorisches); towering St. Stephen's Cathedral; impressive Habsburg sights at the Hofburg (royal apartments, treasury, crypt, and Lipizzaner stallions); sumptuous palaces (including Schönbrunn); a flourishing café culture; and a fabled classical-music tradition, from opera to the Boys' Choir.

▲Bratislava, Slovakia (1 day)

Just down the Danube from Vienna (and on the way to Budapest), this lively capital bustles with colorfully restored historic buildings, a strollable Old Town, and a modern riverbank people zone.

MORE CENTRAL AND EASTERN EUROPE

Consider weaving any of these neighboring countries into your Central European vacation.

Croatia is Central Europe's seafaring Riviera, with inviting beach towns (Hvar, Korčula), bustling port cities (Split), an interior of waterfalls and hill towns, a thriving capital (Zagreb), and delightful Dubrovnik—one of Europe's best-preserved medieval cities.

Bosnia-Herzegovina, with a mountainous landscape and a predominantly Muslim cultural heritage, offers easy access to mosques, minarets, and cobbled bazaars, as well as an epic history.

Montenegro is the land of the "Black Mountain," where soaring cliffs rocket up from the picturesque Bay of Kotor, and the rugged interior hides remote pockets of history.

Bulgaria, a surprising, underrated country, sits at the intersection of the Slavic, Greek, and Muslim worlds, with a mix of busy cities (Sofia, Plovdiv), soulful Orthodox monasteries (Rila), cliff-hanging towns (Veliko Tarnovo), and Black Sea beaches.

Romania, an eclectic crossroads with Roman roots, features a big, scruffy, yet captivating capital (Bucharest); the wooded mountains and plains of Transylvania, with its tidy towns, dramatic castles, and fortified churches; Maramureș, with Europe's most vivid traditional folk life; and Bucovina, with lavishly painted monasteries.

Planning Your Trip

To plan your trip, you'll need to design your itinerary—choosing where and when to go, how you'll travel, and how many days to spend at each destination. For general advice on sightseeing, accommodations, restaurants, and more, see the Practicalities chapter.

DESIGNING AN ITINERARY

As you read this book and learn your options...

Choose your top destinations.

My recommended itinerary (on page 20) gives you an idea of how much you can reasonably see in 21 days, but you can adapt it to fit your own interests and time frame.

Most travelers target a combination of Prague, Budapest, Kraków, and Vienna. But consider working in lesser-known places, too. For example, Ljubljana (Slovenia) and Gdańsk (Poland) are unexpectedly rewarding destinations.

If you'd like to splice in some time in nature, two great options are the wooded Bohemian hills around Český Krumlov, or the alpine thrills of Slovenia's Lake Bled and Julian Alps.

Or, delve more deeply into just one or two countries. You could happily spend a week or two in Poland—connecting the cities of Kraków, Warsaw, Toruń, and Gdańsk, plus side trips.

If you'll spend a week or more in the Czech Republic, Hungary, or a Croatia-Slovenia-Bosnia swing, consider one of my other guidebooks, with more in-depth coverage of those destinations.

Decide when to go.

Central Europe's "tourist season" runs roughly from May through mid-October. Summer has its advantages: the most predictable weather, very long days (light until after 21:00), and the busiest schedule of tourist fun.

In spring and fall—May, June, September, and early October—travelers enjoy fewer crowds and milder weather. This is my favorite time to travel here. However, in cities, conventions can raise hotel prices, especially in September; certain small towns can feel almost deserted before May or after October.

Winter travelers find concert season in full swing, with no tourist crowds (except in always-packed Prague, or during Christmas markets in Kraków, Budapest, and other cities). However, some accommodations and sights are either closed or run on a limited schedule. Confirm your sightseeing plans locally, especially when traveling off-season. The weather can be cold and dreary, and night will draw the shades on your sightseeing before dinnertime.

For weather specifics, see the climate chart in the appendix.

Connect the dots.

Link your destinations into a logical route. Determine which cities you'll fly into and out of. Begin your search for transatlantic flights on Google Flights.

Decide if you'll travel by car, public transportation, or—best for most trips—a combination. A car is a worthless headache in big cities like Prague, Budapest, and Vienna, and the distances between these cities are long—best suited for a train or flight. But there are a few locations where having a car opens up a world of possibilities: road-tripping around the Czech Republic to Český Krumlov, for example, or exploring Slovenia's Julian Alps. Do most of your trip by public transit, then rent a car (or hire a driver) strategically, for a day or two, in places where it's warranted.

To determine approximate travel times between destinations, study the driving maps in the Practicalities chapter or check Google Maps; visit Bahn.com for train schedules. Budget flights can be an alternative to long train rides; check Skyscanner.com for intra-European flights (but keep in mind

Central Europe's Best Three-Week Trip by Public Transportation

Day	Plan	Sleep
1	Fly into Kraków	Kraków
2	Kraków	Kraków
3	Side-trip to Auschwitz-Birkenau Memorial	Kraków
4	Travel to Prague (cheap flight, long train ride, or private driver)	Prague
5	Prague	Prague
6	Prague	Prague
7	Prague (maybe side-trip to Kutná Hora)	Prague
8	To Český Krumlov (by train, bus, or car)*	Český Krumlov
9	Český Krumlov	Český Krumlov
10	Shuttle bus to Vienna	Vienna
11	Vienna	Vienna
12	Vienna	Vienna
13	Train to Budapest (stop in Bratislava en route)	Budapest
14	Budapest	Budapest
15	Budapest	Budapest
16	Budapest (maybe side-trip to Eger)	Budapest
17	Train or bus to Ljubljana	Ljubljana
18	Ljubljana	Ljubljana
19	To Lake Bled (by train, bus, or car)**	Lake Bled
20	Lake Bled and nearby sights**	Lake Bled
21	Fly home from Ljubljana	

* Consider renting a car for a day or two of Czech road-tripping; by car, you can visit Konopiště Castle en route from Prague to Český Krumlov.
** Consider renting a car in Ljubljana or Lake Bled for a day or two of exploring Slovenia's mountains; you could add a day to drive the Julian Alps loop.

Notes: This urban-focused plan spends most nights in cities (except for Český Krumlov and Lake Bled) with side trips to smaller towns.

   Tricky Connections: To connect long distances between stops, get creative. From Kraków to Prague, you could take a 10-hour night train or a complicated daytime connection—or shop around for a cheap flight. Better yet, splurge on a private driver based in Kraków or Prague for this

five-hour drive, and fit in a stop at Auschwitz en route (about $500-700). Train connections between Český Krumlov and Vienna require multiple changes, but shuttle services do the trip affordably in under four hours. From Budapest to Ljubljana, consider the direct train (7.5 hours) or a potentially faster bus (6 hours, www.flixbus.com).

Car Rental Concerns: Typically, you won't pay extra to drop off a car at a different location within the same country, but international drop-offs come with astronomical fees. That's another good reason to connect longer distances by public transit or flights, and rent cars selectively en route. For more on this, see the Practicalities chapter.

Two-Week Variation: If you're tight on time, skip Slovenia (better yet, save it for another trip) and cut out some side trips (Kutná Hora, Eger).

air travel's larger carbon footprint). If you sleep well on trains, a night train can be an efficient option for longer journeys.

Write out a day-by-day itinerary.

Figure out how many destinations you can comfortably fit in your time frame. Don't overdo it—few travelers wish they'd hurried more. Allow enough days per stop (see estimates in "Central Europe's Top Destinations," earlier). Minimize one-night stands. It can be worth taking a late-afternoon drive or train ride to settle into a town for two consecutive nights—and gain a full uninterrupted day for sightseeing. Include sufficient time for transportation; whether you travel by train or car, it'll take you a half-day to get between most destinations.

Staying in a home base (like Prague or Budapest) and making day trips can be more efficient than changing locations and hotels.

Take sight closures into account. Avoid visiting a town on the one day a week its must-see sights are closed. Check if any holidays or festivals fall during your trip—these attract crowds and can close sights. Note major sights where advance tickets are required (or recommended) or a free Rick Steves audio tour is available.

Give yourself some slack. Every trip, and every traveler, needs downtime for doing laundry, picnic shopping, people-watching, and so on. Pace yourself. Assume you will return.

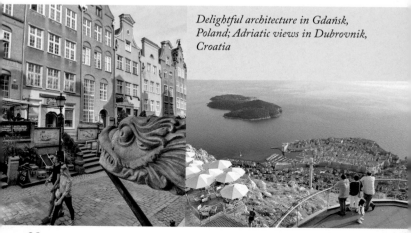

Delightful architecture in Gdańsk, Poland; Adriatic views in Dubrovnik, Croatia

Trip Costs Per Person

Run a reality check on your dream trip. You'll have major transportation costs in addition to daily expenses.

Flight: A round-trip flight from the US to Prague, Budapest, or Vienna costs about $900-1,500, depending on where you fly from and when. Flying into one city and out of another is typically about the same price.

Public Transportation: For a three-week trip, allow $300 per person for buses and second-class trains. In some cases, a short flight can be cheaper than taking the train.

Car Rental: Allow roughly $350-500 per week (booked well in advance), not including tolls, gas, parking, and insurance.

AVERAGE DAILY EXPENSES PER PERSON

$180
Applies to cities, figure on less for towns and across Poland

Lodging
Based on two people splitting the cost of a $150 double room with breakfast
$75

Meals
$15 for lunch, $30 for dinner, and $5 for coffee, beer, or ice cream
$50

City Transit
Buses and taxis/Uber
$15

Sights and Entertainment
This daily average works for most people.
$40

Budget Tips

To cut your daily expenses, take advantage of the deals you'll find throughout Central Europe and mentioned in this book.

City transit passes (for multiple rides or all-day usage) decrease your cost per ride.

Avid sightseers buy combo-tickets or passes that cover multiple museums. If a town doesn't offer deals, visit only the sights you most want to see, and seek out free sights and experiences (people-watching counts).

Some businesses—especially hotels and walking-tour companies—offer discounts to my readers (look for the RS% symbol in the listings in this book).

Reserve your rooms directly with the hotel. Some hotels offer a discount if you pay in cash and/or ▶▶▶

Rick Steves Central Europe

▶▶▶ stay three or more nights (check online or ask).

Rooms can cost less outside of peak season (roughly late October through early April). And even seniors can sleep cheaply in hostels (most have private rooms) for about $30 per person. Or check Airbnb-type sites for deals.

It's no hardship to eat inexpensively in Central Europe. In the less pricey countries (such as Poland), even "fancy" sit-down meals come at a reasonable price. And anywhere you go, you'll find tasty, affordable meals at food stands, bakeries, and takeout shops. Cultivate the art of picnicking in atmospheric settings.

When you splurge, choose an experience you'll always remember, such as a Hungarian thermal bath, a cable-car ride in the Slovenian Alps, or an opera or concert in lavish surroundings. Minimize souvenir shopping; focus instead on collecting wonderful memories. ■

Paprika-flavored goulash in Hungary; cooking class in Poland; sunflower fields near Eger, Hungary

BEFORE YOU GO

You'll have a smoother trip if you tackle a few things ahead of time. For more info on these topics, see the Practicalities chapter and RickSteves.com, which has helpful travel-tip articles and videos.

Make sure your travel documents are valid. If your passport expires within six months of your return date, you need to renew it (allow 12-plus weeks). Be aware of entry requirements; you may need to register with the European Travel Information and Authorization System (ETIAS; quick and easy process, https://travel-europe.europa.eu/etias_en). Get passport and country-specific travel info at Travel.State.gov.

Arrange your transportation. Book your international flights. Overall, Google Flights is the best place to start searching for flights. It's worth thinking about buying essential train tickets online in advance, getting a rail pass (though this is rarely a good value in Central Europe), renting a car, or booking cheap European flights. (You can wing it once you're there, but it may cost more.) Drivers: Consider bringing an International Driving Permit (sold at AAA offices in the US, www.aaa.com) along with your license.

Book rooms well in advance, especially if your trip falls during peak season or any major holidays or festivals.

Reserve ahead for key sights. Reserve online for the Auschwitz-Birkenau Concentration Camp Memorial—slots open up 90 days in advance. At peak times, reserve ahead for the Schindler's Factory Museum and Wieliczka Salt Mine in Kraków. To tour the Hungarian Parliament in Budapest, try to book two weeks ahead. Reservations are smart for Vienna's Schönbrunn Palace and may be required for the Vintgar Gorge near Slovenia's Lake Bled.

Hire guides in advance. Local guides—an exceptional value in these countries—can get booked up. I've listed several favorites. If you want a specific guide, reserve ahead by email.

Consider travel insurance. Compare the cost of insurance to the cost of your potential loss. Understand what protections your credit card might offer and whether your existing insurance (health, homeowners, or renters) covers you and your possessions overseas.

Manage your money. "Tap-to-pay" or "contactless" cards are widely accepted and simple to use. You may need your credit card's PIN for some purchases—request it if you don't have one. Alert your bank that you'll be using your debit and credit cards in Europe. You don't need to bring local cash for your trip; you can withdraw currency from ATMs in each country you visit.

Use your smartphone smartly. Sign up for an international service plan, or rely on Wi-Fi instead. Download any apps you'll want on the road, such as maps, translators, and Rick Steves Audio Europe (see sidebar).

Pack light. You'll walk with your luggage more than you think. I travel for weeks with a single carry-on bag and a day pack. Use the packing checklist in the appendix as a guide.

Rick's Free Audio Tours and Video Clips

Rick Steves Audio Europe, a free app, makes it easy to download my audio tours and listen to them offline as you travel. For this book (look for the ⚲), free audio tours cover sights and neighborhoods in Prague and Vienna. The app also offers my public radio show interviews with travel experts from around the globe. Scan the QR code to find it in your app store, or visit RickSteves.com/AudioEurope.

Rick Steves Classroom Europe, a powerful tool for teachers, is also useful for travelers. This video library contains about 600 short clips excerpted from my public television series. Enjoy these videos as you sort through options for your trip and to better understand what you'll see in Europe. Check it out at Classroom.RickSteves.com.

Travel Smart

Central Europe sometimes intimidates first-time visitors. It shouldn't! These countries are as welcoming and well organized as the rest of the Continent (often more so). If you have a positive attitude, equip yourself with good information (this book), and expect to travel smart, you will.

Read—and reread—this book. Note opening hours of sights, closed days, crowd-beating tips, and whether reservations are required or advisable. Check the latest at RickSteves.com/update. Because this region's history is complicated, study up for a broader understanding.

Be your own tour guide. As you travel, get up-to-date info on sights, reserve tickets and tours, reconfirm hotels and travel arrangements, and check transit connections. Visit local tourist information offices. Upon arrival in a new town, lay the groundwork for a smooth departure; confirm the train, bus, or road you'll take when you leave.

Outsmart thieves. Pickpockets abound in crowded places where tourists congregate. Treat commotions as smokescreens for theft. Keep your passport and backup cash and cards secure in a money belt tucked under your clothes; carry only a day's spending money and a card in your front pocket or wallet. Don't set valuable items down on counters or café tabletops, where they can be quickly stolen or easily forgotten.

Minimize potential loss. Keep expensive gear to a minimum. Bring copies or take photos of important documents (passport and cards) to aid in replacement if they're lost or stolen. Back up photos and devices to the cloud as you travel.

Beat the summer heat. If you wilt easily, choose a hotel with air-conditioning, start your day early, take a midday siesta, and resume your sightseeing later. Seek out museums that are comfortably air-conditioned, and take frequent breaks.

Guard your time and energy. Taking a taxi or Uber can be a good value if it saves you a long wait for a bus or an exhausting walk across town. To avoid long lines, follow my crowd-beating tips, such as buying tickets in advance, or sightseeing early or late.

Be flexible. Even if you have a well-planned itinerary, expect changes, strikes, closures, sore feet, bad weather, and so on. Your Plan B could turn out to be even better.

Attempt the language. Most Central Europeans—especially in the tourist trade and in cities, and just about anyone under age 50—speak English. But if you learn some of their language, even just a few pleasantries, you'll get more smiles and make more friends. Apps such as Google Translate work for on-the-go translation help, but you can get a head start by practicing some survival phrases: You'll find them after the country introductions in this book.

Connect with the culture. Interacting with locals carbonates your experience. Enjoy the friendliness of the Central European people. Ask questions; most locals are happy to point you in their idea of the right direction. Set up your own quest for the best bit of communist kitsch, mug of Czech beer, bowl of borscht, or scenic mountain viewpoint. When an opportunity pops up, make it a habit to say "yes."

Central Europe...here you come!

CZECH REPUBLIC
Česká Republika

CZECH REPUBLIC

Česká Republika

The Czech Republic is geographically small. On a quick visit, you can enjoy a fine introduction while still packing in plenty of surprises. The country has a little of everything for the traveler. Quaint villages? Check. Beautiful landscapes? Check. World-class art? Czech, Czech, and Czech.

While the Czechs have long occupied the lands of the present-day Czech Republic, for most of their history they were treated as second-class citizens, under the thumb of foreign rulers (generally from Germany or Austria). That the Czech nation exists as an independent state today is practically a Cinderella story. So let's get to know the underdog Czechs.

In Czech towns and villages, you'll find a simple joy of life—a holdover from the days of the Renaissance. The deep spirituality of the Baroque era still shapes the national character. The magic of Prague, the beauty of Český Krumlov, and the lyrical quality of the countryside relieve the heaviness caused by the turmoil that passed through here. Get beyond Prague and explore the country's medieval towns. These rugged woods and hilltop castles will make you feel as if you're walking through the garden of your childhood dreams.

Given their imaginative, sometimes fanciful culture, it's no surprise that the Czechs have produced some famously clever writers—from Franz Kafka (who wrote about a man waking up as a giant cockroach) to Karel Čapek (who wrote about artificially created beings he dubbed "roboti," or robots). The unique entertainment form of Black Light Theater—a combination of illusion, pantomime, puppetry, and modern dance—exemplifies Czech creativity (see page 127).

Czechs refuse to dumb things down. Education and intellect are important, and academics are honored in Czech society. At the end of communism, the parliament elected a poet, playwright, and philosopher, Václav Havel, to serve two terms as president.

Beyond his intellect, the masses that took to the streets in 1989 no doubt also appreciated Havel's independent thinking and bold actions (he had been imprisoned by communist authorities

for his activities promoting human rights). Perhaps because they've seen their national affairs bungled by centuries of foreign overlords, many Czechs have a healthy suspicion of authority and an admiration for those willing to flout it.

Other Czechs with a rebellious spirit are national hero Jan Hus (who refused to recant his condemnation of Church corruption and was burned at the stake), contemporary artist David Černý (whose outrageous stunts are always a lightning rod for controversy), and, of course, the man named "the greatest Czech of all time," Jára Cimrman. A fictional character created in the 1960s by a pair of radio satirists, Cimrman has taken on a life of his own—and today is something of a nationwide practical joke. (See the sidebar later in this chapter.)

The Czechs' well-studied, sometimes subversive, often world-weary outlook can be perceived by outsiders as cynicism. Czechs have a sharp, dry, often sarcastic sense of humor and a keen sense of irony. They don't suffer fools lightly...and watching a United Nations of clueless tourists trample their capital city for the past generation hasn't done wonders for their patience. Be one of the very few visitors who bother to learn a few pleasantries—hello, please, thank you—in their language. (See "Czech Language," later.) You'll notice a difference in how you're treated.

Of the Czech Republic's three main regions—Bohemia, Moravia, and small Silesia—the best-known is Bohemia, where Prague is. It has nothing to do with beatnik bohemians; the name comes from the Celtic tribe that inhabited the land before the coming of the Germans and the Slavs. A longtime home of Czechs, Germans, and Jews, Bohemia is circled by a naturally fortifying ring of mountains and cut down the middle by the Vltava River.

Czech Republic Almanac

Official Name: The country's official name is Czechia. It's better known as the Česká Republika, born on January 1, 1993, along with Slovakia, when the nation of Czechoslovakia—formed after World War I and dominated by the USSR after World War II—split into two countries.

Size: 30,450 square miles (slightly smaller than South Carolina).

People: The population is 10.7 million. About 84 percent identify as ethnic Czechs (or Bohemians) and another 5 percent as Moravian. The distinction between the two is blurred, however, as both speak the same language, and many residents of Moravia prefer to identify as Czech.

Before the war in Ukraine, there were 200,000 Ukrainians in the Czech Republic. In 2022, 500,000 more gained refugee status, making Ukrainians by far the largest minority. Other significant minorities are Slovaks and Vietnamese. Only 15 percent of the population identifies with an organized church, primarily the Roman Catholic Church.

Geography: The Czech Republic comprises three regions (called "lands" here)—Bohemia (Čechy), Moravia (Morava), and a small slice of Silesia (Slezsko).

Latitude and Longitude: 50°N and 14°E (similar latitude to Vancouver, British Columbia).

Biggest Cities: Prague (the capital, 1.3 million), Brno (386,000), Ostrava (305,000), and Plzeň (172,000).

Economy: The gross domestic product is about $282 billion (similar to Louisiana). The GDP per capita is approximately $41,000 (compared to $70,000 for the average American).

Currency: 20 Czech crowns (*koruna*, Kč) = about $1.

Government: From 1948 to 1989, Czechoslovakia was a communist state under Soviet control. Since 2004, the Czech Republic has been a member of the EU with a vibrant democracy. Its parliament includes the 200-member Chamber of Deputies (elected every four years) and 81 senators (elected every six years). President Petr Pavel, a former army general, was elected overwhelmingly in 2023 and is committed to a liberal, pro-Western course. The current leadership is a coalition of three right-of-center parties, the Mayors' Party, and the liberal Pirate Party. The opposition consists of a populist centrist party led by a business tycoon, and the extreme far right.

Flag: The Czech flag is red (bottom), white (top), and blue (a triangle along the hoist side).

The winegrowing region of Moravia (to the east) is more Slavic and colorful, and more about the land.

But the country consists of more than rollicking beer halls and gently rolling landscapes. It's also about dreamy wine cellars and fertile Moravian plains, with the rugged Carpathian Mountains on the horizon. Politically and geologically, Bohemia and Moravia are two distinct regions. The soils and climates in which the hops and wine grapes grow are very different...and so are the two regions' mentalities. The boisterousness of the Czech polka contrasts with the melancholy of the Moravian ballad; the political viewpoint of the Prague power broker is at odds with the spirituality of the Moravian bard.

Only a tiny bit of Silesia—around the town of Opava—is part of the Czech Republic today; the rest of the region is in Poland and Germany. People in Silesia speak a wide variety of dialects that mix Czech, German, and Polish.

Most tourists who visit the Czech Republic see only Prague. But if you venture outside the capital, you'll enjoy traditional towns and villages, great prices, a friendly and gentle countryside dotted by nettles and wild poppies, and almost no international tourists. Since the time of the Habsburgs, fruit trees have lined the country roads for everyone to share. Take your pick.

HELPFUL HINTS

Tolls: If you're driving on highways in the Czech Republic, you're required to display a toll sticker. Your rental car may already come with the necessary sticker—ask. For details, see "Tolls" on page 1114.

Rail Passes: The Czech Republic is covered by a Eurail Czech Republic pass and the more expensive Eurail Global Pass. If your train travel will be limited to a handful of rides and/or short distances (for example, within the Czech Republic), you're probably better off without a pass—Czech tickets are cheap to buy as you go. But if you're combining Prague with international destinations, a rail pass could save you money. For more detailed advice on figuring out the smartest rail-pass options for your train trip, visit RickSteves.com/rail.

CZECH HISTORY

The Czechs have always been at a crossroads of Europe—between the Slavic and Germanic worlds, between Catholicism and Protestantism, and between Cold War East and West. As if having foreseen all of this, the mythical founder of Prague—the beautiful princess Libuše—named her city "Praha" (meaning "threshold" in Czech).

Charles IV and the Middle Ages (500s-1300s)

The pagan, Slavic tribes that arrived in this part of Europe in the sixth century AD were first united by the Prague-based Přemysl dynasty. The main figure of this era was Duke Václav (AD 907-935), who was later immortalized in a Christmas carol as "Good King Wenceslas." He converted the Czechs to Christianity and founded a church at Prague Castle, on a bluff overlooking the Vltava River.

In 1004, Bohemia was incorporated into the Holy Roman Empire (an alliance of mostly German-speaking kingdoms and dukedoms). Within 200 years—thanks to its strategic location and privileged status within the empire—Prague had become one of Europe's largest and most highly cultured cities.

The 14th century was Prague's golden age, when Holy Roman Emperor Charles IV (1316-1378) ruled. Born to a Luxembourger nobleman and a Czech princess, Charles IV was an ambitious man on the cusp of the Renaissance. He lived and studied in France and Italy, spoke five languages, and counted Petrarch as a friend—but always felt a deep connection to his mother's Czech roots.

Selecting Prague as his seat of power, Charles imported French architects to make the city a grand capital, founded the first university north of the Alps, and invigorated the Czech national spirit. (He popularized the legend of Wenceslas to give his people a near-mythical, King Arthur-type cultural standard-bearer.) Much of Prague's history and architecture—including the famous Charles Bridge, Charles University, St. Vitus Cathedral, New Town, and Karlštejn Castle—can be traced to this dynamic man's rule.

Jan Hus and Religious Wars (1300s-1600s)

Jan Hus (c. 1369-1415) was a local preacher and professor who got in trouble with the Vatican a hundred years before Martin Luther. Like Luther, Hus preached in the people's language rather than in Latin. To add insult to injury, he spoke out against Church corruption. Tried for heresy and burned in 1415, Hus became both a religious martyr and a national hero. While each age has defined Hus to its liking, the way he challenged authority while staying true to his beliefs has long inspired and rallied the Czech people.

Inspired by Hus' reformist ideas, the Czechs rebelled against both the Roman Catholic Church and German political control. This burst of independent thought led to a period of religious wars. Protestant Czech patriots, like the rough-and-rugged war hero Jan Žižka (often depicted in patriotic art with his trademark eye patch), fought to maintain Czech autonomy. But ultimately, these rebels were overwhelmed by their Catholic opponents. The result of these wars was the loss of autonomy to Vienna.

Ruled by the Habsburgs of Austria, Prague stagnated—except during the rule of King Rudolf II (1552-1612), a Holy Roman Emperor. With Rudolf living in Prague, the city again blossomed as a cultural and intellectual center. Astronomers Johannes Kepler and Tycho Brahe flourished, as did other scientists, and much of the inspiration for Prague's great art can be attributed to the king's patronage.

Not long after this period, Prague entered one of its darker spells. The Thirty Years' War (1618-1648) began in Prague when Czech Protestant nobles, wanting religious and political autonomy, tossed two Catholic Habsburg officials out the window of the castle. (This was one of Prague's many defenestrations—a uniquely Czech solution to political discord, in which offending politicians are literally thrown out the window.) The Czech Estates Uprising lasted two years, ending in a crushing defeat in the Battle of White Mountain (1620), which marked the end of Czech freedom. Twenty-seven leaders of the uprising were executed (today commemorated by crosses on Prague's Old Town Square), most of the old Czech nobility was dispossessed, and Protestants had to convert to Catholicism or leave the country.

Often called "the first world war" because it engulfed so many nations, the result was 300 years of Habsburg rule from afar, as Prague became a German-speaking backwater of Vienna. While the Austrian rule contributed to economic prosperity—and was fairly liberal compared to its Russian and Prussian neighbors—Czechs still tend to despise the Habsburgs.

Czech National Revival (1800s-1918)

The end of Prague as a German city came gradually. During the centuries that the Czech language and culture were suppressed, "Prag" and other cities were populated mainly by German-speaking urbanites, while "backwards" peasants kept the old Czech ways alive in the countryside. But as the Industrial Revolution attracted Czech farmers and country folk to the cities, the demographics of the Czech population centers began to shift. Between 1800 and 1900—though it remained part of the Habsburg Empire—Prague went from being an essentially German town to a predominantly Czech one.

As in the rest of Europe, the 19th century was a time of great nationalism, when the age of divine kings and ruling families came to a fitful end. The Czech spirit was first stirred by the work of historian František Palacký, who dug deep into the Czech archives to forge a national narrative. During this time, Czechs were inspired by the completion of Prague's St. Vitus Cathedral, the symphonies of Antonín Dvořák, and the operas of Bedřich Smetana, which were performed in the new National Theater.

Alphonse Mucha, a prodigiously talented Czech artist who made a name for himself in the high society of turn-of-the-century Paris, embodied this wave of nationalism. When he could have lived out his days in the lap of luxury in Paris or New York City, Mucha chose instead to return to his homeland and spend decades painting a magnum opus celebrating the historical journey of the Czechs and all Slavs—the *Slav Epic*.

After the Habsburgs' Austro-Hungarian Empire suffered defeat in World War I, their vast holdings broke apart and became independent countries. Among these was a union of Czechia, Slovakia, and Ruthenia, the brainchild of a clever politician named Tomáš Garrigue Masaryk (see sidebar on page 122). The new nation, Czechoslovakia, was proclaimed in 1918, with Prague as its capital.

Troubles of the 20th Century (1918-1989)

Independence lasted only 20 years. In the notorious Munich Agreement of September 1938—much to the dismay of the Czechs and Slovaks—Great Britain and France peacefully ceded to Hitler a fringe around the edge of Bohemia called the Sudetenland, populated mainly by people of German descent (see sidebar on page 202). It wasn't long before Hitler seized the rest of Czechia (Slovakia, overrun by local clerical-fascists, declared itself a puppet state) and the Holocaust began. Under the ruthless Nazi governor Reinhard Heydrich, tens of thousands of Jews were sent first to the concentration camp at Terezín, and later to Auschwitz and other death camps. After Heydrich was assassinated by a pair of British-trained Czech agents, the campaign of genocide grew even worse. Out of the 55,000 Jews living in Prague before the war, more than 80 percent perished during the Holocaust; throughout Czechoslovakia, an estimated 190,000 Jews were murdered. Percentagewise, the Roma fared even worse, with 90 percent of the prewar Roma population of Czechia perishing in the Holocaust.

For centuries, Prague's cultural makeup had consisted of a rich mix of Czech, German, and Jewish people—historically, they were almost evenly divided. With the Jewish population decimated, part of that delicate tapestry was gone forever. And after World War II ended, more than two million people of Germanic descent who lived in Czechoslovakia were pushed into Germany. Their forced resettlement—which led to the deaths of untold numbers of Germans (what some today might call "ethnic cleansing")—was demanded by the public and carried out by Czechoslovak president Edvard Beneš, who had ruled from exile in London throughout the war. Today's Czech Republic is largely homogenous—about 90 percent Czechs.

Although Prague escaped the bombs of World War II, it went directly from the Nazi frying pan into the communist fire. A local uprising freed the city from the Nazis on May 8, 1945, but the Soviets "liberated" them on May 9.

While the Soviets had special interest in controlling Czechoslovakia (particularly because of its uranium deposits), Czechoslovakia was represented by an internationally recognized exile government during the war. This government was allowed to come back and rule until the 1946 election. And up until 1948, Czechoslovakia was still a sovereign state (though it was under Soviet pressure) whose elected leaders were responsible for shaping its eventual orientation.

The first mistake was that the government in exile (despite Churchill's warnings) signed a binding cooperation pact with the Soviet Union in 1943. Then the communists won the most seats in the 1946 election—garnering more than 40 percent of the vote in the Czech lands (in Slovakia, they came in second). In 1947, under Soviet pressure, parliament voted against the Marshall Plan. When the country's leaders and electorate realized the communists weren't playing according to any rulebook, it was too late. By 1948, the communists controlled all the powerful ministries and suppressed student-led protests calling for democracy. For more than 40 years, they would not hold a free election.

The early communist era (1948-1968) was a mixture of misguided zeal, Stalinist repressions, and attempts to wed socialism with democracy. The "Prague Spring" period of reform—initiated by a young generation of progressive communists in 1968, led by the charismatic Slovak politician Alexander Dubček—came to an abrupt halt under the treads of Warsaw Pact tanks (for details, see page 93). A wave of protests spread through the country in 1969, as furious young Czechs lit themselves on fire to decry communist

oppression. But the status quo would hold strong for another 20 years.

Every small town had its own set of loudspeakers for broadcasting propaganda. Locals remember growing up with these mouthpieces of government boasting of successes ("This year, despite many efforts of sabotage on the part of certain individuals in service of imperialist goals, we have surpassed the planned output of steel by 195 percent"), calling people to action ("There will be no school tomorrow as all will join the farmers in the fields for an abundant harvest"), or quelling disturbances ("Some citizens may have heard about alien forces in our society taking advantage of this week's anniversary to spread unrest.").

Eventually the Soviet empire crumbled, beginning with reforms in Hungary in the summer of 1989 and culminating in the fall of the Berlin Wall that November. A few weeks later, Czechoslovakia regained its freedom in the student- and artist-powered 1989 "Velvet Revolution," so called because there were no casualties...or even broken windows (see page 96). Václav Havel, a poet, playwright, and philosopher who had been imprisoned by the communist regime, became Czechoslovakia's first postcommunist president.

"It's Not You, It's Me": The Peaceful Breakup (1989-1993)

In the postcommunist age of new possibility, the two peoples of Czechoslovakia began to wonder if, in fact, they belonged together.

Ever since they joined with the Czechs in 1918, the Slovaks felt overshadowed by Prague (unmistakably the political, economic, and cultural center of the country). Slovakia, which in the preceding 50 years had been stripped by Hungary even of the right to run schools in its own language, stood no chance of true independence after World War I. And over the years, the Czechs resented the financial burden of carrying their poorer neighbors to the east.

The dissolution of Czechoslovakia began over a hyphen, as the Slovaks wanted to rename the country Czecho-Slovakia. Ideally, this symbolic move would come with a redistribution of powers: two capitals and two UN reps, but one national bank and a single currency. This idea was rejected, and in June 1992, the Slovak nationalist candidate Vladimír Mečiar fared surprisingly well in the elections—suggesting that the Slovaks were serious about secession. The politicians plowed ahead, getting serious about the split in September 1992. The transition took only three months from start to finish.

The split became official on January 1, 1993, and each country ended up with its own capital, currency, and head of state. For most, the breakup dissolved tensions, and three decades later, Czechs and

Slovaks still feel closer to each other than to any other nationality. It is no surprise that an elected Czech president's first official visit is to Bratislava, and vice-versa.

Since the split, the Czech Republic has had three significant turning points. In March 1999, it joined NATO. On May 1, 2004, the country joined the European Union. Three and a half years later, it entered the Schengen Agreement, effectively erasing its borders for the purposes of work and travel. The Czech Republic had become a fully integrated member of the European community.

The Czech Republic Today (2000 to Present)

After 14 years in office, a term-limited Václav Havel stepped down in 2003. He died in 2011. While he's fondly remembered by Czechs as a great thinker, writer, and fearless leader of the opposition movement during the communist days, many consider him to have been less successful as a president.

The next president, Václav Klaus, had been the pragmatic author of the economic reforms in the 1990s. Klaus' surprising win in the 2003 election symbolized a change from revolutionary times, when philosophers became kings, to modern humdrum politics, when offices gained by bargaining with the opposition (Communist Party votes in parliament were the decisive factor in Klaus' election).

Behind-the-scenes deals in parliament allowed Klaus to be reelected, drawing public outrage and eventually a change in the country's constitution. This led, in January 2013, to the first election of a president directly by the people (rather than by parliament).

The winner then (and again in 2018) was Miloš Zeman, the other political heavyweight of the 1990s. Zeman—a tobacco, pork, and *Becherovka*-powered man of the people—brought the Social Democratic Party back to dominance. Zeman was a controversial figure with slippery politics. He began his career on the left, then abandoned the Social Democrats and swung hard to the right, and fired up his base with populist rhetoric. (If you're thinking "the Czech Donald Trump," you're not far off.)

But during the 2023 election, former army general Petr Pavel convincingly defeated the Zeman-backed candidate, marking a turn away from populism. Pavel started his military career pragmatically as a member of the Communist Party in the 1980s, but later transformed himself into a war hero (having saved a French contingent during the 1990s Yugoslav Wars). After his predecessors' attempts to bring the country closer to Russia and China, President Pavel promised a return to the Western-oriented, human-rights-first approach of Václav Havel.

Jára Cimrman: The Greatest Czech?

"I am such a complete atheist that I am afraid God will punish me." Such is the pithy wisdom of Jára Cimrman, the man overwhelmingly voted the "Greatest Czech of All Time" in a 2005 national poll. Who is Jára Cimrman? A philosopher? An explorer? An inventor? He is all these things, yes, and much more.

Born in the mid-19th century, Cimrman studied in Vienna before journeying the world. He traversed the Atlantic in a steamboat he designed himself, taught drama to peasants in Peru, and drifted across the Arctic Ocean on an iceberg. He invented the lightbulb, but Edison beat him to the patent office by five minutes. It was he who suggested to the Americans the idea for a Panama Canal, though, as usual, he was never credited. Indeed, Cimrman surreptitiously advised many of the world's greats: Eiffel on his tower, Einstein on his theories of relativity, Chekhov on his plays. ("You can't just have *two* sisters," Cimrman told the playwright. "How about three?") Long before the world knew of Sartre or Camus, Cimrman was writing tracts such as *The Essence of the Existence,* which would become the foundation for his philosophy of "Cimrmanism," also known as "nonexistentialism." (Its central premise: "Existence cannot not exist.")

Despite Jára Cimrman's genius, the "Greatest Czech" poll's sponsors had a single objection to his candidacy: He's not real, but the brainchild of Czech humorists Zdeněk Svěrák and Jiří Šebánek, who brought this patriotic Renaissance Man to life in 1967 in a satirical radio play.

How should we interpret the fact that the Czechs chose a fictional character as their greatest countryman over any of their flesh-and-blood national heroes—say, Charles IV (the 14th-century Holy Roman Emperor who established Prague as the cultural and intellectual capital of Europe) or Martina Navrátilová (someone who plays a sport with bright green balls)?

I like to think that the vote for Cimrman says something about the country's enthusiasm for blowing raspberries in the face of authority. From the times of the Czech kings who used crafty diplomacy to keep the German menace at bay, to the days of Jan Hus and his criticism of the Catholic Church, to the flashes of anticommunist revolt that at last sparked the Velvet Revolution in 1989, the Czechs have maintained a healthy disrespect for those who would tell them how to live their lives. Their vote for a fictional personage, says Cimrman's co-creator Svěrák, shows two things about the Czech nation: "That it is skeptical about those who are major figures and those who are supposedly the 'Greatest.' And that the only certainty that has saved the nation many times throughout history is its humor."

However, the Czech president is largely a figurehead. Power rests with the prime minister, who is chosen in the parliamentary elections. Recently, the traditional political parties were challenged by an antiestablishment candidate: food-industry mogul, second-wealthiest Czech, and former secret-police collaborator Andrej Babiš. He's the founder and head of the populist Action of Dissatisfied Citizens party that's considered by critics to be a cross between Vladimir Putin, Silvio Berlusconi, and Viktor Orbán.

Babiš served as prime minister between 2017 and 2021, a term that was plagued with mass public protests, mainly against his massive conflicts of interest. This inspired parties across the political spectrum to band together and eventually defeat Babiš at the polls. In 2022, the new government coalition strongly supported Ukraine and helped steer the rest of the EU to do the same. The government also opened the country's borders—and its purse—to Ukrainian refugees, taking in over a half-million people. Many Czechs saw sharp parallels to the 1968 Soviet crackdown in their own country, so support for Ukrainian refugees came naturally. But the war also caused a surge in energy prices and an inflation rate of 15 percent, posing a major challenge for the government.

Despite recent turmoil, the trajectory of Czech history continues to trend positive. Both in the capital and in rural villages, the country feels more affluent than ever, all while celebrating its inherent Czech-ness.

CZECH CUISINE

The Czechs have one of Europe's most stick-to-your-ribs cuisines. Heavy on meat, potatoes, and cabbage, it's hearty and tasty—designed to keep peasants fueled through a day of hard work. Some people could eat this stuff forever, while others seek a frequent break in the form of international restaurants (bigger towns such as Prague, Český Krumlov, and Kutná Hora have several options).

Soups

Polévka (soup) is the most essential part of a meal. The saying goes: "The soup fills you up, the dish plugs it up." *Pečivo* (bread) may be served with soup, or you may need to ask for it; it's always charged separately depending on how many *rohlíky* (rolls) or slices of *chleba* (yeast bread) you eat.

Some of the thick soups for a cold day are:

Zelná (or **zelňačka**): Cabbage
Čočková: Lentil
Fazolová: Bean
Dršťková: Tripe—delicious if fresh, chewy as gum if not

CZECH REPUBLIC

Czech Dumplings

Czech dumplings (*knedlíky*) resemble steamed white bread. They come in plain or potato (*bramborové*) varieties, are meant to be drowned in gravy (dumplings never accompany sauceless dishes), and are eaten with a knife and fork.

Sweet dumplings, listed in the dessert section on a menu, are a tempting option in summer, when they are loaded with fresh straw-berries, blueberries, apricots, or plums, and garnished with cus-tard and melted butter. Beware, though, that many restaurants cheat by filling the sticky dough with a smattering of jam or fruit preserve; before ordering, ask the waiter for details, or discreetly inspect that plate at your neighbor's table. Dump-lings with frozen fruit lose some of the flavor but are still worth trying.

The lighter soups are:

Hovězí (or **slepičí vývar s nudlemi**): Beef or chicken broth with noodles

Pórková: Leek

Květáková: Cauliflower

Main Dishes

These can either be *hotová jídla* (quick, ready-to-serve standard dishes, in some places available only during lunch hours, generally 11:00-14:30) or the more specialized *jídla na objednávku* or *minutky* (plates prepared when you order).

Below are some popular meat dishes. Note that the word *pečené* (roasted) shows up frequently on menus.

Guláš: Thick, meaty stew

Pečená kachna: Roasted duck

Pečené kuře: Roasted chicken

Smažený řízek: Fried pork fillet, like Wiener schnitzel

Svíčková na smetaně: Beef tenderloin in cream sauce

Vepřové koleno: Pork knuckle

Vepřová pečeně: Pork roast

If you're spending the night out with friends, have a beer and feast on the huge *vepřové koleno*, usually served with mustard *(hořčicí)*, horseradish sauce *(křenem)*, and yeast bread *(chleba)*.

In this landlocked country, fish options are typically limited to *kapr* (carp) and *pstruh* (trout), prepared in a variety of ways and served with potatoes or fries—although Czech perch and Norwegian salmon have cropped up on many local menus.

Vegetarians can go for the delicious *smažený sýr s bramborem* (fried cheese with potatoes) or default to *čočka s vejci* (lentils with fried egg).

Salads and Sides

Starches and Garnishes: *Hotová jídla* come with set garnishes, but if ordering à la carte *(jídla na objednávku)*, you'll typically need to order your garnishes separately (otherwise you'll get only the main dish). In either case, the most common sides are *knedlíky* (bread dumplings), *zelím* (cabbage), and *bramborem* (potatoes).

Salad: *Šopský salát,* like a Greek salad, is usually the best salad option (a mix of tomatoes, cucumbers, peppers, onion, and feta cheese with vinegar and olive oil). The server will bring it with the main dish, unless you specify that you want it before.

Dessert

Consider the following for *moučník* (dessert):

Lívance: Small pancakes with jam and curd

Palačinka: Crêpes served with fruit or jam

Zmrzlinový pohár: Ice-cream sundae

Many restaurants will offer fruit-filled dumplings and different sorts of *koláče* (pastries) and *štrůdl* (apple strudel), but it's much better to get these from a bakery. A *větrník* is a super-decadent, glazed cream puff.

All over Prague's Old Town, you'll find kiosks selling a treat called *trdlo* or *trdelník.* This is a long ribbon of dough wrapped around a stick, slowly cooked on a rotisserie, then rolled in cinnamon, sugar, or other toppings. While these aren't "traditional Czech" (they were imported quite recently from Hungary), they do offer a fresh, sweet treat. Try to get one that's still warm, rather than one wrapped in plastic—it makes a big difference.

BEVERAGES

Coffee: No Czech meal is complete without a cup of coffee. Espresso has become the norm in recent years, and locals drink it with added water and cream on the side. In most places, you'll still find *turecká káva* (Turkish coffee—finely ground coffee that only partly dissolves, leaving "mud" on the bottom; drink it without milk). This is how Czechs used to drink their coffee.

Water: Water comes bottled and generally costs more than beer (tap water is generally not served). Czech mineral waters *(minerálka)* have a high mineral content. They're naturally carbonated because they come from the springs in the many Czech spas (Mattoni, the most common brand, is from Carlsbad). If you want still water, ask for *neperlivá*.

Beer, Wine, and Liqueurs: Bohemia is beer country, with Europe's best and cheapest brew (see the sidebar on page 45). Moravians prefer wine and *slivovice* (SLEE-voh-veet-seh)—a plum brandy so highly valued that it's the de facto currency of the Carpathian Mountains (often used to barter with sheepherders and other mountain folk). *Medovina* ("honey wine") is mead.

In bars and restaurants, you can go wild with memorable liqueurs, most of which cost about a dollar a shot. Experiment. *Fernet,* a bitter drink made from many herbs, is the leading Czech aperitif. Absinthe, made from wormwood and herbs, is a watered-down version of the hallucinogenic drink that's illegal in much of Europe. It's famous as the muse of many artists (including Henri de Toulouse-Lautrec in Paris more than a century ago). *Becherovka,* made of 13 herbs and 38 percent alcohol, was used to settle upset aristocratic tummies and as an aphrodisiac. This velvety drink remains popular today. *Becherovka* and tonic mixed together is nicknamed *beton* ("concrete"). If you drink three, you'll find out why.

CZECH LANGUAGE

Czech is a Slavic language closely related to its Polish and Slovak neighbors. These days, English is widely spoken, and you'll find the language barrier minimal—unless you're dealing with a clerk or service person over age 50.

Czech pronunciation can be tricky. The language has a dizzying array of diacritical marks (little doo-hickeys over some letters that affect pronunciation). Most notably, some letters can be topped with a *háček (č, š, ž, ň, ě)*.

Czech Beer

Czechs are among the world's most enthusiastic beer *(pivo)* drinkers—adults drink an average of 80 gallons a year. The pub

is a place to have fun, complain, discuss art and politics, talk hockey, and chat with locals and visitors alike. *Na zdraví* means "to your health" in Czech. Whether you're in a *restaurace* (restaurant), *hostinec* (pub), or *hospoda* (bar), a beer will land on your table upon the slightest hint to the waiter, and a new pint will automatically appear when the old glass is almost empty (until you tell the waiter to stop). Order beer from the tap *(točené* means "draft"; *sudové pivo* means "keg beer"). More and more pubs are upgrading to beer from the tank *(tankové)*. A *pivo* is large (0.5 liter—17 oz); a *malé pivo* is small (0.3 liter—10 oz).

The Czechs perfected the first Pilsner-style lager, introduced by a Bavarian in nearby Plzeň, and the result, Pilsner Urquell, is on tap in many local pubs. But the Czechs produce plenty of other good beers; most of the famous brands, including Krušovice, Gambrinus, Staropramen, and Kozel, are owned internationally. Budvar, from the town of Budějovice ("Budweis" in German), is the last state-owned brewery. For years, the Czech and the American breweries disputed the "Budweiser" brand name. The solution: Czech Budweiser is sold under its own name in Europe, China, and Africa, while in America it is marketed as Czechvar.

The big degree symbol on beer bottles doesn't indicate alcohol content. Instead, it is a measurement used by brewers to track the density of certain ingredients. As a rough guide, 10 degrees is about 3.5 percent alcohol, 12 degrees is about 4.2 percent alcohol, and 11 and 15 degrees are dark beers. The most popular Czech beers are about as potent as German beers and only slightly stronger than typical American brews. Traditional establishments have beers from only one brewery on tap: one 10-degree, one 12-degree, one dark, and one non-alcoholic beer.

In recent years, Czechs have moved toward local microbrews. More restaurants are making their own beer or serving beer only from independent breweries. Modern beer bars *(pivní bar,* with a range of microbrews on tap) are popping up like crazy. The one word to characterize a successful Czech microbrew is *balance*. While Czechs do like to try new tastes, they are looking for a beer they can spend an evening with, drinking several pints throughout the night.

Here are some clues for Czech pronoun-ciation:

j sounds like "y" as in "yarn"
c sounds like "ts" as in "cats"
č sounds like "ch" as in "chicken"
š sounds like "sh" as in "shrimp"
ž sounds like "zh" as in "leisure"
ň sounds like "ny" as in "canyon"
ě sounds like "yeh" as in "yet"
ď sounds like the "dj" sound in "ledge"

Prague is flooded with tourists, most of whom don't bother to learn a single word of the local language. Study the Czech survival phrases on the following pages and give it your best shot. The locals will appreciate your efforts.

When navigating town, these words might be helpful: *město* (MYEHS-toh, town), *náměstí* (nah-myehs-tee, square), *ulice* (OO-leet-seh, street), *nábřeži* (NAH-bzheh-zhee, embankment road), and *most* (mohst, bridge).

Czech Survival Phrases

The emphasis in Czech words usually falls on the first syllable—but don't overdo it, as this stress is subtle. A vowel with an accent (á, é, í, ú, ý) is held longer. The combination ch sounds like the guttural "kh" sound in the Scottish word "loch." The uniquely Czech ř (as in Dvořák) sounds like a cross between a rolled "r" and "zh"; in the phonetics, it's "zh." Here are a few English words that all Czechs know: super, OK, pardon, stop, menu, problem, and no problem.

Hello. (formal)	Dobrý den.	**doh**-bree dehn
Hi. / Bye. (informal)	Ahoj.	**ah**-hoy
Do you speak English?	Mluvíte anglicky?	mloo-**vee**-teh ahn-**glits**-kee
Yes. / No.	Ano. / Ne.	**ah**-noh / neh
I don't understand.	Nerozumím.	neh-roh-zoo-meem
Please / You're welcome. / Can I help you?	Prosím.	**proh**-seem
Thank you.	Děkuji.	**dyeh**-kwee
Excuse me. / I'm sorry.	Promiňte.	proh-**meen**-teh
Good.	Dobře.	**dohb**-zheh
Goodbye.	Nashledanou.	**nah**-skleh-dah-noh
one / two / three	jeden / dva / tři	**yay**-dehn / dvah / tzhee
hundred / thousand	sto / tisíc	stoh / **tee**-seets
How much?	Kolik?	**koh**-leek
local currency	koruna (Kč)	koh-**roo**-nah
Write it?	Napište to?	**nah**-pish-teh toh
Is it free?	Je to zadarmo?	yeh toh **zah**-dar-moh
Where can I buy / find...?	Kde mohu koupit / najít...?	guh-**deh moh**-hoo **koh**-pit / **nah**-yeet
I'd like... (said by a man)	Rád bych...	rahd bikh
I'd like... (said by a woman)	Ráda bych...	**rah**-dah bikh
We'd like...	Rádi bychom...	**rah**-dyee **bee**-khohm
...a room.	...pokoj.	**poh**-koy
...a ticket to _____.	...jízdenka do _____.	**yeez**-dehn-kah doh _____
Where is...?	Kde je...?	guh-**deh** yeh
...the train station	...nádraží	**nah**-drah-zhee
...the bus station	...autobusové nádraží	**ow**-toh-boo-soh-veh **nah**-drah-zhee
...the tourist information office	...turistická informační kancelář	**too**-rih-stit-skah **een**-for-mahch-nee **kahn**-tseh-lahzh
...the toilet	...véцé	**veht**-seh
men / women	muži / ženy	**moo**-zhee / **zheh**-nee
left / right / straight	vlevo / vpravo / rovně	**vleh**-voh / **fprah**-voh / **rohv**-nyeh
At what time...?	V kolik...?	**fkoh**-leek
...does this open / close	...otevírají / zavírají	**oh**-teh-vee-rah-yee / **zah**-vee-rah-yee
now / soon / later	teď / brzy / později	tedge / **bir**-zih / **pohz**-dyeh-yee
today / tomorrow	dnes / zítra	duh-**nehs** / **zee**-trah

In a Czech Restaurant

I'd like to reserve... (said by a man)	Rád bych zarezervoval... rahd bikh **zah**-reh-zehr-voh-vahl	
I'd like to reserve... (said by a woman)	Ráda bych zarezervovala... **rah**-dah bikh **zah**-reh-zehr-voh-vah-lah	
...a table for one / two.	...stůl pro jednoho / dva. stool proh **yehd**-noh-hoh / dvah	
nonsmoking	nekuřácký **neh**-kuhzh-aht-skee	
Is this table free?	Je tento stůl volný? yeh **tehn**-toh stool **vohl**-nee	
Can I help you?	Mohu vám pomoci? **moh**-hoo vahm poh-**moht**-see	
The menu (in English), please.	Jídelní lístek (v angličtině), prosím. **yee**-dehl-nee **lee**-stehk (**fahn**-gleech-tee-nyeh) **proh**-seem	
Service is / isn't included.	Spropitné je / není zahrnuto. **sproh**-pit-neh yeh / **neh**-nee **zah**-har-noo-toh	
to go	s sebou **seh**-boh	
with / and / or	s / a / nebo suh / ah / **neh**-boh	
ready-to-eat meal	hotová jídla **hoh**-toh-vah **yeed**-lah	
breakfast / lunch / dinner	snídaně / oběd / večeře **snee**-dahn-yeh / **ohb**-yeht / **veh**-cheh-sheh	
appetizers	předkrmy **pzhehd**-krih-meh	
bread / cheese / sandwich	chléb / sýr / sendvič khlehb / seer / **sehnd**-veech	
soup / salad	polévka / salát poh-**lehv**-kah / **sah**-laht	
meat / poultry / fish	maso / drůbež / ryby **mah**-soh / **droo**-behzh / **rih**-bih	
fruit / vegetables	ovoce / zelenina **oh**-voht-seh / **zeh**-leh-nyee-nah	
dessert	dezert **deh**-zehrt	
(tap) water	voda (z kohoutku) **voh**-dah (**skoh**-hoht-koo)	
mineral water	minerální voda **mih**-neh-rahl-nyee **voh**-dah	
carbonated / not carbonated (spoken)	s bublinkami / bez bublinek **sboob**-leen-kah-mee / behz **boo**-blee-nehk	
carbonated / not carbonated (printed)	perlivá / neperlivá **pehr**-lee-vah / **neh**-pehr-lee-vah	
milk	mléko **mleh**-koh	
(orange) juice	(pomerančový) džus (**poh**-mehr-ahn-choh-vee) "juice"	
coffee / tea	káva / čaj **kah**-vah / chai	
wine / beer	vino / pivo **vee**-noh / **pee**-voh	
red / white	červené / bílé **chehr**-veh-neh / **bee**-leh	
sweet / dry	sladké / suché **slahd**-keh / **soo**-kheh	
glass / bottle	sklenka / lahev **sklehn**-kah / **lah**-hehv	
light / dark	světlé / tmavé **svyeht**-leh / **tmah**-veh	
Cheers!	Na zdraví! nah zdrah-**vee**	
Enjoy your meal.	Dobrou chuť. **doh**-broh khoot	
More. / Another.	Více. / Další. **veet**-seh / **dahl**-shee	
The same.	To samé. toh **sah**-meh	
The bill.	Účet. **oo**-cheht	
I'll pay.	Zaplatím. **zah**-plah-teem	
tip	spropitné **sproh**-pit-neh	
Delicious!	Výborné! **vee**-bohr-neh	

PRAGUE

Few cities can match the over-the-top romance and Old World charm...and tourist crowds of Prague. But this fun, historic city is popular for good reason: It's the only Central European capital to escape the bombing of the last century's wars, and it's one of the Continent's best-preserved cities.

Prague is a photographer's delight. As you wind past historic statues and pastel facades adorned with gables, balconies, lanterns, and countless little architectural details, the city itself seems a work of art. Besides its medieval and Baroque look, it's a world of willowy Art Nouveau paintings and architecture. You'll also see rich remnants of its strong Jewish heritage and stark reminders of the communist era. And you'll meet an entrepreneurial mix of locals and expats, each with their own brilliant scheme of how to make money in the tourist trade.

To escape the crowds and have Prague to yourself, seek out the back lanes and pretend you're strolling through the 18th century. Duck into pubs to enjoy the hearty food and good pilsner beer, and tour museums packed with fine art. Attend a concert. You'll leave Prague dreaming of coming back.

PLANNING YOUR TIME

A few days in Prague is plenty of time to experience the city and enjoy some side trips. Even if you're in a rush, allow at least two full days (with three nights) for a good introduction to the city.

Keep in mind that Jewish Quarter sights close on Saturday and Jewish holidays. Some museums, mainly in the Old Town, are closed on Mondays.

PRAGUE

Prague in Two or More Days
Here's my suggested plan for experiencing Prague in two days.

Day 1

9:00	Orient yourself to the city's core with my Old Town and Charles Bridge Walk. Along the way, enter some of the sights (such as the Municipal House) and climb the old tower at either end of the Charles Bridge to enjoy the view.
13:00	Have lunch in the Old Town or Lesser Town.
15:00	Explore the Jewish Quarter.
Evening	Choose between a beer hall, live music, or Black Light Theater.

Day 2

8:00	Zip up to Prague Castle on the tram. Be in the ticket line before 9:00, visit St. Vitus Cathedral before the crowds arrive, then visit the rest of the castle sights.
11:00	As you leave the castle, tour the Lobkowicz Palace.
12:00	Have lunch on Castle Square, at the Strahov Monastery, or in the Lesser Town.
13:30	Explore the Castle Quarter and Lesser Town (options include Loreta Church, Strahov Monastery, Nerudova street, Lesser Town Square, Lennon Wall, and Kampa Island).
15:30	Metro to the Muzeum stop (at the National Museum) and visit Wenceslas Square.
16:30	Tour the Mucha Museum.
Tips:	You could tour the Cold War Museum (on Wenceslas Square) while there, but check tour times in advance and adjust your day plan as needed. If you'd rather sleep in today, flip this plan—visit Wenceslas Square and the Mucha Museum, then tram up to the castle in the early afternoon (after 14:00) as the crowds disperse.

Day 3 and Beyond
With more time, fit in additional museums that interest you. With four days or more, add some of Prague's worthwhile day trips: Kutná Hora (delightful small town with gorgeous cathedral and famous bone church), the Terezín Memorial (Holocaust history), and/or Konopiště Castle (with a lived-in Habsburg interior). Český Krumlov is a bit far for a day trip—it's much better if you stay overnight.

Orientation to Prague

PRAGUE BY NEIGHBORHOOD

Residents call their town "Praha" (PRAH-hah). It's big, with about 1.3 million people—and it boasts one of the largest compact historical centers in Europe.

The Vltava River (VUL-tah-vah) divides the city in two. East of the river are the Old Town and the New Town (with its iconic Wenceslas Square; Václavské Náměstí, vaht-SLAHF-skeh NAH-myehs-tee), the main train station (Hlavní Nádraží, HLAV-nee NAH-drah-zhee), and most of my recommended hotels. To the west of the river is Prague Castle, and below that, the sleepy Lesser Town. Connecting the two halves are several bridges, including the landmark Charles Bridge (Karlův Most, KAR-loov most).

Until about 1800, Prague was four distinct towns with four town squares, all separated by fortified walls. Each town had a unique character, drawn from the personality of its first settlers. Today, much of Prague's charm survives in the distinct spirit of these towns.

Old Town (Staré Město, STAR-eh MYEHS-toh): Nestled in the bend of the river, this is the historic core, almost traffic-free, where most tourists spend their time. It's pedestrian-friendly, with small winding streets, old buildings, shops, and beer halls and cafés. In the center sits the charming Old Town Square (Staroměstské Náměstí, STAR-oh-myehst-skeh NAH-myehs-tee). Slicing east-west through the Old Town is the main pedestrian axis, along Celetná and Karlova streets.

Jewish Quarter (Josefov, YOO-zehf-fohf): Within the Old Town, this area by the river contains a high concentration of old synagogues and sights from Prague's deep Jewish heritage. It also holds the city's glitziest shopping area (with big-name international designers filling gorgeously restored Art Nouveau buildings).

New Town (Nové Město, NOH-vay MYEHS-toh): Stretching south from the Old Town is the long, broad expanse of Wenceslas Square, marking the center of the New Town. Arcing around the Old Town, the New Town cuts a swath from riverbank to riverbank. As the name implies, it's relatively new ("only" 600 years old). It's the neighborhood for noisy traffic, modern buildings, fancy department stores, and a few communist-era sights.

Castle Quarter (Hradčany, HRAD-chah-nee): High atop a

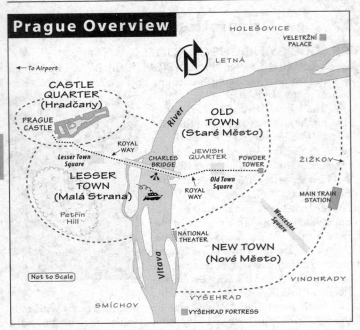

Prague Overview

hill on the west side of the river stands the massive complex of Prague Castle, marked by the spires of St. Vitus Cathedral. For a thousand years, this has been the neighborhood of Czech rulers (including today's president and foreign minister). Consequently, the surrounding area is noble and leafy, with high art and grand buildings, little commerce, and few pubs.

Lesser Town (Malá Strana, MAH-lah STRAH-nah): Nestled at the foot of Castle Hill is this pleasant former town of fine palaces and gardens (and a few minor sights). This is Prague's diplomatic neighborhood, made to feel elegant by stately embassies, but lacking some of the funky personality of the Old Town.

The Royal Way: Cutting through the towns—from the Powder Tower through the Old Town, crossing the Charles Bridge, and winding up to St. Vitus Cathedral—is the ancient path of coronation processions. Today, this city spine (the modern streets of Celetná, Karlova, and Nerudova) is marred by tacky trinket shops and jammed by tour groups—explore beyond it if you want to see the real Prague.

TOURIST INFORMATION

The Old Town has two TIs: on the **Old Town Square** (in the Old Town Hall, just to the left of the Astronomical Clock; Tue-Sun 9:00-19:00, Mon from 11:00) and around the corner from

Havelská Market (at Rytířská 12; daily 9:00-19:00). There's also a TI in the Lesser Town at **Petřín Tower** (daily 9:00-20:30, shorter hours off-season). For general tourist information in English, dial +420 221 714 714 (Mon-Fri 9:00-17:00) or check the useful TI website: www.prague.eu. Look for the helpful transit guide and information on guided walks and bus tours. TIs can also book local guides and concerts.

Monthly event guides include the *Prague Guide* (small fee), and the free *Prague This Month* and *Heart of Europe* (summer only).

Sightseeing Passes: Prague has two pricey passes—the Prague Visitor Pass, offered by the TI, and the **Prague CoolPass** (www.praguecoolpass.com). For most travelers, neither is worth the steep cost (e.g., 2,100 Kč/2 days).

ARRIVAL IN PRAGUE

Most visitors arrive at Prague's main train station (Hlavní Nádraží), on the eastern edge of downtown—a 20-minute walk, short taxi ride, or bus ride to the Old Town Square and many of my recommended hotels. Prague's Václav Havel Airport—12 miles from downtown—is easily connected to the city center by public bus, airport bus, minibus shuttle, and taxis. For details on these options, see Prague Connections, at the end of this chapter.

HELPFUL HINTS

Sightseeing Tips: The Museum of Medieval Art is closed on Mondays, and Jewish Quarter sights are closed on Saturdays. St. Vitus Cathedral at Prague Castle is closed Sunday mornings for Mass.

Rip-Offs: As in any heavily touristed city, in Prague naive tourists can fall victim to con artists. Most scams happen right under your nose: being charged a two-scoop price for one scoop of ice cream, having extra items appear on your restaurant bill, or not getting the correct change. Anytime you pay for something with cash, make a mental note of how much it costs, how much you're handing over, and how much you expect back. Count your change. Don't be in a rush. Wait until you get all the money you're due.

Freestanding ATMs are notorious for bad rates. Use an ATM attached to an actual bank (look for names that include the word *banka* or *spořitelna,* and avoid Euronet machines).

Pickpockets: They're abundant in Prague. They can be little chil-

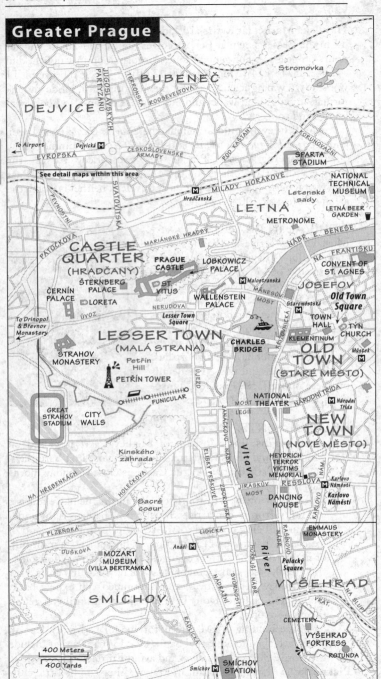

PRAGUE

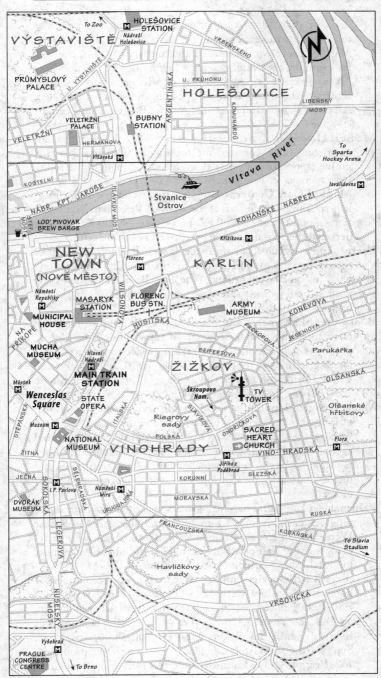

VÝSTAVIŠTĚ

To Zoo

HOLEŠOVICE STATION

Nádraží Holešovice

VRBENSKÉHO

PRŮMYSLOVÝ PALACE

U. VÝSTAVIŠTĚ

U. PRŮHONU

ARGENTINSKÁ

HOLEŠOVICE

KOMUNARDŮ

LIBEŇSKÝ MOST

VELETRŽNÍ PALACE

BUBNY STATION

HERMANOVA

VELETRŽNÍ

Vltavská

Vltava River

To Sparta Hockey Arena

KOSTELNÍ

NÁBŘ. KPT. JÁROŠE

HLÁVKŮV MOST

Štvanice Ostrov

ROHANSKÉ NÁBŘEŽÍ

Invalidovna

ŠTEF. MOST

LOĎ PIVOVAR BREW BARGE

NEW TOWN (NOVÉ MĚSTO)

Florenc

Křižíkova

KARLÍN

Náměstí Republiky

MASARYK STATION

WILSONOVA

FLORENC BUS STN.

ARMY MUSEUM

KONĚVOVA

MUNICIPAL HOUSE

HUSITSKÁ

NA PŘÍKOPĚ

JESENIOVA

MUCHA MUSEUM

Hlavní Nádraží

ŠEIFERTOVA

PROKOPOVA

Parukářka

Můstek

MAIN TRAIN STATION

ŽIŽKOV

OLŠANSKÁ

Wenceslas Square

STATE OPERA

ITALSKÁ

Škroupovo Nám.

SLAVÍKOVA

TV TOWER

Olšanské hřbitovy

ŠTĚPÁNSKÁ

Muzeum

Riegrovy sady

ONDŘIČKOVA

SACRED HEART CHURCH

Flora

ZITNÁ

NATIONAL MUSEUM

POLSKÁ

VINOHRADY

VINO-HRADSKÁ

JEČNÁ

I.P. Pavlova

Jiřího z Poděbrad

SLEZSKÁ

SOKOLSKÁ

BĚLEHRADSKÁ

Náměstí Míru

KORUNNÍ

DVOŘÁK MUSEUM

URUGUAYSKÁ

MORAVSKÁ

RUSKÁ

LEGEROVA

FRANCOUZSKÁ

KODAŇSKÁ

To Slavia Stadium

NUSELSKÝ MOST

Havlíčkovy sady

VRŠOVICKÁ

Vyšehrad

PRAGUE CONGRESS CENTRE

To Brno

dren, or adults dressed as professionals—sometimes even as tourists with jackets draped over their arms to disguise busy fingers. Thieves work crowded and touristy places in teams—for example, they might create a commotion at the door to a Metro or tram car. Assume any big distraction is a smoke-screen for theft, keep things zipped up, and wear a money belt. All of this can sound intimidating, but Prague is safe. Simply stay alert.

Medical Help: For above-standard assistance in English (including dental care), consider the top-quality **Hospital Na Homolce** (appointment—less than 1,000 Kč; daily 8:00-16:00, Roentgenova 2, Praha 5, +420 257 271 111). The **Canadian Medical Care Center** is a small, private clinic with an English-speaking Czech staff at the Nádraží Veleslavín Metro station (appointment—3,000 Kč, house call—4,500 Kč, halfway between the city and the airport, +420 222 300 300).

Useful Apps: Czech Tourism's free **Czech Republic—Land of Stories** app has info on popular destinations and events, along with historical background. The free **Beer Adventures** app guides you on a suds-sampling tour of Prague bars, pubs, and breweries.

Bookstore: Shakespeare and Sons is a friendly English-language bookstore with a wide selection of translations from Czech, the latest publications, and a reading space downstairs overlooking a river channel (daily 11:00-19:00, one block from Charles Bridge on Lesser Town side at U Lužického Semináře 10, +420 257 531 894, www.shakes.cz).

Maps: Google Maps works well here for navigation. A good map of Prague is also helpful. Look for one with trams and Metro lines marked, and tiny sketches of the sights (30-70 Kč; sold at kiosks, exchange windows, and tobacco stands). The *Kartografie Praha* **city map,** which shows all the tram lines and major landmarks, also includes a castle diagram and a street index.

Pharmacies: You'll find handy pharmacies in the Palladium shopping center on Náměstí Republiky and at Palackého 5 near Wenceslas Square (both open 9:00-18:00). A 24-hour pharmacy is at the Na Františku hospital (on the embankment next to Hotel InterContinental, Na Františku 1).

Laundry: A **full-service laundry** near most of my recommended hotels is at Karolíny Světlé 11 (3-hour wash-and-dry, Mon-Fri 7:30-19:00, closed Sat-Sun, 200 yards from Charles Bridge on Old Town side, +420 721 030 446); another laundry is at Rybná 27 (same-day pickup, Mon-Fri 8:00-18:00, closed Sat-Sun, +420 602 511 695); for locations, see the map on page 132. **Prague Andy's Laundromat** offers full service (weekdays

Prague's Best Views

Enjoy the "Golden City of a Hundred Spires" during the early evening, when the light is warm and the colors are rich. Good viewpoints include the following:

- The garden terrace in front of **Strahov Monastery,** above the castle (see page 121)
- The many balconies and spires at **Prague Castle**
- **Villa Richter** restaurant, overlooking the city from just below the castle past the Golden Lane
- The top of either tower on **Charles Bridge**
- **Old Town Square clock tower** (with a handy elevator)
- **Hotel u Prince's** rooftop dining terrace overlooking the Old Town Square (also with an elevator, free but for diners only)
- The steps of the **National Museum** overlooking Wenceslas Square
- The top of the **Žižkov TV tower,** offering spaceship views of the city, in the Žižkov/Vinohrady neighborhood east of the city center (150 Kč for elevator to observatory at 300 feet, free access to Oblaca restaurant at 200-foot level for customers)

only) and self-service (Mon-Fri 9:00-20:00, Sat-Sun from 8:00, last load at 18:30, near Náměstí Míru Metro stop at Korunní 14, Praha 2, +420 733 112 693, www.praguelaundromat.cz).

Bike Rental: Prague's network of bike paths makes bicycles a feasible option for exploring the center of town and beyond (see https://mapa.prahounakole.cz for a map). Two bike-rental shops are located near the Old Town Square: **Praha Bike** (Dlouhá 24, +420 732 388 880, www.prahabike.cz) and **City Bike** (Králodvorská 5, +420 776 180 284, www.citybikeprague.com). They also organize guided bike tours.

Car Rental: You won't want or need to drive within compact Prague, but a car can be handy for exploring the countryside. All the biggies have offices in Prague.

Travel Service and Tours: Magic Praha is a tiny travel service run by Lída Jánská. A Jill-of-all-trades, she can help with accommodations and transfers throughout the Czech Republic, as well as private tours and side trips to historic towns (+420 604 207 225, magicpraha@magicpraha.cz).

GETTING AROUND PRAGUE

You can walk nearly everywhere. Brown street signs (in Czech, but with helpful little icons) direct you to tourist landmarks. For a sense of scale, the walk from the Old Town Square to the Charles Bridge takes less than 10 minutes (depending on crowds).

Prague's Pedestrian Freeways: Four pedestrian thoroughfares cut through the essentially traffic-free center of Prague. You'll find yourself swept along on an international river of touristic humanity on the following streets: **Na Příkopě** ("On the Moat"; from the bottom of Wenceslas Square to the Municipal House and Republic Square), **Celetná** (from Municipal House to the Old Town Square), **Karlova** (from the Old Town Square to

the Charles Bridge), and **Melantrichova/Na Můstku** (from the bottom of Wenceslas Square to the Old Town Square). The shops along these tourist-clogged arteries are generally tourist traps. If you simply walk a block away, you'll find better values and more charming corners.

Commit to Public Transportation: It's worth figuring out the public transportation system, which helps you reach farther-flung sights (such as Prague Castle) and can save time and sweat jumping from spot to spot within the center. The Metro is slick, the trams fun, and Uber quick and easy. Prague's tram system is especially wonderful—trams rumble by frequently and take you just about anywhere.

By Public Transportation

Excellent, affordable public transit (Metro, trams, and buses) is perhaps the best legacy of the communist era. You can find more information and a route planner in English at www.dpp.cz.

Tickets: The Metro, trams, and buses all use the same tickets:
- 30-minute **short-trip ticket** *(krátkodobá),* which allows as many transfers as you can make in a half-hour—30 Kč

- 90-minute **standard ticket** *(základní)*—40 Kč
- **24-hour pass** *(jízdenka na 24 hodin)*—120 Kč
- **3-day pass** *(jízdenka na 3 dny)*—330 Kč

Since Prague is a great walking town, most find that buying a few individual tickets works better than a pass. Tickets are available from several outlets: The official **PID Lítačka app** allows you to purchase mobile tickets, which you can either activate immediately or save to use later. To use a mobile ticket, scan the QR code as you board.

Paper tickets are sold at **hotels, newsstand kiosks, and machines at Metro stops.** Be sure to validate your ticket as you get on the tram or bus, or as you enter the Metro station, by sticking it in the yellow machine, which stamps a time on it. Inspectors routinely ambush ticketless riders (including tourists) and fine them 1,000 Kč on the spot.

For trams and buses, tickets are also sold **on board** at a red ticket machine in the middle of the tram car or bus (tap-to-pay cards only). Tickets bought from these onboard machines have the time printed on them and don't need to be validated.

Trams: Trams run every few minutes in the daytime (a schedule is posted at each stop). Navigate by signs that list the end stations. At the platform, a sign lists all the stops for each tram in order. Remember that trams going one direction leave from one platform, while trams going the other direction might leave from a different platform nearby—maybe across the street or a half-block away. When the tram arrives, open the doors by pressing the green button.

As you go, follow along carefully so you'll be ready when your stop comes up. Newer trams have electronic signs that show either the next stop *(příští)* or a list of upcoming stops. Also, listen to the recorded announcements for the name of the current stop, followed by the name of the stop that's coming up next. (Confused tourists, thinking they've heard their stop, are notorious for rushing off the tram one stop too soon.) It's best to sit on the right near the front, where it's easy to see the sign on the platform of each stop.

Tram #22 (or **#23,** the retro 1960s ver-

Prague Public Transportation

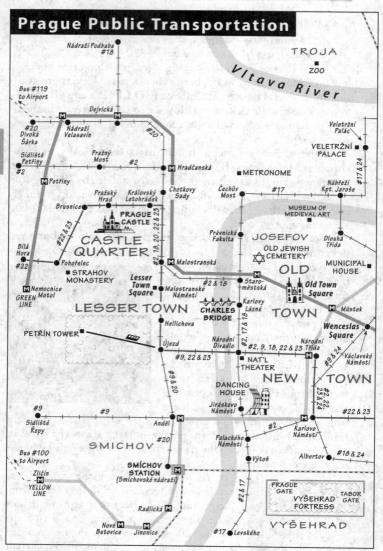

sion) is practically made for sightseeing, connecting the New Town with the Castle Quarter. The tram uses some of the same stops as the Metro (making it easy to get to—or travel on from—the tram route). The most convenient stops are in the New Town (at Národní Třída, between the bottom of Wenceslas Square and the river; and Národní Divadlo, at the National Theater), in the Lesser Town (Malostranské Náměstí, on the Lesser Town Square; and Malostranská Metro stop, near the riverbank), and above Prague

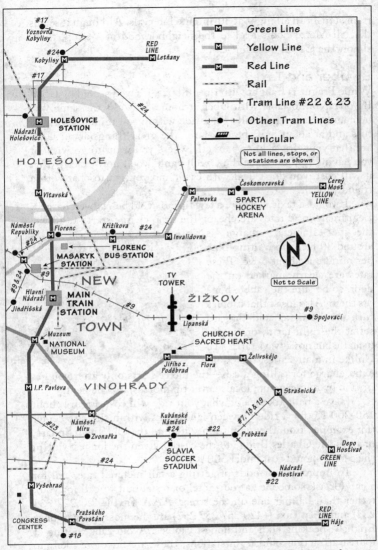

Castle (Královský Letohrádek—for the Summer Palace and scenic entry to Prague Castle; Pražský Hrad—for the main castle entry; and Pohořelec—for the Strahov Monastery).

Metro: The three-line Metro system is handy and simple but doesn't always get you right to the tourist sights (landmarks such as the Old Town Square and Prague Castle are several blocks from the nearest Metro stops). The Metro closes at midnight, but nighttime tram routes (identified with white numbers on blue backgrounds at tram stops) run all night at 30-minute intervals. Although it seems that all Metro doors lead to the neighborhood of Výstup, that's simply the Czech word for "exit."

By Uber and Taxi

While Prague is fraught with rip-off taxis, it's well served by Uber. If you're comfortable with Uber at home, it works the same way here and you can generally get a ride within five minutes with no fuss and at about half the taxi fare. The great things about Uber are that your driver knows exactly where you want to go without you having to pronounce the Czech name, you know exactly what it will cost, you don't deal with cash, and you get to chat with a friendly local.

If you use taxis, here are a few tips to avoid being overcharged. Legitimate local rates are cheap: The drop charge starts at 40 Kč, the per-kilometer charge is around 30 Kč, and waiting time per minute is about 6 Kč. These rates are clearly marked on the door, so be sure the cabbie honors them. Also insist that cabbies turn on the meter and that it's set at the right tariff, or *"sazba"* (usually but not always tariff #1).

Unlike in many cities, there's no extra charge for calling a cab—the meter starts only after you get in. Tip by rounding up; locals never tip more than 5 percent.

Have a ballpark idea of what your ride will cost. Figure about 150-200 Kč for a ride between landmarks within the city center (for example, from the main train station to the Old Town Square, or from the Charles Bridge to the castle). Even the longest ride in the center should cost under 300 Kč.

To improve your odds of getting a fair metered rate, call for a cab (or ask someone at your hotel or restaurant to call for you), rather than hailing one on the street. **AAA Taxi** (+420 222 333 222) and **City Taxi** (+420 257 257 257) are the most likely to have English-speaking staff and honest cabbies. Avoid cabs waiting at tourist attractions and train stations; these are far more likely to be crooked.

If a cabbie surprises you at the end with an astronomical fare, challenge it. Point to the rates on the door. Get your hotel receptionist to back you up. Pull out your phone and threaten to call the police. (Because of legislation to curb dishonest cabbies, the police will stand up for you.) Or simply pay what you think the ride should cost and walk away.

Tours in Prague

∩ To sightsee on your own, download my free Prague City Walk audio tour.

WALKING TOURS

A staggering number of small companies offer walking tours of the Old Town, the castle, and more (check at the TI). Since guiding is a routine side job for university students, you'll generally get hardworking young guides with fine language skills at good prices. While I'd rather go with my own local guide (see below), public walking tours are cheaper (4 hours for about 450 Kč), cover themes you might not otherwise consider, connect you with other English-speaking travelers, and allow for spontaneity. The quality depends on the guide rather than the company. Your best bet is to show up at the Astronomical Clock a couple of minutes before 8:00, 10:00, or 11:00, then chat with a few of the umbrella-holding guides and choose the one you click with.

"Free" Tours: These are not really free—at the end, you're expected to tip your guide (with bills, not coins). Guides are usually expat students who memorize a script and give an entertaining performance as you walk through the Old Town, with little respect for serious history. In general, they're fine for the backpacker and hostel crowd (for whom they're designed).

LOCAL GUIDES

In Prague, hiring a guide is particularly smart (and a ▲▲ experience). Expect to pay around 3,000 Kč for a half-day tour. Because prices are usually per hour (around 850 Kč), not per person, small groups can hire an inexpensive guide for a whole day or for chunks of time over several days. Guides meet you wherever you like and tailor the tour to your interests. Visit websites for details, then make arrangements by email.

Guide Services: These two outfits represent a cadre of top-notch guides.

At **PragueWalker,** Kateřina Svobodová, a hardworking historian-guide who knows her stuff, manages a team of enthusiastic and friendly guides (+420 603 181 300, www.praguewalker.com, katerina@praguewalker.com).

At **Personal Prague Guide Service,** Šárka Kačabová uses her teaching background to help you understand Czech culture, and has a team of personable and knowledgeable guides (RS%—30 minutes free with this book, +420 777 225 205, www.personalpragueguide.com).

Private Guides: These guides generally learned their trade

PRAGUE

Prague at a Glance

Old Town

▲▲▲**Old Town Square** Magical main square of Old World Prague, with dozens of colorful facades, dramatic Jan Hus Memorial, looming Týn Church, and fanciful Astronomical Clock. **Hours:** Týn Church generally open to sightseers Tue-Sat 10:00-13:00 & 15:00-17:00, Sun 10:30-12:00, closed Mon; Astronomical Clock strikes on the hour daily 9:00-23:00, until 20:00 in winter; clock tower open Tue-Sun 9:00-21:00, Mon from 11:00, shorter hours Jan-March. See page 67.

▲▲▲**Charles Bridge** Atmospheric, statue-lined bridge connecting the Old Town to the Lesser Town and Prague Castle. See page 82.

▲▲▲**Jewish Quarter** Finest collection of Jewish sights in Europe, featuring various synagogues and an evocative cemetery. **Hours:** Jewish Museum sights open Sun-Fri 9:00-18:00, Nov-March until 16:30, closed Sat and on Jewish holidays; Old-New Synagogue open Sun-Thu 9:00-18:00, off-season until 17:00, Fri closes one hour before sunset, closed Sat and Jewish holidays. See page 83.

▲▲**Museum of Medieval Art** Best Gothic art in the country, at the former Convent of St. Agnes. **Hours:** Tue-Sun 10:00-18:00, closed Mon. See page 90.

▲**Havelská Market** Colorful open-air market that sells crafts and produce. **Hours:** Daily 9:00-18:00. See page 79.

New Town

▲▲▲**Wenceslas Square** Lively boulevard at the heart of modern Prague. See page 90.

▲▲**Municipal House** Pure Art Nouveau architecture, including Prague's largest concert hall and several eateries. **Hours:** Daily 10:00-18:00, but most of the interior is viewable by tour only. See page 98.

▲**Cold War Museum** Re-creation of a nuclear fallout shelter, in

post-communism but can still share memories of the time before the transition. For even more guides, see www.guide-prague.cz.

Jana Hronková has a natural style—a welcome change from the more strict professionalism of some other guides—and a penchant for the Jewish Quarter (+420 732 185 180, https://praguediscoveries.com). A tour with my co-author, **Honza Vihan,** adds more nuance and context to the history covered in this guide-the basement of a hotel. **Hours:** English tours daily at 11:00, 13:00, 14:30, and 16:00. See page 94.

▲**Mucha Museum** Easy-to-appreciate Art Nouveau works by Czech artist Alphonse Mucha. **Hours:** Daily 10:00-18:00. See page 97.

▲**Museum of Communism** The rise and fall of the regime, from start to Velvet finish. **Hours:** Daily 9:00-20:00. See page 98.

PRAGUE

Lesser Town
▲**Petřín Hill** Lesser Town hill with public art, a funicular, and a replica of the Eiffel Tower. **Hours:** Funicular—daily 8:00-22:00; tower—daily 9:00-21:00, shorter hours off-season. See page 104.

Castle Quarter
▲▲▲**St. Vitus Cathedral** The Czech Republic's most important church, featuring a climbable tower and a striking stained-glass window by Art Nouveau artist Alphonse Mucha. **Hours:** Daily 9:00-17:00, Nov-March until 16:00, closed Sunday mornings for Mass. See page 111.

▲▲**Prague Castle** Traditional seat of Czech rulers, with St. Vitus Cathedral, Old Royal Palace, Basilica of St. George, shop-lined Golden Lane, and lots of crowds. **Hours:** Castle sights—daily 9:00-17:00, Nov-March until 16:00; castle grounds—daily 6:00-22:00. See page 105.

▲▲**Lobkowicz Palace** Delightful private art collection of a Czech noble family. **Hours:** Daily 10:00-18:00. See page 119.

▲**Strahov Monastery and Library** Baroque center of learning, with ornate reading rooms and old-fashioned science exhibits. **Hours:** Daily 9:00-12:00 & 13:00-17:00. See page 121.

▲**Loreta Church** Beautiful Baroque church, a pilgrim magnet for centuries, containing what some believe to be part of Mary's house from Nazareth. **Hours:** Daily 9:00-17:00, Nov-March 9:30-16:00. See page 124.

book (+420 603 418 148, honzavihan@hotmail.com). **Zuzana Tlášková** speaks English as well as Hebrew (+420 774 131 335, tlaskovaz@seznam.cz). **Martin Bělohradský,** formerly an organic chemistry professor, is enthusiastic about fine arts and architecture (+420 723 414 565, martinb5666@gmail.com).

Jana Krátká enjoys sharing Prague's tumultuous 20th-century history with visitors (+420 776 571 538, janapragueguide@gmail.

com). Friendly **Petra Vondroušová** designs tours to fit your interests (+420 602 319 420, www.compactprague.com). **Kamil and Pavlína** run a family business specializing in tours of Prague and beyond. They also provide sightseeing and transport as far as Vienna and Berlin (+420 605 701 861, https://prague-extra.com).

Running Tours Prague are guided by Radim Prahl, a local with an appetite for ultramarathons; he'll run you past monuments, through parks, and down back alleys at your own pace (1,250 Kč for one person, 1,500 Kč for two people; +420 777 288 862, www.runningtoursprague.com).

JEWISH QUARTER TOURS

Jewish guides (of varying quality) lead private three-hour tours in English of the Jewish Quarter. Consider **Wittmann Tours** (4,800 Kč, or 6,800 Kč with Sylvie Wittman herself, plus museum entry fees; +420 603 426 564, www.wittmann-tours.com). They also offer an all-day minibus tour to the Terezín Memorial. Several of the **private guides** recommended earlier also do good tours of the Jewish Quarter.

TOURS OUTSIDE PRAGUE

To get beyond the sights listed in most guidebooks, or for a deeply personal look at the usual destinations, contact **Tom and Marie Zahn.** Tom is American, Marie is Czech, and together they lead family-friendly day excursions (in Prague and throughout the country). Their specialty is Personal Ancestral Tours & History (P.A.T.H.)—with sufficient notice, they can help Czech descendants find their ancestral homes, perhaps even a long-lost relative. Tom and Marie can also help with other parts of your travel in Central and Eastern Europe (US +1 360 450 5959, Czech +420 257 940 113, www.pathways.cz for tours, www.pathfinders.cz for genealogy research).

Reverend Jan Dus, an enthusiastic pastor who lived in the US for several years, now serves a small congregation about 100 miles east of Prague. Jan can design itineraries and likes to help travelers connect with locals in little towns, particularly in northeastern Bohemia and Moravia. He also has an outstanding track record in providing genealogical services (US +1 800 807 1562, www.revjan.com).

Old Town and Charles Bridge Walk

Nestled in the bend of the river is Prague's compact, pedestrian-friendly Old Town. It's also Prague's tourism ground zero, jammed with tasteful landmarks and tacky amusements alike.

A boomtown since the 11th century, the Old Town has long

been the busy commercial quarter, filled with merchants, guilds, students, and supporters of the Church and social reformer Jan Hus (who wanted a Czech-style Catholicism). Here, Prague feels like the Gothic metropolis that it—at its heart—still is.

This walk (rated ▲▲▲) starts in the **Old Town Square.** From here we'll snake through the surrounding neighborhood, get a glimpse of the New Town (at Wenceslas Square), and end on the Charles Bridge—one of the most atmospheric spots in all of Europe.

Length of This Walk: Allow three hours for this walk.

Crowd Warning: Much of this walk is packed with sightseers all day long. A huge bottleneck occurs in front of the Astronomical Clock near the top of each hour.

❷ SELF-GUIDED WALK
• *Begin with the Old Town Square's centerpieces, the...*

❶ Jan Hus and Virgin Mary Monuments

The **Jan Hus Memorial,** erected in 1915, is an enduring icon of the long struggle for (Czech) freedom. In the center, Jan Hus—the

reformer who became the symbol of Czech nationalism—stands tall amid the rising flames. Hus, born in 1369, was a priest who challenged both the Church's and the secular rulers' claim to dominion. His defiant stance—depicted so powerfully in this monument—galvanized the Czech people, who rallied to fight not just for their religious beliefs but also for independence from any human controls.

Hus was arrested, charged with heresy, excommunicated, and, in 1415, burned at the stake. His followers, called Hussites, picked up the torch and fought on for two decades in the Hussite Wars, which killed tens of thousands and left Bohemia a virtual wasteland.

Surrounding Hus' statue are the Hussites who battled the entrenched powers of their time. Look into the faces of these medieval warriors of faith—it was a bitter fight. Two hundred years later, in 1620, a disorganized Czech rebellion was crushed by the united Habsburgs at White Mountain just outside Prague—effectively ending Czech independence and freedom of worship for three centuries.

Each subsequent age has interpreted Hus to its liking: For

PRAGUE

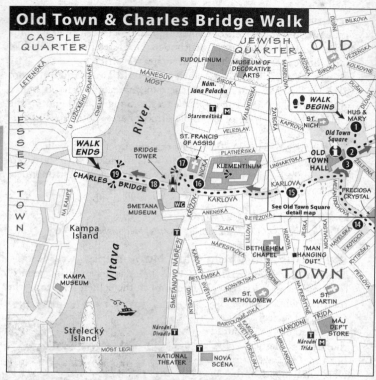

Old Town & Charles Bridge Walk

Protestants, Hus was the founder of the first Protestant church (though he was actually an ardent Catholic); for revolutionaries, this critic of the temporal powers was a proponent of social equality; for nationalists, this Czech preacher was the defender of the language; and for communists, this ideologue was first to preach the gospel of communal ownership (though he never spoke against individual property per se).

Now turn your attention to the **Virgin Mary** atop her sandstone column. Originally erected in 1652, shortly after the Thirty Years' War, the first genuinely Baroque statue in Prague honored Mary as the city's protector. Mary was intended to rally Catholics and non-Catholics alike—just as they had been rallied four years earlier to defend their homes from Swedish invasion. But by the late 19th century, ardent nationalists had come to perceive this delicate, Bernini-inspired Mary as a symbol of the

1. Jan Hus & Virgin Mary Monuments
2. Old Town Square
3. Old Town Hall & Astronomical Clock
4. Týn Church
5. Ungelt Courtyard
6. Church of St. James
7. Celetná Street
8. House of the Black Madonna
9. Estates Theater & Charles University
10. Powder Tower
11. Municipal House
12. Na Příkopě
13. Wenceslas Square
14. Havelská Market
15. Karlova Street
16. Charles IV Statue
17. View from the River
18. Charles Bridge
19. View from Charles Bridge

PRAGUE

militantly Catholic Habsburgs. (Cue installation of the Jan Hus Memorial, with Jan's eyes locked on Mary in a defiant stare-down.)

A few days after the declaration of independence in 1918, a rebellious mob turned on the "Habsburg" Virgin, tearing down the column and breaking the statue. At the time, the majority viewed this act as historical vindication. But pious Catholics (the country remained predominantly Catholic even after independence) felt a sense of injustice: Isn't Mary a symbol of unity and peace?

Under communism there was little chance to restore the monument, but the debate resurfaced after 1989. For 23 years Czech sculptor Petr Váňa worked on a faithful replica. Finally, in 2020, Prague's city council allowed the Virgin to return to her original spot, reigniting the century-old controversy.

It will take time for Prague's citizens to get used to having two monuments in the square. I see Mary's return as a sign of a mature democracy that allows minority voices to be heard, and as a more nuanced reflection of the country's conflicted past.

• *Stepping away from the monuments, stand in the center of the Old Town Square and take a 360-degree...*

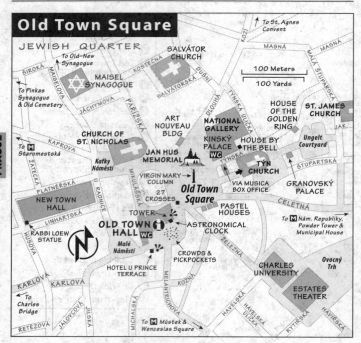

Old Town Square

JEWISH QUARTER

To Old-New Synagogue

To Pinkas Synagogue & Old Cemetery

SALVÁTOR CHURCH

MAISEL SYNAGOGUE

ART NOUVEAU BLDG

NATIONAL GALLERY

CHURCH OF ST. NICHOLAS

KINSKÝ PALACE

HOUSE BY THE BELL

HOUSE OF THE GOLDEN RING

ST. JAMES CHURCH

Ungelt Courtyard

JAN HUS MEMORIAL

Kafky Náměstí

VIRGIN MARY COLUMN

Old Town Square

TÝN CHURCH

VIA MUSICA BOX OFFICE

GRANOVSKÝ PALACE

27 CROSSES

PASTEL HOUSES

NEW TOWN HALL

TOWER

OLD TOWN HALL

ASTRONOMICAL CLOCK

To Nám. Republiky, Powder Tower & Municipal House

RABBI LOEW STATUE

Malé Náměstí

CROWDS & PICKPOCKETS

HOTEL U PRINCE TERRACE

CHARLES UNIVERSITY

Ovocný Trh

ESTATES THEATER

To Charles Bridge

To Můstek & Wenceslas Square

100 Meters

100 Yards

N

PRAGUE

To St. Agnes Convent

❷ Old Town Square Orientation Spin-Tour

Whirl clockwise to get a look at Prague's diverse architectural styles: Gothic, Renaissance, Baroque, Rococo, and Art Nouveau. Prague was largely spared the devastating aerial bombardments of World War II that leveled so many European cities (like Berlin, Warsaw, and Budapest). Few places can match the Old Town Square for Old World charm.

Start with the green domes of the Baroque **Church of St. Nicholas.** Originally Catholic, now Hussite, this church is a popular concert venue. The Jewish Quarter is a few blocks behind the church, down the uniquely tree-lined "Paris Street" (Pařížská)—which also has the best lineup of Art Nouveau houses in Prague.

Spin to the right. Behind the Hus Memorial is a fine yellow building that introduces us to Prague's wonderful world of Art Nouveau: pastel colors, fanciful stonework, wrought-iron balconies, colorful murals—and what are those firemen statues on top doing? Prague's architecture is a wonderland of ornamental details.

Continue spinning a few doors to the right to the large, red-and-tan Rococo **Kinský Palace,** which displays the National Gallery's top-notch temporary exhibits (there's a handy WC in the courtyard).

Immediately to the right of the Rococo palace stands the tower-

Jan Hus and the Early Reformers

Jan Hus (c. 1369-1415) lived and preached more than a century before Martin Luther (1483-1546), but they had many things in common. Both were college professors as well as priests. Both drew huge public crowds as they preached in their university

chapels. Both condemned Church corruption, promoted local religious autonomy, and advocated for letting the common people participate more in worship rituals. Both established their national languages. (It's Hus who gave the Czech alphabet its unique accent marks so that the letters could fit the sounds.) And, by challenging established authority, both got in big trouble.

Hus was born in the small southern Bohemian town of Husinec and moved to Prague to study at the university. He served as a rector at Charles University starting in 1402. Preaching from the pulpit in Bethlehem Chapel (still open to the public), Hus drew inspiration from the English philosopher John Wycliffe (c. 1320-1384), who was an early advocate of reforming the Catholic Church to strip the clergy of its power.

Hus' revolutionary sermons drew huge crowds of reverent but progressive-minded Czechs. He proposed that the congregation should be more involved in worship (for example, be allowed to drink the wine at Communion) and have services and scriptures written in the people's language, not in Latin. Even after he was excommunicated in 1410, Hus continued preaching his message.

In 1414, the Roman Catholic Church convened the Council of Constance to grapple with the controversies of the day. First they posthumously excommunicated Wycliffe, proclaiming him a heretic and exhuming his corpse to symbolically burn at the stake. Then they called Hus to Constance, where on July 6, 1415, they declared him a heretic. After refusing to recant his beliefs and praying that God would forgive his enemies, Hus was tied to a stake and burned alive. But by this time, Hus' challenging ideas had been embraced by many Czechs and sparked the bloodiest civil war in the country's history.

The Council, this early Catholic precursor to the Counter-Reformation, kept things under control for three generations. But in the 16th century, a German monk named Martin Luther found a more progressive climate for these same revolutionary ideas. Thanks to the new printing press and his more widely spoken German language, Luther was able to spread his message cheaply and effectively. While Hus loosened Rome's grip on Christianity, Luther orchestrated the Reformation that finally broke it. Today, both are honored as national heroes as well as religious reformers.

like **House by the Bell,** one of the finest examples of a 13th-century Gothic patrician house anywhere in Europe (also the oldest building on the square).

Farther to the right is the towering, Gothic **Týn Church** (pron. "teen"), with its fanciful twin spires. It's been the Old Town's leading church in every era. In medieval times, it was Catholic. When the Hussites came to dominate the city (c. 1420s), they made it the headquarters of their faith. After the Habsburg victory in 1620, it reverted to Catholicism. The symbolism tells the story: Between the church's two towers, find a golden medallion of the Virgin Mary. Beneath that is a niche with a golden chalice. In Hussite times, the chalice symbolized their cause—that all should be able to take Communion. When the Catholics triumphed, they melted down the original chalice and made it into the golden image of Mary. In 2016, the chalice was returned to the niche.

The row of pastel houses in front of the Týn Church has a mixture of Gothic, Renaissance, and Baroque facades and gables. If you like live music, the convenient **Via Musica box office** near the church's front door has all the concert options; we'll pass it later on this walk.

Spinning right, to the south side of the square, take in more **glorious facades,** each a different color with a different gable on top—step gables, triangular, bell-shaped. The tan 19th-century Neo-Gothic house at #16 has a steepled bay window and a mural of St. Wenceslas on horseback.

Finally, you reach the pointed 250-foot-tall spire marking the 14th-century **Old Town Hall.** At the base of the tower, near the corner of the tree-filled park, find **27 white crosses** inlaid in the pavement. These mark the spot where 27 nobles, merchants, and intellectuals—Protestants *and* Catholics—were beheaded in 1621 after the White Mountain defeat. This is still considered one of the grimmest chapters in the country's history.

• *Around the left side of the tower are two big, fancy, old clock faces being admired by many, many tourists.*

❸ Old Town Hall and Astronomical Clock

The Old Town Hall, with its distinctive trapezoidal tower, was built in the 1350s, during Prague's golden age. First, turn your attention to the famous clock.

Astronomical Clock: See if you can figure out how it works. Of the two giant dials on the tower, the top one tells the time on two rings: The inner one, with Roman numerals, is similar to present-day clocks, while the outer one, numbered 1 through 24 in a strange but readable Bohemian script, rotates to reset each day at sunset. Within the dial is yet another revolving disc, where today's zodiac sign is marked.

If all of this seems complex, it must have been a marvel in the early 1400s, when the clock was installed. Remember that back then, everything revolved around the Earth (the fixed middle background—with Prague marking the center, of course). The clock was heavily damaged during World War II, and much of what you see today is a reconstruction.

The second dial, below the clock, was added in the 19th century. It shows the signs of the zodiac, scenes from the seasons of a rural peasant's life, and a ring of saints' names. There's one for each day of the year, and a marker on top indicates today's special saint. In the center is a castle, symbolizing Prague.

Four statues flank the upper clock. These politically incorrect symbols evoke a 15th-century outlook: The figure staring into a mirror stands for vanity, a Jewish moneylender holding a bag of coins is greed, and (on the right side) a Turk with a mandolin symbolizes hedonism. All these worldly goals are vain in the face of Death, whose hourglass reminds us that our time is unavoidably running out.

The clock strikes the top of the hour and puts on a little **glockenspiel show** daily from 9:00 to 23:00 (until 20:00 in winter). As the hour approaches, keep your eye on Death. First, Death tips his hourglass and pulls the cord, ringing the bell, while the moneylender jingles his purse. Then the windows open and the 12 apostles shuffle past, acknowledging the gang of onlookers. Finally, the rooster at the very top crows and the hour is rung. The hour is often wrong because of Daylight Saving Time (completely senseless to 15th-century clockmakers).

Sights Inside the Old Town Hall: The ornately carved Gothic entrance door to the left of the clock leads to the TI, a pay WC, and the ticket desk for the clock-tower elevator and Old Town Hall tours. Step into the **entry hall** (free). It's beautifully decorated with a 1904 Art Nouveau mosaic that celebrates Prague (Lady Prague on the throne is being honored by characters representing all the nationalities of the Habsburg Empire) and various Czech mythological scenes.

You can pay to see other sights inside. One ticket (300 Kč, sold on floors 1 and 3) covers the tour of the Old Town Hall—you'll see a few sterile rooms and the workings of the Astronomical Clock—as well as the trip up the tower by elevator (from floor 3) for the big view (Tue-Sun 9:00-21:00, Mon from 11:00, shorter hours Jan-March; 45-minute tours usually 4/day in English at 10:00, noon, 14:00, and 16:00—preregister at ticket office).

PRAGUE

• *Now head back across the square to tour the pointy Týn Church. Enter by making your way through the cluster of buildings in front of it. (If the church is closed, try peeking in from the locked gate just inside the door.)*

❹ Týn Church

This is the Old Town's main church (worth ▲). While it has roots dating back to the 1100s, this structure dates from Prague's golden age. It was built around 1360 as the univer-sity church by the same architect who de-signed St. Vitus Cathedral at Prague Castle.

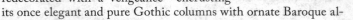

Cost and Hours: 40 Kč requested do-nation; Tue-Sat 10:00-13:00 & 15:00-17:00, Sun 10:30-12:00, closed Mon.

Visiting the Church: The structure is full of light, with soaring Gothic arches. The ornamentation reflects the church's troubled history. Originally Catholic, it was taken over by the Hussites, who whitewashed it and stripped it of Catholic icons. When the Catholic Habsburgs retook the church, they redecorated with a vengeance—encrusting its once elegant and pure Gothic columns with ornate Baroque al-tars and statues of Mary and the saints.

At the front-right corner of the church (to the right of the pulpit), on the pillar is a brown stone slab showing an armored man with a beard and ruff collar, his hand resting on a globe. This is the first modern astronomer, **Tycho Brahe** (1546-1601). Buried here, he was brought to Prague by the Habsburgs.

Now circle around to face the stunning **main altar,** topped with a statue of the archangel Michael with a flaming sword. A painting (on the lower level) shows Mary ascending to heaven, where (in the next painting up) she's to be crowned. To the right of the altar is a statue of one of Prague's patron saints, **John of Nepo-muk**—always easy to identify thanks to his halo of stars.

You're surrounded by the **double-eagle symbol** of the Catho-lic Habsburgs: on the flag borne by a knight statue on the altar, atop the organ behind you (Prague's oldest), and above you on the ceiling.

Leaving the Church: After exiting the church, walk through the **Via Musica** ticket office (on your right; a handy place to get classical-music tickets—see page 127. Leaving at the far end, turn right, where you'll walk by the north (formerly main) entrance to the Týn Church (with the most delicate pieces of Gothic stone ma-sonry in town—all original 14th century).

Look to the left across the street at Granovský Palace, the fine Renaissance building with sgraffiti and openings for muskets. In what was economically the most important place in the Old Town, this was a fortress within a fortified town. Notice the carved, stone gate to a courtyard and also the House of the Golden Ring (to the left).

• *Tucked immediately behind the Týn Church is a welcome oasis of tranquility in the midst of the Old Town Square hubbub—the courtyard called the Ungelt. Through an imposing gate, enter what was once the commercial nucleus of medieval Prague.*

❺ Ungelt Courtyard

This pleasant, cobbled, quiet courtyard of upscale restaurants and shops is one of the Old Town's oldest places. During the Bohemian golden age (c. 1200-1400), the Ungelt was a multicultural hub of international trade. Prague—located at the geographical center of Europe—attracted Germans selling furs, Italians selling fine art, Frenchmen selling cloth, and Arabs selling spices. They converged on this courtyard, where they could store their goods and pay their customs (which is what *Ungelt* means, in German). In return, the king granted them protection, housing, and a stable for their horses. By day, they'd sell their wares on the Old Town Square. At night, they'd return here to drink and exchange news. After centuries of disuse, the Ungelt has been marvelously restored—a great place for dinner, and a reminder that Prague has been a cosmopolitan center for most of its history.

• *Exit the Ungelt at the far end. Just to your left, across the street, is the...*

❻ Church of St. James (Kostel Sv. Jakuba)

Perhaps the most beautiful church interior in the Old Town, the Church of St. James (worth ▲) has been the home of the Minorite

Order almost as long as merchants have occupied the Ungelt. A medieval city was a complex phenomenon: Commerce and a life of contemplation existed side by side.

Step inside (or, if it's locked, peek through the glass door). Artistically, St. James is a stunning example of how simple medieval spaces could be rebuilt into sumptuous feasts of Baroque decoration. The original interior was destroyed by fire in 1689; what's here now is an early-18th-century remodel. The blue light in the altar highlights one of Prague's most venerated treasures—the bejeweled Madonna Pietatis. Above the *pietà*, as if held aloft by hummingbird-like angels, is a painting of the martyrdom of St. James.

Cost and Hours: Free, Tue-Sun 9:30-12:00 & 14:00-16:00, closed Mon.

• *Exiting the church, do a U-turn to the left (heading up Jakubská street, along the side of the church, past some rough-looking bars). After one block, turn right on Templová street. Head two blocks down the street (passing a nice view of the Týn Church's rear end) and go through the arcaded passageway, where you emerge onto ❼ Celetná street (since the 10th century, this has been a corridor in the busy commercial quarter—filled with merchants and guilds). To your right is a striking, angular, cinnamon-colored building called the...*

❽ House of the Black Madonna (Dům u Černé Matky Boží)

Back around the turn of the 20th century, Prague was a center of avant-garde art. Art Nouveau blossomed here, as did Cub-

ism. The House of the Black Madonna's Cubist exterior is a marvel of rectangular windows and cornices—stand back and see how masterfully it makes its statement while mixing with its neighbors...then get up close and study the details. The interior houses a Cubist café (the rec-ommended Grand Café Orient,

one flight up the parabolic spiral staircase)—complete with cube-shaped chairs and square rolls. The Kubista gallery in the far corner shows more examples of this unique style.

• *The long, skinny square that begins just to the left of the Cubist house is the former fruit market (Ovocný Trh). For a peek at the local university and a historic theater, side-trip to the end of this square, then return to this spot.*

❾ Estates Theater and Charles University

The **Estates Theater** (Stavovské Divadlo) is the fancy green-and-white Neoclassical building at the end of the square. Built in the 1780s in a deliberately Parisian style, it was the prime opera venue in Prague at a time when an Austrian prodigy was changing the course of music. Mozart premiered *Don Giovanni* in this building (with a bronze statue of Il Commendatore, a character from that opera, duly flanking the main entrance), and he directed many of his works here. Today, the Estates Theater continues to produce *The Marriage of Figaro, Don Giovanni,* and *The Magic Flute.*

The main building of Prague's **Charles University,** the Karo-linum, is next door (on the right as you face the theater, tucked down a little courtyard). Prague in the late 1500s was one of the most enlightened places in Europe. The astronomers Tycho Brahe (who tracked the planets) and his assistant Johannes Kepler (who formulated the laws of motion) both worked here. Charles University has always been at the center of Czech political thinking and revolutions, from Jan Hus in the 15th century to the passionately patriotic Czech students who swept communists out of power in the Velvet Revolution. The ground-floor Gothic interior of the Karolinum can be visited for free—find the modern main entrance in the little fenced-off courtyard by the lions fountain (just turn left as you walk past the guard).

• *Return to the House of the Black Madonna, then turn right and head up busy Celetná street to the big, black...*

⑩ Powder Tower

The 500-year-old Powder Tower was the main gate of the old town wall. It also housed the city's gunpowder—hence the name. This is the only surviving bit of the wall that was built to defend the city in the 1400s. (Though you can go inside, it's not worth paying to tour the interior.)

• *Pass regally through the Powder Tower, leaving the Old Town. You'll emerge into a big, busy intersection. To your left is the Municipal House, a cream-colored build-*
ing topped with a green dome. Find a spot with a good view of the facade.

⑪ Municipal House (Obecní Dům)

The Municipal House is the "pearl of Czech Art Nouveau." Art Nouveau flourished during the same period as the Eiffel Tower and Europe's great Industrial Age train stations.

The same engineering prowess and technological advances that went into making those huge erector-set rigid buildings were used by artistic architects to create quite the opposite effect: curvy, organically flowing lines, inspired by vines and curvaceous women. Look at the elaborate wrought-iron balcony—flanked by bronze Atlases hefting their lanterns—and the lovely stained glass (as in the entrance arcade). Mosaics and sculptural knickknacks (see the faces above the windows) made the building's facade colorful and joyous.

PRAGUE

Prague: The Queen of Art Nouveau

Prague is Europe's best city for Art Nouveau. That's the style of art and architecture that flourished throughout Europe around 1900. It was called "nouveau"—or new—because it was associated with all things modern: technology, social progress, and enlightened thinking. Art Nouveau was neo-nothing, but instead a fresh answer to all the revival styles of the late 19th century and an organic response to the Eiffel Tower art of the Industrial Age.

By taking advantage of recent advances in engineering, Art Nouveau liberated the artist in each architect. Notice the curves and motifs expressing originality—every facade is unique. Artists such as Alphonse Mucha believed that the style should apply to all facets of daily life. They designed everything from buildings and furniture to typefaces and cigarette packs.

Though Art Nouveau was born in Paris, it's in Prague where you'll find some of its greatest hits: the Municipal House and nearby buildings, Grand Hotel Europa (on Wenceslas Square), the exuberant facades of the Jewish Quarter, the Jerusalem Synagogue, and—especially—the work of Mucha. You can see his stained-glass window in St. Vitus Cathedral (at Prague Castle) and his art at the excellent Mucha Museum (near Wenceslas Square). Mucha's final masterpiece, *The Slav Epic,* is on display in his hometown of Moravský Krumlov.

The Municipal House was built in the early 1900s, when Czech nationalism was at a fever pitch. Having been ruled by the Austrian Habsburgs for the previous 300 years, the Czechs were demanding independence. This building was drenched in patriotic Czech themes, and all the artists and materials used were Czech. Within a few short years, in 1918, the nation of Czechoslovakia was formed—and the independence proclamation was announced to the people right here, from the balcony of the Municipal House.

The Municipal House interior has some of Europe's finest Art Nouveau decor and is worth ▲▲ (for details, see "Sights in the New Town," later). It's free to enter and wander the public areas.
• *Now head west down Na Příkopě.*

⓬ Na Příkopě, the Old City Wall
The street called Na Příkopě was where the old city wall once stood. More specifically, the name Na Příkopě means "On the Moat," and

you're walking along what was once the moat outside the wall. To your right is the Old Town. To the left, the New. The city was protected on two sides by its river and on the other two sides by its walls (marked by the modern streets called Na Příkopě, Revoluční, and Národní Třída). The only river crossing back then was the fortified Charles Bridge.

• *Continue up Na Příkopě street to an intersection (and nearby Metro stop) called Můstek. To your left stretches the vast expanse of the wide boulevard called...*

PRAGUE

⓭ Wenceslas Square

Wenceslas Square—with the National Museum and landmark statue of St. Wenceslas at the very top—is the centerpiece of Prague's New Town (rated ▲▲▲). This square was originally a thriving horse market. Today, it's a world of high-fashion stores, fine old facades and jarringly modern ones, and fast-food restaurants.

• *Let's plunge back into the Old Town and return to the Old Town Square. Turn around, and with your back to Wenceslas Square, head downhill on the street called Na Můstku—"along the bridge"—that crossed the moat (příkopě) we've been following until now. After one touristy block, Na Můstku jogs slightly to the left and becomes Melantrichova. A block farther along, on the left, is the thriving...*

⓮ Havelská Market

This open-air market, offering crafts and produce, was first set up in the 13th century for the German trading community. Though heavy on souvenirs these days, the market (worth ▲) still feeds hungry locals and vagabonds. Lined with inviting benches, it's an ideal place to enjoy a healthy snack—and merchants are happy to sell a single vegetable or piece of fruit. The market is also a fun place to browse for crafts. The cafés in the old arcades offer a relaxing vantage point from which to view the action.

• *Continue along Melantrichova street. Eventually—after passing increasingly tacky souvenir shops—Melantrichova curves right and spills out at the Old Town Square, right by the Astronomical Clock. At the clock, turn left down Karlova street. The rest of our walk follows Karlova to the Charles Bridge. Begin by heading along the top of the Small Market Square (Malé Náměstí, with lots of outdoor tables), then follow Karlova's twisting course—Karlova street signs keep you on track, and*

Karlův Most signs point to the bridge. Or just go generally downhill and follow the crowds.

PRAGUE

⓯ Karlova Street

Although traffic-free, Karlova street is utterly jammed with tourists as it winds toward the Charles Bridge. But the route has plenty of historic charm if you're able to ignore the contemporary tourism. As you walk, notice historic symbols and signs of shops, which advertised who lived there or what they sold. Cornerstones, designed to protect buildings from careening carriages, also date from centuries past.

The **Klementinum** (which once housed the university's library) is the large building that borders Karlova street on the right. Just past the intersection with Liliová, where the street opens into a little square, turn right through the archway (at #1) and into a tranquil courtyard that feels an eternity away from the touristy hubbub of Karlova. You can also visit the Klementinum's impressive ▲ Baroque interior on a guided tour.

• *Karlova street leads directly to a tall medieval tower that marks the start of Charles Bridge. But before entering the bridge, stop on this side of the river. To the right of the tower is a little park with a great view of both the bridge and the rest of Prague across the river.*

⓰ Charles IV Statue: The Bohemian Golden Age

Start with the statue of the bridge's namesake, Charles IV (1316-1378). Look familiar? He's the guy on the 100-koruna bill. Charles was the Holy Roman Emperor who ruled his vast empire from Prague in the 14th century—a high-water mark in the city's history. The statue shows one of Charles' many accomplishments: He holds a contract establishing Charles University, the first in Central Europe. The women around the pedestal

symbolize the school's four traditional subjects: theology, the arts, law, and medicine.

Charles was the preeminent figure in Europe in the late Middle Ages. His domain encompassed the modern Czech Republic and parts of Germany, Austria, Italy, and the Low Countries.

Charles was cosmopolitan. Born in Prague, raised in Paris, crowned in Rome, and inspired by the luxury-loving pope in Avignon, Charles returned home bringing Europe's culture with him. Besides founding Charles University, he built Charles Bridge, much of Prague Castle and St. Vitus Cathedral, and the New

Town (modeled on Paris). His Golden Bull of 1356 served as Europe's constitution for centuries (and gave anti-Semite Charles first right to the property of Jews). Power-hungry, he expanded his empire through networking and shrewd marriages, not war. Charles traded ideas with the Italian poet Petrarch and imported artists from France, Italy, and Flanders. Under Charles, Prague became the most cultured city in Europe. Seemingly the only thing Charles did not succeed in was renaming Prague: He wanted it to be called "New Jerusalem."

Now look up at the **bridge tower** (which you can climb for wonderful views; see next stop). Built by Charles, it's one of the finest Gothic gates anywhere. The statuary shows the 14th-century hierarchy of society: people at street level, above them kings, and bishops above the kings.

• *Stroll to the riverside, belly up to the banister, and take in the...*

⓱ View from the River

Before you are the Vltava River and Charles Bridge. Across the river, atop the hill, is Prague Castle topped by the prickly spires of St. Vitus Cathedral.

Prague Castle has been the seat of power in this region for over a thousand years, since the time of Wenceslas. By some measures, it's the biggest castle on earth.

The **Vltava River** (from Old German "wild waters") is better known by the modern German mutation of the same name, Moldau. It bubbles up from the Šumava Hills in southern Bohemia and runs 270 miles through a diverse landscape, like a thread connecting the Czech people. As we've learned, the Czechs have struggled heroically to carve out their identity while surrounded by mightier neighbors—Austrians, Germans, and Russians. The Vltava is their shared artery.

The **view of Charles Bridge** from here is supremely photogenic. The historic stone bridge, commissioned in 1342, connects the Old Town with the district called the Lesser Town at the base of the castle across the river. The bridge is almost seven football fields long, lined with lanterns and 30 statues, and bookended with medieval towers.

You can climb either tower. The one above you, on the **Old Town side** of the river (Staroměstská Mostecká Věž, 138 steps), rewards you with some of Prague's best views: a stunning vista of the bridge and a perfect panorama that reminds you why Prague is called the "Golden City of a Hundred Spires." On the **Lesser Town side** (Malostranská Mostecká Věž), you can huff up 146 steps for fine views of the bridge, the neighborhood rooftops, and the castle. If you're trying to decide which to climb, consider that for snapping photos, the light is better if you climb the Old Town tower early in the day and the Lesser Town tower late in the day (150 Kč to climb each tower, daily 9:00-21:00, April-May and Sept 10:00-19:00, Oct-March until 18:00).

• *Now wander onto the bridge. Make your way slowly across the bridge, checking out several of the statues, all on the right-hand side.*

⓲ Charles Bridge (Karlův Most)

This much-loved ▲▲▲ bridge offers one of the most pleasant and entertaining strolls in Europe. Musicians, artisans, and a constant parade of people make it a festi-

val every day. You can return to this bridge throughout the day to enjoy its various charms. Early and late, it can be enchantingly lonely. The impressively expressive statues on either side of the bridge depict saints.

Partway along the bridge, on your right, find a small **brass relief** showing a cross with five stars embedded in the wall of the bridge (it's just below the little grate that sits on top of the stone banister). The relief depicts a figure floating in the river, with a semicircle of stars above him. This marks the traditional spot where the Czech patron saint John of Nepomuk is believed to have been tossed off the bridge and into the river.

For the rest of that story, continue past two more statue groups to the bronze Baroque statue of **St. John of Nepomuk,** with the

five golden stars encircling his head. This statue always draws a crowd. John was a 14th-century priest to whom the queen confessed all her sins. According to a 17th-century legend, the king wanted to know his wife's secrets, but Father John dutifully refused to tell. The shiny plaque at the base of the statue shows what happened next: John was tortured and killed by being thrown off the bridge. The plaque shows the heave-ho. When he hit the water, five stars appeared, signifying his purity. Notice the date on the inscription—1683. This oldest statue on the bridge was unveiled on the supposed 300th anniversary of the martyr's death. Traditionally, people believe that touching the St. John plaque will make a wish come true. But you get only one chance in life to make this wish, and you may never tell anyone what that wish is.

• *A good way to end this walk is to enjoy the city and river* ⑲ *view from the bridge.*

From here, you can continue across the bridge to the Lesser Town (Kampa Island, on your left as you cross the bridge, is a tranquil spot to explore; for more details, see "Sights in the Lesser Town," later). You can also hike or take the tram up to the castle (a 10-minute walk to the right is the Malostranská stop for the Metro or for handy tram #22 or #23). Or retrace your steps across the bridge to enjoy more time in the Old Town.

Sights in the Old Town (Staré Město)

My Old Town and Charles Bridge Walk, earlier, covers the main sights in this area: the **Old Town Square, Týn Church, Old Town Hall/Astronomical Clock, Church of St. James,** and **Charles Bridge.** It also points out key landmarks, including **the Ungelt** courtyard, **House of the Black Madonna,** and **Powder Tower.**

Here are some additional sights in the Old Town. ∩ My Prague City Walk audio tour covers some of these.

JEWISH QUARTER (JOSEFOV)

Prague's Jewish Quarter, worth ▲▲▲, is the best place in Europe to learn about this important culture and faith interwoven in the fabric of Central and Eastern Europe. Within a three-block radius, several original synagogues, a cemetery, and other landmarks survive, today collected into one big, well-presented sight known as the Jewish Museum in Prague. The impressive Old-New Synagogue completes the picture. It can get crowded here, so time your visit carefully (early or late is best). For background on typical synagogue architecture, see the sidebar on page 305.

Jewish Museum in Prague (Židovské Muzeum v Praze)

The "museum" consists of four synagogues, a ceremonial hall, and a cemetery—each described later and covered by the same ticket.

Cost and Hours: 400 Kč, 550 Kč combo-ticket includes Old-New Synagogue; open Sun-Fri 9:00-18:00, Nov-March until

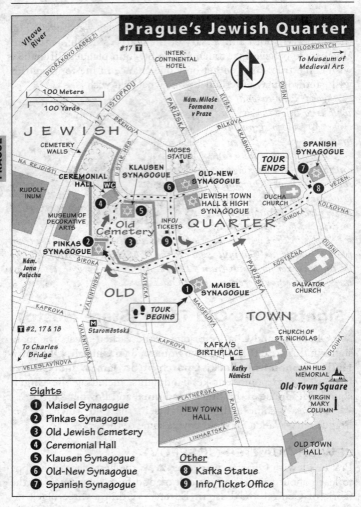

Prague's Jewish Quarter

Sights
1. Maisel Synagogue
2. Pinkas Synagogue
3. Old Jewish Cemetery
4. Ceremonial Hall
5. Klausen Synagogue
6. Old-New Synagogue
7. Spanish Synagogue

Other
8. Kafka Statue
9. Info/Ticket Office

16:30, closed Sat—the Jewish Sabbath—and on Jewish holidays, website lists all closures; 300 Kč audioguide is overkill, +420 222 317 191, www.jewishmuseum.cz.

Buying Tickets and Avoiding Lines: Tickets are sold in person and on the Jewish Museum and Old-New Synagogue websites. In person, buy your ticket at the Maisel or Klausen synagogues or at the Information Center at Maiselova 15 (near the intersection with Široká street). Avoid buying at the Pinkas Synagogue, which tends to have long lines. The Pinkas Synagogue can be packed, especially between 10:00 and 11:30, so consider getting there right as it opens or later in the day.

Dress Code: Men are expected to cover their heads when entering an active synagogue or cemetery. While you'll see many visitors ignoring this custom, it's respectful to bring a cap or borrow a museum-issued yarmulke.

Getting There: The Jewish Quarter is an easy walk from Old Town Square, up delightful Pařížská street (next to the green-domed Church of St. Nicholas). The Staroměstská Metro stop is just a couple of blocks away.

○ Self-Guided Tour: You can see the sights in any order. This tour starts at the Maisel Synagogue; alternatively, you could plan your time around the crowded Pinkas Synagogue. Ideally, be there right as it opens to avoid the crowds.

Maisel Synagogue (Maiselova Synagóga): This pastel-colored Neo-Gothic synagogue, originally built as a private place of worship, now houses an interactive exhibit on Jewish history in the Czech lands up until 1800 and a few precious medieval objects. During the Nazi occupation, employees of the Jewish Museum used this building as a warehouse for a vast collection of Judaica gathered from vanished communities around the country. Rumor had it that Hitler planned to turn this collection into a "Museum of the Extinct Race."

Inside, the interactive exhibit retraces a thousand years of Jewish history in Bohemia and Moravia. Well explained in English, topics include the origin of the Star of David, Jewish mysticism, the Golem legend, the history of discrimination, and the creation of Prague's ghetto. Pre-WWII photographs of small-town synagogues from the region are projected on a large screen. Notice the eastern wall, with the holy ark containing a precious Torah mantel. Look for the banner of the Prague Jewish Butchers Guild, the emblem of the Cobblers Guild, a medieval seal ring, and the bema grillwork from Prague's demolished Zigeuner Synagogue.

Pinkas Synagogue (Pinkasova Synagóga): For many visitors, this house of worship—today used as a memorial to Holocaust victims—is the most powerful of the Jewish Quarter sights.

Enter and go down the steps leading to the **main hall** of this small late-Gothic/early-Renaissance synagogue. Notice the old stone-and-wrought-iron bema in the middle, the niche for the ark at the far end, the crisscross vaulting overhead, and the Art Nouveau stained glass filling the place with light.

But the focus of this synagogue is its walls, inscribed with the handwritten **names** of 77,297 Czech Jews sent to the gas chambers at Auschwitz and other camps. Czech Jews were especially hard hit by the Holocaust. More than 155,000 of them passed through the nearby Terezín camp alone. Most died with no grave marker, but they are remembered here.

The names are carefully organized: Family names are in red,

followed in black by the individual's first name, birthday, and date of death (if known) or date of deportation. You can tell by the dates that families often perished together. The names are gathered in groups by hometowns (listed in gold, as well as on placards at the base of the wall). As you ponder this sad sight, you'll hear the somber reading of the names alternating with a cantor singing the Psalms.

On your way out, watch on the right for the easy-to-miss stairs up to the small **Terezín Children's Art Exhibit.** Well described in English, these drawings were made by Jewish children imprisoned at Terezín, 40 miles northwest of Prague (a worthy day trip from here). This is where the Nazis shipped Prague's Jews for processing before transporting them east to death camps. Thirty-five thousand Jews died at Terezín of disease and starvation, and many tens of thousands more died in other camps. Of the 8,000 children transported from Terezín, only 240 came back. The teacher who led the drawing lessons and hid these artworks believed children could use imagination to liberate their minds from the camp. Their art survives to defy fate.

Old Jewish Cemetery (Starý Židovský Hřbitov): Hiding behind a wall and sitting above the street level, this is where Prague's Jews buried their dead. A stroll through the crooked tombstones is a poignant experience.

Meander along a path through 12,000 evocative tombstones. They're old, eroded, inscribed in Hebrew, and leaning this way and that. A few of the dead have larger ark-shaped tombs. Most have a simple epitaph with the name, date, and a few of the deceased's virtues.

From 1439 until 1787, this was the only burial ground allowed for the Jews of Prague. Over time, the bodies had to be stacked on top of each other—seven or eight deep—so the number of people buried here is actually closer to 85,000. Graves were never relocated because of the Jewish belief that, once buried, a body should not be moved. Layer by layer, the cemetery grew into a small plateau. Tune in to the noise of passing cars outside and you realize that you're several feet above the modern street level—which is already high above the medieval level.

People place pebbles on honored tombstones. This custom, a sign of respect, shows that the dead have not been forgotten and recalls the old days, when rocks were placed upon a sandy gravesite to keep the body covered. Others leave scraps of paper that contain prayers and wishes.

Ceremonial Hall (Obřadní Síň): This rustic stone tower (1911), at the edge of the cemetery, was a mortuary house used to prepare the body and perform purification rituals before burial. The inside is painted in fanciful, flowery Neo-Romanesque style. It's filled with a worthwhile exhibition on Jewish medicine, death, and burial traditions.

Klausen Synagogue (Klauzová Synagóga): This 17th-century synagogue is devoted to Jewish religious practices. The ground-floor displays touch on Jewish holidays. Upstairs, exhibits illustrate the rituals of everyday Jewish life. It starts at birth. There are good-luck amulets to ensure a healthy baby, and a wooden cradle that announces, "This little one will become big." A male baby is circumcised (see the knife). The boy or girl grows to celebrate a coming-of-age Bar or Bat Mitzvah around age 12 or 13. Marriage takes place under a canopy, and the couple sets up their home—the exhibit ends with some typical furnishings.

Note that the Spanish Synagogue—described next—is a few blocks away from the core of the Jewish Quarter. Before heading over there, consider visiting the nearby **Old-New Synagogue** (described at the end of this section).

Spanish Synagogue (Španělská Synagóga): Called "Spanish" though its design is Moorish (which was all the rage when this was built in the 19th century), this has the most opulently decorated interior of all the synagogues. It marked a time of relative wealth and importance for Prague's Jews, who in this era were increasingly welcome in the greater community and (in many cases) adopted a reformed approach to worship. Exhibits explain the lives of Czech Jews in the 19th and early 20th centuries, when they believed they were living their best days yet...unaware that the Holocaust was looming.

The decor is exotic and awe-inspiring. Intricate interweaving designs (of stars and vines) cover every inch of the red-gold and green walls and ceiling. A rose window with a stylized Star of David graces the ark.

The new synagogue housed a new movement within Judaism—a Reform congregation—which worshipped in a more modern way. The bema has been moved to the front of the synagogue, so the officiant faces the congregation. There's also a prominent organ (upper right) to accompany the singing.

Displays of Jewish history bring us through the 18th, 19th, and tumultuous 20th centuries to today. In the 1800s, Jews were increasingly accepted and successful in the greater society. But tolerance brought a dilemma—was it better to assimilate within the dominant culture or to join the growing Zionist homeland movement? To reform the religion or to remain orthodox?

Upstairs, the **balcony exhibits** focus on Czech Jews in the

1900s. Start in the area near the organ, which explains the modern era of Jewish Prague, including the late 19th-century development of Josefov. Then work your way around the balcony, with exhibits on Jewish writers (Franz Kafka), philosophers (Edmund Husserl), and other notables (Freud). This intellectual renaissance came to an abrupt halt with World War II and the mass deportations to Terezín. The final display covers the modern nation of Israel. Finish your visit across the landing in the **Winter Synagogue,** showing a trove of silver—Kiddush cups, Hanukkah lamps, Sabbath candlesticks, and Torah ornaments.

Old-New Synagogue (Staronová Synagóga)

The oldest and most important building in the Jewish Quarter, the Old-New Synagogue goes back at least seven centuries. While the exterior seems simple compared to ornate neighboring townhouses, the interior is atmospherically 13th century.

Cost and Hours: 220 Kč, 550 Kč combo-ticket includes Jewish Museum in Prague; Sun-Thu 9:00-18:00, off-season until 17:00, Fri closes one hour before sunset, closed Sat and on Jewish holidays; +420 222 317 191, www.synagogue.cz.

Visiting the Synagogue: Built in 1270, this is the oldest synagogue in Central Europe (and some say the oldest still-working synagogue in all of Europe). The name may come from the fact that it was "New" when built but became "Old" when other, newer synagogues came on the scene. The exterior is simple, with a unique sawtooth gable. Standing like a reinforced bunker, it feels as though it has survived plenty of hard times.

As you enter, you descend a few steps below street level to the 13th-century street level and the medieval world.

The **interior** is pure Gothic—thick pillars, soaring arches, and narrow lancet windows. If it looks like a church, well, the architects were Christians. The stonework is original, and the woodwork (the paneling and benches) is also old. This was one of the first Gothic buildings in Prague.

Seven centuries later, it's still a working synagogue. There's the stone bema in the middle where the Torah is read aloud, and the ark at the far end, where the sacred scrolls are kept. To the right of the ark, one chair is bigger, with a Star of David above it. This chair always remains empty out of respect for great rabbis of the past. Where's the women's gallery? Here, women worshipped in rooms that flanked the hall, watching the service through those horizontal windows in the walls.

Before leaving, check out the **lobby** (the long hall where you show your ticket). It has two fortified old lockers—in which the most heavily taxed community in medieval Prague stored its money in anticipation of the taxman's arrival.

Prague's Jewish Quarter

Jews first came to Prague in the 10th century. The least habitable, marshy area closest to the bend was allotted to the Jewish community. The Jewish Quarter's main intersection (Maiselova and Široká streets) was the meeting point of two medieval trade routes. For centuries, Jews coexisted—at times tensely—with their non-Jewish Czech neighbors.

During the Crusades in the 12th century, the pope declared that Jews and Christians should not live together. Jews had to wear yellow badges, and their quarter was walled in and became a ghetto (minority neighborhood) of wooden houses and narrow lanes. In the 16th and 17th centuries, Prague had one of the biggest ghettos in Europe, with 11,000 inhabitants. Within its six gates, Prague's Jewish Quarter was a gaggle of 200 wooden buildings.

Faced with institutionalized bigotry and harassment, Jews relied mainly on profits from moneylending (forbidden to Christians) and community solidarity to survive. While their money bought them protection (the kings taxed Jewish communities heavily), it was often also a curse. Throughout Europe, when times got tough and Christian debts to the Jewish community mounted, entire Jewish communities were evicted or killed. The worst pogroms were in 1096 and in 1389, when around 3,000 Jews were killed.

In 1781, Emperor Josef II, motivated more by economic concerns than by religious freedom, eased much of the discrimination against Jews. In 1848, the Jewish Quarter's walls were torn down, and the neighborhood—named Josefov in honor of the emperor who provided this small measure of tolerance—was incorporated as a district of the Old Town.

In 1897, ramshackle Josefov was razed and replaced by a new modern town—the original 31 streets and 220 buildings became 10 streets and 83 buildings. They leveled the medieval-era buildings (except the synagogues) and turned this into perhaps Europe's finest Art Nouveau neighborhood, boasting stately facades with gables, turrets, elegant balconies, mosaics, statues, and all manner of architectural marvels. By the 1930s, Prague's Jewish community was prospering.

But then World War II hit. Of the 55,000 Jews living in Prague in 1939, just 10,000 survived the Holocaust to see liberation in 1945. And in the communist era—when the atheistic regime was also anti-Semitic—recovery was slow.

Today, Prague's Jewish community numbers about 7,000 people. While a modern grid plan has replaced the higgledy-piggledy medieval streets of old, Široká ("Wide Street") remains the main street, and Jewish-themed shops and restaurants add ambience to the neighborhood.

NORTH OF THE OLD TOWN SQUARE, NEAR THE RIVER

Stray just a couple of blocks north of the Old Town Square and you'll find a surprisingly tourist-free world of shops and cafés, pastel buildings with decorative balconies and ornamental statues, winding lanes, cobblestone streets, and mosaic sidewalks. It's also home to this fine, underrated museum.

▲▲Museum of Medieval Art (Středověké umění v Čechách a Střední Evropě)

Prague flourished in the 14th century, and the city has amassed an impressive collection of altarpieces and paintings from that age. Today, this art is housed in the tranquil former Convent of St. Agnes, which was founded in the 13th century by a Czech princess-turned-nun as the first hospital in Prague. A visit here is your best chance to see exquisite medieval art in Prague.

Cost and Hours: 250 Kč; Tue-Sun 10:00-18:00, closed Mon; two blocks northeast of the Spanish Synagogue, along the river at Anežská 12; +420 224 810 628, www.ngprague.cz.

Sights in the New Town (Nové Město)

Enough of pretty, medieval Prague—let's leap into the modern era. The New Town, with Wenceslas Square as its focal point, is today's urban Prague, characterized by bustling boulevards and interesting neighborhoods. Even today, the New Town is separated from the Old Town by a "moat" (the literal meaning of the street called Na Příkopě). As you cross busy Na Příkopě, you leave the medieval cuteness and souvenir shops behind, and enter a town of malls and fancy shops that cater to locals and visitors alike. The New Town is one of the best places to view Prague's remarkable Art Nouveau art and architecture, and to learn more about its communist past.

 Download my Prague City Walk audio tour, which covers some of these sights.

WENCESLAS SQUARE AND NEARBY

These sights are on or within a few blocks of the elongated main square of the New Town.

▲▲▲Wenceslas Square Walk (Václavské Náměstí)

More a broad boulevard than a square, this city landmark is named for St. Wenceslas, whose equestrian statue overlooks the square's top end. Wenceslas Square functions as a stage for modern Czech history: The creation of the Czechoslovak state was celebrated here in 1918; in 1968, the Soviets suppressed huge popular demonstrations (called the Prague Spring) at the square; and in 1989, more than 300,000 Czechs and Slovaks converged here to demand their freedom (in the Velvet Revolution). Today, it's a busy commercial thoroughfare.

● **Self-Guided Walk:** For a taste of Prague's 20th-century history, take a stroll beginning at the top of the square. (To get here quickly, ride the Metro to the Muzeum stop.)

PRAGUE

• *Begin at the big...*

Statue of Duke Wenceslas I: The "Good King" of Christmas-carol fame was actually a wise and benevolent 10th-century

duke. Václav (as he's called by locals) united the Czech people, back when this land was known as Bohemia. A rare example of a well-educated and literate ruler, Wenceslas Christianized and lifted the culture. He astutely allied the powerless Czechs with the Holy Roman Empire of the German nation. And he began to fortify Prague's castle as a center of Czech government. After his murder in 929, Wenceslas was canonized as a saint. He became a symbol of Czech nationalism (and appears on the 20 Kč coin). Later kings knelt before his tomb to be crowned. And he remains an icon of Czech unity whenever the nation has to rally. Like King Arthur in England, Wenceslas is more legend than history, but he symbolizes the country's birth.

The statue is surrounded by the four other Czech patron saints. Notice the focus on books. A small nation without great military power, the Czechs have thinkers as national heroes, not warriors.

And this statue is a popular meeting point. Locals like to say, "I'll meet you under the horse's tail."

• *Circle behind the statue and stand below that tail; turn your attention to the impressive building at the top of Wenceslas Square.*

National Museum: This grand, lavishly restored building dates from the 19th century, when modern nation-states were forming in Europe and the Czech people were still living under the auspices of Austria's Habsburg Empire. Bold structures like this Neo-Renaissance building were a way to show the world that the Czech lands had a distinct culture and a heritage of precious artifacts, and that Czechs deserved their own nation.

Look closely at the columns on the building's facade. Those

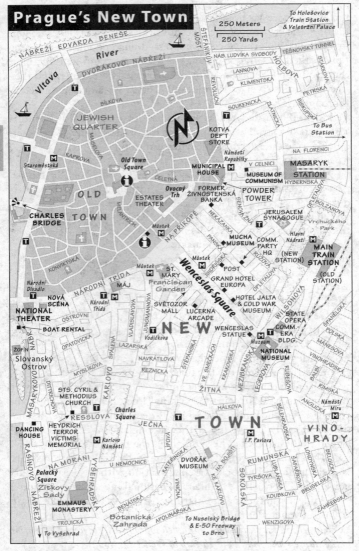

Prague's New Town

light-colored patches (meticulously preserved during the recent renovation) are covering holes where Soviet bullets hit during the 1968 crackdown. The state-of-the-art interior is filled with diverse exhibits ranging from minerals to modern history (250 Kč, daily 10:00-18:00 plus most Wed from 9:00, www.nm.cz).

• *To the left of the National Museum (as you face it) is a...*

   Communist-Era Building: This out-of-place modern struc-

The Prague Spring and Its Fall

In January 1968, the Slovak politician Alexander Dubček replaced the aging apparatchiks at the helm of the Communist Party of Czechoslovakia. Handsome and relatively youthful, Dubček used the brand of a smiling playboy; he appeared on magazine covers in his Speedo, about to dive into a swimming pool. Young Czechs and Slovaks embraced Dubček as a potential hero of liberalization.

In April, Dubček introduced his "Action Program," designed to tiptoe away from strict and stifling Soviet commu-

nism and forge a more moderate Czechoslovak variation. Censorship eased, travel restrictions were relaxed, state companies began forming joint ventures with Western firms, money poured into the sciences, and a newspaper called *Tomorrow* (rather than *Today*) became the most popular in the country. Plays put on at the Semafor Theater (in today's Světozor mall) lampooned Soviet leader Brezhnev and his ilk. During this so-called "Prague Spring," optimism soared.

But then, around midnight on August 20, 1968, the thundering sound of enormous airplanes ripped across the floodlit rooftops of Prague. The Soviets had dispatched over 200,000 Warsaw Pact troops to invade Czechoslovakia, airlifting tanks right into the capital city. Dubček and his team were arrested and taken to Moscow. Czechs and Slovaks took to the streets, boycotting and striking. Tanks rolled through Wenceslas Square, spraying protesters with bullets...some of which are still embedded in the National Museum's pillars. Over the course of the occupation, 72 Czechs and Slovaks were killed.

Dubček stepped down and went into internal exile, and his successor—the hardliner Gustáv Husák—immediately pursued a policy of "normalization." People who refused to sign a petition commending the "Russian Liberation" were fired from their jobs and forced to find worse ones. Some protesters—including Jan Palach—went to the extreme of setting themselves on fire to protest against the regime. Tens of thousands of Czechs and Slovaks reluctantly emigrated to the West, fearing what might come next.

While the ill-fated tale of the Prague Spring is pessimistic, it provides an insightful bookend to what happened 21 years later: The children of the generation that suffered Czechoslovakia's bitterest disappointment ushered in mass demonstrations that ended this dark era.

ture once housed the rubber-stamp Czechoslovak Parliament back when it voted in lockstep with Moscow. Between 1994 and 2008, this building was home to Radio Free Europe. After communism fell, RFE lost some of its funding and could no longer afford its Munich headquarters. In gratitude for its broadcasts—which had kept the people of Eastern Europe in touch with real news—the Czech government offered this building to RFE for 1 Kč a year. But as RFE energetically beamed its American message deep into the Muslim world from here, it drew attention—and threats—from Al-Qaeda. In 2009, RFE moved to a new fortress-like headquarters literally across the cemetery wall from Franz Kafka's grave (an easier-to-defend locale). Now this is an annex of the National Museum.

• *Start walking down Wenceslas Square. Pause about 30 yards along, at the little patch of bushes. In the ground on the downhill side of those bushes is a…*

Memorial to the Victims of 1969: After the Russian crackdown of 1968, a young philosophy student named Jan Palach,

inspired by a video of monks immolating themselves in protest in Vietnam, decided that the best way to stoke the flame of independence was to do the same right here. On January 16, 1969, Palach stood on the steps of the National Museum and ignited his body. He died a few days later. A month later, another student did the same thing, followed by another. Czechs are keen on anniversaries, and 20 years after Palach's defining act, in 1989, hundreds of Czechs gathered here again in protest. A sense of new possibility swept through the city, and 10 months later, the communists were history.

• *Farther down the square, locate the building on the right with the beige travertine facade (and many balconies). This is the…*

Jalta Hotel and Cold War Museum: This building is most representative of the 1950s Neoclassical, Socialist Realist style. Designed at the height of the Cold War as a hotel for VIPs, it came with an underground crisis-fallout shelter that visiting Soviet generals could use as a command center in case nuclear war broke out. The bunkers were recently refurbished back to their original state by a group of Czechoslovak army fans and converted into the ▲**Cold War Museum,** with a command room, hospital room, spying room (showing you how an operator tapped telephone conversations), and an air-filtering facility (visits by tour only, 400 Kč for one-hour tour in English, departing daily at 11:00, 13:00, 14:30, and 16:00 from inside Jalta Hotel, www.en.muzeum-studene-valky.cz).

• *Continue down Wenceslas Square.*

Architecture Along Wenceslas Square: As you walk, you'll notice the architecture is unlike the historic Old Town—nearly everything here is from the past two centuries. Wenceslas Square is a showcase of Prague's many architectural styles: You'll see Neo-Gothic, Neo-Renaissance, and Neo-Baroque from the 19th century. There's curvaceous Art Nouveau from around 1900. And there's the modernist response to Art Nouveau—Functionalism from the mid-20th century, where the watchword was "form follows function" and beauty took a back seat to practicality. You'll see buildings from the 1950s communist era, forgettable glass-and-steel buildings of the 1970s, modern stores from the 2000s, and new construction.

The Velvet Revolution: Opposite Grand Hotel Europa (on the left side of the square), find the Marks & Spencer building and its **balcony** (partly obscured by trees).

Picture the scene on this square on a cold November night in 1989. Czechoslovakia had been oppressed for the previous 40 years by communist Russia. But now the Soviet empire was beginning to crumble, jubilant Germans were dancing on top of the shattered Berlin Wall, and the Czechs were getting a whiff of freedom.

Czechoslovakia's revolution began with a bunch of teenagers, who—following a sanctioned gathering—decided to march on Wenceslas Square (see sidebar). They were surrounded and beaten by the communist riot police, and days later their enraged parents, friends, and other members of the community poured into this square to protest. Night after night, this huge square was filled with more than 300,000 ecstatic Czechs and Slovaks who believed freedom was at hand. Each night they would jingle their key chains in the air as if saying to their communist leaders, "It's time for you to go home now." Finally, they gathered and found that their communist overlords had left—and freedom was theirs.

On that night, as thousands filled this square, a host of famous people appeared on that balcony to greet the crowd. There was a well-known priest and a rock star famous for his rebellion against authority. There was Alexander Dubček, the hero of the Prague Spring reforms of 1968. And there was Václav Havel, the charismatic playwright who had spent years in prison, becoming a symbol of resistance—a kind of Czech Nelson Mandela. Now he was free. Havel's voice boomed over the gathered masses. He proclaimed the resignation of the Politburo and the imminent freedom of the Republic of Czechoslovakia. He pulled out a ring of keys and jingled it. Thousands of keys jingled back in response to indicate time was up.

PRAGUE

The Velvet Revolution of 1989

On the afternoon of November 17, 1989, 30,000 students gathered in Prague's New Town to commemorate the 50th anniversary of the suppression of student protests by the Nazis, which had led to the closing of Czech universities through the end of World War II. Remember, this was just a few weeks after the fall of the Berlin Wall, and the Czechs were feeling the winds of change blowing across Central Europe. The 1989 demonstration—initially planned by the Communist Youth as a celebration of the communist victory over fascism—spontaneously turned into a protest *against* the communist regime. "You are just like the Nazis!" shouted the students. The demonstration was supposed to end in the National Cemetery at Vyšehrad (the hill just south of the New Town). But when the planned events concluded in Vyšehrad, the students decided to march on toward Wenceslas Square...and make some history.

As they worked their way north along the Vltava River toward the New Town's main square, the students were careful to keep their demonstration peaceful. Any hint of violence, the demonstrators knew, would incite brutal police retaliation. Instead, as the evening went on, the absence of police became conspicuous. (In the 1980s, the police never missed a chance to participate in any demonstration...preferably outnumbering the demonstrators.) At about 20:00, as the students marched down Národní Třída toward Wenceslas Square, three rows of police suddenly blocked the demonstration at the corner of Národní and Spálená streets. A few minutes later, military vehicles with fences on their bumpers (having crossed the bridge by the National Theater) appeared behind the marching students. This new set of cops compressed the demonstrators into the stretch of Národní Třída between Voršilská and Spálená. The end of Mikulandská street was also blocked, and police were hiding inside every house entry. The students were trapped.

At 21:30, the "Red Berets" (a special anti-riot commando force known for its brutality) arrived. The Red Berets lined up on both sides of this corridor. To get out, the trapped students had to run through the passageway as they were beaten from the left and right. Police trucks ferried captured students around the corner to the police headquarters (on Bartolomějská) for interrogation.

The next day, university students throughout Czechoslovakia decided to strike. Actors from theaters in Prague and Bratislava joined the student protest. Two days later, the students' parents—shocked by the attacks on their children—marched into Wenceslas Square. Sparked by the events of November 17, 1989, the wave of peaceful demonstrations ended later that year on December 29, with the election of Václav Havel as the president of a free Czechoslovakia.

In previous years, the communist authorities would have sent in tanks to crush the impudent masses. But by 1989, the Soviet empire was collapsing, and the Czech government was shaky. Locals think that Soviet head of state Mikhail Gorbachev (mindful of the Tiananmen Square massacre a few months before) might have made a phone call recommending a nonviolent response. Whatever happened, the communist regime was overthrown with hardly any blood being spilled. It was done through sheer people power—thanks to the masses of defiant Czechs who gathered here peacefully in Wenceslas Square, and Slovaks doing the same in Bratislava. A British journalist called it "The Velvet Revolution," and the name caught on in the West. Locals call it simply "The Revolution."

• *A block from the bottom of Wenceslas Square, look for the gate tucked behind the Jungmann statue on Jungmannovo Náměstí. Head through to find the...*

Franciscan Garden: Ahhh! This garden's white benches and spreading rosebushes are a universe away from the fast beat of the city. The peacefulness reflects the purpose of its Franciscan origin. St. Francis, the founder of the order, thought God's presence could be found in nature. In the 1600s, Prague became an important center for a group of Franciscans from Ireland. Enjoy the herb garden and children's playground. (A WC is just out the far side of the garden.)

• *Exit the garden at the opposite corner from where you entered (past the little yellow gardening pavilion and the herb garden). Continue straight ahead to reach the Old Town or turn right along Na Příkopě street to visit the Mucha Museum, Municipal House, or Museum of Communism. For places farther afield, hop on the Metro at Můstek. The rest of Prague is yours to enjoy.*

▲Mucha Museum (Muchovo Muzeum)

This enjoyable little museum features a small selection of the insistently likeable art of Alphonse Mucha (MOO-kah, 1860-1939), whose florid style helped define what became known as Art Nouveau. It's all crammed into a too-small space, some of the art is faded, and the admission price is steep—but there's no better place to gain an understanding of Mucha's talent, his career, and the influence he's had on the world art scene. And the museum, partly overseen by Mucha's grandson, gives you a peek at some of the posters that made Mucha

PRAGUE

famous. You'll learn how these popular patriotic banners, filled with Czech symbols and expressing his people's ideals and aspirations, aroused the national spirit. Enjoy decorative posters from his years in Paris, including his celebrated ads for the French actress Sarah Bernhardt. Check out the photographs of his models, which Mucha later re-created in pencil or paint, and be sure to see the 30-minute film on the artist's life. Then peruse the well-stocked gift shop.

Cost and Hours: 300 Kč, daily 10:00-18:00, good English descriptions, two blocks off Wenceslas Square at Panská 7, +420 224 233 355, www.mucha.cz.

NEAR NA PŘÍKOPĚ

At the bottom of Wenceslas Square, the street running to the right is called Na Příkopě, meaning "On the Moat." It is a showcase of Art Nouveau: Be sure to keep your eyes up as you stroll here. City tour buses leave from along this street, which also offers plenty of shopping temptations.

▲Museum of Communism (Muzeum Komunismu)

This small museum offers a fascinating look at the "dream, reality, and nightmare" of communism. You'll walk through the years (with good English descriptions) between the 1918 birth of Czechoslovakia and World War II, when the Soviets "liberated" Czechoslovakia from the Nazis. The communists quickly came to power, with statues of Stalin and propaganda permeating Czech society. Then the dark side: attempted escapes, police, interrogation, and torture, as a video on the wall shows images that humanize the tragedy of this period. A section on the eventual fall of communism is inspiring.

Cost and Hours: 380 Kč, daily 9:00-20:00, a block off Republic Square at V Celnici 4, +420 224 212 966, www.museumofcommunism.com.

▲▲Municipal House (Obecní Dům)

The cultural and artistic leaders who financed this Art Nouveau masterpiece (1905-1911) wanted a ceremonial palace to reinforce self-awareness of the Czech nation. While the exterior is impressive, the highlight is the interior—and at least part of it is free. To extend your Art Nouveau bliss, take a guided tour or attend a concert here.

Cost and Hours: The entrance halls and public spaces are free to explore (daily 10:00-

18:00). For an in-depth look at all the sumptuous halls and banquet rooms, join a one-hour **tour** (290 Kč, English tours—usually 3/day departing between 11:00 and 17:00; limited to 35 people—buy your ticket online or from the ground-floor shop where tours depart; Náměstí Republiky 5, +420 222 002 101, www.obecnidum.cz).

Concerts: Performances are held regularly in the lavish Smetana Hall (schedule on website). Note that many concerts are promoted as if they are held in the Municipal House, but are performed in a smaller, less impressive hall in the same building.

Visiting the House: Don't be timid about poking around the interior, which is open to the public. Having lunch or a drink in one of the eateries is a great way to experience the decor, but you can also just glimpse them from the doorway (as you "check out the menu").

Enter under the green, wrought-iron arcade. In the **rotunda,** admire the mosaic floor, stained glass, woodwork doorway, and lighting fixtures. To the left is a recommended **café** *(kavárna)*—a harmony of woodwork, marble, metal, and glittering chandeliers.

From the rotunda, step into the **lobby,** where you can look up the staircase that leads to the main concert hall (no tourist access upstairs). Also in the lobby is the box office, selling concert tickets and guided English tours of the building.

Facing the staircase, go right and head **downstairs**—yes, tourists are welcome there. Admire the colorful tiles in the stairwell and more colorful tiles in the downstairs main room. Look for the plaster model of this building and the adjacent Powder Tower, which shows how the angled facade conceals a surprisingly large performance space. Also check out the **American Bar** (salute the US flags above the bar) and the **Plzeňská Restaurant** (with its dark-wood booths and colorful tile scenes of happy peasants). Finish your tour by going back upstairs to find the **Modernista shop** (tucked to the left as you face the main staircase)—full of fancy teacups and jewelry.

Sights in the Lesser Town
(Malá Strana)

Huddled under the castle on the west bank of the river just over the Charles Bridge, the Lesser Town is a Baroque time capsule. It's the oldest of the four towns that make up Prague, dating to the early 10th century. It's also the best-preserved part of the city, with only a few buildings here dating from after 1800.

Though underappreciated, there is nothing "lesser" about this part of town. If you like hidden, quiet alleyways rather than busy commercial bustle, you'll want to take time to explore the neighborhood.

LESSER TOWN SQUARE AND NEARBY

From the end of the Charles Bridge (with TI in tower), Mostecká street leads two blocks up to the Lesser Town Square (Malostranské Náměstí) and the huge Church of St. Nicholas. This square is split into an upper and lower part by the domineering Church of St. Nicholas. A Baroque plague column oversees the upper square (and a handy Via Musica ticket office is on the uphill side).

Church of St. Nicholas (Kostel Sv. Mikuláše)

When the Jesuits came to Prague, they found the perfect piece of real estate for their church and its associated school—right on the Lesser Town Square. The church (built 1703-1760) is the best example of High Baroque in town.

Cost and Hours: Church—100 Kč, daily 9:00-18:00, Nov-Feb until 16:00; tower climb—100 Kč, daily 10:00-22:00, shorter hours in winter, tower entrance is outside the right transept.

Visiting the Church: The church's interior is giddy with curves and illusions. This is "dynamic Baroque," with circles intersecting circles, creating an illusion of movement. Stand directly under the tallest dome and look up. Spin slowly around, greeting four giant statues—the fathers of the Eastern Church. Look up and see the earthly world merging with heaven above.

The **altar** features a lavish gold-plated Nicholas, flanked by the two top Jesuits: the founder, St. Ignatius Loyola, and his missionary follower, St. Francis Xavier—one killing evil, the other spreading the gospel.

Climb the staircase in the left transept up to the **gallery** for a close-up look at a collection of large canvases and illusionary frescoes by Karel Škréta, who is considered the greatest Czech Baroque painter. At first glance, the canvases are utterly dark, but as sunbeams shine through the window, various parts of the paintings brighten. The church walls seem to nearly fuse with the sky, suggesting that happenings on earth are closely connected to heaven.

Tower Climb: For a good look at the city and the church's 250-foot dome, climb the 215 steps up the bell tower. Closed to the public during the communist period, the deck was used by the secret police to spy on activities at the nearby embassies of the US, Britain, and West Germany. There is a good exhibit in English on this aspect, as well as on the May 5, 1945, uprising against the Nazi occupiers.

Concerts: The church hosts evening classical music concerts; tickets are usually on sale at the church ticket desk (500 Kč, generally nightly at 18:00 except Tue, www.stnicholas.cz).

Nerudova Street

This steep, cobbled street, connecting the Lesser Town Square up to the castle, is named for Jan Neruda, a gifted 19th-century journalist. It's lined with old buildings still sporting the characteristic doorway signs (such as two golden suns, a red lion, a green lobster, or three violins) that once served as street addresses. The surviving signs have been carefully restored and protected by law. They represent the family name, the occupation, or the various passions of the people who once inhabited the houses. In the 1770s, in order to run her empire (and collect taxes) more effectively, Habsburg empress Maria Theresa decreed that house numbers were to be used instead of these quaint names. The neighborhood is filled with noble palaces, now generally used as foreign embassies (the American embassy is a couple of blocks to the left as you hike uphill) and as offices of the Czech Parliament.

Kampa Island

One hundred yards from the castle end of the Charles Bridge, stairs on the left lead down to the main square of Kampa Island (mostly created from the rubble of the Lesser Town, after it was devastated in a 1540 fire). The island features relaxing pubs, a breezy park, hippies, lovers, a fine contemporary art gallery, and river access. At the far end of Kampa Square is the park entrance. Midway through the park (on the left) is the former mill building, Sovovy Mlýny. In it is the

PRAGUE

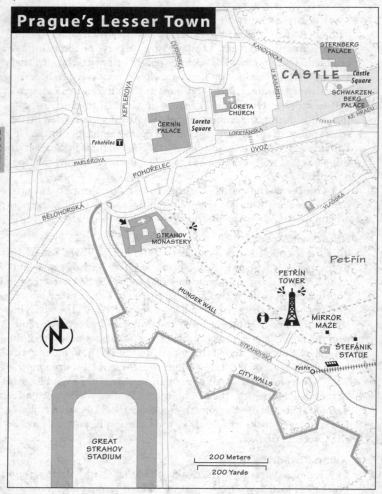

Prague's Lesser Town

STERNBERG PALACE

CASTLE

Castle Square

SCHWARZENBERG PALACE

KE HRADU

ČERNINSKÁ

KANOVNICKÁ

U KASÁREN

KEPLEROVA

LORETA CHURCH

Loreta Square

ČERNÍN PALACE

Pohořelec 🚊

PARLÉŘOVA

LORETÁNSKÁ

ÚVOZ

POHOŘELEC

VLAŠSKÁ

BĚLOHORSKÁ

STRAHOV MONASTERY

Petřín

PETŘÍN TOWER

HUNGER WALL

🛈 ➔ MIRROR MAZE

ŠTEFÁNIK STATUE

STRAHOVSKÁ

Petřín 🚋

CITY WALLS

GREAT STRAHOV STADIUM

200 Meters
200 Yards

Museum Kampa, home to the Jan and Meda Mládek Collection, which features works once prohibited by the former communist regime, as well as other modern artworks (permanent exhibit—190 Kč, all exhibits—350 Kč, daily 10:00-18:00, www.museumkampa.cz).

Returning to Kampa Square, as you leave the park take the first lane on the left, which winds around to a little bridge. The high-water mark at the end of the bridge dates from 1890. The **old water wheel** is the last survivor of many mills that once lined the canal here, powering industry before the arrival of steam power. Each mill had its own protective water spirit or goblin *(vodník)*. Note the one sitting on a tree stump by the wheel.

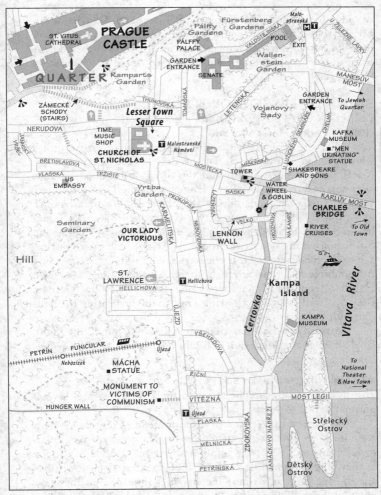

PRAGUE

Lennon Wall (Lennonova Zeď)

Near the old water wheel described earlier and just across the tiny bridge, beneath the trees on the right, is the colorful Lennon Wall.

While V. I. Lenin's ideas hung like a water-soaked trench coat upon the Czech people, singer John Lennon's ideas gave many locals hope and a vision. When Lennon was killed in 1980, this large wall was spontaneously covered with memorial graffiti. Night after night, the police would paint over the "All You Need Is Love" and "Imagine" graffiti. And day after day, it would reappear. Until independence came in 1989, travelers, freedom lovers, and local hippies gathered here. Even today, people come here to imagine. *"John žije"* is Czech for "John lives."

SOUTH OF LESSER TOWN SQUARE
Church of Our Lady Victorious
(Kostel Panny Marie Vítězné)

This otherwise ordinary Carmelite church displays Prague's most worshipped treasure, the Infant of Prague (Pražské Jezulátko). Kneel at the banister in front of the tiny lost-in-gilded-Baroque altar and find the prayer in your language (of the 13 in the folder). Brought to Czech lands during the Habsburg era by a Spanish noblewoman who came to marry a Czech nobleman, the Infant has become a focus of worship and miracle tales in Prague and Spanish-speaking countries. South Americans come on pilgrimage to Prague just to see this one statue. An exhibit upstairs shows tiny embroidered robes given to the Infant, including ones from Habsburg empress Maria Theresa of Austria (1754) and Vietnam (1958), as well as a video showing a nun lovingly dressing the doll-like sculpture.

Cost and Hours: Free, Mon-Sat 9:30-17:00, Sun 13:00-18:00, English-language Mass Sun at 12:00 and Thu at 17:00, Karmelitská 9, www.pragjesu.cz.

▲Petřín Hill (Petřínské Sady)

This hill, topped by a replica of the Eiffel Tower, features several unusual sights.

Monument to Victims of Communism (Pomník Obětem Komunismu): The sculptural figures of this poignant memorial, representing victims of the totalitarian regime, gradually atrophy as they range up the hillside steps. They do not die but slowly disappear, one limb at a time. The statistics inscribed on the steps say it all: From 1948 until 1989, in Czechoslovakia alone, 205,486 people were imprisoned, 248 were executed, 4,500 died in prison, 327 were shot attempting to cross the border, and 170,938 left the country.

Hunger Wall (Hladová Zed'): To the left of the Victims of Communism monument is this medieval defense wall, which was Charles IV's 14th-century equivalent of FDR's work-for-food projects. The poorest of the poor helped build this structure just to eke out a bit of income.

To the right (about 50 yards away) is the base of a handy **funicular** you can ride up the hill to the Petřín Tower (uses tram/Metro ticket, runs daily every 10-15 minutes 8:00-22:00).

Petřín Hill Summit and Tower: The top of Petřín Hill is considered the best place in Prague to take your date for a romantic city view. Built for an exhibition in 1891, the 200-foot-tall Petřín Tower—an elegant pure Art Nouveau steel and wood structure—is one-fifth the height of its Parisian big brother, which was built two years earlier. But, thanks to this hill, the top of the tower sits at the same elevation as the real Eiffel Tower. Before you climb up, appreciate the tower's sinuous curves. Climbing the 400 steps rewards you with amazing views of the city (150 Kč, daily 9:00-21:00, shorter hours off-season). A **mirror maze** next door to the tower is fun for a quick wander if you're already here (75 Kč, same hours as tower).

Sights in the Castle Quarter (Hradčany)

Looming above Prague, dominating its skyline, is the Castle Quarter. Prague Castle and its surrounding sights are packed with Czech history, as well as with tourists. The nearby Strahov Monastery (above the castle) has a fascinating old library and beautiful views over all of Prague.

PRAGUE CASTLE (PRAŽSKÝ HRAD)

This vast and sprawling complex has been the seat of Czech power for centuries. It collects a wide range of sights, including the country's top church, its former royal palace, and an assortment of history and art museums (together rated ▲▲).

Getting There

By Tram: Trams #22 and #23 take you up to the castle. Catch either tram at Národní Třída (between Wenceslas Square and the National Theater in the New Town), in front of the National Theater (Národní Divadlo, on the riverbank in the New Town), or at Malostranská (the Metro stop in the Lesser Town). After rattling up the hill, trams make three stops near the castle:

Pražský Hrad (Prague Castle) offers the quickest commute to the castle—from the stop, simply walk along U Prašného Mostu

PRAGUE

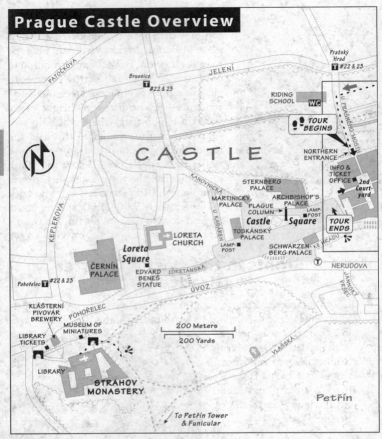

Prague Castle Overview

and over the bridge, past the stone-faced but photo-op-friendly guards at the **northern entrance,** which leads into the castle's Second Courtyard.

Královský Letohrádek (Royal Summer Palace) allows a scenic but slow approach through the Royal Gardens to the bridge near the castle's **northern entrance.**

Pohořelec is best if you'd like to start with the Strahov Monastery, then hike 10 minutes down to Castle Square (by way of Loreta Church) and begin your tour there, at the castle's **main entrance.**

By Taxi or Uber: Ask your driver to drop you at either Pražský Hrad or Královský Letohrádek (see above). Another option is to have them drop you off just under the castle at the top of Nerudova street (at the little square under the staircase), and then climb 200 yards up the pedestrian-only cobblestone street from there.

By Foot: The fairly steep, three-quarter-mile uphill walk from

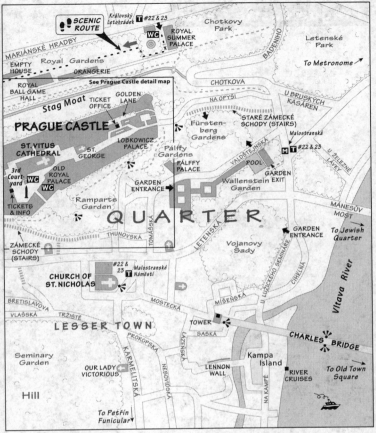

the river takes about 20 minutes. From the Charles Bridge, follow the main cobbled road (Mostecká) to the Lesser Town Square, marked by the huge, green-domed Church of St. Nicholas. From there, hike uphill along Nerudova street. After about 10 minutes, a steep lane on the right leads to Castle Square.

Planning Your Time

Prague Castle is the city's most crowded sight. The grounds become a sea of tourists during peak times (worst 9:30-14:00 in high season). The most cramped area is the free vestibule inside St. Vitus Cathedral; any sight that you pay to enter—including other parts of the cathedral—will be less jammed.

Minimize the effect of crowds and maximize your enjoyment by following one of these plans.

Early-Bird Visit: Leave your hotel no later than 8:00. Ride the tram to the Pražský Hrad stop, look around **Castle Square,**

PRAGUE

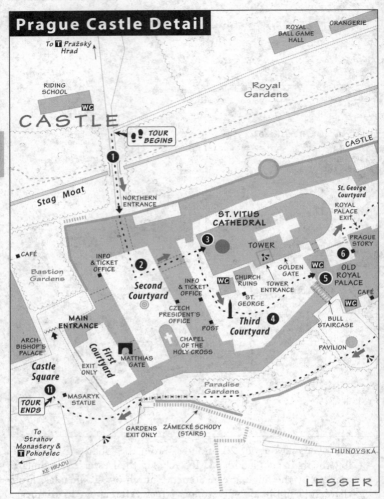

Prague Castle Detail

To **T** Pražský
Hrad

ROYAL
BALL GAME
HALL

ORANGERIE

RIDING
SCHOOL

Royal
Gardens

CASTLE

WC

CASTLE

**TOUR
BEGINS**

❶

Stag Moat

NORTHERN
ENTRANCE

ST. VITUS
CATHEDRAL

St. George
Courtyard

ROYAL
PALACE
EXIT

CAFÉ

Bastion
Gardens

INFO
& TICKET
OFFICE

❷

Second
Courtyard

❸

INFO
& TICKET
OFFICE

WC

TOWER

CHURCH
RUINS
ST.
GEORGE

GOLDEN
GATE

TOWER
ENTRANCE

WC

PRAGUE
STORY

❻

❺

OLD
ROYAL
PALACE

CAFÉ

WC

MAIN
ENTRANCE

CZECH
PRESIDENT'S
OFFICE

POST

Third
Courtyard

❹

BULL
STAIRCASE

ARCH-
BISHOP'S
PALACE

First
Courtyard

EXIT
ONLY

Matthias
Gate

CHAPEL
OF THE
HOLY CROSS

PAVILION

Castle
Square

MASARYK
STATUE

Paradise
Gardens

❶❶

**TOUR
ENDS**

GARDENS
EXIT ONLY

ZÁMECKÉ SCHODY
(STAIRS)

THUNOVSKÁ

To
Strahov
Monastery &
T Pohořelec

KE HRADU

LESSER

and be sure you're in line at the ticket office in the Third Courtyard, across from **St. Vitus Cathedral,** before 9:00. Once you have your ticket, head to the cathedral as soon as possible after it opens at 9:00, and for a few minutes, you'll have the sacred space to yourself...then, on your way out, you'll pass a noisy human traffic jam of multinational tour groups. Visit the rest of the castle sights at your leisure: the Old Royal Palace, the Basilica of St. George, and Lobkowicz Palace.

Afternoon Visit/Adding on Strahov Monastery and Loreta Church: If you're heading to Prague Castle after lunch and want to add on an efficient visit to the sights above the castle, ride the tram to the Pohořelec stop. Tour the Strahov Monastery, then drop

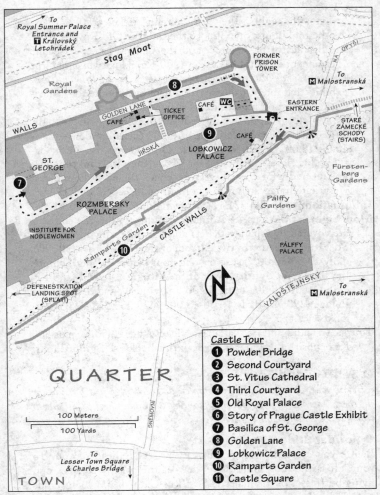

PRAGUE

Castle Tour
1. Powder Bridge
2. Second Courtyard
3. St. Vitus Cathedral
4. Third Courtyard
5. Old Royal Palace
6. Story of Prague Castle Exhibit
7. Basilica of St. George
8. Golden Lane
9. Lobkowicz Palace
10. Ramparts Garden
11. Castle Square

by Loreta Church on your way (downhill) to Castle Square. By the time you hit Castle Square, the crowds should be thinning out. The only risk is running out of time to enter all the sights by closing time.

Nighttime Visit: The castle is least crowded at night. True, the sights are closed, but the castle grounds are free, safe, peaceful, floodlit, and open late. The tiny, normally jammed Golden Lane (medieval merchant street) is empty and romantic at night—and no ticket is required.

Orientation to Prague Castle

Cost: Admission to the castle grounds is free, but you need a ticket to enter the sights. The "Basic circuit" ticket (250 Kč) covers the highlights: St. Vitus Cathedral, the Old Royal Palace, the Basilica of St. George, and the Golden Lane. A second "Permanent exhibitions" ticket (200 Kč) adds two sights (the Prague Castle Picture Gallery and *The Story of Prague Castle* exhibit) that interest those with a healthy appetite for history. Tickets are good for two days.

Hours: Castle grounds—daily 6:00-22:00; castle sights—daily 9:00-17:00, Nov-March until 16:00; castle gardens—daily 10:00-18:00, closed Nov-March. On Sundays, St. Vitus Cathedral is closed until noon for Mass. The cathedral can close unexpectedly for special services (check the event calendar at www.katedralasvatehovita.cz or call +420 724 933 441).

Information: +420 224 371 111, www.hrad.cz.

More Sights at the Castle: Additional sights within the complex are covered by separate tickets and have their own hours: the **St. Vitus Treasury in the Chapel of the Holy Cross** (300 Kč, daily 10:00-18:00, last entry one hour before closing), climbing the **Great South Tower of St. Vitus Cathedral** (150 Kč, daily 10:00-18:00, until 16:00 in winter), and **Lobkowicz Palace** (290 Kč, daily 10:00-18:00, +420 233 312 925, www.lobkowicz.cz).

Tours: An audioguide is available at ticket offices (350 Kč plus 500 Kč deposit). I'd skip it in favor of this book's self-guided tour.

❍ Self-Guided Tour

• *Begin your visit to the castle complex at the bridge just outside the northern entrance. If approaching from Castle Square, join this tour at stop #2, the Second Courtyard.*

❶ Powder Bridge (Prašný Most)

Before you cross the bridge, survey the scene ahead of you. To your left is the most impressive view of the prickly steeples and flying buttresses of the majestic St. Vitus Cathedral, which stands in the middle of the medieval iceberg called Prague Castle. It's a 1,900-foot-long series of courtyards, churches, and palaces, covering 750,000 square feet—by some measures, the largest castle on earth. Crossing the bridge (actually a landfill), look down into the abysmal Stag Moat (Jelení příkop) that naturally protects the fortress from the north.

The stoic **guards** at this northern entrance make a great photo-op, as does the changing of the guard (on the hour). In fact, there's a guard-changing ceremony at every gate. The biggest, most crowded ceremony occurs at noon, at the top gate by Castle Square.

• *Walk through the double gate and emerge into the Second Courtyard. To your right is an information center where you can buy your ticket (or, if lines are long, try the one in the Third Courtyard, then come back to start the tour).*

❷ Second Courtyard

During the 18th century, Empress Maria Theresa commissioned her favorite Italian architect to connect the disparate buildings in the castle grounds into a unified Neoclassical whole. While Maria Theresa never resided here, the imposing—and to this day largely empty—complex was meant to project the aura of undisputed Habsburg power. This included painting the whole thing in the Habsburgs' favorite shade of yellow. Locals still feel uncomfortable in these "Viennese" surroundings and rush through the courtyard to take cover in one of the blessedly medieval interiors.

Before you do the same, note the fountain and Renaissance well in the middle of the square. Just to the left of the well, the modern green awning (with the golden-winged, catlike griffin) marks the entrance to the **offices of the Czech president.** If the president is in town, his flag flies over the roof at the opposite end of the square.

• *Now walk through the passageway (to the left of the president's office) that leads into the Third Courtyard. There you'll see the impressive facade of St. Vitus Cathedral. Even without a ticket, tourists can step into the church entryway for a crowded view of the nave (and a bit of the Mucha stained glass)—but it's worth paying to see the whole church.*

❸ St. Vitus Cathedral (Katedrála Sv. Víta)

This Roman Catholic cathedral, worth ▲▲▲, is the Czech national church—it's where kings were crowned, royalty have their

tombs, the relics of saints are venerated, and the crown jewels are kept. Since AD 920, a church has stood on this spot, marking the very origins of the Czech nation.

The letters below correspond to the cathedral map.

❹ Entrance Facade: The two soaring towers of this Gothic wonder rise 270 feet. The ornate facade features pointed arches, elaborate tracery, Flamboyant pinnacles, a rose window, a dozen statues of saints, and gargoyles sticking out their tongues.

So what's up with the four guys in modern suits carved into

PRAGUE

the stone, as if supporting the big round window on their shoulders? They're the architects and builders who finished the church six centuries after it was started. Even though church construction got underway in 1344, wars, plagues, and the reforms of Jan Hus conspired to stall its completion. Finally, fueled by a burst of Czech nationalism, Prague's top church was finished in 1929 for the 1,000th Jubilee anniversary of St. Wenceslas. The entrance facade and towers were the last parts to be finished.

• *Enter the cathedral. If it's not too crowded in the free entrance area, work your way to the middle of the church for a good...*

❶ View down the Nave: The church is huge—more than 400 feet long and 100 feet high—and flooded with light. Notice the intricate "net" vaulting on the ceiling, especially at the far end. It's the signature feature of the church's chief architect, Peter Parler (who also built the Charles Bridge).

• *Now make your way through the crowds and pass through the ticket turnstile (left of the roped-off area). The third window on the left wall is worth a close look.*

❷ Mucha Stained-Glass Window: This masterful 1931 Art Nouveau window was designed by Czech artist Alphonse Mucha and executed by a stained-glass craftsman.

Mucha's window was created to celebrate the birth of the Czech nation and the life of Wenceslas. The main scene (in the four central panels) shows Wenceslas as an impressionable child kneeling at the feet of his Christian grandmother, St. Ludmila. She spreads her arms and teaches him to pray. Wenceslas would grow up to champion Christianity, uniting the Czech people.

Above Wenceslas are the two saints who first brought Christianity to the region: Cyril (the monk in black hood holding the Bible) and his older brother, Methodius (with beard and bishop's garb). They baptize a kneeling convert.

Follow their story in the side panels, starting in the upper left. Around AD 860 (back when Ludmila was just a girl), these two Greek missionary brothers arrive in Moravia to preach. The pagan Czechs have no written language to read the Bible, so (in the next scene below), Cyril bends at his desk to design the necessary alphabet (Glagolitic, which later developed into Cyrillic), while Methodius meditates. In the next three scenes, they travel to Rome and

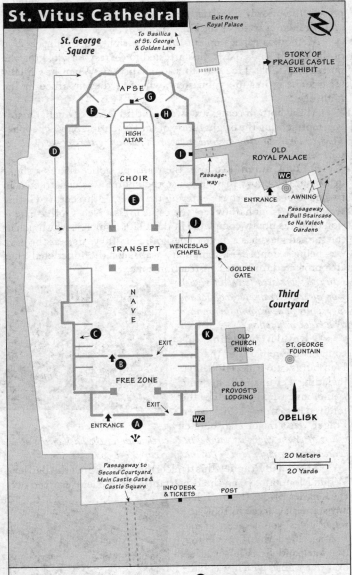

St. Vitus Cathedral

Exit from Royal Palace

St. George Square

To Basilica of St. George & Golden Lane

STORY OF PRAGUE CASTLE EXHIBIT

APSE

G

F

H

HIGH ALTAR

D

I

OLD ROYAL PALACE

CHOIR

Passageway

WC

E

ENTRANCE

AWNING

Passageway and Bull Staircase to Na Valech Gardens

J

TRANSEPT

WENCESLAS CHAPEL

L

GOLDEN GATE

N A V E

Third Courtyard

C

K

OLD CHURCH RUINS

ST. GEORGE FOUNTAIN

EXIT

B

FREE ZONE

OLD PROVOST'S LODGING

OBELISK

EXIT

WC

ENTRANCE

A

20 Meters

20 Yards

Passageway to Second Courtyard, Main Castle Gate & Castle Square

INFO DESK & TICKETS

POST

PRAGUE

A Entrance Facade	**G** Tomb of St. Vitus
B View down the Nave	**H** Tomb of St. John of Nepomuk
C Mucha Stained-Glass Window	**I** Royal Oratory
D Old Church	**J** Wenceslas Chapel
E Royal Mausoleum	**K** Tower Entrance
F Relief of Prague	**L** Last Judgment Mosaic

present their newly translated Bible to the pope. But Cyril falls ill, and Methodius watches his kid brother die.

Methodius carries on (in the upper right), becoming bishop of the Czech lands. Next, he's arrested for heresy for violating the pure Latin Bible. He's sent to a lonely prison. When he's finally set free, he retires to a monastery, where he dies mourned by the faithful.

At the bottom center are two beautiful (classic Mucha) maidens, representing the bright future of the Czech and Slovak peoples.
• *Continue circulating around the church, following the one-way, clockwise route.*

❹ Old Church: Just after the transept, notice there's a slight incline in the floor. That's because the church was constructed in two distinct stages. You're entering the older, 14th-century Gothic section. The front half (where you came in) is a Neo-Gothic extension that was finally completed in the 1920s (which is why much of the stained glass has a modern design). For 400 years—as the nave was being extended—a temporary wall kept the functional altar area protected from the construction zone.

• *In the choir area (on your right), soon after the transept, look for the big, white marble tomb surrounded by a black iron fence.*

❺ Royal Mausoleum: This contains the remains of the first Habsburgs to rule Bohemia, including Ferdinand I, his wife Anne, and Maximilian II. The tomb dates from 1590, when Prague was a major Habsburg city.

• *Just after the choir, as you begin to circle around the back of the altar, watch on your right for the fascinating, carved-wood...*

❻ Relief of Prague: This depicts the aftermath of the Battle of White Mountain, when the Protestant King Frederic escaped over the Charles Bridge (before it had any statues). Carved in 1630, the relief gives you a peek at old Prague. Find the Týn Church (far left) and St. Vitus Cathedral (far right), which was half-built at that time. Back then, the Týn Church was Hussite, so the centerpiece of its facade is not the Virgin Mary (more of a

Catholic figure) but a chalice, a symbol of Jan Hus' ideals. The old city walls—now replaced by the main streets of the city—stand

strong. The Jewish Quarter is the flood-prone zone along the riverside below the bridge on the left—land no one else wanted. The weir system on the river—the wooden barriers that help control its flow—survives to this day.

• *Circling around the high altar, you'll see various...*

Tombs in the Apse: Among the graves of medieval kings and bishops is that of ❻ **St. Vitus,** shown as a young man clutching a book and gazing up to heaven. Why is this huge cathedral dedicated to this rather obscure saint, who was martyred in Italy in AD 303 and never set foot in Bohemia? A piece of Vitus' arm bone (a holy relic) was supposedly acquired by Wenceslas I in 925. Wenceslas built a church to house the relic on this spot, attracting crowds of pilgrims. Vitus became quite popular throughout the Germanic and Slavic lands, and revelers danced on his feast day. (He's now the patron saint of dancers.) At the statue's feet is a rooster, because the saint was thrown into a boiling cauldron along with the bird (the Romans' secret sauce)...but he miraculously survived.

A few steps farther, the big silvery tomb with the angel-borne canopy honors ❼ **St. John of Nepomuk.** Locals claim it has more than a ton of silver.

Just past the tomb, on the wall of the choir (on the right), is another finely carved, circa-1630 **wood relief** depicting an event that took place right here in St. Vitus: Protestant nobles trash the cathedral's Catholic icons after their (short-lived) victory.

Ahead on the left, look up at the ❽ **royal oratory,** a box supported by busy late-Gothic, vine-like ribs. This private box, connected to the king's apartment by an outside corridor, let the king attend Mass in his jammies. The underside of the balcony is morbidly decorated with dead vines and tree branches, suggesting the pessimism common in the late Gothic period, when religious wars and Ottoman invasions threatened the Czech lands.

• *From here, walk 25 paces and look left through the crowds and door to see the richly decorated chapel containing the tomb of St. Wenceslas. Two roped-off doorways give visitors a look inside. The best view is from the second one, around the corner and to the left, in the transept.*

❾ **Wenceslas Chapel:** This fancy chapel is the historic heart of the church. It contains the tomb of St. Wenceslas, patron saint of the Czech nation; it's where Bohemia's kings were crowned; and it houses (but rarely displays) the Bohemian crown jewels. The chapel walls are paneled with big slabs of precious and semiprecious

PRAGUE

stones. The jewel-toned stained-glass windows (from the 1950s) admit a soft light. The chandelier is exceptional. The place feels medieval.

The tomb of St. Wenceslas is a colored-stone coffin topped with an ark. Above the chapel's altar is a statue of Wenceslas, bearing a lance and a double-eagle shield. He's flanked by (painted) angels and the four patron saints of the Czech people. Above Wenceslas are portraits of Charles IV (who built the current church) and his beautiful wife. On the wall to the left of the altar, frescoes depict the saint's life, including the episode where angels arrive with crosses to arm the holy warrior. For centuries, Czech kings were crowned right here in front of Wenceslas' red-draped coffin.

• *Leave the cathedral, turn left (past the WC), and survey the...*

❹ Third Courtyard

The **obelisk** was erected in 1928—a single piece of granite celebrating the 10th anniversary of the establishment of Czechoslovakia and commemorating the soldiers who fought for its independence. It was originally much taller but broke in transit—an inauspicious start for a nation destined to last only 70 years.

From here, you get a great look at the sheer size of St. Vitus Cathedral and its fat green **tower** (325 feet tall). Up there is the Czech Republic's biggest **bell** (16.5 tons, from 1549), nicknamed "Zikmund." You can view the bell as you climb up the 287 steps of the tower to the observation deck at the top (❿ **tower tickets and entry** near sculpture of St. George—a 1960s replica of the 13th-century original).

It's easy to find the church's **Golden Gate** (for centuries the cathedral's main entry)—look for the glittering ❶ **14th-century mosaic of the Last Judgment.** The modern, cosmopolitan, and ahead-of-his-time Charles IV commissioned this monumental decoration in 1370 in the Italian style. Jesus oversees the action, as some go to heaven and some go to hell. The Czech king and queen kneel directly beneath Jesus and six patron saints. On coronation day, royalty would walk under this arch, a reminder to them (and their subjects) that even those holding great power are not above God's judgment.

Across from the Golden Gate, in the corner, notice the copper, scroll-like **awning** supported by bulls. This leads to a fine garden just below the castle. The stairway, garden, and other features around the castle were designed in the 1920s by the Slovene architect Jože Plečnik (see page 753). Around the turn of the 20th century, Prague was considered the cultural standard-bearer of the entire Slavic world—making this a particularly prestigious assignment.

• *In the corner of the Third Courtyard, near the copper awning, is the entrance to the...*

❺ Old Royal Palace (Starý Královský Palác)

The highlight of the palace building (dating from the 12th century), worth ▲▲, is the large **Vladislav Hall**—200 feet long, with an im-

pressive vaulted ceiling of vine-shaped (late-Gothic) tracery. It could be filled with market stalls, letting aristocrats shop without going into town. It was big enough for jousts— even the staircase (which you'll use as you exit) was designed to let a mounted

soldier gallop in. Beginning in the 1500s, nobles met here to elect the king. The tradition survived into modern times. As recently as the 1990s, the Czech parliament crowded into this room to elect their president.

On your immediate right, enter the two small Renaissance rooms known as the **"Czech Office."** From these rooms, two governors used to oversee the Czech lands for the Habsburgs in Vienna. Head for the far room, wrapped in windows. In 1618, angry Czech Protestant nobles poured into these rooms and threw the two Catholic governors out the window. (Amazingly, the two survived.) An old law actually permits this act—called defenestration—which usually targets bad politicians.

As you reenter the main hall, go to the far end and out on the **balcony** for a sweeping view of Prague.

• *The next sight requires the extra "Permanent exhibitions" ticket; if you don't have one, skip down to the Basilica of St. George. Otherwise, as you exit the Royal Palace, hook left around the side of the building and backtrack a few steps uphill to find stairs leading down to...*

❻ The Story of Prague Castle Exhibit (Příběh Pražského Hradu)

This museum of old artifacts (with good English descriptions) is your best look at castle history and its kings, all housed in the cool

Gothic cellars of the Old Royal Palace. Throughout the exhibit, models of the castle show how it grew over the centuries.

• *Directly across the courtyard from the rear buttresses of St. Vitus is a very old church with a pretty red facade. This is the...*

❼ Basilica of St. George (Bazilika Sv. Jiří)

Step into one of the oldest structures (worth ▲) at Prague Castle to see this re-created Romanesque church (a product of a 19th-century "purification" that removed the  layers of Baroque) and the burial place of Czech royalty. The church was founded by Wenceslas' dad before 920, and the present structure dates from the 12th century. (Its Baroque facade and side chapel that survived the purification came later.) Inside, the place is beautiful in its simplicity. Notice the characteristic thick walls and rounded arches. In those early years, building techniques were not yet advanced enough to use those arches for the ceiling—it's made of wood instead.

This was the royal burial place before St. Vitus was built, so the tombs here contain the remains of the earliest Czech kings. Climb the stairs that frame either side of the altar to study the area around the apse. St. Wenceslas' grandmother, Ludmila, was reburied here in 925. Her stone tomb is in the added Gothic chapel just to the right of the altar. Inside the archway leading to her tomb, look for her portrait.

• *Exit the church and continue walking downhill. Notice the basilica's gorgeous Renaissance side entrance, with St. George fighting the dragon in the tympanum. You'll next see the basilica's Romanesque nave and towers—a strong contrast to the lavish painted Baroque facade. To your right, tucked together, you'll see the palaces of Catholic nobility who wanted to be both close to power and able to band together should the Protestants grab the upper hand. Take a left once you have passed the apse of the St. George Basilica, then turn right and then left again to stroll through the...*

❽ Golden Lane

This medieval merchant street, worth ▲, was once lined with the former residences of soldiers and craftsmen. Today, it's filled with touristy shops.

• *At the end of the Golden Lane, walk down the stairway in a tunnel and, keeping the former prison tower to your left, make a sharp right turn through a small gate. Walk across a courtyard and exit to the left to face the...*

❾ Lobkowicz Palace (Lobkowiczký Palác)

This palace, rated ▲▲ and covered by a separate ticket, displays the private collection of a prominent Czech noble family, including paintings, ceramics, and musical scores. The Lobkowiczes' property was confiscated twice in the 20th century: first by the Nazis at the beginning of World War II, and then by the communists in 1948. In 1990, William Lobkowicz, then a Boston real estate broker, returned to Czechoslovakia to fight a legal battle to reclaim his family's property and, eventually, to restore the castles and palaces. The obvious care that went into creating this museum, the collection's variety, and the personal insight it offers into Czech nobility make the Lobkowicz worth an hour of your time. Members of the Lobkowicz family (including William) narrate the delightful, included audioguide. If you visit, use the map that comes with your ticket to focus on the highlights.

• *Once you're done touring the palace, you can exit the castle complex through the gate at the bottom (eastern) end of the castle. A scenic rampart just below the lower gate offers a commanding view of the city. From there, you can either head to the Malostranská tram/Metro station and riverbank, or loop around to Castle Square (where this tour continues).*

To reach Malostranská station, follow the crowds down the 700-some steps of a steep lane called Staré Zámecké Schody ("Old Castle Stairs"). To continue this tour (or to reach Strahov Monastery), take a hard right as you leave the castle gate and stroll through the long, delightful...

❿ Ramparts Garden (Zahrada Na Valech)

This garden comes with commanding views of the city below (free, daily 10:00-18:00 or later, closed Nov-March). Along the way, notice the Modernist layout of the garden, designed by Jože Plečnik of Slovenia. Halfway through the long park is a circular viewpoint. At roughly the same distance under the brick wall of the Royal Palace, find a Baroque column commemorating the miraculous survival of the defenestrated overlords. As you exit the garden at the far end through a narrow gate on top of a wide, monumental staircase, notice the cool wolf snout design of the adjacent doorknob, another Plečnik trademark.

• *Make your way into...*

⓫ Castle Square (Hradčanské Náměstí)

Castle Square was the focal point of premodern power. The **Fighting Titans** sculpture, depicting two triumphant gladiators, marks

the main entry into the residence of
Czech kings. The archbishop lived
(and still lives) in the **Archbishop's
Palace**—the ornate, white-and-yel-
low Rococo building with the oversized facade. Above the doorway is
the family coat of arms of the archbishop that built this palace: three
white goose necks in a red field.
(The portal on the left leads to the

Sternberg Palace art museum, with European paintings.)

Closer to you, near the overlook, the statue of a man in a business suit (marked *TGM*) honors the father of modern Czechoslovakia: **Tomáš Garrigue Masaryk.** At the end of World War I,
Masaryk—a university professor—united the Czechs and Slovaks
into one nation and became its first president.

On the left side of the square, behind the statue, the building with a step-gable roofline is **Schwarzenberg Palace,** where the
aristocrats from Český Krumlov stayed when they were visiting
from their country estates. Notice the envelope-shaped patterns
stamped on the exterior. These Renaissance-era adornments etched
into wet stucco—called sgraffito—decorate buildings throughout
the castle and all over Prague and the Czech Republic. Today,
Schwarzenberg Palace is an art museum with a
collection of Renaissance, Baroque, and Rococo
masterpieces.

The dark gray Baroque sculpture in the
middle of the square is a **plague column.** Erected as a token of gratitude to Mary and the saints
for saving the population from epidemic disease,
these columns are an integral part of the main
squares of many Habsburg towns.

Two more palaces are worth looking at. At
the far-right corner of the square, past the plague
column, is the delightful **Martinický Palace,**
with delicate Renaissance portals and detailed
figural sgraffito depicting the feats of biblical
Joseph and mythic Hercules. The pastel **Toskánský Palace** at the
western end of the square is a beautifully balanced example of Baroque palatial architecture.

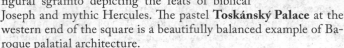

• *From the top corner of Toskánský Palace, you can either continue up
along Loretánská street to the Loreta Church and Strahov Monastery
(both described later), or take the scenic staircase on the left down to the
top of Nerudova street in the Lesser Town.*

SIGHTS ABOVE THE CASTLE

The Strahov Monastery, with its twin Baroque domes, and the pretty Loreta Church sit above the castle and are easy to combine with your castle visit. Visiting the monastery first allows you to walk downhill to the castle (taking in fine views and passing Loreta Church on the way), but it also means you'll wind up at the busiest entrance to the castle. If you anticipate crowds, see the castle sights first, then walk back up to Loreta and Strahov.

Getting There: From central Prague, take tram #22 or #23 to the Pohořelec stop. Follow the tracks for 50 yards, take the pedestrian lane that rises up beside the tram tracks, and enter the fancy gate on the left near the tall red-brick wall. You'll see the twin spires of the monastery; the library entrance is on the little square with the monastery church. From the castle, exit Castle Square past the Toskánský Palace and walk up along Loretánská street to the church and monastery.

▲Strahov Monastery and Library (Strahovský Klášter a Knihovna)

This fine old monastery has perched on the hill just above Prague Castle since the 12th century. Medieval monasteries were a mix of industry, agriculture, and education, as well as worship and theology. In its heyday, Strahov Monastery had a booming economy of its own, with vineyards, a brewery, and a sizable beer hall—all now open once again. You can explore the monastery complex, check out the beautiful old library, and even enjoy a brew (no longer monk-made, but still refreshing).

Cost and Hours: Grounds—free and always open; library—150 Kč, daily 9:00-12:00 & 13:00-17:00, +420 233 107 718; www.strahovskyklaster.cz. Tickets are sold in the small former church to your left just after you pass through the fancy entrance gate. A pay WC is just to the right of the monastery entrance.

Visiting the Monastery and Library: The monastery's **main church,** dedicated to the Assumption of St. Mary, is an originally Romanesque structure decorated by the monks in textbook Baroque (usually closed, but look through the gate inside the front door to see its interior). Notice the grand effect of the Baroque architecture—both rhythmic and theatric. Go ahead, inhale. That's the scent of Baroque.

The **library** is just to the right of the church—head up the stairs for a peek at how enlightened thinkers in the 18th century influenced learning. The **display cases** in the library gift shop show off illuminated manuscripts, described in English. Some are in old Czech, but because the Enlightenment promoted the universality of knowledge (and Latin was the universal language of Europe's educated elite), there was little place for regional dialects—there-

Tomáš Garrigue Masaryk (1850-1937)

Tomáš Masaryk founded the first democracy in Central Europe at the end of World War I, uniting the Czechs and the Slovaks to create Czechoslovakia. Like Václav Havel 70 years later, Masaryk was a politician whose vision extended far beyond the mountains enclosing the Bohemian basin.

Masaryk, from a poor servant family in southern Moravia, earned his PhD in sociology in Vienna, studied in Leipzig, and then became a professor at Charles University of Prague. By then, he was married to American Charlotta Garrigue, a social revolutionary from a Unitarian New York family. Through Charlotta, Masaryk was introduced to America's high society, which proved crucial in 1918 when he successfully campaigned there for the recognition of his new country.

Masaryk was greatly impressed with America, and his admiration for its democratic system (and his wife) became the core of his evolving political creed. He traveled the world and served in the Vienna parliament. At the outbreak of World War I, while most other Czech politicians stayed in Prague and supported the Habsburg Empire, 64-year-old Masaryk went abroad in protest and formed a highly original plan: to create an independent, democratic republic of Czechs and Slovaks. Masaryk and his supporters recruited an army of 100,000 soldiers who were willing to fight with the Allies against the Habsburgs, establishing a strong case to put on official desks in Paris, London, and Washington.

On the morning of October 28, 1918, news of the unofficial capitulation of the Habsburgs reached Prague. Supporters of Masaryk's plan quickly took control of the city and proclaimed the free republic. As the people of Prague tore down double-headed eagles (a symbol of the Habsburgs), the country of Czechoslovakia was born.

On December 21, 1918, four years after he had left the country as a political unknown, Masaryk arrived in Prague as the greatest Czech hero since the revolutionary priest Jan Hus. He told the jubilant crowd, "Now go home—the work has only started." Throughout the 1920s and 1930s, Masaryk was a vocal defender of democratic ideals in Europe against the rising tide of totalitarian ideologies. Today, Masaryk is one of only a few foreign leaders to be honored with a statue in Washington, DC.

fore, few books here are in the Czech language.

Two rooms (seen only from the doors) are filled with 10th-to-17th-century books, shelved under elaborately painted ceilings. The theme of the first and bigger hall is **philosophy**, with the history of the Western pursuit of knowledge painted on the ceiling. The second hall—down a hallway lined with antique furniture—focuses on **theology.** As the Age of Enlightenment began to take hold in Europe at the end of the 18th century, monasteries still controlled the books. Notice the gilded, locked case containing the *libri prohibiti* (prohibited books) at the end of the room, above the mirror. Only the abbot had the key, and you had to have his blessing to read these books—by writers such as Nicolas Copernicus, Jan Hus, and Jean-Jacques Rousseau. Even the French encyclopedia was locked away.

The **hallway** connecting the two library rooms was filled with cases illustrating the new practical approach to natural sciences. In the crowded area near the philosophy hall, find the dried-up elephant trunks (flanking the narwhal or unicorn horn) and one of the earliest models of an electricity generator.

Nearby: That hoppy smell you're enjoying in front of the monastery is the recommended **Klášterní Pivovar,** where they brew beer just as monks have for centuries (in the little courtyard directly across from the library entrance; described on page 147).

Downhill and through the gate opposite where you came in, find the ▲ **monastery garden view terrace** to the right. From the public perch beneath the restaurant tables, you'll have exquisite views over the domes and spires of Prague.

Loreta Square (Loretánské Náměstí)

On the way to Castle Square (from Strahov Monastery, or directly from the tram stop) is Loreta Square, dominated by the beautiful Baroque **Loreta Church** (described later).

Černín Palace, on the uphill (left) side of the square, was the unfortunate site of a modern-day defenestration. On March 10, 1948, soon after the communists took over, popular Czechoslovak politician Jan Masaryk (son of Tomáš Garrigue Masaryk, Czechoslovakia's first president) was found dead in this building's courtyard, below a palace bathroom window. While authorities at the time ruled it a suicide, an independent forensic examination in the 1990s confirmed foul play. The most likely theory is that

Masaryk was killed by the Soviet secret police, who had learned of Masaryk's plans to leave the country and represent it while in exile.

▲Loreta Church

This church has been a hit with pilgrims for centuries, thanks to its dazzling bell tower, peaceful yet plush cloister, sparkling treasury, and much-venerated Holy House. In the middle of the cloister courtyard, you'll find what some pilgrims consider part of Mary's actual home in Nazareth. You'll also see one of Prague's most beautiful Baroque churches, a fine treasury collection (upstairs), and—in a tiny chapel in one corner—"St. Bearded Woman," the patron saint of unhappy marriages.

Cost and Hours: 210 Kč; daily 9:00-17:00, Nov-March 9:30-16:00; audioguide-150 Kč, +420 220 516 740, www.loreta.cz.

Shopping in Prague

Prague's entire Old Town seems designed to bring out the shopper in visitors. **The Ungelt,** the courtyard tucked behind the Týn Church just off the Old Town Square, is packed with touristy but decent-quality shops. **Michalská,** a semihidden lane right in the thick of the tourist zone, has a variety of shops (from the Small Market Square/Malé Náměstí near the Astronomical Clock, go through the big stone gateway marked *459*). On **Havelská** street, you can browse the open-air Havelská Market, a touristy but enjoyable place to shop for inexpensive handicrafts and fresh produce (daily 9:00-18:00, two long blocks south of the Old Town Square). And **Celetná,** exiting the Old Town Square to the right of the Týn Church, is lined with big stores selling traditional Czech goodies.

Na Příkopě, the mostly pedestrianized street following the former moat between the Old Town and the New Town, has the city center's handiest lineup of modern shopping malls. Na Příkopě street opens up into Republic Square (Náměstí Republiky)—boasting Prague's biggest mall, Palladium, hidden behind a pink Neo-Romanesque facade. Across the square is the communist-era, brown, steel-and-glass 1980s department store Kotva ("Anchor") that has been recently remodeled inside.

Národní Třída (National Street), which continues past Na Příkopě in the opposite direction (toward the river), is less touristy and lined with some inviting stores. **Karlova,** the tourist-clogged

drag connecting the Old Town Square
to the Charles Bridge, should be avoided entirely.

Puppets: Czechs have treasured
the art of puppets for centuries. Good
options are **Galerie Michael,** at U
Lužického Semináře 7 in the Lesser
Town and at Jilská 22 in the Old Town
(https://buymarionettes.com); the no-
name **Loutky** ("Puppets") shop at the
top of Nerudova (at #51, www.loutky.
cz); and, in the Ungelt courtyard, **V
Ungeltu** and **Hračky, Loutky.**

Glass and Crystal: Since the Re-
naissance, Prague has been known for its exquisite glass and crystal. Well-respected sources for Czech glass and crystal include
Moser (flagship store at the Černá Růže shopping mall at Na
Příkopě 12, plus a branch on the Old Town
Square, www.moser.com), **Artěl** (see listing
later, under "Art Nouveau Design Shops"),
and **Blue,** specializing in sleek, modern
designs (locations include Malé Náměstí
13, Pařížská 3, Melantrichova 6, Celetná
2, Mostecká 24, and at the airport; https://
bluepraha.cz).

Bohemian Garnets *(Granát):* These
blood-red gemstones have unique refractive
properties. If you buy garnet jewelry, shop
around, use a reputable dealer, and ask for
a certificate of authenticity (glass imitations
are common). Of the many garnet shops,
Turnov Granát Co-op has the largest se-

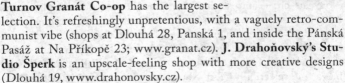

lection. It's refreshingly unpretentious, with a vaguely retro-com-
munist vibe (shops at Dlouhá 28, Panská 1, and inside the Pánská
Pasáž at Na Příkopě 23; www.granat.cz). **J. Drahoňovský's Studio Šperk** is an upscale-feeling shop with more creative designs
(Dlouhá 19, www.drahonovsky.cz).

Costume Jewelry and Beads: You'll see *bižutérie* (costume
jewelry) all over Prague. **AleAle** is run by a couple who use a
3,000-year-old lamp method to make beads, which they combine
with silver to create unique jewelry (Lázeňská 2, www.aleale.cz).
Round, glass beads—sometimes called Druk beads—are popular and range from large marble-sized beads to minuscule "seed
beads." The biggest producer of glass beads is Jablonex, from the
town of Jablonec nad Nisou. **Material,** in the Ungelt courtyard be-

hind the Týn Church, has a fun selection of seed beads, as well as some finer pieces (www.i-material.com).

Organic Cosmetics and Handmade Gifts: Manufaktura is your classy, one-stop shop for good-quality Czech gifts, from organic cosmetics to handicrafts. You'll find many locations near the Old Town Square (at Melantrichova 17, Celetná 12, and Karlova 26), at Republic Square (in the Palladium mall), near the Lesser Town end of the Charles Bridge (Mostecká 17), in the main train station, and even along Prague Castle's Golden Lane (www.manufaktura.çz). **Botanicus** is similar but smaller (in the Ungelt courtyard behind the Týn Church, www.botanicus.cz).

Fashion and Design: Czechs have a unique sense of fashion. One popular trend is garments that are adorned with embroidery, leather, beads, hand-painted designs, or other flourishes—all handmade. The Jewish Quarter's **Pařížská street** has the big-name international designers, but for something more local, focus on some of the side streets that run parallel to Pařížská. One block over, **Elišky Krásnohorské street** features boutiques selling local designs. A block farther east, more boutiques line **Dušní street.** A short walk away, **Dlouhá street**—which exits the Old Town Square near the Jan Hus statue—offers more Czech designers.

Fashionistas are sometimes surprised to learn that the famous and well-respected **Baťa** shoe brand is not Italian but Czech; their seven-story flagship store, on Wenceslas Square (at #6), is nirvana for shoe lovers. Nearby, one of the pavilions inside the Franciscan Garden (hiding just off Wenceslas Square) houses **Bohemania,** a fun and youthful boutique with clothes, jewelry, and other unique pieces (www.bohemania.com). For funky hipster design, Benediktská, a tiny street tucked in a quiet corner of the Old Town, has a little cluster of creative boutiques.

Art Nouveau Design Shops: Prague is Europe's best Art Nouveau city—and several shops sell Art Nouveau glassware, home decor, linens, posters, and other items. **Artěl** is thoughtfully curated (by Lesser Town end of Charles Bridge at U Lužického Semináře 7; www.artelglass.com). **Modernista** (downstairs inside the Municipal House and in the House of the Black Madonna) has a fine selection of Art Nouveau and Art Deco jewelry, glassware, wooden toys, books, and so on. Their flagship store is in the **Modernista Pavilon,** a sleek, gorgeously restored former market hall that's also home to a variety of trendy fashion and home-decor shops, out in the Vinohrady neighborhood (Vinohradská 50, www.modernista.cz). **Kubista,** in the House of the Black Madonna, has a fun-to-peruse selection of Czech Cubist dishes, jewelry, furniture, books, and more (Ovocný Trh 19, www.kubista.cz).

Books, Maps, Posters, and Music: Try **Shakespeare and Sons,** in the Lesser Town (described on page 56). **Kiwi Map Store,**

near Wenceslas Square, is Prague's best source for maps and travel guides (Jungmannova 23). **ProVás** stocks a wide array of unique posters—originals, reprints, and lots of vintage ads from the 1920s (closed Sat-Sun, Rybná 21).

Entertainment in Prague

Prague booms with live and inexpensive theater, classical music, jazz, and pop entertainment. Everything is listed in several monthly cultural-events programs (free at TIs).

Buying Tickets: To understand your options (the street Mozarts are pushing only their own concerts), drop by the **Via Musica**

box office next to the Týn Church on the Old Town Square (daily 10:00-20:00, +420 224 826 440, www.viamusica.cz) or the **Time Music** shop in the Lesser Town Square across from the Church of St. Nicholas (daily 10:00-20:00, +420 257 535 568). If you don't see a posted list of today's events, just ask for it.

Tips: Locals dress up for the more serious concerts, opera, and ballet, but many tourists wear casual clothes (avoid shorts, sneakers, or flip-flops). For church concerts, ticket prices at the door are often soft and negotiable.

THEATER AND CONCERTS

Black Light Theater

A kind of mime/modern dance variety show, Black Light Theater has no language barrier. Unique to Prague, it originated in the 1960s as a playful and mystifying theater of the absurd. Shows last about an hour and a half. Arrive a few minutes early to avoid sitting in the first two rows, which are too close and can ruin the illusion.

Black Light Theatre Srnec: Founded and still run by Jiří Srnec, a visual artist and music composer who invented the Black Light Theater concept in 1961, this troupe offers simple narratives and revels in the childlike, goofy wonder of the effects. The intimate size of the theater also allows for mimes to spontaneously engage with the audience. Their primary show, *Anthology*, traces the development of the art over the past 60 years (600 Kč, generally nightly, on Národní Třída in the same building as the Reduta Jazz Club, Národní 20, +420 774 574 475, www.srnectheatre.com).

Image Theater: This show has more mime and elements of the absurd (and sometimes slapstick), and more dance along with the illusions. They offer the most diverse lineup of programs, including a "best of" (580 Kč, nightly, off Národní Třída 25 in the Metro passageway, +420 222 314 448, www.imagetheatre.cz).

Classical Concerts

Each day, classical concerts designed for tourists fill delightful Old World halls and churches with crowd-pleasing music: Vivaldi, Best of Mozart, Most Famous Arias, and works by the famous Czech composer Antonín Dvořák. Concerts typically cost 400-1,000 Kč and last about an hour. Typical venues include two buildings on the Lesser Town Square (the Church of St. Nicholas and the Prague Academy of Music in Liechtenstein Palace), the Klementinum's Chapel of Mirrors, the Old Town Square (in a different Church of St. Nicholas), and the stunning Smetana Hall in the Municipal House. Musicians vary from excellent to amateurish.

For a memorable venue and top-notch musicians, see a concert at Smetana Hall, the Rudolfinum, or the National Theater—featuring Prague's finest ensembles (such as the Prague Symphony Orchestra or Czech Philharmonic).

The **Prague Symphony Orchestra** plays mainly in the gorgeous Art Nouveau Smetana Hall of the Municipal House. Their ticket office is inside the building, just to the left past the main glass door entrance (Mon-Fri 10:00-18:00, +420 222 002 336, www.fok.cz).

The **Czech Philharmonic** performs in the classical Neo-Renaissance Rudolfinum across the street from the Pinkas Synagogue. Their ticket office is on the right side of the building, under the stairs (250-1,650 Kč, open Mon-Fri 10:00-18:00 and until just before showtime on concert days, on Palachovo Náměstí on the Old Town side of Mánes Bridge, +420 227 059 227, www.ceskafilharmonie.cz).

Both orchestras perform in their home venues about five nights a month from September through June. On most other nights these spaces are rented to agencies that organize tourist concerts of varying quality. Check first whether your visit coincides with either ensemble's performance before settling for any of these substitutes.

You'll find tickets for tourist concerts advertised and sold on the street in front of these buildings. Although the music may not be the finest, these concerts do allow you to experience music in one of Prague's best venues on the night of your choice. This is especially worth considering if you want to enjoy classical music in the Municipal House when the Symphony Orchestra isn't in town (but make sure your concert takes place in Smetana Hall rather than in the smaller and far less spectacular Grégr Hall).

PRAGUE

Opera and Ballet

A handy ticket office for the following theaters (all part of the National Theater group) is directly across the street from the main entrance to the Estates Theater on Železná street.

The **National Theater** (Národní Divadlo), on the New Town side of Legií Bridge, has a stunning Neo-Renaissance interior to match its status as the top venue in the country (300-1,000 Kč, shows from 19:00, weekend matinees also at 14:00, +420 224 901 448, www.narodni-divadlo.cz).

The **Estates Theater** (Stavovské Divadlo) is where Mozart premiered and directed many of his most beloved works. *Don Giovanni*, *The Marriage of Figaro*, and *The Magic Flute* are on the program a couple of times each month (800-1,400 Kč, shows from 20:00, between the Old Town Square and the New Town on a square called Ovocný Trh, +420 224 901 448, www.narodni-divadlo.cz).

The **State Opera** (Státní Opera), formerly the German Theater, recently underwent an expensive remodel to rival the National Theater. Ballets and operas by non-Czech composers are typically performed here (400-1,200 Kč, at 19:00 or 20:00, 4 Wilsonova, on the busy street between the main train station and Wenceslas Square, see map on page 92, +420 224 901 448, www.narodni-divadlo.cz).

MUSIC CLUBS

Young locals keep Prague's many music clubs in business. Most clubs—from rock to folk to jazz—are neighborhood institutions, generally holding 100-200 people. Most have a cover charge.

Old Town: A few blocks from the Old Town Square, **Roxy** features live bands from outside the country twice a week—anything from Irish punk to Balkan brass—and experimental DJs on other nights (Dlouhá 33, www.roxy.cz). **Agharta Jazz Club** showcases some of the best Czech and Eastern European jazz in a cool Gothic cellar just steps off the Old Town Square (Železná 16, www.agharta.cz).

New Town: The scene is young and trendy at **Lucerna Music Bar,** popular for its '80s and '90s video parties on Friday and Saturday nights (in the basement of Lucerna Arcade, Vodičkova 36, www.musicbar.cz). **Reduta Jazz Club** launches you into the 1960s-era classic jazz scene (when jazz provided an escape for trapped freedom lovers in communist times). It features regular performances by top Czech jazz musicians. US president Bill Clinton once played the sax here (on Národní Třída next to Café Louvre, www.redutajazzclub.cz).

The Lesser Town: With its tight, steamy, standing-room-only space, **Malostranská Beseda** is the only club in the center with daily live performances. The crowd tends to be a bit older (Malostranské Náměstí 21, www.malostranska-beseda.cz).

Žižkov: Originally a 1920s movie theater, today **Palác Akropolis** hosts a chill-out lounge, a literary café, and two halls that offer a mix of concerts, disco, and theater (advance ticket sales at café, Mon-Fri 10:00-24:00, Sat-Sun from 16:00, corner of Kubelíkova and Fibichova, under Žižkov TV tower, Metro: Jiřího z Poděbrad, +420 269 330 911, www.palacakropolis.cz).

Sleeping in Prague

Peak months for hotels in Prague are May, June, and September. Easter and New Year's are the most crowded times, when prices are jacked up a bit. Book well in advance for peak season or if your trip coincides with a major holiday or festival (see the appendix). Many apartments in the city center are available for short-term rentals (Airbnb is the largest provider).

OLD TOWN HOTELS AND PENSIONS

You'll pay higher prices to stay in the Old Town, but for many travelers, the convenience is worth the expense. These places are all within a 10-minute walk of the Old Town Square.

$$$$ Hotel Metamorphis is a splurge, with solidly renovated rooms in Prague's former caravanserai (12th-century merchants' hostel). Its breakfast room is in a spacious medieval cellar with modern artwork. Some of the street-facing rooms, located above two popular bars, are noisy at night (Malá Štupartská 5, +420 221 771 011, www.hotelmetamorphis.cz, hotel@metamorphis.cz).

$$$$ Hotel Maximilian is a sleek, mod, 71-room place with Art Deco black design; big, plush living rooms; and all the services and comforts you'd expect in a four-star hotel. It faces a church on a perfect little square just a short walk from the action (Haštalská 14, +420 225 303 111, www.maximilianhotel.com, reservation@maximilianhotel.com).

$$$ Design Hotel Jewel Prague (U Klenotníka), with 11 modern, comfortable rooms in a plain building, is three blocks off the Old Town Square (RS%—use promo code "ricksteves10" online, no elevator, Rytířská 3, +420 224 211 699, www.hoteljewelprague.com, info@jewelhotel.cz).

$$$ The Dominican has 28 luxurious rooms in a still-functional, 14th-century Dominican monastery. Rooms are historical, many with original medieval wooden ceilings, and the hotel has a pleasantly small feel (breakfast-350 Kč extra, for a better deal try the recommended cafés on Řetězová, hotel entrance on Jalovcová, +420 224 248 555, www.axxoshotels.com, reception.dominican@axxoshotels.com).

Sleep Code

Hotels in this book are categorized according to the average price of a standard double room with breakfast in high season. 20 Kč = about $1.

$$$$	**Splurge:** Most rooms over 4,700 Kč (€200)
$$$	**Pricier:** 3,500-4,700 Kč (€150-200)
$$	**Moderate:** 2,300-3,500 Kč (€100-150)
$	**Budget:** 1,200-2,300 Kč (€50-100)
¢	**Backpacker:** Under 1,200 Kč (€50)
RS%	**Rick Steves discount**

Unless otherwise noted, credit cards are accepted and hotel staff speak basic English. Comparison-shop by checking prices at several hotels (on each hotel's own website, on a booking site, or by email). For the best deal, *book directly with the hotel.* Ask for a discount if paying in cash; if the listing includes **RS%,** request a Rick Steves discount.

$$$ Brewery Hotel u Medvídků ("By the Bear Cubs") has 43 comfortable rooms in a big, rustic, medieval shell with dark wood furniture. Upstairs, you'll find lots of beams—or, if you're not careful, they'll find you (RS%—use promo code "oldgott" online, "historical" rooms cost slightly more, apartment available, Na Perštýně 7, +420 224 211 916, www.umedvidku.cz, info@umedvidku.cz, manager Vladimír). The pension runs a popular beer-hall restaurant with live music most Fridays and Saturdays until 23:00—request an inside room for maximum peace.

$$$ Unitas Hotel, in a former convent and communist prison, ironically offers plush comfort and bright, airy rooms. The premises formerly served as interrogation cells for the likes of Václav Havel (Bartolomějská 9, +420 224 230 533, www.unitas.cz, unitas@unitas.cz).

$$ Hotel Haštal is next to Hotel Maximilian (listed earlier) on the same quiet, hidden square. A popular hotel even back in the 1920s, this family-run place has been renovated to complement the neighborhood's vibrant circa-1900 architecture. Its 31 rooms are comfortable and insulated against noise (RS%; free tea, coffee, and wine; air-con, Haštalská 16, +420 222 314 335, +420 725 369 369, www.hastal.com, info@hastal.com).

$$ Green Garland Pension (U Zeleného Věnce), on a central cobbled lane, has a small-place feel rare for the Old Town. Located in a thick 14th-century building with open beams, it has a blond-hardwood charm decorated with a warm and personal touch. The nine clean and simply furnished rooms are two and three floors up, with no elevator (RS%, family room, closed Jan-March, com-

PRAGUE

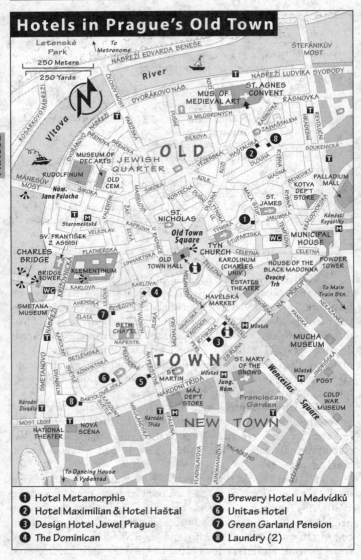

Hotels in Prague's Old Town

1. Hotel Metamorphis
2. Hotel Maximilian & Hotel Haštal
3. Design Hotel Jewel Prague
4. The Dominican
5. Brewery Hotel u Medvídků
6. Unitas Hotel
7. Green Garland Pension
8. Laundry (2)

munication in off-season may be slow, Řetězová 10, +420 222 220 178, www.uzv.cz, pension@uzv.cz).

UNDER THE CASTLE, IN THE LESSER TOWN
Several of these listings are buried on quiet lanes deep in the Lesser Town, among cobbles, quaint restaurants, rummaging tourists, and embassy flags.

$$$$ Hotel Nerudova 211 has eight suites and two apartments situated in a splendid Baroque house once owned—and redesigned—by renowned architect Jan Blažej Santini-Aichel. A thorough restoration highlights the period details, including painted wood ceilings, frescoed walls, and tile stoves. It's a family-run operation, and it shows in the service and attention to detail (family rooms, Nerudova 14, +420 601 211 000, https://nerudova211.com, info@nerudova211.com).

$$$$ Hotel Sax's 22 rooms are decorated in a retro, meet-the-Jetsons fashion. With a fruity atrium and a distinctly modern, stark feel, this is a stylish, no-nonsense place (air-con, elevator, free tea and pastries daily at 17:00, Jánský Vršek 3, +420 775 859 694, www.hotelsax.cz, hotel@sax.cz).

$$$ Hotel Julián is an oasis of professional, predictable decency in an untouristy neighborhood. Its 33 spacious, fresh, well-furnished rooms and big, homey public spaces hide behind a noble Neoclassical facade. The staff is friendly and helpful (RS%, family rooms, air-con, elevator, plush and inviting lobby, summer roof terrace, parking lot; Metro: Anděl, as you leave the Metro station go left and take tram #9, #12, or #20 for two stops; Elišky Peškové 11, Praha 5, +420 257 311 150, www.hoteljulian.com, info@julian.cz). Free lockers and a shower are available for those needing a place to stay after checkout (while waiting for a flight or train, for example).

$$$ Dům u Velké Boty ("House at the Big Boot"), on a quiet square in front of the German Embassy, is the rare quintessential family hotel in Prague: homey, comfy, and extremely friendly. Mellow Kuba, the second generation in charge and a film producer in winter, treats every guest as a (thirsty) friend and always has a supply of good advice and stories. Each of the 12 rooms is uniquely decorated, most in a tasteful, 19th-century Biedermeier style (RS%, cash only, cheaper rooms with shared bath, family rooms, children up to age 10 sleep free—toys provided, Vlašská 30, +420 257 532 088, www.dumuvelkeboty.cz, info@dumuvelkeboty.cz). There's no hotel sign on the house—look for the splendid geraniums in the windows.

$$$ Mooo Apartments, in a meticulously restored 500-year-old house built around a secluded balconied courtyard, offers 13 spacious apartments with kitchenettes (no breakfast, some rooms without air-con, down the staircase from Nerudova at Jánský Vršek 8, +420 277 016 830, www.mooo-apartments.com, castle@mooo-apartments.com). For supplies, use the Žabka convenience store diagonally across the way. Mooo has an additional, larger location in a hip part of the New Town.

$$ Residence Thunovská, just below the Italian embassy on a relatively quiet staircase leading up to the castle, rents six rooms in a house that once belonged to the Mannerist artist Bartholomeus

PRAGUE

Hotels & Restaurants in the Lesser Town & Castle Quarter

Accommodations
1. Hotel Nerudova 211
2. Hotel Sax
3. Hotel Julián
4. Dům u Velké Boty
5. Mooo Apartments
6. Residence Thunovská

Eateries & Entertainment
7. Malostranská Beseda
8. Lokál U Bílé Kuželky
9. St. Martin
10. Vegan's Prague
11. Natureza Vegetarian House
12. U Hrocha
13. Cukrkávalimonáda
14. Café Savoy
15. Pastař
16. Petřínské Terasy
17. Villa Richter
18. Lobkowicz Palace Café
19. Klášterní Pivovar
20. Host Restaurant
21. Hostinec u Černého Vola
22. Malý Buddha
23. U Zavěšenýho Kafe a Divadlo Pokračuje
24. U Labutí
25. Kuchyň
26. Kavárna ve Šternberském Paláci
27. Kavárna Nový Svět

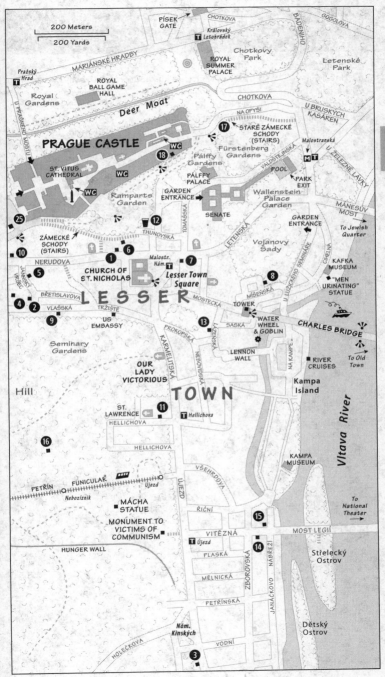

PRAGUE

200 Meters

200 Yards

CHOTKOVA

PÍSEK GATE

GOGOLOVA

BADENIHO

Královský
Letohrádek

ROYAL SUMMER PALACE

Chotkovy Park

Letenské Park

Prašský Hrad

MARIÁNSKÉ HRADBY

ROYAL BALL GAME HALL

CHOTKOVA

Royal Gardens

Deer Moat

NA OPYŠI

U PRAŠNÉHO MOSTU

U BRUSKÝCH KASÁREN

STARÉ ZÁMECKÉ
SCHODY (STAIRS)

17

Malostranská

Fürstenberg Gardens

PRAGUE CASTLE

18

WC

ST. VITUS CATHEDRAL

WC

Pálffy Gardens

Pálffy Palace

VALDŠTEJNSKÁ

POOL

PARK EXIT

U ŽELEZNÉ LÁVKY

25

Ramparts Garden

WC

GARDEN ENTRANCE

SENATE

Wallenstein Palace Garden

GARDEN ENTRANCE

MÁNESŮV MOST

To Jewish Quarter

THUNOVSKÁ

12

10

ZÁMECKÉ SCHODY (STAIRS)

NERUDOVA

6

1

Malostr. Nám.

Vojanovy Sady

CHELINA

U LUŽICKÉHO SEMINÁŘE

KAFKA MUSEUM

5

CHURCH OF ST. NICHOLAS

7

Lesser Town Square

"MEN URINATING" STATUE

LETENSKÁ

JÁNSKÝ VRŠEK

BŘETISLAVOVA

L E S S E R

8

4

2

VLAŠSKÁ

TRŽIŠTĚ

MOSTECKÁ

MÍŠEŇSKÁ

TOWER

CHARLES BRIDGE

9

US EMBASSY

PROKOPSKÁ

13

SASKÁ

WATER WHEEL & GOBLIN

To Old Town

Seminary Gardens

KARMELITSKÁ

LÁZENSKÁ

LENNON WALL

NA KAMPĚ

River Cruises

NEBOVIDSKÁ

OUR LADY VICTORIOUS

Kampa Island

Vltava River

Hill

T O W N

ST. LAWRENCE

11

Hellichova

KAMPA MUSEUM

HELLICHOVA

HELLICHOVA

16

VŠEHRDOVA

FUNICULAR

Újezd

PETŘÍN

Nebozízek

ŘÍČNÍ

To National Theater

MÁCHA STATUE

15

MONUMENT TO VICTIMS OF COMMUNISM

VITĚZNÁ

MOST LEGII

HUNGER WALL

Újezd

14

Střelecký Ostrov

PLASKÁ

MĚLNICKÁ

ZBOROVSKÁ

JANÁČKOVO NÁBŘEŽÍ

PETŘÍNSKÁ

Nám. Kinských

MOLECKOVA

VODNÍ

3

Dětský Ostrov

PRAGUE

Hotels & Restaurants in the New Town & Nearby

Accommodations
1. Hotel Cube
2. Mosaic House
3. Hotel 16
4. Hotel Anna
5. Hostel Elf
6. Sophie's Hostel
7. Czech Inn Hostel

Eateries
8. Restaurace u Pinkasů
9. Café Louvre & Knedlín
10. Kantýna
11. Pivovarský Dům
12. Municipal House Eateries
13. Brasserie La Gare
14. Zvonice
15. ZEM
16. Bistro Muzeum
17. Ovocný Světozor
18. Velryba
19. Oblaca
20. Pivnice u Sadu
21. Kravín
22. Mlsnej Kocour
23. Vinohradský Parlament
24. Bruxx
25. Aromi

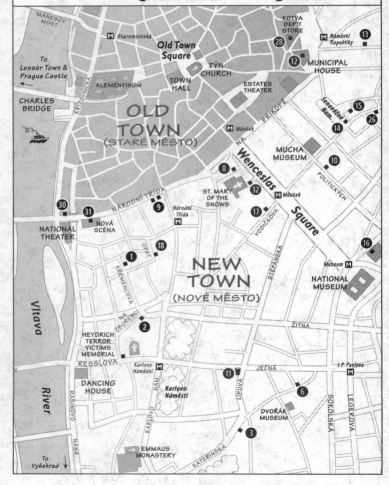

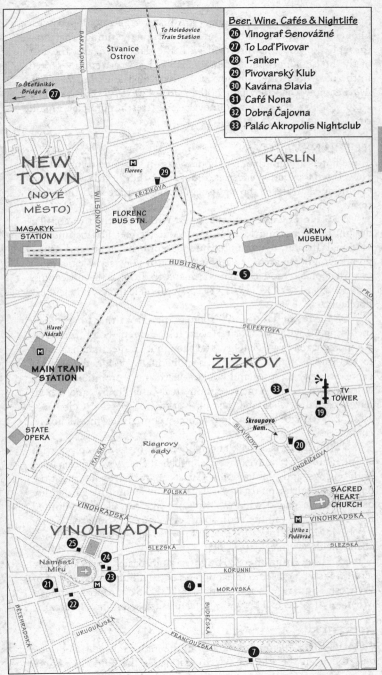

PRAGUE

Beer, Wine, Cafés & Nightlife
- 26 Vinograf Senovážné
- 27 To Loď Pivovar
- 28 T-anker
- 29 Pivovarský Klub
- 30 Kavárna Slavia
- 31 Café Nona
- 32 Dobrá Čajovna
- 33 Palác Akropolis Nightclub

Sprangler. The renovated rooms are historic and equipped with kitchenettes and Italian furniture. The original chimney that runs through the house is inscribed with the date 1577, and the rest of the house is not much younger (RS%, breakfast extra—served in the next-door café, Thunovská 19, look for the *Consulate of San Marino* sign, reception open 9:00-19:00, +420 257 531 189, mobile +420 721 855 880, www.thunovska19.cz, resthunprague@gmail.com).

IN THE NEW TOWN

These hotels are in urban neighborhoods on the outer fringe of the New Town, beyond Wenceslas Square. But they're still within several minutes' walk of the sightseeing zone and are well served by trams.

$$$ Hotel Cube sets itself apart with its distinctive angular design and appealing location, on a quiet street just behind the National Theater, five minutes by foot from the sights and near a popular nightlife area. It's a good option if your style leans more toward cool and modern than warm and traditional (family rooms, Křemencova 18, +420 251 019 811, www.hotelcube.cz, hotelcube@hotelcube.cz).

$$$ Mosaic House's 90 rooms range from tiny to spacious, including 10 with outdoor terraces. It's a "green" hotel, fueled by 100 percent renewable energy, and though it's large, it manages not to feel impersonal: Each room is individually designed, with accents—mainly pictures and books—featuring a prominent Czech cultural figure. The large reception area, café, library, and spa all have a casual, stylish vibe (just off Karlovo Náměstí at Odborů 4, +420 277 016 880, www.mosaichouse.com, info@mosaichouse.com).

$$ Hotel 16 is a sleek and modern business-class place with an intriguing Art Nouveau facade, polished cherry-wood elegance, high ceilings, and 14 fine rooms. Guests are primarily interns at the nearby general hospital (RS%, back rooms facing the garden are quieter, triple-paned windows, air-con, free tea, elevator, limited free parking, 10-minute walk south of Wenceslas Square, Metro: I.P. Pavlova, Kateřinská 16, Praha 2, +420 776 245 960, no website, adam.sneider@vfn.cz).

$$ Hotel Anna offers 26 bright, simple, pastel rooms and basic service. It's a bit closer to the action—just 10 minutes by foot east of Wenceslas Square (elevator, Budečská 17, Praha 2, Metro: Náměstí Míru, +420 222 513 111, www.hotelanna.cz, sales@hotelpro.cz).

HOSTELS

¢ Hostel Elf, a 10-minute walk from the main train station or one bus stop from the Florenc Metro station, is the wildest of these hostels: fun-loving, ramshackle, and covered with noisy, self-in-flicted graffiti. They offer cheap, basic beds; a helpful staff; and use-ful services—free luggage room, no lockout, free tea and coffee, cheap beer, and a terrace (private rooms available, reserve four days ahead, Husitská 11, Praha 3, take bus #133 or #207 from Florenc Metro station for one stop to U Památníku, +420 222 540 963, www.hostelelf.com, info@hostelelf.com).

¢ **Sophie's Hostel,** on a quiet street a 10-minute walk from the top of Wenceslas Square, has a modern design in an Art Nou-veau building. There's a shared kitchen as well as a hearty breakfast prepared by a real chef—not exactly the norm for hostels (private rooms and apartment available, Melounova 2, Praha 2, around the corner from I.P. Pavlova metro stop, +420 210 011 300, https://sophieshostel.com, info@sophieshostel.com).

¢ **Czech Inn Hostel,** two tram stops from Náměstí Míru metro in the expat Vinohrady neighborhood, has a cool design mixing natural wood, lacquered cement, and exposed brick. There's a basement bar that regularly stages concerts and stand-up (cozy private rooms and apartments available, take tram #4 or #22 from Náměstí Míru two stops to Krymská, at Francouzská 76, +420 210 011 110, www.czech-inn.com, info@czech-inn.com).

Eating in Prague

A big part of Prague's charm is found in wandering aimlessly through the city's winding old quarters, marveling at the archi-tecture, watching the people, and sniffing out fun restaurants. In addition to meat-and-potatoes Czech cuisine, you'll find trendy, student-oriented bars and some fine international eateries (in gen-eral, Indian and Italian food tends to be very good, Thai and Viet-namese mediocre, Chinese drowned in soy sauce). For ambience, the options include traditional, dark Czech beer halls; elegant Art Nouveau dining rooms; and modern cafés.

I've listed eating and drinking establishments by neighbor-hood. Most of the options—and highest prices—are in the **Old Town.** For a light meal, consider one of Prague's many cafés.

Generally, if you walk just a few minutes away from the tourist flow, you'll find better value, atmosphere, and service. The more touristy a place is, the more likely you'll pay too much—either in inflated prices or because waiters pad the bill.

Several areas well situated for sightseeing are lined with tour-isty restaurants. While these places are not necessarily bad values, I've listed only a few of your many options—just survey the scene in these spots and choose whatever looks best. **Kampa Square,** just off the Charles Bridge, feels like a quiet, small-town square. **Havelská Market** is surrounded by a mix of fancy restaurants and cheap little eateries. The massive **Old Town Square** is *the* place to nurse a drink or enjoy a meal while watching the tide of people, both tourists and locals, sweep back and forth. **Bethlehem Square,** still part of the Old Town but away from the main tourist flow, is my choice for an atmospheric outdoor evening meal.

EATING TIPS

Paying and Tipping: Look at your itemized bill carefully to make sure you understand each line (especially in touristy spots). Restaurants with sit-down service include a service charge on the bill. On top of that, locals tip by rounding up (usually 5 to 10 percent for good service—but not more).

Smoking in Restaurants: Like most European countries, the Czech Republic does not permit smoking inside restaurants and cafés. It is generally OK, however, to smoke in outdoor seating areas, which nonsmokers may occasionally find unpleasant.

Dining with a View: For great views, consider these options, described later: **Villa Richter** (next to Prague Castle, above Malostranská Metro stop), **Petřínské Terasy** (next to the funicular stop halfway up Petřín Hill), or the **Oblaca** restaurant and café (200 feet up in the Žižkov TV tower east of downtown).

Traditional Czech Places: While many Czechs have gradually come to prefer the cosmopolitan tastes of the world to the mundane taste of pork and sauerkraut, they like to revisit traditional institutions to reconnect with the childhood flavors of tripe soup or goulash. So while "authentic" Czech restaurants in the center have become touristy, they're still great fun, a good value, and enjoyed by locals as well. Expect unadorned spaces, curt service, and reasonably good, inexpensive food.

Cheap-and-Cheery Sandwich Shops: All around town you'll find modern little sandwich shops offering inexpensive fresh-made sandwiches (grilled if you like), pastries, salads, and drinks. You can get the food to go or eat inside at simple tables.

Groceries and Farmers Markets: Ask your hotelier for the location of the nearest grocery store. An even cheaper chain of small grocery stores, with several locations in the Old Town, is Žabka (look for a colored shopping basket sign outside).

Farmers markets crop up around the city and tantalize picnickers. Apart from vegetables, you'll find quality cheeses, juices, cakes, coffee, and more (www.farmarsketrziste.cz). The most central is on **Republic Square** (Náměstí Republiky), just across the street from the Municipal House and the Powder Tower (Mon-Fri until 20:00). The most scenic is the **Náplavka** ("River Landing") market on the Vltava embankment, just south of the Palacký Bridge (Sat 8:00-14:00).

Restaurant Code

Eateries in this book are categorized according to the average cost of a typical main course. Drinks, desserts, and splurge items can raise the price considerably. 20 Kč = about $1.

$$$$ **Splurge:** Most main courses over 475 Kč (€20)
$$$ **Pricier:** 350-475 Kč (€15-20)
$$ **Moderate:** 200-350 Kč (€10-15)
$ **Budget:** Under 200 Kč (€10)

In the Czech Republic, a pub, basic sit-down eatery, and less-touristy café or teahouse is **$**, a typical restaurant—or a fancy café with coffee over 50 Kč and tea over 100 Kč—is **$$**, an up-scale restaurant is **$$$,** and a swanky splurge is **$$$$.**

PRAGUE

THE OLD TOWN

For locations, see the "Restaurants in Prague's Old Town" map.

Traditional Czech

$$ Restaurace u Provaznice ("By the Ropemaker's Wife") has all the Czech classics, peppered with the story of a once-upon-a-time-faithful wife. (Check the menu for details of the gory story.) Natives congregate under bawdy frescoes for the famously good "pig leg" with horseradish and Czech mustard. This is a handy spot on a peaceful lane just a block from the commotion at the bottom of Wenceslas Square (daily, Provaznická 3, +420 224 232 528).

$$ U Medvídků ("By the Bear Cubs") started out as a brewery in 1466 (they still offer a range of their own microbrews, including one of the oldest-ever wheat beers) and is now a flagship beer hall of the Czech Budweiser. The one large room is bright, noisy, and touristy (daily, a block toward Wenceslas Square from Bethlehem Square at Na Perštýně 7, +420 736 662 900).

$ U Zlatého Tygra ("By the Golden Tiger Pub") has long embodied the proverbial Czech pub, where beer turns strangers into kindred spirits as they share their life stories with one another. Today, "The Tiger" is a buzzing shrine to one of its longtime regulars, the writer Bohumil Hrabal, whose fictions immortalize many of the colorful characters that once warmed the wooden benches here (tight seating, daily from 15:00, just a block off Karlova at Husova 17, +420 222 221 111).

$ Restaurace u Betlémské Kaple, behind Bethlehem Chapel, is not "ye olde" Czech. It's peaceful, woody, and spacious. Locals appreciate the cheap lunch deals and fish specialties. Portions are splittable and prices are good (daily, Betlémské Náměstí 2, +420 222 221 639).

$$ Restaurace Mlejnice ("The Mill") is a fun little pub

Restaurants in Prague's Old Town

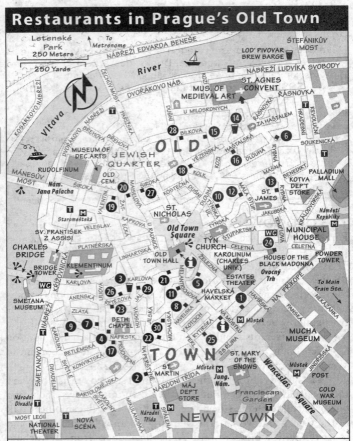

Eateries

1. Restaurace u Provaznice
2. U Medvídků
3. U Zlatého Tygra
4. Restaurace u Betlémské Kaple
5. Restaurace Mlejnice
6. Lokál
7. V Zátiší
8. Kogo Havelská
9. Lehká Hlava
10. Maitrea Vegetarian Rest.
11. Country Life Restaurant
12. Dhaba Beas Cafeteria
13. Indian Jewel
14. James Joyce Irish Pub
15. La Casa Blů
16. Food Lab
17. Alriso Risotteria Italiana
18. Kolkovna
19. Alforno Focacceria Italiana
20. King Solomon Restaurant
21. Hotel u Prince Terasa Roof Terrace

Beer, Wine & Cafés

22. Myslíš?
23. Autentista Wine & Champagne Bar
24. Grand Café Orient
25. Café Café
26. Café Montmartre
27. Kafka Hummus Café
28. Božská Lahvice
29. Crème de la Crème
30. U Zlatého Kohouta

strewn with farm implements and happy eaters, located just out of the tourist crush two blocks from the Old Town Square. They serve traditional specials, hearty salads, and modern Czech plates. Reservations are smart for dinner (daily, between Melantrichova and Železná at Kožná 14, +420 224 228 635, www.restaurace-mlejnice. cz).

$$ Lokál is a hit for its good-quality Czech classics. Filling a long, arched space, the restaurant plays on nostalgia: The stark interior is a deliberate 1980s retro design, and it celebrates the hungry and thirsty working class. The name roughly means "the neighborhood dive"—a reference to the basic canteens of that age. Reservations are smart (daily until late, Dlouhá 33, +420 734 283 874, https://lokal-dlouha.ambi.cz).

Modern and Vegetarian

$$$$ V Zátiší prides itself on being untraditional in every sense, from the ambience and service to the chef's imaginative concoctions. Delicate deer, duck, and fish typically swim in carefully calibrated sauces and come with unusual side dishes (Mon-Sat lunch and dinner, Sun dinner only, Liliová 1, +420 222 221 155).

$$$ Kogo Havelská serves modern takes on traditional Italian cuisine, including perfectly cooked pasta and fish and meats paired with seasonal ingredients. They also make their own bread and desserts (daily, Havelská 29, +420 224 210 259).

$ Lehká Hlava ("Clear Head") is a vegetarian oasis of peace located within 100 yards of the Charles Bridge on a hidden cul-de-sac. Its delightful historic vaulted space, given a retro sci-fi remodel, couldn't feel more distant from the bustle of the ubiquitous crowds. The chef is on a mission to please the senses with a wide-ranging menu of veggie takes on international cuisine. The daily lunch specials are a particularly good value (daily, limited options 15:30-17:30, Boršov 2, +420 222 220 665).

$$ Maitrea Vegetarian Restaurant is a favorite Old Town vegetarian place, where a spirit of wellness and feng shui prevails. The ground floor is fresh and modern. Downstairs is a world of fountains, pillows, and Buddhas. The extensive, creative menu will stoke your appetite (vegan-friendly, daily, cheap lunch specials Mon-Fri, half a block downhill from the Týn Church north door at Týnská 6, +420 221 711 631).

$$ Country Life Restaurant is a cafeteria with a well-displayed buffet of salads and hot veggie dishes. It's midway between the Old Town Square and the bottom of Wenceslas Square. They're serious about their vegetarianism, serving only plant-based, unprocessed, and unrefined food (pay by weight; Mon-Thu 8:30 until 19:00, Fri until 16:00, Sun 11:00-18:00, closed Sat; through courtyard at Melantrichova 15/Michalská 18, +420 224 213 366).

$$ Dhaba Beas Cafeteria is run by a Punjabi chef. Diners grab a steel tray and scoop up whatever looks good—typically various choices of *dal* (lentils) and *sabji* (vegetables) with rice or *chapati* (pancakes). The food is sold by weight—you'll likely spend 200 Kč for lunch. Tucked away in a courtyard behind the Týn Church, this place is popular with university students and young professionals (daily, Týnská 19, +420 608 035 727).

International Eateries and Bars

Dlouhá, the wide street leading away from the Old Town Square behind the Jan Hus Memorial, takes you into a neighborhood west of the Jewish Quarter where you can eat your way around the world. Here are a few favorites from this United Nations of eateries.

Indian: Located in a modern building two blocks behind the Municipal House, **$$$ Indian Jewel** was among the first in a recent wave of quality Indian restaurants to arrive in Prague. They offer Indian classics, vegetarian options, and good-value lunch specials on weekdays. The hardworking owner, Sanjeev, is proud of his rare-in-Prague tandoor oven—ideal for baking authentic breads (daily, Rybná 9, +420 725 107 059).

Irish: $ James Joyce Irish Pub may seem like a strange recommendation in Prague—home of some of the world's best beer—but it has the kind of ambience that locals (and few tourists) seek out. They serve basic pub grub, fish and chips, and curries. Expats have favored this pub for Guinness ever since the Velvet Revolution enabled the Celts to return to one of their original homelands. Worn wooden floors, dingy walls, and the Irish manager transport you right into the heart of blue-collar Dublin (daily until late, U Obecního Dvora 4, +420 224 818 851).

Mexican: One of the last student bastions in the Old Town, **$$ La Casa Blů,** with cheap lunch specials, Mexican plates, Staropramen beer, and greenish mojitos, is your own little pueblo in Prague. Painted in warm oranges and reds, energized by upbeat music, and guarded by creatures from Mayan mythology, La Casa Blů attracts a fiesta of happy eaters and drinkers (daily, Sun from 14:00, on the corner of Kozí and Bílkova, +420 224 818 270).

International Fusion: $$ Food Lab, with a sleek, modern interior, blends tastes from all over the world. Breakfast is sumptuous and the weekly lunch menus are a good value. Dinner portions encourage family-style sharing (daily, Haštalská 4, +420 257 310 713).

Italian near Bethlehem Square: Located on a quiet square near Bethlehem Chapel, **$$$ Alriso Risotteria Italiana** offers creative gluten-free dishes in a classy setting with seating both inside and out. Locals come here for the moist and flavorful rice bread (daily, Betlémské Náměstí 11, +420 222 233 341).

Jewish Quarter

These restaurants are well placed to reenergize after a demanding tour of the Jewish Quarter. Also consider the nearby international eateries listed earlier.

$$$ Kolkovna, the flagship restaurant of a chain allied with Pilsner Urquell, is big and woody yet modern, serving a fun mix of Czech and international cuisine—ribs, salads, cheese plates, and beer. It feels a tad formulaic...but not in a bad way (a bit overpriced, daily, across from Spanish Synagogue at V Kolkovně 8, +420 224 819 701).

$$$ Alforno Focacceria Italiana is a low-key slice of Italy conveniently located across the street from the Pinkas synagogue. You can splurge on fancy fish and meat dishes or opt for relatively affordable pasta dishes and weekday lunch specials (daily, Široká 25, +420 224 818 322).

$$$ King Solomon Restaurant, the oldest kosher restaurant in Prague, serves traditional Jewish dishes in a handsome setting, with an emphasis on roasted, grilled, and braised meats. The daily fixed-price *menu*, available at both lunch and dinner, gives you the chance to sample a range of dishes for a good price (daily, Fri and Sat Shabbat meals by reservation only, Široká 8, +420 224 818 752, www.kosher.cz).

Dining with an Old Town Square View

$$$$ Hotel u Prince Terasa, atop the five-star hotel facing the Astronomical Clock, is designed for foreign tourists. A sleek elevator inside the hotel takes you to the rooftop terrace, packed with tables and an open-air grill. The view is arguably the best in town—especially at sunset. The menu is overpriced, with photos that make ordering easy. Servers can be rude, dishonest, and aggressive. Confirm exact prices before ordering. This place is also great for a drink at sunset or late at night (daily, outdoor heaters, Staroměstské Náměstí 29, +420 737 261 842, www.terasauprince.com).

THE LESSER TOWN

These characteristic eateries are handy for a bite before or after your Prague Castle visit. For locations, see the "Hotels and Restaurants in the Lesser Town and Castle Quarter" map, earlier.

$$ Malostranská Beseda, in the impeccably restored former Town Hall, weaves together an imaginative menu of traditional Czech dishes (both classic and little known), vegetarian fare, and fresh fish. It feels a bit sterile and formulaic, but you can choose among three settings: the ground-floor restaurant on the left, the café on the right (serves meals, but it's OK to have only coffee or cake), or the packed beer hall downstairs, where Pilsner Urquell is served (daily, Malostranské Náměstí 21, +420 257 409 112). The restaurant has a recommended music club upstairs.

$$ Lokál U Bílé Kuželky ("By the White Bowling Pin"), a branch of the Old Town's recommended Lokál restaurant, is the best bet for quick, cheap, well-executed Czech classics on this side of the river (daily until late, Míšeňská 12; from the Charles Bridge, turn right around the U Tří Pštrosů Hotel just before the Lesser Town gate; +420 257 212 014).

$$ St. Martin is the quintessential neighborhood pub/restaurant serving inexpensive dishes (mainly burgers), a variety of beers, and a selection of wines from two family-owned Moravian wineries (daily, tucked away on a little street just above the American embassy at Vlašská 7, +420 257 219 728).

$$ Vegan's Prague, on the top two floors and a tiny terrace of a narrow medieval house, serves vegan variations on Czech classics as well as Asian fare. The setting is a tasteful mix of Renaissance roof beams, Balinese art, and gorgeous vistas (daily, Nerudova 36, +420 735 171 313).

$$ Natureza Vegetarian House, on a quiet walnut-tree-shaded patio next to the Gothic walls of St. Lawrence Church, is a snug, family-run place offering eclectic vegetarian, vegan, and gluten-free food. Choose from soups, salads, veggie burgers, Asian-inspired dishes, burritos, risottos, desserts, and fancy nonalcoholic drinks (daily until 17:00, Hellichova 14, +420 721 678 883).

$ U Hrocha ("By the Hippo"), a small authentic pub with tar dripping from its walls, is packed with beer drinkers. Expect simple, traditional meals—basically meat starters with bread. Just below the castle near the Lesser Town Square (Malostranské Náměstí), it's actually the haunt of many members of parliament, which is around the corner (cash only, daily from 12:00, chalkboard lists daily meals in English, Thunovská 10, +420 257 533 389).

$$ Cukrkávalimonáda ("Sugar, Coffee, Lemonade") is part restaurant and part patisserie, serving big salads, made-to-order sandwiches, artful pastries, and freshly squeezed juice in a setting mixing old and new decor. The bistro—an oasis just a block away from the tourist crush—is 50 yards down the first street to the left after you exit the Charles Bridge (daily 9:00-19:00, Lázeňská 7, +420 257 225 396).

Across the Bridge from the National Theater: Consider these **$$$** elegant choices near the riverfront. **Café Savoy** is the closest you'll get to a Viennese café in Prague—with exquisite dishes mixing French, Viennese, and Czech influences; thoughtful service; and elegant Art Deco surroundings (lunch specials weekdays only, breakfast all day; long hours daily; Vítězná 5, +420 731 136 144). **Pastař** ("The Pasta Maker") is serious about freshly made pasta. Their small menu—Italian with a bit of Czech—includes fine fish and meat dishes as well, and the service is attentive and friendly (daily, Malostranské Nábřeží 558, +420 777 009 108).

Near the Funicular, on Petřín Hill: Halfway up Petřín Hill, **$$ Petřínské Terasy** offers great views over the city from the terrace or woody seating indoors. The menu features traditionally prepared meats (cash only, daily, Petřín 393, +420 257 320 688).

THE CASTLE QUARTER

For locations, see the "Hotels and Restaurants in the Lesser Town and Castle Quarter" map, earlier.

$$$ Villa Richter, at the end of the castle promontory and surrounded by the country's oldest vineyard, is a popular wedding venue—one look at the gorgeous city view tells you why. You can take it all in from the panoramic outdoor seating area while nibbling on "street food" paired with a glass of the vineyard's wine (daily until 19:00, no reservations, past the castle exit gate by the Golden Lane, +420 702 282 402).

$$$ Lobkowicz Palace Café is conveniently located at the far end of the castle near the end of the Golden Lane. There are three seating options—aim for the terrace, which has to-die-for views over the city. A selection of soups, salads, sandwiches, and warm Czech classics is served at the premium prices you'd expect for the location (daily until 18:00, +420 731 192 281).

$$ Klášterní Pivovar ("Monastery Brewery"), founded by an abbot in 1628 and reopened in 2004, has two large rooms and a pleasant courtyard. This is the place, though touristy, to taste a range of unpasteurized beers brewed on the premises, including amber, wheat, and IPA. To accompany the beer, try the strong beer-flavored cheese served on toasted black-yeast bread (daily, Strahovské Nádvoří 301, +420 233 353 155). It's directly across from the entrance to the Strahov Library (don't confuse it with the enormous, tour group-oriented Klášterní Restaurace next door, to the right).

$$$ Host Restaurant is hidden in the middle of a staircase that connects Loretánská and Úvoz streets. This spot, which boasts super views of the Lesser Town and Petřín Hill, has a modern black-and-white design and an imaginative menu (daily; as you go up Loretánská, watch for stairs leading down to the left at #15—just before the arcaded passageway; +420 606 123 449).

$ Hostinec u Černého Vola ("By the Black Ox") is a dingy old-time pub—its survival in the midst of all the castle splendor and tourism is a marvel. It feels like a kegger on the banks of the river Styx, with classic bartenders serving up Kozel beer (traditional "Goat" brand with excellent darks) and beer-friendly gut-bomb snacks (fried cheese, local hot dogs). The pub is located on Loretánská (cash only, daily, 50 yards from Loreta Church, no sign outside, look for the only house on the block without an arcade, English menu on request).

$$ Malý Buddha ("Little Buddha") serves delightful food—especially vegetarian—and takes its theme seriously. You'll step into a mellow, low-lit escape of bamboo and peace, where you'll be served by people with perfect complexions and almost no pulse to the no-rhythm of meditative music. Eating in their little back room is like dining in a temple (cash only, closed Mon, between the castle and Strahov Monastery at Úvoz 46, +420 604 709 379).

$ U Zavěšenýho Kafe a Divadlo Pokračuje ("By the Hanging Coffee" and "The Show Goes On"), just below Loreta Square on the way to the castle, is a creative little pub/restaurant with friendly service that has attracted a cult following among Prague's literati. You can "hang a coffee" here for a local vagabond by paying for an extra coffee on your way out (daily until late, Loretánská 13, +420 733 483 900).

$$ U Labutí ("By the Swans") offers Czech food for a good price in a tranquil courtyard, just across from the Plague Column on Castle Square (daily, Hradčanské Náměstí 11, +420 220 511 191).

$$ Kuchyň ("Kitchen"), just behind the Tomáš Masaryk statue on Castle Square, has a small terrace with great city views. They serve Czech classics with a modern twist (daily, Hradčanské Náměstí 1, +420 736 152 891).

$ Kavárna ve Šternberském Paláci is the locals' getaway from the tourist scene on Castle Square. It's tucked behind the Archbishop's Palace. They serve soup or goulash with bread and drinks in a quiet courtyard at unbeatable prices. Check out the garden with stunning sculptures that's through the door on the left corner of the courtyard (Tue-Sun until 18:00, closed Mon, Hradčanské Náměstí 15, +420 703 372 197).

$ Kavárna Nový Svět ("New World Café"), on a quiet lane down from the Loreta Church, offers a tasty cake-and-coffee break from the tourist crowds, either in a cozy interior or a beautiful garden setting (Tue-Sun until 19:00, closed Mon, Nový Svět 2).

THE NEW TOWN AND NEARBY

For locations, see the "Hotels and Restaurants in the New Town and Nearby" map, earlier.

Traditional Czech

$$ Restaurace u Pinkasů, founded in 1843, is known among locals as the first place in Prague to serve Pilsner beer. It's popular for solid, basic Czech pub grub. You can sit in its traditional interior, in front to watch the street action, or out back in a delightful garden shaded by the Gothic buttresses of the neighborhood church (daily, near the bottom of Wenceslas Square, between the Old Town and New Town, Jungmannovo Náměstí 16, +420 221 111 152).

$$ Café Louvre is an elegant favorite from long ago (it opened in 1902 and maintains its classic atmosphere). It features simple tables, paper tablecloths, and an army of young waiters serving up decent food (Czech classics, vegetarian dishes, lunch specials) at good prices (two-course lunch offered; long hours daily; Národní 22, +420 724 054 055).

$ Knedlín ("The Dumpling Village") is a tiny place that, in keeping with its name, serves 20 kinds of dumplings, both sweet and savory. Having one is an indulgent snack; get two and you're on your way to a meal. Order from the display case and then squeeze yourself in, like filling in a dumpling, at one of the minuscule tables (daily, Národní 24, +420 702 214 518).

$$ Kantýna serves "meat from the bone" (a.k.a., very fresh). A cross between a traditional butcher's shop and a modern pick-from-the-counter canteen, this place offers the best quality fast food for carnivores. They also serve a wide selection of freshly made soups, salads, and traditional desserts (daily, a block off the middle of Wenceslas Square, just down the street from the Mucha Museum at Politických Vězňů 5, no reservations).

$$ Pivovarský Dům ("The Brewhouse"), on the corner of Ječná and Lípová, is popular with locals for its rare variety of fresh beers (yeast, wheat, and fruit-flavored), fine classic Czech dishes, and an inviting interior that mixes traditional and modern (daily, reservations recommended in the evenings, walk up Štěpánská street from Wenceslas Square for 10 minutes, or take tram #22 for two stops from Národní to Štěpánská; Lípová 15, +420 296 216 666, www.pivo-dum.cz).

Art Nouveau Splendor in the Municipal House

$$$ Kavárna Obecní Dům, a dressy café, is drenched in chandeliered, Art Nouveau elegance and offers the best value and experience here. Light, pricey meals and drinks come with great atmosphere and bad service (long hours daily, live piano or jazz trio in the evening, +420 222 002 763).

$$$ Restaurace Obecní Dům, in the next wing, is fine and formal, oozing Mucha elegance and slinky romance. They serve not particularly imaginative modern Czech cuisine with few international touches. You're here more for the ambience than the food (daily, +420 222 002 770).

$$$ The beer cellar is overpriced and generally filled with tour groups (daily).

Other New Town Eateries

Near Masaryk Station: $$$ Brasserie La Gare opened with the mission to serve Czechs authentic French brasserie fare. It prides itself on its grilled fish and meats, and the lunch specials are a good value. The combination of wood-and-bronze interior and an open fire recreates a French-village atmosphere. There's also a French bakery and a deli (daily, V Celnici 3, +420 222 313 712).

At and **Near Jindřišská Tower: $$$$ Zvonice** ("Bellfry") is an over-the-top splurge nested between wooden beams, exposed brick, and a 16th-century bronze bell on the top two floors of the gothic Jindřišská Tower (reached by elevator). The chef specializes in traditional Czech preparations of game, and a few fish and vegetarian options are also available (daily, Jindřišská 33, the tower three blocks from central Wenceslas Square is hard to miss, +420 224 220 009, www.restaurantzvonice.cz).

$$$ ZEM ("Earth," punning on Zen) melds Czech and Japanese influences to produce an "avant-garde" cuisine that puts a premium on creativity. Whether you order yakitori or schnitzel, what arrives on your plate will likely defy expectations. The setting is equally engaging: the artsy 1920s interior has the stagelike open kitchen as its focal point (lunch specials, daily, just behind the Jindřišská Tower three blocks from central Wenceslas Square at Senovážné Náměstí 23, +420 227 344 900).

Near Wenceslas Square: $ Bistro Muzeum, in the former communist parliament building (now part of the National Museum) at Wenceslas Square, offers daily menus, freshly roasted coffee, soups, and sandwiches in a pleasant, kid-friendly setting (daily until 18:00, Vinohradská 1, +420 220 960 458).

$ Ovocný Světozor ("World of Fruit") is a colorful joint that's popular for its ice cream, but they also sell really cheap (and good) Czech-style open-face sandwiches—plus cakes and other desserts. Ask for an English menu (long hours daily, in the Světozor Mall off Wenceslas Square at Vodičkova 39).

Near Národní Třída: $$ Velryba is a low-key, artsy café-restaurant in a cool neighborhood buzzing with students. Here you can enjoy a beer, a burger, and chicken wings five minutes from the Old Town with nary a tourist in sight (daily, Opatovická 24, +420 224 931 444).

Žižkov

$$$ Oblaca ("The Clouds"), the restaurant 200 feet up in the

Žižkov TV tower, is expensive, but it comes with a Sputnik's-eye view. A less pricey café serves breakfast and lunch (open late daily 11:00-24:00, less expensive café open 9:00-16:00, reservations recommended, Mahlerovy Sady 1, Metro: Náměstí Jiřího z Poděbrad, +420 210 320 086, https://towerpark.cz/oblaca, www.towerpark.cz/en/oblaca-restaurant).

$ **Pivnice u Sadu** is the quintessential neighborhood pub, frequented as much by Czechs as by the Americans, Russians, and Slovaks who live in the area. Sit outside in the shade of a wild cherry tree, or in the interior decorated with whatever the neighbors found in their attics and gave to the restaurant (long hours daily, on a round square a block west from Žižkov TV tower at Škroupovo Náměstí 5, Metro: Náměstí Jiřího z Poděbrad, +420 222 727 072).

Vinohrady
Náměstí Míru Square: The area around this square has a wide choice of good restaurants. $$ **Kravín** ("Cowshed") serves Czech classics, pasta, and grilled meats in a red-brick interior. The lunch menu is a good value (daily, Náměstí Míru 18, +420 702 015 054). $$ **Mlsnej Kocour** ("Fussy Cat"), run by the Pilsner brewery, focuses on Czech dishes in modern decor that can feel a bit formulaic (daily, Belgická 42, +420 222 541 584).

$$ **Vinohradský Parlament** specializes in classic Czech cuisine, particularly dumplings. At lunchtime it's the local crowd's first choice for a quick fix (daily, Korunní 1, +420 224 250 403). Nearby $$$ **Bruxx** is a Belgian brasserie with a good-value lunch menu (daily, Náměstí Míru 9, +420 224 250 404) and $$$$ **Aromi** is a high-end Italian restaurant serving meticulously prepared seafood in a fancy setting (lunch and dinner Mon-Fri, dinner only Sat, closed Sun, Náměstí Míru 6, +420 222 713 222).

CRAFT BEER AND WINE BARS
These places give you a good sense of Prague's popular craft beer and wine scenes. For locations, see the "Hotels and Restaurants in the New Town and Nearby" map unless otherwise noted.

$$ **Vinograf Senovážné** is an intimate wine bar with over 500 bottles to choose from and a carefully crafted seasonal food menu that's both creative and eclectic (lunch specials, closed Sun, just behind the Jindřišská Tower, three blocks from central Wenceslas Square at Senovážné Náměstí 23, +420 214 214 681).

$$ **Loď Pivovar** ("The Brewery Barge") brews three staple beers and a range of specials on the premises. The upper deck is effectively an open-air beer garden, the middle deck doubles up as a restaurant with traditional Czech dishes, while the eye-at-water-level bottom deck is a pub that pairs beer with traditional Czech

tapas (daily; at Dvořákovo nábřeží just under the Štefánik Bridge, near the Convent of St. Agnes; +420 773 778 788).

$$ T-anker is a beer terrace sitting on top of the 1970s Kotva department store just off Republic Square. While their *Tanker* beer is specially made for this location, they do a good a job of rotating beers from around Prague and the country on their nine taps. The view of the Old Town towers is unbeatable (daily; either enter through the main doors of Kotva and take the elevator to the fourth floor and then the escalator up one more floor, or take the side entrance from Králodvorská street and then the elevator to the fifth floor; +420 722 445 474).

$$ Pivovarský Klub ("The Brew Club") serves a wide selection of Czech microbrews in a modern, blond-wood restaurant. Every week different beers are featured on tap (daily, evening reservations recommended; about 50 yards on the left along Křižíkova from Florenc Metro station, Křižíkova 17+420 222 315 777; https://pivo-klub.cz).

$$ Myslíš? ("Do You Think?") specializes in Czech microbrews of diverse provenance, ranging from lagers to IPAs to stouts. It's hard to beat the location—a small modern ground floor and a large, cool brick cellar in the heart of the Old Town (vegan lunch served, daily until late, Sat-Sun evening only, Skořepka 3, just around the corner from the Havelská Market—for location, see the "Restaurants in Prague's Old Town" map, +420 774 591 091).

$$ Autentista Wine and Champagne Bar serves a carefully curated list of organic Czech and international wines in a vaulted space with modern design. You can accompany your vino with a selection of cheeses and cured hams (daily from 17:00, Řetězová 10—for location, see the "Restaurants in Prague's Old Town" map, +420 602 587 827).

CAFÉS

The Prague coffeehouse scene is alive and kicking. While some cafés are dripping with history, new ones are popping up almost daily. Cafés in the Old Town and New Town are as much about the ambience as they are about the coffee.

Old Town

For locations, see the "Restaurants in Prague's Old Town" map, earlier.

$$ Grand Café Orient is only one flight up off busy Celetná street, yet a world away from the crush of tourism below. Located in the Cubist House of the Black Madonna, the café is fittingly decorated with a Cubist flair. With its stylish, circa-1910 decor toned to dark green, this space is full of air and light—and a good value as well. The café takes its Cubism seriously: Traditionally round desserts are served square (sandwiches, salads, vanilla squares and other desserts, great balcony seating, long hours daily, Ovocný Trh 19, at the corner of Celetná near the Powder Tower, +420 224 224 240).

$$ Café Café, just off to the right from the main drag connecting the Old Town and Wenceslas Square, serves salads, sandwiches, and cakes in a fancy setting (long hours daily, Rytířská 10, +420 774 331 122).

$$ Café Montmartre, a block and a world away from the tourist crush of Karlova on the quiet Řetězová street, feels like a hidden meeting place for dissident poets from the 1950s (Mon-Fri from 14:00, Sat-Sun from 16:00, Řetězová 7, +420 601 364 137).

$$ Kafka Hummus Café is a stylish pit stop for a dose of coffee and a bite of crunchy falafel or homemade hummus in-between synagogue visits (Mon-Fri until 18:00, Sat-Sun until 20:00, in the Jewish Quarter at Široká 12).

$$ Božská Lahvice ("Divine Bottle") is a café-cum-bookstore in a spacious, light-filled underground space just steps from the Spanish Synagogue. It's a local favorite for wine, coffee, soup, and pierogi in between book browsing (long hours daily, Bílkova 6, +420 734 441 004).

At the intersection of Řetězová and Husova, **Crème de la Crème**'s ice cream is a hit with locals for its fruity and nutty flavors (daily, Husova 12).

New Town

For locations, see the "Hotels and Restaurants in the New Town and Nearby" map on page 136.

$$ Kavárna Slavia, across from the National Theater (facing the Legií Bridge on Národní street), is a fixture in Prague, famous as a hangout for its literary elite. Today, it's past its prime, with a faded Art Deco interior and celebrity photos on the wall. But its iconic status makes it a fun stop for a coffee (long  hours daily, sit as near the river as possible, Smetanovo Nábřeží 2, +420 224 218 493). Notice the *Drinker of Absinthe* painting on the wall (and on the menu)—with the iconic Czech writer struggling with reality.

$$ Café Nona, on the second floor of the new building of the National Theater, takes you back to the 1980s with its fashionably retro design. Sip your coffee and enjoy the view of busy National Street below (long hours daily, Národní 4, +420 775 755 147).

TEAHOUSES

In the 1990s, after the borders opened, many young Czechs ventured beyond Western Europe to places like Southeast Asia, Africa, or Peru. When they returned, many gravitated toward Eastern-style teahouses, where the civilization-weary spirit was soothed by the strong taste of yogi chai and the scent of incense. While the teahouse boom has passed, two fine examples still survive in handy Old Town and New Town locales.

$ **Dobrá Čajovna** ("Good Teahouse"), only a few steps off the bustle of Wenceslas Square, takes you into a peaceful, bamboo-shaded world that elevates tea to a religious ritual. You'll be given an English menu—which lovingly describes each tea—and a bell. The menu lists a world of tea (very fresh, prices by the small pot), "accompaniments" (such as Exotic Miscellany), and light meals "for hungry tea drinkers." When you're ready to order, ring your bell to beckon a tea monk (daily, Sun from 14:00; through a short passageway near the base of Wenceslas Square, opposite McDonald's; at Václavské Náměstí 14, +420 224 231 480). For location, see the "Hotels and Restaurants in the New Town and Nearby" map on page 136).

$ **U Zlatého Kohouta** ("By the Golden Rooster"), nestled in the corner of a picturesque (and well-hidden) Old Town courtyard, feels even more intimate and less formulaic than Dobrá Čajovna. Japanese woodblock prints and old Chinese maps adorn the walls, and the menu ranges from Taiwanese oolongs to Himalayan yogi teas to a Czech grandma's dried-fruit potions. Sit in one of three tiny vaulted rooms or outside in the circa-1800 workaday courtyard with Tibetan prayer flags flapping above (Mon-Fri from 13:00, Sat-Sun from 14:00; from the end of the Havelská Market farthest from the church, take a sharp right and head down a narrow street, then look for a small courtyard entry in the corner on the left at Michalská 3; +420 705 223 526). For location, see "Restaurants in Prague's Old Town" map, earlier.

Prague Connections

BY TRAIN

Prague's **main train station** (Hlavní Nádraží; "Praha hl. n." on schedules) serves all international trains; most trains within the Czech Republic, including high-speed SC Pendolino trains; and buses to and from Nürnberg and Munich. Trains serving Berlin also stop at the secondary **Holešovice station** (Nádraží Holešovice, located north of the river). Both stations have ATMs (best rates) and exchange bureaus (rotten rates). You'll find handy Czech train and bus schedules at https://idos.idnes.cz (for English, click on the drop-down menu in the top-right corner). It's also worth checking the Czech Railways (České Dráhy) website, www.cd.cz, for specific connections.

To get a better geographical picture, remember that the Czech Republic is a country of landlocked, would-be sailors (recall the greeting "*ahoj*"). Accordingly, the four main international rail lines connect Prague to the closest ports on the four seas: the **North Sea Line** to Hamburg (7 hours) via Dresden and Berlin, the **Baltic Line** to Gdańsk (11 hours) via Warsaw, the **Black Sea Line** to Varna (40 hours) via Budapest and Belgrade, and the **Adriatic Line** to Split (20 hours) via Vienna and Zagreb.

Main Train Station (Hlavní Nádraží)

The station is a busy hive of shops and services; posted maps help you find your way. Three parallel tunnels connect the tracks to the arrival hall. Taking any of these, you'll first reach a low-ceilinged corridor with several services: a variety of handy picnic-supply shops and the "official" taxi stands (avoid these rip-off cabbies—explained later).

Continuing straight down past this corridor, you'll reach the main hall, with four Metro entrances in the center (two for each direction; see "Getting from the Main Station to Your Hotel," later). The one good ATM (pink, Unicredit Bank) is under the stairs across from the main ticket office. Avoid the blue-and-yellow Euronet ATMs, which have bad rates. **Lockers** are in the corner under the stairs on the right, and a **Billa supermarket** is in the corner under the stairs to the left.

Buying Tickets: To get the best prices and to ensure you get on your preferred train (some can sell out), buy ahead online at https://idos.idnes.cz. Tickets for Czech Railways (České Dráhy) trains are also sold at www.cd.cz.

To purchase in person, for most trains head for the **CD ticket office**—marked *ČD Centrum*—in the middle of the main hall under the stairs. The regular ticket desks are faster if you already know your schedule and destination, but not all attendants speak good English. For more in-depth questions, look for the tiny **ČD Travel** office, on the left as you enter the main office, which sells both domestic and international tickets, and is more likely to provide help in English (Mon-Fri 9:00-18:00, Sat until 14:00, closed Sun, shorter hours in winter, +420 972 241 861, www.cd.cz).

The **RegioJet travel office,** with desks at both sides of the main ticket office, sells international train tickets from the DB (Deutsche Bahn—German railways) system and offers various DB deals and discounts. RegioJet also runs its own trains to Olomouc and Košice, Slovakia, and sells a variety of domestic (e.g., to Český Krumlov) and international (Vienna) bus tickets without a commission (daily until 19:45, +420 539 000 511, https://regiojet.cz). Despite its name, RegioJet does not sell plane tickets.

The **Leo Express ticket office,** across the hall from the ČD Centrum, sells tickets for its trains to Olomouc and Košice (www.le.cz).

Bus Stops: To reach the bus stops for the AE bus to the airport and the DB buses to Nürnberg and Munich, head upstairs to the Art Nouveau hall (explained later) and head outside.

Deciphering Schedules: Platforms are listed by number and—confusingly—sometimes also by letter. *S (sever)* means "north"—the corridor to the left as you face the tracks; *J (jih)* means "south"—the corridor to the right. But in practice, you can take any corridor and walk along the platform to your train. *B1* means the bus platform (upstairs and out front), while *1B*—used by Leo Express trains—is the shorter track at the far-left end of platform 1.

Getting from the Main Station to Your Hotel

Even though the main train station is basically downtown, getting to your hotel can be a little tricky.

On Foot: Most hotels I list in the Old Town are within a 20-minute walk of the train station. Exit the station into a small park, walk through the park, and then cross the street on the other side. Head down Jeruzalémská street to the Jindřišská Tower and tram stop, walk under a small arch, and then continue slightly to the right down Senovážná street. At the end of the street, you'll see the Powder Tower—the grand entry into the Old Town—to the left. Alternatively, Wenceslas Square in the New Town is a 10-minute walk—exit the station, cross the park, and walk to the left along Opletalova street.

By Metro: The Metro is easy. The entrance is right inside the station's main hall—look for the red *M* with two directions: *Háje* or *Letňany*. To purchase tickets from the machine by the Metro entrance, you'll need a credit card. Validate your ticket in the yellow machines *before* you go down the stairs to the tracks.

To get to hotels in the Old Town, take the Letňany-bound red line from the train station to Florenc, then transfer to the yellow line (direction: Zličín) and get off at either Náměstí Republiky, Můstek, or Národní Třída; these stops straddle the Old Town.

Or you can catch the Háje-bound red line to the Muzeum stop, then transfer to the green line (direction: Nemocnice Motol) and get off at either Můstek or Staroměstská. The next stop, Malostranská, is a 15-minute walk from my recommended hotels in the Lesser Town.

By Taxi or Uber: The fair metered rate into the Old Town is about 200 Kč; if your hotel is farther out or across the river, it should

be no more than 300 Kč. Avoid the "official" taxi stand that's marked inside the station: These thugs routinely overcharge arriving tourists (and refuse to take locals, who know the going rate and can't be fooled). Instead, to get an **honest cabbie**, exit the station's main hall through the big glass doors, then cross 50 yards through a park to Opletalova street. A few taxis are usually waiting there in front of Hotel Chopin, on the corner of Jeruzalémská street. Or call a taxi (operators speak English; AAA Taxi, +420 222 333 222; City Taxi, +420 257 257 257). Before getting into a taxi, always confirm the maximum price to your destination, and make sure the driver turns on the meter. For more pointers on taking taxis, see page 62.

Uber works the same way it does at home and typically costs less than a taxi. Drivers pick up from the small parking lot next to platform 1B.

By Tram: The nearest tram stop is to the right as you exit the station (about 200 yards away). Tram #9 (headed away from railway tracks) takes you to the neighborhood near the National Theater and the Lesser Town but isn't useful for most Old Town hotels.

Holešovice Train Station (Nádraží Holešovice)

This station, slightly farther from the center, is suburban mellow. The main hall has the same services as the main train station, in a more compact area. On the left are international and local ticket windows (open 24 hours) and an information office. On the right is an uncrowded café. Two ATMs are just outside the first glass doors, and the Metro is 50 yards to the right (follow signs toward *Vstup,* which means "entrance"; it's three stops to Hlavní Nádraží—the main station—or four stops to the city-center Muzeum stop).

Taxis and trams are outside to the right (allow 300 Kč for a cab to the center).

Train Connections

All international trains pass through the main station (Hlavní Nádraží); some also stop at Holešovice (Nádraží Holešovice). Direct trains connect Prague to Berlin, Munich, Vienna, Budapest, Kraków, and Warsaw. For tips on rail travel, see the "Transportation" section of the Practicalities chapter.

From Prague's Main Station to Domestic Destinations: Konopiště Castle (train to **Benešov,** 2/hour, 1 hour, then 1.5-mile walk), **Kutná Hora** (hourly, 1 hour), **Český Krumlov** (8/day, 1/day direct, 3 hours), **České Budějovice** (almost hourly, 2.5 hours), **Moravský Krumlov** (8/day, 4 hours, change in Brno), **Olomouc** (at least hourly, 2.5 hours), **Brno** (2/hour, 3 hours).

BY BUS

Prague's main bus station is at Florenc, east of the Old Town (Metro: Florenc). But some connections use other stations, including Roztyly (Metro: Roztyly), Na Knížecí (Metro: Anděl), Holešovice (Metro: Nádraží Holešovice), Hradčanská (Metro: Hradčanská), Zličín (Metro: Zličín), or the main train station (Metro: Hlavní Nádraží). Be sure to confirm which station your bus uses. Check Flixbus (www.flixbus.com) and Eurolines (www.eurolines.de) for international connections.

From Prague by Bus to: Terezín (3-4 direct Mon-Fri, fewer Sat-Sun, 1 hour, more with transfer, departs from Nádraží Holešovice), **Český Krumlov** (hourly, 3 hours, departs from Florenc or Na Knížecí), **Brno** (2/hour from Florenc, 2.5 hours, train is better), **Moravský Krumlov** (1/day, 4 hours, change in Znojmo or Brno, train is better).

BY PLANE
Václav Havel Airport

Prague's modern, tidy, user-friendly Václav Havel Airport is located 12 miles (about 30 minutes) west of the city center. Terminal 2 serves destinations within the EU (no passport controls); Terminal 1 serves everywhere else. The airport has ATMs (avoid the change desks), transportation services (such as city transit and shuttle buses), kiosks selling city maps, and a TI (code: PRG, www.prg.aero).

Getting from the Airport to Your Hotel

Getting between the airport and downtown is easy. Leaving either airport terminal, you have several options, listed below from cheapest to priciest:

Dirt Cheap: Take bus #119 to the Nádraží Veleslavín stop (15 minutes) and then take the Metro into the center (another 10 minutes, 40 Kč, buy tickets at info desk in airport arrival hall). This is also fastest as it avoids traffic jams.

Budget: Take the airport express (AE) bus to the main train station (60 Kč, runs every half-hour daily about 6:00-21:00, 40 minutes, look for the *AE* sign in front of the terminal and pay the driver, www.cd.cz). From the station, you can take the Metro, hire a taxi or Uber, or walk to your hotel.

Moderate: Prague Airport Transfers offers 24-hour shuttle and taxi service (door-to-door shared taxi-290 Kč/person; +420 222 554 211 from Czech Republic or +420 516 340 3070 from US, www.prague-airport-transfers.co.uk). Uber usually costs about half the price of a taxi; drivers pick up in the parking lot facing Terminal 1.

Expensive: Catch a taxi. Cabbies wait at the curb directly in front of the arrival hall. Or book a yellow AAA taxi through their office in the airport hall—you'll get a 50 percent discount coupon for the trip back. AAA taxis wait in front of exit D at Terminal 1 and exit E at Terminal 2 (metered rate, generally 600 Kč to downtown).

BY PRIVATE CAR SERVICE

Mike's Chauffeur Service is a reliable, family-run company with fair and fixed rates around town and beyond. Friendly Mike's motto is, "We go the extra mile for you." If Mike is busy, he'll send one of his colleagues—all of whom speak English (round-trip fares, with waiting time included, prices valid through 2025 with this book: Český Krumlov—4,800 Kč, Terezín—2,400 Kč, Karlštejn—2,400 Kč, Karlovy Vary and Pilsner Urquell brewery in Plzeň—4,800 Kč; surcharge for credit-card payment, these prices for up to 4 people, minibus for up to 7 or 8 also available; +420 602 224 893, www.mike-chauffeur.cz, mike.chauffeur@cmail.cz). On the way to Český Krumlov, Mike will stop for no extra charge at Hluboká Castle and/or České Budějovice, where the original Bud beer is made. Mike can also arrange a local guide for your time in many of these places. And for day trips from Prague, Mike can bring bicycles along and will pedal with you.

Mike also offers "Panoramic Transfers" to **Vienna** (8,000 Kč, depart Prague at 8:00, arrive Český Krumlov at 10:00, stay up to 5 hours, 1-hour scenic Czech riverside-and-village drive, then a 2-hour autobahn ride to your Vienna hotel, maximum 4 people),

Budapest (11,500 Kč via Bratislava or the South Moravia wine country, 6 hours), and **Kraków** (10,800 Kč direct, or 11,500 Kč with a stop at Auschwitz; these prices include all road taxes). Mike can also pick you up in any of these cities and bring you to Prague. Check Mike's website for special deals on last-minute transfers, including super-cheap "deadhead" rides when you travel in the opposite direction of a full-fare client.

NEAR PRAGUE

Kutná Hora • Terezín Memorial • Konopiště Castle

Prague has plenty to keep a traveler busy, but don't overlook the interesting day trips in the nearby Bohemian countryside. Within a short bus or train ride of Prague (in different directions), you'll find a rich medieval town, a sobering concentration camp memorial, and a grand castle.

Kutná Hora

Kutná Hora (KOOT-nah HO-rah) is a refreshingly authentic yet unmistakably gorgeous town that sits on top of what was once Europe's largest silver mine. In its heyday, the mine was so productive that Kutná Hora was Bohemia's "second city" after Prague. Much of Europe's standard coinage was minted here, and the king got a 12 percent cut of every penny. In addition to financing much of Prague's grand architecture, these precious deposits also paid for Kutná Hora's particularly fine cathedral. But by about 1700, the

mining and minting petered out, and the city slumbered.

Once rich, then ignored, Kutná Hora is now appreciated by tourists looking for a handy side trip from Prague. While most visitors come here primarily for the famous, offbeat Sedlec Bone Church, the delightful town itself trumps it—with one of the finest

Day Trips

Czech churches outside Prague (St. Barbara's Cathedral), a breath-taking promenade overlooking the valley, a fascinating silver mine, and a cute, cobbled town center with pretty pastel houses.

All in all, underrated Kutná Hora makes a strong case for the title of "best Czech stop outside of Prague." Unlike dolled-up Český Krumlov, Kutná Hora is a typical Czech town. The shops on the main square cater to locals, and the factory between the Sedlec Bone Church and the train station—since the 1930s, the biggest tobacco processor in the country—is now Philip Morris' headquarters for Central Europe. Kutná Hora is about as close to quintessential Czech life as you can get. Small, untouristy original handicraft shops and many delightful cafés are worthwhile stops on a walk through town.

GETTING TO KUTNÁ HORA

The town is 45 miles east of Prague. Direct trains from Prague stop at Kutná Hora's main train station, two miles from the town center (hourly, 1 hour; some require a transfer in Kolín). From the main station, a local train shuttles visitors in just a few minutes to Sedlec station (near the **Sedlec Bone Church**), then to the central Město station (near the rest of the sights). After getting off at the main station, follow the passage beneath the tracks to the cute little yellow local train. For train schedules, see https://idos.idnes.cz.

From Prague, make sure to buy a round-trip ticket to "Kutná Hora Město" rather than "Kutná Hora hl. n." (the main station)—the price is nearly the same, and this gives you the flexibility to get off and on at any of the three Kutná Hora stations.

PLANNING YOUR TIME

For the most efficient visit, head to the Sedlec Bone Church first, then explore the town center. Kutná Hora is quiet on Sundays, when most shops are closed.

Here's my suggested plan: At Kutná Hora's main train station, transfer to the local train. Get off at its first stop (Kutná Hora Sedlec) and walk five minutes to the Bone Church, stopping at St. Mary's Basilica along the way. After your visit, head to St. Barbara's Cathedral in the town center via public bus or taxi. After touring the cathedral, follow my self-guided walk to the Czech Museum of Silver and take an English-language mine tour (book ahead online or by phone; if you arrive without a reservation, drop by in advance to sign up). At the end of the day, walk to Město station (about 15 minutes) to catch the train back to Kutná Hora's main train station, where you'll transfer to a train back to Prague.

Orientation to Kutná Hora

For a relatively small town (about 20,000 people), Kutná Hora is tricky to navigate: It's long and skinny, with a spaghetti of lanes that stretch from the main train station, past the Bone Church, to the historical center, which sits on the summit of a promontory.

TOURIST INFORMATION

The main TI is on Kollárova street just a few steps from **Palacký Square** (daily 9:00-18:00, shorter hours off-season; +420 327 512 378, www.kutnahora.cz). It also rents bicycles.

Smaller TIs are located near the **Bone Church** (+420 326 551 049) and in front of the **cathedral** (handy WCs, +420 775 363 938).

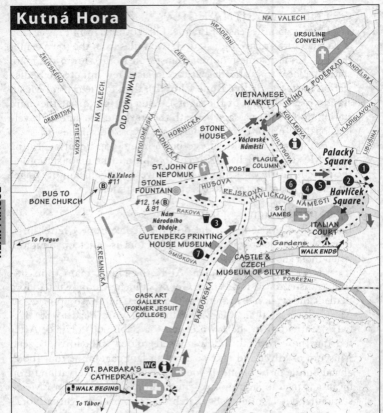

Kutná Hora

ARRIVAL IN KUTNÁ HORA

The **Kutná Hora Sedlec station** is a short walk from the Bone Church. From the station, head one block down the street perpendicular to the tracks heading toward the large St. Mary's Basilica. Cross the main street. Immediately to your left is the TI and the ticket office. Buy your ticket here, then find the Bone Church in the middle of the cemetery directly ahead.

If you're skipping the Bone Church (or not visiting it first), stay on the train to the **Kutná Hora Město station** in the valley. From there, hike up to St. Barbara's Cathedral (about 20 minutes) to find the start of my self-guided Kutná Hora walk.

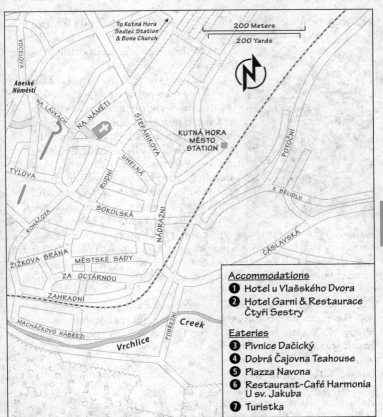

Kutná Hora Walk

Kutná Hora's most famous sight—the Bone Church—is on the outskirts of town (in Sedlec) and listed later. This self-guided walk connects the rest of the sights you'll want to see in a near-loop of the historical center. Before you get too far into the walk, call or drop by the Czech Museum of Silver to book a spot on the mine tour (if you have not already done so on their website). No stop on this walk is more than 10 minutes from the museum, so you can bail out and head for your tour at any point and easily resume the walk later.

• *Begin in the inviting park surrounding the cathedral.*

St. Barbara's Cathedral and Park: Rising like three pointy tents from a forest of buttresses, St. Barbara's strikes an exquisite Gothic profile. This culmination of Czech Gothic architecture was funded with a "spare no expense" attitude by a town riding the crest of a wave of mining wealth. Be sure to tour the **cathedral's interior**

(see listing, later)—but also take the time to do a slow lap around the pristine park that surrounds it.

Behind the church's apse, belly up to the **viewpoint** for an orientation to the city. From left to right, visually trace the historical center that perches along the promontory's crest: The long former Jesuit College now houses a modern art museum. The big, gray building that plunges down the cliff is the town's "little castle" *(Hrádek)*, with the Czech Museum of Silver. And the spire to the right of that bookends this walk. Surveying this scene, think about the history of a town made very, very rich by the glittering deposits it sits upon. Wealthy as it was, this was still an industrial town: The river below was so polluted they called it "Stink" in Czech. Notice the vineyards draping the hill.

• *After circling the church, walk along the grand...*

Terrace: Just before you head along the panoramic promenade, notice the handy TI in the little house on the left. Then

stroll regally along the stately white building, which now houses **GASK,** the contemporary Art Gallery of the Central Bohemian Region (permanent exhibit-100 Kč; Tue-Sun 10:00-18:00, closed Mon year-round and Jan-Feb).

Near the end of the terrace, continue following the broad cobbled footpath downhill...and keep an eye out for an army of white-jacketed, white-helmeted miners trudging up the hill for their daily shift. Or maybe they're tourists, about to explore the former silver mine at the **Czech Museum of Silver,** which occupies the big building on your right (see listing, later). Across the street is the **Gutenberg Printing House Museum,** with an intriguing exhibit on 19th-century printing presses (120 Kč, Thu-Mon 10:00-17:00, Sat until 19:00, closed Tue-Wed).

• *At the little park in front of the Czech Museum of Silver, take the left (level) fork, following* Stone Fountain *signs. When you hit the bigger street (with lots of parked cars), turn left (uphill, on Rejskova) and bear left around the big drab building. You'll emerge into a little square (Rejskovo Náměstí), with a big and impressive...*

Stone Fountain (Kamenná Kašna): The intensive mining under Kutná Hora released arsenic and other toxins, poisoning the water supply. The city struggled with obtaining clean drinking water, which had to be brought  to town by a sophisticated system of pipes, then stored in large tanks. At the end of the 15th century, the architect Rejsek built a 12-sided, richly decorated Gothic structure over one of these tanks. Although no longer functioning, the fountain survives unchanged—the only structure like it in Bohemia.

• *Facing the fountain, hook right around the corner and head down Husova street. On the left, you'll pass the stately town library (Městská Knihovna), then the gorgeous late-Baroque/Rococo Church of St. John of Nepomuk (named for the Czech patron saint). Turn left up the street after this church (Lierova). At the top of the street, turn right on Václavské Náměstí (Kutná Hora's own Wenceslas Square). On your left, you'll spot the frilly decorations on the...*

Stone House (Kamenný Dům): Notice the meticulous detail in the grape leaves, branches, and animals on this house's facade and up in its gable. Talented Polish craftsmen delicately carved the brittle stone into what was considered a marvel of its time. Inside is a moderately interesting museum dedicated to local life from the 17th to 19th century, with a vaulted cellar displaying Gothic masonry (100 Kč, Tue-Sun 9:00-18:00, shorter hours off-season, closed Mon and Dec-March).

• *Continue past the house as the street opens into a leafy and inviting square. For a slice of "authentic Czech" life, continue straight when the street narrows again; a half-block down on your right, under the* tržnice *sign, is the town's humble...*

Vietnamese Market: This double row of stalls selling knock-off Nikes and cheap jeans is as much a part of Czech urban life today as farmers markets (Mon-Fri 7:30-16:45, shorter hours Sat, closed Sun). The stalls are run by Vietnamese immigrants, the Czech Republic's third-largest minority (after Slovaks and Ukrainians). Many came here in the 1970s as part of a communist solidarity program that sent Vietnamese workers to Czech textile factories. They learned the language, adapted to the environment, and, after 1989, set off on a road to entrepreneurial success that allowed them to bring over friends and relatives.

• *Backtrack a few steps uphill, then turn left to walk down through the postcard-perfect Šultysova street, with a towering plague column at its center. Turn left at the street past the column, enjoying the pretty, color-*

ful arcades. You'll emerge into the lively main square.

Palacký Square (Palackého Náměstí): Beautiful but still somehow local, this square enjoys colorful facades, tempting al fresco restaurant tables, and generous public benches.

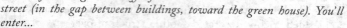

• *Exit the square at the far-right corner, following the traffic-free street (in the gap between buildings, toward the green house). You'll enter...*

Havlíček Square (Havlíčkovo Náměstí): The monuments on this leafy, parklike square are a Who's Who of important Czech patriots.

Straight ahead, the stone statue with his arm outstretched is **Karel Havlíček** (1821-1856), the founder of Czech political journalism (and the square's namesake). From Kutná Hora, Havlíček ran an influential magazine highly critical of the Habsburg government. In 1851, he was forced into exile and detained for five years in the Tirolean Alps under police surveillance. His integrity is reflected by the quote inscribed on the

statue: "You can try to bribe me with favors, you can threaten me, you can torture me, yet I will never turn a traitor." His motto became an inspiration for generations of Czech intellectuals, most of whom faced a similar combination of threats and temptations. Havlíček (whose name means "little Havel") was much revered in the 1970s and 1980s, when the *other* Havel (Václav) was similarly imprisoned for his dissent.

Below and to the right, the bronze, stoutly bearded statue in front of the big building honors the founder of Czechoslovakia, **Tomáš Garrigue Masaryk** (see sidebar on page 122). Circle around behind the pedestal to see the brief inscription tracing the statue's up-and-down history, which parallels the country's troubled 20th-century history: erected by Kutná Hora townspeople on October 27, 1938 (the eve of Czechoslovakia's 20th birthday); torn down in 1942 (by occupying Nazis, who disliked Masaryk as a symbol of Czech independence); erected again on October 27, 1948 (by freedom-loving locals, a few months after the communist coup); torn down again in 1957 (by the communists, who considered Masaryk an enemy of the working class); and erected once again on October

27, 1991. Notice that the Czechs, ever practical, have left a blank space below the last entry.

Masaryk stands in front of the building known as the **Italian Court** (Vlašský Dvůr). Step inside its fine courtyard. This palace, located on the site where Czech currency was once made, became Europe's most important mint and the main residence of Czech kings in the 1400s. It's named for the Italian minters who came to Kutná Hora to teach the locals their trade. Most of

the present-day building is a 19th-century reconstruction. Today, it hosts a moderately interesting museum that includes the Art Nouveau-decorated St. Wenceslas Chapel and displays on minting and local history in an original Gothic hall (120 Kč, daily 9:00-18:00, shorter hours Oct-March, ticket office on second floor inside courtyard).

Exiting the courtyard of the Italian Court, turn right and watch on the wall to your right for a small bronze tablet showing a hand flashing a peace sign, covered with barbed wire. This is an unassuming little **memorial** to the victims of the communist regime's misrule and torture.

Continue straight down the steps into a little park, and then turn right to reach a great **viewpoint.** It overlooks the distinctive roof of the cathedral and the scenic valley below.

• *Your walk is finished. If you're headed for the Czech Museum of Silver, take this scenic route: Walk back up to Havlíček Square, circle around the Italian Court, curl along the downhill side of St. James' Church, and enjoy the views. Eventually the view terrace dead-ends at a little lane that bends right and uphill, depositing you at the museum.*

If you're headed back to Prague, it takes about 15 minutes to walk to the Kutná Hora Město train station from Havlíček Square. Head downhill past the park, which funnels you between two buildings. Take the first left on Roháčova, then the first right on Sokolská. When you reach the wide cross street (Nádražní), turn left and follow the train tracks to the little pink station.

Sights in Kutná Hora

ON THE OUTSKIRTS
▲▲Sedlec Bone Church (Kostnice v Sedlci)
Located about 1.5 miles from the town's historical center, the Sedlec Bone Church sits in a serene graveyard and looks unassum-

ing from the outside. But inside, it's filled with the bones of 40,000 people—stacked into neat, 20-foot-tall pyramids decorating the walls and ceilings. The 14th-century plagues and 15th-century wars provided all the raw material necessary for the monks who made these designs.

Cost and Hours: 160 Kč ticket covers the Bone Church and St. Mary's Basilica, 320 Kč combo-ticket adds St. Barbara's Cathedral; daily 8:00-18:00, March and Oct 9:00-17:00, Nov-Feb 9:00-16:00; good 20 Kč audioguide adds 15 minutes of commentary to make it more meaningful, +420 327 561 143, www.sedlec.info.

Visiting the Church: Stand outside the church. This is a place of reflection. The cemetery here was "seeded" with holy earth brought from Jerusalem, which made this sacred ground. Demand was high, and corpses that could no longer pay the rent (i.e., those who lacked surviving relatives with enough disposable income for post-mortem real estate) were "evicted." What to do with the bones? Recycle them as church decorations with a message.

The monks, who first placed these bones 400 years ago, were guided by the belief that in order to live well, one must constantly remember death (*memento mori*—"what we are now, someday you shall be"). They also wanted to remind viewers that the earthly church was a community of both the living and the dead, a countless multitude that would one day stand before God. Later bone stackers were more interested in design than theology... as evidenced by the many show-off flourishes you'll see around the church.

Approach the church. Ignore the dull upper chapel and head down below (look for the *kostinec* sign). Flanking the stairwell are two giant chalices made of bones (a symbol of Jan Hus' egalitarian approach to worship).

Downstairs, on both sides are giant stacks of bones, reaching the top of the Gothic vaults (there are six such bone-pyramids in this small chapel). The skulls are neatly arranged on top, in the belief that this closeness to God would serve them well when Jesus returns to judge the living and the dead. Straight ahead dangles a chandelier, which supposedly includes at least one of every bone in the human body. In the glass case on the right (by the pillar), see the skulls with gnarly holes and other wounds. These belonged to soldiers who died fighting in the Hussite Wars—a boom time for this cemetery.

Finally, head into the left wing of the church, where you'll find a giant coat of arms of the aristocratic Schwarzenberg family—decorated with the skull of an Ottoman invader (a fearsome foe of the time), whose "eye" is being pecked out by a raven made of human bones.

Your visit is over. Head into town, thankful all of your limbs are intact.

Nearby: You'll pass the magnificent Sedlec **St. Mary's Basilica** as you walk from the train station to the Bone Church. Originally predating both the silver mine and the town of Kutna Hora, St. Mary's was burned down by the Hussites in 1421 and resurrected in the late 1600s by the great Baroque architect Santini. While the interior is not as impressive as St. Barbara's, the stunning golden monstrance holder from the 1300s—in one of the chapels on the left—is worth a peek (160 Kč with Bone Church, 320 Kč combo-ticket with Bone Church and St. Barbara's Cathedral; Mon-Sat 9:00-18:00, Sun from 11:00, shorter hours off-season; +420 326 551 049, www.sedlec.info/en/cathedral).

Getting from the Bone Church to Town: The helpful TI between the Bone Church and St. Mary's can call you a taxi (about 150 Kč to St. Barbara's Cathedral—the start of my self-guided walk, taxi +420 777 239 909 or +420 800 100 512, arrives within 10 minutes). It's also possible by public bus (details at TI) but you'll save time and effort with a quick taxi ride.

IN THE CENTER
▲▲St. Barbara's Cathedral (Chrám Sv. Barbory)
The cathedral was founded in 1388 by miners who dedicated it to their patron saint. The dazzling interior celebrates the town's sources of wealth, with frescoes featuring mining and minting. This church was a stunning feat of architecture by three of Prague's Gothic geniuses: Johann Parler, Matyáš Rejsek, and Benedict Ried. And, like Prague's cathedral, it sat unfinished and sealed off for centuries, until it was finally completed in the early 20th century.

Cost and Hours: 180 Kč, 320 Kč combo-ticket with Bone Church and St. Mary's Basilica; daily 9:00-18:00, shorter hours Nov-March; audioguide-20 Kč, +420 327 515 796, www.khfarnost. cz.

Visiting the Cathedral: While this tour covers the highlights, you'll receive a more detailed flyer at the ticket desk, or you can rent the more in-depth audioguide.

Head inside, walk to the middle of the main nave, and just take it all in. Intricate, lacy vaulting decorates an impossibly high ceiling that's also decorated with the coats of arms of local guilds. This is the epitome of Gothic: a mind-bogglingly tall nave supported by flying buttresses that create space for not one but two

NEAR PRAGUE

levels of big windows, pointed arches where the columns converge, and an overall sense of verticality and light.

The gorgeous **high altar**'s Last Supper scene of carved and painted wood is a neo-Gothic copy of the original. Circle clockwise around the apse, past Baroque altars. In the first chapel (the **St. Catherine chapel**) stands a Gothic Madonna from 1380, the oldest and most precious statue in the cathedral. As you walk, appreciate the fine **stained-glass windows** throughout the church. These are by František Urban, a contemporary of Alphonse Mucha who employed a similarly eye-pleasing Art Nouveau flair.

Continue around the apse. The second-to-last chapel, called the **Smíšek Chapel,** is an artistic highlight. The late-Gothic frescoes—*The Arrival of the Queen of Sheba, The Trial of Trajan,* and especially the fresco under the chapel's window depicting two men with candles—are the only remaining works of a Dutch-trained master in Gothic Bohemia. The final chapel, called the **Miners' Chapel,** has frescoes under the windows showing miners going about their daily labor. Most miners were healthy, unattached men in their 20s. An average of five miners died each day—from cave-ins, collapsing scaffolding, built-up poisonous gases, fires, and so on.

Continue up the side nave. Midway along, look for a wooden **miner statue** on a pillar on your right. He's wearing a typical white miner's coat. White fabric was the cheapest option (as it required no dyes) and was easier to see in the dark. The leather mat wrapped around his waist made it easier for him to slide down chutes inside the mine. His pick-like tool identifies him as the mining foreman.

At the back wall of the long chapel on your left, notice the precious frescoes from 1463 showing two people minting coins.

Loop around the back of the church, coming back up the left nave. You'll pass finely carved wooden **choir benches** that blend, in perfect Gothic harmony, with the church's architecture.

▲Hrádek Castle and the Czech Museum of Silver (České Muzeum Stříbra)

Located in Kutná Hora's 15th-century Hrádek ("little castle"), the Czech Museum of Silver offers a fascinating look at the primary source of local wealth and pride. Over the centuries, this mine produced some 2,500 tons of silver, copper, and zinc. Today, you can visit the facility on a 1.5-hour tour, which lets you spelunk in the former miners' passages that run beneath the entire town center. Note that the tour involves some tight squeezes and may be uncomfortable if you're claustrophobic. Bring warm clothing—mines are cold.

Cost and Tours: The English-language tour (Route II) costs 160 Kč—book ahead (see below). If an English tour is unavailable, book the Czech version; English flyers are provided. Route I, which includes only the aboveground museum, is pointless.

Hours: Tue-Sun 10:00-18:00, April and Oct until 17:00, Nov-Jan until 16:00, closed Mon year-round and Feb-March, last tour 1.5 hours before closing.

Information: +420 327 512 159 or +420 733 420 366, www.cms-kh.cz.

Reservations Recommended: Book a tour slot online two or more days in advance; flag icons indicate which tours are offered in English. It's also possible to call the day before or the morning of your visit (wait through the Czech recording to speak to someone in English). Without reservations, drop by the museum soon after you arrive in Kutná Hora to reserve.

Visiting the Museum and Mine: First, your guide takes you to see an intriguing horse-powered winch that once hoisted 2,000 pounds of rock at a time out of the mine. You'll learn the two methods miners used to extract the precious ore: either by hammering with a chisel or pick, or by setting a fire next to a rock—heating it until it naturally cracked.

Then you'll don a miner's coat and helmet, grab a bulky communist-era flashlight, and walk like the Seven Dwarfs through the town center to a secret doorway. It's time to climb deep into the mine for a wet, dark, and claustrophobic tour of the medieval shafts that honeycomb the rock beneath the town—walking down 167 steps, traversing 900 feet of underground passages, then walking back up 35 steps.

Along the way, you'll see white limestone deposits in the form of mini stalagmites and stalactites, and peer down into a 26-foot-deep pool of crystal-clear water. The mine holds a steady, year-round temperature of 54 degrees Fahrenheit while fat drops of condensation fall continually from the ceiling thanks to the nearly 100 percent humidity. Prepare for the moment when all the lights go out, plunging you into a darkness as total as you'll ever experience. You'll understand why miners relied on their other senses. For instance, when silver was struck, it made a telltale sound and smelled faintly like garlic.

Finally, ascending to ground level, your guide will explain safety mechanisms at the surface and walk you through the smelting and minting processes that turned those raw deposits into coins for an entire continent.

Sleeping and Eating in Kutná Hora

Sleeping: Although one day is enough for Kutná Hora, staying overnight saves you money (hotels are much cheaper here than in Prague) and allows you to better savor the atmosphere of a small Czech town.

$ Hotel u Vlašského Dvora and **Hotel Garni** are two renovated townhouses run by the same management. Furnished in a mix of 1930s and modern style, the hotels come with access to a fitness center and sauna. Hotel Garni is slightly nicer (a few steps off main square at Havlíčkovo Náměstí 513, +420 771 226 021, www.hotelykh.cz).

Eating: $$ Pivnice Dačický has made a theme of its namesake, a popular 17th-century author who once lived here. Solid wooden tables rest under perky illustrations of medieval town life, and a once-local brew, also named after Dačický, flows from the tap. They serve standard Czech fare, as well as excellent game and fish. Service can be slow when a group arrives (daily, Rakova 8, +420 327 512 248, mobile +420 603 434 367).

$$ Dobrá Čajovna Teahouse offers the chance to escape—not to medieval times, but to an Orient-themed paradise. Filled with tea cases, water pipes, and character, this place is an ideal spot to dawdle away the time that this ageless town has reclaimed for you. They serve Indian vegetarian plates and filled pita breads (daily 14:00-22:00, Havlíčkovo Náměstí 84, +420 777 028 481).

$ Restaurace Čtyři Sestry ("At the Four Sisters") is a family restaurant with a changing rotation of Czech classics, chef's specials, and vegan fare attracting largely a local crowd. Sit in the modern interior or in the shady courtyard behind the restaurant (long hours Mon-Sat, until 16:00 on Sun, on Havlíčkovo Náměstí, right above Hotel Garni, +420 327 512 749).

$$ Piazza Navona, which obnoxiously advertises itself as "the only true Italian restaurant in town," draws loyal customers thanks to its decent food and superb outside seating on the main square (daily, Palackého Náměstí 90, +420 327 512 588).

$$ Restaurant-Café Harmonia U sv. Jakuba fills the need if you are open to a European rendition of Mexican food. Sit in the bright red-and-green interior or on the pleasant outdoor patio (daily, Husova 9, +420 327 512 275).

$ Turistka is a charming café that bakes its own goodies and serves an excellent breakfast (Tue-Sun 9:00-18:00, closed Mon, between St. Barbara's Cathedral and the silver mine at Barborská 29).

Kutná Hora Connections

To return to Prague, hop on a local train from Kutná Hora Město station, near the historical center (or Kutná Hora Sedlec station if you end your day at the Bone Church), and take it to the Kutná Hora main station for your train transfer to Prague. From the main station, trains to Prague run hourly; some require a quick and easy transfer in Kolín. For train schedules, see https://idos.idnes.cz.

Terezín Memorial

Terezín (TEH-reh-zeen), an hour by bus from Prague, was originally a fortified town named after Habsburg empress Maria Theresa (it's called "Theresienstadt" in German). It was built in the 1780s with state-of-the-art, star-shaped walls designed to keep out the Prussians. Ironically, the town's medieval walls, originally meant to keep Germans out, were later used by Germans to keep the Jews in.

In 1941, the Nazis removed the town's 7,000 inhabitants and brought in 58,000 Jews, creating a horribly overcrowded ghetto. As the Nazis' model "Jewish town" for deceiving Red Cross inspectors, Terezín fostered the illusion that its Jewish inmates lived relatively normal lives—making the sinister truth all the more cruel.

Compared to other such sights (such as Auschwitz or Mauthausen), Terezín (worth ▲▲) feels different: First, the memorial focuses less on the Nazis' ruthless and calculated methods, and instead celebrates the arts and culture that thrived here despite the conditions—imbuing the place with a tragic humanity. Second, the various museums, memorials, and points of interest are spread over a large area in two distinct parts: a drab grid of a town and the original fortress (across the river, a short walk away). This means you're largely on your own to connect the dots and flesh out the story (use my self-guided tour to help).

GETTING THERE

The camp is about 40 miles northwest of Prague. It's most convenient to visit Terezín by **bus** (described next) or **tour bus** (various tour companies in Prague offer full-day tours to Terezín, including Wittman Tours, www.wittmann-tours.com).

Buses to Terezín leave from Prague's Holešovice train station (Nádraží Holešovice, on Metro line C). When you get off the Metro (coming from the city center), head toward the front of the train, go upstairs, turn right, and walk to the end of the corridor. You'll see bus stands directly ahead, outside the station. The Terezín bus departs from platform 7 (direction: Litoměřice; direct buses Mon-Fri at 9:00, 10:10, and 11:00, Sat at 9:30 and 10:30, Sun at 10:30, 1 hour, pay driver). You'll arrive in Terezín at the public bus stop on the main square, around the corner from the Museum of the Ghetto. Some buses also stop earlier, by the Small Fortress. The driver and fellow passengers may tell you to get off there, but my self-guided tour works best if you begin at the stop in town (after the bus passes a field of crosses on your right and travels across the river).

For schedules see https://idos.idnes.cz—you want "Terezín Litoměřice." Be sure to check the return schedule, too—the bus for Prague leaves from Terezín's main square and takes about an hour (pay driver).

PLANNING YOUR TIME

Because the sights are scattered, plan on lots of walking, and give yourself plenty of time: Three hours is enough for a minimal visit; allow four hours to see everything, and more like five to really delve in. Your understanding of Terezín becomes immeasurably deeper with the help of a local guide (for a list of Prague-based guides, see page 63).

ORIENTATION TO TEREZÍN

Cost: The 280 Kč combo-ticket includes all parts of the camp.

Hours: Most sights, including the Museum of the Ghetto, Magdeburg Barracks, and Hidden Synagogue, are open daily 9:00-18:00, Nov-March until 17:30. The Columbarium and Crematorium are closed Sat. The Crematorium is open Sun-Fri 10:00-18:00, Nov-March until 16:00; the Small Fortress is open daily 8:00-18:00, Nov-March until 16:30.

Information: +420 416 724 535, mobile +420 604 241 179, www.pamatnik-terezin.cz.

Visitor Information: In Terezín town, the **TI** is located at the exit from town toward Litoměřice. It has handy information (such as the Prague bus schedule and directions to town landmarks) and helpful staff who speak English (daily 9:00-17:00, Dukelských hrdinů 43, +420 775 711 881, www.terezin.cz).

Tours: Use the form at www.pamatnik-terezin.cz to reserve a guided tour in English (included in entry).

Eating: Avoid the stale sandwiches in the **Museum of the Ghetto**'s dingy basement cafeteria. The **Small Fortress** has a **$** cafeteria. In Terezín town, **$ Atypik Restaurant** offers Czech canteen classics popular with students and museum employees, served on an airy terrace or in the cramped interior with a peek into the kitchen (Mon-Fri 9:30-21:00, Sat-Sun 11:00-18:00, Máchova 91, +420 607 554 945).

BACKGROUND

Terezín was the Nazis' model "Jewish town," a concentration camp dolled up for propaganda purposes. Here, in a supposedly "self-governed Jewish resettlement area," Jewish culture seemed to thrive, as "citizens" put on plays and concerts, published a magazine, and raised their families. But it was all a carefully planned deception, intended to convince Red Cross inspectors that Jews were being treated well. The Nazis even coached prisoners on how to answer the inspectors' anticipated questions.

The Nazi authorities also used Terezín as a place to relocate elderly and disabled Jews from throughout the Third Reich—so the ghetto was filled with prisoners not only from the Czech lands, but from all over Europe.

In the fall of 1944, the Nazis began transporting Jews from Terezín to even more severe death camps (especially Auschwitz) in large numbers. Virtually all Terezín's Jews (155,000 over the course of the war) ultimately ended up dying—either here (35,000) or in extermination camps farther east.

One of the notable individuals held at Terezín was Viennese artist Friedl Dicker-Brandeis. This daring woman, a leader in the Bauhaus art movement, found her life's calling in teaching children freedom of expression. She taught the kids in the camp to distinguish between the central things—trees, flowers, lines—and peripheral things, such as the conditions of the camp. In 1944, Dicker-Brandeis volunteered to be sent to Auschwitz after her husband was transported there; she was killed a month later.

Of the 15,000 children who passed through Terezín from 1942 to 1944, fewer than 100 survived. The artwork they created at Terezín is a striking testimony to the cruel horror of the Holocaust. In 1994, Hana Volavková, a Terezín survivor and the director of the Jewish Museum in Prague, collected the children's artwork and poems in the book *I Never Saw Another Butterfly*.

⊙ SELF-GUIDED TOUR

The Terezín experience consists of two parts: the walled town of Terezín, which became a Jewish ghetto under Hitler; and (a half-mile walk east, across the river) the Small Fortress, which was a Gestapo prison camp for mostly political prisoners of all stripes (including non-Jewish Czechs). The complete tour involves about four miles of walking (including the walk from the town to the Small Fortress, then back again to catch your return bus to Prague). Pace yourself. If you want to cut it short, I've suggested sections that you could skip.

Terezín Town

• *The bus from Prague drops you off at Terezín town's spacious...*

❶ Main Square (Náměstí Československé Armády): Today,

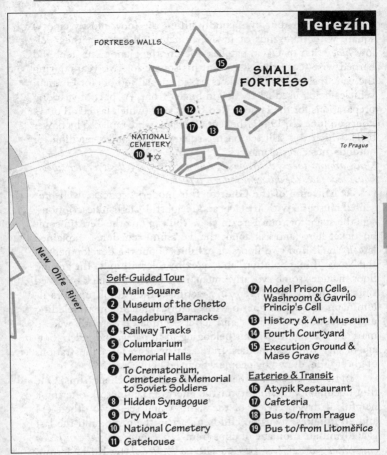

Terezín

FORTRESS WALLS

SMALL FORTRESS

NATIONAL CEMETERY

New Ohře River

To Prague

NEAR PRAGUE

<u>Self-Guided Tour</u>
1. Main Square
2. Museum of the Ghetto
3. Magdeburg Barracks
4. Railway Tracks
5. Columbarium
6. Memorial Halls
7. To Crematorium, Cemeteries & Memorial to Soviet Soldiers
8. Hidden Synagogue
9. Dry Moat
10. National Cemetery
11. Gatehouse
12. Model Prison Cells, Washroom & Gavrilo Princip's Cell
13. History & Art Museum
14. Fourth Courtyard
15. Execution Ground & Mass Grave

<u>Eateries & Transit</u>
16. Atypik Restaurant
17. Cafeteria
18. Bus to/from Prague
19. Bus to/from Litoměřice

Terezín feels like a workaday, if unusually tidy, Czech town, with a tight grid plan hemmed in by its stout walls. And for much of its history, that's exactly what it was. But when Hitler annexed Czechoslovakia, he evicted the residents to create a ghetto for Jews forcibly transplanted here from Prague and elsewhere. Be-

cause it started out as a pretty town, rather than a gloomy prison or custom-built concentration camp, the Nazi authorities cultivated Terezín as a "model" to illustrate to the outside world how good the Jews had it here.

Begin your tour by mentally filling the (now mostly empty) square with thousands of Jewish inmates, all wearing their yellow *Juden* Star of David patches. Picture the giant circus tent and barbed-wire fence that stood on this square for two years during the war. Inside, Jewish workers boxed special motors for German vehicles being used on the frigid Soviet front. As part of yearlong preparations for the famous Red Cross visit (which lasted all of six hours on June 23, 1944), the tent and fence were replaced by flower beds (which you still see on the square today) and a pavilion for outdoor music performances.

• *Just around the corner from the bus stop, in the yellow former school-house that faces the adjacent square, is the...*

❷ Museum of the Ghetto: This modern, concise, well-presented museum, with artifacts and insightful English descriptions, sets the stage for your Terezín visit. You can buy the Terezín combo-ticket here (and ask about the day's film schedule—explained later). You'll find two floors of **exhibits** about the development of the Nazis' "Final Solution" and Terezín's role within it. The ground floor includes some evocative memorials (such as a stack of seized suitcases and a list of Terezín's victims). The exhibit upstairs illuminates life in the ghetto with historical documents (including underground publications and letters—inmates were allowed to mail one per month), items belonging to inmates, and video footage of survivors' testimonies. In the stairwell are large illustrations of ghetto life, drawn by people who lived here.

In the basement is a theater showing four excellent **films.** One film documents the history of the ghetto (31 minutes), offering a helpful, if dry, overview of the sights you'll see. Two others (14 and 20 minutes) focus on children's art in the camp, and the last is a 10-minute montage of clips from *Der Führer schenkt den Juden eine Stadt (The Führer Gives a City to the Jews),* by Kurt Gerron. Gerron, a Berlin Jew, was a 1920s movie star who appeared with Marlene Dietrich in *Blue Angel.* Deported to Terezín, Gerron in 1944 was asked by the Nazis to produce a propaganda film. The resulting film depicts healthy (i.e., recently arrived) "Jewish settlers" in Terezín happily viewing concerts, playing soccer, and sewing in their rooms—yet an unmistakable, deadly desperation radiates from their pallid faces. The only moment of genuine emotion comes toward the end, when a packed room of children applauds the final lines of the popular anti-Nazi opera *Brundibár:* "We did not let ourselves down, we chased the nasty Brundibár away. With a happy song, we won it all." Even the Nazis were not fooled: Gerron and his wife were shipped to Auschwitz, and the film was never shown in public.

• *To learn more about living conditions in the camp, return to the main square and continue straight past it, along Tyršova street. A few blocks down, just before the wall, on the left you'll find the...*

❸ **Magdeburg Barracks:** Peek inside the large courtyard, then continue upstairs and follow the one-way, counterclockwise loop.

First you'll see a meticulously restored dormitory, complete with three-tiered beds, suitcases, eyeglasses, dolls, chessboards, sewing kits...and utterly no privacy. After Terezín's residents were evicted and Jews were imported in huge numbers, every available space was converted from single-family apartments to outrageously cramped slumber mills like this. Jaunty music lures you around the corner to the first of several rooms celebrating the arts here at Terezín. You'll see exhibits on composers, artists, and writers who expressed their creativity even in these horrifying conditions. These include profiles of individuals and a wide variety of stirring illustrations of life in the ghetto. Near the end is a room reproducing the camp cabaret stage, where inmates entertained each other.

• *With limited time or energy, consider skipping the next several stops, which take a long, if poignant, detour outside the walls. Jump ahead to the moat (see "Dry Moat," later) by leaving the barracks, turning right, and walking 100 yards to a brick gate. (If you do decide to skip the following stops, you can easily fit in the Hidden Synagogue at the end, before hopping on your bus back to Prague, as it's one block from the main square.)*

To continue the full tour, exit the barracks, turn left, and walk until you dead-end at the city wall. Turn right and walk along the inside of the stout wall to the far corner. Slicing through the hole in the wall are the remnants of...

❹ **Railway Tracks:** In the early years of the camp, Jews arrived at the train station in the nearby town of Bohušovice and then had to walk the remaining 1.5 miles to Terezín. This was too public a display for the Nazis, who didn't want townspeople to observe the transports and become suspicious (or to try to interact with the inmates in any way). So the prisoners were forced to construct a

railway line that led right to Terezín...and then back out again to Auschwitz.

• *Follow the tracks outside the wall.*

❺ **Columbarium and** ❻ **Memorial Halls:** Exiting the wall, on the left is a Columbarium, where the Nazis deposited cardboard boxes containing the ashes of dead prisoners. The Germans originally promised that the remains would be properly buried after the war, but in 1945, to erase evidence, the ashes of Terezín victims were dumped into the Ohře River. Farther along, past the little pension/café and across the bridge, on the right you will find Jewish and Christian ceremonial halls and the main morgue.

• *When the main road swings right, take the left turn (marked* Krematorium*) and walk past bucolic vegetable plots and fruit gardens, and along a driveway lined with pointy poplar trees, to reach the...*

❼ **Crematorium and Cemeteries:** The low-lying yellow building (to the left of the monumental menorah) is the **crematorium,** where Nazis burned the bodies of those who died here. Step inside to see a small exhibit on death and burial in the ghetto (explaining that, over time, single graves in coffins gave way to mass graves, then to simply burning bodies en masse and dumping the ashes in the river). Then head into the chilling main

chamber, where four ovens were kept busy cremating bodies.

Outside, surrounding the crematorium is a **Jewish cemetery** with the bodies of those who had died before cremation became the norm. Farther to the right (as you face the crematorium) is a **Russian cemetery** and a **Memorial to Soviet Soldiers.** The Soviets liberated Terezín without a fight as the Nazis retreated, on May 8, 1945. But just days before, an epidemic of typhus had spread through the camp. In the weeks after the war ended, scores of Soviet soldiers and medical workers who tried to contain the epidemic died, along with hundreds of former prisoners.

• *Retrace your steps back through the wall, and continue straight ahead past the train tracks, up Dlouhá street. After three blocks, watch on the left for the low-profile green house at #17. Walk through the corridor to reach the fascinating...*

❽ **Hidden Synagogue:** Inside you'll find a courtyard; the bakery that used to be here hid the synagogue behind it. This is the only one of the camp's eight hidden synagogues that survived. The atmospheric space is still inscribed with two Hebrew captions, which are translated as "May my eyes behold, how You in compassion return to Sinai," and "If I forget Jerusalem, may my tongue rot and my right arm fall off." These words indicate that the prayer room belonged to a congregation of Zionists (advocates of a Jewish state), who, one would expect, were specifically targeted by the Nazis.

Upstairs, a few prisoners lived in a tight attic space. Even though the cramped rooms (reconstructed with period items) seem impossibly small, they were a far better accommodation than the mass housing in which most prisoners were interned. It's thought that a group of craftsmen who labored in a nearby workshop were "lucky" enough to live here.

• *Leaving the synagogue house, turn right, and at the corner, turn left to pop out at the main square. To proceed to the Small Fortress, head down Tyršova as if you're going to the Magdeburg Barracks. Before you get there, turn left along the park, then continue one block up Palackého to the brick gate. You'll cross a bridge over a...*

❾ Dry Moat: Imagine this moat filled with plots of vegetables, grown by starving Jews for well-fed SS officers. Turn left and walk along the moat. The top of the fortification walls on the other side were once equipped with benches and pathways.

• *When you reach the main road, turn right across the New Ohře River (the original course of the river was diverted here when Terezín was built). After about five minutes, you'll come to a blocked-off, tree-lined driveway and the prison camp.*

Terezín Prison Camp

• *On the right side of the driveway is the wedge-shaped...*

❿ National Cemetery: The remains of about 10,000 victims of Terezín (including 2,386 individual graves; the rest were moved here from mass graves elsewhere) fill this cemetery, which was created after the war's end. The sea of headstones powerfully illustrates the scope of the crime that took place here. Notice that, in addition to the giant Star of David (closer to the fortress), a cross towers over the cemetery. This is a reminder that you've left the Jewish ghetto and are about to enter a very different part of the Terezín complex. From 1940 to 1945, this fortress functioned as a Gestapo prison, through which 32,000 inmates passed (of whom nearly 10 percent died here)—chiefly members of the Czech resistance and communists. While the majority of the camp's victims weren't Jewish, the 1,500 Jews interned here were treated with particular severity.

• *Now head under the black-and-white-striped gate.*

⓫ Gatehouse: Inside

the gate, on the left, is a modest museum about the pre-WWII history of this fortress. If you need a break before continuing, you could pause at the handy cafeteria. The wood-and-metal chandeliers inside were produced by Jewish workers for the SS officers who once dined in these two rooms.

• *Continuing into the central part of the fortress, watch on the left for a turnstile into a long, skinny side courtyard. Go in and head to the end of the courtyard, under the notorious* Arbeit Macht Frei *sign painted above an arched gate (a postwar replica of the viciously sarcastic "Work will set you free" sign that was displayed at all camps). Go under this gate to reach a courtyard ringed with...*

⓱ Model Prison Cells: Step into some of the barracks on the right side of the courtyard to see tight, triple-decker bunks where prisoners were essentially

stacked at bedtime. Halfway down the courtyard, under the *Block-A* sign, peek into the medical cell.

At the far end, the **washroom** in the right-hand corner (by #15) was built solely for the purpose of fooling Red Cross inspectors. Go ahead, turn the faucets: No pipes were ever installed to bring in water.

The shower room two doors to the left, on the other hand, was used to fool the Jews. Here they got used to the idea of communal bathing, so they wouldn't be suspicious when they were later taken to similar-looking installations at Auschwitz. (There were no gas chambers at Terezín—most of the deaths here were caused by malnutrition, disease, and, to a lesser extent, execution.)

Before the Nazis, the Austrian monarchy used the Small Fortress as a prison. In the little side courtyard next to the shower room, look for a ghostly doorway with a plaque that recalls the most famous prisoner from that time, Bosnian Serb **Gavrilo Princip,** whose assassination of Archduke Franz Ferdinand and his wife Žofie in 1914 sparked World War I. Princip died here in 1918 of tuberculosis; of the six Sarajevo conspirators imprisoned here, only two survived.

• *Return through the* Arbeit Macht Frei *gate, then back out into the fortress' central yard. Turn left and continue deeper into the complex. The large building on your right is marked by* Muzeum *signs.*

⓭ History and Art Museum: The ground floor of this building features an exhibit about the Nazi-era history of the Small Fortress. Photographs and brief descriptions identify many of the individuals who were imprisoned—and in many cases, executed. Upstairs is a gallery of paintings by prominent Czech artists, mostly focusing on themes of camp life (and a few about the Spanish Civil War).

• *Back out in the main yard, continue straight ahead, through two gateways in a row. You'll emerge into the wide, eerie...*

⓮ Fourth Courtyard: Here you'll have more opportunities to step into former prison cells that flank the yard; some of these house temporary exhibits.

At the far end, you'll find a plaque in the ground listing the 17 countries whose citizens perished at Terezín.

• *Returning to the fortress' main yard once more, turn right and follow the long buildings. Turn right to find the...*

⓯ Execution Ground and Mass Grave: This is where firing squads executed somewhere between 200 and 300 of Hitler's enemies. Many of Terezín's victims were buried in mass graves along the fortress ramparts. After the war, these remains were moved to the National Cemetery we saw on the way into the fortress.

• *Our tour ends here. As you ponder Terezín, remember the message of all such memorials: Never again.*

Konopiště Castle

Konopiště (KOH-noh-peesh-tyeh) was the Neo-Gothic residence of the Archduke Franz Ferdinand d'Este—the heir to the Austro-Hungarian Empire, whose assassination sparked World War I. Located 30 miles south of Prague, it's workable either as a day trip or on the way to Český Krumlov. While it's the least visually arresting of the castles near Prague, its interior has some captivat-

ing stories to tell about its former inhabitants. Enjoyable for anyone, Konopiště is worth ▲ for most. But it's a must for Habsburg aficionados—historians find it worth ▲▲▲.

Construction of the castle began in the 14th century, but today's exterior and furnishings date from about 1900, when Franz Ferdinand renovated his new home. As one of the first castles in Europe to have an elevator, a WC, and running water, Konopiště shows "modern" living at the turn of the 20th century.

Those who lived at Konopiště played a role in one of the most important moments in European history: Franz Ferdinand's assassination in Sarajevo (chillingly illustrated by items displayed inside the castle). The shooting eventually meant the end of the age of hereditary, divine-right, multiethnic empires—and the dawn of a Europe of small, nationalistic, democratic nation-states. Historians get goose bumps at Konopiště, where if you listen closely, you can almost hear the last gasp of Europe's absolute monarchs.

The castle interior is only viewable via a guided tour. There are several tour options, but the best is Route 3 (limited space, so book online or call ahead to reserve—see "Orientation to Konopiště," later).

GETTING THERE

By Train: Trains from Prague's main station drop you in Benešov (2/hour, 1 hour, https://idos.idnes.cz); a well-marked trail goes from the station to the castle (1.5 miles). To walk to the castle, as you exit the Benešov train station, turn left and walk along the street parallel to the railroad tracks. Turn left at the first bridge you see crossing over the tracks. Along the way you'll see trail markers on trees, walls, and lampposts—one yellow stripe between two white stripes. Follow these markers. As you leave town, watch for a marker with an arrow pointing to a path in the woods. Take this path to bypass the castle's enormous parking lot, which is clogged with souvenir shops and bus fumes.

By Car: Konopiště is about a 45-minute drive from Prague and a two-minute detour off of the main route to Český Krumlov (head east toward Brno on the D-1 expressway; take exit #21 toward *Benešov/České Budějovice/Linz;* after about 9 miles (15 kilometers) watch for the Konopiště turnoff on the right). Bypass the first, giant parking lot (ringed by restaurants); a bit farther along, on the left near the lake, is a smaller lot that's closer to the castle. From either lot, hike uphill about 10-15 minutes to Konopiště.

ORIENTATION TO KONOPIŠTĚ

Cost and Tours: The recommended Route 3 is 370 Kč in English. Routes 1 and 2 are 270 Kč apiece. All tickets are 30 Kč cheaper if you join a Czech-speaking tour (but renting the English audioguide costs 50 Kč—effectively negating most of your savings).

Hours: May-Aug Tue-Sun 10:00-17:00; Sept 9:00-16:00; April and Oct-Nov until 15:00; closed Mon year-round and Dec-March.

Information: +420 317 721 366, www.zamek-konopiste.cz.

Reservations Recommended: Space on Route 3 is limited to eight people per hour: It's smart (and worth the small extra charge) to reserve a spot in advance on their website, or by calling one day ahead or on the morning of your visit.

VISITING THE CASTLE

While there are three tour options, **Route 3** is the most intimate and interesting. It takes you through the rooms where Franz Ferdinand, his Czech bride Žofie, and their three kids lived while waiting for Uncle Franz Josef to expire. When the communists took over, they simply threw drop cloths over the furniture and let the place sit, untouched, for decades. Now everything has been meticulously restored (with the help of 1907 photographs)—launching you right into a turn-of-the-20th-century time capsule.

The tour takes you through halls upon halls of hunting trophies (each one marked with the place and date of the kill), paint-

ings of royal relatives (including an entire wall of Italian kings—relations of Franz Ferdinand's Neapolitan mother), and photographs of the many places they traveled and the three kids as they grew up. The tour includes Franz Ferdinand's dressing room (with his actual uniform and his travel case all packed up and ready to go); his private study (which feels like he just stepped away from his desk for a cup of coffee); the living room (with 1,180 pairs of antlers on the walls); the private dining room (with the table set for an intimate family dinner for five); the master bedroom (with its huge bed); the children's bedrooms, playrooms, and classroom (with their toys and books still on the shelves); three bathrooms with running water and flushing toilets; and—in the final room—a glass display case containing the dress Žofie was wearing that fateful day in Sarajevo (including her still blood-stained corset). Down the hall are the royal couple's death masks, Franz Ferdinand's bloody suspenders, and the actual bullet that ended Žofie's life.

Route 2—which covers the oldest wing of the castle—is also

NEAR PRAGUE

NEAR PRAGUE

Archduke Franz Ferdinand (1863-1914)

Archduke Franz Ferdinand was born to the brother of the Habsburg emperor (Franz Josef) and a Neapolitan princess. After his cousin died under "mysterious circumstances," Franz Ferdinand was thrust into the role of heir apparent to the throne of the Austro-Hungarian Empire—one of the biggest realms Europe has ever seen. But he had to be patient: His uncle Franz Josef took the throne in 1848 and would hold onto it for nearly 70 years. In fact, he outlived his nephew.

While he waited, Franz Ferdinand kept himself busy by spending time at his bachelor pad in Konopiště. At a ball in Vienna, he met a gorgeous but low-ranking Czech countess, Žofie Chotková. The couple danced all night. After long years of secret courtship, Franz Ferdinand announced his intentions to marry Žofie. His uncle was displeased—Žofie was an aristocrat, not a princess as expected as the spouse for the heir apparent. Franz Josef insisted that Žofie could never be an empress and none of their children could inherit the throne. These family squabbles cemented Franz Ferdinand and Žofie's preference for living at Konopiště.

While waiting for a succession that would never arrive, Franz Ferdinand threw himself into his hobbies with zeal. He traveled around the world twice—partly for diplomatic reasons, but largely to pursue his passion for exotic hunting. Shooting anything in sight—deer, bears, tigers, elephants, and crocodiles—he killed about 300,000 animals, a few thousand of which stare morbidly at you from the walls at Konopiště. Franz Ferdinand and Žofie were also devoted parents, raising three children: Žofie, Max, and Ernesto.

In the Kaiser's Pavilion on the grounds of Konopiště, Franz Ferdinand met with German Kaiser Wilhelm and tried to talk him out of plotting a war against Russia. Wilhelm argued that a war would benefit both Germany and Austria: Germans wanted colonies, and the Austro-Hungarian Empire could use a war to divert attention from its domestic problems. But Franz Ferdinand foresaw war as suicidal for Austria's overstretched monarchy.

Soon after, Franz Ferdinand and Žofie went to Sarajevo, in the Habsburg-annexed territories of Bosnia and Herzegovina. There Gavrilo Princip, a Bosnian Serb separatist, shot the Habsburg archduke who so loved shooting, and Žofie. Franz Ferdinand's assassination ironically gave the Germans (and their allies in the Austro-Hungarian administration) the pretext to go to war against Serbia and its ally, Russia. World War I soon broke out. The event Franz Ferdinand had tried to prevent was, in fact, sparked by his death.

worth considering and provides the most comprehensive look into the castle, its history, and celebrated collections. You'll see the oversized elevator (with a couch to make the family comfortable on the 45-second ride upstairs), the library, and the staggeringly large armory collection. **Route 1,** covering some other rooms, the hunting hall, and the balcony, is the least interesting.

Other Sights at the Castle: Your tour ticket includes two quirky additional sights that are worth poking into. **Franz Ferdinand's Shooting Range,** just off of the castle courtyard, offers a quick glimpse at the emperor-in-waiting's elaborate system of moving targets; a video demonstrates how the various targets would move around to keep his skills sharp. The **Museum of St. George,** tucked beneath the long terrace (around the side of the palace), displays Franz Ferdinand's collection of hundreds of sculptures and paintings of St. George slaying the dragon...taking a theme to an extreme.

While the stretch between the parking lot and the castle entrance is overrun by tour groups, the **gardens** and the **park** are surprisingly empty. In the summer, the flowers and goldfish in the rose garden are a big hit with visitors. The peaceful 30-minute walk through the woods around the lake (wooden bridge at the far end) offers fine castle views.

Tucked away in the bushes behind the pond is a pavilion coated with tree bark, a perfect picnic spot. This simple structure, nicknamed the **Kaiser's Pavilion,** was the site of a fateful meeting between the German Kaiser Wilhelm and the Archduke Franz Ferdinand.

Eating at Konopiště Castle: $$ Zámecká Restaurace sits under the hill halfway between the parking lot and the lake. Known for its affordable game, this is an appropriate culinary tie-in after touring the hunting-obsessed archduke's quarters (daily until 16:00, July-Aug until 18:00, +420 602 296 039). Or consider bringing picnic supplies from Prague (or buy them at the grocery store by the Benešov train station) and enjoy the peace and thought-provoking ambience of a **picnic** in the shaded Kaiser's Pavilion. Or eat cheaply on Benešov's main square (try **$ U Zlaté Hvězdy**—"The Golden Star").

NEAR PRAGUE

ČESKÝ KRUMLOV

Krumau

Surrounded by mountains, lassoed by its river, and dominated by its castle, this town mesmerizes visitors. When you see its awe-inspiring castle, delightful Old Town of cobbled lanes and shops, and easy canoeing options, you'll understand why having fun is a slam-dunk here. Romantics are floored by Český Krumlov's spectacular setting; you could spend all your time doing aimless laps from one end of town to the other.

The sharp bends in the Vltava provide natural moats, so it's no wonder Český Krumlov has been a choice spot for eons. Celtic tribes settled here a century before Christ. Then came Germanic tribes. The Slavic tribes arrived in the ninth century. The Rožmberks (Rosenbergs)—Bohemia's top noble family—ran the city from 1302 to 1602. You'll spot their rose symbol all over town.

The 16th century was the town's golden age, when Český Krumlov hosted artists, scientists, and alchemists from across Europe. In 1588, the town became home to an important Jesuit college. In 1602, the Rožmberks ran out of money to fund their lavish lifestyles, so they sold their territory to the Habsburgs—who ushered in a more Germanic period. After that, as many as 75 percent of the town's people were German—until 1945, when most Germans were expelled (for more on this era and its repercussions, see the sidebar later in this chapter).

Český Krumlov's rich mix of Gothic, Renaissance, and Baroque buildings is easy to miss. As you wander, be sure to look up...notice the surviving details in the fine stonework and pretty gables. Step into shops. Snoop into back lanes and tiny squares. Gothic buildings curve with the winding streets. Many precious Gothic and Renaissance frescoes were whitewashed in Baroque times (when the colorful trimmings of earlier periods were long out of style). Today, these frescoes are being rediscovered and restored.

Český Krumlov is a huge tourist magnet, which makes things colorful and easy for travelers. It can feel like a medieval theme park—but, fortunately, there are still a few hidden nooks and sleepy back alleys to savor. And a half-day float on the river can help you relax into the local pace.

PLANNING YOUR TIME

It's easy to enjoy Český Krumlov without ever paying to enter a sight (morning and evening are best for strolling without crowds). But a tour of the Baroque Theater at the castle is worth considering—book ahead for an English tour (see "Sights in Český Krumlov," later, for details), then build your day around your visit time. While you're at it, consider booking an English tour of the castle interior. Visits to the synagogue and Seidel Photo Studio Museum bring more recent history alive.

If the outdoors is your thing, a paddle down the river is a highlight, and a walk up to the Křížový Vrch (Hill of the Cross) rewards you with a fine view of the town and its unforgettable riverside setting.

Many sights are closed on Monday, though the major attraction—the town itself—is always open. Evenings are for atmospheric dining and drinking.

Orientation to Český Krumlov

Český Krumlov (CHESS-key KROOM-lohv) means, roughly, "Czech Bend in the River." Calling it "Český" for short sounds silly to Czech speakers (since dozens of Czech town names begin with "Český")—rather, they call it "Krumlov."

The city is extremely easy to navigate. The twisty Vltava River, which makes a perfect *S* through the town, ropes the Old Town into a tight peninsula. Above the Old Town is the Castle Town. Český Krumlov's one main street starts at the isthmus and winds through the peninsula, crossing a bridge before snaking through the Castle Town, the castle complex (a long series of courtyards), and the castle gardens high above. I've narrated this route on my self-guided walk. The main square, Náměstí Svornosti—with the TI, ATMs, and taxis—dominates the Old Town and marks the center of the peninsula. My recommended restaurants, hotels, and sights are all within a 5-to-10-minute walk of this square.

TOURIST INFORMATION

The helpful **city TI** is on the main square (daily 9:00-18:00, June-Aug until 19:00, shorter hours in winter, +420 380 704 622, www.ckrumlov.info). The 129 Kč *City Guide* book includes a schematic town-and-castle map. The TI has a baggage-storage desk and can check train and bus schedules. Ask about concerts, city walking tours in English, and canoe trips on the river. The **castle TI,** which provides information about castle tours but does not sell tickets, is in the castle's lowest courtyard (daily 9:00-18:00, +420 380 725 110).

    Český Krumlov Card: This 400 Kč card, sold at the TI and participating sights, covers entry to the Round Tower and Castle Museum (but not castle tours), the Museum of Regional History, the Seidel Photo Studio Museum, and the Monastery Museum. Do the math to decide if it makes sense for you.

ARRIVAL IN ČESKÝ KRUMLOV

By Train: The train station is a 20-minute walk from town (turn right out of the station, then walk downhill onto a steep cobbled path leading to an overpass into the town center). Taxis are standing by to zip you to your hotel (about 100 Kč), or call +420 602 113 113.

    By Bus: The bus station is just three blocks away from the Old Town. Follow signs for *Centrum*. Figure on 60 Kč for a taxi from the station to your hotel.

    By Car: Parking lots ring the town center, each one marked by a blue *P* sign. If your hotel is in the mostly traffic-free center, you'll be allowed to drive in (gingerly passing hordes of tourists) and park on the main square just long enough to drop off your bags and get directions to one of the outer lots. The flow of traffic is one-way: Enter at the east end of town, on Horní street, then exit across two bridges at the south end of town, on Linecká street (get details from your hotel before you arrive).

HELPFUL HINTS

Festivals: Locals and visitors alike drink oceans of beer and celebrate the town's medieval roots at big events such as the Five-Petalled Rose Festival (Slavnosti Pětilisté Růže), where blacksmiths mint ancient coins, jugglers swallow fire, mead flows generously, and pigs are roasted on open fires (late June, www.ckrumlov.info). The summer also brings a top-notch international music festival, with performances in pubs, cafés, and the castle gardens (mid-July-mid-Aug, www.festivalkrumlov.cz).

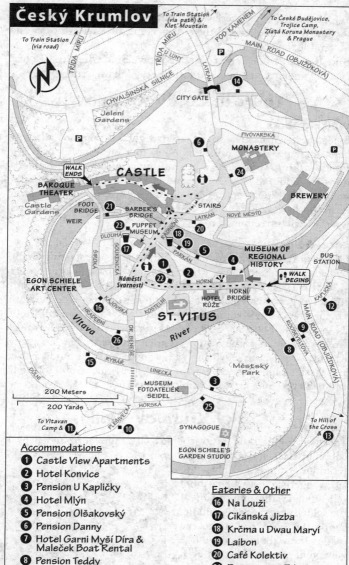

Český Krumlov

Accommodations

1. Castle View Apartments
2. Hotel Konvice
3. Pension U Kapličky
4. Hotel Mlýn
5. Pension Olšakovský
6. Pension Danny
7. Hotel Garni Myší Díra & Maleček Boat Rental
8. Pension Teddy
9. Pension Anna
10. Pension Athanor
11. To Penzion Weber
12. Pension Gardena
13. To Pension Kříž
14. Hostel 99 & Hospoda 99 Rest.
15. Hostel Postel

Eateries & Other

16. Na Louži
17. Cikánská Jizba
18. Krčma u Dwau Maryí
19. Laibon
20. Café Kolektiv
21. Restaurace Zdroj
22. Krčma Šatlava
23. Krumlovská Picka & CK Shuttle Office
24. Dobrá Čajovna
25. Pražírna Ideál
26. Vltava Sport Service (Boats/Bikes)

During St. Wenceslas celebrations, the square becomes a medieval market and the streets come alive with theater and music (late Sept).

Bike Rental: You can rent bikes at **Vltava Sport Service** (see listing under "Canoeing and Rafting the Vltava," later).

Tours in Český Krumlov

Walking Tours

Since the town itself, rather than its sights, is what it's all about here, taking a guided walk is the key to a meaningful visit. The **Free Walking Tour** offers a general town introduction. Reservations are required: Book online and meet in front of the TI on the main square (tip expected—about 200-400 Kč/person depending on group size, daily at 14:00, also at 10:30 in high season, 2 hours, www.wisemanfreetour.com).

Local Guides

Oldřiška Baloušková studied in California before starting a family back in her hometown, which she knows through and through (1200 Kč/1.5-hour tour, +420 737 920 901, oldriskab@gmail.com). **Jiří (George) Václavíček,** a gentle and caring man who perfectly fits mellow Český Krumlov, is a joy to share this town with (600 Kč/hour, +420 603 927 995, www.krumlovguide.com). **Karolína Kortusová** is an enthusiastic, experienced guide. Her company, Krumlov Tours, can set you up with a good local tour guide, palace and theater admissions, river trips, and more (guides-600 Kč/hour, +420 723 069 561, https://krumlovtours.com).

Český Krumlov Walk

The town's best sight is its cobbled cityscape, surrounded by a babbling river and capped by a dramatic castle. Most of Český

Krumlov's modest sights are laced together in this charming self-guided walk from the top of the Old Town, down its middle, across the river, and up to the castle. The walk begins at a fine viewpoint...and ends at an even better one. I've divided it into two parts: downhill, through the Old Town to the river; then uphill, ascending through the castle complex on the other side. You can also do the two parts on different days. The second half of the walk makes a useful spine for organizing a visit to the castle quarter. To trace the route of this walk, see the "Český Krumlov" map.

A Town Transformed by Tourism

A visit to Český Krumlov can actually be fascinating *not* for seeing any semblance of local life (the town's original residents more or less cleared out in 1945) and instead for seeing how tourism has transformed this living piece of history. Today, Czechs are about as entitled to claim Český Krumlov as their own as are the throngs of mesmerized visitors. To put things in perspective: The town center has fewer than 20 permanent residents...and receives two million visitors a year.

To highlight this demographic trend, an artist in 2018 hired families to live in four Old Town apartments (the job description included sipping coffee outside, hanging laundry out the windows, and encouraging their kids to play in the street). Locals (who say they rarely go into the Old Town, as there is "no one to meet there anymore") shook their heads, and a Prague-based newspaper reported (with perhaps a dose of Schadenfreude) that only one particularly resilient family lasted a whole month on the job.

THE OLD TOWN

• *Start at the bridge over the isthmus, which was once the fortified grand entry gate to the town. For the best view, step down to the little terrace in front of the restaurant gate.*

Horní Bridge: From this "Upper Bridge," note the natural fortification provided by the tight bend in the river. Trace the river to your right, where it curves around the last building in town, with a smokestack. This is the Pivovar Český Krumlov Brewery, makers of the hometown brew (with tours—see listing under "Sights in Český Krumlov," later). Behind that, on the horizon, is a pile of white apartment high-rises—built in the last decade of the communist era to solve a housing shortage (many homes were demolished after their German owners were forced out at the end of World War II). To the left of the brewery stands a huge monastery (with the pointy red steeple; today, this hosts the Monastery Museum). Behind that, on Kleť Mountain—the highest hilltop—stands a TV tower and a world-class astronomical observatory and research center.

Head back up to the middle of the bridge. Look down and left, then down and right. Notice how the Vltava wraps entirely around the town center. Rafters take about a half-hour to circle around the Old Town peninsula, beginning and ending under this bridge.

• *Head into town on...*

Horní Street: As you step off the bridge, Český Krumlov's aptly named "Upper Street" passes the **Museum of Regional His-**

tory on the right (see "Sights in Český Krumlov," later). Just past the museum, a little garden overlook affords a fine castle view.

Immediately across the street (on the left), notice the Renaissance facade of **Hotel Růže:** This former Jesuit college hides a beautiful courtyard, now filled with artistic vendor stands. Pop inside to shop or just admire its decoration of faux sgraffito "bricks," made by scratching into an outer layer of one color of plaster to reveal a different color beneath. This style was all the rage during the town's boom time, and we'll see several more examples on this walk.

• *Walk another block down the main drag until you reach steps on the left leading to the...*

Church of St. Vitus: Český Krumlov's main church was built as a bastion of Catholicism in the 15th century, when the Roman Catholic Church was fighting the Hussites. Step inside (generally open daily 9:00-16:30, Sunday Mass at 9:30, daily Mass at 17:00 in the winter chapel, +420 380 711 336). The 17th-century Baroque high altar shows a totem of religious figures: the Virgin Mary (crowned in heaven), St. Vitus (above Mary), and, way up on top, St. Wenceslas, the patron saint of the Czech people, long considered their ambassador in heaven. The canopy in the back, though empty today, once supported a grand statue of a Rožmberk atop a horse. The statue originally stood at the high altar. (Too egotistical for Jesuits, it was later moved to the rear of the nave and then lost for good.) While the 1906 Neo-Gothic main organ has been renovated, it's the cute little circa-1716 Baroque beauty that gets more attention—deservedly so.

• *Continuing on Horní street, you'll come to the...*

Main Square (Náměstí Svornosti): Lined with a mix of Renaissance and Baroque homes of burghers (all built on 12th-century Gothic foundations), the main square has a grand charm. The Town Hall (the crenellated white building on the right) flies both the Czech flag and the town flag, which shows the rose symbol of the Rožmberk family, who ruled the town for 300 years.

Imagine the history that this square has seen: In the 1620s, the town was held by the (very Catholic) Habsburgs, just as Lutheran Protestantism was rising to threaten Catholic Europe. Krumlov was a seat of Jesuit power and learning, and the intellectuals of the Roman church allegedly burned books on this square. Later, when there was a bad harvest, locals blamed witches—and burned them, too. Every so often, terrible plagues rolled through the countryside. In a nearby village, all but two residents were killed by a plague.

But the plague stopped before devastating the people of Český Krumlov, and in 1715—as thanks to God—they built the plague monument that stands on the square today (on the left). Much later, in 1938, Hitler stood right here before a backdrop of

long Nazi banners to celebrate the annexation of the Sudetenland. And in 1968, Russian tanks spun their angry treads on the roads to this square to intimidate locals who were demanding freedom.

• *From the main square, walk down Radniční street (on the right, just past the Town Hall) and cross the...*

Barber's Bridge (Lazebnický Most): This wooden bridge, decorated with two 19th-century statues, connects the Old Town and the Castle Town. On the right side stands a statue of St. John of Nepomuk, who's also depicted by a prominent statue on Prague's Charles Bridge. Among other responsibilities, he's the protector against floods. In the great floods in August 2002, the angry river submerged the bridge (but removable banisters minimized the damage). Stains just above the windows of the adjacent building show how high the water rose.

• *The second part of the walk involves lots of uphill hiking—but it's worth it to see the castle courtyards and dramatic views.*

KRUMLOV CASTLE

Big and imposing, the town castle boasts several fine courtyards, spectacular viewpoints, and gorgeous gardens—all of which are open to the public, free to enter, and fun to roam (though some areas may be closed on Mon). This part of the walk focuses on those public spaces, leading you from Barber's Bridge, through the heart of the castle, and up to a picturesque viewpoint just before the gardens. The castle also has several individual sights (Round Tower, Castle Museum, Upper Castle, Baroque Theater) that can be laced into this walk but require paid admission and/or a reserved tour (for details, see listings under "Sights in Český Krumlov," later).

• *Cross the bridge and head up shop-lined Latrán street, which bends to the right. Just after that bend, look for the stairs on your left (in front of the gray-and-white building). Head up, passing under a stone arch with the wood-carved rose symbol of the Rožmberk family. You'll emerge into the castle's...*

First (Lower) Courtyard: This is just the first of many courtyards that bunny-hop up through the castle complex. This was the site for workers and industry (stables, smithy, brewery, pharmacy, and so on)—convenient for aristocratic needs, but far enough away to keep noises and smells at bay.

Looking up, you can't miss the strikingly colorful **Round Tower** that marks the location of the first castle, built here to guard the medieval river crossing. It features a colorfully restored 16th-century Renaissance paint job, fancy astrological decor, terra-cotta symbols of the zodiac, and a fine arcade.

• *Head up to the former drawbridge. Look over the sides of the bridge. Spot any bears?*

Bear Pits (Medvědí Příkop): These hold a family of European brown bears, as they have since the Rožmberks added bears to their coat of arms in the 16th century to demonstrate their (fake) blood relation to the distinguished Italian Orsini family (whose name means "bear-like"). Featured on countless coats of arms, bears have long been totemic animals for Europeans. Pronouncing the animal's real name was taboo in many cultures, and Czechs still refer to bears only indirectly. For example, in most Germanic languages, the word "bear" is derived from "brown," while the Slavic *medvěd* literally means "honey eater."

Near the top of the bridge, notice the gently worded sign suggesting that—rather than toss down your junk-food leftovers—you add a few coins in the collection slot to finance "more varied meals and delicacies" for the bears.

• *Continue through the gateway into the...*

Second Courtyard: Here you'll spot more of the sgraffito (Renaissance faux features scraped into wet plaster) that decorates much of the castle. To your left, at the bottom of the courtyard, is the entrance to the **tower climb** and the **Castle Museum.** Farther up on the left is the **ticket office** for castle tours, including the Baroque Theater—stop in now (if you haven't already) to see about a tour.

• *From here, things get steep as we enter the...*

Heart of the Castle Complex: Head up the bridge, noticing the little view terrace on the left—the first of several along here. You'll emerge into the **Third Courtyard,** then (after a corridor) the **Fourth Courtyard.** Nicely preserved paintings enliven their blocky facades. Wrapped around these courtyards is the castle proper, a mighty Renaissance building sometimes called the Upper Castle (interiors open to visitors—notice the meeting points for various tour options). Continuing straight out through the end of the Fourth Courtyard, you'll cross the breathtaking **Cloak Bridge**—a triple-decker, statue-lined, covered bridge spanning a vast gorge and connecting the castle firmly with the gardens that sprawl behind it. Enjoy the views—but, believe it or not, even better ones are coming up.

Notice the **Baroque Theater,** at the far end of the bridge, which still uses traditional methods for moving scenery and producing sound effects. Aspects of this back-in-the-day stagecraft still survive on Broadway today. This is one of only two such original theaters in Europe.

• *After the bridge, continue uphill through the...*

Fifth Courtyard: Really more of a pathway, this connects the castle to its gardens. Walk along the white wall—with peekaboo windows—until you are almost at the gate up top. High on the wall to the right, notice the **sundial.** Check the time: It's dead-on... except for Daylight Saving Time, which was unknown to medieval timekeepers. Notice that the sundial cuts into one of the faux windows, painted on the lower level of the building to create Renaissance symmetry.

Now step through the low-profile door directly across from the sundial. You'll emerge at a spectacular **viewpoint** that takes in the entire town, its curving river, and even the colorful tower and most of the castle complex you just came through. Jockey your way through the selfie-snapping crowd and drink it in. (Or literally drink, at the little adjacent bar.)

• *Our walk is finished. But if you still have stamina, you can consider exploring the* **castle gardens**—*they're just uphill, through the gate from the Fifth Courtyard.*

Sights in Český Krumlov

KRUMLOV CASTLE COMPLEX
(KRUMLOVSKÝ ZÁMEK)

No Czech town is complete without a castle—and now that the nobles are gone, their mansions are open to us common folk. Český Krumlov is no different. Its immense Krumlov Castle complex, one of the largest in Central Europe, perches on a rock promontory overlooking the Vltava River and the town. The original Gothic castle took shape here in the 13th century, and eventually the Rožmberk, Eggenberg, and Schwarzenberg families each inherited it in turn. In successive waves of additions and renovations, they built it into the splendid Renaissance/Baroque property you see today.

The following sights are listed in the order you'll reach them as you climb up through the complex (ideally following my self-guided walk, earlier). The Round Tower and Castle Museum can be visited at your leisure, while other castle interiors—including the excellent Baroque Theater—can be seen only with a guided tour (see next). On a quick visit, the only sight I'd bother paying admission for is the theater.

Reservations Recommended: It's worth booking ahead to guarantee a slot on an English-language tour of the **Upper Castle interior** or the **Baroque Theater** (the theater is the castle attraction most likely to sell out). Book at least a day ahead on the castle website. You'll be issued an eticket with your selected tour time. Print the ticket or have it accessible on your mobile device, and be in the correct courtyard a few minutes before your appointed time, or you'll be locked out.

Reservations can also be made in person at the castle ticket office, or by phone.

Information: +420 380 704 721, www.zamek-ceskykrumlov.cz.

▲Round Tower (Zâmecká Věž) and Castle Museum (Hradní Muzeum)

These two sights share a ticket office at the bottom of the castle's middle courtyard. While neither is a must, both are worth considering if you want a peek inside the castle without committing to a guided tour.

Colorfully impressive from the outside, the **tower** is also fun to climb. Twist up the 163 well-worn wood and stone steps to the top, where you'll be rewarded with grand 360-degree views over the town, the rest of the castle complex, and happy boaters floating on the river.

The exhibits at the **Castle Museum** focus on key moments in the lives of the town's various ruling families: Rožmberks, Eggenbergs, and Schwarzenbergs. Be sure to download the free mobile guide onto your phone before you enter. You'll see a hall of aristocratic portraits; the offices, bedrooms, and dining rooms of the various inhabitants; and a modest religious treasury, armory, and musical instruments collection. At the end, you can sit in old-timey cinema seats and watch archival footage of the castle's residents from the 1920s and 1930s.

Cost and Hours: Combo-ticket for tower and museum—180 Kč; both open daily 9:00-16:30, June-Aug until 17:30, shorter hours and closed Mon in winter; last entry one hour before closing. This ticket is not sold online.

▲Upper Castle (Horní Hrad)

While the Upper Castle grounds are free to explore, you'll need to take a tour to access the interiors. Two different tour routes give

you a glimpse of the places where the Rožmberks, Eggenbergs, and Schwarzenbergs dined, studied, worked, prayed, entertained, and slept. (By European standards, the castle's not much, and the tours move slowly.) Imagine being an aristocratic guest here, riding the dukes' assembly line of fine living: You'd promenade through a long series of elegant spaces and dine in the sumptuous dining hall before enjoying a concert in the Hall of Mirrors, which leads directly to the Baroque Theater (described next). After the play, you'd go out into the château garden for a fireworks finale.

Cost and Hours: Choose from Tour I (Baroque and Renaissance rooms, of the most general interest) or Tour II (19th-century castle life). Tours cost 240 Kč, leave regularly, and are conducted in Czech, English, and occasionally German (note that the English tours often book up). Tour I runs Tue-Sun 9:00-16:00, longer hours June-Aug; Tour II runs Sat-Sun 9:00-16:00, Tue-Sun July-Aug, longer hours in summer. It's smart to book ahead—see "Reservations Recommended," earlier.

▲▲Baroque Theater (Zámecké Divadlo)

Europe once had several hundred Baroque theaters. Using candles for light and fireworks for special effects, most burned down. Today, only two survive in good shape and are open to tourists: one at Stockholm's Drottningholm Palace, and one here, at Krumlov Castle. During the 45-minute tour, you'll sit on benches in the theater and then go under the stage to see the wood-and-rope contraptions that enabled scenes to be scooted in and out within seconds (while fireworks and smoke blinded the audience). It's a lovely little theater with an impressive 3-D effect that makes the stage look deeper than it really is, but don't bother with the tour unless you

The Expulsion
of Ethnic Germans from Czechoslovakia

For seven centuries, Czech- and German-speaking people jointly inhabited and cultivated the lands of Bohemia, Moravia, and Silesia. Then, during the 19th century, the growing importance of ethnic identity resulted in tensions between these communities and fierce competition between their institutions. This situation was made worse by the German- and Hungarian-dominated Habsburg monarchy, which treated local Slavs as second-class citizens.

The end of World War I handed the Slavs an unprecedented opportunity to claim the land for themselves. The principle that gave countries such as Poland, Czechoslovakia, and Yugoslavia independence was called "self-determination": Each nation had the right to its own state within the area in which its people formed the majority. But the peoples of this part of Europe had mixed over the centuries, making it impossible to create functioning states based purely on ethnicity. In Bohemia—which became Czechoslovakia—the borders were drawn along historical boundaries. While the country was predominantly Slavic, areas with overwhelming German majorities remained.

Amid an economic downturn, ethnic Germans were swayed by Nazi propaganda. In 1935, 63 percent of Germans in Czechoslovakia voted for the Sudeten Nazi Party, enabling Hitler to appeal to international powers on their behalf, using the principle of self-determination. The 1938 Munich Agreement ceded the German-speaking areas of Czechoslovakia to the Third Reich, and ethnic Czechs were forced to leave.

Over the course of World War II, many Czechs came to believe that peaceful coexistence with Germans in a single state was impossible. As the war wound down, Czechoslovakia's exiled president Edvard Beneš traveled to Washington and Moscow, securing backing for a state-organized expulsion of more than 2.2 million ethnic Germans. From 1945 to 1946, Czechoslovak soldiers carried out the "transfer" orders: They typically entered a German-speaking town or village, took a few prisoners, and threat-

can snare a spot on an English one. The theater is used only once a year for an actual performance, attended by Baroque theater enthusiasts.

Cost and Hours: 280 Kč, tours Tue-Sun May-Oct, no tours Nov-April; English departure generally at 10:00. Due to the theater's fragility, groups are limited to 20 people, and English tours generally sell out. Reserve ahead—see "Reservations Recommended," earlier.

ened to execute the hostages unless everyone of German descent left. The expulsions sometimes turned violent: In June 1945, some 2,000 ethnic German civilians, including children, were executed near the town of Saatz.

While Beneš and most Czechs considered the expulsion of ethnic Germans revenge for the war and historical injustices, the communists saw a future opportunity: The emptied region was to become a revolutionary laboratory. Ironically, the Czechs regained "their" land but eroded their freedom; meanwhile, the Germans lost the land of their ancestors but gained a chance to build a prosperous democracy.

For the next 40 years, the "transfer" of ethnic Germans was a taboo subject, as the communist anti-Nazi propaganda machine rolled on as if the war never ended. After 1989, the issue was reluctantly broached by politicians on both sides of the border, as it threatened to derail otherwise strong relations between the Czech and German governments. Toward 2004, tensions again rose, as Czech politicians resisted demands for reparations from Sudeten Germans in Berlin and Brussels, who thought repayment should be a precondition to Czech entry into the European Union.

Over the last decade, the subject finally became depoliticized. Former German residents have begun visiting their old homes, sharing stories of their trauma with young Czechs, who—having grown confident in their freedom—are able to take a more nuanced view of their country's history. In 2015, the Sudeten German Association stepped back from its support for repatriates' legal claims. A year later, the Czech Minister of Culture Daniel Herman delivered a speech at the annual Sudeten German convention in Nürnberg, addressing the audience as "dear compatriots" and expressing regret over the events of 1945-46. An act that would have amounted to political suicide just 10 years earlier was positively received by the Czech public. Seventy years after a traumatic divorce, a door to reconciliation finally opened.

Castle Gardens (Zámecká Zahrada)

This lovely, 2,300-foot-long garden crowns the castle complex. It was laid out in the 17th century, when the noble family would have it lit with 22,000 oil lamps, torches, and candles for special occasions. The lower part is geometrical and symmetrical—French garden-style. The upper part is wilder—English garden-style. Both are delightful.

Cost and Hours: Free, open May-Sept daily 8:00-19:00, April and Oct until 17:00, closed Nov-March.

OTHER SIGHTS IN TOWN
▲Seidel Photo Studio Museum
(Museum Fotoateliér Seidel)

This fully preserved, meticulously renovated 1905 Art Nouveau villa featuring original furnishings, a garden, and 100-year-old photo equipment offers a welcome respite from the crowds and the ubiquitous Middle Ages. The museum, set in the home and studio of Josef Seidel (1859-1935) and his son František (1908-1997), features more than 100,000 of their original photographs of life in this mountainous region—Šumava, or Böhmerwald (Bohemian Forest)—between 1880 and 1950.

Josef Seidel was unique among his contemporaries in focusing his photography on just one region, and was the first in the country to use autochrome. Allowed to remain in Český Krumlov during and after World War II at a time when many Germans in the country were expelled, František continued his father's photography business, remaining here until his death in 1997. After his wife died in 2003, the town bought the house and converted it into a delightful museum and a cultural center for cross-cultural understanding. Restored, functional equipment offers hands-on experience with the process of photography during the late 19th and early 20th centuries. You can literally smell the history.

Cost and Hours: 170 Kč, includes English audioguide; Tue-Sun 9:00-12:00 & 13:00-16:00; across the river south of Old Town at Linecká 272, +420 736 503 871, www.seidel.cz.

Synagogue

Completed in 1910 in a mixture of architectural styles, this synagogue served the small Jewish community of Český Krumlov and neighboring villages. In 1938, there were 200 congregants here, but only two members of the area's Jewish community survived after World War II. Terribly run-down for decades after the war, the synagogue was restored to its former glory in 2015 by the Prague Jewish community, with funding from the European Union and German and Austrian sponsors. It contains an exhibit on its history and hosts concerts and contemporary art exhibits.

Cost and Hours: Free; Tue-Sun 10:00-16:00, closed Mon; shorter hours off-season, across the river south of Old Town at Za Soudem 282, +420 604 217 174, www.synagoga-krumlov.cz.

Eating: The **$ Café Synagoga,** with an assortment of cakes, occupies the former basement residence of the rabbi's family and an adjacent peaceful garden (daily 10:00-18:00, closed Oct-April).

Museum of Regional History
(Regionální Muzeum v Českém Krumlově)

This small museum gives you a quick look at regional costumes, tools, and traditions. When you pay, pick up the English translation of the displays (it also includes a lengthy history of Krumlov). Start on the top floor, where you'll see a Bronze Age exhibit, old paintings, a glimpse of noble life, and a look at how the locals rafted lumber from the Böhmerwald Mountains all the way to Vienna (partly by canal). Don't miss the fun-to-study ceramic model of Český Krumlov in 1800 (note the extravagant gardens high above the town). The lower floor comes with fine folk costumes and domestic art.

Cost and Hours: 60 Kč, Tue-Sun 9:00-12:00 & 12:30-17:00, July-Aug until 18:00, closed Mon year-round, Horní 152, +420 380 711 674, www.muzeumck.cz.

Puppet Museum and Fairy Tale House
(Muzeum Loutek a Pohádkový Dům)

In three small rooms, you'll view fascinating displays of more than 200 movable creations (overwhelmingly of Czech origin, but also some from Burma and Rajasthan). At the model stage, children of any age can try their hand at pulling the strings on their favorite fairy tale.

Cost and Hours: 100 Kč, daily 10:00-17:00, Nov-March 11:00-16:00, +420 723 325 262, Radniční 29, www.krumlovskainspirace.cz.

▲Pivovar Český Krumlov Brewery Tour

This may be one of the most intimate brewery tours in this land that so loves its beer. Tucked into a river bend on the edge of town,
Český Krumlov's spunky little brewery has an authenticity that can't be matched by the big, soulless corporate breweries (such as Pilsner Urquell, in Plzeň, or the Czech Budweiser, in nearby České Budějovice). This is your chance to learn about the beer-making process at a facility where they're still

using the same giant copper vats from 1915. While some of the facility has recently been modernized (and ongoing works may reroute the tour a bit), you'll still see lots of vintage equipment, including the original brew house (still in service), the fermentation vats, the cellars used for aging, and the bottling plant. Your tour ends with a visit to the pub, where you can sample some brews, including a

CESKÝ KRUMLOV

"smoky" dark beer (Nakouřený Švihák), made with malt that tastes like salami and then aged for 100 days.

Cost and Hours: Tours are by appointment only, 1,250 Kč for groups of 1-4 people, 250 Kč/person for larger groups, includes three tastes. Reserve at least two days ahead by phone or email, +420 775 733 462, www.pivovarceskykrumlov.cz, tours@pivovarck.cz.

Getting There: It's just a short stroll up Nové Město street from the main drag below the castle. During ongoing reconstruction, you may instead have to loop around town to the back entrance on Pivovarska—about a 10-minute walk.

Křížový Vrch (Hill of the Cross)

For an easy 30-minute hike up to the hill with commanding views, walk to the end of Rooseveltova street, cross at the traffic light, then head straight for the first (empty) chapel-like Station of the Cross. Turning right, it's easy to navigate along successive Stations of the Cross until you reach the white church on the hill (closed to the public), set in the middle of wild meadows. Looking down into the valley at the medieval city nestled within the S-shaped river, framed by the rising hills, it's hard to imagine any town with a more powerful *genius loci* (spirit of the place). The view is best at sunset.

▲▲▲Canoeing and Rafting the Vltava

For a quintessentially Czech experience, join the locals for a paddle down the Vltava River, the country's most popular place for boating. Novices and hearty paddlers alike can spend as little as 30 minutes to a full day easing into a mellow, drifting mindset—stopping for a snack or a *pivo* at one of the many pubs and cafés along the way.

Rental companies all over town offer the same basic fleet: fiberglass canoes for two to three people, and rubber rafts for two to six people. While the canoes are faster and more agile, they require some experience to navigate a few whitewater areas. The rafts, meanwhile, are slower and easy to navigate, even for newcomers. A map, a waterproof bag, and all the necessary gear are included. With limited time, you can start from town and paddle as far as you like, then head back (see later for details). Plan to spend at least three hours on the river to fully appreciate the experience.

Rental Companies: Ingetour launches and picks up in each of the most useful locations (Krumlov Vltavan, Krumlov Trojice,

Zlatá Koruna, Boršov) and runs a regular bus connecting them (Zlatá Koruna and Boršov are also connected by regular bus and train). You can end your paddle at any of their locations without committing from the start. While it's best to reserve ahead, you can often just show up (www.ingetour.cz). Ingetour, like many other companies, also offers guided day trips. Other options are **Maleček** (Rooseveltova 28, +420 602 744 074, www.malecek.cz) and **Vltava Sport Service** (Hradební 60, +420 380 711 988, www.ckvltava.cz). Vltava Sport Service offers a boat-and-bike option, boating down to Zlatá Koruna Abbey and cycling back via Dívčí Skála castle (Maiden's Rock).

Downstream from Český Krumlov (1-7 hours): This plan allows you to paddle for as long as you want. Start at the Vltavan campsite above Český Krumlov, where most rental com-
panies are based (it's easiest to
arrange a ride there with your
rental company). From here,
it's about an hour (with some
challenging sections) to the
Trojice campsite at the other
end of Český Krumlov (you
can bail out here if you've had
enough). Two hours more brings you to **Zlatá Koruna Monastery,** a beautifully set Gothic monastery (see listing under "Near Český Krumlov," next). While many end their trip at the monastery (bus and train stations are close by), those who venture farther into the nature reserve that follows are rewarded with spectacular scenery and minimal river traffic. The water on this section also flows faster, so it is more fun. It can take close to four hours to reach the next stop in **Boršov.** To return to Český Krumlov from Boršov, you can take the Ingetour bus (last departure at 16:30) or the train (5-minute walk from dock; trains every 2 hours; 30 minutes).

NEAR ČESKÝ KRUMLOV
Zlatá Koruna Monastery (Klášter Zlatá Koruna)

This Cistercian abbey was founded in the 13th century by a Bohemian king to counter the growing influence of the Vítek family, the ancestors of the mighty Rožmberks. As you enter the grounds, notice the magnificent central linden tree, with its strange, cape-like leaves; it's said to have been used by the anti-Catholic Hussites when they hanged the monks. There are several tours: The one-hour tour takes you through the rare two-storied Gothic Chapel of the Guardian Angel, the main church, and the cloister; the 10-minute tour takes you to the abbey chapel, with the original Gothic Zlatá

ČESKÝ KRUMLOV

ČESKÝ KRUMLOV

Roma in Central Europe

Numbering 12 million, the Roma people constitute a bigger European nation than the Czechs, the Hungarians, or the Dutch. (The term "Gypsies," previously the common name for this group, is now considered derogatory and inaccurate.)

Descended from several low north-Indian castes, the Roma began to migrate through Persia and Armenia into the Ottoman Empire a thousand years ago. Known for their itinerant lifestyle, expertise in horse trading, skilled artisanship, and flexibility regarding private property, the Roma were both sought out and suspected in medieval Europe.

The Industrial Revolution threatened the Roma's traditional livelihoods, making their wandering lifestyle difficult to sustain. In the 1940s, Hitler sent hundreds of thousands of Roma to the gas chambers. In the occupied Protectorate of Bohemia and Moravia (Czechoslovakia minus the Sudetenland that had been annexed to Germany), Hitler had the help of Czech policemen who ran the two Roma "transfer" camps in Lety and Hodonín, where hundreds died even before being transported to Auschwitz. Only 10 percent of the protectorate's 5,000-strong prewar Roma population survived.

After the war, tens of thousands of Roma from eastern Slovakia were relocated into the Sudetenland. At this time, the communist governments in Eastern Europe required Roma to speak the country's major language, settle in towns, and work in new industrial jobs. Rather than producing well-adjusted citizens, the result was an erosion of time-honored Roma values, as the policy shattered traditionally cohesive communities. It left the new Roma generation prone to sexual, alcohol, and drug abuse, and filled state-run orphanages with deprived Roma toddlers.

When the obligation and right to work disappeared with the communist regimes in 1989, rampant unemployment and dependence on welfare joined the list of Roma afflictions. As people all over Central Europe found it difficult to adjust to the new economic realities, they again turned on the Roma as scapegoats. Many Roma now live in segregated ghettos. Those who make it against the odds and succeed in mainstream society typically do so by turning their backs on their Roma heritage.

In this context, the Roma in Český Krumlov are a surprising success story. The well-integrated, proud Roma community here (numbering 1,000, or 5 percent of the town's population) is considered a curious anomaly even by experts. Their success could be due to a number of factors: the legacy of the multicultural Rožmberks, the fact that almost everyone in Český Krumlov is a relative newcomer, or maybe how local youngsters, regardless of skin color, tend to resolve their differences over a beer in the local "Gypsy Pub" (Cikánská Jizba), with a trendy Roma band setting the tune.

Koruna Madonna, the most treasured painting in the region; and the 30-minute tour combines highlights of both.

Cost and Hours: 180 Kč for one-hour tour in Czech, generally runs every half-hour, pick up English leaflet; 60 Kč for 10-minute abbey chapel tour; 140 Kč for 30-minute sacral tour; main tour runs June-Aug Tue-Sun 9:00-16:30, closed Mon, shorter hours in spring and fall, closed Nov-March; +420 380 743 126, www.klaster-zlatakoruna.cz.

Getting There: Drivers can reach the abbey in about 10 minutes from Český Krumlov (head north out of town and follow route #39). But it's more fun to get there by raft or canoe—the abbey is directly above the river at the end of a three-hour float (see "Canoeing and Rafting the Vltava," earlier).

Sleeping in Český Krumlov

Český Krumlov is filled with small pensions and hostels. Summer is busy all around. Plan to book months ahead to stay near the center, and at least a year ahead for places in the heart of town. Though I usually recommend booking directly with hotels, many of these small pensions are easier to book through Booking.com. My favorite neighborhood is called Plešivecká; it's in the historic part of town, just a five-minute walk from the center, yet somehow away from all the tourist commotion.

IN AND NEAR THE OLD TOWN

$$$ Castle View Apartments rents seven diverse apartments. These are the best-equipped rooms I've found in town—the bathroom floors are heated, all come with kitchenettes, and everything's done just right. Their website describes each stylish apartment; the "view" ones really do come with eye-popping vistas (RS%, apartment sleeps up to 6, breakfast at a nearby hotel, Šatlavská 140, +420 731 108 677, www.castleview.cz, info@castleview.cz).

$ Hotel Konvice is run by a German couple—and their three children—with a personal touch. Each room is uniquely decorated (a block above the main square at Horní 145, +420 380 711 611, https://en.stadthotel-krummau.de, hotelkonvice@quick.cz).

$ Pension U Kapličky, on a quiet street adjacent to a chapel and a city park, consists of two artistically designed apartments in an unusually shaped medieval house. Jitka, a teacher of stone carving at the local arts academy and one of the last old-timers still calling central Český Krumlov home, lives downstairs and bakes pastries for breakfast (reserve months ahead, Linecká 60, +420 606 434 090, https://ukaplicky.ckrumlov.cz, ukaplicky@ckrumlov.cz).

BELOW THE MAIN SQUARE

Secluded Parkán street, which runs along the river below the square, has a hotel and a row of small pensions. These places have a family feel and views of the looming castle above.

$$$ Hotel Mlýn, at the end of Parkán, is a tastefully furnished hotel with 50 rooms and all the amenities (elevator, pay parking, Parkán 120, +420 380 731 133, www.hotelmlyn.eu, info@hotelmlyn.eu).

$$ Pension Olšakovský, which has a delightful breakfast area on a terrace next to the river, treats visitors as family guests (free parking, Parkán 114, +420 792 311 040, www.olsakovsky.cz, office@olsakovsky.cz).

AT THE BASE OF THE CASTLE

A quiet, cobbled pedestrian street (Latrán) runs below the castle just over the bridge from the Old Town. Lined with cute shops, it's a 10-minute walk downhill from the train station.

$ Pension Danny is a little funky place, with homey rooms and a tangled floor plan above a restaurant (in-room breakfast, Latrán 72, +420 603 210 572, www.pensiondanny.cz, recepce@pensiondanny.cz).

BETWEEN THE BUS STATION AND THE OLD TOWN

Rooseveltova street, midway between the bus station and the Old Town (a four-minute walk from either), is lined with several fine little places. The key here is tranquility—the noisy bars of the town center are out of earshot.

$$ Hotel Garni Myší Díra ("Mouse Hole") hides 11 bright and woody Bohemian contemporary rooms overlooking the Vltava River just outside the Old Town (includes transfer to/from bus or train station, free parking, Rooseveltova 28, +420 380 712 853, www.hotelmysidira.cz). The no-nonsense reception, which closes at 20:00, runs a recommended boat rental company (Maleček, at the same address).

$ Pension Teddy offers three deluxe rooms that share a balcony overlooking the river and have original 18th-century furniture. Or stay in one of four modern-style rooms, some of which also face the river (cash only, staff may be unhelpful, pay parking, Rooseveltova 38, +420 724 003 981, www.penzionteddy.cz, info@penzionteddy.cz).

$ Pension Anna is well run, with two doubles, six apartments, and a restful little garden. Its apartments are spacious suites, with a living room and stairs leading to the double-bedded loft. The upstairs rooms can get stuffy during the summer (pay parking, Rooseveltova 41, +420 380 711 692, www.pensionanna-ck.cz, info@

pensionanna-ck.cz). If you book a standard double and they bump you up to an apartment, don't pay more than the double rate.

IN THE PLEŠIVECKÁ NEIGHBORHOOD

To reach this historical part of town—one of the last genuine-feeling neighborhoods in Český Krumlov—cross the Dr. Beneše Bridge, then climb the stairs directly ahead of you. These lead into a small, quiet square, with a couple of hotels and cafés. Take the street diagonally to the left (Plešivecká), which descends back toward the river, where you'll find more local life. You'll need to book up to a year in advance to stay in this neighborhood. A handy Coop supermarket is at the end of Plešivecká street.

$$ Pension Athanor is situated in a historic house on a quiet square (Plešivecké Náměstí 271, +420 720 611 712, www.apartmanyathanor.cz, info@apartmanyathanor.cz).

$ Penzion Weber is a family-run operation with a pleasant little garden overlooking the river (Plešivecká 129, +420 605 162 478, www.penzionweber.cz, weber.f@seznam.cz).

OUTSIDE THE CITY CENTER

$$ Pension Gardena has 16 spacious, airy rooms in two adjacent, tactfully renovated historical buildings. A family business with a garden, it's on the way into town from the bus station just a hundred yards above Horní Bridge (Kaplická 21, +420 380 711 028, mobile +420 607 873 974, www.pensiongardena.com, gardena@seznam.cz).

$ Pension Kříž, with five rooms in a new house, is tucked away in a quiet, modern villa district under the Křížový Vrch (Hill of the Cross), just a five-minute walk from Horní Bridge (Křížová 71, +420 775 421 012, www.penzion-kriz.cz, ubytovani@penzion-kriz.cz).

HOSTELS

¢ Hostel 99's picnic-table terrace looks out on the Old Town. While the gentle sound of the river gurgles outside your window late at night, you're more likely to hear a youthful international crowd having a great time (cash only, private rooms available, laundry, recommended Hospoda 99 restaurant, 10-minute downhill walk from train station or two bus stops to Spicak; Věžní 99, +420 797 631 820, www.restaurant-99.com, hostel99@hostel99.cz).

¢ Hostel Postel is a small, artsy place with just 15 beds huddled down by the river, sleeping two to six people per room (Rybářská 35, +420 776 720 722, www.hostelpostel.cz, info@hostelpostel.cz).

Eating in Český Krumlov

With a huge variety of creative little restaurants, Český Krumlov
is a fun place to eat. In peak season, the good places fill up fast, so
make reservations or eat early.

IN AND NEAR THE OLD TOWN

$$ Na Louži seems to be everyone's favorite Czech bistro, with
40 seats (many at shared tables) in one 1930s-style room decorated
with funky old advertisements. They serve good, inexpensive, un-
pretentious local cuisine and hometown beer on tap (daily, near the
Egon Schiele Art Center at Kájovská 66, +420 380 711 280, www.
nalouzi.com).

$$ Cikánská Jizba ("Gypsy Pub") is a Roma tavern filling one
den-like, barrel-vaulted room. The Roma staff serves Slovak-style
food (most of the Czech Republic's Roma population came from
Slovakia). While this rustic little restaurant—which packs its 10
tables under a mystic-feeling Gothic vault—won't win any culinary
awards, you never know what festive and musical activities will
erupt, particularly on Friday and Saturday nights, when the band
Cindži Renta ("Wet Rag") performs here (closed Sun, 2 blocks toward castle from main square at Dlouhá 31, +420 722 236 615).

$$ Krčma u Dwau Maryí ("Tavern of the Two Marys") is a
characteristic old place with idyllic riverside picnic tables, serving
medieval Czech cuisine and drinks. The fascinating menu explains
the history of the house and makes a good case that the food of
the poor medieval Bohemians was tasty and varied. Buck up for
buckwheat, millet, greasy meat, or the poor-man's porridge (daily,
Parkán 104, +420 380 717 228).

$$ Laibon is a top choice for filling vegetarian meals, from
Indian dal and vegetables to burritos, couscous, or Slovak gnocchi
with sheep milk cheese. Settle down in the meditative inside or
head out onto the castle-view river terrace and observe the raft-
and-canoe action while you eat (daily, Parkán 105, +420 775 676
654).

$$ Café Kolektiv tries to inject some modern sophistication
into this old town. It has a stark minimalist interior, a chalkboard
menu, well-executed light café fare with some international flavors,
a good cocktail selection, and stylish—if stuffy—service (daily
until 18:00, Latrán 13, across from the castle stairs, +420 776 626
644).

$$ Restaurace Zdroj, with fine outdoor riverside seating and
a somewhat less inviting interior, is *the* place in town to taste fresh
carp, trout, or pike perch. They also offer non-fish daily specials
(daily, on the island by the millwheel, +420 724 149 771).

$$$ Krčma Šatlava is an old prison gone cozy, with an open fire, big wooden tables under a rustic old medieval vault, and tables outdoors on the pedestrian lane. It's great for a late drink or roasted game (cooked on an open spit). *Medovina* is hot honey wine (daily, on Šatlavská, follow lane leading to the side from  TI on main square, +420 380 713 344).

$ Krumlovská Picka, a tiny, atmospheric place on the island by the millwheel, offers takeout pizza and freshly baked-and-filled baguettes. Cuddle near the oven inside or picnic on the outside terrace (daily, closed off-season, Dlouhá 97, +420 777 804 638).

OUTSIDE THE CITY CENTER

$$ Hospoda 99 Restaurace serves good, cheap soups, salads, and meals. It's the choice of hostelers and locals alike for its hamburgers, vegetarian food, Czech dishes, and cheap booze (daily, at Hostel 99, Věžní 99, +420 380 713 813). This place is booming until late, when everything else is hibernating.

$ Dobrá Čajovna, at the base of the castle, is a typical example of the quiet, exotic-feeling teahouses that flooded Czech towns in the 1990s as alternatives to smoky, raucous pubs. Though directly across from the castle entrance, it's a world away from the tourist hubbub. With its meditative karma inside and a peaceful terrace facing the monastery out back, it provides a relaxing break (daily, Latrán 54).

IN THE PLEŠIVECKÁ NEIGHBORHOOD

Good traditional eateries with outdoor seating line the Vltava in the Plešivecká neighborhood; just cross the Dr. Beneše Bridge and head right along the river.

$ Pražírna Ideál ("Ideal Roastery"), on the corner of Linecká just past the Seidel Photo Studio Museum, is a tiny local place far away from the crowds and dead serious about the quality of its cakes and fair-trade brews (daily 9:30-19:00, Horská 70).

Český Krumlov Connections

BY PUBLIC TRANSPORTATION

Most trains to and from Český Krumlov require a transfer in the city of **České Budějovice,** a transit hub just to the north. Buses, on the other hand, are direct, if less comfortable. Bus and train timetables are available at https://idos.idnes.cz.

If you have time in České Budějovice between connections, consider a visit to the town's gigantic medieval main square, Náměstí Přemysla Otakara II (about a six-block walk from the station). Store your bags in lockers at the train station, then exit the station to the right, cross the street at the crosswalk, and head straight down Lannova třída (which becomes Kanovnická street) to the square.

By Train
From Český Krumlov by Train to: České Budějovice (11/day, 45 minutes), **Prague** (9/day, 1/day direct, 3 hours), **Vienna** (8/day with changes in Budějovice and České Velenice, 5 hours), **Budapest** (6/day with changes in Budějovice and Linz, 7 hours).

By Bus
The state-of-the-art bus station is a five-minute walk above town (bus info +420 380 711 190). Regiojet (www.regiojet.com), Flixbus (www.flixbus.cz), and Leo Express (www.leoexpress.com) have online reservation systems, the newest buses, and a free drink for passengers.

From Český Krumlov by Bus to: Prague (at least hourly, 3 hours; tickets can also be bought at the Český Krumlov TI), **České Budějovice** (transit hub for other destinations such as Třeboň, Telč, and Třebíč—hourly, 30 minutes).

BY SHUTTLE SERVICE
From Český Krumlov to Austria and Beyond: Several companies offer handy shuttle service. The best of the bunch is CK Shuttle, with free Wi-Fi on board and affordable fares: 1,200 Kč per person one-way to **Vienna** (3.5 hours), **Salzburg** (3 hours), **Hallstatt** (3 hours), or **Prague** (2.5 hours). They can also take you to Linz (where you can hop on the speedy east-west main rail line through Austria), Budapest, Munich, and other places. They offer door-to-door service to and from your hotel (office at Dlouhá 95, www.ckshuttle.cz). Another reliable option is Sebastian Tours (higher prices, +420 607 100 234 or mobile +420 608 357 581, www.sebastianck-tours.com, pensionsebastiantours@gmail.com).

POLAND
Polska

POLAND

Polska

Poland is a land of surprises. Some travelers may still imagine this place as a backwards, impoverished land of rusting factories, smoggy cities, and gloomy citizens—only to be left speechless when they step into Kraków's vibrant main square, Gdańsk's colorful Royal Way, or Warsaw's trendy hipster zones. Today's Poland has a vibrant urbanity, an enticing food and design culture, dynamic history, and kindhearted locals.

The Poles are a proud people—as moved by their spectacular failures as by their successes. Their quiet elegance has been tempered by generations of abuse by foreign powers.

In a way, there are two Polands: lively, cosmopolitan urban centers; and countless tiny farm villages in the countryside. A societal tension exists between city-dwelling progressives and what they call the "simple people" of Poland: salt-of-the-earth Poles descended from generations of farmers, who still live an uncomplicated, agrarian lifestyle and tend to be politically conservative and staunchly Euroskeptic.

Poland is arguably Europe's most devoutly Catholic country. Even compared to other nominally Catholic countries, travelers are struck by how the Poles' faith pervades their lives and worldviews. This is probably because the Catholic faith has united and sustained the Poles through many tough times. Squeezed between Protestant Germany (Prussia) and Eastern Orthodox Russia, Poland wasn't even a country for generations (during the Partitions, 1795-1918)—but  its Catholicism helped keep its spirit alive. Then, under communism, Poles found their religion a source of both strength and rebellion—they could express dissent against the atheistic regime by going to church. Be sure to step into some serene church interiors. These aren't museums—you'll almost certainly see locals engrossed

in prayer. (Visit with respect: Maintain silence, and if you want to take pictures, do so discreetly.)

Much of Poland's story is a Jewish story. Starting in the Middle Ages, Poland was a magnet for Jewish refugees because of its relatively welcoming policies. "Relatively" is the operative word. Polish history is rife with pogroms and other acts of violence, and Jewish people were forbidden from owning land; that's why they settled mostly in cities.

Jewish cultural life in Poland blossomed in the early 20th century. Before World War II, 80 percent of Europe's Jews lived in this country. Warsaw was the world's second-largest Jewish city (after New York), with 380,000 Jews (out of a total population of 1.2 million). But the Holocaust (and a later Soviet policy of sending "troublemaking" Jews to Israel) decimated the Jewish population.

This tragic chapter, combined with postwar border shifts and population movements, made Poland one of Europe's most ethnically homogeneous countries. Today, 97 percent of citizens are ethnic Poles; only a few thousand Polish Jews remain, along with small minorities of Ukrainians and Germans.

Poland has long been staunchly pro-America. Of course, their big neighbors (Russia and Germany) have been their historic enemies. And when Hitler invaded in 1939, the Poles felt let down by their supposed European friends (France and Britain), who declared war on Germany but provided virtually no military support to the Polish resistance. America, meanwhile, is seen as the big ally from across the ocean—and the home of the largest population of Poles outside of Poland.

Poles may strike some visitors as brusque. Among older generations, this may be a holdover from challenging communist times.

And it may help to know that, because of the plainspoken cadence of Polish, Poles speaking English sometimes sound more impatient or gruff than they realize. Part of the Poles' charm is that they're not as slick and self-assured as many Europeans: They're kind, soft-spoken, and quite shy. On a recent train trip in Poland, I offered my seatmate a snack—and spent the rest of the trip enjoying a delightful conversation with a new friend.

HELPFUL HINTS

Price Ranges: Many hotels and restaurants in Poland fall in this book's lower price ranges (**$** and **$$**). This is a reflection not of quality but of the value of Poland compared to other destinations in Central Europe. A **$$** hotel or restaurant in Poland can often meet or exceed the caliber of a **$$$$** place in Prague or Vienna. Don't be put off by seemingly low prices: Even elegant choices don't break the bank here, and frugal travelers can order high on the menu.

Restroom Signage: To confuse tourists, the Poles have devised a secret way of marking their WCs. You'll see doors marked with *męska* (men) and *damska* (women)—but even more often, you'll simply see a triangle (for men) or a circle (for women).

Train Tickets: It's easiest to buy train tickets online at www.intercity.pl; while not particularly user-friendly, it's in English and workable with a little patience (it helps to create a log-in). Tickets are emailed, and you can simply show them on your phone to the conductor. At train stations, you'll see both ticket machines and staffed windows *(kasy)*. These may be marked (sometimes only in Polish) for domestic tickets, international tickets, and so on; ask to make sure you're in the right line. Leave plenty of time to buy your ticket.

Train Station Lingo: "PKP" is the abbreviation for Polish National Railways ("PKS" is for buses). In larger towns with several train stations, you'll normally use the one called Główny (meaning "Main"—except in Warsaw, where it's *Centralna*). *Dworzec główny* means "main train station." Most stations have several platforms *(peron),* each of which has two tracks *(tor)*. Departures are generally listed by the *peron*, so keep your eye on both tracks for your train. Arrivals are *przyjazdy*, and departures are *odjazdy*. Left-luggage counters or lockers are marked *przechowalnia bagażu*. On arriving at a station, to get

Poland Almanac

Official Name: Rzeczpospolita Polska (Republic of Poland), or Polska for short.

Snapshot History: This thousand-year-old country has been dominated by foreign powers for much of the past two centuries, finally achieving true independence (from the Soviet Union) in 1989.

People: As of mid-2023, this stands at over 41 million people (slightly less than California)—which includes at least 1.5 million recent arrivals from Ukraine who may not become permanent residents. Four out of every five Poles are practicing Catholics.

Latitude and Longitude: 52°N and 20°E (similar latitude to Berlin, London, and Edmonton, Alberta).

Area: 121,000 square miles, the same as New Mexico.

Geography: Because of its overall flatness, Poland has been a corridor for invading armies since its infancy. The Vistula River (650 miles) runs south-to-north up the middle of the country, passing through Kraków and Warsaw, and emptying into the Baltic Sea at Gdańsk. Poland's climate is generally cool and rainy—40,000 storks love it.

Biggest Cities: Warsaw (the capital, 1.8 million), Kraków (800,000), and Łódź (660,000).

Economy: The gross domestic product is $1.1 trillion, with a GDP per capita of $29,500. The 1990s saw an aggressive and successful transition from state-run socialism to privately owned capitalism.

Currency: 1 złoty (zł, or PLN) = 100 groszy (gr) = about 25 cents; 4 zł = about $1.

Government: Poland's mostly figurehead president selects the prime minister and cabinet, with legislators' approval. They govern along with a two-house legislature (Sejm and Senat) of 560 seats. Prime Minister Mateusz Morawiecki represents the majority political party, the right-wing Law and Justice (Prawo i Sprawiedliwość, or PiS for short). President Andrzej Duda, formerly of PiS (but currently a conservative-leaning independent), was narrowly reelected to a second five-year term in 2020.

Flag: The upper half is white, and the lower half is red—the traditional colors of Poland. Poetic Poles claim the white represents honor, and the red represents the blood spilled by the Poles to protect that honor. The flag sometimes includes a coat of arms with a crowned eagle (representing Polish sovereignty). Under Soviet rule, the crown was removed from the emblem, and the eagle's talons were trimmed. On regaining its independence, Poland coronated its eagle once more.

into town, follow signs for *wyjście* (sometimes followed by *do centrum* or *do miasta*).

Transit Route Planner: For a good public transit route planner for most Polish cities, try https://jakdojade.pl. You can also buy transit tickets on the Jakdojade app.

Easter Revelry: This is a major holiday in Poland, rivaling Christmas in importance. Expect most businesses to close from Friday or Saturday through Monday (which is also a national holiday). If you're in town for Easter, take part in some of the special traditions: All week, churches feature specially decorated chapels and altars. On Saturday, Poles bring lovingly decorated baskets of food to be blessed at church (Święconka). On Easter Sunday, Poles attend Mass and celebrate with an hours-long breakfast (the sour soup *żurek* is one of many traditional dishes). Monday is Śmigus-Dyngus, when people throw water at their loved ones (no joke).

Busy May: May 1 is May Day and May 3 is Constitution Day; this usually causes virtually the entire country to close down for a week. Later in the month, younger kids get out of school, so families go on vacation (Kraków is one of the most popular domestic destinations).

POLISH HISTORY

Poland is flat. Glancing at a topographical map of Europe, it's easy to see the Poles' historical dilemma: The path of least resistance from northern Europe to Russia leads right through Poland. Over the years, many invaders—from Genghis Khan to Napoleon to Hitler—have taken advantage of this fact. The country has been called "God's playground" for the many wars that have rumbled through its territory. Poland has been invaded by Soviets, Nazis, French,

Austrians, Russians, Prussians, Swedes, Teutonic Knights, Tatars, Bohemians, Magyars—and, about 1,300 years ago, Poles.

Medieval Greatness

The first Poles were the Polonians ("people of the plains"), a Slavic band that arrived here in the eighth century. In 966, Mieszko I, duke of the Polonian tribe, adopted Christianity and founded the Piast dynasty, which would last for more than 400 years. Centuries before Germany, Italy, or Spain first united, Poland was born.

Poland struggled against two different invaders in the 13th

Top 10 Dates That Changed Poland

AD 966: The Polish king Mieszko I is baptized a Christian, symbolically uniting the Polish people and founding the nation.

1385: The Polish queen Jadwiga marries a Lithuanian duke, starting the two-century reign of the Jagiełło family.

1410: Poland defeats the Teutonic Knights at the Battle of Grunwald, part of a golden age of territorial expansion and cultural achievement.

1572: The last Jagiellonian king dies, soon replaced by bickering nobles and foreign kings. Poland declines.

1795: In the last of three Partitions, the country is divvied up by its more-powerful neighbors: Russia, Prussia, and Austria.

1918: Following World War I, Poland finally reclaims its land and sovereignty.

1939: The Free City of Danzig (today's Gdańsk) is invaded by Nazi Germany, starting World War II. At war's end, the country is "liberated" (i.e., occupied) by the Soviet Union. After the war, Poland's borders and population shift significantly westward.

1980: Lech Wałęsa and the Solidarity trade union lead a successful strike, demanding more freedom from the communist regime.

1989: Poland gains independence under its first president—Lech Wałęsa. Fifteen years later, Poland joins the European Union.

2010: President Lech Kaczyński and 95 other high-level government officials are killed in a plane crash in Smoleńsk, Russia.

century: the Tatars (Mongols who ravaged the south) and the Teutonic Knights (Germans who conquered the north). But despite these challenges, Poland persevered. The last king of the Piast dynasty was also the greatest: Kazimierz the Great, who famously "found a Poland made of wood and left one made of brick and stone," and helped bring Poland (and its then-capital, Kraków) to international prominence. The progressive Kazimierz also invited Europe's much-persecuted Jews to settle here, establishing Poland as a relative haven for the Jewish people, which it would remain until the Nazis arrived.

Kazimierz the Great died at the end of the 14th century without a male heir. His grand-niece, Princess Jadwiga, became "king" (the Poles weren't ready for a "queen") and married Lithuanian prince Władysław Jagiełło, uniting their countries against a common enemy, the Teutonic Knights. Their marriage marked the beginning of the Jagiellonian dynasty and set the stage for Poland's golden age.

During this time, Poland expanded its territory, the Polish nobility began to acquire more political influence, Italy's Renaissance (and its architectural styles) became popular, and the Toruń-born astronomer Nicholas Copernicus shook up the scientific world with his bold new heliocentric theory. Up on the Baltic coast, the port city of Danzig (today's Gdańsk) took advantage of its Hanseatic League trading partnership to become one of Europe's most prosperous cities.

Foreign Kings and Partitions

When the Jagiellonians died out in 1572, political power shifted to the nobility. Poland became a republic of nobles governed by its wealthiest 10 percent—the *szlachta*, who elected a series of foreign kings. In the 16th and 17th centuries, with its territory spanning from the Baltic Sea to the Black Sea, the Polish-Lithuanian Commonwealth was the largest state in Europe.

But over time, many of the elected kings made selfish or poor diplomatic decisions and squandered the country's resources. To make matters worse, the nobles' parliament (Sejm) introduced the concept of *liberum veto* (literally "I freely forbid"), whereby any measure could be vetoed by a single member. This policy, which effectively demanded unanimous approval for any law to be passed, paralyzed the Sejm's already-waning power.

Sensing the Commonwealth's weakness, in the mid-17th century forces from Sweden rampaged through Polish and Lithuanian lands in the devastating "Swedish Deluge." While Poland eventually reclaimed its territory, a third of its population was dead. The Commonwealth continued to import self-serving foreign kings, including Saxony's Augustus the Strong and his son, who drained Polish wealth to finance vanity projects in their hometown of Dresden.

By the late 18th century, the Commonwealth was floundering...and surrounded by three land-hungry empires (Russia, Prussia, and Austria). The Poles were unaware that these neighbors had entered into an agreement now dubbed the "Alliance of the Three Black Eagles" (all three of those countries, coincidentally, had that same symbol); they began to circle Poland's white eagle. Stanisław August Poniatowski, elected king with Russian support in 1764, would be Poland's last.

Over the course of less than 25 years, Russia, Prussia, and Austria divided Polish territory among themselves in a series of three Partitions. In 1772 and again in 1790, Poland was forced into ceding large chunks of land to its neighbors. Desperate to reform their government, Poles enacted Europe's first democratic constitution (and the world's second, after the US Constitution) on May 3, 1791—still celebrated as a national holiday. This visionary document protected the peasants, dispensed with both *liberum veto* and the election of the king, and set up something resembling a modern nation. But the constitution alarmed Poland's neighbors, who swept in soon after with the third and final Partition in 1795. "Poland" disappeared from Europe's maps, not to return until 1918.

Even though Poland was gone, the Poles wouldn't go quietly. As the Partitions were taking place, Polish soldier Tadeusz Kościuszko (also a hero of the American Revolution) returned home to lead an unsuccessful military resistance against the Russians in 1794.

Napoleon offered a brief glimmer of hope to the Poles in the early 19th century, when he marched eastward through Europe and set up the semi-independent "Duchy of Warsaw" in Polish lands. But that fleeting taste of freedom lasted only eight years, until Napoleon's defeat at Waterloo. The Congress of Vienna, which again redistributed Polish territory to Prussia, Russia, and Austria, is sometimes called (by Poles) the "Fourth Partition." In a classic case of "my enemy's enemy is my friend," the Poles still have great affection for Napoleon for how fiercely he fought against their mutual foes.

The Napoleonic connection also established France as a safe haven for refugee Poles. After another failed uprising against Russia in 1830, many of Poland's top artists and writers fled to Paris— including pianist Fryderyk Chopin and Romantic poet Adam Mickiewicz (whose statue adorns Kraków's main square and Warsaw's Royal Way). These Polish artists tried to preserve the nation's spirit with music and words; those who remained in Poland continued to fight with swords and fists. By the end of the 19th century, the image of the Pole as a tireless, idealistic insurgent emerged. During this time, some Romantics—with typically melodramatic flair—dubbed Poland "the Christ of nations" for the way it was misunderstood and persecuted by the world, despite its nobility.

Poles didn't just flock to France during the Partitions. Untold numbers of Polish people uprooted their lives to pursue a better future in the New World. About 10 million Americans have Polish ancestry, and most of them came stateside from the mid-19th to early 20th century. Because the sophisticated and educated tended to remain in Poland, these new arrivals were mostly poor farmers who were (at first) unschooled and didn't speak English, placing them on a bottom rung of American society. It was during this time that the tradition of insulting "Polack jokes" emerged. Some claim these originated in Chicago, which was both a national trendsetter in humor and a magnet for Polish immigrants. Others suggest that German immigrants to America imported cruel stereotypes of their Polish neighbors from the Old World. Either way, the jokes became more vicious through the 20th century, until the Polish government actually lobbied the US State Department to put a stop to them.

As the map of Europe was redrawn following World War I, Poland emerged as a reborn nation, under the war hero-turned-head of state, Marshal Józef Piłsudski. The newly reformed "Second Polish Republic," which patched together the bits and pieces of territory that had been under foreign rule for decades, enjoyed a diverse ethnic mix—including Germans, Russians, Ukrainians, Lithuanians, and an enormous Jewish minority. A third of Poland spoke no Polish.

This interwar period was particularly good to Poland's Jews. They were, for the first time, legally protected citizens of Poland, with full voting rights. Cities like Warsaw, Kraków, and Wilno (today's Vilnius, Lithuania)—where Jews made up a quarter to a third of the population—saw the blossoming of a rich Jewish culture.

Meanwhile, the historic Baltic port city of Gdańsk—which was bicultural (German and Polish)—was granted the special "Free City of Danzig" status to avoid dealing with the prickly issue of whether to assign it to Germany or Poland. But the peace was not to last.

World War II

On September 1, 1939, Adolf Hitler began World War II by attacking Danzig to bring it into the German fold. Before the month was out, Hitler's forces had overrun Poland, and the Soviets had taken over a swath of eastern Poland (today part of Ukraine, Belarus, and Lithuania).

In their *Drang nach Osten* ("March to the East"), the Nazis considered the Poles *slawische Untermenschen*, "Slavic sub-humans" who were useful only for manual labor. Poland was also home to a huge population of Jewish people. Nazi Germany annexed Polish regions that it claimed historic ties to, while the rest (including "Warschau" and "Krakau") became a puppet state ruled by the *Generalgouvernement* and Hitler's handpicked governor, Hans Frank. The Nazis considered this area *Lebensraum*—"living space" that wasn't nice enough to actually incorporate into Germany but served perfectly as extra territory for building things that Germans didn't want in their backyards...such as notorious death camps, including Auschwitz-Birkenau.

The Poles anxiously awaited the promised military aid of France and Britain; when help failed to arrive, they took matters into their own hands, forming a ragtag "Polish Home Army" and staging incredibly courageous but lopsided battles against their powerful German overlords (such as the Warsaw Uprising). Throughout the spring of 1945, as the Nazis retreated from their failed invasion of the Soviet Union, the Red Army gradually "liberated" the rubble of Poland from Nazi oppression—guaranteeing it another four decades of oppression under another regime.

During World War II, occupied Poland had the strictest laws in the Nazi realm: Along with Serbia, this was the only place where, if you were caught trying to help Jews escape, your entire family could be executed. And yet, many Poles risked their lives to help escapees. Of course, many other Poles looked the other way, and some willingly participated in Nazi atrocities. Poland (whose current government would rather forget some of this nuance) is still coming to grips with its role in the Holocaust.

But there's no denying that Poland was horrifically scarred by World War II. With six million deaths over six years—including both Polish Jews and ethnic Poles—Poland suffered the worst per-capita losses of any nation. By the war's end, one out of every five Polish citizens was dead—and 90 percent of those killed were civilians. While the human and infrastructure loss of World War II was incalculable, that war's cultural losses were also devastating—for example, some 60,000 paintings were lost.

At the war's end, the victorious Allies shifted Poland's borders significantly westward—folding historically German areas into Polish territory and appropriating previously Polish areas for the USSR. This prompted a massive movement of populations—which today we'd decry as "ethnic cleansing"—as Germans were forcibly removed from western Poland, and Poles from newly Soviet territory were transplanted to Poland proper. Entire cities were repopulated (such as the formerly German metropolis of Breslau, which was renamed Wrocław and filled with refugee Poles from Lwów, now Lviv, in Ukraine). After millions died in the war, millions more were displaced from their ancestral homes. When the dust settled, Poland was almost exclusively populated by Poles.

Saddle on a Cow: Poland Under Communism

Poland suffered horribly under the communists. A postwar intimidation regime was designed to frighten people "on board" and coincided with government seizure of private property, rationing, and food shortages. The country enjoyed a relatively open society under Premier Władysław Gomułka in the 1960s, but the impractical, centrally planned economy began to unravel in the 1970s. Stores were marked by long lines stretching around the block.

The little absurdities of communist life—which today seem almost comical—made every day a struggle. For years, every elderly woman in Poland had hair the same strange magenta color. There was only one color of dye available, so if you had dyed hair, the

The Heritage of Communism

While communism is an ugly memory for most Poles, those who were teenagers when it ended—with only gauzy memories of communist times and no experience grappling with its adult realities—have some nostalgia. A friend who was 13 in 1989 recalled those days this way:

"My childhood is filled with happy memories. Under communism, life was family-oriented. Careers didn't matter. There was no way to get rich, no reason to rush, so we had time. People always had time.

"But there were also shortages. We stood in line not knowing what would be for sale. We'd buy whatever shoes were available and then trade for the right size. At grocery stores, vinegar and mustard were always on the shelf, along with plastic cheese to make it seem less empty. We had to carry ration coupons, which we'd present when buying a staple that was in short supply. We didn't necessarily buy what we needed—just anything that could be bartered  on the black market. I remember my mother and father had to 'organize' for special events...somehow find a good sausage and some Coca-Cola.

"Instead of a tidy roll of toilet paper, bathrooms came with a wad of old newspapers. Sometimes my uncle would bring us several toilet paper rolls, held together with a string— the best gift anyone could give.

"Boys in my neighborhood collected pop cans. Cans from other countries represented a world of opportunities beyond our borders. Parents could buy these cans on the black market, and the few families who were allowed to travel returned home with a treasure trove of cans. One boy up the street from me went to Italy and proudly brought home a Pepsi can. Everyone wanted to see this huge status symbol. But a month later, communism ended, you could buy whatever you wanted, and everyone's can collections were worthless.

"We had real chocolate only for Christmas. The rest of the year, we got something called 'chocolate-like product,' which was sweet, dark, and smelled vaguely of chocolate. And we had oranges from Cuba for Christmas, too. Everybody was excited when the newspapers announced, 'The boat with the oranges from Cuba is just five days away.' The smell of Christmas was so special: chocolate and oranges. Now we have that smell every day. Still, my happiest Christmases were under communism."

choice was simple: Let your hair grow out (and look clownishly half red and half white), or line up and go red.

During these difficult times, the Poles often rose up—staging major protests in 1956, 1968, 1970, and 1976. Stalin famously noted that introducing communism to the Poles was like putting a saddle on a cow.

When an anticommunist Polish cardinal named Karol Wojtyła (later known as St. John Paul II) was elected pope in 1978, then visited his homeland in 1979, it was a sign to his compatriots that change was in the air. In 1980, Lech Wałęsa, an electrician at the shipyards in Gdańsk, became the leader of the Solidarity movement, the first workers' union in communist Eastern Europe. After an initial 18-day strike at the Gdańsk shipyards, the communist regime gave in, legalizing Solidarity.

But the union grew too powerful, and the communists felt their control slipping away. On Sunday, December 13, 1981, Po-

land's head of state, General Wojciech Jaruzelski, appeared on national television to declare martial law in order to "forestall Soviet intervention." (Whether the Soviets actually would have invaded remains a hotly debated issue.) Tanks ominously rolled through the streets of Poland on that snowy December morning, and the Poles were terrified.

Martial law lasted until 1983. Each Pole has chilling memories of this frightening time. During riots, the people would flock into churches—the only place they could be safe from the ZOMO (riot police). People would go for their evening walks during the 19:30 government-sanctioned national news as a sign of protest. But Solidarity struggled on, going underground and becoming a united movement of all demographics, 10 million members strong (more than a quarter of the population).

In July 1989, the ruling Communist Party agreed to hold open elections (reserving 65 percent of representatives for themselves). Their goal was to appease Solidarity, but the plan backfired: Communists didn't win a single contested seat. These elections helped spark the chain reaction across Eastern Europe that eventually tore down the Iron Curtain. Lech Wałęsa became Poland's first postcommunist president.

Poland in the 21st Century

When 10 new countries joined the European Union in May 2004,

Poland was the most ambivalent of the bunch. After centuries of being under other empires' authority, the Poles were hardly eager to relinquish some of their hard-fought autonomy to Brussels. Many Poles thought that EU membership would make things worse (higher prices, a loss of traditional lifestyles) before they got better. But most people agreed that their country had to join to thrive in today's Europe.

The most obvious initial impact of EU membership was the droves of job-seeking young Poles who migrated to other EU countries (mostly the UK, Ireland, and Sweden, which were the first to waive visa requirements for Eastern European workers). Many found employment at hotels and restaurants. In the mid-aughts, visitors to London and Dublin noticed a surprising language barrier at hotel front desks, and Polish-language expat newspapers joined British gossip rags on newsstands. Those who remained in Poland were concerned about the "brain drain" of bright young people flocking out of their country. But with the 2008 economic crisis, quite a few Polish expats returned home. Britain's departure from the EU (2020's Brexit) slammed the door shut on that already-waning British-Polish connection—though a large number of Polish expats remain in the UK.

Poland is by far the most populous of the Central European EU members, with over 41 million people (about the same as Spain, or about half the size of Germany). This makes Poland the sixth largest of the 26 EU member states—giving it serious political clout, which it has already asserted...sometimes to the dismay of the EU's more established powers.

On the American political spectrum, Poland may be the most conservative country in Europe. This is partly due to the outsize influence of Catholicism on political discourse, and partly because Poles are phobic when it comes to "big government"—after being subjugated and manipulated by so many foreign oppressors over the centuries.

Since the early 2000s, the country's right wing has been represented by a pair of twin brothers, Lech and Jarosław Kaczyński. (The Kaczyński brothers were child actors who appeared in several popular movies together.) Their conservative Law and Justice Party (PiS for short) is pro-tax cuts, fiercely Euroskeptic (anti-EU), and very Catholic. In the 2005 presidential election, Lech Kaczyński emerged as the victor, then took the controversial step of appointing his identical twin brother Jarosław as Poland's prime minister.

The political pendulum swung back toward the left in October 2007, when the Kaczyński brothers' main political rival, the pro-EU Donald Tusk, led his Civic Platform Party to victory in the parliamentary elections. The name Kaczyński loosely means "duck"—so the Poles quipped that they were led by "Donald and the Ducks."

Tragically, the levity wasn't to last. On April 10, 2010, a plane carrying President Lech Kaczyński and a large contingent of Poland's leaders crashed in a thick fog near the city of Smoleńsk, Russia. All 96 people on board—including top government, military, and business officials, high-ranking clergy, and others—were killed, plunging the nation into a period of stunned mourning. Poles wondered why, yet again, an unprecedented tragedy had befallen their nation. (Ironically, the group's trip was intended to put a painful chapter of Poland's history to rest: a commemoration of the Polish officers and enlisted men killed in the Soviet massacre at Katyń.)

Over the last decade, the political pendulum has just kept on swinging, as key governmental posts have gone back and forth between the two dominant parties—the Civic Platform (which controlled parliament 2007-2015) and Law and Justice (2015-present).

Since taking power, Law and Justice—chaired by Jarosław Kaczyński—has come under fire for policies that many observers consider borderline-authoritarian (in the vein of Viktor Orbán's Fidesz in Hungary, or Donald Trump in the US). They've packed the ostensibly autonomous Constitutional Tribunal with party loyalists; purged opposition Supreme Court judges, civil servants, and military leaders; levied fines against critical news coverage in a manner that threatens freedom of the press; and removed the director of the Museum of the Second World War in Gdańsk—deeming the exhibit "not Polish enough" and installing a new director who altered many of the exhibits. Because of these and other concerns, in late 2017, the EU initiated Article 7 of the EU Treaty for the first time—stripping Poland of some of its voting rights within the EU.

And yet, at the same time, Donald Tusk—Poland's former prime minister and most high-profile left-leaning politician—has become a major player in the EU government, serving two terms as the president of the European Council (2014-2019). It remains to be seen where the Polish political pendulum swings next. But one thing is clear: The Poles are making their presence felt in European politics.

Invasion of Ukraine

When Vladimir Putin's Russia invaded Ukraine in February 2022, millions of Ukrainians fled to neighboring countries—and more than eight million of them crossed the border into Poland. Even a year and a half later, an estimated 1.5 million Ukrainians were still in Poland.

However, this was not a chaotic "refugee crisis," with sprawl-

Bar Mleczny (Milk Bar)

When you see a "bar" in Poland, it doesn't mean alcohol—it means cheap grub. Eating at a *bar mleczny* (bar MLECH-neh) is an essential Polish sightseeing experience. These cafete-
rias, which you'll see all over
the country, are a remarkably
affordable way to get a good
meal...and, with the right attitude, a fun cultural experience.

In the communist era, the
government subsidized milk
bars, allowing workers to enjoy
a meal out. The name comes
from the cheese cutlets that
were sold here, back in a time
when good meat was rare. The
tradition (and name) continues today, as milk-bar prices remain astoundingly low: a filling meal for under $10. And, while
communist-era fare could be gross, today's milk-bar cuisine is
typically great.

Milk bars usually offer many of the traditional tastes listed
in the "Polish food" section. Common items are soups (such as
żurek and *barszcz*), a variety of cabbage-based salads, *kotlet*
(fried pork chops), pierogi (similar to ravioli, with various fillings), and *naleśniki* (pancakes). You'll see glasses of juice, as
well as bottles of water and Coke.

There are two broad categories of milk bars: updated,
modern cafeterias that cater to tourists (English menus),
add some modern twists to their traditional fare, and charge
about 50 percent more; and time-machine dives that haven't
changed for decades. At truly traditional milk bars, the service
is aimed at locals, which means limited English and a confusing ordering system.

Every milk bar is a little different, but here's the general
procedure: Head to the counter, wait to be acknowledged,
and point to what you want. Handy vocabulary: *to* (sounds like
"toe") means "this"; *i* (pronounced "ee") means "and."

If the milk-bar server asks you any questions, you have
three options: Nod stupidly until they just give you something,
repeat one of the things they just said (assuming they've
asked you to choose between two options, like meat or cheese
in your pierogi), or hope that a kindly English-speaking Pole
in line will leap to your rescue. If nothing else, ordering at a
milk bar is an adventure in gestures. Smiling seems to slightly
extend the patience of milk-bar staffers.

Once your tray is all loaded up, pay the cashier, do a double-take when you realize how cheap your bill is, then find a
table. After the meal, bus your own dishes to the little window.

ing tent cities and desperately miserable people camped out in squalor at borders, as we saw with Syrian refugees in southeastern Europe in the fall of 2015. Rather, Poland absorbed these new arrivals smoothly, with locals opening up their homes to take in strangers in need. Across the political divide, Poles were united on the importance of helping their neighbors. People here justifiably feel great pride in how their country rose to the occasion when faced with an unprecedented humanitarian crisis.

The resolution of this latest chapter of Poland's story is not yet known. As the war in Ukraine drags on, more refugees are deciding to—at least for now—make new lives, putting down roots in Poland.

As time wears on, popular opinion is mixed. When I traveled around Poland in 2022 and 2023, most Poles I spoke with were proud of what they'd done for the Ukrainians. But some did raise concerns, including worry that this influx from a foreign (albeit similar) culture might lead to unwanted cultural shifts in the greater society. Others groused that generous policies designed to help the new arrivals (for example, free passage on public transportation) were not sustainable long-term. A few also noted that Ukraine has never formally apologized for WWII-era atrocities against the Poles (the so-called "Volhynian Slaughter," in which tens of thousands of Polish civilians were ethnically cleansed by Ukrainian partisans in Nazi-occupied territory).

Still others pointed out that Poland lost approximately as many people when the country joined the EU and bright young workers moved to other European lands to find better employment. When viewing things from a historical perspective, Poland is simply replenishing its population.

Poland's tourism industry also took a hit with the war, as many international visitors stayed away—perhaps not realizing that, as a member of NATO and the EU, Poland is in an entirely different geopolitical situation than Ukraine, at far lower risk of invasion. As Poles who work in tourism are still waiting to recoup their losses from the double-whammy of the Covid-19 pandemic and the Ukraine war, it's clear to any visitor that the country is a safe, fascinating, rewarding place to visit.

POLISH FOOD

Polish food is hearty and tasty—most classic dishes were created to provide calories for working fields and farms. Because Poland is north of the Carpathian Mountains, its weather tends to be chilly, limiting the kinds of fruits and vegetables that flourish here. As in other northern European countries (such as Ukraine, Russia, or Scandinavia), dominant staples include potatoes, dill, berries, beets, and rye. Much of what you might think of as "Jewish cuisine" turns up on Polish menus (gefilte fish, potato pancakes, chicken soup, and so forth)—which makes sense, given that Poles and Jews lived in the same area for centuries.

For such a big country, you'll find that menus are quite similar nationwide. Any regional variations were papered over during the communist period, when "Polish cuisine" was legally standardized. (Restaurants—which were rare—were obligated to meticulously follow recipes from one official, government-issued cookbook.) Over the last generation, some of this regional variation is beginning to return—especially in Gdańsk on the Baltic coast, with access to more seafood and influence from Scandinavian chefs—but you'll still find a lot of consistency from place to place.

Polish soups are a highlight; they claim to have more than 200 types. The most typical are *żurek* and *barszcz*. *Żurek* (often translated as "sour soup" on menus) is a thickened, light-colored soup made from a sourdough or rye base, usually containing a hard-boiled egg and pieces of *kiełbasa* (sausage).

Barszcz, better known to Americans as borscht, is a savory beet soup that you'll see in several varieties: *Barszcz czerwony* (red borscht) is a thin, flavorful broth with a deep red color, sometimes containing dumplings *(uszkami)* or a hard-boiled egg. *Barszcz ukraiński* (Ukrainian borscht) is thicker, with cream and vegetables (usually cabbage, beans, and carrots). Confusingly, there's another type of "borscht" that has no beets at all: *barszcz biały* ("white borscht"), which is very similar to the sour soup *żurek*.

In summer, try the "Polish gazpacho"—*chłodnik*, a savory cream soup with beets, onions, and radishes that's served cold. I had never met a Polish soup I didn't like...until I was introduced to *flaki* (sometimes *flaczki*)—tripe soup.

Another Polish dish that may be familiar is pierogi. These ravioli-like dumplings come with various fillings. The most traditional are minced meat, sauerkraut, mushroom, cheese, and blueberry; many restaurants also experiment with more exotic fillings. Pierogi are often served with specks of fatty bacon to add flavor. Pierogi are a budget traveler's dream: Restaurants serving them are everywhere, and they're generally cheap, tasty, and very filling.

Bigos is a rich and delicious sauerkraut stew cooked with meat, mushrooms, and whatever's in the pantry. It's sort of the Polish version of chili—it's a beloved comfort food, especially in the cold of winter, and everyone has their own recipe. *Gołąbki* is a dish of cabbage leaves stuffed with minced meat and rice in a tomato or mush-room sauce. *Kotlet schabowy* (fried pork chop) is another favorite.

Kaczka (duck) is popular, as is freshwater fish: Look for *pstrąg* (trout) and *węgorz* (eel). Carp *(karp)* is also common, especially at Christmas. Traditionally, people would bring home a live carp be-fore the holiday, then keep it in the bathtub until it was time to eat. One Polish friend explained that she came to think of the carp as a family pet; at Christmas, her parents told her it had swum away, down the drain...at exactly the same time they were sitting down for a fish dinner. (She became a vegetarian for 20 years, and still won't touch carp. She terms this affliction "carp-al trauma syn-drome.") On the Baltic Coast (such as in Gdańsk), you'll also see *łosoś* (salmon), *śledź* (herring), and *dorsz* (cod).

Poles eat lots of potatoes, which are served with nearly every meal. Look for *placki ziemniaczane*—potato pancakes.

Some dreary old foods are newly hip in today's Poland. Her-ring-and-vodka bars are trendy. The Polish street food *zapiekan-ka*—a toasted baguette with melted cheese, rubbery mushrooms from a can, and a drizzle of ersatz ketchup—began life as a "hard-ship food" under communism, as a pale imitation of pizza. These days it has been reborn as a street-food staple; *zapiekanka* vendors top them with a world of creative flavors. The bagel-like bread rings you'll see sold on the street, *obwarzanki* (singular *obwarzanek*), are also cheap, and usually fresh and tasty. And, as throughout Europe, gourmet hamburgers are in—including a trend for vegan burgers.

Poland has good pastries—look for a *cukiernia* (pastry shop). The classic Polish treat is *pączki*, glazed jelly doughnuts. They can have different fillings, but most typical is a wild-rose jam.

Szarlotka is apple cake—sometimes made with chunks of ap-ples (especially in season), sometimes with apple filling. *Sernik* is cheesecake, *makowiec* is a poppy-seed roll, and *winebreda* is like a Danish. *Napoleonka* is a French-style treat with layers of crispy wa-fers and custard. A *mazurek* could be vaguely compared to a "des-sert pizza"—a dense, sweet flatbread smothered with even sweeter spreads (often chocolate or caramel) and other toppings. The yeast or sponge cake called *babka* literally means "grandma"—it's named for the Bundt-pan shape, which resembles a traditional woman's skirt. A *babeczka* ("little grandma") is a smaller version, like a cup-cake.

Lody (ice cream) is popular. The tall, skinny cones of soft-serve ice cream are called *świderki*, sometimes translated as "American ice cream." The most beloved traditional candy is *ptasie mleczko* (birds' milk), which is semisour marshmallow covered with choco-late. E. Wedel is the country's top brand of chocolate, with outlets in all the big cities.

Thirsty? *Woda* is water, *woda mineralna* is bottled water

Poland's "Other" Cuisines: Georgian and Ukrainian

With the influx of war refugees from Ukraine—many of whom have decided to put down roots in their adopted homeland— Poland's culinary scene is also evolving. In addition to traditional Polish fare, travelers can look for restaurants serving two other cuisines: Georgian and Ukrainian.

Keep an eye out for **Georgian** restaurants and bakeries (look for *gruzińska*). Throughout the former USSR—including in Ukraine—food from Georgia, the former Soviet satellite in the Caucasus, is a beloved, flavorful change of pace from the dominant local fare. (Compare it to Mexican cuisine in the US, or Indian food in Britain.) Even before the arrival of Ukrainian refugees, Georgian food was catching on in Poland—and now that trend is accelerating.

Georgian food is utterly delicious, with a more vibrant and varied flavor profile than most Polish cooking. Herbs, spices, walnuts, and plums are major ingredients. Popular items include *khachapuri* (hot bread filled with cheese and other fillings, somewhat like a calzone, sometimes topped with a fried egg), *chinkhali* or *khinkali* (a hearty filled dumpling gathered into a thick, doughy "handle" and dipped into sauces), *kharcho* (a spicy broth with lots of meat and onions), *satsivi* (diced chicken in a spicy yellow sauce), and Georgian-style salad— typically tomato, cucumber, onion, and herbs, mixed up with a walnut paste. Because this cuisine is relatively new even for Poles, many Georgian restaurants have enticing and educational picture menus. If you have yet to try a Georgian meal... do it here.

Ukrainian cuisine has many similarities to Poland's own cooking, but with a regional spin: Staples include "Ukrainian-style" borscht, a red beet stew thick with vegetables and beans; the pierogi-like *varenyky;* and cabbage rolls (like a Polish *gołąbki*) called *holubtsi*. Other mainstays are the filled rolls called *pyrizhky;* the polenta-like cornmeal dish *banosh,* with meat and other flavorings mixed in; and *syrnyky,* deep-fried cheese-curd pancakes with berry sauce. Rye, which thrives in the Ukrainian climate, is a dominant flavor. Some Ukrainian restaurants also feature Georgian dishes, thanks to that cuisine's popularity there.

As you consider where to eat, consider going beyond Polish fare—and the ubiquitous Italian places—to try some of these unique cuisines that you may not find back home.

(*gazowana* is with gas, *niegazowana* is without), *kawa* is coffee, *herbata* is tea, *sok* is juice, and *mleko* is milk. Żywiec, Okocim, and Lech are the best-known brands of *piwo* (beer).

Wódka (vodka) is a Polish staple—the word means, roughly, "precious little water." Poles take vodka seriously and control its production assiduously. Its ingredients are domestically grown, and pure vodka contains some combination of just six ingredients: potatoes, rye, wheat, barley, oats, and the wheat-rye hybrid triticale. Quality vodkas have different flavor profiles depending on how the distiller has blended these ingredients; for example, potato gives an oily consistency, rye is sweeter and warming, and wheat is also sweet but lighter—ideal for summery mixed drinks.

Żubrówka, the most famous brand of vodka, comes with a blade of grass from the bison reserves in eastern Poland (look for the bison on the label). The bison "flavor" the grass...then the grass flavors the vodka. Poles often mix Żubrówka with apple juice, and call this cocktail *szarlotka* ("apple cake").

Traditionally, vodka is shot rather than sipped, and it's chased not by another drink but by salty, greasy food: pickles, lard, herring, potato pancakes, or steak tartare (but never just bread, which soaks up the spirit and keeps it in the stomach). For "Cheers!" say, *"Na zdrowie!"* (nah ZDROH-vyeh).

Other distillates are also popular, both traditional (Polish gins, whiskeys, and aqua vita, here called *okowita*) and more creative options—hipster-run artisanal distilleries are popping up all over. *Nalewka*, essentially a fruit-infused brandy (like a cordial), is typically made by macerating fruit with sugar, then pouring over vodka or firewater; it's often aged, and can be used for medicinal purposes. The sour cherry version, *wiśniówka*, is newly trendy—you'll see little pubs selling it all over Poland. Another "health" drink is the brandy called Krupnik: Poles swear that if you're getting a cold, mixing a slug of Krupnik with hot water and a squeeze of lemon will fix you right up.

Unusual nonalcoholic drinks to try if you have the chance are *kwas* (a cold, fizzy, Ukrainian-style beverage made from day-old rye bread) and *kompot* (a hot drink made from stewed berries). Poles are unusually fond of carrot juice (often cut with fruit juice); Kubuś is the most popular brand.

"Bon appétit" is *"Smacznego"* (smatch-NEH-goh). To pay, ask for the *rachunek* (rah-KHOO-nehk).

POLISH LANGUAGE

Polish is closely related to its neighboring Slavic languages (Slovak and Czech), with the biggest difference being that Polish has lots of fricatives (hissing sounds—"sh" and "ch"—often in close proximity).

POLAND

Polish intimidates Americans with long, difficult-to-pronounce words. But if you take your time and sound things out, you'll develop an ear for it. One rule of thumb that helps: The stress is generally on the next-to-last syllable.

Polish has some letters that don't appear in English, and some letters and combinations are pronounced differently than in English:

ć, ci, and **cz** all sound like "ch" as in "church"
ś, si, and **sz** all sound like "sh" as in "short"
ż, ź, zi, and **rz** all sound like "zh" as in "leisure"
dż and **dź** both sound like the "dj" sound in "jeans"
ń and **ni** sound like "ny" as in "canyon"
ę and **ą** are pronounced nasally, as in French: "e*n*" and "a*n*"
c sounds like "ts" as in "cats"
ch sounds like "kh" as in the Scottish "loch"
j sounds like "y" as in "yellow"
w sounds like "v" as in "Victor"
ł sounds like "w" as in "with"

So to Poles, "Lech Wałęsa" isn't pronounced "lehk wah-LEH-sah," as Americans tend to say—but "lehkh vah-WEHN-sah."

The Polish people you meet will be impressed and flattered if you take the time to learn a little of their language. To get started, check out the selection of Polish survival phrases on the following pages.

As you're tracking down addresses, these words will help: **miasto** (mee-AH-stoh, town), **plac** (plahts, square), **rynek** (REE-ne-hk, big market square), **ulica** (OO-leet-sah, road), **aleja** (ah-LAY-yah, avenue), and **most** (mohst, bridge). And that long word you see everywhere—**zapraszamy**—means "welcome."

Polish Survival Phrases

Keep in mind a few Polish pronunciation tips: w sounds like "v," ł sounds like "w," ch is a back-of-your-throat "kh" sound (as in the Scottish "loch"), and rz sounds like the "zh" sound in "pleasure." The vowels with a tail (ą and ę) have a slight nasal "n" sound at the end, similar to French.

Hello. (formal) / Goodbye.	Dzień dobry. / Do widzenia. jehn **doh**-brih / doh veed-**zay**-nyah
Hi. / Bye. (informal)	Cześć. cheshch
Do you speak English? (asked of a man)	Czy Pan mówi po angielsku? chih pahn **moo**-vee poh ahn-**gyehl**-skoo
Do you speak English? (asked of a woman)	Czy Pani mówi po angielsku? chih **pah**-nee **moo**-vee poh ahn-**gyehl**-skoo
Yes. / No.	Tak. / Nie. tahk / nyeh
I (don't) understand.	(Nie) rozumiem. (nyeh) roh-**zoo**-myehm
Please. / You're welcome. / Can I help you?	Proszę. **proh**-sheh
Thank you (very much).	Dziękuję (bardzo). jehn-**koo**-yeh (**bard**-zoh)
Excuse me. / I'm sorry.	Przepraszam. psheh-**prah**-shahm
No problem.	Żaden problem. **zhah**-dehn **proh**-blehm
Good.	Dobrze. **dohb**-zheh
one / two / three	jeden / dwa / trzy **yeh**-dehn / dvah / tzhih
hundred / thousand	sto / tysiąc stoh / **tih**-shants
How much?	Ile? **ee**-leh
local currency	złoty (zł) **zwoh**-tih
Is it free?	Czy to jest za darmo? chih toh yehst zah **dar**-moh
Is it included?	Czy jest to wliczone? chih yehst toh vlee-**choh**-neh
Where can I find / buy...?	Gdzie mogę dostać / kupić...? guh-**dyeh moh**-geh **doh**-statch / **koo**-peech
I'd like... (said by a man)	Chciałbym... **khchaw**-beem
I'd like... (said by a woman)	Chciałabym... **khchah**-wah-beem
...a room.	...pokój. **poh**-kooey
...a ticket to _____.	...bilet do _____. **bee**-leht doh _____
Where is...?	Gdzie jest...? guh-**dyeh** yehst
...the train station	...dworzec kolejowy **dvoh**-zhehts koh-leh-**yoh**-vih
...the bus station	...dworzec autobusowy **dvoh**-zhehts ow-toh-boos-**oh**-vih
...the tourist information office	...informacja turystyczna een-for-**maht**-syah too-ris-**titch**-nah
...the toilet	...toaleta toh-ah-**leh**-tah
men / women	męska / damska **mehn**-skah / **dahm**-skah
left / right / straight	lewo / prawo / prosto **leh**-voh / **prah**-voh / **proh**-stoh
At what time...?	O której godzinie...? oh kuh-**too**-ray gohd-**zhee**-nyeh
...does this open / close	...będzie otwarte / zamknięte **bend**-zheh oht-**vahr**-teh / zahm-**knyehn**-teh
today / tomorrow	dzisiaj / jutro jee-**shī** / **yoo**-troh

In a Polish Restaurant

I'd like to reserve... (said by a man)	Chciałbym zarezerwować... khchaw-beem zah-reh-zehr-voh-vahch
I'd like to reserve... (said by a woman)	Chciałabym zarezerwować... khchah-wah-beem zah-reh-zehr-voh-vahch
We'd like...	Chcielibyśmy... khchehl-ee-bish-mih
...a table for one person / two people.	...stolik na jedną osobę / dwie osoby. stoh-leek nah yehd-now oh-soh-beh / dvyeh oh-soh-bih
The menu (in English), please.	Menu (po angielsku), proszę. meh-noo (poh ahn-gyehl-skoo) proh-sheh
service (not) included	usługa (nie) wliczona oos-woo-gah (nyeh) vlee-choh-nah
cover charge	wstęp vstenp
"to go"	na wynos nah vih-nohs
with / without	z / bez z / behz
and / or	i / lub ee / loob
milk bar (cheap cafeteria)	bar mleczny bar mletch-nih
fixed-price meal (of the day)	zestaw (dnia) zehs-tahv (dih-nyah)
specialty of the house	specjalność zakładu speht-syahl-nohshch zah-kwah-doo
daily special	danie dnia dah-nyeh dih-nyah
breakfast / lunch / dinner	śniadanie / obiad / kolacja shnyah-dahn-yeh / oh-bee-aht / koh-laht-syah
appetizers	przystawki pshih-stahv-kee
bread / cheese / sandwich	chleb / ser / kanapka khlehb / sehr / kah-nahp-kah
soup / salad	zupa / sałatka zoo-pah / sah-waht-kah
meat / poultry	mięso / drób myehn-soh / droob
fish / seafood	ryba / owoce morza rih-bah / oh-voht-seh moh-zhah
fruit / vegetables	owoce / warzywa oh-voht-seh / vah-zhih-vah
dessert	deser deh-sehr
(tap) water	woda (z kranu) voh-dah (skrah-noo)
mineral water	woda mineralna voh-dah mee-neh-rahl-nah
carbonated / not carbonated	gazowana / niegazowana gah-zoh-vah-nah / nyeh-gah-zoh-vah-nah
milk	mleko mleh-koh
(orange) juice	sok (pomarańczowy) sohk (poh-mah-rayn-choh-vih)
coffee / tea	kawa / herbata kah-vah / hehr-bah-tah
wine / beer / vodka	wino / piwo / wódka vee-noh / pee-voh / vood-kah
red / white	czerwone / białe chehr-voh-neh / bee-ah-weh
glass / bottle	szklanka / butelka shklahn-kah / boo-tehl-kah
Cheers!	Na zdrowie! nah zdroh-vyeh
More. / Another.	Więcej. / Inny. vyehnt-say / een-neh
The same.	Taki sam. tah-kee sahm
the bill / I'll pay.	rachunek / Ja płacę. rah-khoo-nehk / yah pwaht-seh
tip	napiwek nah-pee-vehk
Delicious!	Pyszne! pish-neh

KRAKÓW

Kraków is easily Poland's best destination: a beautiful, user-friendly, old-fashioned city buzzing with history, enjoyable sights, tourists, and college students. Even though the country's capital moved from here to Warsaw more than 400 years ago, Kraków remains Poland's cultural and intellectual center. Increasingly (and justifiably) popular, Kraków is giving Prague a run for its money on the "must visit" tourist route.

What's so special about it? First off, Kraków is simply charming; more than any town in Europe, it seems made for aimless strolling. And its historic walls and former moat corral an unusually full range of activities and interests: bustling university life, thought-provoking museums, breathtaking churches that evoke a powerful faith (and include many sights relating to Poland's favorite son, St. John Paul II), sprawling parks that invite you to relax, vivid artifacts of Poland's Jewish heritage, and a burgeoning foodie and nightlife scene. Nearby, there are compelling side trips to the most notorious Holocaust site anywhere (Auschwitz-Birkenau), a communist planned workers town (Nowa Huta), and a mine filled with salty statues (Wieliczka). With so many opportunities to learn, to have fun, or to do both at once, it's no surprise that Kraków has become a world-class destination.

PLANNING YOUR TIME

Don't skimp on your time in Kraków. It takes a minimum of two days to experience the city, and a third (or even a fourth) day lets you dig in and consider a world of fascinating side trips.

Almost everyone coming to Kraków also visits the Auschwitz-Birkenau Concentration Camp Memorial—and should. As it's about an hour and a half away, this demands the better part of a day. Visiting Auschwitz requires a reservation, which you need to book long in advance (see the next chapter).

If you have only two full days (the "express plan"), start off with my self-guided walk through the Old Town and a quick stroll up to Wawel Castle, then head over to the Schindler's Factory Museum and wind down your day in Kazimierz. Your second day is for side-tripping to Auschwitz. This plan gives you a once-over-lightly look at Kraków but leaves almost no time for entering the sights.

More time buys you the chance to relax, enjoy, and linger: Tackle the Old Town and Wawel Castle on the first day, Kazimierz and museums of your choice on the second day, and Auschwitz (and other side trips) with additional days. If you have a special interest, you could side-trip to the St. John Paul II pilgrimage sites on the outskirts of town, or to the communist architecture of the Nowa Huta suburb. Wieliczka Salt Mine is another crowd-pleasing, half-day option.

Regardless of how long you stay, your evening choices are many and varied: Savor the Main Market Square over dinner or a drink, take in a jazz show, do a pub crawl through the city's many youthful bars and clubs (best in Kazimierz), or enjoy traditional Jewish music and cuisine (also in Kazimierz).

Orientation to Kraków

Kraków (Poles say KROCK-oof, but you can say KRACK-cow; it's sometimes spelled "Cracow" in English) is mercifully compact, flat, and easy to navigate. While it's Poland's second-biggest city (with 780,000 people), the tourist's Kraków feels small—from the main square, you can walk to just about everything of interest in less than 15 minutes. Just to the south is Poland's primary waterway, the Vistula River (Wisła, VEES-wah).

Most sights—and almost all recommended hotels and restaurants—are in the **Old Town** (Stare Miasto, STAH-reh mee-AH-stoh), which is surrounded by a greenbelt called the Planty (PLAHN-tee). In the center of the Old Town lies the Main Market Square (Rynek Główny, REE-nehk GWOHV-neh)—it's such an important landmark, I call it simply "the Square." At the Old Town's northeast corner, just outside the ring road, is the main train station. And at the southern end of the Old Town, on the riverbank, is the hill called **Wawel** (VAH-vehl)—with a historic castle, museums, and Poland's national church.

About a 20-minute walk (or quick tram/taxi ride) southeast of the Square is the neighborhood called **Kazimierz** (kah-ZHEE-mehzh)—with Jewish landmarks and Holocaust sites (including the Schindler's Factory Museum) and the city's best food and nightlife area.

A few more attractions are just beyond the core, including the St. John Paul II pilgrimage sites (in the Łagiewniki neighborhood), the communist-planned town of Nowa Huta, Wieliczka Salt Mine, and the Kościuszko Mound.

The southern mountains are not far away, and Kraków fills a shallow, bowl-shaped valley ringed by hills—which means the city has a tendency to trap fog and, sometimes, smog.

TOURIST INFORMATION

Kraków has many helpful TIs, called InfoKraków (https:// infokrakow.pl). Four branches are in or near the Old Town (most are open daily 9:00-17:00, but some have slight variations):

• In the **Planty** park, between the main train station and Main Market Square (open later in July-Sept—until 19:00, in a round kiosk at Ulica Szpitalna 25, +48 533 818 291)

• On **Ulica Św. Jana,** just north of the Main Market Square (specializes in concert tickets, daily year-round 9:00-17:00, at #2, +48 533 826 409)

• In the **Cloth Hall** right on the Main Market Square (at #1/3, +48 530 290 661)

• Just west of **Wawel Hill** (also covers the entire region, Powiśle 11, +48 533 826 031)

Other TI branches are in **Kazimierz** (Ulica Józefa 7, +48 533 834 969) and the **airport** (daily 9:00-19:00, +48 533 825 344). There's a "TI" marked inside the **Wyspiański Pavilion,** but it's really more of a gift shop (called "Kraków Story") that can answer a few questions. Note that the TIs sell tickets for only one tour company, Kraków Booking; for additional options, see "Tours in Kraków," later, and look around online.

Sightseeing Pass: The TI's **Kraków Tourist Card** includes admission to 40 city museums (basically everything except the Wawel Hill sights and Wieliczka Salt Mine)—but unless you're sightseeing like mad, it's unlikely you'd save money with the card. Given how walkable Kraków is, the version that does not include public transit is a better value than the one that does.

Warning: Many private travel agencies, room-booking services, and tour operators masquerade as TIs, with deceptive *i* signs. If I haven't listed them in this section, they're not a real TI.

Museum of Kraków (Muzeum Krakowa) Visitors Center: Facing the Main Market Square is an information office and ticket desk for the Museum of Kraków, where you can prebook tickets for the popular Schindler's Factory Museum and Rynek Underground Museum. If you've arrived in town to find online tickets already sold out, additional tickets often become available here for

Kraków's Old Town

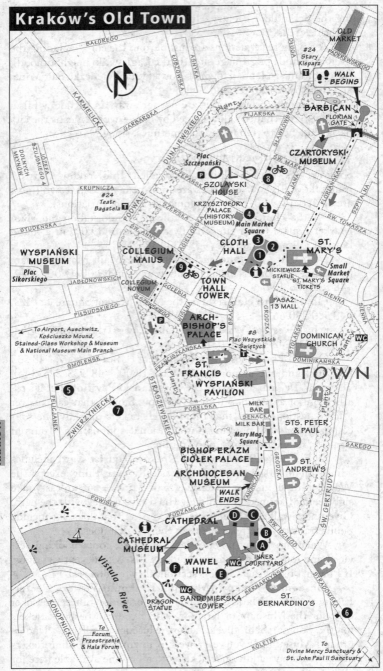

OLD MARKET

BAŁOREGO

KARMELICKA

GARBARSKA

DŁUGA
PADEREWSKIEGO

#24 Stary Kleparz
T
WALK BEGINS

Planty

BARBICAN

PIJARSKA

FLORIAN GATE

SŁAWKOWSKA

ŚW. MARKA

CZARTORYSKI MUSEUM

Plac Szczepański
P
OLD

SZOLAYSKI HOUSE

KRUPNICZA
#24 Teatr Bagatela
T

STUDENSKA

ŚW. JANA

KRZYSZTOFORY PALACE (HISTORY MUSEUM)
4
Main Market Square

ŚW. TOMASZA

WYSPIAŃSKI MUSEUM

Plac Sikorskiego

COLLEGIUM MAIUS

ŚW. ANNY

JAGIELLOŃSKA

CLOTH HALL
3
2
1
ST. MARY'S

Small Market Square

MICKIEWICZ STATUE
ST. MARY'S TICKETS

9

JABŁONOWSKICH

COLLEGIUM NOVUM

TOWN HALL TOWER

BRACKA
GRODZKA

SIENNA

PASAŻ 13 MALL

PIŁSUDSKIEGO

GOLĘBIA

OLSZEWSKIEGO

P

ARCH-BISHOP'S PALACE

WIŚLNA

#8 Plac Wszystkich Świętych
T

DOMINICAN CHURCH
WC

To Airport, Auschwitz,
Kościuszko Mound,
Stained-Glass Workshop & Museum
& National Museum Main Branch

SMOLEŃSK

FRANCISZKAŃSKA

ST. FRANCIS

TOWN

STRASZEWSKIEGO

WYSPIAŃSKI PAVILION

DOMINIKAŃSKA
STOLARSKA

5

7

Planty

POSELSKA

MILK BAR

SENACKA

MILK BAR

STS. PETER & PAUL

SAREGO

ZWIERZYNIECKA

FELICJANEK

Mary Mag. Square

BISHOP ERAZM CIOŁEK PALACE

ARCHDIOCESAN MUSEUM

WALK ENDS

GRODZKA

ST. ANDREW'S

ŚW. IDZIEGO

KANONICZA

POWIŚLE

PODZAMCZE

D
C

B

A

CATHEDRAL

ŚW. IDZIEGO

BERNARDYŃSKA

STRADOMSKA

ŚW. GERTRUDY

CATHEDRAL MUSEUM

WAWEL HILL

F
E
WC

INNER COURTYARD

ST. BERNARDINO'S

Vistula River

DRAGON STATUE

WC
SANDOMIERSKA TOWER

6

KONOPNICKIEJ

To Forum,
Przestrzenie
& Hala Forum

KOLETEK

To Divine Mercy Sanctuary &
St. John Paul II Sanctuary

KRAKÓW

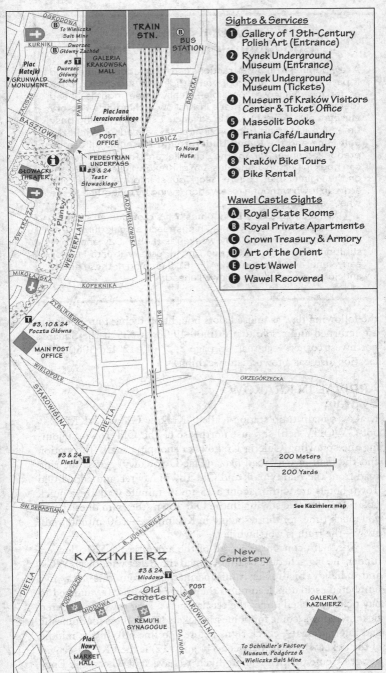

Sights & Services

1. Gallery of 19th-Century Polish Art (Entrance)
2. Rynek Underground Museum (Entrance)
3. Rynek Underground Museum (Tickets)
4. Museum of Kraków Visitors Center & Ticket Office
5. Massolit Books
6. Frania Café/Laundry
7. Betty Clean Laundry
8. Kraków Bike Tours
9. Bike Rental

Wawel Castle Sights

A. Royal State Rooms
B. Royal Private Apartments
C. Crown Treasury & Armory
D. Art of the Orient
E. Lost Wawel
F. Wawel Recovered

OGRODOWA
To Wieliczka Salt Mine
Dworzec Główny Zachód
KURNIKI
TRAIN STN.
BUS STATION
Plac Matejki
GRUNWALD MONUMENT
#3 Dworzec Główny Zachód
GALERIA KRAKOWSKA MALL
ZACISZE
BASZTOWA
PAWIA
Plac Jana Jeziorańskiego
BOSACKA
POST OFFICE
LUBICZ
To Nowa Huta
PEDESTRIAN UNDERPASS
SŁOWACKI THEATER
#3 & 24 Teatr Słowackiego
Planty
ŚW. KRZYŻA
WESTERPLATTE
RADZIWIŁŁOWSKA
MIKOŁAJSKA
KOPERNIKA
ŻYBLIKIEWICZA
BLICH
#3, 10 & 24 Poczta Główna
MAIN POST OFFICE
WIELOPOLE
GRZEGÓRZECKA
STAROWIŚLNA
DIETLA
200 Meters
200 Yards
#3 & 24 Dietla
KRAKÓW
ŚW. SEBASTIANA
See Kazimierz map
ŚW. SEBASTIANA
B. JOSELEWICZA
KAZIMIERZ
New Cemetery
DIETLA
PODBRZEZIE
#3 & 24 Miodowa
MIODOWA
POST
Old Cemetery
STAROWIŚLNA
GALERIA KAZIMIERZ
REMU'H SYNAGOGUE
Plac Nowy
DAJWÓR
MARKET HALL
To Schindler's Factory Museum, Podgórze & Wieliczka Salt Mine

Don't Miss Out!
Book Key Sights in Advance

A few popular Kraków attractions can fill up at busy times, and it pays to reserve ahead. If you're going to **Auschwitz,** book as far in advance as possible—ideally three months ahead (details in the next chapter). In Kraków, **Schindler's Factory Museum** also sells out well in advance. Especially during busy times, it's also smart to book several days ahead for **Wieliczka Salt Mine** and the **Rynek Underground Museum.** All can be prebooked online. Or, for the Schindler and Rynek sights, you can book in person at the Museum of Kraków ticket office right on the Main Market Square (see "Tourist Information"); if you arrive in town without a reservation, swing by that office to see what's available.

What constitutes **"busy times"?** It's crowded all summer long, and weekends anytime. Things reach a peak during Poland's long summer holiday weekends (Labor Day and Constitution Day, May 1-3; Corpus Christi, usually in late May or early June; and Assumption, Aug 15). If coming at these times, anticipate crowds and book well ahead.

the following day, as unused slots bought up by big tour operators are returned and resold (daily 10:00-19:00, at #35 at the Square's northwest corner—see map on page 242, +48 12 426 5060). This location also has a town history exhibit.

ARRIVAL IN KRAKÓW
By Train

Kraków's main train station (called "Kraków Główny," KROCK-oof GWOHV-neh) sits just northeast of the Old Town, adjoining the sprawling Galeria Krakowska shopping mall. The station and the mall face a broad plaza (Plac Dworcowy) across the ring road from the Planty park and Old Town. My recommended Old Town hotels are within about a 15-to-20-minute walk, or a quick taxi ride. (If you're staying in the Old Town, the tram doesn't save you much time; for those staying in Kazimierz—a 30-minute walk away—the tram is worthwhile.)

The main concourse has all of the amenities: ATMs, lockers (under the big schedule board between the ticket windows), WCs, and a handy Biedronka minisupermarket. From this area, five numbered escalators lead up to the train platforms. If you need to buy tickets, tucked under the escalators is a long row of numbered ticket windows (some for domestic tickets only, others for domestic and international—check signs before you line up). In the middle of the ticket windows (between #11 and #12) is the PKP Passenger Service Center, which is more likely to have staff who speak English. There are ticket machines around this area, or you can buy most tickets online (www.intercity.pl).

Getting Between the Station and Downtown: The easiest option is to take a **taxi;** they wait in the parking lot on the station's rooftop—go up the stairs or elevator from your platform (15-20 zł into town; for a fair rate, be sure to take a taxi marked with a company name and telephone number). Or order an **Uber,** which is often cheaper (see "Getting Around Kraków," later).

If you prefer to walk or take a tram, you'll be funneled through the Galeria Krakowska shopping mall. Begin by following *Exit to the City* signs. Once inside the mall, continue straight ahead. To **walk,** follow *Old Town* signs, which eventually route you to the left. You'll pop out at a big plaza where you'll continue straight, taking the broad ramp down into a pedestrian underpass beneath the ring road, emerging into the Planty. The Main Market Square is straight ahead (look for the twin spires of St. Mary's Church).

If you'd rather take a **tram,** continue straight ahead through the mall, following signs for *Exit Pawia street.* Emerging here, you'll see the Dworzec Główny Zachód tram stop; tram #3 in the direction of Nowy Bieżanów stops at the eastern edge of the Old Town (Poczta Główna stop) before continuing to Kazimierz (Miodowa stop).

There is a **shortcut** to avoid going through the sprawling and sometimes congested mall: The modern train station is attached to the old station (the yellow building facing the big plaza, now hosting art exhibitions) by a sidewalk under a green canopy. This can save you a little walking (and a lot of shopping temptations). It's tricky to find from inside the station: Go behind the Biedronka supermarket, near track 1, and exit toward Lubicz street. Walk up the ramp and follow the green canopy to the plaza.

To get **from town to the station** (or to the bus station behind it), head to the northeast corner of the Planty, take the underpass beneath the ring road, walk across the plaza and into the Galeria Krakowska mall, and once inside, follow signs to *Railway Station* and *Station Hall.*

By Bus

The bus station is directly behind the main train station. When arriving by bus, first head into the train station, then continue through it, following the directions given earlier for arrival by train.

To get *to* the bus station from the Old Town (for example, to catch a bus to Auschwitz), walk all the way through to the far end of the train station area (past platform 5, exit marked for *Bus Station*). The bus terminal (marked *Dworzec Autobusowy*) is upstairs. Inside are the standard amenities (lockers and WCs), domestic and international ticket windows, and an electronic board showing

Kraków: A Snapshot History

Kraków grew wealthy from trade in the late 10th and early 11th centuries. Traders who passed through were required to stop here and sell their wares at a reduced cost. Local merchants re-sold those goods with big price hikes...and Kraków thrived. In 1038, it became Poland's capital.

Tatars invaded in 1241, leaving the city in ruins. Krakovians re-built their streets in a near-perfect grid, unlike the narrow, maze-like lanes of most medieval towns. The destruction also paved the way for the spectacular Main Market Square—still Kraków's best feature.

King Kazimierz the Great sparked Kraków's golden age in the 14th century (see the sidebar, later). In 1364, he established the university that still defines the city (and counts Copernicus and St. John Paul II among its alumni).

But Kraków's power waned as Poland's political center shift-ed to Warsaw. In 1596, the capital officially moved north. And with the Partitions of the late 18th century, Poland disappeared from the map and Kraków became a provincial backwater of Vienna.

After Napoleon briefly reshuffled Europe in the early 19th century, Kraków was granted the status of a relatively indepen-dent city-state for about 30 years. The Free City of Kraków, a tiny sliver wedged between three of Europe's mightiest empires, enjoyed an economic boom that saw the creation of the Planty park, the arrival of gas lighting and trams, and the construction of upscale suburbs outside the Old Town. Only after the unsuccess-ful Kraków Uprising of 1846 was the city forcefully brought back into the Austrian fold. But despite Kraków's reduced prominence, Austria's comparatively liberal climate allowed the city to become a haven for intellectuals and progressives (including a young rev-

the next several departures. Some bus departures, marked on the board with a *G*, leave from the upper *(gorna)* stalls, which you can see out the window. Other bus departures, marked with a *D*, leave from the lower *(dolna)* stalls in the garage beneath your feet; to find these, use the stairs or the elevator right in the middle of the bus terminal. Because the bus station area can be challenging to navi-gate, leave yourself plenty of time before departure.

By Car

Centrum signs lead you into the Old Town—you'll know you're there when you hit the ring road that surrounds the Planty park. Parking garages surround the Old Town. Your hotelier can advise you on directions and parking.

By Plane

The modern **John Paul II Kraków-Balice Airport** is about 10 miles

olutionary thinker from Russia named Vladimir Lenin).

The Nazis overran Poland in September 1939, installing the *Generalgouvernement,* a ruling body headed by Hans Frank. Germany wanted to quickly develop "Krakau" into their Polish capital. They renamed the Main Market Square "Adolf-Hitler-Platz," tore down statues of Polish figures (including the Adam Mickiewicz statue that dominates the Main Market Square today), and invested heavily in construction and industrialization (opening the door for Oskar Schindler to take over a factory from its Jewish owners). The German "New Order" included seizing businesses, rationing, and a strict curfew for Poles and Jews alike. A set of "Jewish laws" targeted, then decimated, Poland's huge Jewish population.

Kraków's cityscape emerged from World War II virtually unscathed. But when the communists took over, they decided to give intellectual (and potentially dissident) Kraków an injection of Soviet values. They built Nowa Huta, an enormous steelworks and planned town for workers, on the outskirts, dooming Kraków to decades of smog.

St. John Paul II was born (as Karol Wojtyła) in nearby Wadowice and served as archbishop of Kraków before being called to Rome. Today, the hometown boy-turned-saint draws lots of pilgrims and is, for many, a big part of the city's attraction. Saintly ties aside, Kraków might be the most Catholic town in Europe's most Catholic country; be sure to visit a few of its many churches.

In recent years, the city's Kazimierz district has come back to life—both with Jewish-themed cultural sights and with lively bars, food trucks, and restaurants. This mingling of the historic with the contemporary typifies a city that always has been Poland's heartbeat.

west of the center (code: KRK, www.krakowairport.pl). The easiest way downtown is to hop on the slick and speedy **train** (follow *Kolej do Centrum* signs up the ramp, then across the sky bridge to the parking garage; 17 zł, 1-2/hour, 18 minutes to Kraków's main train station—see arrival instructions earlier, under "By Train"). There's also a **taxi** stand in front of the terminal; the official rate for the 30-minute ride into town should be about 110 zł. You can also order an Uber (typically cheaper than a taxi) or arrange a taxi transfer in advance (such as with recommended driver Andrew Durman, listed under "Tours in Kraków," later).

Many budget flights—including some on Wizz Air and Ryanair—use the **International Airport Katowice in Pyrzowice** (Międzynarodowy Port Lotniczy Katowice w Pyrzowicach, code: KTW, www.katowice-airport.com). This airport is about 18 miles from the city of Katowice, which is about 50 miles west of Kraków. Direct buses run sporadically between Katowice Airport and Kraków's main train station area (60 zł, trip takes 1.75 hours, generally scheduled to meet incoming flights, www.matuszek.com. pl). You can also take the bus from Katowice Airport to Katowice's train station (hourly, 50 minutes), then take the train to Kraków (hourly, 1.5 hours). Wizz Air's website (www.wizzair.com) is useful for figuring out your connection.

HELPFUL HINTS

Exchange Rate: 1 złoty (zł, or PLN) = about 25 cents; 4 zł = about $1.

Book Ahead: In Kraków, you're wise to book in advance your visits to the popular Schindler's Factory Museum, Wieliczka Salt Mine, and Rynek Underground Museum (see details in each listing)—and you definitely need to book well ahead for a visit to Auschwitz (see next chapter). That and perhaps a fancy dinner and any tour you hope to take is all you need to concern yourself with in advance.

Sightseeing Tips: Aside from the churches, most major sights are managed by one of three organizations: the **National Museum in Kraków,** mainly art collections (www.mnk.pl); **Museum of Kraków/Muzeum Krakowa,** mainly historical exhibits (including Schindler's Factory and Rynek Underground Museum, www.muzeumkrakowa.pl); and the many underwhelming sights at **Wawel Castle** (www.wawel.krakow.pl). All three organizations tend to tinker with hours, closed days, and free days. Before heading out, check the "Kraków at a Glance" sidebar, later, and confirm with the websites above.

Many sights are **closed** on Monday, but others remain open: Wieliczka Salt Mine, all the churches, Jagiellonian University Museum, Jewish-themed sights in Kazimierz, and a few of the sights at Wawel Castle (morning only). On Tuesday, the Wawel Castle sights close early, but the cathedral remains open. On Saturday, most of Kazimierz's Jewish-themed sights are closed. On Sunday, churches have limited hours for sightseers (for example, Wawel Cathedral opens at 12:30).

Also be aware of days that certain sights are **free:** On Tuesday, the National Museum branches (including the Czartoryski Museum, Wyspiański Museum, and Gallery of 19th-Century Polish Art in the Cloth Hall) are free, but some are open limited hours; the Rynek Underground Museum is also free (but open shorter hours and crowded). On Monday, the Schindler's Factory Museum is free, open only in the morning, and extremely crowded.

Bookstore: For an impressive selection of new and used English books, try **Massolit Books,** just west of the Old Town. They also have a café with drinks and light snacks, and a good children's section (daily 10:00-20:00, Ulica Felicjanek 4, +48 12 432 4150, www.massolit.com).

Laundry: The inviting **Frania Café,** a short walk from Wawel Castle (on the way to Kazimierz), is a café/pub with washers and dryers (pay more for full service), relaxing ambience, a full bar serving espresso drinks and laundry-themed hard drinks, an enticing menu, long hours, and a friendly staff (daily 7:30-22:00, Stradomska 19, +48 783 945 021, www.pralniasamoobslugowa.pl).

Betty Clean is a full-service laundry that's slightly closer to the Old Town, but expensive (priced per item not per load, takes 24 hours—or pay extra for express service, Mon-Fri 8:00-18:00, Sat 10:00-14:00, closed Sun, just outside the Planty park at Ulica Zwierzyniecka 6, +48 12 423 0848).

For locations, see the "Kraków's Old Town" map.

GETTING AROUND KRAKÓW

Kraków's top sights and best hotels are easily accessible by foot. You'll need wheels only if you're going to outlying areas (Kazimierz, Nowa Huta, John Paul II pilgrimage sites, and so on).

By Public Transit

Trams and buses zip around Kraków's urban sprawl. The same tickets work system-wide and are based on how long the ride takes: 4 zł/20 minutes *(20-minutowy)*, 6 zł/1 hour *(60-minutowy)*. You can also get tickets good for 24 hours (17 zł), 48 hours (35 zł), and 72 hours (50 zł). Buy tickets at kiosks, at the machines you'll see at bigger stops, or on board (look for a machine; if not, buy your ticket from the driver). Some machines take credit cards, others only cash. You can also buy tickets on the Jakdojade app, which works in other Polish cities as well. Always validate a single-ride ticket when you board the bus or tram. For a good route planner, see Jakdojade.pl.

Tram #3 is particularly handy. It goes from the side of the train station (Dworzec Główny Zachód) to the ring road in front of the station (Dworzec Główny), then stops at the eastern edge of the Old Town (Poczta Główna, at the main post office) before continuing to Kazimierz (Miodowa is at the north end, near Ulica Szeroka; Św. Wawrzyńca is at the south end, near the old tram depot) and Podgórze, near the Schindler's Factory Museum (Plac Bohaterow Getta). **Tram #24** is also useful: It stops at the western edge of the Old Town (Teatr Bagatela), then loops around the northern edge to stop near the Barbican (Stary Kleparz) before meeting up with tram #3 in front of the train station (Dworzec Główny) and continuing on to Kazimierz and Podgórze (same stops as listed above).

By Taxi or Uber

Only take cabs that are clearly marked with a company logo and telephone number. Legitimate Kraków taxis start at 9 zł and charge about 3 zł per kilometer—or more at night—while unofficial taxis charge whatever they like. Rides generally cost around 20-25 zł but can take longer than you'd expect: Due to the Old Town's many traffic restrictions and pedestrian zones, a "short ride across town" may require looping all the way around the ring road. You're more likely to get the fair metered rate by calling a cab, rather than taking one waiting at tourist spots. Well-established companies include **iCar** (+48 12 653 55 55), **Megataxi** (+48 12 19625), **Radio Taxi** (+48 12 19191), and **Barbakan** (+48 12 19661).

Uber is typically cheaper than Kraków's official taxis (though prices can spike during busy "surge" periods). Be aware that, while some taxi companies are allowed to pick up and drop off within Kraków's highly restricted Old Town, Ubers generally can't—so you may need to walk to the ring road. In my experience, Polish Uber drivers (and their cars) are a bit less polished and professional than those back home—but they're cheap, usually friendly, and handy.

By Bike

The riverfront bike path is enticing on a nice day; the Planty park, while inviting, can be a bit crowded for biking. **KRK Bike Rental** is very central and affordably rents a variety of bikes, from city touring bikes to electric models (daily 9:00-21:00, less in bad weather, closed Nov-March, Ulica Św. Anny 4, +48 509 267 733, www.krkbikerental.pl).

Tours in Kraków

Local Guides

I've enjoyed working with several wonderful Kraków guides. Prices are standard and affordable (500 zł/half-day, 900 zł/day), and some of them have cars for day-tripping into the countryside for an extra charge.

Tomasz Klimek (+48 605 231 923, tomasz.klimek@interia.pl) and his business partner **Monika Prylinska** (+48 693 648 528, monikaprylinska@gmail.com) are both top-notch guides; together they run Kraków Urban Tours (see later), but you can also hire them one-on-one (500 zł/half-day, 900 zł/day, slightly more with a car).

Two other great guides are **Anna Bakowska** (+48 604 151 293, leadertour@wp.pl) and **Marta Chmielowska** (+48 603 668 008, martachm7@gmail.com).

I wouldn't bother hiring a guide for the trip to Auschwitz—

only official Auschwitz guides can legally give tours on-site, so you'll wind up joining one of the tours once there; instead, it's a better value to hire a driver (like Andrew or Chester, listed next).

Drivers

Since Kraków is such a useful home base for day trips, it can be handy to splurge on a private driver for door-to-door service. **Andrew (Andrzej) Durman,** a Pole who lived in Chicago and speaks fluent English, is a gregarious driver, translator, miracle worker, and all-around great guy. While not a licensed tour guide, Andrew is an eager conversationalist and loves to provide lively commentary while you roll. Although you can hire Andrew for a simple airport transfer or an Auschwitz day trip, he also enjoys tackling more ambitious itineraries, from helping you explore your Polish ancestry to taking you on multiday journeys around Poland and beyond. These prices are transportation only for up to 4 people: 600 zł to Auschwitz, 350 zł to Wieliczka Salt Mine, 120 zł for transfer from Kraków-Balice Airport, or 800 zł for an all-day trip into the countryside—such as into the High Tatras or to track down your Polish roots near Kraków (more to cover gas costs for trips longer than 100 km one-way; long-distance transfers for up to 4 people to Prague, Budapest, Vienna, or Berlin for 2,500 zł—or 300 zł extra if he makes longer stops en route or picks you up there; all prices higher for bigger van, +48 602 243 306, andrew@tour-service.pl). If he's busy, Andrew may send you with one of his English-speaking colleagues, such as Karol or Stefan.

Local guide Marta Chmielowska's husband, **Czesław** (a.k.a. Chester), can also drive you to nearby locations (650 zł for all-day trip to Auschwitz, 400 zł to Wieliczka Salt Mine, or a very long day combining Wieliczka and Auschwitz for 1,000 zł; 2,400 zł for a transfer to Prague; to book, see Marta's contact information, earlier).

Kraków Urban Tours

This company, run by recommended guides Tomasz and Monika (who also guide tours for me in Europe), works hard to put travelers in touch with genuine cultural experiences that many tourists miss. In addition to a variety of local walking tours—including a "Greatest Hits" Old Town walk (€50) and a food tour (€90)—they've curated some special experiences that offer more cultural intimacy. For example, their pierogi-making class begins at the Kleparz farmers market, where you'll personally shop for the ingredients, then heads to a local home (rather than a classroom or restaurant) to make pierogi just like Babcia used to make (€70/person for a 4-plus-hour experience). They also have tours to Nowa Huta to learn about the communist period; all-day trips into the mountains around Zakopane; a "Made in Kraków" shopping tour

Kraków at a Glance

▲▲▲**Main Market Square** Stunning heart of Kraków and a people magnet any time of day; the centerpiece Cloth Hall features souvenirs and museum upstairs. See page 262.

▲▲**St. Mary's Church** Landmark church with extraordinary wood-carved Gothic altarpiece. **Hours:** Mon-Sat 11:30-17:45, Sun from 14:00. See page 259.

▲▲**St. Francis Basilica** Lovely Gothic church with some of Poland's best Art Nouveau. **Hours:** Mon-Sat 10:00-16:00, Sun 13:00-15:30; open longer hours for services and prayer. See page 268.

▲▲**Wawel Cathedral** Poland's national church, with tons of tombs, a crypt, and a climbable tower. **Hours:** Mon-Sat 9:00-17:00, Sun from 12:30; Nov-March daily until 16:00; cathedral museum closed Sun off-season; tower climb in summer only. See page 274.

▲▲**Wawel Castle Grounds** Historic hilltop with views, castle, cathedral, courtyard with chakras, and a passel of museums. **Hours:** Grounds open daily 6:00 until dusk, but some museums closed Mon. See page 279.

▲▲**Gallery of 19th-Century Polish Art** Worthwhile collection of paintings by should-be-famous artists, upstairs in the Cloth Hall. **Hours:** Tue-Sun 10:00-18:00, closed Mon. See page 284.

▲▲**Czartoryski Museum** Eclectic collection of historic bric-a-brac and art, including Leonardo's stunning *Lady with an Ermine*. **Hours:** Tue-Sun 10:00-18:00, closed Mon. See page 288.

▲▲**Stanisław Wyspiański Museum** Small but delightful collection of the great Młoda Polska (Art Nouveau) master. **Hours:** Tue and Fri-Sun 10:00-17:00, closed Mon and Wed-Thu. See page 292.

that helps you find locally made, meaningful items to take home; an innovative pinhole photography tour; and a handmade souvenir workshop with proceeds that support local homelessness-relief charities. You can either join a scheduled tour with other travelers or (for a higher cost) book a private experience. It's fun to peruse their offerings (+48 665 015 665, www.krakowurbantours.com, info@krakowurbantours.com).

Walking Tours

A variety of interchangeable companies run daily city walking tours in English in summer. Most do a three-hour tour of the Old

▲▲**Rynek Underground Museum** Exhibit on medieval Kraków filling excavated cellars beneath the Main Market Square. **Hours:** Mon & Wed-Thu 10:00-19:00 (closed second Mon of each month), Tue until 14:00, Fri-Sun until 20:00. See page 294.

▲▲**Wieliczka Salt Mine** Medieval salt mine on the outskirts of the city (and time-consuming to visit) featuring an underground world of salty caverns and hand-hewn salt sculptures. **Hours:** Tours at the top of each hour, daily 8:00-18:00, shorter hours off-season. See page 324.

▲▲**Schindler's Factory Museum** Building where Oskar Schindler saved over 1,000 Jewish workers, now an engaging exhibit about Kraków's WWII experience. **Hours:** Mon 10:00-14:00, Tue-Sun until 18:00 (closed first Tue of the month). See page 312.

▲▲**Old Jewish Cemetery** Poignant burial site in Kazimierz, with graves from 1552 to 1800. **Hours:** Sun-Fri 9:00-16:00, sometimes until 18:00 May-Sept, closes earlier in winter and by sundown on Fri, closed Sat. See page 301.

▲**New Jewish Cemetery** Graveyard with tombs from after 1800, partly restored after Nazi desecration. **Hours:** Sun-Fri 8:00-16:00, closed Sat. See page 309.

▲**Pharmacy Under the Eagle** Small but evocative, with interactive exhibits about the Holocaust in Kraków. **Hours:** Wed-Sun 10:00-17:00; closed Mon-Tue. See page 311.

▲**Stained-Glass Workshop and Museum** Stained-glass factory offering tours and hands-on classes. **Hours:** Tours Tue-Sat at 12:00 and 15:00, classes by appointment. See page 298.

KRAKÓW

Town as well as a three-hour tour of Kazimierz, the Jewish district (expect to pay about 70 zł per tour). Guide quality can be variable and the scene is continually evolving; it's best to pick up local fliers (the TI works exclusively with one company, Kraków Booking, but hotel reception desks generally have more options), then choose the one that fits your interests and schedule. For a more established outfit, consider Kraków Urban Tours, earlier. You'll also see ads for "free" tours—which are not really free (the guide gets paid only if you tip generously).

Food Tours

Kraków Urban Tours, described earlier, offers casual evening food walks that basically assemble a full meal with a little sightseeing thrown in (at 18:00, €90, 3 hours, www.krakowurbantours.com, info@krakowurbantours.com).

Another fine choice is **Eat Polska,** which smartly connects food to culture and history, making the experience equal parts informative and delicious (about €80 for a food tour or a vodka tasting with hearty food pairings, get details and book at www.eatpolska.com).

Crazy Guides

This irreverent company offers tours to the communist suburb of Nowa Huta and other outlying sights. For details, see page 328.

Bike Tours

Kraków Bike Tours is a well-established operation that runs daily four-hour bike tours in English, with 25 stops in the Old Town, Kazimierz, and Podgórze (€24, you can pay extra to use an electric bike, July-Sept daily at 10:00 and 15:00, spring and fall only 1/day at 10:00, confirm details and prebook online, office in the court-yard at Sławkowska 11, +48 510 394 657, www.krakowbiketour.com).

Bus Tours to Auschwitz or Wieliczka

As Kraków is so easily enjoyed on foot, taking a bus tour doesn't make much sense in town. But they can be handy for reaching out-lying sights. Various tour companies run itineraries to Auschwitz (6 hours), Wieliczka Salt Mine (4 hours), and other regional side trips (each itinerary around 140-170 zł).

Given the difficulty of reserving your own appointment at Auschwitz (explained in the next chapter), one of these bus tours—which include a guided tour of the camp—may be your most con-venient option. **See Kraków** (www.seekrakow.com) and **Discover Cracow** (www.discovercracow.com) typically use smaller 19-seat minibuses. They sometimes offer hotel pickup, which seems con-venient, but you'll waste a lot of time driving around the city to other hotels. **Kraków Booking** (which has a monopoly at the TI; www.krakowbooking.com) and **Cracow City Tours** (www.cracowcitytours.com) use larger 50-seat buses with a central pickup point near the Old Town.

At any company, the on-bus guiding is hit-or-miss but largely irrelevant since you'll be handed off to an official Auschwitz guide once at the camp. Note that the many tour offices and faux-TIs you'll see around town simply sell tickets for these companies. If you waited too long to reserve at Auschwitz and are desperate to get in at short notice, try dropping into various agencies around town to see if anyone has space.

Buggy Tours

You'll see (and hear) horse-drawn buggies that trot around Kraków from the Main Market Square. The going rate is a hefty 300 zł for a 30-minute tour to the castle and back (though prices can be soft when it's not too busy). After dark, they're lit up like fanciful Cinderella coaches—a memorable scene, all lined up in front of St. Mary's Church.

Golf-Cart Tours

Several outfits around town (including on the Square) offer tours on a golf cart with recorded commentary. Given the limits on car traffic in the old center, this can be a handy way to connect the sights for those with limited mobility. Generally, you'll pay about 250 zł for a 30-minute tour around the Old Town; to extend the trip to Kazimierz, it's 500 zł; and adding the Podgórze former Jewish ghetto and Schindler's Factory costs a total of 750 zł (these prices are for the entire golf cart, up to 5 people). Prices tend to be soft—try haggling.

Kraków's Royal Way Walk

This self-guided walk is designed to link up most of Kraków's major sights (see the map on page 242). Much of the walk follows a route called the "Royal Way" because the king used to follow this same path when he returned to Kraków after a journey. After the capital moved to Warsaw, most kings still used Wawel Cathedral for important events. In fact, from 1320 to 1795, nearly every Polish king traversed Kraków's Royal Way at least twice: on the day he was crowned and on the day he was buried. You could sprint through this walk in about an hour and a half (less than a mile altogether), but it's much more fun if you take it like the kings did...slowly.

• *Begin just outside the main gate (the Florian Gate) at the north end of the Old Town. Face the tall, rectangular tower marking the town entrance.*

▲City Walls and Barbican (Barbakan)

Tatars—those battle-hardened invaders from Central Asia—destroyed Kraków in 1241. To better defend their rebuilt city, Krakovians built this **wall.** The original rampart had 47 watchtowers and eight gates. (You'll find a bronze model of the wall just to the right of the tower.)

Now turn around. The big, round defensive fort standing outside the wall is the **Barbican,** built to provide extra fortification to weak sections—namely, the gates. Imagine how it looked in 1500, when the Barbican stood outside the town moat with a long bridge leading to the Florian Gate—the city's main entryway. Today, you can pay a small fee to scramble along the passages and fortifications of the Barbican, though there's little to see inside, other than a small but good exhibit giving you a sense of how

the walls were designed. The same ticket also lets you climb up onto the surviving stretch of Old Town walls flanking the Florian Gate (entry from inside walls).

• *The greenbelt within which the Barbican sits is called the...*

▲▲Planty

By the 19th century, Kraków's no-longer-necessary city wall had fallen into disrepair. As the Austrian authorities were doing all

over their empire, they decided to tear down what remained, fill in the moat, and plant trees. (The name comes not from the English "plant" but from the Polish *plantovac,* or "flat"—because they flattened out this area to create it.) Today, the Planty is a beautiful park that stretches 2.5 miles around the entire pe-

rimeter of Kraków's Old Town. To give your Kraków visit an extra dimension, consider a quick bike ride around the Planty (best early in the morning, when it's less crowded) with a side trip along the parklike riverbank near Wawel Castle; you'll see bike-rental places around the Old Town (including KRK Bike Rental, mentioned in "Getting Around Kraków," earlier).

Circle around the left side of the Barbican. On your left, keep an eye out for a unique monument depicting an elderly, bearded man in the corner of a huge frame. This honors **Jan Matejko,** arguably Poland's most beloved painter, who specialized in giant-scale epic historical scenes several times larger than this frame. We'll hear Matejko's name many more times on this walk.

As you continue around the Barbican, look down to see the much lower ground level around its base—making it easy to imagine that the Planty was once anything but flat.

• *Across the busy street from the Barbican, standing in the middle of the long park, is the...*

Grunwald Monument

This memorial honors one of the most important battles in the history of a nation that has seen more than its share: the Battle of Grunwald on July 15, 1410, when Polish and Lithuanian forces banded together to finally defeat the Teutonic Knights, who had been running roughshod over the lands along the Baltic. Lying dramatically slain at the base of this monument, like a toppled Goliath, is the defeated Grand Master of the Teutonic Knights— German crusaders who had originally been brought to Poland as mercenaries. It's easy to see this vanquished statue as a thinly veiled metaphor for one of Poland's powerful, often domineering neighbors. When the Nazis took power here, this statue was one of the first things they tore down. When they left, it was one of the first things the Poles put back up.

• *If you'd like to see a slice of Krakovian life, side-trip one block to the left of the monument, to the local farmers market. It hides a block behind the busy ring road.*

The Old Market (Stary Kleparz)

The colorful Old Market offers a refreshing dash of Kraków that has nothing to do with history or tourism. It's just lots of hard-scrabble people selling what they grow or knit, and lots of others buying. Wander around as if on a cultural scavenger hunt. Find the freshest doughnuts *(pączki)*, the most popular bakery, the villager selling slippers she knitted, the smelliest smoked-fish stand, and the old man with the smoked cheese (Mon-Sat 7:00-18:00—but busiest and most interesting in the morning, closed Sun).

• *Now retrace your steps to the Barbican and enter the Old Town by walking through the...*

Florian Gate (Brama Floriańska)

As you approach the gate, look up at the **crowned white eagle**, representing courage and freedom—the historic symbol of the Polish people.

Inside the gate, notice the little chapel on the right with a replica of the famous **Black Madonna of Częstochowa,** the most important religious symbol among Polish Catholics. The original, located in Częstochowa (70 miles north of Kraków), is an Eastern Orthodox-style icon of mysterious origin with several mystical legends attached to it. After the icon's believed role in protecting a monastery from

Swedish invaders in the mid-17th century, it was named "Queen and Protector of Poland."

Once through the gate, look back at it. High above is **St. Florian,** patron of the fire brigade. As fire was a big concern for a wooden city of the 15th century, Florian gets a place of honor.

You'll often see traditionally clad **musicians** near the gate, performing their lilting folk melodies for tips.

• *You're standing at the head of Kraków's historic (and now touristic) gamut...*

▲Floriańska Street (Ulica Floriańska)

In good weather, hanging on the inside of the city wall in both directions is a makeshift **art gallery,** where—traditionally—starv-

ing students hawk the works they've painted at the Academy of Fine Arts (across the busy street from the Barbican). The entrance to get on top of the wall—covered by the Barbican ticket—is at the left end of this gallery. If you detoured just a little farther along the wall, to the brick skybridge, you'd reach the entrance to the **Czartoryski Museum,** an eclectic collection of artifacts, including a famous portrait (no, not *that* one) by Leonardo da Vinci...see page 288).

Now begin strolling down **Floriańska street** (floh-ree-AHN-skah). Notice that all over town, storefronts advertising themselves as "tourist information" offices are actually tourist sales agencies (see a list of legitimate TIs on page 241). Along with the fast-food joints, also notice some uniquely Polish snacks: The various pizza and kebab windows also sell *zapiekanka*—a toasted baguette with toppings, similar to a French bread pizza. Or, for an even quicker bite, buy an *obwarzanek* (ring-shaped, bagel-like roll, typically fresh) from a street vendor; many still use their old-fashioned blue carts. Pijana Wiśnia (on the right at #36) sells the sour-cherry liqueur called *wiśniówka;* while this is a very old drink, it's newly trendy—you'll see shops like

this one all over Poland.

About halfway down the first block, on the left (at #45, round green sign), look for **Jama Michalika** ("Michael's Cave"). Around the turn of the 20th century, this dark, atmospheric café was a hangout of the *Młoda Polska* (Young Poland) movement—the Polish answer to Art Nouveau. The walls are papered with sketches from poor artists—local bohemians who couldn't pay their tabs. Today, it hosts a folk troupe that performs traditional music and dance with dinner many evenings (see listing under "Entertainment in Kraków"). Poke around inside this circa-1900 time warp and appreciate this unique art gallery. (For a real time warp, notice the smokers in their own hazy room up front.)

Tourist-clogged Floriańska has more than its share of tacky amusements: wax museum, "Beer House," Thai spa, "I Heart Kraków" shop, and Candy Cat bulk-candy store. But there are some real family-run businesses mixed in: For example, about a block farther down, at #20 (on the right), **Staropolskie Trunki** ("Old Polish Drinks") offers an education in vodka, with a long bar and countless vodkas and liquors—all open and ready to be tasted. They don't carry any big brand names; these are all locally made. They can help you navigate your options—let them know if you like sweet, dry, and so on (four tastes for 25 zł with an explanation from the bartender, daily 10:00-late).

• *Continue into the Main Market Square, where you'll run into...*

▲▲St. Mary's Church (Kościół Mariacki)

A church has stood on this spot for 800 years. The original church was destroyed by the first Tatar invasion in 1241, but all subsequent versions—including the current one—have been built on the same foundation. You can look down the sides to see how the Main Market Square has risen about seven feet over the centuries.

How many church towers does St. Mary's have? Technically, the answer is one. The shorter tower belongs to the church; the

taller one is a municipal watchtower, from which you'll hear a bugler playing the hourly *hejnał* song. According to Kraków's favorite legend, during that first Tatar invasion, a town watchman saw the enemy approaching and sounded the alarm. Before he could finish the tune, an arrow pierced his throat—which is why, even today, the *hejnał* stops suddenly partway through. Today's buglers—12 in all—are firemen first, musicians second. Each one works a 24-hour shift up there, playing the *hejnał* four times on the hour—with one bugle call for each direction. (It's even broadcast on national Polish radio at noon.) While you're in Kraków, you'll certainly hear one of these tiny, hourly, broken performances.

To see one of the most finely crafted Gothic altarpieces anywhere, it's worth paying admission to enter the church. The front door is open 14 hours a day and is free to those who come to pray, but tourists use the door around the right side (buy your ticket across the little square from this door). The panels of the altarpiece are opened with fanfare each day at 11:50.

Cost and Hours: 15 zł, Mon-Sat 11:30-17:45, Sun from 14:00.

Visiting the Church: Inside, you're struck by the lavish decor. This was the church of the everyday townspeople, built out of a spirit of competition with the royal high church at Wawel Castle.

At the altar is one of the best medieval **woodcarvings** in existence—the exquisite, three-part altarpiece by German Veit Stoss (Wit Stwosz in Polish). Carved  over 12 years and completed in 1489, it's packed with emotion rare in Gothic art. Get as close as you can and study the remarkable details. Stoss used oak for the structural parts and linden trunks for the figures. The open altar depicts the Dormition (death—or, if splitting theological hairs, heavenly sleep) of the Virgin. The artist catches the apostles around Mary, reacting in the seconds after she collapses. Mary is depicted in three stages: At the bottom, her body goes limp in the arms of her panicking followers. In the middle, her soul—radiating beams of light—is being escorted to heaven by Jesus. And, at the very top (in the cupola above the frame), Mary sits upon a heavenly throne as she's crowned by Jesus. The six scenes on the sides are the Annunciation, birth of Jesus, visit by the Three Magi, Jesus' Resurrection, his Ascension, and Mary becoming the mother of the apostles at Pentecost.

When the Nazis invaded Poland, they made a list of artistic masterpieces they planned to plunder and take home to Germany—and this altarpiece was on it. It was dismantled and taken to Nürnberg, where it was hidden away in a cellar and managed to survive that city's destruction. After the war, it was returned here and painstakingly reassembled.

There's more to St. Mary's than the altar. While you're admiring this church's art, notice the flowery Neo-Gothic painting covering the choir walls. Stare up into the starry, starry blue ceiling. As you wander around, consider that the church was renovated a century ago by three Polish geniuses from two very different artistic generations: the venerable positivist Jan Matejko and his Art Nouveau students, Stanisław Wyspiański and Józef Mehoffer

Kazimierz the Great (1333-1370)

Out of the many centuries of Polish kings, only one earned the nickname "great," and he's the only one worth remembering: Kazimierz the Great.

K. the G., who ruled Poland from Kraków in the 14th century, was one of those larger-than-life medieval kings who left his mark on all fronts—from war to diplomacy, art patronage to womanizing. His scribes bragged that Kazimierz "found a Poland made of wood, and left one made of brick and stone." He put Kraków on the map as a major European capital. He founded many villages (some of which still bear his name—including one that's an important neighborhood of Kraków) and replaced wooden structures with stone ones (such as Kraków's Cloth Hall). Kazimierz also established the Kraków Academy (today's Jagiellonian University), the second-oldest university in Central Europe. And to protect all of these new building projects, he heavily fortified Poland by building a series of imposing forts and walls around its perimeter. If you have a 50 zł note, take a look at it: That's Kazimierz the Great on the front, and on the back you'll see his capital, Cracovia, and the most important town he founded, Casmirus.

Most of all, Kazimierz is remembered as a progressive, tolerant king. In the 14th century, other nations were deporting—or even interning—their Jewish subjects, who were commonly scapegoated for anything that went wrong. But the enlightened Kazimierz created policies that granted Jews more opportunities (often related to banking and trade) and allowed them a chance for higher social standing—establishing the country as a safe haven for Jews in Europe.

Kazimierz the Great was the last of Poland's long-lived Piast dynasty. Although he left no male heir—at least, no legitimate one—Kazimierz's advances set the stage for Poland's golden age (14th-16th century). After his death, Poland united with Lithuania (against the common threat of the Teutonic Knights), the Jagiellonian dynasty was born, and Poland became one of Europe's mightiest medieval powers.

(we'll learn more about these two later on our walk). The huge silver bird under the organ loft in back is that symbol of Poland, the crowned white eagle.

Tower Climb: For the best view in town, you can climb 271 steep, claustrophobic stairs to the top of the taller tower to visit the *hejnał* fireman (20 zł, pay at the ticket office for the church, departs at :05 and :30 past each hour; May-Sept Tue-Sat 10:00-17:30, Sun from 13:00, closed Mon; on good-weather days in shoulder season, open only Thu-Sat; closed off-season and in bad weather).

• *Leaving the church, notice the neck clamps dangling from the exterior walls near the side door. If you were leaving Mass in centuries past,*

*there would be criminals chained here for public humiliation. You'd spit
on them before turning right and stepping into one of the biggest market
squares anywhere.*

▲▲▲Main Market Square (Rynek Główny), a.k.a. "The Square"

Kraków's marvelous Square, one of Europe's most gasp-worthy
public spaces, bustles with street musicians, colorful flower stalls,

cotton-candy vendors, loiter-
ing teenagers, the local break-
dancing troupe, businesspeople
commuting by foot, gawking
tourists, soap-balloon-blowers,
and the lusty coos of pigeons.
The Square is where Kraków
lives. It's often filled with various special events, markets, and
festivals. The biggest are the seasonal markets around Easter and
Christmas, but you're likely to stumble on something special going
on just about any time of year (especially June through Aug).

The Square was established in the 13th century, when the city
had to be rebuilt after being flattened by the Tatars. At the time,
it was the biggest square in medieval Europe. It was illegal to sell
anything on the street, so everything had to be sold here on the
Main Market Square. It was divided into smaller markets, such
as the butcher stalls, the ironworkers' tents, and the still-standing
Cloth Hall (described later).

Notice the modern **fountain** with the glass pyramid at this
end of the Square. A major excavation of the surrounding area created a museum of Kraków's medieval history that literally sprawls
beneath the Square (for more on the recommended **Rynek Underground Museum,** see page 294).

The statue in the middle of the Square is a traditional meeting
place for Krakovians. It depicts Romantic poet **Adam Mickiewicz**
(1789-1855), who's considered the "Polish Shakespeare." His epic
masterpiece, *Pan Tadeusz,* is still regarded as one of the greatest
works in Polish literature. A wistful, nostalgic tale of Polish-Lithuanian nobility, *Pan Tadeusz* stirred patriotism in a Poland that had
been dismantled by surrounding empires through a series of three
Partitions.

The Square is so beautiful partly because the Old Town was
spared the bombs of World War II. The Nazis considered Kraków
a city with Germanic roots and wanted it saved. But they were
quick to destroy any symbols of Polish culture or pride. The statue

The Młoda Polska (Young Poland) Art Movement

Polish art in the late 19th century was ruled by positivism, a school with a very literal, straightforward focus on Polish history. But when the next generation of Kraków's artists came

into their own in the early 1900s, they decided that the old school was exactly that. Though moved by the same spirit and goals as the previous generation—evoking Polish patriotism at a time when their country was being occupied—these new artists used very different methods. They were inspired by a renewed appreciation of folklore and peasant life. Rather than being earnest and literal (an 18th-century Polish war hero on horseback), the new art was playful and highly symbolic (the artist frolicking in a magical garden in the idyllic Polish countryside). This movement became known as Młoda Polska (Young Poland)—Art Nouveau with a Polish accent.

Stanisław Wyspiański (vees-PAYN-skee, 1869-1907) was the leader of Młoda Polska. He produced beautiful artwork, from simple drawings to the stirring stained-glass images in Kraków's St. Francis Basilica. Wyspiański was an expert at capturing human faces with realistic detail, emotion, and personality. The versatile Wyspiański was also an accomplished stage designer and writer. His patriotic play *The Wedding*—about the nuptials of a big-city artist and a peasant girl—is regarded as one of Poland's finest dramas. In Kraków, you can tour the Wyspiański Museum and see his works in St. Francis Basilica and other churches; he's also well represented in Warsaw's National Museum.

Józef Mehoffer (may-HOH-fehr), Wyspiański's good friend and rival, was another great Młoda Polska artist. Mehoffer's style is more expressionistic and abstract than Wyspiański's, often creating an otherworldly effect. See Mehoffer's work in Kraków's St. Francis Basilica and at the artist's former residence (see the Józef Mehoffer House), and in Warsaw at the National Museum.

Other names to look for include **Jacek Malczewski** (mahl-CHEHV-skee), who specialized in self-portraits, and **Olga Boznańska** (bohz-NAHN-skah), the movement's only prominent female artist. Both are featured in Warsaw's National Museum; Malczewski's works also appear in Kraków's Gallery of 19th-Century Polish Art.

KRAKÓW

of Adam Mickiewicz, for example, was pulled down immediately after occupation.

At the far end of the Square, you'll see the tiny, cubical, copper-domed **Church of St. Adalbert,** one of the oldest churches in Kraków (10th century). This Romanesque structure predates the Square. Like St. Mary's (described earlier), it seems to be at an angle because it's aligned east-west, as was the custom when it was built. (In other words, the churches aren't crooked—the Square is. Any other "crooked" building you see around town predates the 13th-century grid created during the rebuilding of Kraków.)

Drinks are reasonably priced at cafés on the Square (figure 15-20 zł for a coffee, soft drink, beer, or wine; and about 30 zł for a fancier cocktail). Find a spot where you like the view and the chairs, then sit and sip. Order a coffee, Polish *piwo* (beer, such as Żywiec, Okocim, or Lech), or a shot of *wódka* (Żubrówka is a quality brand; for more on Polish drinks, see page 233). For a higher vantage point, the Cloth Hall's **Café Szał terrace**—overlooking the Square and St. Mary's Church—offers one of the best views in town (daily, enter through Gallery of 19th-Century Polish Art entrance).

As the Square buzzes around you, imagine this place before 1989. There were no outdoor cafés, no touristy souvenir stands, and no salespeople hawking cotton candy or neon-lit whirligigs. The communist government shut down all but a handful of the businesses. They didn't want people to congregate here—they should be at home, because "a rested worker is a productive worker." The buildings were covered with soot from the nearby Lenin Steelworks in Nowa Huta. The communists denied the pollution, and when the student "Green Brigades" staged a demonstration in this Square to raise awareness in the 1970s, they were immediately arrested. How things have changed.

• *The huge, yellow building right in the middle of the Square is the...*

▲▲Cloth Hall (Sukiennice)

In the Middle Ages, this was the place where cloth sellers had their market stalls. Kazimierz the Great turned the Cloth Hall into a

permanent structure in the 14th century. In 1555, it burned down and was replaced by the current building. The crowned letter *S* (at the top of the gable above the entryway) stands for King Sigismund the Old, who commissioned this version of the hall. As Sigismund fancied all things Italian (including women—

he married an Italian princess), this structure is in the Italianate Renaissance style. Sigismund kicked off a nationwide trend, and you'll still see Renaissance-style buildings like this one all over the country, making the style typically Polish. We'll see more works by Sigismund's imported Italian architects at Wawel Castle.

The Cloth Hall is still a functioning market—selling mostly souvenirs, including wood carvings, chess sets, jewelry (especial-

ly amber), painted boxes, and trinkets. Cloth Hall prices are slightly inflated, but still cheap by American standards. You're paying a little extra for the convenience and the atmosphere, but you'll see locals buying gifts here, too.

Pay WCs are at each end of the Cloth Hall. The upstairs of the Cloth Hall is home to the excellent **Gallery of 19th-Century Polish Art** (enter behind the statue of Adam; for a self-guided tour, see page 285).

• *Browse through the Cloth Hall passageway. As you emerge into the sleepier half of the Square, the big tower on your left is the...*

Town Hall Tower

This is all that remains of a town hall building from the 14th century—when Kraków was the powerful capital of Poland. (To visualize the intact structure, look for the bronze model to the right of the stairs.) After the 18th-century Partitions of Poland, Kraków's prominence took a nosedive. As the town's importance crumbled, so did its town hall. It was cheaper to tear down the building than to repair it, and all that was left standing was this nearly 200-foot-tall tower. In summer, you can climb the tower, stopping along the way to poke around an exhibit on Kraków history, but the views from up top are disappointing (18 zł, free on Mon, open March-Oct Mon 11:00-15:00, Tue-Sun until 18:00, likely closed off-season).

Nearby: The **gigantic head** at the base of the Town Hall Tower is a sculpture by contemporary artist Igor Mitoraj, who studied here in Kraków. Typical of Mitoraj's works, the head is an empty shell that appears to be wrapped in cloth. While some locals enjoy having a work

KRAKÓW

by their fellow Krakovian in such a prominent place, others disapprove of its sharp contrast with the Square's genteel Old World ambience. Tourists enjoy playing peek-a-boo with the head's eyes.

• *When you're finished on the Square, we'll head toward Wawel Hill. The official Royal Way makes a beeline for the castle, but we'll take a scenic detour to see some less touristy back streets, visit Kraków's historic university and one of its best churches, and go for a quick walk through the Planty park.*

Exit the square at the corner nearest the Town Hall Tower—basically, in the direction the giant head is looking—then turn right along Ulica Św. Anny. After one block, turn left onto Jagiellońska street. Enter the courtyard of the big, red-brick building on your right.

Jagiellonian University and the Collegium Maius

Kraków had the second university in Central Europe (founded in 1364, after Prague's). Over the centuries, Jagiellonian U. has boasted such illustrious grads as Copernicus and St. John Paul II. And today, the city's character is still defined largely by its huge student population (numbering around 150,000). Many of the university buildings fill the area to the west of the Old Town, so you'll see more students (and fewer tourist traps) in this part of town than elsewhere.

This building—called the Collegium Maius—is the historic heart of Kraków's university culture. It dates from the 15th century. In the Middle Ages, professors were completely devoted to their scholarly pursuits. They were unmarried and lived, ate, and slept here in an almost monastic environment. They taught downstairs and lived upstairs. In many ways, this building feels more like a monastery than a university. While this courtyard is the most interesting part, you can also tour the interior. The courtyard also hosts free temporary exhibits; look for posters.

The university also comes with some chilling history. On November 6, 1939, the occupying Nazis called all professors together for a meeting. With 183 gathered unknowingly in a hall, they were unceremoniously loaded into trucks and sent to concentration camps, where many were killed. Hitler knew: If you want to decapitate a culture, you kill its intelligentsia.

Before you leave, if you're a fan of rich, thick hot chocolate, enjoy a cup at **Kawiarnia U Pęcherza** (down the stairs near the entrance)—widely regarded as the best in town.

If it's open, head down the *sgraffito*-lined passage on the side of the courtyard (it's on your left as you enter the courtyard). You'll emerge into the **Professors' Garden,** a tranquil space filled with red brick, ivy, stony statues, and inviting benches (open daily 9:00-18:30 or until dusk, closed off-season).

• *Exit the garden through the fancy gate and turn right on Jagiellońska. Spot any students? You'll follow this for two more blocks, passing the much larger and newer, but still red-brick,* **Collegium Novum** *building—the modern administrative headquarters of Jag U., built in the late 19th century to commemorate the 500th anniversary of the building we just left.*

Jagiellońska dead-ends at a dynamic statue on a pillar. Turn left into the inviting **Planty**—*the ring park we saw at the start of this walk. You'll stroll about five minutes through the Planty—dodging bikes and hearing the rattle of trams through the trees—with the Old Town buildings on your left and the ring road through the park on your right. When you reach a street with tram tracks, cross it and turn left. Pause in the park just before the church and take note of the light-yellow building on the left (across the street), with a picture of St. John Paul II smiling down from above the stone doorway.*

Archbishop's Palace

This building was St. John Paul II's residence when he was the archbishop of Kraków. And even after he became pope, it remained his home-away-from-Rome for visits to his hometown. After a long day of saying formal Mass during his visits to Kraków, he'd wind up here. Weary as he was, before going to bed he'd stand in the window above the entrance for hours, chatting casually with the people assembled below—about religion, but also about sports, current events, and whatever was on their minds.

In 2005, when the pope's health deteriorated, this street filled with his supporters, even though he was in Rome. For days, somber locals focused their vigil on this same window, their eyes fixed on a black crucifix that had been placed here. At 21:37 on the night of April 2, 2005, the pope passed away in Rome. Ten thousand Krakovians were on this street, under this window, listening to a Mass broadcast on loudspeakers from the church. When the priest announced the pope's death, every single person simultaneously fell to their knees in silence. For the next several days, thousands of the faithful continued to stand on this street, staring intently at the window where they last saw the man they considered to be the greatest Pole.

• *Now go through the back door of one of Kraków's finest churches...*

▲▲St. Francis Basilica (Bazylika Św. Franciszka)

This beautiful Gothic church, which was St. John Paul II's home church while he was archbishop of Kraków, features some of Poland's best Art Nouveau in situ (in the setting for which it was intended). After an 1850 fire, it was redecorated by the two leading members of the Młoda Polska (Young Poland) movement: Stanisław Wyspiański and Józef Mehoffer. The glorious decorations inside this church are the result of their great rivalry run amok.

Cost and Hours: Free; open for visitors Mon-Sat 10:00-16:00, Sun 13:00-15:30; longer hours for services and prayer.

Visiting the Basilica: Step through the door and let your eyes adjust to the low light. Take a few steps up the nave, pausing at the third pew on the left. On the back of this pew, notice the **silver plate** labeled "Jan Paweł II"—marking JPII's favorite place to pray when he lived in the Archbishop's Palace across the street. Just beyond, on the left, you'll see a painting of Poland's premier pontiff.

Now walk another 20 feet down the nave and notice the painting on the right, with an orange-and-blue background. This depicts **St. Maksymilian Kolbe,** the Catholic priest who sacrificed his own life to save a fellow inmate at Auschwitz in 1941 (notice the *16670*—his concentration camp number—etched into the background; read his story on page 365). Kolbe is particularly beloved here, as he actually served at this church.

Now turn around and look up above the door you entered. There, in all its glory, is the stained-glass window titled *God the Father Let It Be,* created by the great Art Nouveau artist Stanisław Wyspiański—and regarded by some as his finest masterpiece. (For more on Wyspiański, see page 263.) The colors beneath the Creator change from yellows and oranges (fire) to soothing blues (water), depending on the light. Wyspiański was supposedly inspired by Michelangelo's vision of God in the Sistine Chapel, though he used a street beggar to model God's specific features. Wyspiański also painted the delightful floral stained-glass windows that line the nave, high up—fitting for a church dedicated to a saint so famous for his spiritual connection to nature.

Now turn back around to face the main altar and head into the **chapel** on the left. This important chapel houses a replica of the Shroud of Turin—which, since it touched the original shroud, is also considered a holy relic (displayed along the left side of the chapel). At the main altar in this chapel, notice the plaques honoring Michał Tomaszek and Zbigniew Strzałkowski. These two Polish priests traveled to Peru as missionaries. There, they (along with an Italian priest) were murdered by communist guerrillas calling themselves the Shining Path. Today, they are considered martyrs.

Before leaving this chapel, look high on the walls at the glorious Stations of the Cross. These were painted by **Józef Mehoffer**—
a friend and rival of Wyspiański—as a response to Wyspiański's work.

Now head back into the nave, turn left, and walk toward the main altar. (If a service is going on, you may not be able to get very far—just look from here.) On the walls, notice Wyspiański's gorgeous Art Nouveau floral patterns.

Up in the apse, take a moment to appreciate the Wyspiański-designed **stained-glass windows** flanking the high altar. On the right is St. Francis, the church's namesake, holding up his hands to show the stigmata on his palms. On the left is the Blessed Salomea—a medieval Polish woman who became queen of Hungary but later returned to Poland and entered a convent after her husband's death. Notice she's dropping a crown—repudiating the earthly world and giving herself over to the simple, stop-and-smell-God's-roses lifestyle of St. Francis. Salomea (who's buried in a side chapel) founded this church. Notice also the Mucha-like paintings by Wyspiański on the pilasters between the windows... yet one more sumptuous Art Nouveau detail in this church that's so rich with them.

• *Head back outside. If no services are going on, you can slip out the side door, to the left of the altar. Otherwise, head back out the way you came and hook right. Either way, you're heading to the right along Franciszkańska street. After passing a few monuments and a tram stop, turn right down busy...*

Grodzka Street

Now you're back on the Royal Way proper. At the corner of Grodzka street stands the modern, copper-colored **Wyspiański Pavilion.**

Karol Wojtyła (1920-2005): The Greatest Pole

The man who became St. John Paul II began his life as Karol Wojtyła, born to a military officer and his wife in the town of Wadowice near Kraków on May 18, 1920. Karol's mother died when he was only nine years old, and his older brother was gone just a few years later. At age 18, Karol moved with his father to Kraków to study philosophy and drama at Jagiellonian University.

Young Karol was gregarious and athletic—an avid skier, hiker, swimmer, and soccer goalie—but his real passion was acting. During the Nazi occupation in World War II, he worked in a quarry to avoid being sent to a labor camp in Germany. In defiance of the Nazis, he secretly studied theology and appeared in illegal underground theatrical productions. When the war ended, he resumed his studies, now at the theology faculty.

After graduating in 1947, Wojtyła swiftly rose through the ranks of the Catholic Church hierarchy. By 1964, he was archbishop of Kraków, and just three years later, he became the youngest cardinal ever. Throughout the 1960s, he fought an ongoing battle with the regime when they refused to allow the construction of a church in the Kraków suburb of Nowa Huta. After years of saying Mass for huge crowds in open fields, Wojtyła finally convinced the communists to allow the construction of the Lord's Ark Church in 1977. A year later, Karol Wojtyła was called to the papacy—the first non-Italian pope in more than four centuries. In 1979, he paid a visit to his native Poland. In a series of cautiously provocative speeches, he demonstrated to his countrymen the potential for mass opposition to communism.

Imagine you're Polish in the 1970s. Your country was devastated by World War II and has struggled under an oppressive regime ever since. Food shortages are epidemic. Lines stretch around the block even to buy a measly scrap of bread. Life is bleak, oppressive, and hopeless. Then someone who speaks your language—someone you've admired your entire life, and one of the only people you've seen successfully stand up to the regime—becomes one of the world's most influential people. A Pole like

Step inside (daily 9:00-20:00) to see three recent stained-glass windows based on designs Wyspiański once submitted for a contest to redecorate Wawel Cathedral. Although these designs were rejected back then, they were finally realized on the hundredth anniversary of his death (in 2007). Visible from inside the building during the day, and gloriously illuminated to be seen outside the building at night, they represent three Polish historical figures: the gaunt St. Stanisław (Poland's first saint), the skeletal Kazimierz the Great (in the middle), and the swooning King Henry the Pious.

you is the leader of a billion Catholics. He makes you believe that the impossible can happen. He says to you again and again: *"Nie lękajcie się"*—"Have no fear." And you begin to believe it.

From his bully pulpit, the pope had a knack for cleverly challenging the communists—just firmly enough to get his point across but stopping short of jeopardizing the stature of the Church in Poland. Gentle but pointed wordplay was his specialty. The inspirational role he played in the lives of Lech Wałęsa and the other leaders of Solidarity emboldened them to rise up; it's no coincidence that the first successful trade union strikes in the Soviet Bloc took place shortly after John Paul II became pope. Many people (including Mikhail Gorbachev) credited John Paul II for the collapse of Eastern European communism.

Even as John Paul II's easy charisma attracted new worshippers to the Church (especially young people), his conservatism on issues such as birth control, homosexuality, and female priests pushed away many Catholics. Under his watch, the Church struggled with pedophilia scandals. Many still fault him for turning a blind eye and not putting a stop to these abuses much earlier. By the end of his papacy, John Paul II's failing health and conservatism had caused him to lose stature in worldwide public opinion.

And yet, approval of the pope never waned in Poland. His compatriots—even the relatively few atheists and agnostics—saw John Paul II both as the greatest hero of their people...and as a member of the family, like a kindly grandfather. When Pope John Paul II died on April 2, 2005, the mourning in his homeland was particularly deep and sustained. Musical performances of all kinds were canceled, and the irreverent MTV-style music channel simply went off the air out of respect.

A speedy nine years after his death, Karol Wojtyła became St. John Paul II in April 2014. Out of 265 popes, few have been given the title "great," but there's already talk in Rome of increasing their ranks. Someday soon we may speak of this man as "St. John Paul the Great." His fellow Poles already do.

If you're not churched out, you can dip into the **Dominican Church**—just a block away, to your left (described later).

Now continue down Grodzka street. This lively thoroughfare, connecting the Square with Wawel, is teeming with shops—and some of Kraków's best restaurants (see "Eating in Kraków," later). Survey your options now and choose (and maybe reserve) your favorite for dinner tonight. This street is also characterized by its fine arcades over the sidewalks. While this might seem like a charming Renaissance feature, the arcades were actually added by the Nazis after they invaded in 1939; they wanted to convert Kraków into a city befitting its status as the capital of their Polish puppet state.

This is also a good street to find some of Kraków's **milk bars.** The most traditional one is about two blocks down, on the right (at #45), with a simple *Bar Mleczny* sign. These government-subsidized cafeterias are the locals' choice for a quick, cheap, filling, lowbrow lunch. Prices are deliriously cheap (soup costs about a dollar), and the food isn't bad.

• *One more block ahead, the small square on your right is...*

Mary Magdalene Square (Plac Św. Marii Magdaleny)

This square offers a great visual example of Kraków's deeply religious character. In the Middle Ages, Kraków was known as "Little Rome" for its many churches. Today, there are 142 churches and monasteries within the city limits (32 in the Old Town alone)— more per square mile than anywhere outside of Rome. You can see several of them from this spot: The nearest, with the picturesque white facade and row of saints out front, is the Roman-style **Church of Saints Peter and Paul** (Poland's first Baroque church, and a popular tourist concert venue). The statues lining this church's facade are the 11 apostles (minus Judas), plus Mary Magdalene, the square's namesake. The next church to the right, with the twin towers, is the Romanesque **St. Andrew's** (now with a Baroque interior). Dating from the rough-and-tumble 11th century, it was designed to double as a place of last refuge—notice the arrow slits around the impassable lower floor. According to legend, a spring inside this church provided water to citizens who holed up here during the Tatar invasions. The church was spared, but that didn't save the rest of Kraków from being overrun by marauding armies. Imagine this stone fortress of God being the only building standing amid a smoldering and flattened Kraków after the 13th-century destruction.

If you look farther down the street, you can see three more churches. And even the square next to you used to be a church, too—it burned in 1855, and only its footprint survives.

• *Go through the square and turn left down...*

Kanonicza Street (Ulica Kanonicza)

With so many churches around here, the clergy had to live somewhere. Many lived on this well-preserved street—supposedly the oldest street in Kraków. As you walk, look for the cardinal hats over three different doorways. The **Hotel Copernicus,** on the left at #16, is named for a famous guest who stayed here five centuries ago. Directly across the street at #17, the **Bishop Erazm Ciołek**

Palace hosts a good exhibit of medieval art and Orthodox icons. Next door, the yellow house at #19 is where Karol Wojtyła lived for 10 years after World War II—long before he became St. John Paul II. Today, this building houses the **Archdiocesan Museum,** which is the top spot in the Old Town to learn about Kraków's favorite son. Both of these sights are described later, under "Sights in Kraków."

• *This marks the end of Kanonicza street—and the end of our self-guided walk. But there's still much more to see. Across the busy street, a ramp leads up to the most important piece of ground in all of Poland: Wawel.*

Sights in and near the Old Town

WAWEL HILL

Wawel (VAH-vehl), a symbol of Polish royalty and independence, is sacred territory to every Polish person. A castle has stood here since the beginning of Poland's recorded history. Today, Wawel—awash in tourists —is the most visited sight in the country. Crowds and an overly complex admissions system for the hill's many historic sights can be exasperating. Thankfully, a stroll through the cathedral and around the castle grounds—with the help of

the following commentary—is enough. I've described these sights in the order of a handy self-guided walk. The many museums on Wawel (all described in this section) are mildly interesting but can be skipped (grounds open daily from 6:00 until dusk, inner courtyard closes 30 minutes earlier). In May and June, it's mobbed with students, as it's a required field trip for Polish schoolkids.

Wawel Sights: The sights you'll enter at Wawel are divided into two institutions, cathedral and castle, each with separate tickets. Tickets for the castle sights are sold at two points (at the long line at the top of the ramp; or with no line at the top of the hill, across the central square). To enter the most important sight—the cathedral—buy your ticket at the office across from the cathedral entrance.

• *From Kanonicza street—where my self-guided Old Town walk ends—head up the long ramp to the castle entry.*

Entry Ramp

Huffing up this ramp, it's easy to imagine how this location—rising

KRAKÓW

above the otherwise flat plains around Kraków—was both strategic and easy to defend. When Kraków was part of the Habsburg Empire in the 19th century, the Austrians turned this castle complex into a fortress, destroying much of its delicate beauty. When Poland regained its independence after World War I, the castle was returned to its former glory. The bricks you see on your left as you climb the ramp bear the names of Poles from around the world who donated to the cause.

The jaunty equestrian statue ahead is **Tadeusz Kościuszko** (1746-1817). If that name seems familiar, it's because Kościuszko was a hero of the American Revolution and helped design West Point. When he returned to his native Poland, he fought bravely but unsuccessfully against the Russians (during the Partitions that would divide Poland's territory among three neighboring powers). Kościuszko also gave his name to several American towns, a county in Indiana, a brand of mustard from Illinois, and the tallest mountain in Australia.

• *Hiking through the Heraldic Gate next to Kościuszko, you pass the ticket office (if you'll be going into the museums, use the other ticket office, with shorter lines, on the top of the hill—see "Tickets and Reservations," later). As you crest the hill and pass through the stone gate, on your left is...*

▲▲Wawel Cathedral

Poland's national church is its Westminster Abbey. While the history buried here is pretty murky to most Americans, to Poles, this church is *the* national mausoleum. It holds the tombs of nearly all of Poland's most important rulers and greatest historical figures.

Cost and Hours: 22 zł ticket includes cathedral entry, tower climb, crypt, royal tombs, the John Paul II Wawel Cathedral Museum, and the Archdiocesan Museum not far away (described later). Buy this ticket at the house across from the cathedral entry—marked *KASA*—where you can also rent an audioguide. The cathedral is open Mon-Sat 9:00-17:00, Sun from 12:30 (except the cathedral museum is closed Sun off-season), Nov-March daily until 16:00 (+48 12 429 9516, www.katedra-wawelska.pl).

Cathedral Exterior

Before entering, go around to the far side of the cathedral to take in its profile. This uniquely eclectic church is the product of centuries of haphazard additions—it's surrounded by some 17 chapels and towers that were grafted on to the original, Romanesque, 12th-century core. (The white base of the nearest tower is original. Anything at Wawel that's made of white limestone like this was probably part of the earliest Romanesque structures.) In a sense, when you're looking at the cathedral, you're barely seeing the "cathedral" at all—just these many addenda. To give you a sense of the historical sweep, scan the chapels from left to right: 14th-century Gothic, 12th-century Romanesque (the base of the tower), 17th-century Baroque (the inside is Baroque, though the exterior is a copy of its Renaissance neighbor), 16th-century Renaissance, and 18th- and 19th-century Neoclassical. (This variety in styles is even more evident in the chapels' interiors, which we'll see soon.)

Pay attention to the two particularly interesting domed chapels to the right of the tall tower. The gold one is the Sigismund Chapel, housing memorials to the Jagiellonian kings—including Sigismund the Old, who was responsible for Kraków's Renaissance renovation in the 16th century. The Jagiellonian Dynasty was a high point in Polish history. During that golden 16th century, Poland was triple the size it is today, stretching all the way to the Ottoman Empire and the Black Sea. Poles consider the Sigismund Chapel, made with 80 pounds of gold, to be the finest Renaissance chapel north of the Alps. The copper-domed chapel next to it, home to the Swedish Vasa dynasty, resembles its neighbor (but it's a copy built 150 years later, and without all that gold).

Go back around and face the church's **front entry** for more architectonic extravagance. The tallest tower, called the Sigismund Tower, has a clock with only an hour hand. Climbing a few steps into the entry, you see Gothic chapels (with pointy windows) flanking the door, a Renaissance ceiling, lavish Baroque decoration over the door, and some big bones (a simple whale rib and two vertebrae). In the Middle Ages, these were thought to have been the bones of the mythic Wawel dragon and put here as an oddity to be viewed by the public. (Back

then, there were no museums, so unusual items like these were used to lure people to the church.) The door is the original from the 14th century, with fine wrought-iron work. The K with the crown stands for Kazimierz the Great. The black marble frame is made of Kraków stone from nearby quarries.

KRAKÓW

Cathedral Interior

The cathedral interior is slathered in Baroque memorials and tombs, decorated with tapestries, and soaked in Polish history. The ensemble was designed to help keep Polish identity strong through the ages. It has...and it still does.

After you step inside, you'll follow the one-way, clockwise route that leads you through the choir, then around the back of the apse, then back to the entry.

At the entry, look straight ahead to see the silver tomb under a **canopy,** inspired by the one in St. Peter's Basilica at the Vatican. It contains the remains of the first Polish saint, Stanisław (from the 11th century). In front of the canopy, look for a metallic reliquary that's shaped like a book with its pages being ruffled by the wind (labeled, in Latin, *Sanctus Johannes Paulus II*). The glass capsule in the reliquary holds a drop of St. John Paul II's blood. It takes this shape because of what believers consider a highly significant moment during his memorial service: Before a crowd of thousands on St. Peter's Square in Rome, a book was placed on John Paul II's simple wooden coffin. As the service processed, its pages were ruffled back and forth by the wind, until they were finally slammed shut...as if the Holy Spirit were "closing the book" on his life.

Go behind this canopy into the ornately carved **choir** area. For 200 years, the colorful chair to the right of the high altar has been the seat of Kraków's archbishops, including Karol Wojtyła, who served here for 14 years before becoming pope. It's also here that Polish royal coronations took place.

Now you'll continue into the left aisle. Straight ahead is the entrance to the **Sigismund Tower;** to ascend it, you'll climb 70 claustrophobic wooden stairs to the 11-ton Sigismund Bell and pleasant views of the steeples and spires of Kraków.

Before moving on, there's another small sight back toward where you entered the church: Look for the low-profile staircase and descend into the little **crypt** (with a rare purely Romanesque interior), which houses the remains of Adam Mickiewicz, the Romantic poet whose statue dominates the Main Market Square; and another beloved Romantic poet and playwright, Juliusz Słowacki. You'll also find a white marble monument to Fryderyk Chopin (who's buried in Paris), put here on the 200th anniversary of his birth in 2010.

Now continue around the apse (behind the main altar). After looping around to the right, as you head back up the far aisle, look for the red-marble tomb (on the right) of The Great One—**Kazimierz,** of course. Look for *Kazimierz III Wielki*. At his feet you can see a little animal that was originally intended to be a lion, but because local craftspeople lacked a model, it wound up looking more like a beaver with a lion's mane. This is an allusion to a famous saying about Kazimierz, the nation-builder: He found a Poland made of wood, and left one made of brick and stone. The belt Kazimierz wears represents the fortifications he built in a ring around his Polish realm.

You may notice that there's one VIP (Very Important Pole) who's missing...Karol Wojtyła, a.k.a. John Paul II. Even so, a few more steps toward the entrance, on the left, is the **Chapel of St. John Paul II.** The late pontiff left no specific requests for his body, and the Vatican controversially (to Poles, at least) chose to entomb him in Vatican City, instead of sending him back home to Wawel. While Karol Wojtyła's remains are in St. Peter's Basilica, this chapel was recently converted to honor him—with a plaque in the floor and an altar with his picture. Someday, Poles hope, he may be moved here (but, the Vatican says, don't hold your breath).

Back out in the main church, about 10 steps farther on the right, is the white sarcophagus of **St. Jadwiga** (with a dog at her feet). This 14th-century "king" of Poland advanced the fortunes of her realm by partnering with the king of Lithuania. The resulting Jagiellonian dynasty fought off the Teutonic Knights, helped Christianize Lithuania, and oversaw a high-water

mark in Polish history. (Despite the queen's many contributions, the sexism of the age meant that she was considered a "king" rather than a "queen.") She was sainted by Pope John Paul II in 1997.

Across from Jadwiga, peek into the gorgeous 16th-century **Sigismund Chapel,** with its silver altar (this is the gold-roofed chapel you just saw from outside). Locals consider this the "Pearl of the Polish Renaissance" and the finest Renaissance structure outside Italy.

Next, look into the **Vasa Chapel** (past the side door, also on the left): Remember that its exterior matches the restrained, Renaissance style of the Sigismund Chapel, but the interior is clearly Baroque, slathered with gold and silver—quite a contrast.

To the left of the main door, take a look at the Gothic **Holy Cross Chapel,** with its seemingly Orthodox-style 14th-century frescoes.

In the back corner of the church—on the other side of the main door—is the entrance through the Czartoryski Chapel to the **royal tombs.** (You'll exit outside the church, so be sure you're done in here first.) Once downstairs, the first big room, an original Romanesque space called St. Leonard's Crypt, houses Poland's greatest war heroes: Kościuszko (of American Revolution fame), Jan III Sobieski (who successfully defended Vienna from the Ottomans; he's in the simple black coffin with the gold inscription *J III S*), Sikorski, Poniatowski, and so on. Poles consider this room highly significant as the place where St. John Paul II celebrated his first Mass after becoming a priest (in November 1946).

Then you'll wander through several rooms of second-tier Polish kings, queens, and their kids. Head down more stairs into a stark corridor, where you'll run into the plaque honoring the Polish victims of the Katyń massacre in the USSR during World War II. Stepping into the next room, you'll see the tomb of President Lech Kaczyński and his wife Helena, who were among the 96 Polish politicians killed in a tragic 2010 plane crash at Smoleńsk, where the diplomats had planned to attend a ceremony memorializing the Katyń massacre. Up a few stairs is the final grave, belonging to Marshal Józef Piłsudski, the WWI hero who later seized power and was the de facto ruler of Poland from 1926 to 1935. His tomb was moved here so the rowdy soldiers who came to pay their respects wouldn't disturb the others.

• *Exit near the Kaczyński tomb. To visit the cathedral's museum (covered by the same ticket), cross the little square and head up the stairs next to the statue of St. John Paul II.*

John Paul II Wawel Cathedral Museum

This small museum fills four rooms with artifacts relating to both the cathedral and St. John Paul II. Downstairs is the Royal Room, with vestments, swords, regalia, coronation robes, and items that were once buried with the kings, as well as early treasury items (from the 11th through 16th century). Upstairs is the "Papal Room" with items from St. John Paul II's life: his armchair, vestments, caps, shoes, and miter (pointy pope hat), plus souvenirs from his travels. (If you're into  papal memorabilia, the collection at the nearby Archdiocesan Museum—covered by the same ticket and described later—is better.) The adjoining room holds a later treasury collection (17th through 20th century).

Cost and Hours: Same ticket and hours as the cathedral (see earlier), except the museum is closed Sun off-season.

• *When you're finished with the cathedral sights, stroll around the...*

▲▲Wawel Castle Grounds

In the rest of the castle, you'll uncover more fragments of Kraków's history and have the opportunity to visit several museums. I consider the museums skip-pable, but if you want to visit them, buy tickets before you enter the inner courtyard. Read the descriptions on page 282 to decide which, if any, museums appeal to you.

◐ **Self-Guided Tour:** This guided stroll, which doesn't enter any of the admission-charging attractions, is plenty for most visitors.

• *For a historical orientation, stand with the cathedral to your back, and survey the empty field between here and the castle walls.*

Gothic Church Ruins: This hilltop has seen lots of changes over the years. Kazimierz the Great turned a small fortress into a mighty Gothic castle in the 14th century. But that original fortress burned to the ground in 1499, and ever since, Wawel has been in flux. For example, in the grassy field, notice the foundations of two Gothic churches that were destroyed when the Austrians took over Wawel in the 19th century and needed a parade ground for their troops. (They built the red-brick hospital building beyond the field, now used by the Wawel administration.)

• *Facing the cathedral, look right to find a grand green-and-pink entry-way. Go through here and into the palace's dramatically Renaissance-style...*

Inner Courtyard: If this space seems to have echoes of Florence, that's because it was designed and built by young Florentines after Kazimierz's original castle burned down. As with the Cloth Hall, recall that Sigismund the Old married an Italian princess (Bona Sforza, from the famous Milanese family). Along with his bride, he imported Italian architecture, fashion (low-cut dresses), and food (tomatoes and potatoes, which had arrived in Italy from the New World).

The courtyard has three distinct levels: The ground floor housed the private apartments of the higher nobility (governors and castle administrators), the middle level held the private apartments of the king, and the top floor—much taller, to allow more light to fill its large spaces—were the public state rooms of the king. (They

KRAKÓW

have the opposite problem in Italy, where the goal is shade rather than sunshine, so the lower floors are taller—the reverse of what you see here.)

The wing to the right of where you entered is fascist in style (notice the column-like grooves around the windows). It was built

as the headquarters of the notorious Nazi governor of German-occupied Poland, Hans Frank. (He was tried and executed in Nürnberg after the war.)

At the right end of the courtyard is a false wall, designed to create a pleasant Renaissance symmetry, and also to give the illusion that the castle is bigger than it is. Looking through the windows, notice that there's nothing but air on the other side. When foreign dignitaries visited, these windows could be covered to complete the illusion. The entrances to most Wawel museums are around this courtyard, and some believe that you'll find something even more special: chakra.

Adherents to the Hindu concept of **chakra** believe that a powerful energy field connects all living things. Some believe that, mirroring the seven chakra points on the body (from head to groin), there are seven points on the surface of the earth where this energy is most concentrated: Delhi, Delphi, Jerusalem, Mecca, Rome, Velehrad...and Wawel Hill—specifically over there in the corner (immediately to your left as you enter the courtyard—the stretches of wall flanking the door to the baggage-check room, and all the way to the door in the corner). Look for peaceful people (here or elsewhere on the castle grounds) with their eyes closed. One thing's for sure: They're not thinking of Kazimierz the Great. The smudge marks on the wall are from people pressing up against this corner, trying to absorb some good vibes from this chakra spot.

The Wawel administration seems creeped out by all this. They've done what they can to discourage this ritual (such as putting up information boards right where the power is supposedly most focused), but believers still gravitate from far and wide to hug the wall. Give it a try...and let the chakra be with you. (Just for fun, ask a Wawel tour guide about the chakra, and watch her squirm—they're forbidden to talk about it.)

• If you want to visit some of the **castle museums** (you can enter most of them from this courtyard), you'll first need to buy tickets elsewhere. Stick with me for a little longer to finish our tour of the grounds, and we'll wind up near a ticket office.

Head slightly downhill through the square, across to the gap in the buildings beyond the field, to the...

Viewpoint over the Vistula: Belly up to the wall and enjoy the panorama over the **Vistula River** and Kraków's outskirts. The "Polish Mississippi"—which runs its entire course in Polish lands—is the nation's artery for trade and cultural connection. It stretches 650 miles from the foothills of the Tatra Mountains in southern Poland, through many of the country's major cities (Kraków, Warsaw, Toruń), before emptying into the Baltic Sea in Gdańsk.

From this viewpoint, you can see some unusual landmarks, including the odd wavy-roofed building just across the river (which houses the Manggha Japanese art gallery) and the biggest conference center in Poland (to the left of the wavy building). A bit farther to the left is an eyesore of a communist concrete hotel, now home to a very cool summertime "beach bar" with a Ferris wheel (the Forum Przestrzenie, described on page 340). To the right, the suspiciously symmetrical little bulge that tops the highest hill on the horizon is the artificial Kościuszko Mound (described later). And on a particularly crisp day, far in the distance (beyond the wavy building), you can see the Tatra Mountains marking the border of Slovakia.

Now look directly below you, along the riverbank (to the left), to find a fire-belching monument to the **dragon** that was instrumental in the founding of Kraków. Once upon a time, a prince named Krak founded a town on Wawel Hill. It was the perfect location—except for the fire-breathing dragon that lived in the caves under the hill and terrorized the town. Prince Krak had to feed the dragon all of the town's livestock to keep the monster from going after the townspeople. But Krak, with the help of a clever shoemaker, came up with a plan. They stuffed a sheep's skin with sulfur and left it outside the dragon's cave. The dragon swallowed it and, before long, developed a terrible case of heartburn. To put the fire out, the dragon started drinking water from the Vistula. He kept drinking and drinking until he finally exploded. The town was saved, and Kraków thrived. Today, visitors enjoy watching the dragon blow fire into the air (about every four minutes; can vary from a big plume to a tiny puff).

If you'd like a higher viewpoint on the riverfront, you can pay a few złoty to climb 137 stairs to the top of **Sandomierska Tower** (at the far end of the hill,

KRAKÓW

past the visitors center, no elevator; open only in summer). But I'd skip it—the view from up top is only through small windows.

• *Our Wawel tour is finished. If you'd like to explore some of the museums, you can buy your tickets in the nearby visitors center (head back into the main Wawel complex—with the empty field—and turn right); here you'll also find WCs, a café, and a gift shop. Or you can head to the riverfront park: Walk downhill (through the Dragon's Den, or use the main ramp and circle around the base of the hill) to reach the embankment—a delightful place to simply stroll and relax, with beautiful views back on the castle complex.*

Wawel Castle Museums

Wawel Castle offers a dizzying array of museums, exhibits, and attractions, all covered by separate tickets. Visitors stand before a long, pointlessly complicated menu of options, puzzling over how to spend their time and money. But here's the good news: Most, arguably all, of the Wawel Castle sights are skippable. While some of the castle's fine artifacts and pretty rooms are appealing to Poles, most casual visitors find that the best visit is simply to enjoy the cathedral and the castle grounds (following my self-guided tour, earlier). But in case you'd like to dig deeper, here's the scoop.

Tickets: Each sight has its own ticket (prices listed later); English descriptions are posted, and you can rent an audioguide for 12 zł that covers a few of the sights. Sort through your choices and buy tickets at the visitors center at the far corner of the castle grounds (across the field from the cathedral, in the big red-brick building). You can't buy tickets at the door of any sight, so choose and buy your tickets here at the start of your visit. The number of tickets per sight are limited and come with an assigned entry time (though ticket-checkers tend to be pretty flexible). It's possible to reserve ahead online or by phone (see the official website for details)...but I wouldn't bother. Frankly, if they're sold out, you're not missing much.

Hours: The hours of the various exhibits change frequently and there can be exceptions from sight to sight; for the latest, see www.wawel.krakow.pl. But in general, most of these sights should be open Tue 9:30-14:00, Wed-Sun until 17:00. Most sights are closed Mondays, but some are open and free Monday mornings until 13:00 (these rotate every few months).

Sights: Unless you're a Poland completist, the only Wawel attraction really worth considering is the first one.

To see the **Royal State Rooms** (Komnaty Królewskie), costing 35 zł and worth ▲, you climb up to the top floor and wander through some halls with antique furniture to reach the Throne Room, with 30 carved heads in the ceiling. According to legend, one of these heads got mouthy when the king was trying to pass

judgment—so its mouth has been covered to keep it quiet. Continue into some of the palace's finest rooms, with 16th-century Brussels tapestries (140 of the original 300 survive), remarkably decorated wooden ceilings, and gorgeous leather-tooled walls. Wandering these halls with their period furnishings, you get a feeling for the 16th- and 17th-century glory days of Poland, when it was a leading power in Central Europe. The Senate Room, with its throne and elaborate tapestries, is the climax.

The **Royal Private Apartments** (Prywatne Apartamenty Królewskie) are similar to the State Rooms and essentially redundant. Touring these, you'll see a columned hall, some Meissen porcelain, and a variety of artwork (30 zł).

The **Crown Treasury** (Skarbiec Koronny) shows off an impressive collection of regalia: giant banners (some dating back to the 16th century); swords, scepters, helmets, shields, and kingly chain mail; exquisite items gifted to Jan III Sobieski in thanks for defeating the Ottomans in the 1683 Battle of Vienna (including a sumptuous mantle from King Louis XIV and a comically oversized coronation sword from the pope); a rustic table loaded down with gold, silver, and enamel tankards; and lots of other fancy items once belonging to Polish royals (35 zł).

The **Armory** (Zbrojownia) is a decent collection of swords, saddles, and shields; ornately decorated muskets, crossbows, and axes; and cannons (20 zł).

The small **Art of the Orient** (Sztuka Wschodu) exhibit displays Ottoman swords, carpets, banners, vases, and other items dating from Jan III Sobieski's victory in the Battle of Vienna (20 zł).

The **Lost Wawel** (Wawel Zaginiony) exhibit traces the history of the hill and its various churches and castles. You'll see a model of the entire castle complex in the 18th century (pre-Austrian razing) then walk through scarcely explained excavations of a 10th-century church. On the way, you'll see models of the cathedral at various stages, and a display of tiles from 16th-century stoves that once heated the place (15 zł).

The **Wawel Recovered** (Wawel Odzyskany) exhibit is a more modern look at the evolution of this hilltop—with more models and reconstructions than actual foundations (15 zł).

There are also **temporary exhibits,** a separate ticket to walk along the castle's **first-floor galleries,** access to the **Royal Gardens**

KRAKÓW

on the hillsides below the castle, and likely even more by the time you read this.

Eating: Various light eateries circle the castle courtyard, but if you just want a drink, it's hard to beat the cheap self-service snack bar next to the Lost Wawel entrance, with fine views across to the cathedral.

KRAKÓW'S ART MUSEUMS

Kraków's National Museum (Muzeum Narodowe) is made up of a series of small but interesting art collections scattered throughout the city (http://mnk.pl). These are some of the most engaging sights in town; you can find details on current exhibitions at the National Museum website. An 80 zł **combo-ticket,** called a *karnet,* covers the permanent collections in all of these museums (good for your entire stay)—worth considering if you'll be visiting more than three of them. National Museum branches are usually free to enter one day a week—likely Tuesday, but check the website.

▲▲Gallery of 19th-Century Polish Art (Galeria Sztuki Polskiej XIX Wieku)

This small and surprisingly enjoyable collection of works by obscure Polish artists fills the upper level of the Cloth Hall. While you probably won't recognize any of the Polish names in here—and this collection isn't quite as impressive as Warsaw's National Gallery—many of these paintings are just plain delightful. It's worth a visit to see some Polish canvases in their native land and

to enjoy views over the Square from the hall's upper terraces.

Cost and Hours: 32 zł, free on Tue; open Tue-Sun 10:00-18:00, closed Mon; entrance on side of Cloth Hall facing Adam Mickiewicz statue, +48 12 424 4600.

Background: During the 19th century—when every piece of art in this museum was created—there was no "Poland." The country had been split up among its powerful neighbors in a series of three Partitions and would not appear again on the map of Europe until after World War I. Meanwhile, the 19th century was a period of national revival throughout Europe, when various previously marginalized ethnic groups began to take pride in what made them different from their neighbors. So the artists you see represented here were grappling with trying to forge a national identity at a time when they didn't even have a country. You'll sense a pessimism that comes from people who feel abused by foreign powers, mingled with a resolute spirit of national pride.

⊘ Self-Guided Tour: The collection fills just four rooms: two small rooms in the center and two big halls on either side. On a quick visit, focus on the highlights in the big halls I mention here.

Entering the Cloth Hall, buy your ticket and head up the stairs (or use the elevator). The obligatory coat check is on floor 1, and the museum is on floor 2. Between them, peek out onto the inviting **café terrace** for a fine view of the Square and St. Mary's (then return here after your museum visit for a scenic drink.)

The first two small rooms contain little of interest. You enter **Room I** (Bacciarelli Room), with works from the Enlightenment; straight ahead is **Room II** (Michałowski Room), featuring Romantic works from 1822 to 1863. The larger, twin halls on either side merit a linger.

Siemiradzki Room (Room III, on the right): This features art of the Academy—that is, "conformist" art embraced by the art critics of the day. Entering the room, turn right and survey the canvases counterclockwise. The space is dominated by the works of Jan Matejko, a remarkably productive painter who specialized in epic historical scenes that also commented on his own era.

• *Circling the room, look for these paintings.*

Jan Matejko, *Wenyhora:* The first big canvas (immediately on your right as you enter, next to the door) is Matejko's depiction of Wenyhora, a late-18th-century Ukrainian soothsayer who, according to legend, foretold Poland's hardships—the three Partitions, Poland's pact with Napoleon, and its difficulties regaining nationhood. Like many Poles of the era, Matejko was preoccupied with Poland's tragic fate, imbuing this scene with an air of inevitable tragedy.

Jacek Malcezewski, *Death of Ellenai:* A similar gloominess is reflected in this canvas. The main characters in a Polish Romantic poem, Ellenai and Anhelli, have been exiled to a remote cabin in Siberia (in Russia, one of the great powers occupying Poland). Just when they think things can't get worse...Ellenai dies. Anhelli sits immobilized by grief.

• *A few canvases down, dominating the right side of the hall, is...*

Jan Matejko, *Tadeusz Kościuszko at Racławice:* One of the heroes of the American Revolution, now back in his native Poland fighting the Russians, doffs his hat after his unlikely victory at the Battle at Racławice. In this battle (which ultimately had little bearing on Russia's drive to overtake Poland), a ragtag army of Polish peasants defeated the Russian forces. Kościuszko is clad in an

KRAKÓW

American uniform, indicating Matejko's respect for the American ideals of democracy and self-determination.

• *Dominating the far wall is...*

Henryk Siemiradzki, *Nero's Torches:* On the left, Roman citizens eagerly gather to watch Christians being burned at the stake

(on the right). The symbolism is clear: The meek and downtrodden (whether Christians in the time of Rome, or Poles in the heyday of Russia and Austria) may be persecuted now but have faith that their noble ideals will ultimately prevail.

• *On the next wall, find...*

Pantaleon Szyndler, *Bathing Girl:* This piece evokes the orientalism popular in 19th-century Europe, when romanticized European notions of the Orient (such as "harem slave girls") were popular artistic themes. Already voyeuristic, the painting was originally downright lewd until Szyndler painted over a man leering at the woman from the left side of the canvas.

• *The huge canvas on this wall is...*

Jan Matejko, *The Prussian Homage:* The last Grand Master of the fearsome Teutonic Knights swears allegiance to the Polish king in 1525. This historic ceremony took place in the Main Market Square in Kraków, the capital at the time. Notice the Cloth Hall balustrade and the spires of St. Mary's Church in the background. Matejko has painted his own face on one of his favorite historical figures, the jester Stańczyk at the foot of the throne.

• *Continue the rest of the way around the room. Keep an eye out for Tadeusz Ajdukiewicz's portrait of Helena Modrzejewska, a popular actress of the time, attending a party in this very building. Finally, backtrack through Room I and continue straight ahead into the...*

Chełmoński Room (Room IV): Featuring works of the late 19th century, this section includes Realism and the first inklings of Symbolism and Impressionism. Just as elsewhere in Europe (including Paris, where many of these painters trained), artists were beginning to throw off the conventions of the Academy and embrace their own muse.

• *As you turn right and proceed counterclockwise through the room, the first stretch of canvases features landscapes and genre paintings. Among these, about halfway down, a particularly fine canvas is...*

Wladyslaw Malecki, *A Gathering of Storks:* The majestic birds stand under big willows in front of the setting sun. Even seemingly innocent wildlife paintings have a political message: Storks are particularly numerous in Poland, making them a subtle patriotic symbol.

• *A few canvases down, find...*

Józef Brandt, *A Meeting on a Bridge:* This dramatic painting shows soldiers and aristocrats pushing a farmer into a ditch—a comment on the state of the Polish people at that time. Just to the right, see Brandt's *Fight for a Turkish Standard*. This artist specialized in battle scenes, frequently involving a foe from the East—as was often the reality here along Europe's buffer zone with Asia.

• *A few more canvases to the left of Brandt's works is...*

Samuel Hirszenberg, *School of Talmudists:* Young Jewish students pore over the Talmud. One of them, deeply lost in thought, may be pondering more than ancient Jewish law. This canvas suggests the inclusion of Jews in Poland's cultural tapestry during this age. While still subject to pervasive bigotry here, many Jewish refugees found Poland to be a relatively welcoming, tolerant place to settle on a typically hostile continent.

• *Dominating the end of the room is...*

Józef Chełmoński, Four-in-Hand: In this intersection of worlds, a Ukrainian horseman gives a lift to a pipe-smoking nobleman. Feel the thrilling energy as the horses charge directly at you through splashing puddles.

• *Heading back toward the entrance, on the right wall, watch for...*

Witold Pruszkowski, *Water Nymphs:* Based on Slavic legends (and wearing traditional Ukrainian costumes), these mischievous, siren-like beings have just taken one victim (see his hand in the foreground) and are about to descend on another (seen faintly in the upper-right corner).

Beyond this painting are some travel pictures from Italy and France (including some that are very Impressionistic, suggesting a Parisian influence).

• *Flanking the entrance/exit door are two of this room's best works. First, on the right, is...*

Władysław Podkowiński, Frenzy: This gripping painting's title *(Szał),* tellingly, has also been translated as *Ecstasy* and *Insanity.* A pale, sensuous woman—possibly based on a socialite for whom the artist fostered a desperate but unrequited love—clutches an all-fired-up black stallion that's frothing at the mouth. This sexually charged painting caused a frenzy indeed at its 1894 unveiling, leading the unbalanced artist to attack his own creation with a knife (you can still see the slash marks in the canvas).

• *And finally, on the other side of the door is...*

Jacek Malczewski, *Introduction:* A young painter's apprentice on a bench contemplates his future. Surrounded by nature and with his painter's tools beside him, it's easy to imagine this as a self-portrait of the artist as a young man...wondering if he's choosing the correct path. Malczewski was an extremely talented Młoda Polska artist who tends to be overshadowed by his contemporary, Wyspiański. Viewing this canvas—and others by him—makes me feel grateful that he decided to stick with painting.

▲▲Czartoryski Museum (Muzeum Czartoryskich)

This eclectic collection, originally assembled by a precocious aristocrat to celebrate Poland's cultural heritage, is best known to visitors for one painting: Leonardo

da Vinci's masterful *Lady with an Ermine*—which alone warrants the ▲▲ rating. The museum also has an excellent (and rare) Rembrandt landscape. The rest of the collection is a historical jumble: decorative arts, tapestries, treasury items, Meissen porcelain figures, old flags and banners, portraits of kings and aristocrats, majolica pottery, ornate suits of armor, a ceremonial Turkish tent from the 1683 siege of Vienna, and more Czartoryski family portraits than anyone not named Czartoryski would ever care to see. I'd suggest a quick stroll through the rest of the collection, then linger over the Rembrandt and (especially) the stunning Leonardo. Oh, baby!

Cost and Hours: 38 zł, free on Tue; Tue-Sun 10:00-18:00, closed Mon; a short walk from the Florian Gate at Pijarska 15—enter near the brick skybridge, +48 12 370 54 66, http://mnk.pl.

Background: The museum's collection came about, in part, thanks to Poland's 1791 constitution (Europe's first), which inspired Princess Izabela Czartoryska to begin gathering bits and bobs of Polish history and culture. Soon after, when the Partitions dismantled the country, Izabela doubled down on this pursuit—assembling proud Polish bric-a-brac with the motto, "The past for the future," looking ahead to a time when Poland would be reconstituted. That would not happen within her lifetime; she fled with the collection to Paris after the 1830 insurrection. Her son, Adam Czartoryski—who purchased the Leonardo for his mom as a gift—was so influential during this period of exile that he was sometimes called the "uncrowned king of Poland." It took 45 years after the family fled for Izabela's grandson to return the collection to its present Kraków location. During World War II, the Nazis hauled the collection to Germany; although most of it has been returned, some pieces are still missing. The dusty old museum got a serious upgrade starting in 2010 and finally reopened in 2019.

◐ Self-Guided Tour: There are some basic English descriptions, but for the full story, invest in the somewhat long-winded but insightful audioguide (10 zł). Or just follow this selective self-guided commentary for an efficient visit. Spoiler alert: The two all-star paintings are essentially the last things you'll see on this tour. (If you'd like to get to them faster, consider skipping floor 1 and heading right up to floor 2, then speeding through the first few rooms.)

From the ticket desk, head through the lovely courtyard and take the stairs or elevator up to floor 1. You'll begin in two **Rooms of the Czartoryskis,** with portraits and busts of the members of this illustrious family, who were VIPs about two centuries ago. (Their red family crest—with a horseback knight raising his sword—decorates the windows.) You'll see their fancy sabers, ornate jackets and gowns, and a pair of ceremonial keys.

The next few rooms display Princess Czartoryska's collection of Polish artifacts roughly chronologically, by dynasty. In the **Room of the Jagiellonian Dynasty**—tucked among altar paintings, tapestries, tattered flags, and other precious objects—look for the 10 small portraits of the Jagiełło clan in a single frame, done by the workshop of Lucas Cranach the Younger (see his trademark, the small winged lion, in the corner of each one). The **Room of the Vasa Dynasty** is more militaristic, as this was a time of warfare—hence the emphasis on weaponry over simple beauty.

The **Room of the Victory of Vienna** commemorates that fateful battle in 1683, when the Polish King Jan III Sobieski led a pan-European army to success in defending the Austrian capital against an Ottoman siege. The room's centerpiece is a ceremonial tent and a Persian carpet like the ones used by the Ottomans in that battle. On display are actual weapons and equipment (shields, sabers, and saddles) used by the troops that day. Notice the winged hussar suit of armor—those rattling feathers made a fearsome sound when charging full-tilt on horseback. You'll also see Sobieski's ornate divinative shield and a ceremonial saber presented to him by the pope.

The **Room of the Saxons** illustrates how Poland's next dynasty—the Wettins (imported from Dresden, in today's Germany)—squandered their country's resources, ultimately hastening

KRAKÓW

its decline: Notice the expensive Meissen porcelain favored by the Wettins, and the wine glasses, goblets, and plates they used for one of their favorite pastimes...feasting.

The **Room of the Enlightenment**—a bright era for many European lands—coincides with Poland's darkest moment, when the country was chopped up and divided among land-hungry neighbors in a series of three Partitions. The large portrait shows Stanisław August Poniatowski, Izabela Czartoryska's cousin and the final Polish king, who took the throne at age 32 and presided over both Europe's first democratic constitution in 1791...and, just a few years later, the fall of his nation. One case displays his ceremonial swords and medals; the other shows some of his belongings: cane, fan, flute, and powder horn.

Then you'll enter a dimly lit wing with liturgical paraments (amber cross, vestments), then "Pompa Funebris," illustrating the pomp surrounding funeral rituals (see the tattered tombstone banner from 1660, and nearby, the smaller coffin portraits).

The last section on this floor shows off three rooms of **"Oriental Art"**: first from Persia (carpet) and India (bronze statues), then from China (fans, porcelain, a giant bronze dragon), then from Japan (find the display case of *netsuke*—minuscule sculptures carved in ivory or wood).

Now head upstairs to level 2 and cross over the skybridge—looking down over the beautifully restored courtyard at the center of the complex.

While downstairs was mainly about Poland, this floor showcases **European art.** The Antiquity Parlor features paintings, sculptures, and tapestries inspired by ancient Greece and Rome; the Medieval Parlor has gilded altarpieces and other church art; and Northern European Art from the 15th to the 17th century displays...well, exactly that, including some Habsburg portraits.

Finally, we come to the room called Age of the Rembrandt Period. Ignore all the also-rans in this room (for now) and head straight across to the dramatically lit painting: **Rembrandt van Rijn's** *Landscape with the Good Samaritan* (1638). This small, detailed painting depicting the popular parable is one of only a few known landscapes by Rembrandt. In the right foreground, the Samaritan helps the wounded man onto his horse as a little boy watches. To the left, much farther down the road (just beyond the waterfall), find the two tiny figures walking—the priest and the Levite who passed the injured man. The murky colors make it a little tricky to pick out all the details, but Rembrandt's trademark dramatic lighting creates a powerful scene.

There's a small, dimly lit room off of this Rembrandt hall—if you're not looking for it, it's easy to miss. But don't miss it! This is the room where you'll find **Leonardo da Vinci's** *Lady with an*

Ermine. This small (21 x 16 inches) but magnificently executed portrait of a 16-year-old young woman is a rare surviving work by one of history's greatest minds.

Spend some time lingering over the canvas (dating from 1489 or 1490). The subject is likely Cecilia Gallerani, the young mistress of Ludovico Sforza, the duke of Milanand Leonardo's employer. The ermine (white during winter) suggests chastity—thus bolstering Cecilia's questioned virtue—but is also a naughty reference to the duke's nickname, Ermellino—notice that his mistress is sensually, ahem, "stroking the ermine."

Painted before the *Mona Lisa*, the portrait was immediately recognized as revolutionary. Cecilia turns to look at someone, her gaze directed to the side. Leonardo catches this unguarded, informal moment, an unheard-of gesture in the days of the posed, front-facing formal portrait. Her simple body language and faraway gaze speak volumes about her inner thoughts and personality. Leonardo tweaks the generic Renaissance "pyramid" composition, turning it to a three-quarters angle, and softens it with curved lines that trace from Cecilia's eyes and down her cheek and sloping shoulders before doubling back across her folded arms. The background—once gray and blue—was painted black in the 19th century.

Using special lights and cameras, conservators have been able to virtually peel back layers of paint to see earlier "drafts" of the painting (Leonardo was known to tinker with his works over time). They've revealed that the ermine was likely not included in the original version. Perhaps Leonardo added it later as a nod to the duke.

Lady with an Ermine is a rare surviving portrait in oil by Leonardo. She's better preserved than her famous cousin in Paris *(Mona Lisa)*, and—many think—simply more beautiful. Can we be sure it's really by the enigmatic Leonardo? Yep—the master's fingerprints were found literally pressed into the paint (he was known to work areas of paint directly with his fingertips).

After this grand finale, you'll pass through the **Polish Hall**—painted a patriotic Polish red—displaying mementos of historical figures and events: gilded shields honoring mighty leaders, small sarcophagi with the remains of great Poles, portraits of monarchs, and flags and banners from the battlefield.

You'll finish by walking through some **temporary exhibits.** The museum also has an exhibit called **The Origins: Ancient Art**

KRAKÓW

Gallery—with items from Egypt, Greece, and Rome—but it costs extra and isn't worth it for most visitors.

Before you depart, ponder this: The museum technically owns a third masterpiece, **Raphael's** *Portrait of a Young Man,* but its whereabouts are unknown. Arguably one of the most famous and most valuable stolen paintings of all time, it's quite likely a self-portrait (but possibly a portrait of Raphael by another artist), depicting a Renaissance dandy, clad in a fur coat, with a self-satisfied smirk. Painted in 1513 or 1514 and purchased by a Czartoryski prince around the turn of the 19th century, the work was seized by the occupying Nazis during World War II. Along with the paintings by Leonardo and Rembrandt, this Raphael decorated the Wawel Castle residence of Nazi governor Hans Frank. But when Frank and the Nazis fled the invading Red Army at the end of the war, many of their pilfered artworks were lost—including the Raphael.

▲▲Stanisław Wyspiański Museum (Muzeum Stanisława Wyspiańskiego)

One of the great joys of travel is getting to know supremely talented artists you'd never heard of back home. And if you give Stanisław Wyspiański a chance, he may tick that box for you. This concise, beautiful museum assembles many of Wyspiański's best works, offering an ideal introduction to this leader of the Młoda Polska movement (Poland's answer to Art Nouveau; see the sidebar on page 263). If you enjoyed Wyspiański's stained glass and wall paintings in St. Francis Basilica, you'll find even more to like here.

Cost and Hours: 18 zł, free on Tue, audioguide available; Tue and Fri-Sun 10:00-17:00, closed Mon and Wed-Thu; a five-minute walk outside the Planty and west of the Old Town at Plac Sikorskiego 6, +48 12 433 57 60, http://mnk.pl.

Visiting the Museum: With just a few rooms spread over three floors, the museum is easy to see. Most of Wyspiański's works are not paintings or sculptures, but pastels, drawings, and designs for his grand-scale stained-glass windows; as these are fragile, specific items get shuffled in and out of the collection and some things mentioned here may not be on view. (You'll notice some of the more delicate works even have rolled-up curtains hanging above them so they can be covered for protection as needed.)

A dynamic bust of Wyspiański greets you outside the door. Inside, buy your ticket and head into the lone exhibition room on the main floor: **At Home,** featuring an array of landscapes of the countryside around Kraków (plus his iconic pastel of St. Mary's spires viewed from the balcony of the Cloth Hall); Toulouse-Lautrec-like portraits of Wyspiański's contemporaries (including one showing his friend and rival Josef Mehoffer—twice on a single portrait); a variety of self-portraits at various ages (from fresh-faced student, to young and hungry artist, to fatherly family man); and—perhaps most beautiful—intimate portraits of his family members in everyday poses that capture the universality of human experience. These works showcase the personality and endearing behavior of wife Helen, daughter Helenka, and sons Mietek and Staś.

Next head upstairs to level 1. The first room, **Elements,** is devoted to the stunning decorations Wyspiański created for St. Francis Basilica. The theme: a Franciscan love of nature. The centerpiece is a gigantic, life-sized design for his masterpiece—the *God the Father Let It Be* stained-glass window—displayed on a massive roller. Examine the designs for other windows and for the beautiful floral wall decorations. If you've seen these in situ—hanging high on dimly lit walls—this is a wonderful opportunity to examine the details up close.

Next, hook left into the room marked **Apollo Christ.** The focal point here is Wyspiański's design for a window he created for Kraków's House of the Medical Society—titled *Apollo, Copernicus' System.* In addition to Wyspiański's mastery of religious themes, he was captivated by the ancient world, especially the Greeks. Notice how this design juxtaposes the story of Apollo, with a pose resembling Jesus' Crucifixion, all wrapped up in the medieval breakthrough of a scientist who studied here in Kraków.

Also in this room, you'll find some of the plays Wyspiański wrote (and a costume he designed for one of them), designs for his stained-glass windows inside St. Mary's and the Dominican Church (both described elsewhere in this chapter), and some decorative arts handmade by Wyspiański—such as a bench and a tapestry with flowers.

Now cross over—again past the giant *God the Father* roller—to the next section, **Wawel Castle: Drama of Kings.** Yet another of Wyspiański's passions was the evocative architecture of the churches and castles of the Middle Ages. In this room, you'll see some sketches he made of such structures, both in Poland and abroad, and costume sketches (and an actual crown) he designed for a play he wrote about this era. In the center of the room is a model for an imaginative upgrade to Wawel Castle, which would have transformed it into the "Polish Acropolis" he felt it could and should become. (There's even a Circus Maximus-like elongated stadium at the foot of the hill.) If you've been to Wawel, you know that these plans never materialized.

Also in this room are two more large-scale masterpieces. One is Wyspiański's design *(Polonia)* for a stained-glass window in Lviv Cathedral (today in Ukraine, then part of Poland), and another is a hauntingly beautiful wintertime scene of the Planty, with black naked branches of trees lining a boulevard to a mirage-like Wawel Castle, hovering in the distance.

Now use the elevator (or stairs) to go down two floors, to level -1. Here are the two final, small exhibits: First is **My Books,** displaying books that Wyspiański wrote, designed illustrations for, or both. Then comes **Metamorphoses,** a deep dive into the plays that Wyspiański wrote (including another costume he designed). In this room, look for the VR headsets; you can sit down, strap one on, and go for a virtual "flight" over Kraków, zooming in for up-close visits to the locations that inspired many of the works we've seen here.

Leaving the museum, it's hard to shake the feeling that there must be many other artists whose fame will never reach the level of their talent. But at least for you and Wyspiański, that's no longer the case.

Bishop Erazm Ciołek Palace (Pałac Biskupa Erazma Ciołka)

This branch of the National Museum features two separate art collections. Upstairs, the extensive "Art of Old Poland" section shows off works from the 12th through the 18th century, with room after room of altarpieces, sculptures, paintings, and more. The "Orthodox Art of the Old Polish Republic" section on the ground floor offers a taste of the remote eastern reaches of Poland, with icons and other ecclesiastical art from the Orthodox faith. You'll see a sizeable section of the iconostasis (wall of icons) from the town of Lipovec. Both collections are covered by the same ticket and are very well presented in a modern facility. Items are labeled in English, but there's not much description beyond the rentable audioguide.

Cost and Hours: 18 zł, free on Tue; open Tue 10:00-18:00, Wed-Sun until 16:00, closed Mon; Kanonicza 17, +48 12 424 9371.

More National Museum Branches

While less interesting than the branches listed earlier, the National Museum's **Main Branch** (Gmach Główny) is worth a visit for museum completists. It features 20th-century Polish art and compelling temporary exhibits (a few blocks west of the Main Market Square at Aleja 3 Maja 1).

The **Szołayski House** (Kamienica Szołayskich), just one short block from the Main Market Square, features high-quality temporary exhibits; art lovers can check what's on (Plac Szczepański 9).

OTHER OLD TOWN ATTRACTIONS

▲▲Rynek Underground Museum (Podziemia Rynku)

In the early 2000s, a renovation of the Main Market Square's pavement unearthed a wealth of remains from previous structures. Now you can do some urban spelunking with a visit to this high-tech medieval-history museum, which is literally underground—beneath all the photo-snapping tourists on the Square above.

Cost and Hours: 32 zł, free on Tue; open Mon and Wed-Thu

10:00-19:00 (but closed the second Mon of each month), Tue until 14:00, Fri-Sun until 20:00, last entry 1.25 hours before closing, Rynek Główny 1, +48 12 426 5060, www.podziemiarynku.com.

Crowd-Beating Tips: This museum can sell out on busy days (especially on Tuesdays—when it's free and closes early—and on summer weekends). Because it's popular with school groups, late afternoons and evenings are quieter. At busy times, it's wise to book ahead online; alternatively, you can buy advance tickets in person at the Museum of Kraków office nearby, at the northwest corner of the Square (see "Tourist Information," earlier).

Visiting the Museum: The **entrance** faces St. Mary's and the pyramid-shaped fountain on the east side of the Cloth Hall (near

the fountain), but the **ticket office** is around on the opposite side of the same building. If you already have your tickets, just go to the entrance; if you need to buy tickets, circle around to the ticket office (see locations on page 242).

Once **inside,** climb down a flight of stairs and follow the numbered panels—1 to 70—through the exhibit (all in English). Modern museum technology illuminates life and times in medieval Kraków: Touchscreens let you delve into topics that intrigue you, 3-D virtual holograms resurrect old buildings, and video clips illustrate everyday life on unexpected surfaces (such as a curtain of fog).

All of this is wrapped around large chunks of early structures that still survive beneath the Square; several "witness columns" of rock and dirt are accompanied by diagrams helping you trace the layers of history. Interactive maps emphasize Kraków's Europe-wide importance as an intersection of major trade routes, and several models, maps, and digital reconstructions give you a good look at Kraków during the Middle Ages—when the Old Town looked barely different from today. You'll see a replica of a blacksmith's shop and learn how "vampire prevention burials" were used to ensure that the suspected undead wouldn't return from the grave. In the middle of the complex, look up through the glass of the Square's fountain to see the towers of St. Mary's above. Under the skylight is a model of medieval Kraków. While it looks much the same as today, notice a few key changes: the moat ringing the Old Town, where the Planty is today; and the several smaller market halls out on the Square.

Deeper in the exhibit, explore the long corridors of ruined buildings that once ran alongside the length of the Cloth Hall. There are many intriguing cases showing artifacts that shops would have sold (jewelry, tools, amber figurines, and so on). Also in this area, you'll find a corridor with images of the Square all torn up for the renovation, plus a series of five modern brick rooms, each showing a brief, excellent film outlining a different period of Kraków's history. These "Kraków Chronicles" provide a big-picture context to what otherwise seems like a loose collection of cool museum gizmos, and also help you better appreciate what you'll see outside the museum's doors.

Nearby: At the northwest corner of the Square, the **Krzysztofory Palace** (at #35) is the headquarters of Museum of Kraków. At the entrance is a visitors center where you can get information and book tickets and reservations for a variety of these sights (see "Tourist Information," earlier). The building also has a city **history museum,** which offers a sprawling lesson on two floors (28 zł, free on Tue, open daily 10:00-19:00, last entry 1.25 hours before closing, Rynek Główny 35, +48 12 426 5060). While the exhibits try hard, this is best left to serious historians or those looking for a mildly engaging rainy-day activity. In the basement, you'll find paintings, sculptures, suits of armor, busts of royalty, and old street signs; the most interesting section, at the end, is a film showing a virtual reconstruction of medieval Kraków. Upstairs, there are themed rooms (such as "spirituality" and "academia") to complete the story. You'll finish with a walk through a gigantic version of the nativity scenes that are featured in a festival each December.

Jagiellonian University Museum: Collegium Maius

Kraków's historic university building sits in a quiet area a short walk from the Square. While the atmospheric courtyard itself—described earlier in "Kraków's Royal Way Walk"—is worth ▲, the interior is less compelling. They routinely change details for how you enter—sometimes it's with a student guide, other times you're free to roam with an audioguide—but either way, you'll likely see the library, refectory (with a gorgeously carved Baroque staircase), treasury (including Polish filmmaker Andrzej Wajda's honorary Oscar), assembly hall, some old scientific instruments, and other academic artifacts.

Cost and Hours: 15 zł, free on Wed afternoons; guided tours depart 2/hour Mon-Fri 10:00-13:00; unaccompanied visits with audioguide Mon-Fri 13:00-17:00, Sat 10:00-15:00; closed Sun;

two short blocks west of the Square at Jagiellońska 15, +48 12 663 1448, www.maius.uj.edu.pl).

Dominican Church, a.k.a. Holy Trinity Church (Bazylika Trójcy Świętej)

In most towns, this church would be something special. In church-crazy Kraków, it's an also-ran. Still, it's easy to see (just a couple of blocks south of the Square) and worth a peek.

Cost and Hours: Free but donation requested, daily 6:30-13:00 & 16:00-20:00, facing Plac Dominikański at Stolarska 12.

Visiting the Church: Inside, you'll find a Neo-Gothic space that was rebuilt after a devastating 1850 fire. The unique metal chandeliers are one of many modern flourishes added during the late-19th-century restoration of the church. Climb the staircase in the left aisle to reach the chapel of St. Hyacinth. Locally known as St. Jacek, this early Dominican leader—called the "Apostle of the North"—is also the patron saint of pierogi (stuffed dumplings, similar to ravioli). During a famine, St. Jacek supposedly invented pierogi and—in a loaves-and-fishes-type miracle—produced plateful after plateful, feeding the desperate locals. His image adorns Kraków's annual Pierogi Cup contest, and to this day, when old-fashioned Poles are surprised, they might exclaim, *"Święty Jacek z pierogami!"* ("St. Jacek and his pierogi!"). Back down in the main part of the church, stroll slowly past the gorgeously carved wooden seats of the choir area (behind the altar); then, at the main altar, identify the three parts of the Trinity: Jesus (short beard), God (long beard), and Holy Spirit (beardless dove).

Archdiocesan Museum (Muzeum Archidiecezjalne)

This museum, in a building where St. John Paul II lived both as a priest and as a bishop, is a handy place to learn more about Kraków's favorite son (without making the long trip to the St. John Paul II Sanctuary on the outskirts or his family home museum in Wadowice—both described later). The exhibition includes John Paul II's personal effects, including clothes, handwritten notes, travel gear, bike, kayak, and skis—reminding visitors that he was one sporty pope. Then you'll tour the lavish private apartments where he lived from 1958 until 1967, as archbishop of Kraków. Throughout the collection are many portraits and photographs of the late pontiff—making his cult of personality almost palpable.

Cost and Hours: 10 zł or included in Wawel Cathedral ticket—see earlier, Tue-Sun 10:00-17:00, closed Mon, Kanonicza 19, +48 12 421 8963, www.archimuzeum.pl.

▲Stained-Glass Workshop and Museum (Pracownia i Muzeum Witrażu)

This fascinating, offbeat attraction sits on a busy urban street about a 10-minute walk beyond the Planty west of the Old Town. Its centerpiece is the actual stained-glass workshop, from 1902, where Stanisław Wyspiański and other great artists created windows that decorate many Kraków churches. I like how this place approaches a very old craft with a fresh, youthful enthusiasm. You can take a tour of the production facility, including a demonstration of stained glass being created by hand; you can join a workshop to make your own stained-glass creation; or you can just come and hang out in their chill, easygoing café, decorated with some beautiful samples. Check the schedule and book ahead online, for either the tour or the workshop.

Cost and Hours: 50 zł for a 45-minute tour including a demo, usually Tue-Sat at 12:00 and 15:00; tour plus window-making workshop around 300 zł, longer courses also available; café open Tue-Sat 11:30-13:30 & 14:30-16:30, Sat 10:00-17:00, closed Sun-Mon; kitty-corner from National Museum main branch at Aleja Zygmunta Krasińskiego 23, +48 512 937 979, www.muzeumwitrazu.pl.

Sights in Kazimierz

The neighborhood of Kazimierz (kah-ZHEE-mehzh), 20 minutes by foot or 5 minutes by tram southeast of Kraków's Old Town,

is the historic heart of Kraków's once-thriving Jewish community. After years of neglect, the district began a rejuvenation in the early 2000s. Today, while not quite as slick and polished as Prague's Jewish Quarter, Kazimierz's assortment of synagogues, cemeteries, and museums helps visitors appreciate the neighborhood's rich Jewish legacy. At the same time, Kazimierz also happens to be the city's edgy, hipster culture center—jammed with colorful bars, cre-

ative eateries, and designer boutiques. This unlikely combination—where somber synagogues coexist with funky food trucks—makes Kazimierz a big draw among all types of travelers.

Planning Your Visit: Try to visit any day except Saturday, when most Jewish-themed sights are closed (except the Old Synagogue and Galicia Jewish Museum). Monday comes with a few closures of non-Jewish sights: the Ethnographic Museum and Museum of Engineering and Technology. On Monday, the Schindler's Factory Museum is free, but it's open shorter hours and is more crowded than usual. It's always smart to **book ahead for the Schindler's Factory Museum,** which often sells out. For more suggestions on what to do in Kazimierz, see the Shopping, Entertainment, Sleeping, and Eating sections.

Etiquette: To show respect, men cover their heads while visiting a Jewish cemetery or synagogue. Most sights offer loaner yarmulkes, or you can wear your own hat.

Getting to Kazimierz: From Kraków's Old Town, it's about a 20-minute **walk.** From the Main Market Square, head down Ulica Sienna (near St. Mary's Church) and through the Planty park. When you hit the busy ring road, bear right and continue down Starowiślna for 15 more minutes. The **tram** shaves off a few minutes: Find the stop along the ring road, on the left-hand side of Ulica Sienna (across the street from the Poczta Główna, or main post office). Catch tram #3 or #24, and ride two stops to Miodowa. Walking or by tram, at the intersection of Starowiślna and Miodowa, you'll see a tiny park across the street and to the right. To reach the heart of Kazimierz—Ulica Szeroka—cut through this park. The same trams continue to the sights in Podgórze (including the Schindler's Factory Museum), described later.

To return to the Old Town, catch tram #3 or #24 from the intersection of Starowiślna and Miodowa (kitty-corner from where you got off the tram).

Information: An official **TI** is at Ulica Józefa 7.

KAZIMIERZ WALK

This self-guided walk, worth ▲▲, is designed to help you get your bearings in Kazimierz, connecting both its Jewish sights (mostly in "Part 1") and its eclectic other attractions, from trendy bars to underrated museums ("Part 2"). Allow about an hour for the entire walk, not counting museum, cemetery, and synagogue visits along the way. From the end of the walk, you can easily cross the river to this area's biggest sight, the Schindler's Factory Museum.

Part 1: Jewish Heritage on Ulica Szeroka

• *We'll start on Ulica Szeroka ("Broad Street")—the center of the neighborhood, which feels like more of an elongated square than a "street."*

Begin at the bottom (southern) edge of the small, fenced, grassy park, near the strip of restaurants. In the park with the tall trees, look for the low-profile, stone...

Kazimierz Monument

You're standing in the historical heart of Kraków's Jewish community. In the 14th century, King Kazimierz the Great enacted policies that encouraged Jews fleeing other kingdoms to settle in Poland—including in Kraków. He also founded this town, which still bears his name. Originally, Jews lived in the Old Town, but they were scapegoated after a 1495 fire and forced to relocate to Kazimierz. Back then, Kazimierz was still a separate  town, divided by a wall into Christian (west) and Jewish (east) neighborhoods. Ulica Szeroka was the main square of the Jewish community. Over time, Jews were more or less accepted into the greater community, and Jewish culture flourished here.

All that would change in the mid-20th century. The **monument** honors the "65 thousand Polish citizens of Jewish nationality from Kraków and its environs"—more than a quarter of the city's pre-WWII population—who were murdered by the Nazis during the Holocaust. When the Nazis arrived, they immediately sent most of Kraków's Jews to the ghetto in the eastern Polish city of Lublin. Soon after, they forced Kraków's remaining 15,000 Jews into a walled ghetto at Podgórze, across the river. The Jews' cemeteries were defiled, and their buildings were ransacked and destroyed. In 1942, the Nazis began transporting Kraków's Jews to death camps (including Płaszów, just on Kraków's outskirts; and Auschwitz-Birkenau).

Only a few thousand Kraków Jews survived the war. During the communist era, this waning population was ignored or mistreated. After 1989, interest in Kazimierz's unique Jewish history was faintly rekindled. But it was only when Steven Spielberg chose to film *Schindler's List* here in 1993 that the world took renewed interest in Kazimierz. (A local once winked to me, "They ought to build a statue to Spielberg on that square.") Although the current Jewish population in Kraków numbers only 200, Kazimierz has become an internationally known destination for those with an interest in Jewish heritage.

• *Facing the park, look to the left. The arch with the Hebrew characters marks the entrance to the...*

Kazimierz Walk

1. Kazimierz Monument
2. Old Jewish Cemetery & Jan Karski Statue
3. Old Shop Fronts
4. Hamsa Rest. & Jarden Bookshop
5. Klezmer-Hois Restaurant
6. New Jewish Cemetery
7. Rubinstein Birthplace
8. Popper Synagogue
9. Old Synagogue
10. Food Trucks
11. Isaac Synagogue
12. Plac Nowy
13. Meiselsa & Bożego Ciała Streets
14. Schindler's List Passage
15. Ulica Józefa
16. Plac Wolnica
17. Ethnographic Museum
18. Old Tram Depot
19. Museum of Engineering & Technology
20. Judah Square
21. Galicia Jewish Museum

▲▲Old Jewish Cemetery (Stary Cmentarz)

This small cemetery was used to bury members of the Jewish community from 1552 to 1800. With more than a hundred of the top Jewish intellectuals of that age buried here, this is considered one of the most important Jewish cemeteries in Europe.

Cost and Hours: 10 zł includes cemetery and attached Remu'h Synagogue; hours vary with demand—especially outside peak season—but generally open Sun-Fri 9:00-16:00, can be open until 18:00 May-Sept, closes earlier off-season and by sundown on Fri, closed Sat year-round, Ulica Szeroka 40.

Visiting the Cemetery: Walk under the arch, pay the admission fee, step into the cemetery, and survey the tidy rows of headstones. This early Jewish resting place (later replaced by the New Cemetery, described later) was desecrated by the Nazis during the Holocaust. In the 1950s, it was discovered, excavated, and put back together as you see here. Shattered gravestones form a mosaic **wall** around the perimeter.

Notice that many graves have a curved top or are engraved with an arch-like pattern—suggesting passage into another realm. As in all Jewish cemeteries and memorials, you'll see many small stones stacked on the graves. The tradition comes from placing stones—representing prayers—over desert graves to cover the body and prevent animals from disturbing it.

Behind the little synagogue to the left, in the elevated, fenced area near the tree, the tallest **tombstone** belonged to Moses Isserles (a.k.a. Remu'h), an important 16th-century rabbi. He is believed to have been a miracle worker, and his grave was one of the only ones that remained standing after World War II. Notice the written prayers crammed into the cracks and crevices of the tombstone.

Near the gate to the cemetery, step into the tiny **Remu'h Synagogue** (c. 1553, covered by cemetery ticket). Tight and cozy, this has been carefully renovated and is fully active. Notice the original 16th-century frescoed walls and ceilings, and the historic donation box at the door. For more on typical synagogue architecture, see the sidebar.

• *Back outside, turn left and continue up to the top of...*

Ulica Szeroka

Just above the cemetery gate, notice a bronze statue of a gentleman seated on a bench. This is a tribute to **Jan Karski** (1914-2000), a Catholic Pole and resistance fighter who published his eyewitness account *The Story of a Secret State* about the Holocaust in 1944. Karski—the ultimate whistleblower—was one of the first people who spoke out about Nazi atrocities, at a time when even many world leaders had only an inkling about what was happening in Hitler's realm. Karski's revelations, so shocking as to be literally unbelievable to many, went ignored by some key leaders—arguably extending the horrors of the Holocaust.

Just above that, at the top corner of the square, notice the side street with a row of rustic old Jewish **shop fronts,** which evoke the bustle of prewar Kazimierz. The Jewish names—Rattner, Weinberg, Nowak, Holcer—stand testament to the lively soul of this neighborhood in its heyday. This lane leads to Miodowa street, which you can follow left to reach two of Kazimierz's lesser-known synagogues (Tempel and Kupa, both described later).

The building at the top of the square houses the recommended **Hamsa** restaurant (with modern Israeli food) and **Jarden Bookshop,** which serves as an unofficial information point for the neighborhood and sells a wide variety of fairly priced books on Kazimierz and Jewish culture in the region (daily, Ulica Szeroka 2).

Kitty-corner from the bookshop, notice **Klezmer-Hois**—one of many restaurants offering live traditional Jewish klezmer music nightly in summer (for more on klezmer music and details on your options, see "Entertainment in Kraków," later).

The **New Jewish Cemetery**—less touristed and a striking contrast to the Old Jewish Cemetery we just saw—is a worthwhile detour, about a five-minute walk away (and described later in this section). To get there, cut through the grassy little lot between Jarden Bookshop and Klezmer-Hois, turn right, cross the busy street, then go through the railway underpass.

When you're ready to move on, do a 180 and head back downhill on Ulica Szeroka. You'll pass the little park again, then come to a row of lively, mostly Jewish-themed **restaurants** with outdoor tables. Some places along here typically feature outdoor klezmer music in good weather—allowing you to get a taste of this unique musical form before committing to a full meal.

Halfway down this side of the square, the green house at #14 is where **Helena Rubinstein** was born in 1870. At age 31, she emigrated to Australia, where she parlayed her grandmother's traditional formula for hand cream into a cosmetics empire. Many cosmetics still used by people worldwide today were invented by Rubinstein, who was just one of many illustrious Jewish residents of Kazimierz.

Two doors past the Rubinstein house, notice the round arch marking the courtyard of the **Popper Synagogue,** which is now home to an extensive bookstore that's worth a peek (daily).

Continue past the restaurants to the very bottom of Ulica Szeroka and pause at the steps before heading down into the sunken area around the Old Synagogue. To the synagogue's left, notice a short, reconstructed stretch of Kazimierz's 14th-century **town wall,** with a roofed rampart on top. This is a reminder that medieval Kazimierz was a separate city from Kraków. It's easy to read some history into a map of Kazimierz (you'll find one on the big panel in front of the Old Synagogue, down the stairs): Today's Starowiślna and Dietla streets—which frame off Kazimierz in a triangle of land hemmed in by the riverbank—were once canals (Kazimierz was built on an island). When King Kazimierz the Great—who reportedly didn't care much for Krakovians—founded this district in 1335, he envisioned it as a separate town to rival Kraków. It wasn't until around 1800 that the two towns merged.

• *The building at the bottom of the square is the...*

Old Synagogue (Stara Synagoga)

The oldest surviving Jewish building in Poland (15th century) sits eight steps below street level. Jewish structures weren't allowed to be taller than Christian ones— and so, in order to have the proper proportions, the synagogue's "ground floor" had to be underground. Today, the synagogue houses a good three-room museum on local Jewish culture, with informative English descriptions and a well-preserved main prayer hall (18 zł, free on Mon; Mon 10:00-14:00, Tue-  Sun until 17:00; shorter hours off-season; Ulica Szeroka 24, +48 12 422 0962).

• *A few more Jewish sights can be found in the surrounding streets; I'll point these out in "Part 2," though the rest of this walk focuses on a more recent chapter of the neighborhood.*

Part 2: Contemporary Kazimierz

• *Stand with your back to the Old Synagogue, at the top of the stairs, and turn left, heading up the little alley next to Szeroka 28—called Lewkowa.*

Hipster Kazimierz

Follow Lewkowa between some old buildings. When you pop out into an open area, angle right, then continue straight along Ulica Ciemna. Soon you'll hit an inviting little **pod of food trucks.** Pause here—perhaps while nursing an açaí smoothie, a Thai-style rolled ice cream, or a taco—and ponder the explosion of youthful culture that's taken place in Kazimierz over the last generation.

At the end of World War II, Kazimierz was badly damaged

The Synagogue

A synagogue is a place of public worship, where Jews gather to pray, sing, and read from the Torah. Most synagogues have similar features, though they vary depending on the congregation.

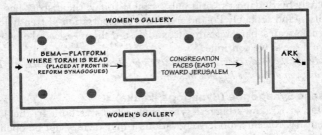

The synagogue generally faces, at least symbolically, toward Jerusalem (in Kraków, worshippers face east). At the east end is an alcove called the **ark,** which holds the Torah. These scriptures (the first five books of the Christian Old Testament) are written in Hebrew on scrolls wrapped in luxuriant cloth. The other main element of the synagogue is the **bema,** an elevated platform from which the Torah is read aloud (the equivalent of a pulpit in a Christian church). In traditional Orthodox synagogues, the bema is near the center of the hall, and the reader stands facing the same direction as the congregation. In other branches of Judaism, the bema is at the front, and the reader faces the worshippers. Orthodox synagogues have separate worship areas for men and women, usually with women in the balcony.

The synagogue walls might be decorated with elaborate patterns of vines or geometric designs, but never statues of people, which could be considered idol worship. A lamp above the ark is always kept lit, as it was in the ancient temple of Jerusalem, and candelabras called menorahs also recall the temple. Other common symbols are the two tablets of the Ten Commandments given to Moses, or a Star of David, representing the Jewish king's shield.

At a typical service, the congregation arrives at the start of Sabbath (Friday evening). As a sign of respect toward God, men don yarmulkes (small round caps). As the cantor leads songs and prayers, worshippers follow along in a book of weekly readings. At the heart of the service, everyone stands as the Torah is ceremoniously paraded, unwrapped, and placed on the bema. Someone—the rabbi, the cantor, or a congregant—reads the words aloud. The rabbi ("teacher") might give a commentary on the Torah passage.

KRAKÓW

and depopulated. And so it remained for generations, as the communist authorities brushed Jewish heritage under the rug. By the early 2000s, Kazimierz's artistically dilapidated buildings, low rents, and easy proximity to the Old Town became enticing to creative young people. A variety of artsy entrepreneurs took root here, beginning with a cluster of ramshackle, rustic bars (inspired partly by Budapest's "ruin pub" scene). Today, the district has the city's (and probably Poland's) highest concentration of trendy food trucks, cafés, bars, restaurants, and design shops—several of which we'll see as we continue.

• *From the food trucks, continue straight ahead (on Izaaka street). This leads you along the left side of...*

Isaac Synagogue (Synagoga Izaaka)

One of Kraków's biggest synagogues, this was built in the 17th century. Recently under renovation, it may or may not be open to visitors. If you can get inside, notice how the walls in the prayer hall are decorated with giant paintings of prayers for worshippers who couldn't afford to buy books.

• *Just past Isaac Synagogue is the heart of Kazimierz's nightlife zone (also bustling by day). Dive in, passing some characteristic cafés. Then jog right at the glitzy Plac Nowy 1 beer hall to reach...*

Plac Nowy

Kazimierz's endearing "new" market square, Plac Nowy (plats NOH-vee), retains much of the gritty flavor of the district before tourism and gentrification. The circular brick building in the center is a slaughterhouse where Jewish butchers would properly kill livestock, kosher-style. Today, its windows are filled with little stand-up eateries, most of them featuring the traditional, local, pizza-like *zapiekanki*. Circle the market hall and browse for a snack (for more on the Plac Nowy scene, see "Eating in Kraków," later). This square is also ringed by several fun and funky bars—enjoyable by day but hopping at night.

• *Leave Plac Nowy along Meiselsa street (to the left from where you entered, past the yellow Jewish Cultural Center). After one block, pause at the intersection of...*

Meiselsa and Bożego Ciała Streets

The Holocaust was a dark chapter that dominates Kazimierz's history. But this intersection is a reminder that, up until the Nazis arrived, Kazimierz was a place where Jews and Christians lived side by side in relative har-

mony. Notice the street names, which mix Jewish and Catholic namesakes: Ulica Meiselsa ("Meisels Street"—honoring a deeply respected 19th-century rabbi) and Ulica Bożego Ciała ("Corpus Christi Street"—named for the towering brick church you can see just ahead). As if to celebrate the ecumenism of this intersection, a street artist has painted a graffiti Gene Kelly on the wall...very "happy again" indeed that Kazimierz is blossoming and full of life.
• *Backtrack a few steps up Meiselsa and duck into the courtyard on the right, under the dilapidated arch.*

Schindler's List Passage

This courtyard is a popular tour-ist spot thanks to its brush with fame as a location for some key scenes in *Schindler's List* (find the black-and-white stills from the movie—and actual historic pho-tos—partway down on the right). Spielberg connection aside, this is a particularly evocative setting to nurse a relaxing drink in the at-mospheric beer garden.
• *Carry on all the way through the passage. You'll emerge at...*

Ulica Józefa: Design Street

This street has Kazimierz's highest concentration of funky, one-off boutiques: jewelry, fashion, housewares, and more. It's a great place to browse. There's also a TI just across the street.
• *When you're ready to move along, take Ulica Józefa right a few steps to the intersection with Ulica Bożego Ciała, turn left, and follow it a long block. You'll pass Corpus Christi Church on your left, then arrive at...*

Plac Wolnica

Remember that Kazimierz was originally a separate town from Kraków. This was its main market square, designed to one-up its crosstown rival—right down to the dramatic, red-brick Catholic church on the corner (Corpus Christi).

The former Kazimierz Town Hall at the far end of the square houses an unusually good **Ethnographic Museum** (Muzeum Etnograficzne)—worth ▲. If you're interested in Polish folk cul-ture, it's worth a visit (18 zł, free on Tue, open Tue-Sun 10:00-19:00, closed Mon, Ulica Krakowska 46, +48 12 430 6023, www.etnomuzeum.eu). On the ground floor, you'll find models of tra-ditional rural Polish homes, as well as musty replicas of the in-teriors (like an open-air folk museum moved inside). The exhibit continues upstairs, where each in a long lineup of traditional Polish

KRAKÓW

folk costumes is identified by specific region. Follow the one-way route through exhibits on village lifestyles, rustic tools, and musical instruments (including a Polish bagpipe). A highlight is the explanation of traditional holiday celebrations—from elaborate crèche scenes at Christmas to a wall of remarkably painted Easter eggs. Some items are labeled in English, but it's mostly in Polish. The top floor features temporary exhibits.

• *There's more to see in Kazimierz. But if you're pooped, several trams run from here back to Wawel Castle, then on to the Plac Wszystkich Świętych stop in the heart of the Old Town (catch tram from along Krakowska street, behind the Ethnographic Museum).*

To continue the walk from Plac Wolnica, head up Ulica Św. Wawrzyńca (at the corner where you entered the square, with the Corpus Christi Church on your left).

Ulica Św. Wawrzyńca: Industrial Kazimierz

By the late 19th century, Kazimierz was not just a Jewish cultural hotspot but also a center of local industry. (It's no coincidence that Oskar Schindler had his factory near here.) After the church, on your left, look for the glass-and-steel arched roof of the Industrial Age **old tram depot,** which now houses a recommended brewpub. In sunny summer weather, the pebbly courtyard is filled with happy drinkers.

Across the street, notice the many tram tracks leading into a courtyard with several more storage sheds for local trams. This gorgeously restored complex now houses the **Museum of Engineering and Technology** (Muzeum Inżynierii i Techniki)—yet another of Kraków's many engaging, well-presented museums (closed Mon, Ulica Św. Wawrzyńca 15, www.mit.krakow.pl).

Continue along Ulica Św. Wawrzyńca a few more steps. At the intersection with Wąska, **Judah Square** (Skwer Judah) is a vacant lot with a gaggle of enticing food carts watched over by a giant mural. Commissioned for Kraków's Jewish Cultural Festival in 2013, the illustration was painted by Israeli street artist Pilpeled. It shows a young boy who feels small and scared but lionhearted nevertheless—a poignant symbol for the Holo-

caust survivors of Kazimierz. If you're ready for a meal or snack, you'll find several good options here.

• *A half-block farther down Ulica Św. Wawrzyńca is another place for refreshment, the recommended Craftownia (Polish microbrews on tap, on the left at #22). Next you'll reach the intersection with Dajwór street.*

Turn left here and walk a few steps up the street; on the right, you'll find the...

Galicia Jewish Museum (Galicja Muzeum)

This museum, worth ▲ and housed in a restored Jewish furniture factory, focuses on the present rather than the past. The permanent "Traces of Memory" photographic exhibit shows today's remnants of yesterday's Judaism in the area around Kraków (a region known as "Galicia"). From abandoned synagogues to old Jewish gravestones flipped over and used as doorsteps, these giant postcards of Jewish artifacts (with good English descriptions) ensure that an important part of this region's heritage won't be forgotten. Temporary exhibits complement this permanent collection (20 zł, daily 10:00-18:00, one block east of Ulica Szeroka at Ulica Dajwór 18, +48 12 421 6842, www.galiciajewishmuseum.org). The museum also serves as a sort of cultural center, with a good bookstore and café.

• *Our Kazimierz orientation walk is finished. From here, you have several options. To **return to Ulica Szeroka**, where we began, walk up Dajwór street past the museum, then angle left through the park at the reconstructed chunk of town wall—you'll wind up at the Old Synagogue.*

*For the next two options, you'll first head back down to Ulica Św. Wawrzyńca, turn left, and walk one more block to the intersection with Starowiślna street. Just to the left on Starowiślna, look for the tram stops. The tram stop on the far side of the street takes you **back to the Old Town** (tram #3 or #24). From the tram stop on the near side of the street, tram #3 or #24 zips you to the **sights in Podgórze**—including Ghetto Heroes' Square and the Schindler's Factory Museum (both described later). You can also reach the Podgórze sights on foot by turning right on Starowiślna and crossing the bridge (about a 10-minute walk).*

MORE JEWISH SIGHTS IN KAZIMIERZ

In addition to the sights connected by the walk above, here's another cemetery and a few more synagogues to round out your Jewish Kazimierz experience.

▲New Jewish Cemetery (Nowy Cmentarz)

This burial place—much larger than the Old Jewish Cemetery—has graves of those who died after 1800. It was vandalized by the Nazis, who sold many of its gravestones to stonecutters and used others as pavement in their concentration camps. Many have since been cemented back in their original positions, while others—which could not be replaced—have been used to create the moving mosaic wall and Holocaust monument (on the right as you enter). Most gravestones are in one of four languages: Hebrew (generally the oldest, especially if there's no other language, though some are newer "retro" tombstones), Yiddish (sounds like a mix of Ger-

man and Hebrew and uses the
Hebrew alphabet), Polish (Jews
who assimilated into the Polish
community), and German (Jews
who assimilated into the German community). The earliest
graves are simple stones, while
later ones imitate graves in Polish Catholic cemeteries—larger,
more elaborate, and with a long
stone jutting out to cover the

body. Notice that some new-looking graves have old dates. These
were most likely put here well after the Holocaust (or even after the
communist era) by relatives of the dead.

Cost and Hours: Free, Sun-Fri 8:00-16:00, closed Sat. It's
tricky to find: Go under the railway tunnel at the east end of Ulica
Miodowa and turn right as you emerge; look for the gate with the
small *cmentarz żydowski* sign.

Synagogues

In addition to the three synagogues mentioned on the Kazimierz
Walk (Old Synagogue, Isaac, and Remu'h), others welcome visitors. Each of these charges a small admission fee and is closed Saturdays. The **High Synagogue**—so called because its prayer room is
upstairs—displays changing exhibits, most of which focus on the
people who lived here before the Holocaust (Ulica Józefa 38). **Tempel Synagogue** (Synagoga Templu) has the grandest interior—big
and dark, with elaborately decorated, gilded ceilings and balconies (corner of Ulica Miodowa and Ulica Podbrzezie). The **Jewish
Community Centre** next door offers activities both for members of
the local Jewish community and for tourists (lectures, genealogical
research, Friday-night Shabbat meals, Hebrew and Yiddish classes,
and so on; https://linktr.ee/jcckrakow). Nearly across the street,
the smaller **Kupa Synagogue** (Synagoga Kupa)—clean and brightly decorated—sometimes hosts temporary exhibits (Miodowa 27).

NEAR KAZIMIERZ: PODGÓRZE

The neighborhood called Podgórze (POD-goo-zheh), directly
across the Vistula from Kazimierz, has one of Kraków's most famous sights: Schindler's Factory Museum. I've listed the area's
sights in the order you'll reach them as you come from Kazimierz
or the Old Town.

Background: This is the neighborhood where the Nazis
forced Kraków's Jews into a ghetto in early 1941. (*Schindler's List*
and the films in the Pharmacy Under the Eagle museum depict
the sad spectacle of Jews loading their belongings onto carts and

trudging over the bridge into Podgórze.) Non-Jews who had lived here were displaced to make way for the new arrivals. The ghetto was surrounded by a wall with a fringe along the top that resembled Jewish gravestones—a chilling premonition. A short section of this wall still stands along Lwowska street. The tram continued to run through the middle of Podgórze, without stopping—giving Krakovians a harrowing glimpse at the horrifying conditions inside the ghetto.

Getting There: To go directly to Ghetto Heroes' Square, continue through Kazimierz on tram #3 or #24 (described earlier, under "Getting to Kazimierz") to the stop called Plac Bohaterow Getta. Or you can ride the tram or walk 10 minutes across the bridge from the end of my Kazimierz Walk.

Ghetto Heroes' Square (Plac Bohaterow Getta)

This unassuming square is the focal point of the visitor's Podgórze. Today, the square is filled with a monument consisting of 68 empty

metal chairs—representing the 68,000 people deported from here. This is intended to remind viewers that the Jews of Kazimierz were forced to carry all of their belongings—including furniture—to the ghetto on this side of the river. It was also here that many Jews waited to be sent to extermination camps. The small, gray building at the river end of Ghetto Heroes' Square feels like a train car inside, evocative of the wagons that carried people from here to certain death.

▲Pharmacy Under the Eagle (Apteka pod Orłem)

This small but good museum, on Ghetto Heroes' Square, tells the story of Tadeusz Pankiewicz, a Polish Catholic pharmacist who chose to remain in Podgórze when it became a Jewish ghetto. During this time, the pharmacy was an important meeting point for the ghetto residents, and Pankiewicz and his staff heroically aided and hid Jewish victims of the Nazis. (Pankiewicz survived the war and was later acknowledged by Israel as one of the "Righteous Among the Nations"—non-Jews who risked their lives to help the Nazis' victims during World War II. You'll see his medal on display in the white memorial room at the end of the museum.) Today, the pharmacy hosts an exhibit about the Jewish ghetto.

Cost and Hours: 18 zł, free on Wed; open Wed-Sun 10:00-17:00, closed Mon-Tue; Plac Bohaterow Getta 18, +48 12 656 5625.

KRAKÓW

Visiting the Museum: You'll enter into the re-created pharmacy, where the "windows" are actually screens that show footage from the era. Push buttons, pull out drawers, answer the phone—it's full of interactive opportunities to better understand ghetto life. You'll learn about people who worked in the pharmacy (including riveting interviews with eyewitnesses—some in English, others subtitled) and hear Pankiewicz telling stories about that tense time. You'll also learn a bit about the pharmacy business from that period.

▲▲Schindler's Factory Museum (Fabryka Emalia Oskara Schindlera)

One of Europe's top museums about the Nazi occupation fills some of the factory buildings where Oskar Schindler and his Jewish employees worked. The museum tells the wartime story not only of Schindler and his workers but also of all of Kraków. It's loaded with in-depth information (all in English), and touchscreens invite you to learn more and watch eyewitness interviews. Scattered randomly between the exhibits are replicas of everyday places  from the age—a photographer's shop, a tram car, a hairdresser's salon—designed to give you a taste of 1940s Kraków. Note that you'll see nothing of the actual factory or equipment, as the threat of the advancing Red Army forced Schindler to move his operation lock, stock, and barrel to Nazi-occupied Czechoslovakia in 1944.

Cost and Hours: 32 zł, free on Mon; open Mon 10:00-14:00, Tue-Sun until 18:00 (except closed the first Tue of each month), last entry 1.5 hours before closing; +48 12 257 1017, www.muzeumkrakowa.pl.

Book Ahead: It's always wise to book ahead for this very busy and popular sight, which frequently sells out. To get your choice of time slots, book at least several days in advance—the sooner, the better—at www.bilety.mhk.pl. (For Mondays, when it's free and extremely busy, you may not be able to prebook online; check the website for the latest policy.) Or, if you arrive in Kraków without a ticket and it's already sold out, stop by the Museum of Kraków Visitors Center on the Main Market Square (see "Tourist Information" on page 241). Ideally, swing by that office the day before you'd like to tour the museum; that's when unsold tickets, previously bought up by local agencies, are returned and become available to procrastinators.

Crowd-Beating Tips: Once inside, the museum can be un-

KRAKÓW

pleasantly congested. For a more leisurely experience, the best strategy is to arrive right when it opens, or later in the day—if you have an average appetite for information, planning to arrive 2 hours before closing time should be about right.

Getting There: It's in a gloomy industrial area a five-minute walk from Ghetto Heroes' Square (Plac Bohaterow Getta): Go up Kącik street (to the left of the big, glass skyscraper), go under the railroad underpass, and continue two blocks, past MOCAK (the Museum of Contemporary Art in Kraków, described later) to the second big building on the left (Ulica Lipowa 4). Look for signs to *Emalia*.

Visiting the Museum: Entering on the ground floor, you'll find special exhibits and a "film café" (interesting for fans of the movie) with refreshments. Then head upstairs to the first floor.

First Floor: The 35-minute **film**, called *Lipowa 4* (this building's address), sets the stage with interviews of both Jews and non-Jews describing their war-

time experience (find it just off the museum's first, circular room; subtitled in English, it runs continuously).

From here, the one-way route winds through the permanent exhibit, called **"Kraków Under Nazi Occupation 1939-1945."** First, while pleasant music plays, "stereo-

scopic" (primitive 3-D) photos of prewar Kraków capture an idyllic age when culture flourished and the city's Jews (more than one-quarter of the population) blended more or less smoothly with their Catholic-Pole neighbors. But then, a video explains the Nazi invasion of Poland in early September of 1939: It took them only a few weeks to overrun the country (which desperately awaited the promised help of their British and French allies, who never arrived).

Through the next several rooms, watch the film clip of SS soldiers marching through the Main Market Square—renamed "Adolf-Hitler-Platz"—and read stories about how the Nazis' *Generalgouvernement* attempted to reshape the life of its new capital, "Krakau." (Near the tram car, look for the decapitated head of the Grunwald monument, which had been a powerful symbol of a Polish military victory over German forces.) You'll see the story of a newly German-owned shop selling Nazi propaganda and learn how professors at Kraków's Jagiellonian University were arrested to prevent them from fomenting rebellion among their students. During

KRAKÓW

Oskar Schindler (1908-1974) and His List

Steven Spielberg's instant-classic, Oscar-winning 1993 film, *Schindler's List,* brought the world's attention to the inspiring story of Oskar Schindler, the compassionate German business-man who did his creative best to save the lives of the Jewish work-ers at his factory in Kraków. Spielberg chose to film the story right here in Kazimierz, where the events actually unfolded.

Oskar Schindler was born in 1908 in the Sudetenland (cur-rently part of the Czech Republic, then predominantly German). Early on, he displayed an idiosyncratic interpretation of ethics that earned him both wealth and enemies. As Nazi aggressions escalated, Schindler (who was very much a Nazi) carried out es-pionage against Poland; when Germany invaded the country in 1939, Schindler smelled a business opportunity. Early in the Nazi occupation of Poland, Schindler came to Kraków and lived in an apartment at Ulica Straszewskiego 7 (a block from Wawel Castle). He took over the formerly Jewish-owned Emalia factory at Ulica Lipowa 4, which produced metal pots and pans that were dipped into protective enamel; later, the factory also began producing ar-maments for the Nazi war effort. The factory was staffed by about 1,000 Jews from the nearby Płaszów Concentration Camp, which was managed by the ruthless SS officer Amon Göth (depicted in *Schindler's List*—based on real events—shooting at camp inmates for sport from his balcony).

At a certain point, Schindler began to sympathize with his Jewish workers, and he increasingly did what he could to protect them and offer them better lives. Schindler fed them far better than most concentration-camp inmates and allowed them to sell some of the pots and pans they made on the black market to make money. After he saw many of his employees and friends murdered during an SS raid in 1943, he ramped up these efforts. He would come up with bogus paperwork to classify those threat-

this time, even Polish secondary schools were closed—effectively prohibiting learning among Poles, whom the Nazis considered in-ferior. But Polish students continued to meet clandestinely with their teachers. You'll also see images of Hans Frank—the hated puppet ruler of Poland—moving into the country's most important symbol of sovereignty, Wawel Castle.

The exhibit also details how early Nazi policies targeted Jews with roundups, torture, and execution. (Down the staircase is an eerie simulation of a cellar prison.) As the Nazis ratcheted up their genocidal activities, troops swept through Kraków on March 3, 1941, forcing all the remaining Jews in town to squeeze into the newly created Podgórze ghetto. At the bottom of the stairs, look for the huge pile of plunder—Jewish wealth stolen by the Nazis.

Second Floor: Climb upstairs using the long **staircase,** which

ened with deportation as "essential" to the workings of the factory—even if they were unskilled. He sought and was granted permission to build a "concentration camp" barracks for his workers on the factory grounds, where they lived in far better conditions than those at Płaszów. These lucky few became known as *Schindlerjuden*—"Schindler's Jews."

As the Soviet army encroached on Kraków in October 1944, word came that the factory would need to be relocated west, farther from the front line. While Schindler could easily have simply turned his workers over to the concentration camp system and certain death—as most other industrialists did—he decided to bring them with him to his new factory at Brünnlitz (Brněnec, in today's Czech Republic). He assembled a list of 700 men and 300 women who worked with him, along with 200 other Jewish inmates, and at great personal expense, moved them to Brünnlitz. At the new factory, Schindler and the 1,200 people he had saved produced grenades and rocket parts—virtually all of them, the workers later claimed, mysteriously defective.

After the war, Schindler—who had spent much of his fortune protecting his Jewish workers—hopped around Germany and Argentina, repeatedly attempting but failing to break back into business (often with funding from Jewish donors). He died in poverty in 1974. In accordance with his final wishes, he was buried in Jerusalem, and today his grave is piled high with small stones left there by appreciative visitors. He has since been named one of the "Righteous Among the Nations" for his efforts to save Jews from the Holocaust. Thomas Keneally's 1982 book *Schindler's Ark* brought the industrialist's tale to a wide audience that included Steven Spielberg, who vaulted Schindler to the ranks of a cultural icon.

KRAKÓW

was immortalized in a powerful scene in *Schindler's List*. At the top of the stairs on the right is a small room that served as "Schindler's office" for the film (though it's been determined that his actual office was elsewhere; we'll see it soon).

You'll walk through a corridor lined by a replica of the wall that enclosed the **Podgórze ghetto** and see poignant exhibits about the horrific conditions there (including a replica of the cramped living quarters). The Nazis claimed that Jews had to be segregated here, away from the general population, because they "carried diseases."

Continue into the office of Schindler's secretary, with exhibits about Schindler's life and video touchscreens that play testimonial footage of Schindler's grateful employees. Then proceed into the actual **Schindler's office.** The big map (with German names for cities) was uncovered when the factory was being restored. Because Schindler's short tenure here was the only time in the factory's history that these Polish place names would appear in German, it's believed that this map was hung over his desk. Facing the map is a giant monument of enamel pots and pans, like those that were made in this

factory. There are 1,200 pots—one for each Jewish worker that Schindler saved. Inside the monument, the walls are lined with the names on Schindler's famous list. The creaky floorboards are intentional: a reminder that the Nazis knew every step you took.

Proceeding through the exhibit, you'll learn more about everyday life—both for ghetto dwellers and for everyday non-Jewish Krakovians, including the Polish resistance (see the Home Army's underground print shop). More eyewitness accounts relate the terrifying days of March 13 and 14, 1943, when the Podgórze ghetto was liquidated, sending survivors to the nearby Płaszów Concentration Camp. The replica of the Płaszów quarry, where inmates were forced to work in

unimaginably difficult conditions, provides a poignant memorial for those who weren't fortunate enough to wind up on Schindler's list.

Now head all the way back down to the ground floor.

Ground Floor: Exhibits here capture the uncertain days near the end of the war in the summer of 1944, when Nazis arrested between 6,000 and 8,000 suspected saboteurs after the Warsaw Uprising and sent them to Płaszów (see the replica of a basement hideout for 10 Jews who had escaped the ghetto); and later, when many Nazis had fled Kraków, leaving residents to await the Soviet Union's Red Army (see the replica air-raid shelters). The Red Army arrived here on January 18, 1945—at long last, the five years, four months, and twelve days of Nazi rule were over. The Soviets caused their own share of damage to the city before beginning a whole new occupation that would last for generations...but that's a different museum.

Finally, walk along the squishy floor—evoking how life for anyone was unstable and unpredictable during the Nazi occupation—into the **Hall of Choices.** The six rotating pillars tell the stories of people who chose to act—or not to act—when they witnessed atrocities. Think about the ramifications of the choices they made...and what you would have done in their shoes. The final room holds two books: a white book listing those who tried to help, and a black book listing Nazi collaborators. Exiting the museum, notice the portraits of Oskar Schindler's workers who lived long and happy lives after the war.

Nearby: Before heading back to downtown Kraków, consider paying a visit to the superb **Museum of Contemporary Art in Kraków** (Muzeum Sztuki Współczesnej w Krakowie)—or MOCAK for short—that fills the warehouse buildings once occupied by Schindler's workers, behind this main building (closed Mon, www.mocak.pl). Or, for a glass of wine, head just a few doors down from the museum to find the delightful **Krakó Slow Wines** (marked *Lipowa 6F*). This mellow, inviting wine bar and shop is well stocked with wines mostly from Central Europe (daily, +48 669 225 222.

John Paul II Pilgrimage Sights

Catholics coming to Kraków eager to walk in the footsteps of St. John Paul II appreciate the city's dazzling churches and its Archdiocesan Museum. And for most, that's enough. But true pilgrims head for worthwhile sights outside the city center: two sanctuaries related to John Paul II on the outskirts of Kraków and the St. John Paul II Family Home Museum in the town of Wadowice, an hour's drive away.

Sanctuaries in Kraków
The two biggest, most impressive JPII destinations are about four miles south of Kraków's Old Town, in the Łagiewniki neighborhood. While the main attraction here for pilgrims is the John Paul II Sanctuary, historically and geographically you'll come first to the Divine Mercy Sanctuary—so I've covered that first. The sights aren't worth the trek for the merely curious, but they offer a glimpse of the deep faith that characterizes the Polish people.

Getting There: A **taxi** or **Uber** from downtown takes 20-30 minutes and makes things easy. By public transit, you can take **tram #8** from Plac Wszystkich Świętych in the Old Town (next to St. Francis Basilica) or **tram #10** from the Poczta Główna stop, along the Planty at the eastern edge of the Old Town; on either tram, ride about 20 minutes and get off at the Łagiewniki SKA stop. From there, take the pedestrian underpass, turn right, cross the train tracks, and huff a few minutes uphill along the wall to find the entrance to the complex. (You can see the glass steeple of the church from the tram stop—a handy visual landmark.)

After touring the Divine Mercy sights, you'll head to the St. John Paul II Sanctuary—a 15-minute walk or a short, inexpensive taxi or Uber trip. To go directly to the John Paul II Sanctuary from the Old Town, take tram #10 and ride it all the way to the Sanktuarium Bożego Miłosierdzia stop.

Divine Mercy Sanctuary
(Sanktuarium Bożego Miłosierdzia)

This complex, built around a humble red-brick convent, honors the early 20th-century St. Faustina, who saw a miraculous vision of Jesus that became a powerful religious symbol for many Catholics. Today, pilgrims from around the world revere the relics both of Faustina and of John Paul II (who advocated for her sainthood), and learn more about her story from the convent's present-day sisters—many of whom speak English.

Background: One cold and blustery evening in 1931, Sister Faustina Kowalska (1905-1938) answered the convent doorbell to find a beggar asking for some food. Faustina brought some soup to the man, who revealed his true nature: a figure of Jesus Christ clad in a white robe, with one hand raised in blessing and the other touching his chest. Emanating from his chest were twin beams of light: red (representing blood, the life of souls) and white (water, which through baptism washes souls righteously clean). Transformed by her experience, Faustina worked with an artist to create a painted version of the image—called the Divine Mercy—which is one of the most important symbols of Polish Catholicism.

Always frail in health, Faustina died at 33—the same age as Jesus. The story of Faustina deeply moved a young Karol Wojtyła. When he became pope, he dedicated the first Sunday after Easter as the day of Divine Mercy worldwide. In 2000, he made his fellow Krakovian the first Catholic saint of the third millennium. To properly revere the newly important St. Faustina, a futuristic church and visitors center was built alongside her original convent.

Cost and Hours: All parts of the complex are free to enter, but donations are happily accepted. Each part has slightly different hours (listed later; www.faustyna.pl). Note that the daily 15:00 "Hour of Mercy" service—in both the chapel and the modern church—is worth planning around.

Visiting the Complex: Entering the complex through the

side gate, look uphill to find a **walkway** with flags from around the world and plaques translating the Divine Mercy's message—"Jesus, I trust in you"—in dozens of languages.

Just before entering the **original chapel,** look up and to the right—the window with the flowers marks the cell where Faustina died. Inside the chapel (daily 6:00-21:15), the altar to the left of the main altar displays an early copy of Faustina's Divine Mercy painting. Her relics are in the white case just below; in the white kneeler just in front of the chapel, notice the little reliquary holding one of her bones (which worshippers can embrace as they pray).

Leaving the chapel, turn left and go to the far end of the accommodations building. Enter the door on the right to find the **replica of Faustina's cell.** While this is a newer building, here they've created Faustina's convent cell, including many of her personal effects. Drop a coin in the slot for an evocative headphone description of these items, and of the vision of Jesus that put her convent on the map (usually open daily 8:30-18:00).

From here, head downhill and circle around the large brick building—passing (on the right) an area for outdoor Mass.

Dominating the campus is the futuristic, glass-and-steel **main church,** which was consecrated by Pope John Paul II on his final visit to Poland in 2002 (daily 7:00-20:00). The lower level has a variety of small chapels, each one donated by Catholic worshippers in a different country (Germany, Hungary, Slovakia, and so on)—and each with a dramatically different style.
The central chapel on this level has a modern altar and another bone of St. Faustina. Upstairs, the main sanctuary is a sleek cylindrical space with wooden sunbeams sharply radiating from the altar area. That altar—framed by the gnarled limbs of windblown trees, representing the suffering of human existence—contains a replica of the Divine Mercy painting, flanked by the woman who saw the vision (Faustina, on the right) and the Polish pope who made it a worldwide phenomenon (John Paul II, on the left).

Head back out to the terrace surrounding the church. The bold **tower**—as tall as St. Mary's on Main Market Square—has an elevator to a glassed-in viewpoint offering panoramas over the Divine Mercy campus, the adjacent John Paul II Sanctuary complex, and—on the distant horizon—the spires of Wawel Cathedral and Kraków's Old Town (daily 8:00-19:00). Near the base of the tower

KRAKÓW

is a **canopy** where Mass is said on Divine Mercy Sunday each year, before a crowd of 100,000 who fill the fields below.

Connecting to the St. John Paul II Sanctuary: You can see the rectangular, brick tower of the JPII Sanctuary from the Divine Mercy Sanctuary; it's about a 15-minute walk through the park (downhill, then uphill). Alternatively, you can make a short, inexpensive trip in a taxi (see if any are waiting at the parking lot in front of the sanctuary's hotel—the boxy, white building; otherwise, ask the receptionist to call one, or order an Uber).

St. John Paul II the Great Sanctuary (Sanktuarium Św. Jana Pawła II Wielkiego)

This complex, funded entirely by private donors, celebrates the life and sainthood of Kraków's favorite son. A visit has two parts: the giant sanctuary (church) and the nearby museum.

Cost and Hours: Sanctuary—free, daily 7:30-19:00, until 18:00 in winter, www.sanktuariumjp2.pl; museum—15 zł, daily 9:00-17:00.

Sanctuary of St. John Paul II the Great: This hypermodern church is big and splendid. In the **downstairs** area, the cen-

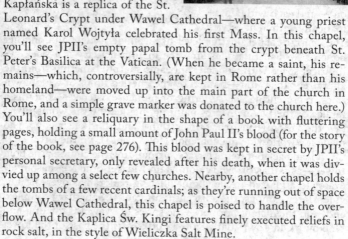

tral chapel features paintings of JPII's papal visits to various pilgrimage sites, both in Poland (Częstochowa) and abroad (Fátima, Lourdes). Ringing that central area is a variety of interesting smaller chapels.

On the outer wall, look for three in particular: The Kaplica Kapłańska is a replica of the St. Leonard's Crypt under Wawel Cathedral—where a young priest named Karol Wojtyła celebrated his first Mass. In this chapel, you'll see JPII's empty papal tomb from the crypt beneath St. Peter's Basilica at the Vatican. (When he became a saint, his remains—which, controversially, are kept in Rome rather than his homeland—were moved up into the main part of the church in Rome, and a simple grave marker was donated to the church here.) You'll also see a reliquary in the shape of a book with fluttering pages, holding a small amount of John Paul II's blood (for the story of the book, see page 276). This blood was kept in secret by JPII's personal secretary, only revealed after his death, when it was divvied up among a select few churches. Nearby, another chapel holds the tombs of a few recent cardinals; as they're running out of space below Wawel Cathedral, this chapel is poised to handle the overflow. And the Kaplica Św. Kingi features finely executed reliefs in rock salt, in the style of Wieliczka Salt Mine.

Head upstairs to the sleek, modern **main sanctuary.** The concrete structure supports large walls, providing a canvas for dynamic mosaics of Bible stories. Above the main altar, in the middle, you'll see the Three Kings delivering their gifts to the Baby Jesus and the Virgin Mary—with St. John Paul II serenely overlooking the scene. Other scenes include Adam and Eve, Jesus calming the storm, the wedding feast at Cana, and the Last Supper. In the back-left corner, a smaller chapel displays the blood-spattered vestments that St. John Paul II was wearing on May 13, 1981, when he was shot by a would-be assassin.

The sanctuary anchors a sprawling complex of conference facilities and other attractions for pilgrims. Poke around. The museum, described next (and on the right as you exit the sanctuary's main door), is the sight most worth visiting.

St. John Paul II Museum: This collects many of the gifts bestowed on the beloved pope (African carved masks and ivory tusks; Latin American tapestries; the key to the city of Long Branch, New Jersey; a pair of glass doves of peace given to him—perhaps with a touch of irony—by US vice president Dick Cheney), ornate worship aids (chalices, crosses, and so on), and modern art that celebrates the modern pope and his life's work. There are also personal items, from his papal ski and hiking gear to the place settings from his Vatican dinner table to his stylish red leather shoes. You'll also see the throne from his last visit to Poland in 2002, and a replica of the humble room across the street from St. Francis Basilica where he stayed on visits back to his homeland.

Returning to Kraków: Taxis may be waiting at the sanctuary; otherwise, you can ask the museum desk to call one for you (or order an Uber). Or, you can walk downhill through the park to find the Sanktuarium Bożego Miłosierdzia stop; tram #10 goes back to the Old Town.

Wadowice—St. John Paul II's Hometown

Karol Wojtyła was born and lived until age 18 in Wadowice (VAH-doh-veet-seh, pop. 20,000), about 30 miles southwest of Kraków. This working-class town, known for its woodworkers and factories, seems an unassuming place to have produced such a globally influential figure. And today, it's a place of pilgrimage for admirers of the man young "Lolek" would become.

Getting There: Wadowice is about an hour's drive from Kraków. As it's roughly in the same direction as Auschwitz, a local guide or driver can help you connect both places for one very busy day of contrasts—though you'll want to time things carefully. (If using public transit, doing both is not realistic.) Buses run frequently from Kraków to Wadowice's train station (about 1.25

hours one-way, departs every 20 minutes); from there, you can walk about 10 minutes to the main square and museum.

Visiting Wadowice: The town of Wadowice has a beautifully restored **main market square** (Plac Jana Pawła II). Information

panels around the square tell the story of the local boy done very, very good, and plaques in the cobbles list the cities and countries John Paul II visited. At the top of the square (opposite the church), the green *cukiernia* (pastry shop) sells the local cream cake, *kremówki*, which the pope raved about—having a slice is practically obligatory on a visit to Wadowice.

The square is dominated by the pretty Baroque steeple of the home **church** of young Karol Wojtyła (officially the Basilica of the Presentation of the Blessed Virgin Mary). Today, a larger-than-life statue of John Paul II stands outside that church, whose outer walls are plastered with plaques, photos, and information boards about the saint. Inside the church, in the chapel left of the main altar, you can see the font where he was baptized (a photo of him visiting the font as pope hangs on the wall nearby). He also took his First Communion and served as an altar boy here.

Immediately to the right of the church, across a narrow lane, stands the house where Karol Wojtyła was born and grew up—now an impressive museum.

▲▲St. John Paul II Family Home Museum

This thoughtfully presented multimedia museum tells the story of Karol Wojtyła, his journey to the papacy, and his legacy. It fills four

floors of the tenement building where his family lived through his adolescence. Worth ▲▲▲ for the faithful, it's engaging and informative to anyone—though detractors will note the complete omission of any criticism. The museum is essentially an exercise in lionizing a giant historical figure, and that it does very well; it's a well-executed combination of important artifacts and stirring storytelling.

Cost and Hours: 39 zł includes audioguide, free on Tue; April-Oct Wed-Mon 9:00-18:00, Tue from 12:00, Nov-March until 16:00, May-Sept open until 19:00 Fri-Sun, closed last Tue of month year-round; last entry 1.25 hours before closing; on the main square next to the town church at Ulica Kościelna 7, +48 33 823 2662, https://domjp2.pl). Be sure to book ahead online to visit on Tuesdays, when the museum is free and very busy.

Tours: You can see the museum on your own (with an audioguide) or join a guided tour. If you already know the story of John Paul II, you may prefer to see it on your own to linger over the riveting exhibits—which offer lots to unpack—at your own pace. A tour is handy for those looking for an efficient introduction (or a refresher) on his life story. English tours run irregularly—check and book ahead on the website.

Visiting the Museum: You'll begin with a wall of photographs featuring Karol Wojtyła's parents and his youth—back when he was known as Lolek. The apartment in this tenement building was above a Jewish-run general store; that storefront has been re-created in the entryway. Inside is an homage to the approximately 20 percent of young Karol's neighbors who were Jewish, many of whom died in the Holocaust. You'll also see a hologram reconstruction of the town synagogue (destroyed by the Nazis) and footage of John Paul II's historic visits to the Rome synagogue and the Wailing Wall in Jerusalem. (As pope, he was noted for his ecumenism—which the museum credits partly to his many Jewish friends and neighbors here in Wadowice.)

Next, you'll learn of Karol's deep spiritual ties to the nearby village of Kalwaria Zebrzydowska, which he visited more than 100 times. And you'll see the skis and hiking gear he used to explore the nearby hills.

Upstairs is the three-room **apartment** where Karol's family lived. Most of the furniture is from the period, but not actually the family's; a few exceptions are in glass cases. You'll see the parlor; the bedroom, where Karol was born and which he later shared with his father (see the two single beds); and the kitchen. The kitchen table looks out at a sundial on the side of the adjacent church. The motto Karol saw there every day—"Time flies; eternity dwells"—became one of his mantras. Perhaps this soulfulness at such a young age was inspired by the many losses in his life: He lost his mother at age 9, his brother at age 12, and his father at age 20.

Then you'll step into the **museum** proper. The large red room covers the 40 years Karol Wojtyła spent in Kraków—from his time as a student, and then as a priest, archbishop, and cardinal, until he was called to the papacy. These stages are represented by the various robes, actually worn by him, displayed here.

Next, the replica of St. Peter's boat marks his transition to the papacy. You'll see a room about the attempt on his life in 1981 (the actual handgun used is in a glass case in the floor); a hall commemorating his eight pilgrimages home to Poland (the first three

KRAKÓW

while it was still controlled by the communists); a rotunda with a replica of the Jubilee Doors at St. Peter's Basilica in Rome, under a dome supported by giant illustrated versions of his encyclicals; and a room documenting the staggering 129 countries Pope John Paul II visited during his 104 pilgrimages. In the floor, transparent boxes hold soil from many of these countries (commemorating the pope's tradition of kissing the ground in each place), and a nearby display case shows off some unusual mementos from those travels: an embroidery with the Lord's Prayer in Inuit, a Congolese statue of Jesus with strongly African features, a Marvel comic book about the life of John Paul II, and a Burger King-branded cardboard periscope for catching a glimpse of the Popemobile over the crowds.

Use the elevator to descend to the basement and continue the visit. You'll see the kayak he took on camping trips with his students in the 1970s, and a room dedicated to the World Youth Days he was instrumental in creating. (Conspicuously absent is any mention of John Paul II's inaction when it came to protecting children who were molested by priests on his watch.)

The exhibit ends with the final days of John Paul II's earthly life; you'll see his bedside clock, stopped at the hour of his death, and a Bible displaying the final words he heard (as a nun was reading to him when he died). The red hall features a backup copy of the book of his funeral Mass, which famously flipped closed in the wind; and actual red robes worn by attendees. Then, the white room commemorates his sainthood—with an illustration of St. John Paul II surrounded by some of the many people he himself had sainted as pope; and walls of letters left behind by visitors to Rome around the time of his funeral, asking for his intercession.

Rounding out the museum are some temporary exhibits. You'll return onto the square where young Karol Wojtyła spent his childhood. Now...time for some cream cake. Lolek would have wanted it that way.

Sights Outside Kraków

The following sights—an impressive salt mine, a purpose-built communist town, and an unusual earthwork—require a bus, tram, or train ride to reach. Also near Kraków are the St. John Paul II Family Home Museum in Wadowice (described above) and the poignant memorial at Auschwitz-Birkenau Concentration Camp (covered in the next chapter).

▲▲Wieliczka Salt Mine (Kopalnia Soli Wieliczka)

Wieliczka (veel-EECH-kah), a salt mine southeast of Kraków, is beloved by Poles. Hundreds of feet beneath the ground, the mine is filled with sculptures that miners have lovingly carved out of the

salt. You'll explore this unique gallery—learning both about the art
and about medieval mining techniques—on a required tour. Though
the sight is a bit overrated, it's
unique and practically obligatory if
you're in Kraków for a few days. In
my experience, about half of those
who visit love Wieliczka, while half
feel it's a waste of time—but it can
be hard to predict which half you're
in. Read this description before you
decide. And expect a lot of walking.

Cost and Hours: The standard
"Tourist Route" costs 126 zł and is by guided tour only. English-
language tours leave at the top of each hour, daily 8:00-18:00 (these
are first and last tour times), with shorter hours off-season. More
in-depth routes (such as the interactive "Miners' Route," where
visitors wear coveralls and helmets and operate some of the old
equipment) are explained on the website.

Information: The mine is in the town of Wieliczka at Ulica
Daniłowicza 10 (+48 12 278 7302, www.kopalnia.pl).

Crowd-Beating Tips: This popular sight can be packed, and
there's a strict limit on how many people can be in the mine at once.
It's busiest between 10:00 and 16:00—try to arrive before or after
those times (the ticket office opens at 7:30; since the last English
tour leaves at 18:00 in summer, arriving in the afternoon can be
a good way to stretch your sightseeing day). It's most crowded on
weekends and in the summer and overrun on long holiday weekends. Given the possibility of selling out, it's smart to **book an
entry time** on the website in advance (no extra charge).

Getting There: The salt mine is 10 miles from Kraków. By
far the easiest option is to hop on **train SKA1** at Kraków's main
train station (2/hour, 7 zł, 25 minutes, get off at Wieliczka Rynek-
Kopalnia; from there, walk up through the parking lot and follow
signs to the Daniłowicza shaft and entrance, about 5 minutes). In
a pinch, you can take **bus #304** (at the Dworzec Główny Zachód
stop, on Ogrodowa street, at the opposite side of Galeria Krakowska mall from the train station); while these depart frequently, they
take longer (about 40 minutes) and are subject to traffic delays. **Private drivers** also make this trip (see page 251).

Visitor Information: While taking pictures is allowed, flash
photos often don't turn out, thanks to the irregular reflection of
the salt crystals. Dress warmly—the mine is a constant 57 degrees
Fahrenheit. Before entering, you'll have to check large bags.

Eating: There's a good little **$ cafeteria** deep down in the

KRAKÓW

mine, at the end of the tour route. Up at the surface is a wide range of eateries, from snack stands to sit-down restaurants.

Background: Going all the way back to Neolithic times, prehistoric tribes gathered salt from springs in this area. In the 1280s, Wieliczka Salt Mine began producing salt in earnest. Under Kazimierz the Great, one-third of Poland's income came from these precious deposits—back in an age when salt was called "white gold" and was extremely valuable for its ability to preserve foods. (The Romans even paid workers in salt—*salarium,* the origin of our word "salary.") The mines were so important that Kazimierz the Great enacted laws protecting the miners—the first known instance of worker-protection laws in Europe. Wieliczka was controlled by the Polish crown and, after the Partitions, by the Austro-Hungarian Empire (which outfitted miners with military-style uniforms). During this time, around the Industrial Revolution (and under efficient Austrian management), the mine hit peak productivity.

Wieliczka miners spent much of their lives underground, leaving for work before daybreak and returning after sundown, rarely emerging into daylight. To pass the time, beginning in the 17th century, miners carved figures, chandeliers, and even entire underground chapels out of the salt. For many modern visitors, these carvings are the most memorable part of Wieliczka.

Until just a few years ago, the mine still produced salt. Today's miners—about 400 of them—primarily work on maintaining the 200 miles of chambers. This entire network is supported by pine beams—over time, the salt strengthens the wood (some you'll see are more than 200 years old), whereas metal would rust. Per tradition, the wood beams are painted white to reflect the dim light of the miners' oil lamps. Today, visitors see only about 1.5 percent of the sprawling mines. (You would not want to visit the original medieval mines, which have tunnels only about three feet tall.)

Visiting the Mine: For the main tour ("Tourist Route"), head for the Daniłowicz shaft, and buy your ticket if you haven't already. At the appointed time, find the English tour area to wait for your guide, who leads you 380 steps down a winding staircase. If you've always wanted to experience true vertigo, peer between the banisters on your way down. Once at level 1, you begin a 1.5-mile stroll, generally downhill (more than 800 steps down altogether), past 20 of the mine's 2,000 chambers (with signs ex-

plaining when they were dug), finishing 443 feet below the surface (at level 3). When you're done, an elevator beams you back up.

As you spelunk, your guide offers a canned commentary about the history of the mines. You'll learn how the miners lived and worked, using horses who spent their entire adult lives without ever seeing the light of day. You'll see the gigantic horse-pulled wheels used to operate lifts within the mines and find out why igniting pockets of methane gas near the ceiling was the most dangerous part of the job (the mortality rate for miners was about 1 in 10). All along the way, you'll walk through tunnels caved out of the rock salt; although it can be dark in color (mixed with other minerals such as sandstone and gypsum), it's about 90 percent pure salt. To transport the salt out of the mine, the miners would either carve it into big blocks or crush it and pour it into barrels.

The tour takes you through vast underground caverns, past subterranean lakes (32 percent salt—like the Black Sea, the maximum allowed by nature), and introduces you to some of the mine's many sculptures. You'll see Copernicus (who actually visited here in the 15th century), an army of salt elves, the Polish military hero Józef Piłsudski, and this region's favorite son, St. John Paul II.

Expect to be wowed by the enormous **Chapel of St. Kinga,** carved over three decades in the early 20th century. Look for the salt-relief carving of the Last Supper (its 3-D details are astonishing, considering it's just six inches deep). The chapel is still used for services every Sunday morning at 7:30.

From there, you'll see a few more chambers, including one with a big lake and a brief sound-and-light show. Your tour finishes in a deep-down shopping zone about 1.5 hours after you started. From here you can decide whether to return to the surface or add on the Mine Museum.

Returning to the Surface: You'll loop around through a handy cafeteria, then take an old-school elevator through the Daniłowicz shaft, back up to where you began. (If it's extremely busy, they may send you up the modern Regis shaft, which pops you out closer to the town center of Wieliczka—about a 10-minute walk through a pretty park back to the entrance building.)

Optional Add-On—Mine Museum: If you're not pooped, you can tack on a visit to the museum (included in your ticket)—which adds about an hour and a mile more walking. While overkill for most, the museum provides a bit more historical context. A guide will take you through the exhibits, showing you the fancy Habsburg-era miner uniforms; historic maps and etchings of the networks of mines, and cutaway scenes of life below the surface; tools and mining equipment (including a variety of Aladdin-style oil lamps, and huge slings used to lower horses into the mines); a photo gallery of famous visitors, including kings, queens, popes, presidents, and Lech Wałęsa; and a remarkably detailed model of the town of Wieliczka circa 1645.

Nearby: Near the parking lot, you'll see the **"Graduation Tower,"** a modern fort-like structure with a wooden walkway up top. The tower is designed to evaporate and then condense the supposedly very healthy brine from deep underground. The resulting moist, salty air is used to treat patients with lung problems. While locals are prescribed visits here, for most tourists it's not worth the extra money.

▲Nowa Huta

Nowa Huta (NOH-vah HOO-tah, "New Steel Works"), an enormous planned workers' town five miles east of central Kraków, offers a glimpse into the stark, grand-scale aesthetics of the communists. Although challenging to appreciate on your own, it's particularly well suited to a guided tour (options noted below). While Nowa Huta is lost on many visitors, it's a must for those curious for a look at large-scale artifacts of the communist period.

Getting There: Tram #4 goes from near Kraków's Old Town (catch the tram on the ring road near Kraków's main train station, at the Dworzec Główny stop) along John Paul II Avenue (Aleja Jana Pawła II) to Nowa Huta's main square, Plac Centralny (about 30 minutes total), then continues a few minutes farther to the main gate of the Tadeusz Sendzimir Steelworks—the end of the line. From there, it returns to Plac Centralny and back to Kraków.

Tours: For a thoughtful look at Nowa Huta, book with **Kraków Urban Tours** (see page 251). Or, for something looser and more off-the-wall, consider Mike Ostrowski's **Crazy Guides,** which offers private tours to Nowa Huta in genuine communist-era vehicles (mostly Trabants and Polski Fiats) with a laid-back hipster guide (€110/2 people for a 1.5-hour tour by car; €155/2 people for 2.5-hour version that adds a walking tour; see www.crazyguides. com for other options and to book, +48 500 091 200). If you're already hiring a **local guide** or **private driver** in Kraków, consider paying a little extra to add a quick spin through Nowa Huta.

Background: Nowa Huta was the communists' idea of paradise. It's one of only three towns outside the Soviet Union that were custom-built to showcase socialist ideals. (The others are Dunaújváros—once called Sztálinváros—south of Budapest, Hungary; and Eisenhüttenstadt—once called Stalinstadt—near Brandenburg, Germany.) Completed in just 10 years (1949-1959), Nowa Huta was built here primarily because the Soviets felt that smart and sassy Kraków needed a taste of heavy industry. Farmers and villagers were imported to live and work in Nowa Huta. Many new residents, who weren't accustomed to city living, brought along their livestock (which grazed in the fields around unfinished buildings).

For commies, Nowa Huta was idyllic: Dad would cheerily ride the tram into the steel factory, mom would dutifully keep house, and the kids could splash around at the artificial beach and learn how to cut perfect red stars out of construction paper. But Krakovians had the last laugh: Nowa Huta, along with Lech Wałęsa's shipyard in Gdańsk, was one of the home bases of the Solidarity strikes that eventually brought down the regime. Now, with the communists long gone, Nowa Huta remains a major suburb of Poland's cultural capital, with a whopping 200,000 residents.

Touring Nowa Huta: Nowa Huta's focal point used to be known simply as **Central Square** (Plac Centralny), but in a fit of poetic justice, it was later renamed for the anticommunist crusader, Ronald Reagan.

A map of Nowa Huta looks like a clamshell: a semicircular design radiating from Central/Reagan Square. Numbered streets fan out like spokes on a wheel, and trams zip workers directly to the immense factory.

Nowa Huta's designers found inspiration in a surprising source: the Italian Renaissance (which, thanks to the textbook Renaissance design of the Cloth Hall and other landmarks, Soviet architects considered typically Polish). Notice the elegantly predictable arches and galleries that would make Michelangelo proud. The settlement was loosely planned on the gardens of Versailles (both with axes radiating from a central hub).

Nowa Huta was delightfully orderly, primly painted, impeccably maintained, and downright beautiful...if a little boring. It was practical, too: Each of the huge apartment blocks is a self-contained unit, with its own grassy inner courtyard, school, and shops. Each is labeled with *Os.* (meaning "section"), plus a name and a number. Driveways, which appear to dead-end at underground garage doors, lead to vast fallout shelters.

Wander around. Poke into the courtyards, which often are filled with green parks, cheerful playgrounds, and ventilation for the fallout shelters beneath. The enclosed architecture makes you feel safe...but also *monitored*.

Reflect on what it would be like to live here. It may have been more pleasant than you imagine; the looming buildings are packed with happy little apartments filled with color, light, and warmth. These days, Nowa Huta is a very desirable place to live, partly because everything is smartly designed to be close at hand and easily connected to the city center by public transit—precisely what today's urban planners aspire to.

For those interested to learn more, Museum of Kraków operates a **Nowa Huta Museum** (Muzeum Nowej Huty) along the main road south of Central/Reagan Square (closed Mon-Tue, Os. Centrum E 1, www.muzeumkrakowa.pl).

The wide boulevard running northeast of Central/Reagan Square, now called Solidarity Avenue (Aleja Solidarności, lined with tracks for tram #4), leads to the **Tadeusz Sendzimir Steelworks.** Originally named for Lenin, this factory was supposedly built using plans stolen from a Pittsburgh plant. It was designed to be a cog in the communist machine—reliant on iron ore from Ukraine and therefore worthless unless Poland remained in the Soviet Bloc. Down from as many as 40,000 workers at its peak, the steelworks now employs about 10,000. Today, there's little to see other than the big sign, stern administration buildings, and smokestacks in the distance. Examine the twin offices flanking the sign—topped with turrets and a decorative frieze inspired by Italian palazzos, these continue the Renaissance theme of the housing districts.

Another worthwhile sight in Nowa Huta is the **Lord's Ark Church** (Arka Pana, several blocks northwest of Central/Reagan Square on Ulica Obrońców

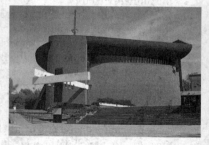

Krzyża). Back when he was archbishop of Kraków, Karol Wojtyła fought for years to build a church in this most communist of communist towns. When the regime refused, he insisted on conducting open-air Masses before crowds in fields, until the communists finally capitulated. No "official" building supplies were allowed to be used; all materials had to be sourced through back channels. Consecrated in 1977, the Lord's Ark Church has a Le Corbusier–esque design that looks like a fat, exhausted Noah's Ark resting on Mount Ararat—encouraging Poles to persevere through the deluge of communism. Inside, the giant crucifix depicts Christ in agony...while also, seemingly, about to take flight. The Carrara marble altar was donated by Italian Catholics.

Kościuszko Mound (Kopiec Kościuszki)

On a sunny day, the parklands west of the Old Town are a fine place to get out of the city and commune with Krakovians at play. On the outskirts of town is the Kościuszko Mound, a nearly perfectly conical hill erected in 1823 to honor Polish and American military hero Tadeusz Kościuszko. The mound incorporates soil that was brought here from battlefields where the famous general fought, both in Poland and in the American Revolution. Later, under Habsburg rule, a citadel with a chapel was built around the mound, which provided a fine lookout over this otherwise flat terrain. And more recently, the hill was reinforced with steel and cement to prevent it from eroding away. You'll pay to enter the walls and walk to the top—up a curlicue path that makes the mound resemble a giant soft-serve cone—and inside you'll find a modest Kościuszko museum. While not too exciting, this is a pleasant place for an excursion on a nice day.

Cost and Hours: 24 zł, includes museum, mound open daily 9:00-dusk, museum open daily 9:30-19:00—shorter hours off-season, café, +48 12 425 1116, www.kopieckosciuszki.pl.

Getting There: Ride tram #1 (from in front of the Wyspiański Pavilion or the main post office) to the end of the line, called Salwator. From here, you can either follow the well-marked path uphill for 20 minutes or hop on bus #100 to the top.

Shopping in Kraków

Two of the most popular Polish souvenirs—amber and pottery—come from areas far from Kraków. You won't find any great bargains on those items here, but several shops specializing in them are listed below. Somewhat more local are the many wood carvings you'll see.

The **Cloth Hall,** smack-dab in the center of the Main Market Square, is the most convenient place to pick up Polish souvenirs. It has a good selection at respectable prices (summer Mon-Fri 9:00-18:00, Sat-Sun until 15:00—but many stalls remain open later; winter Mon-Fri 9:00-16:00, Sat-Sun until 15:00).

Jewelry

The popular **amber** *(bursztyn)* you'll see sold around town is found on northern Baltic shores; if you're also heading to Gdańsk, wait until you get there (for more on amber, see page 471). One unique alternative that's a bit more local is **"striped flint"** *(krzemień pasiasty),* a stratified stone that's polished to a high shine. It's mined in a very specific subregion near Kraków. Each piece has its own unique wavy, sandy patterns.

Jewelry shops abound in the Old Town. For a good selection of striped flint, amber, and other jewelry, try the no-name shop on **Plac Mariacki,** the little square facing the side entrance of St. Mary's Church; they also have a selection of Polish folk costumes in the basement (at #9—look for *Amber Souvenir* in window). A few

Kraków's Old Town Shopping & Entertainment

OLD MARKET

DŁUGA

PADEREWSKIEGO

KARMELICKA

ŁOBZOWSKA

ASNYKA

#24 Stary Kleparz

SŁAWKOWSKA

BARBICAN

FLORIAN GATE

PIJARSKA

CZARTORYSKI MUSEUM

GARBARSKA

DUNAJEWSKIEGO

Planty

SZUJSKIEGO

DOLNYCH MŁYNÓW

JÓZEFA

SW. MARKA

200 Meters

200 Yards

KRUPNICZA

Plac Szczepański

OLD 5 4

SW. JANA

FLORIAŃSKA

18

SZPITALNA

SZOLAYSKI HOUSE

24

#24 Teatr Bagatela

PODWALE

SZEWSKA

SZCZEPAŃSKA

KRZYSZTOFORY PALACE (HISTORY MUSEUM)

Main Market Square

SW. TOMASZA

STUDENSKA

JAGIELLOŃSKA

7

19

ST. MARY'S

WYSPIAŃSKI MUSEUM

Plac Sikorskiego

COLLEGIUM MAIUS

SW. ANNY

CLOTH HALL 1

20

21

Small Market Square

JABŁONOWSKICH

COLLEGIUM NOVUM

TOWN HALL TOWER

15

22 2

23

SIENNA

PIŁSUDSKIEGO

GOŁĘBIA

OLSZEWSKIEGO

8

16

11

6

BRACKA

GRODZKA

SIENNA

ARCH-BISHOP'S PALACE

DOMINIKAŃSKA

STOLARSKA

DOMINICAN CHURCH

WC

← To Airport, Auschwitz, Kościuszko Mound, Stained-Glass Workshop & Museum & National Museum Main Branch

WISLNA

FRANCISZKAŃSKA

#8 Plac Wszystkich Świętych

TOWN

SMOLEŃSK

17

ST. FRANCIS

Planty

Planty

WYSPIAŃSKI PAVILION

STRASZEWSKIEGO

POSELSKA

ZWIERZYNIECKA

FELICJANEK

MILK BAR

SENACKA

STS. PETER & PAUL 14

Mary Mag. Square

SAREGO

BISHOP ERAZM CIOŁEK PALACE

GRODZKA

ST. ANDREW'S

KANONICZA

ARCHDIOCESAN MUSEUM

POWIŚLE

PODZAMCZE

SW. IDZIEGO

SW. GERTRUDY

CATHEDRAL

CATHEDRAL MUSEUM

WAWEL HILL

WC

INNER COURTYARD

Vistula River

WC

DRAGON STATUE

SANDOMIERSKA TOWER

BERNARDYŃSKA

ST. BERNARDINO'S

STRADOMSKA

KONOPNICKIEJ

To 25 ↓

KOLETEK

KRAKÓW

Shopping

1. Cloth Hall
2. Plac Mariacki Jewelry
3. Ceramika Bolesławiecka
4. Dekor Art
5. Mila & Chopin Gallery/Royal Chamber Orchestra Hall
6. Folkstar
7. Krakuska
8. Szambelan
9. To Ulica Józefa Shops
10. Kacper Global Shoes
11. Pasaż 13 Mall
12. Galeria Krakowska
13. Galeria Kazimierz

Entertainment

14. Sts. Peter & Paul Church
15. St. Adalbert Church
16. Polonia House/Dom Polonii
17. Kraków Philharmonic
18. Jama Michalika
19. Jazz Club u Muniaka
20. Harris Piano Jazz Bar
21. Pod Baranami
22. Buddha Nightclub
23. Vodka Café Bar
24. Staropolskie Trunki (Vodka Tasting)
25. To Forum Przestrzenie & Hala Forum

KRAKÓW

more jewelry and design shops cluster along Sławkowska street, which runs north from the Main Market Square.

Polish Pottery

"Polish pottery," with distinctive blue-and-white designs, is made in the region of Silesia, west of Kraków (in and around the town of Bolesławiec). But assuming you won't be going there, you can browse one of the shops in Kraków. **Ceramika Bolesławiecka,** on a busy urban street between the Old Town and Kazimierz, has a tasteful, affordable selection of pottery that's oriented more toward locals than tourists (closed Sun, Starowiślna 43). In the Old Town—and with inflated prices to match—two places face each other across Sławkowska street, just a block north of the Square: **Dekor Art** at #11 and **Mila** at #14.

A Taste of Local Culture

While tacky souvenir shops abound in the streets near the Square, two locally run places sell mementos more closely tied to Polish culture. **Folkstar,** along Grodzka street just south of the Square, has all manner of products adorned with the exuberantly colorful floral folk patterns of the local countryside (daily, Grodzka 14). **Krakuska,** named for (and run by) female Krakovians, is a lovingly cluttered hole-in-the-wall with more folk items (daily, Szewska 9).

Szambelan, a block south of the Main Market Square, is a fun concept for vodka lovers: Peruse the giant casks of three dozen different flavored vodkas, buy an empty bottle, and they'll fill and seal it to take home (daily, Gołębia 2 at the corner with Bracka).

Designer Shops along Ulica Józefa, in Kazimierz

As the epicenter of Kraków's hipster scene, Kazimierz is the best place in town to browse one-off boutiques (both design and fashion). Several good options line up along Ulica Józefa, mostly concentrated along a two-block stretch. Head just one block south from Plac Nowy on Estery street, turn right, and survey the possibilities (mostly on the left side of the street). You'll find jewelry boutiques, vintage ware, fascinating works by untrained artists, clothing and housewares from local designers, and much more.

Polish Leather Shoes

Kacper Global has a large outlet selling colorful, made-in-Poland shoes in styles from athletic to casual to stylish. They're located in the area between Wawel Castle and Kazimierz—a handy add-on if you're heading to either place (closed Sun, Stradomska 21, https://kacperglobal.pl).

Shopping Malls

A small but swanky mall called **Pasaż 13** is a few steps off the southeast corner of the Main Market Square, where Grodzka street enters the square. Enter the mall under the balcony marked *Pasaż 13.* You'll find a cool brick-industrial interior, with upscale international chains...and not much that's Polish (daily).

Two enormous shopping malls lie just beyond the tourist zone. The gigantic **Galeria Krakowska,** with nearly 300 shops, shares a square with the train station (daily, kids' play area upstairs from the main entry). Only slightly smaller is **Galeria Kazimierz** (daily, just a few blocks east of the Kazimierz sights, along the river at Podgórska 24).

Entertainment in Kraków

As a town full of both students and tourists, Kraków has plenty of fun options, especially at night.

IN THE OLD TOWN
For locations of the following places, see the "Kraków's Old Town Shopping and Entertainment" map, earlier).

Main Market Square
Intoxicating as the Square is by day, it's even better at night...pure enchantment. Have a meal or sip a drink at an outdoor café, or just grab a bench and enjoy the scene. There's often live al fresco music coming from somewhere (either at restaurants, at a temporary stage set up near the Town Hall Tower, or from talented buskers). You could spend hours doing slow laps around the Square after dark and never run out of diversions. For a great view over the Square at twilight, nurse a drink at **Café Szał**—on the Cloth Hall's upper terrace (long hours, enter through Gallery of 19th-Century Polish Art).

Concerts
You'll find a wide range of musical events, from tourist-oriented Chopin concerts and classical "greatest hits" selections in quaint old ballrooms and churches, to folk-dancing shows, to serious philharmonic performances. The best all-around site for concert information is KrakowCulture.pl; also look for the hefty, free quarterly magazine *Kraków Culture* (at the TI). Other good listings can be found at CracowConcerts.com and Facebook.com/orkiestrasm. Hotel lobbies are stocked with fliers, but to get all of your options, visit the TI north of the Square on Ulica Św. Jana, which specializes in cultural events.

Popular Classical Concerts: The three main choices are organ concerts in churches (usually at 17:00), orchestral or chamber music, or Chopin (either can happen anytime between 18:00 and 20:00). The going rate for most concerts is around 60-70 zł. Many are held in churches (such as **Sts. Peter and Paul** on Ulica Grodzka and **St. Adalbert** on the Square). You'll also find concerts in fancy mansions on or near the Main Market Square (including the **Polonia House/Dom Polonii** upstairs from Wierzynek restaurant at #14, near Ulica Grodzka; and the **Chopin Gallery**—also billed as the **Royal Chamber Orchestra Hall**—just up Sławkowska street from the Square at #14). Occasionally in summer, they're held in various gardens around town.

Serious Concerts: The **Kraków Philharmonic** (Filharmonia im Krakowie) puts on concerts aimed at local music lovers rather than tourists—more serious than crowd-pleasing—in a 700-seat hall just west of the Planty (Zwierzyniecka 1, + 48 506 625 430, www.filharmonia.krakow.pl).

Folk Music: Various venues present a small, hardworking ensemble of colorfully costumed Krakovian singers, dancers, and musicians who put on a fun little folk show as you dine. While this is obviously a very touristy scene, it's fun if you approach it with the right spirit—and the performers try hard to involve members of the audience in the polkas and circle dances. The Old Town lineup changes from year to year; start by checking at the historic **Jama Michalika,** with its dusty old Art Nouveau interior right along Floriańska street (150 zł includes dinner; Wed and Sat at 19:00; Floriańska 45, +48 12 422 1561, www.cracowconcerts.com). If you have a car, you can reach a more rustic venue 30 minutes outside the city: **Skansen Smaków,** filling a log cabin-like building, has shows each Thursday night (170 zł, book ahead, +48 12 357 1006, www.skansensmakow.pl).

Jazz

Kraków has a surprisingly thriving jazz scene. Several popular clubs hide on the streets surrounding the Main Market Square (open nightly, most shows start around 21:30, sometimes free or a cover of 20-30 zł for better shows). **Jazz Club u Muniaka** is the most famous and best for all-around jazz in a sophisticated cellar environment (Ulica Floriańska 3, +48 12 423 1205, www.jazzumuniaka.club). **Harris Piano Jazz Bar,** right on the Square (at #28), is more casual and offers a mix of traditional and updated "fusion" jazz, plus blues (+48 12 421 5741, www.harris.krakow.pl).

Nightlife in the Old Town

The entire Old Town is crammed with nightclubs and discos pumping loud music on weekends. On a Saturday, the pedestrian streets can be more crowded at midnight than at noon. Most of these nightspots are garden-variety dance clubs, lacking any personality or creativity. Worse, to save money, young locals stand out in front of nightclubs to drink their own booze (BYOB) rather than pay high prices for the drinks inside—making the streets that much more crowded and noisy. For low-key hanging out, people choose a café on the Square; otherwise, they head for Kazimierz, with a more interesting variety of nightspots.

That said, there are a few places right around the Square—in addition to the jazz options listed earlier—that are worth checking out.

First, at the southwest corner of the Square, go down the corridor with the Starbucks at #27, then find the staircase that descends to **Pod Baranami** ("Under the Rams"). This historic spot—once home to a subversive, counterculture cabaret show (and still hosting occasional performances)—feels like a mysterious speakeasy where well-dressed grown-ups meet to sip cocktails and relive their younger days. Cozy tables sprawl through several rooms (daily, +48 12 421 25 00, www.piwnicapodbaranami.pl).

Across the Square, on the east side (where it meets Grodzka street), are two more places worth checking out. At #6, head into the passage to find the **Buddha** nightclub, with comfy lounge sofas under awnings in an immaculately restored old courtyard. For something funkier and even more local, go down the passage at #19, which runs a surprisingly long distance through the block—passing a shot bar called Szototo. Soon you'll start to see tables for the **Herring Embassy;** you'll eventually emerge at **Stolarska street,** a still enjoyable but far less touristy scene (for more on the Herring Embassy and Stolarska, see pages 348-349).

If you have (or would like to cultivate) an appreciation for vodka, stop by the **Vodka Café Bar,** serving more than 100 types of vodkas, liquors, and hard drinks. You can buy a tasting flight board with six small shots; they'll help you narrow down your options. It's a mellow, uncluttered space that lets you focus on the vodka and the company (daily from 15:00, weekends from 13:00, Mikołajska 5).

IN KAZIMIERZ

Aside from the Old Town's gorgeous Square, Kraków's best area to hang out after dark is Kazimierz. Although this is also the former Jewish quarter, the Jewish Sabbath has nothing to do with the bar scene here. You can, however, still hear traditional Jewish music called klezmer. For tips on enjoying a concert of klezmer music, see the sidebar.

Bars and Clubs

Squeezed between centuries-old synagogues and cemeteries are enticing hangouts running the full gamut from sober and tasteful to wild and clubby. The classic recipe for a Kazimierz bar: Find a dilapidated old storefront, fill it with ramshackle furniture, turn the lights down low, pipe in old-timey jazz music from the 1920s, and sprinkle with alcohol. Serves one to two dozen hipsters. After

Kazimierz Entertainment & Nightlife

New Cemetery

NEW CEMETERY ENTRANCE

(#3 & 24 from Old Town)

(#3 & 24 to Old Town)

POST

TEMPEL SYNAGOGUE

KUPA SYNAGOGUE

Old Cemetery

REMU'H SYNAGOGUE

Ulica Szeroka

WALL

To Podgórze

Plac Nowy

ISAAC SYNAGOGUE

HIGH SYNAGOGUE

OLD SYNAGOGUE

GALICIA JEWISH MUSEUM

To Wawel Hill

CORPUS CHRISTI CHURCH

MUSEUM OF ENGINEERING & TECHNOLOGY

KAZIMIERZ

Plac Wolnica

ETHNO-GRAPHIC MUSEUM

100 Meters

100 Yards

(#6, 8, 10 & 13 to Castle & Old Town)

Vistula River

NADWIŚLAŃSKA

PIWNA

JÓZEFIŃSKA

WĘGIERSKA

STAROMOSTOWA

BOLESŁAWA LIMANOWSKIEGO

100 Meters

100 Yards

1. Klezmer-Hois Restaurant
2. Awiw Restaurant & Other Live Outdoor Klezmer
3. Plac Nowy 1 Bar
4. Alchemia
5. Mleczarnia
6. Nova Resto Bar
7. Singer
8. Warsztat
9. Eszeweria
10. Kolanko No. 6

a few clubs of this type caught on, a more diverse cross-section of nightspots began to move in, including some loud dance clubs. The whole area is bursting with life. For locations, see the map on this page.

On and near Plac Nowy: The highest concentration of bars rings the Plac Nowy market square. Do a loop to browse your options. **Plac Nowy 1** specializes in Polish microbrews and upmarket

Klezmer Music in Kazimierz

On a balmy summer night, Kazimierz's main square, Ulica Szeroka, is filled with the haunting strains of klezmer—traditional Jewish music from 19th-century Poland, generally with violin, string bass, clarinet, and accordion. Skilled klezmer musicians can make their instruments weep or laugh like human voices. There are two main ways to enjoy some klezmer music: at a restaurant or at a concert.

Restaurants: Several eateries on Ulica Szeroka offer klezmer music, typically starting between 19:00 and 20:00. The musicians move from room to room, and the menus tend to be a mix of traditional Jewish and Polish cuisine (which are quite similar). But don't come here just for the food—it's an afterthought to the music. While most places claim to do concerts "nightly year-round," they can be canceled anytime it's slow (especially off-season)—confirm ahead.

Some old-school restaurants offer reasonably priced food but charge 40 zł per person for the music. Probably your best choice is the well-established **$$$ Klezmer-Hois,** filling a venerable former Jewish ritual bathhouse and making you feel like you're dining in a rich grandparent's home (daily 8:00-22:00, at #6, +48 12 411 1245, www.klezmer.pl).

Some restaurants with outdoor seating on Ulica Szeroka offer "free" al fresco klezmer music for customers (though the food tends to be that much more expensive). Because the music is free, anybody (at neighboring restaurants, or simply strolling past) can enjoy a taste of klezmer. Just show up, comparison-shop music and menus, and—if you like what you hear—pick a place for dinner or a drink. **$$$ Awiw** (at #13, overpriced food) is one such option.

Within the **Old Town,** there are also sometimes klezmer concerts at Sławkowska 14 (a.k.a. the Royal Chamber Orchestra Hall, www.cracowconcerts.com). However, for most visitors it's worth the easy trek to Kazimierz to enjoy a concert.

Don't worry too much about seeking out a particular musician—they are equally good, and each brings a unique style to the music. Many venues share musicians, so on any given night it's hard to predict who's performing where. Bottom line: If you're interested in klezmer music, you can't go wrong in Kazimierz.

KRAKÓW

pub grub in a bright, sleek (and arguably "un-Kazimierz") setting. Across the square, **Alchemia,** one of the first—and still one of the best—bars in Kazimierz, is candlelit, cluttered, and claustrophobic, with cavelike rooms crowded with rickety old furniture, plus a cellar used for live performances (Estery 5, www.alchemia.com.pl). Late at night, the little windows in the Plac Nowy **market hall** do a big business selling *zapiekanki* (baguette with toppings) to hungry bar-hoppers.

On Rabina Meiselsa street, just a half-block off Plac Nowy, under the arch to a characteristic courtyard is **Mleczarnia,** a beer garden with rickety tables squeezed under the trees and its cozy old-fashioned pub across the street (at #20).

Near Isaac Synagogue: A block east of Plac Nowy, a few more places cluster on the wide street in front of Isaac Synagogue. The huge **Nova Resto Bar** dominates the scene with a long covered terrace, a vast interior, and seating in their courtyard. This feels upscale and a bit pretentious compared to many of the others, but it's the place to be seen (Estery 18, www.novarestobar.pl). Facing Nowa are some smaller, more accessible options: **Singer** is classy and mellow, with most of its tables made of old sewing machines (Estery 20), while **Warsztat** has an exploding-instruments-factory ambience (Izaaka 3, www.restauracjawarsztat.pl).

On Józefa Street: Yet more good bars are just a short block south. Along Józefa, you'll find a pair of classic Kazimierz joints: **Eszeweria,** which wins the "best atmosphere" award, feels like a Polish speakeasy that's been in mothballs for the last 90 years—a low-key, unpretentious, and inviting hangout (Józefa 9). A block up, **Kolanko No. 6** has a cozy bar up front, a pleasant beer garden in the inner courtyard, and a fun events hall in back (Józefa 17, www.kolanko.net).

Beach Bar on the Riverbank

South of the river, roughly between Kazimierz and Wawel Castle, **Forum Przestrzenie** fills a dilapidated concrete hotel—a mostly abandoned dinosaur from communist times. But now the
ground floor has been taken
over by a lively hipster bar—especially appealing in the balmy
summer months, when comfy
low-slung chairs sprawl across a
tidy lawn and a pebbly "beach"
with views across the Vistula to
Wawel Castle. They serve cof-

fee, wine, beer, summery cocktails, and a wide variety of bar food. A few artists and designers also have boutiques here, and in the summer, they have live music and DJs (open daily in good weather until late, skip the trip if it's not nice out, Ulica Marii Konopnickiej 28, +48 515 424 724, www.forumprzestrzenie.com). The enticing **Hala Forum** food hall is next door, and you may also see a Ferris wheel and/or a hot-air balloon ride nearby—making this lively scene easy to spot from afar.

Sleeping in Kraków

Kraków has ample accommodation choices, and healthy competition keeps prices reasonable and makes choosing a hotel fun rather than frustrating. I've focused my accommodations in two areas: in and near the Old Town; and in Kazimierz, a hipper, more affordable neighborhood that's home to both the old Jewish quarter and a thriving dining and nightlife zone.

Both neighborhoods can suffer from discos that thump loud music on weekend nights to attract roving gangs of rowdy drinkers. I've tried to avoid the areas most plagued by noise, but to help your odds, ask for a quiet room when you reserve...and bring earplugs.

IN AND NEAR THE OLD TOWN

Most of my listings are inside (or within a block or two of) the Planty park that rings the Old Town. Sleeping inside the Old Town comes with pros (maximum atmosphere; handy location for sightseeing and dining) and cons (high prices; the potential for noise—especially on weekends—as noted earlier). Places just outside the Old Town are still handy, but quieter and cheaper. If you need a room in a pinch, several slick, international chains (Ibis, Mercure, Puro) have branches near the train station.

$$$$ Hotel Copernicus is the top splurge inside Kraków's Old Town, with 29 rooms in a historic shell on one of the finest, most serene streets in the historical center. The service is polished—verging on snobby—and the rooms are decorated with heavy beams, hand-painted frescoes, and antique furniture (aircon, elevator, Kanonicza 16, +48 12 424 3400, www.hotel.com.pl, copernicus@hotel.com.pl).

$$$ Donimirski Boutique Hotels are a reliably comfortable option that set the bar for quality and value (www.donimirski. com). All have friendly staff, discounts for my readers, and classy little extras that add up to a memorable hotel experience. **Hotel Polski Pod Białym Orłem** ("White Eagle") has 60 classic rooms conveniently located near the Florian Gate just inside the Old Town walls (RS%, apartments available, air-con, elevator, Ulica Pijarska 17, +48 12 422 1144, hotel.polski@donimirski.com). **Hotel Gródek** offers 23 rooms a three-minute walk behind St. Mary's Church, on a quiet dead-end street overlooking the Planty park (RS%, air-con, elevator, pay parking, Na Gródku 4, +48 12 431 9030, grodek@donimirski.com). They also have a six-room annex, **Hotel Pugetów,** that can be rented by a small group (Ulica Starowiślna 15A, pugetow@donimirski.com).

$$ Hotel Senacki is a business-class place renting 20 comfortable rooms between Wawel Castle and the Main Market Square. The staff is warm, professional, and conscientious, and the loca-

---

Sleep Code

Hotels in this book are categorized according to the average price of a standard double room with breakfast in high season. 4 zł = about $1.

$$$$	**Splurge:** Most rooms over 900 zł (€200)
$$$	**Pricier:** 700-900 zł (€150-200)
$$	**Moderate:** 500-700 zł (€100-150)
$	**Budget:** 250-500 zł (€50-100)
¢	**Backpacker:** Under 250 zł (€50)
RS%	**Rick Steves discount**

Unless otherwise noted, credit cards are accepted and hotel staff speak basic English. Comparison-shop by checking prices at several hotels (on each hotel's own website, on a booking site, or by email). For the best deal, *book directly with the hotel.* Ask for a discount if paying in cash; if the listing includes **RS%**, request a Rick Steves discount.

---

tion is perfect, making this an ideal spot to stay. Top-floor "attic" rooms have low beams, skylight windows, and a flight of stairs after the elevator (air-con, elevator to all but the attic rooms, ask about nearby pay parking, Ulica Grodzka 51, +48 12 422 7686, www.hotelsenacki.pl, senacki@hotelsenacki.pl).

$$ Grand Ascot Hotel sits just beyond the end of the lively, pedestrianized Krupnicza dining drag—a pleasant walk away from the Old Town. With 63 business-class rooms over a plush lobby, it feels a bit posh yet reasonably priced (family rooms, air-con, elevator, sauna and fitness area, Józefa Szujskiego 4, +48 12 446 7600, www.grandascot.pl, rezerwacja@grandascot.pl).

$$ Hotel Wawel has 39 rooms on a well-located street that's quieter than the Old Town norm. It's colorful and serene; above the swanky marble lobby are hallways creatively painted with the history of the building and images from around Kraków. Out back, a fountain gurgles in a cute little courtyard (air-con, elevator—but doesn't go to top floor, Ulica Poselska 22, +48 12 424 1300, www.hotelwawel.pl, hotel@hotelwawel.pl).

$$ Bracka 6, conveniently located one short block off the Main Market Square, is a sort of a hybrid between a hotel and an apartment house. The 16 stylish rooms—with sleek lines, lots of glass, and exposed brick—each have a kitchen, so breakfast is optional and extra (at a nearby café). The lack of full hotel amenities keeps the prices affordable for this level of modern elegance. In this central location, request a quieter room in back (air-con, elevator, laundry service, limited reception hours—let them know when you're arriving, Bracka 6, +48 608 000 609, www.bracka6.pl, info@bracka6.pl).

$ Hotel Wielopole sits a block outside the Planty, on the way to the lively Kazimierz district. Its 35 tight rooms are tucked down a side street just past the main post office, facing a big Holiday Inn. The staff are proud of their attentive service, and they post an informative little newsletter daily (air-con, elevator, Italian restaurant in cellar, Wielopole 3, +48 12 422 1475, www.wielopole.pl, office@wielopole.pl).

$ Hotel Amber sits on a dreary urban street just outside the Planty park but still less than a 10-minute walk from the Square. Run by the same company as Hotel Wielopole (described above), it has an equally pleasant emphasis on welcoming service. The hotel has two parts: 18 perfectly fine, if smallish, rooms in the original building; and 20 slightly more upscale rooms in the newer "design" section. Both parts share a small gym, sauna, and garden in back (air-con, elevator, Garbarska 8-10, +48 12 421 0606, www.hotel-amber.pl, office@hotel-amber.pl).

$ Cracowdays is the farthest of my listings from the center of town, about a 15-minute walk away (a tram can cut a few minutes off the trek). But it's also a notch more refined than the places listed previously. It sits in a pleasant residential neighborhood west of the Main Market Square, with eight beautifully decorated and thoughtfully tended rooms, all sharing a central kitchen (plus two stand-alone studio apartments in another building). Owner Magdalena, a great traveler, prides herself on creating an atmosphere where fellow wanderers can feel welcome far from home (air-con, Grabowskiego 7, +48 604 460 860, www.cracowdays.com, reservation@cracowdays.com).

$ Kraków for You Apartments offers 16 studios and one- and two-bedroom units with kitchenettes around a courtyard along one of Kraków's most happening streets, just a few steps off the Main Market Square. A few of their rooms are elsewhere in the Old Town (reception open daily 10:00-20:00, request quieter courtyard room, lots of stairs with no elevator, go down the passage at Grodzka 4, +48 660 541 085, www.krakowforyou.com, info@krakowforyou.com, Mikołaj).

¢ Globtroter Guest House offers 17 basic, somewhat stuffy, rustic-feeling rooms with high ceilings and big beams around a serene garden courtyard. Marek (Mark) conscientiously focuses on value—keeping prices reasonable by not offering needless extras (RS%, 2 people can cram into a single to save money, family rooms, breakfast at nearby café extra, pay laundry service, fun 700-year-old brick cellar lounge, go down passageway at #7 at the square called Plac Szczepański, +48 12 422 4123, www.globtroter-krakow.com, globtroter@globtroter-krakow.com).

KRAKÓW

Kraków's Old Town Hotels & Restaurants

OLD MARKET

200 Meters
200 Yards

To 11

#24 Stary Kleparz

BARBICAN

FLORIAN GATE

27 CZARTORYSKI MUSEUM 27

17

10

6

31 30

KRUPNICZA

#24 Teatr Bagatela

Plac Szczepański

13

OLD

SZOLAYSKI HOUSE

25

KRZYSZTOFORY PALACE (HISTORY MUSEUM)

Main Market Square

20

STUDENSKA

WYSPIAŃSKI MUSEUM

Plac Sikorskiego

COLLEGIUM MAIUS

29

CLOTH HALL

ST. MARY'S

23

Small Market Square

24

3

COLLEGIUM NOVUM

TOWN HALL TOWER

ST. ADALBERT'S

16

8

PASAŻ 13 MALL

12

21

DOMINICAN CHURCH

WC

To Airport, Auschwitz, Kościuszko Mound, Stained-Glass Workshop & Museum & National Museum Main Branch

ARCH- BISHOP'S PALACE

#8 Plac Wszystkich Świętych

ST. FRANCIS

WYSPIAŃSKI PAVILION

14

28 18

7

TOWN

SENACKA

STS. PETER & PAUL

5

Mary Mag. Square

BISHOP ERAZM CIOŁEK PALACE

ARCHDIOCESAN MUSEUM

1

15

ST. ANDREW'S

19

22

CATHEDRAL

CATHEDRAL MUSEUM

WAWEL HILL

WC

INNER COURTYARD

ST. BERNARDINO'S

WC

SANDOMIERSKA TOWER

DRAGON STATUE

Vistula River

To Forum Przestrzenie & Hala Forum

KRAKÓW

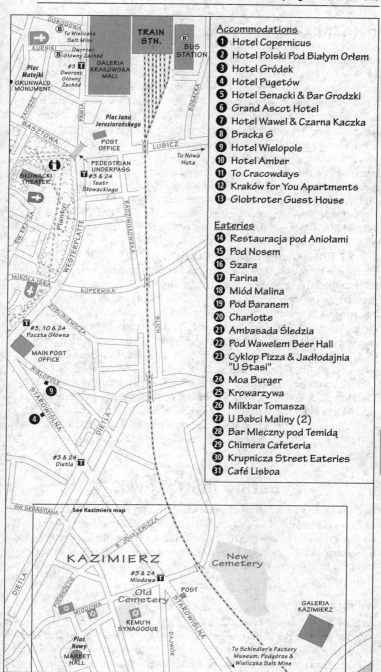

Accommodations

1. Hotel Copernicus
2. Hotel Polski Pod Białym Orłem
3. Hotel Gródek
4. Hotel Pugetów
5. Hotel Senacki & Bar Grodzki
6. Grand Ascot Hotel
7. Hotel Wawel & Czarna Kaczka
8. Bracka 6
9. Hotel Wielopole
10. Hotel Amber
11. To Cracowdays
12. Kraków for You Apartments
13. Globtroter Guest House

Eateries

14. Restauracja pod Aniołami
15. Pod Nosem
16. Szara
17. Farina
18. Miód Malina
19. Pod Baranem
20. Charlotte
21. Ambasada Śledzia
22. Pod Wawelem Beer Hall
23. Cyklop Pizza & Jadłodajnia "U Stasi"
24. Moa Burger
25. Krowarzywa
26. Milkbar Tomasza
27. U Babci Maliny (2)
28. Bar Mleczny pod Temidą
29. Chimera Cafeteria
30. Krupnicza Street Eateries
31. Café Lisboa

KRAKÓW

IN KAZIMIERZ

Kazimierz is both Kraków's Jewish heart and soul, and its trendiest eating and nightlife zone. Sleeping here puts you in close proximity to synagogues and klezmer concerts, as well as to food trucks and hip nightclubs (expect some noise, especially on weekends). Keep in mind that, while pleasant in its own right, Kazimierz is a 20-minute walk or a 5-minute tram ride from Kraków's atmospheric old center (for details on getting to Kazimierz from the Old Town, see page 299). For locations, see the map on page 352.

$$$ Metropolitan Boutique Hotel is an upscale refuge a block before the heart of Kazimierz (just off the busy road on the way to Kraków's Old Town). Its 59 rooms—with exposed brick and slick modern style—sit along a somewhat dreary but conveniently located side street (air-con, elevator, gym, Joselewicza 19, +48 12 442 7500, www.hotelmetropolitan.pl, hotel@hotelmetropolitan. pl).

$$ Rubinstein Residence sits right in the middle of Ulica Szeroka—surrounded by klezmer restaurants and synagogues, in the heart of the neighborhood. It fills a painstakingly restored old townhouse (parts of it dating to the 15th century) with heavy wood beams and 30 swanky rooms—some of them palatial suites that incorporate old features like frescoes and pillars. The rooftop terrace—open to the public, with views over Kazimierz and to the Old Town—sets this place above (air-con, elevator, Szeroka 12, +48 12 384 0000, www.rubinstein.pl, recepcja@rubinstein.pl).

¢ Residence Tournet, well run by friendly Piotr and Sylwia Działowy, is your cheap-and-cheery option, offering 18 colorful, perfumed rooms near the edge of Kazimierz toward Wawel Castle (elevator plus a few stairs, reception open 7:00-22:00, Ulica Miodowa 7, +48 12 292 0088, www.accommodation.krakow.pl, tournet@nocleg.krakow.pl).

Eating in Kraków

Kraków has a wide array of great restaurants. As the food scene changes constantly, I've chosen established places that have a proven track record. In my listings, you'll find a mix of old-school Polish eateries and modern alternatives (which are still rooted in the local tradition). You could also consider a food tour (see "Tours in Krakow" near the beginning of this chapter).

IN THE OLD TOWN

Kraków's Old Town is loaded with dining options. All of these eateries (except the milk bars) are likely to be booked up on weekends—always reserve ahead. It's tempting to dine on the Main Market Square; however, most restaurants here cater mainly to

---

Restaurant Code

Eateries in this book are categorized according to the average cost of a typical main course. Drinks, desserts, and splurge items (steak and seafood) can raise the price considerably. 4 zł = about $1.

$$$$ **Splurge:** Most main courses over 90 zł (€20)
$$$ **Pricier:** 70-90 zł (€15-20)
$$ **Moderate:** 50-70 zł (€10-15)
$ **Budget:** Under Under 50 zł (€10)

In Poland, a milk bar or takeout spot is **$**; a basic sit-down eatery is **$$**; a casual but more upscale restaurant is **$$$**; and a swanky splurge is **$$$$**.

---

tourists and—other than Szara, recommended below—don't provide the best value for the money. To enjoy the same experience more affordably, have just a drink on the Square and dine elsewhere.

$$$ Restauracja pod Aniołami ("Under Angels") offers a dressy, candlelit atmosphere on a wonderful covered patio or in a deep, steep, romantic cellar with rough wood and medieval vaults. Peruse the elaborately described menu of medieval nobles' dishes. The cuisine is traditional Polish, with an emphasis on grilled meats and trout (on a wood-fired grill). Every meal begins with *smalec* (spread made with lard, fried onion, bacon, and apple). Don't go here if you're in a hurry—only if you want to really slow down and enjoy your dinner. Reservations are smart (daily from 13:00, Ulica Grodzka 35, +48 12 421 3999, www.podaniolami.pl).

$$$$ Pod Nosem ("Under the Nose") is a worthwhile splurge for refined, updated Polish cuisine in a sophisticated, untouristy atmosphere. It's tucked at the far end of sleepy Kanonicza lane, just beyond the tourists and before Wawel Castle. In a tight dining room that skips the kitsch, they offer an extensive wine list and a short menu of artfully executed Polish dishes (daily, Kanonicza 22, +48 12 376 0014, www.kanonicza22.com).

$$$$ Szara owns a prime location right on the Main Market Square, in the 14th-century Kamienica Szara ("Grey House"). The restaurant is a well-regarded option for a higher-end meal of elevated Polish cuisine, with a short menu of meat and fish dishes. The interior feels rich and dressy, with gilded vaults and Józef Mehoffer-painted ceilings soaring overhead, and the outdoor tables own a prime location facing the Square. If you're looking to splurge memorably for a special occasion, this is a fine choice (daily, Rynek Główny 6, +48 12 421 6669, www.szara.pl).

$$ Czarna Kaczka ("Black Duck") features Polish fare with an emphasis on duck (of course) and dumplings. The cozy, steamy, arched interior is a central choice for traditional food done well, but not too rustic. As it fills up, book ahead (daily from 13:00, next to Hotel Wawel at Poselska 22, +48 500 195 149, https://czarnakaczka.pl).

$$$ Farina, specializing in international/Mediterranean fish and seafood dishes from chef Monika Turasiewicz, is a dressy, upscale-feeling, well-established choice for a memorable meal. It's smart to reserve ahead (closed Mon, Św. Marka 16, +48 519 399 474, https://farina.com.pl).

$$ Miód Malina ("Honey Raspberry") is an acceptably kitschy Polish-Italian fusion restaurant filled with the comforting aroma of its wood-fired oven. The menu is mostly Polish, with a few Italian dishes thrown in. Sit in the cozy, warmly painted interior or out in the courtyard (reservations smart, daily, Ulica Grodzka 40, +48 12 430 0411, www.miodmalina.pl).

$$$ Pod Baranem ("Under the Ram") is a solid midrange bet for well-executed, traditional Polish food. Respected by locals, it sits just outside the tourist chaos, quietly facing the Planty near Wawel Castle. Several cozy rooms—tasteful but not stuffy—sprawl through a homey old building (daily from 13:00, Św. Gertrudy 21, +48 12 429 4022, www.podbaranem.com).

Youthful Style at Plac Szczepański: While seemingly every corner of the Old Town is jammed with tourists, the pleasant square called Plac Szczepański—tucked at the northwest corner of the Old Town—feels more like the terrain of university students. While just two short blocks from the Square, this small array of cafés and galleries has a vibe that's more Warsaw-urbane than ye olde Kraków. Among these, **$ Charlotte** is a winner—it's a classy, French-feeling bakery/café/wine bar. They make their own breads and pastries in the basement (with lots of seating—you can watch the bakers work if you come early enough in the morning), cultivate a stay-awhile coffeehouse ambience upstairs, and throw in a few square-facing sidewalk tables to boot. The food is light café fare—sandwiches, pastries, and salads—rather than a filling dinner (daily, Plac Szczepański 2, +48 12 431 5610).

On Stolarska Street: Stolarska street, a neatly pedestrianized, oddly untrammeled "embassy row" just a block away from the Main Market Square, is worth exploring for a meal or a drink. Stolarska has a fun variety of more locals-oriented bars and cafés. Begin at the Small Market Square (Mały Rynek) behind St. Mary's Church and head south. On the left, look for the ridiculously long sign that perfectly identifies the business: *Pierwszy Lokal Na Stolarskiej Po Lewej Stronie Idąc Od Małego Rynku* ("The first pub on the left side of Stolarska coming from the Small Market Square"). Notice that this once-sleepy street is lined with embassies and consulates—it's easy to spot the flags of Germany, the US, and France. On the left, in the stretch of cafés under canopies, you'll see the **$$ Ambasada Śledzia** ("Herring Embassy"), with a divey, youthful atmosphere and a "Polish tapas" approach: A dozen different types of herring and other light meals, plus a variety of vodka to wash it down, are posted on the menu. You'll order at the bar, then find a table or take it to go (daily, Stolarska 8). Across the street and 50 paces back up, the Pasaż Bielaka (look for the low-profile stone doorway at #5) runs through the middle of the block all the way out to the Main Market Square (emerging at Rynek Główny #19); in here is another sprawling branch of the Herring Embassy.

Beer Hall: The rollicking Czech-style **$ Pod Wawelem** ("Under Wawel") is right on the Planty park near Wawel Castle. It's packed with locals seeking big, sloppy, greasy portions of meaty fare, with giant mugs of various beers on tap (including Polish and Bavarian). Choose between the bustling interior and the outdoor terrace right on the Planty. Locals come here not for a romantic dinner but for a rowdy evening out with friends (different specials every day—such as giant schnitzel, pork ribs, or roasted chicken; daily, Ulica Św. Gertrudy 26-29, +48 12 421 2336).

Pizza: Cozy and charming **$ Cyklop** has good wood-fired pizzas, with 10 tables wrapped around the cook and his busy oven (daily, near St. Mary's Church at Mikołajska 16, +48 12 421 6603).

Burgers (and Vegan Burgers): Gourmet hamburgers are all the rage in Poland. One of the best options in the center is **$ Moa Burger,** with a dozen different types of big, sloppy, "New Zealand-style" hamburgers. Order at the counter, then find a seat at a shared table. This isn't "fast food"—everything is made to order (daily, Mikołajska 3, +48 12 421 2144). For vegan burgers, a handy place in the center is **$ Krowarzywa** (a pun roughly meaning both "Cow Alive" and "Cow Vegetable")—with a hip atmosphere and an enticing menu of meatless options (daily, Sławkowska 8, +48 531 777 136).

Milk Bars and Other Quick, Cheap, Traditional Eats

Kraków is a good place to try the cheap cafeterias called "milk bars." For pointers on eating at a milk bar, review the sidebar on page 230.

$ Milkbar Tomasza is an upgraded milk bar popular with local students. Modern and relatively untouristy, it serves big, splittable portions of high-quality food—a mix of Polish and international—plus breakfast dishes all day (great big salads, daily specials, open Tue-Sun until 18:00, closed Mon, Ulica Tomasza 24, +48 12 422 1706).

$ U Babci Maliny ("Granny Raspberry"), with a grinning Granny on the sign, is well established and much appreciated for its big portions of flavorful traditional food. One location, frequented almost entirely by Krakovians and designed for university students and staff, is tucked into an inner courtyard of the Science Academy. Find the door at Sławkowska 17, then make your way into the inner courtyard, with an entrance to a rustic cellar where it looks like a kitschy cottage bomb went off. Another location is across the street from the National Theater building at Szpitalna 38. The main floor, also done up in gaudy cottage style, is self-service and budget priced, while the cellar—with a drawing-room vibe—has table service and slightly higher prices (both are open daily). Both locations have walls of photos of the owner posing with bodybuilders and ultimate fighters...not quite in keeping with the country theme.

$ Jadłodajnia "U Stasi" is a throwback that makes you feel like you're in on Kraków's best-kept secret. Its hidden location—tucked at the far end of the passage with the recommended Cyklop pizzeria—attracts a wide range of loyal local clientele, from hardscrabble seniors to politicians, artists, and actors. They're all here for well-executed, unpretentious, home-style Polish lunch grub. There can be a bit of a language barrier, so go with the flow: Pick up the English menu as you enter, find a table, wait for them to take your order, enjoy your meal, then pay as you leave. This is an excellent value and a real, untouristy Polish experience. The short menu changes every day—and when they're out, they're out (Mon-Fri until 17:00, closed Sat-Sun, Mikołajskiej 16).

Throwback Milk Bars on Grodzka Street: Just a couple of blocks south of the Main Market Square, on busy Ulica Grodzka, two classic milk bars somehow survive the onslaught of the modern world. First, at the corner with Senacka, is the remarkably basic and traditional milk bar, **$ Bar Mleczny pod Temidą.** The next best thing to a time machine to the communist era, this place has grumpy monolingual service, a mostly local clientele, and cheap but good food (daily). A few more

steps down, also on the right (just before the two churches), **$ Bar Grodzki** is a single tight little room with shared tables. They specialize in tasty potato pancake dishes *(placki ziemniaczane)*. Order high on the menu and try the rich and hearty "Hunter's Delight"— potato pancake with sausage, beef, melted cheese, and spicy sauce. The English menu posted by the counter makes ordering easy. Order, sit, and wait to be called to fetch your food (daily).

$ **Chimera Cafeteria,** just off the Main Market Square, is a handy spot for a quick lunch in the center. It serves fast traditional meals to a steady stream of students. You'll order at the counter—choose a big plate (6 items) or medium plate (4 items) and select from an array of salads and main dishes by pointing to what you'd like. Then eat on their quiet, covered garden courtyard (good for vegetarians, daily, near the university at Ulica Św. Anny 3). I'd skip their expensive full-service restaurant (in the basement), which shares an entryway.

Lively Student Zone Just West of the Old Town

A few minutes' walk west of the Old Town is a trendy, energetic neighborhood with more students than tourists. If ye olde Kraków is getting a little olde, this area is a closer, easier escape than Kazimierz. The spine of this zone is **Krupnicza street,** a pedestrianized strip that begins just across the ring road from the Planty. To get here, head out Szewska street from the middle of the Square (to the west), cross the busy ring road, and fork left at the Teatr Bagatela. Several eateries along here are worth considering: $ **Meat & Go,** a cellar restaurant with hearty meat dishes (at #3 on the right); a pod of $ **food trucks** (just beyond #6 on the left, under the mural); $$ **Dynia,** with a hip brick interior and an inviting garden courtyard (at #20 on the left); and $ **Meho Café,** a casual place with drinks, light food, and delightful seating in the garden behind the Józef Mehoffer House Museum (at #26 on the left). At the end of the street, hook right to find the best place in the area for a sweet treat: $ **Café Lisboa,** which serves great coffee and excellent *pastéis de nata*, the national dessert of Portugal—made by a Pole who went to Belém to learn how to make it just right (Dolnych Młynów 3).

IN KAZIMIERZ

The entire district is bursting with lively cafés and bars—it's a happening night scene. For locations, see the map on page 352.

Fast and Cheap

Kazimierz has some great takeout and street food—handy for a lunch break from daytime sightseeing here, or for an affordable dinner break from bar-hopping.

$ **Food Trucks:** Kazimierz has two pods of fun-to-browse food trucks—most open daily for lunch and dinner. **Judah Square,** named for its big graffiti mural by an Israeli street artist, is tucked at the southern fringe of the tourists' Kazimierz, near the old tram depot (corner of Św. Wawrzyńca and Wąska). Mainstays here include Andrus (super-decadent and gooey roasted pork sandwiches), Boogie Truck burgers, Yatai sushi, Belgian-style fries, Pan Kumpir baked potatoes, and the beloved Chimney Cake Bakery, which

Kazimierz Hotels & Restaurants

Accommodations

1. To Metropolitan Boutique Hotel
2. Rubinstein Residence
3. Residence Tournet

Eateries

4. Judah Square Food Trucks
5. Isaac Synagogue Food Trucks
6. Plac Nowy Eateries
7. Bagelmama
8. Stara Zajezdnia
9. Craftownia
10. Lody Tradycyjna Receptura
11. Good Lood
12. Bottiglieria 1881
13. Karakter
14. Kuchnia u Doroty
15. Hummus Amamamusi
16. Hamsa Restaurant

rotisserie-roasts dough and sugar into a sweet and crunchy cake, then fills it with ice cream and other toppings—a Hungarian treat. Right in the heart of the tourist zone, another food truck pod fills a vacant lot **behind Isaac Synagogue,** just steps from Ulica Szeroka. Here you'll find painted-wooden-pallet furniture, hammocks, twinkle lights, and a mellow vibe. Likely options include hot dogs, Mexican tacos, açaí smoothies, burgers, veggie wraps, Thai ice cream, and—of course—more chimney cakes. Note that any and all of these could reshuffle their carts—or be gone entirely, replaced by a ritzy new building—at any moment. But it's clear that, in general, Kazimierz's food-truck scene is here to stay.

Polish Fast Food on Plac Nowy: The centerpiece of the Plac Nowy market is a circular brick slaughterhouse, which has recently been taken over by Kazimierz foodies. Each of the shop windows—which once housed butchers and basic Polish grub—is now operated by a different pop-up eatery, most of them serving the Poles' beloved *zapiekanki:* toasted baguettes with cheese, ketchup, and a bewildering array of other toppings. You can take a spin around the building to survey your options—noting where the lines are longest (locals know which *zapiekanek* is best).

Bagels: A casual shop popular with expats and locals, **$ Bagelmama** is run by an American named Nava (who once worked as a private chef for tennis star John McEnroe). The bagels come dressed with a wide variety of spreads, and they also sell sandwiches, soups, salads, desserts, and fresh juices. You can eat in or get it to go (Mon-Fri until 16:00, Sat-Sun until 17:00, Ulica Dajwór 10, +48 12 346 1646).

Beer: Beer lovers find two different experiences along Św. Wawrzyńca. **$$ Stara Zajezdnia** ("Old Tram Depot") fills exactly that—a cavernous old industrial hall—with tables and happy drinkers, draining huge mugs of the five different types of beer brewed on the premises. (You can also order a sampler.) In good weather, the vast courtyard out front becomes an idyllic, self-service beer garden filled with relaxing lounge chairs (Św. Wawrzyńca 12, +48 664 323 988). For craft beer aficionados, **Craftownia** has 18 Polish microbrews on tap (and many more by the bottle) in a nondescript setting (daily from 14:00, Św. Wawrzyńca 22, +48 515 010 565).

Hip Bars with Food: Several of the bars listed under "Entertainment in Kraków," earlier, serve decent food. If you're looking for classic ramshackle Kazimierz ambience first and something to munch on second, consider these **$$** options: **Alchemia** (daily, Estery 5), **Kolanko No. 6** (daily, Józefa 17), and **Warsztat** (daily, Izaaka 3). For locations, see the "Kazimierz Entertainment and Nightlife" map, earlier.

Ice Cream: True to its name, **Lody Tradycyjna Receptura** has some of the best "ice cream from a traditional recipe" in Kraków—if not in Poland. The straightforward, seasonal flavors—just a few varieties—are made fresh each morning and sold until they run out. Locals line up here—and if you have a sweet tooth, you should, too (daily, Starowiślna 83). **Good Lood** (a pun on *lody*—ice cream) is newer and hipper but based on the same concept: creative flavors made fresh daily. Once they're out...they're out (daily, Plac Wolnica 11).

Dining in Kazimierz

In addition to its hip, fast, and cheap eateries, Kazimierz is emerging as a foodie hotspot for sit-down, take-your-time meals. In fact, this neighborhood owns Kraków's only Michelin star (at the first listing, below).

$$$$ Bottiglieria 1881—a chic, sophisticated restaurant tucked unassumingly just off Plac Wolnica—recently earned a Michelin star. Chef Przemysław Klima delicately constructs fixed-price menus of modern Polish and international fare. The cellar is stocked with wines from all over the world (with an emphasis on Italian). As this is one of Kraków's top "destination" restaurants, be sure to book ahead (closed Sun-Mon, Bochenska 5, +48 660 661 756, www.1881.com.pl).

$$$ Karakter, a short walk from the core of Kazimierz, feels lively, trendy, fresh, and upmarket. They take a meat-focused, international approach, but with ample Polish influences. You'll peruse a tempting menu of everything from pastas, mussels, and steaks to more innovative dishes like horse tenderloin tartare or beef tongue in wasabi sauce (Mon dinner only, Tue-Sun lunch and dinner, Brzozowa 17, +48 795 818 123).

$ Kuchnia u Doroty is a hidden gem for affordable, authentic, Grandma-style Polish food with zero pretense. Tucked along a forgotten side street at the edge of Kazimierz, its no-frills, welcoming interior is a haven for those seeking hearty local cuisine at a great value (cheap daily specials, open daily, Augustiańska 4, +48 517 945 338).

Middle Eastern: Hole-in-the-wall **$ Hummus Amamamusi** is a bar selling creamy, top-quality homemade hummus with various toppings, bread, and veggies. They also make their own soft drinks and have great coffee. The delicious food here is worth the short walk from the core of Kazimierz (daily until 17:00, Meiselsa 4, +48 533 306 288). **$$$ Hamsa,** with a prime location at the top of Ulica Szeroka and lots of tempting tables out front, offers "hummus and happiness," with an updated take on Israeli food (that's Middle Eastern, not traditional Jewish fare). Don't come here for matzo balls and klezmer music, but for an enticing menu of *mezes* (small plates, like hummus and various dips) and grilled meat dishes in a modern, hip atmosphere (daily, Ulica Szeorka 2, +48 515 150 145).

Kraków Connections

For getting between Kraków and **Auschwitz,** see the next chapter. To confirm rail journeys, check specific times at the main train station or online (www.intercity.pl). You can also buy tickets on this website; you'll be sent an eticket, which you can show to the conductor on board.

From Kraków by Train to: **Warsaw** (about hourly, 2.5 hours, slick EIC express train, requires seat reservation), **Gdańsk** (6/day direct, 5.5 hours on EIC express, plus night train, 9 hours), **Toruń** (7/day, 5.5 hours, most transfer at Warsaw's Zachodnia station), **Prague** (2/day direct, 7.5 hours, plus 1 night train, 10 hours; additional connections may be possible with change in Katowice and other points; some connections are operated by private Czech rail company Leo Express, www.leoexpress.com), **Berlin** (2-3/day, 9-10 hours with change at Warsaw's Zachodnia station, more options with multiple changes), **Budapest** (2/day direct—one during the day in 9 hours, the other overnight in 10 hours; additional connections possible with changes; also consider long-distance bus, www.flixbus.com), **Vienna** (2/day direct—1 during the day in 6 hours, the other overnight in 8.5 hours; additional connections possible with changes).

By Bus: For certain journeys between major cities—both domestic and international—you can save time and money by taking a bus instead of a train. Check your options with Flixbus (www.flixbus.com).

KRAKÓW

AUSCHWITZ-BIRKENAU

The unassuming regional capital of Oświęcim (ohsh-VEENCH-im) was the site of one of humanity's greatest crimes: the systematic murder of at least 1.1 million innocent people. From 1940 until 1945, Oświęcim was the home of Auschwitz, the biggest, most notorious concentration camp in the Nazi system. Today, Auschwitz is the most poignant memorial anywhere to the victims of the Holocaust.

"Auschwitz" (OWSH-vits) actually refers to a series of several camps in German-occupied Poland—most importantly Auschwitz I, in the town of Oświęcim (50 miles west of Kraków), and Auschwitz II—Birkenau (about 1.5 miles west of Oświęcim). Visitors generally start with Auschwitz I, then ride a shuttle bus to Birkenau. **Auschwitz I,** where public transportation from Kraków arrives, has the main museum building, the *Arbeit Macht Frei* gate, and indoor museum exhibits in former prison buildings. **Birkenau** (BEER-keh-now), on a much bigger scale and mostly outdoors, has the infamous guard tower, a vast field with ruins of barracks, a few tourable barracks, the notorious "dividing platform," a giant monument flanked by remains of destroyed crematoria, and a prisoner processing facility called "the Sauna."

A visit here is obligatory for Polish 14-year-olds; students usually come again during their last year of school. And it's an important pilgrimage for school groups from other countries. Many visitors leave flowers and messages; one message—from a German visitor—reads, "Nations who forget their own history are sentenced to live it again."

GETTING THERE

To reach Auschwitz from Kraków, it's easiest to join a package tour or hire a private guide or driver (1.5-hour drive each way). But the trip is also doable by train or bus (allow about 2 hours each way). For details, see "Auschwitz Connections," at the end of this chapter.

Orientation to Auschwitz

Cost: Most of the time, you're required to join a guided tour of Auschwitz I for 90 zł. (Alternatively, you could join a "study tour," or hire your own guide—see the "Guided Tours at Auschwitz" sidebar.) At off-peak times (April-Sept after 16:00, March and Oct after 15:00, Feb after 14:00, Jan and Nov after 13:00, Dec after 12:00), the tour is not required—you are allowed to visit on your own for free, though donations are appreciated. For any visit, **reservations are required** to enter Auschwitz I (see later). Any time of year, Birkenau grounds can be toured without a guide.

Hours: The museum opens daily at 7:30. Closing times change with the season: June-Aug at 19:00, April-May and Sept at 18:00, March and Oct at 17:00, Feb at 16:00, Jan and Nov at 15:00, and Dec at 14:00. These are "last entry" times; the grounds at Auschwitz I stay open 1.5 hours later (though many buildings—including the national memorials—close promptly at these times). The grounds at Birkenau, where most groups end their visits, may stay open even later.

Information: +48 33 844 8100, www.auschwitz.org.

Why Visit Auschwitz?

Why visit a notorious concentration camp on your vacation? Auschwitz-Birkenau is one of the most moving sights in Europe, and certainly the most important of all the Holocaust memorials. Seeing the camp can be difficult: Many visitors are overwhelmed by sadness and anger, as well as inspiration at the remarkable stories of survival. Auschwitz survivors and victims' families want tourists to come here and experience the scale and the monstrosity of the place. In their minds, a steady flow of  visitors will ensure that the Holocaust is always remembered—so nothing like it will ever happen again.

Auschwitz isn't for everyone. But I've never met anyone who toured Auschwitz and regretted it. For many, it's a profoundly life-altering experience—at the very least, it will forever affect the way you think about the Holocaust.

Mandatory Reservations: With well over one million visitors each year, Auschwitz struggles with crowds. Reservations are required—even if you're visiting late in the day, on your own. Book as soon as your dates are set—ideally weeks in advance—at https://visit.auschwitz.org. Entrance slots for individuals typically become available 90 days before the date of visit (and can fill quickly, especially for May and June, when school groups crowd the site). These details can change—confirm on the website.

If an English tour isn't available for your preferred date, consider booking one in a foreign language; once inside, you can use this chapter's self-guided tour.

After you've booked your reservation, you'll be sent a barcode; to get in, you'll need both the barcode (on your phone) and an ID for each person in your group. (This system, while cumbersome, prevents scalpers from buying up tickets and reselling them at inflated prices.)

Last-Minute Options: I don't recommend arriving in Kraków without an advance ticket. But if you do, there are a couple of last-minute options: You can book a **day tour** through a private company in Kraków, which includes both transportation and a tour of the camp (see the "Guided Tours at Auschwitz" sidebar). Or take your chances and **just show up**—a few tickets are reserved for same-day visitors. The visitors center opens at 7:30; typically, the later you arrive, the longer the wait. You can pass any wait time by first going to Birkenau, which has less strict timing requirements.

Getting from Auschwitz I to Birkenau: Buses shuttle visitors two miles between the camps (free, typically every 10-20 minutes, schedule posted at bus stops at each site, timed to correspond with tours). Taxis are also standing by (about 20-25 zł). Or you can walk the 30-40 minutes between the camps, which gives you a chance for reflection. Along the way, you'll pass the Judenrampe, an old train car like the ones used to transport prisoners.

Services: The visitors center at Auschwitz I has an information desk, bookshops, baggage storage (large bags must be checked), and WCs. The guard tower at Birkenau has another bookshop and more WCs.

Eating: You'll find eating options at the visitors center; additional choices are nearby.

Expect Changes: The Auschwitz museum is continually maintained and updated. Some things may be different than described here, but everything is well signposted.

Etiquette: The camp encourages visitors to remember that Auschwitz is the place where more than a million people lost their lives. Behave and dress here as you would at a cemetery. Photos are allowed inside some buildings, as posted.

Auschwitz Tour

Although most visitors will (and should) take a guided tour, the self-guided commentary below is worth reading before your visit to get your head around the history and the scope of what you're about to experience. If you visit on your own without a tour, read the text ahead of time, then use it to guide you through the camp.

Regardless of how you arrive, you'll begin at the new visitors center for Auschwitz I. This area can be crowded and chaotic; show your ticket, go through the security checkpoint, and get oriented. When ready, you'll go through an underground tunnel and arrive at the main entrance building. This is where the tour begins. You'll start with an eight-minute **movie,** which offers a concise history of the camp and sets the stage for what you'll see.

• *To begin your visit, stand by the main building and look over the grassy field to get oriented.*

AUSCHWITZ I

Before World War II, this camp was a base for the Polish army. When Hitler occupied Poland, he took over these barracks and

AUSCHWITZ-BIRKENAU

turned the site into a concentration camp for his Polish political
enemies. The location was ideal:
The industrial city of Oświęcim
was already an established rail
junction, with good connections to Germany and the rest
of Europe. (In fact, in the decades leading up to the war, tens
of thousands of Polish families
emigrating to North America

came through Oświęcim.) Nearby rivers also provided natural protective boundaries.

An average of 14,000 prisoners were kept at this camp at one
time. (Birkenau could hold up to 100,000.) In 1942, Auschwitz
became a death camp for the extermination of European Jews
and others whom Hitler considered "undesirable." By the time the
camp was liberated in 1945, at least 1.1 million people had been
murdered here—approximately 960,000 of them Jewish.

• *Go closer to the camp entrance, approaching the notorious...*

"Arbeit Macht Frei" Gate

Although this gate imparts the message "Work Sets You Free," it's
cruelly ironic. The only way out of the camp for the prisoners was
through the crematorium chimneys. Note that the "B" was welded
on upside down by belligerent inmates, who were forced to make
this sign (and much of the camp). The sign is a replica; the original
was stolen one night in December 2009, then recovered two days
later, cut up into several pieces. The original is now safely in the
museum's possession but no longer displayed.

Just inside the gate and to the right, the camp orchestra (made
up of prisoners) used to play marches; having the prisoners march
made them easier to count.

• *From the gate, proceed straight up the "main street" of the camp.*

You'll pass two rows of barracks. The first one holds a variety
of national memorials. We'll circle back here later, if you'd like to
enter some of them. The second row of barracks holds the main
museum exhibitions. Blocks 4 and 5 focus on how Auschwitz
prisoners were killed. Blocks 6, 7, and 11 explore the conditions
for prisoners who survived here a little longer than most. In each
block, arrows guide you on a one-way route through the numbered
rooms; in many cases, exhibits are both downstairs and upstairs—
don't miss these.

• *Start with the third block you come to, on your right.*

Guided Tours at Auschwitz

While you can see it on your own (using this chapter's self-guided tour), most visitors take a guided tour—in fact, these are required at peak times. Even during these busy times, you can enter Birkenau without a guide.

Organized Museum Tours: The Auschwitz Museum's excellent guides are serious and frank historians who feel a strong sense of responsibility about sharing the story of the camp. The regularly scheduled 3.5-hour English tour covers Auschwitz and Birkenau (90 zł; 130 zł for 6-hour "study tour"). These tours must be prebooked at https://visit.auschwitz.org. Arrive for your scheduled tour 30 minutes early.

Private Official Museum Guides: If you have a special interest or a small group, it's affordable and worthwhile to hire one of the museum's guides for a private tour. Choose between the basic 3.5-hour tour (620 zł) or a longer "study tour" (800 zł/6 hours, 890 zł/spread over 2 days); rates are higher for more than 10 people. Because English-speaking guides are limited, reserve as far in advance as possible—ideally, when time slots open up 90 days ahead—at https://visit.auschwitz.org.

Day Tours from Kraków: Various Kraków-based companies sell round-trip tours from Kraków to Auschwitz, which include a guided tour of the camp (typically around 140-170 zł). I can't vouch for their quality, but the main outfits are **See Kraków** (www.seekrakow.com), **Discover Cracow** (www.discovercracow.com), **Kraków Booking** (www.krakowbooking.com), and **Cracow City Tours** (www.cracowcitytours.com)—for details, see page 254.

Local Guides and Drivers from Kraków: For easy transportation to Auschwitz-Birkenau, hire a Kraków-based guide or driver (about 600-700 zł per carload). They will clearly explain how to reserve a time slot for entry, then provide an easy, no-stress connection between your hotel and the museum, with commentary about what you're seeing in the countryside en route. I've listed my favorite guides and drivers on page 251.

Block 4: Extermination

In Room 1, a map identifies the countries from which Auschwitz prisoners were brought—as far away as Norwegian fjords and Greek isles. In an alcove along the side of the room is an urn filled with ashes, a symbolic memorial to all the camp's victims. At the end of the hall is a giant photo of arriving prisoners from Hungary.

Room 2 shows photographs of Jewish ghettos from all over Europe being "liquidated"—that is, the residents assembled and deported to various concentration camps. Thanks to its massive occupancy, Auschwitz was a destination for many.

Room 3 displays rare photos of scenes inside the camp. To pre-

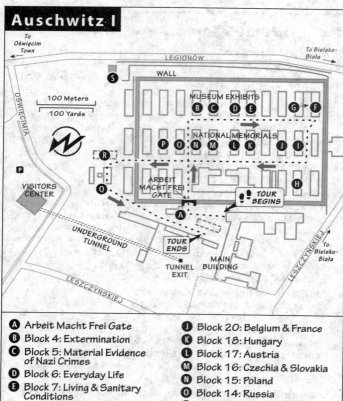

Auschwitz I

To Oświęcim Town

To Bielsko-Biała

LEGIONÓW

WALL

100 Meters
100 Yards

MUSEUM EXHIBITS
B **C** **D** **E** **G** **F**

NATIONAL MEMORIALS
P **O** **N** **M** **L** **K** **J** **I**

S Camp Commander's Home

R Gallows

Q Crematorium

ARBEIT MACHT FREI GATE

H

A

TOUR BEGINS

TOUR ENDS

P VISITORS CENTER

OŚWIĘCIMIA

UNDERGROUND TUNNEL

TUNNEL EXIT

MAIN BUILDING

To Bielsko-Biała

LESZCZYŃSKIEJ

A Arbeit Macht Frei Gate	**J** Block 20: Belgium & France
B Block 4: Extermination	**K** Block 18: Hungary
C Block 5: Material Evidence of Nazi Crimes	**L** Block 17: Austria
D Block 6: Everyday Life	**M** Block 16: Czechia & Slovakia
E Block 7: Living & Sanitary Conditions	**N** Block 15: Poland
F Block 11: The Death Block	**O** Block 14: Russia
G Execution Courtyard	**P** Block 13: Roma (Gypsy)
H Block 27: Jewish Memorial	**Q** Crematorium
I Block 21: Netherlands	**R** Gallows
	S Camp Commander's Home

vent a riot, the Nazis claimed at first that this was only a transition camp for resettlement in Eastern Europe.

Upstairs in Room 4 is a model of a Birkenau crematorium. People entered on the left, then undressed in the underground rooms (hanging their belongings on numbered hooks and encouraged to remember their numbers to retrieve their clothes later). They then moved into the "showers" and were killed by Zyklon-B gas (hydrogen cyanide), a German-produced

Chilling Statistics: The Holocaust in Poland

The majority of people murdered by the Nazis during the Holocaust were killed right here in Poland. For centuries, Poland was known for its relative tolerance of Jews, and right up until the beginning of World War II, Poland had Europe's largest concentration of Jews: 3,500,000. Throughout the Holocaust, the Nazis murdered 4,500,000 Jews in Poland (many of them brought in from other countries) at camps, including Auschwitz, and in ghettos such as Warsaw's.

By the end of the war, only 300,000 Polish Jews had survived—less than 10 percent of the original population. Many of these survivors were granted "one-way passports" (read: deported) to Israel, Western Europe, and the US by the communist government in 1968 (following a big student demonstration with a strong Jewish presence). Today, only about 10,000 Jews live in all of Poland.

cleaning agent that is lethal in high doses. This efficient factory of murder took about 20 minutes to kill 8,000 people in four gas chambers. Elevators brought the bodies up to the crematorium. Members of the *Sonderkommand*—Jewish inmates who were kept isolated and forced by the Nazis to work here—removed the corpses' gold teeth and shaved off their hair (to be sold) before putting the bodies in the ovens. It wasn't unusual for a *Sonderkommand* worker to discover a wife, child, or parent among the dead. A few of these workers committed suicide by throwing themselves at electric fences; those who didn't were systematically executed by the Nazis after a two-month shift. Across from the model of the crematorium are empty canisters of Zyklon-B.

Across the hall in the dimly lit Room 5 is one of the camp's most powerful exhibits: a wall of actual victims' hair—4,400 pounds of it. Also displayed is cloth made of the hair, used to make Nazi uniforms. The Nazis were nothing if not efficient...not even human body parts could be wasted.

Back downstairs in Room 6, you may see an exhibit on the plunder of victims' personal belongings. People being transported here were encouraged to bring luggage—and some victims had even paid in advance for houses in their new homeland. After they were killed, everything of value was sorted and stored in warehouses that prisoners named "Canada" (after a country they associated with great wealth). Although the Canada warehouses were destroyed, you can see a few of these items in the next building.

• *Head next door, to the left.*

AUSCHWITZ-BIRKENAU

Block 5: Material Evidence of Nazi Crimes

The exhibits in this block consist mostly of piles of the victims' goods, a tiny fraction of everything the Nazis stole. As you wander through the rooms, you'll see eyeglasses, fine Jewish prayer shawls, crutches and prosthetic limbs (the first people the Nazis exterminated were mentally and physically ill German citizens), and a pile of pots and pans.

Then, upstairs, you'll witness a seemingly endless mountain of shoes, children's clothing, and suitcases with names of victims—many marked *Kind*, or "child." Visitors often wonder if the suitcase with the name "Frank" belonged to Anne, one of the Holocaust's most famous victims. After being discovered in Amsterdam by the Nazis, the Frank family was transported here to Auschwitz, where they were split up. Still, it's unlikely this suitcase was theirs. Anne Frank and her sister Margot were sent to the Bergen-Belsen camp in northern Germany, where they died of typhus shortly before the war ended. Their father, Otto Frank, survived Auschwitz and was found barely alive by the Russians, who liberated the camp in January 1945.

• *Cross over to the next block.*

Block 6: Everyday Life

Although the purpose of Auschwitz was to murder its inmates, not all were killed immediately. After an initial evaluation, about 20 percent of prisoners were registered and forced to work. (This did not mean they were chosen to live—just to die later.) This block shows various aspects of daily existence at the camp.

The halls are lined with photographs of victims, each identified with a name, birthdate, occupation, date of arrival at Auschwitz, date of death, and camp registration number. The dates reveal that these people survived here an average of two to three months. Similar photographs hang in several other museum buildings; as with the plundered items in the last

19472
DĄBROWSKI JAN
ur. 8.2.1920 r., robotnik,
przybył 30.7.1941, zginął we wrześniu 1942.

block, keep in mind that these represent only a tiny fraction of the masses of people murdered at Auschwitz. In fact, most of the faces you see in these halls are non-Jewish Poles, who were among the early inmates at the camp. Later—when new arrivals were predominantly Jewish—photographing each prisoner became too expensive, so they were tattooed instead.

The room on the right displays drawings of the arrival process. One end of the room displays actual camp uniforms. After the ini-

St. Maksymilian Kolbe (1894-1941)

Among the many inspirational stories of Auschwitz is that of a Polish priest named Maksymilian Kolbe. Before the war, Kolbe traveled as a missionary to Japan, then worked in Poland for a Catholic newspaper. While he was highly regarded for his devotion to the Church, some of his writings had an unsettling anti-Semitic sentiment. But during the Nazi occupation, Kolbe briefly ran an institution that cared for refugees—including Jews.

In 1941, Kolbe was arrested and interned at Auschwitz. When a prisoner from Kolbe's block escaped in July of that year, the Nazis punished the remaining inmates by selecting 10 of them to be put in the Starvation Cell until they died—based on the Nazi "doctrine of collective responsibility." After the selection had been made, Kolbe offered to replace a man who expressed concern about who would care for his family. The Nazis agreed. (The man Kolbe saved is said to have survived the Holocaust.)

All 10 of the men—including Kolbe—were put into Starvation Cell 18. Two weeks later, when the door was opened, only Kolbe had survived. The story spread throughout the camp and Kolbe became an inspiration to the inmates. To squelch the hope he had given the others, Kolbe was executed by lethal injection.

In 1982, Kolbe was canonized by the Catholic Church. Some critics—mindful of his earlier anti-Semitic rhetoric—still consider Kolbe's sainthood controversial. But most Poles feel he redeemed himself through this noble act at the end of his life.

tial selection, those chosen to work were showered, shaved, and photographed. Pictures show the tattoos used to register prisoners: on the chest, on the arm, or—for children—on the leg. A display shows the symbols that prisoners had to wear to show their reason for internment—Jew, Roma (Gypsy), homosexual, political prisoner, and so on.

Across the hall, Room 4 shows the starvation that took place here. The 7,500 survivors that the Red Army found when the camp was liberated were essentially living skeletons (the "healthier" inmates had been forced to march to Germany). Of those liberated, one-fifth died soon after of disease and starvation.

In Room 5, you can see scenes from the prisoner's workday (sketched by survivors after liberation). Prisoners worked as long as the sun shone—8 hours in winter, up to 12 hours in summer—mostly on farms or in factories.

Another room is about Auschwitz's child inmates, 20 percent of the camp's victims. Blond, blue-eyed children were either "Germanized" in special schools or, if younger, adopted by German families. Dr. Josef Mengele conducted gruesome experiments here on children, especially twins and triplets, ostensibly to find ways to increase fertility for German mothers.

• *Next up is...*

Block 7: Living and Sanitary Conditions

Tours sometimes skip this block because it's a bottleneck, and most of what you'll see inside is similar to exhibits elsewhere in the camp. The focus is on the living conditions of prisoners held in these barracks—at first about 700 per building, and eventually up to 1,000. As you progress down the hall, you'll see how conditions grew more and more unpleasant: At first, the floor was strewn with hay, or with straw-filled mattresses. Later, three-tiered bunk beds (with two or eventually three prisoners per bed) were crammed into each room. You'll also see the washrooms (with trough-like sinks) and the latrines (with individual toilets—rather than the long, communal benches we'll see later at Birkenau). The Block Elder's Room showed how supervisors—selected from among the prisoners—had special privileges.

• *Blocks 8-10 are vacant (medical experiments were carried out in Block 10). Block 11 was the most notorious of all.*

Block 11: The Death Block

Head into the **"Death Block"** (#11), from which nobody ever left alive. Death here required a "trial"—but it was never a fair trial.

Room 2 (on the left as you enter) is where these sham trials were held, lasting about two minutes each. In Rooms 4 and 5, you can see how prisoners lived in these barracks—more three-level bunks, with three prisoners sleeping in each bed (they had to sleep on their sides so they could fit). In Room 6, people undressed before they were executed.

In the **basement,** you'll see several types of cells. In the Standing Cells (#22), four people would be forced to stand together for hours at a time (amid bricks that went all the way to the ceiling then). In the Dark Cell (#20), which held up to 30, there was only a small window for ventilation—and if it became covered with snow, the prisoners suffocated. The Starvation Cell (#18) held prisoners selected to starve to death when a fellow prisoner escaped; Maksymilian Kolbe spent two weeks here to save another man's life (see sidebar on Kolbe). The basement is also where Nazi scientists carried out the first tests of Zyklon-B.

If the **upstairs** is open, you'll find gallows and a bench used for administering lashes. Filling this floor are exhibits on various forms of punishment, mostly focusing on resistance within the camp, escapees, and local Poles who were executed—either for trying to assist the prisoners or for fighting with Nazi officers.

Finally, step into the walled-in **courtyard** between Blocks 10 and 11. The wall at the far end is where the Nazis shot several thousand political prisoners, leaders of camp resistance, and religious leaders. Notice that the windows are covered so that nobody could witness the executions. Also take a close look at the memorial—the back of it was made of a material designed by Nazis to catch the bullets without a ricochet. Inmates were shot at short range—about three feet. There are usually fresh flowers and other memorials placed at this poignant location.

• *Leaving Block 11, proceed straight ahead, between the buildings, to the other row of barracks. Several of these blocks house...*

National Memorials

These exhibits were created not by museum authorities but by representatives of the home countries of the camps' victims. As these memorials overlap with the general exhibits and are designed for Europeans to learn more about the victims from their own homelands, most visitors skip this part of the site. On the other hand, while the main museum exhibits await renovation and modernization, the displays in these national memorials tend to be slicker and better-presented than the ones we just saw. As you walk along this street toward our next stop (the crematorium), consider stepping into the ones that interest you.

The first one you see is the memorial to **Jewish** victims (Block 27), and this powerful memorial may be the one most worth entering. The entryway displays the words *SHOAH—Holocaust*. A large room with black-and-white footage captures the joyful flowering of Jewish culture in the interwar period—when Europe and the Mediterranean basin had some 10.8 million Jews. Upstairs, clips of Hitler speeches spout the hateful propaganda that led to the Holocaust. The "Geography of Murder" room shows the locations of death camps and killing sites where Jews were murdered. You'll watch eyewitness testimony from survivors and see art penciled on blank walls that was inspired by actual children's art from concentration camps. The final room contains the gigantic Book of Names—individually listing each and every one of the nearly 6 million Jews murdered in the Holocaust. The book practically fills an entire room.

Most of the other national memorials are on the right side

of the street. Across from the Jewish memorial, Block 21 honors **Dutch Jews,** including perhaps the most famous Dutch victim of the concentration camp, Anne Frank.

Block 20, a former hospital block, is shared by **Belgium** and **France.** A room near the entrance explains how some prisoners were killed by lethal injection, with portraits and biographical sketches of victims. Upstairs is the powerful Belgium exhibit, with a room featuring victims' portraits. Block 18 holds a very modern, conceptual exhibit about **Hungary**'s victims, with an eerie heart-beat sound pervading the space; Block 17 memorializes victims from **Austria.** Across from this block, notice the long **gallows** used for mass hangings and the **wooden guard booth** where the SS took roll call. If someone was missing, the entire group had to stand at attention—perhaps for hours—until that person was located. Block 16 contains a well-presented exhibit about **Czech** and **Slovak** victims.

Block 15 honors victims from **Poland,** focusing on the 1939 Nazi invasion of the country, which resulted in the immediate internment of Polish political prisoners. Exhibits explain the process of "Germanization"—such as renaming Polish streets with German names—and (upstairs) the underground resistance that fought to get back some control over Poland.

Block 14 is the **Russian** national memorial. However, this one's a bit controversial: While Russia claims to have lost "Russian" Jews to the Holocaust, virtually all of them were technically Polish Jews who had been living within Russia. (They spoke Polish, not Russian.) To sidestep the hot topic of how to identify these victims, this memorial focuses not on victims, but on the Russian liberation of the camp.

Block 13 houses the **Roma (Gypsy)** exhibit. You'll learn that the Roma, along with the Jews, were considered no better than "rats, bedbugs, and fleas," and explore elements of the so-called *Zigeunerfrage*—the "Gypsy question" about what to do with this "troublesome" population.

• *At the end of this row of barracks, you reach a guard tower and a barbed-wire fence. Jog a few steps to the right, through the hole in the fence, then angle left toward the earthen mound with the giant, ominous brick chimney. Enter on the right side.*

Crematorium

You'll enter into the big **"shower room."** Up to 700 people at a time could be gassed here. People undressed outside, or just inside the door. Look for the vents in the ceiling—this is where the SS men dropped the Zyklon-B.

In the adjacent room is a replica of the **furnace.** This facility could burn 340 bodies a day—so it took two days to burn all of the bodies from one round of executions. (The Nazis didn't like this "inefficiency," so they built four more huge crematoria at Birkenau.)

• *Exiting the crematorium, you're facing the main building where we began the tour. But first, circle around to the opposite side of the crematorium—near where you entered—for the closest thing this story has to a happy ending.*

Shortly after the war, camp commander Rudolf Höss was tried, convicted, and sentenced to death. Survivors requested that he be executed at Auschwitz, and in 1947, he was hanged here. The **gallows** are preserved behind the crematorium, about a hundred yards from his home where his wife—who is said to have loved her years here—raised their children in a villa maintained by enslaved people and furnished with possessions of the dead.

• *Take your time with Auschwitz I. When you're ready, continue to the second stage of the camp—Birkenau.*

AUSCHWITZ II—BIRKENAU

In 1941, realizing that the original Auschwitz camp was too small to meet their needs, the Nazis began a second camp in some nearby farm fields. The original plan was for a camp that could hold 200,000 people, but at its peak, Birkenau (Brzezinka) held about 100,000. They were still adding onto it when the camp was liberated in 1945.

• *Train tracks lead past the main building and into the camp. The first sight that greeted prisoners was the...*

Guard Tower

If you've seen *Schindler's List*, the sight of this icon of the Holocaust—shown in stirring scenes from the movie—may make you queasy.

Go through the gate to survey the camp: a vast field of chimneys and a few intact wooden and brick barracks. Some of the barracks were destroyed by Germans. Most were dismantled to be used for fuel and building materials shortly after the war. But the first row has been reconstructed (using components from the original structures). The train tracks lead straight back to the dividing platform, and then dead-end at the ruins of the crematorium and camp monument at the far side.

• *Turn right (passing the WCs) and walk through the barbed-wire fence to reach the...*

Auschwitz II – Birkenau

Legend:
- ① Guard Tower, Viewpoint, WC & Bookstore
- ② Latrine & Restored Barracks
- ③ Dividing Platform
- ④ Crematoria Ruins (4)
- ⑤ Monument
- ⑥ "The Sauna"
- ⑦ "Canada" Foundations
- ⑧ Brick Barracks
- ⑨ Shuttle Bus to Auschwitz I

☐ Foundations
▬ Existing Buildings

200 Meters
200 Yards

Wooden Barracks

The first of these barrack buildings was the **latrine:** The front half of the building contained washrooms, and the back was a row of toilets. There was no running water, and prisoners were in charge of keeping the latrine clean. Because of the resulting unsanitary conditions and risk of disease, the Nazis were afraid to come in here—so the latrine became the heart of the black market and the inmates' resistance movement.

The third barrack was a **bunkhouse.** Each inmate had a personal number, a barrack number, and a bed number.

Inside, you can see the bunks (angled so that more could fit). An average of 400 prisoners—but up to 1,000—would be housed in each of these buildings. These wooden structures, designed as stables by a German company to fit 51 horses (look for the horse-tying rings

on the wall), came in prefab pieces that made them cheap and convenient. Two chimneys connected by a brick duct provided a little heat. The bricks were smoothed by inmates who sat here to catch a bit of warmth.

• *Return to the train tracks and follow them toward the monument about a half-mile away, at the back end of Birkenau. At the intersection of these tracks and the perpendicular gravel road (halfway to the monument)—now marked by a lonely train car—was the gravel pitch known as the...*

Dividing Platform

A Nazi doctor would stand facing the guard tower and evaluate each prisoner. If he pointed to the right, the prisoner was sentenced to death, and trudged—unknowingly—to the gas chamber. If he pointed to the left, the person would be registered and live a little longer. It was here that families from all over Europe were torn apart forever. (Photographs near the wooden building show the sad scene.)

Now carry on along the train tracks. As you walk on the camp's only road, imagine the horror of this place—all the barracks packed with people, smoke billowing from the busy crematoria.

• *At the end of the tracks, go 50 yards to the left and climb the three concrete steps to view the ruins of the...*

Crematorium

This is one of four crematoria here at Birkenau, each with a capacity to cremate more than 4,400 people per day. At the far-right end of the ruins, see the stairs where people entered the rooms to undress. They were given numbered lockers, conning them into thinking they were coming back. (The Nazis didn't want a panic.) Then they piled into the "shower room"—the underground passage branching away from the memorial—and were killed. Their bodies were burned in the crematorium (on the left), giving off a scent of sweet almonds (from the Zyklon-B). Beyond the remains of the crematorium is a hole—once a gray lake where tons of ashes were dumped.

This efficient factory of death was destroyed by the Nazis as the Red Army approached, leaving the haunting ruins you see today.

When the Soviets arrived on January 27, 1945, the nightmare of Auschwitz-Birkenau was over. The Polish parliament voted to turn these grounds into a museum so that the world would understand, and never forget, the horror of what happened here.

• *At the back of the camp stands the...*

Monument

Built in 1967 by the communist government in its heavy "Socialist Realist" style, this monument represents gravestones and the chimney of a crematorium. The plaques, written in each of the languages spoken by camp victims (including English, far right), explain that the memorial is "a cry of despair and a warning to humanity."

• *With more time, you could continue deeper into the...*

Rest of the Camp

There's much more to see for those who are interested—Birkenau sprawls for a frightening distance. One worthwhile extension is  the reception and disinfection building that prisoners called **"the Sauna"** (the long building with four tall chimneys). It was here that prisoners would be forced to strip and be deloused; their belongings were seized and taken to the "Canada" warehouses (described earlier) to be sorted. Walking through here (on glass floors designed to protect the original structure below), you'll see artifacts of the grim efficiency with which prisoners were "processed"—their heads were shaved, they were tattooed with a serial number, and they were assigned uniforms and wooden clogs to wear. Portraits at the end of the building humanize those who passed through here. Look for the cart, which was used to dispose of ashes.

In front of the Sauna is a field of foundations of the **"Canada" warehouses.** Nearby are the other two destroyed **crematoria.**

• *On your way back out of the camp, consider detouring to the right to look inside one of the...*

Brick Barracks

Enter one of these buildings. The supervisors lived in the two smaller rooms near the door. Farther in, most barracks still have the wooden bunks that held about 700 people per building. Four

On the Way to Auschwitz: The Polish Countryside

You'll spend an hour or two gazing out the window as you drive or ride to Auschwitz—offering a good look at the Polish countryside. Ponder these thoughts about what you're passing...

The small houses you see are traditionally inhabited by three generations at the same time. Nineteenth-century houses (the few that survive) often sport blue stripes, which in those days announced that a daughter was eligible for marriage. Once they saw these blue lines, local boys were welcome to come a-courtin'.

Some of the houses are bigger, very boxy, and have almost flat roofs rather than angled ones. These prefab homes generally date from the communist period and are sturdily built (of concrete) so they can handle the heavy snow loads in winter. While some have been nicely colorized, most are a drab gray or beige.

Big churches mark small villages. In fact, Polish Catholics like to show off their civic and spiritual pride by building wildly imaginative churches. Like in the US, tiny roadside memorials and crosses indicate places where fatal accidents have occurred.

Polish farmers traditionally had small lots that were notorious for not being very productive. These farmers somewhat miraculously survived the communist era without having to merge their farms. For years, they were Poland's sacred cows: producing little, paying almost no tax, and draining government resources. But after Poland joined the European Union in 2004, many had to collectivize their farms after all.

Since most people don't own cars, bikes are common and public transit is excellent. There are lots of bus stops, as well as minibuses that you can flag down. The bad roads are a legacy of communist construction, exacerbated by heavy truck use and brutal winters.

Poland has more than 2,000 counties, or districts, each with its own coat of arms; you'll pass several along the way. The forests are state owned, and locals enjoy the right to pick berries in the summer and mushrooms in the autumn (you may see people—often young kids—selling their day's harvest by the side of the road). The mushrooms are dried and then boiled to make tasty soups in the winter.

or five people slept on each bunk; the floor was reserved for new arrivals. There were chamber pots at either end of the building. After a Nazi doctor died of typhus, sanitation improved, and these barracks got running water.

Auschwitz Connections

The Auschwitz Museum is in the town of Oświęcim, about 50 miles west of Kraków. The drive takes around 1.5 hours, depending on traffic. By public transit, it's about 2 to 2.5 hours each way, including travel time to and from the bus or train station.

FROM KRAKÓW TO AUSCHWITZ

The easiest way to reach Auschwitz is with a **package tour** or **private guide or driver;** both of these options are described on page 250.

If you're using public transportation, here are your choices (each option costs around 20 zł):

The most comfortable public transit option is to take a **public bus** (hourly, 1.5 hours, get current schedule at any Kraków TI, buses depart from Kraków's main bus station behind the train station, run by Lajkonik). Look for buses to "Oświęcim" (not necessarily "Auschwitz"). Note that these buses can be full, and there's no way to reserve a seat—line up early (generally about 15 minutes ahead). Be sure the driver knows you're heading to the *Muzeum*. Once in Oświęcim, buses stop first at the train station, then continue on to the museum's visitors center.

Your other option is to ride the **train** to Oświęcim (about 4/ day direct, 2 hours), but be aware that it takes about 20-25 minutes to walk from the train station to the camp/visitors center. Instead, you can take a taxi (likely around 20 zł).

RETURNING FROM AUSCHWITZ TO KRAKÓW

Upon arrival at Auschwitz I, plan your departure by visiting the information desk. They can give you a schedule of departures and explain where the bus leaves from. If you intend to stay late into the afternoon, make a point of figuring out the last bus or train back to Kraków. Plan accordingly, and remember to allow enough time to make it from Birkenau back to Auschwitz I to catch your ride.

WARSAW

Warszawa

Warsaw (Warszawa, vah-SHAH-vah in Polish) is Poland's capital and biggest city. It's huge, famous, and important...but not particularly romantic. If you're looking for Old World quaintness, head for Kraków. If you're tickled by spires and domes, get to Prague. But if you want to experience a truly 21st-century city, Warsaw's your place.

A decade ago, Warsaw was dreary and uninviting. But things have changed here dramatically. The Varsovians (as locals are called) are chic and sophisticated, and here by choice; according to some studies, as many as 8 out of every 10 Varsovians weren't born in Warsaw. Young professionals dress and dine as well as the Parisians and Milanese, and they've mastered the art of navigating an urban jungle in heels or a man bun. Today's Warsaw has gleaming new office towers, glitzy shopping malls, swarms of international

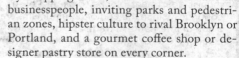

businesspeople, inviting parks and pedestrian zones, hipster culture to rival Brooklyn or Portland, and a gourmet coffee shop or designer pastry store on every corner.

Stroll down revitalized boulevards that evoke the city's glory days, pausing at an outdoor café to sip coffee and nibble at a *pączek* (the classic Polish jelly doughnut). Drop by a leafy park for an al fresco Chopin concert, packed with patriotic Poles. Commune with the soul of Poland at the city's many state-of-the-art museums—take your pick: Poland's artists (National Museum), its favorite composer (Chopin Museum), its dramatic histo-

Warsaw History: Ebbs and Flows

Warsaw has good reason to be a city of the future: The past hasn't been very kind. Historically, Warsaw has seen wave after wave of foreign rulers and invasions—especially during the last hundred years. But in this horrific crucible, the enduring spirit of the Polish people was forged. Years ago, one proud Varsovian told me, "Warsaw is ugly because its history is so beautiful."

Founded around 1300, Warsaw gradually gained importance through the late Middle Ages. In the mid-16th century, it became the seat of the Sejm (parliament of nobles), and it took over as seat of the royal court (and therefore Poland's capital) in 1596.

The city's golden age was between the World Wars, when Poland—newly reconstituted after a century and a half of foreign rule under the Partitions—was proudly independent. Interwar Warsaw saw a flourishing of commerce, construction, and the arts almost unmatched in Europe at that time, when it was also the largest and most culturally rich Jewish city in Europe.

This age of optimism was cut brutally short by the city's darkest days, as the Nazis occupied the city (and all of Poland) at the outbreak of World War II. First, its Jewish residents were forced into a tiny ghetto. They rose up...and were slaughtered (the Ghetto Uprising—see page 419). Then, in the war's waning days, its surviving residents rose up...and were slaughtered (the Warsaw Uprising—see page 426). Fed up with the troublesome Varsovians, Hitler sent word to systematically demolish the entire city, block by block. At the war's end, Warsaw was virtually gone. An estimated 800,000 residents were dead—nearly two out of every three souls.

The Poles almost gave up on what was then a pile of rubble, planning to build a brand-new capital city elsewhere. But ultimately, they decided to rebuild, creating a city of contrasts: painstakingly restored medieval lanes and retrofitted communist apartment blocks (*bloki* in Polish). And its evolution continues. Since the end of communism, Warsaw has become a hub of international trade and diplomacy—adding sleek skyscrapers to its skyline. Finally emerging from the gloom of the 20th century, Warsaw is no longer ugly. The city—and its history—are more beautiful than ever.

ry (Museum of Warsaw and Warsaw Uprising Museum), its dedication to the sciences (Copernicus Science Center), and its Jewish story (Museum of the History of Polish Jews). You can also dig into one of Europe's most interesting foodie scenes, where a world of wildly creative chefs open new restaurants all the time—at budget prices. If you picture a dreary metropolis, think again. Warsaw is full of surprises.

PLANNING YOUR TIME

One day is the absolute minimum to get a quick taste of Warsaw—but you'll have to sightsee very selectively. The city can easily fill two or three days, and even then you'll need to pick and choose. Review your museum-going options to decide how much time you need.

No matter how long you stay, get your bearings by taking a stroll through Polish history, following my Royal Way Walk from Palm Tree Circle to the Old Town. With more time, extend your stroll on my Old Town Walk for a sampling of Warsaw's historic core. Then visit other sights according to your interests and time: Jewish history, the Warsaw Uprising, Polish artists, royalty, hands-on science gizmos, hipster hangouts, or Chopin. To slow down and take a break from the city, relax in Łazienki Park.

For dinner, buck the tourist trend by leaving the overpriced Old Town and riding a tram or the Metro, or taking a taxi or an Uber to the hip Śródmieście district, which has the highest concentration of quality eateries.

Orientation to Warsaw

Warsaw sprawls with 1.8 million residents. Everything is on a big scale—it seems to take forever to walk just a few "short" blocks.

Get comfortable with public transportation (or taxis or Uber) and plan your sightseeing to avoid backtracking.

The tourist's Warsaw blankets a mild hill on the west bank of the Vistula River (in Polish: Wisła, VEES-wah). To break things into manageable chunks, I think of the city as three major zones (from north to south):

The **Old Town and Royal Way,** at Warsaw's northern edge, is the most touristy area. Here you'll find the Old Town (Stare Miasto, STAH-reh mee-AH-stoh), the adjacent and nearly-as-old New Town (Nowe Miasto, NOH-vay mee-AH-stoh), the Royal Castle on Castle Square (Plac Zamkowy, plahts zahm-KOH-veh), and the historical artery called the Royal Way (Trakt Królewski, shwock kroh-LEHV-skee). This bustling strip has strollable boulevards, genteel cafés, expansive squares and parks, and stately landmarks both historic and faux-historic (much of this area was rebuilt after World War II).

Warsaw Overview

Eateries & Shopping
1. Hala Koszyki Food Hall
2. Plac Zbawiciela Eateries
3. Beirut & other Poznańska Eateries
4. Mokotowska Street (Shopping)

POLISH HISTORY MUSEUM (UNDER CONSTRUCTION)

CYTADELA

SŁOMIŃSKIEGO

Vistula River

GDAŃSKI BRIDGE

WYBRZEŻE GDAŃSKIE

To Centrum Praskie Koneser, Polish Vodka Museum & i

SKOCZYLASA
JAGIELLOŃSKA
TARGOWA

Wileński

See the Central Warsaw map

KONWIKTORSKA SANGUSZKI
BONIFRATERSKA
FRANCISZKAŃSKA
FRETA

New Town Square

NEW TOWN

DEFENSIVE WALL

Old Town Square

WYBRZEŻE HELSKIE

WYBRZEŻE KOŚCIUSZKOWSKIE

PRAGA MUSEUM

PRAGA

To Mus. of Hist. of Polish Jews & Former Ghetto

ŚWIĘTOJERSKA

BARBICAN

Krasińskich Garden

GEN. ANDERSA

DŁUGA

MIODOWA

OLD TOWN

Castle Square

ROYAL CASTLE

ŚLĄSKO-DĄBROWSKI BRIDGE

OKRZEI
WYBRZEŻE SZCZECIŃSKIE

ST. ANNE'S

ROYAL WAY

To National Stadium

Ratusz M

SOLIDARNOŚCI

NATIONAL THEATER & OPERA

WIERZBOWA

RADZIWIŁŁ PALACE

HOTEL BRISTOL

KAROWA

BROWARNA

DOBRA

COPERNICUS SCIENCE CENTER

ŚWIĘTOKRZYSKI BRIDGE

ORLA
SENATORSKA

Piłsudski Square

KRAKOWSKIE PRZEDMIEŚCIE

CZACKIEGO

KRÓLEWSKA

Saxon Garden

WARSAW UNIVERSITY

ELEKTROWNIA POWIŚLE

Centrum Nauki Kopernik M

PTASIA

OBOŻNA

GRZYBOWSKA

HOLY CROSS

Nowy Świat- Uniwersytet M

TAMKA

CHOPIN MUSEUM

FONIATOWSKIEGO BRIDGE

Świętokrzyska M

ŚWIĘTOKRZYSKA

NOWY ŚWIAT

FOKSAL

To Warsaw Uprising Museum

GALERIA CENTRUM MALL

CHMIELNA

SMOLNA

JERUSALEM AVE.

PALACE OF CULTURE & SCIENCE

E. PLATER

ZŁOTA

Centrum M

WIDOK

JEROZOLIMSKIE

PALM TREE CIRCLE

NATIONAL MUSEUM

LUDNA

NOWOGRODZKA

ŻURAWIA

Three Crosses Square

CENTRAL TRAIN STATION

AL. NIEPODLEGŁOŚCI

CHAŁUBIŃSKIEGO

WSPÓLNA

HOŻA

POZNAŃSKA

MARSZAŁKOWSKA

WILCZA

ROYAL WAY

KRUCZA

3

4

PIĘKNA

AL. UJAZDOWSKIE

ROZBRAT

KOSZYKOWA

PIĘKNA

Constitution Square

MOKOTOWSKA

1

ŚRÓDMIEŚCIE

NOWOWIEJSKA

2

Plac Zbawiciela

Politechnika

Łazienki Park

CHOPIN MONUMENT & CONCERTS

PALACE ON THE WATER

WAWELSKA

0.5 Kilometer

0.5 Mile

ROYAL WAY

To Wilanów Palace B

BELWEDER

AL. ARMII LUDOWEJ

WARSAW

"**Palm Tree Circle**" is my nickname for the center of the city, near the traffic circle with a fake palm tree—where busy Jerusalem Avenue (Aleja Jerozolimskie, ah-LAY-uh yeh-ro-zoh-LIM-skyeh) crosses the shopping street called Nowy Świat (NOH-veh SHVEE-aht). Nearby are some good accommodations, trendy upscale eateries, pedestrianized shopping streets and glitzy malls, the National Museum (Polish art), the Palace of Culture and Science (communist-era landmark skyscraper), and the central train station (Warszawa Centralna).

The **Śródmieście** (SHROD-myesh-cheh, "Downtown") district, to the south, is a mostly residential zone with the city's best restaurant and nightlife scene and some good accommodations. The only real sight here is lush Łazienki Park, with its summertime al fresco Chopin concerts.

In sprawling Warsaw, many more sights—including some major ones—lie outside these three areas, but all are within a long walk or a short ride on public transit or in a taxi/Uber. These include the Museum of the History of Polish Jews and the Warsaw Uprising Museum (to the west) and the Copernicus Science Center (to the east, along the river). Across the river is the hardscrabble but gentrifying Praga district.

TOURIST INFORMATION

Warsaw's TI is helpful, but the locations are less than handy: one at the **Palace of Culture and Science** (enter on the side facing the train station, on Emilii Plater; daily 9:00-19:00, Oct-April until 18:00) and the other across the river in Praga, at the trendy **Koneser Center** (same hours, Plac Konesera 2). There's also a privately run TI partner on Castle Square, but it's a souvenir shop first and far less helpful—drop by here only if you want to grab some brochures (Plac Zamkowy 1/13). The general information number for all TIs is +48 503 033 720. All information is also available online (www.warsawtour.pl).

Sightseeing Pass: Busy sightseers might consider the **Warsaw Pass,** which covers admission to most major sights, the best hop-on, hop-off bus tour, and a Chopin concert, but no city transit (149 zł/24 hours, 199 zł/48 hours, 239 zł/72 hours, sold at the TI). If your museum-going plans are ambitious, do the math.

ARRIVAL IN WARSAW
By Train

Most trains arrive at the **central train station** (Warszawa Centralna, vah-SHAH-vah tsehn-TRAHL-nah), a communist-era monstrosity that has been renovated with surprising grace. (Don't get off at Warszawa Zachodnia or Warszawa Wschodnia—the

Western and Eastern stations, respectively—which are far from the tourist area.)

Warszawa Centralna can be tricky to navigate: Three parallel concourses run across the tracks, accessed by three different sets of escalators from each platform, creating a subterranean maze (with well-signed lockers, ticket windows, and lots of shops and eateries). Be patient: To get your bearings, ride up on your platform's middle escalator, then look for signs to the wide-open **main hall** (follow signs for *hala główna/main hall*). Here you'll

find a row of ticket windows, eateries, waiting areas (upstairs), and (from outside, near the taxi stand) views of the adjacent Palace of Culture and Science and Złota 44 skyscrapers. If you have a little time to kill, walk across the street to the super-modern Złote Tarasy shopping mall.

Getting into Town: To reach the tourist zone and most of my recommended hotels, a taxi/Uber is the easiest choice, while the bus is more economical (but more challenging to find).

Taxis wait outside the main hall. To get a fair fare, look for one with a company logo and telephone number, and ask for an estimate up front (the ride should cost no more than about 20-30 zł for most of my recommended hotels). You can also order an **Uber,** but it can be tricky to identify a pick-up location near the station— consider walking out to a busy road with pullouts and ordering it from there.

From the station, **bus #175** or **#128** takes you to the Royal Way and Old Town in about 10 minutes. (Credit-card-operated ticket machines are at major bus stops and often on board; for details on getting tickets, see "Getting Around Warsaw," later.) You can catch either bus in front of the skyscraper with the Hotel Marriott, across busy Jerusalem Avenue from the station. Because it's hard to find this stop from the station's mazelike corridors, it's probably simplest to ascend to street level (on the Aleja Jerozolimskie side) and cross surface streets to reach the well-marked Marriott tower. Both buses terminate just off Piłsudski Square, a five-minute walk from the Old Town. **Bus #160** also goes to the Old Town (though not via the Royal Way), but it departs from the opposite side of the station: To find its stop from the main hall, go out the side door toward *Ulica Emilii Plater.*

Buying Train Tickets: Lining one wall of the main arrival hall *(hala główna)* are 16 ticket windows; window #1 is for information. There are also ticket machines throughout the station, and you can book online at Intercity.pl. If buying tickets in person, allow plenty of time to wait in line. At one corner of the main hall, the InfoDworzec office can help you get oriented to the station but doesn't sell tickets (daily 7:00-21:00). Remember: Even if you have a rail pass, a reservation is still required on many express trains (including EIC trains to Kraków or Gdańsk). If you're not sure, ask. To get to your train, first find your way to the right platform (*peron*, as noted on schedules), then keep an eye on both tracks (*tor*) for your train.

By Plane
Fryderyk Chopin International Airport
Warsaw's Fryderyk Chopin International Airport (Lotnisko Chopina Waszawa, code: WAW, www.lotnisko-chopina.pl) is about six miles southwest of the center.

To get into town, you can take the train or bus (similar prices, around 5 zł). The train is faster, but the bus makes more stops in the city center and may get you closer to your hotel. From the arrivals area, just follow signs to either option.

The **train** departs about twice hourly and takes 20-30 minutes. The line into town is operated by two different companies (SKM and KM)—take whichever one departs first. Be ready for your stop: Half the trains make fewer stops and take you to Centralna station; others make a few more stops and use the Warszawa Śródmieście station—which feeds into the same underground passages as Centralna (these trains also continue one more stop to the Warszawa Powiśle station, which is closer to Nowy Świat and nearby hotels). Whether arriving at Centralna station or Warszawa Śródmieście, see the "By Train" arrival instructions, earlier.

Bus #175 departs from the curb in front of arrivals every 15-20 minutes and runs into the city center (Centralna station, the Royal Way, and Piłsudski Square near the Old Town, 30-45 minutes depending on traffic; buy ticket from machine before you board).

For a **taxi,** head to the official taxi stand. Taxis have a fixed rate of about 50 zł to most downtown hotels (trip takes 30 minutes depending on traffic). It's generally cheaper to order an **Uber** (except at very busy times).

Modlin Airport
Modlin Airport (code: WMI, www.modlinairport.pl), about 21 miles northwest of the city center, primarily serves budget airlines (especially Ryanair). A **taxi** into downtown Warsaw should be about 150 zł (the maximum legitimate fare is 200 zł, or 250 zł at night). There may be a direct **bus** operated by Flixbus (www.flixbus.com), or you can take the well-coordinated **bus-plus-train connection:** Take a shuttle bus to Modlin's main train station, then hop on a

train to Warszawa Centralna station (about 20 zł total, runs about hourly, 1-1.5 hours total, www.mazowieckie.com.pl).

GETTING AROUND WARSAW

Sprawling Warsaw can be exhausting to get around. Get comfortable with public transportation and taxis/Uber.

By Public Transit: Warsaw's efficient, affordable public transportation network includes buses, trams, and the two-line Metro (transit info: www.wtp.waw.pl). Everything is covered by the same tickets. Most rides within the tourist zone take less than 20 minutes, so the default is the 3.40-zł 20-minute ticket *(bilet 20-minutowy)*. For longer journeys, a single ticket *(bilet jednorazowy)* covers any trip up to 75 minutes for 4.40 zł. A 24-hour travelcard *(bilet dobowy)*—which pays for itself if you take at least five trips—costs 15 zł. Ticket machines, which are at most major stops and on board many buses and trams, are easy to use; they have English instructions and take credit cards. Be sure to validate your ticket as you board by inserting it into the little yellow box. You can also buy tickets on the Jakdojade app, which has a route finder.

Most of the city's major attractions line up on a single axis, the Royal Way, which is served by several different buses (but no trams). **Bus #175**—particularly useful on arrival—links Chopin Airport, the central train station, the Royal Way, and the Old Town (it terminates at Piłsudski Square, about a five-minute walk from Castle Square). Once you're in town, the designed-for-tourists **bus #180** conveniently connects virtually all the significant sights and neighborhoods: the former Jewish Ghetto and Museum of the History of Polish Jews, Castle Square/the Old Town, the Royal Way, Łazienki Park, and Wilanów Palace (south of the center). This user-friendly bus lists sights in English on the posted schedule inside (other buses don't). **Bus #111** is another handy option for those going to the Jewish Museum; from there, it runs parallel to the bus #180 route, cutting over to the Royal Way just south of Piłsudski Square, then down to Nowy Świat, before turning off to the east with a stop in front of the National Museum and then over the river.

Bus routes beginning with "E" (marked in red on schedules) are express, so they go long distances without stopping (these don't run July-Aug). Note that on Saturdays and Sundays in summer (May-Sept), the Nowy Świat-Krakowskie Przedmieście section of the Royal Way is closed to traffic, so the above routes detour along a parallel street.

Trams are useful for reaching the trendy Śródmieście district in the south. Several trams run along the north-south Marszałkowska corridor, with stops at Plac Konstytucji (Constitution Square, the heart of the Śródmieście) and at Plac Zbawiciela (with a cluster of great eateries).

Warsaw's two-line **Metro** system, designed for commuters, can be useful for hops between certain sights—especially line 2, which runs east to west; its most convenient stops are Rondo Daszyńskiego (near the Warsaw Uprising Museum), Świętokrzyska (where you can transfer to line 1), Nowy Świat-Uniwersytet (in the middle of the Royal Way, near the Copernicus Monument), Centrum Nauki Kopernik (on the riverbank, near the Copernicus Science Center), Stadion Narodowy (National Stadium, across the river), and Wileński (near the heart of the Praga district). The north-south line 1, which stops at the train station (Centrum), is less useful for visitors.

By Taxi: Use only cabs that are clearly marked with a company logo and telephone number; official cabs have a mermaid decal on the front door (or call your own: Locals like City Taxi, +48 19459; MPT Radio Taxi, +48 19191; or Ele taxi, +48 22 811 1111). All official taxis have similar rates: 8 zł to start, then 3 zł per kilometer (4.50 zł after 22:00, on weekends, or in the suburbs). **Uber** also works well in Warsaw and is typically cheaper than a taxi.

Tours in Warsaw

Walking Tours

Each year, new companies crop up offering walking tours in Warsaw. These tend to have one of two approaches: a "free" tour of the main sights (with generous tipping expected); or communism-themed tours, often with a ride to a gloomy apartment-block area for a taste of the Red old days. The TI and most hotels have brochures. Survey the latest offerings, do some homework (check online reviews), and pick a tour that suits your interests.

Private Guides

Having a talented local historian as your guide in this city, with such a complex and powerful story to tell, greatly enhances your experience. I've worked with two great guides, who charge around 750 zł for a four-hour walking tour: **Jola Postrzygacz** (+48 602 252 707, jolanta@postrzygacz.pl) and **Hubert Pawlik** (various tours, includes options by car, see descriptions on his website, +48 502 298 105, www.warsaw-citytours.com, guide@warsaw-citytours.com).

Food Tours

Eat Polska does excellent food and vodka tours around this fast-changing foodie mecca. A top-quality guide will take your small group to a variety of restaurants and bars around the city, with tasting samples at each one. The guides provide insightful context

Central Warsaw

Accommodations

1 Hotel Indigo
2 Between Us B&B & Między Nami
3 Chopin Boutique
4 Apple Inn
5 Oki Doki City Hostel
6 Hotel Bristol
7 Hotel Le Régina
8 Duval Apartments
9 Castle Inn
10 To Hotel Nobu

Eateries

11 Bibenda
12 Soul Kitchen
13 Le Cabaret
14 Drugie Dno
15 Żywioły
16 Kamanda Lwowska
17 A. Blikle
18 E. Wedel Pijalnia Czekolady
19 Elektrownia Powiśle Eateries
20 Warszawa Powiśle
21 Browary Warszawskie Eateries
22 Fabryka Norblina Eateries
23 To Centrum Praskie Koneser Eateries
24 Żyto & Freta 33
25 Pyzy, Flaki Gorące!
26 Zapiecek (5)

Rondo Babka

PARKING LOT WITH FORMER GHETTO WALL

UMSCHLAGPLATZ MONUMENT

FORMER SS HQ

STAWKI

MURANÓW
(Former Jewish Ghetto)

NISKA

DUBOIS

BUNKER

MUSEUM OF THE HISTORY OF POLISH JEWS

GHETTO HEROES SQUARE

Muranów

Plac Krasinskich

M. ANIELEWICZA

ZAMENHOFA

KARMELICKA

Nalewki

Zamenhofa

Krasińskich Garden

GEN. WŁ. ANDERSA

KONWIKTORSKA

SANGUSZKI

MIĘDZYPARKOWA

Z. SŁOMIŃSKIEGO

FRANCISZKAŃSKA

Ratusz M

Plac Bankowy

SOLIDARNOŚCI

ELEKTORALNA

PTASIA

FOOTBRIDGE OF REMEMBRANCE

PL. MIROWSKI

AL. JANA PAWŁA II

WALICÓW

GRZYBOWSKA

CHŁODNA

NOŻYK SYNAGOGUE

Plac Grzybowski

TWARDA

ŚWIETOKRZYSKA

GRZYBOWSKA

ŻELAZNA

PROSTA

GHETTO WALL FRAGMENT

ŁUCKA

WRONIA

PANSKA

SIENNA

ZŁOTE TARASY MALL

Dworzec Centralny Bus #160

PRZYOKOPOWA

TOWAROWA

Muzeum Powstania Warszawskiego

WARSAW UPRISING MUSEUM

Rondo Daszynskiego M

Rondo Daszyńskiego

PROSTA

MIEDZIANA

ZŁOTA

CHMIELNA

VARSO TOWER

CENTRAL TRAIN STATION

Dw. Centralny

Dworzec Centralny Bus #175

400 Meters

400 Yards

WARSAW

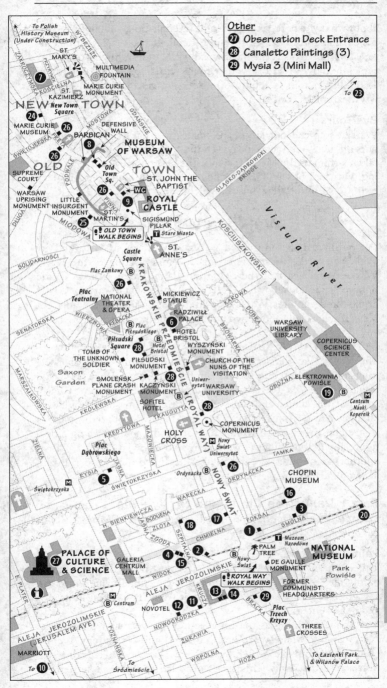

Other

㉗ Observation Deck Entrance
㉘ Canaletto Paintings (3)
㉙ Mysia 3 (Mini Mall)

about what you're tasting, making this educational about both Polish cuisine and Polish culture in general. If you have a serious interest in food, this is the most worthwhile tour in town (food tours typically daily at 13:00, vodka tours with food pairings daily at 17:00, either tour is about 400 zł/person, get details and book at www.eatpolska.com).

Bus Tours

Warsaw's spread-out landscape makes it a natural for a hop-on, hop-off bus—although heavy traffic may make you wish you'd taken a tram or the Metro instead. The best choice is CitySightseeing, with red buses (85 zł/24 hours, 90 zł/48 hours, two routes). Skip City-Tour (yellow buses), which is less reliable.

Walks in Warsaw

I've outlined two self-guided walks in Warsaw. The Royal Way Walk covers the most interesting one-mile section of the Royal Way—in the heart of the city, from Palm Tree Circle to Castle Square. It's followed by the Old Town Walk, which starts in Castle Square and explores Warsaw's Old Town, ending in the adjacent New Town. Allow about two hours to do both walks back-to-back.

ROYAL WAY WALK

The Royal Way (Trakt Królewski) is the six-mile route that the kings of Poland used to travel from their main residence (at Castle Square in the Old Town) to their summer home (Wilanów Palace, south of the center and not worth visiting). This busy boulevard changes names from Nowy Świat to Krakowskie Przedmieście as it stretches from south to north. Not counting sightseeing stops, figure about 30 minutes to walk along Nowy Świat ("Part 1"), then another 45 minutes along Krakowskie Przedmieście to the Old Town ("Part 2").

Part 1: Palm Tree Circle and Nowy Świat

• *Start this walk at the traffic circle officially named for Charles de Gaulle but colloquially known as...*

Palm Tree Circle

This is one of the city's main intersections, marked by the iconic palm tree. Stand near the communist-era monument under the spruce trees (on the curb, kitty-corner from the biggest building) and get oriented.

You're standing at the intersection of two major boulevards: **Nowy Świat** (where we're heading next) and **Jerusalem Avenue** (Aleja Jerozolimskie, which heads from Warszawa Centralna station across the river). This street once led to a Jewish settlement

Warsaw at a Glance

▲▲▲**Museum of the History of Polish Jews** Exceptional, expansive exhibit on the full Jewish experience through Polish history. **Hours:** Wed-Mon 10:00-18:00, Sat until 20:00, closed Tue. See page 418.

▲▲**Castle Square** Colorful spot with whiffs of old Warsaw—Royal Castle, monuments, and a chunk of the city wall—and cafés just off the square. See page 397.

▲▲**Royal Castle** Warsaw's best palace, rebuilt after World War II, but retaining its former opulence and many original furnishings. **Hours:** Tue-Sun 10:00-18:00, Oct-April until 17:00, closed Mon year-round. See page 403.

▲▲**Old Town Market Square** Re-creation of Warsaw's glory days, with lots of colorful architecture. See page 400.

▲▲**National Museum** Collection of mostly Polish art, with unknown but worth-discovering works by Jan Matejko and the Młoda Polska (Art Nouveau) crew. **Hours:** Tue-Sun 10:00-18:00, Fri until 20:00, closed Mon. See page 409.

▲▲**Warsaw Uprising Museum** State-of-the-art space tracing the history of the Uprising and celebrating its heroes. **Hours:** Wed-Mon 8:00-18:00, Sat-Sun from 10:00, closed Tue. See page 425.

▲**Copernicus Science Center** Spiffy science museum with well-explained, hands-on exhibits in English; Warsaw's best family activity. **Hours:** Mon-Thu 8:00-18:00, Fri until 20:00, Sat-Sun 9:00-19:00. See page 414.

▲**Łazienki Park** Lovely, sprawling green space with Chopin statue, peacocks, and Neoclassical buildings. **Hours:** Always open; wonderful outdoor Chopin concerts mid-May-late Sept generally Sun at 12:00 and 16:00. See page 428.

▲**Museum of Warsaw** In-depth treatment of the history of Warsaw, with excellent movie in English. **Hours:** Tue- Fri 9:00-17:00, Thu until 19:00, Sat-Sun 11:00-18:00, closed Mon. See page 407.

▲**Marie Skłodowska-Curie Museum** Honors the great Polish scientist who studied radiation, in her birth home. **Hours:** Tue-Sat 12:00-18:00, closed Sun-Mon. See page 408.

called New Jerusalem. Like so much else in Warsaw, it's changed names many times. Between the World Wars, it became "May 3rd Avenue," celebrating Poland's 1791 constitution (Europe's first). But this was too nationalistic for the occupying Nazis, who called it simply Bahnhofstrasse ("Train Station Street"). Then the communists switched it back to "Jerusalem," strangely disregarding the religious connotations of that name. (Come on, guys—what about a good, old-fashioned "Stalin Avenue"?) The strikingly wide boulevards were part of the city's post-WWII Soviet rebuilding. Communist urban planners felt that eight-to-twelve-lane roads were ideal for worker pageantry like big May Day parades...and, when the workers weren't happy, for Soviet tanks to thunder around, maintaining order.

You can't miss the giant **palm tree** in the middle of Jerusalem Avenue. When a local artist went to the real Jerusalem, she was struck by the many palm trees—and wanted to erect one along Warsaw's own little stretch of "Jerusalem." This artificial palm tree went up in 2002 as a temporary installation. It was highly controversial, dividing the neighborhood. One snowy winter day, the pro-palm tree faction—who appreciated the way the tree spiced up this otherwise dreary metropolis—camped out here in bikinis and beachwear to show their support. They prevailed, and the tree is now a permanent fixture.

The big, blocky building across the street (on the left side of the intersection) was the **headquarters of the Communist Party,** built in 1948. *Nowy Świat* translates as "New World," inspiring a popular communist-era joke: What do you see when you turn your back on the Communist Party? A "New World." Ironically, when the economy was privatized in 1991, this building became home to Poland's stock exchange. And then the country's only dealership for Ferraris—certainly not an automobile for the proletariat—moved in downstairs.

On the corner in front of the former Communist Party HQ, a statue of **Charles de Gaulle** strides confidently up the street. A gift from the government of France, this celebrates the military tactician who came to Warsaw's rescue when the Red Army invaded from the USSR after World War I.

To the left of the Communist Party building is the vast **National Museum**—a good place for a fascinating lesson in Polish art (see the self-guided tour later, under "Sights in Warsaw").

Before walking down Nowy Świat, notice the small but powerful **monument** near you. In 1956, this was dedicated to the "Poles who fought for People's Poland"—with a strong communist connotation. In a classic example of Socialist Realism, the communists

appropriated a religious theme that Poles were inclined to embrace (this pietà composition)...and politicized it. But in 2014, the statue was rededicated to the "*partyzantom* who fought for free Poland in World War II." "Partisan" was a bad word in the 1950s, when it was used to describe the soldiers of the Polish Home Army—which fought against both the Nazis and the Soviets.

• *From here, turn your back to the Communist Party building and head into a new world—down Nowy Świat—to the first intersection. As you stroll, notice how massive, intense Warsaw suddenly becomes more intimate and accessible.*

Nowy Świat

This charming shopping boulevard, lined with boutiques, cafés, and restaurants, feels upscale and elegant. Before World War II, Nowy Świat was Warsaw's most popular neighborhood. And today, once again, rents are higher here than anywhere else in town. While most tourists flock into the Old Town, Varsovians and visiting businesspeople prefer this zone and farther south.

The city has worked hard to revitalize this strip with broad sidewalks, flower boxes, old-time lampposts, and strict restrictions on traffic (only buses and taxis—and on summer weekends, it's entirely traffic-free).

Look down the street and notice the harmonious architecture. In the 1920s, this street was anything but cohesive: an eclectic and decadent strip of Art Deco facades, full of individualism. Rather than rebuild in that "trouble-causing" style, the communists used an idealized, more conservative, Neoclassical style, which feels more like the 1820s than the 1920s.

Ulica Chmielna, the first street to the left, is an appealing pedestrian street leading to Emil Wedel's chocolate heaven (a five-minute walk away—down Chmielna and then right on Szpitalna street; described later, under "Eating in Warsaw"). Between here and the Palace of Culture and Science stretches one of Warsaw's top shopping neighborhoods (culminating at the Galleria Centrum mall).

Across the street from Chmielna (on the right) is the restaurant street called **Foksal.** On a balmy summer evening, this street is filled with chatty al fresco diners. For more ideas on eating along either of these streets—Foksal or Chmielna—see page 436.

A few steps farther down Nowy Świat, on the left, look for the recommended **A. Blikle** pastry shop and café—a venerable spot for Polish sweets, especially *aczki* (rose-flavored jelly dough-nuts). Don't miss the chance to sample this distinctly Polish treat. Step inside for a dose of the 1920s: good-life Art Deco decor and historical photos. Or, if you're homesick for Starbucks, drop in to one of the second-wave coffee shops that line this stretch of Nowy Świat—many with American-style lattes "to go."

A half-block down the street (on the left, at #39) is a rare sur-viving bit of preglitz Nowy Świat: Bar Mleczny Familijny, a clas-sic **milk bar**—a government-subsidized cafeteria filled with locals seeking a cheap meal (an interesting cultural artifact, but not rec-ommended for a meal; for more about milk bars, see the sidebar on page 230). But don't be surprised if it's gone by the time you visit; in this high-rent district, it's unlikely that these few remaining hold-overs from the old days will survive for much longer.

Eat and shop your way along Nowy Świat. About one more block down, **Ordynacka street** (on the right) leads downhill to the Chopin Museum, worth considering for musical pilgrims.

Keep going. At the intersection with busy Świętokrzyska is a handy **Metro stop** for the M2 line; you can use this to reach the Warsaw Uprising Museum to the west, or the Copernicus Science Center or Praga district to the east.

• *Continuing straight along Nowy Świat through a duller stretch, you'll walk alongside a hulking, gloomy building on your left before popping out in a pleasant square with a big statue of Copernicus.*

Part 2: Krakowskie Przedmieście

• *The street name changes to Krakowskie Przedmieście (meaning, rough-ly, "suburb in the direction of Kraków") at the big...*

Copernicus Statue

This statue, by the great Danish sculptor Bertel Thorvaldsen, stands in front of the Polish Academy of Science. **Mikołaj Kopernik** (1473-1543) was born in Toruń and went to college in Kraków. The Nazis stole his statue and took it to Germany (which, like Poland, claims Copernicus as its own). Now it's back where it belongs. The concentric circles radiating from the front of the

statue represent the course of the planets' orbits, from Mercury to Saturn.

Just to Copernicus' left is a low-profile, black-marble **Chopin bench**—one of many scattered around the center. These benches mark points related to his life (in this case, his sister lived across the street). Each of these benches plays Chopin's music with the push of a button (though because of passing traffic, this one is tough to hear).

Directly in front of the statue, in the glass case, find a replica of a **Canaletto painting** of this same street scene in 1778 and compare it to today's reality. As the national archives were destroyed, city builders referred to historic paintings like these for guidance after World War II. You'll see other Canaletto replicas like this one scattered around the city.

• *Across from Copernicus, the Church of the Holy Cross is worth a look.*

Church of the Holy Cross (Kościół Św. Krzyża)

We'll pass many churches along this route, but the Church of the Holy Cross is unique (and free to enter). Composer **Fryderyk Chopin's heart** is inside one of the pillars of the nave (first big pillar on the left, look for the marker). After two decades of exile in France, Chopin's final wish was to have his heart brought back to his native Poland after his death. During World War II, the heart was hidden away in the countryside for safety.

Check out the bright gold chapel, located on the left as you face the altar, near the front of the church. It's dedicated to a saint whom Polish Catholics believe helps them with **"desperate and hopeless causes."** People praying here are likely dealing with some tough issues. The beads draped from the altarpieces help power their prayers, and the many little brass plaques are messages of thanks for prayers answered.

In the back-left corner (as you face the altar) is a chapel dedicated to Poland's favorite son, **St. John Paul II.** His ghostly image appears out of the wall; beneath him is a rock inscribed with the words *Tu es Petrus* (Latin for "You are Peter"—what Jesus said when he made St. Peter the first-ever pope), embedded with a capsule containing JPII's actual blood.

Just opposite, in the back-right corner, behind the giant barbed wire, is a memorial to the 22,000 Polish POWs—mostly officers and prominent civilians—massacred by Soviet soldiers in 1940 near **Katyń,** a village in today's Russia. Stalin was determined

WARSAW

to decapitate Poland's military intelligentsia in a ruthless mass kill-ing, which Poles have never forgotten.

Leaving the church, notice the 19th-century, bronze-and-granite **statue of Christ bearing the cross** along the balustrade. In front, a placard reads, "Lift up your hearts." Even as Warsaw bore the burden of Russian occupation, this statue inspired them to remain strong and not lose hope.

• *Cross the street (appreciating how pedestrian-friendly it is—crossing here used to be a real-life game of Frogger), and continue left.*

Warsaw University

A long block up the street on the right, you'll see the gates (marked *Uniwersytet*) to the main campus of **Warsaw University,** found-ed in 1816. This lively student district has plenty of bookstores *(księgarnia)* and cafeterias.

Keep strolling, appreciating the fine facades. The 18th century was a time of great political decline for Poland, as a series of in-competent foreign kings mishandled crises and squandered funds. But ironically, it was also Warsaw's biggest economic boom time. Along this boulevard, aristocratic families of the period built **man-sions**—most of them destroyed in World War II and rebuilt since. Some have curious flourishes (just past the university on the right, look for the doorway supported by four bearded brutes admiring their overly defined abs...it's supposed to be a six-pack, but I count ten). Over time, many of these families donated their mansions to the university.

• *The bright-yellow church a block up from the university, on the right, is the...*

Church of the Nuns of the Visitation
(Kośicół Sióstr Wizytek)

This Rococo confection from 1761 is the only church on this walk that survived World War II, and is notable because Chopin was briefly the organist here.

The monument in front of the church commemorates **Cardi-nal Stefan Wyszyński,** who was the head of the Polish Catholic Church from 1948 to 1981. The communist authorities opposed the Church but also realized it would be risky for them to shut down the churches in such an ardently religious country. The Com-munist Party and the Catholic Church coexisted tensely in Poland, and when Wyszyński protested a Stalinist crackdown in 1953, he was arrested and imprisoned. Three years later, in a major victory for the Church, Wyszyński was released. He continued to fight the communists, becoming a great hero of the Polish people in their struggle against the regime—so much so, he's been called the "un-crowned king of Poland."

Across the street is another then-and-now Canaletto illustration.

• *Farther up (on the right, past the park) is the elegant, venerable...*

Hotel Bristol

A striking building with a round turret on its corner, the Hotel Bristol was used by the Nazis as a VIP hotel and bordello, and survived World War II.
If you wander through any fancy Warsaw lobby... make it this one. Step in like you're staying here and explore its fine public spaces, with fresh Art Deco and Art Nouveau flourishes. The café in front retains its Viennese atmosphere, but the *pièce de résistance* is the stunning Column Bar deeper in, past the dramatically chandeliered lounge.

• *Leave the Royal Way briefly here for a worthwhile detour. With the corner turret of Hotel Bristol at your back, cross the street and bear left between the buildings—passing the fancy Raffles Europejski Hotel. You'll pop out at a vast expanse. Continue straight ahead across the street and stand at the edge of...*

Piłsudski Square (Plac Marszałka Józefa Piłsudskiego)

The oversized, empty-feeling Piłsudski Square (pew-SOOD-skee) has been important Warsaw real estate for centuries, constantly changing with the times. In the 1890s, the Russians who controlled this part of Poland began construction of a huge and magnificent Orthodox cathedral on this spot. But soon after it was completed, Poland regained its independence, and anti-Russian sentiments ran hot. So in the 1920s, just over a decade after the cathedral went up, it was torn down. During the Nazi occupation, this square took the name "Adolf-Hitler-Platz." Under the communists, it was Zwycięstwa, meaning "Victory" (of the Soviets over Hitler's fascism).

When the regime imposed martial law in 1981, the people of Warsaw silently protested by filling the square with a giant cross made of flowers. The huge **plaque** in the ground near the road commemorates two monumental communist-era Catholic events on this square: John Paul II's first visit as pope to his homeland on June 2, 1979; and the May 31, 1981, funeral of Cardinal Stefan Wyszyński, whom we met across the street. The **cross** nearby also honors the 1979 papal visit, with one of his most famous and inspiring quotes to his countrymen: "Let thy spirit descend, let thy spirit descend, and renew the face of the earth—of *this* earth" (meaning Poland, in a just-barely-subtle-enough dig against the communist regime that was tolerating his visit).

Now walk deeper into the square and stand in the center, near the giant **flagpole,** with the Royal Way at your back, for this quick spin tour orientation: Ahead are the Tomb of the Unknown Soldier and Saxon Garden; 90 degrees to the right is the old National Theater, eclipsed by a modern business center/parking garage; another 90 degrees to the right is a statue of Piłsudski (which you passed to get here); and 90 more degrees to the right is the Sofitel—formerly the Victoria Hotel, the ultimate plush, top-of-the-top hotel where all communist-era VIPs stayed.

In front of the hotel, the monument that resembles a **giant black staircase** commemorates the 2010 crash in Smoleńsk, Russia, of a plane carrying 96 top government officials, including President Lech Kaczyński. There were no survivors. (A week later, the funeral for Kaczyński on this square drew more than 100,000 mourners.) Now look to the left to see a giant statue of Kaczyński at the edge of the square—striding in this direction, with his hand over his heart. You'll see lots of relatively new Kaczyński memorials throughout Warsaw (and Poland). On the one hand, it's a shocking trauma for a nation to lose a president unexpectedly midterm—think of all the things named for JFK in the US. On the other hand, the party Kaczyński co-founded (Law and Justice) still holds power in Poland—in fact, his twin brother is its chairman—so it's also politically expedient for them to lionize him as a martyr.

To the right of the hotel, on the horizon, you can see Warsaw's quickly expanding skyline. The imposing Palace of Culture and Science, which once stood alone over the city, is now joined by a cluster of glittering postcommunist skyscrapers, giving Warsaw a Berlin-esque vibe befitting its important role as a business center of Central Europe.

Deeper into the square, you may see fences on either side, or you may see a sprawling **construction zone.** The city is finally getting around to rebuilding some of the buildings that were leveled by the Nazis: the Saski Palace, the Brühl Palace, and three tenement houses that once fronted Królewska street. (The colonnade straight ahead—described below—was once part of the Saski Palace.) If the fences are still up, peer through the holes to see the brick foundations they've already excavated.

If it's accessible, walk to the fragment of colonnade by the park that marks the **Tomb of the Unknown Soldier** (Grób Nieznanego Żołnierza). The Saski Palace (this is all that's left) was built by the Saxon prince electors (Dresden's Augustus the Strong and his son), who became kings of Poland in the 18th century. After the palace was destroyed in World War II, this fragment was kept to memorialize Polish soldiers. The names of key battles over 1,000 years are etched into the columns, the urns contain dirt from major Polish battlefields, and two soldiers stand stiffly at attention. Every hour on the hour, they do a crisp Changing of the Guard—which, poignantly, honors those who have perished in this country, so shaped by wars against foreign invaders.

Just behind the tomb is the stately **Saxon Garden** (Ogród Saski), inhabited by genteel statues, gorgeous flowers, and a spurting fountain. This park was also built by the Saxon kings of Poland. Like most foreign kings, Augustus the Strong and his son cared little for their Polish territory, building gardens like these for themselves instead of investing in more pressing needs. Poles

say that foreign kings such as Augustus did nothing but "eat, drink, and loosen their belts" (it rhymes in Polish). According to Poles, these selfish absentee kings were the culprits in Poland's eventual decline. But they do appreciate having such a fine venue for a Sunday stroll.

Walk back out toward the Royal Way, stopping at the statue you passed earlier. In 1995, the square was again renamed—this time for **Józef Piłsudski** (1867-1935), the guy with the big walrus mustache. With the help of a French captain named Charles de Gaulle (whom we met earlier), Piłsudski forced the Russian Bolsheviks out of Poland in 1920 in the so-called "Miracle on the Vistula." Piłsudski is credited with creating a once-again-independent Poland after more than a century of foreign oppression, and he essentially ran Poland as a virtual dictator after World War I. Of course, under the communists, Piłsudski was swept under the rug. But

since 1989, he has enjoyed a renaissance as many Poles' favorite prototype anticommunist hero. His name adorns streets, squares, and bushy-mustachioed monuments all over the country.

• *Return to Hotel Bristol, turn left, and continue your Royal Way walk.*

Radziwiłł Palace

Next door to the hotel, you'll see
the huge Radziwiłł Palace. The
Warsaw Pact was signed here
in 1955, officially uniting the
Soviet satellite states in a military alliance against NATO.
This building has also, from
time to time, served as the Polish "White House." Along the
street in front of the palace is

another monument to the 2010 Smoleńsk plane crash, which effectively decapitated Poland's leadership.

• *Beyond Radziwiłł Palace, on the right, you'll reach a park with a...*

Statue of Adam Mickiewicz

Poland's national poet, Adam Mickiewicz spearheaded Poland's
cultural survival during more than a century when the country disappeared from maps—absorbed by Austria, Prussia, and Russia.
This was an age when underdog nations (and peoples without nations) all over Europe had their own national revival movements.
The statue was erected in 1898 with permission from the Russian
czar, as long as the people paid for it themselves. It's still an important part of community life: Polish high school students have a
big formal ball (like a prom) 100 days before graduation. After the
ball, if students come here and hop around the statue on one leg,
it's supposed to bring them good luck on their finals. Mickiewicz,
for his part, looks like he's suffering from a heart attack—perhaps
in response to the impressively ugly National Theater and Opera a
block in front of him.

• *Continue to the end of the Royal Way, marked by the big pink palace.
Just before the castle, on your right, is...*

St. Anne's Church

This Rococo church has playful Corinthian capitals inside and out
and a fine pulpit shaped like the prow of a ship—complete with
a big anchor. The richly orna-
mented apse, behind the altar,
survived World War II. This
church offers organ concerts
nearly daily in summer (see "Entertainment in Warsaw," later).

For a scenic finale to your
Royal Way stroll, climb the 150
steps of the **view tower** by the
church (10 zł, generally open
daily 10:00-18:00, later in summer, closed in bad winter weather).

You'll be rewarded with excellent views—particularly of Castle Square and the Old Town. From up top, visually retrace your steps along the Royal Way, and notice the emerging skyline surrounding the Palace of Culture and Science. The tower also affords a good look at the Praga district across the river, where the Red Army waited for the Nazis to level Warsaw during the uprising. Help was so close at hand...but stayed right where it was.

• *Just across from the view tower entrance, look for another Chopin bench (in front of #79). From St. Anne's Church, it's just a few more steps to Castle Square and the start of my Old Town Walk.*

OLD TOWN WALK

In 1945, not a building remained standing in Warsaw's "Old" Town (Stare Miasto). Everything you see here is rebuilt, mostly finished by 1956. Some think the Old Town seems artificial, in a Disney World kind of way. For others, the painstaking postwar reconstruction feels just right, with Old World squares and lanes charming enough to give Kraków a run for its money.

This concise walk, which can be done in about 45 minutes (and is a natural continuation of the Royal Way Walk outlined earlier), offers a quick overview of Warsaw's rebuilt historic core. We'll begin at Castle Square; wind through the streets and squares of the Old Town; pop out at the far side, at the Barbican; and have the opportunity to venture a few minutes farther, into the pretty and mellow New Town. For those looping back, there's also an optional, lightly guided return to this point via sleepy back streets.

• *Begin by standing on the gateway square to the Old Town, at the base of the tall pillar.*

Castle Square (Plac Zamkowy)

This beautiful square (rated ▲▲) is packed with Polish history. Get comfy for a quick overview:

Historically, the Polish kings called Kraków home. But things began to change in 1572, with the expiration of the second great Polish dynasty—the Jagiellonians. Rather than elevate another Polish aristocratic family to the throne, the Polish nobility decided to keep power in their own hands. From that point on, Poland was ruled by the Sejm, or Republic of Nobles—consisting of the kingdom's wealthiest 10 percent. The Sejm elected various foreign kings for limited stints on their throne. While this system kept Poland under its own control (to a degree), it wound up being unworkable: Poor choices of sovereigns, coupled with in-fighting among the nobles, paralyzed Poland and ultimately led to it being wiped from the map of Europe for a century and a half.

The guy on the 72-foot-tall **pillar** is Sigismund III, the first Polish king from the Swedish Vasa dynasty (or Waza in Polish). In 1596, it was Sigismund who relocated his royal seat from Kraków to Warsaw: Warsaw was the meeting point of the Sejm, and it was closer to the center of 16th-century Poland (which had expanded to the east).

Turn your attention to the big, pink **Royal Castle**. A castle has stood here since Warsaw was founded around 1300, but it grew much more important after Warsaw became the capital: It was both the meeting place of the Sejm and the residence of the king...sort of like Buckingham Palace and the Houses of Parliament rolled into one. The palace reached its peak under Stanisław August Poniatowski—the final Polish king—who imported artists and architects to spiff up the interior.

During World War II, Luftwaffe bombs all but obliterated the palace—only one wall remained standing. Reconstruction stalled because Stalin considered it a palace for the high-class elites. It was finally rebuilt in the more moderate 1970s, funded by local donations. The castle's opulent interior is well worth touring—see listing later, under "Sights in Warsaw." (I'll wait while you tour the castle...then let's meet out here to resume the walk.)

Along the right side of the castle, notice the **two previous pillars** lying on their sides. The first one, from 1644, was falling apart and had to be replaced in 1887 by a new one made of granite. In 1944, a Nazi tank broke this second pillar—a symbolic piece of Polish heritage—into the four pieces (still pockmarked with bullet holes) that you see here today. As Poland rebuilt, its citizens put Sigismund III back on his pillar. Past the pillars are views of Warsaw's red-and-white National Stadium across the river—built for the Euro Cup soccer tournament in 2012.

Across the square from the castle, you'll see the partially re-constructed **defensive wall**. This rampart once enclosed the entire Old Town. Like all of Poland, Warsaw has seen invasion from all sides.

Explore the café-lined lanes that branch off Castle Square. Street signs indicate the year that each lane was originally built.

The first street is **Ulica Piwna** ("Beer Street"). If you take a little detour up this street, you'll find **St. Martin's Church** (Kościół Św. Martina, on the left). Run by Franciscan nuns, this church has a simple, modern interior. Walk up the aisle and find the second pillar on the right. Notice the partly destroyed crucifix—it's the only church artifact that survived World War II. Across the street and closer to Castle Square, admire the carefully carved doorway of the house called *pod Gołębiami* ("Under Doves")—dedicated to the memory of an old woman who fed birds amidst the Old Town rubble after World War II.

Back on Castle Square, find the white **plaque** on the wall (at Plac Zamkowy 15/19). It explains that 50 Poles were executed by Nazis on this spot on September 2, 1944. You'll see plaques like this all over the Old Town, each one commemorating victims or opponents of the Nazis. The brick planter under the plaque is often filled with fresh flowers to honor the victims.

• *Leave the square at the far end, on* **St. John's street** *(Świętojańska). On the plaque under the street name sign, you can guess what the dates mean, even if you don't know Polish: This building was constructed from 1433 to 1478, destroyed in 1944, and rebuilt from 1950 to 1953.*

Partway down the street on the right, you'll come to the big brick...

Cathedral of St. John the Baptist (Katedra Św. Jana Chrzciciela)

This cathedral-basilica is the oldest (1370) and most important church in Warsaw. Superficially unimpressive, the church's own archbishop admitted that it was "modest and poor"—but "the historical events that took place here make it magnificent" (much like Warsaw itself). Poland's constitution was consecrated here on May 3, 1791. Much later, this church became the final battleground of the 1944 Warsaw Uprising—when a Nazi "tracked mine" (a huge bomb on tank tracks—this one appropriately named *Goliath*) drove into the church and exploded, massacring the rebels. You can still see part of that tank's tread hanging on the outside wall of the church (through the passage on the right side, between the buttresses).

Cost and Hours: Cathedral—free, crypt—5 zł, both open to tourists Mon-Sat 10:00-17:00, Sun from 15:00, closed during services and summertime organ concerts (see "Entertainment in Warsaw," later).

Visiting the Cathedral: Head inside. Typical of brick churches, it has a "hall church" design, with three naves of equal height. In the back-left corner, find the chapel with the tomb of Cardinal Stefan Wyszyński—the great Polish leader who, as Warsaw's archbishop, morally steered the country through much of the Cold War. (Notice the request to pray for his beatification, as Poles would love to see him become a saint.) Nearby, the crypt holds graves of several important Poles, including Stanisław August Poniatowski (the last Polish king) and Nobel Prize-winning author Henryk Sienkiewicz. Then head up the nave to the main altar, which holds a copy of the Black Madonna—proclaimed "everlasting queen of Poland" after a victory over the Swedes in the 17th century. The original Black Madonna is in Częstochowa (125 miles south of Warsaw)—a mecca for Slavic Catholics, who visit in droves in hopes of a miracle. In the chapel left of the high altar, look for the crucifix ornamented with real human hair.

Nearby: Those interested in Cold War espionage may want to seek out a nearby exhibit about **Ryszard Kukliński** (1930-2004), a Polish military officer who worked closely with USSR authorities...all the while collecting priceless intelligence for the CIA. Kukliński's story, with many twists and turns, is riveting. The excellent exhibit about this superspy was recently slated to be folded into a brand-new **Cold War Museum,** which you'll likely find in the streets immediately behind the cathedral (for the latest, see www.muzeumzimnejwojny.com).

• *Continue up the street and enter Warsaw's grand...*

Old Town Market Square (Rynek Starego Miasta)

For two centuries, this was a gritty market square. Sixty-five years ago, it was a pile of bombed-out rubble. And today, like a phoenix from the ashes, it's risen to remind residents and tourists alike of the prewar glory of the Polish capital (which is why it's rated ▲▲).

Head to the **mermaid fountain** in the middle of the square. The mermaid is an important symbol in Warsaw—you'll see her everywhere. Legend has it that a mermaid *(syrenka)* lived in the Vistula River and protected the townspeople. While this siren supposedly serenaded the town, she's most appreciated for her strength (hence the sword). This square seems to declare that life goes on in Warsaw, as it always has. Children frolic here, oblivious to the turmoil their forebears withstood. When the fountain gurgles, the kids giggle.

Each of the square's four sides is named for a prominent 18th-century Varsovian: Kołłątaj, Dekert, Barss, and Zakrzewski. These men served as "Presidents" of Warsaw (mayors, more or less), and Kołłątaj was also a framer of Poland's 1791 constitution. Take some time to explore the square. Enjoy the colorful architecture. Notice that many of the buildings were intentionally built to lean out into the square—to approximate the higgledy-piggledy wear and tear of the original buildings.

If you'd like to learn more about Warsaw's history, visit the Museum of Warsaw on the Dekert (north) side of the square (described later, under "Sights in Warsaw").

• *Exit the square on Nowomiejska (at the mermaid's 2 o'clock, next to the Museum of Warsaw, under the second-story niche sculpture of St. Anne). After a block, you'll reach the **Barbican** (Barbakan). This defensive gate of the Old Town, similar to Kraków's, protected the medieval city from invaders. Once you've crossed through the Barbican, you're officially in Warsaw's...*

New Town (Nowe Miasto)

This 15th-century neighborhood is "new" in name only: It was the first part of Warsaw to spring up outside the city walls (and is therefore slightly newer than the Old Town. The New Town is a fun place to wander: only a little less charming than the Old Town, but with a more real-life feel—people live and work here. While busy sightseers may choose to skip the New Town, if you stick with me for a few minutes longer, it's worth the extra time. Continue straight ahead from the Barbican on Nowomiejska, which becomes Freta. As you proceed deeper into the New Town, you can feel the tourism slowly melt away. You'll pass an outpost of the E. Wedel chocolate  empire, and some funky galleries and boutiques. On the right is the informative **museum about Marie Skłodowska-Curie,** who grew up in this neighborhood (at #16; see listing later, under "Sights in Warsaw").

Just beyond, for some modern "design"-oriented souvenirs, watch on the left for the endearing **Love Poland Design shop** (at #29/31)...pierogi pillow, anyone?

That shop also marks the entrance to the mellow, easy-to-like **New Town Square** (Rynek Nowego Miasta). A few recommended restaurants line its top edge, and its bottom is dominated by the distinctive green dome of St. Kazimierz Church. While just a short walk from the Old Town, this feels a world apart—a fine spot to relax in the heart of this giant city, enjoy an al fresco meal, sit on a bench, do some people-watching...and just enjoy.

• *To finish our walk with a scenic overview, cross through to the bottom end of the square and turn left, then right (with the green dome on your right). Keep going with the red-brick St. Mary's Church (Kościół*

WARSAW

Mariacki) on your left-hand side. Soon you'll emerge at a park with a monument and an overlook.

The **Marie Skłodowska-Curie monument** honors the woman whose museum we passed earlier. Maria Skłodowska (1867-1934) grew up in this neighborhood at a time when Warsaw was under Russian control, so women were not allowed to pursue a university education. Instead, she left in 1891 for Paris, where—while studying at the Sorbonne—she met and fell in love with a fellow scientist named Pierre Curie. The two wed and became part-

ners in life and in research (and the Polish "Maria" became French "Marie").

They were the first to identify and explain the phenomenon of radioactivity, and they discovered two new elements: polonium (which Marie named after her native land—in the monument she's holding an object that represents that discovery) and radium. They were awarded the Nobel Prize in Physics; later, Marie also won a Nobel Prize in Chemistry, for how her discoveries revolutionized the world's understanding of how the elements function.

After Pierre died in a horse-cart accident, Marie took over his professorship at the Sorbonne and continued her research; among other accomplishments, she founded the Radium Institute, which still carries out important cancer research. (Marie and Pierre were the first to treat certain tumors with radiation.) Few scientists of her generation had so great an impact on our understanding of the world than this brilliant woman from Warsaw.

Madame Curie is looking out over a **panorama** of the Vistula River and Warsaw's more rugged and wild eastern embankment. Down below is an inviting park with a "multimedia fountain" that performs a sound-and-light show on weekends in the summer (ask the TI for the schedule)—which can be viewed from either up here or down along the river. Speaking of which, notice the inviting promenade that runs along the Vistula—in good weather, it's packed with locals enjoying their city. Why not join them?

• *Our walk is finished. You can head back the way you came to reach the Old Town Square. Or, to see a side of the Old Town that many tourists miss, consider this scenic detour back to Castle Square.*

Optional Return Detour: From the Barbican to Castle Square

Go back through the Barbican and over the little bridge, turn right, and walk along the houses that line the inside of the wall. You'll pass a leafy garden courtyard on the left—a reminder that people actually live in the tourist zone within the Old Town walls. Just beyond the garden on the right, look for the carpet-beating rack, used to clean rugs (these are common fixtures in people's backyards). Go left into the square called Szeroki Dunaj ("Wide Danube"), walk to its end, then turn right at Wąski Dunaj ("Narrow Danube").

After about 100 yards, you'll pass the city wall. Just to the right (outside the wall), you'll see the monument to the **Little Insurgent** of 1944, a child wearing a grown-up's helmet and too-big boots, and carrying a machine gun. Children—especially Scouts (Harcerze)—played a key role in the resistance against the Nazis. Their job was mainly carrying messages and propaganda.

Continue around the wall, admiring more public art. Circling all the way back around, soon before you hit the giant pillar, look for the statue honoring **Jan Zachwatowicz** (1900-1983)—the architect who oversaw the rebuilding of Old Warsaw after World War II. If you've enjoyed your visit, offer him a thank-you to end this tour.

Sights in Warsaw

THE OLD TOWN
These sights are linked by my Old Town Walk, earlier.

▲▲Royal Castle (Zamek Królewski)
Warsaw's Royal Castle, dominating Castle Square at the entrance to the Old Town, has the most opulent interior in Poland. Many

of its furnishings are original (hidden away when it became clear the city would be demolished in World War II). A visit to the castle is like perusing a great Polish history textbook. In fact, you'll likely see grade-school classes sitting cross-legged on the floors. Watching the teachers quizzing eager young history buffs, try to imagine what it's like to be a young Pole growing up in a country with such a tumultuous history. The "Royal Route" (the lavish apartments) is worth paying for, but unless you're an art lover, I'd skip the extra cost of the Gallery of Masterpieces. Wednesday is a good day to visit—it's free, and although some royal rooms are closed, enough are open to make a visit worthwhile.

Cost and Hours: Royal Route—50 zł, Gallery of Masterpieces—40 zł, more for special exhibits, free on Wed (when some royal rooms are closed); open Tue-Sun 10:00-18:00, Oct-April until 17:00, closed Mon year-round, last entry one hour before closing; Plac Zamkowy 4, +48 22 355 5170, www.zamek-krolewski.pl.

Tours: The castle's well-produced audioguide is included in the ticket price (10 zł on Wed, when entry is free). Good English information is posted throughout. For an efficient visit, use my commentary to follow the one-way route through the castle.

Services: A public WC is on the courtyard just around the corner of the castle, with more inside and downstairs.

Visiting the Castle: Because the castle visitor route often changes, it's possible you won't see the rooms in this exact order; match the labels in each room to the corresponding text below.

Entering the courtyard, find the ticket office, then cross to the opposite side to enter. (Downstairs are the mandatory coat check and the audioguide desk.) In the lobby, turn left, pass the gift shop and café, then follow *Castle Route* signs upstairs.

The first big room is the **Council Chamber,** where a "Permanent Council" consisting of the king, 18 senators, and 18 representatives met to chart Poland's course. Next is the **Great Assembly Hall,** heavy with marble and chandeliers. The statues of Apollo and Minerva flanking the main door are modeled after King Stanisław August Poniatowski and Catherine the Great of Russia, respectively. (The king enjoyed a youthful romantic dalliance with Catherine on a trip to Russia, and never quite seemed to get over her...much to his wife's consternation, I'm sure.)

Step into the **Knights' Hall,** with yet more busts and portraits of VIPs—Very Important Poles. The statue of Chronos—god of time, with the globe on his shoulders—is actually a functioning clock, though now it's stopped at 11:15 to commemorate the exact time in 1944 when the Nazis bombed this palace to bits. Attached to this hall is the **Marble Room,** with more portraits of Polish greats ringing the top of the room. Above the fireplace is a portrait of Stanisław August Poniatowski (the last Polish king).

Next, step into the **Throne Room.** Notice the crowned white eagles, the symbol of Poland, decorating the banner behind the throne. The Soviets didn't allow anything royal or aristocratic, so postwar restorations came with crownless eagles. Only after 1989 were these eagles crowned again. Peek into the **Conference Room,** with portraits of Russia's Catherine the Great, England's George III, and

France's Louis XVI—in whose esteemed royal league Poniatowski liked to consider himself.

Pass through four more grand rooms: the King's Study, Dressing Room, and Bedchamber (with a gorgeous green silk canopy over the bed), then the Old Audience Chamber. Finally, you'll enter the **Canaletto Room,** filled with canvases of late 18th-century Warsaw painted in exquisite detail by this talented artist. (This Canaletto, also known for his panoramas of Dresden, was the nephew of another more famous artist with the same nickname, known for painting Venice's canals.) Paintings like these helped post-WWII restorers resurrect the city from its rubble. Straight ahead as you enter, on the lower wall, the biggest canvas features the view of Warsaw from the Praga district across the river; pick out the few landmarks that are still standing (or, more precisely, have been resurrected). The castle you're in dominates the center of the painting, overlooking the river. Notice the artist's self-portrait in the lower left. On the facing wall is Canaletto's depiction of the election of Stanisław August Poniatowski as king, in a field outside Warsaw (notice the empty throne in the middle of the group). Among the assembled crowd, each flag represents a different Polish province.

From here, look left of the big "view of Warsaw" painting into the **side chapel,** reserved for the king. In a box to the left of the altar is the heart of Tadeusz Kościuszko, a hero of both the American Revolution and the Polish struggle against the Partitions (for more about the Partitions, see page 222).

As you cross over to the other part of the castle, you'll pass through the **Four Seasons Gallery** (with some fine but faded Gobelin tapestries) before entering a few rooms occupied by the houses of parliament—a reminder that this "castle" wasn't just the king's house but also the meeting place of the legislature. In the giant red room called the **New Deputies' Chambers,** notice the maps over the doors showing Poland's constantly in-flux borders—a handy visual aid for the many school groups that visit here.

After several rooms, you'll reach the grand **Senators' Chamber,** with the king's throne, surrounded by different coats of arms. Each one represents a region that was part of Poland during its golden age, back when it was united with Lithuania and its territory stretched from the Baltic to the Black Sea (see the map on the wall between the doors). In this room, Poland adopted its

1791 constitution (notice the replica in the display case to the left of

the throne). It was the first in Europe, written soon after America's and just months before France's. And, like the Constitution of the United States, it was very progressive, based on the ideals of the Enlightenment. But when the final Partitions followed in 1793 and 1795, Poland was divided between neighboring powers and ceased to exist as a country until 1918—so the constitution was never fully put into action.

At the end of this impressive chamber, you'll turn right into a room with two giant canvases by the great historical painter **Jan Matejko,** showing a very high point and a very low point in Polish history (for more on Matejko, see page 410). First, on the right wall, the *Constitution of 3 May 1791* shows the giddy procession (with the Marshall of the Sejm crowd-surfing through the Old Town, and this castle in the background) heading up the street to the Cathedral of St. John the Baptist to consecrate the first constitution in Europe. But from there, Poland's fortunes tumbled dramatically. Straight ahead from where you entered, *Rejtan—The Fall of Poland* shows the nobleman Tadeusz Rejtan (on the right) lying in front of a door and pulling his shirt open in violent protest against his colleagues in the Sejm debating the First Partition in 1773, which ceded some Polish territory to neighboring Russia, Prussia, and Austria. Two Partitions later, Poland was erased from the map of Europe for a century and a half.

In the next room is another Matejko painting (on the right): *Stefan Batory at Pskov,* in which the Polish king negotiates with Ivan the Terrible's envoys to break their siege of a Russian town. Notice the hussars—fearsome Polish soldiers wearing winged armor.

From here, you'll work your way back down to the lobby where you began. There you'll also find the entrance to another sight...

Gallery of Masterpieces: This gallery of paintings, sculpture, and decorative arts may please art lovers, but it's not essential viewing for most. Inside is a fine cabinet of silver and crystal, and the 36 paintings of the Lanckrońoski Collection. In the final room, take your time appreciating two canvases by Rembrandt (both from 1641). *Girl in a Picture Frame* is exactly that—except that she's "breaking the frame" by resting her hands on a faux frame that Rembrandt has painted inside the real one...shattering the fourth wall in a way that was unusual for the time. The other, *A Scholar at His Writing Table,* shows the hirsute academic glancing up from his notes. Circle around behind the canvases to see X-rays of the paintings, which have helped experts better understand the master's techniques.

Other Castle Sights: Consider a detour to the **Kubicki Arcades** (Arkady Kubiciego), the impressively excavated arcades deep beneath the castle. From the entrance lobby, head downstairs to the

area with the cloakroom, bathrooms, and bookshop, then find the long escalator that takes you down to the arcades. It's free to wander the long, cavernous, and newly clean and gleaming space, made elegant by grand drapes.

The **"Tin-Roofed Palace"** (Pałac pod Blachą) features an extensive oriental carpet collection and seven unimpressive apartments of Prince Józef Poniatowski, the king's brother; it's not worth the 30 zł extra.

▲Museum of Warsaw (Muzeum Warszawy)

Four adjoining townhouses on the north side of the Old Town Square have been connected and turned into this in-depth museum that tells the story of Warsaw. While there's too much detail for a casual visitor's attention span, it's well presented and offers some interesting insight into this great city.

Cost and Hours: 25 zł, includes audioguide, free on Tue; open Tue-Fri 9:00-17:00, Thu until 19:00, Sat-Sun 11:00-18:00, closed Mon; Rynek Starego Miasta 28–42, +48 22 277 4300, www. muzeumwarszawy.pl.

Visiting the Museum: The permanent collection, called "Warsaw in 23 Rooms," offers exactly that. Pick up the detailed map and the dense-but-informative audioguide, and head down into the cellars for an orientation to the city's history—with a timeline, lots of graphs, maps, and helpful models of key landmarks. Then head upstairs and weave your way through the labyrinthine collection; your geo-tagged audioguide knows (roughly) where you are and offers commentary.

Back up on the ground floor, in the courtyard, you'll find architectural decorations from city buildings, as well as the original mermaid statue from the square. Then work your way up through four floors: Floor 1 has a photography gallery, paintings of Warsaw, and a model of the Old Town in the late 18th century. Floor 2 features bronzes, silverwork, portraits of important Varsovians, and clothing. Floor 3 has a moving collection of "relics" from the difficult WWII days and a more lighthearted exhibit on "Warsaw packaging"—with nostalgic vintage advertising. Floor 4 features antique clocks and the "Schiele Room"—named not for the artist, but for the local merchant family whose furnishings and personal objects you can see here. You can continue all the way up into the attic ("viewing platform") to look down over the square, and to see panoramas of the Old Town's rooftops.

The museum sporadically presents a poignant 20-minute film

WARSAW

(in English) tracing the tragic WWII experience of this city—from a thriving interwar metropolis, to a bombed-out wasteland, to the focus of a massive rebuilding effort. This only runs a couple of times each week; consider calling or dropping by to find out when, so you can time your visit accordingly (10 zł).

▲Marie Skłodowska-Curie Museum

Maria Skłodowska (1867-1934)—who, as Marie Curie, would go on to accomplish many firsts, including pioneering the study of radioactivity and becoming the only person to win Nobel Prizes in two different disciplines—was born in this building and grew up in the neighborhood before she moved to Paris to study. This concise, endearing museum is happy to introduce visitors to Madame Curie's world and work. Just a few rooms on one floor, it's made meaningful by the good included audioguide.

Cost and Hours: 11 zł, free on Tue; open Tue-Sat 12:00-18:00, closed Sun-Mon; Ulica Freta 16, +48 22 831 8092, www.mmsc.waw.pl.

Visiting the Museum: Buy your ticket, pick up your audioguide, and head upstairs to tour the exhibit. First you'll learn about Maria Skłodowska's childhood (with lots of black-and-white photos). Then you'll step into a re-creation of the glass-roofed Parisian shed where she and her husband, Pierre, conducted early experiments. You'll see old instruments and equipment, and learn more about the couple and their revolutionary discoveries. On the wall are copies of the two Nobel Prizes she won—one jointly with Pierre, the other solo (later, other members of her family would also go on to win Nobels). Then you'll walk through a room of biographical panels describing different stages of her life—for example, during World War I, where she contributed to the war effort by operating a mobile X-ray unit to treat injured soldiers. Finally, you'll see a re-creation of a drawing room like the one she grew up in, including items from her family. A short film provides a recap of all you've learned about this remarkable, often unheralded scientist. Downstairs are temporary exhibits and a well-stocked shop of Skłodowska swag (say that three times fast).

Polish History Museum

This ambitious new museum is being built north of the New Town, at Warsaw's Citadella. The project has been ongoing for years; it could open as early as 2024. Once open, this promises to become a big and important draw for all visitors—especially Poles. To check on the progress, see MuzHP.pl. They're also planning a Polish Army Museum nearby.

NEAR PALM TREE CIRCLE

These sights are in the city center, near Palm Tree Circle—where Jerusalem Avenue crosses Nowy Świat.

East of the Royal Way (Toward the River)
▲▲National Museum (Muzeum Narodowe)

A celebration of underrated Polish artists, this museum offers a surprisingly engaging and—if you follow my tour—concise overview of this country's impressive painters (many of whom are unknown outside their home country). A modern, state-of-the-art exhibition space allows these unsung canvases to really belt it out.

Cost and Hours: 25 zł, more for temporary exhibits, permanent collection free on Tue; Tue-Sun 10:00-18:00, Fri until 20:00, closed Mon, last entry 45 minutes before closing; one long block east of Nowy Świat at Aleja Jerozolimskie 3, bus #111 stops right out front, +48 22 629 3093, www.mnw.art.pl.

◉ Self-Guided Tour: The collection fills several separate galleries. The museum's strongest point—and the bulk of this tour—is its 19th-century Polish art. But before diving in, consider some of the other collections.

Overview: To get your bearings, pick up a floor plan as you enter. On the ground floor are Ancient Art (from Greek pieces to artifacts left by early Polish tribes), the Faras Gallery (highlighting the museum's fine collection of archaeological findings from that ancient Egyptian city), and a good collection of Medieval Art, which gathers altarpieces from churches around Poland—organized both chronologically and geographically—and displays some of the most graphic crucifixes and pietàs I've seen.

Upstairs (floor 1) is the excellent Gallery of 19th-Century Art, which is described by the tour below. Nearby, through the gift shop, is the worthwhile 20th- and 21st-Century Art collection, with an impressive array of Modern and Postmodern Polish artists, including photographers and filmmakers. The underwhelming Gallery of Old Masters fills floor 2.

To cut to the chase, focus on the **Gallery of 19th-Century Art.** We'll start with the granddaddy of Polish art, Jan Matejko.

• *From the entrance lobby, head up the left staircase, then turn left across the mezzanine and ascend a few more stairs to enter the collection. Matejko is hiding at the far end of this wing: Entering the collection, angle right, then left, heading all the way to the room at the far end, which is dominated by a gigantic battlefield canvas. (If you get lost, ask the attendants, "mah-TAY-koh?")*

Jan Matejko: While not the most talented of artists—he's a fairly conventional painter, lacking a distinctive, recognizable style—Matejko more than made up for it with vision and productivity. His typically super-sized paintings are steeped in proud

Jan Matejko (1838-1893)

Jan Matejko (yawn mah-TAY-koh) is Poland's most important painter, period. In the mid-to-late 19th century, the nation of Poland had been dissolved by foreign powers, and Polish artists struggled to make sense of their people's place in the world. Rabble-rousing Romanticism seemed to have failed (inspiring many brutally suppressed uprisings), so Polish artists and writers turned their attention to educating the people about their history, with the goal of keeping their traditions alive.

Matejko was at the forefront of this so-called "positivist" movement. He saw what the tides of history had done to Poland and was determined to make sure his countrymen learned from it. He painted two types of works: huge, grand-scale epics depicting monumental events in Polish history; and small, intimate portraits of prominent Poles. Polish schoolchildren study history from books with paintings of virtually every single Polish king—all painted by the incredibly prolific Matejko.

Matejko is not admired for his technical mastery or for the literal truth of his works—he was notorious for fudging historical details to give his canvases a bit more propagandistic punch. But he is revered for the emotion behind—and inspired by—his works. His paintings are utilitarian, straightforward, and dramatic enough to stir the patriot in any Pole. The intense focus on history by Matejko and other positivists is one big reason why today's Poles are still so in touch with their heritage.

You'll see Matejko's works in Warsaw's National Museum and Royal Castle, as well as in Kraków's Gallery of 19th-Century Polish Art (above the Cloth Hall). You can also visit his former residence in Kraków.

Polish history. Matejko's biggest work here—in fact, the biggest canvas in the whole building—is the enormous *Battle of Grunwald.* This epic painting commemorates one of Poland's high-water marks: the dramatic victory of a Polish-Lithuanian army over the Teutonic Knights, who had been terrorizing northern Poland for decades (for more on the Teutonic Knights, see page 521). On July 15, 1410, some 40,000 Poles and Lithuanians (led by the sword-waving Lithuanian in red, Grand Duke Vytautas) faced off against 27,000 Teutonic Knights (under their Grand Master, in white) in one of the medieval world's bloodiest battles. Matejko plops us right in the thick of the battle's climax, painting life-size figures and framing off a 32-foot-long slice of the two-mile battle line.

In the center of the painting, the Teutonic Grand Master is about to become a shish kebab. Duke Vytautas leads the final charge. And waaaay up on a hill (in the upper-right corner, on horseback, wearing a silver knight's suit) is Władysław Jagiełło, the first king of the Jagiellonian dynasty...ensuring his bloodline will survive another 150 years.

Matejko spent three years covering this 450-square-foot canvas in paint. The canvas was specially made in a single seamless piece. This was such a popular work that almost as many fans turned out for its unveiling as there are figures in the painting.

From Poland's high point in the *Battle of Grunwald*, look over your right shoulder for another, much smaller Matejko canvas, **Stańczyk,** to see how Poland's fortunes shifted drastically a century later. This more intimate portrait depicts a popular Polish figure: the court jester Stańczyk, who's smarter than the king, but not allowed to say so. This complex character, representing the national conscience, is a favorite symbol of Matejko's. Stańczyk slumps in gloom. He's just read the news (on the table beside him) that the city of Smoleńsk has fallen to the Russians after a three-year siege (1512-1514). The jester had tried to warn the king to send more troops, but the king was too busy partying (behind the curtain). The painter Matejko—who may have used his own features for Stańczyk's face—also blamed the nobles of his own day for fiddling while Poland was partitioned.

More Matejkos fill this room. On the left wall as you face *Grunwald* is a self-portrait of the gray-bearded artist (compare his features to Stańczyk's), flanked by Matejko's portraits of his children and his wife.

On the final wall is a smaller but very dramatic scene, *The Sermon of Piotr Skarga*. In the upper-right corner, this charismatic, early 17th-century Jesuit priest waves his arms to punctuate his message: Poland's political system is broken. Skarga is addressing fat-cat nobles and the portly King Sigismund III Vasa (seated and wearing a ruffled collar), who were acting in their own self-interests instead of prioritizing what was best for Poland. Notice that Skarga's audience isn't hearing his ravings—they seem bored, bugged, or both. The king is even taking a nap. They should have listened: Poland's eventual decline is often considered the fault of its unworkable political system. After the Partitions, the ahead-of-his-time Skarga was rehabilitated as a visionary who should have been heeded. Notice that, like Stańczyk, Skarga is a self-portrait of Matejko.

• *Leaving Matejko, we'll pass through several more rooms of lesser-known Polish painters to the opposite wing, where we'll meet several of Matejko's students—each of whom developed his own style and left his mark on the Polish art world. On the way, I'll point out a few canvases worth a pause.*

Other Polish Painters: First, head back down the long cor-

WARSAW

ridor the way you came (passing some Matejko copycats), cutting through a corner of the Portrait Gallery. When you reach the door you came in, bear right to stay inside the gallery. At the end of that first, large room, you'll find some battle scenes by **Józef Brandt** (1845-1915)—the only painter who rivaled Matejko in capturing epic warfare on canvas. Many of Brandt's scenes focus on confronting an enemy from the east, which was Poland's lot for much of its history. His biggest work here, *Rescue of Tatar Captives*, is typical of his scenes.

Continue straight into the next room, with some fine landscape scenes. This room (the partition in the middle) also has works by the talented **Józef Chełmoński** (1849-1914): *Indian Summer* and (around back) *Storks*—a young boy and his grandfather look to the sky as a formation of storks flies overhead. Storks, which are rare in many places but abundant in Poland, are a proud national symbol.

Turn right and go through one more long room, watching for **Aleksander Gierymski**'s (1850-1901) small, evocative, personality-filled *Jewish Woman Selling Oranges* (on the left wall).

• *You'll emerge into a big, violet-walled room that kicks off the collection of...*

Młoda Polska: Matejko's pupils took what he taught them and incorporated the Art Nouveau styles that were emerging around Europe to create a new movement called "Young Poland" (see page 263). This room features works by two of the movement's big names.

On the left wall are paintings by **Jacek Malczewski** (1854-1929), some of them depicting the goateed, close-cropped artist in a semisurrealistic, Polish countryside context. Malczewski painted more or less realistically, but enjoyed incorporating one or two subtle, symbolic elements evocative of Polish folkloric tradition—magical realism on canvas. *The Death of Ellenai* (1907) shows the pivotal scene in Juliusz Słowacki's epic 1838 poem, *Anhelli*, in which a young nobleman exiled from Poland during the Partitions is forced to make his way through the wastelands of Siberia. When his young and idealistic travel companion, Ellenai, perishes, Anhelli kisses her feet and abandons all hope.

Most of the works on the opposite wall are by **Józef Mehoffer** (1869-1946), who paints with brighter colors in a more stylized form, with more abstraction. Mehoffer's hypnotic *Strange Garden* (from 1902-1903) is a bucolic vision of blue-clad Mary Poppinses, nude cherubs, lots of flowers...and a gigantic, hovering, golden dragonfly that places the otherwise plausible scene in the realm of pure fantasy. In the middle of the room, the small version of Auguste Rodin's *The Kiss* reminds us how this emotion-conveying style, called Symbolism, was also finding expression elsewhere in Europe.

The next room, at the end of the hall, features some lesser-known painters from the age. Among these, **Olga Boznańska** (1865-1940) is worth lingering over: Her gauzy, almost Impressionistic portraits skillfully capture the humanity of each subject.

Head back into the Malczewski/Mehoffer room and find the small, darkened adjoining rooms. The first one features additional Malczewski paintings; the second is a treasure trove of works by the founder and biggest talent of Młoda Polska, **Stanisław Wyspiański** (1869-1907). The specific items in this room are subject to change—as Kraków, which owns the best collection of hometown boy Wyspiański, shuffles his works in and out of special exhibitions—but you'll likely see both paintings and pastel works by this Art Nouveau juggernaut. Wyspiański also designed stage sets and redecorated some important churches; some of the large pastel-on-paper works you may see here were used as studies for those projects. And you'll likely see some self-portraits and portraits of his wife and children.

Pondering the works here—and throughout the museum—think about how such a talented artist from a small country can be left out of textbooks across the ocean. The rest of the museum is yours to explore. If you're craving lesser works by more recognizable names, they're upstairs.

Chopin Museum (Muzeum Fryderyka Chopina)

The reconstructed Ostrogski Castle houses this museum honoring Poland's most famous composer, with manuscripts, letters, and original handwritten compositions. You'll learn about Chopin's early life in Żelazowa Wola and Warsaw; see a replica of his drawing room in Paris, and his last piano, which he used for composing during the final two years of his life (1848-1849); and

learn about the women who loomed large in his life (including his older sister Ludwika, his mother Justyna, and George Sand—the French author who took a male pseudonym in order to be published, and who was romantically linked with Chopin). Listening stations give you the chance to deepen your appreciation for Chopin's talent. While this is all riveting to Chopin devotees, casual fans may find the museum falls a bit short in igniting enthusiasm for the composer—for that, it's worth attending a concert, either here or elsewhere in Warsaw (see "Entertainment in Warsaw," later).

Cost and Hours: 25 zł, free (and crowded) on Wed; open Tue-

Sun 10:00-18:00, closed Mon, last entry 45 minutes before closing; 3 blocks east of Nowy Świat at Ulica Okólnik 1, +48 22 441 6251, https://muzeum.nifc.pl.

Concerts: Under the palace is a **concert hall,** which hosts a variety of performances from May through September—ranging from frequent weekend piano recitals to "young talents" afternoon concerts by local music students. Some are included in museum entry, while others require a separate ticket. Check the schedule and book at Bilety.nifc.pl.

Nearby: The park next to the museum surrounds the Chopin University of Music; hanging out here, you'll often hear students rehearsing inside.

Other Chopin Sight: The composer's tourable **birth house** is in a park in Żelazowa Wola, 34 miles from Warsaw. While interesting to Chopin devotees, it's not worth the trek for most (closed Mon, details at museum website, +48 46 863 3300).

▲Copernicus Science Center (Centrum Nauki Kopernik)

This facility, a wonderland of completely hands-on scientific doodads that thrill kids and kids-at-heart, is a futuristic romper room. (For kids, it's worth at least ▲▲.)

Filling two floors of an industrial-mod, purpose-built space, this is Warsaw's best family activity. Exhibits are described in both Polish and English, and there are frequent demonstrations and special events—ask when you buy your ticket, or check their website.

Cost and Hours: 40 zł, 28 zł for kids, slightly more on weekends; Mon-Thu 8:00-18:00, Fri until 20:00, Sat-Sun 9:00-19:00, last entry one hour before closing; Wybrzeże Kościuszkowskie 20, +48 22 596 4100, www.kopernik.org.pl.

Crowd-Beating Tips: This popular attraction can be busy on weekends and school holidays. If you anticipate crowds, book ahead on their website to secure your preferred entry time.

Getting There: It's an easy downhill walk from Warsaw's Royal Way, but the hike back up is fairly steep. Near the modern bridge—about a five-minute walk from the museum—are a Metro stop and a bus stop (both called Centrum Nauki Kopernik). Metro line 2 connects the science center to the National Stadium, the Royal Way (near the Copernicus statue), and the Warsaw Uprising Museum.

Visiting the Center: The science center is a sprawling, two-floor playhouse of hands-on, interactive exhibits. The specifics are always in flux, so pick up a map as you enter and just enjoy exploring. Kids love trying out the various tools and machines, playing with the air cannons, and running a slinky down an inclined treadmill. On the main floor is a special area for kids under five (called "Buzzz!"). Every visitor finds their own highlights, but favorites include the talking Copernicus robot and the "High Voltage Theater." The attached planetarium has a constantly changing schedule of performances (these cost extra and run about hourly at :30 past the hour, in Polish with English headset, ask for schedule and book at main ticket desk).

Nearby: The **riverside embankment** near the center has a few areas that are fun to stroll; it was created when the busy riverfront highway was rerouted into an underground tunnel. A giant Warsaw mermaid raises her sword at passing joggers, cyclists, and rollerbladers. From here, you have good views of the modern Holy Cross Bridge (Most Świętokrzyski) and the National Stadium, proudly wrapped in the patriotic red and white of the Polish flag. These riverbanks are a popular hangout by day and after dark; in the summer, a stroll along here reveals a world of picnics, family outings, and impromptu parties.

Also don't miss the postindustrial, futuristic **Elektrownia Powiśle** dining and shopping complex, just across the street from the museum (described later, under "Eating in Warsaw").

West of the Royal Way (near Centralna Station)
Palace of Culture and Science
(Pałac Kultury i Nauki, or PKiN)

This massive skyscraper, dating from the early 1950s, is still one of the tallest buildings in Europe (760 feet with the spire). While you can ride the lift to its top for a commanding view, the highlight is simply viewing it up close from ground level.

Viewing the Skyscraper: This building was a "gift" from Stalin that the people of Warsaw couldn't refuse. Varsovians call it "Stalin's Penis"... using cruder terminology than that. (There are seven such "Stalin Gothic" erections in Moscow.) If it feels like an Art Deco Chicago skyscraper, that's because the architect was inspired by the years he spent studying and working in  Chicago in the 1930s. Because it was to be "Soviet in substance, Polish in style," Soviet architects toured Poland to absorb local culture before starting the project. Notice the frilly decorative friezes that top each level—evocative of Poland's many Renaissance buildings (such as Kraków's Cloth Hall). The clock was added in 1999 as part of the millennium celebrations. Since the end of communism, the younger generation doesn't mind the structure so much—and some even admit to liking it for the way it enlivens the predictable glass-and-steel skyline springing up around it.

Everything about the Pałac is big. Approach it from the east side (facing the busy Marszałkowska street and the slick Galeria Centrum shopping mall). Stand in front of the granite tribune where communist VIPs surveyed massive May Day parades and pageantry on the once-imposing square, which today holds a sloppy parking lot. From there, size up the skyscraper—its grand entry flanked by massive statues of Copernicus on the right (science) and the great poet Mickiewicz on the left (culture). It's designed to show off the strong, grand-scale Soviet aesthetic and architectural skill. The Pałac contains various theaters (the culture), museums of evolution and technology (the science), a congress hall, a multiplex, an observation deck, and lots of office space. With all this Culture and Science under one Roof, it's a shame that only the ground-floor lobby (which feels like stepping into 1950s Moscow and is free to enter) and the 30th-floor observatory deck are open to the public (25 zł to zip up on retrofitted Soviet elevators, daily 10:00-20:00, may be open later in summer, www.pkin.pl).

Nearby: Behind the Pałac sprawls Warsaw's new skyline of glittering skyscrapers. **Varso Tower,** which opened in 2022, finally eclipsed the Pałac's height record, at 1,020 feet tall (the tallest building in the EU). But the most interesting skyscraper is **Złota 44,** with its dramatic swooping lines rising high into the air. This was designed by Poland-born architect Daniel Libeskind, perhaps best known for Berlin's Jewish Museum and for his role as master architect in redeveloping the World Trade Center site in New York City. The tower's shape evokes an eagle (a symbol for Poland) just beginning to take flight. At its base—and immediately behind Centralna station, easy to check out while waiting for your train— is **Złote Tarasy shopping mall,** featuring a funky, undulating glass-and-steel roof (https://zlotetarasy.pl).

JEWISH WARSAW

In the early 1600s, an estimated 80 percent of all Jews lived in Poland—then the largest country in Europe. And particularly between the two World Wars, Jewish culture flourished here. But after centuries of dwelling in relative peace in tolerant and pragmatic Poland, Warsaw's Jews suffered terribly at the hands of the Nazis. Several sights in Warsaw commemorate those who were murdered, and those who fought back. Because the Nazis leveled the ghetto, there is nothing left except the street plan, a few scattered monuments, and the heroic spirit of its former residents. However, the top-notch Museum of the History of Polish Jews is a magnet for those interested in this chapter of Polish history.

Getting There: To reach Ghetto Heroes Square and the museum from the Old Town, you can hop in a **taxi** or an **Uber,** or take a **bus** (to the Nalewki-Muzeum stop; bus #180 is particularly useful; bus #111 reaches this stop from farther south—Piłsudski Square, Nowy Świat, Palm Tree Circle, and the National Museum). You can also **walk** there in about 15 minutes: Go through the Barbican gate two blocks into the New Town, turn left on Świętojerska, and walk straight 10 minutes—passing the green-glass Supreme Court building. En route, at the corner of Świętojerska and Nowiniarska, watch for the pattern of bricks in the sidewalk, marking *Ghetto Wall 1940-1943*.

▲Ghetto Heroes Square (Plac Bohaterow Getta)

The square is in the heart of what was the Jewish ghetto—now surrounded by bland Soviet-style apartment blocks. After the uprising, the entire ghetto was reduced to dust by the Nazis, leaving the communists to rebuild to their own specifications. Today, the district is called Muranów ("Rebuilt").

The **monument** in the middle of the square commemorates those who fought and died "for the dignity and freedom of the Jew-

ish Nation, for a free Po-land, and for the liberation of humankind." The statue features heroic Jewish men who knew that an inglori-ous death at the hands of the Nazis awaited them. Flames in the background show Nazis burning the ghetto. The opposite side features a sad procession of Jews trudging to concen-tration camps, with subtle Nazi bayonets and helmets moving things along.

As you face the monument, look through the trees to the right to see a seated statue. **Jan Karski** (1914-2000) was a Catholic Pole and resistance fighter who traveled extensively through Poland during the Nazi occupation, collected evidence, and then reported on the Warsaw Ghetto and the Holocaust to the leaders of the Western Allies (including a personal meeting with FDR). In 1944, while the Holocaust was still going on, Karski published his eye-witness account, *The Story of a Secret State* (which you can see on this statue's armrest). After the war he became a US citizen, and in 2012 President Barack Obama awarded him a posthumous Presidential Medal of Freedom.

The huge, glassy building facing the monument from across the square is the Museum of the History of Polish Jews (described next).

▲▲▲Museum of the History of Polish Jews (Muzeum Historii Żydów Polskich, a.k.a. POLIN)

This world-class attraction thoughtfully traces the epic, millennium-long story of Jews in Poland. This is not a "Holocaust museum"; rather, it provides stirring, comprehensive documentation of the very rich Polish Jewish experience across the centuries. In-depth, engaging, vividly illustrated, and eloquently presented, the exhibits present a powerful context for the many Jewish cultural sites around Poland—offering insights both for  people familiar with the story and for those who aren't. The museum is at once expansive and intimate, with ample descriptions, videos, and touchscreens; you could spend all day here, but two hours is the minimum. Its name, POLIN, means "rest here" in Hebrew and also evokes birdsong. It wins my vote for the best museum in Poland, and it's easily Europe's best Jewish museum—and a strong contender for the best European historical museum, period. The building also hosts cultural events and temporary exhibits.

Cost and Hours: Core exhibition—45 zł, includes essential audioguide, more for temporary exhibits; Wed-Mon 10:00-18:00, Sat until 20:00, closed Tue, last entry two hours before closing; Anielewicza 6, +48 22 471 0300, www.polin.pl.

Visiting the Museum: Before entering, view the building's striking **exterior** (designed by Finnish architect Rainer Mahlamäki). You'll enter (and go through a security checkpoint) at the large, asymmetrical hole in the side of the building. Once you're inside, the symbolism becomes clear: This represents Moses parting the Red Sea. (While the main exhibit covers the thousand years of Jews in Poland, this goes back even further—to the Jewish origin story.)

Buy your tickets for the core exhibition and pick up the invaluable 60-stop audioguide, which helps provide a concise structure for your exploration of the sprawling exhibitions. The main floor has a children's area and the good **$ Warsze** café, with a tempting cafeteria line of Polish and Jewish classics.

WARSAW

Warsaw's Jews and the Ghetto Uprising

From the Middle Ages until World War II, Poland was a relatively safe haven for Europe's Jews. While other kings were imprisoning and deporting Jews in the 14th century, the progressive king Kazimierz the Great welcomed Jews into Poland, even granting them special privileges (see page 261).

By the 1930s, there were more than 380,000 Jews in Warsaw—nearly a third of the population (and the largest concentration of Jews in any European city). The Nazis arrived in 1939. Within a year, they had pushed all of Warsaw's Jews into one neighborhood and surrounded it with a wall, creating a miserably overcrowded ghetto (crammed with an estimated 460,000 people, including many from nearby towns). There were nearly 600 such ghettos in cities and towns all over Poland.

By the summer of 1942, more than a quarter of the Jews in the ghetto had either died of disease, committed suicide, or been murdered. The Nazis started moving Warsaw's Jews (at the rate of 5,000 a day) into what they claimed were "resettlement camps." Most of these people—300,000 in all—were actually murdered at Treblinka or Auschwitz. Finally, the waning population—now about 60,000—began to get word from concentration camp escapees about what was actually going on there. Spurred by this knowledge, Warsaw's surviving Jews staged a dramatic uprising.

On April 19, 1943, the Jews attacked Nazi strongholds. The overwhelming Nazi war machine—which had rolled over much of Europe—imagined they'd be able to put down the rebellion easily. Instead, they struggled for a month to finally crush the Ghetto Uprising. The ghetto's residents and structures were "liquidated." About 300 of Warsaw's Jews survived, thanks in part to a sort of "underground railroad" of courageous Varsovians.

Warsaw's Jewish sights are emotionally moving, but even more so if you know some of their stories. You may have heard of **Władysław Szpilman,** a Jewish concert pianist who survived the war with the help of Jews, Poles, and even a Nazi officer. Szpilman's life story was turned into the Oscar-winning film *The Pianist,* which powerfully depicts events in Warsaw during World War II.

Less familiar to non-Poles—but equally affecting—is the story of Henryk Goldszmit, better known by his pen name, **Janusz Korczak.** Korczak wrote imaginative children's books that are still enormously popular among Poles. He worked at an orphanage in the Warsaw ghetto. When his orphans were sent off to concentration camps, the Nazis offered the famous author a chance at freedom. Korczak turned them down, choosing to die at Treblinka with his children.

WARSAW

Then head downstairs and follow the one-way route. In this high-tech, interactive space, exhibits in eight galleries mingle with actual artifacts to bring history to life.

You'll begin by passing through a simulated forest—evocative of legends about the Jews' arrival in Poland—to reach the **First Encounters** exhibit. Here you'll learn how Jewish merchants made their way to Poland in the 10th century (with maps of their trade routes and samples of what they sold). The story is told partly from the perspective of Ibrahim ibn Yakub, a Sephardic Jew who penned early travelogues about Europe. Look for the display case that holds a coin from the ninth century, with Hebrew characters, that was minted in Poland. In 1264, Duke Bolesław the Pious—the first of many tolerant Polish rulers—extended rights and protections to his Jewish subjects, allowing them to thrive. In the next room, on the left wall are illustrations of the leading Polish cities of the time, and on the right wall are Polish medieval monarchs, with in-depth explanations of each one's policies toward their Jewish subjects.

Next, the **Paradisus Iudaeorum** explains how, as Jews became more established in Polish society in the 15th and 16th centuries,

they enjoyed better and better living conditions. (Meanwhile, anti-Semites bitterly complained that Poland was becoming a "Jewish Paradise"—the name of this exhibit.) The centerpiece here is a gigantic, interactive model of Kraków and its Jewish quarter, Kazimierz. In the library section, you can flip through virtual pages of books from the era—representing the flourishing of education during this time. Poland was a rare place where books would actually be printed in Hebrew.

Continuing into the next area, you'll enter a dark hallway that explains the Khmelnytsky Uprising—a mid-17th-century Cossack rebellion against the Polish lords and the Jews who served them. This brought a new wave of pogroms and 10,000 Jewish deaths, mainly in present-day Ukraine.

After the uprising, Polish lords invited Jews to privately owned market towns—called *shtetls*—to help reestablish the economy. **The Jewish Town** offers a fascinating look at different walks of life in a typical Jewish community: the market,

where Jews and Christians could mingle at the tavern; the home, where a family would live, work, eat, and sleep in a single room; the cemetery (touchscreens invite you to learn about the symbolism of Jewish tombstones); and the synagogue, with a gloriously colorful replica of a ceiling and bema (prayer platform) from a wooden synagogue from the village of Gwoździec—dripping with symbolism that's explained on nearby touchscreens. The depictions of "exotic" animals were influenced by Ottoman art and painted by local artists, who had never actually seen these beasts—leading to several errors, including an elephant with claws and an "ostrich" that looks more like an eagle. An exhibit also traces the mid-18th-century rise of Hasidism—a mystical branch of Judaism—in the eastern Polish lands (today's Ukraine).

With the Partitions of the late 18th century (when Polish territory was divided among neighboring powers), the Jewish population—who had spent centuries carving out a vital niche in a united Poland—now found themselves split among three different empires (symbolized by giant portraits of the rulers of Prussia, Russia, and Austria, all facing the Polish throne).

Encounters with Modernity examines how Jews in different parts of the Polish lands had very different experiences. Some were required by the new authorities to adopt surnames for the first time. Flippable panels illustrate how Russian authorities required both men and women to change their traditional clothing. You'll see a replica salon of a wealthy Jewish family who mingled with elites, and learn about the debate at that time of what the role of Jews in society should be (illustrated by a fine collection of items from Jewish ceremonies commemorating rites of passage). You'll also learn about the competing movements within Judaism that emerged during this era: Hasidism, led by charismatic Tzadiks who promised a closer spiritual connection to God, and the more reform-minded Haskalah, an intellectual approach inspired by the Enlightenment.

A mesmerizing, painterly film follows a day in the life of a young student at a *yeshiva* (school). A railway station represents the Industrial Revolution, when the world got smaller. You'll learn how some Jews worked hard to integrate with their dominant cultures (such as the painter Maurycy Gottlieb). This period also saw the emergence of modern anti-Semitism, including a brutal pogrom in Warsaw in 1881. As Jews sought to define a modern Jewish identity in the late 19th century, many emigrated—some to North or South America, and still others to the Holy Land (the beginnings of Zionism).

All of this sets the stage for World War I, when Jews were drafted into various armies—and often forced to fight one another. But at war's end, Poland was reconstituted as an independent nation. You'll step out onto **The Jewish Street,** which re-creates an interwar shopping street from a Jewish community. ("The Jewish Street" was also slang for the Jewish world in general.) It was between the world wars—when a newly independent Poland extended full citizenship and voting rights to its Jewish citizens—that Jewish cultural life flourished as never before. Three million Jews lived in Poland—including one-third of Warsaw's population. You'll see re-created Warsaw sites relating to newspapers, cinema, writers, and artists; and you'll learn about Jewish tourism of the era (when middle-class Jews would travel around Poland and Europe to visit Jewish cultural sites). Don't miss the mezzanine area, with exhibits about education and reform—including bilingual schooling (Yiddish and Polish), the beloved educator and author Janusz Korczak, and the debate over "ghetto benches" (segregated seating areas in schools).

This was also a time of rising anti-Semitism, segregation, boycotts, and anti-Jewish quotas. After one more nostalgic stroll down "The Jewish Street," you come to September 1, 1939, when the Nazis invaded Poland. They stripped Jews of their rights and possessions; humiliated, labeled, tortured, and executed them; and eventually implemented the **Holocaust.**

The exhibit traces, step by step, the escalation of the Nazis' "Final Solution," with a focus on events here in Warsaw: forcing Jews into a ghetto (you'll walk across a platform representing the bridge that connected the two parts of the ghetto, offering Jewish people fleeting glimpses of "normal" life going on outside their walls), the liquidation of the ghetto and the movement of Warsaw's Jews to the death camp at Treblinka, and the Ghetto Uprising, a desperate last stand in which the dwindling number or Warsaw's Jews put up a valiant, but ultimately doomed, fight. Making these stories personal are contemporaneous diaries, documents, and photographs.

The exhibit poses difficult questions about how non-Jewish Poles helped—or did not help—the Jews who were gradually disappearing from their cities. And it explains how a sort of "underground railroad" worked at great peril to save as many Jews as possible—as depicted in the movie *The Pianist.* (Look for the chess set carved by a Jew in hiding.) All told, 9 out of every 10 Polish Jews were murdered in the Holocaust. Only about 300,000 survived.

Finally, **The Postwar Years** follows Holocaust survivors in the years just after the war, when, astonishingly, they were scapegoated for war crimes. About 150,000 more (half the total survivors) fled to the newly created state of Israel, and those who remained had to navigate an unfriendly, anti-Semitic communist regime. In 1968, the communists launched an "anti-Zionist" campaign; eventually around 15,000 Polish Jews lost their citizenship and left for Israel,

Western Europe, and the US. Not until the fall of communism could the rest finally enter a world of new possibilities. The final room poses a powerful question: Given this rich yet traumatic history, what is the future for Jews in Poland?

The creation of this museum—the first time that the full story of the Jews of Poland has ever been told in such a mainstream way, and in all its epic scope—represents a critical milestone in celebrating a culture that has survived a harrowing history.

Ghetto Walking Tour

For a poignant stroll through what was the ghetto, with faint echoes of a tragic history, take this brief, lightly guided walk for a few blocks. The neighborhood itself is drab and boxy, though increasingly gentrified. It was rebuilt in characterless communist style after it was leveled during the Holocaust. You'll have to work hard to resurrect the memory of what went on here.

Stand along the street facing the back side of the monument, with the museum behind it. Turn right and walk along Zamenhofa—which, like many streets in this neighborhood, is named for a hero of the Ghetto Uprising. From here, you'll follow a series of three-foot-tall, black stone memorials to uprising heroes—the **Path of Remembrance.** Like stations of the cross, each recounts an event of the uprising. Every April 19th (the day the uprising began), huge crowds follow this path.

In a block and a half, just beyond the corner of Miła (on the left, partly obscured by some bushes), you'll find a **bunker** where about 100 organizers of the uprising hid (and where they committed suicide when the Nazis discovered them on May 8, 1943).

Continue following the black stone monuments up Zamenhofa (which becomes Dubois), then turn left at the corner, onto broad and busy Stawki. The ugly gray building on your left (a half-block down at #5, near the tram stop) was the **headquarters of the SS** within the ghetto. This is where the transportation of Warsaw's Jews to concentration camps was organized.

Using the crosswalk at the tram stop, cross Stawki and proceed straight ahead into the gap between the two buildings. At the back of this parking lot is a surviving part of the red-brick **ghetto wall,** with a few remaining scraps of 1940s barbed wire.

Farther up Stawki street, on the right, is the finale of this walk: the **Umschlagplatz** monument. That's German for "transfer place," and it marks the spot where the Nazis brought Jewish families to prepare them to be loaded onto trains bound for Treblinka or Auschwitz. This was the actual site of the touching scene in the film *The Pianist* where the grandfather shares bits of chocolate with his family before being forever separated. In the walls of the monument are inscribed the first names of some of the victims.

Other Warsaw Ghetto Sights

There are several other powerful sights relating to the ghetto, but they're spread far and wide around the city. Ideally, join a tour or hire a guide to weave them together. Here are some of the key locations; the first two are closer to the Palace of Culture and Science, while the final one is west of the Museum of the History of Polish Jews.

A rare, small surviving section of the **ghetto wall** that surrounded Warsaw's Jews during the Nazi occupation is behind a stretch of humdrum buildings just west of the Palace of Culture and Science. Enter through the passage at Ulica Złota 62 and bear right; you'll find it tucked back in a courtyard.

The **Nożyk Synagogue,** just north of the Palace of Culture and Science, is the only synagogue that survived World War II; it's relatively new, dating from 1902 (Twarda 6). After the liquidation of the ghetto, the building was kept intact to use as stables by occupying Nazi forces. Rebuilt in 1983, it's still used today as a place of worship and gathering, and is not typically open to the public.

Several blocks northeast, a monument called the **Footbridge of Remembrance** (Kładka Pamięci) spans Chłodna street near the intersection with Żelazna street. This recalls the wartime period when the walled Jewish ghetto included a corridor where local trams could pass through. In order to cross between the "Large Ghetto" (to the north of here) and the "Small Ghetto" (to the south), Jews had to walk over a footbridge—giving them a cruelly enticing glimpse of the "outside world." (This scene was vividly staged in *The Pianist,* and there's a conceptual re-creation of the bridge in the Museum of the History of Polish Jews.) A few steps up Chłodna street is a different monument from a different era, honoring Jerzy Popiełuszko, the outspoken, pro-Solidarity priest who was murdered by the communist secret police during martial law in 1984; he lived in the house at #15.

WARSAW UPRISING SIGHTS

For those interested in the 1944 Warsaw Uprising, it's worth visiting two sights: one a monument, the other a museum. Neither is right along the main tourist trail; the monument is closer to the core sightseeing zone, while the museum is a subway, tram, or taxi/Uber ride away.

Warsaw Uprising Monument

The most central sight related to the Warsaw Uprising is the monument at Plac Krasińskich (intersection of Ulica Długa and

Miodowa, one long block and about a five-minute walk southwest of the New Town Square). Larger-than-life soldiers and civilians race for the sewers in a desperate attempt to flee the Nazis. Just behind the monument is the oxidized-copper facade of Poland's Supreme Court.

▲▲Warsaw Uprising Museum (Muzeum Powstania Warszawskiego)

Thorough, modern, and packed with Polish field-trip groups, this museum celebrates the heroes of the uprising (or, as this museum calls it, the Warsaw Rising). It's a bit cramped, and finding your way through the exhibits can be confusing, but it works hard to illuminate this complicated chapter of Warsaw's history. The location is inconvenient (a taxi/Uber or public transit ride west of Centralna station) and, because it takes some time to visit, may not be worth the trek for those with a casual interest. But history buffs find it worthwhile.

Cost and Hours: 30 zł, free on Mon; open Wed-Mon 8:00-18:00, Sat-Sun from 10:00, closed Tue; +48 22 539 7947, www.1944.pl.

Audioguide: The informative, two-hour audioguide is ideal if you want to delve into the whole story (10 zł, rent it in the gift shop). But the museum is so well described, you can just wander aimlessly and be immersed in the hellish events.

Eating: The museum's $ café is oddly pleasant, serving drinks and light snacks amidst genteel ambience from interwar Warsaw. In summer you can dine on a peaceful terrace. You'll also find a few business lunch-type places in the surrounding office zone.

Getting There: The museum is on the western edge of downtown—a long, dull walk—at Ulica Przyokopowa 28. While it's easiest to reach by taxi or Uber (figure about 10 minutes and 20 zł from the Royal Way), you can get close on public transit: Ride the Metro or a bus to Rondo Daszyńskiego, or a tram to the Muzeum Powstania Warszawskiego stop. From any of these, it's a short walk to the museum (can be tricky to find, as it's tucked around on the back side of the block).

Visiting the Museum: Buy your ticket at the little house at the far end of the entrance courtyard (marked *kasa*), then head into the main hall. The high-tech main exhibit sprawls across three floors. It tells the story of the uprising chronologically, with a keen focus on military history. The exhibit covers several topics but doesn't provide a big-picture narrative; to fully understand the context of what you're seeing, read the sidebar before your visit.

As you enter, the **Room of the Little Insurgent** on the right is a children's area, reminding visitors young and old that Varsovian kids played a role in the Warsaw Uprising, too.

WARSAW

The Warsaw Uprising

By the summer of 1944, it was becoming clear that the Nazis' days in Warsaw were numbered. The Red Army drew near, and by late July, Soviet tanks were within 25 miles of downtown Warsaw.

The Varsovians could simply have waited for the Soviets to cross the river and force the Nazis out. But they knew that Soviet "liberation" would also mean an end to Polish independence. The Polish Home Army numbered 400,000—30,000 of them in Warsaw alone—and was the biggest underground army in military history. The uprisers wanted Poland to control its own fate, and they took matters into their own hands. The symbol of the resistance was an anchor made up of a *P* atop a *W* (which stands for *Polska Walcząca*, or "Poland Fighting"—you'll see this icon all around town). Over time, the Home Army had established an extensive network of underground tunnels and sewers, which allowed them to deliver messages and move around the city without drawing the Nazis' attention. These tunnels gave the Home Army the element of surprise.

On August 1, 30,000 Polish resistance fighters launched an attack on their Nazi oppressors. They poured out of the sewers and caught the Nazis off guard. The ferocity of the Polish fighters stunned the Nazis. But the Nazis regrouped, and within a few days, they had retaken several areas of the city—murdering tens of thousands of innocent civilians as they went. In one notorious incident, some 5,500 Polish soldiers and 6,000 civilians who were surrounded by Nazis in the Old Town were forced to flee through the sewers; many drowned or were shot. (This scene is depicted in the Warsaw Uprising Monument on Plac Krasińskich.)

Two months after it had started, the Warsaw Uprising was over. The Home Army called a cease-fire. About 18,000 Polish uprisers had been killed, along with nearly 200,000 innocent civilians. An infuriated Hitler ordered that the city be destroyed—which it was, systematically, block by block, until virtually nothing remained.

Through all of this, the Soviets stood still, watched, and waited. When the smoke cleared and the Nazis left, the Red Army marched in and claimed the wasteland that was once called Warsaw. After the war, General Dwight D. Eisenhower said that the scale of destruction here was the worst he'd ever seen. The communists later tracked down the surviving Home Army leaders, killing or imprisoning them.

Depending on whom you talk to, the desperate uprising of Warsaw was incredibly brave, stupid, or a little of both. As for the Poles, they remain fiercely proud of their struggle for freedom. In 2004, 60 years after the uprising, the Warsaw Uprising Museum opened to document and commemorate this tragedy.

WARSAW

The **ground floor** sets the stage with Germany's invasion and occupation of Poland. The Generalgouvernement (Nazi puppet government of occupied Poland, ruled by Hans Frank in Kraków) wasted no time in asserting its control over the Poles; you'll learn how they imprisoned and executed priests, professors, and students. You'll also hear the story of the earlier, smaller uprisings that preceded the Warsaw Uprising, including the Poland-wide Operation Tempest (Burza) in 1943. During those earliest rebellions, Warsaw was intentionally left out of the fray...but only for the time being. The print shop shows how propaganda was spread during the occupation despite the watchful eye of the Nazis.

To keep with the chronological flow, skip the middle floor for now and ride the elevator to the **top floor** (#2), which covers the main part of the uprising. You'll meet some of the uprising's heroes and learn about their uniforms, weapons, and methods. The room in the middle, with felt drapes, tells the story of the Wola Massacre, in which some 40,000 residents of that Warsaw neighborhood were executed in just three days. Beyond that, the "Kino Palladium" movie screen shows fascinating Home Army newsreel footage from the period (with English subtitles). To the right of the screen, you'll walk through a simulated sewer, reminiscent of the one that many Home Army soldiers and civilians used to evade the Germans. Imagine terrified troops quietly traversing a sewer line like this one more than a mile long (but with lower ceilings)—and doing it while knee-deep in liquid sewage. At the end of the "sewer," stairs lead down to the middle floor.

The **middle floor** focuses on the grueling aftermath of the uprising. The later days of the uprising are outlined, battle by battle. A chilling section describes how Warsaw became a "city of graves," with burial mounds and makeshift crosses scattered everywhere. One room honors the Field Postal Service, which, at great personal risk, continued mail delivery of both military communiqués and civilian correspondences. Many of these brave "mailmen" were actually Scouts who were too young to fight. Nearby, another room recreates a clandestine radio broadcast station set up in a living room. If you need a break, look for the red corridor leading through the USSR section to the **café** and WC.

End your visit by walking down the stairs into the **main hall,** which is dominated by two large-scale exhibits: a replica of an RAF Liberator B-24 J, used for airborne surveillance of wartime Warsaw; and a giant movie screen showing more newsreels assembled by the Home Army's own propaganda unit during the uprising. Under the screen, behind the black curtains, an exhibit tells the story of Germans in Warsaw, along with another, more claustrophobic walk-through sewer.

Also in the main hall, look for the entrance to the seven-minute 3-D film *City of Ruins (Miasto Ruin)*, with virtual aerial footage of the postwar devastation. This gives you a look at the reality of the thousand people (nicknamed "Robinson Crusoes") who lived in bombed-out Warsaw immediately after the war. It's worth waiting in line to see this powerful film.

The **park** surrounding the building features several thought-provoking sights. A Chevy truck armored by the Home Army is both a people's tank and an example of how outgunned they were. Along the back is the Wall of Memory, a Vietnam War Memorial-type monument to soldiers of the Polish Home Army who were killed in action. You'll see their rank and name, followed by their code name, in quotes. The Home Army observed a strict policy of anonymity, forbidding members from calling each other by anything but their code names. The bell in the middle is dedicated to the commander of the uprising, Antoni Chruściel (code name "Monter").

SOUTH OF THE CENTER
▲Łazienki Park (Park Łazienkowski)

The huge, idyllic Łazienki Park (wah-ZHYEN-kee) is where Varsovians go to play. The park is sprinkled with fun Neoclassical buildings, strutting peacocks, and young Poles in love. It was built by Poland's very last king (before the final Partition), Stanisław August Poniatowski, to serve as his summer residence and provide a place for his citizens to relax.

On the edge of the park (along Belwederska) is a **monument to Fryderyk Chopin.** The monument, in a rose garden, is flanked by platforms, where free summer piano **concerts** of Chopin's music are given weekly (mid-May-late Sept only, generally Sun at 12:00 and 16:00—confirm at TI). The statue shows Chopin sitting under a wind-blown willow tree. Although he spent his last 20 years and wrote most of his best-known music in France, his inspiration came

from wind blowing through the willow trees of his native land, Poland. The Nazis were quick to destroy this statue, which symbolizes Polish culture. They melted the original (from 1926) down for its metal. Today's copy was recast after World War II. Savor this spot; it's great in summer, with roses wildly in bloom, and in autumn, when the trees provide a golden backdrop for the romantic statue.

Venture down into the ravine and to the center of the park, where (after a 10-minute hike) you'll find King Poniatowski's strik-

ing **Palace on the Water** (Pałac na Wodzie)—liter-ally built in the middle of a river. Nearby, you'll spot a clever amphitheater with seating on the riverbank and the stage on an island. The king was a real man of the Enlightenment, host-

ing weekly Thursday dinners here for artists and intellectuals. But Poland's kings are long gone, and proud peacocks now rule this roost.

Getting There: The park is just south of the city center on the Royal Way. Buses #116 and #180 run from Castle Square in the Old Town along the Royal Way directly to the park (get off at the stop called Łazienki Królewskie, by Belweder Palace—you'll see Chopin squinting through the trees on your left). Maps at park entrances locate the Chopin monument, the Palace on the Water, and other park attractions.

EAST OF THE CENTER: THE PRAGA DISTRICT

If you're in Warsaw for a longer stay, or are curious to see an emerg-ing hipster zone, cross the river to the Praga district. Praga was spared the worst of the WWII bombs; in fact, this is where the Red Army watched and waited as Hitler's forces leveled the historic city center. And today, Praga's relatively low rents and easy access to downtown make it a popular place for creative young Poles to live, eat, and party.

From Castle Square, the Śląsko-Dąbrowski Bridge rumbles over the Vistula (with ample tram and bus connections) right to the heart of this "other side of the river" neighborhood. (The Wileński stop, on the M2 Metro line, is also handy.) You can stroll along the traditional-feeling main drag, **Targowa**—a wide street with easy tram access, local shops and cafés, and Praga's own history museum (closed Mon, www.muzeumpragi.pl). Or, for a look at contempo-rary Praga, walk 10 minutes east to the postindustrial **Centrum Praskie Koneser**—a former distillery that has been transformed into a hip dining and entertainment complex (for an events calen-dar, see www.koneser.eu). Wander through the red-brick buildings to find a tempting place for a meal. Or, if you need an excuse to cross the river, sign up for a tour and tasting at the **Polish Vodka Mu-**

WARSAW

seum—filling one part of the former Koneser distillery. After a tour and a look at both old and new methods for making vodka, you'll enjoy an educational tasting designed to train your palate (closed Mon, smart to book ahead at www.muzeumpolskiejwodki.pl).

Shopping in Warsaw

You'll notice that many Varsovians are chic, sophisticated, and very well dressed. To see where they outfit themselves, go window-shopping. **Mysia 3** is a super-hip mini mall with three concise floors dedicated to mostly Polish fashion designers, but also has cutting-edge housewares and decor (daily, across Jerusalem Avenue from Nowy Świat, inside the former communist propaganda office at Mysia 3, www.mysia3.pl). Warsaw's main "fashion row" is a bit farther south, in the Śródmieście district. **Mokotowska street,** which angles northeast from trendy Plac Zbawiciela, is lined with dozens of chichi boutiques, jewelry shops, shoe stores, designer pastry shops, hair salons, and hipster barbers. The highest concentration is a few short blocks north of Plac Zbawiciela, north of Piękna. If you enjoy this zone, the area immediately to the west—along Wilcza and Poznańska streets—has more of the same.

Entertainment in Warsaw

Warsaw fills the summer with live music. In addition to more serious options (opera, symphony, etc.), consider these crowd-pleasing choices.

CHOPIN

My favorite Warsaw music option is to enjoy a Chopin performance. There's nothing like hearing Chopin's compositions passionately played by a teary-eyed Pole who really feels the music. The best option is the outdoor concert in front of the big Chopin statue in **Łazienki Park,** but it is held only one day a week in summer (free, mid-May-late-Sept generally Sun at 12:00 and 16:00, www. lazienki-krolewskie.pl; for more on this option, see the Łazienki Park listing on page 428).

If you're not in town on a Sunday, the next best thing is the **Chopin Salon.** Jarek Chołodecki, who runs the recommended Chopin Boutique lodging, hosts an intimate piano concert in his delightful salon nightly at 19:00. The performance can cover a range of musical styles and composers—but generally there are piano pieces featuring Chopin. The concert lasts around 45 minutes and is followed by wine, homemade cakes, and social time. A small group of locals and travelers gathers around Jarek's big, shiny Steinway grand to hear great music by talented young artists in a great city (70 zł, half-price for hotel guests, Ulica Smolna 14, reservations required, +48 22 829 4801, www.bbwarsaw.com).

The **Chopin Museum** features a variety of quality piano recitals—including several presented by local music students. These typically take place from May through September, and many are included in the museum's admission price (for details, see the museum listing on page 413).

Additionally, various **touristy Chopin concerts** are popping up all over the city; figure 85 zł for a piano performance set in a drawing room or small theater. Ask at the TI for the latest fliers.

OTHER MUSIC

Two big, historic churches in and near the Old Town put on 30-minute **organ concerts** most days. Choose between the Cathedral of St. John the Baptist, with an austere brick interior, right in the heart of the Old Town (25 zł, Mon-Sat at 12:00, no concerts Sun); and the frilly, Rococo St. Anne's Church, with a more sumptuous interior, just outside the Old Town (25 zł, May-early Oct Mon-Sat at 12:00, no concerts Sun). Both are run by the same company (+48 501 158 477, www.kapitula.org).

Free outdoor **jazz concerts** take place each Saturday in summer right on the Old Town Square (July-Aug at 19:00). In the summer, in good weather, the recommended Chopin Boutique hotel hosts **rooftop concerts** with sweeping views over Warsaw; the music varies, but it's often smooth jazz (free, usually May-Sept daily at 16:00, confirm schedule at https://bbwarsaw.com).

LIVELY HANGOUT ZONES

The Old Town and New Town are totally for tourists. To find some more interesting areas to explore and hang out after dark, your first stop should be **Plac Zbawiciela** in Śródmieście and the surrounding streets (see page 438). Locals also enjoy spending a balmy afternoon or evening on the **Vistula riverbanks.** Long ignored by Varsovians, the left (west) bank has undergone a dramatic renovation, with beautiful parklike embankments ideal for strolling. Meanwhile, the right (east) bank is still rugged and undeveloped, with forests and natural beaches; the biggest beach is around the eastern base of the Poniatowski Bridge (where Jerusalem Avenue crosses the river).

Sleeping in Warsaw

Warsaw is affordable for a European capital—for what you'd spend on a decent midrange room in Rome or Amsterdam, you can get a palatial room in a top-end hotel here. That said, two of my Warsaw favorites—Chopin Boutique and Duval Apartments—are both affordable and characteristic, making them great all-around choices.

I've arranged my listings by neighborhood. For locations, see the "Central Warsaw" map, earlier. Keep in mind that in the Old Town, you'll rarely see a local, while in Śródmieście, you'll rarely see a tourist. Choose your Warsaw experience.

NEAR PALM TREE CIRCLE (NOWY ŚWIAT AND JERUSALEM AVENUE)

Considering how spread out Warsaw is, this is a convenient location for reaching various sights around the city. While comfortable inside, these hotels are in big buildings on uninspiring urban streets.

$$ Hotel Indigo, part of a high-end chain, surrounds a sleek and glassy atrium with 60 posh rooms at reasonable prices. A row of nearby nightclubs can generate lots of noise on the weekends—ask for a quieter room, and pack earplugs (air-con, elevator, Smolna 40, +48 22 418 8900, www.indigowarsaw.com, reservation@indigowarsaw.com).

$$ Between Us B&B is an inviting home-away-from-home for hipsters in Warsaw. Beata rents three trendy rooms above a recommended café centrally located in downtown Warsaw. As this place books up early, reserve far ahead (on second floor, no elevator, check in at Między Nami café downstairs, Bracka 20, +48 22 828 5417 or +48 603 096 701, www.between-us.eu, info@between-us.eu).

$ Chopin Boutique offers comfort, class, personality, hospitality, and value in an ideal location. Jarek Chołodecki, who lived near Chicago for many years, returned to Warsaw and converted this beautifully renovated apartment building into a bed-and-breakfast with 38 endearingly creaky, creatively decorated, antique-furnished rooms. Quirky, charming Jarek is a good host (you'll feel like you're staying with your Warsaw sophisticate cousin), and his staff provide  a warm professionalism. You'll enjoy breakfast at big communal tables in the cellar restaurant, escape from the city in the garden courtyard, and have the opportunity to take in a nightly Chopin concert in the ground-floor salon—see "Entertainment in Warsaw," earlier. Jarek prides himself on his hotel's eco-friendliness and sustainability—with solar panels on the roof and much of the produce grown on the premises (RS%, elevator, free loaner bikes, rooftop deck with sweeping views over Warsaw, some rooms have street noise—ask for a quieter one in back, Ulica Smolna 14, +48 22 829 4801, https://bbwarsaw.com, info@bbwarsaw.com).

$ Apple Inn, with 10 tight, modern rooms that have small windows high above the streets of Warsaw, is your cheap-and-cheery option in the center. It's in the attic of the former Jabłkowski Brothers department store—and, since *jabłko* means "apple," the name is a clever pun (air-con, shared kitchen and library, sometimes unstaffed—clearly communicate your arrival time, Chmielna 21, unit 22B—ride elevator to fourth floor, +48 601 746 006, www.appleinn.pl, Marta).

¢ Oki Doki City Hostel, on a pleasant square a few blocks in front of the Palace of Culture and Science, is colorful, creative, and easygoing. Each of its 37 rooms was designed by a different artist with a special theme—such as Van Gogh, Celtic spirals, heads of state, or Lenin. It's run by Ernest—a Pole whose parents loved Hemingway—and his wife Łucja, with help from their sometimes-jaded staff (private rooms available, up lots of stairs with no elevator, Plac Dąbrowskiego 3, +48 22 828 0122, www.okidoki.pl, okidoki@okidoki.pl).

In Śródmieście ("Downtown"): Foodies, people who hate tourists, and travelers who really want to disappear into Warsaw choose to sleep in Śródmieście, a 10-to-15-minute walk (or quick tram ride) south of Jerusalem Avenue. **$$$$ Hotel Nobu,** part of a high-end international chain, is a sophisticated home base in urbane Śródmieście. Its 117 rooms come in two types: The majority are sleek Asian minimalism, with bare-concrete hallways and well-decorated rooms. The rest are in a historic hotel building next door, with classic Art Deco style (air-con, elevator, Wilcza 73, nearest tram/bus stop at Koszykowa, +48 22 551 8888, https://warsaw.nobuhotels.com).

IN OR NEAR THE OLD TOWN

The Old Town area has some fine splurges and easy access to the romantic, rebuilt historic core. But it's less handy to Warsaw's trendier side.

$$$$ Hotel Bristol is Warsaw's top splurge—as much a landmark as a hotel (see description on page 393), this classic address on the Royal Way is where you're likely to spot visiting dignitaries and celebrities. (Just inside the round entrance on the corner, find the wall of brass knobs identifying past VIP guests—from Pablo Picasso to Ed Sheeran.) The public spaces are palatial, with sumptuous Art Deco lounges, bars, and coffee shops that make you want to dress up just to hang out. And the 206 rooms are fresh, elegant, and well equipped. If you like a posh home base, check the rates here first—you may be surprised at how affordable opulence can be (air-con, classy old vintage elevator, gym, swimming pool, sauna, Krakowskie Przedmieście 42, +48 22 551 1000, www. hotelbristolwarsaw.pl, bristol@luxurycollection.com).

$$$ Hotel Le Régina, part of the Mamaison group, is another tempting splurge, buried in the quiet and charming New Town (just north of the Old Town, a short walk away). From elegant public spaces to its 61 rooms, everything here is done with class (air-con, elevator, exercise room, pool, Kościelna 12, +48 22 531 6000, www.mamaisonleregina.com, reservations.leregina@ mamaison.com).

$ Duval Apartments, named for a French woman who supposedly had an affair with the Polish king in this building, offers four nicely appointed rooms above a café and teahouse (called Same Fusy) a few steps off the square in the Old Town. Each spacious room has a different theme: traditional Polish, Japanese, glass, or retro. Offering B&B comfort with hotel anonymity, this is a solid value in a dreamy location. Especially on busy weekends, there may be some noise from revelers in the street out front—light sleepers can request a quieter back room (lots of stairs with no elevator, no breakfast—but ample options nearby, between the Barbican and Old Town Square at Nowomiejska 10, +48 608 679 346, www. duval.net.pl, duval@duval.net.pl). Arrange a meeting time with Agnieszka or Marcin when you reserve.

$ Castle Inn, sitting on Castle Square at the entrance to the Old Town, is run by the owners of Oki Doki Hostel (described earlier). Each of its 22 creative and colorful rooms has different decor. While not plush, it's central and well priced (portable air-con in "deluxe" rooms in summer—otherwise no air-con, lots of stairs and no elevator, can be noisy—request quiet room, Świętojańska 2, +48 22 425 0100, www.castleinn.pl, castleinn@castleinn.pl).

Eating in Warsaw

Warsaw is, quite unexpectedly, one of Central Europe's best food cities...not that the tourists who stick to the kitschy Old Town restaurants would know. While there are some fine places in the historic center to sample traditional Polish food, that's better done in Old World Kraków; in Warsaw, don't be shy about exploring some local neighborhoods to find a more eclectic, modern, cosmopolitan food scene. Prices are low, so even a "splurge" restaurant lets you experience high-end

cuisine for a fraction of the cost of a similar place in a Western European capital.

But be warned: The food scene here changes at a bewildering pace. What's hot and new one year is shuttered the next. Don't be surprised if some places I list here are closed when you visit. On the upside, that means there's always something new to check out. Ask around, and do some research to find out what's trending right now.

Unless otherwise noted, see the "Central Warsaw" map, earlier, for locations.

NEAR PALM TREE CIRCLE (NOWY ŚWIAT AND JERUSALEM AVENUE)

These practical options are right in the middle of your sightseeing plans. The clientele is a mix of local yuppies, savvy business travelers, and tourists smart enough to steer clear of Old Town restaurants.

Nowogrodzka Street

This otherwise unassuming street, one block south of busy Jerusalem Avenue, is a burgeoning foodie strip for local urbanites. The best choice here is **$$ Bibenda,** a rustic-trendy bar with cocktails and an enticing seasonal menu of Polish fusion dishes. The creative chefs use Polish classics as a starting point, then jazz them up with elements borrowed from corresponding dishes in other cultures. For example, you might see fried chicken (a Polish staple) marinated in buttermilk (from the American south) with a raspberry/chipotle glaze (from Mexico). Or perhaps a *gołąbki* (Polish cabbage roll) done in the style of a Turkish *dolma* (stuffed grape leaves). Or perhaps a beet salad with Sicilian citrus and radicchio. You may not see these exact dishes, as the menu changes constantly, but what you eat will invariably be creative, delicious, and surprisingly affordable. They have outstanding craft cocktails, too. They don't take reservations, so arrive early or line up (Mon dinner only, Tue-Sun lunch from 13:00 and dinner, Nowogrodzka 10, +48 502 770 303, www.bibenda.pl).

Also along Nowogrodzka, you'll find **$$$ Soul Kitchen,** a more upscale-feeling place with international cuisine in a sophisticated cellar (daily, downstairs at #18A, +48 519 020 888, www.soulkitchen.pl); **$$ Le Cabaret,** a dressy, grown-up-feeling "jazz café bistro" with a throwback-upscale interior, a short menu of hot and cold small plates, and live jazz music (daily, at #4A, +48 536 976 403); and **$ Drugie Dno,** an industrial microbrew taproom with bare brick, eight beers on tap, and affordable burgers (daily from 16:00, at #4, +48 22 625 3709, www.drugiedno.pl).

Near the Heart of Nowy Świat

The first cross street you reach on Nowy Świat (coming from Jerusalem Avenue) has a concentration of dining options in both directions. To the right (east, toward the river) runs **Foksal street,** lined with an ever-changing lineup of lively, contemporary eateries where diners cram the al fresco tables. This enticing strip feels generic and a bit touristy. (The recommended Kamanda Lwowska, described below, is a bit farther down Foksal.) To the left (west, toward the Palace of Culture and Science) runs **Chmielna street.** This grubby urban corridor has an entirely different vibe: Rather than upscale sit-down places, it's an intriguing lineup of hole-in-the-wall and takeaway joints: Vietnamese, kebabs, pizza slices, Belgian fries, bubble tea, fancy ice cream, and so on.

After a couple of blocks, Chmielna opens up into a lovely traffic-free square (with modern benches) at **Szpitalna street.** Here the vibe changes again, with some appealing, upmarket, hangout hipster cafés where you can grab a good drink or a bite: The sleek and modern **$$ Żywioły** ("Elements") bakery, filling the ground floor of the modernized Jabłkowski Brothers department store building, is a good and obvious choice (daily, straight ahead at Chmielna 19, +48 501 984 040, www.zywioly.pl); just to the left, find the hipper **$ Między Nami,** with ramshackle secondhand furniture, a short but tempting menu, and an ambience that encourages hanging out (closed Sun, Bracka 20, downstairs from recommended Between Us B&B, +48 22 828 5417, www.miedzynamicafe.com). Emil Wedel's chocolate heaven, described later under "Classic Polish Treats," is a block north.

Very Traditional Polish Food: $$ Kamanda Lwowska is the best spot in central Warsaw for big portions of homestyle Polish cooking. It's named for the former Polish city that's now in Ukraine (Lwow, a.k.a. Lviv). It has a few outdoor seats in a parklike setting and a charming, cluttered old cellar with just a touch of kitsch. The friendly and fun staff serves up well-executed Polish classics (daily from 13:00, Foksal 10, +48 22 828 1031, www.kamandalwowska.pl).

Classic Polish Treats: *Pączki* and Chocolate

These places are on or close to the busy Nowy Świat boulevard.

A. Blikle, Poland's most famous pastry shop, serves a wide variety of delicious treats. This is where locals shop for cakes when they're having someone special over for coffee. The specialty is *pączki* (PONCH-kee), the quintessential Polish doughnut, filled with rose-flavored jam. You can get your goodies "to go" in the shop, or pay double to enjoy them with coffee in the swanky, classic café with indoor or outdoor seating (daily, Nowy Świat 35, +48 22 828 6601). They also have a sit-down restaurant, but I come here only for the *pączki*. You'll see many other A. Blikle branches around town, but this is the original.

E. Wedel Pijalnia Czekolady thrills chocoholics. Emil Wedel made Poland's favorite chocolate, and today, his former residence houses this chocolate shop and genteel café. This is the spot for delicious pastries and a *real* hot chocolate—*czekolada do picia* ("drinking chocolate"), a cup of melted chocolate, not just hot chocolate milk. Or, if you fancy chocolate mousse, try *pokusa*. Wedel's was *the* Christmas treat for locals under communism. Cadbury bought the company when Poland privatized, but they kept the E. Wedel name, which is close to all Poles' hearts...and taste buds (daily, Szpitalna 8, +48 22 827 2916, www.wedelpijalnie.pl).

IN POWIŚLE, NEAR THE RIVERBANK

The low-lying Powiśle neighborhood—squeezed in the little canyon between the Royal Way and the river—is trendy, thanks partly to its proximity to the inviting riverbank parks and Copernicus Science Center. These places aren't worth a big detour, but a trip here lets you escape the congested urban center, explore a quieter side of town, and combine a meal with a stroll along the river.

Elektrownia Powiśle is a sprawling, futuristic complex that fills a former electric plant across the street from the Copernicus Science Center. It preserves an original red-brick hall, newly adorned with lots of steel, glass, and steampunk accents. The core of the complex is dedicated to dining, surrounded by a sprawling designer mall (if you're in the market for modern Polish fashion or upmarket tennis shoes, this is the place). The **$ food hall** is a handy place to browse for a meal—the eclectic lineup includes everything from microbrews, smash burgers, and gourmet hot dogs to sushi, ramen, dim sum, and tacos. There are also a few attached **$$-$$$$ sit-down restaurants.** Even if you're not looking for a meal, the dramatic old-meets-new architecture makes this worth a stroll-through (closed Sun, Dobra 42, www.elektrowniapowisle. com).

$ Warszawa Powiśle is a café/bar occupying the old, communist-style ticket office for the suburban train station of the same name. Tucked along a picturesque bike lane beneath the towering legs of a bridge, its sidewalk is jammed with cool Varsovians and in-the-know visitors. I'd skip the basic food (light sandwiches, dumplings) and instead

just enjoy the vibe with a drink (daily, Kruczkowskiego 3B, +48 22 474 4084).

IN ŚRÓDMIEŚCIE ("DOWNTOWN")

Warsaw's Śródmieście district is the epicenter of Polish hipster/foodie culture—where you'll find young Varsovian foodies digging into affordable dishes at the trendiest new places. This area is a 15-minute walk south of Jerusalem Avenue and also well served by public transportation (several trams run frequently along the main north-south Marszałkowska corridor to Plac Zbawiciela); the Politechnika Metro stop is also nearby. Listed next are a few different restaurant-hunting zones, with a handful of specific recommendations. For locations of the places listed in this section, see the "Warsaw Overview" map, on page 378.

Hala Koszyki

This trendy food hall (pronounced koh-SHEE-kee), which opened in 2016 in a renovated brick market hall from 1906, is your handiest one-stop shop for sampling Warsaw's current dining scene. Outside—sandwiched between the two brick entrances—is a sprawling zone of al fresco tables amidst lush trees strewn with twinkle lights. Inside, you'll find more than a dozen entirely different eateries, covering all of the culinary bases: Spanish  tapas, sushi, Indian, Latin American, Italian, Thai, hummus bar, dim sum, beer hall, tea salon, gourmet chocolates, *gelateria*, Portuguese, the grotesquely over-the-top "Jeff's American Food," and more (most are **$-$$**). It's anchored by the big bar in the middle, surrounded by communal seating.

The upper level, ringed by design studios, has quieter seating and views over the action. The complex also has some serious sit-down eateries, including **$$$ Ćma** ("Moth"), with updated Polish fare and occasional DJs (daily, Koszykowa 63, www.koszyki.com). They also have live performances (ranging from concerts for kids to Polish stand-up comedy)—check the website for details.

On Plac Zbawiciela

Named "Holiest Savior Square" for the looming church, this is a dizzying six-way intersection with a big traffic circle ringed by hulking old colonnades. To get a quick taste of the Śródmieście scene, come here first and just do a slow loop around the circle, surveying your options. Starting to the right of the steeple and moving clockwise, here are a few options you'll see (all open daily): **$$ Izumi Sushi, $ Karma** coffee shop (drinks, sandwiches, and salads), and **$$ Tuk Tuk** Thai street food are all popular, with great seating out on the square. Continuing two crosswalks around the circle, you'll cross Mokotowska; looking left here, you may spot a line of people at **Sucré**—an unpretentious hole-in-the-wall serving all-natural, homemade ice cream. The next section (after Mokotowska)

has **Pałaszowanie,** serving cheap but creative *zapiekanki* (French bread pizza), followed by the trendy **$$ Charlotte** designer bakery and wine bar, with homemade treats and sandwiches at tables spilling out all over the square. Up above, **Plan B** is a hipster dive bar with drinks, snacks, and views down over the square; this is where revelers head at 2 in the morning, after the restaurants are closed (find the graffiti-slathered staircase up just past Charlotte).

On and near Poznańska Street
A few short blocks west of Plac Zbawiciela, this street is also lined with trendy and youthful eateries (especially around the intersection with Wilcza street; the nearest tram/bus stop is Hoża, and it's also not far from Plac Konstytucji). Strolling this strip, you'll find several enticing options. **$$ Beirut,** a rustic and casual bar serving up good Middle Eastern food, is the culinary anchor of this neighborhood—always packed and lively. The hummus bar, on the left, has a wide variety of *meze*s (small plates) and grilled meats, while the "Kraken Rum Bar" on the right has fish dishes (portions are modest—plan to share a few, order at the counter then find a table, daily, Poznańska 12). **$$ Tel Aviv,** with gluten-free and vegan Middle Eastern food across the street, is the upscale and more user-friendly answer to Beirut...and enjoys handling its overflow (daily, Poznańska 11). A few steps away, at the intersection with Wilcza, is **$$$$ Nolita,** one of Warsaw's top-end, white-tablecloth, fine-dining splurges (closed Sun-Mon, Sat dinner only, Wilcza 46, www.nolita.pl).

OTHER HIP, POSTINDUSTRIAL HANGOUTS
In addition to **Hala Koszyki** (in Śródmieście) and **Elektrownia Powiśle** (near the river and Copernicus Science Center)—both recommended above—Warsaw has several other trendy food-and-drink zones that fill rejuvenated former industrial com-

WARSAW

plexes. Scattered around the city, these capitalize on a Poland-wide obsession with postindustrial hipness; if you're near any of them, or if you're simply interested in exploring a different chunk of this sprawling city, these are worth a browse. At each, you'll find a range of options, from food-hall counters slinging tempting global cuisine, to sit-down splurges, to convivial pubs. All have eateries that are open daily; for the current lineup, see the websites.

Browary Warszawskie, near the Warsaw Uprising Museum in the Wola district west of downtown, fills the former home of Haberbusch and Schiele—Poland's largest brewery in the 19th century. Leveled in World War II, now it's been rebuilt in modern style under the name "Warsaw Breweries" (Grzybowska 60, www.browarywarszawskie.com.pl).

Fabryka Norblina, also in Wola, is the former factory of Norblin, a huge facility that produced metal items in the 19th and early 20th centuries. Now it's a thriving entertainment zone, with ample bars, restaurants, and "Food Town," with two dozen global food counters. If you'd like to learn more about the complex's industrial history, they also have a museum and guided tours (Żelazna 51/53, www.fabrykanorblina.pl).

Centrum Praskie Koneser—or Koneser Center for short—offers a good excuse to visit the Praga district, across the river (described on page 429). In addition to housing the Polish Vodka Museum, this former distillery complex has a wide array of dining, drinking, and entertainment venues (Plac Konesera 8, https://koneser.eu).

IN OR NEAR THE OLD TOWN

The restaurants within the Old Town and surrounding streets are 100 percent for tourists. Dining right on the Old Town Market Square is exorbitantly expensive, but could be worth it for those who treasure a romantic memory. Still, I'd rather walk a block or two to one of these options. The first two are on the New Town Square—an enjoyable five-minute stroll beyond the Barbican; with each step, you feel the tourist-to-local ratio dropping.

$$ Żyto is a cozy, stylish spot facing the New Town Square, where you can sample Ukrainian cuisine. Perusing the menu is actually educational: You'll see Ukrainian spins on what you might think are "Polish" dishes, like pierogi; and you'll notice influences from other parts of that huge country—Hungarian-style *borgacz,* Georgian-style salad with walnut paste, and so on (daily, Freta 29/31, +48 575 806 296). For more on Ukrainian food, see page 234.

$$ Freta 33, next door, has decent international fare (such as pastas), fine outdoor seating, and a contemporary subway-tile

WARSAW

interior. It feels modern and hip for this ye olde neighborhood (daily, Freta 33, +48 22 635 0931).

$ Pyzy, Flaki Gorące! is close to Castle Square, but just across the street from the Old Town wall, which helps it feel less touristy. The name—meaning "Hot Dumplings and Tripe!"—is also the menu. Cozy and casual, with a dash of trendy and kitschy, it's a fine spot for updated-traditional Polish flavors. Most of the dishes—dumplings with various toppings, soups (including the namesake tripe soup, *flaki po warszawsku*), and herring—all come in jars, a homage to Poland's historic propensity for preserving foods through the long, hard winters. They also have flatbreads with very Polish toppings (daily, Podwale 5, +48 722 255 245, www.pyzyflakigorace.pl).

$ Zapiecek, with a half-dozen locations in and near the Old Town, is a kitschy chain serving up cheap and cheery traditional Polish dishes. Yes, it's definitely touristy. But the prices are reasonable, and the food is better and more authentic than it has any right to be. They proudly make their prizewinning pierogi by hand every morning. If you need a quick, traditional meal anywhere near the Old Town, you could do much worse (handiest location faces the Cathedral of St. John the Baptist at Świętojańska 13, others are on the main drag through the New Town at Freta 1 and Freta 18, two more on the Royal Way at Nowy Świat 64 and Krakowskie Przedmieście 55, all open long hours daily).

Warsaw Connections

Almost all trains into and out of Warsaw go through hulking Warszawa Centralna station (described earlier, under "Arrival in Warsaw," including ticket-buying tips).

If you're heading to Gdańsk, note that the red-brick Gothic city of Toruń and the impressive Malbork Castle are both on the way but are on separate train lines—making it difficult to do both en route (see the Gdańsk and Pomerania chapters). Also be aware that EIC and IC express trains to many destinations—including Kraków and Gdańsk—require seat reservations, even if you have a rail pass.

You can buy most tickets online (www.intercity.pl). To confirm rail journeys, check specific times online or at the station.

From Warszawa Centralna Station by Train to: Kraków (about hourly, 2.5 hours), **Gdańsk** (hourly, 3 hours), **Malbork** (hourly, 2.5 hours), **Toruń** (every 2 hours direct, 3 hours on express IC train, more with changes), **Prague** (2/day direct, more with change in Ostrava, 8.5 hours), **Berlin** (4/day direct, 6.5 hours, no direct night train), **Budapest** (1/day direct, 11.5 hours;

1/day overnight, 13 hours; more with change in Břeclav, Czech Republic), **Vienna** (2/day direct, 7.5 hours; plus 1 night train, 11.5 hours).

By Bus: Flixbus—described on page 1108—runs bus routes throughout Poland and to international destinations (www.flixbus.pl).

GDAŃSK & THE TRI-CITY

Gdańsk (guh-DAYNSK), on the Baltic Coast of Poland, may be *the* great undiscovered Central European destination—rich with history and culture, slathered with gorgeous architecture old and new, loaded with world-class museums and great restaurants...and just plain fun.

Exploring Gdańsk is a delight. It feels like Poland's answer to Amsterdam or Scandinavia. The historical center is a gem, with block after block of red-brick churches and narrow, colorful, ornately decorated Hanseatic burghers' mansions. The riverfront embankment, with its trademark medieval crane, oozes salty maritime charm. Gdańsk's history is also fascinating—from its 17th-century golden age to the headlines of the late 20th century, big things happen here. You might even see ol' Lech Wałęsa still wandering the streets. And yet Gdańsk is also unmistakably a city of the future, with state-of-the-art construction projects popping up all over.

Gdańsk and two nearby towns (Sopot and Gdynia) together form an area known as the "Tri-City," offering several day-trip opportunities north along the coast (see page 503). The belle époque seaside resort of Sopot beckons to holidaymakers, while the modern burg of Gdynia sets the pace for today's Poland. Beyond the Tri-City, the sandy Hel Peninsula is a popular spot for summer sunbathing, and Malbork Castle (covered in the next chapter) is an easy half-hour train ride away.

PLANNING YOUR TIME

Gdańsk, with more than its share of great sights (and tempting side trips), demands two full days—which also makes the long trip up here more worthwhile. (Add a night in Toruń, while you're at it.) If you're in a rush and have a limited appetite for sightseeing, you could squeeze it into one day. If you have more time, Gdańsk will fill it.

Gdańsk sightseeing has three major components: the Royal Way (historic main drag with good museums); the river embankment, leading to the WWII history museum; and the modern shipyard where Solidarity was born (with a fascinating museum). If you have just one (very busy) day, follow my self-guided walk through the Main Town and then out to the Solidarity sights, followed by a spin through the WWII museum (closed Mon) and a stroll along the riverfront back into town.

With two days, I'd devote one day to the Main Town, riverbank, and WWII museum; and a second day to the Solidarity sights, rounding out your time with other attractions: Art lovers enjoy the National Museum (with a stunning altar painting by Hans Memling), history buffs make the pilgrimage to Westerplatte (where World War II began), castle fans side-trip to Malbork, and church and pipe-organ fans might visit Oliwa Cathedral in Gdańsk's northern suburbs (on the way to Sopot).

If you have more time, consider the wide variety of side trips. The most popular option is the half-day round-trip to Malbork Castle (30-45 minutes each way by train, plus two or three hours to tour the castle—see next chapter). It only takes a quick visit to enjoy the resort town of Sopot (25 minutes each way by train), but on a sunny day, that town's beaches may tempt you to laze around longer. Gdynia is skippable, but it does have one great sight (the Emigration Museum) and rounds out your take on the Tri-City. If you have a full day and great weather, and you don't mind fighting the crowds for a patch of sandy beach, go to Hel.

Gdańsk gets very busy in late June, when school holidays begin, and it's crowded with (mostly German, Norwegian, and Swedish) tourists from July to mid-September—especially during St. Dominic's Fair (Jarmark Św. Dominika, three weeks from late July to mid-Aug), with market stalls, concerts, and other celebrations.

Closed (and Free) Days: Most sights in Gdańsk close one day each week, typically either Tuesday (Museum of Gdańsk branches) or Monday (other museums). And some sights are free one day each week—for example, the Museum of Gdańsk branches are free on Monday. Check these details when planning your sightseeing (as these days tend to change from year to year). If you're in town when major museums are closed, good alternatives include visiting churches (including St. Mary's) or the European Solidarity Center. If side-tripping anywhere, check ahead for closed days: For example, Malbork Castle's interiors and Gdynia's Emigration Museum are closed on Mondays.

Orientation to Gdańsk

With 460,000 residents, Gdańsk is part of the larger urban area known as the Tri-City (Trójmiasto, total population of one million).

But the tourist's Gdańsk is compact, welcoming, and walkable—virtually anything you'll want to see is within a 20-minute stroll of everything else.

Focus on the Main Town (Główne Miasto), home to most of the sights described, including the spectacular Royal Way main drag, Ulica Długa. The Old Town (Stare Miasto) has a handful of old brick buildings and faded, tall, skinny houses—but the area is mostly drab and residential, and not worth much time. Just beyond the northern end of the Old Town (about a 20-minute walk from the heart of the Main Town) is the entrance to the Gdańsk Shipyard, with the excellent European Solidarity Center and its top-notch museum. From here, shipyards sprawl for miles.

Crossing the River: In addition to the big, permanent bridge in front of the Green Gate, Gdańsk has two pedestrian bridges in the tourist zone: a **swing bridge** near the Crane (connecting to the sleek modern strip on Granary Island) and a **drawbridge** farther north (just beyond the carousel on Fishmarket Square). Both bridges are available to pedestrians from :30 past each hour until the top of the hour; when the clock approaches :00, you'll hear a siren and a recorded warning to clear the bridges so they can open for boat traffic. Then, after 30 minutes, they click back into place for pedestrians again. If exploring across the river, keep an eye on the time...unless you don't mind taking a longer route back. You may also see a small **ferry** (named the *Motława*, like the river) that occasionally shuttles visitors back and forth on the extremely quick crossing between the Crane and the old granaries across the way (small fee, operated by the Maritime Museum).

Language Barrier: The second language in this part of Poland is German, not English. As this was a predominantly German city until the end of World War II, German tourists flock here in droves. But you'll win no Polish friends if you call the city by its more familiar German name, Danzig.

Cruise Crowds: Gdańsk is an increasingly popular cruise destination, with about 100 ships calling here each year (most dock at the nearby city of Gdynia, and passengers take a bus or train in). During summer daytime hours, the town is filled with little excursion groups.

TOURIST INFORMATION

Gdańsk has two different TI organizations. Most helpful is the **regional TI,** which occupies the Upland Gate, at the start of my self-guided walk (daily 9:00-18:00, off-season until 17:00, +48 58 732 7041, www.pomorskie.travel). The **city TI** is conveniently located at the bottom end of the main drag, at Długi Targ 28 (just to the left as you face the river gate; daily 9:00-17:00, +48 58 301 4355, www.visitgdansk.com). There's also a TI desk at the airport, and there may be one in the future at the Solidarity Center.

Sightseeing Pass: Busy sightseers should consider the **Tourist Card,** which includes entry to several sights in Gdańsk, Gdynia, and Sopot, and discounts at others (such as 20 percent off the European Solidarity Center). Check the list of what's covered, and do the arithmetic (65 zł/24 hours, 85 zł/48 hours, 105 zł/72 hours, pay more to add local transit, sold only at TIs).

ARRIVAL IN GDAŃSK

By Train at Gdańsk's Main Train Station (Gdańsk Główny): If you're on a PKP train, get off at the Gdańsk Główny stop. This
station is a pretty brick palace on the western edge of the old center. (To save money, architects in Colmar, France, copied this exact design to build their city's station.) As this station has been under construction, details may be in flux. But generally, trains to other parts of Poland (marked *PKP*) typically use platforms 1 or 2; regional trains with connections to the Tri-City (marked *SKM*) use platform 3. The bus station (Dworzec PKS) is behind the train station, accessible via the pedestrian tunnel that connects the platforms.

To **walk** into town, use the pedestrian underpass to go beneath the busy road; from
where you emerge, it's a 10-to-15-minute walk to the heart of town and most hotels (bear right from the underpass and head for all the red-brick church towers). Considering the stairs and the distance, it's easier—and affordable—to hop in a **taxi** or request an **Uber** (about 20-25 zł); from the tunnel under the tracks, exit toward *ul. Podwale Grodzkie* to pop out at the busy road, where you can meet your Uber or find a taxi.

By Train at Gdańsk Śródmieście: If you're arriving in

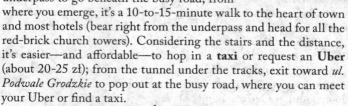

Gdańsk on a commuter SKM train, consider getting off at the Gdańsk Śródmieście station, which is a slightly shorter walk to the start of my Gdańsk Walk. From Gdańsk Śródmieście, use the underpass to reach the gigantic Forum shopping mall. Walk straight through the mall to the far end; after exiting, if you look to the right, you'll see a pedestrian underpass leading to the Upland Gate and the start of my walk.

By Plane: Gdańsk's architecturally impressive, user-friendly airport, named for Lech Wałęsa, is about five miles west of the city center (code: GDN, www.airport.gdansk.pl). From the arrivals area, follow signs to the handy train, which zips to the main train station in about 30 minutes (5 zł, 1-2/hour). Public **bus** #210 also heads to the main train station; you can get off one stop earlier, at Hucisko, for a slightly shorter walk to the main part of town (5 zł, buy ticket at machine before boarding, 2/hour Mon-Fri, hourly Sat-Sun, 40 minutes). The 25-minute **taxi** ride into town should cost around 60-80 zł; an **Uber** typically costs less (except during peak times).

GETTING AROUND GDAŃSK

Nearly everything is within easy walking distance of my recommended hotels, but public transportation can be useful for reaching outlying sights such as Oliwa Cathedral, Westerplatte, Sopot, Gdynia, and Hel (specific transportation options for these places are described in each listing).

By Public Transportation: Gdańsk's trams and buses work on the same tickets: single-ride ticket—4.80 zł, 24-hour ticket—18 zł. Major stops have user-friendly ticket machines, which take credit cards; otherwise, buy tickets *(bilety)* at kiosks marked *RUCH*. In the city center, the stops worth knowing about are Plac Solidarnośći (near the European Solidarity Center), Gdańsk Główny (in front of the main train station), and Brama Wyżynna (near the Upland Gate and the Gdańsk Śródmieście commuter train station).

By Taxi or Uber: Taxis cost about 8 zł to start, then 2-3 zł per kilometer (a bit more at night). However, taxis waiting at stands often have inflated rates; it's safer to call a cab (try Neptun, +48 19686 or +48 585 111 555; EcoCar, +48 123 456 789; or Dajan, +48 58 19628). Uber works well in Gdańsk and is typically cheaper than a taxi.

Tours in Gdańsk

Private Guides

Hiring a local guide is an exceptional value. **Agnieszka Syroka**—personable and knowledgeable—is a wonderful guide (750 zł/half-day tour, more for all day, +48 502 554 584, www.tourguidegdansk.

Gdańsk at a Gdlance

▲▲▲Gdańsk Walk Stroll down the city's colorful showpiece main drag, ending at the famous shipyards and the European Solidarity Center. See page 449.

▲▲▲Solidarity Sights and Gdańsk Shipyard Home to the beginning of the end of Eastern European communism, with a towering monument and excellent museum. **Hours:** Memorial and shipyard gate—always open. European Solidarity Center exhibit—Mon-Fri 10:00-19:00, Sat-Sun until 20:00; Oct-April Wed-Mon 10:00-17:00, Sat-Sun until 18:00, closed Tue. See page 474.

▲▲Main Town Hall Ornate meeting rooms, town artifacts, and tower with sweeping views. **Hours:** June-Sept Tue-Sun 10:00-18:00, Mon from 12:00; Oct-May Wed-Mon 10:00-16:00, Thu until 18:00, closed Tue. See page 468.

▲▲Artus Court Grand meeting hall for guilds of golden-age Gdańsk, boasting an over-the-top tiled stove. **Hours:** Same as Main Town Hall. See page 470.

▲▲St. Mary's Church Giant red-brick church crammed full of Gdańsk history. **Hours:** Mon-Sat 8:00-17:30, Sun from 13:00, until 18:30 in July-Aug, tower typically open later in summer but generally closed in winter. See page 460.

▲▲Museum of the Second World War Poland's definitive museum on the most devastating conflict in human history. **Hours:** Tue 10:00-16:00, Wed-Sun 10:00-18:00 (until 20:00 in July-Aug), closed Mon year-round. See page 485.

▲Amber Museum High-tech exhibit of valuable golden globs of petrified tree sap. **Hours:** July-Aug Mon 12:00-20:00, Tue-Sun 10:00-20:00; Sept-June Wed-Mon 10:00-18:00, closed Tue. See page 470.

▲Uphagen House Tourable 18th-century interior, typical of the pretty houses that line Ulica Długa. **Hours:** Same as Main Town Hall. See page 468.

▲St. Bridget's Church Home church of Solidarity, with poignant memorials and a massive amber altar. **Hours:** Mon-Sat 10:00-18:30, Sun from 13:30. See page 465.

com, syroka.agnieszka@gmail.com). Other guides include **Izabella Daszkiewicz** (similar rates, +48 506 511 752, gedanka@op.pl, www.gedanka.pl) and **Jacek "Jake" Podhorski,** who teaches economics at the local university (500 zł/4 hours, more for all day and/or with his car, +48 603 170 761, jacek.podhorski@ug.edu.pl).

Gdańsk Walk

In the 16th and 17th centuries, Gdańsk was the wealthiest city in the Polish lands, with gorgeous architecture (much of it in the Flemish Mannerist style) rivaling that in the two historic capitals, Kraków and Warsaw. During this golden age, Polish kings would visit this city of well-to-do Hanseatic League merchants and gawk along the same route trod by tourists today.

The following self-guided walk—rated ▲▲▲—introduces you to the best of Gdańsk. It bridges the two historic centers (the Main Town and the Old Town), dips into St. Mary's Church (the city's most important church), and ends at the famous shipyards and Solidarity Square (where Poland began what ultimately brought down the USSR). I've divided the walk into two parts (making it easier to split up, if you like): The first half focuses on a loop through the Main Town, with most of the high-profile sights; while the second part carries on northward, through the less touristy (but still interesting) Old Town to the shipyards.

PART 1: THE MAIN TOWN
• *Begin at the west end of the Main Town, just beyond the last gate at the edge of the busy road—across from the mega-shopping mall.*

❶ Upland Gate (Brama Wyżynna)
The Main Town's fortifications were expanded with a Renaissance wall bound by the Upland Gate (built in 1588). "Upland" refers to the low hills you see beyond—considered high country in this flat region. Standing with your back to the busy arterial (which traces the old moat), study the gate. Find its three coats of arms (the black eagle for Royal Prussia, the crowned white eagle for Poland, and the two crosses for Gdańsk). Recall that this city has, for almost the entirety of its history before the mid-20th century, been bicultural: Germanic and Polish, coexisting more or less peacefully. Also notice the little wheels that once hoisted a drawbridge.

GDAŃSK & THE TRI-CITY

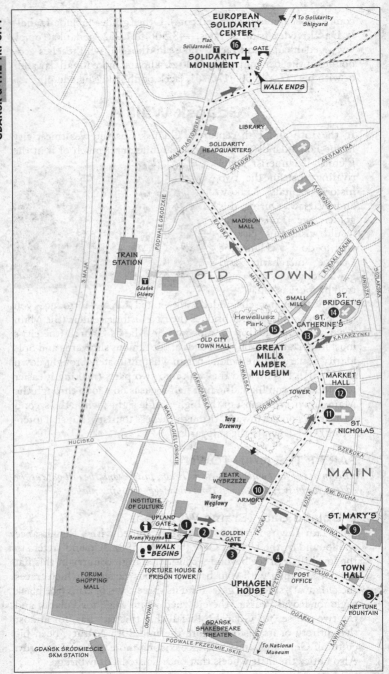

EUROPEAN
SOLIDARITY
CENTER

→ To Solidarity
Shipyard

Plac
Solidarności

16 SOLIDARITY
MONUMENT

GATE

WALK ENDS

LIBRARY

SOLIDARITY
HEADQUARTERS

WAŁY PIASTOWSKIE

WAŁOWA

AKSAMITNA

PODWALE GRODZKIE

MADISON
MALL

KAŁESKA

MŁYNY

J. HEWELIUSZA

RYBAKI GÓRNE

STOLARSKA

JAGIELLIN

MNISZKI

TRAIN
STATION

3 MAJA

Gdańsk
Główny

OLD TOWN

Heweliusz
Park

SMALL
MILL

ST.
BRIDGET'S **14**

15

ST.
CATHERINE'S

13

KATARZYNKI

OLD CITY
TOWN HALL

KOWALSKA

GREAT
MILL &
AMBER
MUSEUM

WAŁY JAGIELLOŃSKIE

GARNCARSKA

PODWALE

TOWER

MARKET
HALL **12**

11

ST.
NICHOLAS

HUCISKO

Targ
Drzewny

SZEROKA

TEATR
WYBRZEŻE

Targ
Węglowy

MAIN

ŚW. DUCHA

INSTITUTE
OF CULTURE

10

ARMORY

TRACKA

KOZIA

ST. MARY'S **9**

UPLAND
GATE

ℹ

1

2

GOLDEN
GATE

PIWNA

FORUM
SHOPPING
MALL

Brama Wyżynna T

WALK
BEGINS

3

4

DŁUGA

TOWN
HALL

TORTURE HOUSE &
PRISON TOWER

UPHAGEN
HOUSE

POCZTOWA

POST
OFFICE

OGARNA

5

NEPTUNE
FOUNTAIN

ŁAWNICZA

OKOPOWA

GDAŃSK
SHAKESPEARE
THEATER

ZBYTKI

→ To National
Museum

GDAŃSK ŚRÓDMIEŚCIE
SKM STATION

PODWALE PRZEDMIEJSKIE

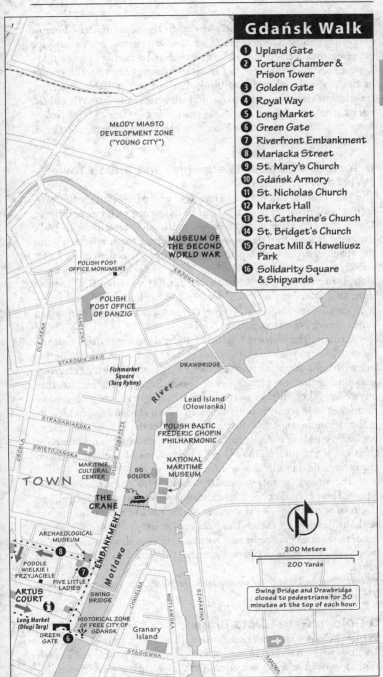

Gdańsk Walk

1. Upland Gate
2. Torture Chamber & Prison Tower
3. Golden Gate
4. Royal Way
5. Long Market
6. Green Gate
7. Riverfront Embankment
8. Mariacka Street
9. St. Mary's Church
10. Gdańsk Armory
11. St. Nicholas Church
12. Market Hall
13. St. Catherine's Church
14. St. Bridget's Church
15. Great Mill & Heweliusz Park
16. Solidarity Square & Shipyards

MŁODY MIASTO DEVELOPMENT ZONE ("YOUNG CITY")

MUSEUM OF THE SECOND WORLD WAR

POLISH POST OFFICE MONUMENT

POLISH POST OFFICE OF DANZIG

KROSNA

OLEJARNA

TANECZNA

STAROMIEJSKIE

Fishmarket Square (Targ Rybny)

DRAWBRIDGE

River

Lead Island (Ołowianka)

STRAGANIARSKA

POLISH BALTIC FREDERIC CHOPIN PHILHARMONIC

GROBLA

ŚWIETOJAŃSKA

MARITIME CULTURAL CENTER

DŁUGIE POBRZEŻE

SS SOŁDEK

NATIONAL MARITIME MUSEUM

TOWN

THE CRANE

EMBANKMENT

ARCHAEOLOGICAL MUSEUM

8

PODOLE WIELKIE I PRZYJACIELE

7

FIVE LITTLE LADIES

ARTUS COURT

1

Long Market (Długi Targ)

SWING BRIDGE

HISTORICAL ZONE OF FREE CITY OF GDAŃSK

GREEN GATE

6

Motława

CHMIELNA

MOTŁAWSKA

Granary Island

SZAFARINA

STAGIEWNA

ŁASOWA

200 Meters

200 Yards

Swing Bridge and Drawbridge closed to pedestrians for 30 minutes at the top of each hour.

Now look across the busy street, to the supermodern **Forum shopping center.** Controversial for its over-the-top design (and for covering over a historic canal), this replaced a ragtag old flea market area. A lion—symbol of Gdańsk—perches high on the corner of the rust-colored main building. I'm not in the habit of telling travelers to visit shopping malls...but this one really is worth a peek.

• *It's a straight line from here to the river. Walk around the arch (which houses a good TI—find the entrance on the back side) to the next arch, just a few steps ahead.*

❷ Torture Chamber (Katownia) and Prison Tower (Wieża Więzienna)

The tall, Gothic brick gate before you was part of an earlier protective wall made useless after the Renaissance walls were built in 1588. The evocative passage is generally open (and free) to walk through. Inside, find gargoyles (on the left, a town specialty) and the shackles from which prisoners were hung (on the right). Look waaaay up at the inside of the high gable to find the headless man, identifying this as the torture chamber. (If you stand in just the right spot, you can "reattach" his head to his body.) This old jail—with its 15-foot-thick walls—was used as a prison even in modern times, under Nazi occupation.

Leaving the Torture Chamber and Prison Tower through the far end, look to your left (100 yards away) to see a long, brick building with four fancy, uniform gables. This is the **armory** *(zbrojownia),* one of the finest examples of Dutch Renaissance architecture anywhere. Though this part of the building appears to have the facades of four separate houses, it's an urban camouflage to hide its real purpose from potential attackers. But there's at least one clue to what the building is really for: Notice the exploding cannonballs at the tops of the turrets. (We'll get a better look at the armory from the other side, later in this walk.)

The round, pointy-topped tower next to the armory is the **Straw Tower** (Baszta Słomiana). Gunpowder was stored here, and the roof was straw—so if it exploded, it could easily blow its top without destroying the walls. And to the left you'll see the sleek, modern **Teatr Wybrzeże** performing arts complex—one of many new venues that have opened around this cultural hub in recent years.

• *Straight ahead, the final and fanciest gate between you and the Main Town is the...*

❸ Golden Gate (Złota Brama)

While the other gates were defensive, this one's purely ornamental. The four women up top represent virtues that the people of Gdańsk should exhibit toward outsiders (left to right): Peace, Freedom,

Prosperity, and Fame. The gold-lettered inscription, a psalm in medieval German, compares Gdańsk to Jerusalem: famous and important. Directly above the arch is the Gdańsk coat of arms: two white crosses under a crown on a red shield. We'll see this symbol all over town. Photographers love the view of the Main Town framed in this arch. Inside the arch, you may see old photos showing the 1945 bomb damage. Heartbreaking aerial views of the city in 1945 illustrate how 80 percent of its buildings were in ruins.

• *Passing through the Golden Gate, you reach the Main Town's main drag.*

❹ The Royal Way

Before you stretches Ulica Długa (cleverly called the "Long Street")—the main promenade of what, 600 years ago, was a tremendously wealthy city, thanks to its profitable ties to the Hanseatic League of merchant cities. This promenade is nicknamed the "Royal Way" because (just as in Warsaw and Kraków) the king would follow this route when visiting town.

Walk half a block and then look back at the Golden Gate. The women on top of this side represent virtues the people of Gdańsk should cultivate in themselves (left to right): Wisdom, Piety, Justice, and Concord (if an arrow's broken, let's take it out of the quiver and fix it). The inscription—sharing a bit of wisdom as apropos today as it was in 1612—reads, "Concord makes small countries develop, and discord makes big countries fall." Gdańsk was cosmopolitan and exceptionally tolerant in the Middle Ages, attracting a wide range of people, including many who were persecuted elsewhere: Jews, Scots, Dutch, Flemish, Italians, Germans, and more. Members of each group brought with them strands of their culture, which they wove into the tapestry of this city—demonstrated by the eclectic homes along this street. Each facade and each gable was different, as nobles and aristocrats wanted to display their wealth. On one visit, a traveler seeing this street for the first time gasped to me, "It's like stepping into a Fabergé egg."

During Gdańsk's golden age, these houses were taxed based on frontage (like the homes lining Amsterdam's canals)—so they were built skinny and deep. The widest houses belonged to the super-elite. Different as they are from the outside, every house had the same general plan inside. Each had three parts, starting with the front and moving back: First was a fancy drawing room, to show off for visitors. Then came a narrow corridor to the back rooms—often

Gdańsk History

Visitors to Gdańsk are surprised at how "un-Polish" the city's history is. In this cultural melting pot of German, Dutch, and Flemish merchants (with a smattering of Italians and Scots), Poles were only a small part of the picture until the city became exclusively Polish after World War II. However, in Gdańsk, cultural backgrounds traditionally took a back seat to the bottom line. Wealthy Gdańsk was always known for its economic pragmatism— no matter who was in charge, merchants here made money.

Gdańsk is Poland's gateway to the waters of Europe, where its main river (the Vistula) meets the Baltic Sea. The town was first mentioned in the 10th century and was seized in 1308 by the Teutonic Knights (who called it "Danzig"; for more on the Teutonic Knights, see page 521). The Knights encouraged other Germans to settle on the Baltic coast, and gradually turned Gdańsk into a wealthy city. In 1361, Gdańsk joined the Hanseatic League, a trade federation of mostly Germanic merchant towns that provided mutual security. By the 15th century, Gdańsk was a leading member of this mighty network, which virtually dominated trade in northern Europe (and also included Toruń, Kraków, Lübeck, Hamburg, Bremen, Bruges, Bergen, Tallinn, Novgorod, and nearly a hundred other cities).

In 1454, the people of Gdańsk rose up against the Teutonic Knights, burning down their castle and forcing them out of the city. Three years later, the Polish king borrowed money from wealthy Gdańsk families to hire Czech mercenaries to take the Teutonic Knights' main castle, Malbork (described in the next chapter). In exchange, the Gdańsk merchants were granted special privileges, including exclusive export rights. Gdańsk now acted as a middleman for much of the trade passing through Polish lands, and paid only a modest annual tribute to the Polish king.

The 16th and 17th centuries were Gdańsk's golden age. Now a part of the Polish kingdom, the city had access to an enormous hinterland of natural resources to export—yet it maintained a privileged, semi-independent status. Like Amsterdam, Gdańsk became a progressive and booming merchant city. Its mostly Germanic and Dutch burghers imported Dutch, Flemish, and Italian architects to give their homes an appropriately Hanseatic flourish. At a time of religious upheaval in the rest of Europe, Gdańsk became known for its tolerance—a place that opened its doors to all visitors (many Mennonites and Scottish religious refugees emigrated here). It was also a haven for great thinkers, including philosopher Arthur Schopenhauer, women's rights activist Käthe Schirmacher, and scientist Daniel Fahrenheit (who invented the mercury thermometer).

Along with the rest of Poland, Gdańsk declined in the late 18th century and became part of Prussia (today's northern Germany) during the Partitions. But the people of Gdańsk—even those of German heritage—had taken pride in their independence and weren't enthusiastic about being ruled from Berlin. After World War I, in a unique compromise to appease its complex ethnic makeup, Gdańsk once again became an independent city-state: the Free City of Danzig (about 750 square miles, populated by 400,000 ethnic Germans and 15,000 Poles). Like a holdover from medieval fiefdoms in modern times, it even issued its own currency (the Gulden) and stamps. Danzig, along with the so-called Polish Corridor connecting it to Polish lands, effectively cut off Germany from its northeastern territory. On September 1, 1939, Adolf Hitler started World War II when he invaded Gdańsk in order to bring it back into the German fold. Later, nearly 80 percent of the city was destroyed when the Soviets "liberated" it from Nazi control.

After World War II, Gdańsk officially became part of Poland and was painstakingly reconstructed. In 1970, and again in 1980, the shipyard of Gdańsk witnessed strikes and demonstrations that would lead to the fall of European communism. Poland's great anticommunist hero and first postcommunist president, Lech Wałęsa, still lives here. When he flies around the world to give talks, he leaves from Gdańsk's "Lech Wałęsa Airport."

A city with a recent past that's both tragic and uplifting, Gdańsk celebrated its 1,000th birthday in 1997. Very roughly, the city has spent about 700 years as an independent entity, and about 300 years under Germanic overlords (the Teutonic Knights, Prussia, and the Nazis. But today, Gdańsk is decidedly its own city. And, as if eager to prove it, Gdańsk has made big improvements at a stunning pace: mu-  seums (the European Solidarity Center and WWII museum), cultural facilities (the Shakespeare Theater), sports venues (a stadium that resembles a blob of amber, built for the 2012 Euro Cup tournament), and an ongoing surge of renovation and refurbishment that has the gables of the atmospheric Hanseatic quarter gleaming once again.

along the side of an inner courtyard. Because the houses had only a few windows facing the outer street, this courtyard provided much-needed sunlight to the rest of the house. The residential quarters were in the back, where the family actually lived: bedroom, kitchen, office. To see the interior of one of these homes, pay a visit to the interesting **Uphagen House** (at #12, on the right, a block and a half in front of the Golden Gate; described later).

Pause in front of Uphagen House, look around, and ponder this beautiful street's very ugly history. At the end of World War II, the Royal Way was in ruins. That epic war actually began here, in what was then the "Free City of Danzig." Following World War I, nobody could decide what to do with this influential and multi-ethnic city. So, rather than assign it to Germany or Poland, it was set apart as its own little autonomous statelet. In 1939, Danzig was 80 percent German-speaking—enough for Hitler to consider it his. And so, on September 1 of that year, the Nazis seized it in one day with relatively minor damage (though the attack on the Polish military garrison on the city's Westerplatte peninsula lasted a week).

But six years later, when the Soviets arrived (March 30, 1945), they devastated the city. This was the first traditionally German city that the Red Army took on their march toward Berlin. And, while it was easy for the Soviets to seize the almost empty city, the commander then insisted that it be leveled, building by building—in retaliation for all the pain the Nazis had caused in Russia. (Soviets didn't destroy nearby Gdynia, which they considered Polish rather than German.) Soviet officers turned a blind eye as their soldiers raped and brutalized residents. An entire order of horrified nuns committed suicide by throwing themselves into the river.

It was only thanks to detailed drawings and photographs that these buildings could be so carefully reconstructed. Notice the cheap plaster facades done in the 1950s—rough times under communism, in the decade after World War II. (Most of the town's medieval brick was shipped to Warsaw for a communist-sponsored "rebuild the capital first" campaign.) While the fine facades were restored, the buildings behind the facades were completely rebuilt to modern standards.

Just beyond Uphagen House, on the left at #73, **Grycan** has been a favorite for ice cream here for generations. Just a few doors down, also on the left, are some of the most striking **facades** along the Royal Way. The blue-and-white house with the three giant heads is from the 19th century, when the

hot style was eclecticism—borrowing bits and pieces from various architectural eras. This was one of the few houses on the street that survived World War II.

At the next corner on the right is the huge, blocky, red **post office,** which doesn't quite fit with the skinny facades lining the rest of the street. Step inside. With doves fluttering under an airy glass atrium, the interior's a class act.

A few doors farther down on the left, just past #62/63, notice the **colorful scenes** over the windows. These are slices of life from 17th-century Gdańsk: drinking, talking, shopping, playing music. The ship is a *koga,* a typical symbol of Hanseatic ports like Gdańsk.

Across the street and a few steps down are the fancy facades of three houses belonging to the very influential medieval **Ferber family,** which produced many burghers, mayors, and even a bishop. On the house with the little dog over the door (#29), look for the heads in the circular medallions. These are Caesars of Rome. At the top of the building is Mr. Ferber's answer to the constant question, "Why build such an elaborate house?"—*PRO INVIDIA,* "For the sake of envy."

A few doors down on the right (at #33/34), is Gdańsk's most scenically situated milk bar, **Bar Mleczny Neptun.** Back in communist times, these humble cafeterias were subsidized to give workers an affordable place to eat out. To this day, they offer simple and very cheap grub.

Before you stands the **Main Town Hall** (Ratusz Głównego Miasta) with its mighty brick clock tower. Consider climbing its observation tower and visiting its superb interior, which features ornately decorated meeting rooms for the city council (described later, under "Sights in Gdańsk").

As you stroll along this street—and throughout your time in Gdańsk—you'll periodically hear cheerful **carillon music** playing from the top of the Main Town Hall tower. This 14-bell instrument, which dates from 1561, chimes throughout the day, providing a lovely soundtrack to a Gdańsk visit. On Saturdays at noon, there's a longer concert (www.carillongdansk.pl).

• *Just beyond the Main Town Hall, Ulica Długa widens and becomes...*

❺ Long Market (Długi Targ)

Step from the Long Street into the Long Market and do a slow, 360-degree spin to appreciate the amazing array of proud architecture. The centerpiece of this square is one of Gdańsk's most important landmarks, the statue of **Neptune**—god of the sea. He's a fitting symbol for a city that dominates the maritime life of Poland. Behind him is another worthwhile museum, the **Artus Court**. Step up to the magnificent door on the right side and study the golden relief just above, celebrating the Vistula River (in so many ways the lifeblood of the Polish nation): Lady Vistula is exhausted after her heroic journey and is finally carried by Neptune to her ultimate destination, the Baltic Sea. (This is just a preview of the ornate art that fills the interior of this fine building—described later.)

Midway down the Long Market (on the right, across from the Hard Rock Café) is a glass case with the **thermometer and barometer of Daniel Fahrenheit.** Although that scientist was born here—his birth house is just a few blocks away—he did his groundbreaking work in Amsterdam.

• *At the end of the Long Market is the...*

❻ Green Gate (Zielona Brama)

This huge gate (named for the Green Bridge just beyond) was built as a residence for visiting kings...who usually preferred to stay back by Neptune instead (maybe because the river, just on the other side of this gate, stank).

A few steps down the skinny lane to the left is the endearing little **Historical Zone of the Free City of Gdańsk** museum, which explains the interwar period when "Danzig" was an independent and bicultural city-state (described later). During this period, four out of five people living in the free city identified themselves not as Germans or Poles but as "Danzigers."

• *Now go through the gate, walk out onto the Green Bridge, anchor yourself in a niche on the left, and look downstream.*

❼ Riverfront Embankment

The Motława River—a side channel of the mighty Vistula—flows into the nearby Baltic Sea. This port was the source of Gdańsk's phenomenal golden-age wealth. This embankment was jam-packed in its heyday, the 14th and 15th centuries. It was so crowded with boats that you would hardly have been able to see the water, and boats had to pay a time-based moorage fee for tying up to a post.

Look back at the **Green Gate** and notice that these bricks are much smaller than the locally made ones we saw earlier on this walk. These bricks are Dutch: Boats from Holland would come here empty of cargo but with a load of bricks for ballast. Traders filled their ships with goods for the return trip, leaving the bricks behind.

See any pirate ships? The old-fashioned **galleons** and other tour boats depart hourly for a fun cruise to Westerplatte (where on

September 1, 1939, Germans fired the first shots of World War II) and back. Though kitschy, the galleons are a fun way to get out on the water (see details on page 493).

Across the river is **Granary Island** (Wyspa Spichrzów), where grain was stored until it could be taken away by ships. Before World War II, there were some 400 granaries here; almost all were destroyed...and this island remained rubble until the mid-2010s, when developers began erecting a passel of modern new buildings (evoking the old Gdańsk gables) and wrapped the island in a scenic boardwalk—a wonderful place for a stroll. While there's not much sightseeing value along here, it's a delightful place to promenade, enjoy views back on the historic skyline across the river, and perhaps browse for a meal or drink. The three older-looking granaries downstream, in the distance on the next island, house exhibits for the National Maritime Museum (described later).

From your perch on the bridge, look down the embankment (about 500 yards, on the left) and find the huge wooden **Crane** (Żuraw) bulging over the water. This monstrous 15th-century crane—a rare example of medieval port technology—was once used for loading and repairing ships...beginning a shipbuilding tradition that continued to the days of Lech Wałęsa. The crane mechanism was operated by several workers scrambling around in giant hamster wheels. Treading away to engage the gears and pulleys, they could lift 4 tons up 30 feet, or 2 tons up 90 feet.

Near the Crane, notice the white, modern **swing bridge** that makes it easier for pedestrians to do a loop along both embankments. At the top of each hour, it swings parallel to the river to allow boats to pass, making it inaccessible for 30 minutes. (The similar white drawbridge, farther downstream, works on the same schedule.) You'll hear a big commotion every time it's about to swing; watch the tourists scurry.

• *Walk along the embankment about halfway to the Crane. Along the way, you may pass the moorings for* ***excursion boats*** *heading to the Westerplatte monument. (Or these may be farther down along the embankment, beyond the Crane.)*

Pause when you reach the big brick building with green window frames and a tower. This red-brick fort houses the ***Archaeological Museum*** *(described later). Its collection includes the five ancient stones in a small garden just outside its door (on the left). These are the* ***Prussian***

Hags—*mysterious sculptures from the second century AD (a.k.a. "Five Little Ladies," each described in posted plaques).*

Turn left through the gate in the middle of the brick building. You'll find yourself on the most charming lane in town...

❽ Mariacka Street

The calm, atmospheric "Mary's Street" leads from the embankment to St. Mary's Church. Stroll the length of it, enjoying the most romantic lane in Gdańsk. (If you need a coffee break, the recommended Drukarnia—on the right—is tops.) The **porches** extending out into the street, with access to cellars underneath, were a common feature in Gdańsk's golden age. For practical reasons, after the war, these were restored only on this street and a few others. Notice how the porches are bordered with fine stone relief panels and gargoyles attached to storm drains. If you get stuck there in a hard rainstorm, you'll understand why in Polish these are called "pukers." Enjoy a little amber comparison-shopping. As you stroll up to the towering brick St. Mary's Church, imagine the entire city like this cobbled lane of proud merchants' homes, with street music, delightful facades, and brick church towers high above.

Look up at the church tower viewpoint—filled with people who hiked 409 steps for the view. Our next stop is the church, which you'll enter on the far side under the tower. Walk around the left side of the church, appreciating the handmade 14th-century bricks on the right and the plain post-WWII facades on the left. (Reconstructing the Royal Way was better funded. Here, the priority was simply getting people housed again.) In the distance is the fancy facade of the armory (where you'll head after visiting the church).

• *But first, go inside...*

❾ St. Mary's Church (Kościół Mariacki)

Of Gdańsk's 13 medieval red-brick churches, St. Mary's (rated ▲▲) is the one you must visit. It's the largest brick church in the world—with a footprint bigger than a football field (350 feet long and 210 feet wide), it can accommodate 20,000 standing worshippers.

Cost and Hours: Church entry—likely free for now, tower climb—16 zł, Mon-Sat 8:00-17:30, Sun from 13:00, until 18:30 in July-Aug, tower typically open later in summer but generally closed in winter.

➲ **Self-Guided Tour:** Inside, sit directly under the fine carved and painted 17th-century

Protestant pulpit, two-thirds of the way down the nave (on the left side), to get oriented.

Overview: Built from 1343 to 1502 by the Teutonic Knights (who wanted a suitable centerpiece for their newly captured main city), St. Mary's remains an important symbol of Gdańsk. The church started out Catholic, became Lutheran in the mid-1500s, and then became Catholic again after World War II. (Remember, Gdańsk was a Germanic city before World War II and part of the big postwar demographic shove, when Germans were sent west and Poles from the east relocated here. Desperate, cold, and homeless, the new Polish residents moved into what was left of the German homes.) While the church was originally frescoed from top to bottom, the Lutherans whitewashed the entire place. Today, some of the 16th-century whitewash has been peeled back (behind the high altar—we'll see this area soon), revealing a bit of the original frescoes. The floor is paved with 500 gravestones of merchant families. Many of these were cracked when bombing sent the brick roof crashing down in 1945.

Most Gothic churches are built of stone in the basilica style—with a high nave in the middle, shorter aisles on the side, and flying buttresses to support the weight. (Think of Paris' Notre-Dame.) But with no handy source of stone available locally, northern Polish churches are built of brick, which won't work with the basilica design. So, like all Gdańsk churches, St. Mary's is a "hall church"—with three naves the same height and no exterior buttresses.

Also like other Gdańsk churches, St. Mary's gave refuge to the Polish people after the communist government declared martial law in 1981. When a riot broke out and violence seemed imminent, people flooded into churches, knowing that the ZOMO riot police wouldn't dare follow them inside.

Most of the church decorations are original. A few days before the Soviets arrived to "liberate" the city in 1945, locals—knowing what was in store—hid precious items in the countryside. Take some time now to see a few of the highlights.

• *From this spot, you can see most of what we'll visit in the church: As you face the altar, the astronomical clock is at 10 o'clock, the Ferber family medallion is at 1 o'clock, the Priests' Chapel is at 3 o'clock (under a tall, colorful window), and the magnificent 17th-century organ is directly behind you (it's played at each Mass and during free concerts on Fri in summer).*

Pulpit: For Protestants, the pulpit is important. Designed as an impressive place from which to share the Word of God in the people's language, it's located mid-nave so all can hear.

• *Opposite the pulpit is the moving...*

Priests' Chapel: The 1965 statue of Christ weeping commem-

GDAŃSK & THE TRI-CITY

orates 2,779 Polish chaplains executed by the Nazis. See the grainy black-and-white photo of one about to be shot, above on the right.

• *Head up the nave to the...*

High Altar: The main altarpiece, beautifully carved in 1517, is a triptych showing the coronation of Mary. She is surrounded by the Trinity: flanked by God and Jesus, with the dove representing the Holy Spirit overhead. The church's medieval stained glass was destroyed in 1945. Poland's biggest stained-glass window, behind the altar, is from 1980.

• *Directly to the right of the altar, high on a pillar, find the big, opulent family marker.*

Ferber Family Medallion: The falling baby (under the crown) is Constantine Ferber. As a precocious child, li'l Constantine leaned out his window on the Royal Way to see the king's processional come through town. He slipped and fell but landed in a salesman's barrel of fish. Constantine grew up to become the mayor of Gdańsk.

• *Now circle around behind the altar, on the right side. Search high above you, on the walls to your right, to spot those restored pre-Reformation frescoes. Behind the altar, look for a...*

Glass Case: This case was designed to hold Hans Memling's *Last Judgment* painting, which used to be in this church but is currently being held hostage by the National Museum (described later, under "Sights in Gdańsk"). To counter the museum's claim that the church wasn't a good environment for such a precious work, the priest had this display case built—but that still wasn't enough to convince the museum to give the painting back. (You'll see a smaller replica of the painting elsewhere in the church.) For years, the case was simply empty; more recently, finally taking the hint, the local priest has begun to display a few vestments and ecclesiastical gear here.

• *Now circle back the way you came to the area in front of the main altar and turn right into the transept. High on the wall to your right, look for the...*

Astronomical Clock: This 42-foot-tall clock is supposedly the biggest wooden clock in the world. Below it is an elaborate circular calendar that, like a medieval computer, calculates on which day each saint's festival day falls in different years (see the little guy on the left, with the pointer). Above are zodiac signs and the time (back then, the big hand was all you needed). Way up on top, Adam and Eve are naked and ready to ring the bell. Adam's been swinging his clapper at the top of the hour since 1473; these days, you'll hear the clock clang on the quarter-hour, with a big show each day at 11:55.

• *A few steps in front of the clock is a modern chapel with the...*

Memorial to the Polish Victims of the 2010 Smoleńsk Plane

Crash: The gold-shrouded Black Madonna honors the 96 victims of an air disaster that killed much of Poland's government—including the president and first lady—during a terrible storm over Russia. The main tomb is for Maciej Płażyński, from Gdańsk, who was leader of the parliament. On the left, the jagged statue has bits of the wreckage and lists each victim by name.

• *Head a few steps back toward the entrance, then look back at one of the nearby pillars to find a large painting (facing the back of the church).*

Replica of *Last Judgment* Altarpiece: This is a smaller, mustier replica of the exquisite, priceless altarpiece housed in the National Museum. If you're not planning to go see it at the National Museum, you could read the description on page 491 now.

• *In the back-left corner of the church are stairs—lots and lots of stairs—leading to the...*

Church Tower: You can climb 409 steps to burn off some pierogi and *pączki*, and to earn a grand city view. It's a long hike (and you'll know it—every 10th step is numbered). But because the viewpoint is surrounded by a roof, the views are distant and may not be worth the effort. The first third is up a tight, medieval spiral staircase. Then you'll walk through the eerie, cavernous area between the roof and the ceiling before huffing up steep concrete steps that surround the square tower (as you spiral up, up, up around the bells). Finally, you'll climb a little metal ladder and pop out at the viewpoint.

• *Leaving the church, angle left and continue straight up atmospheric **Ulica Piwna** ("Beer Street")—a lovely lane lined with bars, cafés, and restaurants—toward the sprightly facade of the armory.*

❿ The Gdańsk Armory (Zbrojownia)

The 1605 armory, which we saw from a distance at the start of this walk, is one of the best examples of Dutch Renaissance architecture in Europe. Athena, the goddess of war and wisdom, stands in the center, amid motifs of war and ornamental pukers.

• *If you want to make your walk a loop, you're just a block away from where we started (to the left). Or, to continue through the Old Town to the European Solidarity Center's fine museum, follow the second part of this walk.*

PART 2: THROUGH THE OLD TOWN TO THE SHIPYARDS

The second part of this walk works its way out of the Main Town and heads into the Old Town, toward Solidarity Square and the shipyards. We'll walk along this street (which changes names a couple of times) nearly all the way. The walk ends at the European Solidarity Center's fine museum. You'll want plenty of time to tour the museum and linger over its exhibits, so if you're already pooped or it's getting late in the day, consider finishing this walk another time.

• *Facing the armory, turn right and head up Kołodziejska, which quickly becomes Węglarska. After two blocks (that is, one block before the big market hall), detour to the right down Świętojańska and use the side door to enter the brick church.*

⓫ St. Nicholas Church (Kościół Św. Mikołaja)

Near the end of World War II, when the Soviet army reached Gdańsk on its march westward, they were given the order to burn all the churches. Only this one survived—because it happened to be dedicated to Russia's patron saint. As the best-preserved church in town, it has a more dazzling interior than the others, with lavish black-and-gold Baroque altars.

• *Backtrack out to the main street and continue along it, passing a row of seniors selling their grown and foraged edibles. Immediately after the church is Gdańsk's...*

⓬ Market Hall

Built in 1896 and renovated in 2005, Gdańsk's market hall is fun to explore. Step inside (closed Sun) and appreciate the delicate steel-and-glass canopy overhead. Browse the market stalls; the meat is downstairs, and the veggies are outside on the adjacent square. As this was once the center of a monastic community, the basement has the graves of medieval Dominican monks, which were exposed when the building was refurbished: Peer over the glass railing and you'll see some of those scant remains.

Across the street from the Market Hall, a round, red-brick **tower,** part of the city's protective wall back in 1400, marks the end of the Main Town and the beginning of the Old Town.

• *Carry on. For an ice cream break, watch on the right (after crossing the street) for the recommended Paolo Gelateria. Another block up the street, on the right, is the huge...*

⓭ St. Catherine's Church (Kościół Św. Katarzyny)

"Katy," as locals call it, is the oldest church in Gdańsk, proud of its carillon (there's a small Clock Tower Museum in the tower, and you can hear carillon concerts on Fridays at 11:00; see www.carillongdansk.pl). In May of 2006, a carelessly discarded cigarette caused the church roof to burst into flames. Local people ran into the church and pulled everything outside, so nothing valuable was damaged; even the carillon bells were saved. However, the roof and wooden frame were totally destroyed. The people of Gdańsk were determined to rebuild this important symbol of the city. Within days of the fire, fundraising concerts were held to scrape together most of the money needed to raise the roof once more. Step inside.

The austere interior is evocative, with still-bare-brick walls that almost seem intentional—as if they're trying for an industrial-mod look.

• *The church hiding a block behind Katy—named for Catherine's daughter Bridget—has important ties to Solidarity and is worth a visit. Go around the right side of Katy and skirt the parking lot to find the entrance, on the side of the church near the far end.*

⓮ St. Bridget's Church (Kościół Św. Brygidy)

This was the home church of Lech Wałęsa during the tense days of the 1980s. The church and its priest, Henryk Jankowski, were particularly aggressive in supporting the ideals of Solidarity. Jankowski became a vocal advocate for the movement. In gratitude for the church's support, Wałęsa named his youngest daughter Brygida. Rated ▲, it's the city's second-most worthwhile church to enter, after St. Mary's.

Cost and Hours: 5 zł, Mon-Sat 10:00-18:30, Sun from 13:30.

Visiting the Church: Head inside. For your visit, start at the high altar, then circle clockwise back to the entry.

The enormous, unfinished **high altar** is made entirely of amber—more than a thousand square feet of it. Features that are already in place include the Black Madonna of Częstochowa, a royal Polish eagle, and the Solidarity symbol (tucked below the Black Madonna). The structure, like a scaffold, holds pieces as they are completed and added to the ensemble; as it grows,

it also spreads to adjacent walls, as if a slow-moving fungus. The giant bronze statues below the altar depict Cardinal Stefan Wyszyński (on the left, the head of the Polish Catholic Church through much of the communist period) and St. John Paul II (on the right).

The wrought-iron gate of the adjacent **Chapel of Fatima** (right of main altar) recalls great battles and events in Polish history from 966 to 1939, with important dates boldly sparkling in gold. Some say the Polish Church is too political. Others argue that it was only through a politically engaged Church that this culture survived the Partitions of Poland over a century and a half, plus the brutal antireligious policies of the communist period. The national soul of the Polish people—whether religious or not, and for better or for worse—is tied up in the Catholic faith.

Henryk Jankowski's tomb—a white marble box with dark-red trim—is along the same wall, but closer to the back of the church. Jankowski was a key figure during Solidarity times; the tomb proclaims him *Kapelan Solidarności* ("Solidarity Chaplain"). But his public standing took a nosedive near the end of his life—thanks to ego-driven projects like his amber altar, as well as accusations of anti-Semitism and corruption. Forced to retire in 2007, Jankowski died in 2010.

In the rear corner, where a figure lies lifeless on the floor under a wall full of wooden crosses, is the tomb of Solidarity martyr **Jerzy Popiełuszko.** A courageous and famously outspoken Warsaw priest, in 1984 Popiełuszko was kidnapped, beaten, and murdered by the communist secret police. Notice that the figure's hands and feet are bound—as his body was found. The crosses on the wall above are historic—each one was carried at various strikes against the communist regime. The communists believed they could break the spirit of the Poles with brutality—like the murder of Popiełuszko. But it only made the rebels stronger and more resolved to ultimately win their freedom.

Under the choir loft, step into the evocative chapel with **memorials** to other 20th-century Polish martyrs.

Near the exit, on a monitor, a fascinating 12-minute **video** shows great moments of this church, with commentary by Lech Wałęsa himself.

• *Return to the main street, turn right, and continue on. The big brick building ahead on the left, with the many windows in its roof, is the Great Mill. Walk just beyond the building and look down at the canal that once powered it.*

⓮ The Great Mill and Heweliusz Park

This huge brick building dates from the 14th century. Look at the waterfalls and imagine standing here in 1400—with the mill's 18

wheels spinning 24/7, powering grindstones that produced 20 tons of flour a day. Like so much else here, the mill survived until 1945. Today this building houses the **Amber Museum**—a starkly modern exhibit filling this old shell with countless examples of those precious deposits (described later).

Heweliusz Park, just beyond the mill, is worth a look. Just steps into the family-friendly park is a **fountain** that brings shrieks of joy to children on hot summer days. On the adjacent corner, notice a branch of the popular **Pellowski bakery**—a handy place to pick up a *pączek* (jelly doughnut) to enjoy at one of the benches.

Venturing farther into the park, in the distance is the **Old City Town Hall** (Dutch Renaissance style, from 1595). The monument near the top of the park honors the 17th-century astronomer **Jan Heweliusz.** He's looking up at a giant, rust-colored wall with a map of the heavens. Heweliusz built the biggest telescopes of his era to better appreciate and understand the cosmos. Behind the mill stands the **miller's home**—its opulence indicates that, back in the Middle Ages, there was a lot of money in grinding.

• *To get to the shipyards, keep heading straight up Rajska. You'll pass the modern Madison shopping mall. After another long block, jog right, passing to the right of the big, ugly, and green 1970s-era skyscraper. On your right, marked by the famous red logo on the roof, is today's* **Solidarity headquarters** *(which remains the strongest trade union in Poland, with 700,000 members, and is also active in many other countries). On the corner in front of the Solidarity building, look for two big chunks of* **wall:** *a piece of the Berlin Wall, and a stretch of the shipyard wall that Lech Wałęsa scaled to get inside and lead the strike. The message: What happened behind one wall eventually led to the fall of the other Wall.*

From here, hike on (about 200 yards) toward the huge, rust-colored building in the distance, angling left at the roundabout to reach the trio of tall, skinny crosses in front of it.

⑯ Solidarity Square and the Shipyards

Three tall crosses mark Solidarity Square and the rust-colored European Solidarity Center (with an excellent museum). For the exciting story of how Polish shipbuilders set in motion events that led to the end of the USSR, turn to page 474.

Sights in Gdańsk

MAIN TOWN (GŁÓWNE MIASTO) AND OLD TOWN (STARE MIASTO)

The following sights are listed roughly in the order you'll see them on the self-guided walk.

Museum of Gdańsk

The Museum of Gdańsk has four excellent branches—the Uphagen House, Main Town Hall, Artus Court, and Amber Museum—and a few lesser ones. Along with St. Mary's Church (described earlier), these are the four most important interiors in the Main Town. They are covered by separate tickets.

Cost: 22 zł each for Uphagen House, Main Town Hall, or Artus Court, 32 zł for Amber Museum. All are typically free on Mondays.

Hours: The **Uphagen House, Main Town Hall,** and **Artus Court** have the same hours, which are notoriously changeable but generally around June-Sept Tue-Sun 10:00-18:00, Mon from 12:00; Oct-May Wed-Mon 10:00-16:00, Thu until 18:00, closed Tue. The **Amber Museum** has different hours: July-Aug Mon 12:00-20:00, Tue-Sun 10:00-20:00; Sept-June Wed-Mon 10:00-18:00, closed Tue.

Information: The museums share a phone number and website (central +48 58 767 9100, www.muzeumgdansk.pl).

▲Uphagen House (Dom Uphagena)

This interesting place, at Ulica Długa 12, is your chance to glimpse what's behind the colorful facades lining this street. It's the only grand Gdańsk mansion rebuilt as it was before 1945, and it has the typical configuration of three parts: dolled-up visitors' rooms in front, a corridor along the courtyard, and private rooms in the back. The finely decorated salon was used to show off for guests. You'll see several examples of "Gdańsk-style furniture," characterized by three big, round feet along the front, lots of ornamentation, and usually a virtually impossible-to-find lock (sometimes hidden behind a movable decoration). Passing into the dining room, note the knee-high paintings of hunting and celebrations. Along the passage to the back, each room has a theme: butterflies in the smoking room, flowers in the next room, birds in the music room. In the private rooms at the back, the decor is simpler.

Back downstairs, you'll see the rustic working rooms: a humble bedroom, the kitchen, and the pantry. Step out into the courtyard to appreciate how it carves a little fresh air and sunshine out of a densely packed city. Back inside, look for the cross-section model showing the three parts of the house you just walked through. You'll exit through a room with photos of the house before the war, which were used to reconstruct what you see today.

▲▲Main Town Hall (Ratusz Głównego Miasta)

This landmark building contains remarkable decorations from Gdańsk's golden age. You can also climb 293 concrete steps to the top of the **tower** for commanding views (15 zł extra, closed Oct-April).

Visiting the Main Town Hall: Buy your ticket on the ground floor, which also houses a space for temporary exhibits. Then walk through the courtyard and up the stairs to the historic rooms. First you'll be directed to the room on your left, the **Great Weta Hall**—a meeting room with big portraits and big windows.

Then, returning to the room where you first entered, ogle the finely crafted spiral staircase. The ornately carved wooden **door** is all-original, from the 1600s. Above the door are two crosses under a crown. This seal of Gdańsk is being held—as it's often depicted—by a pair of lions. The felines are stubborn and independent, just like the citizens of Gdańsk. The surface of the door is carved with images of crops. Around the frame of the door are mermen, reminding us that this agricultural bounty, like so many of Poland's resources, is transported on the Vistula and out through Gdańsk.

Step through the ornate door into the **Red Hall,** where the Gdańsk city council met in the summertime. (The lavish fireplace, with another pair of lions holding the coat of arms of Gdańsk, was just for show. There's no chimney.) City council members would sit in the seats around the room, debating city policy. Marvel at the 17th-century inlaid wood panels (just overhead) showing slices of local life. Paintings on the wall above represent the seven virtues that the burghers meeting in this room should possess.

The exquisite ceiling—with 25 paintings in total—is all about theology. Including both Christian and pagan themes, the ceiling was meant to inspire the decision makers in this room to make good choices. Study the oval painting in the middle (from 1607)—the museum's highlight. It shows the special place Gdańsk occupies between God, Poland, and the rest of the world. In the foreground, the citizens of Gdańsk go about their daily lives. Above them, high atop the arch, God's hand reaches down (from within clouds of Hebrew characters) and grasps the Main Town Hall's steeple. The rainbow arching above also symbolizes God's connection to Gdańsk. Mirroring that is the Vistula River, which begins in the mountains of southern Poland (on the right), runs through the country, and exits at the sea in Gdańsk (on the left, where the rainbow ends).

Continue into the less impressive **Winter Hall,** with another fireplace (this one actually hooked up to a chimney) and another coat of arms held by lions. The desk behind glass belonged to Paweł Adamowicz, who served as the president (mayor) of Gdańsk during the tumultuous transitional period from 1998 through 2019—when he was, shockingly, stabbed during a charity event and died at age 53. You can see a photo of this beloved local politician on the wall behind.

From here, head up another flight of stairs to a series of rooms with **temporary exhibits.** Then, up yet another flight, is a fascinating exhibit about Gdańsk's time as a **"free city"** *(wolne miasto)* between the World Wars—when, because of its delicate ethnic mix of Poles and Germans, it was too precarious to assign it to either country. You'll see border checkpoints, uniforms, signs in German (the predominant language of "Danzig"), and reconstructed rooms (homes and shops) from the era.

Near the end of this section, you have the option to climb up to the top of the **tower**. Otherwise, head back down and out the way you came.

▲▲Artus Court (Dwór Artusa)

In the Middle Ages, Gdańsk was home to many brotherhoods and guilds (like businessmen's clubs). For their meetings, the city pro-

vided this elaborately decorated hall, named for King Arthur—a medieval symbol for prestige and power. Just as in King Arthur's Court, this was a place where powerful and important people came together. Of many such halls in Baltic Europe, this is the only original one that survives (in the tall, white, triple-arched building behind Neptune statue at Długi Targ 43; enter through the door to the left of the big arches).

Visiting the Artus Court: In the grand hall, various **cupboards** line the walls. Each organization that met here had a place to keep its important documents and office supplies. Suspended from the ceiling are seven giant, elaborate **model ships** that depict Baltic vessels, symbolic of the city's connection to the sea.

In the far-back corner is the museum's highlight: a gigantic **stove** decorated with 520 colorful tiles featuring the faces of kings, queens, nobles, mayors, and burghers—a mix of Protestants and Catholics, as a reminder of Gdańsk's religious tolerance. Almost all the tiles are original, having survived WWII bombs.

Notice the huge **paintings** on the walls above, with 3-D animals emerging from flat frames. Hunting is a popular theme in local artwork. Like minting coins, hunting was a privilege usually reserved for royalty, but it was extended in special circumstances to the burghers of special towns...like Gdańsk. These "paintings" are new, digitally generated reproductions of the originals, which were damaged in World War II.

The next room—actually in the next building—is a typical **front room** of the burghers' homes lining Ulica Długa. Ogle the gorgeously carved wooden staircase, the Gdańsk-style cupboards, and three more model ships. A series of rooms with more artifacts leads to the exit.

▲Amber Museum (Muzeum Bursztynu)

This collection is displayed in a sleek, glossy, state-of-the-art space inside the very creaky and historic Great Mill, a short walk from the Main Town (and on the way to the Solidarity Sights, at Wielkie Młyny 16). The museum tells the story of the precious yellow

All About Amber

Poland's Baltic seaside is known as the Amber Coast. You can see amber (bursztyn) in Gdańsk's Amber Museum, in the collection at Malbork Castle (see the Pomerania chapter), and in shop windows everywhere.

This fossilized tree resin originated here on the north coast of Poland 40 million years ago. Scientists debate exactly what caused this sudden proliferation of sap—it may have been caused by shifting weather conditions, or in response to a new parasite or disease. Later—starting around 2.5 million years ago—Ice Age glaciers spread amber even further around the Baltic region. Then came human beings, who have been drawn to amber since the Stone Age. Archaeologists have found Roman citizens (and their coins) buried with crosses made of amber.

Almost 75 percent of the world's amber comes from northern Poland. It can be foraged, mined by digging deep holes, "fished" using nets, or accessed using hydraulic technology. And occasionally, it simply washes up on the beaches after a winter storm.

While we think of amber as simply yellow, it comes in some 300 distinct shades, from yellowish white to yellowish black, from opaque to transparent. Darker-colored amber is generally mixed with ash and sand—making it more fragile, and generally less desirable. Lighter amber is mixed with gasses and air bubbles. Some of the elaborate amber sculptures you'll see are joined with "amber glue"—melted-down amber mixed with an adhesive agent. More recently, amber craftsmen are combining amber with silver to create artwork—a method dubbed the "Polish School."

Dating back at least to the 16th century, some people believe that amber—specifically, the succinic acid found in white amber—has medicinal properties. A traditional cure for arthritis pain is to pour strong vodka over amber, let it set, and then rub it on sore joints. Other remedies call for mixing amber dust with honey or rose oil. It sounds superstitious, but users claim that it works.

deposits that the Baltic Sea is known for. But while the items displayed here are dazzling, the place is a bit light on actual information—this collection is all about ogling amber.

Visiting the Museum: From ye olde Gdańsk, you'll step through the creaky doors into a different world: glassy black surfaces that reflect the yellows, oranges, and browns of the amber everywhere you look. Buy your ticket and head up to tour the exhibit, which fills two floors upstairs.

Floor 1 covers the geology and history of amber. Timelines date back eons, and case after case of jagged chunks of raw amber illustrate the wide range of colors. One case shows smooth-polished amber with inclusions trapped inside (like those dino-DNA mosquitoes in *Jurassic Park*). You'll also learn about the various methods for finding amber (including special nets) and about its importance to golden-age Gdańsk. Touchscreens strain to explain the story of amber, but the information is pretty thin.

Floor 2 ("Amber in Culture") is simply a showcase of objects created from amber, including altars, chests, necklaces, brooches, chess sets, tankards, candelabras, miniatures, a bowl of fruit, pipes, clocks, an entire table, contemporary jewelry, and a working guitar—all beautifully lit, and all made or decorated with amber.

Back downstairs, the exit is through the extremely well-stocked gift shop (of course); there's also a handy café.

Other Museums in the Main Town

With so many worthwhile sights in town, you'll have your hands full with the biggies. But if you have a special interest, these museums are also worth considering for a visit:

The **Historical Zone of the Free City of Gdańsk** (Strefa Historyczna Wolne Miasto Gdańsk), tucked just off the main drag near the Green Gate, is the best place to learn about the fascinating period between World Wars I and II, when Gdańsk was not part of Germany or Poland but the self-governing Free City of Danzig. This modest museum earnestly shows off artifacts from the time—photos, stamps, currency (the Gulden), maps, flags, promotional tourist leaflets, and other Danzig artifacts (closed Mon, down the little alley just in front of the Green Gate at Warzywnicza 10A, +48 58 320 2828, www.strefahistorycznawmg.pl).

The **Archaeological Museum** (Muzeum Archeologiczne) is worth a quick peek: distinctive urns with cute faces (which date from the Hallstatt Period and were discovered in slate graves around Gdańsk), Bronze and Iron Age tools, before-and-after photos of WWII Gdańsk, and a reconstructed 12th-century Viking-like Slavonic longboat. You can also climb the building's tower, with good views up Mariacka street toward St. Mary's Church (closed Mon, Ulica Mariacka 25, +48 58 322 2100, www.archeologia.pl).

The **National Maritime Museum** (Narodowe Muzeum

Morskie) is an eclectic collection spread among several buildings on either side of the river. The main point of interest is the medieval Crane that dominates Gdańsk's historic waterfront; this recently reopened after a restoration. Next door is the skippable Maritime Cultural Center—of interest only to nautical nuts. Across the river, more exhibits fill the three rebuilt old granaries, and you can also crawl through the holds and scramble across the deck of a decommissioned steamship called the *Sołdek*—the first postwar vessel built at the Gdańsk shipyard (closed Mon, Ulica Ołowianka 9, +48 58 301 8611, www.nmm.pl).

Theater lovers may enjoy seeing the **Gdańsk Shakespeare Theater** (Teatr Szekspirowski), at the southern edge of the Main Town. As early as the 17th century, theater troupes from England would come to this cosmopolitan trading city to perform. In 1993, local actors revived the tradition with an annual Gdańsk Shakespeare Festival. In 2014, the city built the state-of-the-art Gdańsk Shakespeare Theater to honor its connection to the Bard. The architecture is minimalist, blocky, black brick (with a few symbolic faux buttresses to echo the gables of the surrounding buildings). The main theater can be modified to create three different types of performance spaces (proscenium, thrust stage, and theater-in-the-round)—and even has a retractable roof to wash the actors with direct sunlight. The theater hosts a wide variety of performances and festivals, and still does some Shakespeare in English during the annual Shakespeare Festival in summer. Call or check their website for details on tours and upcoming performances (Bogusławskiego 1, +48 58 351 0101, www.teatrszekspirowski.pl).

▲Fishmarket Square (Targ Rybny)

If out for a stroll, make your way just five minutes along the embankment past the Crane and swing bridge to this square, where a kid-friendly carousel spins next to a big Hilton hotel. It's no longer an actual fish market, and there's not much sightseeing here. But this vantage point offers great views up and down the river: Across the way, on Lead Island (Ołowianka), is the stately home of the Baltic Philharmonic, with its sail-like adornment, along with a giant Ferris wheel and a photo-op *GDAŃSK* sign. Downriver (to the left) you can see how the city is growing in that direction, with modern residential and commercial developments sprawling up the riverbank. Farther downstream (not visible from here) is Westerplatte, the point where World War II began. And upriver (to the right), you can see the three reconstructed old granaries and giant ship of the Maritime Museum, and beyond that, the swing bridge and Gdańsk's slick new city-center Granary Island development. This is a fine spot to find a bench and enjoy the buzz of a proud historic city on the rise.

SOLIDARITY AND THE GDAŃSK SHIPYARD

Gdańsk's single most memorable experience is exploring the ship-yard (Stocznia Gdańska) that witnessed the beginning of the end of communism's stranglehold on Central and Eastern Europe. Taken together, the sights in this area are worth ▲▲▲. Here in the former industrial wasteland that Lech Wałęsa called the "cradle of freedom," this evocative site tells the story of the brave Polish shipyard workers who took on—and ultimately defeated—an Evil Empire. A visit to the Solidarity (Solidarność) sights has two main parts: Solidarity Square (with the memorial and gate in front of the shipyard), and the outstanding museum inside the European Solidarity Center.

Getting to the Shipyard: These sights cluster around Solidar-ity Square (Plac Solidarności), at the north end of the Old Town, about a 20-minute walk from the Royal Way. For the most interest-ing approach, follow Part 2 of my self-guided walk (earlier), which ends here. Or take tram #7 or #8 from the Brama Wyżynna stop (near the Upland Gate) or the train station to the Plac Solidarości stop.

Background: After the communists took over Central and Eastern Europe at the end of World War II, oppressed peoples throughout the Soviet Bloc rose up in different ways. The most dramatic uprisings—Hungary's 1956 Uprising (see page 590) and Czechoslovakia's 1968 "Prague Spring" (see page 93)—were bru-tally crushed under the treads of Soviet tanks. The formula for freedom that finally succeeded was a patient, nearly decade-long series of strikes and protests spearheaded by Lech Wałęsa and his trade union, called Solidarność—"Solidarity." (The movement also benefited from good timing, as it coincided with the *perestroika* and *glasnost* policies of Soviet premier Mikhail Gorbachev.) While politicians tussled from their plush offices, imagine the courage it took for Wałęsa and his fellow workers to fight communism on the front lines—armed with nothing more than guts.

▲▲▲Solidarity Square (Plac Solidarności) and the Monument of the Fallen Shipyard Workers

The seeds of August 1980 were sown a decade before. Since be-coming part of the Soviet Bloc, the Poles staged frequent strikes, protests, and uprisings to secure their rights, all of which were put down by the regime. But the bloodiest of these took place in De-cember of 1970—a tragic event memorialized by the **three-crosses monument** that towers over what's now called Solidarity Square.

The 1970 strike was prompted by price hikes. The communist government set the prices for all products. As Poland endured dras-tic food shortages in the 1960s and 1970s, the regime frequently announced what it called "regulation of prices." Invariably, this

meant an increase in the cost of essential foodstuffs. (To be able to claim "regulation" rather than "increase," the regime would symbolically lower prices for a few select items—but these were always nonessential luxuries, such as elevators and TV sets, which nobody could afford anyway.) The regime was usually smart enough to raise prices on January 1, when the people were fat and happy after Christmas, and too hungover to complain. But on December 12, 1970, bolstered by an ego-stoking visit by West German chancellor Willy Brandt, Polish premier Władysław Gomułka increased prices. The people of Poland—who cared more about the price of Christmas dinner than relations with Germany—struck back.

A wave of strikes and sit-ins spread along the heavily industrialized north coast of Poland, most notably in Gdańsk, Gdynia, and Szczecin. Thousands of angry demonstrators poured through the gate of this shipyard, marched into town, and set fire to the Communist Party Committee building. In an attempt to quell the riots, the government-run radio implored the people to go back to work. On the morning of December 17, workers showed up at shipyard gates across northern Poland, and were greeted by the army and police. Without provocation, the Polish army opened fire on the workers. While the official death toll for the massacre stands at 44, others say the true number is much higher. The monument, with a trio of 140-foot-tall crosses, honors those lost to the regime that December.

Go to the middle of the **wall** behind the crosses, to the monument of the worker wearing a flimsy plastic work helmet, attempting to shield himself from bullets. Behind him is a list—pockmarked with symbolic bullet holes—of workers murdered on that day. *Lat* means "years old"—many teenagers were among the dead. The quote at the top of the wall is from St. John Paul II, who was elected pope eight years after this tragedy. The pope was known for his clever way with words, and this very carefully phrased quote—which served as an inspiration to the Poles during their darkest hours—skewers the regime in a way subtle enough to still be tolerated: "Let thy spirit descend, and renew the face of the earth—of *this* earth" (that is, Poland).

Stretching to the left of this center wall are plaques representing labor unions from around Poland—and around the world (look for the Chinese characters)—expressing solidarity with these workers. To the right is an enormous Bible verse: "May the Lord

Lech Wałęsa

In 1980, the world was turned on its ear by a walrus-mustachioed shipyard electrician. Within three years, this seemingly run-of-the-mill Pole had precipitated the collapse of communism, led a massive 10 million-member trade union with enormous political impact, been named *Time* magazine's Man of the Year, and won a Nobel Peace Prize.

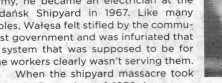

Lech Wałęsa was born in Popowo, Poland, in 1943. After working as a car mechanic and serving two years in the army, he became an electrician at the Gdańsk Shipyard in 1967. Like many Poles, Wałęsa felt stifled by the communist government and was infuriated that a system that was supposed to be for the workers clearly wasn't serving them.

When the shipyard massacre took place in December of 1970 (see page 474), Wałęsa was at the forefront of the protests. He was marked as a dissident, and in 1976, he was fired. Wałęsa hopped from job to job and was occasionally unemployed—under communism, a rock-bottom status reserved for only the most despicable derelicts. But he soldiered on, fighting for the creation of a trade union and building up quite a file with the secret police.

In August 1980, Wałęsa heard news of the beginnings of the Gdańsk strike and raced to the shipyard. In an act that has since become the stuff of legend, Wałęsa scaled the shipyard wall to get inside.

Before long, Wałęsa's dynamic personality won him the unofficial role of the workers' leader and spokesman. He negotiated with the regime to hash out the August Agreements, becoming a rock-star-type hero during the so-called "16 Months of Hope"... until martial law came crashing down in December 1981. Wałęsa was arrested and interned for 11 months in a country house. After

give strength to his people. May the Lord bless his people with the gift of peace" (Psalms 29:11).

Inspired by the brave sacrifice of their true comrades, shipyard workers rose up here in August 1980, formulating the **"21 Points"** of a new union called Solidarity. Their demands included the right to strike and form unions, the freeing of political prisoners, and an increase in wages. The 21 Points are listed in Polish on the panel at the far end of the right wall, marked *21 X TAK* ("21 times yes"). An unwritten precondition to any agreement was the right for the workers of 1980 to build a memorial to their comrades slain in 1970. The government agreed, marking the first time a communist

being released, he continued to struggle underground, becoming a symbol of anticommunist sentiment.

Finally, the dedication of Wałęsa and Solidarity paid off, and Polish communism dissolved—with Wałęsa rising from the ashes as the country's first postcommunist president. But the skills that made Wałęsa a rousing success at leading an uprising didn't translate well to the president's office. Wałęsa proved to be a stubborn, headstrong politician, frequently clashing with the parliament. He squabbled with his own party, declaring a "war at the top" of Solidarity and rotating higher-ups to prevent corruption and keep the party fresh. He also didn't choose his advisors well, enlisting old friends as staffers who wound up immersed in scandal. His overconfidence was his Achilles' heel, and his governing style verged on authoritarian.

Unrefined and none too interested in scripted speeches, Wałęsa was a simple man who preferred playing Ping-Pong with his buddies to attending formal state functions. Though lacking a formal education, Wałęsa had unsurpassed drive and charisma... but that's not enough to lead a country—especially during an impossibly complicated, fast-changing time.

Wałęsa was defeated at the polls, by the Poles, in 1995, and when he ran again in 2000, he received a humiliating 1 percent of the vote. Since leaving office, Wałęsa has kept a lower profile but still delivers speeches worldwide. Many poor Poles grumble that Lech, who started life simple like them, has forgotten the little people. But his fans point out that he gives much of his income to charity. And on his lapel, he still always wears a pin featuring the Black Madonna of Częstochowa—the most important symbol of Polish Catholicism.

Poles say there are at least two Lech Wałęsas: the young, bombastic, working-class idealist Lech, at the forefront of the Solidarity strikes, who will always have a special place in their hearts; and the failed President Wałęsa, who got in over his head and tarnished his legacy.

regime ever allowed a monument to be built to honor its own victims. Wałęsa called it a harpoon in the heart of the communists. The towering monument, with three crucified anchors on top, was designed, engineered, and built by shipyard workers. The monument was finished just four months after the historic agreement was signed.

• *Now continue to the gate and peer through into...*

Gdańsk Shipyard (Stocznia Gdańska) Gate #2

When a Pole named Karol Wojtyła was elected pope in 1978—then visited his homeland in 1979—he inspired 40 million fellow citizens to believe that impossible dreams can come true. Prices continued to go up, and the workers continued to rise up. By the summer of 1980, it was clear that the dam was about to break.

In August, crane operator Anna Walentynowicz was fired unceremoniously just short of her retirement. (For more on Walen-

tynowicz, see the sidebar.) This sparked a strike in the Gdańsk Shipyard (then called the Lenin Shipyard) on August 14, 1980. An electrician named Lech Wałęsa had been fired as an agitator years before. But on hearing news of the strike, Wałęsa went to the shipyard and climbed over the wall to get inside, soon taking over leadership for the strike.

These were not soldiers, nor were they idealistic flower children. The strike participants were gritty, salt-of-the-earth manual laborers: forklift operators, welders, electricians, machinists. Imagine being one of the 16,000 workers who stayed here for 18 days during the strike—hungry, cold, sleeping on sheets of Styrofoam, inspired by the new Polish pope, excited about finally standing up to the regime...and terrified that at any moment you might be gunned down, like your friends had been a decade before.

Workers, afraid to leave the shipyard, communicated with the outside world through this gate—spouses and siblings showed up here and asked for a loved one, and those inside spread the word until the striker came forward. Occasionally, a truck pulled up inside the gate, with Lech Wałęsa standing atop its cab with a megaphone. Facing the thousands of people assembled outside the gate, Wałęsa gave progress reports on the negotiations and pleaded for supplies. The people of Gdańsk responded, bringing armfuls of bread and other food to keep the workers going. Solidarity.

During the strike, two items hung on the fence. One of them (which still hangs there today) was a picture of Pope John Paul II—a reminder to believe in your dreams and have faith in God (for more on the Pope and his role in Solidarity, see page 270). The other item was a makeshift list of the strikers' 21 Points—demands scrawled in red paint and black pencil on pieces of plywood. (A replica now hangs above and on the right; the original is in the museum.)

• *Walk through the passage at the right end of the gate and enter the former shipyard.*

There's not much to see today, but during its peak from 1948 to 1990, the **shipyard** churned out over a thousand ships and employed 16,000 workers. About 60 percent of these ships were ex-

The Women of Solidarity

Anna Walentynowicz (1929-2010) worked as a welder and a crane operator at the Lenin Shipyard. While she began her ca-

reer as an exemplary socialist worker, the 1970 massacre of workers soured her on the communist regime. She joined an illegal trade union, distributed a workers' newsletter to agitate for change, and spoke up when a supervisor stole money from a workers' fund.

In the summer of 1980, at age 60, Walentynowicz was fired just a few months shy of her planned retirement. As the earliest strikes that would grow into Solidarity gained momentum, the rehiring of Walentynowicz was one of the strikers' 21 Points. Before Wałęsa became "the face of Solidarity," that face belonged to Walentynowicz. (Ultimately, Walentynowicz was reinstated and retired with her full pension.)

Another influential founder of Solidarity was shipyard nurse **Alina Pienkowska** (1952-2002). As the strike began, authorities cut off all phone lines—except the one to the clinic, which Pienkowska used to reach out to like-minded colleagues around Poland.

Just a few days into the strike, the authorities agreed to some of the workers' lesser demands; Lech Wałęsa, among others, chalked this up as a success and began to wind down the protests. Many of the strikers began to leave the shipyard and head for home.

But Pienkowska was aware that what had begun here in Gdańsk was already spreading across Poland. On a loudspeaker, she implored her fellow workers to stick to their strike, alongside other trade unions across Poland that had already begun to join their cause. In fact, so determined were Pienkowska and Walentynowicz to fully live the idea of "solidarity" that they locked the shipyard gates to prevent more workers from leaving. Because of these brave and principled women, many of the strikers decided to stay, and even many of those who left returned the next day (reportedly at the urging of their wives) to carry on—transforming what could have ended as a historical footnote into a world-changing event.

Tragically, both women met untimely deaths. Pienkowska died of cancer in 2002, at age 50. And Walentynowicz was aboard the plane filled with Polish politicians and other influential figures that crashed in Smoleńsk, Russia, on April 10, 2010. But their legacy lives on. While Lech Wałęsa became the movement's public face, Walentynowicz and Pienkowska are considered the conscience, heart, and soul of Solidarity. Both were ultimately awarded the Order of the White Eagle—Poland's highest honor.

ported to the USSR—and so, when the Soviet Bloc broke apart in the 1990s, they lost a huge market. Today, the facilities employ closer to 1,200 workers...who now make windmills.

Before entering the museum, take a look around. This part of the shipyard, long abandoned, is being redeveloped into a **"Young City"** (Młode Miasto), with shopping, restaurants, offices, and homes. Rusting shipbuilding equipment is being torn down, and old brick buildings are being converted into gentrified flats. Farther east, the harborfront is also being rejuvenated, creating a glitzy marina and extending the city's delightful waterfront people zone farther and farther to the north.

• *The massive, rust-colored European Solidarity Center, which faces Solidarity Square, houses the museum where we'll learn the rest of the story.*

▲▲▲European Solidarity Center (Europejskie Centrum Solidarności)

Europe's single best sight about the end of communism is made even more powerful by its location: in the very heart of the place

where those events occurred. Filling just one small corner of a huge, purpose-built educational facility, the permanent exhibition uses larger-than-life photographs, archival footage, actual artifacts, interactive touchscreens, and a state-of-the-art audioguide to eloquently tell the story of the end of Eastern European communism.

Cost and Hours: 30 zł, includes audioguide; Mon–Fri 10:00–19:00, Sat–Sun until 20:00; Oct–April Wed–Mon 10:00–17:00, Sat–Sun until 18:00, closed Tue; last entry one hour before closing, Plac Solidarności 1, +48 58 772 4000, www.ecs.gda.pl.

◉ Self-Guided Tour: First, appreciate the architecture of the **building** itself. From the outside, it's designed to resemble the rusted hull of a giant ship—seemingly gloomy and depressing. But step inside to find an interior flooded with light, which cultivates a surprising variety of life—in the form of lush gardens that make the place feel like a very expensive greenhouse. You can interpret this symbolism a number of ways: Something that seems dull and dreary from the outside (the Soviet Bloc, the shipyards themselves, what have you) can be full of brightness, life, and optimism inside.

In the lobby, buy your ticket for the permanent exhibit and pick up the essential, included audioguide. The exhibit has much to see, and some of it is arranged in a conceptual way that can be tricky to understand without a full grasp of the history. I've outlined the basics in this self-guided tour, but the audioguide can illuminate more details—including translations of films and eye-witness testimony from participants in the history.

Notice that the center also hosts temporary exhibits (filling a ground-floor space beneath the escalators), a "Play Department" area for kids, a simple $ café, and, back near the entrance, the more upscale $$ AmberSide restaurant. (For more eating options near-by, see page 502.)

• *The permanent exhibit fills seven lettered rooms—each with its own theme—on two floors upstairs. From the lush lobby, head up the escalator and into...*

The Birth of Solidarity (Room A): This room picks up right in the middle of the dynamic story we just learned out on the square. It's August 1980, and the shipyard workers are rising up. You step straight into a busy shipyard: punch clocks, workers' lockers, and—up on the ceiling—hundreds of plastic helmets. A big **map** in the middle of the room shows the extent of the shipyard in 1980. Near-by stands a small **truck;** Lech Wałęsa would stand on top of the cab of a truck like this one to address the nervous locals who had amassed outside the shipyard gate, awaiting further news.

In the middle of the room, carefully protected under glass, are those original **plywood panels** onto which the strikers scrawled their 21 demands and then lashed to the gate. Just beyond that, a giant video screen and a map illustrate how the strikes that began here spread like a virus across Poland. At the far end of the room, behind the partition, stand **two tables** that were used during the talks to end the strikes (each one with several actual items from that era, under glass).

After 18 days of protests (notice the dates marked on the floor), the communist authorities finally agreed to negotiate. On the afternoon of August 31, 1980, the Governmental Commission and the Inter-Factory Strike Committee (MKS) came together and signed the August Agreements, which legalized Solidarity—the first time any communist government had permitted a workers' union. As Lech Wałęsa sat at a big table and signed the agreement, other union reps tape-recorded the proceedings and played them later at their own factories to prove that the unthinkable had hap-pened. Take a moment to linger over the rousing **film** that plays on the far wall, which begins with the strike, carries through with the tense negotiations that a brash young Lech Wałęsa held with the authorities, and ends with the triumphant acceptance of the strik-ers' demands. Lech Wałęsa rides on the shoulders of well-wishers out to the gate to spread the good news. The gate opens, the strikers file out, and the crowd cheers: "Leszek! Leszek!" (Lech-y! Lech-y!) The shipyard gate opens, and—finally!—the strikers get to return to the outside world.

• *Back by the original 21 demands, enter the next exhibit...*

The Power of the Powerless (Room B): This section traces the roots of the 1980 strikes, which were preceded by several far-less successful protests. It all begins with a kiss: a giant photograph of Russian premier Leonid Brezhnev mouth-kissing the Polish premier Edward Gierek, with the caption **"Brotherly Friendship."** Soviet premiers and their satellite leaders really did greet each other "in the French manner," as a symbolic gesture of their communist brotherhood.

Working your way through the exhibit, you'll see the door to a **prison cell**—a reminder of the intimidation tactics used by the Soviets in the 1940s and 1950s to deal with their opponents as they exerted their rule over the lands they had liberated from the Nazis.

The typical **communist-era apartment** is painfully humble. After the war, much of Poland had been destroyed, and population shifts led to housing shortages. People had to make do with tiny spaces and ramshackle furnishings. Communist propaganda blares from both the radio and the TV.

A map shows **"red Europe"** (the USSR plus the satellites of Poland, Czechoslovakia, Hungary, and East Germany), and a **timeline** traces some of the smaller Soviet Bloc protests that led up to Solidarity: in East Germany in 1953, in Budapest and Poznań in 1956, the "Prague Spring" of 1968, and other 1968 protests in Poland.

In the wake of these uprisings, the communist authorities cracked down even harder. Peek into the **interrogation room,** with a wall of file cabinets and a lowly stool illuminated by a bright spotlight. (Notice that the white Polish eagle on the seal above the desk is missing its golden crown—during communism, the Poles were allowed to keep the eagle, but its crown was removed.)

The next exhibit presents a day-by-day rundown of the **1970 strikes,** from December 14 to 22, which resulted in the massacre of the workers who are honored by the monument in front of this building. In the glass case, the leather jacket with bullet holes was worn by a 20-year-old worker who was killed that day. A wall of mug shots gives way to exhibits chronicling the steady rise of dissent groups through the 1970s, culminating in the June 1976 protests in the city of Radom (prompted, like so many other uprisings, by unilateral price hikes). On your way out of this section, you pass through a mock-up of a grocery store from the period...with empty shelves.

• *Loop back through Room A and proceed straight ahead into...*

Solidarity and Hope (Room C): While the government didn't take the August Agreements very seriously, the Poles did...and before long, 10 million of them—one out of every four, or effectively half the nation's workforce—joined Solidarity. So began what's often called the **"16 Months of Hope."** Newly legal, Solidarity continued to stage strikes and make its opposition known. Slick Solidarity posters and children's art convey the childlike enthusiasm with which the Poles seized their hard-won kernels of freedom. The communist authorities' hold on the Polish people began to slip. Support and aid from the outside world poured in, but the rest of the Soviet Bloc looked on nervously, and the Warsaw Pact army assembled at the Polish border and glared at the uprisers. The threat of invasion hung heavy in the air.

• *Exiting this room, head up the staircase and into...*

At War with Society (Room D): In this black room, you're greeted by a wall of TV screens delivering a stern message. On Sunday morning, December 13, 1981, the Polish head of state, **General Wojciech Jaruzelski**—wearing his trademark dark glasses—appeared on national TV and announced the introduction of **martial law.** Solidarity was outlawed, and its leaders were arrested. Frightened Poles heard the announcement and looked out their windows to see Polish Army tanks rumbling through the snowy streets. (On the opposite wall, see footage of tanks and heavily armed soldiers intimidating their countrymen into compliance.) Those who were children at the time recall turning on their televisions for a beloved Sunday-morning cartoon show, *Teleranek,* and instead seeing this chilling message. Jaruzelski claimed that he imposed martial law to prevent the Soviets from invading. Today, many historians question whether martial law was really necessary, though Jaruzelski remained unremorseful through his death in 2014.

Continuing deeper into the exhibit, you come to a **prisoner transport.** Climb up inside to watch chilling scenes of riots, demonstrations, and crackdowns by the ZOMO riot police. In one gruesome scene, a demonstrator is quite intentionally run over by a truck. From here, pass through a gauntlet of *milicja* riot-gear shields to see the truck crashing through a gate. Overhead are the uniforms of nine striking miners from the **Wujek mine** who were massacred on December 16, 1981 (their names are projected on the pile of coal below). The regime called this event "pacification."

Martial law was a tragic, terrifying, and bleak time for the Polish people. It did not, however, kill the Solidarity movement, which continued its fight after going underground. Passing prison cells, you'll see a wall plastered with handmade, underground posters and graffiti. Notice how in this era, **Solidarity propaganda** is much more primitive; circle around the other side of the wall to see several presses that were actually used in clandestine Solidarity print shops during this time. The outside world sent messages of support as well as supplies—represented by the big wall of cardboard boxes. This approval also came in the form of a Nobel Peace Prize for Lech Wałęsa in 1983; you'll see video clips of his wife accepting the award on his behalf (Wałęsa feared that if he traveled abroad to claim it, he would not be allowed back into the country). On the other side of the room is an exhibit about Pope John Paul II's visit in the very tense days of 1983.

• *But even in these darkest days, there were glimmers of hope. Enter...*

The Road to Democracy (Room E): By the time the pope visited his homeland again in 1987, martial law had finally been lifted, and Solidarity—still technically illegal—was gaining momentum, gradually pecking away at the communists. Step into the small inner room with footage of the **pope's third pilgrimage** to his homeland in 1987, by which time (thanks in no small part to his inspirational role in the ongoing revolution) the tide was turning.

Step into the room with the big, white **roundtable.** With the moral support of the pope and the entire Western world, the brave Poles were the first European country to throw off the shackles of communism when, in the spring of 1989, the "Roundtable Talks" led to the opening up of elections. The government arrogantly called for parliamentary elections, reserving 65 percent of seats for themselves.

In the next room, you can see Solidarity's strategy in those **elections:** On the right wall are posters showing Lech Wałęsa with each candidate. Another popular "get out the vote" measure was the huge poster of Gary Cooper—an icon of America, which the Poles deeply respect and viewed as their friendly cousin across the Atlantic—except that, instead of a pistol, he's packing a ballot. Rousing reminders like this inspired huge voter turnout. The communists' plan backfired, as virtually every open seat went to Solidarity. It was the first time ever that opposition candidates had taken office in the Soviet Bloc. On the wall straight ahead, flashing a V-for-*wiktoria* sign, is a huge photo of Tadeusz Mazowiecki—an early leader of Solidarity, who became prime minister on June 4, 1989.

• *For the glorious aftermath, head into the final room.*

The Triumph of Freedom (Room F): This room is dominated by a gigantic **map of Central and Eastern Europe.** A countdown clock on the right ticks off the departure of each country from communist clutches, as the Soviet Bloc "decomposes." You'll see how the success of Solidarity in Poland—and the ragtag determination of a scruffy band of shipyard workers right here in Gdańsk—inspired people all over Central and Eastern Europe. By the winter of 1989, the Hungarians had opened their borders, the Berlin Wall had crumbled, and the Czechs and Slovaks had staged their Velvet Revolution. (Small viewing stations that circle the room reveal the detailed story for each country's own road to freedom.) Lech Wałęsa—the shipyard electrician who started it all by jumping over a wall—became the first president of postcommunist Poland. And a year later, in Poland's first true elections since World War II, 29 different parties won seats in the parliament. It was a free-election free-for-all.

In the middle of the room stands a white wall with **inspirational quotes** from St. John Paul II and Václav Havel—the Czech poet-turned-protester-turned-prisoner-turned-president—which are repeated in several languages. On the huge wall, the **Solidarity "graffiti"** is actually made up of thousands of little notes left behind by visitors to the museum. Feel free to grab a piece of paper and a pen and record your own reflections.

• *Finally, head downstairs into a peaceful space.*

Culture of Peaceful Change (Room G): Many visitors find that touring this museum—with vivid reminders of a dramatic and pivotal moment in history that took place in their own lifetimes and was brought about not by armies or presidents but by everyday people—puts them in an emotional state of mind. Designed for silent reflection, this room overlooks the monument to those workers who were gunned down in 1970. It shows footage of Pope John Paul II; Lech Wałęsa; Martin Luther King, Jr.; and others who dedicated their lives to peaceful change.

• *For an epilogue, continue deeper into the former shipyard to see one more important landmark from 1980. Exit the building the way you came in and turn left. The path leads to a low-profile, red-brick building about 80 yards ahead, the...*

Sala BHP

This is the building where the communists sat down across the table from Lech Wałęsa and his team and worked out a compromise (as seen in the videos inside the European Solidarity Center). Entering, turn left into the Small Hall to see shipyard photos, banners, office equipment, and other memorabilia from the time. The other side of the building (right from the entrance) is the actual, larger hall where those fateful meetings took place, with a long table set up on the stage. You'll see a model of the shipyard, circa 1980, and models of the various ships that were built here.

Cost and Hours: Free, daily 10:00-18:00, Oct-April until 16:00, www.salabhp.pl.

NORTH OF THE MAIN TOWN
▲▲Museum of the Second World War (Muzeum II Wojny Światowej)

In 2017, Poland's definitive WWII museum opened in a state-of-the-art, purpose-built facility a 10-minute walk north of Gdańsk's Main Town. It uses artifacts, creative design, insightful storytelling, and ample archival footage to tell the story of the war that began right at Gdańsk's doorstep—focusing on the Polish experience, but also expanding its focus to other aspects of the conflict. At more than 50,000 square feet, it's one of the biggest historical exhibits in the world. (Pace yourself.) While those with a limited appetite for history may find it overwhelming, even those with a casual interest will be glad they invested two or three hours touring its exhibits.

As impressive as the museum is, it could have been that much better. The original design presented an ambitiously global, yet personal, perspective on the war—carefully calibrated to be evenhanded and international in its outlook. But as it neared completion, ruling politicians from the nationalistic Law and Justice Party deemed it too paci-fistic and "not Polish enough"—it needed to be more bombastic and emotional. They replaced

the museum director and his staff, and hired a new director who changed several exhibits to be more singularly patriotic—playing up the "martyrdom" aspect of Poland's role in the war. In the end, it's sad to think that this museum could have been Europe's best WWII museum—if only trained historians had been allowed to control it, rather than politicians. For that reason, I rate it ▲▲ rather than ▲▲▲.

Cost and Hours: 29 zł, free on Tue, essential audioguide-12 zł; Tue 10:00-16:00, Wed-Sun 10:00-18:00 (until 20:00 in July-Aug), closed Mon year-round, last entry one hour before closing; Plac Władysława Bartoszewskiego 1, +48 58 760 0960, www.muzeum1939.pl.

Getting There: It's a short walk north of the historical center. The most appealing approach is to walk north along the riverfront promenade all the way to its end; you'll see the giant, rust-red, glassy tower on your left.

Visiting the Museum: As you approach, appreciate the sym-bolic architecture of the site. The ground level—nicely landscaped, with inviting slingback chairs in the summer—represents the pres-ent. The museum's exhibit space is entirely underground—repre-senting the past. And the tower rising above represents the future. All of the buildings are clad in rusted steel—the material of choice in this shipbuilding city.

Head down the stairs at the base of the tower, go inside, and take the elevator down to level -3. This area has ticket desks, a cloakroom, WCs, a **$** bistro, a shop, a cinema, temporary exhibits, and the entrance to the permanent exhibition. For a more serious meal, you can ride the elevator up to floor 4 to find an affordable, bright **$** restaurant with views over the city.

When you buy your ticket, spring for the **audioguide,** which helpfully navigates the highlights of the sprawling exhibits and translates some of the films. It's geo-tagged, so it knows where you are and informs you accordingly.

Ticket and audioguide in hand, head through the turnstile. A long **corridor** stretches to your right; 18 clearly numbered exhibition halls weave in and out of this corridor, chronologically telling the story. As you crisscross through the corridor, take a moment to ponder its exhibits about everyday life in wartime, covering such topics as food and cooking, fashion and style, the black market, travel, and music.

Before heading into the main exhibition, consider turning left, into the **Time Travel** exhibit. Designed for Polish kids, it follows two children and their everyday life, before, during, and after the war—with the same apartment re-created for each time period.

The first part of the exhibit is straight ahead from the entrance turnstile: A movie that sets the stage by recapping the events of World War I and the interwar period.

Now proceed down the corridor and work your way chronologically through the numbered exhibits. Section **01**—spread across three smaller rooms—traces the rise of communism in the Soviet Union (the quern stone was used for grinding grain by ethnic Poles in Ukraine, many of whom perished under Stalin's policies), fascism in Italy (the Fiat embodies the populism—a car in every driveway—that drove Mussolini's propaganda), and Nazism in Germany (with a bust and posters of Hitler, some hateful anti-Semitic propaganda, a Hitler Youth uniform, and a clip from Leni Riefenstahl's *Triumph of the Will*).

Section **02** is a reconstructed Polish street from the interwar period. (Remember this.) The next hallway outlines the rise of imperialism in Japan, Franco's ascent in Spain, and Germany's dismantling of the Versailles system that ended the conflict of World War I. Gdańsk—then called Danzig—held a unique position: It was a free city, with Germany on one side and Poland on the  other. As Hitler rose, Western Europeans already knew that Danzig would be a bulwark against his aggression (see the stone border marker)—giving rise to the slogan "Die for Danzig." On the wall in the next room—wallpapered with giant swastikas and hammer-

and-sickles—find a replica of the secret Molotov-Ribbentrop Pact between the USSR and Nazi Germany, agreeing to divide Poland down the middle...and clearing the way for invasion.

In section **03,** you'll learn how that invasion took place on September 1, 1939, when Hitler invaded Poland (en route to Danzig) and quickly overran the country—the first use of his relentless Blitzkrieg ("Lightning War") strategy. One exhibit explains the first volley of that war, in which 200 Poles defended the military transit depot Westerplatte against 3,000 Nazi troops for seven days. You'll learn about the brutal Nazi atrocities from that first invasion, including photos of bombed-out cities. One of the museum's highlights is the film *Siege*, shot and narrated by American correspondent Julien Bryan, who was in Warsaw during the invasion and witnessed the Nazis bombarding a church during Mass, the bombing of a maternity ward, and a village of peasants machine-gunned from the air while digging up potatoes. You'll learn how soon, the Soviet Union also invaded, per their secret agreement—meeting the Nazis in the middle and splitting Poland in half (see the huge map on the wall).

Across the main corridor, section **04** outlines Soviet conquests in other parts of Europe (Finland, the Baltic states, Romania). Section **05** (with a JU-87 dive bomber suspended from the wall) explains how this was a new kind of war, relying heavily on air warfare (Hitler's Luftwaffe).

Back across the corridor, section **06** documents the ruthlessness of the Nazis, including their starvation of Soviet POWs (the "Hunger Plan" that killed more than three million captured troops), the 871-day Siege of Leningrad (today's St. Petersburg, where one million civilians starved to death), and air raids that killed another one million civilians.

Across the corridor, section **07** considers how totalitarian regimes recruited collaborators in the countries they occupied—employing methods from propaganda to intimidation. You'll see a replica of a "Red Corner"—a wood-paneled workers' meeting hall, draped in communist propaganda, that you'd find in any workplace or institution. A film on Soviet propaganda methods explains Stalin's philosophy of "national in form, Soviet in content"—appropriating locally beloved symbols but infusing them with a communist agenda.

Crossing the hall, giant letters spell out *TERROR*. Here, first bear left into section **08,** which explains how totalitarian regimes rounded up and executed elites (such as the USSR's

Katyń Massacre of Polish intelligentsia, close to the heart of every Pole). The room with a vast map on the floor illustrates forced resettlement; the doors lining the walls have exhibits explaining specific examples. You'll learn how heavily the occupying forces relied on forced labor—essentially exploiting 20 million slaves—including workers here in Gdańsk (the metal plates in revolving cases were used to keep track of workers). This section also has a powerful exhibit on daily life in Nazi concentration camps, with many powerful objects: striped uniforms and wooden clogs, a homemade nativity scene and tiny figures carved from a toothbrush by prisoners, a violin, and a baby's christening gown. You'll also see a wheelchair from a psychiatric hospital near Gdańsk. All of its inmates were executed.

As you circle back to the giant *TERROR* letters, section **09** explores the methodical implementation of the Holocaust, includ-

ing a train car used to transport prisoners. A wall of suitcases is a reminder of how prisoners were stripped of belongings on arrival. Nearby, a controversial exhibit touts the Poles who risked their lives to save their Jewish neighbors—with no mention of the Poles who looked the other way, or even collaborated with the Nazi occupiers. With this in mind, you'll walk through a room displaying photographs of hundreds of Jewish Holocaust victims. Section **10** considers other instances of ethnic cleansing during World War II, including Serbs killed in the Nazi puppet state of Croatia and Poles killed in Ukraine.

Section **11**—with the giant letters *OPÓR* ("Resistance")—explains the various ways that occupied peoples rose up. Poland maintained a government in exile, and a military that participated in Allied offensives (Poles were the first to reach the top of Monte Cassino in Italy)—essentially a continuation of prewar statehood, despite occupation. You'll learn about both civilian resistance movements and partisan fighting forces on the battlefields (such as Tito's Partisans in Yugoslavia). This section also honors various uprisings against totalitarian regimes.

Section **12** features the clandestine front—spies, espionage, and the battle over secrets. In a room with an actual Enigma machine, you'll learn how it was Polish mathematicians who first broke the Nazis' secret code...then furnished that breakthrough to the British. Today, Alan Turing and the other codebreakers at Britain's Bletchley Park get virtually all of the credit for the tens of thousands of lives that were saved. (Many Poles believe that the breaking of the Enigma code was Poland's single most important contribution to winning the war.)

Section **13** considers the ways that countries mobilize—economically and societally—in times of war. Wartime brought about such innovations as the jet engine, the computer, and the nuclear bomb. While the Nazis relied on slave labor to build armaments, the Allies mobilized female citizens...and outproduced their enemies three-to-one. In this section, you'll see a Sherman Firefly tank (built in the UK).

The very brief section **14** explains how the tide of war turned toward the Allies, while section **15** considers the postwar reality—which was cooked up even before Hitler was dead, when Churchill, FDR, and Stalin met in Yalta, agreeing to divvy up Europe after their victory. (Many Poles still consider this a betrayal: After their suffering and valiant contributions, they were effectively left to the whim of the USSR.) The postwar period was bittersweet: victory parades celebrating the defeat of evil, but also a Poland left in ruins, the rise of a ruthless Soviet empire in Eastern Europe, and a series of forced population resettlements (to match the new borders) that uprooted millions. The bright-white room commemorates the first-ever use of nuclear weapons: the bombing of Hiroshima (see the shards of pottery, symbolizing the devastation).

Section **16** shows the same city street we saw earlier—but now in ruins, presided over by a Soviet tank. Giant panels (added later) emphasize how Poland lost more lives per capita than any other nation in this conflict. Next, a map in the floor illustrates postwar forced population shifts, and a mockup of a courtroom considers both the triumphs and the failings of the postwar justice system: Yes, high-profile war criminals were prosecuted.

But the overflowing file cabinet on the dark side of the room is a reminder of the many lower-level war criminals who were never brought to justice.

Cross the destroyed street to section **17,** with photos of cities that were left in ruins at war's end; and section **18,** divided by a symbolic "Iron Curtain"—a reminder that World War II was only the beginning of a painful chapter for Poland and all of Central and Eastern Europe.

Just before you exit, playing overhead is a cheaply produced, rabble-rousing, hyperbolic, nakedly patriotic **movie** called *The Unconquered*...a sad reminder of the way a wonderful museum was mucked up by politics. (Before the right-wing government fired the museum director, this film was very different—ending the exhibit on a pensive note, with as many questions as answers. Now, it sends Polish visitors out into the world entirely assured of their own righteousness.)

Despite its shortcomings, the Museum of the Second World War is a powerful and comprehensive look at the most devastating conflict in human history, from the perspective of the country that was perhaps the most devastated by it.

Nearby: A short walk over a canal (across the Więcierze Bridge) from the museum is the **Polish Post Office of Danzig** (on Plac Obrońców Poczty Polskiej). History buffs recognize this landmark as part of the initial Nazi attacks on September 1, 1939, which began World War II. The post office—which was a nerve center for local Polish intelligence officers—was attacked by Nazi forces and defended by Polish officers. After 15 hours of fighting, everyone inside was dead or had fled; those who escaped were later executed. This event was immortalized in the 1959 Günter Grass historical novel *The Tin Drum.* The stately brick building is now a museum, and in the plaza out front is the giant and dramatic **Monument to the Defenders of the Polish Post Office** (from 1979): An angel hands a rifle down to a fallen fighter to continue the struggle; overhead, stylized birds flutter their wings dramatically into the sky.

SOUTH OF THE MAIN TOWN

A 10-minute walk south of the Main Town, this sight rounds out the Gdańsk experience for those with a special interest in art.

National Museum in Gdańsk (Muzeum Narodowe w Gdańsku)

This art collection, housed in what was a 15th-century Franciscan monastery, is worth ▲▲ to art lovers for one reason: Hans Memling's glorious *Last Judgment* triptych altarpiece, one of the two most important pieces of art to be seen in Poland (the other is Leonardo da Vinci's *Lady with an Ermine,* in Kraków's Czartoryski Museum). If you're not a purist, you can settle for seeing the much smaller replica in St. Mary's Church. But if medieval art is your bag, it's worth a visit.

Cost and Hours: 15 zł, free on Fri; open Tue-Sun 11:00-18:00, closed Mon, last entry 45 minutes before closing; walk 10 minutes due south from Ulica Długa's Golden Gate, after passing the Shakespeare Theater take the pedestrian underpass beneath the big cross street, then continue down the busy street until you see signs for the museum; Ulica Toruńska 1, +48 58 301 6804, www.mng.gda.pl.

Visiting the Museum: Find the **altarpiece by Hans Memling** (c. 1440-1494)—from where you enter, it's usually at the top of the stairs and to the right. The history of the painting is as interesting as the work itself. It was commissioned in the mid-15th century by the Medicis' banker in Florence, Angelo di Jacopo Tani. The ship delivering the painting from Belgium to Florence was hijacked by a Gdańsk pirate, who brought the altarpiece to his hometown to be displayed in St. Mary's Church. For centuries, kings, emperors, and czars admired it from afar, until Napoleon seized it in the early 19th century and took it to Paris to hang in the Louvre. Gdańsk finally got the painting back, only to have it exiled again—this time into St. Petersburg's Hermitage Museum—after World War II. On its return to Gdańsk in 1956, this museum claimed it—though St. Mary's wants it back.

Have a close look at Memling's well-traveled work. It's the end of the world, and Christ rides in on a rainbow to judge humankind. Angels blow reveille, waking the dead, who rise from their graves. The winged archangel Michael—dressed for battle and wielding the cross like a weapon—weighs the grace in each person, sending them either to the fires of hell (right panel) or up the sparkling-crystal stairway to heaven (left).

It takes all 70 square feet of paneling to contain this awesome scene. Jam-packed with dozens of bodies and a Bible's worth of symbolism, and executed with astonishing detail, the painting can keep even a non-art lover occupied. Notice the serene, happy expressions of the righteous, as they're greeted by St. Peter (with his giant key) and clothed by angels. And pity the condemned, their faces filled with terror and sorrow as they're tortured by grotesque devils more horrifying than anything Hollywood could devise.

Tune in to the exquisite details: the angels' robes, the devils' genetic-mutant features, the portrait of the man in the scale (a Medici banker), Michael's peacock wings. Get as close as you can to the globe at Christ's feet and Michael's shining breastplate: You can just make out the whole scene in mirror reflection. Then back up and take it all in—three panels connected by a necklace of bodies that curves downward through hell, crosses the earth, then rises up to the towers of the New Jerusalem. On the back side of the triptych are reverent portraits of the painting's patron, Angelo Tani, and his new bride, Catarina.

Beyond the Memling, the remainder of the collection isn't too thrilling. The rest of the upstairs has more Flemish and Dutch art, as well as paintings from Gdańsk's golden age and various works by Polish artists. The ground floor features a cavernous, all-white cloister filled with Gothic altarpiece sculptures, gold and silver wares, and Gdańsk-style furniture.

OUTER GDAŃSK

These two sights—worthwhile only to those with a particular interest—are each within the city limits of Gdańsk, but they take some serious time to see round-trip.

Oliwa Cathedral (Katedra Oliwska)

The suburb of Oliwa, at the northern edge of Gdańsk, is home to this visually striking church. The quirky, elongated facade hides a surprisingly long and skinny nave. The ornately decorated 18th-century organ over the main entrance features angels and stars that move around when the organ is played. While locals are proud of this place, it takes some effort to reach—worthwhile only if you can make it to a concert.

Concerts: The animated organ performs its 20-minute show frequently, especially in summer (in high season, concerts at the top of most hours—confirm schedule online or at Gdańsk TI before making the trip, www.archikatedraoliwa.pl). Note that on Sundays and holidays, there are no concerts before 15:00.

Getting There: Oliwa is about six miles northwest of central Gdańsk, on the way to Sopot and Gdynia. To reach Oliwa from Gdańsk's main train station, you have two options: Ride **tram #6** or **#12**, get off at the Oliwa stop, and walk a few minutes through the park to the church (about 30 minutes total); or take an **SKM commuter train** to the Gdańsk Oliwa stop (15 minutes), then walk 15 minutes (or take a taxi) to Oliwski Park and the cathedral.

Westerplatte

World War II began on September 1, 1939, when Adolf Hitler sent the warship *Schleswig-Holstein* to attack this Polish munitions depot, which was guarding Gdańsk's harbor. Though it gives serious WWII history buffs goosebumps, casual visitors will find little to see here aside from a modest museum, a towering monument, and some old bunkers. For many, the reason to "go to Westerplatte" isn't for the destination, but for the chance to get there on a little cruise down the river...perhaps on a "pirate ship."

Getting There: The most enjoyable option is to ride a replica **17th-century galleon,** either the *Galeon Lew* ("Lion Galleon") or the *Czarna Perła* ("Black Pearl"). These over-the-top-touristy boats depart hourly from the embankment in the heart of Gdańsk (you can't miss them) for a lazy 1.5-hour round-trip cruise to Westerplatte and back. Alternatively, you can choose to get off at Westerplatte and return on a later boat. You'll see more industry than scenery, but it's a fun excuse to set sail (80 zł round-trip, 60 zł one-way, the two boats take turns departing at the top of each hour in season, +48 601 629 191, https://perlalew.pl). Two duller alternatives leave from nearby: big, modern **Żegluga Gdańska** boats (www.zegluga.pl); or cheaper but less frequent city-run **ZTM**

"ferry trams" *(tramwaj wodny),* which depart from the embankment on the south side of the bridge (3-4/day). Another option is to take **bus** #106 or #138 from the main train station (about 30 minutes to Westerplatte).

Shopping in Gdańsk

The big story in Gdańsk is **amber** *(bursztyn),* a fossil resin available in all shades, shapes, and sizes (see the "All About Amber" sidebar, earlier). The best place to browse and buy amber is along the atmospheric Ulica Mariacka (between the Motława River and St. Mary's Church). This pretty street, with old-fashioned balconies and dozens of display cases, is fun to wander even if you're not a shopper.

To avoid rip-offs—such as amber that's been melted and reshaped—always buy it from a shop, not from someone standing on the street. (But note that most shops also have a display case and salesperson out front, which are perfectly legit.) Prices everywhere are about the same, so instead of seeking out a specific place, just window shop until you see what you want. Styles range from gaudy necklaces with huge globs of amber, to tasteful smaller pendants in silver settings, to cheap trinkets. All shades of amber—from near-white to dark brown—cost about the same, but you'll pay more for inclusions (bugs or other objects stuck in the amber).

Gdańsk also has several modern shopping malls, most of them in the Old Town or near the main train station. The most impressive is the Forum, across the street from the Upland Gate; the Madison shopping center is between the Main Town and the Solidarity shipyard.

Entertainment in Gdańsk

Strolling the Embankments: This city feels made to order for simply strolling. Before or after dinner, you'll find yourself doing laps up and down both sides of the embankment and along the Royal Way. You'll pass plenty of tempting spots for a dessert or a drink (for ideas, see below).

Live Music: Check the schedule for the **Polish Baltic Philharmonic,** officially named for Fryderyk Chopin, which performs in the red-brick hall across the embankment from Fishmarket Square (near the drawbridge; www.filharmonia.gda.pl).

Drinks: As a lively town with lots of both tourists and students, Gdańsk has plenty of rowdy bars that fill up on weekends. But it also has some more refined watering holes that enjoy showing off special local liquors. Better restaurants are likely to have two hard drinks that are distinctly Gdańsk: **Goldwasser** is a sweet, faintly anisey liqueur flecked with actual gold (similar to Gold-schläger). **Machandel,** a juniper-based liquor, is served chilled in a shot glass with a dried plum on a toothpick. According to local superstition, for good luck, you're supposed to drink the shot, chase it with the dried plum, then break the toothpick.

While those are quite traditional, Gdańsk also has a new generation of producers creating all manner of distillates that go beyond the stereotypical "Polish vodka." **Podole Wielkie i Przyjaciele** is an inviting, educational, and fun place to sample some locally made options. They specialize in *okowita*—a.k.a. aqua vita, "water of life"—usually based on wheat, barley, rye, or potato and infused with various flavors. They grow everything on their own farm, about 50 miles outside the city. They've also got a unique line of liquor distilled from various beers. The *i przyjaciele* in their name means "and friends," and they also carry some different drinks made by other local producers—ranging from gin and whiskey to more traditional vodka. You can stop in to do a tasting (priced per shot)—they enjoy guiding visitors through their options. The well-stocked shop has bottles generally in the 160-300-zł range (Mon-Sat until 21:00, Sun until 20:00, Chlebnicka 37/38, +48 730 850 066, www.podolewielkie.pl).

Sleeping in Gdańsk

The high season is generally May through September; at all of these places, you'll pay a bit less off-season. Many hotels are booked up (mostly with German and Scandinavian tourists) in peak season—reserve ahead.

IN THE MAIN TOWN

The Main Town is convenient for sightseeing, but some places come with nighttime noise—particularly in summer, when loud bars and discos keep things lively. Request a quiet room...and pack earplugs.

$$ Gotyk House is a small hotel that's comfortable while still respecting the sanctity of Gdańsk's oldest house (and supposedly the residence of Copernicus' longtime lover). You can't get more central in this city; the chimes from St. Mary's Church, next door, provide a pleasant soundtrack. The original, historic building has five rooms (air-con only on top floor); a modern annex out back holds six additional rooms with air-conditioning and more refined touches. Neither building has an elevator, so be ready for stairs (Ulica Mariacka 1, +48 58 301 8567, www.gotykhouse.eu, reservation@gotykhouse.eu).

$ Hotel Admirał is simply practical: a big, solidly built, business-class place with 44 comfortable rooms tucked in a peaceful residential alley at the north end of the embankment, just a few

GDAŃSK & THE TRI-CITY

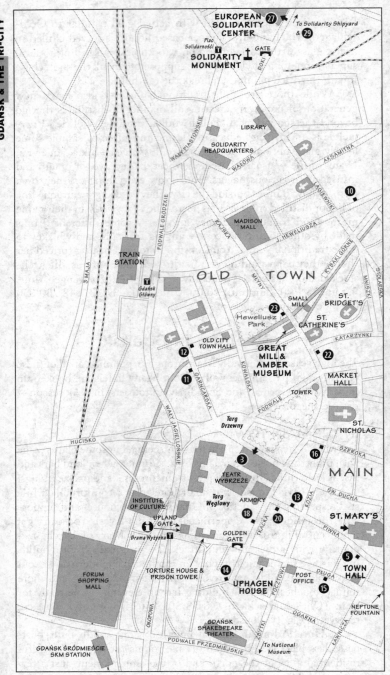

EUROPEAN SOLIDARITY CENTER 27

To Solidarity Shipyard & 29

Plac Solidarności

SOLIDARITY MONUMENT

GATE DOKI

LIBRARY

SOLIDARITY HEADQUARTERS

WAŁOWA

AKSAMITNA

ŁAGIEWNIKI

10

WAŁY PIASTOWSKIE

PODWALE GRODZKIE

KAŁŻA

MADISON MALL

J. HEWELIUSZA

RYBAKI GÓRNE

MNISZKI

STOLARSKA

OLD TOWN

TRAIN STATION

Gdańsk Główny

3 MAJA

MŁYNY

SMALL MILL

ST. BRIDGET'S

ST. CATHERINE'S

KATARZYNKI

23

Heweliusz Park

OLD CITY TOWN HALL

12

KOWALSKA

GREAT MILL & AMBER MUSEUM

22

MARKET HALL

11

GARNCARSKA

TOWER

PODWALE

ST. NICHOLAS

WAŁY JAGIELLOŃSKIE

Targ Drzewny

HUCISKO

SZEROKA

16

MAIN

3

TEATR WYBRZEŻE

ŚW. DUCHA

KOZA

13

ST. MARY'S

INSTITUTE OF CULTURE

Targ Węglowy

ARMORY

18

TKACKA

20

UPLAND GATE

Brama Wyżynna

GOLDEN GATE

PIWNA

DŁUGA

5

TOWN HALL

FORUM SHOPPING MALL

TORTURE HOUSE & PRISON TOWER

14

POCZTOWA

UPHAGEN HOUSE

POST OFFICE

15

NEPTUNE FOUNTAIN

OKOPOWA

GDAŃSK SHAKESPEARE THEATER

ZBYTKI

OGARNA

ŁAWNICZA

GDAŃSK ŚRÓDMIEŚCIE SKM STATION

PODWALE PRZEDMIEJSKIE

To National Museum

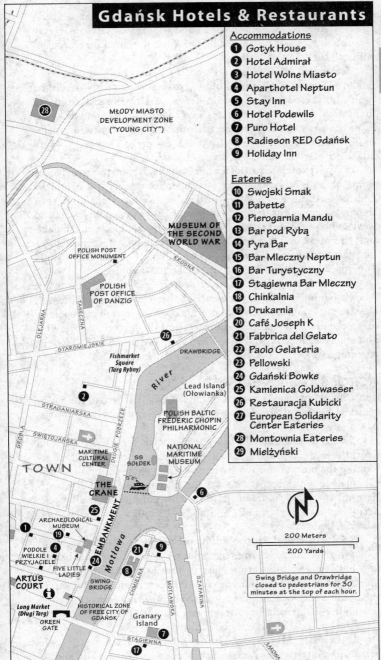

Gdańsk Hotels & Restaurants

Accommodations
1 Gotyk House
2 Hotel Admirał
3 Hotel Wolne Miasto
4 Aparthotel Neptun
5 Stay Inn
6 Hotel Podewils
7 Puro Hotel
8 Radisson RED Gdańsk
9 Holiday Inn

Eateries
10 Swojski Smak
11 Babette
12 Pierogarnia Mandu
13 Bar pod Rybą
14 Pyra Bar
15 Bar Mleczny Neptun
16 Bar Turystyczny
17 Stągiewna Bar Mleczny
18 Chinkalnia
19 Drukarnia
20 Café Joseph K
21 Fabbrica del Gelato
22 Paolo Gelateria
23 Pellowski
24 Gdański Bowke
25 Kamienica Goldwasser
26 Restauracja Kubicki
27 European Solidarity Center Eateries
28 Montownia Eateries
29 Mielżyński

MŁODY MIASTO DEVELOPMENT ZONE ("YOUNG CITY")

MUSEUM OF THE SECOND WORLD WAR

POLISH POST OFFICE MONUMENT

POLISH POST OFFICE OF DANZIG

KROSNA

STAROMIEJSKIE

OLEJARNA

TANECZNA

DRAWBRIDGE

Fishmarket Square (Targ Rybny)

River

Lead Island (Ołowianka)

POLISH BALTIC FRÉDÉRIC CHOPIN PHILHARMONIC

STRAGANIARSKA

GROBLA

ŚWIĘTOJAŃSKA

DŁUGIE POBRZEŻE

MARITIME CULTURAL CENTER

NATIONAL MARITIME MUSEUM

SS SOŁDEK

TOWN

THE CRANE

EMBANKMENT

Mottawa

ARCHAEOLOGICAL MUSEUM

PODOLE WIELKIE I PRZYJACIELE

FIVE LITTLE LADIES

ARTUS COURT

SWING BRIDGE

CHMIELNA

MOTŁAWSKA

SZAFARINA

Long Market (Długi Targ)

GREEN GATE

HISTORICAL ZONE OF FREE CITY OF GDAŃSK

Granary Island

STĄGIEWNA

ŁAMONA

200 Meters

200 Yards

Swing Bridge and Drawbridge closed to pedestrians for 30 minutes at the top of each hour.

steps off Fishmarket Square. Reliably comfortable, if not fancy, and conveniently located, this is a handy home base (air-con, elevator, Tobiasza 9, +48 58 320 0320, www.admiralhotel.pl, recepcja@admiralhotel.pl).

$ Hotel Wolne Miasto ("Free City") offers lush, wood-carved public spaces with photos of old Gdańsk and 68 richly decorated rooms on the edge of the Main Town, just two blocks from the main drag. It's above a popular disco that gets noisy on weekends (Thu-Sat nights), so it's especially important to request a quieter room when you reserve (elevator, Ulica Świętego Ducha 2, +48 58 305 2255, www.hotelwm.pl, rezerwacja@hotelwm.pl).

$ Aparthotel Neptun lacks personality but owns a great location—on a slightly dreary side street between delightful Mariacka and the bustling Royal Way. While it's just a few steps to most of the town's big sights, it's just far enough away to avoid crowds and weekend noise. The 39 rooms and apartments are modern, efficient, well equipped, and forgettable...but well priced for the central location (air-con on top floor only, elevator, spa, Grzaska 1, +48 604 466 466, www.apartneptun.com, info@apartneptun.com).

$ Stay Inn couldn't be more central—facing the side of St. Mary's Church, right in the heart of the Main Town. Although the street it's on is quieter than most, a downstairs pub can be noisy on weekends. The place feels modern, and the 45 rooms are stylish and colorful (air-con, elevator, Piwna 28, +48 58 354 1543, www.stayinngdansk.com, booking@stayinngdansk.com).

ACROSS THE RIVER

These hotels are across the river from the Main Town, in the thriving new Granary Island area—still a short and easy walk to the Main Town sights.

$$$ Hotel Podewils is the top choice for a friendly, Old World splurge. Filling a storybook-cute house from 1728, overlooking the marina and across the river from a fine panorama of the Gdańsk embankment, it's classy. The public spaces and 10 rooms have all the modern amenities, but with plush, almost Baroque, decor (air-con, Szafarnia 2, +48 58 300 9560, www.podewils.pl, gdansk@podewils.pl).

$$ Puro Hotel, in the middle of Granary Island, is part of a Norwegian chain. It's big (eight floors), splashy, and fills brand-new buildings with towering glass atriums, a big restaurant, and a top-floor bar. The 211 rooms are modern, practical, and stylish; for the quality and location, it's a great value for those wanting a big hotel (air-con, elevator, spa, Stągiewna 26, +48 58 563 5000, www.purohotel.pl, gdansk@purohotel.pl).

Other Big Hotels on Granary Island: Each year, more brand-new international chain hotels open on Granary Island. If you're looking for big-hotel predictability (with air-con, elevators, etc.), consider two places filling sleek new buildings right along the embankment facing the Main Town: the smaller **$$ Radisson RED Gdańsk** (30 rooms, Chmielna 2, +48 58 600 2810, www. radissonhotels.com) and the gigantic **$ Holiday Inn** (240 rooms, Chmielna 1, +48 58 733 4000, www.ihg.com).

Eating in Gdańsk

With its heritage as a wealthy trading city, Gdańsk has its own distinct cuisine. While much of Poland—with its roots in poverty—dines on hearty, rustic countryside dishes, the Hanseatic merchants here preferred to flaunt their wealth with rich foods, lots of butter, and lively imported spices. For example, they favored deer (hunted—a pastime of the rich) over beef or pork (farm raised—a duty of the poor). This is perhaps best demonstrated by the local Goldwasser liqueur, with flecks of actual gold—see "Entertainment in Gdańsk," earlier. And, of course, you'll also find excellent Baltic seafood here on the north coast: Herring *(śledź)* is popular, as is cod *(dorsz)*.

IN THE MAIN TOWN AND OLD TOWN

My recommendations are scattered around the city center, all within about a 15-minute walk of each other and all near the main sightseeing zones. I've covered the scenic options along the embankment in a separate section.

$$ Swojski Smak ("Taste of Home"), tucked away from the touristy town center on a nondescript residential street partway to the Solidarity shipyards, is an intriguing combination of new and old. The menu is classic Polish fare, just like Babcia used to make: pierogi, hearty soups, potato pancakes, and a long list of nostalgic "dishes from childhood." But the setting is modern, industrial, and funky, with raw brick and a youthful, trendy vibe. They also pride themselves on their extensive selection of vodkas and good cakes (daily, Heweliusza 25/27, +48 58 320 1912, www.swojskismak.pl).

$ Babette is a delightful lunch or early dinner spot that feels both traditional and modern...trendy yet accessible. They serve a range of soups, stews, sides, and spreads, all with fresh-baked bread. Order at the counter, then find a table in the cozy contemporary café setting and dig in. It's an ideal spot for a hearty, quick, delicious meal (daily until 19:00, Garncarska 4/6, +48 535 717 766, www.pracowniababette.pl).

$ Pierogarnia Mandu, a few steps away from Babette, serves a wide variety of pierogi—all handmade (see them working through the window), with modern flourishes. Hiding in a nondescript residential zone between the train station and the main tourist area, it's worth seeking out for pierogi, plus a variety of other international dumplings. Book ahead to avoid waiting in line at the door. Don't come here in a hurry—it can take some time for your dumplings to be made to order (daily, Elżbietańska 4, +48 58 300 0000, www. pierogarnia-mandu.pl).

Potatoes!: Two places—each just a block off the main drag (in opposite directions)—offer tasty, hearty, affordable potato dishes. **$ Bar pod Rybą** ("Under the Fish") is nirvana for fans of baked potatoes *(pieczony ziemniak)*. They offer more than 20 varieties, piled high with a wide variety of toppings and sauces, from Mexican beef to herring to Polish cheeses. They also serve fish dishes with salad and potatoes, making this a cheap place to sample local seafood. The interior has big, comfy couches, and the outdoor seating fills a big stone balcony on atmospheric Piwna street (daily, Piwna 61, +48 58 305 1307, www.barpodryba.pl). **$ Pyra Bar** is another potato-based eatery; in addition to baked potatoes, they also have individual-sized casseroles (similar to a gratin) and potato pancakes—all available with a wide range of toppings. I'd skip the dull interior; eat here only if you can enjoy the lovely outdoor seating on a characteristic corner. Pick a table, then go inside to order at the bar (daily, Garbary 6/7, +48 58 301 9282, www.pyrabar.pl).

Milk Bars: Gdańsk has several classic, basic, fill-the-tank milk bars that are handy for grabbing a quick meal. **$ Bar Mleczny Neptun** owns a prime location, right on the main drag facing the Main Town Hall (daily until 19:00, Ulica Długa 33, +48 58 301 4988). **$ Bar Turystyczny** ("Tourist") is misnamed—it's beloved by locals and always jammed (daily until 18:00, on the way between the Main Town and the Solidarity sights at Szeroka 8, +48 58 301 6013). **$ Stągiewna Bar Mleczny,** in the middle of Granary Island across the river, is a classy, updated, modern milk bar with appealing outdoor seating (daily until 18:00, Stągiewna 15, +48 570 112 222). For more on milk bars, see page 230.

Georgian: $$ Chinkalnia, part of a Ukrainian chain that's now opening up locations around Poland, is an excellent place to sample Georgian food in a central setting, a half-block off the Royal Way. Choose between the cozy Georgian-village interior, or outdoor tables on a characteristic street. The photographic menu offers a user-friendly introduction to this delicious cuisine; for starters, the namesake *chinkali* are handheld dumplings (daily, Tkacka 6, +48 573 189 707). For a quick primer on Georgian food, see page 234.

Coffee: $ Drukarnia ("Printer") is the best spot in town for gourmet coffee in a modern, trendy setting that still melds well with the tradition all around it. The industrial-mod interior fills two floors, and the outdoor seating occupies a stone balcony at a prime location along Gdańsk's loveliest street, Mariacka. In addition to coffee and creative tea drinks, they have craft beers, breakfast, and other light bites—sandwiches and cakes (daily, Mariacka 36, +48 510 087 064).

Hipster Bar/Café: Café Joseph K, on charming Piwna street, is a popular hangout for coffee, craft beer, and creative cocktails. Similar to Drukarnia (but edgier and less coffee focused), they have a modern interior and stay-awhile outdoor tables. Locals marvel at how this place attracts revelers both young and old, with a mix of light communist-era kitsch and a trendy currency (long hours daily, Piwna 1, +48 572 161 510).

Ice Cream: The people of Gdańsk—and its many visitors—seem obsessed with ice cream *(lody)*. There are two good options offering better quality: **Fabbrica del Gelato,** tucked between giant hotels on a back street of Granary Island, is run by mother-and-son team Natalja and Boris, who trained with Italian experts and now enjoy creating their own delicious, often creative flavors (daily, Chmielna 3/4, +48 530 181 917). **Paolo Gelateria** is another good choice, also with some interesting flavors (the chocolate and mushroom is strangely delicious), on the way between the Main Town and the Solidarity sights (daily, across from the Great Mill/Amber Museum at Podwale Staromiejskie 96, +48 504 222 651).

***Pączki* and Other Pastries: Pellowski,** with multiple locations, is a small chain that locals swear by for pastries, especially *pączki* (jelly doughnuts). There's a handy one at the Heweliusz Park next to the Amber Museum.

On the Riverfront Embankment

Perhaps the most appealing dining zone in Gdańsk stretches along the riverfront embankment near the Crane. On a balmy summer evening, the outdoor tables here are enticing. This area is popular—consider scouting a table during your sightseeing, and reserve your choice for dinner later that night. These places are slightly pricier than other options in town, but worth considering for the views and ambience—especially if

it's nice enough to sit outside. While these choices line up along the Main Town side of the river, you'll find plenty more options—generally trendier and more international—across the river.

$$ Gdański Bowke is rollicking and ye olde, with model ships hanging from the rafters and a lively energy. The menu of classic local dishes looks like a big, vintage newspaper. They brew their own beer, and often have live music out on the embankment (daily, Długie Pobrzeże 11, +48 58 380 1111).

$$$ Kamienica Goldwasser is a classy choice, offering more elevated Polish and international cuisine in a posh European setting. Choose between cozy, romantic indoor seating on several levels, or scenic outdoor seating (daily, occasional live music, Długie Pobrzeże 22, +48 58 301 8878).

$$ Restauracja Kubicki, along the water just past the Hilton, has a long history (since 1918), but a recent remodel has kept the atmosphere—and its food—feeling fresh. This is a good choice for high-quality Polish and international cuisine in a fun, sophisticated interior that's a clever mix of old and new (daily, Wartka 5, +48 58 301 0050).

NEAR THE SOLIDARITY SHIPYARD

This zone is still being developed, but some interesting dining options are opening up for those visiting the monuments and museum.

The **European Solidarity Center** itself has both a basic **$** café and a nicer sit-down **$$** restaurant.

A thriving new food hall, **Montownia,** may be open by the time you visit. This former industrial complex has been completely rejuvenated as a super-trendy commercial hub with more than 20 eateries (www.montowniafoodhall.pl; about a five-minute walk straight ahead, as you exit the European Solidarity Center).

And then there's a completely unexpected, hidden gem of a wine bar in the middle of industrial blight. If you leave the European Solidarity Center to the left, pass the Sala BHP, cross the wide street, and angle left through the parking lot to the run-down-looking, red-brick building, you'll discover **$$ Mielżyński**—a posh, upscale, inviting wine shop with an industrial-hip wine bar upstairs. They serve both Polish and international wines in a sophisticated setting, paired with thoughtfully crafted dishes. This is a classy oasis for in-the-know wine lovers willing to go looking for it (daily, Ulica Doki 1, +48 500 019 898, www.mielzynski.pl).

Gdańsk Connections

BY TRAIN

Gdańsk is well connected to the Tri-City via commuter SKM trains (explained later, under "Getting Around the Tri-City"). It's also connected to Warsaw and Kraków by the high-speed EIC line (which requires reservations). Given the distance between Gdańsk and other Polish destinations, also consider domestic flights: LOT has easy flights between Gdańsk and Kraków for not much more than a train ticket.

From Gdańsk by Train to: Malbork (2/hour, about half are express EIC trains that take 30 minutes, the rest are slower regional trains that take around 45 minutes), **Toruń** (4/day direct, 2.5 hours; more with a change in Bydgoszcz or Iława, 3 hours), **Warsaw** (hourly, 3 hours on express EIC train), **Kraków** (6/day direct, 5.5 hours, plus 9-hour night train), **Berlin** (1/day direct, 6 hours; 3/day, 7.5 hours, change in Poznań).

BY BOAT

Boats depart from Gdańsk's embankment to nearby destinations, including **Westerplatte** (the monument marking where World War II started—see page 493) and **Hel** (the beachy peninsula, described later; most boats take about 2 hours and are operated by Żegluga Gdańska, www.zegluga.pl). Some boats go only in the summertime (July-Aug), while others continue into the shoulder season; if connections from Gdańsk are limited, you may find more options from Gdynia. Boats generally don't run in winter (Nov-March). As schedules are changeable, confirm your plans carefully at the TI.

BY CRUISE SHIP

A few cruise ships (under 800 passengers) dock in **Gdańsk,** near the Westerplatte monument (described earlier; connected to the center by 45-minute pleasure-boat trip or 30-minute ride on bus #106 or #138 to the Brama Wyżynna stop at the start of my self-guided walk; some cruise lines also offer a direct shuttle into town).

Many cruises advertising a stop in "Gdańsk" actually dock in the nearby town of **Gdynia** (described later in this chapter).

The Tri-City (Trójmiasto)

Gdańsk is the anchor of the three-part metropolitan region known as the Tri-City (Trójmiasto). The other two parts are as different as night and day: Sopot, a swanky resort town, and Gdynia, a practical, nose-to-the-grindstone business center. The Tri-City as a whole is home to bustling industry and a sprawling university, with several campuses and plenty of well-dressed, English-speaking students. Beyond the Tri-City, the long, skinny Hel Peninsula—a sparsely populated strip of fishing villages and fun-loving beaches—arches dramatically into the Baltic Sea.

Sopot—boasting sandy beaches, tons of tourists, and a certain elegance—is the most appealing day-trip option. Gdynia is less romantic, but comes with an excellent Emigration Museum

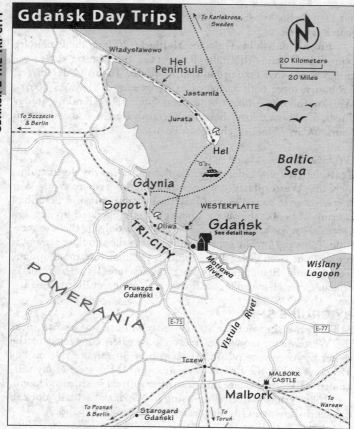

and offers a glimpse into workaday Poland. Hel, which requires the better part of a day to visit, is worthwhile only if you've got perfect summer weather and a desire to lie on the beach.

GETTING AROUND THE TRI-CITY

Gdańsk, Sopot, and Gdynia are connected by two different types of trains, both of which use Gdańsk's main train station: regional commuter trains (*kolejka*, operated by SKM) and trains operated by Poland's national railway (PKP). The SKM trains are cheaper, a bit slower, and more frequent than long-distance PKP trains. Trains to Hel are always operated by PKP.

Buying Tickets: Confusingly, SKM trains and PKP trains are covered by different tickets, which cost about the same (figure around 4-6 zł one-way between Gdańsk and Gdynia). Check posted schedules or look online to figure out which train works for you. For an SKM train, you can just hop on board, then pay the attendant in the first car (credit cards OK). For PKP trains, buy your ticket at a machine or ticket window before you board. Note that some special PKP trains require reservations, which cost extra.

Using the Right Stop: Each city has multiple stops. Remember, in Gdańsk, use either Gdańsk Główny (the main station for SKM and PKP) or Gdańsk Śródmieście (SKM only). For Sopot, use the stop called simply Sopot. For Gdynia, it's Gdynia Główna (the main station).

Boat Alternative: For a more romantic—and much slower—approach, consider a boat (see "Gdańsk Connections," earlier).

Sopot

Sopot (SOH-poht), dubbed the "Nice of the North," was a celebrated haunt of beautiful people during the 1920s and 1930s, and it remains a popular beach getaway to this day.

Sopot was created in the early 19th century by Napoleon's doctor, Jean Georges Haffner, who believed Baltic Sea water to be therapeutic. By the 1890s, it had become a fashionable seaside resort. This gambling center boasted enough high-roller casinos to garner comparisons to Monte Carlo.

The casinos are gone, but the health resorts remain, and you'll still see more well-dressed people here per capita than just about anywhere else in the country. While it's not quite Cannes, Sopot feels relatively high class. But even so, a childlike spirit of summer-vacation fun pervades this St-Tropez-on-the-Baltic, making it an all-around enjoyable place.

You can get the gist of Sopot in just a couple of hours. Zip in on the train, follow the main drag to the sea, wander the pier, get your feet wet at the beach, then head back to Gdańsk. Why not come here in the late afternoon, enjoy those last few rays of sunshine, stay for dinner, and then take a twilight stroll on the pier?

Orientation to Sopot

The main pedestrian drag, Monte Cassino Heroes street (Ulica Bohaterów Monte Cassino), leads to the Molo, the longest pleasure pier in Europe. From the Molo, a broad, sandy beach stretches in each direction. Running parallel to the surf is a tree-lined, people-filled path made for strolling.

Tourist Information: The TI is in front of the train station at Dworcowa 4 (daily 9:00-17:00, +48 501 590 773, www.sopot.pl). A second branch is near the base of the Molo at Plac Zdrojowy 2 (closed Sat-Sun).

Arrival in Sopot: From the SKM station, exit to the left and walk down the street. After a block, you'll see the PKP train station on your left. Continue on to the can't-miss-it main drag, Ulica Bohaterów Monte Cassino (marked by the big red-brick church steeple). Follow it to the right, down to the seaside.

Sights in Sopot

▲Monte Cassino Heroes Street
(Ulica Bohaterów Monte Cassino)

Nicknamed "Monciak" (MOHN-chak) by locals, this in-love-with-life promenade may well be Poland's most manicured street (and is named in honor of the Polish soldiers who helped the Allies pry Italy's Monte Cassino monastery from Nazi forces during World War II). The street is lined with happy tourists, trendy cafés, al fresco restaurants, movie theaters, and late 19th-century facades (known for their wooden balconies). The most popular building along here (on the left, about halfway down) is the so-called **Crooked House** (Krzywy Domek), a trippy, Gaudí-inspired building that looks like it's melting. Hard-partying Poles prefer to call it the "Drunken House," and say that when it looks straight, it's time to stop drinking.

Molo (Pier)

At more than 1,600 feet long, this is Europe's longest wooden entertainment pier. While you won't find any amusement-park rides, you will be surrounded by vendors, artists, and Poles having the time of their lives. Buy a *gofry* (Belgian waffle topped with whipped cream and fruit) or an oversized cloud of *wata cukrowa* (cotton candy), grab your partner's hand, and stroll with gusto (small entry fee, open long hours daily, www.molo.sopot.pl).

Climb to the top of the Art Nouveau lighthouse for a waterfront panorama. Scan the horizon for sailboats and tankers. Any pirate ships? For a jarring reality check, look over to Gdańsk. Barely visible from the Molo are two of the most important sites in 20th-century history: the towering monument at Westerplatte, where World War II started; and the cranes rising up from the Gdańsk Shipyard, where Solidarity was born and European communism began its long goodbye.

In spring and fall, the Molo is a favorite venue for pole vaulting—or is that Pole vaulting?

The Beach

Yes, Poland has beaches. Nice ones. When I heard Sopot compared to places like Nice, I'll admit that I scoffed. But when I saw those stretches of inviting sand as far as the eye can see, I wished I'd packed my swim trunks. (You could walk from Gdańsk all the way to Gdynia on beaches like this.) The sand is finer than anything I've seen in Croatia...though the water's not exactly crystal-clear. Most of the beach is public, except for a small private stretch in front of the Grand Hotel Sopot. Year-round, it's crammed with locals. At these northern latitudes, the season for bathing is brief and crowded.

Overlooking the beach next to the Molo is the **Grand Hotel Sopot.** It was renovated to top-class status just recently, but its history goes way back. They could charge admission for a multiroom suite that has hosted the likes of Adolf Hitler, Marlene Dietrich, and Fidel Castro (but not all at the same time). With all the trappings of Sopot's belle époque—dark wood, plush upholstery, antique furniture—this room had me imagining Hitler sitting at the desk, looking out to sea, and plotting the course of World War II.

Gdynia

Compared to its flashier sister cities, straightforward Gdynia (guh-DIN-yah) is all business. Gdynia is less historic than Gdańsk or Sopot, as it was built almost entirely in the 1920s to be Poland's main harbor after "Danzig" became a free city. Called "The Gateway to Poland," the city's waterfront is built on large concrete piers (a communist-style fountain in the middle of the park marks the original coastline). Although nowhere near as attractive as Gdańsk or Sopot, Gdynia has an upscale, modern feel and a lovely waterfront promenade (www.gdynia.pl).

Gdynia is a major business center and—thanks to its youthful, progressive city government—has edged ahead of the rest of Poland economically. It enjoys one of the highest income levels in the country. The fine Modernist architecture of the downtown has been renovated, and Gdynia is becoming known for its top-tier shopping—all the big designers have boutiques here. If a Pole has been shopping on Świętojańska street in Gdynia, it means that he or she has some serious złoty.

Because Gdańsk's port is relatively shallow, the biggest cruise ships must put in at Gdynia...leaving confused tourists to poke around town looking for some medieval quaintness before coming to their senses and heading for Gdańsk. Gdynia is also home to a major military harbor and an important NATO base.

To get a taste of Gdynia, take the train to the Gdynia Główna station, follow signs to *wyjście do miasta*, cross the busy street, and walk 15 minutes down Starowiejska. When you come to the intersection with the broad Świętojańska street, turn right (in the direction the big statue is looking) and walk two blocks to the tree-lined park on the left. Head through the park to the Southern Pier (Molo Południowe). This concrete slab—not nearly as charming as Sopot's wooden-boardwalk version—features a modern shopping mall and a smattering of sights, including an aquarium and a pair of permanently moored museum boats.

The big sightseeing draw in Gdynia is at the fairly distant Nabrzeże Francuskie (French Quay, where cruise ships arrive—handy for cruisers but a taxi or Uber ride away for tourists coming on the train). Here you'll find the excellent Emigration Museum, telling the story of Poles who left through Gdynia to find a better life in the New World.

Sights in Gdynia

▲▲Emigration Museum (Muzeum Emigracji)

This museum, right next to Gdynia's cruise terminal, fills the former Marine Station building at the address Polska 1. This building opened in 1933, becoming the main port of departure for Polish American Lines passenger steamers to New York City and Quebec. For a time, vast numbers of Poles emigrated to the New World through right here. (Before that time, they mostly went through Hamburg or Bremen.) After World War II, the

Iron Curtain slammed shut, the line was severed, and the Marine Station remained bombed out for decades. Now it has been renovated and hosts a high-tech, engaging museum that tells the story of the 3.5 million Poles who left their homeland in search of a better life between the mid-19th century and World War II. Concise yet informative, engaging, and all in English, the exhibit is a delight for anyone, and worth ▲▲▲ for Polish Americans.

Cost and Hours: 18 zł, free on Wed; open Tue 12:00-20:00,

Wed-Sun 10:00-18:00, closed Mon; good 10-zł audioguide, www.polska1.pl.

Getting There: It's a 25-minute, dreary walk from Gdynia's main train station. The taxis waiting out front overcharge; you'll get a more reasonable price if you order an Uber or call for a taxi (try Hallo Express, +48 602 119 190). Or you can take a bus: #119 and #133 go from near the station to the Dworzec Morski/Muzeum Emigracji stop.

Visiting the Museum: Buy your ticket on the main floor, where you'll also find WCs, a café, and a museum shop. Then head upstairs, through the middle of the cavernous building, to find the exhibit entrance. Inside, the permanent exhibition tells the story of Polish emigration. You'll see photos of famous Poles who left (from Kościuszko to Chopin), and learn about the various waves of emigration throughout Polish history and what sparked each one: the Partitions in the late 18th century, failed uprisings in 1830 and 1864, and the potato famine (Poland suffered like Ireland did—the wall of potatoes symbolizes how important this staple was to peasant life). The Industrial Revolution sparked a different kind of (internal) emigration, as rural farming families moved into the cities for work.

The exhibit introduces the Sikora family and follows their emigration from Chmielnik to Chicago, by way of the port of Bremen. You'll learn how the "emigration industry" operated: Steamer lines conducted a medical examination of each passenger before they left Europe—because if they were rejected upon examination once they arrived in the New World, the company had to pay to ship them back. Exhibits include a mock-up of a train station, the deck of an Atlantic steamship, a cross-section of life below decks, and a peek into a tight sleeping quarters, crammed with bunks where the poorest passengers would spend 10 days on turbulent seas. Finally, you arrive in New York City. Imagine seeing a wall of skyscrapers after a long journey from a thatched village. The train car is a reminder that from New York, new arrivals spread out across North America. Chicago is famous for its huge Polish émigré population, but you'll learn that many Poles also went to Brazil ("Brazilian Fever").

You'll learn about the history of Gdynia (a purpose-built port, created entirely after World War I) and see a giant replica of the MS *Stefan Bathory*—a passenger steamer that was built here. (Sadly, when transatlantic travel

ended after World War II, ships like this one were scrapped.) In the World War II section, trees cut down to their stumps represent the forced displacement of populations during and after the war. You'll learn about the "Polish diaspora" around the world (Chicago, Rio, Britain, Australia). At the end of World War II, Polish officers who had fought alongside the Western Allies were warned not to return to Poland—where they'd be executed as potential rabble-rousers against the Soviet regime. So they stayed where they were, creating a new wave of "emigration." The exhibit ends with a kitschy look at Poland under communism (and Solidarity).

Exiting the exhibit, step out onto the long terrace that looks out over the cruise port. While it serves tourists today, this port evokes the millions of brave Poles who left behind everything they knew, set sail across a dangerous ocean, and had the courage to seek a new life in a New World.

ARRIVING BY CRUISE IN GDYNIA

Many Northern European cruises include a stop at "Gdańsk"; most of these actually put in at Gdynia's sprawling port. And, while Gydnia's town center is relatively manicured and pleasant, its port area is the opposite. Cruise ships are shuffled among hardworking industrial piers with few amenities. Port information: www.port. gdynia.pl.

Each of the port's many piers is named for a country or region. Most cruise ships use **French Quay** (Nabrzeże Francuskie), which is also home to Gdynia's best sight, the **Emigration Museum.** This deserves at least an hour of your time—or more, if you have Polish ancestry—and is a good place to spend any remaining time before "all aboard."

To get from your cruise ship to Gdańsk, the best option is a **shuttle bus-plus-train connection.** The shuttle drops you off at Skwer Kociuski, in downtown Gdynia (5-10-minute trip). From here, it's about a 15-minute walk to the train station (Dworzec Główna), then a 30-to-40-minute ride into Gdańsk (for details on various train options, see "Getting Around the Tri-City," earlier). If you're taking an SKM train that uses the Gdańsk Śródmieście stop, get off there for a quicker walk into the town center; otherwise, use the main Gdańsk Główny stop. Returning to Gdynia on the train, you want the Gdynia Główna stop.

Some cruise lines may offer a **direct shuttle bus** all the way to Gdańsk, which can be worth paying for, in the interest of efficiency.

Taxi drivers line up to meet arriving cruise ships. Cabbies here are usually unofficial (and therefore can set their own, inflated rates). It's worth ordering an Uber or calling for a taxi to get legitimate rates. Taxi drivers generally take euros, though their off-the-cuff exchange rate may not be favorable.

For more details on Gdynia's port—and several others on the Baltic, North Sea, and beyond—pick up the *Rick Steves Scandinavian and Northern European Cruise Ports* guidebook.

Hel Peninsula (Mierzeja Helska)

Out on the edge of things, this slender peninsula juts 20 miles into the ocean, providing a sunny retreat from the big cities—even as it shelters them from Baltic winds. Trees line the peninsula, and the northern edge is one long, sandy, ever-shifting beach.

On hot summer days, Hel is a great place to frolic in the sun with Poles. Sunbathing and windsurfing are practically religions here. Small resort villages line Hel Peninsula: Władysławowo (at the base), Chałupy, Kuźnica, Jastarnia, Jurata, and—at the tip—a town also called Hel. Beaches right near the towns can be crowded in peak season, but you're never more than a short walk away from your own stretch of sand. There are few permanent residents, and the waterfront is shared by budget campgrounds, hotels hosting middle-class families, and mansions of Poland's rich and famous (former president Aleksander Kwaśniewski has a summer home here).

The easiest way to go to Hel—aside from coveting thy neighbor's wife—is by boat (see "Gdańsk Connections," earlier). Most trains and buses to Hel depart from Gdynia, so you'll likely need to transfer there if coming from Gdańsk. On sunny summer days—when Hel is notorious for its hellish traffic jams—overland transit is crowded and slow. The bus that connects Władysławowo to the outlying towns and beaches of Hel is—no joke!—bus #666.

POMERANIA

Malbork Castle • Toruń

The northwestern part of Poland—known as Pomerania (Pomorze, as in "along the sea")—is red-brick fairy tale country. While the region has nothing to do with excitable little dogs, it does offer two of Poland's top attractions outside of the big cities: Malbork, the biggest Gothic castle in Europe, is one of the best castles in Central Europe. And farther south, the Gothic town of Toruń—the birthplace of Copernicus—holds hundreds of beautiful buildings...and, it seems, even more varieties of tasty gingerbread. The story of this region—which was part of the German world for much of its history—is tied inexorably to the Teutonic Knights, who ruled over this northern swath of present-day Poland and fortified their holdings with elegant red brick...still the hallmark of Pomerania.

Be prepared for a higher language barrier here; unlike Kraków and Warsaw, English is not the default. While they do get foreign visitors, most are Germans or Scandinavians—Americans make up a tiny percentage of the mix.

PLANNING YOUR TIME

Malbork works well as a side trip from Gdańsk (frequent trains, 30-45 minutes each way), and it's also on the main train line from Gdańsk to Warsaw. And Toruń is well worth a stroll or an overnight if you want to sample a smaller Polish city. Unfortunately, Toruń is on a different train line than Malbork—visiting both in one day makes for a very long day. Consider doing Malbork as a side trip from Gdańsk, then visit Toruń on the way to or from Warsaw. If opting for this plan, Toruń is also a delightful place to settle in for the night.

Malbork Castle

Malbork Castle is soaked in history. The biggest brick castle in the world, the largest castle of the Gothic period, and one of Europe's most imposing fortresses, it sprawls on a marshy plain at the edge of the town of Malbork, 35 miles southeast of Gdańsk. This was the headquarters of the Teutonic Knights, the Germanic band of ex-Crusaders who dominated northern Poland in the Middle Ages. It's worth ▲▲▲ for castle lovers, or ▲▲ for anyone.

Touring the massive castle, you'll see good exhibits on amber and armor, walk through vast halls with graceful Gothic arches and fan vaulting, learn a bit about the Teutonic Knights, and see enough red brick to last a lifetime. Visiting the whole place is a bit exhausting, but this chapter's self-guided tour helps you focus on the highlights.

GETTING THERE

Malbork is conveniently located right on the express train line between Gdańsk and Warsaw. Coming by train from Gdańsk, be ready for grand views of the castle on your right as you cross the Nogat River. Bag storage is available at the station's lockers (next to the exit doors).

Figure around 20 zł for a **taxi** or **Uber** to the castle. Or it's an easy, 15-minute, mostly downhill **walk:** Leave the station to the right, walk straight past the bus stops, and go through the pedestrian underpass beneath the busy road (by the red staircase). Ascending the stairs on the other side, turn right and follow the busy road (noticing peek-a-boo views on your right of the castle's main tower). Take the first right and head down Kościuszki, the main shopping street (partway down on the right, a fancy peach-colored building houses the TI). Near the bottom of Kościuszki, at the fountain and the McDonald's, jog right, then—at the roundabout—turn left to cross the moat. The castle ticket office will be on your right.

If you want to avoid the uphill walk back to the station, ask the info desk clerk in the castle ticket office to call a (fairly priced) taxi for you.

POMERANIA

ORIENTATION TO MALBORK CASTLE

Cost: The main "historical route" costs 80 zł and includes an audioguide. On Mondays, and after hours on other days—when the interiors are closed—you can pay 40 zł for a "green route" that includes only the exteriors.

Hours: The main "historical route" is open Tue-Sun 9:00-19:00 (Oct-April until 15:00), last entry two hours before closing. If you come on Mon, or after the last entry time Tue-Sun (17:00-18:30 in season and 13:00-14:30 off-season), you can get into the exteriors-only "green route." The grounds stay open one hour later (until 20:00 in season, 16:00 off-season).

Information: +48 55 647 0978, www.zamek.malbork.pl.

Crowd-Beating Tips: The castle is busiest at midday, when there can be a line for tickets. If you anticipate crowds—or arrive to see a line—you can use your phone to buy a ticket on their website.

Tours: You're required to visit either with a guided tour or with an audioguide. Effectively, most visitors simply borrow an included audioguide—then either use it, or ignore it and follow my self-guided tour. You can ask about the availability of an English tour, but these are relatively rare.

Eating: At the castle courtyard, **$ Restauracja Piwniczka** has stick-to-your-ribs, beer-hall fare served in atmospheric cellars or at outdoor tables. Several cheap **$ food stands** cluster outside the castle (by the river). To escape the crowds, after your castle visit you can take the footbridge across the river, then turn right along the opposite riverbank and go through the long parking lot to reach **$ Bistro na Fali,** perched on a small hill looking back over the castle (daily, Wałowa 10, +48 534 610 670, www. bistronafali.pl).

Best Views: The views of massive Malbork are stunning—especially at sunset, when its red brick glows. Be sure to walk out across the footbridge over the Nogat River. The most scenic part of the castle is the twin-turreted, riverside Bridge Gate, which used to be connected by a bridge to the opposite bank.

BACKGROUND

When the Teutonic Knights were invited to Polish lands in the 13th century to convert neighboring pagans, they found the perfect site for their new capital here, on the bank of the Nogat River.

Construction began in 1274. After the Teutonic Knights conquered Gdańsk in 1308, the order moved its official headquarters from Venice to northern Poland, where they remained for nearly 150 years. They called their main castle Marienburg, the "Castle of Mary," in honor of the order's patron saint. Poles call it "Malbork."

At its peak in the early 1400s, Malbork was both the imposing home of a seemingly unstoppable army and Europe's final bastion of chivalric ideals. Surrounded by swamplands, with only one gate in need of defense, it was a tough nut to crack. Malbork Castle was never taken by force in the Middle Ages, though it had to withstand various sieges by the Poles during the Thirteen Years' War (1454-1466)—including a campaign that lasted more than three years. Finally, in 1457, the Polish king gained control of Malbork by buying off Czech mercenaries guarding the castle. Malbork became a Polish royal residence for 300 years. But when Poland was partitioned in the late 18th century, this region went back into German hands. The castle became a barracks, windows were sealed up, delicate vaulting was damaged, bricks were quarried for new buildings, and Malbork deteriorated.

In the late 19th century, Romantic German artists and poets rediscovered the place. An architect named Konrad Steinbrecht devoted 40 years of his life to Malbork, painstakingly resurrecting the palace's medieval splendor. A half-century later, the Nazis used the castle to house POWs. Hitler—who, like many Germans, had a soft spot for Malbork's history—gave the order to defend it to the last man. About half of the castle was destroyed by the Soviet army, who saw it as a symbol of long-standing German domination. But it was restored once again, and today Malbork has been returned to its Teutonic glory.

⊙ SELF-GUIDED TOUR

The official "historical tour" of Malbork lasts about three hours; my tour of the highlights takes about half that long, unless you linger. Use the map in this section to navigate. The castle complex is a bit of a maze, with multiple entrances and exits for each room, often behind closed (but unlocked) doors. Don't be shy about grabbing a medieval doorknob and letting yourself in. If you're here on a Monday or after hours, on a "green route" ticket, you won't have access to many of the indoor areas described on this tour.

Entering the Castle Complex

From the ticket office, exit straight ahead and belly up to the brick wall by the bronze model for a panoramic view of the giant complex. Slowly pan across one of Europe's most intimidating fortresses—home to the Grand Master, monks, and knights of the Teutonic Order. The High Castle (where the monks lived) is on

Malbork Castle

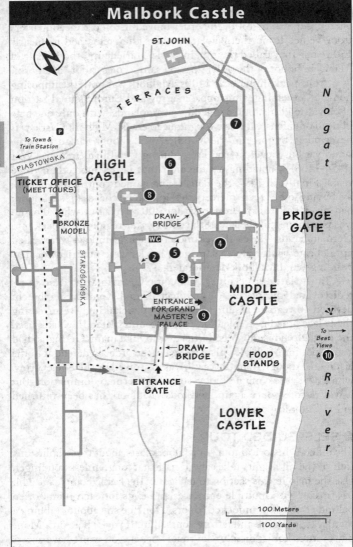

1 Amber Exhibition (downstairs)
2 Armory (upstairs)
3 "Boiler Room" (downstairs)
   & Grand Refectory (upstairs)
4 Grand Master's Palace
5 Grand Master Statues

6 Well
7 Dansker Tower
8 St. Mary's Church
9 Restauracia Piwniczka
10 To Bistro na Fali

the left, marked by the 30-foot-tall statue of Mary at the end of St. Mary's Church. To the right is the Middle Castle, where the knights lived. We'll loop around the right end (Middle Castle), working our way inside and ending at the High Castle.

The bronze **model** shows the realm of the Teutonic Knights at their peak—stretching from Gdańsk in the north to Toruń to the south, and, waaaay up on the northeast, the city of Kłajpeda, today part of Lithuania. For more than a century (1308-1410), the Teutonic Knights were a formidable presence. For more on this history, see the sidebar later in this chapter.

• *Now turn right and cross the drawbridge under the brick tower. Keep going alongside the moat, turning left to cross another drawbridge into the castle ward. Ahead and to the right, the long, low-lying building was the Lower Castle, where servants and support staff lived. Just before that, on the left, is yet another drawbridge. Show your ticket here and cross partway over the bridge—pausing just outside the brick gate.*

Entrance Gate

Above the door to the brick gate is a sculpture of the Virgin Mary with Baby Jesus, next to a shield and helmet. The message is two-fold: This castle is protected by Mary, and the Teutonic Knights are here to convert pagans—by force, if necessary.

From the drawbridge, look right to observe the formidable fortifications. The Teutonic Knights connected nearby lakes to create a system of canals, forming a moat around the castle that could be crossed only by drawbridge. The rooster-capped corner tower (which contains a toilet) is connected by a sky bridge to the fancy Gothic 14th-century facade of the brick infirmary—kept at a distance for disease control.

Continue farther, until you're inside the gate structure itself. Imagine the gate behind you slamming shut. Look up to see wooden chutes where archers are preparing to rain arrows down on you. Your last thought: Maybe we should have left the Teutonic Knights alone after all.

Before you're pierced by arrows, read the castle's history in its walls: The foundation is made of huge stones—rare in these marshy lands—brought from Sweden. But most of the castle, like so many other buildings in northern Poland, was built with handmade red brick. Throughout the castle, the darker-colored, rougher brick is original, and the lighter-colored, smoother brick was used during later restorations (in the 19th century, and again after World War II). Marvel at the ironclad doors and the heavy portcullis.

Venture through two more enclosed spaces, watching for the holes in the wall (for more guards and soldiers). Ponder the fact that you must pass through five separate, well-defended gates to reach the...

POMERANIA

POMERANIA

Middle Castle (Zamek Średni)

This part of Malbork, built at an uphill incline to make it even more imposing, was designed to impress. Knights and monks lived here.

Let's get oriented: To your left is the east wing, where visiting monks would sleep. Today, this houses the Amber Exhibition (ground floor) and the armory (upstairs). To the right (west) as you enter the main courtyard is the Grand Refectory (closer to the entrance) and the Grand Master's Palace (the taller, squarer building at the far end).

• *Enter the ground floor of the building on the left (go through the small door and take a few steps down). Here you'll tour the...*

Amber Exhibition

Amber, precious petrified tree sap, is found here in Poland; for a primer, read the "All About Amber" sidebar on page 471. You'll start 42 million years ago and follow the story of amber, then walk down the dimly lit corridor, checking out huge chunks of raw amber and illuminated displays of inclusions (bugs and other organic objects stuck in the amber, à la *Jurassic Park*). Some of the ancient amber artifacts displayed here are up to 3,000 years old, found in graves.

At the end of the corridor, U-turn and work your way back up a parallel hall, lined with all manner of exquisite amber creations: boxes, brooches, necklaces, chess sets, pipes, miniature ships, wine glasses, and belts for skinny-waisted, fashion-conscious women. Many of the finely decorated jewelry boxes and chests have ivory, silver, or shell inlays—better for contrast than gold. The portable religious shrines and altars allowed travelers to remain reverent on the road and still pack light. Notice the wide range of amber colors—from opaque white to transparent yellow to virtually black.

• *Exit at the far end. As you emerge into the Middle Castle courtyard, go up the wooden staircase on your right, go inside, turn left and walk to the end of the long hall, and go up the stairs. Here you'll find the...*

Armory

This enjoyable, well-displayed collection includes an impressive array of swords, armor, and other armaments. Look for the 600-year-old "hand-and-a-half" swords—too big to be held in one hand. Tucked behind the cannons is a giant shield. A row of these shields could be lined up to form a portable wall—called a phalanx—to protect the knights. In the big room with the decoratively hilted swords, look for the terrifying "flame-bladed sword." You'll also see pikes, maces, crossbows, rifles, and horse armor. And in the room with the body armor, the centerpiece is a suit of armor from the hussars—Polish horse-back knights. Equipped with wings, it created a terrifying sound when the horses were galloping.

• *At the end of the armory, head down the modern stairs and back outside (a handy WC is straight ahead). Cross the main courtyard, angling downhill, and enter the smaller courtyard through the passage next to the stubby, dark-wood-topped tower. Find the (unlabeled and sometimes closed) door to a dark, steep flight of stairs that leads down into the...*

"Boiler Room"

The Teutonic Knights had a surprisingly sophisticated method for heating this huge complex. You see a furnace down below and a holding area for hot rocks above. The radiant heat given off by the rocks spread through the vents without also filling them with smoke (illustrated by a chart on the wall). This is one of 11 such "boiler rooms" in the castle complex. As you tour the rest of the castle, keep an eye out for saucer-sized heating vents in the floor.

• *Climb back up the stairs, take an immediate left through a tiny arch, and then go left again, up through the second door (not down through the first door, which takes you out of the castle). This leads into the...*

Grand Master's Palace

This was one of the grandest royal residences in medieval Europe, used in later times by Polish kings and German kaisers. (Today, it's sometimes used for special exhibitions.)

• *From the kitchen—with its huge chimney (wow!)—turn left into the big and bright...*

Grand Refectory: With remarkable palm vaulting and grand frescoes, this dining hall hosted feasts for up to 400 people to celebrate a military victory or to impress visiting dignitaries. In the floor, notice the 36 heating vents—which are directly above the boiler room you just visited—designed to keep the VIPs warm.

• *At the far end of the refectory, climb the stairs into the...*

Private Rooms of the Grand Master:

Though the Teutonic Order dictated that the monks sleep in dormitories, the Grand Master made an exception for himself—with this suite of private rooms. This area is a bit of a maze, so stick with me (or just wander around looking for each of these rooms): From the hall where you enter, bear left into another hall, with show-off decor—including some 15th-century original frescoes of wine leaves and grapes.

Go through the door to the left of the fireplace into the Grand Master's **bedroom,** decorated with (now very faint) frescoes of four virgins—female martyrs. Beyond that is the green-walled **study** of the Grand Master.

Continue through the study and you'll step into the Top Knight's dining room, the **Winter Refectory,** with fewer windows (better insulation) and more of the little heating vents in the floor. The walls are draped with tapestries, which also helped warm things up a bit.

For a dramatic contrast, continue into the next room—the **Summer Refectory.** With big stained-glass windows and deli-cate vaulting supported by a single central pillar, this room was clearly not designed with defense in mind. In fact, medieval Polish armies focused their attacks on this room. On one legendary occasion, the attackers—tipped off by a spy—knew that an important meeting was going on here and fired a cannonball into the room. It just missed the pillar. (You can see where the cannonball hit the wall, just above the fireplace.) The ceiling eventually did collapse during World War II.

Continue through the Summer Refectory, stepping out into a hallway. Turn right, noticing the washbasin and trough along the corridor. Anyone wanting an audience with the Grand Master had to wash both his hands and his feet. Farther along, find the stairs down (on your left).

• *Take those stairs back out in the courtyard. On your right are four...*

Grand Master Statues

Though this was a religious order, these powerful guys look more like kings than monks. From left to right, shake hands with Hermann von Salza (who was Grand Master when the Teutonic Knights came to Poland), Siegfried von Feuchtwangen (who actually moved the T. K. capital from Venice to Malbork, and who conquered Gdańsk for the knights—oops, can't shake his hand, which was supposedly chopped off by Soviet troops), Winrich von

The Teutonic Knights

The Order of the Teutonic Knights began in the Holy Land in 1191, during the Third Crusade. These militarized German monks built hospitals and cared for injured knights. When the Crusades ended in the 12th century, the knights returned to Europe and reorganized as a chivalric order of Christian mercenaries—pagan-killers for hire.

In 1226, a northern Polish duke called in the Teutonic Knights to subdue a tribe of pagans who had been attacking his lands. Clad in their white cloaks with skinny black crosses,

the Teutonic Knights spent 60 years "saving" the pagans by turning them into serfs or massacring them.

Job done, the Teutonic Knights decided to stick around. With the support of the pope and the Holy Roman Emperor (who were swayed by the knights' religious zeal), the knights built one of Europe's biggest and most imposing fortresses: Malbork. In 1308, they seized large parts of northern Poland (including Gdańsk), cutting off Polish access to the Baltic Sea. The knights grew rich from Hanseatic trade, specializing in amber, grain, and timber. By the late 14th century, the Teutonic Knights had grown to become Europe's largest-ever monastic state and were threatening to overtake Lithuania.

Inspired by a mutual desire to oust the Teutonic Knights, the Poles and the Lithuanians teamed up. In 1386, Polish princess Jadwiga married Lithuanian prince Władysław Jagiełło, kick-starting a grand new dynasty: the Jagiellonians.

Every Pole knows the date July 15, 1410: the Battle of Grunwald. King Władysław Jagiełło and Lithuanian grand duke Vytautas the Great led a ragtag army of some 40,000 soldiers—Lithuanians, Poles, other Slavs, and even speedy Tatar horsemen—against 27,000 Teutonic Knights. At the end of the day, some 18,000 Poles and Lithuanians were dead—but so were half of the Teutonic Knights, and the other half had been captured. Poland and Lithuania were victorious.

The Battle of Grunwald marked the beginning of the end for the Teutonic Knights, who were conclusively defeated during the Thirteen Years' War (1454-1466). The order officially dissolved in 1575, when they converted to Protestantism and much of their land was folded into Prussia. Later, 19th-century Polish Romantics reimagined the Teutonic Knights as an early symbol of Germanic oppression—poignant among Poles, who suffered through a new round of German abuse in World War II. Some conspiracy theorists believe the Teutonic Knights are still very much active...but that's another story.

POMERANIA

Kniprode (who oversaw Malbork's golden age and turned it into a castle fit for a king), and Markgraf Albrecht von Hohenzollern (the last Grand Master before the order dissolved and converted to Protestantism).

• *We're heading into the final section of the castle. Before we do, it's a good time for a break—WCs and eateries are in this courtyard. When you're ready, continue into the High Castle. To the right of the Grand Masters, cross over the...*

Drawbridge

As you cross, notice the extensive system of fortifications and moats protecting the innermost part of the castle just ahead. Once inside the gate, on your left is a door leading to a green zone that runs around the High Castle. Here you'll see a collection of stone catapult balls that were actually fired at this castle when it was under siege. (Look high above to see the dents such stones can make.) This is a fun area to explore on your way back out of the castle...if you're not castled out by that point.

Continue straight ahead from the drawbridge, into a passage that's lined with holes to the sides (for surveillance) and with chutes up above (to pour scalding water or pitch on unwanted visitors). It's not quite straight—so a cannon fired here would hit the side wall of the passage, rather than enter the High Castle and its central courtyard...which is what you're about to do now.

High Castle (Zamek Wysoki)

This is the heart of the castle and its oldest section. From this spot, the Teutonic Knights governed their vast realm—the largest monk-ruled territory in European history. As much a monastery as a fortress, the High Castle was off-limits to all but 60 monks of the Teutonic Order and their servants. (The knights stayed in the Middle Castle.) Here you'll find the monks' dormitories, chapels, church, and refectory. As this was the nerve center of the Teutonic Knights, it was also their last line of defense. They stored enormous amounts of food here in case of a siege.

In the middle of the High Castle courtyard is a **well**—an essential part of any inner castle, especially one as prone to sieges as Malbork. At the top is a sculpture of a pelican. Because this noble bird was believed to kill itself to feed its young (notice that it's piercing its own chest with its beak), it was often used in the Middle Ages as a symbol for the self-sacrifice of Jesus.

• *Take some time to explore the...*

POMERANIA

Ground Floor

Immediately to your left is a door leading to the **prison,** with small "solitary confinement" cells near the entrance. Diagonally across the courtyard, hiding in the far corner, is an exhibit on **stained-glass windows** from the castle church.

Back near where you entered the courtyard, step into the **kitchen.** This exhibit—with a long table piled with typical ingredients from that time—gives you a feel for medieval monastery life. The monks who lived here ate three meals a day and drank lots of beer (made here) and wine (imported from France, Italy, and Hungary). A cellar under the kitchen was used as a simple refrigerator—big chunks of ice were cut from the frozen river in winter, stored in the basement, and used to keep food cool in summer. Behind the long table, see the big dumbwaiter (with shelves for hot dishes), which connects this kitchen with the refectory upstairs. Step into the giant stove and peer up into the biggest chimney in the castle.

• *Now go back out into the courtyard and climb up the stairs near where you first entered.*

Middle Floor

• *From the top of the stairs, the first door on the left (with the colorfully painted arch) leads to the most important room of the High Castle, the...*

Chapter Room: Monks gathered here after Mass, and it was also the site for meetings of Teutonic Knights from throughout the realm. If a Grand Master was killed in battle, the new one would be elected here. Carvings above each chair indicated the status of the man who sat there. The big chair belonged to the Grand Master. Notice the little windows high on the wall above his chair, connecting this room to the church next door. Ecclesiastical music would filter in through these windows; imagine the voices of 60 monks bouncing around with these acoustics.

While monks are usually thought to pursue simple lives, the elegant vaulting in this room is anything but plain. The 14th-century frescoes (restored in the 19th century) depict Grand Masters. In the floor are more vents for the central heating.

• *Leave the Chapter Room and walk straight ahead, imagining the monk-filled corridors of Teutonic times. The first door on the right is the...*

Treasury: As you explore the five rooms of the tax collector and the house administrator, notice the wide variety of safes and other lock boxes. Documents, amber, and coins were kept behind heavily armored and well-locked doors.

• *Continue around the cloister. At the end of the corridor, spot the little devil (see photo next page) at the bottom of the vaulting (on the right, just above your head). He's pulling his beard and crossing his legs—pointing you down the long corridor leading about 100 yards away from the cloister to the...*

Dansker Tower: From the devil's grimace, you might have guessed that this tower houses the latrine. Four wooden toilet stalls filled this big room. Where one is missing, you can look down to see how the "toilets" simply dropped the waste into the moat. For obvious sanitary (and olfactory) reasons, this potty tower is set apart from the main part of the castle. The bins above the toilets were filled with cabbage leaves, to be used by the T. K. as TP (and as an organic form of Preparation H). This tower could also serve as a final measure of defense—it's easier to defend than the entire castle. Food was stored above, just in case. More info on this grand castle WC is on the wall.

• *Return down the long corridor. Before the end, on the right-hand side of the long passage, a door leads into the...*

Church Exhibition: Once dormitories for the monks, these three rooms now display a wide range of relics from the church. In the last room, on the far wall, is the artistic highlight of the castle: a finely carved and gilded three-panel altarpiece from 1504 featuring the coronation of Mary. Mary's face is mesmerizing. Characteristic of the late Gothic period, the robes seem to fly unrealistically (as if they were bent metal).

• *Back out in the main cloister, turn right and continue to the end, arriving at the...*

Golden Gate: This elaborate doorway—covered in protective glass—marks the entrance to St. Mary's Church. Before entering, examine this rare original **door.**

Ringed with detailed carvings from the New Testament and symbolic messages about how monks of the Teutonic Order should live their lives, it's a marvelous example of late 13th-century art. At the bottom-left end of the arch, find the five wise virgins who, having filled their lamps with oil and conserved it wisely, are headed to heaven. On the right, the five foolish virgins who overslept and used up all their oil are damned, much to their dismay.

Step inside **St. Mary's Church** to appreciate a glorious Gothic interior—recently reopened after a lengthy restoration. Straight ahead from where you entered, look for the 14th-century cross, which was partly burned when the castle was destroyed. Throughout the space, notice how the restorers intentionally used different materials to distinguish repairs from different eras:

the brighter plaster dates from the recent work, while the darker plaster (closer to the area where you entered) is from the 19th century.

• *Back outside, go through the narrow door next to the Golden Gate and hike up the tight spiral staircase to the final set of exhibits.*

Top Floor

Walk through a space with temporary exhibits. At the end, descend into the **monks' common room** (left, at the bottom of the stairs). Over the fireplace is a relief depicting the Teutonic Knights fighting the pagans. To the left and above (see the stone windows) is a balcony where musicians entertained the monks after a meal.

The next, very long room, with seven pillars, is the **refectory,** where the monks ate in silence. Along the right-hand wall are

lockable storage boxes for tableware. At the end of this room, just beyond another ornate fireplace, notice the grated hole in the wall. This is where the dumbwaiter comes up from the kitchen (which we saw below). Beyond this room is an exhibit about the architectural renovation of the castle.

• *Your Malbork tour ends here. You leave the way you came. En route, you can walk around terraces lining the inner moat, between the castle walls (stairs lead down off the drawbridge, by the catapult balls). It's hardly a must-see, but it's pleasant enough, with the Grand Master's garden, a cemetery for monks, and the remains of the small St. Anne's Chapel (with Grand Master tombs).*

MALBORK CONNECTIONS

From Malbork by Train to: Gdańsk (2/hour, 30 minutes on express EIC train, 45 minutes on slower regional train), **Toruń** (about every 2 hours, 2.5 hours, change in Iława), **Warsaw** (hourly, 2.5 hours on express EIC train).

Toruń

Toruń (TOH-roon) is a living fairy tale that feels like Poland's best-kept secret...and one of Europe's, too. This pretty, lazy Goth-ic town, conveniently located about halfway between War-saw and Gdańsk, is well worth a few hours to stroll the lively streets, ogle the huge red-brick buildings, and savor the flavor of perhaps Poland's most livable city. You won't regret spending the night...but when it's time to leave, you may regret spending just one.

With about 210,000 residents and 30,000 students (at Coper-nicus University), Toruń is a thriving burg. Like Kraków (and un-like most other Polish cities), Toruń escaped destruction during World War II and remains well preserved today. Locals brag that their city is a "mini Kraków." But that sells both cities short. Toruń lacks Kraków's over-the-top romanticism, and its sights are quickly exhausted. On the other hand, Toruń may well be Poland's most user-friendly city: tidy streets with a sensible grid plan, wide pe-destrian boulevards crammed with locals who greet each other like they're long-lost friends, and an easygoing ambience that seems to say, "Hey—relax." It's jammed with Polish school groups and fami-lies, and some in-the-know Germans...but few Americans.

Toruń clings fiercely to its two claims to fame: It's the proud birthplace of the astronomer Copernicus (Mikołaj Kopernik), and home to a dizzying variety of gingerbread treats (*piernika;* pyer-NEE-kah).

Orientation to Toruń

Everything in Toruń worth seeing is in the walled Old Town, climbing up a gentle hill from the Vistula River. The broad, traffic-free main drag, Ulica Szeroka (called Różana at the entrance of town), bisects the Old Town, running parallel to the river. You can walk from one end of the town center to the other in about 15 minutes.

The helpful **TI** is right where the main square meets the main walking street, Ulica Szeroka (daily 10:00-17:00, closed Sun in winter, Ulica Szeroka 43, +48 56 621 0930, www.visittorun.com).

ARRIVAL IN TORUŃ

Toruń's main train station (Toruń Główny) is across the river from the Old Town, about a mile away. The tidy main hall sits between tracks 1 and 2. Lockers are between the food hall and track 2.

To reach the Old Town, you can take a **taxi**—they wait out the door from the main hall (figure 20-25 zł or less to Plac Rapackiego, the start of my Toruń Walk, or most recommended hotels). To go by **bus**, first buy a single ticket from the Relay kiosk inside the station (about 4 zł), then use the escalators, stairs, or elevator to descend to the pedestrian underpass and exit toward *Ul. Kujawska* (past platform 4). You'll surface near an old steam locomotive; nearby is the stop for bus #27 to Plac Rapackiego, the first stop after the long bridge. (Buses #11 and #14 also make this trip.) To return to the station, catch the bus across the busy road from where you got off. Note: Public transit is free for anyone over age 65 (just show your passport if asked).

Alternate Train Station: Some (but not all) trains also stop at **Toruń Miasto** station, which is a bit closer to the Old Town (about a 15-minute walk along the river). Check schedules carefully to see if your train stops here; those overnighting in town may find it more convenient.

Toruń Walk

This lazy, low-impact self-guided walk takes you through the heart of Toruń—showing you pretty much everything you'd want to see on a brief visit. With no stops, you could do it all in about 45 minutes.

• *Coming from the train station, the bus stop is at...*

Plac Rapackiego

The park that rings Toruń—once the site of the medieval city wall—is an inviting people zone. From the bus stop, walk straight ahead through the park, toward town. You'll pass a borrow-a-bike station and a futuristic sculpture, labeled *Solimnia Regit,* honoring hometown boy Copernicus' heliocentric theory...more on him later. The big, historic, ornately gabled building on your left is the Collegium Maximum, the historic headquarters of Toruń's prestigious university.

Carry on straight ahead, going below the narrow house marked *1936* and the adjoining local Solidarity headquarters. Under the tower, you'll find some remaining tram tracks, commemorating the line that ran along the city's main drag from 1936 until 1970. You'll pop out on the town's main drag.

• *Continue one block straight along the main street to reach the bustling...*

POMERANIA

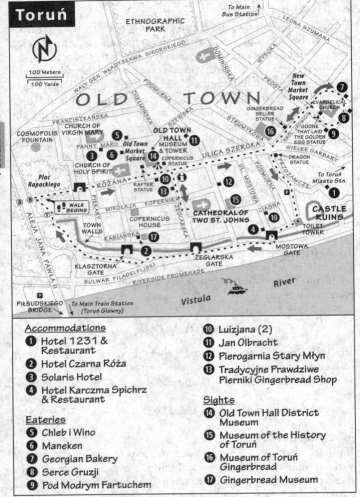

Toruń

Accommodations
1. Hotel 1231 & Restaurant
2. Hotel Czarna Róża
3. Solaris Hotel
4. Hotel Karczma Spichrz & Restaurant

Eateries
5. Chleb i Wino
6. Maneken
7. Georgian Bakery
8. Serce Gruzji
9. Pod Modrym Fartuchem
10. Luizjana (2)
11. Jan Olbracht
12. Pierogarnia Stary Młyn
13. Tradycyjne Prawdziwe Pierniki Gingerbread Shop

Sights
14. Old Town Hall District Museum
15. Museum of the History of Toruń
16. Museum of Toruń Gingerbread
17. Gingerbread Museum

Old Town Market Square (Rynek Staromiejski)

This square is surrounded by huge brick buildings and outdoor restaurants buzzing with lively locals (for tips, see "Eating in Toruń," later).

The **Old Town Hall** (Ratusz Staromiejski) fills the middle of the square. Like the Cloth Hall in Kraków, this building began life as a general market. Toruń is, at its heart, a trading city, and benefitted tremendously from its membership in the Hanseatic League—a trade union of Northern European maritime cities. Toruń's prime position on the Vistula River, navigable by oceangoing vessels, put it on the map and allowed it to prosper. The Old Town Hall contains a fine, if dated, museum, and you can pay to climb its tower for a town view. To escape the square's bustle, you can step into this building's serene brick courtyard, with the ticket office and museum entrance (for details, see "Sights in Toruń," later).

The ornate, dark-red building with the pointy spires facing the Old Town Hall is the **Artus Court,** marking the location where the medieval town council and merchants' guilds met. While the town was founded in 1231, the current building is Neo-Gothic, dating from 1891; inside its dramatic, vertical, covered courtyard, you'll find a New Orleans-themed restaurant (seriously...see "Eating in Toruń," later). In the pavement directly in front of this building, plaques celebrate famous people who were born here or have ties to this town...sort of a Toruń walk of fame.

Toruń seems to specialize in statues that spin fanciful tales. The first of these is at the nearest corner of the Old Town Hall. Look for the fountain with the guy playing a violin. This is a **rafter** *(retman)*—one of the medieval lumberjacks who lashed tree trunks together and floated them down the Vistula to Gdańsk. This particular rafter came to Toruń when the town was infested with frogs. He wooed them with his violin and marched them out of town. (Hmm...sounds like a certain pied piper...)

Standing by the fountain, look in the direction the rafter's bow is pointing. Two doors to the right of the giant Artus Court, at the very top of the skinny greenish building, spy the silhouette of a **cat.** According to local legend, while prowling the rooftops in the 17th century, this cat saw an invading Swedish army. So, he began howling loudly, waking the town just in time to prepare for the battle.

Now walk along the front of the Old Town Hall. At the far corner, the bigger statue depicts **Mikołaj Kopernik,** known internationally as Nicolaus Copernicus (1473-1543). This Toruń-born son of aristocrats turned the world on its ear when he suggested that the sun, not the earth, is the center of the universe (the "heliocentric theory"). Toruń is seriously proud of this local boy done good—he's the town mascot, as well as the namesake of the local university. Among its fields of study, Copernicus U. has a healthy astronomy program. There's a planetarium in the Old Town (just past the far corner of the square) and a giant radio telescope on the outskirts. Despite all the local fuss over Copernicus, there's some dispute about his "nationality": He was born in Toruń, but at a time when it was the predominantly German town of "Thorn." So, is he Polish...or German? (For more on Copernicus, you can visit his birth house—now a museum—two blocks away; described later, under "Sights in Toruń.") Either way, this statue is the town's top selfie spot—you'll see Polish families lining up to snap the perfect photo.

Copernicus faces a shiny **donkey** at the corner of Szeroka and Żeglarska streets. Notice the sharp ridge on the donkey's back, which recalls a humiliating punishment. Centuries ago, delinquents and petty criminals needing to be set straight would be forced to straddle this donkey—after townspeople had tied heavy stones to their feet, weighing them down painfully.

• *But you're on vacation—and, rather than humiliation, you get gingerbread. Follow your nose to the right, down Żeglarska street, which is lined with...*

Gingerbread Shops

For Poles, Toruń is synonymous with gingerbread *(piernika)*—you'll smell its heavenly scent all over town. When Chopin visited, most of his impressions of Toruń revolved around gingerbread. Today, this Toruń treat can be topped with different kinds of jams or glazes, and/or dipped in chocolate. But historically, gingerbread was more straightforward—and a valuable commodity. The honey used in its dough and for glazing acted as a preservative, allowing gingerbread to be traded far and wide. And its spices aid digestion, so it served a medicinal purpose as well. Thanks to Hanseatic League connections, Toruń's bakers had access to exotic, imported spices such as white ginger, cinnamon, clove, anise, citrus skins, cardamom, and peppercorns (for which *piernika* is named). Traditionally, gingerbread dough was pressed into wooden molds, giving each cookie a distinctive shape.

While you'll spot a half-dozen options for buying gingerbread within a few steps of here, I like the one marked **Tradycyjne Prawdziwe Pierniki** (on the right, at #25). This shop has a fun system: All the varieties cost the same, so you can assemble just the mix you like by pointing. *Róża* is rose, *malina* is raspberry, *czarna porzeczka* is black currant, *morela* is apricot, and—of course—*czekolada* is chocolate.

• *A few steps down and across the street is the...*

Cathedral of Two Saint Johns (Katedra Św. Jana Chrzciciela i Jana Ewangelisty)

Dedicated in the 12th century to both John the Baptist and John the Evangelist, this is the parish church of the Old Town. Its massive bulk dominates the view of Toruń from across the river. From street level, appreciate the architectural heaviness: The marshy land lacked big stones, so instead of flying buttresses, medieval engineers employed an overbuilt brick structure so they could go big.

If it's open, step into the interior, with graceful Gothic austerity—delicate ribs and whitewashed walls. The gravestones of big shots pave the floor. Each trade guild had its own chapel, with its own fancy altar. On the wall to the left of the main altar, notice the finely restored 13th-century *Last Judgment* fresco. As you leave, head to the back-right corner (opposite where

you came in) and find the colorful baptismal font where, in 1473, Copernicus was baptized (free entry, tower climb extra, irregular hours).

• *Having satisfied your ginger tooth and seen the town's most important church, head back to the square and that painful donkey, turn right, and join the human stream down the appropriately named...*

Ulica Szeroka ("Wide Street")

This intoxicating-in-good-weather pedestrian promenade leads through the heart of town. Embedded in the paving bricks are the coats of arms of Toruń's medieval trading partners. On each side of the street is an eclectic commotion of fun facades and intriguing shops. Stow your guidebook for a few minutes and just stroll and window-shop. I'll meet you just before you get to

a clock tower in the middle of the street.

About 30 yards before the road forks at the stately, white Empik building, look down narrow **Przedzamcze street** to the right to see fragments of the town wall. This marks the border between the Old Town and the New Town (chartered only about 30 years later—both in the 13th century). While these areas are collectively known today as the unified "Old Town," they were quite different in the Middle Ages—each with its own market square and separated by a wall. Because the New Town lacked the easy access to the river, most of its residents were craftspeople who supplied the traders in the Old Town.

At the start of Przedzamcze street, on the left, notice the small, fenced stretch of stream that runs underground through town. Next to the stream is another legendary monument: a **dragon.** As the plaque explains, back in 1746, locals swore in official

POMERANIA

records that they saw a real-life, six-foot-long dragon right about here.

• *Across Szeroka street from Przedzamcze, Strumykowa street leads to the better of Toruń's two gingerbread museums (described later).*

Let's take a quick spin through the New Town. Bear left at the clock tower to head up Królowej Jadwigi street. At the first street on the left, look for the green statue of the **gingerbread seller** *(piernikarka)—with lots of goodies in her basket.*

Another block straight ahead, you pop out at...

New Town Market Square (Rynek Nowomiejski)

This sleepy, inviting square is nearly as appealing as its Old Town counterpart. Its centerpiece is an angular and austere **Evangelical Church**—a reminder that this northern part of Poland, with its Prussian roots, isn't just for Catholics.

At the near end of the church, look for yet another fairy-tale statue—this time, one that may be more familiar: the **Goose That Laid the Golden Egg.**

Do a slow spin around the square, surveying options for a meal (either now or later—for recommendations, see "Eating in Toruń," later). In addition to a historic pub, the far corner of the square has a surprising concentration of Georgian restaurants, from the republic in the Caucasus. If you haven't tried this delicious cuisine before, now's a good chance. (For more on Georgian food, see page 234.)

• *When you're ready, we'll backtrack through town for our final stop—a look at the castle where Toruń began.*

Head out of the square the way you came, on Królowej Jadwigi, just two short blocks to the intersection at the clock tower. Bear right here, then turn left down Przedzamcze—passing the dragon and his stream that we saw earlier. We'll follow that (underground) stream down toward the river. When you reach the parking lot, bear left under the stubby, standalone brick gate. Emerging on the other side, you'll see an old mill straight ahead and a crenellated brick tower on your right. You're standing in the middle of what's left of...

Toruń Castle

This castle, built by the Teutonic Knights who were so influential in northern Poland in the Middle Ages (see page 521), was destroyed in the 15th century by the locals—who, aside from a heap of bricks, left only the tower that housed the Teutonic toilets. You can pay to enter the ruins nearby—basically just foundations—but there's little to see. However, what survives is one of the better toilet towers in Europe—which was connected to the castle by an elevated walkway and located far enough away to keep things hygienic. (Notice how it was positioned to drop into the dragon's stream—which you can see uncovered here again.) The old mill next to the toilet is now a recommended hotel and restaurant named 1231, for the date the Teutonic Order arrived here.

• *Our walk is over. You can backtrack the way you came and explore more of the city (including the sights listed next). Or you can take a quick riverside stroll: Go under the toilet tower and down to the Vistula River, turn right, and stroll along the castle and 14th-century city walls back to your starting point (and the bus stop back to the station). The road is called Bulwar Filadelfijski—for Toruń's sister city in Pennsylvania.*

Sights in Toruń

Toruń is more about strolling than it is about sightseeing—the town's museums are underwhelming. Aside from its half-dozen red-brick churches (any of which are worth dropping into), the following attractions are worth considering on a rainy day.

Hours: Almost all of these sights—everything except the second Gingerbread Museum—are operated by the city and have the same hours: Tue-Sun 10:00-18:00, Oct-April until 16:00, closed Mon year-round (www.muzeum.torun.pl).

City History Museums

Toruń operates two different history museums. Both show off intimate bits and pieces of history—from pewter tankards to old gingerbread molds—that show the richness of this traders' city. They're essentially redundant—pick one.

The **Old Town Hall District Museum,** inside the centerpiece building on the main square, has more impressive spaces—including Gothic corridors and royal meeting rooms upstairs. But the collection is dusty and challenging to appreciate. The highlight is the Gothic Gallery on the main floor—featuring medieval church art saved from the region's churches, with lots of Marys (the patron of the Teutonic Order), and a close-up look at some 14th-century stained glass. You can also pay to climb the 176 narrow wooden steps to the top of the **tower** for great views over the city center (36.50 zł combo-ticket covers museum and tower, 22.50 zł for one or the other, tower open until 20:00 in May-Sept).

A few blocks away, the **Museum of the History of Toruń** fills an old red-brick granary with four floors of well-explained artifacts, colorful exhibits, and English translations. While the space is less impressive, it's a more meaningful experience. Your ticket includes an informative, 13-minute 3-D movie (with English subtitles) about the town's history on the top floor (19.50 zł, Łazienna 16).

Gingerbread Museums

Toruń has various gingerbread experiences (mainly oriented to Polish school groups and families) that enjoy teaching about this important local product. Buying and sampling gingerbread is the only "essential" Toruń experience, but these options round out your visit nicely. Unlike cookies, you should choose just one.

The **Museum of Toruń Gingerbread,** just off the main drag at the far end of town, is more of a traditional museum. It fills the historic red-brick Weese family gingerbread factory, established in 1885. (The company still makes gingerbread, in a modern plant on the outskirts.) After watching a brief film, you'll walk through three floors of quaint, modern exhibits that trace the history of gingerbread: artifacts (molds, ovens) in the cellar, a recreated late 19th-century street on the upper floor, and an interesting overview of the gingerbread-making process on the main floor. For a separate fee, they offer hands-on **gingerbread demonstrations**—predominantly in Polish, but if the guide speaks some English, they may add some extra commentary for you (36.50 zł combo-ticket includes museum and demo, 22.50 zł for one or the other, Strumykowa 4).

The **Gingerbread Museum** (Muzeum Piernika), between the main square and the river, is popular with kids and with anyone wanting an English demonstration rather than a traditional museum. Costumed medieval bakers spend about an hour walking you through the traditional process of rolling, cutting out, baking, and tasting your own batch of gingerbread cookies. After aging for 12 weeks to achieve the proper consistency, the dough bakes for only 12 minutes—or, according to medieval bakers, about 50 Hail Marys (34 zł, daily 10:00-18:00, Polish tours at the top of each hour, English tours about once daily—likely at 14:00 but confirm ahead, in peak times it's smart to reserve online in advance, Rabiańska 9, +48 56 663 6617, www.muzeumpiernika.pl).

Old Toruń Gingerbread (Piernikarnia Starotoruńska), a block above the main square, is similar to the Gingerbread Museum, with costumed bakers and a hands-on demonstration, but feels less crowded and less commercial. English demonstrations are sporadic; call or email ahead to see if one is scheduled (32 zł, daily 10:00-18:00, Francziskańska 16, +48 56 621 1019, zwiedzajtorun@gmail.com).

Copernicus House (Dom Kopernika)

Filling a pair of gabled brick buildings between the main square and the river, this museum celebrates the hero of Toruń. As much about medieval Toruń as about the famous astronomer and sprawling over several floors, the exhibits loosely explain Nicolaus Copernicus' life and achievements, with several re-created Gothic rooms. However, it's not engaging and fails to do justice to this very important native son; ultimately, it's a big disappointment and skippable for casual visitors. If you do visit, I wouldn't bother paying the additional fee for the "4-D cinema"—while it provides a weighty introduction to astronomy and astrophysics, from the Big Bang to the plight of Pluto, it barely mentions Copernicus.

Cost and Hours: 22.50 zł, 4-D cinema-22.50 zł, Kopernika 15, +48 566 605 613.

Other Toruń Museums

Toruń is a popular destination for Polish families, and the TI loves to suggest attractions for those with more time. The **"Mill of Knowledge"** is a hands-on science museum designed for kids, with six floors of interactive exhibits. The **Travelers Museum** focuses on Toruń native Tony Halik, who hosted a travelogue TV show that was many Poles' gateway to the world. The **Toruń Fortress Museum,** just north of the Old Town, offers a glimpse inside the city's impressive red-brick fortifications. The city has two **open-air folk museums:** one just north of the Old Town, and a better one, called Olender, a few miles south of the river. And in the park ringing the Old Town, just a two-minute walk from the bus stop, is the **Fontanna Cosmopolis,** a dancing fountain that thrills kids with a little music-and-lights show each evening (generally runs May-Oct, get details at TI).

Sleeping in Toruń

$$ Hotel 1231 is trying to go high-class in this small town. It has 22 modern rooms filling a restored 13th-century mill at the bottom of town, next to the old toilet tower, with 20 additional sleek rooms in an annex. They also have a restaurant, bar, fitness center, sauna, "golf simulator," and other amenities—all run with a whiff of pretense (air-con, elevator, Przedzamcze 6, +48 56 619 0910, www.hotel1231.pl, recepcja@hotel1231.pl).

$ Hotel Czarna Róża ("Black Rose") feels fresh and modern, with 23 rooms on a back street. About half of the rooms are in the older building and cheaper, while the rest are pricier, as they have an elevator, air-con, and river views (Rabiańska 11, +48 56 19637, https://hotelczarnaroza.pl, hotel@hotelczarnaroza.pl).

$ Solaris Hotel, beautifully located just steps off the main square, has 23 conventional, cozy rooms tucked into a historic town house. It's quirky but central and friendly (air-con, elevator, Panny Marii 9, +48 56 471 3042, https://hotelsolaris.pl, recepcja@hotelsolaris.pl).

$ Hotel Karczma Spichrz ("Granary") has 24 rooms in a renovated old granary, and 20 more in a newer annex. Rustic and creaky, it has huge wooden beams around every corner (low ceilings, thin floors and walls can be noisy, air-con, elevator, a block off the main drag toward the river at Ulica Mostowa 1, +48 56 657 1140, www.spichrz.pl, hotel@spichrz.pl).

Eating in Toruń

Toruń is a great place to eat, with lots of tempting options—including several non-Polish, international choices. In this gingerbread-crazy town, look for various drinks, dishes, and desserts with that distinctive flavor (including gingerbread beer).

Old Town Market Square: The square surrounding the Old Town Hall is ringed with stay-awhile al fresco tables, any of which is a good choice for a scenic meal; most are open long hours daily. Favorites include **$$ Chleb i Wino** ("Bread and Wine"), which feels a bit more upscale, with Polish and Mediterranean dishes; and **$ Maneken,** the original outpost of a popular chain, which serves savory crêpe dishes in a convivial, trendy-feeling interior.

New Town Market Square: This out-of-the-way square is especially sleepy at night. There are some great choices here, including three Georgian restaurants. The **$ Georgian bakery** at #26 is handy for picking up a quick and tasty meal. Of the sit-down places, **$ Serce Gruzji** is charming, tasty, and family run (closed Mon, at #1, +48 787 383 665). A few steps away, **$$ Pod Modrym Fartuchem** ("Blue Apron Inn") fills a charming gabled house with cozy tables, ye olde ambience, and traditional food—continuing a legacy that dates back to 1489 (daily, at #8, +48 533 331 985).

Cajun: Luizjana, named for the US state, serves Cajun cooking that's better than it has any right to be, and offers a nice break from traditional Polish fare. They have two locations (both open daily for lunch and dinner); I'd opt for the one that fills the (covered) courtyard of the Artus Court, facing the Old Town Hall. This beautiful space is a lovely spot for a meal, and the New Orleans soundtrack is lively...even if it feels a bit out of place (Ulica Rynek Staromiejski 6, +48 883 117 711). The other location is on a more humdrum side street, with indoor and outdoor tables (Mostowa 10, http://restauracjaluizjana.pl).

Brewery: $ Jan Olbracht, filling a characteristic old brick building a short walk off the main drag, is a glitzy microbrewery with five beers on tap (you can order a sampler) plus pub grub (daily, Szczytna 15, +48 797 903 333, www.browar-olbracht.pl). Roughly across the street is a classic milk bar, Pod Małgośka.

Traditional Restaurants in Hotels: The recommended **$$ Spichrz** and **$$$ 1231** hotels both have traditional restaurants in historic spaces, with tempting menus of stick-to-your-ribs traditional fare. Spichrz is a bit ye olde and more casual; 1231 feels more upscale (see contact information earlier).

Hearty Pierogi: Pierogarnia Stary Młyn ("Old Mill"), on a side street near the history museum, has an over-the-top-rustic interior (and some outdoor tables) and a long menu of pierogi—boiled, baked, pan-fried—with various fillings (daily, Łazienna 28, +48 566 210 309). This is a small chain, with a few other locations as well.

Toruń Connections

Toruń is a natural stopover on the way between Warsaw and Gdańsk. The connection to Warsaw or Gdańsk is quick and easy; to reach Malbork, you'll usually need to change.

From Toruń by Train to: Warsaw (every 2 hours direct, 3 hours on express IC train), **Gdańsk** (4/day direct, 2.5 hours; additional options with a change in Bydgoszcz or Iława, 3 hours), **Malbork** (about every 2 hours, 2.5 hours, change in Iława), **Kraków** (1/day direct, 6.5 hours; more options with a change in Warsaw: 7/day, 6 hours), **Berlin** (4/day, 6 hours, change in Poznań).

By Bus: If heading to **Gdańsk,** consider buses operated by Flixbus, which are cheaper than the train (www.flixbus.com).

HUNGARY

Magyarország

HUNGARY

Magyarország

Hungary is an island of Asian-descended Magyars in a sea of Slavs. Even though the Hungarians have thoroughly integrated with their Slavic and German neighbors in the millennium-plus since they arrived, there's still something about the place that's distinctly Magyar (MUD-jar). Here in quirky, idiosyncratic Hungary, everything's a little different from the rest of Europe in terms of history, language, culture, customs, and cuisine—but it's hard to put your finger on exactly how.

Just a century ago, this country controlled half of one of Europe's grandest realms: the Austro-Hungarian Empire. Today, perhaps clinging to their former greatness, many Hungarians remain old-fashioned and nostalgic. With their dusty museums and bushy moustaches, they love to remember the good old days. Buildings all over the country are marked with plaques boasting *MŰEMLÉK* ("historical monument").

Thanks to this focus on tradition, the Hungarians you'll encounter are generally polite, formal, and professional. Hungarians have class. Everything here is done with a proud flourish. When a server comes to your table in a restaurant, they'll say, *"Tessék parancsolni"*—literally, "Please command, sir." The standard greeting, *"Jó napot kívánok,"* means, "I wish you a good day." Women sometimes hear the even more formal greeting, *"Kezét csókolom"*—"I kiss your hand." And when your train or bus makes a stop, you won't be alerted by a mindless, blaring beep but instead by peppy music.

Hungarians are also orderly and tidy...in their own sometimes unexpected ways. Yes, Hungary has its share of litter, graffiti, and crumbling buildings, but you'll find great reason within the chaos. The Hungarian railroad has a long list of discounted fares—for seniors, kids, dogs...and monkeys. (It could happen.) My favorite town name in Hungary: Hatvan. This means "Sixty" in Hungarian...and it's exactly 60 kilometers from Budapest. You can't argue with that logic.

Hungary's tradition of orderly, left-brained thinking has produced titans of science, technology, and industry: Edward Teller ("father of the hydrogen bomb"), John von Neumann (computer

science pioneer), George Soros (billionaire investor), and Ernő Rubik (creator of the famous cube). Hungarians' enjoyment of a mind-bending puzzle is also evident in their fascination with chess, which is played in cafés, parks, and baths. Locals joke that Hungarians are so clever that they can enter a revolving door behind you and exit in front of you.

Like their Viennese neighbors, Hungarians appreciate the good life. Budapesters cultivate a genteel café culture, whiling away afternoons at coffeehouses while nursing a drink and dessert. And they revere classical music, having produced many great composers (including Béla Bartók, Zoltán Kodály, and Franz Liszt).

While one in five Hungarians lives in Budapest, the countryside plays an important role in the country's economy—this has always been a highly agricultural region. The sprawling Great Hungarian Plain (Puszta) that makes up a vast swath of Hungary is the country's breadbasket. You'll pass through fields of wheat and corn, but the grains are secondary to Hungarians' (and tourists') true love: wine. Hungarian winemaking standards plummeted under the communists, but many vintner families have reclaimed their land, resumed their traditional methods, and are making wines worthy of pride once more. (For details, see the "Hungarian Wines" sidebar, later.)

Somehow Hungary, at the crossroads of Europe, has managed to become cosmopolitan while remaining perfectly Hungarian. The Hungarians—like Hungary itself—are a cross-section of Central European cultures: Magyars, Germans, Czechs, Slovaks, Poles, Serbs, Jews, Ottomans, Romanians, Roma (Gypsies), and

HUNGARY

Hungary Almanac

Official Name: Magyarország (Hungary).

Size: 36,000 square miles, similar to Indiana or Maine. Population 10 million.

Geography: Hungary sits in the Carpathian Basin, bound by the Carpathian Mountains (in the north) and the Dinaric Mountains (in the south). Though it's surrounded by mountains, Hungary itself is relatively flat, with some gently rolling hills. The Great Hungarian Plain—beginning on the east bank of the Danube in Budapest—stretches all the way to Asia. Hungary's two main rivers—the Danube and Tisza—run north-south through the country, neatly dividing it into three regions.

Latitude and Longitude: 47°N and 20°E; similar latitude to Seattle, Paris, and Vienna.

Biggest Cities: Budapest (the capital, nearly 2 million), Debrecen (in the east, 205,000), and Miskolc (in the north, 165,000).

Economy: The gross domestic product is $325 billion, with a per capita GDP of about $33,000. Grains, metals, machinery, and automobiles are major exports, and about one-quarter of trade is with Germany. Inflation has been a problem in recent years, with relatively large fluctuations in the exchange rate.

Currency: 350 forints (Ft, or HUF) = about $1.

Government: The single-house National Assembly (199 seats) is the only ruling branch directly elected by popular vote. The legislators in turn select the figurehead president (currently Katalin Novák, the first woman to hold that office) and the ruling prime minister (Viktor Orbán); both belong to the far right, nativist Fidesz party.

Flag: Three horizontal bands, top to bottom: red (representing strength), white (faithfulness), and green (hope). It often includes the Hungarian coat of arms: horizontal red-and-white stripes (on the left); the patriarchal, or double-barred, cross (on the right); and the Hungarian crown (on top).

The Average János: The typical Hungarian eats a pound of lard a week (they cook with it). The average family has three members and spends almost three-fourths of its income on housing. According to a condom-company survey, the average Hungarian has sex 131 times a year (behind only France and Greece), making them Europe's third-greatest liars.

---

many others. Still, no matter how many generations removed they are from Magyar stock, there's something different about Hungarians. It's a unique European culture that's a pure joy to discover.

HELPFUL HINTS

First Name Last: Hungarians list a person's family name first, and the given name is last—just as in many other Eastern cultures (think of Kim Jong-un). So the composer known as "Franz Liszt" in German is "Liszt Ferenc" in his homeland.

Toll Sticker: Driving on Hungarian expressways requires a toll sticker. Ask about this when you rent your car (if it's not already included, you'll have to buy one). For details, see "Tolls" on page 1114.

HUNGARIAN HISTORY

The Hungarian story—essentially the tale of a people finding their home—is as epic as any in Europe. Over the course of a millennium, a troublesome nomadic tribe that was the scourge of Europe gradually assimilated with its neighbors and—through a combination of tenacity and diplomacy—found itself controlling a vast swath of Central Europe.

Locals toss around the names of great figures such as Kossuth, Széchenyi, and Nagy as if they're talking about old friends. Take this crash course so you can keep up.

The story begins long, long ago and far, far away...

Welcome to Europe

The land we call Hungary has long been considered the place—culturally and geographically—where the West (Europe) meets the East (Asia). The Roman province of Pannonia once extended to the final foothills of the Alps that constitute the Buda Hills, on the west side of the Danube. Across the river, Rome ended and the barbarian wilds began. From here, the Great Hungarian Plain stretches in a long, flat expanse all the way to Asia—hemmed in to the north by the Carpathian Mountains. (Geologists consider this prairie-like plain to be the westernmost steppe in Europe—resembling the terrain that covers much of Central Asia.) After Rome collapsed and Europe fell into the Dark Ages, Hungary became the territory of Celts, Vandals, Huns, and Avars...until some out-of-towners moved into the neighborhood.

The seven nomadic Magyar tribes, led by the mighty Árpád (and, according to legend, guided by the mythical Turul bird),

thundered into the Carpathian Basin in AD 896. But after their long and winding westward odyssey, the Great Hungarian Plain felt comfortingly like home to the Magyars—reminiscent of the Asian steppes of their ancestors.

The Magyars would camp out in today's Hungary in the win-

HUNGARY

ters, and in the summers, they'd go on raids throughout Europe. They were notorious as incredibly swift horsemen whose use of stirrups allowed them to easily outmaneuver foes and victims. From Italy, France, Germany's Rhine, and the Spanish Pyrenees, all the way to Constantinople (modern-day Istanbul)—the Magyars had the run of the Continent.

For half a century, the Magyars ranked with the Vikings as the most feared people in Europe. To Europeans, this must have struck a chord of queasy familiarity: a mysterious and dangerous eastern tribe running roughshod over Europe, speaking a gibberish language, and employing strange, terrifying, relentless battle techniques. No wonder they called the new arrivals "Hun-garians."

Planted in the center of Europe, the Magyars effectively drove a wedge in the middle of the sprawling Slavic populations of the Great Moravian Kingdom (basically today's "Central Europe"). The Slavs were split into north and south—a division that persists today: Czechs, Slovaks, and Poles to the north; and Croats, Slovenes, Serbs, Bosniaks, and Bulgarians to the south. (You can still hear the division caused by the Magyars in the language: While Czechs and Russians call a castle *hrad*, Croats and Serbs call it *grad*.)

After decades of terrorizing Europe, the Magyars were finally defeated by a German and Czech army at the Battle of Augsburg in 955. Géza, Grand Prince of the Hungarians—realizing that if they were to survive, his people had to put down roots and get along with their neighbors—made a fateful decision that would forever shape Hungary's future: He adopted Christianity; baptized his son, Vajk; and married him to a Bavarian princess at a young age.

On Christmas Day in the year 1000, Vajk changed his name to István (Stephen) and was symbolically crowned by the pope. At

István's request, a Venetian missionary, Gerardo di Sagredo, came to Buda to help convert the Hungarians. But he was martyred for his efforts, becoming known to Hungarians as St. Gellért. The domestication of the nomadic Magyars was difficult—due largely to the resistance of István's uncles—but was ultimately successful. Hungary became a legitimate Christian kingdom, welcomed by its neighbors. Under kings such as László I, Kálmán "the Book Lover," and András II, Hungary entered a period of prosperity. Medieval Hungary ruled a vast empire—including large parts of today's Slovakia, Romania (Transylvania), Serbia (Vojvodina), and Croatia.

The Tatars, the Ottomans, and Other Outsiders (AD 1000-1686)

One of Hungary's earliest challenges came at the hands of fellow invaders from Central Asia. Through the first half of the 13th century, the Tatars—initially led by Genghis Khan—swept into Eastern and Central Europe from Mongolia. In the summer of 1241, Genghis Khan's son and successor, Ögedei Khan, broke into Hungarian territory. The Tatars sacked and plundered Hungarian towns, laying waste to the kingdom. It was only Ögedei Khan's death in early 1242—and the ensuing dispute about succession—that saved the Hungarians, as Tatar armies rushed home and the Mongolian Empire contracted. The Hungarian king, Béla IV, was left to rebuild his ruined kingdom—creating some of the first stout hilltop castles that still line the Danube.

Each of Béla's successors left his own mark on Hungary, as the Magyar kingdom flourished. When the original Árpád dynasty died out in 1301, they imported French kings (from the Naples-based Anjou, or Angevin, dynasty) to continue building their young realm. King Károly Róbert (Charles Robert) won over the Magyars, and his son Nagy Lajos (Louis the Great) expanded Hungarian holdings.

This was a period of flux for all of Central Europe, as the nearby Czech and Polish kingdoms also saw their long-standing dynasties expire. For a time, royal intermarriages juggled the crowns of the region between various ruling families. Most notably, for 50 years (1387-1437) Hungary was ruled by Holy Roman Emperor Sigismund of Luxembourg, whose holdings also included the Czech lands, parts of Italy, much of Croatia, and more.

For more than 150 years, Hungary did not have a Hungarian-blooded king. This changed in the late 15th century, when a shortage of foreign kings led the enlightened King Mátyás (Matthias) Corvinus to ascend to the throne. The son of popular military hero János Hunyadi, King Matthias fostered the arts, sparked a mini-Renaissance, and successfully balanced foreign threats to Hungarian sovereignty (the Habsburgs to the

north and west, and the Ottomans to the south and east). Under Matthias, Hungarian culture and political power reached a peak.

But even before the reign of "good king Mátyás," the Ottomans (from today's Turkey) had already begun slicing their way through the Balkan Peninsula toward Central Europe. In 1526, the Ottomans entered Hungary when Sultan Süleyman the Magnificent killed Hungary's King Lajos II at the Battle of Mohács. By 1541, they took Buda. The Ottomans would dominate Hungarian life (and history) until the 1680s—nearly a century and a half.

The Ottoman invasion divided Hungary into thirds: Ottoman-occupied "Lower Hungary" (more or less today's Hungary); rump "Upper Hungary" (basically today's Slovakia), with its capital at Bratislava (which they called "Pozsony"); and the loosely independent territories of Transylvania, ruled by Hungarian dukes. During this era, the Ottomans built some of the thermal baths that you'll still find throughout Hungary.

Ottoman-occupied Hungary became severely depopulated, and many of its towns and cities fell into ruins. While it was advantageous for a Hungarian subject to adopt Islam (for lower taxes and other privileges), the Ottomans rarely forced conversions—unlike the arguably more oppressive Catholics who controlled other parts of Europe at the time. Ottoman rule meant that Hungary took a different course than other parts of Europe during this time. Hungarians fully enjoyed the Renaissance but missed out on other major European historical events—from the Age of Discovery and Age of Reason to the devastating Catholic-versus-Protestant wars that plagued much of the rest of Europe.

Crippled by the Ottomans and lacking power and options, desperate Hungarian nobles offered their crown to the Austrian Habsburg Empire in exchange for salvation from the invasion. The Habsburgs instead used Hungary as a kind of buffer zone between the Ottoman advance and Vienna. And that was only the beginning of a very troubled relationship between the Hungarians and the Austrians.

Habsburg Rule, Hungarian National Revival, and Revolution (1686-1867)

In the late 17th century, the Habsburg army, starting from Vienna, began a sustained campaign to push the Ottomans out of Hungary in about 15 years. They finally wrested Buda and Pest from the Ottomans in 1686. The Habsburgs repopulated the cities with Germans, while Magyars reclaimed the countryside.

The Habsburgs governed the country as an outpost of Austria. The Hungarians—who'd had enough of foreign rule—fought them tooth and nail. Countless streets, squares, and buildings throughout the country are named for the "big three" Hungarian patriots who resisted the Habsburgs during this time: Ferenc Rákóczi (who led the unsuccessful War of Independence in 1703-1711), István Széchenyi (a wealthy count who funded grand structures to give his Magyar countrymen something to take pride in), and Lajos Kossuth (who led the Revolution of 1848).

The early 19th century saw a thawing of Habsburg oppression. Here as throughout Europe, "backward" country traditions began to trickle into the cities, gaining more respect and prominence. It was during this time of reforms that Hungarian (rather than German) became the official language. It also coincided with a Romantic Age of poets and writers (such as Mihály Vörösmarty and Sándor Petőfi) who began using Hungarian to create literature for the first time. By around 1825, the Hungarian National Revival was underway, as the people began to embrace the culture and traditions of their Magyar ancestors. Like people across Europe—from Ireland to Italy, and from Prague to Scandinavia—the Hungarians were rediscovering what made them unique.

In March of 1848, a wave of Enlightenment-fueled nationalism that began in Paris ignited a revolutionary spirit in cities such as Vienna, Milan...and Budapest. On March 15, the Revolution of 1848 began with Petőfi reading a rabble-rousing poem on the steps of the National Museum in Pest.

In the spring of 1849, the Hungarians mounted a bloody but successful offensive to take over a wide swath of territory, including Buda and Pest. But in June, Franz Josef enlisted the aid of his fellow divine monarch, the Russian czar, who did not want the Magyars to provide an example for his own independence-minded subjects. Some 200,000 Russian reinforcements flooded into Hungary, crushing the revolution by August. After the final battle, the Habsburgs executed 13 Hungarian generals, then celebrated by clinking mugs of beer. Until very recently, clinking beer mugs was considered, by traditional Hungarians, just bad style.

For a while, the Habsburgs cracked down on their unruly Hungarian subjects. After a critical military loss to Bismarck's Prussia in 1866, Austria understood that it couldn't control its rebellious Slavic holdings all by itself.

And so, just 18 years after crushing the Hungarians in a war, the Habsburgs handed them the reins. With the Compromise *(Ausgleich)* of 1867, Austria granted Budapest the authority over the eastern half of their lands, creating the so-called Dual Monarchy of the Austro-Hungarian Empire. Hungary was granted their much-prized "home rule," where most matters were administered from Budapest rather than Vienna. The Habsburg emperor, Franz Josef, agreed to a unique "king and emperor" *(König und Kaiser)* arrangement, where he was emperor of Austria but only king of

Hungary. In 1867, he was crowned Hungarian king in both Buda (at Matthias Church) and Pest (on today's March 15 Square). The insignia "K+K" *(König und Kaiser)*—which you'll still see everywhere—evokes these grand days.

Budapest's Golden Age (1867-1918)

The *Ausgleich* marked a turning point for the Hungarians, who once again governed their traditional holdings: large parts of today's Slovakia, Serbia, and Transylvania, and smaller parts of today's Croatia, Slovenia, Ukraine, and Austria. To better administer their sprawling realm, in 1873, the cities of Buda, Pest, and Óbuda merged into one mega-metropolis: Budapest.

Serendipitously, Budapest's new prominence coincided with the 1,000th anniversary of the Hungarians' ancestors, the Magyars, arriving in Europe. The year 1896 saw an over-the-top millennial celebration for which many of today's greatest structures were created.

No European city grew faster in the second half of the 19th century than Budapest; in the last quarter of that century alone, Budapest doubled in size, building on the foundation laid by Széchenyi and other patriots. By 1900, the city was larger than Rome, Madrid, or Amsterdam. But before long, the Hungarians began to make the same mistakes the Habsburgs had—trampling on the rights of their minorities and enforcing a policy of "Magyarization" that compelled subjects from all ethnic backgrounds to adopt the Hungarian language and culture. Soon the golden age came crashing to an end, and Hungary plunged into its darkest period.

The Crisis of Trianon (1918-1939)

World War I marked the end of the age of divine monarchs, as the Romanovs of Russia, the Ottomans of Asia Minor, and the Habsburgs of Austria-Hungary saw their empires break apart. Hungary, which had been riding the Habsburgs' coattails for the past half-century, now paid the price.

As retribution for their role on the losing side of World War I, the 1920 Treaty of Trianon (named for the palace on the grounds of Versailles where it was signed) reassigned two-thirds of Hungary's former territory and half of its population to Romania, Ukraine, Czechoslovakia, and Yugoslavia.

The Treaty of Trianon had a huge impact on Hungarian history—and on the Hungarian psyche. Not unlike the overnight construction of the Berlin Wall, towns along the new Hungarian borders were suddenly divided down the middle. Many Hungarians found themselves unable to visit relatives or commute to jobs that were in the same country the day before. This sent hundreds of

Pre-Trianon Hungary

thousands of Hungarian refugees—now "foreigners" in their own towns—into Budapest, sparking a bittersweet boom in the capital.

To this day, the Treaty of Trianon is regarded as one of the greatest tragedies of Hungarian history. Like the Basques and the Serbs, the Hungarians feel separated from each other by circumstances outside their control. Today, more than two million ethnic Hungarians live outside Hungary (mostly in Romania)—and many Hungarians believe that these lands should still belong to the Magyars. The sizeable Magyar minorities in neighboring countries have often been mistreated—particularly in Romania (under Ceaușescu), Yugoslavia (under Milošević), and Slovakia (under Mečiar). You'll see maps, posters, and bumper stickers with the distinctive shape of a much larger, pre-WWI Hungary. (More recently, Hungary's current leadership has learned that stoking resentment about Trianon can help further its political agenda.)

After Trianon, the newly shrunken Kingdom of Hungary had to reinvent itself. The Hungarian crown sat unworn in the Royal Palace, as if waiting for someone worthy to claim it. The WWI hero Admiral Miklós Horthy had won many battles with the Austro-Hungarian navy. Though the new Hungary had no sea and no navy, Horthy retained his rank and ruled the country as a regent. A popular joke points out that during this time, Hungary was a "kingdom without a king" and a landlocked country ruled by a sea admiral. This sense of compounded deficiency pretty much sums up the morose attitude Hungarians have about those gloomy post-Trianon days.

A mounting financial crisis and lingering resentment about the strict post-WWI reparations made Hungary fertile ground for some bold new fascist ideas.

World War II and the Arrow Cross
(1939-1945)

As Adolf Hitler rose to power in Germany, some other countries that had felt mistreated in the aftermath of World War I—including Hungary—saw Nazi Germany as a vehicle to greater independence. Admiral Horthy joined forces with the Nazis with the hope that they might help Hungary regain the crippling territorial losses of Trianon. In 1941, Hungary (somewhat reluctantly) declared war on the Soviet Union in June—and against the US and Britain in December.

Being an ally to the Nazis, rather than an occupied state, also allowed Hungary a certain degree of self-determination through the war. And, although Hungary had its own set of anti-Semitic laws and was complicit in the mass murder of Jews lacking citizenship and living within their borders, the majority of its sizeable Jewish population was spared from immediate deportation to Nazi concentration camps. Winning back chunks of Slovakia, Transylvania, and Croatia in the early days of World War II also bolstered Hungarian acceptance of the Nazi alliance.

As Nazism took hold in Germany, Hungary's homegrown fascist movement—spearheaded by the Arrow Cross Party (Nyilaskeresztes Párt)—gained popularity as well. As Germany increased its demands for Hungarian soldiers and food, Admiral Horthy resisted...until Hitler's patience wore thin. In March 1944, the Nazis invaded and installed the Arrow Cross in power. The Arrow Cross made up for lost time, immediately beginning a savage campaign to execute Hungary's Jews—not only sending them to death camps but also butchering them in the streets. As the end of the war neared, Hungarian Nazi collaborators resorted to desperate measures, such as lining up Jews along the Danube and shooting them into the river. Hungary lost nearly 600,000 Jews to the Holocaust.

The Soviet Army eventually "liberated" Hungary, but at the expense of Budapest: A months-long siege, from Christmas 1944 to mid-February 1945, reduced the proud city to rubble. One out of every ten Hungarian citizens perished in the war.

Communism...with a Pinch of Paprika (1945-1989)

After World War II, Hungary was gradually compelled to adopt Moscow's system of government. The Soviet-puppet hardliner premier, Mátyás Rákosi, ruled Hungary with an iron fist. Everyday people were terrorized by the KGB-style secret police (called the ÁVO, later ÁVH) and intimidated into accepting the new regime. Non-Hungarians were deported, potential and actual dissidents disappeared into the horrifying gulag system of Siberia (and similar forced-work camps in Hungary), food shortages were epidemic, people were compelled to spy on their friends and families, and countless lives were ruined. Coming on the heels of Trianon and two devastating world wars, communist rule was a blow that Hungary is still recovering from.

Beginning on October 23, 1956, the Hungarians courageously staged a monumental uprising, led by Communist Party reformer Imre Nagy. Initially, it appeared that one of the cells on the Soviet Bloc might win itself the right to semiautonomy. But Moscow couldn't let that happen. In a Tiananmen Square-style crackdown, the Soviets sent in tanks to brutally put down the uprising and occupy the city. When the dust settled, 2,500 Hungarians were dead and 200,000 fled to the West. (If you know any Hungarian Americans, their families more than likely fled in 1956.) Nagy was arrested, given a sham trial, and executed in 1958. For more on these events, see the "1956" sidebar on page 590.

The Hungarians were devastated. They were frustrated that the Suez Canal crisis distracted the world from their uprising. Many felt betrayed that the US—which spoke so boldly against the Soviet Union—did not offer them military support (contrary to the promises of the American-operated Radio Free Europe). While the US and its Western allies understandably did not want to turn the Cold War hot, the Hungarians felt abandoned.

Weeks after the uprising came the now-legendary "Blood in the Water" match at the Melbourne Olympics. Soviet satellite states were often ordered to "throw" matches to allow the USSR's athletes to prevail. On December 6, 1956, Moscow issued such a decree to the Hungarian men's water polo team in their semifinal against the Soviet Union. The Hungarians refused and played their hearts out. The game turned violent, and in one indelible image, a Hungarian athlete emerged from the pool with blood pouring from a gash above his right eye. The Hungarians won 4-0 and went on to take the gold.

After the uprising, the USSR installed János Kádár—a colleague of Nagy's who was loyal to Moscow—to lead Hungary. For a few years, things were bleak as the secret police ratcheted up their efforts against potential dissidents. But in the 1960s, Kádár's reformist tendencies began to cautiously emerge. Seeking to gain the support of his subjects (and avoid further uprisings), Kádár adopted the optimistic motto, "If you are not against us, you are with us." While still mostly cooperating with Moscow, Kádár gradually allowed the people of Hungary more freedom than citizens of neighboring countries had—a system dubbed "goulash communism."

The "New Economic Mechanism" of 1968 partly opened Hungary to foreign trade. People from other Warsaw Pact countries—Czechs, Slovaks, and Poles—flocked to Budapest's Váci Utca to experience "Western evils" unavailable to them back home, such as Adidas sneakers and Big Macs. People half-joked that Hungary was the happiest barrack in the communist camp.

In the late 1980s, the Eastern Bloc began to thaw. And Hungary—which was always skeptical of the Soviets—was one of the first satellite states that implemented real change. In February 1989, the Hungarian communist parliament, with little fanfare, essentially voted to put an expiration date on their own regime. There were three benchmarks in that fateful year: May 2, when Hungary was the first Soviet Bloc country to effectively open its borders to the West (by removing its border fence with Austria); June 16, when communist reformer Imre Nagy and his comrades were given a proper, ceremonial reburial on Heroes' Square; and August 19, when, in the first tentative steps toward the reunification of Europe, Hungarians and Austrians came together in a field near the town of Sopron for the so-called "Pan-European Picnic." (Some 900 East Germans seized this opportunity to make a run for the border...and slipped into the West when Hungarian border guards refused orders to shoot defectors.) On October 23—the anniversary of the 1956 Uprising—the democratic Republic of Hungary triumphantly replaced the People's Republic of Hungary.

Hungary Today: Capitalism, EU Membership, and Orbán (1989-Present)

The transition from communism to capitalism was not easy. While many Hungarians were eager for the freedom to travel and pursue the interests that democracy allowed them, many others struggled to cope with the sudden reduction of government-provided services.

In 2004, Hungary joined the European Union. And since then, it seems Hungary has often been in the international news.

The Hungarian Socialist Party (MSzP), which took control of parliament in 2002, stubbornly maintained and even extended some social programs, despite worries that mounting public debt would bankrupt the country.

As a result, rampant inflation continued to wrack the country. In late 2008, with Prime Minister Ferenc Gyurcsány warning of "state bankruptcy"

and a currency collapse, Hungary received a $25 billion bailout package from the EU, International Monetary Fund, and World Bank. Gyurcsány resigned in early 2009, acknowledging that he was getting in the way of Hungary's economic recovery.

Viktor Orbán, of the nationalistic, right-wing Fidesz Party, became prime minister in May 2010. Fidesz stands for traditional Christian and Hungarian values, economic interventionism, and severe skepticism about immigration and European Union membership.

Orbán seized on his two-thirds coalition majority to adopt a new, Fidesz-favorable constitution that stripped away checks and balances and entrenched party leaders in institutions that had previously been considered apolitical. Almost immediately, international observers—including the EU and US—grew concerned.

Fidesz has taken other actions that many consider troubling markers of illiberalism and a threat to open society. In early 2011, they created a new FCC-like media authority with broad latitude for suppressing material that it considers inappropriate. In 2020, Fidesz ended legal recognition of transgender people, and in 2021, they enacted "anti-pedophile" laws designed to discriminate against LGBTQ+ citizens. And over time, they've slowly nationalized the school system—ensuring that the same Fidesz-approved textbooks are now used in every school in Hungary.

Reinterpreting Hungarian history in a way that flatters Hungary (while leaving out complicated or uncomfortable details) is another hallmark of Fidesz. With a "Make Hungary Great Again" attitude, they've rehabilitated some figures (such as Miklós Horthy, who forged an alliance with Hitler's Nazi Germany), while brushing aside other, less Fidesz-friendly figures (such as the communist reformer Imre Nagy, the hero of the 1956 Uprising). Fidesz has renamed more than two dozen streets, squares, and other features of Budapest, and they've removed or replaced several old monuments—including a beloved statue of Nagy that once stood proudly near the Parliament.

At the same time, Fidesz has been proactive about funneling European Union funds into public-works projects, and Budapest has made remarkable progress in renovating formerly dreary streets and squares.

Orbán outrages younger, EU-supporting, highly educated Hungarians who believe in an open society and liberal democracy. However, he has hit upon a successful formula for staying in power without their votes: He was decisively reelected in 2018 and again in 2022. He's sometimes compared to his fellow nativist and traditionalist, Donald Trump. But Orbán possesses greater intelligence and self-control, and a savvy ability to suspend his own ego when it serves his political ends—making him even more challenging for opponents to dislodge.

Now essentially guaranteed to remain in power at least through 2026, Viktor Orbán stands as the poster boy of a pan-national movement of traditionalism and nativism. As he pulls Hungary farther from the tenets of liberal democracy, an open society, and the stated aims and values of the European Union, it remains to be seen whether Hungary's political pendulum will swing back toward the center.

HUNGARIAN CUISINE

Hungarian cuisine is the undisputed best in Central Europe. It delicately blends Magyar peasant cooking (with rich spices), refined by the elegance of French preparation, with a delightful smattering of flavors from the vast, multiethnic Austro-Hungarian Empire (including Germanic, Balkan, Jewish, and Carpathian). Everything is heavily seasoned: with paprika, tomatoes, and peppers of every shape, color, size, and flavor.

An *étterem* ("eatery") is a nice sit-down restaurant, while a *vendéglő* is usually more casual. A *bisztró* is a simple eatery with a concise but well-executed menu. A *söröző* ("beer place") is a pub that sells beer and pub grub. A *kávéház* ("coffeehouse") is where Hungarians gather to meet friends, get a caffeine fix...and sometimes to have a meal. Other cafés serve only light food, or sometimes only desserts. But if you want a wide choice of cakes, look for a *cukrászda* (pastry shop—*cukor* means "sugar").

When foreigners think of Hungarian cuisine, what comes to mind is goulash. But tourists may find "real Hungarian goulash" isn't the thick stew that they were expecting. The word "goulash" comes from the Hungarian *gulyás leves*, or "shepherd's soup"—a tasty, rustic, nourishing dish originally eaten by cowboys and shepherds on the Great Hungarian Plain. Here in its homeland, it's a clear, spicy broth with chunks of meat, potatoes, and other vegetables. Elsewhere (such as in neighboring Germanic and Slavic countries), the word "goulash" does describe a thick stew. The hearty Hungarian stew called *pörkölt* is probably closer to what most people think of as goulash.

Aside from the obligatory *gulyás*, make a point of trying another unusual Hungarian specialty: cold fruit soup *(hideg gyümölcs leves)*. This sweet, cream-based treat—generally eaten before the meal, even though it tastes more like a dessert—is usually made with *meggy* (sour cherries), but you'll also see versions with *alma* (apples), *körte* (pears), and other fruits. It may be harder to find outside of summer.

Other Hungarian soups *(levesek)* include *bableves* (bean soup), *zöldségleves* (vegetable soup), *gombaleves* (mushroom soup), *halászlé* (fish broth with paprika), and *húsleves* (meat or chicken soup).

Hungarians adore all kinds of meat. *Hús* or *marhahús* is beef, *csirke* is chicken, *borjú* is veal, *kacsa* is duck, *liba* is goose, *sertés* is

pork, *sonka* is ham, *kolbász* is sausage, *szelet* is schnitzel (*Bécsi szelet* means Wiener schnitzel)—and the list goes on. One trendy ingredient you'll see on menus is *mangalica*. This uniquely Hungarian, free-range woolly pig (basically a domesticated boar) is high in unsaturated fat. *Libamáj* is goose liver, which is a

local delicacy (anything prepared "Budapest style" is topped with goose liver). Lard is used extensively in cooking, making Hungarian cuisine very rich and filling.

Meat is often covered with delicious sauces or garnishes, from rich cream sauces to spicy pastes to fruit jam. For classic Hungarian flavors, you can't beat chicken or veal *paprikás* (described in the "Paprika Primer" sidebar).

Vegetarians have a tricky time in traditional Hungarian restaurants, many of which offer only a plate of deep-fried vegetables. A traditional Hungarian "salad" is composed mostly or entirely of pickled vegetables (cucumbers, cabbage, peppers, and others); even many modern restaurants haven't quite figured out how to do a good, healthy, leafy salad. Fortunately, many modern, trendy eateries in the capital offer excellent vegetarian options.

Starches *(köretek)* can include *nokedli* (small, boiled "drop noodles"), *galuska* (noodles), *burgonya* (potatoes), *sült krumpli* (French fries), *krokett* (croquettes), or *rizs* (rice). *Kenyér* (bread) often comes with the meal. A popular snack—especially to accompany a wine tasting—is a *pogácsa,* a little ball of cheesy fried dough.

Sometimes your main dish will come with steamed, grilled, or deep-fried vegetables. A common side dish is *káposzta* (cabbage, often prepared like sauerkraut). You may also see *töltött káposzta* (cabbage stuffed with meat) or *töltött paprika* (stuffed peppers). *Lecsó* (LEH-choh) is the Hungarian answer to ratatouille: a richly flavorful stew of tomatoes, peppers, and other vegetables.

Thin, crêpe-like pancakes *(palacsinta)* are usually a starter, but sometimes served as a main dish. A delicious traditional dish is *Hortobágyi palacsinta* (Hortobágy pancakes). This is a savory crêpe

Paprika Primer

The quintessential ingredient in Hungarian cuisine is paprika. In Hungarian, the word *paprika* can mean both peppers (red or green) and the spice that's made from them. Peppers can be stewed, stuffed, sautéed, baked, grilled, or pickled. For seasoning, red shakers of dried paprika join the salt and pepper on tables.

There are more than 40 varieties of paprika spice, with two main types: hot (*csípős* or *erős*) and sweet (*édesnemes* or simply *édes;* sometimes also called *csemege*—"delicate"). Hungarians typically cook with sweet paprika to add flavor and color. Then, at the table, they put out hot paprika so each diner can adjust the heat to his or her preferred taste.

On menus, anything cooked *paprikás* (PAW-pree-kash) comes smothered in a spicy red paprika gravy, thickened with sour cream. Most often you'll see this option with *csirke* (chicken) or *borjú* (veal), and it's generally served with dumpling-like boiled egg noodles called *nok-edli*. This dish is *the* Hungarian staple.

To add even more kick to your food, ask for a jar of the bright-red, sambal-like paste called *Erős Pista* (EH-rewsh PEESH-taw). Literally "Spicy Steve," this Hungarian answer to Tabasco is best used sparingly. Or try *Édes Anna* (AY-desh AW-naw, "Sweet Anna"), a variation that's more sweet than spicy. You'll also see tubes of *Gulyáskrém* (a bright-orange, sweet-but-not-hot paste for jazzing up soups) and *Piros Arany* ("Red Gold," a deep-red, intensely flavorful, spicy paste). These—along with paprika—make a fun and tasty souvenir.

wrapped around a tasty meat filling and drenched with creamy paprika sauce.

Pancakes also appear as desserts, stuffed and/or covered with fruit, jam, and other toppings. Most famous is the *Gundel palacsinta,* stuffed with walnuts and raisins in a rum sauce, topped with chocolate sauce, and flambéed.

Cakes and pastries are a big deal in Hungary. Try the *Dobos torta* (a many-layered chocolate-and-vanilla cream cake), *flódni* (layer cake of Jewish origin, with apples, walnuts, and poppy seeds), *Rákóczi turós* (sweet cheese curd cake with jam), *somlói galuska* (rum-soaked sponge cake), *krémes* (delicate custard wafer cake), anything with *gesztenye* (chestnuts), and *rétes* (strudel with various fillings, including *túrós,* curds). And many *cukrászda* also serve *fa-*

gylalt (ice cream, *fagyi* for short), sold by the *gomboc* (ball).

When the server comes to take your order, they might say *"Tessék"* (TEHSH-shayk), or maybe the more formal *"Tessék parancsolni"* (TEHSH-shayk PAW-rawn-chohl-nee)— "Please command, sir." When they bring the food, they will probably say, *"Jó étvágyat!"* (yoh AYT-vah-yawt)—"Bon appétit." When you're ready for the bill, you can simply say, *"Fizetek"* (FEE-zeh-tehk)—"I'll pay."

Drinks

Kávé (KAH-vay) and *tea* (TEH-aw) are coffee and tea. (Confusingly, *tej* is not tea—it's milk.) As for water (*víz*, pronounced "veez"), it comes as *szódavíz* (soda water, sometimes just carbonated tap water) or *ásványvíz* (spring water, more expensive).

Hungary is first and foremost a wine country. For the complete rundown on Hungarian wines, see the sidebar.

Hungary isn't particularly well known for its beer (*sör*, pronounced "shewr"), but Dreher and Borsodi are two of the better brands. *Világos* is lager; if you prefer something darker, look for *barna* (brown). I've recommended some places to try Hungarian microbrews in Budapest (see "Entertainment in Budapest" in the Budapest chapter) and in Eger.

Hungary is almost as proud of its spirits as its wines. The local firewater, *pálinka*, is a powerful schnapps made from various fruits (most often plum, *szilva;* or apricots, *barack*). Also look for the pear-flavored Vilmos brandy.

Unicum is a unique and beloved Hungarian bitter liquor made of 40 different herbs and aged in oak casks. Look for the round bottle with the red cross on the label. The flavor is powerfully unforgettable—like Jägermeister, but harsher. Unicum started out as a medicine and remains a popular digestif for easing an upset stomach. Purists claim it's better to drink it at room temperature, but novices find it easier to slug back when chilled. If the original Unicum overwhelms your palate, try one of the newer variations: Unicum Next, with more of a citrus flavor; Unicum Szilva (with a golden plum on the label), which is aged in plums that cut some of the bitterness with a rich sweetness; or Unicum Barista, infused with coffee (www.zwack.hu).

If you're drinking with some new Magyar friends, impress them with the standard toast: *Egészségedre* (EH-gaysh-shay-geh-dreh; "to your health").

Hungarian Wines

Wine *(bor)* is an essential part of Hungarian cuisine.

Whites *(fehér)* can be sweet *(édes),* half-dry *(félszáraz),* or dry *(száraz).* Whites include the standards (riesling, chardonnay), as well as some wines made from more typically Hungarian grapes: ***leányka*** ("little girl"), a half-dry, fairly heavy, white table wine; ***cserszegi fűszeres,*** a spicy, light white that can be fruity; the half-dry, full-bodied ***hárslevelű*** ("linden leaf"); the dry, light, refreshing ***furmint;*** and the dry ***kéknyelű*** ("blue stalk").

Reds *(vörös)* include familiar varieties (cabernet sauvignon, cabernet franc, merlot, pinot noir), and some that are less familiar. Spicy, medium-bodied, somewhat fruity ***kékfrankos*** ("blue Frankish") is perhaps the most common Hungarian red wine grape. ***Kekporto*** is better known as *blauer Portugieser* in German-speaking countries. In Eger, try **Bull's Blood,** a.k.a. Egri Bikavér, a distinctive blend of reds—typically with a *kékfrankos* base—that comes with a fun local legend (see page 702).

The most famous Hungarian wine is Tokaji Aszú, a sweet, late-harvest, honey-colored dessert wine made primarily from furmint grapes. It's a D.O.C. product, meaning that to have that name, it must be grown in a particular region. Tokaj is a town in northeastern Hungary, while aszú is a "noble rot" grape. The wine's unique, concentrated flavor—rich and sweet without being syrupy—is made possible by a fungus *(Botrytis cinerea)* that thrives on the grapes in the late fall. The grapes are left on the vine, where they burst and wither like raisins before they are harvested in late October and November. This sucks the water out of the grape, leaving behind a very high sugar content and a deep golden color. The best-quality Tokaji Aszú wines are numbered either five or six, indicating how many eight-gallon tubs *(puttony)* of these "noble rot" grapes were added to the base wine—the higher the number, the sweeter the wine.

Other variations on Tokaji, which mix that concentrated flavor with wine made from the later-harvest plump grapes, can be less sweet.

Except for Bull's Blood and Tokaji Aszú, Hungarian wines are not widely available in the US. If you'd like to assemble a variety to ship home, the Tasting Table Wine Shop in Budapest works with an importer to make things easier (see page 671). And for a great introduction to Hungarian wines, consider the guided tastings offered by Taste Hungary (see page 651).

HUNGARIAN LANGUAGE

Even though Hungary is surrounded by Slavs, Hungarian is not at all related to the Slavic languages (such as Polish, Czech, or Croatian). In fact, Hungarian isn't related to *any* European language, except for very distant relatives Finnish and Estonian. This can make it sound extremely "foreign" to outsiders. (Words can be quite long, because Hungarian is agglutinative: To create meaning, you start with a root word and then tack on suffixes—sometimes resulting in a pileup of extra sounds.) But it's a highly rational language—the basics are easier to grasp than they may seem at first.

One easy word is *"Szia"* (SEE-yaw), which means both hello and goodbye (like "ciao" or "aloha"). Hungarians also have a charming habit of using the English word "hello" for both "hi" and "bye." You might overhear a Hungarian end a telephone conversation with a cheery "Hello! Hello! Hello!" Another handy word that Hungarians (and people throughout Central Europe) understand is *Servus* (SEHR-voos, spelled *Szervusz* in Hungarian)—the old-fashioned greeting from the days of the Austro-Hungarian Empire. If you draw a blank on how to say hello, just offer a cheery, *"Servus!"*

Üdvözöljük a Vásárcsarnokban!
Új nyitva tartás:
Hétfő:................06-17
Kedd-Péntek:....06-18
Szombat:..........06-15
Vasárnap:..........Zárva

Hungarian pronunciation is clear and predicable, as long as you remember a few key rules. First, the emphasis always goes on the first syllable, and the following syllables are more monotone—giving the language a distinctive cadence that Hungary's neighbors love to tease.

Several letters sound different in Hungarian than in other languages. For example, *s* alone is pronounced "sh," while *sz* is pronounced "s." This explains why you'll hear in-the-know travelers pronouncing Budapest as "BOO-daw-pesht." You might catch the *busz* up to Castle Hill—pronounced "boose." And "Liszt" is easier to pronounce than it looks: It sounds just like "list." To review:

s sounds like "sh" as in "shirt"

sz sounds like "s" as in "saint"

Hungarian has a set of unusual palatal sounds that don't quite have a counterpart in English. To make these sounds, gently press the thick part of your tongue to the roof of your mouth (instead of using the tip of your tongue behind your teeth, as we do in English):

gy sounds like "dg" as in "hedge"

ny sounds like "ny" as in "canyon" (not "nee")

ty sounds like "tch" as in "itch"

cs sounds like "ch" as in "church"

As for vowels: The letter *a* almost sounds like *o* (aw, as in "hot"), but with an accent *(á)*, it brightens up to the more standard "ah." Likewise, while *e* sounds like "eh," *é* sounds like "ay." An accent *(á, é, í, ó, ú)* indicates that you linger on that vowel but not necessarily that you stress that syllable. Like German, Hungarian has umlauts *(ö, ü)*, meaning you purse your lips when you say that vowel: Roughly, *ö* sounds like "ur" and *ü* sounds like "ew." A long umlaut *(ő, ű)* is the same sound, but you hold it a little longer. Words ending in *k* are often plural.

Here are a few other letters that sound different in Hungarian than in English:

c and **cz** both sound like "ts" as in "cats"

zs sounds like "zh" as in "leisure"

j and **ly** both sound like "y" as in "yellow"

OK, maybe it's not *that* simple. But you'll get the hang of it, and Hungarians will appreciate your efforts.

One more tip: Hungarians list a person's family name first—so the composer Franz Liszt is called "Liszt Ferenc" in his homeland.

For a complete list of Hungarian survival phrases, see the following pages. As you navigate, remember these key Hungarian terms: *tér* (pronounced "tayr," square), *utca* (OOT-zaw, street), *út* (oot, boulevard), *körút* (KUR-root, ring road), *híd* (heed, bridge), and *város* (VAH-rohsh, town). To better match what you'll see locally, in the following chapters I've mostly used these Hungarian terms (instead of the English equivalents).

Hungarian Survival Phrases

In Hungarian, the letter a is pronounced "aw," while á is a brighter "ah." In the phonetics, dj is pronounced like the j in "jeans."

Hello. (formal)	Jó napot kívánok.	yoh **nah**-poht **kee**-vah-nohk
Hi. / Bye. (informal)	Szia. / Hello.	**see**-yaw / "Hello"
Do you speak English?	Beszél angolul?	beh-sayl **awn**-goh-lool
Yes. / No.	Igen. / Nem.	**ee**-gehn / nehm
I (don't) understand.	(Nem) értem.	(nehm) **ayr**-tehm
Please. / You're welcome.	Kérem. / Szívesen.	**kay**-rehm / **see**-veh-shehn
Thank you (very much).	Köszönöm (szépen).	**kur**-sur-nurm (**say**-pehn)
Excuse me. / I'm sorry.	Bocsánat.	**boh**-chah-nawt
No problem.	Semmi gond.	**sheh**-mee gohnd
Good.	Jól.	yohl
Goodbye.	Viszontlátásra.	**vee**-sohnt-lah-tahsh-raw
one / two / three	egy / kettő / három	edj / **keh**-tur / **hah**-rohm
four / five / six / seven	négy / öt / hat / hét	naydj / urt / hawt / hayt
eight / nine / ten	nyolc / kilenc / tíz	nyolts / **kee**-lehnts / teez
hundred / thousand	száz / ezer	sahz / **eh**-zehr
How much?	Mennyi?	**mehn**-yee
forint (local currency)	forint (Ft)	**foh**-reent
Where is it?	Hol van?	hohl vawn
Is it free (no charge)?	Ingyen van?	een-**jehn** vawn
Where can I find / buy...?	Hol találok / vehetek...?	hohl **taw**-lah-lohk / **veh**-heh-tehk
I'd like / We'd like...	Kérnék / Kérnénk...	**kayr**-nayk / **kayr**-naynk
...a room.	...egy szobát.	edj **soh**-baht
...a ticket (to ____).	...egy jegyet (____-ig).	edj **yehdj**-yeht (____-ig)
Is it possible?	Lehet?	leh-**heht**
Where is the ____?	Hol van a ____?	hohl vawn aw ____
big train station (in Budapest)	pályaudvar	**pah**-yood-vawr
small train station (elsewhere)	vasútállomás	**vaw**-shoot-ah-loh-mahsh
bus station	buszpályaudvar	**boos**-pah-yood-vawr
tourist information office	turista információ	**too**-reesh-taw een-for-maht-see-yoh
toilet	toalet / WC	**toh**-aw-leht / **vayt**-say
men / women	férfi / női	**fayr**-fee / **nur**-ee
left / right	bal / jobb	bawl / yohb
straight	egyenesen	**edj**-eh-neh-shehn
At what time...?	Mikor...?	**mee**-kor
...does this open / close	...nyit / zár	nyit / zahr
Just a moment.	Egy pillanat.	edj **pee**-law-nawt
now / soon / later	most / hamarosan / később	mohsht / **haw**-maw-roh-shawn / **kay**-shurb
today / tomorrow	ma / holnap	maw / **hohl**-nawp

In a Hungarian Restaurant

I'd like to reserve a table for one / two people.	Szeretnék foglalni egy asztalt egy / két fő részére. seh-reht-nayk fog-lawl-nee edj aws-tawlt edj / kayt few ray-say-reh
Is this table free?	Ez az asztal szabad? ehz oz aws-tawl saw-bawd
Can I help you?	Tessék? tehsh-shayk
The menu (in English), please.	Kérem az (angol), étlapot kay-rehm oz (awn-gohl) ayt-law-poht
service (not) included	a számla a felszolgálási díjat (nem) tartalmazza aw sahm-law aw fehl-sohl-gah-lah-shee dee-yawt (nehm) tawr-tawl-maw-zaw
"to go"	elvitelre ehl-vee-tehl-reh
with / without	_____-val / nélkül _____ vawl / nayl-kewl
and / or	és / vagy aysh / vawdj
breakfast / lunch / dinner	reggeli / ebéd / vacsora reh-geh-lee / eh-bayd / vah-choh-rah
fixed-price meal (of the day)	(napi) menü (naw-pee) meh-new
daily special	napi ajánlat naw-pee aw-yahn-lawt
main courses	főételek fur-ay-teh-lehk
appetizers	előételek eh-lur-ay-teh-lehk
bread / cheese	kenyér / sajt kehn-yayr / shayt
sandwich	szendvics send-veech
soup	leves leh-vehsh
salad	saláta shaw-lah-taw
meat / poultry	hús / szárnyasok hoosh / sahr-nyaw-shohk
fish	halak haw-lawk
seafood	tengeri halak tehn-geh-ree haw-lawk
fruit / vegetables	gyümölcs / zöldség jewm-urlch / zulrd-shayg
dessert	desszert deh-sehrt
vegetarian	vegetáriánus veh-geh-tah-ree-ah-noosh
(tap) water	(csap) víz (chawp) veez
mineral water	ásványvíz ash-vawn-veez
milk / (orange) juice	tej / (narancs) lé tay / (naw-rawnch) lay
coffee / tea	kávé / tea kah-vay / teh-aw
beer / wine	sör / bor shohr / bohr
red / white	vörös / fehér vur-rursh / feh-hayr
sweet / dry / semi-dry	édes / száraz / félszáraz ay-dehsh / sah-rawz / fayl-sah-rawz
glass / bottle	pohár / üveg poh-hahr / ew-vehg
Cheers!	Egészségedre! eh-gaysh-shay-geh-dreh
More. / Another.	Még. / Máskikat. mayg / mah-shee-kawt
The same.	Ugyanazt. oodj-aw-nawst
Bill, please. (literally, "I'll pay.")	Fizetek. fee-zeh-tehk
tip	borravaló boh-raw-vaw-loh
Bon appétit!	Jó étvágyat! yoh ayt-vah-yawt
Delicious!	Finom! fee-nohm

BUDAPEST

Budapest—Europe's most underrated big city—is a unique metropolis at the heart of a unique nation. Feel your stress ebb away as you soak in hundred-degree water, surrounded by opulent Baroque domes (and happy Hungarians). Ogle richly decorated interiors, evoking a proud nation's bygone glory days. Dive into a bowl of goulash, the paprika-flavored peasant soup. Take an after-dinner stroll along the Danube, immersed in a grand city that's bathed in floodlights.

With nearly two million people (3.3 million in the outlying area), Budapest feels oversized. That's because, like Vienna, the city was built as the head of a much larger empire than it now governs. But once you understand how Budapest is laid out, it's easy to grasp. And visitors who get comfortable with the Metró, trams, and buses have the city by the tail (see "Getting Around Budapest," later).

PLANNING YOUR TIME

Budapest demands at least two full days—and that assumes you'll be selective and move fast. To slow down and really dig into the city, give it a third or fourth day. Adding more time allows for day trips.

Below are some possible plans, depending on the length of your trip. Each evening, you have a range of options: savoring good restaurants, attending an opera or concert, enjoying a romantic river cruise, relaxing in a thermal bath (some are open after hours), exploring the city's ruin pubs and other nightlife, or simply strolling the floodlit Danube embankments and bridges.

Budapest in Two Days

You'll only have time to squeeze in one or two big sights; the most worthwhile are the Parliament (book tickets ahead online), the Great Synagogue, the Opera House, and the House of Terror.

Day 1: Spend the day in Pest. Begin at the Parliament and stroll through Leopold Town, then walk through Downtown Pest, ending at the Great Market Hall. Then circle around the Small Boulevard to Deák Tér (perhaps stopping en route at the Great Synagogue) and consider walking up Andrássy Út to Heroes' Square and City Park. Or, if you're exhausted already, just take the M1/yellow Metró line to Hősök Tere and ogle the Heroes' Square statues and Vajdahunyad Castle. In the late afternoon, reward yourself with a soak at Széchenyi Baths.

Day 2: In the morning, tackle any Pest sights you didn't have time for yesterday. After lunch, ride bus #16 or #216 from Deák Tér to Buda's Castle Hill. Finally, head back to Pest for dinner.

Budapest in Three or More Days

Day 1: Get your bearings in Pest. Begin by strolling through Leopold Town (including a tour of the Parliament—book tickets ahead online), followed by a walk up Andrássy Út (including touring the Opera House and the House of Terror) to Heroes' Square and City Park. End your day with a soak at the Széchenyi Baths.

Day 2: Delve deeper into Pest, starting with a stroll through Downtown Pest. After visiting the Great Market Hall, circle around the Small Boulevard to explore the Great Synagogue and Jewish Quarter. If you'd like to squeeze in another spa, cross the river to Buda for a soak at the Gellért or Rudas baths.

Day 3: Use the morning to see any remaining Pest sights. Then, after lunch, take bus #16 or #216 from Deák Tér to Castle Hill.

With More Time: If you have a fourth day, spread the day 1 activities over more time, circle back to any sights you've missed, and consider heading out to Memento Park to see a collection of old communist statues.

Orientation to Budapest

Budapest is split down the center by the Danube River. On the east bank is flat **Pest** (pronounced "pesht"), and on the west bank is hilly **Buda.** (A third part of the city, **Óbuda,** is north of Buda.)

Bridges: Buda and Pest are connected by a series of characteristic bridges. From north to south, there's the low-profile **Margaret Bridge** (Margit Híd, crosses Margaret Island), the iconic **Chain Bridge** (Széchenyi Lánchíd), the white and modern **Elisabeth**

Bridge (Erzsébet Híd), and the green **Liberty Bridge** (Szabadság Híd). Four more bridges lie beyond the tourist zone.

Districts: Budapest uses a district system (like Paris and Vienna). There are 23 districts *(kerület)*, identified by Roman numerals. For example, Castle Hill is in district I, central Pest is district V, and City Park is in district XIV. Addresses often start with the district's Roman numeral.

Pest: Central Pest, along a gentle bend in the Danube, has two main parts—**Downtown Pest** (Belváros, BEHL-vah-rohsh) and, just to the north, the banking and government center called **Leopold Town** (Lipótváros, LEE-poht-vah-rohsh). You can walk from the northern end of Leopold Town (the Parliament area) to the southern end of Downtown Pest (the Great Market Hall) in about 30 minutes.

Pest is surrounded by four concentric ring roads *(körút)*. Downtown Pest is corralled within the Kiskörút, or **"Small Boulevard."** More attractions lie between there and the Nagykörút, or **"Great Boulevard."** Arterial boulevards, called *út*, stretch from central Pest into the suburbs. These include the wide, genteel, entertaining **Andrássy Út** (AWN-drah-shee oot), with many of my recommended accommodations, restaurants, nightlife, and sightseeing.

More key sights lie along the **Small Boulevard** (connected by trams #47, #48, and #49), including the Great Synagogue, the National Museum, and the Great Market Hall.

Several other points of interest are spread far and wide along the **Great Boulevard** (circled by trams #4 and #6). From north to south, it passes Margaret Island (the city's playground, in the middle of the Danube); the Nyugati/Western train station; the Oktogon intersection, where it crosses Andrássy Út; the opulent New York Café, with the Keleti/Eastern train station just up the street; and the intersection with Üllői Út, near the Holocaust Memorial Center and the Applied Arts Museum.

Buda: Two steep hills rise up from Buda's riverbank—**Castle Hill** (Várhegy, VAHR-hehj), marked by the domes and steeples

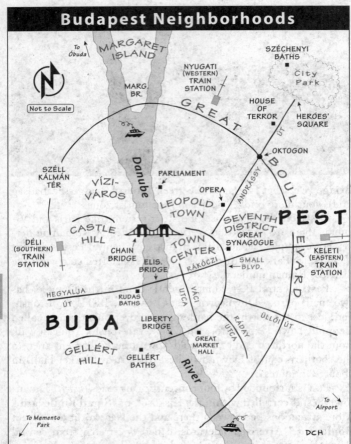

Budapest Neighborhoods

of the Castle District; and **Gellért Hill,** flanked by thermal baths (Rudas at the southern base of the hill, and Gellért at the northern base) and capped by a grand viewpoint. The pleasant **Víziváros** (VEE-zee-vah-rohsh, "Water Town") residential neighborhood is squeezed between the castle and the Danube.

Central Buda is surrounded by a ring road, and the busy Hegyalja Út rumbles through the middle of the tourists' Buda (between Castle and Gellért Hills). Behind Castle and Gellért hills is of little interest to tourists (except for the Déli/Southern train station).

The square called **Batthyány Tér,** at the north end of Víziváros, is a hub for the neighborhood, with a handy Metró stop (M2/red line), tram stops, market hall, and eateries. Just north of Castle Hill is Széll Kálmán Tér, another transit hub for Buda, with a Metró station (M2/red line), several tram stops, and the giant Mammut shopping mall.

TOURIST INFORMATION

The city of Budapest has just one official TI in Downtown Pest. It's in the brightly colored kiosk on Városháza Park, near the Deák Tér transit hub (daily 9:00-19:00, Károly Körút, www.budapestinfo. hu). You may also find TI "mobile info points" in highly trafficked areas.

Sightseeing Passes: The **Budapest Card** includes all public transportation, walking tours of Buda and Pest, admission to a handful of sights (including the National Museum, National Gallery, and Memento Park), a shuttle bus up to the castle, and 10-50 percent discounts on many other major museums, thermal baths, and attractions (€29/24 hours, €43/48 hours, €56/72 hours, longer versions available, www.budapest-card.com). If you take advantage of the included walking tours, the Budapest Card can be a good value for a very busy sightseer—do the math. Buy it online, then exchange the digital voucher for your card when you get to town. You can also purchase the card at the TI, at service points for BKK (the public transit authority), at many hotels, and at other locations around Budapest.

ARRIVAL IN BUDAPEST
By Train

Budapest has three major train stations (*pályaudvar,* abbreviated *pu.*): Keleti ("Eastern") station, Nyugati ("Western") station, and Déli ("Southern") station; a fourth, suburban station—Kelenföld—is a common transfer point for destinations to the south (including Pécs). Before departing Budapest, it's essential to confirm which station your train leaves from.

The taxi stands in front of each train station are notorious for ripping off tourists. Instead, use **public transportation** (each station is on at least one Metró line and well served by various buses and trams); order a **taxi** using the **Bolt app** (see "Getting Around Budapest—By Taxi," later); or, if you must use a taxi, call for one rather than hopping into one parked outside (call +36 1 211 1111 or +36 1 266 6666, and tell the English-speaking dispatcher where you are). For tips on all of this—and on using the Metró system to connect into downtown Budapest—see "Getting Around Budapest," later.

Getting Hungarian Cash on Arrival: At the train stations, it can be tricky, if not impossible, to find a reputable ATM. (The few that you see are most likely operated by Euronet—an exchange bureau that offers worse rates and higher fees than a bank-to-bank transaction.) Ideally, get to your hotel, then get advice on finding

Snapshot History of Budapest

Budapest is a rich cultural stew made up of Hungarians, Germans, Slavs, and Jews, with a dash of Turkish paprika, all simmered for centuries in a thermal bath. Each group has left its mark, but through it all, something has remained that is distinctly...Budapest.

Budapest sits on a thin layer of earth covering thermal springs. Those waters attracted the ancient Romans, who, 2,000 years ago, established Aquincum just north of today's city center.

In AD 896, a nomadic group from Central Asia called the Magyars took over the Carpathian Basin (roughly today's Hungary). After running roughshod over Europe, the Magyars—the ancestors of today's Hungarians—settled down, adopted Christianity, and became fully European. The twin towns of Buda and Pest emerged as the leading cities of Hungary. Gradually Buda and Pest became both a de facto capital and a melting pot for the peoples of Central and Eastern Europe.

In the 16th century, the Ottomans invaded. They occupied Budapest (and much of Hungary) for nearly a century and a half, introducing their way of life and practices—such as soaking in thermal baths. Finally, the Habsburg monarchs from neighboring Austria liberated Hungary—and kept it for themselves.

After many decades of Hungarian uprisings, the Compromise of 1867 created the Austro-Hungarian Empire; six years later, the cities of Buda, Pest, and Óbuda merged to become Budapest, which governed a sizeable chunk of Eastern Europe. For the next few decades, Budapest boomed and Hungarian culture blossomed. A flurry of construction surrounded the year 1896—Hungary's 1,000th birthday.

But with World War I, Budapest's fortunes reversed: Hungary lost the war and two-thirds of its land. Hungary again backed a loser in World War II; the ruins of Budapest were claimed by the Soviets, who introduced communism to the country. Although a bold uprising in 1956 was brutally put down, a milder "goulash communism" eventually emerged here. Budapest became a place where other Eastern Bloc residents could experiment with "Western evils," from Big Macs to Nikes.

By the end of communism in 1989, the city's rich architectural heritage was in shambles. Forever torn between a nostalgic instinct to cling to past glory days and a modern drive to innovate, Budapest has reinvented its cityscape with a mix of old and new. The latest chapter in Budapest's history has been written by Prime Minister Viktor Orbán, who has overseen an unprecedented burst of urban renewal but also a rise in authoritarianism and emotionally charged nationalism.

Budapest's uniquely epic history—still a work in progress—has shaped a glorious metropolis that fascinates both Hungarians and tourists alike.

an ATM run by a real bank. These days, credit cards are widely accepted (for example, using the BudapestGO app for buying transit tickets, or the Bolt app for hailing a taxi); in fact, some short-term visitors get by without withdrawing any cash at all.

Keleti/Eastern Station

Keleti train station (Keleti Pu.) is south of City Park, east of central Pest. The station faces a plaza called Baross Tér, with stops for two different Metró lines (M2/

red and M4/green).

The long **tracks 6-9** stretch all the way to the front doors of the station, which exit toward Baross Tér and the Metró stops. **Tracks 1-5** and **10-13** are set back from the main entrance on either side.

Along **track 6,** a side door leads to a beautifully restored arrivals hall and an exit to a taxi stand (avoid it).

To **get into town by Metró,** head out the big front doors into the giant plaza, then take any of the staircases down into the lower area of the square; once down there, bear left to reach the M2/red Metró line, or right to reach the M4/green Metró line. For a taxi, order one using the Bolt app or by calling.

Nyugati/Western Station

Nyugati train station (Nyugati Pu.) is the most central of Budapest's stations, facing the Great Boulevard on the northeast edge of downtown Pest.

Most trains use the shorter **tracks 1-9,** which are set back from the main entrance. From the head of these tracks, use the stairs or escalator just inside the doors to reach an underpass and the Metró (M3/ blue line). Or exit straight

ahead into a small parking lot with buses, taxis, and—around to the right—the WestEnd City Center shopping mall. (The useful trams around the Great Boulevard are outside the main door, at the head of the longer tracks 10-13.)

Tracks 10-13 extend all the way to the main entrance. From here, exit straight ahead out the main entrance and you'll be on Teréz Körút, the very busy Great Boulevard ring road. In front of the building are a stand selling heavenly smelling, cheap portions

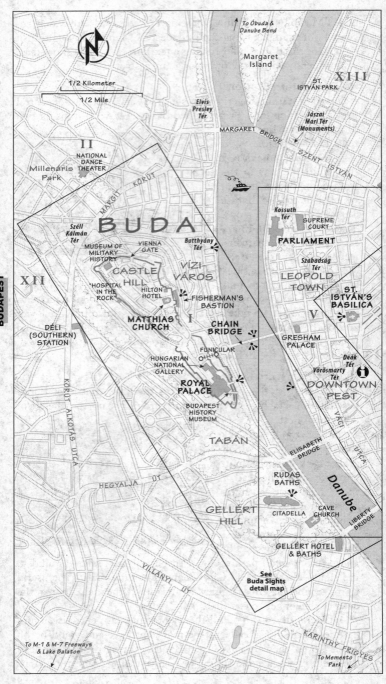

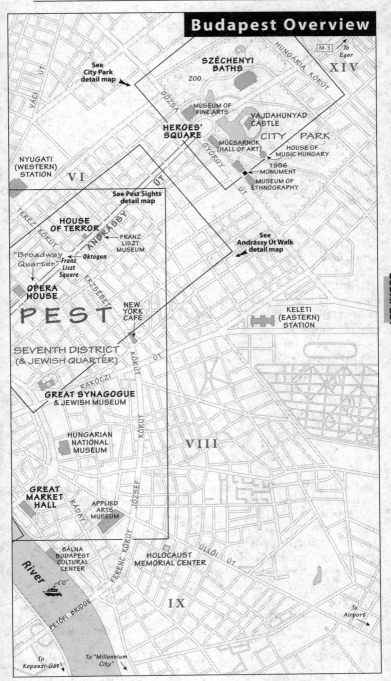

Budapest Overview

BUDAPEST

of *kürtőskalács* chimney cakes, and the stop for the handy trams #4 and #6 (which zip around the Great Boulevard); and to the right are stairs leading to an underpass (use it to avoid crossing this busy intersection, or to reach the Metró's M3/blue line).

Beyond track 13, set back again from the main entrance, are four more platforms—**tracks 14-17.** From here, it's easiest to simply walk along track 13 to the main entrance.

Déli/Southern Station

Tucked behind Castle Hill on the Buda side, this station is dreary. From the tracks, go straight ahead into the vast main hall, with well-marked domestic and international ticket windows. Downstairs, you'll find several shops and eateries, and access to the very convenient M2/red Metró line, which takes you to several key points in town: Batthyány Tér (on the Buda embankment, at the north end of the Víziváros neighborhood), Deák Tér (the heart of Pest, with connections to two other Metró lines), and Keleti train station (where you can transfer to the M4/green Metró line).

By Plane

Budapest's **Liszt Ferenc Airport** is 10 miles southeast of the center (code: BUD, www.bud.hu); some Hungarians may still call the airport by its former name, "Ferihegy." The airport's lone passenger terminal is called "Terminal 2." The terminal has two adjacent parts, which you can walk between in just a few minutes: the smaller Terminal 2A is for flights to/from EU/Schengen countries (no passport control required), while Terminal 2B is for flights to/from other countries.

All flights feed into the same baggage claim area. Exiting baggage claim, you'll find the desk for booking an airport shuttle, the kiosk for booking a taxi into town (outside, at the curb), and the ticket machines and stop for the public bus (also outside, past the taxi kiosk).

Getting Between the Airport and Downtown Budapest: The handiest public transit option is **express bus #100E,** which departs frequently and heads directly downtown, stopping only at three key Metró stations in central Pest: Astoria, Kálvin Tér, and Deák Tér (1,500 Ft, runs about every 10 minutes, 40-60 minutes depending on traffic). **Bus #200E** is cheaper (covered by a standard transit ticket or pass), but it goes only as far as the Kőbánya-Kispest Metró station, where you'll need to transfer to get farther into town.

The **miniBUD airport shuttle** is a decent value for door-to-door minibus service, though it's the slowest choice: You may have to wait for other arrivals to show up, and then you'll make multiple stops around town. Still, it's cost-effective for those not in a hurry who want an easy transfer (to the city center: €20/1 person, €23/2 people; takes about 30-60 minutes depending on hotel location, plus waiting time; +36 1 550 0000, www.minibud.hu; if arranging a minibus transfer *to* the airport, book it at least 24 hours in advance).

The fastest, priciest option is to take a **taxi.** Főtaxi has a monopoly at the taxi stand out front; figure about €30 (or around 12,000 Ft) to downtown, depending on traffic.

By Car

Avoid driving in Budapest if you can. Especially during rush hour (7:00-9:00 and 16:00-18:00), congestion is maddening. Don't drive down roads marked with a red circle, or in lanes marked for buses; these can be monitored by traffic cameras, and you could be mailed a ticket.

There are three concentric ring roads, all of them slow: the Small Boulevard (Kiskörút), Great Boulevard (Nagykörút), and outermost Hungária Körút. Farther out, the M-0 expressway makes a not-quite-complete circle around the city center.

Parking: While in Budapest, unless you're heading to an out-of-town sight (such as Memento Park), park the car at or near your hotel and take public transportation. Within the Great Boulevard, it's generally free to park on the street from 20:00 until 8:00 the next morning (farther out, it's free after 18:00). But in some heavily touristed areas, you may have to pay around the clock. Always check signs carefully, and confirm with a local (such as your hotelier) that you've parked appropriately. Also, be sure to park within the lines—otherwise, your car is likely to get "booted" (with a giant red brace on your wheel). A guarded parking lot is safer but more expensive (ask your hotel or look for the blue *P*s on maps). As rental-car theft can be a problem, ask at your hotel for advice.

HELPFUL HINTS

Sightseeing Strategies: Just about everything in Budapest is walkable, but distances can be far. Plan your sightseeing geographically to minimize backtracking. Public transit and taxis save valuable time.

Keep in mind that (aside from the Gellért and Rudas Baths) Buda's sightseeing is mostly concentrated on Castle Hill, and can easily be done in less than a day, while Pest deserves as much time as you're willing to give it. Save relatively laid-back Buda for when you need a break from the big city.

Rip-Offs: Budapest is quite safe for a city of its size. Occasionally tourists run into con artists or pickpockets; wear a money belt and secure your valuables in touristy places and on public transportation.

Restaurants on the Váci Utca shopping street are notorious for overcharging tourists. Anywhere in Budapest, avoid restaurants that don't list prices on the menu. Check your bill carefully. Most restaurants add a 12 percent service charge; if you don't notice this, you might accidentally double-tip (for more on tipping, see page 1099). Also, at Váci Utca and at train stations, avoid using the rip-off currency exchange booths (such as Euronet, Interchange, or Checkpoint). It's better to simply get cash from an ATM associated with a major bank (including OTP, MKB, K&H, and various big international banks).

For tips on outsmarting cabbie crooks, see "Getting Around Budapest—By Taxi," later.

Medical Help: Near Buda's Széll Kálmán Tér, **FirstMed Centers** is a private, pricey, English-speaking clinic (by appointment or urgent care, call first, Hattyú Utca 14, 5th floor, district I, M2: Széll Kálmán Tér, +36 1 224 9090, www.firstmedcenters. com). The word for hospital is *kórház*.

Money: The Hungarian forint (Ft) has been volatile in recent years, so many businesses list their prices in the more stable euro currency. As rough shorthand, remember that 350 Ft is about €1.

English Bookstore: Bestsellers has a fine selection of new books, mostly in English; it's near St. István's Basilica (Mon-Fri 10:00-18:30, Sat 11:00-18:00, closed Sun, Október 6 Utca 11—see map on page 667, +36 1 312 1295).

Pharmacies: The helpful **BENU Gyógyszertár** pharmacy is dead-center in Pest, between Vörösmarty and Széchenyi squares. They have a useful directory that lists the Hungarian equivalent of US prescription medicines (Mon-Fri 8:00-20:00, closed Sat-Sun, Dorottya Utca 13, district V, M1: Vörösmarty Tér, for location see map on page 658, +36 1 317 2374). Each district has one 24-hour pharmacy (these should be noted outside the entrance to any pharmacy).

Laundry: The self-service launderette chain **Bubbles** is open 24/7, unstaffed, automated, and takes credit cards. The most convenient location is near the Small Boulevard, at the inner edge of the Seventh District, at Paulay Ede 3, M1: Bajcsy-Zsilinszky Út; check their website for others (www.bubbles.hu). **Laundry Budapest,** also in the Seventh District, is another good choice with lots of machines (daily 9:00-24:00, last wash at 22:00, Dohány Utca 37, near M2: Blaha Lujza Tér, +36 1 781 0098, www.laundrybudapest.hu). For locations, see the map on page 664.

For full service, **Vajnóczki Tisztítószalon** is a block from the Oktogon (next-day service, Mon-Fri 8:00-18:00, Sat until

Tonight We're Gonna Party Like It's 1896

Visitors to Budapest need only remember one date: 1896. For the millennial celebration of their ancestors' arrival in Europe, Hungarians threw a blowout party. In the thousand years between 896 and 1896, the Magyars had gone from being a nomadic Central Asian tribe that terrorized the Continent to sharing the throne of one of the most successful empires Europe had ever seen.

On New Year's Day morning, 1896, church bells clanged through the streets of Buda and Pest. That June, the Habsburg royal couple Franz Josef and Sisi were among the 5.7 million people who came to enjoy the Hungarian National Exhibition at City Park. At Vérmező Park (behind Castle Hill), whole oxen were grilled on the spit to feed commoners.

Budapest used its millennial celebration as an excuse to build monuments and buildings appropriate for the co-capital of a huge empire, including these landmarks:

- **Heroes' Square** and **Millennium Monument**
- **Vajdahunyad Castle** (in City Park)
- **Parliament** building (96 meters tall, 96 front steps)
- **St. István's Basilica** (also 96 meters tall)
- M1/yellow Metró line, a.k.a. *Földalatti* ("Underground")
- **Great Market Hall** (and four other market halls)
- **Andrássy Út** and most of the fine buildings lining it
- **Opera House**
- A complete rebuilding of **Matthias Church** (on Castle Hill)
- **Fisherman's Bastion** (by Matthias Church)
- Green **Liberty Bridge** (then called Franz Josef Bridge)

The key number in Hungary is 96—even the national anthem takes 96 seconds. But it turns out that the date was wrong: A commission—convened to establish the exact year of the Magyars' debut—determined it happened in 895. But city leaders knew they'd never make an 1895 deadline, and requested the finding be changed to 896.

13:00, closed Sun, Szófia Utca 8—see map on page 655, +36 1 342 3796).

Bike Rental: Budapest isn't the easiest place for cyclists. But as the city adds more bike lanes and traffic-free zones, those comfortable with urban cycling may be tempted. The city transit authority has a subsidized public bike network called **Bubi** (for "**Bu**dapest **Bi**kes"). Bike stations are scattered throughout town; you can rent and pick a bike up at any station and drop it off at any other, for affordable rates (for prices and details, see http://molbubi.bkk.hu).

Drivers: Friendly, English-speaking **Gábor Balázs** can drive you around the city or into the surrounding countryside (€20/

hour, 3-hour minimum in city, 4-hour minimum in country-side, +36 20 936 4317, bgabor.e@gmail.com). **Zsolt Gál** and his team offer transfers, side-trips, and longer trips to Prague or Vienna (+36 70 452 4900, forma111562@gmail.com). Note that these are drivers, not tour guides. For a licensed tour guide who also does countryside driving trips, see "Tours in Budapest," later.

Best Views: Budapest is a city of marvelous vistas. Some of the best are from the Citadella fortress (high on Gellért Hill, may be under renovation), the promenade in front of the Royal Palace and the Fisherman's Bastion on top of Castle Hill, and the embankments or many bridges spanning the Danube (especially the Chain Bridge). The classic Parliament view is from across the river, along the Buda embankment near Batthyány Tér (the light is best late in the day). Don't forget the view from the tour boats on the Danube—particularly lovely at night.

GETTING AROUND BUDAPEST

Budapest sprawls. Connecting your sightseeing just on foot is tedious and unnecessary. It's crucial to get comfortable with the well-coordinated public trans-portation system: Metró lines, trams, buses, and trolley buses. (Taxis can get you everywhere else.) Budapest's transit system website is www.bkk.hu.

Tickets

The same tickets work for the entire transit system.

You can buy **paper tickets** at kiosks, Metró ticket windows, or user-friendly machines. As prices are affordable and it can be frustrating to find a ticket machine, I generally invest in a multiday ticket to have the freedom of hopping on at will.

Or you can download the **BudapestGO mobile app,** which offers real-time route planning and lets you buy tickets and passes directly through the app (for the same prices as the paper tickets).

Your ticket options are as follows:

• **Single ticket** (*vonaljegy*, for a ride of up to an hour on any means of transit; transfers allowed only within the Metró system)—350 Ft (or 450 Ft if bought from the driver)

• **Short single Metró ride** (*Metrószakaszjegy*, 3 stops or fewer on the Metró)—300 Ft

• **Transfer ticket** (*átszállójegy*—travel up to 90 minutes, including one transfer between Metró and bus)—530 Ft

• **Pack of 10 single tickets** (*10 darabos gyűjtőjegy*), which can be shared—3,000 Ft (note that these must stay together as a single pack—they can't be sold separately)

• Unlimited multiday travel cards for Metró, bus, and tram, including a **24-hour travelcard** (*24 órás jegy*, 2,500 Ft/24 hours), **72-hour travelcard** (*72 órás jegy*, 5,500 Ft/72 hours), and **seven-day travelcard** (*hetijegy*, 6,500 Ft/7 days)

• **24-hour group travel card** (*csoportos 24 órás jegy*, 5,000 Ft), covering up to five adults—a great deal for groups of three to five people

• **Budapest Card,** which combines a multiday ticket with sightseeing discounts (see "Tourist Information," earlier)

Always validate single-ride tickets as you enter the bus, tram, or Metró station (stick it in the elbow-high box). On older buses and trams that have little red validation boxes, stick your ticket in the black slot, then pull the slot toward you to punch holes in your ticket. Multiday tickets only need to be validated once. The stern-looking people waiting as you enter or exit the Metró want to see your validated ticket. Cheaters are fined 12,000 Ft on the spot, and you'll be surprised how often you're checked. All public transit runs from 4:30 in the morning until 23:50; a few designated night buses and trams operate overnight.

Handy Terms: *A* ____ *felé* means "in the direction of ___." *Megálló* means "stop" or "station," and *Végállomás* means "end of the line."

By Metró

Riding Budapest's efficient Metró, you really feel like you're down in the guts of the city. There are four lines:

• **M1/yellow**—The first subway line on the Continent, this line runs beneath Andrássy Út from the center to City Park. Dating from 1896, "the Underground" (Földalatti) is so shallow that you must follow the signs on the street (listing end points—Mexikói Út Felé takes you toward City Park) to gauge the right direction, because there's no underpass for switching platforms. Though recently renovated, the M1 line retains its old-time atmosphere.

• **M2/red**—Built during the communist days, it's more than 100 feet deep and designed to double as a bomb shelter. Going under the Danube to Buda, the M2 connects the Déli/Southern train station, Széll Kálmán Tér (where you catch bus #16, #16A, or #116 to the top of Castle Hill), Batthyány Tér (Víziváros and the HÉV suburban railway), Kossuth Tér (behind the Parliament), Astoria (near the Great Synagogue on the Small Boulevard), and the Keleti/Eastern train station (where it crosses the M4/green line).

• **M3/blue**—This line makes a broad, boomerang-shaped swoop north to south on the Pest side. Key stops include the Nyugati/Western train station, Ferenciek Tere (in the heart of Down-

BUDAPEST

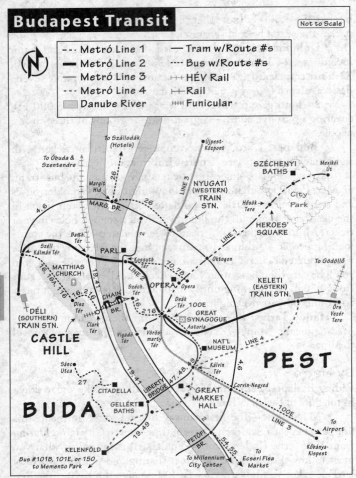

Budapest Transit

Not to Scale

Legend:
- --- Metró Line 1
- — Metró Line 2
- Metró Line 3
- --- Metró Line 4
- Danube River
- — Tram w/Route #s
- --- Bus w/Route #s
- +++ HÉV Rail
- + Rail
- +++ Funicular

town Pest), Kálvin Tér (near the Great Market Hall and many recommended hotels; this is also where it crosses the M4/green line), and Corvin-negyed (near the Holocaust Memorial Center).

• **M4/green**—This line runs from southern Buda to the Gellért Baths, under the Danube to Fővám Tér (behind the Great Market Hall) and Kálvin Tér (where it crosses the M3/blue line), then up to Rákóczi Tér (on the Grand Boulevard) and the Keleti/Eastern train station (where it crosses the M2/red line).

The three lines—M1, M2, and M3—cross only once: at the **Deák Tér** stop (often signed as *Deák Ferenc Tér*) in the heart of Pest, near where Andrássy Út begins.

Aside from the historic M1 line, most Metró stations are at

intersections of ring roads and other major thorough-fares. You'll usually exit the Metró into a confusing underpass. Directional signs indicate which streets, addresses, and tram or bus stops are near each exit.

By HÉV

Budapest's suburban rail system, or HÉV (pronounced "hayv," stands for Helyiérdekű Vasút, "Railway of Local Interest"), branches off to the outskirts and beyond. On a short visit, it's un-likely that you'll need to use it, unless you're heading to the Óbuda neighborhood (for its museums), the charming Danube Bend town of Szentendre, or the royal palace at Gödöllő.

The H5 (purple) HÉV line that begins at Batthyány Tér in Buda's Víziváros neighborhood heads through Óbuda to Szenten-dre; from the station at Örs Vezér Tere, the H8 (pink) line runs east to Gödöllő.

The HÉV is covered by standard transit tickets and passes for rides within the city of Budapest (such as to Óbuda). But if going beyond—such as to Szentendre or Gödöllő—you'll have to pay more.

By Tram

Budapest's trams are handy and frequent, taking you virtually any-where the Metró doesn't. Here are some trams you might use:

Tram **#2** follows Pest's Danube embankment, parallel to Váci Utca. From north to south, it begins at the Great Boulevard (Jászai Mari Tér, near Margaret Bridge and stops on either side of the Par-liament (north side near the visitors center/Országház stop, as well as south side near the Kossuth Tér Metró stop), Széchenyi István Tér and the Chain Bridge, Vigadó Tér, and the Great Market Hall (Fővám Tér stop).

Trams **#19** and **#41** run along Buda's Danube embankment from Batthyány Tér (with an M2/red Metró station, and HÉV trains to Óbuda and Szentendre). From Batthyány Tér, these trams run (north to south) through Víziváros, with several helpful stops: Clark Ádám Tér (the bottom of the Castle Hill funicular, near the stop for bus #16 or #216 up to Castle Hill), Várkert Bazár (Castle Park with escalators and elevators up to the Royal Palace), Rudas Gyógyfürdő (Rudas Baths), then around the base of Gellért Hill to Szent Gellért Tér (Gellért Baths and M4/green Metró station).

Trams **#4** and **#6** zip around Pest's Great Boulevard ring road

BUDAPEST

(Nagykörút), connecting Nyugati/Western train station and the Oktogon with the southern tip of Margaret Island and Buda's Széll Kálmán Tér (with M2/red Metró station, and buses up to the castle). At night, this route is replaced by bus #6.

Trams **#47**, **#48**, and **#49** connect the Gellért Baths in Buda with Pest's Small Boulevard ring road (Kiskörút), with stops at the Great Market Hall (Fővám Tér stop), the National Museum (Kálvin Tér stop), the Great Synagogue (Astoria stop), and Deák Tér (end of the line).

By Bus and Trolley Bus

I use the Metró and trams for most of my Budapest commuting. But some buses are useful for shortcuts within the city, or for reaching outlying sights. Note that the transit company draws a distinction between gas-powered "buses" and electric "trolley buses" (powered by overhead cables). Unless otherwise noted, the following are standard buses:

Buses **#16**, **#16A**, **#116**, and **#216** all head up to the top of Castle Hill (get off at Dísz Tér—the closest stop to the Royal Palace). Buses #16 and #216 make several handy stops in Pest (Deák Tér, Széchenyi István Tér), then cross the Chain Bridge for more stops in Buda (including Clark Ádám Tér, at the Buda end of the Chain Bridge on its way up to the castle). From Széll Kálmán Tér, behind Castle Hill, buses #16, #16A, and #116 head up to the castle.

Trolley buses **#70** and **#78** zip from near the Opera House (intersection of Andrássy Út and Nagymező Utca) to the Parliament (Kossuth Tér).

Bus **#26** begins at Nyugati/Western train station and heads around the Great Boulevard to Margaret Island, making several stops along the island.

Bus **#27** runs from either side of Gellért Hill to just below the Citadella fortress at the hill's peak (Búsuló Juhász stop).

Bus **#100E** is a handy, speedy express bus connecting Liszt Ferenc Airport to Deák Tér, with only two other stops en route (Astoria and Kálvin Tér Metró stops).

Buses **#101B**, **#101E**, and **#150** run from Kelenföld (the end of the line for the M4/green Metró line) to Memento Park.

By Taxi

Budapest strictly regulates its official taxis, which must be painted yellow and have yellow license plates. These taxis are required to charge identical rates: a drop rate of 1,100 Ft, and then 440 Ft/ kilometer, plus 110 Ft/minute for wait time. A 10 percent tip is expected. A typical ride within central Budapest shouldn't run more than 2,000-3,000 Ft.

If you take an unofficial taxi, there's a very high probability you'll get ripped off with much higher rates. Unfortunately, cabbie crooks hang out at places frequented by tourists (such as at train stations). If you wave down a cab on the street, be sure it has a yellow license plate; otherwise, it's not official. Better yet, do as the locals do and call a cab from a reputable company: **City Taxi** (+36 1 211 1111), **Taxi 6x6** (+36 1 266 6666), or **Főtaxi** (+36 1 222 2222). Most dispatchers speak English; hotels and restaurants are often happy to call one for you.

Bolt App: Many popular ride-hailing apps (including Uber, Lyft, and FreeNow) don't operate in Hungary. However, the similar Bolt app lets you request a regular taxi at the regular rates. The app allows you to pay by credit card (consider downloading it before your trip).

Tours in Budapest

Local Guides

While guides might be available last-minute, it's better to book them in advance. These guides, who have all been indispensable help in writing and updating this book, have the same rates (€150/ half-day, €300/full day): **Péter Pölczman** is an exceptional guide who really puts you in touch with the Budapest you came to see (+36 20 926 0557, www.budapestyourself.com, peter.polczman@ gmail.com). **Andrea Makkay** has professional polish and a smart understanding of what visitors really want to experience (+36 20 962 9363, www.privateguidebudapest.com, andrea.makkay@ gmail.com). **George Farkas** is well attuned to the stylish side of this fast-changing metropolis (+36 70 335 8030, georgefarkas@ gmail.hu). **György Ujlaki** has a passion for history, food, wine, and culture, and is enjoyable to simply spend time with (+36 30 407 9875, gujlaki@gmail.com). **Eszter Bokros** brings enthusiasm to sharing her city (+36 70 625 6655, eszterbokros1@gmail.com).

Elemér Boreczky, a retired university professor, doesn't lead conventional walking tours but enjoys chatting with curious visitors about Budapest's rich cultural history. Reach out to Elemér if you'd enjoy an unconventional "tour" that's essentially a graduate-level seminar on the nuances of this grand city (+36 30 491 1389, boreczky.elemer@gmail.com).

BUDAPEST

Walking Tours

Budapest's best-established walking-tour company is **Absolute Tours,** run by Oregonian Ben Frieday. Their 3.5-hour All in One walking tour offers a good overview of the city (daily at 10:00). They also have a Buda Castle walk, a nighttime walk that also includes a boat trip, and private tours (RS%—enter code "RICK" when booking, +36 20 929 7506, www.absolutetours.com).

▲▲Danube Boat Tours

Cruising the Danube, while touristy, is a fun and convenient way to get a feel for the city's grand layout. The most established company, **Legenda Cruises,** is a class act that runs well-maintained, glassed-in panoramic boats day and night. All of their cruises include a free drink and romantic headphone commentary. By night, TV monitors show the interiors of the great buildings as you float by.

I've negotiated a special RS% discount with Legenda for my readers—but you must book directly and ask for the Rick Steves price (20 percent discount). By **day,** the 75-minute Duna Bella cruise costs €10.80 for Rick Steves readers; if you want, you can hop off at Margaret Island to explore on your own, then return after 45 minutes on a later cruise (departs every 45 minutes, in winter runs 1-2/day with no Margaret Island stop). By **night,** the one-hour "Danube Legend" cruise (with no Margaret Island visit) costs €15.20 for Rick Steves readers (4/day, 2/day in winter). On weekends, it's smart to book ahead for the evening cruises.

The Legenda dock is in front of the Marriott on the Pest embankment (find pedestrian access under tram tracks at downriver end of Vigadó Tér, district V, M1: Vörösmarty Tér, +36 1 266 4190, www.legenda.hu). Competing river-cruise companies are nearby, but given the quality and the discount, Legenda offers the best value.

Bus Tours

Various companies run hop-on, hop-off bus tours, which make 12 to 16 stops as they cruise around town on a two-hour loop with headphone commentary (generally around €35/24 hours). Most companies also offer a wide variety of other tours, including dinner boat cruises and trips to the Danube Bend.

Private Tours into the Hungarian Countryside

The Hungarian countryside is well worth exploring. If you'd like a taste without driving yourself, hire **Ádám Kiss,** a licensed guide who lives in the folk-museum village of Hollókő. Ádám can pick you up in Budapest (at your hotel or the airport) and drive you to your choice of countryside destinations ($200/day, plus travel costs; for example, for an all-day visit to Hollókő and Eger for two people, you'd pay about $400 total for round-trip transportation, guiding, admissions, and lunch). Ádám also enjoys helping people track down their roots in the Hungarian countryside. Contact him for pricing (+36 20 379 6132, adamtheguide@gmail.com).

Sights in Pest

Most of Pest's top sights cluster in five neighborhoods: **Leopold Town** and **Downtown Pest** (together forming the city's central core); the **Jewish Quarter,** just outside the inner ring road; along the grand boulevard **Andrássy Út;** and at that boulevard's end, near **Heroes' Square and City Park.**

Several other excellent sights are not contained in these areas and are covered in greater depth in this chapter: along the **Small Boulevard** (Kiskörút), along the **Great Boulevard** (Nagykörút), and along the boulevard called **Üllői Út.**

Sightseeing Tips: Budapest boomed in the late 19th century, after it became the co-capital of the vast Austro-Hungarian Empire. Most of its finest buildings (and top sights) date from this age. To appreciate an opulent interior—a Budapest experience worth ▲▲▲—prioritize touring either the Parliament or the Opera House. The Opera tour is more crowd-pleasing, while the Parliament tour is grander and a bit drier (with a focus on history and parliamentary process). "Honorable mentions" go to the interiors of St. István's Basilica, the Great Synagogue, the Párisi Udvar or New York Café coffeehouses (both require the purchase of a drink), and both the Széchenyi and the Gellért Baths.

LEOPOLD TOWN (LIPÓTVÁROS)

The Parliament building, which dominates Pest's skyline, is the centerpiece of the city's banking and business district. Called Lipótváros ("Leopold Town"), this snazzy "uptown" quarter features some of the best of Budapest's many monuments. Below, I've linked up the top sights in Leopold Town as a self-guided walk, starting at the grandiose Parliament building and ending at the Chain Bridge.

BUDAPEST

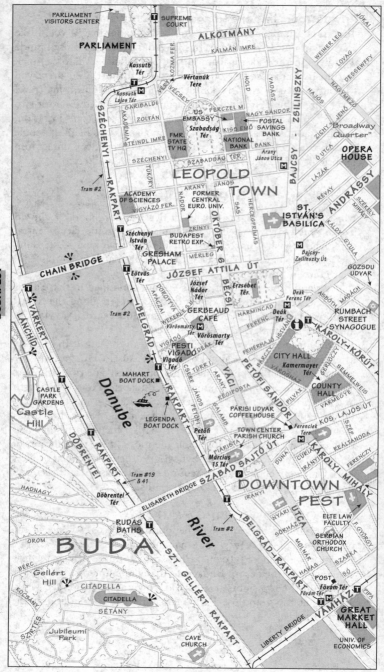

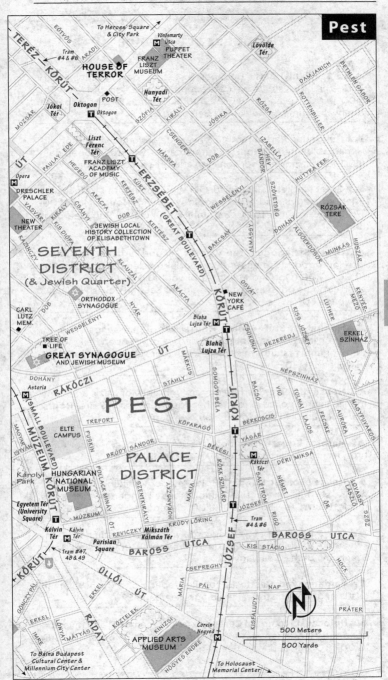

Pest

BUDAPEST

TERÉZ KÖRÚT
EÖTVÖS
ARADI
Tram #4 & 6
To Heroes' Square & City Park
Vörösmarty Utca
PUPPET THEATER
HOUSE OF TERROR
FRANZ LISZT MUSEUM
Lövölde Tér
DAMJANICH
BETHLEN GÁBOR
ROTTENBILLER
Hunyadi Tér
MOZSÁR
Jókai Tér
Oktogon
POST
Oktogon
SZOFIA
KIRÁLY
JÓSIKA
RÓZSA
IZABELLA
HEY
SÁNDOR
SZÖVETSÉG
HÚTYRA FER.
ÚT
CSENGERY
HÁRSFA
Liszt Ferenc Tér
FRANZ LISZT ACADEMY OF MUSIC
ERZSÉBET
DOB
KERTÉSZ
KÚRT
ERZSÉBET (GREAT BOULEVARD)
PAULAY EDE
HEGEDÜ
AKÁCFA
WESSELÉNYI
DOHÁNY
ALSÓERDŐSOR
MUNKÁS
HUSZÁR
RÓZSÁK TERE
Opera
DRESCHLER PALACE
VASVÁRI
KIRÁLY
KIS DIÓFA
CSÁNYI
DOB
JEWISH LOCAL HISTORY COLLECTION OF ELISABETHTOWN
BARCSAY
OSVÁT
NEW YORK CAFÉ
KISS JÓZSEF
KENYÉR-MEZŐ
LUTHER
NEW THEATER
KAZINCZY
SEVENTH DISTRICT (& Jewish Quarter)
KLAUZÁL
NYÁR
AKÁCFA
KÖRÚT
Blaha Lujza Tér
CSOKONAI
BEZERÉDJ
VIG
NÉPSZÍNHÁZ
ERKEL SZÍNHÁZ
CARL LUTZ MEM.
DOB
ORTHODOX SYNAGOGUE
WESSELÉNYI
ÚT
MÁRKUS
Blaha Lujza Tér
PACSÓ
TOLNAI LAJOS
FECSKE
AURÓRA
NAGYFUVAROS
TREE OF LIFE
GREAT SYNAGOGUE AND JEWISH MUSEUM
STÁHLY
SOMOGYI BÉLA
DOHÁNY
Astoria
RÁKÓCZI
(SMALL BOULEVARD)
MÚZEUM KÖRÚT
MAGYAR
ISTVÁN
ELTE CAMPUS
TREFORT
PUSKIN
BRÓDY SÁNDOR
POLLÁCK MIHÁLY
SZENTKIRÁLYI
P E S T
KŐFARAGÓ
BÉKÉSI
RÖKK SZILÁRD
MÁRIA
KÖRÚT
BÉRKOCSIS
YÁSÁR
SALÉTROM
NÉMET
Rákóczi Tér
DÉRI MIKSA
LÓVÁSZ LÁSZLÓ
ŐR
SZÍSZ
Károlyi Park
HUNGARIAN NATIONAL MUSEUM
MÚZEUM
HORÁNSZKY
PALACE DISTRICT
JÓZSEF
RIGÓ
Tram #4 & 6
Egyetem Tér (University Square)
Kálvin Tér
REVICZKY
Mikszáth Kálmán Tér
KRÚDY LŐRINC
JÓZSEF
KIS STÁCIÓ
BAROSS UTCA
HOCK
Tram #47, 48 & 49
Parisian Square
BAROSS UTCA
CSEPREGHY
PÁL
NAP
PRÁTER
KÖRÚT
ÜLLŐI ÚT
ERKEL
KÖZTELEK
MÁRIA
KISFALUDY
RÁDAY
GÖNCZY PÁL
ERKEL
LÓNYAI
MÁTYÁS
KINIZSI
APPLIED ARTS MUSEUM
Corvin-Negyed
HŐGYES ENDRE
N
500 Meters
500 Yards
IMRE
To Bálna Budapest Cultural Center & Millennium City Center
To Holocaust Memorial Center

Budapest at a Glance

Pest

▲▲▲Széchenyi Baths Budapest's steamy soaking scene in City Park—the city's single best attraction. **Hours:** Mon and Wed-Thu 7:00-19:00, Tue and Fri 8:00-20:00, Sat-Sun 9:00-20:00, may be open later summer weekends. See page 621.

▲▲Hungarian Parliament Vast riverside government center with remarkable interior. **Hours:** Visitors center with tours open daily 8:00-18:00; shorter hours on Mon and off-season. See page 588.

▲▲Great Market Hall Colorful Old World mall with produce, eateries, souvenirs, and great people-watching. **Hours:** Mon 6:00-17:00, Tue-Fri until 18:00, Sat until 15:00, closed Sun. See page 604.

▲▲Great Synagogue The world's second largest, with fancy interior, good museum, and memorial garden. **Hours:** Sun-Thu 10:00-20:00 (Oct and March-April until 18:00), Fri 10:00-16:00; shorter hours off-season; always closed Sat and Jewish holidays. See page 606.

▲▲Hungarian State Opera House Neo-Renaissance splendor and affordable opera. **Hours:** Lobby/box office open daily 10:00-19:00 or until first intermission; English tours usually daily at 13:30, 15:00, and 16:30. See page 610.

▲▲House of Terror Harrowing remembrance of Nazis and communist secret police in former headquarters/torture site. **Hours:** Tue-Sun 10:00-18:00, closed Mon. See page 613.

▲▲Heroes' Square Mammoth tribute to Hungary's historic figures, fronted by art museums. See page 617.

▲▲House of Music Hungary Boldly modern building in City Park with a stirring, interactive exhibit about Hungarian and world music. **Hours:** Tue-Sun 10:00-18:00, closed Mon. See page 618.

▲▲City Park Budapest's backyard, with Art Nouveau zoo, Transylvanian Vajdahunyad Castle replica, amusement park, and Széchenyi Baths. See page 620.

▲▲Vajdahunyad Castle Epcot-like replica of a Transylvanian castle and other historical buildings. See page 620.

▲▲Holocaust Memorial Center Excellent memorial and museum honoring Hungarian victims of the Holocaust. **Hours:** Tue-Sun 10:00-18:00, closed Mon. See page 621.

▲**St. István's Basilica** Budapest's largest church, with a saint's withered fist and great city views. **Hours:** Mon 9:00-16:30, Tue-Sat 9:00-17:45, Sun 13:00-17:45, panorama terrace and treasury open daily until 19:00. See page 598.

▲**Hungarian National Museum** Expansive collection of fragments from Hungary's history. **Hours:** Tue-Sun 10:00-18:00, closed Mon. See page 605.

▲**Rumbach Street Synagogue** Moorish-style synagogue with a grand interior, balcony views, and an exhibit on Hungarian Jews. **Hours:** Sun-Thu 10:00-20:00 (Oct and March-April until 18:00), Fri 10:00-16:00; Nov-Feb Sun-Thu 10:00-16:00, Fri until 14:00; closed Sat year-round and on Jewish holidays. See page 609.

▲**Margaret Island** Budapest's traffic-free urban playground, with spas, ruins, gardens, a game farm, and fountains, set in the middle of the Danube. See page 600.

Buda
▲▲**Matthias Church** Landmark Neo-Gothic church with gilded history-book interior and revered 16th-century statue of Mary and Jesus. **Hours:** Mon-Sat 9:00-17:00, Sun from 13:00. See page 629.

▲▲**Gellért Baths** Touristy baths in historic Buda hotel. **Hours:** Daily 9:00-19:00. See page 633.

▲▲**Rudas Baths** Half-millennium-old Turkish dome over a series of hot-water pools. **Hours:** Daily 6:00-20:00, nighttime bathing Fri-Sat 22:00-late. See page 634.

▲**Hungarian National Gallery** Top works by Hungarian artists, housed in the Royal Palace. **Hours:** Tue-Sun 10:00-18:00, closed Mon. See page 626.

▲**Hospital in the Rock and Nuclear Bunker** Fascinating underground network of hospital and bomb-shelter corridors from World War II and the Cold War. **Hours:** Daily 10:00-19:00. See page 632.

Day Trips from Budapest
▲▲**Memento Park** Larger-than-life communist statues collected in one park, on the outskirts of town. **Hours:** Daily 10:00-sunset. See page 677.

▲▲Hungarian Parliament (Országház)

With an impressive facade and an even more extravagant interior, the oversized Hungarian Parliament dominates the Danube riverbank. A hulking Neo-Gothic base topped by a soaring Neo-Renaissance dome, it's one of the city's top landmarks. Touring the building offers the chance to stroll through one of Budapest's most dazzling interiors.

Cost and Hours: 10,000 Ft for a required 45-minute tour in English (with a tour guide or an audioguide); visitors center open with frequent tour departures daily 8:00-18:00; Nov-April 8:00-16:00 (Fri-Sun until 18:00 in April). On Mondays when parliament is in session (generally about two times per month Sept-May), there are no tours after 10:00.

Information: +36 1 441 4904, www.parlament.hu.

Advance Tickets Recommended: Tickets come with an appointed tour time and usually sell out—sometimes two weeks in advance (even sooner at busy times). Book ahead through the official website (www.jegymester.hu/parlament). Select "Parliament Visit," then a date and time of an English tour; some are with an audioguide, while others have a tour guide (same price).

If you can't get tickets online, additional same-day tickets are typically available each morning. These are released shortly after 8:00 and can be booked online or purchased in person—but come early, as they're often sold out by 9:00.

After booking, you'll be sent an eticket (print it if you can). At your appointed time, head to the Parliament visitors center—a modern, underground space at the northern end of the long Parliament building (look for the statue of a lion on a pillar). If you can't print your ticket, arrive early and go to the information desk (not the ticket desk, which can have long lines) to ask them to print it for you.

Getting There: Ride tram #2 to the Országház stop, which is next to the visitors center entrance (Kossuth Tér 1, district V). You can also ride the M2/red Metró line to Kossuth Tér, then walk to the other end of the Parliament building to find the visitors center.

Background: The Parliament was built from 1885 to 1902 to celebrate the Hungarian millennium year of 1896. Its elegant, frilly spires and riverside location were inspired by its counterpart in London (where the architect studied). When completed, the Parliament was a striking and cutting-edge example of the mix-and-match Historicist style of the day. The building is at once grandly ambitious and a hodgepodge of various influences—a Neo-Gothic palace topped with a Neo-Renaissance dome, which once had a huge, red communist star on top of the tallest spire. Fittingly, it's the city's top icon. The best views of the Parliament are from across the Danube—especially in the late-afternoon sunlight.

Visiting the Parliament: The visitors center has WCs, a café, a gift shop, and the Museum of the History of the Hungarian National Assembly. Also in the lobby is a brief but fun **virtual reality ride** in a hot-air balloon, which whisks you for about five minutes over the rooftop of the still-under-construction Parliament building, circa 1894 (2,500 Ft).

With your ticket in hand, be at the security checkpoint inside the visitors center at least five minutes before your tour departure time.

On the 45-minute tour, your guide will explain the history and symbolism of the building's intricate decorations and offer a lesson in the Hungarian parliamentary system. You'll also see dozens of bushy-mustachioed statues illustrating the occupations of workaday Hungarians through history.

You'll see the building's monumental entryway and 96-step grand staircase—slathered in gold foil and frescoes, and bathed in shimmering stained-glass light. Then you'll gape up under the ornate gilded dome for a peek at the heavily guarded Hungarian crown, which is overlooked by statues of 16 great Hungarian monarchs, from St. István to Habsburg empress Maria Theresa. Finally, you'll walk through a cushy lounge—across one of Europe's largest carpets—to see the legislative chamber.

• *The vast square behind the Parliament is studded with attractions. Stay where you are for a quick...*

Kossuth Tér Spin-Tour

This square is sprinkled with interesting monuments and packed with Hungarian history. But it's gone through a lot of changes in the last few years, under the steady guidance of the ruling Fidesz party, led by Viktor Orbán. A nativist, nationalistic party, which swept to power after Hungarians grew weary of the bumblings of the poorly organized, shortsighted left-wing opposition party, Fidesz has exerted its influence over every walk of Hungarian life... beginning with the look of this building and square, and the monuments around it. The square itself used to be a more higgledy-piggledy mix of ragged asphalt, parks, monuments, and trees. But Fidesz wanted the mighty Parliament building to stand bold and unobstructed. Several older monuments (including, ironically, an "eternal" flame honoring victims of the communists) were swept away. Trees were cut down overnight, before would-be protesters could make a peep. And today the square has a scrubbed-clean look that some critics consider borderline-fascist.

BUDAPEST

1956

The year 1956 is etched into the Hungarian psyche. In that year, the people of Budapest staged the Soviet Bloc's first major uprising against the communist regime. It also marked the first time that the Soviets implicitly acknowledged, in brutally putting down the uprising, that the people of Eastern Europe were not "communist by choice."

The seeds of revolution were sown with the death of a tyrant: Josef Stalin passed away on March 5, 1953. Suddenly the choke hold that Moscow had on its satellite states loosened. During this time of "de-Stalinization," Hungarian premier Imre Nagy presided over two years of mild reform, before his political opponents (and Moscow) became nervous and demoted him. (You can read more about Nagy later in this chapter.)

In 1955, Austria declared its neutrality in the Cold War. This thrust Hungary to the front line of the Iron Curtain and raised the stakes both for Hungarians who wanted freedom and for Soviets who wanted to preserve their buffer zone. When Stalin's successor, Nikita Khrushchev, condemned Stalin's crimes in a "secret speech" to communist leaders in February 1956, it emboldened the Soviet Bloc's dissidents. A workers' strike in Poznań, Poland, in October inspired Hungarians to follow their example.

On October 23, 1956, the Hungarian uprising began. A student union group gathered in Budapest at 15:00 to articulate a list of 16 demands against the communist regime. Then they marched toward Parliament, their numbers gradually swelling. One protester defiantly cut the Soviet-style insignia out of the center of the Hungarian flag, which would become the uprising's symbol.

By nightfall, some 200,000 protesters filled Kossuth Tér behind Parliament, calling for Imre Nagy, the one communist leader they believed could bring change. Nagy finally appeared around 21:00. Ever the pragmatic politician, he implored patience. Following the speech, a large band of protesters took matters into their own hands, marched to City Park, and tore down the hated Stalin statue that stood there (see page 682).

Another group went to the National Radio building to read their demands on the air. The ÁVH (communist police) refused to let them do it and eventually opened fire on the protesters. The peaceful protests evolved into an armed insurrection, as frightened civilians gathered weapons and supplies.

Overnight, Moscow decided to intervene. Budapesters awoke on October 24 to find Red Army troops occupying their city. That morning, Imre Nagy—who had just been promoted again to prime minister—promised reforms and tried to keep a lid on the simmering discontent.

The next day, October 25, a huge crowd gathered on Kossuth Tér behind the Parliament to hear from Nagy. In the hubbub, shots rang out as Hungarian and Soviet soldiers opened fire on the (mostly unarmed) crowd. Of the victims, 72 deaths are known by name, but likely hundreds more were injured or perished.

The Hungarians fought back with an improvised guerilla resistance. They made use of any guns they could get their hands on, as well as Molotov cocktails, to strike against the Soviet occupiers. Combatants included many adolescents (the celebrated "Pest Youth"). The fighting tore apart the city, and some of the fallen were buried in impromptu graves in city parks.

Political infighting in Moscow paralyzed the Soviet response, and an uneasy cease-fire fell over Budapest. For 10 tense days, it appeared that the Soviets might allow Nagy to push through some reforms. Nagy, a firmly entrenched communist, had always envisioned a less repressive regime...but within limits. While he was at first reluctant to take on the mantle of the uprising's leadership, he gradually began to echo what he was hearing on the streets. He called for free elections, the abolishment of the ÁVH, the withdrawal of Soviet troops, and Hungary's secession from the Warsaw Pact.

But when the uprisers attacked and killed ÁVH officers and communist leaders in Budapest, it bolstered the case of the Moscow hardliners. On November 4, the Red Army launched a brutal counterattack in Budapest that left the rebels reeling. At 5:20 that morning, Imre Nagy's voice came over the radio to beg the world for assistance. Later that morning, he sought asylum at the Yugoslav Embassy across the street from City Park. He was never seen alive in public again.

János Kádár—an ally of Nagy's who was palatable to the uprisers, yet firmly loyal to Moscow—was installed as prime minister. The fighting dragged on for about another week, but the uprising was eventually crushed. By the end, 2,500 Hungarians and more than 700 Soviets were dead, and 20,000 Hungarians were injured. Communist authorities arrested more than 15,000 people, of whom at least 200 were executed (including Imre Nagy). Anyone who had participated in the uprising was blacklisted; fearing this and other forms of retribution, some 200,000 Hungarians fled to the West.

Though the 1956 Uprising met a tragic end, within a few years Kádár did succeed in softening the regime, and the milder, so-called "goulash communism" emerged. And today, even though the communists are long gone, the legacy of 1956 pervades the Hungarian consciousness. Some Budapest buildings are still pockmarked with bullet holes from '56, and many Hungarians who fled the country in that year still have not returned. October 23 remains Hungary's most cherished holiday.

BUDAPEST

Look to the right end of the Parliament. Poking up is a **pillar** topped by a lion being strangled and bitten by a giant snake (a typically heavy-handed Fidesz monument). This pillar marks the entrance to the Parliament visitors center.

Looking a bit farther to the right, at the end of the park you'll see a **monument to Lajos Kossuth,** the square's namesake, who led the 1848 Revolution against the Habsburgs.

The street that leaves this square behind Kossuth's left shoulder is Falk Miksa Utca, Budapest's **"antique row"**—a great place to browse for nostalgic souvenirs.

Panning right from the Kossuth statue, across the tram tracks you'll see a stately palace. The design was the first runner-up for the Parliament building, so they built it here, to house the **Supreme Court.**

To the right, the **Ministry of Agriculture** was the second runner-up for the Parliament. Today it features a very low-profile, but poignant, **monument to the victims of the 1956 Uprising** against Soviet rule: At the right end of the protruding arcade, notice that the walls are pockmarked with little metal dollops. Two days into the uprising, on October 25, the ÁVH (communist police) and Soviet troops on the rooftop above opened fire on demonstrators gathered in this square—massacring many and leaving no doubt that Moscow would not tolerate dissent. In the monument, each of the little metal knobs represents a bullet.

In the foreground, between you and the two big palaces, is a long, rectangular reflecting pond—a memorial to the people killed by government troops when they revolted here in 1956.

Between those two hulking buildings, notice a long, somber ramp that leads down toward an eternal flame—flickering behind giant stone plinths. This so-called **Memorial of National Solidarity** (Összetartozás Emlékhelye) commemorates the Treaty of Trianon, which stripped Hungary (one of the losers of World War I) of two-thirds of its historic territory. The walls of the ramp are etched with the names of cities and towns that were once part of a much larger, pre-Trianon Hungary. At the base, the flame is surrounded by seven jagged plinths—representing the seven countries that currently own some piece of what was once Hungary.

Spin farther to the right, where a dramatic **equestrian statue of Ferenc Rákóczi** stands in the park. Rákóczi valiantly—but unsuccessfully—led the Hungarians in their War of Independence (1703-1711) against the Habsburgs.

Now walk toward the far-left side of the Parliament (toward the river). Just before reaching the corner of the building, find the underground memorial marked *1956* (free, closed Mon). Head down the **stairs** to find a **memorial to the 1956 Uprising** that began on this very square. Follow the red line on the floor—first right, and then left. You'll see photos of the events, good English descriptions, and video interviews of eyewitnesses to the massacre on this square on October 25, 1956 (as well as other government mass shootings around Hungary that fall). At the end of the hall is a memorial tomb to those killed by Hungarian secret police, and the symbol of the uprising: a tattered Hungarian flag with a hole cut out of the center.

If you're interested in this grand building's history, a similar underground exhibit on the opposite side (find the stairs down, back toward Kossuth) is a **lapidarium** *(kőtár),* holding some original statues and adornments that once encrusted the Parliament (free, closed Mon).

• *Now let's take a quick...*

Monuments Stroll

Budapest is a city of great monuments, and some of the most vivid are on or near this square.

• *Circle around the left side of the giant Parliament building, passing another statue on a pillar, and walk all the way to the banister overlooking a spectacular view of Buda. Walk along the banister to the left until you come upon a statue of a young man, lost deep in thought, gazing into the Danube.*

Attila József (1905-1937): This beloved modern poet lived a tumultuous, productive, and short life before he took his own life at age 32. József's poems of life, love, and death—mostly written in the 1920s and 1930s—are considered the high point of Hungarian literature. His birthday (April 11) is celebrated as National Hungarian Poetry Day.

Here József reenacts a scene from one of his best poems, "At the Danube." It's a hot day—his jacket lies in a heap next to him, his shirtsleeves are rolled up, and he cradles his hat loosely in his left hand. In the poem, József uses the Danube as a metaphor for life—for the way it has interconnected cities and also times—as he reflects that his ancestors likely pondered the Danube from this same spot.

• *Stand along the railing in front of József, just above the busy road. If you visually trace the Pest riverbank to the left about 100 yards, just before the tree-filled, riverfront park, you can barely see several low-profile dots lining the embankment. This is a...*

Holocaust Monument: Consisting of 60 pairs of iron shoes, this monument commemorates the Jews who were killed when the Nazis' puppet government, the Arrow Cross, came to power in Hungary in 1944. While many Jews were sent to concentration camps, the Arrow Cross massacred some of them right here, shooting them and letting their bodies fall into the Danube.

BUDAPEST

Imre Nagy (1896-1958)

The Hungarian politician Imre Nagy (IHM-reh nodge), now thought of as an anticommunist hero, was actually a lifelong communist. In the 1930s, he allegedly worked for the Soviet secret police. In the late 1940s, he quickly moved up the hierarchy of Hungary's communist government, becoming prime minister during a period of reform in 1953. But when his proposed changes alarmed Moscow, Nagy was quickly demoted.

When the 1956 Uprising broke out, Nagy was drafted to become the head of the movement to soften the severity of the communist regime. Some suspect that Nagy himself didn't fully grasp the dramatic sea change represented by the uprising. When he appeared at the Parliament building on the night of October 23 to speak to the reform-craving crowds for the first time, he began by addressing his compatriots with, "Dear comrades..." When the audience booed, he amended it: "Dear friends..." The crowd went wild.

But the optimism was short lived. The Soviets violently put down the uprising, arrested and sham-tried Nagy, executed him, and buried him disgracefully, face down in an unmarked grave. The regime forced Hungary to forget about Nagy.

Later, when communism was in its death throes in 1989, the Hungarian people rediscovered Nagy as a hero. His body was located, exhumed, and given a ceremonial funeral at Heroes' Square. This event is considered a pivotal benchmark in that year of tremendous change. By the year's end, the Berlin Wall would fall, and the Czechs and Slovaks would stage their Velvet Revolution.

The next chapter in Nagy's legacy has been written by Fidesz, who have recently reversed the rehabilitation of Nagy's image. Because Nagy's ties to communism place him firmly on the left, Fidesz views him as an ideological enemy. The 2018 removal of the Nagy statue facing the Parliament is just the latest in a long, sad history of this great reformer being exploited as a political pawn.

• *For a closer look at the shoes, use the crosswalk (50 yards to your right) to cross the busy embankment road and follow the waterline.*

When you're ready to move on, turn your back to the Danube and walk directly inland, following the tram tracks past an entrance to the Metró. From the back corner of Kossuth Tér, veer right, to a little tree-filled park.

Vértanúk Tere and the Missing Imre Nagy Monument: This small square is dominated by yet another recent monument—this one with a generic, chain-mailed Lady Hungaria honoring **Victims of the Red Terror** (A Nemzet Vértanúinak), when approximately 500 Hungarians lost their lives (including former prime minister

István Tisza) during a brief period of communist rule at the end of World War I. Around back, a valiant hero fights a dragon; this is a vague and generic monument to *all* victims of communism.

But the more significant story is the monument you *won't* see on this square: a stirring homage to the 1956 hero Imre Nagy. Even in this city of abundant monuments, the Nagy statue was a favorite, with powerful symbolism: Nagy, standing on a bridge—representing his dream of creating a system that would bridge stifling Soviet-style communism and a more humane worldview—was literally keeping a watchful eye on the Parliament across the square. One night in 2018 it was removed, with no warning and under cover of darkness, by Fidesz authorities who couldn't get past Nagy's association with communism (even if he was a reformer). It has since been relocated to Jászai Mari

Tér (described later, on page 601). Nagy is internationally lauded as a Hungarian hero and a martyr of the USSR. If wanting to honor "victims of communism"...why not simply keep that statue where it was?

• *Go up the short, diagonal street beyond Vértanúk Tere, called Vécsey Utca. After one block, you emerge into...*

▲Szabadság Tér ("Liberty Square")

One of Budapest's most genteel squares, this space is marked by a controversial monument to the Soviet soldiers who liberated

Hungary at the end of World War II, and ringed by both fancy old apartment blocks and important buildings (such as the former Hungarian State Television headquarters, the US Embassy, and the National Bank of Hungary). A fine café, fun-filled playgrounds, statues of prominent Americans (Ronald Reagan and Harry Hill Bandholtz), and yet another provocative monument (to the Hungarian victims of the Nazis) round out the square's landmarks.

Ronald Reagan: When Fidesz took power in 2010, they quickly began rolling back previous democratic reforms and imposing alarming constraints on the media. Many international ob-

BUDAPEST

Kolodko Minis

Since 2010, Ukrainian-born artist Mihály Kolodko has quietly scattered a series of small cast-bronze statues all over the cityscape of Budapest—known collectively as "Kolodko Minis," each no larger than a Barbie doll. Originally, the artist was drawn to this mini-medium because it was much simpler than getting commissions and permissions for large-scale works. But now Kolodko's distinctive style has made him an in-demand artist (www.kolodkoart.com).

Kolodko's subjects run the gamut, thematically. Many of them are historical: Franz Josef relaxing in a hammock; Franz Liszt sitting on his suitcase at the airport named for him; a drunken Roman legionnaire; a tiny tank to commemorate the 1956 Uprising; and a wind-up Trabant (the car from communist times). Kolodko often celebrates Jewish culture in his sculptures. You'll find Zionist pioneer Tivadar (a.k.a. Theodor) Herzl (near the Great Synagogue); WWII paratrooper Hannah Szenes; Harry Houdini; and pianist Rezső Seress. And some pointed additions popped up after Russia's 2022 invasion of Ukraine: Vladimir Putin piloting a warship, and a Russian soldier plundering someone's pantry.

Others are from pop culture: Kermit the Frog, Ratatouille the culinary rat, Mr. Bean's teddy bear (attached to the wall of the former British Embassy—a commentary on Brexit), a balloon-dog homage to Jeff Koons, a Rubik's Cube (invented by a Hungarian), a urinal (à la Marcel Duchamp), or characters from Hungarian cartoons—Mekk Elek the handyman goat, Főkukac the happy worm, and Kockásfülű Nyúl the checkered-ear rabbit.

And some are simply whimsical, such as a dead squirrel, still clutching a handgun, outlined in chalk. There's also a variety of distinctly Hungarian dogs—such as the Puli and the Viszla.

With its many ostentatious buildings, Budapest is a city that trains visitors to expand their scope—to look up, zoom out, and take it all in. But the Kolodko Minis encourage you to do just the opposite: Focus in on details.

There are about two dozen Kolodko Minis all around the city. I've pointed out a few in this book, but part of the fun is tracking them down yourself. You can find articles that list them and explain their significance, and most of the statues are on Google Maps (search for "Kolodko Mini"). Just be prepared to hunt...these can be as easy to miss as they are satisfying to discover.

servers—including the US government—spoke out against what they considered an infringement on freedom of the press. In an effort to appease American concerns, Prime Minister Orbán erected this statue—and then, perhaps not quite grasping the subtleties of American politics, invited then-Secretary of State Hillary Clinton to the unveiling. It's fun to watch the steady stream of passersby (both Hungarians and tourists) do a double-take, chuckle, then snap a photo with The Gipper.

• *Now enjoy a slow stroll to the far end of the square, where you'll find...*

George H. W. Bush: In 1989, Bush became the first sitting US president to visit Hungary, shortly before the fall of the Iron Curtain, and just days after the death of the Hungarian premier János Kádár. He was giving a speech on Kossuth Tér in the pouring rain, but the paper with his prepared remarks became soaked and unreadable...so instead, he delivered an impromptu speech that wowed the crowd.

• *At the opposite end of Liberty Square from where you entered, you'll find a lively playground in one corner. Along the bottom of this side of the square, near the fountain, look for the...*

Monument to the Hungarian Victims of the Nazis: This heavy-handed Fidesz production commemorates the German invasion of Hungary on March 19, 1944. Standing in the middle of a broken colonnade, an immaculate angel holds an orb with a double cross (part of the crown jewels and a symbol of Hungarian sovereignty). Overhead, a mechanized-looking black eagle (symbolizing Germany) screeches in, its talons poised to strike.

Like so many recent additions to this area, this monument was instantly controversial for the way it whitewashes Hungarian history. Viewing this, you might imagine that Hungary was a peaceful land that was unwittingly caught up in the Nazi war machine. In fact, the Hungarian government was an ally of Nazi Germany for more than three years before this invasion.  And there's no question that, after the invasion, many Hungarians enthusiastically collaborated with their new Nazi overlords.

Mindful of the old adage about people who forget their own history, locals have created a **makeshift counter-memorial** to the victims of the World War II-era Hungarians (not just Germans) in front of this official monument.

On a lighter note, the **fountain** that faces the monument is particularly entertaining. Sensors can tell when you're about to walk through the wall of water…and the curtain of water automatically parts just long enough for you to pass.

• *From the monument, continue two blocks straight ahead, up Herceg-prímás Utca. You'll emerge into a broad plaza in front of…*

▲St. István's Basilica (Szent István Bazilika)

Budapest's biggest church celebrates St. István, Hungary's first Christian king. You can see his withered, blackened, millennium-old fist in a gilded reliquary. Or you can zip up on an elevator (or climb up stairs partway) to a panorama terrace with views over the rooftops of Pest. The skippable treasury has ecclesiastical items, historical exhibits, and artwork (reached by elevator, to the right as you face the church). The church also hosts regular organ concerts (advertised near the entry).

Cost and Hours: Basilica—2,000 Ft, open to tourists Mon 9:00-16:30, Tue-Sat 9:00-17:45, Sun 13:00-17:45; panorama terrace and treasury—3,200 Ft, open daily until 19:00; 4,500 Ft ticket covers all three; periodic concerts inside the basilica (see page 648); Szent István Tér, district V, M1: Bajcsy-Zsilinszky Út or M3: Arany János Utca.

Visiting the Church: Though it looks grand and old, this church only dates back about 130 years—like so many Budapest landmarks, it was built around the millennial celebrations of 1896.

Buy your tickets in the shop around the right side of the church. Then head up the grand stairs. The entrance to the interior is to the left, and to the right is the access to the treasury and the panoramic tower (both skippable).

St. István's interior is dimly lit but gorgeously restored; all the gilded decorations glitter in the low light. You'll see not Jesus but St. István (Stephen), Hungary's first Christian king, glowing above the high altar.

Stand in the back and enjoy the glittering entirety of the interior. The church's main claim to fame is the **"holy right hand"** of **St. István.** The sacred fist—a somewhat grotesque, 1,000-year-old withered stump—is inside a jeweled box. Pop in a 200 Ft coin for two minutes of light.

• *From here, you're very close to the boulevard called Andrássy Út, which leads to the Opera House, House of Terror, and City Park (all described later). To get there, walk around the right side of the basilica and turn right on busy Bajcsy-Zsilinszky Út; Andrássy Út begins across the street, on your left.*

*But for now, we'll head to the Danube for a good look at the mighty Chain Bridge. From the square in front of the basilica, walk straight down Zrínyi Utca. (Note that about a block off Zrínyi Utca is the **Budapest Retro Experience**—a kitschy, engaging, but ultimately lightweight look at life during communist times—from Zrínyi Utca, turn left onto Október 6). Otherwise, continue down Zrínyi Utca, which deadends at the big traffic circle called Széchenyi István Tér. Turn left and walk a half-block to the entrance (on the left) of the...*

Gresham Palace

This was Budapest's first building in the popular Historicist style—but it also incorporates elements of Art Nouveau. Budapest boomed at a time when ar-

chitectural eclecticism—mashing together bits and pieces of different styles—was in vogue. But because much of the city's construction was compressed into a short window of time, even these disparate styles enjoy an unusual harmony. Damaged in World War II, the building was an eyesore for decades. In 1999, the Gresham Palace was meticulously restored to its former glory and converted to a luxury hotel. Even if you can't afford to stay here (see "Sleeping in Budapest," later), saunter into the lobby and absorb the gorgeous details (Széchenyi Tér 5, district V, M1: Vörösmarty Tér or M2: Kossuth Tér).

• *Be sure to get a good look at the Gresham Palace's fine facade. This also puts you right next to the grand...*

Chain Bridge (Széchenyi Lánchíd)

One of the world's great bridges connects Pest's Széchenyi Tér and Buda's Clark Ádám Tér. This historic, iconic bridge, guarded by lions (symbolizing power), is Budapest's most enjoyable and convenient bridge to cross on foot.

Until the mid-19th century, only pontoon barges spanned the Danube between Buda and Pest. In the winter, the pontoons had to be pulled in, leaving locals to rely on ferries (in good weather) or a frozen river. People often walked across the frozen Danube, only to get stuck on the other side during a thaw, with nothing to do but wait for another cold snap.

Count István Széchenyi was stranded for a week trying to get to his father's funeral. After missing it, Széchenyi commissioned Budapest's first permanent bridge—which was also a major symbolic step toward the unification of Buda and Pest. The Chain Bridge was built by Scotsman Adam Clark between 1842 and 1849, and it immediately became an important symbol of Budapest. The biggest and longest span of its day, the Chain Bridge was a model for famous suspension bridges that followed, including the Golden Gate in San Francisco and the Verrazano-Narrows in New York.

Széchenyi—a man of the Enlightenment—charged both commoners and nobles a toll for crossing his bridge, making it an emblem of equality in those tense times. Like all the city's bridges, the Chain Bridge was destroyed by the Nazis at the end of World War II, but it was quickly rebuilt.

• *As you look out to the Danube from here, to the right you can see the tip of...*

▲Margaret Island (Margitsziget)

In the Middle Ages, this island in the Danube (just north of the Parliament) was known as the "Isle of Hares." In the 13th century, a desperate King Béla IV swore that if God were to deliver Hungary from the invading Tatars, he would dedicate his youngest daughter Margaret to the Church. When the Tatars left, Margaret was shipped to a nunnery here. Margaret embraced her new life as a castaway nun and later refused her father's efforts to force her into a politically expedient marriage with a Bohemian king. As a reward for her faith, she became St. Margaret of Hungary.

Today, while the island officially has no permanent residents, urbanites flock here to relax in a huge, leafy park. No cars are allowed on the island—just public buses. The island rivals City Park as the best spot in town for strolling, jogging, biking (you can rent a bike at Bringóhintó, with branches at both ends of the island), and people-watching. Rounding out the island's attractions are an iconic old water tower, the remains of Margaret's convent, a rose garden, a game farm, and a "musical fountain" that performs to the strains of Hungarian folk tunes.

Getting There: Bus #26 begins at Nyugati/Western train station, crosses the Margaret Bridge, then drives up through the middle of the island—allowing visitors to easily get from one end to the other (3-6/hour). **Trams** #4 and #6, which circulate around the Great Boulevard, cross the Margaret Bridge and stop at the southern tip of the island, a short walk from some of the attractions. It's otherwise a long but scenic **walk** between Margaret Island and other points in the city.

• On the Pest embankment, just across the bridge from Margaret Island, are the...

Monuments of Jászai Mari Tér

This otherwise nondescript square is home to several evocative memorials. It's a few minutes' walk north of the Parliament area (along antiques-lined Falk Miksa Utca), and it's the northern terminus of scenic tram #2 (and also on the route of Great Boulevard trams #4 and #6).

The main draw is the **statue of Imre Nagy**—the great communist reformer who reluctantly led Hungary's 1956 Uprising (see the sidebar on page 594). The statue depicts Nagy standing on a bridge, symbolizing the middle path he sought between stifling, Soviet-style communism and a freer society.

Just toward the river from Nagy, tucked right up against the bridge to Margaret Island, you'll see a long, black, marble wall. This is a monument to the victims of a horrific accident that occurred in May 2019, when a sightseeing boat called *Hableány (Mermaid)* ran into a Viking cruise ship under this bridge, killing 26 tourists and two crew members.

For a cheerier tribute, head a block away from the river on the busy ring road and pause at Falk Miksa Utca to see **Columbo,** the Hungarian-American actor Peter Falk.

DOWNTOWN PEST (BELVÁROS)

Pest's Belváros ("Inner Town") is its gritty urban heart—simultaneously its most beautiful and ugliest district. You'll see fancy facades, some of Pest's best views from the Danube embankment, richly decorated old coffeehouses that offer a whiff of the city's golden age, and a cavernous, colorful market hall filled with Hungarian goodies. But you'll also experience crowds, grime, and pungent smells like nowhere else in Budapest. Atmospherically shot through with the crumbling elegance of former greatness, Budapest is a place where creaky old buildings and sleek modern ones feel equally at home. This is a city in transition. Enjoy the rough edges while you can. They're being sanded off at a remarkable pace—and soon, tourists like you will be nostalgic for the "authentic" old days.

Below, I've linked the main landmarks in the Town Center with walking directions, starting at the square called Vörösmarty Tér and ending at the Great Market Hall.

▲Vörösmarty Tér

The central square of the Town Center, dominated by the venerable Gerbeaud coffee shop and a giant statue of the revered Romantic poet Mihály Vörösmarty, is the hub of Pest sightseeing.

BUDAPEST

At the north end of the square is the landmark **Gerbeaud café** and pastry shop. Between the world wars, the well-to-do ladies of Budapest would meet here after shopping their way up Váci Utca. Today, it's still *the* meeting point in Budapest... for tourists, at least. Consider stepping inside to appreciate the

elegant old decor, or for a cup of coffee and a slice of cake. Better yet, hold off for now—even more appealing cafés are nearby (see "Budapest's Café Culture," on page 673).

The yellow **M1 Metró stop** in front of Gerbeaud is the entrance to the shallow *Földalatti*, or "underground"—the first subway on the Continent (built for the Hungarian millennial celebration in 1896). Today, it still carries passengers to Andrássy Út sights, running under that boulevard all the way to City Park.

Walk to the far end of the square and look up the street that's to your left. This traffic-free street (Deák Ferenc Utca)—also known as **"Fashion Street,"** with top-end shops—is the easiest and most pleasant way to walk to Deák Tér and, beyond it, through Erzsébet Tér to Andrássy Út.

• *Extending straight ahead from Vörösmarty Tér is a broad, bustling, pedestrianized shopping street.*

Váci Utca

Dating from 1810-1850, Váci Utca (VAHT-see OOT-zaw) is one of the oldest streets of Pest. *Váci Utca* means "street to Vác"—a town 25 miles to the north. This has long been the street where the elite of Pest would go shopping, then strut their stuff for their neighbors on an evening promenade. Today, the tourists do the strutting here—while the Hungarians go to American-style shopping malls.

This boulevard—Budapest's tourism artery—was a dreamland for Eastern Bloc residents back in the 1980s. It was here that they fantasized about what it might be like to be free, while drooling over Nikes, Adidas, and Big Macs before any of these "Western evils" were introduced elsewhere in the Warsaw Pact region. In fact, partway down the street (on the right, at Régi Posta Utca) is **the first McDonald's behind the Iron Curtain,** where people from all over the Eastern Bloc flocked to dine. Since you had to wait in a long line—stretching around the block—to get a burger, it wasn't "fast food"...but at least it was "West food."

Ironically, this street—once prized by Hungarians and other Eastern Europeans because it felt so Western—is what many foreign tourists today mistakenly think is the "real Budapest." Visitors mesmerized by this stretch of souvenir stands, tourist-gouging eateries, and upscale boutiques are likely to miss some more interesting and authentic areas just a block or two away. Don't fall for this trap. You can have a fun and fulfilling trip to this city without ever setting foot on Váci Utca.

• *For a more appealing people zone than Váci Utca, detour from Vörösmarty Tér a block toward the river, to the inviting...*

Danube Promenade

Some of the best views in Budapest are from this walkway facing Castle Hill—especially this stretch, between the white Elisabeth Bridge (left) and the iconic Chain Bridge (right). This is a favorite place to promenade *(korzó)*, strolling aimlessly and greeting friends.

Dominating this part of the promenade is the Neo-Romantic-style **Pesti Vigadó**—built in the 1880s and recently restored. Charmingly, the word *vigadó*—used to describe a concert hall—literally means "joyous place." In front, the playful statue of **the girl with her dog** captures the fun-loving spirit along this drag.

At the gap in the railing, notice the platform to catch **tram #2**, which goes frequently in each direction along the promenade—a handy way to connect riverside sights in Pest. It's also incredibly scenic. Take it once between the Great Market Hall (to the left) and the Parliament (to the right) just for fun.

• *About 30 more yards toward the Chain Bridge, find the little statue wearing a jester's hat. She's playing on the railing, with the castle behind her.*

The **_Little Princess_** is one of Budapest's symbols and a favorite photo-op for tourists. While many of the city's monuments have interesting backstories, more recent statues (like this one) are simply whimsical and fun.

• *Now walk along the promenade to the left (toward the white bridge). Directly in front of the corner Starbucks*

in the Marriott Hotel (and the nearby Shakespeare statue), *watch for the easy-to-miss stairs leading down under the tram tracks to a crosswalk that leads safely across the busy road to the riverbank. From the top of these stairs, look along the river.*

Lining the **embankment** are several long boats: Some are excursion boats for sightseeing trips up and down the Danube (especially pleasant at night), while others are overpriced (but scenic) restaurants. Kiosks along here dispense info and sell tickets for the various boat companies—look for Legenda Cruises (recommended earlier, under "Tours in Budapest"; their dock is just downstream from here—go down the stairs, cross the road, then walk 100 yards left).

• *From here, both the promenade and Váci Utca cut south through downtown. At the end of this zone is one of Budapest's top attractions.*

▲▲Great Market Hall (Nagyvásárcsarnok)

"Great" indeed is this gigantic marketplace. The Great Market Hall still keeps local shoppers happy, even as it has evolved into one of

the city's top tourist attractions. Goose liver, embroidered tablecloths, golden Tokaji Aszú wine, pickled peppers, communist-kitsch T-shirts, savory *lángos* pastries, patriotic green-white-and-red flags, and paprika of every degree of spiciness...if it's Hungarian, you'll find it here. Come to shop for souvenirs, to buy a picnic, or just to rattle around inside this vast, picturesque, Industrial Age hall (Mon 6:00-17:00, Tue-Fri until 18:00, Sat until 15:00, closed Sun, Fővám Körút 1, district IX, M4: Fővám Tér or M3: Kálvin Tér).

Visiting the Market Hall: Step inside the market and get your bearings: The cavernous interior features three levels. The ground floor has produce stands, bakeries, butcher stalls, heaps of paprika, goose liver, and salamis. Upstairs are stand-up eateries and souvenirs. And in the basement are a supermarket, a fish market, and piles of pickles.

Stroll along the market's "main drag" (straight ahead from the entry), enjoying the commotion of produce stands and vendors selling authentic Hungarian products. About halfway along, you'll see **paprika** on both sides. As you browse, note that there are two types of paprika: sweet (*édes,* used for flavor) and hot (*csípős,* used sparingly to add some kick). While you're at it, pick up some spicy pastes (which hold their flavor better than the fast-degrading powders): the spicy *Erős Pista,* the sweet *Édes Anna,* the soup-enhancing *Gulyáskrém,* and the intensely spicy condiment called, simply, "Red Gold" *(Piros Arany).*

After you've worked your way to the far end of the hall, take the escalator to the upper level. This is a convenient place to look for **souvenirs**—with a wide selection of items that are traditional (embroidery) and not-so-traditional (commie-kitsch T-shirts). While the quality is typically low and there are no bargains here, the prices are slightly better than out along Váci Utca. For tips, see "Shopping in Budapest," later.

As you move closer to the front half of the market, the left wall is lined with fun, cheap, stand-up, Hungarian-style fast-food joints and six-stool pubs. However, 90 percent of the clientele is tourists—with correspondingly high prices. I don't recommend this area for a meal, but you can walk along here to get a glimpse of traditional foods. Many stands sell the deep-fried snack called *lángos* (LAHN-gohsh)—similar to elephant ears, but savory rather than sweet. The most typical version is *sajtos tejfölös*—with sour cream and cheese. You can also add garlic *(fokhagyma)*. At the far end of the upper gallery, the **Fakanál Étterem** cafeteria above the main entrance is very touristy but handy and decent.

For a less glamorous look at the market, head down the escalators near the front of the market (below the restaurant) to the basement. Stop at one of the **pickle stands** and take a look. Hungarians pickle just about everything: peppers and cukes, of course, but also cauliflower, cabbage, beets, tomatoes, garlic, and so on.

Nearby: The **Bálna Budapest** shopping mall and cultural center stands along the riverbank behind the Great Market Hall. The complex was created by bridging a pair of circa-1881 brick warehouses with a swooping glass canopy that earns its name, "The Whale" *(bálna)*. It's a mix of shops, offices, eateries, and conference rooms (a three-minute stroll beyond the back door of the Great Market Hall; www.balnabudapest.hu).

NATIONAL MUSEUM AND PALACE DISTRICT

The Hungarian National Museum and Great Synagogue are along the Small Boulevard, between the Liberty Bridge/Great Market Hall and Deák Tér. The former Jewish Quarter, which sprawls behind the Great Synagogue, is also known as the Seventh District, one of Budapest's most happening nightlife zones, with a fun selection of ruin pubs (for details, see "Nightlife in Budapest," later).

▲Hungarian National Museum (Magyar Nemzeti Múzeum)

One of Budapest's biggest museums features all manner of Hungarian historic bric-a-brac, from the Paleolithic age to a more recent infestation of dinosaurs (the communists). Artifacts are explained by good, if dry, English descriptions. The museum adds substance to your understanding of Hungary's story—but it helps to have a pretty firm foundation

BUDAPEST

first (read "Hungarian History" on page 543). The most engaging part is room 20, where you'll find items from the communist period—including both pro- and (illegal) anti-Party propaganda. The exhibit ends with video footage of the 1989 end of communism—demonstrations, monumental parliament votes, and a final farewell to the last Soviet troops leaving Hungarian soil. The impressive Neoclassical building itself is historic: The 1848 Revolution against Habsburg rule was proclaimed from the front steps.

Cost and Hours: 2,900 Ft, more for temporary exhibits; Tue-Sun 10:00-18:00, closed Mon; near Great Market Hall at Múzeum Körút 14, district VIII, M3: Kálvin Tér, +36 1 327 7773, www.hnm.hu.

Nearby: The streets behind the National Museum—where locals far outnumber tourists—are part of the up-and-coming **Palace District.** For a nice taste of this area, stop by the Tasting Table wine shop to sample some Hungarian wines (see listing on page 671); or wander over to the delightful, leafy, no-name square where Baross Utca meets Reviczky Utca—with a bookseller kiosk, a lively al fresco café, and a distinctly Parisian ambience.

▲▲Great Synagogue (Nagy Zsinagóga)

Also called the Dohány Street Synagogue, Budapest's gorgeous synagogue is the biggest in Europe and the second biggest in the world (after the Temple Emanu-El of New York). A visit here has three parts: touring its ornately decorated interior; exploring the attached museum, which offers a concise lesson in the Jewish faith; and lingering in the evocative memorial garden, with its weeping willow *Tree of Life* sculpture and other poignant monuments.

Cost and Hours: 9,000 Ft for Great Synagogue, museum, and garden, includes free tour (about 2/hour); Sun-Thu 10:00-20:00 (Oct and March-April until 18:00), Fri 10:00-16:00; Nov-Feb Sun-Thu 10:00-16:00, Fri until 14:00; closed Sat year-round and Jewish holidays; Dohány Utca 2, district VII, near M2: Astoria or the Astoria stop on trams #47, #48, and #49, +36 1 343 0420, www.dohany-zsinagoga.hu.

❂ **Self-Guided Tour:** The synagogue's striking **exterior** captures the rich history of the building and the people it represents: The synagogue was completed in 1859 just outside what was then the city limits. Although Budapest's Jews held fast to their own faith, they also wished to demonstrate their worth and how well integrated they were with the greater community.

The two tall towers are not typical of traditional synagogues. The Moorish-flavored architecture is a sign of the Historicism of the time, which borrowed eclectic elements from past styles. Specifically, it evokes the Sephardic Jewish culture that flourished in Iberia; many Hungarian Jews are descended from that group, who fled here after being expelled from Spain in 1492. To some, the towers evoke Moorish minarets. Others note how these towers—along with the rosette (rose window)—helped the synagogue resemble Christian churches of the time. In fact, when it was built, the synagogue was dubbed by one cynic "the most beautiful Catholic synagogue in the world."

Step **inside.** Notice that the synagogue interior feels like a church with the symbols switched—with a basilica floor plan, a nave with two side aisles, two pulpits, and even a pipe organ. The organ—which Franz Liszt played for the building's inauguration—is a clue that this synagogue belonged to the most progressive of the three branches of Judaism here at the time. (Orthodox Jews would never be permitted to do the "work" of playing an organ on the Sabbath.)

In the ark, at the front of the main aisle, 25 surviving Torah scrolls are kept. Catholic priests hid these scrolls during World War II (burying them temporarily in a cemetery). The two-tiered balconies on the sides of the nave were originally for women, who worshipped separately from the men.

Ponder this building's recent history: Although it survived World War II, the Great Synagogue sat neglected for 40 years. But in 1990, it was painstakingly rebuilt, largely with financial support from the Hungarian American cosmetics magnate Estée Lauder. Theodor (Tivadar) Herzl, a pioneer of Zionism, was born in a house next door to the Great Synagogue (now gone). Other people of Hungarian Jewish descent include big names from every walk of life: Harry Houdini (born Erich Weisz), Elie Wiesel, Joseph Pulitzer, Tony Curtis (and his daughter Jamie Lee), George Cukor, Goldie Hawn, George Soros, Peter Lorre, and Eva and Zsa Zsa Gabor. A visit to the Great Synagogue and surrounding Jewish Quarter offers insight into this vital facet of Hungarian history and contemporary life.

• *When you're finished inside, exit through the main doors, turn right, and go to the opposite end of the front arcade. Enter the building, then head upstairs (by stairs or elevator) to the...*

BUDAPEST

Hungarian Jewish Museum (Magyar Zsidó Múzeum): This small but informative museum illuminates the Jewish faith, displaying a wide range of artifacts and succinct but engaging English explanations. The collection is always somewhat in flux, but typically you'll see objects representing the stages of Jewish life: a day, a week, a year, a lifetime. Everyday items reveal how Judaism was interwoven with all aspects of life. It also explains the major holidays of the Jewish calendar—from Rosh Hashanah and Yom Kippur to Purim and Hanukkah. One of the museum's prized pieces—typically displayed on the top floor—is a third-century tombstone from the Roman province of Pannonia (today's Hungary), roughly etched with a menorah.

• *Exiting back into the front courtyard, go down the passageway between the synagogue and the museum (straight ahead from the security checkpoint) to reach the...*

Memorial Garden: During the Soviet siege that ended the Nazi occupation of Budapest in the winter of 1944-1945, many Jews in the ghetto here died of exposure, starvation, and disease. Soon after the Soviets liberated the city, an estimated 2,281 Jews were buried here—considered Hungary's largest mass grave from the Holocaust. The trees and headstones (donated by survivors) were added later. The pillars you'll pass have historical photos of the synagogue and Jewish Quarter.

• *Reaching the end of the corridor, walk out to the garden behind the synagogue, where you'll find the...*

Tree of Life: Created by renowned artist Imre Varga, this weeping willow, cast in steel, was erected in 1990, soon after the fall of communism made it possible to acknowledge the Holocaust. The willow makes an upside-down menorah, and each of the 4,000 metal leaves is etched with the name of a Holocaust victim. New leaves are added all the time, donated by families of the victims.

• *Immediately behind the synagogue is the...*

Garden of the Just: This is a symbolic grave for the many diplomats from other nations who saved Hungarian Jews. The most famous of these—and the biggest name on the monument—is **Raoul Wallenberg** (1912-1947). An improbable hero, this ne'er-do-well Swedish playboy from a prominent family was sent as a diplomat to Hungary because nobody else wanted the post. He was empowered by the Swedish government to do whatever he could—bribe, threaten, lie, or blackmail—to save as many Jews as possible from the Nazis. He surpassed everyone's low expectations by dedicating (and ultimately sacrificing) his life to the cause. By giving Swedish passports to Jews and admitting them to safe houses, he succeeded in rescuing tens of thousands of people from certain death. Shortly after the Soviets arrived, Wallenberg was arrested, accused of being a US spy, sent to a gulag...and never seen alive again.

(Later, Russian authorities acknowledged he was executed in 1947, in Moscow's Lubyanka prison.)

The grave is also etched with the names of other "Righteous Among the Nations" who went above and beyond to save Jews. According to the Talmud, "Whoever saves one life, saves the world entire."

Other Jewish Quarter Sights

While this area was shrouded in soot and gloom during the communist period, today Budapest's Jewish Quarter is coming back to life. You'll find monuments and artifacts of Jewish history in these streets—but you sometimes have to hunt for them a bit.

Orthodox Synagogue: This colorfully decorated space is just two blocks behind the Great Synagogue. Built in the Vienna-inspired Secession style in 1912, this temple stood damaged and deserted for decades after World War II until being renovated in 2006. Today, it invites visitors to see its colorful, sumptuously decorated interior (1,000 Ft; unpredictable hours but likely Sun-Thu 10:00-17:30, Fri until 16:00; Oct-April Sun-Thu 10:00-16:00, Fri until 13:30; closed Sat year-round; enter down little alley, Kazinczy Utca 27, district VII, M2: Astoria).

Gozsdu Udvar: This long series of courtyards burrows through the middle of a city block, between Dob Utca 16 and Király Utca 13. When this neighborhood hosted a fast-growing Jewish population and space was at a premium, courtyards like this one were filled with community life: restaurants, shops, and other businesses.

After decades of neglect, this passage was spruced up and opened to the public. This genteel space—which evokes the golden age of Jewish life in Budapest—is once again filled with cafés and bars, and after hours it's a bustling nightlife hub.

▲Rumbach Street Synagogue: This exquisite synagogue, designed by Otto Wagner, recently reopened after an extensive refurbishment—and it's once again gleaming. The Moorish-style house of worship is a fascinating counterpoint to the Great Synagogue and complements it in many ways. The concise but compelling museum exhibit on the third floor is the best in town for understanding the history of Hungarian Jews (3,000 Ft; Sun-Thu 10:00-20:00 (Oct and March-April until 18:00), Fri 10:00-16:00; Nov-Feb Sun-Thu 10:00-16:00, Fri until 14:00; closed Sat year-

BUDAPEST

round and Jewish holidays; from the *Tree of Life* monument, it's two blocks down Rumbach Utca toward Andrássy Út, district VII, M2: Astoria or M1/M2/M3: Deák Tér and exit for Király Utca).

Jewish Local History Collection of Elisabethtown: This endearingly humble (but lovingly presented) exhibit offers a more intimate look at the lives of the Jewish people who once resided in this neighborhood. They've reconstructed an old building (formerly a ruin pub) and refurnished a middle-class Jewish family apartment upstairs. At the back of the building is a much smaller, more modest one-room apartment belonging to a poor Zionist printer and his family. English information is sparse, but you may be able to borrow an English audioguide (900 Ft; Sun-Thu 14:00-18:00, Fri 10:00-14:00, closed Sat, likely shorter hours in Nov-March; Csányi Utca 5, district VII, M1: Oktogon, +36 1 369 3688, www. erzsitt.hu).

ANDRÁSSY ÚT

Connecting Downtown Pest to City Park, Andrássy Út is Budapest's main boulevard, lined with plane trees, shops, theaters, cafés, and locals living very well. Budapesters like to think of Andrássy Út as the Champs-Elysées and Broadway rolled into one. While that's a stretch, it is a good place to stroll, get a feel for today's urban Pest, and visit a few top attractions on the way to Heroes' Square and City Park.

I've arranged these sights in the order you'll reach them if you walk up the boulevard from where it begins, near Deák Tér. The handy M1/yellow Metró line runs every couple of minutes just under the street, making it easy to skip several blocks ahead, or to backtrack (stops marked by yellow signs).

• *Three blocks up Andrássy Út on the left is the...*

▲▲Hungarian State Opera House
(Magyar Állami Operaház)

The Neo-Renaissance home of the Hungarian State Opera features performances (almost daily except during outdoor music

season, late June-early Sept) and delightful tours. The building dates from the 1890s, not long after Budapest had become co-capital of the Habsburg Empire. The Hungarians wanted to put their city on the map as a legitimate European capital, and that meant they needed an opera house. Emperor Franz Josef provided half the funds...on the condition that it be smaller than the

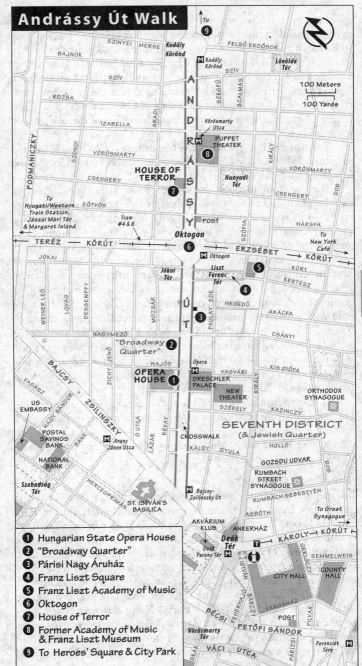

Andrássy Út Walk

To 9

FELSŐ ERDŐSOR

Kodály Körönd

KODÁLY KÖRÖND M

LÖVÖLDE TÉR

SZINYEI MERSE

BAJNOK

SZÍV

SZEGFŰ SZALMÁS

SZÍV

100 Meters
100 Yards

ROZSA

IZABELLA

ARADI

VÖRÖSMARTY UTCA

PUPPET THEATER 8

KIRÁLY

VÖRÖSMARTY

SZÖNDI

VÖRÖSMARTY

CSENGERY

HOUSE OF TERROR 7

HUNYADI TÉR

CSENGERY

DOB

PODMANICZKY

To Nyugati/Western Train Station, Jászai Mari Tér & Margaret Island

EÖTVÖS

POST

SZÓFIA

HÁRSFA

To New York Café

TERÉZ — KÖRÚT Tram #4 & 6

Oktogon 6

ERZSÉBET KÖRÚT

JÓKAI

OKTOGON M

WEINER LEO

LOVAG

DESSEWFFY

JÓKAI TÉR

MOZSÁR

Liszt Ferenc Tér 5

KÜRT

KERTÉSZ

4

HEGEDŰ

AKÁCFA

PAULAY EDE

3

CSÁNYI

NAGYMEZŐ

"Broadway Quarter" 2

ZICHY JENŐ

HAJÓS

Opera

ÚT

BAJCSY

ZSILINSZKY

VADÁSZ

NAGY SÁNDOR

OPERA HOUSE 1

OPERA M

DRESCHLER PALACE

VASVÁRI

KIS DIÓFA

ORTHODOX SYNAGOGUE

US EMBASSY

O UTCA

LÁZÁR

RÉVAY

NEW THEATER

SZÉKELY

KIRÁLY

KAZINCZY

POSTAL SAVINGS BANK

BANK

ARANY JÁNOS UTCA M

CROSSWALK

SEVENTH DISTRICT
(& Jewish Quarter)

NATIONAL BANK

KÁLDY

GYULA

HOLLÓ

GOZSDU UDVAR

Szabadság Tér

HERCEGPRÍMÁS

ST. ISTVÁN'S BASILICA

BAJCSY-ZSILINSZKY ÚT M

RUMBACH STREET SYNAGOGUE

RUMBACH SEBESTYÉN

DOB

ASBÓTH

To Great Synagogue

AKVÁRIUM KLUB

ANKERHÁZ

Deák Ferenc Tér M

Deák Tér M T

KÁROLY — KÖRÚT

SEMMELWEIS

CITY HALL

COUNTY HALL

NYÁRI

FEHÉRHAJÓ

BÁRCZY

VÁROSHÁZ

GERLÓCZY

Vörösmarty Tér

BÉCSI

PETŐFI SÁNDOR

POST

PILVAX

Ferenciek Tére M

DEÁK

VÁCI UTCA

PÁRIZSI

BUDAPEST

1 Hungarian State Opera House
2 "Broadway Quarter"
3 Párisi Nagy Áruház
4 Franz Liszt Square
5 Franz Liszt Academy of Music
6 Oktogon
7 House of Terror
8 Former Academy of Music & Franz Liszt Museum
9 To Heroes' Square & City Park

opera house in his hometown of Vienna. And so, Miklós Ybl designed a building that would exceed Vienna's famous Staatsoper in opulence, if not in size. (Franz Josef was reportedly displeased.) It was built using almost entirely Hungarian materials. After being damaged in World War II, it was painstakingly restored decades later. Today, with lavish marble-and-gold-leaf decor, a gorgeous gilded interior slathered with paintings of Greek myths, and high-quality performances at bargain prices, this is one of Europe's finest opera houses.

You can drop in whenever the box office is open to ogle the ostentatious **lobby** (daily 10:00-19:00 or until the first intermission, Andrássy Út 22, district VI, M1: Opera).

The one-hour **tours** of the Opera House are a must for music lovers and enjoyable for anyone, though the quality of the guides varies: Most spout plenty of fun, if silly, legends, but others can be quite dry. You'll see the main entryway, the snooty lounge area, some of the cozy but plush boxes, and the lavish auditorium. You'll find out why clandestine lovers would meet in the cigar lounge, how the Opera House is designed to keep the big spenders away from the rabble in the nosebleed seats (still the case today), and how to tell the difference between real marble and fake marble. The tour ends with a brief 10-minute performance on the grand staircase (7,000 Ft; English tours usually daily at 13:30, 15:00, and 16:30; prebook tour tickets on the official Opera website (www.opera.hu) or in person at the box office; wise to prebook on weekends, when tours can sell out a day or so ahead; on weekdays, you can generally just show up 15-20 minutes before the tour).

To experience the Opera House in action, take in an excellent and affordable performance (see "Entertainment in Budapest," later).

• *The Opera House marks the beginning of an emerging dining-and-nightlife neighborhood dubbed the...*

"Broadway Quarter"

The major cross street, **Nagymező Utca,** features a chic cluster of restaurants, bars, and theaters (especially on the left side of Andrássy). This is an enjoyable place to stroll on a summer evening. While you might be tempted to attend a show along Budapest's answer to Broadway, note that most of the plays and musicals here are in Hungarian only. Many of my recommended restaurants (described later, under "Eating in Budapest") are in this neighborhood.

A half-block down on the right (at #39) is a grand old early 20th-century building marked **Párisi Nagy Áruház** (Paris Department Store). One of the city's first department stores, this was a popular shopping stop for years, even through communism. Inside and upstairs is a gorgeous old frescoed ballroom, called Lotz Hall, which is sometimes home to a café; if you'd like a coffee break, consider heading inside and up the escalator to check if it's open.

• *Just after the end of the block is a popular outdoor dining area.*

Franz Liszt Square (Liszt Ferenc Tér)

This leafy square is surrounded by hip, expensive cafés and restaurants. (The best is the recommended restaurant **Menza.**)

Strangely, neither the statue on this square nor the one facing it, across Andrássy Út, is of Franz Liszt. But deeper in the park, you'll find a modern statue of Liszt energetically playing an imaginary piano. And at the far end of the square, fronting a gorgeous piazza, is the **Franz Liszt Academy of Music,** founded by and named for this half-Hungarian, half-Austrian composer who had a Hungarian name and passport. Liszt loved his family's Magyar heritage (though he didn't speak Hungarian) and spent his final six years in Budapest. His Academy of Music has been stunningly restored inside and out—step into the magnificent lobby. This space, though smaller, gives the Opera House a run for its money...and speaking of money, the concerts here are even cheaper than at the already reasonably priced Opera (for details on performances, and for more on Liszt, see "Entertainment in Budapest," later).

• *One block up from Franz Liszt Square is the gigantic crossroads known as the...*

Oktogon

This vast intersection with its corners snipped off—where Andrássy Út meets the Great Boulevard ring road (Nagykörút)—was called Mussolini Tér during World War II, then November 7 Tér in honor of the Bolshevik Revolution. Today, kids have nicknamed it American Tér for the fast-food joints littering the square and streets nearby.

From here, if you have time to delve into workaday Budapest, hop on tram #4 or #6, which trundle in both directions around the ring road. For a short detour to the most opulent coffee break of your life, head for the recommended **New York Café** (described later, under "Eating in Budapest"). Just get on a tram to the right (tram #6 toward Móricz Zsigmond Körtér or tram #4 toward Fehérvári Út) and get off at the Wesselényi Utca stop.

• *There's one more major sight between here and Heroes' Square. Walk two more blocks up Andrássy Út to reach the...*

▲▲House of Terror (Terror Háza)

The building at Andrássy Út 60 was home to the vilest parts of two destructive regimes: first the Arrow Cross (the Gestapo-like enforcers of Nazi-occupied Hungary), then the ÁVO and ÁVH secret police (the insidious KGB-type wing of the Soviet satellite government). Now re-envisioned as the "House of Terror," this building uses highly conceptual, bombastic exhibits to document the ugliest moments in Hungary's difficult 20th century.

Cost and Hours: 4,000 Ft, Tue-Sun 10:00-18:00, closed Mon, audioguide-2,000 Ft, Andrássy Út 60, district VI, M1: Vörösmarty Utca—*not* the Vörösmarty Tér stop, +36 1 374 2600, www.terrorhaza.hu.

Tours: The English audioguide, good but plodding and almost too thorough, can be difficult to hear over the din of Hungarian soundtracks in each room (2,000 Ft).

Background: In the lead-up to World War II, Hungary initially allied with Hitler—both to retain a degree of self-determination and to try to regain its huge territorial losses after World War I's devastating Treaty of Trianon (see page 548). But in March 1944, the Nazi-affiliated Arrow Cross Party was forcibly installed as Hungary's new government. The Nazi surrogates deported nearly 440,000 Jewish people to Auschwitz, murdered thousands more on the streets of Budapest, and executed hundreds in the basement of this building.

When the communists moved into Hungary after the war, they took over the same building as headquarters for their secret police (the ÁVO, later renamed ÁVH). To keep dissent to a minimum, the secret police terrorized, tried, deported, or executed anyone suspected of being an enemy of the state.

Visiting the Museum: The **atrium** features a Soviet T-54 tank, and a vast wall covered with 3,200 portraits of people who were murdered by the Nazis or the communists in this very building. The one-way exhibit begins two floors up, then spirals down to the cellar.

Upstairs sets the stage for Hungary's 20th century: its territorial losses after World War I; its alliance with, then invasion by, the Nazis; and its "liberation," then occupation, by the USSR. After passing through a room displaying uniforms and other gear belonging to Hungarian Nazis, you'll reach the room devoted to the **Gulag**—a network of secret Soviet prison camps, mostly in Siberia. These were hard-labor camps where potential and actual dissidents were sent to punish them and make an example of those who would dare to defy the regime.

The **Changing Clothes** room satirizes the readiness of many Hungarians to align themselves with whomever was in power. The room on **The Fifties** examines the gradual insinuation of the communist regime into the fabric of Hungary. Their methods ranged from already-marked ballots to glossy propaganda. Behind the distorted stage is the dark underbelly of the regime: the constant surveillance that bred paranoia among the people. The **Resistance** room—empty aside from three very different kitchen tables—symbolizes the way that resistance to the regime emerged in every walk of life. The exhibit continues downstairs, where the **Resettlement and Deportation** section explains the ethnic cleansing that took place throughout Central and Eastern Europe in the years following World War II. In Hungary alone, 230,000 Germans were uprooted and deported.

In **Surrender of Property and Land,** we learn that under communism, the Hungarian people had to survive on increasingly sparse rations. Enter the labyrinth of pork-fat bricks, which remind old-timers of the harsh conditions of the 1950s. So often, dinner was simply lard on bread.

The next room examines the **ÁVO,** the communist secret police who intimidated the common people of Hungary. Before they were finished, the ÁVO/ÁVH imprisoned, abused, or murdered one person from every third Hungarian family. After passing through the office of Gábor Péter (the first director of the ÁVO), you'll reach the **"Justice"** exhibit, which explores "show trials"— high-profile, loudly publicized, and completely choreographed trials of people who had supposedly subverted the regime. The burden of proof was on the accused, not on the accuser, and coerced confessions were fair game. From 1945 until the 1956 Uprising, more than 71,000 Hungarians were accused of political crimes, and 485 were executed.

Next you'll encounter bright and cheery communist **Propaganda.** The poster about the Amerikai Bogár warns of the threat of the "American Beetle," which threatened Hungarian crops. When a potato beetle epidemic hit, rather than acknowledging their own fault, the communists blamed an American conspiracy. Rounding out this floor are sections on **"Hungarian Silver"** (actually aluminum—lampooning the lowbrow aesthetic of that era) and **Religion** (those who were publicly faithful were discriminated against, closely supervised by the secret police, and often arrested). Then you'll board an elevator. As it descends, you'll watch a video about the grotesque execution process.

When the door opens, you're in the **Prison Cellar.** In the large room after the cells, you'll see a stool with a lamp; nearby are the **torture** devices. The bucket and hose were used to revive torture victims who had blacked out. After the torture room, a small room on the right contains a **gallows** that was used for executions.

The room commemorating the **1956 Uprising** features a symbol of that uprising—a Hungarian flag with a hole cut out of the middle (a hastily removed Soviet emblem) and the slogan *Ruszkik*

BUDAPEST

Haza! ("Russkies go home!"). For more on '56, see the sidebar on page 590. After a sobering room that displays six symbolic gallows, the **Emigration** room features a wall of postcards. More than 200,000 Hungarians simply fled the country after the uprising. The **Hall of Tears** memorial commemorates all the victims of the communists from 1945 to 1967 (when the final prisoners were released from this building). The **Room of Farewell** shows the festive and exhilarating days in 1991 when the Soviets departed, making way for freedom; the reburial of the Hungarian hero, Imre Nagy, at Heroes' Square; and the dedication of this museum.

The chilling finale: walls of photographs of the **"Victimizers"**—members and supporters of the Arrow Cross and ÁVO, some of whom are still living and who were never brought to justice.

• *Across the street and a few steps up Andrássy Út is the...*

Franz Liszt Museum

In this surprisingly modest apartment where the composer once resided, you'll find a humble but appealing collection of artifacts. A pilgrimage site for Liszt fans, it's housed in the former Academy of Music, which also hosts Saturday-morning concerts (see "Entertainment in Budapest," later).

Cost and Hours: 3,000 Ft; Mon-Fri 10:00-18:00, Sat 9:00-17:00, closed Sun; Vörösmarty Utca 35, district VI, M1: Vörösmarty Utca—*not* Vörösmarty Tér stop, +36 1 322 9804, www.lisztmuseum.hu.

• *While you can walk from here to Heroes' Square (visible in the distance, about a 15-minute walk), there's less to see along the rest of Andrássy Út. If you prefer, hop on the Metró here and ride it three stops to Hősök Tere.*

HEROES' SQUARE AND CITY PARK

The grand finale of Andrássy Út, at the edge of the city center, is also one of Budapest's most entertaining quarters. Here you'll find the grand Heroes' Square, dripping with history; the vast tree-filled expanse of City Park, dressed up with fanciful buildings that include an Art Nouveau zoo and a replica of a Transylvanian castle; and, tucked in the middle of it all, Budapest's finest thermal spa and single best experience, the Széchenyi Baths. Over time, the vision is to relocate many of Budapest's leading museums to this park—creating a kind of museum quarter.

▲▲Heroes' Square (Hősök Tere)

Built in 1896 to celebrate the 1,000th anniversary of the Magyars' arrival in Hungary, this vast square culminates at a bold Millennium Monument. Stand-ing stoically in its colon-nades are 14 Hungarian leaders who represent the whole span of this nation's colorful and illustrious history. In front, at the base of a high pillar, are the seven original Magyar chieftains, the Hungarian War Memorial, and young
Hungarian skateboarders of the 21st century. Look for names you may recognize: István, Béla IV, Mátyás Corvinus. The sculptures on the top corners of the two colonnades represent, from left to right: Work and Welfare, War, Peace, and the Importance of Packing Light. The square is also flanked by a pair of museums.

Museums on Heroes' Square: The **Museum of Fine Arts** (Szépművészeti Múzeum) is Budapest's best chance to appreciate some European masters. You'll see mostly Germanic, Dutch, Belgian, and Spanish art, plus lesser works by the likes of Dürer, the Bruegels, Murillo, Velázquez, El Greco, Goya, and more (4,200 Ft; Tue-Sun 10:00-18:00, closed Mon, last entry one hour before closing; Dózsa György Út 41, +36 1 469 7100, www.szepmuveszeti. hu). Facing the Museum of Fine Arts from across Heroes' Square, the **Műcsarnok** ("Hall of Art") rotates temporary exhibits by contemporary artists—of interest only to art lovers (price varies depending on the exhibits; Tue-Sun 10:00-18:00 except Thu 12:00-20:00, closed Mon; Dózsa György Út 37, +36 1 460 7000, www. mucsarnok.hu).

• *With the road on your right and the Műcsarnok museum on your left, carry on straight ahead. Soon you'll see a huge metallic box rising from the grassy park.*

Museum of Ethnography (Néprajzi Múzeum)

This striking building juxtaposes vivid objects from world cultures in surprising ways. In the lobby is a fascinating, free-to-view model of Budapest in the 1910s, and another model showing the ambitious plans for redeveloping City Park. But the building itself overshadows the exhibits, with its sloping U-shaped design and a rooftop you can walk all over.

Cost and Hours: Free to enter building and see city model, permanent exhibit—1,700 Ft, Tue-Sun 10:00-18:00, closed Mon, Dózsa György Út 35, +36 1 474 2100, www.neprajz.hu.

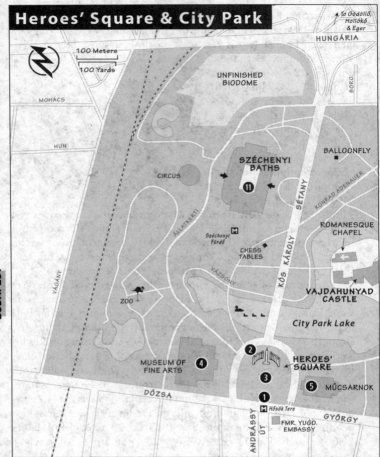

Heroes' Square & City Park

To Gödöllő, Hollókő & Eger

HUNGÁRIA

BORO.

100 Meters
100 Yards

MOHÁCS

HUN

UNFINISHED BIODOME

BALLOONFLY

SZÉCHENYI BATHS

CIRCUS

⓫

KONRAD ADENAUER SÉTÁNY

ROMANESQUE CHAPEL

ÁLLATKERTI

Széchenyi Fürdő Ⓜ

KÓS KÁROLY

VAJDAHUNYAD CASTLE

CHESS TABLES

VÁSONY

VÁGÁNY

ZOO

City Park Lake

❷

MUSEUM OF FINE ARTS ❹

HEROES' SQUARE

❸

❺ MŰCSARNOK

DÓZSA

❶

Ⓜ Hősök Tere

ANDRÁSSY ÚT

FMR. YUGO. EMBASSY

GYÖRGY

BUDAPEST

• In the middle of the building's two halves stands the dramatic **1956 monument,** honoring the 1956 Uprising, when the Hungarian people stood up against Soviet rule. Standing at the back of the monument—with the road behind you—look through the trees to see the wavy yellow roofline. Walk through the park to reach the...

▲▲House of Music Hungary (Magyar Zene Háza)

This striking building—shaped like a "Tree of Life"—hosts three different music venues and an excellent exhibit called Dimensions of Sound. Equipped with an audioguide, you'll explore the history of music in Hungary and around the world, from the Magyar folk music of the countryside, to the evolution of church music, to the famous composers of the Romantic era, to the TV and movie

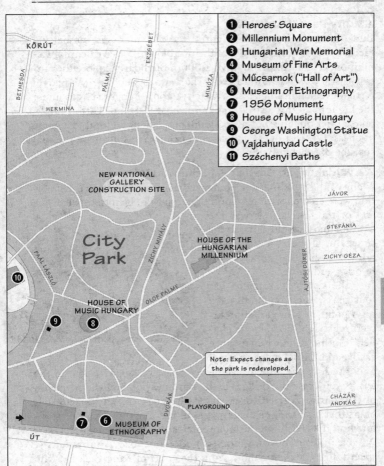

1. Heroes' Square
2. Millennium Monument
3. Hungarian War Memorial
4. Museum of Fine Arts
5. Műcsarnok ("Hall of Art")
6. Museum of Ethnography
7. 1956 Monument
8. House of Music Hungary
9. George Washington Statue
10. Vajdahunyad Castle
11. Széchenyi Baths

NEW NATIONAL GALLERY CONSTRUCTION SITE

City Park

HOUSE OF THE HUNGARIAN MILLENNIUM

HOUSE OF MUSIC HUNGARY

Note: Expect changes as the park is redeveloped.

PLAYGROUND

MUSEUM OF ETHNOGRAPHY

BUDAPEST

soundtracks of today. There are also temporary exhibits and the Hangdóm (Sound Dome), a trippy sound-and-light show.

Cost and Hours: 3,400 Ft, Hangdóm and temporary exhibits covered by separate tickets, Tue-Sun 10:00-18:00, closed Mon, Olof Palme Sétány 3-5, +36 70 799 9449, www.zenehaza.hu.

• *Exiting the House of Music, turn right and walk around its back side (toward the small lake). You'll pass a statue of George Washington (funded and erected in 1906 by Hungarians who emigrated to the US). Imagine Washington turned right, strode toward the snack-and-drink stand, then turned left along the path under the trees (passing the bridge with a yellow railing). Continue until you reach the concrete bridge about 150 yards down that path. This takes you into the heart of...*

▲▲City Park (Városliget)

Budapest's not-so-central "Central Park," which sprawls beyond Heroes' Square, was the site of the overblown 1896 Millennial Exhibition, celebrating Hungary's 1,000th birthday. Explore the fantasy castle of Vajdahunyad. Visit the animals and ogle the playful Art Nouveau buildings inside the city's zoo, or enjoy a circus under the big top. Go for a stroll, rent a rowboat, eat some cotton candy, take a brief ride in a hot-air balloon, or challenge a local to a game of chess. Or, best of all, take a dip in Budapest's ultimate thermal spa, the Széchenyi Baths.

▲▲Vajdahunyad Castle (Vajdahunyad Vára)

Many of the buildings for Hungary's Millennial National Exhibition were erected with temporary materials, to be torn down at the

end of the festival—as was the case for most world fairs at the time. But locals so loved Vajdahunyad Castle that it was rebuilt in brick and stone.

The complex actually has four parts, each representing a high point in Hungarian architectural style: Romanesque chapel, Gothic gate, Renaissance castle, and Baroque palace.

The first part you'll reach (the ornate yellow mansion on the left as you cross the bridge) is the Baroque home of the **Museum of Hungarian Agriculture** (Magyar Mezőgazdasági Múzeum). It brags that it's Europe's biggest agriculture museum, but most visitors find the lavish interior more interesting than the exhibits.

Facing the museum entry is a monument to **Anonymous**—specifically, the Anonymous from the court of King Béla IV, who penned the first Hungarian history in the Middle Ages. This clever approach to depicting an unknown historical figure—whose features are barely visible under his heavy hood—is a favorite photo op.

Next up, on the right you'll see a replica of a 13th-century Romanesque Benedictine **chapel.** Consecrated as an actual church, this is a popular spot for weddings on summer weekends.

In the middle of the complex are the distinctly **Transylvanian-style trapezoidal towers.** The section on the left (around the tallest tower, in the middle of the complex) is Renaissance, while the one on the right is Gothic. The Gothic part is a replica of a famous castle in Transylvania that once belonged to the Hunyadi family; this castle loaned its name to the entire complex.

• *The park's highlight is the big yellow building across the street from Vajdahunyad Castle...*

▲▲▲Széchenyi Baths (Széchenyi Fürdő)

Visiting the Széchenyi Baths is my favorite activity in Budapest. It's the ideal way to reward yourself for the hard work of sightseeing

while enjoying a culturally enlightening experience. Soak in hundred-degree water, surrounded by portly Hungarians squeezed into tiny swimsuits, while jets and cascades pound away your tension. Go for a vigorous swim in the lap pool, giggle and bump your way around the whirlpool, take a dip in water green with minerals, feel the underwater jets tickle your legs, or challenge the locals to a game of Speedo-clad chess. And it's all surrounded by an opulent yellow palace with shiny copper domes. The bright blue-and-white of the sky, the yellow of the buildings, the turquoise of the water...Budapest simply doesn't get any better (for all the details, see "Experiences in Budapest," later).

NEAR ÜLLŐI ÚT

The following museum is near the city center, on the boulevard called Üllői Út. You could stroll there in about 10 minutes from the Small Boulevard ring road (walking the length of the Ráday Utca café street gets you very close), or hop on the M3/blue Metró line to Corvin-Negyed (just one stop beyond Kálvin Tér).

▲▲Holocaust Memorial Center (Holokauszt Emlékközpont)

This sight honors the nearly 600,000 Hungarian victims of the Nazis...one out of every 10 Holocaust victims. The impressive modern complex (with a beautifully restored 1920s synagogue as its centerpiece) is a museum of the Hungarian Holocaust, a monument to its victims, a space for temporary exhibits, and a research and documentation center of Nazi atrocities. Interesting to anybody, but essential to those interested in the Holocaust, this is Budapest's best sight about that dark time—and one of Europe's best, as well.

BUDAPEST

Cost and Hours: 2,400 Ft; Tue-Sun 10:00-18:00, closed Mon, last entry one hour before closing; Páva Utca 39, district IX, M3: Corvin-Negyed, +36 1 455 3333, www.hdke.hu.

Getting There: From the Corvin-Negyed Metró stop, use the exit marked *Holokauszt Emlékközpont* and take the left fork at the exit. Walk straight ahead two long blocks, then turn right down Páva Utca.

Visiting the Center: You'll pass through a security checkpoint to reach the courtyard. Inside, a black marble wall is etched with the names of victims. Head downstairs to buy your ticket.

The excellent permanent exhibit, called "From Deprivation of Rights to Genocide," traces (in English) the gradual process of disenfranchisement, marginalization, exploitation, dehumanization, and eventually extermination that befell Hungary's Jews as World War II wore on. The finale is the interior of the **synagogue,** now a touching memorial filled with glass seats, each one etched with the image of a Jewish worshipper who once filled it. Up above, on the mezzanine level, you'll find temporary exhibits and an information center that helps descendants of Hungarian Jews track down the fate of their relatives.

Nearby: A few blocks away (at Üllői Út 33) is the fanciful, late-19th-century **Applied Arts Museum**—a green-roofed castle that's worth a quick look (from the outside, at least) for architecture fans (museum closed for renovation, likely at least through 2024).

Sights in Buda

Nearly all of Buda's top sights are concentrated on or near its two riverside hills: Castle Hill and Gellért Hill.

Two other major attractions—the part of town called **Óbuda** ("Old Buda") and **Memento Park** (filled with communist-era monuments)—are on the Buda side of the river but away from the center. These sights, along with several others, are described under "Day Trips from Budapest," at the end of the chapter.

CASTLE HILL (VÁRHEGY)

Once the seat of Hungarian royalty, and now the city's highest-profile tourist zone, Castle Hill is a historic spit of land looming above the Buda bank of the Danube. Scenic from afar, but (frankly) a bit soulless up close, it's best seen quickly. I've listed these sights in order from south to north and linked them together with a self-guided walk. All around the hilltop, "old" buildings from various eras are in the process of being rebuilt from scratch—part of a castle-renewal scheme called the National Hauszmann Program. This controversial initiative of the Fidesz government is an effort

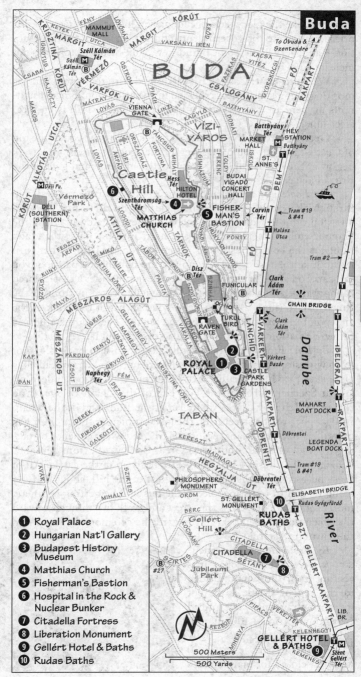

Buda

1 Royal Palace
2 Hungarian Nat'l Gallery
3 Budapest History Museum
4 Matthias Church
5 Fisherman's Bastion
6 Hospital in the Rock & Nuclear Bunker
7 Citadella Fortress
8 Liberation Monument
9 Gellért Hotel & Baths
10 Rudas Baths

BUDAPEST

to both evoke the glory days of Hungarian history and reclaim this prime real estate for government offices. Expect to see construction—and, very likely, some brand-new, faux-historic buildings not mentioned here.

When to Visit: Castle Hill is jammed with tour groups in the morning, but it's much less crowded in the afternoon. Since restaurants up here are touristy and a bad value, Castle Hill is an ideal after-lunch activity.

Getting There: The Metró and trams won't take you to the top of Castle Hill, but you have several other good options. This walk begins at the big Turul bird statue by the monumental gate of the Royal Palace.

On Foot: For a free and scenic approach, you can walk up through the castle gardens called Várkert Bazár (trams #19 and #41 stop right in front). From the monumental gateway facing the Danube embankment, head up the stairs into the park, then look right for the covered escalator. From its top, you can either turn left to hike the rest of the way up (on the switchback path), or you can carry on straight ahead to find an elevator (under a rust-colored canopy) that zips you right up to the view terrace in front of the Royal Palace (floor 2). From here, you can begin the walk at the viewpoint in front of the palace, then see the Turul bird statue and funicular station on your way back across the hill later.

By Bus: From Pest, it's usually fastest to hop on bus **#16** or **#216** with stops near the Deák Tér Metró hub (on Harmincad Utca alongside Erzsébet Tér; use exit "E" from the station underpass) and at Széchenyi Tér, at the Pest end of the Chain Bridge. (You can also catch it at Clark Ádám Tér at the Buda end of the Chain Bridge—across the street from the lower funicular station.) Or you can go via Széll Kálmán Tér (on the M2/red Metró line, or by taking tram #4 or #6 around Pest's Great Boulevard); from here, bus #16, as well as buses **#16A** and **#116,** head up to the castle. All of these buses stop at Dísz Tér, at the crest of the hill, about halfway along its length (most people on the bus will be getting off there, too). From Dísz Tér, cross the street and walk five minutes toward the green dome, then bear left toward the ceremonial gate to find the Turul bird statue.

By Funicular: The funicular (*sikló,* SHEE-kloh) lifts visitors from the Chain Bridge to the top of Castle Hill, but it's an outrageously overpriced two-minute trip (4,100 Ft, not covered by transit pass, daily 8:00-22:00, departs every 5-10 minutes, closed for maintenance

every other Mon). It leaves you right at the Turul bird statue. Unless you enjoy throwing money at nostalgia, I'd skip this and either walk or hop on bus #16 or #216 across the roundabout (described earlier).

By Castle Bus: An oversized golf cart labeled "official Budapest castle bus" runs every 15 minutes from points at the base of the castle (including near the bottom station of the funicular, and in front of the Várkert Bazár) up to essentially the same stops the public bus uses at the top of the castle. While handy, this is a pricey little tourist trip (4,000 Ft round-trip)—worth taking only if you have a Budapest Card, which covers it.

• *Begin the walk at the big statue of the...*

Turul Bird

This mythical bird of Magyar folktales supposedly led the Hungarian migrations from the steppes of Central Asia in the ninth

century. He dropped his sword in the Carpathian Basin, indicating that this was to be the permanent home of the Magyar people. While the Hungarians have long since integrated into Europe, the Turul remains a symbol of Magyar pride. During a surge of nationalism in the 1920s, a movement named after this bird helped revive traditional Hungarian culture. And today, the bird is invoked by right-wing nationalist politicians.

If you hear a commotion while enjoying the view, it may be the **changing of the guard** ceremony that takes place at

the Sándor Palace next to the funicular station, at the top of each hour.

• *We'll return this way later. But for now, go through the monumental gateway by the Turul and climb down the stairs, then walk along the broad terrace in front of the...*

Royal Palace (Királyi Palota)

The imposing palace on Castle Hill barely hints at the colorful story of this hill since the day the legendary Turul dropped his sword. It was once the top Renaissance palace in Europe...but that was several centuries and several versions ago. In the early 15th century, the Renaissance King Mátyás (Matthias) Corvinus converted a humble medieval palace on this site into one of Europe's most extravagant residences, putting Buda and Hungary on the map. Just a few decades later, invading Ottomans occupied Buda and turned the palace into a military garrison. When the Habsburgs laid siege to the hill for 77 days in 1686, gunpowder stored in the cellar exploded, destroying the palace. The Habsburgs took the hill, but Buda was deserted and in ruins. The palace was rebuilt, then damaged again during the 1848 Revolution, then repaired again. As World War II drew to a close, Budapest became the front line between the Nazis and the approaching Soviets.

The Red Army laid siege to the hill for 100 days. They eventually succeeded in taking Budapest...but the city—and the hill—were devastated.

The current palace—a historically inaccurate, post-WWII reconstruction—is a loose rebuilding of previous versions. It's big but soulless. The most prominent feature of today's palace—the green dome—didn't even exist in earlier versions. Fortunately, the palace does house some worthwhile museums (described later), and boasts the fine terrace you're strolling on, with some of Budapest's best views.

• *Behind the big equestrian statue is the main entrance to the...*

▲Hungarian National Gallery (Magyar Nemzeti Galéria)

This museum is the best place in Hungary to appreciate the works of homegrown artists, and to get a peek into the often-morose Hungarian worldview. The collection—which will eventually move to the New National Gallery in City Park—includes a remarkable group of 15th-century, wood-carved altars from Slovakia (then "Upper Hungary"); piles of gloomy canvases dating from the dark days after the failed 1848 Revolution; several works by two great Hungarian Realist painters, Mihály Munkácsy and László Paál; and paintings by the troubled, enigmatic, and recently in-vogue Post-Impressionist Tivadar Csontváry Kosztka. The collection's highlights can be viewed quickly.

Cost and Hours: 3,800 Ft, Tue-Sun 10:00-18:00, closed Mon, café, in the Royal Palace—enter from terrace by Eugene of Savoy statue, district I, +36 20 439 7325, www.mng.hu.

• *Head back outside and face the palace. Go through the passage to the right of the National Gallery entrance (next to the café). You'll emerge into a courtyard decorated with a gorgeous fountain dedicated to King Matthias Corvinus (see the sidebar). Go around the right side of the fountain and through the passage, into the palace courtyard. At the far end of this too-big space is the entrance to the...*

Budapest History Museum (Budapesti Történeti Múzeum)

This earnest collection strains to bring the history of this city to life. It's a deep dive: If Budapest really intrigues you, this is a fine

Mátyás (Matthias) Corvinus: The Last Hungarian King

The Árpád dynasty—descendants of the original Magyar tribes—died out in 1301. For more than 600 years, Hungary would be ruled by elected foreign rulers... with one exception.

In the mid-15th century, the Hungarian military general János Hunyadi enjoyed great success on the battlefield against the Ottomans (including a pivotal victory in 1456's Battle of Belgrade). Meanwhile, Hungary's imported kings kept dying unexpectedly. Finally, the Hungarian nobility took a chance on a Hungarian-born ruler and offered the throne to Hunyadi's son, Mátyás (or Matthias in English). According to legend, they sent a raven with a ring in its mouth to notify Matthias, who was away in Prague. He returned to Buda, and took the raven both as his symbol and as his royal nickname: Corvinus (Latin for "raven").

Matthias Corvinus (r. 1458-1490) became the first Hungarian-descended king in more than 150 years. Progressive and well educated in the Humanist tradition, Matthias Corvinus was the quintessential Renaissance king. A lover of the Italian Renaissance, he patronized the arts and built palaces legendary for their beauty. As a benefactor of the poor, he dressed as a commoner and ventured into the streets to see firsthand how the nobles of his realm treated his people.

A strong, savvy leader, Matthias created Central Europe's first standing army—30,000 mercenaries known as the Black Army. No longer reliant on the nobility for military support, Good King Matthias was able to drain power from the nobles—earning him the nickname the "people's king."

Matthias was also a shrewd military tactician. Realizing that skirmishing with the Ottomans would squander his resources, he made peace with the sultan to stabilize Hungary's southern border. Then he swept north, invading Moravia, Bohemia, and even Austria. By 1485, Matthias moved into his new palace in Vienna, and Hungary was enjoying a golden age.

But just five years later, Matthias died mysteriously at the age of 47, and his empire disintegrated. Before long the Ottomans flooded back into Hungary, and the country entered a dark period. It is said that when Matthias died, justice died with him. To this day, Hungarians rank him the greatest of all kings, and they sing of his siege of Vienna in their national anthem. They're proud that for a few decades they had a truly Hungarian king—and a great one at that.

BUDAPEST

place to explore its history. Otherwise, skip it. The dimly lit fragments of 14th-century sculptures, depicting early Magyars, allow you to see how Asian those original Hungarians truly looked. The "Light and Shadow" exhibit deliberately but effectively traces the union between Buda and Pest. Rounding out the collection are exhibits on prehistoric residents and a sprawling cellar that unveils fragments from the oh-so-many buildings that have perched on this hill over the centuries. You can pay extra for a glimpse at St. Stephen's Hall, a (small) reconstructed royal room.

Cost and Hours: Main exhibit—2,400 Ft; St. Stephen's Hall—3,500 Ft; ticket covering both—4,500 Ft; both open Tue-Sun 10:00-18:00, Nov-Feb until 16:00, closed Mon year-round; district I, +36 1 487 8800, www.btm.hu.

• *From the palace courtyard, it's time to...*

Walk to Matthias Church

Leaving the palace courtyard, walk straight up the slight incline with the rebuilt Hungarian Royal Guard building on your left.

You'll pass under a gate with a raven holding a ring in its mouth—a symbol of King Matthias.

Just beyond the gate, you may see a construction zone (or some recently completed faux-historic buildings) on your left. This is one of many areas where

historical buildings are being rebuilt, decades after being destroyed by WWII bombs, as part of the National Hauszmann Program.

Turn your attention to the buildings across the field on your right. The big white building near the funicular station is the **Sándor Palace,** the Hungarian president's office (with the hourly changing of the guard out front). The yellow building on its left is the former **Court Theater** (Várszínház), which has seen many great performances over the centuries—including a visit from Beethoven in 1800. Several years ago, Prime Minister Viktor Orbán apparently grew jealous of the president's swanky digs, kicked out the dancers, and moved his office from the Parliament to here.

Soon you reach a cross street, at a place called **Dísz Tér** (Parade Square), with convenient bus stops for connecting to other parts of Budapest. Cross the street and carry on straight, gently uphill, on **Tárnok Utca,** bearing right at the park. After being destroyed by Ottomans, streets like this one were rebuilt in sensible Baroque, lacking the romantic time-capsule charm of a medieval old town.

As you continue along, ponder the fact that miles of **caves** were burrowed under Castle Hill—carved out by water, expanded by the Ottomans, and used by locals during the siege of Buda at the end of World War II. You can tour one nearby (the Hospital in the Rock, described later).

On the left, the **Prima grocery store** sells reasonably priced cold drinks and picnic fixings. A good spot for dessert is just up the little lane in front of the grocery store, under the passage called Balta Köz: **Rétesbár,** selling strudel *(rétes)* with various fillings.

Just beyond the grocery store, a warty plague column from 1713 marks **Szentháromság Tér** (Holy Trinity Square), the main square of old Buda.

• *Dominating the square is...*

▲▲Matthias Church (Mátyás-Templom)

Arguably Budapest's finest church inside and out, this historic house of worship—with a frilly Neo-Gothic spire and gilded Hun-

garian historical motifs slathered on every interior wall—is Castle Hill's best sight. From the humble Loreto Chapel (with a tranquil statue of the Virgin that helped defeat the Ottomans), to altars devoted to top Hungarian kings, to a replica of the crown of Hungary, every inch of the church oozes history.

Cost and Hours: 2,500 Ft; Mon-Sat 9:00-17:00 (may close Sat afternoons in summer for weddings), Sun from 13:00; Szentháromság Tér 2, district I, +36 1 488 7716, www.matyas-templom.hu.

Background: Budapest's best church has been destroyed and rebuilt several times in the 800 years since it was founded by King Béla IV. Today's version—renovated at great expense in the late 19th century and restored after World War II—is an ornately decorated lesson in Hungarian history. The church's unofficial namesake isn't a saint, so it can't be formally named for him. Its official name is the Church of Our Lady or the Coronation Church, but everyone calls it Matthias Church, for Matthias Corvinus, the popular Renaissance king who got married here—twice.

Visiting the Church: Examine the **exterior.** While the nucleus of the church is Gothic, most of what you see outside—including the frilly, flamboyant steeple—was added for the 1896 millennial celebrations. At the top of the stone corner tower facing the river, notice the raven—the ever-present symbol of King Matthias Corvinus.

BUDAPEST

Buy your ticket across the square from the church's side door, at the ticket windows embedded in the wall. Then enter the church. There are good English descriptions posted throughout.

The sumptuous **interior** is wallpapered with gilded pages from a Hungarian history textbook. Different eras are represented by symbolic motifs. For example, check out the back wall next to the stairs by the side entrance: This giant coat of arms of beloved King Matthias Corvinus represents the Renaissance.

Work your way clockwise around the church. The first chapel (in the back corner, to the left as you face the closed main doors)— the **Loreto Chapel**—holds the church's prize possession: a 1515 statue of Mary and Jesus. Anticipating Ottoman plundering, locals walled over its niche. The occupying Ottomans used the church as their primary mosque—oblivious to the precious statue hidden behind the plaster. Then, a century and a half later, during the siege of Buda in 1686, gunpowder stored in the castle up the street detonated, and the wall crumbled. Mary's triumphant face showed through, terrifying the Ottomans. Supposedly this was the only part of town taken from the Ottomans without a fight.

Facing the doors, look about four paces to the right. At the top of the stout pillar, a **carved capital** shows two men gesturing excitedly at a book. Dating from 1260, these carvings are some of the earliest surviving features in this church, which has changed much over the centuries.

As you look down the **nave,** notice the banners. They've hung here since the Mass that celebrated Habsburg monarch Franz Josef's coronation at this church on June 8, 1867. In a sly political compromise to curry favor in the Hungarian part of his territory, Franz Josef was "emperor" *(Kaiser)* of Austria, but only "king" *(König)* of Hungary. (If you see the old German phrase "K+K"—still used today as a boast of royal quality—it refers to this *"König und Kaiser"* arrangement.) So, after F. J. was crowned emperor in Vienna, he came down the Danube and said to the Hungarians, "King me."

Now stand at the modern altar in the middle of the church, and look down the nave to the **main altar.** Mary floats above it all, and hovering over her is a full-scale replica of the Hungarian crown, which was blessed by Pope John Paul II. More than a millennium after István, Mary still officially wears this nation's crown.

Left of the altar is the **László Chapel,** venerating a great Christian knight who fought pagans in the 11th century.

Climb the circular staircase (in the front-left corner) up to the **gallery.** Walk along the royal oratory to a small mezzanine that overlooks the altar area—giving you a better look at the altar's details. Then head back along the gallery. In the room with a small organ is a statue of Sisi—Empress Elisabeth—who practically has a cult following among Hungarians. From here, huff up even more steps to a few more modest exhibits and great views down over the nave.

Back down at ground level, you exit the church under a replica of a fine Gothic **tympanum.** The weathered original is on display below, offering an unusual close-up look. The carved scene celebrates the centrality of the book in spreading the word of God.

• *Back outside, at the end of the square next to Matthias Church, is the...*

Fisherman's Bastion (Halászbástya)

Seven pointy domes and a double-decker rampart run along the cliff in front of Matthias Church. Evoking the original seven Magyar tribes, and built for the millennial celebration of their arrival, the Fisherman's Bastion is one of Budapest's top landmarks. While some suckers pay for the views from here, you can enjoy virtually the same view through the windows next to the bastion café for free.

Cost and Hours: 1,200 Ft, buy ticket at ticket office along the park wall across the square from Matthias Church, daily 9:00-20:00; after closing time and off-season, no tickets are sold, but bastion is open and free to enter; Szentháromság Tér 5, district I.

• *Between the bastion and the church stands a...*

Statue of St. István

Hungary's first Christian king tamed the nomadic, pagan Magyars and established strict laws and the concept of private property. In the late 900s, Géza, Grand Prince of the Hungarians, lost a major battle against the forces of Christian Europe—and realized that he must raise his son Vajk (c. 967-1038) as a Catholic and convert his people, or they would be forcefully driven out of Europe. Vajk took the Christian name István (EESHT-vahn, "Stephen") and was baptized in the year 1000. The reliefs on this statue show the commissioners of the pope crowning St. István, bringing Hungary into the fold of Christendom. This pragmatic move put Hungary on the map as a fully European kingdom, forging alliances that would endure for centuries. Without this pivotal event, Hungarians believe that the Magyar nation would have been lost.

• *Head down the charming little street (called Szentháromság Utca) that leads away from Matthias Church. Halfway down this street on the right, look for the venerable, recommended Ruszwurm café—the oldest in Budapest. Then continue out to the terrace and appreciate views of the Buda Hills—the "Beverly Hills" of Budapest, draped with orchards, vineyards, and the homes of the wealthiest Budapesters.*

If you go down the stairs or elevator here, then turn right up the street, you'll reach the entrance of the...

▲Hospital in the Rock and Nuclear Bunker (Sziklakórház és Atombunker)

Sprawling beneath Castle Hill is a 25,000-square-foot labyrinthine network of hospital and fallout-shelter corridors built during the mid-20th century. This lively and engaging tour balances out an otherwise sedate Castle Hill visit. While pricey, a visit here is a must for healthcare workers and WWII buffs.

Cost and Hours: 8,000 Ft for required one-hour tour, daily 10:00-19:00, English tours generally run at the top of each hour, last tour departs at 18:00, gift shop like an army-surplus store, Lovas Utca 4C, district I, +36 70 701 0101, www.sziklakorhaz.eu.

Visiting the Hospital and Bunker: First you'll watch a 10-minute movie (with English subtitles) about the history of the place. Then, your guide leads you through the tunnels to see perfectly preserved WWII and 1960s-era medical supplies and equipment, most still in working order. More than 200 wax figures engagingly bring the various hospital rooms to life: giant sick ward, operating room, and so on. On your way to the fallout shelter, you'll pass the decontamination showers, and see primitive radiation detectors and communist propaganda showing comrades how to save themselves in case of capitalist bombs or gas attacks. In the bunker, you'll also tour the mechanical rooms that provided water and ventilation to this sprawling underground city, and you'll learn about the atom bomb explosions in Hiroshima and Nagasaki.

• *Our Castle Hill walk is finished. If you're ready to head back down to the river (and the Víziváros neighborhood), you can exit down the big staircase below the Fisherman's Bastion.*

From the northern end of the hill, you can head out through the Vienna Gate and follow the road downhill to bustling Széll Kálmán Tér and its handy Metró stop (M2/red line).

GELLÉRT HILL (GELLÉRTHEGY) AND NEARBY

Gellért Hill rises from the Danube just downriver from the castle. When King István converted Hungary to Christianity in the year 1000, he brought in
Bishop Gellért, a monk from Venice, to tutor his son. But some rebellious Magyars put the bishop in a barrel, drove long nails in from the outside, and rolled him down this hill... tenderizing him to death. Gellért became the patron saint of Budapest and gave his name to the hill that killed him. Today, the hill is a fine place to commune with nature on a hike or jog, followed by a restorative splash in either the elegant Gellért Baths (in the Gellért Hotel) or the Turkish-style Rudas Baths (both worth ▲▲ and described later, under "Experiences in Budapest").

Citadella

This strategic, hill-capping fortress was built by the Habsburgs after the 1848 Revolution to keep an eye on their Hungarian subjects. Like so many things in Budapest, it was badly damaged in World War II and never properly restored until now. The Fidesz party is rebuilding it top to bottom as a symbol of Hungarian might. Sometime in 2024 (perhaps later), it's expected to reopen with a view platform and a museum about Hungary's fight for freedom across the centuries, against various foreign oppressors. Before making the trip up here, check locally to make sure it's open.

The hill is crowned by the **Liberation Monument**, featuring a woman holding aloft a palm branch. Locals call it "the lady with the big fish" or "the great bottle opener." A heroic Soviet soldier, who once inspired the workers with a huge red star from the base of the monument, is now in Memento Park (see Memento Park listing, later, under "Day Trips from Budapest").

Getting There: It's a steep hike up from the river to the Citadella. Bus #27 cuts some time off the trip, taking you up to the Búsuló Juhász stop (from which it's still an uphill hike to the fortress). You can catch bus #27 from either side of Gellért Hill.

▲▲Gellért Baths

Located at the famous and once-exclusive Gellért Hotel, right at the Buda end of the Liberty Bridge, this elegant bath complex has long been the city's top choice for a swanky, hedonistic soak. It's also awash in tourists, and the Széchenyi Baths beat it out for pure fun...but the Gellért Baths' mysterious thermal spa rooms and giddy outdoor wave pool make it an enticing option. Note that the attached hotel is scheduled for a major renovation; they hope to keep the baths open, but confirm before visiting (for details on visiting the baths, see "Experiences in Budapest," in the next section).

▲▲Rudas Baths

Along the Danube toward Castle Hill from Gellért Baths, Rudas (ROO-dawsh) offers Budapest's most old-fashioned, Turkish-style bathing experience. The historic main pool of the thermal bath section sits under a 500-year-old Ottoman dome. On weekdays, it's a nude, gender-segregated experience, while on weekends, it becomes more accessible (and mixed). Rudas also has a ho-hum swimming pool, and a state-of-the-art "wellness" section, with a variety of modern massage pools, a "sauna world," and an inviting hot tub/sun deck on the roof with a stunning Budapest panorama (for details, see "Experiences in Budapest," next).

Experiences in Budapest

THERMAL BATHS (FÜRDŐ)

Relaxing in Budapest's thermal baths is the city's top attraction. Bathing with the Magyars is far less daunting than it might sound.

Hungary's thermal baths are like your local swimming pool—except the water is 100 degrees, there are jets and bubbles to massage away your stress, and you're surrounded by ornate architecture and by potbellied Hungarians. (And yes, you can wear your swimsuit.)

All this fun goes way back. The Carpathian Basin—which makes up most of Hungary—is a thin crust covering a vast reservoir of hot water. Budapest alone has 123 natural springs and some two dozen thermal baths.

Those steamy springs have shaped Hungary's history and culture. The Romans took advantage of those waters to build baths. Centuries later, the occupying Ottomans revived the custom. And today, thermal baths are still a fixture of Hungarian life.

The baths are administered and subsidized for patients as a part of the national health-care system. Doctors prescribe treatments that include massage, soaking in baths of various heat and mineral compositions, and swimming laps.

But increasingly, Hungary is playing up the fun side of their hot water. Adventure water parks are springing up all over the country, and many staid old baths have been updated to add "well-

Useful Bath Words

English	Hungarian
Bath	*Fürdő* (FEWR-dur)
Men	*Férfi* (FAYR-fee)
Women	*Női* (NUR-ee)
Changing cabin	*Kabin* (KAW-been)
Locker	*Szekrény* (SEHK-rayn)
Ticket office	*Pénztár* (PAYNZ-tar)
Thermal bath	*Gyógyfürdő* (JOHDGE-fewr-dur) or *Gőz* (gurz)

ness centers" with jets, waterfalls, and currents. Some stately spas are even open late at night, transformed with thumping music and flashing lights.

Where else can you spend a couple of hours soaking in a hot bath and chalk it up to a culturally broadening experience? Overcome your jitters and dive in.

Baths Orientation

Some tourists may feel trepidation at the thought of bathing alongside locals. Relax! If you go into it with an easygoing attitude, I promise you'll have a blast. The system has been modernized, and most bath attendants speak enough English to help you find your way.

Cost and Hours Warning: Baths are forever tinkering with their opening hours. Any cost and hours information in this book could change by the time you visit, so confirm the details before planning your trip to the baths (see www.spasbudapest.com).

Dress Code: While Budapest has some mostly nude, gender-segregated Turkish baths, the ones I describe here are less intimidating: You're expected to wear a swimsuit the entire time, even in rare cases (such as certain days at Rudas) when parts of the baths are all-male or all-female.

You're officially required to wear **flip-flops** ("slippers"), though this rule is unevenly enforced. Regardless, it's a good idea for both sanitary and safety reasons. If you don't have any, you can buy them at the baths (see later).

What to Bring: If you have them, bring a swimsuit, towel, flip-flops, bottle of water, soap and shampoo, comb or brush, swim cap if you want to do laps, plastic bag for your wet swimsuit, and maybe sunscreen and leisure reading. Hotels sometimes frown on guests taking their room towels to the baths; try asking nicely if they offer loaner towels for this purpose. A swim cap is required in lap pools; you can buy a flimsy one there, or try to grab a shower cap from your hotel.

Buying Towels, Flip-Flops, and Swimsuits at the Baths: If you didn't bring along one of these items, you'll need to buy it at the baths. Some baths have an expensive "spa shop" in the lobby, but you may be able to buy what you need once inside for less (ask when you buy your ticket). Figure about 6,000 Ft for a towel or a swimsuit, 4,000 Ft for flip-flops, and 2,000 Ft for a swim cap.

Entry Procedure: Credit cards are accepted. Don't bother with "prepaid" bath tickets advertised around town.

All of Budapest's baths use the same easy system: When you pay, you'll be given a waterproof wristband that you'll need to keep on. Touch it to the panel on the turnstile to enter, then again to be assigned a changing cabin, then again to unlock your cabin. At most baths (except Rudas), the door of your cabin should lock automatically when you close it. If you paid for a locker, choose any empty one and touch it with your wristband to lock it; from then on, it can only be locked and unlocked with the same wristband. If you forget the number of your cabin or locker, just touch your wristband to the panel, and it'll remind you.

Lockers and Cabins: The main choice when buying your ticket is locker or cabin. The (default) locker price is slightly cheaper and gives you access to a gender-segregated, gymnasium-type locker room (which often has communal cabins where modest bathers can change). A cabin is all yours, offering more privacy for changing and a lockable door. I've found both cabins and lockers to be safe, but storing valuables here is at your own risk (if you're nervous, you can pay to rent a safe).

Main Pools: Each bath complex has multiple pools. Big pools with cooler water are for serious swimming, while the smaller, hotter thermal baths (*gyógyfürdő*, or simply *gőz*) are for relaxing, enjoying the jets and current pools, and playing chess. The water bubbles up from hot springs at 77° Celsius (170° Fahrenheit), then is mixed with cooler water to achieve the desired temperatures. Most pools are marked with the water temperature in Celsius (cooler pools are about 30°C/86°F, warmer pools are closer to 36°C/97°F or 38°C/100°F, and the hottest are 42°C/108°F). Locals hit the cooler pools first, then work their way up to the top temps.

Other Bath Features: Most thermal baths also have a dry sauna, a wet steam room, a cold plunge pool, and sunbathing areas. Some baths have fun flourishes: bubbles, whirlpools, massage jets, waterfalls, wave pools, and so on. Be aware that the various water features sometimes take turns running. If a particularly fun feature of the pool doesn't seem to be working, just give it a few minutes.

Kids: At many baths, children under 14 are not allowed in the indoor thermal pools. At baths with lots of fun outdoor options (like Széchenyi), kids can still have a fun time, but at Gellért in the winter, when the wave pool is closed, most of the complex is essentially off-limits to kids. If traveling with children, carefully check the latest policies on the bath's website.

Massages: Don't expect a relaxing, pampering experience. The list of options can be confusing. Generally speaking, these are organized into two categories: **"classical"** (the basic, medical-grade rubdown—figure 10,000 Ft/20 minutes, 15,000 Ft/45 minutes) and **"premium"** or **"VIP"** (longer and more pampering—20,000 Ft/1 hour).

Other helpful terms: A **"relax massage"** or **"aroma massage"** is a restful rubdown, typically using oil. A **"refreshing massage"** is similar but may involve more pressure and/or last longer. A **"scrub massage"** or **"skin-firming massage"** is intended to exfoliate your skin and involves some very hard scrubbing. On busy days (especially Mon, Fri, and Sat), you may have to wait an hour or two; at other times, you may be able to get your massage immediately.

The Baths

Of Budapest's two-dozen thermal baths, the three listed here are the best known, most representative, and most convenient for first-timers. If you're trying to choose, consider this: The **Széchenyi Baths** are big, fun, and beautiful—*the* classic Budapest bathing experience. Széchenyi can also be crowded, a little chaotic, and therefore less relaxing. And because of its size, it's more challenging to navigate. The **Gellért Baths** feel a bit more upscale and genteel, attracting a more sedate, older clientele. The indoor baths here are among Budapest's most beautiful, but the outdoor areas are less inviting and fun than Széchenyi. In general, there's less to "do" at Gellért (especially off-season), but it's very relaxing. The **Rudas Baths** are two baths in one: a historic, 500-year-old, Turkish-bath-like thermal section that feels ancient and extremely atmospheric; and a completely modern, almost clinical-feeling "wellness" section. It's also (relatively) less crowded with tourists than the first two. For more information on all of Budapest's baths, see www.spasbudapest.com.

Széchenyi Baths (Széchenyi Fürdő)

The big, yellow, copper-domed building in the middle of City Park, Széchenyi (SAY-chayn-yee) is easily worth ▲▲▲. Although it's increasingly popular with tourists, you'll still see a fair number of Hungarians here. Magyars of all shapes and sizes stuff themselves into tiny swimsuits and strut their stuff. Bankers and homemakers float blissfully in the warm water. Intellectuals and roly-poly elder statesmen stand in chest-high water around chessboards and

ponder their next moves. This is
Budapest at its best.

Cost: 9,400 Ft for ticket
and locker (in gender-segregated locker room), 1,000 Ft more
for personal changing cabin,
cheaper if you arrive two hours
before closing, 1,500 Ft more on
weekends (Fri-Sun). Regardless
of which entrance or ticket you
use, the price includes both the outdoor swimming pool area and
the indoor thermal bath and sauna.

Hours: Mon and Wed-Thu 7:00-19:00, Tue and Fri 8:00-
20:00, Sat-Sun 9:00-20:00, last entry one hour before closing. On
some summer weekends, the baths may be open later (see "Night
Bathing," below).

Information: +36 1 363 3210, www.szechenyibath.hu.

Location and Entrances: In City Park at Állatkerti Körút
11, district XIV, M1: Széchenyi Fürdő. The huge bath complex
has three entrances. The **"ther-**

mal bath entrance" is the
grand main entry, facing south
(roughly toward Vajdahunyad
Castle). The **"swimming pool
entrance,"** facing the zoo on the
other side of the complex, can be
busier, but makes it quick and
easy to find the outdoor pools.
A third, smaller **"medical en-
trance"**—open only when things are very busy—is between the
other two (and near the Metró station). If there's a long line at one
of the entrances, check the others.

Massage: In the lobby, an English menu lists a wide array
of massages and other treatments. In addition to the standard options, you'll see offers of various special "VIP" or "private" packages
(including some that give you access to an adjoining palm house,
called "Dayspalm").

Night Bathing: The baths are a joy in the evening, when both
the price and the crowds are reduced. Additionally, Széchenyi is
open late into the night on weekends for a "sparty" event, where the
bath complex basically becomes one big hot-water dance club (€65,
most Saturdays starting at 22:00, tickets sell out so book ahead at
https://szechenyibath.com/sparties).

Entering the Baths: These instructions assume that you're
using the **swimming pool entrance.** First, in the grand lobby, pay
the cashier, then touch your wristband to the turnstile and enter.

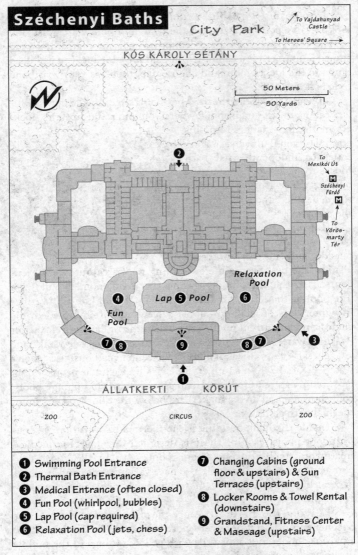

Szechenyi Baths

City Park

To Vajdahunyad Castle
To Heroes' Square

KÓS KÁROLY SÉTÁNY

50 Meters
50 Yards

To Mexikói Út
M Széchenyi Fürdő M
To Vörös-marty Tér

Relaxation Pool

Lap **5** Pool

4 Fun Pool

6

7 **8** **9** **8** **7** **3**

1

ÁLLATKERTI KÖRÚT

ZOO CIRCUS ZOO

BUDAPEST

1 Swimming Pool Entrance
2 Thermal Bath Entrance
3 Medical Entrance (often closed)
4 Fun Pool (whirlpool, bubbles)
5 Lap Pool (cap required)
6 Relaxation Pool (jets, chess)
7 Changing Cabins (ground floor & upstairs) & Sun Terraces (upstairs)
8 Locker Rooms & Towel Rental (downstairs)
9 Grandstand, Fitness Center & Massage (upstairs)

Straight ahead is a row of private changing cabins. If you go **up the stairs,** you'll find more changing cabins, "solarium" sun terraces, a fitness center, and a grandstand overlooking the main pool. (It's worth heading upstairs just to snap some photos of the outdoor complex before you change.) If you go **down the stairs,** you'll find a long hallway lined with hairdryers and mirrors, which leads to locker rooms at each end.

If you paid for a **cabin,** head to the cabins on the main floor, look for an electronic panel on the wall, and hold your wristband against this panel for a few seconds—you'll automatically be assigned a number for a cabin. If you paid for a **locker,** you can head down to the locker room and choose one, then use your wristband to lock it.

If you're using the **thermal bath entrance,** the layout is similar: cabins on the main floor where you enter and upstairs, lockers in the basement. From this entrance, you'll traverse a long series of indoor thermal bath rooms to make your way to the outdoor pools (from the locker room, bear left and circle around the complex).

Taking the Waters: The bath complex has two parts, outside and inside. For most visitors, the best part is the swimming pool area **outside.** Orient yourself to the three pools (facing the main, domed building): The pool to the left is for **fun** (cooler water—30°C/86°F, warmer in winter, lots of jets and bubbles, lively and often crowded, includes circular current pool). The pool on the right is for **relaxation** (warmer water—38°C/100°F, mellow atmosphere, a few massage jets, chess). The **main (lap) pool** in the center is all business (cooler water—28°C/82°F in summer, 26°C/79°F in winter, people doing laps, swim cap required). Stairs to saunas (with cold plunge pools, cold showers, and an ice maker) are below the doors to the indoor thermal bath complex.

Inside the main building is the thermal bath section, a series of indoor pools; each of these is designed for a specific medical treatment. You'll also find steam rooms with an 18°C/64°F cold plunge pool nearby. The pools also have varying types and amounts of healthy minerals—some of which can make the water quite green and/or stinky.

Leaving the Bath: If you're heading to the Metró, the Széchenyi Fürdő station is very close but easy to miss: It's basically a pair of nondescript stairwells with yellow railings in the middle of the park, roughly toward Heroes' Square from the thermal bath entrance (look for the low-profile, yellow *Földalatti* sign; to head for downtown, take the stairwell marked *a Vörösmarty Tér Felé*).

Gellért Baths (Gellért Fürdő)

The ▲▲ baths at Gellért (GEH-layrt) Hotel feel more upscale than Széchenyi. Gellért's indoor thermal pools are Budapest's most atmospheric—with exquisite porcelain details and an air of mystery.

Its outdoor zone—mostly for sunbathing, and with just one smallish hot pool—is less interesting than Széchenyi, with one exception: It has a deliriously enjoyable wave pool that'll toss you around like a queasy surfer (summer only). The hotel is slated for an extensive years-long renovation, which may begin in 2024; they're hoping to keep the baths open for some or all of that time, but anticipate changes (and construction chaos)—it's best to check first before making the trip here.

Cost: 9,400 Ft for ticket and locker, 1,000 Ft more for a personal changing cabin; 1,500 Ft extra on weekends (Fri-Sun).

Hours: Daily 9:00-19:00, last entry one hour before closing.

Information: +36 1 466 6166 ext. 165, http://gellertspa.com.

Location: It's on the Buda side of the green Liberty Bridge (M4: Szent Gellért Tér; or take trams #47, #48, and #49 from Deák Tér in Pest, or trams #19 and #41 along the Buda embankment from Víziváros below the castle, Gellért Tér stop). The hotel's main entrance faces the Danube and the tram and Metró stops. To find the baths entrance, circle around the right side of the huge building—it's under a giant stone arch (Kelenhegyi Út 4, district XI).

Entering the Baths: The entrance doors are flanked by ticket windows; just past those, on the right, is an info desk with English-speaking staff.

After buying your ticket, put on your wristband and glide through the swanky lobby. You'll use the swimming pool entrance, on your right, under the grand dome. Go down the stairs, pass through a long corridor, then climb up the stairs. If you paid for a cabin, you'll find a maze of them at the first landing; for a locker, proceed up one more flight to find the locker rooms. If you need to buy a towel or swimsuit, look for the desk near the entrance to the changing-cabin area.

Taking the Waters: From the locker room, look for signs *to the effervescent bath-pool* (for the indoor section) or *to the swimming-pool with artificial waves* (for the outdoor section).

Gellért Baths

30 Meters
30 Yards

10 Wave Pool

9

WC

Jubileumi Park

7 **8**

9

6 Pool

CAFÉ

7 Thermal **5** P o o l **7** Baths

8 **8**

To Cave Church

3 **WC** **WC** **4**

2 **1**

TICKETS

BATHS ENTRANCE

HOTEL

To Castle Hill

BARTÓK BÉLA

HOTEL ENTRANCE

#19, 41, 47, 48, 49

Gellért Tér **T**

Szent Gellért Tér

SZENT GELLÉRT TÉR

To Liberty Bridge

Szent Gellért Tér **M**

KEMENES UTCA

KELENHEGYI ÚT

BUDAPEST

1 Lobby
2 Swimming Pool Entrance
3 Men's Locker Room (lower level)
4 Women's Locker Room (lower level)
5 Cool-Water Swimming Pool

6 Hot-Water Swimming Pool
7 Thermal Baths (3)
8 Saunas (3)
9 Sunbathing Areas (2)
10 Wave Pool

Inside, the central, genteel-feeling hall is home to a cool-water swimming pool (swim cap required) and a crowded hot-water pool (36°C/97°F). This is used for swimming laps and for periodic water-exercise classes. On sunny days, they crank open the retractable roof. Back toward the main hall are doors to the thermal baths. These were once segregated into men's and women's sections. To reach them, you'll walk through a hall of curtained massage cabins. These grand old halls are the most atmospheric part of the bath— slathered with colorful porcelain decorations. The former men's

section is both hotter and more beautifully decorated than the women's section. I'd focus on the former men's section, which has big pools at either end. At the far end of the bath are a steam room (45-50°C/113-122°F) and a cold plunge pool (18°C/64°F). Back out near the changing cabins is a dry sauna (50-70°C/122-158°F). If you paid for a massage, you'll report to the massage room in this section.

Outside, you'll find several sunbathing areas. There's just one warm thermal pool (36°C/97°F)—follow *adventure pool* signs up and to the right. Near the pool is a Finnish-style woody sauna and a big barrel-shaped plunge pool with cold water.

But the main outdoor attraction is the big, unheated wave pool in the center (generally closed Oct-April, weather dependent). The swells in the deeper area are fun and easy to float on, but the crashing waves at the shallow end are vigorous, if not dangerous.

Rudas Baths (Rudas Fürdő)

To get to the Turkish roots of Budapest's obsession with thermal baths, head for Rudas (ROO-dawsh). Worth ▲▲, it's the most his-

toric, local, and potentially intimidating of the three baths I list—but it may also be the most rewarding, as it offers the most variety.

Rudas has two main sections: the dark, historic, mysterious-feeling Turkish-style thermal bathing zone; and the modern, fun wellness/"sauna world"/swimming pool section. However, on certain days and times the thermal section is open only to men or only to women (see "Hours," later). On Friday and Saturday nights, the thermal section becomes a modern nightclub until the wee hours.

Overview: Rudas' **thermal section** feels more like the classic Turkish baths of yore—with an octagonal central pool under a fine 500-year-old dome first built by the Ottomans. These baths are not about splashy fun—there are no jets, bubbles, or whirlpools. Instead, Rudas is about history and about serious temperature mod-

BUDAPEST

ulation—stepping your body temperature up and down between very hot and very cold.

The **wellness area**—with a handful of relaxing jet pools—is the modern, accessible yin to the thermal baths' antique yang. The main reason to visit this section is the rooftop terrace, where you can sunbathe or soak while looking out over sweeping views of the Budapest skyline. The wellness area is also attached to a "sauna world" (with a half-dozen different wet or dry hot rooms) and a swimming pool for laps.

Cost: "All-in" ticket includes entire complex for 8,600 Ft weekdays, 12,200 Ft weekends; 1,000 Ft extra for private, lockable changing cabin; when the thermal baths are gender-segregated (see below), you can buy a ticket for just the thermal or wellness area (5,900 Ft each).

Hours: Daily 6:00-20:00, last entry one hour before closing. Wellness area mixed gender every day. Thermal section open only to men all day Mon and Wed plus Thu-Fri mornings; only open to women all day Tue; open to everyone Thu-Fri afternoons and Sat-Sun all day. Night bathing (described later) is also mixed gender.

Information: +36 1 375 8373, www.rudasbaths.com.

Location: It's in a low-profile building at the foot of Gellért Hill, just south of the white Elisabeth Bridge (Döbrentei Tér 9, district I). Trams #19 and #41, which run along the Buda embankment, stop right out front (Rudas Gyógyfürdő stop). Those trams also work from Szent Gellért Tér, as do trams #56 and #56A or bus #7. From Pest, you can ride bus #7 from Astoria or Ferenciek Tere to the Rudas Gyógyfürdő stop.

Eating: There's a fine **$$ bistro** on the wellness side, which welcomes both fully dressed customers and those wearing swimsuits. There's also a little cocktail counter up at the rooftop sunbathing/soaking zone, and another basic food-and-drinks counter in the lobby.

Night Bathing: The baths are open—to both men and women, in swimsuits—with a dance hall ambience Fri-Sat 22:00-late (12,600 Ft).

Entering the Baths: If you paid for a private cabin, you'll enter on the main floor into a corridor of cabins. Otherwise, you'll go upstairs to a modern locker room, with men and women mixed (but with private cabins to change in).

Taking the Waters: Remember, Rudas has two distinct areas with entirely different protocols: the thermal bath section and the wellness/"sauna world"/swimming pool section. With the "all-in" ticket, you can float freely between them.

Thermal Bath: The central chamber, under an original 35-foot-high Turkish dome supported by eight pillars, is the historic core of the baths. This area is all about modulating your body temperature—pushing your body to its limit with heat, then dousing off quickly with a bucket of cold water, then heating up again, and so on. Pools of different temperatures let you do this as gradually or quickly as you like.

Along one wall are entrances to the wet sauna (*nedves gőzkamra*, to the left), with 50°C (122°F) scented steam; and the dry sauna (*hőlégkamra*, to the right), with three progressively hotter rooms ranging from 45°C (113° F) to 72°C (161°F). Near the entrance to each one is a shower or a bucket of frigid water (if you're overheated, pull the rope for immediate relief...your skin won't stop tingling for several minutes).

Surrounding this central chamber are hallways with other areas: resting rooms, tanning beds *(szolarium)*, massage rooms, a cold plunge pool, and a scale to see how much sweat you've lost.

To move between the thermal bath and wellness sections, you'll cross through the lobby.

Wellness/Sauna/Pool: First you'll walk along the swimming pool (for laps, swim cap required); upstairs from here is an outdoor sun terrace. Once you're in the far building, upstairs is the "sauna world," where you can move between a variety of steam rooms and dry saunas.

At the far end is the wellness area. The first room, with a huge window looking out over the busy embankment road, has three pools of different temperatures, all with powerful massage jets. In the cold plunge pool, notice the ice maker that continually drops in a cube or two, every few seconds.

But the real highlight of the wellness area is upstairs: At the end of the room, find the staircase and head on up, passing the bistro on your way to the rooftop terrace. Whether soaking in rays on the sun deck or taking a dip in the thermal pool, you're surrounded by the bustle of the city.

Entertainment in Budapest

Budapest is a great place to catch a good—and inexpensive—musical performance. In fact, music lovers from Vienna make the three-hour trip here just to take in a fine opera in a luxurious setting at a bargain price. To sort out your options, see the resources listed below, including the good classical music schedules at MuzsikaKalendarium.hu.

Locals dress up for the more "serious" concerts and opera, but many tourists wear casual clothes—as long as you don't show up in shorts, sneakers, or flip-flops, you'll be fine.

The following **helpful websites** offer current advice on cultural events and nightlife in Budapest: WeLoveBudapest.com, Funzine.

hu, MuzsikaKalendarium.hu (classical music), and XpatLoop.com (by and for expats living here).

For concerts and events, you can buy **tickets** direct on the websites for various venues, but you may be redirected to Jegymester.hu (sort of the Ticketmaster of Hungary, and a good place to survey what's on) or Kulturinfo.Jegy.hu.

What's on can vary by **season.** Some of the best nightclubs and bars are partly or entirely outdoors, so they're far more enjoyable in the summer. Meanwhile, the Hungarian State Opera, the Puppet Theater, and other indoor cultural events tend to take a summer break from late June into early September (though that's prime time for outdoor music).

For a list of some local **festivals,** which often include excellent live music, see "Holidays & Festivals" in the appendix.

A Night at the Opera

Take in an opera by one of the best companies in Europe, in one of Europe's loveliest opera houses, for bargain prices. The Hungarian State Opera usually performs Tuesdays through Sundays (except late June through early September; no performances Mon). Most productions are at the stunning and historic main Hungarian State Opera House (Andrássy Út 22, district VI, M1: Opera, see page 610), but some take place at less impressive venues—make sure you're clear on the location before you book. Most performances are in the original language with Hungarian and English supertitles.

Tickets: Seats range from about 5,200 to 30,000 Ft; they can be booked most easily online, but be sure to use the official Opera website (www.opera.hu) rather than a third-party scalper site. You can also just drop by the Opera House once you're in town and see what's available (daily 10:00-19:00, or until the first intermission). However, tickets often sell out in advance.

Cheap Seats: The best music deal in Europe may be the "cheap seats," which cost 1,800 Ft. There are two types of these tickets. **Obstructed-view** seats are typically in the back of the many small boxes that line the sides of the Opera House; basically, you can choose whether to sit and see nothing or stand and crane your neck to see about half the stage. These tickets go on sale with the other types of tickets and can be booked online.

Same-day standing tickets are located at the very top of the auditorium, wedged between a rail and a velvet-covered bench, al-

lowing you to lean through the performance. Most also have a partially obstructed view of the stage (though big TV screens on the
walls let you see what you're missing). There are 84 standing spaces,
and tickets go on sale two hours before show time and must be purchased in person at the Opera House box office. For popular shows
that are otherwise sold out, these are a hot commodity; it's wise
to line up at the theater 10 to 15 minutes before they go on sale.

While opera lovers should splurge on better seats, if you're
simply curious for a peek inside this grand space, these cheap seats
are a bargain—much cheaper than the guided tour, and offering a
chance to see the venue in action. If your appetite for opera is limited, slipping out at intermission is less than a capital offense.

House of Music Hungary (Magyar Zene Háza)

This architecturally bold venue in City Park is a musical twofer.
First, it has a 300-seat theater that hosts a wide variety of musical performances, plus a smaller lecture hall and an open-air stage
under a canopy of gilded "leaves." Classical, jazz, traditional folk,
electronica, sacred music—the program here has all the bases covered. And second, it's a museum with high-tech, exuberant exhibits that celebrate Hungarian and international music. Music lovers
should drop by to tour the exhibits and check what's on while in
town (see www.zenehaza.hu; in the middle of City Park at Olof
Palme Sétány 3-5, +36 70 799 9449). For a more in-depth description of this facility, see page 618.

Other Venues

Budapest has many other grand spaces for enjoying a performance.
You can find details for each of these on their websites.

The **Franz Liszt Academy of Music** (Liszt Ferenc
Zeneművészeti Egyetem, a.k.a. Zeneakadémia), on Franz Liszt
Square, hosts high-quality professional concerts every night. Restored to its stunning late-19th-century splendor, this venue rivals
even the Opera House for opulence—if attending a concert, make
sure it's in the Grand Hall, or Nagyterem (just off of Andrássy Út at
Liszt Ferenc Tér 8, district VI, M1: Oktogon, www.zeneakademia.
hu). They also do one-hour guided tours of the theater in English
(5,300 Ft, includes brief concert by a student, usually 1/day—typically at 14:30).

The **former Academy of Music** (Régi Zeneakadémia)—just
up Andrássy Út near the House of Terror—houses the Franz Liszt
Museum and hosts performances on Saturday mornings at 11:00
(4,000 Ft, Vörösmarty Utca 35, www.lfze.hu).

The **Pesti Vigadó** ("Pest Concert Hall"), gorgeously restored
and sitting proudly on the Pest embankment, is another fine place
for a concert in elegant surroundings (Vigadó Tér 2, https://vigado.
hu).

The city's two finest churches—both with sumptuous interiors—host tourist-oriented concerts. Most of the shows in **St. István's Basilica** are organ concerts—often scheduled for Monday afternoons, and sometimes also Friday evenings or at other times (check both www.organconcert.hu and www.budapestxplore.com; second option offers RS%—10 percent discount for direct bookings). Up on Castle Hill, **Matthias Church** hosts a variety of touristy shows, from organ recitals to string orchestras (check www.matyas-templom.hu; additional concerts may be found at www.concertsinbudapest.com).

In the Seventh District/Jewish Quarter, the **Rumbach Street Synagogue** is a beautiful space to enjoy a concert (there's no consolidated website for these shows, but keep an eye out for this as a venue in event listings). The **National Dance Theater** (Nemzeti Táncszínház) puts on performances ranging from ballet to folk to contemporary in their main venue at Millenáris Park, just north of Castle Hill (Kis Rókus Utca 16-20, M2: Széll Kálmán Tér, +36 1 434 5900, www.dancetheatre.hu). They also do some performances at Müpa Budapest.

The **Millennium City Center** complex, sitting on the Pest riverbank near the Rákóczi Bridge south of downtown (district IX), is a state-of-the-art facility with multiple venues. **Müpa Budapest,** short for Művészetek Palotája (Palace of Arts), features art installations as well as musical performances in two venues: the 1,700-seat Béla Bartók National Concert Hall and the 460-seat Festival Theater (www.mupa.hu).

Tourist Folklore Concerts: Hungária Koncert typically offers a performance about once weekly (likely Sat, Easter-Oct only, in the Aranytíz Kultúrház near the Chain Bridge at Arany János 10, RS%—10 percent discount if you book direct, +36 1 317 2754 or +36 1 317 1377, www.budapestxplore.com).

Nightlife in Budapest

In addition to strolling the floodlit promenades and taking an after-hours dip at a thermal bath (Széchenyi and Rudas are both partly open late—see "Experiences in Budapest," earlier), here are some ideas for nighttime fun.

Yuppie Drinking Zones

The plaza in front of **St. István's Basilica** is Budapest's most fashionable locale for a glass of wine. Of the many upscale restaurants and bars in this area, DiVino—a bar with contemporary decor and a wide range of Hungarian wines by the glass—is a good choice (see "Eating in Budapest," later).

Franz Liszt Square (Liszt Ferenc Tér), a leafy and inviting zone just off Andrássy Út, is lined with mostly tourist-oriented bars. The pedestrianized **Ráday Utca,** near Kálvin Tér just north of the Great Market Hall, has a similar scene.

For something a bit more genteel—evocative of this city's late-19th-century golden age—locals pass their evenings sipping wine or nibbling dessert at a **café** (see "Budapest's Café Culture" on page 673).

Ruin Pubs

These lively pubs *(romkocsmák)* are filled with ramshackle second-hand furniture, a bohemian-junkyard vibe—and plenty of drinkers having the time of their  lives. Most of the clientele are in their 20s or 30s, but hip oldsters feel perfectly welcome. While some ruin pubs are edgy and high-energy, others are more fit for a hammock. To seek out your ideal ruin pub, know the terminology. A ruin pub may bill itself as a *mulató* (club, usually higher energy) or a *kávézó* (coffeehouse, usually mellower). Many have a *kert* ("garden"), filling deteriorating buildings' courtyards with quirky décor and artful graffiti. Others have a *tető* ("rooftop"). The bigger ruin pubs often have a bouncer stationed outside—but curious travelers are more than welcome. For more info, including additional listings, see RuinPubs.com.

Ruin Pubs in the Seventh District: Budapest's Seventh District—the historic Jewish Quarter, behind the Great Synagogue—teems with clubs, bars, and creative little hole-in-the-wall eateries. Why are so many of these funky bars concentrated in the Jewish Quarter? Because it's conveniently central, yet it remained largely deserted and dilapidated after the commu-  nists took over—keeping rents very low and fostering just the right rickety-chic vibe for ruin pub purveyors.

While this scene changes constantly, here are a few good choices. If you only have time and interest for one, head straight to the first and best, Szimpla. This area can be very lively any night of the week, but it's best Thursday through Saturday. During the peak of summer (July-Aug), most Budapesters are out of town on holiday, making this scene even more touristy. **Szimpla**

BUDAPEST

Kert ("Simple Garden") sprawls through an old building and spills out into a shoddy courtyard. Surrounding the garden is a warren of tiny rooms. There's live music in a soundproof concert room and a selection of decent food (daily, Kazinczy Utca 14, www.szimpla. hu). **Telep** ("Site") is a tumble-down secondhand bar steps from Gozsdu Udvar. There's an art gallery upstairs and often live music (daily, Madách Imre Út 8, just off Rumbach Utca). **Csendes** ("Silent"), with two adjacent branches, is a mellower ruin pub tucked behind Károlyi Park, right in the core of Downtown Pest. The junk-cluttered main "art bar" is at Ferenczy István Utca 5. The Csendes Társ ("Silent Partner") wine bar—a bit more upmarket and snooty—has delightful outdoor tables across the street at the gate to the park and is typically open only in good weather (daily, Magyar Utca 16).

Nearby: While it's not a ruin pub per se, if you're exploring the area, be sure to poke your way down the extremely lively series of courtyards called **Gozsdu Udvar**—jammed with lively bars, cafés, and restaurants.

Summer Terraces (Tető) and Rooftop Bars

In addition to *kert* ("garden"), a key term for enjoying Budapest in the summer is *tető* ("roof"). Rooftop terraces offer laid-back scenery high above the congested city. Most roof terraces are open only in the summer (typically May-Sept) and in good weather, and they start serving drinks and light food around midafternoon. Several offer live music.

360 Bar is on the roof of the old Párisi Nagy Áruház (Andrássy Út 39, M1: Opera, www.360bar.hu).

High Note SkyBar has point-blank views of St. István's. Don't miss the glassed-in passage that leads to spiral stairs up to the two towers—both of which offer even higher, better views (atop the Aria Hotel at Hercegprímás Utca 5, district V, www. highnoteskybar.hu).

Solid Wine Bar, above the recommended Rum Hotel in Downtown Pest, overlooks University Square and comes with a younger but still upscale atmosphere (closed Sun-Mon, Királyi Pál Utca 4, district V, M3/M4: Kálvin Tér, www.solidbudapest.com).

The Duchess, on top of the Matild Palace Hotel, feels well dressed and high-end, with live DJs on weekends and sprawling indoor and outdoor areas—including some with grand views over the Elisabeth Bridge and across the Danube (daily from 17:00, Váci

Utca 36, right next to M3: Ferenciek Tere, +36 70 402 4900, www.
theduchessbudapest.com).

At Buda Castle: White Raven Skybar, on top of the landmark Hilton Hotel at the castle, has pricey drinks, bar snacks, and
stunning views over the colorful rooftop and curlicue spire of the
Matthias Church next door and across the river to Pest. Reservations are essential (inside the Hilton at Hess András Tér 1, district
I, +36 30 676 2620, www.whiteravenskybar.com).

Local Craft Beer and Hungarian Wine

Craft Beer: Budapest has an increasing number of pubs specializing in both Hungarian and international microbrews. **Grav-
ity Brewing** is behind the Great Market Hall (closed Sun-Mon,
Lónyay Utca 22, +36 30 144 8404, www.gravitybp.com). In central Pest, just a few steps from the Deák Tér transit hub, stop by
Madhouse—a big, industrial-feeling gastropub (daily, Anker Köz
1, +36 70 621 0741, www.madhousebudapest.hu). On the Buda
side, **Keg Sörművház,** a long block up from the Gellért Baths (and
Szent Gellért Tér tram and Metró stop), is a nondescript craft beer
cellar (daily, Orlay Utca 1, www.kegsormuvhaz.hu).

Wine: If you prefer grapes to hops, there are several great
spots to sample Hungarian wine. **DiVino Wine Bar** has two locations where you can taste a wide variety—in a trendy wine bar
with grand views of St. István's Basilica or tucked down the chaotic
and lively Gozsdu Udvar passage in the Seventh District. Or, for a
more refined experience, check out **Taste Hungary**'s guided wine
tastings (www.tastehungary.com) and their lovely **Tasting Table**
wine bar and shop (Bródy Sándor Utca 22, near M2: Astoria). For
more on these places, see "Eating in Budapest," later.

Shopping in Budapest

Perhaps Budapest's most appealing street for shoppers is the city's
"antique row," Falk Miksa Utca, just north of the Parliament.

If you just want a few light mementos, Budapest's most convenient—if touristy—shopping venue is the **Great Market Hall**
(described on page 604). In addition to all the colorful produce and
spices downstairs, the upstairs gallery is full of fiercely competitive
souvenir vendors. The **Bálna ("Whale") Cultural Center,** which
sits along the Danube just behind the Great Market Hall, has a
few more options—and the architecture is interesting. **Váci Utca**
features the city's highest prices and worst values.

Up at Buda Castle, **Castellum** gallery showcases the work of
40 local artists and artisans (closed Wed-Thu, kitty-corner from
recommended Ruszwurm café at Úri Utca 26, +36 30 656 1213).

BUDAPEST

Budapest has an excellent **English bookstore,** Bestsellers. For details, see "Helpful Hints," earlier.

Hours: Smaller shops tend to be open Monday through Friday from 10:00 to 18:00 (sometimes later—until 20:00 or 21:00—on Thursday) and Saturday from 10:00 to 13:00 or 14:00, and are closed Sunday. Big malls have longer hours.

Bargaining: At touristy markets (but not established shops), haggling is common for pricier items (more than about 4,000 Ft)—but you'll likely get the merchant to come down only about 10 percent (maybe 20 percent for multiple items). If you pay with a credit card, you're less likely to snare a discount.

VAT Refunds and Customs Regulations: For tips on getting a VAT (value-added tax) refund and getting your purchases through customs, see the "Money" section of the Practicalities chapter.

Souvenir Ideas

Budapest's best souvenirs are edible or drinkable. That quintessential Hungarian spice, **paprika,** is sold in metal cans, linen bags, or porcelain vases—and often accompanied by a tiny wooden scoop. Also look for a variety of paprika-infused pastes—sold in jars or tubes—used to spice up any recipe. (Remember that only sealed containers will make it through customs.) For more, see "Paprika Primer" on page 556.

Special drinks are a fun souvenir but tricky to bring home (you'll have to wrap them very carefully and put them in your checked luggage). Good choices include the unique Hungarian spirit **Unicum,** which comes in many variations; various flavors of the local brandy called *pálinka;* or a bottle of Hungarian **wine** (such as the famous Tokaji Aszú). For more on these drinks, see page 557.

Another popular item is a hand-embroidered **linen tablecloth.** If the thread is thick and the stitching is very even, it was probably done by machine and is less valuable.

Fans of **communist kitsch** can look for ironic T-shirts that poke fun at that bygone era. A good selection is at the Memento Park gift shop, which also sells communist memorabilia.

For a wearable souvenir, **Tisza shoes** (Tisza Cipő) are retro and hip. Their flagship store is along the Small Boulevard near the Great Synagogue (at Károly Körút 1, www.tiszacipo.hu).

Hipster Design and Vintage

Budapest has plenty of fun and idiosyncratic design, home decor, and vintage shops. Many intriguing boutiques have emerged in the **Seventh District/"Ruin Pub" zone.** Scout the possibilities on Király (with an emphasis on home decor), Dob, Rumbach, Dohány, Wesselényi, Kazinczy, and neighboring streets. **Printa,** a print shop, is one reliable place to get a taste of the neighborhood's vendors. **Szimpla**—the original ruin pub—hosts a colorful farmers market each Sunday (9:00-15:00, Kazinczy Utca 14, www.szimpla. hu). Very nearby—just across Andrássy Út from the Seventh District—you'll also find a smattering of intriguing shops along **Hajós Utca,** behind the Opera House.

Sleeping in Budapest

Most travelers find staying in Pest more convenient than sleeping in Buda. Pest has most of the worthwhile sightseeing and nearly all the best restaurants. It also has more Metró and tram stops, making it a snap to get around. Pest feels more lively and local than stodgy, touristy Buda, but it's also more urban. If you don't enjoy big cities, consider sleeping in Buda instead. If you're near the river in Buda, you may have great views across to the Parliament.

In Budapest, most hotels quote rates in euros for the convenience of international guests, and I've ranked them the same way. (Outside of the capital, hotels more often quote rates in forints.) The rate will automatically be converted to forints when you pay. If the credit card reader gives you a choice of currencies, choose forints rather than dollars to avoid excessive conversion fees. The majority of hotels don't include the 4 percent tourist tax in their rates.

PEST

I've arranged my listings by neighborhood, clustered around the most important sightseeing sectors.

Near Andrássy Út

Andrássy Boulevard is handy, local-feeling, and endlessly entertaining. With its ample restaurants, upscale-residential vibe, and easy connection to downtown (via the M1/yellow line), it's the neighborhood where I prefer to sleep.

$$$$ Hotel Moments has 99 Art Deco rooms, a pristine atrium with iron railings, professional service, and a good location at the downtown end of Andrássy Út—making this a fine choice at a high price point. Because it's surrounded by busy streets, light sleepers may be bothered by passing traffic (air-con, elevator, free coffee bar, Andrássy Út 8, district VI, M1: Bajcsy-Zsilinszky Út, +36 1 611 7000, www.hotelmomentsbudapest.hu, reservation@hotelmoments.hu).

$$ K+K Hotel Opera has 200 predictably solid business-class rooms, a great breakfast buffet, and helpful, professional service. Its biggest advantage is the outstanding location, wonderfully situated beside the Opera House and just steps from Andrássy Út and its handy Metró line (air-con, elevator, pay parking garage, Révay

---

Sleep Code

Hotels in this book are categorized according to the average price of a standard double room with breakfast in high season. These ranges apply to cities; you may pay less in towns. 350 Ft = about $1.

$$$$ **Splurge:** Most rooms over €200 (80,000 Ft)
$$$ **Pricier:** €150-200 (60,000-80,000 Ft)
$$ **Moderate:** €100-150 (40,000-60,000 Ft)
$ **Budget:** €50-100 (20,000-40,000 Ft)
¢   **Backpacker:** Under €50 (20,000 Ft)
RS%   **Rick Steves discount**

Unless otherwise noted, credit cards are accepted and hotel staff speak basic English. Comparison-shop by checking prices at several hotels (on each hotel's own website, on a booking site, or by email). For the best deal, *book directly with the hotel.* Ask for a discount if paying in cash; if the listing includes **RS%**, request a Rick Steves discount.

Utca 24, district VI, M1: Opera, +36 1 269 0222, www.kkhotels. com, reservations.opera@kkhotels.com).

$$ Casati Budapest Hotel is a solid value and conveniently located a block off Andrássy Út (across the boulevard from the Opera House, and then down a side street). This classy, Swiss-run hotel has 25 rooms in four different styles, ranging from "classic" to "cool" (review your options online and choose your favorite). Many rooms surround a peaceful courtyard—in this potentially noisy neighborhood, it's worth requesting one of these (air-con, elevator, free sauna and fitness room, Paulay Ede Utca 31, district VI, M1: Opera, +36 1 343 1198, www.casatibudapesthotel.com, info@ casatibudapesthotel.com).

$ Budapest Bed and Breakfast—run with care by András (OHN-drash) and Timea—has five simple yet well-equipped rooms farther from the center, in the quiet diplomatic quarter halfway between the Oktogon and City Park (air-con, a long block off Andrássy Út at Benczúr Utca 3, district VI, M1: Kodály Körönd, +36 30 964 7287, butterflyhomebandb@gmail.com). They also rent rooms in Downtown Pest, near the Great Market Hall (see Butterfly Home Danube B&B, later).

In the Seventh District/Jewish Quarter: A short walk from Andrássy Út, **$$ ROOMbach Hotel Budapest Center**—tucked down a gloomy but central street facing the Rumbach Street Synagogue—has 99 sleek, basic, smallish rooms with a stylish industrial design. It feels modern and solid, and the triple-glazed windows do their best to keep out the ruin-pub noise (air-con, elevator, pay parking, Rumbach Sebestyén Utca 14—for location see the map on

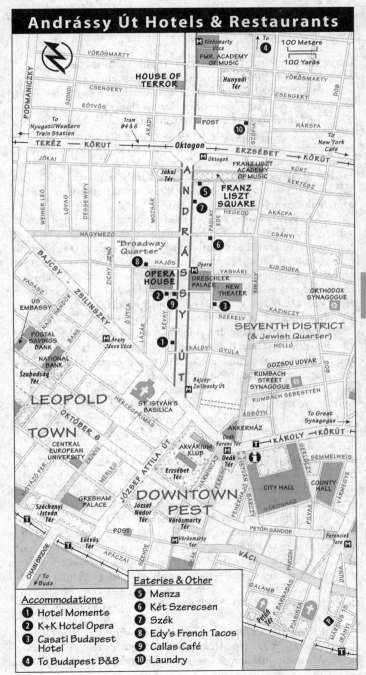

Andrássy Út Hotels & Restaurants

BUDAPEST

Accommodations
1 Hotel Moments
2 K+K Hotel Opera
3 Casati Budapest Hotel
4 To Budapest B&B

Eateries & Other
5 Menza
6 Két Szerecsen
7 Szék
8 Edy's French Tacos
9 Callas Café
10 Laundry

page 664, +36 1 413 0253, www.roombach.com, hotel@roombach.com).

Downtown Pest (Belváros), near Váci Utca

Most hotels on the very central and convenient Váci Utca come with overly inflated prices. But these less expensive options—just a block or two off Váci Utca—offer better value.

$$$ Hotel Rum is a sleek retreat overlooking the rejuvenated University Square in the heart of Downtown Pest. Its 40 sterile but trendy, industrial-mod, "New York-style" rooms come with concrete floors, subway tile, and open shelving. The top-floor wine bar has great views (air-con, elevator, Királyi Pál Utca 4, district V, M3/M4: Kálvin Tér, +36 1 424 9060, www.hotelrumbudapest.com, hello@hotelrumbudapest.com).

$$ Emerald Hotel is a big modern building wrapped almost entirely around an old church, so many of the rooms face a quiet courtyard. It's a rare combination of extremely central (a short walk from the Deák Tér transit hub, in the heart of Downtown Pest) yet peaceful and removed. Its 160 units include compact, stylish rooms and larger suites. The breakfast room is also sharp and contemporary, with black-and-gold accents (family rooms, air-con, elevator, Városház Utca 20, district V, M1/M2/M3: Deák Tér, +36 70 645 9590, www.emeraldhotel.hu, info@emeraldsuites.hu).

$ Gerlóczy Café & Rooms, which also serves good coffee and meals in its recommended café, is an exceptional value—the best spot in central Budapest for affordable elegance. The 19 rooms, set around a classy old spiral-staircase atrium with a stained-glass ceiling, are thoughtfully appointed (some street noise, air-con, elevator, just off Városház Utca at Gerlóczy Utca 1, district V, M3: Ferenciek Tere or M2: Astoria or M1/M2/M3: Deák Tér, +36 1 501 4000, www.gerloczy.hu, info@gerloczy.hu).

$ Butterfly Home Danube B&B, run by András and Timea (from the Budapest Bed and Breakfast, listed earlier), has eight rooms and Danube views near the Great Market Hall (air-con, elevator, Fővám Tér 2-3, 2nd floor, suite #2, district V, M4: Fővám Tér, +36 30 964 7287, butterflyhomebandb@gmail.com).

$ Katona Apartments, with five simple units just around the corner from busy Ferenciek Tere, is conscientiously run by János and Virág. It's a family-friendly budget option in the very center of the city, facing a drab—but appealingly quiet—central courtyard (no breakfast but kitchenette, air-con, elevator, Petőfi Sándor Utca 6, +36 70 221 1797, www.katonaapartments.hu, info@katonaapartments.hu).

In the Palace District: The up-and-coming Palace District is a formerly genteel zone that sprawls around and behind the National Museum, just across the Small Boulevard from Downtown

Pest. **$$$ Brody House,** a hipster hangout with ample public spaces, began as an art gallery that provided a place for its guests to crash and has evolved into a comfortable, full-service B&B. With a trendy, scuffed, ruin-pub vibe, it's classy yet ramshackle. It fills three spacious floors of a townhouse with eight rooms that all ooze a funky, idiosyncratic style (air-con in most rooms, two stories up with no elevator, Bródy Sándor Utca 10, district VIII, M3/M4: Kálvin Tér, +36 1 266 1211, www.brody.house, reception@brody. house).

Leopold Town

These options are within a short walk of St. István's Basilica and the touristy dining zone that surrounds it. For locations, see the map on page 667.

$$$$ Four Seasons Gresham Palace is unquestionably Budapest's top hotel. Stay here only if money is truly no object. You'll sleep in what is arguably Budapest's finest Art Nouveau building. Damaged in World War II, the Gresham Palace sat in disrepair for decades. Today, it sparkles from head to toe, and every detail in its lavish public spaces and 179 rooms is perfectly in place. Even if you're not sleeping here, dip into the lobby to soak in the elegance (air-con, elevator, top-floor spa, Széchenyi Tér 5, district V, between M1: Vörösmarty Tér and M2: Kossuth Tér, +36 1 268 6000, www.fourseasons.com/budapest, budapest.reservations@ fourseasons.com).

$$$$ Prestige Hotel, on a quiet side street around the corner from the Gresham Palace, is a suitably plush alternative for those seeking elegance at a lower price. Its 85 rooms surround a pristine white lobby with a giant twinkling chandelier, and high-end restaurants are just steps away (air-con, elevator, Vigyázó Ferenc Utca 5, district V, +36 1 920 1000, www.prestigehotelbudapest.com, prestigebudapest@zeinahotels.com).

$$ Cortile Hotel, the trendier little sister of Casati Hotel (listed earlier), has 39 rooms and a delightful rooftop swimming pool and bar. The decor has a cheery nature theme—each room is either sky, flora, moss, or terra—and the "no kids" policy attracts a hip, young (or young-at-heart) clientele seeking comfort and class. While the narrow street it's on can be noisy on weekends (request a quieter courtyard room), it's an easy walk to the Opera House or St. István's (air-con, elevator, Dessewffy Utca 14, district VI, M3: Arany János Utca, +36 1 604 9339, www.cortilebudapesthotel.com, info@cortilebudapesthotel.com).

BUDA
Víziváros

The Víziváros neighborhood—or "Water Town"—is the lively part

BUDAPEST

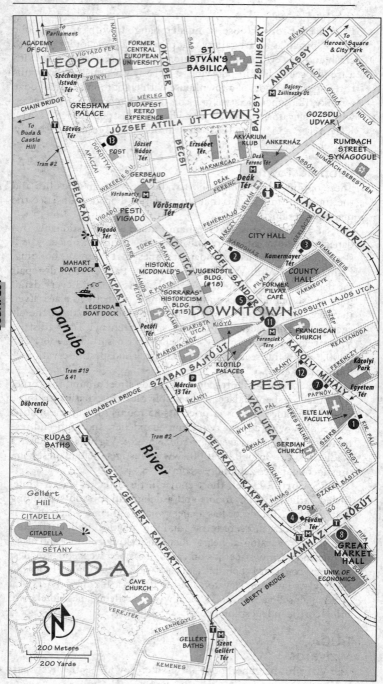

BUDAPEST

Downtown Pest Hotels & Restaurants

Accommodations
1 Hotel Rum
2 Emerald Hotel
3 Gerlóczy Café & Rooms
4 Butterfly Home Danube B&B
5 Katona Apartments
6 Brody House

Eateries & Other
7 Belvárosi Disznótoros
8 Great Market Hall
9 Tasting Table Wine Shop
10 To Rosenstein
11 Párisi Udvar
12 Centrál Kávéház
13 Pharmacy

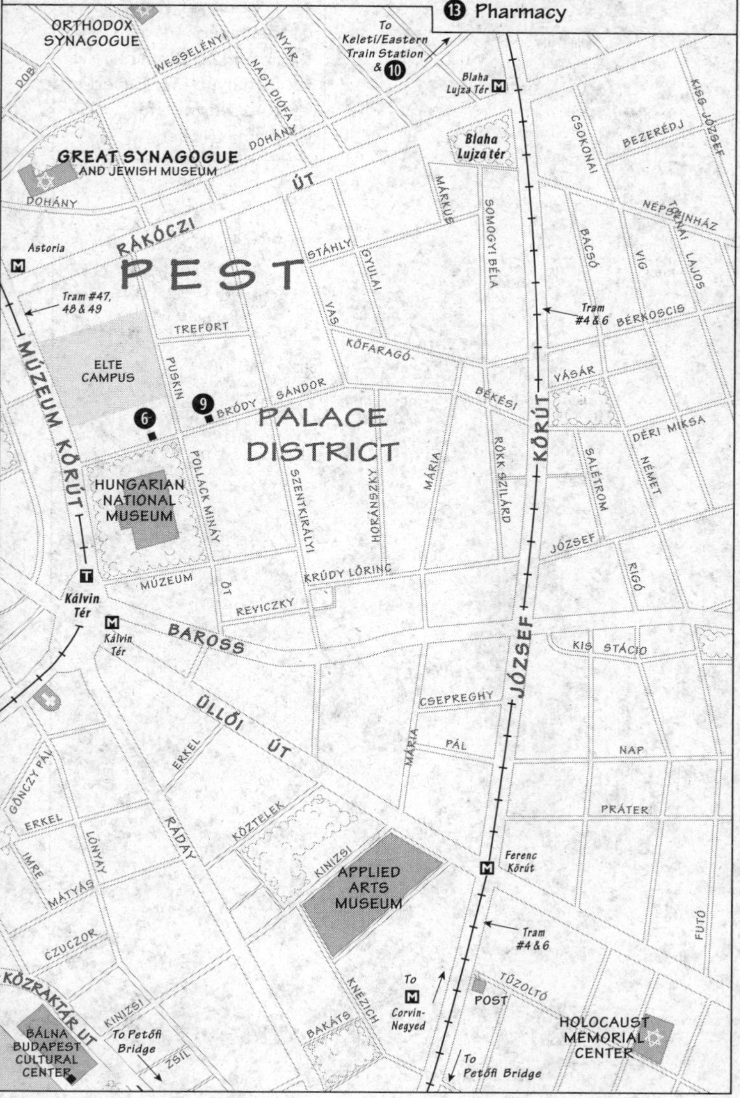

ORTHODOX SYNAGOGUE

To Keleti/Eastern Train Station & 10

Blaha Lujza Tér

GREAT SYNAGOGUE AND JEWISH MUSEUM

Blaha Lujza tér

DOHÁNY

Astoria

RÁKÓCZI ÚT

PEST

Tram #47, 48 & 49

Tram #4 & 6

ELTE CAMPUS

6 9 BRÓDY SÁNDOR

PALACE DISTRICT

HUNGARIAN NATIONAL MUSEUM

KÁLVIN TÉR

Kálvin Tér

BAROSS

ÜLLŐI ÚT

APPLIED ARTS MUSEUM

Ferenc Körút

Tram #4 & 6

To Corvin-Negyed

POST

To Petőfi Bridge

KÖZRAKTÁR UT

BÁLNA BUDAPEST CULTURAL CENTER

To Petőfi Bridge

HOLOCAUST MEMORIAL CENTER

BUDAPEST

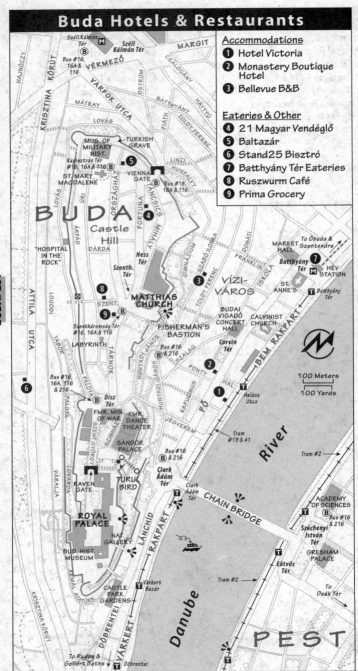

Buda Hotels & Restaurants

Accommodations
1. Hotel Victoria
2. Monastery Boutique Hotel
3. Bellevue B&B

Eateries & Other
4. 21 Magyar Vendéglő
5. Baltazár
6. Stand25 Bisztró
7. Batthyány Tér Eateries
8. Ruszwurm Café
9. Prima Grocery

BUDAPEST

of Buda squeezed between Castle Hill and the Danube, where fishermen and tanners used to live. Víziváros is the most pleasant and convenient area to stay on the Buda side of the Danube, with fine views across the river toward the Parliament building and bustling Pest. Trams #19 and #41 zip along the embankment in either direction, stopping right in front of the first two places listed below. Batthyány Tér, a few minutes' walk away, is a handy center with lots of restaurants, a Metró stop (M2/red line), and the HÉV train to Óbuda and Szentendre. All of these are in district I.

$$$ Hotel Victoria, with 27 stylish, spotless, business-class rooms—each with a grand river view—is a class act. This tall, narrow place (three rooms on each of nine floors) is run with pride and attention to detail by on-the-ball, father-and-son managers Zoltán and Oliver, along with their friendly staff. They also have a few cheaper rooms, facing the street in back. This gem is easily your best choice in this part of Buda (air-con, elevator, free sauna, reserve ahead for pay parking garage, Bem Rakpart 11, +36 1 457 8080, www.victoria.hu, victoria@victoria.hu). The painstakingly restored 19th-century Hubay Palace behind the hotel (entrance next to reception) is used for concerts and other events. It feels like a museum, with inlaid floors, stained-glass windows, and stuccoed walls and ceilings.

$$ Monastery Boutique Hotel offers 47 rooms in an actual Capuchin monastery attached to a church. The rooms—half of which overlook a very quiet courtyard—are modern, tasteful, and stylish, while respecting the history of the building. Although this is not directly on the river, it's just a block away and well priced for the quality (air-con, elevator, Fő Utca 30, +36 1 770 8210, www.monasteryhotel.hu, info@monasteryhotel.hu).

$ Bellevue B&B hides in a quiet residential area on the Víziváros hillside, just below the Fisherman's Bastion staircase. This gem is owned by retired economist Lajos (LIE-yosh) Szuhay, who lived in Canada for four years, and his right-hand man, Bálint. The breakfast room and some of the six straightforward, comfortable rooms have views across the Danube to the Parliament and Pest. Lajos and Bálint love to chat and pride themselves on offering genuine hospitality and a warm welcome—let them know what time you're arriving (cash only, air-con; M2: Batthyány Tér plus a 10-minute uphill walk, or bus #16 or #216 from Deák, Széchenyi, or Clark Ádám squares to Dónati Utca plus a 2-minute walk uphill, then downhill—they'll email you detailed directions; Szabó Ilonka Utca 15/B, +36 30 964 7287, www.bellevuebudapest.com, bellevuebudapestbandb@gmail.com).

Eating in Budapest

Budapest may be one of Europe's most underrated culinary destinations. Hungarian cuisine is excellent—rich, spicy, smooth, and delicious. And Budapest specializes in trendy restaurants that mix Hungarian flavors with international flair, making the food here even more interesting and fun to sample. And while it's not exactly a budget travel destination anymore, prices remain reasonable for such high quality.

EATING TIPS

I rank eateries from $ budget to $$$$ splurge. For a rundown of Hungarian cuisine and beverages, see page 554.

Tipping: Most restaurants in Budapest automatically add a service charge to the bill (look for "service," "tip," *felszolgálási díj*, or *szervízdíj*); if it's been included, an additional tip is not necessary. Otherwise, round up about 10-12 percent.

Dining Hours: Most Hungarians dine between 19:00 and 21:00, peaking around 20:00; trendy zones such as St. István Square and Franz Liszt Square, which attract an after-work crowd, are lively earlier in the evening.

PEST

I've listed these options by neighborhood, emphasizing the areas with the best and most interesting choices, for easy reference with your sightseeing.

Seventh District (Ruin-Pub Zone and Jewish Quarter)

Along with the rise of "ruin pubs" (see "Nightlife in Budapest," earlier), the Seventh District has seen the arrival of a world of great restaurants. Many places feature Jewish food, which comes in two broad categories: traditional (matzo ball soup) and Israeli (hummus, *shakshuka*—tomato-poached eggs—and other Middle Eastern fare).

$$ Mazel Tov, one of Budapest's trendiest eateries (reserve ahead or line up), fills a dilapidated old building at the edge of the ruin-pub zone. Stepping across the tattered threshold, you emerge into an airy, vinestrewn, bare-brick courtyard where twinkle lights are strung over the hardworking open kitchen. With a wink to this district's Jewish origins, they serve creative cocktails and Israeli/Middle Eastern dishes like kebabs, shawarma, falafel, tabbouleh, and *shakshuka*. The joyful atmosphere captures Budapest's thriving foodie energy (daily, Akácfa Utca 47, between M1: Opera and M2: Blaha Lujza Tér, +36 70 626 4280, www.mazeltov.hu).

$$ Dobrumba, close to the Great Synagogue and giving

Restaurant Code

Eateries in this book are categorized according to the average cost of a typical main course. Drinks, desserts, and splurge items can raise the price considerably. 350 Ft = about $1.

$$$$ **Splurge:** Most main courses over 8,000 Ft (€20)
$$$ **Pricier:** 6,000-8,000 Ft (€15-20)
$$ **Moderate:** 4,000-6,000 Ft (€10-15)
$ **Budget:** Under 4,000 Ft (€10)

In Hungary, takeout food or a cafeteria-type place is **$**, an unpretentious sit-down eatery is **$$**, an upmarket but still casual restaurant is **$$$**, and a swanky splurge is **$$$$**.

Mazel Tov a run for its money, feels trendy and slightly ramshackle but still open and inviting. The menu—inspired by the Middle East, the Mediterranean, and the Caucasus—has an enticing variety of hot and cold *meze* (small plates), plus main dishes. The food is vibrantly flavored and delicious, but space is limited—reserve ahead (daily, Dob Utca 5, M1/M2/M3: Deák Tér, +36 30 194 0049, www.dobrumba.hu).

$$$$ Stand, operated by celebrity chefs Szabina Szulló and Tamás Széll, is the refined choice in this neighborhood, with a fixed-price menu of modern Hungarian and international dishes. The proud owner of two Michelin stars, it's considered one of Budapest's top restaurants. You'll dine in a clean, contemporary setting with an open kitchen and impeccable service. Book far ahead (dinner only Tue-Sat—last seating at 20:00, closed Sun-Mon, Székely Mihály Utca 2, M1: Opera, +36 30 785 9139, www.standrestaurant.hu). They also run a more casual and affordable bistro across the river in Buda called Stand25 (see listing, later).

$$ Macesz Bistro ("Matzo") is a grandma's-dining-room-cozy corner restaurant serving traditional Jewish and Hungarian dishes, with a few modern flourishes. The setting is more elegant than many of the funky spots in the Seventh District, and they have a good wine list (daily, Dob Utca 26, M1: Opera, +36 1 787 6164).

$$ Kőleves ("Stone Soup"), next door to Macesz Bistro and filling an old kosher sausage factory, feels more casual and youthful. While the menu emphasizes Jewish and Hungarian dishes, other types are also mixed in (daily, Kazinczy Utca 41, M1: Opera, +36 20 213 5999). In good weather, they also have an adjacent garden courtyard.

$$$ KönyvBár & Restaurant is refined, mellow, and creative. The small dining room feels like a sleek, minimalist library, and the menu has a fun literary theme (*könyv* means "book"). As

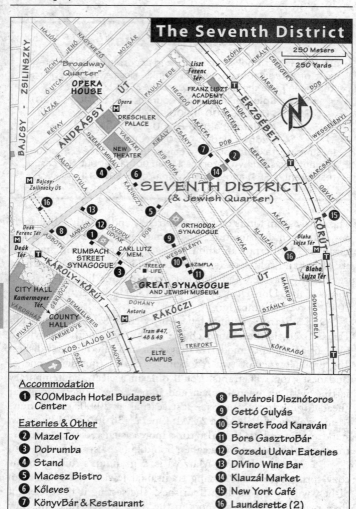

The Seventh District

250 Meters
250 Yards

Accommodation

1 ROOMbach Hotel Budapest Center

Eateries & Other

2 Mazel Tov
3 Dobrumba
4 Stand
5 Macesz Bistro
6 Kőleves
7 KönyvBár & Restaurant
8 Belvárosi Disznótoros
9 Gettó Gulyás
10 Street Food Karaván
11 Bors GasztroBár
12 Gozsdu Udvar Eateries
13 DiVino Wine Bar
14 Klauzál Market
15 New York Café
16 Launderette (2)

it's small and all indoors, it can get warm. Bibliophiles should reserve ahead for an appealing dining experience (Wed-Thu dinner only, Fri-Sat lunch and dinner, closed Sun-Tue, Dob Utca 45, between M1: Opera and M2: Blaha Lujza Tér, +36 20 922 7027, www.konyvbar.hu).

$ Belvárosi Disznótoros ("Downtown Pig Feast") is a pork-centric place named for the traditional feast that follows the slaying of a pig. For an affordable, filling meal, choose from a wide variety of sausages and other meaty fare, priced by the weight, plus hearty sides (the fried cheese is popular). One display case features cooked food, while the other has marinated chicken they can throw on the grill (daily, just a few steps off the M1/M2/M3: Deák Tér transit hub at Király Utca 1/d, +36 70 709 8570, www.belvarosidisznotoros.hu). They have another location in Downtown Pest (see listing, later).

$ Gettó Gulyás is *the* place for stew. They have about a dozen different types, plus a few soups, pickled items, and a handful of pricier main courses, not to mention a decent wine list. Choose between the semi-industrial, bar-like interior or the outdoor stools (daily, Wesselényi Utca 18, M1/M2/M3: Deák Tér, +36 20 376 4480).

Food Trucks and Street Food: Just a couple of doors down from Szimpla (the oldest and best of the ruin pubs—see page 649), the **$ Street Food Karaván** fills a gravel lot with an array of creative food trucks and picnic tables. Options range from burgers and Mexican to vegan, goulash, and *lángos* (like a savory elephant ear). For dessert, try *kürtőskalács*—a delicious "chimney cake." This is a fun, lively scene for the indecisive (daily 11:30-late, Kazinczy Utca 18, M2: Astoria). Several other tempting takeaway places line this street, including **$ Bors GasztroBár** (on the other side of Szimpla), which serves up grilled baguettes with a variety of tasty toppings, plus soups, in a hip and casual setting with no seating (daily, Kazinczy Utca 10, M2: Astoria, +36 30 698 9075).

Gozsdu Udvar: This passage—which laces together a series of courtyards as it runs under apartment blocks through this busy district—is jammed with bars and restaurants. The thriving and youthful scene sprawls for blocks, with options including a branch of DiVino Wine Bar (described later), all-day breakfast joints, homemade pasta bars, karaoke rooms...and even Hungarian cuisine.

Market Hall with Cheap Eats: At the northern edge of the ruin-pub zone is the **$ Klauzál Market,** a neighborhood market hall built in 1897. With soaring steel girders over pristinely restored food stalls and a handy Spar supermarket, it's a fine place to browse for a picnic or grab some street food (most vendors open until about 17:00, supermarket open later, Klauzál Tér 6, runs through the block between Klauzál Utca and Akácfa Utca, between M1: Opera and M2: Blaha Lujza Tér).

Near Andrássy Út

For locations, see the "Andrássy Út Hotels and Restaurants" map on page 655. Note that the Seventh District eateries (in the previous section) are also nearby.

$$ Menza (the old communist word for "School Cafeteria") is the only restaurant worth considering on touristy Franz Liszt Square. With recycled 1970s-era furniture and an orange-brown-gray color scheme, it should win a design award for its postmodern parody of an old communist café—half kitschy-retro, half contemporary-stylish. With tasty and well-priced updated Hungarian and international cuisine, embroidered leather-bound menus, brisk but efficient service, and indoor and outdoor seating,

it's a classic—book ahead (daily, halfway up Andrássy Út at Liszt Ferenc Tér 2, district VII, M1: Oktogon, +36 1 413 1482, www.menza.co.hu).

$$ Két Szerecsen ("Two Saracens") is named for a historic coffee shop at this location that a trader filled with exotic goods. It stays true to that eclectic spirit by featuring a wide variety of cuisines—from Mediterranean to Asian—and has good indoor and outdoor seating, relatively small portions, and a menu that offers something for everyone. Book ahead for this popular place (daily, a block off Andrássy Út at Nagymező Utca 14, district VI, M1: Opera, +36 1 343 1984, https://ketszerecsen.hu/en).

$$$ Szék ("sayk")—the Hungarian name for Transylvania— fills a stylish space right along Andrássy Út, but the menu features traditional flavors: *csorba* (pronounced "chorba"), a hearty soup made with a fermented-bran base; *mics* ("meech"), little mincemeat sausages; and even a "Carpathian Burger." The cuisine is elevated and delicious, and while some of the flavors are similar to classic Hungarian food, it uses recipes that you won't find at many other restaurants (daily, Andrássy Út 41, between M1: Opera and M1: Oktogon, +36 1 721 3154, www.szekrestaurant.hu).

$ Edy's French Tacos is handy if you need a quick bite close to the Opera House. Edy likes to explain that in France, "tacos" are wrapped in a tortilla and grilled flat. (If you try to tell him that's a "burrito," he'll happily set you straight.) You can design your own taco, then eat it at one of the tables in the small interior, or get it to go (closed Mon, Hajós Utca 19, M1: Opera).

Near St. István's Basilica

The streets in front of St. István's Basilica are jammed with upscale, tourist-oriented eateries (district V). They skew pricey—this is a neighborhood where restaurants shooting for a Michelin star set up shop (and a few have succeeded). But I've also scouted some budget choices, sometimes a little farther afield. For locations, see the "Leopold Town Hotels and Restaurants" map; these are all roughly between M1/M2/M3: Deák Tér, M1: Bajcsy-Zsilinszky Út, and M3: Arany János Utca.

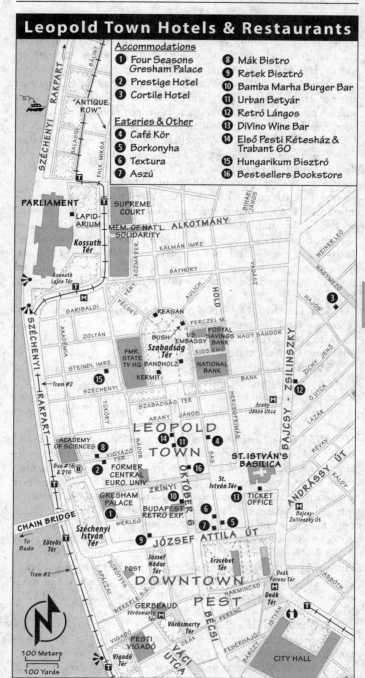

Leopold Town Hotels & Restaurants

Accommodations

1. Four Seasons Gresham Palace
2. Prestige Hotel
3. Cortile Hotel

Eateries & Other

4. Café Kör
5. Borkonyha
6. Textura
7. Aszú
8. Mák Bistro
9. Retek Bisztró
10. Bamba Marha Burger Bar
11. Urban Betyár
12. Retró Lángos
13. DiVino Wine Bar
14. Első Pesti Rétesház & Trabant 60
15. Hungarikum Bisztró
16. Bestsellers Bookstore

BUDAPEST

$$ Café Kör ("Circle"), a mainstay of quality and value, seems oblivious to the trends swirling around this fast-evolving zone. It's a sophisticated but unstuffy neighborhood favorite, serving up mostly Hungarian and some global fare in a tasteful, tight, one-room interior and at a few sidewalk tables. They have good salads and enticing daily specials, and for most meals you can get a smaller portion for a reduced price. It's wise to book ahead (closed Sun, Sas Utca 17, +36 1 311 0053).

$$$$ Borkonyha ("Winekitchen"), with a Michelin star, serves up top-quality modern Hungarian cuisine ("Hungarian dishes—but less paprika, less fat"). And, as the name implies, they're evangelical about high-quality Hungarian wines—with several dozen types sold by the glass. The menu—especially the adventurous chalkboard specials—ventures into "nose-to-tail" cooking, using ingredients you won't find everywhere. The decor is sophisticated black, white, and gold—a dressy place where wine snobs feel at home—and they also have sidewalk seating out front. Reservations are essential (Mon-Fri dinner only, Sat lunch and dinner, closed Sun, Sas Utca 3, +36 1 266 0835, www.borkonyha. hu).

$$$ Textura, across the street, is Borkonyha's side restaurant, offering a more relaxed and youthful environment and a more affordable taste of their cooking (closed Sun, Sas Utca 6, +36 30 787 1051, www.texturaetterem.hu).

$$$ Aszú, along the same street, is another high-end place that's trying to compete with its neighbors. It has a more stylized, modern interior and its own take on elevated Hungarian fare with fusion embellishments (daily, Sas Utca 4, +36 1 328 0360, www. aszuetterem.hu).

$$$$ Mák Bistro is unsnooty despite its Michelin star, and has a loyal following (reservations are essential). It feels like a well-kept secret, tucked down a forgotten side street parallel to the bustling Zrínyi Utca pedestrian drag. Inside, it has a lively brasserie ambience under white-painted brick vaults. The short, carefully selected seasonal menu is based on what's fresh (Wed-Fri dinner only, Sat lunch and dinner, closed Sun-Tue, Vigyázó Ferenc 4, +36 30 723 9383, www.mak.hu).

$$ Retek Bisztró ("Radish"), owned by the people from Hungarikum Bisztró (described later), highlights traditional Hungarian cuisine with some modern pizzazz, in a cheery and floral environment, under high arches (daily, Nádor Utca 5, +36 20 253 5596, www.retekbisztro.hu).

$ Bamba Marha Burger Bar offers a Hungarian take on burgers—using locally sourced beef from *szürkemarha*, the indigenous gray longhorn cattle. (The other word in the name—*bamba*—means, basically, dummy; it's a play on "mad cow.") Part of a small chain, this location is handy for its relatively low prices compared to the many high-end options in the area (daily, Október 6 Utca 6, www.bambamarha.hu).

$$$ Urban Betyár, an immersive Hungarian-culture experience that borders on a theme-park vibe, is touristy—but in a way that makes you not want to look away. Stop in for a meal (Hungarian classics done reasonably well) or at least a coffee, and explore the sprawling folk museum that fills the basement (from the main floor, look for the giant old wine press to find the spiral stairs down to this time-warp zone). The tone is set by the life-sized *betyár*—an old-school Hungarian outlaw—with his puli dog out front (daily, Október 6 Utca 16, +36 1 796 3285, www.urbanbetyar. com). Rounding out their Hungarian-culture theme, they also own the **Trabant 60** bar (with a retro-communism theme) and the recommended **Első Pesti** strudel shop (described below)—both next door.

$ Retró Lángos, across a busy boulevard from the back of the basilica, is a handy and casual place to try *lángos*—the big, hearty Hungarian fry bread with a wide variety of toppings. They have about two dozen different types, from the classic sour cream and garlic to creative variations, plus some *palacsinta* (crepe) options. Order inside, then take a seat, either in the sprawling interior wrapped around the busy kitchen or at an outdoor table. After eating one of these, you won't need to eat again for, oh, about a week (daily, Bajcsy-Zsilinszky Út 25, +36 30 824 2679, www.retrolangos. hu).

$$ DiVino Wine Bar serves more than 100 types of Hungarian wine, listed by region on the chalkboard—all available by the glass or bottle. While a bit commercial, it's still a handy spot to sample local wines—and the views gazing up at the basilica are superb (daily from 16:00, St. István Tér 3, +36 70 935 3980). They have another location—less scenic and a bit more serious about its wine—in the Seventh District's Godszu Udvar corridor (similar hours, Király Utca 13).

Homemade Strudel: See how strudel *(rétes)* is made at **Első Pesti Rétesház,** a folkloric favorite among fans of this treat. Step inside to watch them roll out the long, paper-thin sheets of dough, then wrap them around a variety of fillings. Get a piece to go at the takeaway counter, or sit and enjoy your *rétes* with a cup of coffee (daily, also has a full food menu of traditional Hungarian dishes, Október 6 Utca 22, +36 1 428 0134).

Downtown Pest (Belváros), near Váci Utca

When you ask locals about good places to eat on Váci Utca, they just roll their eyes. But wander a few blocks off the tourist route, and you'll discover a few alternatives with fair prices and better food. In addition to these choices, you'll find recommendations in the "Budapest's Café Culture" section, later. For locations, see the "Downtown Pest Hotels and Restaurants" map on page 659.

$$ Gerlóczy Café, tucked on a peaceful little square next to the giant City Hall, features attentive service and a concise, tasty menu of French, Hungarian, and other cuisine. The clientele is a mix of tourists and upscale-urban Budapesters, including local politicians and actors from nearby theaters. With a take-your-time ambience that's almost Parisian—and with live piano music on weekends after 19:00—this is a classy, particu-

larly inviting spot (good breakfasts, weekday lunch specials, long hours daily, two blocks from Váci Utca, just off Városház Utca at Gerlóczy Utca 1, district V, M3: Ferenciek Tere, +36 1 501 4000).

$ Belvárosi Disznótoros ("Downtown Pig Feast"), described earlier under the Seventh District, also has this very central outpost with shorter hours (Mon-Fri until 18:00, Sat until 17:00, closed Sun, Károlyi Mihály Utca 17, +36 70 602 2775).

Great Market Hall: At the far south end of Váci Utca, you can eat a quick lunch on the upper floor of the Great Market Hall

(Nagyvásárcsarnok). Unfortunately, eateries here cater almost entirely to tourists. But if you're nearby and hungry, here are some options inside the Great Market Hall: **$$ Fakanál Étterem**—the glassed-in, sit-down cafeteria above the main entrance—is touristy, but offers acceptable food, good seating (including some tables overlooking the thriving market hall), and live "Gypsy" music most days during prime lunch hours (closed Sun). The **$ sloppy, stand-up stalls** upstairs along the right side of the building are cheaper, but quality can vary. A favorite is the heavy fry bread called *lángos*. The basic one—slathered with sour cream, cheese, and (if you dare) garlic—is affordable, but order carefully, or they could add piles of toppings to triple or quadruple your bill. Another fine option is to use the market to assemble a **picnic;** get whatever else you need at the Aldi supermarket in the basement (market hall open Mon 6:00-17:00, Tue-Fri until 18:00, Sat until 15:00, closed

BUDAPEST

Sun; supermarket open longer hours, Fővám Körút 1, district IX, M4: Fővám Tér).

Nearby Wine Shop: Tasting Table (run by Taste Hungary) has a well-stocked wine shop on a quiet street in the Palace District, behind the National Museum. You can peruse wines from more than 200 different Hungarian producers, then order a glass or a flight; buy a bottle to consume on your trip; or ship home a handpicked selection. The knowledgeable staff is helpful (Mon-Sat 12:00-20:00, closed Sun, Bródy Sándor Utca 22, M2: Astoria or M3/M4: Kálvin Tér, +36 30 690 4913).

Elsewhere in Pest

Near Liberty Square: $$ Hungarikum Bisztró, tucked in an unassuming neighborhood between big government ministries, is my pick for classic Hungarian cuisine. Rather than gouging tourists, the youthful owners consider themselves ambassadors for the dishes their grandma raised them on. The mellow, unpretentious interior complements the strictly old-fashioned cuisine. Reservations are required (daily, Steindl Imre Utca 13—see map on page 667, district V, M2: Kossuth Lajos Tér, +36 1 797 7177, www.hungarikumbisztro.hu).

Near Keleti/Eastern Train Station: $$ Rosenstein is worth a trip out to the otherwise humdrum area surrounding Keleti station. Run by father-and-son team Tibor and Robert Rosenstein, it's an unpretentious space (the main-floor dining room has slightly more character than the cellar) on a nondescript street. But it's well known simply for the food: Everything on the menu, featuring Hungarian and Jewish dishes, is delicious. Reserve ahead (closed Sun, Mosonyi Utca 3, district VIII, M2: Keleti pu., +36 1 333 3492, www.rosenstein.hu).

BUDA

Eateries up on Castle Hill are generally overpriced and touristy—as with Váci Utca, locals never eat here. The Víziváros ("Water Town") neighborhood, between the castle and the river, is a bit better. Even if you sleep in Buda, try to dine in Pest—that's where you'll find the city's best restaurants. The restaurants listed here are all in district I. For locations, see the "Buda Hotels and Restaurants" map on page 660.

Castle Hill

For a quick bite, visit the handy, affordable **Prima grocery store** (daily, on Tárnok Utca facing Szentháromság Tér). For coffee and cakes, try the historic **Ruszwurm** (described later, under "Budapest's Café Culture"). If you'd rather have a meal—and don't want to head down to Víziváros—try the following choices:

$$$ 21 Magyar Vendéglő ("21 Hungarian Kitchen") features traditional Hungarian fare that's updated for the 21st century. While the mod interior is pleasant, it's also fun to sit out on pretty Fortuna Utca (near the north end of the hill). Like all restaurants on Castle Hill, it's pricey, but this is a rare castle-zone eatery that takes pride in its food rather than being a crank-'em-out tourism machine (daily, Fortuna Utca 21, +36 1 202 2113).

$$$ Baltazár, near the ruins of St. Mary Magdalene Church (a few short blocks from the main sights), is trying to inject some youthful liveliness into the staid, sleepy north end of Castle Hill. It's a fun choice, with bright, brash decor, pleasant outdoor seating, and a wood-fired charcoal grill that churns out smoky dishes (daily, Országház Utca 31, +36 1 300 7050).

Worthwhile Splurge behind Castle Hill: $$$ Stand25 Bisztró, tucked just behind Castle Hill, is worth reserving ahead for a memorable meal. An outpost of the recommended Stand, which has two Michelin stars (see listing earlier, under the Seventh District), it's mostly a lunch spot but also open for weekend dinners. Reservations for either are recommended (Mon-Thu lunch only, Fri-Sat lunch and dinner, closed Sun, Attila Út 10, +36 30 961 3262, www.stand25.hu). From the funicular station near the Chain Bridge at the base of the hill, it's on the other side of the busy tunnel; nearby buses zip you through in a couple of minutes.

Batthyány Tér and Nearby

This bustling square—the transportation hub for Víziváros (on the M2 line)—is overlooked by a modernized, late-19th-century market hall (today housing a big Spar supermarket and various shops). Several worthwhile, affordable eateries cluster around this square.

$ Nagyi Palacsintázója ("Granny's Pancakes")—just to the right of the market hall entrance—serves up cheap sweet and savory crêpes *(palacsinta)* to a local crowd (open daily 24 hours, individual crêpes are small—order a combo for a filling meal, ask for English menu, Batthyány Tér 5).

As you face the market hall, go up the street that runs along its left side (Markovits Iván Utca) to reach more good **$** eateries: Look for **Coyote Coffee and Deli** and (at the end of the block on the right) **Édeni Végan,** a self-service, point-and-shoot vegetarian cafeteria (both open daily).

HUNGARIAN STREET FOOD

For a lighter meal, keep an eye out for these two local specialties:

Lángos is a popular snack—a savory deep-fried flatbread similar to an elephant ear or Native American fry bread. Sold at stands on the street, at the recommended Retró Lángos, and upstairs in the Great Market Hall, the most typical version is spread with cheese and sour cream, and sometimes topped with garlic.

Kürtőskalács is a "chimney cake" pastry twisted around a spindle, rolled in sugar, and then slowly baked on a rotisserie until it's coated in a caramelized crust. They roll it in toppings (cinnamon, coconut, chocolate) and hand it over hot. A basic and perfectly delicious version should run you no more than 700-800 Ft; but in touristy zones, you'll see stands charging double (or more). One tourist-baiting gimmick is to load up the *kürtőskalács* with ice cream, whipped cream, flavored syrups, and other toppings...as an excuse to raise the price even higher. For the real deal, look for the vendors at the start of Andrássy Út, in front of the Nyugati/Western train station, along Váci Utca near March 15 Square, and in the Seventh District's food-truck zone.

BUDAPEST'S CAFÉ CULTURE

In the late 19th century, a vibrant café culture boomed in Budapest, just as it did in Vienna and Paris. The *kávéház* ("coffeehouse") was a local institution. By 1900, Budapest had more than 600 cafés. Locals, many of whom had moved to the city from the countryside, didn't want to pay to heat their homes during the day. Instead, for the price of a cup of coffee, they could come to a café to enjoy warmth, companionship, and loaner newspapers.

Realizing that these neighborhood living rooms were breeding grounds for dissidents, the communists closed the cafés or converted them into *eszpresszós* (with uncomfortable stools instead of easy chairs) or *bisztrós* (stand-up fast-food joints with no chairs at all). But after 1989, nostalgia brought back *kávéház* culture—both as a place to get coffee and food, and as a social institution. While some serve only coffee and cakes, most serve light meals, and some offer full meals.

Over-the-Top Opulence

In Downtown Pest: $$$$ Párisi Udvar ("Paris Passage") fills a stunning former shopping arcade in the heart of the city. Once

borderline-abandoned and closed for years, a grand hotel has restored it to its previous elegance. Entering from Ferenciek Tere, you'll first hit the café under a towering rotunda twinkling with stained glass, where you can order a drink or dessert. Deeper into the arcade, it becomes a full-service restaurant. As you sip, scrutinize the symbolism carved into the lavish decor of this Beaux-Arts space: The honeybees represent wealth, while the monkeys remind us of our humble beginnings. As with New York Café (see next), it's worth overspending to travel back to a more elegant time. Unlike New York Café, this place feels a bit less discovered (daily, Ferenciek Tere 10, district V, right outside the exit for M3: Ferenciek Tere, +36 70 702 4088, www. parisipassage.hu).

On the Great Boulevard: $$$$ New York Café was originally built in 1894 by a big American insurance company (who believed that having the most extravagant café imaginable for their clients would inspire confidence). This fanciful, over-the-top explosion of Neo-Baroque and Neo-Renaissance epitomizes the "mix and match, but plenty of everything" Historicist style of the day. In the early 20th century, artists, writers, and musicians came here to sip overpriced coffee and bask in opulence. Now it's overrun by gawking, selfie-taking tourists...but still visually magnificent. Expect a line (no reservations possible before 18:00). It's snooty and greedy, but it's still a magnificent space to nurse a coffee or a dessert (daily, inside the Anantara New York Palace Hotel at Erzsébet Körút 9, district VII, +36 1 886 6167, www.newyorkcafe.hu). Take the M2/red Metró line to Blaha Lujza Tér and exit toward *Erzsébet Körút,* then walk a block. You can also take tram #4 or #6 from the Oktogon (at Andrássy Út) around the Great Boulevard to the Wesselényi Utca stop. For location, see the map on page 664.

Neighborhood Coffeehouses
Next to the Opera House: $$$ Callas straddles these two categories in both price and elegance. It boasts ideal outdoor seating facing the Opera House and one of the finest Art Nouveau interiors in town, with gorgeous Jugendstil chandeliers. While they do serve meals, most locals come here for coffee and cakes (daily, Andrássy Út 20—see the map on page 655, district VI, M1: Opera, +36 1 354 0954).

In Downtown Pest: $$ Gerlóczy Café nicely recaptures Budapest's early-1900s ambience, with loaner newspapers on racks, marble tables, red-leather benches, a management that encourages loitering, and rich but not ostentatious decor (see restaurant listing, earlier). **$$ Centrál Kávéház** is another venerable favorite. While I'd skip the food, it has an enjoyable and atmospheric two-story interior and is great for a drink (daily, Károlyi Mihály Utca 9, district

V, M3: Ferenciek Tere, +36 1 266 2110). For locations of both, see the map on page 659.

In Buda, on Castle Hill: $$ Ruszwurm lays claim to being Budapest's oldest café (since 1827). Tiny but classy, with old-style Biedermeier furnishings and fine sidewalk seating, it upholds its venerable reputation with pride. Its dead-central location—a block in front of Matthias Church in the heart of the castle district—means that it's a popular tourist spot (though it remains dear to locals' hearts). Look for gussied-up locals chatting here after the Sunday morning Mass (daily until 19:00, Szentháromság Utca 7—see map on page 660).

Budapest Connections

BY TRAIN

Hungary's train network is run by MÁV (Magyar Államvasutak). From centrally located Budapest, train lines branch out across Hungary like spokes on a wheel. Most connections between outlying cities aren't direct—you often end up having to go back through Budapest. While Hungary's trains are generally good, some are old and fairly slow; major routes use faster, newer, and slightly more expensive InterCity trains (marked with an "IC" or a boxed "R" on schedules). To ride an InterCity train, you must pay extra for a required reservation.

If traveling to international destinations such as Bratislava or Vienna, other trains are faster and more direct than the InterCity. Between Budapest and Bratislava, EuroCity (EC) trains are fastest and most direct. If traveling from Budapest to Vienna, Austrian RailJet (RJ) trains are fastest and direct, and don't require seat assignments (but advance-purchase discounts lock you into a specific departure).

Warning: Trains can be very crowded on weekends, when it's smart to book a reservation for any train trip.

For timetables, the first place to check is Germany's excellent all-Europe site, www.bahn.com. You can also check Hungary's own timetable website at http://elvira.mav-start.hu. For general rail information in Hungary, call +36 1 444 4499.

Remember that Budapest has three major train stations (*pályaudvar*, abbreviated *pu.*): Keleti ("Eastern") station, Nyugati ("Western") station, and Déli ("Southern") station.

Buying Train Tickets: For domestic tickets and most international journeys, it's easiest to book **online** on the Hungarian Railways website: www.mavcsoport.hu. You can send an eticket to your phone (you may have to create a login to do this); then, on the train, just flash your eticket to the conductor, who may ask to see your ID. More complicated international journeys—such as ones involving transfers—may need to be purchased in person at a train station ticket office.

If buying tickets **at the station,** simply use the ubiquitous MÁV ticket machines. If you need help, look for a staffed ticket desk—marked *pénztár* or *jegypénztár.* Sometimes international tickets are sold only at a special window (marked *nemzetközi*).

Other key words: *Vágány* (track), *induló vonatok* (departures), and *érkező vonatok* (arrivals).

From Budapest by Train to: Eger (every 2 hours direct, 2 hours, more with transfer in Füzesabony, usually from Keleti/ Eastern station), **Pécs** (every 2 hours direct, 3 hours; a few more connections possible with transfer at suburban Kelenföld station), **Sopron** (every 2 hours direct, 2.5 hours, more with transfer at Kelenföld), **Visegrád** (trains arrive at Nagymaros-Visegrád station, across the river—take shuttle boat to Visegrád; 1-2/hour, 45 minutes, from Nyugati/Western station), **Esztergom** (hourly, 1 hour, usually from Nyugati/Western station; but Esztergom's train station is far from the basilica, making the bus—described later—a better option), **Kecskemét** (hourly, 1.5 hours), **Szeged** (hourly, 2.5 hours).

Bratislava (*Pozsony* in Hungarian, every 2 hours direct, 2.5 hours; more with changes), **Vienna** (*Bécs* in Hungarian, every 2 hours direct on express Railjet, 2.5 hours; more with changes), **Prague** (5/day direct, 6.5 hours), **Kraków** (1/day, 9 hours, change in Bohumin), **Zagreb** (2/day direct, 5.5 hours), **Ljubljana** (1/day direct, 8.5 hours), **Cluj-Napoca** (hub for Transylvania in Romania, 2/day direct, 7.5 hours), **Munich** (every 2 hours direct on express RailJet, 7 hours).

By HÉV: Budapest has its own suburban rail network, called HÉV. For tourists, this is mostly useful for reaching **Szentendre** (from M2: Batthyány Tér) and **Gödöllő** (from M2: Örs Vezér Tere).

BY BUS

Buses can be relatively inexpensive, but are typically slower and less convenient than trains. The only bus you're likely to take is the one to **Eger** (2/hour, 2 hours), which leaves from the Stadionok bus station (at the M2/Metró red line stop of the same name). You can search bus schedules at the website www.menetrendek.hu.

BY PLANE

For information about Budapest's Liszt Ferenc Airport, see "Arrival in Budapest—By Plane" on page 572.

ROUTE TIPS FOR DRIVERS

For pointers on driving into (and parking in) Budapest, see "Arrival in Budapest—By Car" on page 573. Remember, to use Hungary's expressways, you'll need to buy a toll sticker (see page 1114). To get out of town, here are some pointers.

To Eger and Other Points East: Head out of the city center on Andrássy Út, circling behind Heroes' Square to access Kós Károly Sétány through the middle of City Park. You'll pass Széchenyi Baths on the left, then (exiting the park) go over the Hungária Körút ring road, before getting on M-3. This expressway zips you conveniently to Eger (exit #114 for Füzesabony; go north on road 33, then follow road 3, then road 25 into Eger).

To Bratislava, Vienna, and Other Points West: From central Pest, head over the Danube on the white, modern Elisabeth Bridge (Erzsébet Híd). Once in Buda, the road becomes Hegyalja Út; simply follow *Bécs–Wien* signs to get on M-1.

Day Trips from Budapest

On a visit of a few days, Budapest will keep even the most avid sightseer busy. And after Budapest, Eger, covered in the next chapter, is one of the best Hungarian towns. But for a longer stay, a few outlying sights are worth considering. I've listed them here roughly in order of proximity to downtown Budapest.

▲▲Memento Park (a.k.a. Statue Park)

When regimes fall, so do their monuments...literally. Just think of all the statues of Stalin and Lenin that crashed to the ground in late 1989, when people throughout Eastern Europe couldn't wait to get rid of those reminders of their oppressors. But some clever entrepreneur hoarded Budapest's, collecting them in a park in the countryside just southwest of the city—where tourists flock to get a taste of the communist era. Though it can be time-consuming to visit,

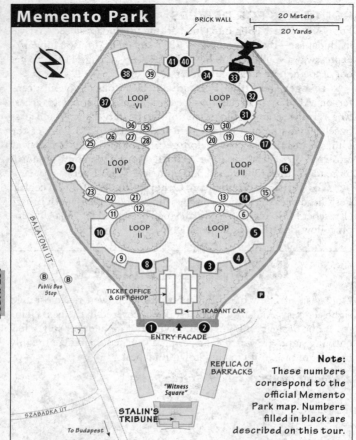

Memento Park

BRICK WALL

20 Meters
20 Yards

LOOP VI
LOOP V
LOOP IV
LOOP III
LOOP II
LOOP I

BALATONI ÚT

Public Bus Stop

TICKET OFFICE & GIFT SHOP

TRABANT CAR

ENTRY FACADE

REPLICA OF BARRACKS

"Witness Square"

STALIN'S TRIBUNE

SZABADKA ÚT

To Budapest

BUDAPEST

P

7

Note: These numbers correspond to the official Memento Park map. Numbers filled in black are described on this tour.

this collection is worth ▲▲▲ for those fascinated by Hungary's commie past. You'll see the great figures of the Soviet Bloc—both international (Lenin, Marx, and Engels) and Hungarian (local bigwig Béla Kun)—as well as gigantic, stoic figures representing Soviet ideals.

Cost and Hours: 3,000 Ft, daily 10:00-18:00, Nov-April until 16:00, six miles southwest of city center at the corner of Balatoni Út and Szabadka Út, district XXII; ride the Metró then bus (for details, see below); +36 1 424 7500, www.mementopark.hu.

Getting There: It's in the countryside six miles southwest of the city center, at the corner of Balatoni Út and Szabadka Út, in district XXII.

Public transit is a bit complicated, but workable: Ride the Metró's M4/green line to its end at Kelenföld. Follow signs to

Őrmező and *Péterhegyi Út* (exit B). Emerging in this bus-stop zone, consult the electronic board. You want bus #101B or #101E, which zip to Memento Park in about 10 minutes (every 10-20 minutes, Mon-Fri only). Bus #150 takes longer (about 20 minutes), but it's the only option on weekends (2-4/hour, runs daily). On any bus, be sure the driver knows where you want to get off.

A round-trip **taxi,** including about an hour of waiting time at the park, should cost around 25,000 Ft (ask your hotel to call one for you; confirm the price before leaving).

If you'd like to be picked up in the city center and brought to Memento Park in a **Trabant**—the classic communist-era car with loads of kitsch value—you can book that on the official website (€150, more with a guided tour, total experience is about three hours).

Visitor Information: The English guidebook, *In the Shadow of Stalin's Boots,* is informative.

Tours: English tours depart from the entrance and last 70 minutes (7,200 Ft, typically available Thu-Sun at 11:00—but check times and prebook on their website).

Background: Under the communists, creativity was discouraged. The primary purpose of art was to further the goals of the state. Promoting **Socialist Realist** art served to encourage complicity with the brave new world the communists were forging. It was also a break with the "decadent" bourgeois art that came before it (Impressionism, Post-Impressionism, and other modern -isms). From 1949 until 1956, Socialist Realism was legally enforced as the sole artistic style of the Soviet Bloc.

As propaganda was an essential weapon in the Soviet arsenal, the regime made ample use of Socialist Realist art. Aside from a few important figureheads, individuals didn't matter. Individual characteristics and distinguishing features were unimportant; people were represented as automatons serving their nation. Artistic merit was virtually ignored. Most figures are trapped in stiff, unnatural poses that ignore the 3,000 years of artistic evolution since the Egyptians. Sculptures and buildings alike from this era were designed to evoke feelings of power and permanence.

Visiting the Park: The numbers here match the statue labels in the park and on the official park map. You're greeted by three of the Communist All-Stars: ❶ **Vladimir Lenin,** a leader of Russia's Bolshevik Revolution; and ❷ **Karl Marx** and **Friedrich Engels,** the German philosophers whose *Communist Manifesto* first articulated the principles behind communism in 1848. Inside the gate, buy your ticket and head into the park. The six walkways branching off the main road all loop you right back to where you started—representing the endless futility of communism. Work your way clockwise around the park, starting with Loop I.

Liberation Monuments (Loop I): Dominating this loop is a ❸ **giant soldier** holding the Soviet flag. Typical of Socialist Realist art, the soldier has a clenched fist (symbolizing strength) and a face that is inspired by his egalitarian ideology.

To the left of this soldier, ❹ **two comrades** stiffly shake hands: the Hungarian worker thrilled to meet the Soviet soldier—protector of the proletariat. Beyond them is a ❺ **long wall,** with a triumphant worker breaking through the left end—too busy doing his job to be very excited.

Crossing the "main street," you'll see a group of statues commemorating a key communist holiday.

April 4, 1945 (Loop II): On this date, the Soviets forced the final Nazi soldier out of Hungary. The tall panel nearest the entrance shows a Hungarian woman and a Soviet woman setting free the ❽ **doves of peace.**

At the back of the loop, the ❿ **Hungarian worker and Soviet soldier** are absurdly rigid even though they're trying to be dynamic. (Even the statues couldn't muster genuine enthusiasm for communist ideals.) Cross over and head up to the next loop.

Heroes of the Workers' Movement (Loop III): Look for the ⓮ bust of the Bulgarian communist leader **Georgi Dimitrov**—one of communist Hungary's many Soviet Bloc comrades. At the back of this loop are ⓰ three blocky portraits. The middle figure is the granddaddy of Hungarian communism: **Béla Kun.** To the left is one of the park's best loved, most photographed, and most artistic statues: ⓱ **Vladimir Lenin,** in his famous "hailing a cab" pose. Cross over—passing the giant red star made of flowers.

More Communist Heroes (Loop IV): This group is dominated by a ㉔ dramatic, unusually emotive sculpture by a genuine artist, **Imre Varga** (see pages 608 and 682). Designed to commemorate the 100th anniversary of Béla Kun's birth, this clever

statue reinforces the communist message: Under the able leadership of Béla Kun, the crusty, bourgeois old regime of the Habsburg Empire (on the left, with the umbrellas) was converted into the workers' fighting force of the Red Army (on the right, with the bayonets). And yet, those silvery civilians in back seem more appealing than the lunging soldiers in front. And notice the lamppost next to Kun: In Hungarian literature, a lamppost is a metaphor for the gallows. This reminds viewers that Kun was ultimately executed by communists in the Soviet Union during Stalin's purges of the late 1930s.

Communist Concepts (Loop V): Look for a rusty pair of ❸❶ **workers' hands** holding a sphere. This represented the hard-won ideals of communism, carefully protected by the hands—but also held out for others to appre-

ciate. The ❸❷ **monument to Hungarian soldiers** honors those who fought against the fascist Francisco Franco in the Spanish Civil War. Dominating this group is a ❸❸ **communist worker** charging into the future, clutching the Soviet flag. To the left is a monument to the communist version of the Boy Scouts: the elementary-school-age ❸❹ **Little Drum-**

mers and the older **Pioneers.** While these organizations existed before the communists, they were slowly infiltrated and turned into propaganda machines. These kids were sent to camp to be properly raised as good little communists; many later forgot the brainwashing but still had fond memories of the socializing.

More Communist Concepts (Loop VI): The ❸❼ long, **white wall** at the back of this section tells quite a story (from left to right): The bullet holes lead up to a jumbled, frightful clutter representing World War II. Then comes the bright light of the Soviet system, and by the end everyone's properly regimented and looking boldly to the future (and enjoying a bountiful crop, to boot). The names in the center represent "heroes" who stayed true to the ideology, party, and nation and died in "defense of proletarian power" in 1956.

Next is a ❸❽ **fallen hero** with arm outstretched, about to collapse to the ground—mortally wounded yet victorious. This monument to "the Martyrs of the Counter-Revolution" also commemorates those who died attempting to put down the 1956 Uprising.

Dead End: The main path dead-ends at the wall, symbolizing life's frustrations under communism. Here stand statues of two Soviet officers who negotiated with the Nazis to end
the WWII siege of Budapest.
⓵ **Captain Miklós Steinmetz**
(on the right) was killed by a
Nazi land mine, while ⓶ **Ilja
Ostapenko** (on the left) was
shot under mysterious circumstances as he returned from the
successful summit. Both became heroes for the communist cause.

Return to the entry gate and head out across the parking lot.

Stalin's Tribune: This section of the complex is a re-cre-ation of the giant grandstand that once stood along "Parade Street." Hungarian and Soviet leaders stood here, at the feet of a giant Stalin statue, to survey military and civilian proces-sions. But during the 1956 Uprising, protesters cut Stalin off at the knees...leaving only the boots. (The entire tribune was later dismantled, and Stalin disappeared without a trace.) Behind the tribune, stairs lead up to a view over the park. In front of the tribune are **barracks,** reminiscent of the ramshackle bar-racks where political prisoners lived in communist-era work camps. These hold special exhibits. Sit down for the creepy film, *The Life of an Agent*—a loop of four training films that were actually used to teach novice spies about secret-police methods and policies.

Óbuda

"Old Buda," just north of Buda, is the oldest part of Budapest, with roots going back to Celtic and Roman times. It has vari-ous sights that cluster around the Szentlélek Tér stop of the HÉV suburban train line (catch the HÉV from the Batthyány tér Metró stop in Buda). The most interesting museum displays works by Hungarian sculptor **Imre Varga**, who worked from the 1950s through the 1990s, and created many popular sculp-tures in Budapest and throughout Hungary. You'll also find a museum filled with eye-popping, colorful paintings by **Victor Vasarely,** the founder of Op Art. If you ride the HÉV farther north to the Aquincum stop, you'll reach an archaeological

museum at the remains of the 2,000-year-old Roman town of
Aquincum and its amphitheater. All of these sights are closed
on Mondays.

Gödöllő Royal Palace

Holding court in an unassuming town on the outskirts of Budapest, this pink Baroque palace was once the residence of
Habsburg emperor Franz Josef and his wife, Empress Elisabeth—better known to her beloved Hungarian subjects as Sisi
(see page 881). While the Habsburg sights in Vienna and near
Prague are better, this is the best place in Hungary to learn about
its former monarchs.

Cost and Hours: 4,200 Ft for permanent exhibit (main
palace apartments); daily 10:00-18:00, off-season shorter hours
and may close Sat-Sun, last entry one hour before closing; tel.
28/410-124, www.kiralyikastely.hu.

Getting There: Take the M2/red Metró line to Örs Vezér
Tere, then catch the HÉV suburban train to Gödöllő—figure
about one hour each way from downtown Budapest.

The Danube Bend

This string of three river towns north of Budapest offers a convenient day-trip getaway for urbanites who want to commune with
nature. While I find "the Bend" less than thrilling, it's undeni-
ably convenient to reach from the capital by train or boat; these
destinations make for handy stopovers if you're driving between
Budapest and Bratislava or Vienna.

Szentendre is a colorful, "Balkans in miniature" artist colony. With a tidy main square, a few engaging art galleries, and
several Orthodox churches built by the Serbs and Greeks who
settled the town, it offers a relaxing escape from the city. This is
the easiest pleasant small town to reach from Budapest—which
means it's also deluged by tourists. To reach Szentendre, hop on
the HÉV suburban train at Budapest's Batthyány tér Metró (the
same one that goes to Óbuda, described earlier).

Visegrád offers a small riverside museum at the scant remains of a Renaissance palace built by King Matthias Corvinus, and a dramatic hilltop castle with fine views over the Bend.
While you can get here by boat or by train (to the Nagymaros-
Visegrád station, then boat across the river), it's not worth the
trip unless you're driving.

Esztergom Basilica is Hungary's biggest and most important church, built on the site where István, Hungary's first
Christian king, was crowned in AD 1000. Packed with history,
it looms grandly above the Danube (free to enter basilica; 1,500
Ft for the treasury; 1,600 Ft for the "tourist areas" (including

BUDAPEST

the crypt, panorama hall, and top of the dome); 2,900 Ft for everything; daily 8:00-19:00, off-season typically until 17:00, www.bazilika-esztergom.hu). The easiest way to reach it is by bus from Budapest's Újpest-Városkapu bus station (at the Metró stop of the same name); trains and other buses from Budapest take you to the far end of town, an inconvenient 45-minute walk to the basilica.

EGER

Eger (EH-gehr) is a county-seat town in northern Hungary, with about 60,000 people and a thriving teacher-training college. While you've probably never heard of Eger, among Hungarians, the town has various claims to fame. Its powerful bishops have graced it with gorgeous churches. It has some of the best and most beloved spas in this hot-water-crazy country (including some worth-a-detour options in the nearby countryside). And, perhaps most of all, Eger makes Hungarians proud as the town that, against all odds, successfully held off the Ottoman advance into Europe in 1552. This stirring history makes Eger a field trip mecca for Hungarian schoolkids. If the town is known internationally for anything, it's for the surrounding wine region (its best-known red wine is Bull's Blood, or Egri Bikavér).

And yet, refreshingly, enchanting Eger remains mostly off the tourist trail. Egerites go about their daily routines amidst lovely Baroque buildings, watched over by one of Hungary's most important castles. Everything in Eger is painted with vibrant colors, and even the communist apartment blocks seem quaint. The sights are few but fun, the ambience is great, and  strolling is a must. It all comes together to make Eger an ideal taste of small-town Hungary.

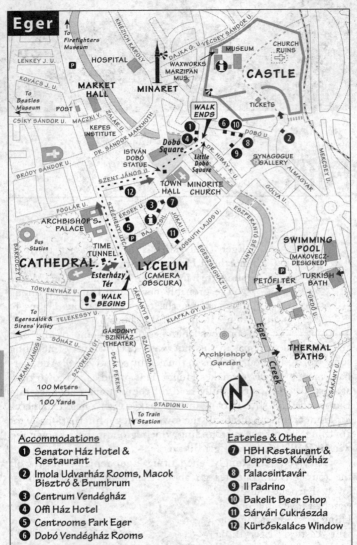

Accommodations
1. Senator Ház Hotel & Restaurant
2. Imola Udvarház Rooms, Macok Bisztró & Brumbrum
3. Centrum Vendégház
4. Offi Ház Hotel
5. Centrooms Park Eger
6. Dobó Vendégház Rooms

Eateries & Other
7. HBH Restaurant & Depresso Kávéház
8. Palacsintavár
9. Il Padrino
10. Bakelit Beer Shop
11. Sárvári Cukrászda
12. Kürtőskalács Window

PLANNING YOUR TIME

Mellow Eger is a fine side trip from Budapest. It's a doable round-trip in a single day (about two hours by train, car, or bus each way), but it's much more satisfying and relaxing to spend the night.

Get oriented with my self-guided town walk, including visits to the cathedral and the Lyceum's fine old library and thrillingly low-tech camera obscura. Have a memorable lunch on the square, then hike up to the castle for views over town. In the late afternoon, unwind at a thermal bath—either in Eger or in the countryside. Round out your day with dinner on the square or a visit to Eger's touristy wine caves in the Sirens' Valley.

In July and August (when Hungarians prefer to go to Lake Balaton), Eger is busy with international visitors; in September and October, around the wine harvest, most of the tourists are Hungarians.

Orientation to Eger

Eger Castle sits at the top of the town, hovering over Dobó Square (Dobó István Tér). Two blocks west of Dobó Square—away from the castle—is the main pedestrian drag, Széchenyi Utca, where you'll find the Lyceum and the cathedral. A few blocks south from the castle (along the small creek) is Eger's thermal bath complex.

TOURIST INFORMATION

Staff at Eger's TI (TourInform) are eager to answer your questions (Mon-Fri 9:00-17:00, Sat until 13:00, closed Sun, Bajcsy-Zsilinszky Utca 9, +36 36 517 715, http://www.visiteger.com).

ARRIVAL IN EGER

By Train: Eger's tiny train station is less than a mile south of the center. The baggage-deposit desk is along the platform by track 1, between the WCs. **Taxis** generally wait out front; try to take one marked with a company name and number. It's about a 15-minute **walk** to the center: Leave the station straight ahead, walk one block, take the hard right turn with the road, and then continue straight (along busy Deák Ferenc Utca) about 10 minutes until you run into the cathedral. To cut your walk time in half, you could take a **bus** partway: Buy a ticket at the newsstand inside the station, go a block straight out the front door, and hop on bus #11, #12, or #14; get off when you reach the big yellow cathedral.

By Car: In this small town, most hotels provide parking or help you find a lot. For a short visit, head for the pay parking garage near the market hall (just north of the main square), or park in the pay lot near the thermal bath complex and swimming pool on Petőfi Sándor Tér (a 10-minute walk south of the main square).

GETTING AROUND EGER

Everything of interest in Eger is within walking distance. But a taxi can be helpful to reach outlying sights, including the Sirens' Valley wine caves and the thermal baths in the countryside (try City Taxi, +36 36 555 555).

HELPFUL HINTS

Blue Monday: Note that the Lyceum's library and the Kepes Institute are closed on Mondays. But you can still visit the cathedral, swim in the thermal bath, explore the market, tour the castle (museums closed Mon off-season), and enjoy the local wine.

Market: Eger has a humble, old-fashioned Market Hall (Piaccsarnok), which offers a taste of local life. This ramshackle hall is a totally untouristy scene, with rough plastic tubs piled high with an abundance of fresh local produce (opens daily at 6:00; while open weekday afternoons, it's best in the mornings).

Nightlife: Things quiet down pretty early in this sedate town. Youthful student bars and hangouts cluster along the main "walking street," Széchenyi Utca (especially Fri and Sat nights). Older travelers may feel more at home on Little Dobó Square, with schmaltzy live music until 21:00 or 22:00 in summer; wine bars nearby may stay open later.

Eger Town Walk

Charming Eger is a delight to stroll. This walk begins near two of the city's main landmarks—in an area more local than touristy—then heads to its delightful main square before winding up to its castle. It includes pretty much anything you'd want to see in town and takes less than an hour, not including sightseeing stops (at the Lyceum and castle).

• *We'll begin on the parklike square called Eszterházy Tér, at the southern edge of the town center—between the cathedral (with two yellow rectangular towers and a dome) and the Lyceum (with a tall tower capped by an oxidized copper bulb). To get here from the main square, angle up Bajcsy-Zsilinszky Utca, passing a fine Art Nouveau facade and the TI.*

Eszterházy Tér

This square is named for Bishop Károly Eszterházy (1725-1799), who helped put Eger on the map during his 40 years in power. Eszterházy had serious clout, which he wielded to transform Eger from a provincial town into a beautiful small city—with lovely architecture that far exceeded its lowly position.

Face the blocky building at the bottom of the square—the **Lyceum,** or teacher-training college. Eszterházy wanted a university in Eger, but Habsburg empress Maria Theresa refused to allow it. And so, instead, Eszterházy built the most impressive teacher-training college on the planet—and stocked it with the best books and astronomical equipment that money could buy. The Lyceum still trains local teachers (enrollment: about 2,000). Tourists also roam the halls of the Lyceum; they come to visit its classic old library and its astronomy museum (which has a fascinating camera obscura), both tucked away in the big, confusing building. For details, see "Sights in Eger," later.

Now turn 180 degrees and face the cathedral, up the grand staircase at the opposite end of the square. The palace that sprawls to the right is the residence of the archbishop. And on the right side of the steps is the entrance to the **Time Tunnel** (Időalagút), a guided tour of the archbishop's former wine cellar network (4,500 Ft, schedule posted at door; most tours in Hungarian with a smidge of English, but there are occasional English tours; check schedule and book ahead at www.idoalagut.hu, +36 70 414 5004).

Head up the grand staircase. You'll pass saints István and László—Hungary's first two Christian kings—and then the apostles Peter and Paul.

• *At the top of the stairs, gape up at...*

Eger Cathedral

The second-biggest church in Hungary (after Esztergom's—see page 683) is worth ▲▲. The cathedral was built in the 1830s by an

Austrian archbishop who had previously served in Venice and who thought Eger could use a little more class. The colonnaded Neoclassical facade, painted a pretty Habsburg yellow, boasts some fine Italian sculpture.

Cost and Hours: 300-Ft donation requested; Mon-Sat 8:30-18:00, Sun 13:00-18:00; Pyrker János Tér 1.

Organ Concerts: The cathedral organ on occasion will boom out a glorious 30-minute concert—most often summer Sundays at 12:45, but likely also at other times in high season (look for posted schedule).

Visiting the Cathedral: As you head inside, look near the back-left corner for the statue of **Szent Rita,** a local favorite (that's the 15th-century saint Rita of Cascia, from Italy). The votive plaques that say *köszönöm* and *hálából* are offering "thanks" and "gratitude" for prayers answered.

Across from Rita is a statue honoring St. Maksymilian Kolbe (1894-1941), a Polish priest who was executed at Auschwitz; around the corner from him (in the corridor) is another 20th-century martyr, the Hungarian cardinal József Mindszenty (1892-1975), who ran afoul of the communist authorities and lived in the US embassy in Budapest until he escaped to Austria.

Now walk down the nave, to the first collection box. Then, turning back to face the door, look up at the ornate **ceiling fresco:** On the left, it shows Hungarians in traditional dress; and on the right, the country's most important historical figures. At the bottom, you see this cathedral, celestially connected with St. Peter's in Rome (opposite). This symbol of devotion to

the Vatican was a brave statement when it was painted in 1950. The communists were closing churches in other small Hungarian towns, but the Eger archbishop had enough clout to keep this one open.

Continue to the transept, stopping directly underneath the main dome. The **stained-glass windows** decorating the north and south transepts were donated to the cathedral by a rich Austrian couple to commemorate the 1,000th anniversary of Hungary's conversion to Christianity—notice the dates: 1000 (when St. István converted the Magyars to Christianity) and 2000.

Turning to leave, notice the enormous **organ**—Hungary's second largest—above the door (try to catch an organ concert—see details earlier).

• *Head back out of the church and down the stairs. When you reach the Lyceum, turn left and walk down...*

Széchenyi Utca

This is Eger's main walking street, lined with colorful townhouses, cafés, and eateries. You'll find that the businesses are mostly oriented to locals (especially students), with a few touristy spots mixed in.

One block down the street, on the left, step through the gate into the grand garden courtyard of the **Archbishop's Palace.** In the peaceful garden, observe the statue on the left, honoring St. István (see page 631), and on the right, a statue for St. Erzsébet (Elisabeth), whose smuggled bread for the poor changed to roses when she was caught—notice the roses in her apron. You can pay to enter the palace itself, with fine old halls described by the dryly informative audioguide (2,000 Ft, includes audioguide; open Tue-Sun 10:00-18:00, cheaper and open until 16:00 Oct-March, closed Mon year-round). As you walk through the bishop's apartments, you'll see vestments, a model of the cathedral, chalices, rare books, a picture gallery, and a balcony looking down into the bishop's private chapel. However, it's pretty dull, and other sights in Eger are more interesting.

Back out on Széchenyi Utca, continue one more block, then

turn right down Szent János Utca (at the McDonald's). Enjoy Eger's pedestrianized core for one long block—noticing that these streets, too, are populated almost entirely by Egerites, despite being just a few steps off the main square. Near the end of the street, on the right at #10, look for the *kürtőskalács* window, selling that heavenly scented Hungarian sweet street food.

• *You'll pop out at...*

Dobó Square (Dobó István Tér)

Dobó Square—worth ▲▲—is the heart of Eger. Ringed by pretty Baroque buildings and watched over by Eger's historic castle, this

square is one of the most pleasant spots in Hungary.

Looking to the left, you'll spot a huge *EGER* sign—marking a second, adjoining square along the town creek. If you walk past the sign and keep going just a couple of minutes, you'll run into the

rustic town market (described earlier, under "Helpful Hints").

Dominating the main square are the twin towers of the exquisitely photogenic **Minorite Church**—often said to be the most beautiful Baroque church in Hungary. The shabby interior is less in-

teresting but has some appealing details. Go inside (free, daily 9:30-17:30). Notice that each of the hand-carved wooden pews has a different motif. Pay close attention to the side altars that flank the nave: The first set (left and right) are 3-D illustrations, painted to replicate the wood altars that burned in a fire; the next set is real. And looking up at the faded ceiling frescoes, you'll see (in the second one from the entrance) the church's patron: St. Anthony of Padua, who's preaching God's word to the fishes after the townspeople refused to hear him.

The green, arcaded building to the right of the Minorite Church is the **Town Hall,** next to an old-fashioned pharmacy.

Walk to the dynamic statue in the middle of the square, which depicts **István Dobó** (EESHT-vahn DOH-boh). The square's namesake and Eger's greatest hero, Dobó defended the city—and all of Hungary—from an Ottoman invasion in 1552 (see his story in the sidebar). Next to Dobó is his co-commander, István Mekcsey.

EGER

István Dobó and the Siege of Eger

In the 16th century, Ottoman invaders swept into Hungary. They easily defeated a Hungarian army—in just two hours—at the Battle of Mohács in 1526.

When Buda and Pest fell to the Ottomans in 1541, Eger became the last line of defense. István Dobó and his second-in-command, István Mekcsey, were put in charge of Eger's forces. They prepared the castle for a siege and waited.

On September 11, 1552—after a summer spent conquering more than 30 other Hungarian fortresses on their march northward—40,000 Ottomans arrived in Eger. Only about 2,000 Egerites (soldiers, their wives, and their children) remained to protect their town. The Ottomans expected an easy victory, but the siege dragged on for 39 days. Eger's soldiers fought valiantly, and the women of Eger also joined the fray, pouring hot tar down on the Ottomans. Gergely Bornemissza, sent to reinforce the people of Eger, startled the Ottomans with all manner of clever and deadly explosives. His "fire wheel"—a barrel of gunpowder studded with smaller jars of explosives—would be lit and rolled downhill to wreak havoc until the final, deadly explosion. Ultimately, the Ottomans left in shame, Eger was saved, and Dobó was a national hero.

The unfortunate epilogue: The Ottomans came back in 1596 and succeeded in conquering an Eger Castle guarded by unmotivated mercenaries. The Ottomans controlled the region for close to a century.

In 1897, a castle archaeologist named Géza Gárdonyi moved from Budapest to Eger, where tales of the siege captured his imagination. Gárdonyi wrote a book about István Dobó and the 1552 Siege of Eger called *Egri Csillagok* ("Stars of Eger," translated into English as *Eclipse of the Crescent Moon,* available at local bookstores and souvenir stands). The book—a favorite of many Hungarians—is taught in schools, keeping the legend of Eger's heroes alive today.

And right at their side is one of the brave women of Eger—depicted here throwing a pot down onto the attackers.

Behind the statue of Dobó is a bridge over the stream that bisects the city. Just before you reach that bridge, look to the left and you'll see the northernmost Ottoman **minaret** in Europe—once part of a mosque, it's now a tourist attraction.

At the bridge, pause and look down at little **Eger creek** below street level. Notice the finely manicured trail that runs along the creek, beckoning to strollers and cyclists. If you follow this creek to the right, in less than 10 minutes you'll reach Eger's excellent thermal-bathing complex (described later, under "Experiences in Eger"). Like much of Hungary, this part of Eger sits on deposits of natural thermal water...can you detect a faint whiff of sulfur?

Across the bridge is the charming **Little Dobó Square** (Kis-Dobó Tér), the most atmospheric place in Eger for an al fresco drink or meal. The wine bar on the square offers tastings, and you'll find more options just up the street.

• *Our brief orientation walk is over. The town's most prominent sight—the castle—is just overhead, hovering over Little Dobó Square. To reach it, bear right at the top of the square, then turn right on Dobó Utca. Follow this pleasant street—lined with an ever-changing array of gift shops, wine bars and wine shops, eateries, and other tourist-oriented businesses—a few short blocks. Soon you'll reach a little park (with a lute-playing figure on a bench); the ramp up to the castle is just beyond this, on the left.*

Sights in Eger

▲EGER CASTLE (EGRI VÁR)

The great St. István—Hungary's first Christian king—founded a church on this hill a thousand years ago. The church was destroyed by Tatars in the 13th century, and this fortress was built to repel another attack. Most importantly, this castle is Hungary's Alamo, where István Dobó defended Eger from the Ottomans in 1552—as depicted in the relief just outside the entry gate.

These days, it's usually crawling with field-tripping schoolchildren from all over the country. (Every Hungarian sixth grader reads *Eclipse of the Crescent Moon*, which thrillingly recounts the heroic siege of Eger.) For those of us who didn't grow up hearing the legend of István Dobó, the complex is hard to appreciate, and English information is sparse. Most visitors find that the most rewarding plan is simply to stroll up, wander the grounds, play "king of the castle" along the ramparts, and enjoy the sweeping views over Eger's rooftops. I'd skip the "casements tour," which costs extra and is in Hungarian only.

Cost and Hours: 3,600 Ft, 1,500-Ft "walking ticket" gets you into the castle grounds after the museums have closed—a good option; waxworks costs 600 Ft extra; castle grounds open daily 8:00-22:00, Nov-March until 21:00; exhibits open mid-March-Oct daily 10:00-18:00, off-season until 16:00 and closed Mon; +36 36 312 744, www.egrivar.hu. The entrance ramp to the castle is at the end of Dobó István Utca, a short walk from Little Dobó Square.

Visiting the Castle: Buy your ticket at the lower gate, then hike up the entry ramp and through the inner gate into the main courtyard—with grassy fields, souvenir stands, and easy access to the ramparts.

Get your bearings by walking up to the round turret with the tall Hungarian flag, to the left as you enter, and take a visual tour over the rooftops of Eger. (If you've completed my Eger Town Walk, this is a fun recap.)

Looking left, spot what looks like a church tower with the feathers of an arrow vertically embedded in the top, next to a big, wooden, bulbous building. This is the Aladár Bitskey Pool, designed by the great Organic architect Imre Makovecz. It anchors Eger's delightful thermal bath area—well worth considering for a break from sightseeing.

Panning 90 degrees to the right, look down over Eger's charming main square, with the twin towers of the Minorite Church. Just beyond, see the round dome and two rectangular towers of the cathedral, and the boxy Baroque tower with a copper bulb on top—that's the Lyceum, with its prized camera obscura. Széchenyi Utca—the main walking street—stretches from these two buildings to the right, to the twin yellow church spires.

Looking farther right, try to spot Eger's minaret (which may be hidden behind the turret)—the northernmost Ottoman minaret still standing in Europe. And all around you are the wooded Bükk Hills, which hide an important wine-growing region.

Now head into the castle proper. Face straight ahead from where you entered. The **round tower** on your left usually holds good temporary exhibitions, down deep inside. And off on the right, just inside the wall, you may see an **archery** exhibit where you can pay to test your skill shooting old-fashioned bows and crossbows.

Now walk straight ahead, through the corridor with the little information window, and emerge into a pink, Gothic-style courtyard. Immediately to your left, notice the entrance to the **dungeon.** While the "casements" you may see advertised are not worth paying extra for, hiking down into this dungeon—covered by your castle ticket—is a similar experience. The long building on the left, next to the dungeon entrance, has the **$$ 1552 Restaurant,** serving up big plates of hearty traditional food; upstairs are temporary exhibits.

Straight ahead, upstairs in the building with the Gothic arches, is the castle's **museum** (with English descriptions). You'll see some architectural decorations, swords and suits of armor, and models of the castle through history—including one illustrating the Ottoman siege of Eger. Also inside are some paintings and a screen showing a classic movie that dramatizes the siege, adding to its legend. The most interesting exhibit is a small side room with objects the Ottomans left behind: weapons, everyday items (pots, bowls), a carpet, and some turban-shaped gravestones.

Head through the little gap between the two buildings of the courtyard to find the **waxworks,** or "Panoptikum." Run separately

from the castle sights, this costs 600 Ft extra. And, while it's kind of silly, it's fun for kids or kids at heart. You'll see a handful of eerily realistic heroes and villains from the siege of Eger (including István Dobó himself, and the leader of the Ottomans sitting in his colorful tent). A visit to the waxworks also lets you scramble through a segment of the tunnels that run inside the castle walls (a plus, since it's not really worth it to wait around through the similar, Hungarian-language casemates tour).

From here, you can explore the **grounds,** including the remains of a once-grand cathedral, a smaller rotunda dating from the days of St. István (10th or 11th century; at the far-right corner as you enter), and the ruins of some old Turkish baths (not worth the extra ticket price).

SIGHTS IN THE LYCEUM (LÍCEUM)

Eger's teacher-training college fills a historic old building that—among all the students, classrooms, and professors' offices—houses

two sights worth a look: a glorious Baroque library, with shelves of historic books and a frescoed ceiling; and the "Magic Tower," with some scientific exhibits and a working camera obscura (Eszterházy Tér 1). While both are inside the same building, they are treated as separate sights.

Cost and Hours: Library—1,200 Ft, open Tue-Sat 9:30-15:30, closed Sun-Mon, also generally closed off-season (since there's no heating); Magic

EGER

Tower—2,000 Ft, Tue-Sun 10:00-16:00, closed Mon, shorter hours (likely weekend mornings only) off-season; www.varazstorny.hu.

▲▲Baroque Library

First, visit the Lyceum's old-fashioned Baroque library one floor up: From the main entry hall, cut through the middle of the courtyard,

go up the stairs to the next floor, and look for Room 223, marked *Biblioteca Eszterhazyana* (it's on the right side of the complex as you face it from the entrance). This library houses 60,000 books (here and in the two adjoining rooms, with several stacked two deep), all cataloged carefully. This is no easy task, since they're in over 30 languages—from Thai to Tagalog—and are shelved according to size rather than topic. Only one percent of the books are in Hungarian—but half of them are in Latin. The shelves are adorned with golden seals depicting some of the great minds of science, philosophy, and religion. Marvel at the gorgeous ceiling fresco, dating from 1778. To thank the patron of this museum, say *köszönöm* to the guy in the second row up, to the right of the podium (above the entry door, second from left, not wearing a hat)—that's Bishop Károly Eszterházy, who founded the Lyceum and for whom the library is named. A portrait of him often stands on an easel at ground level. And the display cases ringing the room show off treasures from the collection—they are changed every year, to avoid exposing any books to sunlight for too long.

▲Magic Tower (Varázstorony)

Turn right as you leave the library to find the staircase that leads up the misnamed "Magic Tower," which is really all about science (*Varázstorony,* follow signs several flights up). First you'll reach the **Astronomical Museum.** Some dusty old stargazing instruments occupy one room, as well as a meridian line in the floor (a dot of sunlight dances along this line each day around noon). Across the hall is a fun, interactive **magic room,** where you can try out scientific experiments—such as using air pressure to make a ball levitate or sending a mini "hot-air balloon" up to the ceiling.

A few more flights up is the Lyceum's treasured **camera obscura**—one of just two originals surviving in Europe (the other is in Edinburgh). You'll enter a dark room and gather around a big, bowl-like canvas, where the guide will fly you around the streets of Eger (presentations about 2/hour, maybe more when busy). Fun as it is today, this camera must have astonished viewers when it was built in 1776—well before anyone had seen "moving pictures." It's a bit of a huff to get up here (nine flights of stairs, 302 steps)—but the camera obscura, and the actual view of Eger from the outdoor terrace just outside, are worth it.

Experiences in Eger

AQUA EGER

Swimming and water sports are as important to Egerites as good wine. They're proud that many of Hungary's Olympic medalists in aquatic events have come from the surrounding county. The town's Aladár Bitskey swimming pool—arguably the most striking building in this part of Hungary—is practically a temple to water sports.

Eger also has several appealing thermal bath complexes: one right in town, and two more a few miles away (near the village of Egerszalók). Budapest offers classier bath experiences, but the Eger options are modern, fully accessible, and far less crowded with American tourists—making them, for some travelers, an all-around better experience. Before you go, be sure to read the thermal bath tips on page 635.

Baths and Pools in Eger

All of these are managed by the same organization (www. egertermal.hu). Bring your swimsuit, a towel, and flip-flops (or buy them at the pool).

Getting There: Eger's bathing complex is a pleasant walk (less than 10 minutes) from the center of town. From the bridge on Dobó Square, follow the creek four blocks south (look for signs to *Strand*). When you reach Petőfi Tér, you're in the aquatic area. The swimming pool is on your left (look for the unique steeple), and the thermal bathing complex is straight ahead; to reach the main entrance, continue straight into the park, then look for the entrance on your left, over a bridge, marked by a big dome. The Turkish bath entrance is around the other side of the complex.

Aladár Bitskey Swimming Pool (Bitskey Aladár Uszoda)

This striking swimming pool was designed by Imre Makovecz, the father of Hungary's Organic architectural style (see sidebar). The building is worth a peek—and you can swim in it, too.

Cost and Hours: 1,200 Ft, Mon-Fri 6:00-21:00, Sat-Sun 7:30-18:00, Frank Tivadar Utca, +36 36 511 810.

EGER

▲Eger Thermal Bath (Eger Termálfürdő)

For a refreshing break from the sightseeing grind, consider a splash at the spa. This is a wonderful opportunity to try a Hungarian bath: fun, accessible, and frequented mostly by locals. Note that there are two adjoining sections: the sprawling indoor/outdoor thermal bath section and the smaller Turkish bath. Each has its own ticket, but it's possible to move between them. If you're going to be at the bath complex for less than 2.5 hours, it's cheaper to enter through the Turkish bath section (see details later).

Cost and Hours: 3,200 Ft, plus 1,800 Ft to add Turkish bath; daily 9:00-19:00, may be open later in summer and have shorter hours off-season, last entry one hour before closing; Petőfi Tér 2, main entrance is through Archbishop's Garden (Érsekkert), +36 36 510 558.

Taking the Waters: Eger's bath complex uses a similar wristband system to the one in Budapest. After paying, you are issued a wristband that you'll use to access your locker. The complex is huge, with a wide array of different pools, each one labeled with its depth and temperature. The best part is the double-domed, indoor-outdoor adventure bath, right at the main entrance (a very comfortable 34°C/93°F). Its cascades, jets, bubbles, geysers, and powerful current pool will make you feel like a kid again. The adjoining pool is warmer (36-38°C/97-100°F) and the most popular area to hang out—Egerites sit peacefully, ignore the slight stink, and feel their arthritis ebb away. Sprawling in both directions are additional pools—for kids, for swimming laps, and for hanging out. The waterslides at the right end (with your back to the main dome) are open only in summer, while the Turkish bath is in a smaller domed building at the opposite end, to the left.

▲Turkish Bath (Török Fürdő)

Eger's beautifully refurbished Turkish-style bath—small but elegant—is tucked in one corner of the thermal bath complex. The underside of the central dome—over a 30°C/86°F pool—glitters with golden tile. Surrounding that are hotter mineral pools (34-36°C/93-97°F), as well as a sauna, steam bath, and aroma bath. This area connects to the thermal bath complex through a turnstile, and uses the same wristband system (Turkish bath entrance is around the left side as you approach the bath complex from the center).

Cost and Hours: The 2,700-Ft Turkish bath ticket is a great deal—it covers you for up to 2.5 hours in both the Turkish bath and the thermal bath area. (If you buy your bath ticket at the main entrance, then want to enter the Turkish bath, you'll be charged an extra entry fee—a poor value.) The Turkish bath is also open later: daily until 21:00 (Mon-Tue from 16:30, Wed-Thu from 15:00, Fri from 13:00, Sat-Sun from 9:00; +36 36 510 522). If you visit late in the day, a good strategy is to enter and change at the Turkish bath (entrance at Fürdő Utca 3), head over to the thermal complex

first, then move back into the Turkish bath when the rest is closed.

Baths near Eger, in Egerszalók

Two more thermal baths—Salt Hill and Demjén Cascade—sit in the countryside outside Eger, flanking a rocky hill between the villages of Egerszalók and Demjén. While these baths lack the old-fashioned class of the Budapest options, they more than compensate with soggy fun. Here's a fun and very hedonistic afternoon plan: Take the bus or taxi to the spa, taxi back to Eger's Sirens' Valley for some wine-cave hopping, then taxi back to your Eger hotel.

Getting There: Both baths are about a mile outside the village of Egerszalók, which is itself about three miles from Eger. **Drivers** leave Eger to the south, toward *Kerecsend*/Route 25; at the roundabout on the outskirts of town, turn right toward *Egerszalók* and *Demjén*. A few minutes later, watch (on the left) for the easy-to-miss turnoff to Saliris Resort (park along the road)—or, for Demjén Cascade, carry on past this, turn left at the T intersection, and head into Demjén village.

Without a car, you can take a public **bus** from Eger's bus station to the baths (take bus going toward Demjén; for Salt Hill, get off at the *Egerszalók Gyógyfürdő* stop—tell the bus driver "EH-gehr-saw-lohk FEWR-dur"—just after leaving the town of Egerszalók; for Demjén Cascade, get off at the entrance to Demjén village; bus runs 9/day Mon-Sat, fewer on Sun, 20-minute trip). Check the return bus information carefully (especially on weekends, when frequency plummets). Or you can take a **taxi** from Eger (+36 36 555 555 for a return taxi from Egerszalók).

Nearby Wineries: The village of Egerszalók has several fine wineries, including the excellent **St. Andrea**—fun to combine with your bath visit (for details, see the "Wineries near the Baths in Egerszalók" section, later).

EGER

▲▲Salt Hill Thermal Spa (at the Saliris Resort)

For decades, Egerites would come to this "salt hill" (a natural terraced formation caused by mineral-rich spring water running down the hillside) in the middle of nowhere and cram together to baste in pools of hot water. Today, the gigantic Saliris Resort hotel and spa complex, built near those original formations, offers a world of hot-water fun tucked into a scenic valley. With 12 indoor pools and five outdoor ones—many cleverly overlapping one another on several levels—these baths are worth the trip outside Eger.

Cost and Hours: 7,200 Ft all day, cheaper for less than 3 hours or if arriving late in the afternoon; 2,750 Ft extra for sauna world; open Sun-Thu 10:00-20:00, Fri-Sat until 21:00, sauna world open daily 11:00-19:30; +36 36 688 500, http://salirisresort.hu/en.

Visiting the Bath: This complex uses the same system as at Eger's thermal baths: Press your wristband against a computer screen to be assigned a locker, change in the private cabin, and then have fun.

From the locker room, a blue carpet leads you out to the pools. Take some time to explore the sprawling complex. The two main pools—warm (32-34°C/90-93°F) and hot (35-39°C/95-102°F)—extend both inside and outside and cascade over several levels. Outside, down on the lower level, is a vast kiddie pool.

Tucked around the right side of the building (as you face the complex) is the "sauna world," with five different types of saunas, some quieter soaking pools, and a clothing-optional outdoor area with wood cabin-type huts that contain Finnish and Russian saunas.

▲Demjén Cascade Thermal Spa

Just over the hill from Salt Hill Thermal Spa, Demjén Baths was recently converted into a high-end resort. The original "thermal valley" *(termál völgy)* part of the complex—pretty but unpretentious, with nicely rustic wooden buildings and pools—is reasonably priced and open long hours, making it popular with locals.

Hungary's Organic Architecture

Hungary's postcommunist generation has embraced a unique, eye-catching style of architecture, called Organic, which was developed and championed by Imre Makovecz (1935-2011).

In his youth, Makovecz pursued a flowing style that was intentionally at odds with the rigid right angles of communist architecture. He was inspired by the Art Nouveau of a "decadent" golden age and by pioneering architects from other countries (including American Frank Lloyd Wright, who employed a more angular style but a similar aesthetic of fitting his works to their surroundings).

After being blacklisted by the regime for his adherence to his architectural vision—and for his nationalistic politics—Makovecz ramped up his pursuit of something new. Makovecz made do with sticks, rocks, and other foraged building materials. He was also inspired by Transylvanian village architecture: whitewashed walls with large, overhanging mansard roofs (resembling a big mushroom).

After the fall of the regime, Makovecz swiftly became Hungary's premier architect. He believed that a building should be a product of its environment, rather than a cookie-cutter copy. Organic buildings use indigenous materials (especially wood) and take on unusual forms—often inspired by animals or plants—that blend in with the landscape. These buildings look like they're rising up out of the ground, rather than plopped down on top of it. Makovecz preferred to work in small communities such as Eger (see photo on page 697) instead of working for large corporations. Makovecz wanted his creations—from churches, thermal baths, and campgrounds to cultural centers, restaurants, and bus stations—to represent the civic pride of the local community. For more on Makovecz, visit www.makovecz.hu.

Jets, fountains, and other "adventure bath"-type features are rare, and the goal here is simply stewing in pools of warm water. A separate "aquapark" section adds waterslides and a diving pool, for an extra charge. But the big draw for thermal-bathing enthusiasts is the newer "cave bath" *(barlangfürdő)*—a subterranean complex of pools, channels, waterslides, hidden grottoes, eerie mood lighting, and a sci-fi/fantasy theme. While the Salt Hill spa described earlier is still a more enjoyable all-around experience, those intrigued by the novelty of an underground thermal playland might prefer to check out Demjén.

Cost and Hours: 8,500 Ft for everything, cheaper for just parts of the complex; Mon-Thu 10:00-21:00, Fri 10:00-22:00, Sat 9:00-22:00, Sun 9:00-21:00; mobile +36 30 853 7419, www.demjencascade.hu.

EGER WINE

Eger is at the heart of one of Hungary's best-known wine regions, internationally famous for its **Bull's Blood** (Egri Bikavér). You'll likely hear various stories as to how Bull's Blood got its name during the Ottoman siege of Eger. My favorite version: The Ottomans were amazed at the ferocity displayed by the Egerites and wondered what they were drinking that boiled their blood and stained their beards so red...it must be potent stuff. Local merchants, knowing that the Ottomans were Muslim and couldn't drink alcohol, told them it was bull's blood. The merchants made a buck, and the name stuck.

Creative as these stories are, they're all bunk—the term dates only from 1851. Egri Bikavér is a blend (everyone has their own recipe), so you generally won't find it at small producers. It begins with a base of *kékfrankos* grapes, typically blended with cabernet sauvignon, merlot, and *kékoportó*.

But Bull's Blood is just the beginning of what the Eger wine region offers. Although Eger is better known for its reds, 42 of the 62 regional varieties are white. (For details, see the the "Hungarian Wines" sidebar on page 558.)

Tasting Local Wine: While it would be enjoyable to drive around the Hungarian countryside visiting a few wineries (and I've recommended one great choice, St. Andrea), the most accessible way to get a quick taste of local wine is at a wine shop in town. Several cluster on Little Dobó Square (Kis-Dobó Tér) and just uphill, along Dobó István Utca. As specific shops tend to come and go, I'd simply stroll this area looking for signs advertising tastings or small glasses of wine, and find a clerk who speaks enough English to help you navigate your choices.

Sirens' Valley (Szépasszony-völgy)

When the Ottoman invaders first occupied Eger, some residents moved into the valley next door, living in caves dug into the hillside. Eventually the Ottomans were driven out, the Egerites moved back to town, and the caves became wine cellars. (Most Eger families who can afford it have at least a modest vineyard in the countryside.) There are more than 300 such caves in the valley to the southwest of Eger, several of which are open for visitors.

Getting to the Sirens' Valley: The valley is on the southwest outskirts of Eger—a long walk or an easy and affordable taxi ride.

Visiting the Sirens' Valley: The best selection of these caves (about 50) is in the Sirens' Valley (on local directional signs, the "Nice Woman Valley"). While the valley can feel vacant and dead, if you visit when it's busy it can be a fun scene—locals showing off their latest vintage, with picnic tables and tipsy tourists spilling out into the street. At some places, you'll be offered free samples; others have a menu for tastes or glasses of wine. While you're not expected to buy a bottle, it's a nice gesture if you've spent a while at one cave (and it's usually quite affordable). Some of the caves are fancy and finished, staffed by multilingual waiters in period costume. Others feel like a dank basement, with grandpa leaning on his moped out front and a monolingual granny pouring the wine inside.

This experience is a strange mix of touristy and local, but not entirely accessible to non-Hungarian-speakers—it works best with a bunch of friends and an easygoing, sociable attitude (cellars generally open 10:00-21:00 in summer, best June-Aug in the late afternoon and early evening, plus good-weather weekends in the shoulder season; it's sleepy and not worth a visit off-season, when only a handful of cellars remain open for shorter hours).

Wineries near the Baths in Egerszalók

The village of Egerszalók, near the Salt Hill and Demjén Cascade thermal baths, has a variety of fun wineries. The most interesting, and well worth a visit for wine lovers, is **St. Andrea.** This slick, modern, Napa Valley-esque facility offers cellar tours and tastings of their excellent wines, which show up on fine restaurant menus across Hungary. They focus on blends that highlight the unique properties of this region, and produce some good, pungent whites with volcanic qualities. While it may be possible to simply drop in for a tasting, it's better to call ahead and let them know you're coming (tastings from 7,000 Ft/person; Mon-Sat 10:00-18:00, closed Sun; Ady Endre Út 88 in Egerszalók, +36 36 474 018, www.standrea.hu, kostolas@standrea.hu). It's most practical with a car (or by taxi), but you can also walk there from the bus stop in Egerszalók's town center (about a half-mile; head down Ady Endre Út, toward the baths).

Sleeping in Eger

I've focused my listings on quaint, well-located hotels. There's no real "luxury" in this town—just bigger, tour-oriented places on the outskirts. Elevators are rare—expect to climb one or two flights of stairs to reach your room. Most of these hotels are in pedestrian zones, so get detailed driving and parking instructions from your

EGER

hotel; many offer free or cheap parking, but it's often a block or two away. Most hotels quote their rates in euros but prefer to be paid in forints.

$ Senator Ház Hotel is a classic small, family-run hotel. Though the 11 rooms are a bit worn, this place is cozy and well run by András and Csöpi Cseh and their right-hand man, Peter. It feels trapped in a nostalgic time warp, with oodles of character, all the right quirks, and a picture-perfect location just under the castle on Little Dobó Square (RS%, air-con, free parking a block away, Dobó István Tér 11, +36 36 411 711, www.senatorhaz.hu, info@senatorhaz.hu). The Cseh family also runs **$ Pátria Vendégház**—with two doubles and two luxurious apartments around a courtyard nearby.

$ Imola Udvarház is a "dessert hotel" with 15 rooms and apartments—some with kitchen, living room, bedroom, and bathroom—all decorated in modern Ikea style. They're roomy and well maintained, with a great location near the castle entrance, and the free on-site parking garage makes this a good choice for drivers (air-con, Tírodi Sebestyén Tér 4, +36 36 516 180, www.imolaudvarhaz.hu, info@imolaudvarhaz.hu).

$ Centrum Vendégház, at the bottom of the main square, has eight simple rooms and apartments around a courtyard. It's basic but comfortable, with parquet floors and traditional furnishings, and well run by László and Timea. Check in at the little grocery store on the ground floor (breakfast extra, Bajcsy-Zsilinszky 17, mobile +36 30 591 3131, www.cve.hu, info@centrum-vendeghaz-eger.hu).

$ Offi Ház Hotel shares Little Dobó Square with Senator Ház (listed above). Its five rooms are classy and romantic but dated and a bit tight, with slanted ceilings. Communication can be tricky (German helps), but the location is superb (air-con, Dobó István Tér 5, +36 36 518 210, www.offihaz.hu, offihaz@upcmail.hu, Offenbächer family).

$ Centrooms Park Eger, an annex for the larger Hotel Park at the edge of town, is impersonal but indeed central, with 21 spartan but sleepable rooms right in the middle of town (breakfast extra and served at main hotel—better to just eat at a café on the square, air-con, Érsek Utca 4, +36 36 522 255, www.centroomseger.hu, info@centroomseger.hu).

¢ Dobó Vendégház, run by warm Marianna Kleszo, has seven basic but colorful rooms just off Dobó Square. Marianna speaks nothing but Hungarian but gets simple reservation emails translated by a friend (cash only, air-con in some upstairs rooms, free parking, Dobó Utca 19, +36 36 421 407, www.dobovendeghaz.hu, info@dobovendeghaz.hu).

EGER

Eating in Eger

$$ Macok Bisztró, near the base of the ramp up to the castle, is every foodie's choice for the best spot in town—with modern, upscale cuisine and a more sophisticated dining experience. It has a classy interior, inviting tables filling a patio, a mix of Hungarian and international dishes, and an extensive wine list (daily, Tinódi Sebestyén Tér 4, +36 36 516 180, www.imolaudvarhaz.hu).

$ Brumbrum is the cheaper, more casual side-restaurant of Macok. They offer tasty, unpretentious, street-food-inspired plates of Hungarian and international fare, pizza by the slice, a variety of wines, and craft beer, all in an industrial-mod setting with subway tile and raw plywood (Wed-Sat lunch and dinner, Sun until 18:00, closed Mon-Tue, same contact information as above).

$$ HBH Restaurant (named for the Hofbräuhaus beer on tap) offers traditional Hungarian dishes, either in a brick-and-wood dining room or—better—at fine outdoor tables at the bottom of the main square (on weekends, reserve a view table in advance). While the service can be curt, the lengthy, well-described menu and good wine list make this a fine choice for a classic Hungarian meal (daily, at the bottom of Dobó Square at Bajcsy-Zsilinszky Utca 19, +36 36 515 516, www.hbh-eger.hu).

$$ Palacsintavár ("Pancake Castle"), near the ramp leading up to the castle, isn't your hometown IHOP. They serve up inventive, artfully presented crêpe-wrapped main courses to a mostly student clientele. The spacious interior is decorated with old cigarette boxes, rock music plays on the soundtrack, and the outdoor tables are appealing (closed Mon, Dobó Utca 9, +36 36 413 980, www.palacsintavar.hu).

$$ Restaurant Senator Ház, on Little Dobó Square, offers the best setting for al fresco dining in town, with good Hungarian and international food. Sure, you're paying a bit extra for the setting—but it's worth it for the postcard-perfect outdoor seating, from which you can survey the Little Dobó Square action (daily, cheesy live music on summer evenings, same contact information as hotel). Neighboring restaurants (such as Offi Ház) offer the same ambience.

$$ Depresso Kávéház brings a touch of modern hipness to Eger's stately main square. Despite its downer name, this young, fresh café features a wide variety of coffee drinks, wine, breakfasts, and a short menu of light meals (sandwiches, quiches, etc.). It owns a great location on the square—with fine outdoor tables facing the castle—and also has a bright, open interior (Wed-Sun lunch and dinner, Mon lunch only, closed Tue, Érsek Utca 14, mobile +36 30 886 6742, www.depresso.hu).

$ Il Padrino is a popular place for simple, cheap, tasty pizzas.

EGER

It's tucked down a non-touristy street a block over from the main square, with a kitschy interior and breezy outdoor tables (daily, Fazola Henrik Utca 1, mobile +36 20 547 9959, www.padrinopizza. hu).

Wine and Beer: To sample either of these, begin on Little Dobó Square and head up Dobó István Utca. You'll pass a few **wine bars** featuring local wines, plus **Bakelit,** a shop selling a dizzying array of Hungarian and international craft beers (daily, Dobó Utca 17, www.bakelitbeer.com).

Student Eats on Széchenyi Utca: To browse for an affordable, forgettable meal, go for a walk on Eger's main walking street, which begins at the cathedral. You'll find a row of lowbrow student eateries serving a variety of pizza, gyros, and burgers, plus lots of bakeries and bars with food. A few tourist-oriented places are mixed in.

Dessert: *Cukrászdák* (pastry shops) line the streets of Eger. For a more local scene, find the tiny **Sárvári Cukrászda,** a block behind the Lyceum. Their pastries are good, but Egerites line up here for homemade gelato (daily, Kossuth Utca 1, between Jókai Utca and Fellner Utca). You'll spot several ice cream parlors in this town, where every other pedestrian seems to be licking a cone. Another good option is the *kürtőskalács* **window** on Szent János Utca, where you can step up and grab a piping-hot chimney cake that's slow-cooked on a rotisserie, then rolled in toppings (daily, Szent János Utca 10).

Eger Connections

BY TRAIN

The only major destination you'll get to directly from Eger's train station is **Budapest** (every 2 hours direct to Budapest's Keleti/ Eastern Station, 2 hours; more frequent and faster with a change in Füzesabony—see below). For other destinations, you'll connect through Füzesabony or Budapest.

Eger is connected to the nearby junction town of **Füzesabony** (FEW-zesh-aw-bone) by frequent trains (13/day, 17 minutes). In Füzesabony, you can transfer to Budapest on either a slower milk run train or a speedier InterCity train (a little pricier, as it requires a supplement, but gets you to Budapest in just under 2 hours total).

BY BUS

Eger's bus station is right in town, a five-minute uphill walk behind Eger's cathedral and the Archbishop's Palace: Go behind the cathedral and through the park, and look for the modern, green, circular building. Blue electronic boards in the center of the station show upcoming departures.

From Eger to Budapest: The direct Eger-Budapest bus service runs twice an hour, is about the same price as the train, and can be a bit faster (express bus—1 hour 50 minutes, regular bus—2 hours 10 minutes). While Eger's bus station is closer to the town center than its train station, this bus takes you to a less central point in Budapest (near Budapest's Stadionok bus station, on the M2/red Metró line).

To the Thermal Baths near Egerszalók: Buses from the same station also connect Eger to the thermal baths near Egerszalók (Salt Hill and Demjén Cascade; see "Getting There" on page 699). However, buses marked for *Egerszalók* do not actually go to the spa; instead, you need a bus going *beyond* Egerszalók, marked for *Demjén*.

EGER

SLOVENIA

Slovenija

SLOVENIA

Slovenija

Tiny, overlooked Slovenia is one of Europe's most unexpectedly charming destinations. At the intersection of the Slavic, Germanic, and Italian worlds, Slovenia is an exciting mix of the best of each culture. Though it's just a quick trip away from the tourist throngs in Croatia, Venice, Munich, Salzburg, and Vienna, Slovenia has stayed mostly off the tourist track—making it a handy detour for in-the-know travelers. Be warned: Everyone I've met who has visited Slovenia wishes they'd allotted more time for this endearing, underrated land.

Today, it seems strange to think that Slovenia was ever part of Yugoslavia. Both in the personality of its people and in its landscape, Slovenia feels more like Austria. Slovenes are more industrious, organized, and punctual than their fellow former Yugoslavs... yet still friendly, relaxed, and Mediterranean. Locals like the balance. And it's beautiful: Slovenia's rolling countryside is dotted with quaint alpine villages and the spires of miniature Baroque churches, against a backdrop of snowcapped peaks.

Only half as big as Switzerland, Slovenia is remarkably diverse for its size. Travelers can hike on alpine trails in the morning and explore some of the world's best caves in the afternoon, before relaxing with a glass of local wine and a seafood dinner while watching the sun set on the Adriatic.

Slovenia enjoys a prosperity unusual for a formerly communist country. The Austro-Hungarian Empire left it with a strong work ethic and an impressive industrial infrastructure, which the Yugoslav government expanded. By 1980, 60 percent of all Yugoslav industry was in little Slovenia (which had only 8 percent of Yugoslavia's population and 8 percent of its territory). Of the 13 new nations that have joined the European Union since 2004, Slovenia was the only one rich enough to enter as a net donor (with a higher

per-capita income than the average), and the first one to join the euro currency zone (it adopted the euro in January 2007).

The country has a funny way of making people fall in love with it. Slovenes are laid-back, easygoing, stylish, and fun. They won't win any world wars (they're too well adjusted to even try)... but they're exactly the type of people you'd love to chat with over a cup of coffee.

The Slovenian language is as mellow as the people. While Slovenes use Serb, German, and English curses in abundance, the worst they can say in their native tongue is, "May you be kicked by a hen." For "Darn it!" they say, "Three hundred hairy bears!" In bad traffic, they might mutter, "The street is white!" (If you want to get a local hopping mad—normally a difficult feat—all you have to do is mistake their beloved homeland for Slovakia.)

Coming from such a small country, locals are proud of the few things that are distinctly Slovenian, such as the roofed hayrack. Because of the frequent rain-fall in the mountainous northwest, the hayracks are covered by a roof that allows the hay to dry thoroughly. The most traditional kind is the *toplar*, consisting of two hayracks connected by one big roof. It looks like a skinny barn

with open, fenced sides. Hay hangs on the sides to dry; firewood, carts, tractors, and other farm implements sit on the ground inside; and dried hay is stored in the loft above. But these wooden *top-larji* are firetraps, and a stray bolt of lightning can burn one down in a flash. So in recent years, more farmers have been moving to single hayracks *(enojni)*; these are still roofed, but have posts made of concrete rather than wood. You'll find postcards and miniature wooden models of both kinds of hayracks (a fun souvenir).

Another uniquely Slovenian memento is a creatively decorated front panel from a beehive *(panjske končnice)*. Slovenia has a

strong beekeeping tradition, and beekeepers believe that painting the fronts of the hives makes it easier for bees to find their way home. Replicas of these panels are available at gift shops all over the country. (For more on the panels and Slovenia's beekeeping heritage, see page 810.)

Slovenia is also the land of polka. Slovenes boldly claim that polka music was invented here, and singer/accordionist Slavko Avsenik—from the village of Begunje near Bled—cranked out popular oompah songs that made him a superstar in Germany and other alpine lands. You'll see the Avsenik ensemble (now led by Slavko's grandson) and other oompah bands on Slovenian TV, where hokey Lawrence Welk-style shows remain an institution.

Most visitors to Slovenia are, in my experience, completely charmed by the place. And now, at long last, the country is slowly being discovered. Some of its biggest destinations (especially Lake Bled) can feel unpleasantly jammed in the summertime. And yet, it still feels untrampled compared to more famous stops, and there's plenty of Slovenia to go around. Visit soon, before the cat is fully out of the bag. Give yourself enough time to go beyond the big-name "whistle-stop" destinations and dig a little deeper into this wonderful land.

HELPFUL HINTS

Farm Stays: To really stretch your euros, try one of Slovenia's more than 400 farmhouse B&Bs, called "tourist farms" *(turistične kmetije)*—similar to *agriturismi* in Italy. These are actual working farms (often organic) that sell meals and/or rent rooms to tourists to help make ends meet. You can use a tourist farm as a home base to explore the entire country: The farthest reaches of Slovenia are only a day trip away. A comfortable, hotelesque

Slovenia Almanac

Official Name: Republika Slovenija, or simply Slovenija.

Size: At 7,800 square miles, it's about the size of New Jersey, but with one-fourth the population. Slovenia's two million people are 83 percent ethnic Slovenes who speak Slovene, plus a smattering of Serbs, Croats, and Muslim Bosniaks. Almost 60 percent of the country is Catholic.

Geography: Tiny Slovenia has four extremely different terrains and climates: the warm Mediterranean coastline; the snowcapped, forested alpine mountains in the northwest; the moderate-climate, central limestone plateau; and, to the east, a corner of the Great Hungarian Plain.

Latitude and Longitude: 46° N and 14° E (latitude similar to Lyon, France; Montreal, Canada; and Bismarck, North Dakota).

Biggest Cities: Nearly one in five Slovenes live in the two biggest cities: Ljubljana (280,000) and Maribor (158,000).

Snapshot History: After being dominated by the Germanic world for centuries, Slovenian culture proudly emerged in the 19th century. In the aftermath of World War I, Slovenia merged with its neighbors to become Yugoslavia, then broke away and achieved independence in 1991.

Economy: Slovenia has a gross domestic product of around $84 billion and a per-capita GDP of $40,000 (the highest, by far, of the former Yugoslavia). Slovenia's economy is based largely on manufactured metal products (trucks and machinery).

Currency: Slovenia uses the euro (€1 = about $1.10).

Government: The country is led by the prime minister (currently Robert Golob, leader of the left-wing Freedom Movement), who governs along with the figurehead president (the center-left Nataša Pirc Musar, the first woman to hold this position). The National Assembly consists of 90 elected legislators; a second house of parliament, the National Council, has much less power.

Flag: Three horizontal bands of white (top), blue, and red. A shield in the upper left shows Mount Triglav, with a wavy-line sea below and three stars above.

double with a private bathroom—plus a traditional Slovenian dinner and a hearty breakfast—can cost as little as €60.

Toll Sticker: To drive on Slovenia's expressways *(avtocesta)*, you'll need to display a toll sticker. If renting your car in Slovenia, make sure it comes with a sticker; if you're driving in from elsewhere, you can buy one at a gas station, post office, or some newsstands (watch for *vinjeta* signs at gas stations as you approach the border). For details, see "Tolls" on page 1114.

SLOVENIAN HISTORY

Slovenia has a long and unexciting history as part of various larger empires. After Illyrian, Celtic, and Roman settlements came and went, this region became populated by Slavs—the ancestors of today's Slovenes—in the late sixth century. Charlemagne's Franks conquered the tiny land in the eighth century, and Slovenia became a backwater of the Germanic world—first as a holding of the Holy Roman Empire, and later as part of the Habsburg Empire. But even as the capital, Ljubljana, was populated by Austrians (who called the city Laibach), the Slovenian language and cultural traditions survived in the countryside.

Through the Middle Ages, much of Slovenia was ruled by the Counts of Celje (highly placed vassals of the Habsburgs). In this era before modern nations—when shifting allegiances and strategic marriages dictated the dynamics of power—the Counts of Celje rose to a position of significant influence in Central and Eastern Europe. Celje daughters intermarried with some of the most powerful dynasties in the region: the Polish Piasts, the Hungarian Anjous, and the Czech Přemysls. Before long, the Counts of Celje had emerged as the Habsburgs' main rivals.

In the 15th century, Count Ulrich II of Celje married into Serbia's ruling family and managed to wrest control of Hungary's massive holdings. Had he not been assassinated in 1456, this obscure Slovenian line—rather than an obscure Austrian one—might have emerged as the dominant power in the eastern half of Europe. (Instead, the Habsburgs consolidated their vanquished foe's fiefdoms into their ever-growing empire.) In homage, the three yellow stars of the Counts of Celje's seal still adorn Slovenia's coat of arms.

Soon after, with Slovenia firmly entrenched in the Counter-Reformation holdings of the Habsburg Empire, the local Reformer Primož Trubar (1508-1586) strove both to put the Word of God into the people's hands and to legitimize Slovene as a written language. This Slovenian answer to Martin Luther secretly translated the Bible into Slovene in Reformation-friendly Germany, then smuggled copies back into his homeland.

Over the next several centuries, much of Slovenia was wracked by Habsburg-Ottoman wars, as the Ottomans attempted to push north through this territory to reach Vienna. Slovenia also found itself caught in the crossfire between Austria and Venice. Seemingly exhausted by all this warfare—and by their own sporadic, halfhearted, and unsuccessful uprisings against Habsburg rule—Slovenia languished.

When the port city of Trieste (then in Slovenian territory) was granted free status in 1718, it boosted the economy of Slovenian lands. The Enlightenment spurred a renewed interest in the Slovenian culture and language, which further flourished when Napoleon named Ljubljana the capital of his "Illyrian Provinces"—Slovenia's own mini empire, stretching from Austria's Tirol to Croatia's Dalmatian Coast. During this brief period (1809-1813), the long-suppressed Slovene language was used for the first time in schools and the government. This kicked off a full-throated national revival movement—asserting the worthiness of the Slovenian language and culture compared to the dominant Germanic worldview of the time. Inspired by the patriotic poetry of France Prešeren (1800-1849), Slovenian pride surged.

The last century saw the most interesting chapter of Slovenian history. Some of World War I's fiercest fighting occurred at the Soča (Isonzo) Front in northwest Slovenia—witnessed by young Ernest Hemingway, who drove an ambulance there. During World War II, Slovenia was divided among Nazi allies Austria, Italy, and Hungary—and an estimated 20,000 to 25,000 Slovenes perished in Nazi- and Italian-operated concentration camps.

As Yugoslavia entered its golden age under war hero Marshal Tito, Slovenia's valuable location where Yugoslavia meets Western Europe (a short drive from Austria or Italy)—and the diligent national character of the Slovenian people—made it a prime candidate for industrialization.

After Tito's death, in 1980, the various Yugoslav republics struggled to redefine their role in the union. While many factions reverted to age-old, pre-Tito nationalistic fervor, the Slovenes increasingly focused on their own future...and began to press for real reforms of the communist system. Slovenia had always been Yugoslavia's smallest, northernmost, most prosperous republic. Slovenes realized that Yugoslavia needed Slovenia much more than Slovenia needed Yugoslavia.

In 1988, the iconoclastic Slovenian magazine *Mladina* pushed the boundaries of Yugoslavia's nominally "free" press, publishing articles critical of the Yugoslav People's Army. Four young reporters (including Janez Janša, who would later become Slovenia's prime minister) were tried, convicted, and imprisoned, spurring outrage among Slovenes. A few months later, the Slovenian delegation defiantly walked out of the Yugoslav League of Communists Congress.

The first-ever free elections in Slovenia on April 8, 1990, ended communist rule and swept reformer Milan Kučan into the presidency. Kučan pursued a Swiss-style confederated relationship with his fellow Yugoslav republics, but he met with resistance from his counterparts, who were more focused on their own ethnic self-interests. Later that year, in a nationwide referendum, 88 percent of Slovenes voted for independence from Yugoslavia.

And so, concerned about the nationalistic politics of Serbian strongman Slobodan Milošević and seeking the opportunity for true democracy and capitalism, Slovenia seceded. Because more than 90 percent of the people here were ethnic Slovenes—and because Slovenia was careful to respect the rights of its minority populations—the break with Yugoslavia was simple and virtually uncontested. Its war for independence lasted just 10 days and claimed only a few dozen lives.

In May 2004, Slovenia became the first of the former Yugoslav republics to join the European Union. The Slovenes have been practical about this move, realizing it's essential for their survival as a tiny nation in a modern world. But there are tradeoffs, and "Euroskeptics" are down on EU bureaucracy. As borders disappear, Slovenes are experiencing more crime. Traditional farms are grappling with strict EU standards. Slovenian businesses are having difficulty competing with big German and other Western European firms. Before EU membership, only Slovenes could own Slovenian land, but now wealthy foreigners are buying property, driving up the cost of real estate. Still, overall, most Slovenes feel that EU membership was the right choice.

After independence, Slovenia impressed its European neighbors with its powerhouse economy and steady growth. However, the 2008 global financial crisis revealed that some of the affluence was deceptive: Many of Slovenia's biggest companies had been running up huge debts, which were assumed by Slovenia's big banks, devastating the economy.

In recent years, Slovenes have grown weary of a string of corrupt and incompetent politicians. One case study is Janez Janša, sometimes called the "Slovenian Trump," who became prime minister for the second time in 2011, was swept out of office amid a wave of protests, and eventually received a prison sentence for corruption. Janša returned as prime minister in 2020, but his party was soundly defeated in the 2022 elections. By contrast, a popular figure—at least in Ljubljana—is the visionary mayor Zoran Janković, who has reshaped the capital during his tenure.

In 2015, Slovenia became the focal point of a Europe-wide debate when a flood of refugees from Syria and other nations showed up at its border. Like its neighbors Croatia and Hungary, Slovenia grappled with the challenge of caring for the new arrivals even as it

Pršut

In Slovenia, Croatia, and Montenegro, *pršut* (purr-SHOOT) is one of the essential food groups. This air-cured ham (like Ital-

ian prosciutto) is soaked in salt and sometimes also smoked. Then it hangs in open-ended barns for up to a year and a half, to be dried and seasoned by the howling Bora wind. Each region produces a slightly different *pršut*. In Dalmatia, a layer of fat keeps the ham moist; in Istria, the fat is trimmed, and the *pršut* is drier.

Since Slovenia and Croatia joined the European Union, strict new standards have been imposed. Separate rooms must be used for the slaughter, preparation, and curing of the ham. While this seems fair enough for large producers, small family farms that want to make just enough *pršut* for their own use—and maybe sell one or two ham hocks to neighbors—find they must invest thousands of euros to be compliant.

facilitated their passage to wealthy Northern European countries. News reports suggested that Slovenia responded to this humanitarian crisis with pragmatic compassion.

While many refugees expressed relief at what a friendly and competent place Slovenia was, those of us who already loved the country were hardly shocked. The Slovenes are adjusting to the 21st century with their characteristic sense of humor and easygoing attitude, just as they've done throughout their history.

SLOVENIAN FOOD

Slovenes brag that their cuisine melds the best of Italian and German cooking—but they also embrace other international influences, especially French. Slovenian cuisine features many pan-Balkan elements: The savory phyllo-dough pastry *burek* is the favorite fast food here, and when Slovenes host a backyard barbecue, they grill up *čevapčiči* and *ražnjiči*, topped off with

the eggplant-and-red-bell-pepper condiment *ajvar*. Slovenia enjoys Italian-style dishes, with a pizza or pasta restaurant on seemingly every corner. Hungarian food simmers in the northeast (where many Magyars reside). And in much of the country, particularly near the mountains, traditional Slovenian food has a distinctly Germanic vibe—including the "four S's": sausages, schnitzels, strudels, and sauerkraut.

Traditional Slovenian meals come with a hearty helping of groats—a grainy mush made with buckwheat, barley, or corn. Buckwheat, which thrives in this climate, often appears on Slovenian menus. You'll also see plenty of *štruklji*, a dumpling-like savory layer cake that can be stuffed with cheese, meat, or vegetables. *Repa* is turnip prepared like sauerkraut. Among the hearty soups in Slovenia is *jota*—a staple for Karst peasants, made from *repa*, beans, vegetables, and often sausage.

Slovenia also has some good pastas. In addition to the familiar Italian-style pastas you'd find anywhere (gnocchi, called *njoki* here, tend to be popular and good), you may see some regional variations. *Fuži*, from Istria, in the southwest, are similar to penne but typically hand-rolled. *Žlikrofi*, from Idrija, are ravioli-like filled dumplings.

The cuisine of Slovenia's Karst region (the arid limestone plain south of Ljubljana) is notable. The small farms and wineries of this region have been inspired by Italy's Slow Food movement—their owners believe that cuisine is meant to be gradually appreciated, not rushed. The Karst's tasty air-dried ham *(pršut)*, available throughout the country, is worth seeking out (see sidebar). Istria (the peninsula just to the south of the Karst, in southern Slovenia and Croatia) produces truffles that, locals boast, are as good as those from Italy's Piedmont region. And in the hills just northwest of the Karst, the Goriška Brda wine region—surrounded on three sides by Italy—is a magnet for in-the-know foodies seeking top-quality wines and affordable high cuisine.

Voda is water, and *kava* is coffee. Radenska, in the bottle with the three little hearts, is Slovenia's best-known brand of mineral water—good enough that the word *Radenska* is synonymous with bottled water all over Slovenia. It's not common to ask for (or receive) tap water, but you can try requesting *voda iz pipe*.

Adventurous teetotalers should forgo the Coke and sample Cockta, a Slovenian cola with an unusual flavor (which supposedly comes from berry, lemon, orange, and 11 herbs). Originally called "Cockta-Cockta," the drink was introduced during the communist period as an alternative to the difficult-to-get Coca-Cola. This local variation developed a loyal following...until the Iron Curtain fell and the real Coke became readily available. Cockta sales plummeted. But in recent years—prodded by the slogan "The Taste of Your Youth"—nostalgic Slovenes are drinking Cockta once more.

The premier Slovenian brand of *pivo* (beer) is Union (OO-nee-

Slovenian Wines

It should come as no surprise that Slovenia produces excellent *vino* (wine). After all, this little country abuts well-respected wine-growing neighbors Italy and Hungary. In fact, Slovenia's winemaking tradition originated with its pre-Roman Illyrian and Celtic inhabitants, meaning that wine has been grown much longer here than in most of Europe. Wine standards plummeted with Yugoslav-era collectivization, but since independence, ambitious vintner families have been determined to bring quality back to Slovenian wines—with impressive results.

The best-known wine-growing region is **Primorska,** in the western hills between Ljubljana and the Adriatic. With a Mediterranean climate (hence its name: "by the sea"), Primorska is best known for its reds. Primorska's Goriška Brda ("Hillsides of Gorica") shares the terroir of Italy's Friuli/Venezia Giulia region (and its much-vaunted, DOC-classified Collio Goriziano wines). This area produces some of Slovenia's most respected wines, made mostly with internationally known grapes such as merlot and cabernet sauvignon. Goriška Brda also produces a good white using the *rebula* grape (in Italian, *ribolla gialla*). A bit farther south, the Karst grows lots of *refošk (refosco)* grapes, which thrive in iron-rich red soil *(terra rossa)*. The extremely full-bodied, "big" *teran* is infused with a high lactic acid content that supposedly gives the wine healing properties. Nearby coastal areas (around Koper) also grow *refošk,* along with the white *malvazija* grape.

To the northeast, near Hungary, the **Podravje** region (the Drava River Valley) is dominated by white grapes—especially *laški riesling* (Welsh riesling) and *renski riesling* (what we'd call simply riesling). In Ptuj or Maribor, local menus list wines produced on the steeper right bank of the Drava River (Haloze) and the left bank (Slovenske Gorice, "Slovenian Hills").

And finally, a bit to the south of Podravje is the **Posavje** region (the Lower Sava River Valley, bordering Croatia). This area, which is still focused on quantity over quality, produces both white and red wines; it's known mostly for the light, russet-colored *cviček* wine (a blend of red and white grapes).

With any Slovenian wine, *vrhunsko* (premium) is a mark of quality, *kakovostno* is a notch down, and *namizno* is a table wine. Other key terms are *suho* (dry), *sladko* (sweet), and *pol-* (half).

One Slovenian wine that has gotten the world's attention recently is **orange wine** (or amber wine). Orange wines go back some 6,000 years but were revived a few decades ago by a Slovenian vintner just across the border in Italy's Friuli-Venezia Giulia. Now produced in the Primorska region, orange wine is essentially a white wine that's processed like a red wine, which means it's left to age with its grape skins to impart a unique color and flavor. Orange wines are best drunk at a temperature somewhere between a chilled white and a room-temperature red; are typically robust, both fruity and dry; and pair well with strong flavors.

ohn), but you'll also see a lot of Laško (LASH-koh), whose mascot is the Zlatorog (or "Golden Horn," a mythical chamois-like animal). For the full story on Slovenian wines, see the sidebar.

Regardless of what you're drinking, to toast, say, *"Na ZDROW-yeh!"*—if you can't remember it, think of "Nice driving!"

Slovenia's national dessert is *potica*, a rolled pastry with walnuts and sometimes also raisins. Although traditionally eaten at Christmas, it's available year-round. Slovenes eat it from the hard outer crust in, saving the nutty center for last. Locals brag that Ljubljana has the finest gelato outside Italy—which, after all, is just an hour down the road. And I agree.

SLOVENIAN LANGUAGE

While the casual tourist won't notice, Slovene is markedly different from the languages spoken in the other former Yugoslav republics. Serbian and Croatian are mutually intelligible; Slovene is gibberish to Serbs and Croats. Most Slovenes, on the other hand, know Serbo-Croatian because, a generation ago, everybody in Yugoslavia had to learn it.

Linguists have identified some 46 official dialects of Slovene, and there are probably another 100 or so unofficial ones. Locals can instantly tell which city—or sometimes even which remote mountain valley—someone comes from by their accent.

The tiny country of Slovenia borders Italy and Austria, with important historical and linguistic ties to both. For self-preservation, Slovenes have always been forced to function in many different languages. All of these factors make them excellent linguists. Most young Slovenes speak flawless English effortlessly—then admit that they've never set foot in the United States or Britain, but love watching American movies and TV shows (which are always subtitled, never dubbed).

In Slovene, *c* is pronounced "ts" (as in "cats"). The letter *j* is pronounced as "y"—making "Ljubljana" easier to say than it looks (lyoob-lyee-AH-nah). Slovene only has one diacritical mark: the *strešica*, or "little roof." This makes *č* sound like "ch," *š* sound like "sh," and *ž* sound like "zh" (as in "measure"). The letter *v* is pronounced like "u"—so the Slovenian word *avto* sounds like "auto," and the mountain Triglav is pronounced "TREE-glau" (rhymes with "cow").

The only trick: As in English, which syllable gets the emphasis is unpredictable.

Learn some key Slovene phrases (see the Slovene survival phrases on the next page). You'll make more friends and your trip will go more smoothly.

Slovene Survival Phrases

In the phonetics, ī sounds like the long i in "light," and bolded syllables are stressed. The vowel "eh" sometimes sounds closer to "ay" (depending on the speaker).

Hello. (formal)	Dober dan.	**doh**-behr dahn
Hi. / Bye. (informal)	Živjo.	**zheev**-yoh
Do you speak English?	Ali govorite angleško? **ah**-lee goh-voh-**ree**-teh ahn-**glehsh**-koh	
Yes. / No.	Ja. / Ne.	yah / neh
I (don't) understand.	(Ne) razumem.	(neh) rah-**zoo**-mehm
Please. / You're welcome.	Prosim.	**proh**-seem
Thank you (very much).	Hvala (lepa).	**hvah**-lah (**leh**-pah)
I'm sorry. / Excuse me.	Oprostite.	oh-proh-**stee**-teh
No problem.	Ni problema.	nee proh-**bleh**-mah
Good.	Dobro.	**doh**-broh
Goodbye.	Na svidenje.	nah **svee**-dehn-yeh
one / two / three	ena / dve / tri	**eh**-nah / dveh / tree
hundred / thousand	sto / tisoč	stoh / **tee**-sohch
How much?	Koliko?	**koh**-lee-koh
local currency	euro	**ee**-oo-roh
Write it?	Napišite?	nah-**peesh**-ee-teh
Is it free?	Ali je brezplačno?	**ah**-lee yeh brehz-**plahch**-noh
Is it included?	Ali je vključeno?	**ah**-lee yeh vuk-**lyoo**-cheh-noh
Where can I find / buy...?	Kje lahko najdem / kupim...? kyeh **lah**-koh **nī**-dehm / **koo**-peem	
I'd like / We'd like...	Želel / Želeli bi...	zheh-**lehl** / zheh-**leh**-lee bee
...a room.	...sobo.	**soh**-boh
...a ticket to ____.	...vozovnico do ____. voh-**zohv**-neet-soh doh ____.	
Is it possible?	Ali je možno?	**ah**-lee yeh **mohzh**-noh
Where is...?	Kje je...?	kyeh yeh
...the train station	...železniška postaja zheh-**lehz**-neesh-kah pohs-**tī**-yah	
...the bus station	...avtobusna postaja	ow-toh-boos-nah pohs-**tī**-yah
...tourist information	...turistično informacijski center too-**rees**-teech-noh een-for-maht-**see**-skee **tsehn**-tehr	
...the toilet	...vece (WC)	**veht**-seh
men / women	moški / ženski	**mohsh**-kee / **zhehn**-skee
left / right / straight	levo / desno / naravnost **leh**-voh / **dehs**-noh / nah-**rahv**-nohst	
At what time?	Ob kateri uri...?	ohb kah-**teh**-ree **oo**-ree
...does this open / close	...se odpre / zapre	seh ohd-**preh** / zah-**preh**
(Just) a moment.	(Samo) trenutek.	(sah-**moh**) treh-**noo**-tehk
now / soon / later	zdaj / kmalu / pozneje zuh-**dī** / kuh-**mah**-loo / pohz-**neh**-yeh	
today / tomorrow	danes / jutri	**dah**-nehs / **yoo**-tree

In a Slovene Restaurant

I'd like to reserve...	Rezerviral bi...	reh-zehr-**vee**-rahl bee
We'd like to reserve...	Rezervirali bi...	reh-zehr-vee-**rah**-lee bee
...a table for one / two.	...mizo za enega / dva.	
	mee-zoh zah **eh**-neh-gah / dvah	
Is this table free?	Ali je ta miza prosta?	
	ah-lee yeh tah **mee**-zah **proh**-stah	
Can I help you?	Izvolite?	eez-**voh**-lee-teh
The menu (in English), please	Jedilni list (v angleščini), prosim.	
	yeh-**deel**-nee leest (vuh ahn-**glehsh**-chee-nee) **proh**-seem	
service (not) included	postrežba (ni) vključena	
	post-**rehzh**-bah (nee) vuk-**lyoo**-cheh-nah	
cover charge	pogrinjek	poh-**green**-yehk
to go	za s sabo	zah **sah**-boh
with / without	z / brez	zuh / brehz
and / or	in / ali	een / **ah**-lee
fixed-price meal (of the day)	(dnevni) meni	
	(duh-**new**-nee) meh-**nee**	
specialty of the house	specialiteta hiše	speht-see-ah-lee-**teh**-tah **hee**-sheh
half portion	polovična porcija	poh-loh-**veech**-nah **port**-see-yah
daily special	dnevna ponudba	duh-**new**-nah poh-**nood**-bah
fixed-price meal for tourists	turistični meni	
	too-**rees**-teech-nee meh-**nee**	
breakfast / lunch / dinner	zajtrk / kosilo / večerjo	
	zī-turk / koh-**see**-loh / veh-**chehr**-yoh	
appetizers	predjedi	prehd-yeh-**dee**
bread / cheese	kruh / sir	krooh / seer
sandwich	sendvič	**send**-veech
soup / salad	juha / solata	**yoo**-hah / sol-**lah**-tah
meat / poultry	meso / perutnina	meh-**soh** / peh-root-**nee**-nah
fish / seafood	riba / morska hrana	**ree**-bah / **mor**-skah **hrah**-nah
fruit / vegetables	sadje / zelenjava	**sahd**-yeh / zeh-lehn-**yah**-vah
dessert	sladica	slah-**deet**-sah
(tap) water	voda (iz pipe)	**voh**-dah (eez **pee**-peh)
mineral water	mineralna voda	mee-neh-**rahl**-nah **voh**-dah
milk	mleko	**mleh**-koh
(orange) juice	(pomarančni) sok	(poh-mah-**rahnch**-nee) sohk
coffee / tea	kava / čaj	**kah**-vah / chī
wine / beer	vino / pivo	**vee**-noh / **pee**-voh
red / white	rdeče / belo	ahr-**deh**-cheh / **beh**-loh
glass / bottle	kozarec / steklenica	
	koh-**zah**-rehts / stehk-leh-**neet**-sah	
Cheers!	Na zdravje!	nah **zdrow**-yeh
More. / Another.	Še. / Še eno.	sheh / sheh **eh**-noh
The same.	Isto.	**ees**-toh
Bill, please.	Račun, prosim.	rah-**choon proh**-seem
tip	napitnina	nah-peet-**nee**-nah
Delicious!	Odlično!	ohd-**leech**-noh

LJUBLJANA

Ljubljana (lyoob-lyee-AH-nah) is irresistible. With a lazy Old Town clustered around a castle-topped hill, Slovenia's capital is often likened to Salzburg. It's an apt comparison—but only if you inject a healthy dose of fun-and-breezy Adriatic culture, add a Slavic accent, and replace favorite son Mozart with local architect Jože Plečnik.

Ljubljana feels smaller than its population of 280,000. With several clusters of good museums that try hard—but have only so much to say—it does its best to please sightseers. But ultimately, this town is all about ambience. The idyllic, cobbled core of Ljubljana is slathered with one-of-a-kind architecture. Festivals fill the summer, and people enjoy a Sunday stroll any day of the week. Fashion boutiques and al fresco cafés jockey for control of the Old Town, while the leafy riverside promenade crawls with stylishly dressed students sipping *kava* and polishing their near-perfect English. Laid-back Ljubljana is the kind of place where graffiti and crumbling buildings seem elegantly atmospheric instead of shoddy. And even those shoddy buildings have been getting a facelift recently. At the same time, city leadership has been creating gleaming traffic-free zones left and right—turning what was already an exceptionally livable city into a pedestrians' paradise.

Batted around by history, Ljubljana has seen cultural influences from all sides—most notably Prague, Vienna, and Venice. This has left the city a happy hodgepodge of cultures. Being the midpoint between the Slavic, Germanic, and Italian worlds gives Ljubljana a special spice.

The Story of Ljubljana

In ancient times, Ljubljana was on the trade route connecting the Mediterranean (just 60 miles away) to the Black Sea. (Toss a bottle off the bridge here, and it can float to the Danube and, eventually, all the way to Russia.) Legend has it that Jason and his Argonauts founded Ljubljana on their way home with the Golden Fleece. Some stories say Jason slayed a dragon here, while others attribute that feat to St. George; the dragon is the city mascot.

During the Neolithic and Bronze ages, the area's earliest inhabitants lived in rustic houses on tall wooden piles in the marshy lands surrounding today's city center. Sometimes called "crannog dwellers" (after similar homes in the Scottish Highlands), these ancient Ljubljanans left behind precious few artifacts, save for half of a wooden wheel and axle (on display at the City Museum).

The area was later populated by the Illyrians and Celts, and was eventually Romanized before being overrun by Huns, only to be resettled by Slavs—the ancestors of today's Slovenes.

In 1335, Ljubljana fell under the Habsburg emperors, who called it Laibach and steered its development for the next six centuries. Slovenian language and culture were considered backward, as most of Laibach's inhabitants spoke German and lived essentially Austrian lifestyles. This Austrian vibe persists today, thanks to abundant Austrian Baroque and Viennese Art Nouveau architecture.

Napoleon named Ljubljana the capital of his Illyrian Prov-

PLANNING YOUR TIME

Ljubljana deserves at least a full day. Rather than checking off a list of museums, spend most of your time strolling the pleasant town center, exploring the many interesting squares and architectural gems, browsing the produce market, shopping at the boutiques, and sipping coffee at sidewalk cafés along the river.

Here's the best plan for a low-impact sightseeing day: Begin on Prešeren Square, the heart of the city, and follow my "Ljubljana Walk" through town—including a browse through the riverside market area. Then wander south through the Krakovo gardens to tour the Jože Plečnik House. In the afternoon, commit some quality time to people-watching at a riverside café, window shopping at some colorful boutiques in the Old Town, or enjoying more sightseeing (good options include the City Museum of Ljubljana; the Serbian Orthodox Church and Tivoli Park, with the Contemporary History Museum, west of downtown; or the Slovenian Ethnographic Museum and other sights in Metelkova, north of downtown).

Ljubljana is sleepy on Sundays: Many shops are closed and the produce market is quiet, but museums are generally open, a mod-

inces, a realm that stretched from the Danube to Dubrovnik and from Austria to Albania (1809-1813). For the first time, the Slovene language was taught in schools, awakening a newfound pride in Slovenian cultural heritage.

In the mid-19th century, the railway connecting Vienna to the Adriatic (at Trieste) was built through town—and Ljubljana boomed. An earthquake rocked the city in 1895, damaging many buildings. Emperor Franz Josef took pity on the city and invested generously in its reconstruction. Ljubljana was made over with Art Nouveau flair. A generation later, architect Jože Plečnik bathed the city in his distinctive classical-meets-modern style.

In World War II, Slovenia was occupied first by the Italians, then by the Nazis. The Nazis couldn't suppress Ljubljana's resistance—so they fenced off the entire city and made it a giant prison, allowing in only basic food shipments. But the Slovenes continued to slip in and out of town undetected, allowing them to agitate through the end of the war.

In 1991, Ljubljana became the capital of one of Europe's youngest nations. Today the city is filled with university students, making it feel very youthful. Ljubljana is on the cutting edge when it comes to architecture, urban planning, public art, fashion, and trendy pubs—a trend encouraged by its larger-than-life mayor, Zoran Janković.

est flea market stretches along the riverfront, and the TI's walking tour still runs. The city is also relatively quiet in August, when the students are on break and locals head to beach resorts.

From late spring through early fall, foodies should aim to be in Ljubljana on a Friday to enjoy the fun "Open Kitchen" street-food festival (see "Eating in Ljubljana," later).

Orientation to Ljubljana

Ljubljana's central zone is compact, and with a little wandering, you'll quickly get the hang of it. The Ljubljanica River—lined with cafés, restaurants, and a buzzing outdoor market—bisects the city, making a 90-degree turn around the base of a castle-topped hill. Most sights are either along or just a short walk from the river. Visitors enjoy the distinctive bridges that span the Ljubljanica, including the landmark Triple Bridge (Tromostovje) and pillared Cobblers' Bridge (Čevljarski Most)—both designed by Jože Plečnik. Between these two is a plain bridge (with great views) called Brv. The center of Ljubljana is Prešeren Square, watched over by a big statue of Slovenia's national poet, France Prešeren.

I've organized the sights in this chapter based on which side of the river they're on: the east (castle) side of the river, where Ljubljana began, which has more medieval charm; and the west (Prešeren Square) side of the river, which has a more Baroque/Art Nouveau feel and most of the urban sprawl. At the northern edge of the tourist's Ljubljana is the train station and Metelkova museum and nightlife zone, at the southern edge are the garden district of Krakovo and the Jože Plečnik House, and at the western edge is Tivoli Park.

Ljubljana's Two Big Ps: You'll hear the following two easy-to-confuse names constantly during your visit. Mind your Ps, and your visit to Ljubljana becomes more meaningful: **Jože Plečnik** (YOH-zheh PLAYCH-neek, 1872-1957) is the architect who shaped Ljubljana, designing nearly all the city's most important landmarks. **France Prešeren** (FRAHN-tseh preh-SHAY-rehn, 1800-1849) is Slovenia's greatest poet and the namesake of Ljubljana's main square.

TOURIST INFORMATION

Ljubljana's helpful, businesslike TI is centrally located facing the **Triple Bridge,** across from Prešeren Square (Mon-Sat 8:00-18:00—may stay open until 19:00 in summer, Sun 8:00-15:00, Stritarjeva 1, +386 1 306 1215, www.visitljubljana.com).

The **Ljubljana Tourist Card,** which includes access to public transportation and covers entry to many city museums as well as the TI's walking tours and boat trips, could save busy sightseers some money (€36/24 hours, €44/48 hours, €49/72 hours).

ARRIVAL IN LJUBLJANA

By Train: Ljubljana's train station (Železniška Postaja) is at the northern edge of the city center. Emerging from the passage up to track 1a, turn right and walk under the long canopy to find the yellow arrivals hall. Everything is well signed in English; most services are in or near the big ticket office at the front of the station. Arrivals are *prihodi,* departures are *odhodi,* and track is *tir.*

You can **walk** to any of my recommended hotels within about 20 minutes (often less). To reach Prešeren Square at the city's center, exit the station to the right and walk a long block along the busy Trg Osvobodilne Fronte (or "Trg O.F." for short, with the bus station in the middle). After passing the bus stalls, turn left across Trg O.F. and go down Miklošičeva (look for the building with the round, red-brick columns). This takes you past some of Ljubljana's most appealing architecture to Prešeren Square.

Avoid unscrupulous **taxis** waiting to spring on unsuspecting tourists at the station—call one that charges fair rates instead (less than €10 to any of my recommended hotels). Waiting just a few more minutes for your cab could easily save you €10 or more. See "Getting Around Ljubljana—By Taxi," later, for recommended taxi companies. (Uber doesn't operate in Slovenia.)

By Bus: Ljubljana's bus station (Autobusna Postaja) is a low-profile building (with ticket windows, a bakery, and newsstands) in the middle of Trg O.F., right in front of the train station. To reach the city center from here, follow the directions under "By Train," earlier.

By Car: Ljubljana is not car-friendly; much of the central zone along the river is entirely traffic-free. Even several blocks of the main thoroughfare, Slovenska Cesta—north of Congress Square, between Šubičeva Ulica and Gosposvetska Cesta—are closed to all traffic except buses. To reach the southern part of the city when entering downtown from the north, you need to circumnavigate the core by looping east along Resljeva Cesta, over the Dragon Bridge by the market, and through the tunnel beneath the castle; from here, Karlovška Cesta cuts back west over the river to the southern stretch of Slovenska Cesta.

Ask your hotel about parking—most have some available, usually for a price. There are two central parking lots, one beneath **Congress Square** and one called **N.U.K. II,** near the National and University Library. Both lots are accessible on Slovenska Cesta only from the south—if coming from the north, see previous directions for looping around town. Another handy lot is **Kapitelj,** just southeast of the Dragon Bridge. If staying overnight, plan to pay about €25-30.

Paid street parking downtown is marked by blue lines (look for meters); these spaces are free Saturdays after 13:00 and all day Sunday. For cheaper parking and longer stays, you can park along the river just south of downtown (in zone 3, south of St. James Bridge—see the "Ljubljana" map). Along here, parking is less than €1/hour, and free on weeknights between 17:00 and 7:00 and all day Sat-Sun.

There's a huge **gas station** on Tivolska Cesta (just west of the train station, near the big Pivovarna Union brewery). It's handy if you're returning a rental car in central Ljubljana.

By Plane: See "Ljubljana Connections" at the end of this chapter.

LJUBLJANA

Ljubljana

To Contemporary History Museum

Tivoli Park

To Pivovarna Union Brewery

GOSPOSVETSKA

KERSNIKOVA ULICA

SLOVENSKA CESTA

CIGALETOVA

Ajdovščina Park

Miklošičev Park

DALMATINOVA ULICA

TIVOLSKA

SERBIAN ORTHODOX CHURCH

NATIONAL GALLERY

ŠTEFANOVA ULICA

CANKARJEVA CESTA

THE SKYSCRAPER

SLOVENSKA CESTA

NAZORJEVA ULICA

GRAND HOTEL UNION

MODERN ART MUSEUM

NATIONAL THEATER

POST

ČOPOVA ULICA

FRANCISCAN CHURCH

US EMBASSY

TOMŠIČEVA

ULICA

Prešeren Square

SLOVENIAN NATIONAL MUSEUM & NATURAL HISTORY MUSEUM

Trg Narodni Herojev

GUBIČEVA

PARLIAMENT

Square of the Republic

UNDER-PASS

MEM. TO THE VICTIMS OF ALL WARS

TRIPLE BRIDGE

MUSEUM ZONE & TIVOLI PARK WALK

ANCHOR

WOLFOVA

BRV BRIDGE

Ribji Square

ERJAVČEVA CESTA

Congress Square

River

TWIN OFFICE TOWERS

SLOVENSKA CESTA

OLD

PREŠERNOVA

GREGORČIČEVA ULICA

ULICA

ULICA

COBBLERS BRIDGE

IGRIŠKA ULICA

VEGOVA

UNIVERSITY

Novi Trg

STARI TRG

MEŠTNI TRG

RIMSKA CESTA

French Revolution Square

NATIONAL & UNIVERSITY LIBRARY

FOUNTAIN

AŠKERČEVA

SLOVENSKA CESTA

N.U.K. II

KRIŽANKE THEATER

GOSPOSKA

CITY MUSEUM

BREG

Ljubljanica

LEVITSKOV TRG

KEBER

ZOISOVA CESTA

ST. JAMES BRIDGE

ROMAN CITY WALL

MIRJE

Krakovo Gardens

EMONSKA CESTA

Krakovo Gardens

FOOTBRIDGE

BARJANSKA CESTA

KRAKOVO

REČNA UL.

GRADAŠKA ULICA

PLEČNIK HOUSE

EIPPROVA ULICA

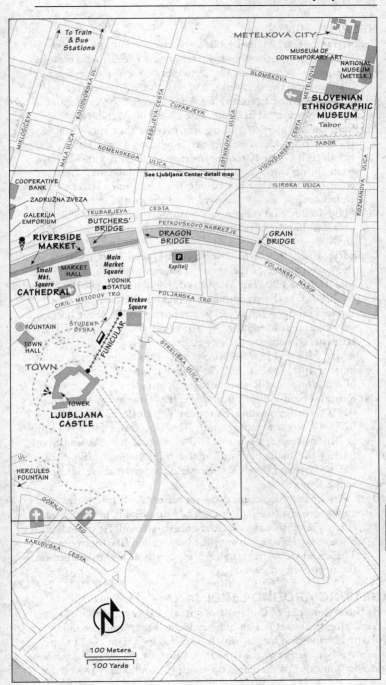

HELPFUL HINTS

Pedestrian Safety: Many Ljubljana residents commute by bike—and they're not shy about whizzing past pedestrians, even in seemingly "pedestrian-only" areas. Stay out of the designated bike lanes on the sidewalks, and stay aware everywhere.

Closed Days: Most Ljubljana museums (except the castle and a few less-important museums) are closed on Mondays.

Markets: In addition to the regular **market** that sprawls along the riverfront (described in my "Ljubljana Walk," later), the wonderful **Open Kitchen** street-food festival runs Fridays from spring through fall (see "Eating in Ljubljana," later). A colorful **flea market** hops along the Ljubljanica River's Breg embankment, across the river from the castle, every Sunday (8:00-14:00), and on summer Saturdays a lively and colorful **arts and handicrafts market** runs in the same place (8:00-16:00).

Laundry: The handy self-service **Speed Queen** launderette is at the western edge of the center, a short walk from downtown (daily 6:00-24:00, Trg Mladinskih Delovnih Brigad 10, +386 64 229 007). The recommended **Hostel Celica** also has self-service laundry—but hostel guests have priority (cheap but not very central at Metelkova 8). For pricey full service, try **Tekstilexpress,** between the city center and Tivoli Park (takes 24 hours, Mon-Fri 7:00-18:00, Sat 9:00-13:00, closed Sun, Cankarjeva 10B, +386 1 252 7354). For locations, see the "Ljubljana Hotels and Restaurants" map, later.

Car Rental: Handy options include **Hertz** (Trdinova 9, +386 1 434 0147, www.hertz.com), **Europcar** (Miklošičeva 15, +386 59 077 040, www.europcar.com), **Avis** (in Grand Hotel Union at Miklošičeva 3, +386 1 421 7340, www.avis.com), and **Sixt** (facing the main platform at the train station, +386 1 234 4650, www.sixt.com). You can also rent from these agencies at the airport.

Best Views: The **Skyscraper's observation deck** offers the best views in town (see listing under "More Sights in Ljubljana," later). Views from the **castle** are nearly as good. At street level, my favorite views are from the bridge called **Brv** (between the Triple and Cobblers' bridges)—especially at night—and from the river promenade.

GETTING AROUND LJUBLJANA

By Bus: Almost all of Ljubljana's sights are easily accessible by foot. And using the buses is a bit of a headache: First, you have to buy a plastic Urbana card for €2, which you then load with credit to pay for rides (you can't pay the driver). A ride costs €1.30 (valid for up to 90 minutes, card shareable by multiple people). Buy the card at the TI, where you can return it to reclaim your €2 at the end of your trip. Transit info: www.lpp.si.

By Taxi: Always call for a cab, or you'll get ripped off. Legitimate taxis usually start at about €2, and then charge €1.50 per kilometer. But many unscrupulous cabbies legally charge far more and tack on bogus additional "surcharges." (Because fares are unregulated, even if they use the meter you'll still pay way too much.) However, if you call a reputable taxi company, Ljubljana is a good taxi town—a ride within the city center (such as from the station to a hotel) should run less than €10. Good companies include **Laguna** (+386 1 511 2314 or mobile +386 31 492 299), **Metro Taxi** (80 1190 from a Slovenian phone, or mobile +386 41 240 200), and **Cammeo** (+386 1 777 1212). Dispatchers speak English, and your hotel, restaurant, or the TI can call a cab for you.

By Bike: Ljubljana is a cyclist's delight, with lots of well-marked bike lanes. It's easiest to rent bikes at the TI (€6/2 hours, €10/4 hours, €14/day). Like many European cities, Ljubljana has a subsidized borrow-a-bike program (called BicikeLJ) with more than 60 locations around the city center. Once you register online with a credit card, rides are free or very cheap (free for the first hour, €1 for the second, €2 for the third, and so on). If you're planning on doing lots of biking, it's worth the hassle to sign up (http://en.bicikelj.si).

By Shuttle: A fleet of green electric carts, called **Kavalirs,** shuttle anyone (even tourists) around the traffic-free downtown pedestrian zone for free. Just wave one down and tell them where you want to go (or phone them at +386 31 666 331 or +386 31 666 332).

Tours in Ljubljana

To help you appreciate Ljubljana, taking a walking tour—either through the TI or by hiring your own local guide—is worth ▲▲.

Walking Tours

The TI organizes excellent two-hour guided town walks of Ljubljana in English, led by knowledgeable guides (€17, daily at 11:00). In summer, they offer a second tour each afternoon at 14:00 that includes a boat trip (€22). Tours meet at Town Hall, around the corner from the Triple Bridge and TI. They also offer a variety of themed tours, including ones that focus on the architectural works of Jože Plečnik. For details and to book, check www.visitljubljana.com, or ask at the TI.

Local Guides

Having an expert show you around his or her hometown for two hours for €100 has to be the best value going (extra for more than two people). **Marijan Kriškovič,** who leads tours for me throughout Europe, is an outstanding guide (+386 40 222 739, kriskovic@ yahoo.com). **Barbara Jakopič,** thoughtful and extremely knowl-edgeable, also leads my tours (+386 40 530 870, jakopic_b@yahoo. com). You can also book a guide through the TI (at least 24 hours in advance).

Boat Cruise

A boat trip on the Ljubljanica River is more romantic than thrill-ing. You'll see multiple companies hawking these €10, one-hour cruises all along the river in the center. But if you'd like some com-mentary en route, it's best to take the TI's version, which is nar-rated by a live guide (€15, 2/day in summer, get details at TI). Most other companies don't have any commentary, though some may have recorded spiels (ask before you buy).

Excursions from Ljubljana

Many worthwhile sights near Ljubljana are tricky to reach by pub-lic transportation. Popular options include the caves at Škocjan and Postojna, Predjama Castle, Lipica Stud Farm, Lake Bled, and the coastal town of Piran. It's possible to link up several of these in a (long) day on a 10-hour excursion, for around €90-100. Three relatively well-established outfits are **Roundabout** (www.travelroundabout.com), **Slovenia Explorer** (www.slovenia-explorer.com), and **To Do in Slovenia** (www.todoinslovenia.com). **Nature Adventures** focuses on active trips including rafting, para-gliding, skydiving, and horseback riding (www.adventures-nature. com).

Ljubljana Walk

This walk—which meanders in a big loop on both sides of the river—offers an orientation for your Ljubljana wanderings. The whole walk takes about 1.5 hours (without entering sights). You'll end just a few steps from where you begin, but along the way I'll point out a few possible detours. (Ljubljana is so small and enjoy-able to stroll that you'll be doing lots of circling back.)

• *Begin on the main square right in the center of Ljubljana, marked by the can't-miss-it pink church.*

PREŠEREN SQUARE AREA

▲▲Prešeren Square (Prešernov Trg)

This square is the heart of Ljubljana. The city's meeting point is the large **statue of France Prešeren,** Slovenia's greatest poet, whose works include the lyrics to the Slovenian national anthem (and whose silhouette adorns Slovenia's €2 coin). The statue shows Prešeren, an important catalyst of 19th-century Slovenian nation-alism, being inspired from above by a Muse. This statue provoked

Ljubljana at a Glance

▲▲▲People-Watching Ljubljana's single best activity is sitting at an outdoor café along the river and watching the vivacious, stylish, fun-loving Slovenes strut their stuff.

▲▲Riverside Market Lively market area in the Old Town with produce, clothing, and souvenirs. **Hours:** Best in the morning, especially Sat; market hall open Mon-Fri 7:00-16:00, Sat until 14:00, closed Sun. See page 738.

▲▲Serbian Orthodox Church of Sts. Cyril and Methodius Beautifully decorated house of worship giving insight into the Orthodox faith. **Hours:** Daily 8:00-19:00. See page 757.

▲▲National and University Library Jože Plečnik's pièce de résistance, with an intriguing facade, piles of books, and a bright reading room. **Hours:** Main staircase open Mon-Fri 10:00-18:00, Sat until 14:00, closed Sun except in summer; student reading room open to the public mid-July-mid-Aug Mon-Sat 10:00-18:00, Sun 11:00-19:00, rest of year Sat 14:30-18:00. See page 745.

▲▲Jože Plečnik House Final digs of the famed hometown architect who shaped so much of Ljubljana, explained by an enthusiastic guide. **Hours:** Tue-Sun 10:00-18:00, English tours begin at the top of each hour, last tour departs at 17:00, closed Mon. See page 752.

▲▲Slovenian Ethnographic Museum Engaging, well-presented collection celebrating Slovenian culture. **Hours:** Tue-Sun 10:00-18:00, closed Mon. See page 760.

▲Cathedral Italian Baroque interior and bronze doors with intricate, highly symbolic designs. **Hours:** Generally daily 11:00-18:00 but opens Tue at 14:00 and Sun at 13:30, on weekends closes for an hour around 15:30. See page 741.

▲Ljubljana Castle Tower with good views and so-so 3-D film. **Hours**: Castle daily 9:00-21:00, grounds until 23:00, both have shorter hours Oct-May. See page 749.

▲Contemporary History Museum Baroque mansion in Tivoli Park, with exhibit highlighting Slovenia's last 100 years. **Hours:** Tue-Sun 10:00-18:00, Thu until 20:00 June-Aug, closed Mon. See page 758.

▲City Museum of Ljubljana Modern, high-tech exhibit covering the city's history. **Hours:** Tue-Sun 10:00-18:00, Thu until 21:00, closed Mon. See page 747.

a scandal and outraged the bishop when it went up a century ago—a naked woman sharing the square with a church! To ensure that nobody could be confused about the woman's intentions, she's conspicuously depicted with typical Muse accessories: a laurel branch and a cloak. Even so, for the first few years citizens covered the scandalous statue with a tarp each night. And the model who posed for the Muse was the subject of so much criticism that no one in Slovenia would hire her—so she emigrated to South America and never returned.

Stand at the base of the statue to get oriented. The bridge crossing the Ljubljanica River is one of Ljubljana's top landmarks, Jože

Plečnik's **Triple Bridge** (Tromostovje). The middle (widest) part of this bridge already existed, but Plečnik added the two side spans to more efficiently funnel the six streets of traffic on this side of the bridge to the one street on the other side. (Now, delightfully, there's no car traffic at all.) The bridge's Venetian vibe is intentional: Plečnik recognized that Ljubljana, located midway between Venice and then-capital Vienna, is itself a bridge between the Italian and Germanic worlds. Across the bridge are the TI, WCs, ATMs, the market and cathedral (to the left), and the Town Hall (straight ahead).

Now turn 90 degrees to the right and look down the first street after the riverbank. Find the orange woman in the picture frame on the upper floor of the first yellow house. This is **Julija Primic,** the unrequited love of Prešeren's life. Tour guides spin romantic tales about how the two met. But the truth is that Prešeren was a teacher in the Primic household when he was in his 30s and she was 4. Later in life, she inspired him from afar—as she does now, from across the square. Julija may have been his muse, but it's not clear how she felt about Prešeren (she married a wealthy Bavarian).

When Ljubljana was hit by an earthquake in 1895, locals

took the opportunity (using an ample rebuilding fund from the Austro-Hungarian Empire) to remake their city in style. Today, Ljubljana—especially the streets around this square—is an architecture-lover's paradise. The **Hauptmann House,** to the right of Julija, was the only building on the square to survive the quake. A few years later, the owner redecorated it in the then-trendy Viennese Art Nouveau style you see today, using bright colors (his family sold dyes). All that remains of the original structure is the little Baroque balcony above the entrance.

Just to the right of the Hauptmann House is a car-sized **model** of the city center—helpful for orientation. The street next to it is **Čopova,** once the route of Ljubljana's Sunday promenade. A century ago, locals would put on their Sunday best and stroll from here to Tivoli Park, listening to musicians and dropping into cafés along the way. Plečnik called it the "lifeline of the city," connecting the green lungs of the park to this urban center.

Continue looking to the right, past the big, pink landmark **Franciscan Church of St. Mary** (not much to see inside). Farther right, the character-istic glass awning marks **Galerija Emporium**—the first big post-quake department store, today government-protected. At the top of the building is Mercury, god of commerce, watching over the square that has been Ljubljana's

commercial heart since the city began. (If you look carefully, you can see the mustachioed face of the building's owner hiding in the folds of cloth by Mercury's left foot.) Because this area was across the river from medieval Ljubljana (beyond the town's limits...and the long arm of its tax collector), it was the best place to buy and sell goods. Today, this sumptuously restored building houses a top-end fashion mall, making it the heart of Ljubljana's boutique culture. Step inside for a glimpse of the grand staircase.

The street between Galerija Emporium and the pink church is **Miklošičeva Cesta,** which connects Prešeren Square to the train station.

• *Go a short block up this street to see some striking architecture.*

Miklošičeva Cesta

When Ljubljana was rebuilding after the 1895 earthquake, town architects and designers envisioned this street as a showcase of its new Art Nouveau image. Ahead on the left is the prominent **Grand Hotel Union,** with a stately domed spire on the corner.

Ljubljana Center

To Tivoli Park

NAZORJEVA ULICA

ČOPOVA ULICA

SLOVENSKA CESTA

POST

GRAND HOTEL UNION

COOPERATIVE BANK

ZADRUŽNA ZVEZA

MIKLOŠIČEVA

FRANCISCAN CHURCH

GALERIJA EMPORIUM

CITY MODEL

Prešeren Square

FRANCE PREŠEREN STATUE

HAUPTMANN HOUSE

JULIJA RELIEF

TRIPLE BRIDGE

LJUBLJANA WALK BEGINS

CONE

To Square of the Republic & Museum Zone & Tivoli Park Walk

MEM. TO THE VICTIMS OF ALL WARS

ZVEZDA KAVARNA

WOLFOVA

OLD

WC (IN UNDERPASS)

ROMAN CITIZEN STATUE

ANCHOR

WALK ENDS

Congress Square

BRV BRIDGE

Ribji Square

FOUNTAIN OF 3 RIVERS

Town Square

TOWN HALL

River

ROMANTIKA GELATO

BEST RIVERBANK CAFÉS

TOWN

GUJŽINA GALERIJA IDRIJSKE ČIPKE

HONEY HOUSE

DOBROTE DOLENJSKE

PIRANSKE SOLINE

MESTNI TRG

ULICA

UNIVERSITY

VEGOVA

GOSPOSKA

COBBLERS' BRIDGE

CHA

CAFETINO

LE POTICA

ROMANTIKA GELATO

OSEM

ALTROKÈ

STARI TRG

TURJAŠKA

Novi Trg

WC

French Revolution Square

NATIONAL & UNIVERSITY LIBRARY (N.U.K.)

KEBER UL.

BREG

Ljubljanica

CITY MUSEUM

KRIŽANKE THEATER

HERCULES FOUNTAIN

GORNJI

STIŠKA ULICA

P N.U.K. II

EMONSKA

To Plečnik House & Trnovo Church

Levitskov Trg

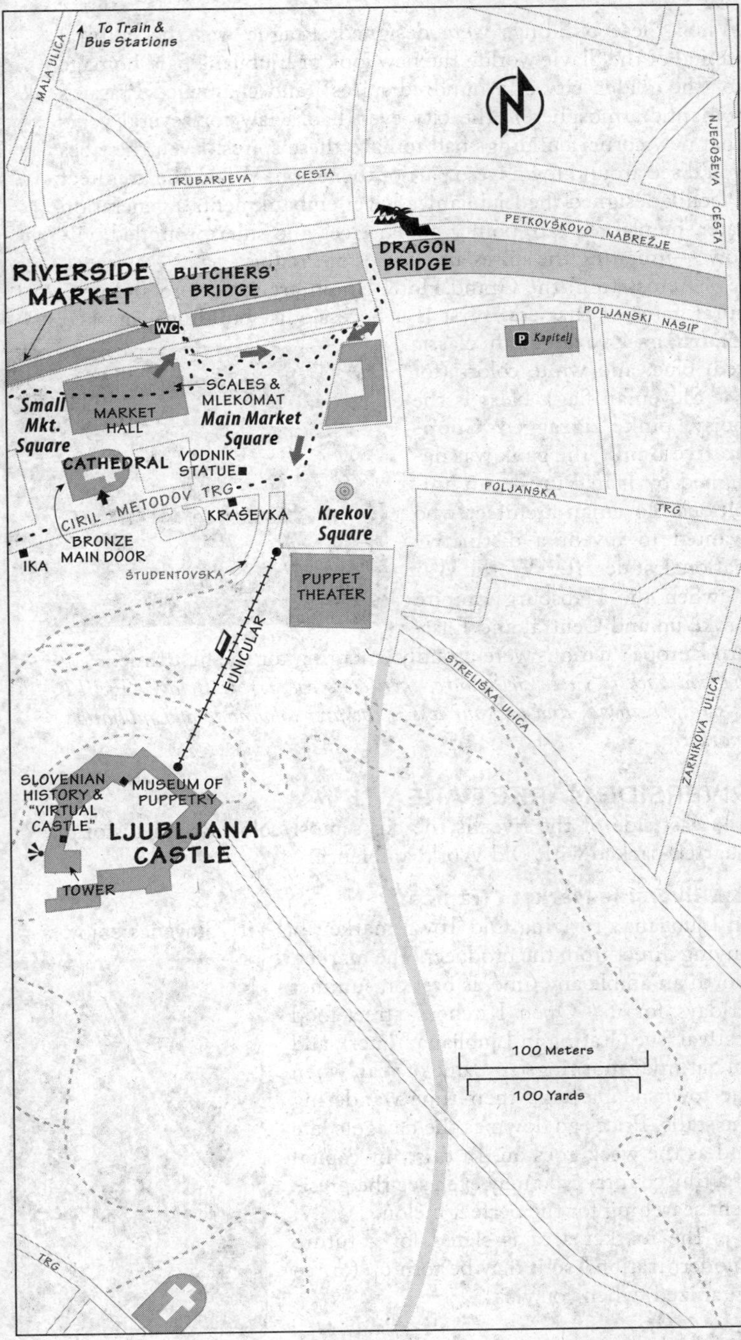

To Train &
Bus Stations

MALA ULICA

TRUBARJEVA CESTA

NJEGOŠEVA CESTA

DRAGON
BRIDGE

PETKOVŠKOVO NABREŽJE

RIVERSIDE
MARKET

BUTCHERS'
BRIDGE

WC

POLJANSKI NASIP

P Kapitelj

SCALES &
MLEKOMAT

Small
Mkt.
Square

MARKET
HALL

Main Market
Square

CATHEDRAL

VODNIK
STATUE

POLJANSKA TRG

CIRIL - METODOV TRG

KRAŠEVKA

Krekov
Square

IKA

BRONZE
MAIN DOOR

ŠTUDENTOVSKA

PUPPET
THEATER

STRELIŠKA ULICA

ZARNIKOVA ULICA

FUNICULAR

SLOVENIAN
HISTORY &
"VIRTUAL
CASTLE"

MUSEUM OF
PUPPETRY

LJUBLJANA
CASTLE

TOWER

100 Meters

100 Yards

TRG

LJUBLJANA

When these buildings were designed, Prague was the cultural capital of the Slavic world. The new look of Ljubljana paid homage to "the golden city of a hundred spires" (and channeled Prague's romantic atmosphere). The city even had a law for several years that new corner buildings had to have these spires. Even the trees you'll see around town were part of the vision. When the architect Plečnik designed the Ljubljanica River embankments a generation later, he planted tall, pointy poplar trees and squat, rounded willows—imitating the spires and domes of Prague.

Across from the Grand Hotel Union are two more architectural gems of that era: First is a Secessionist building—marked
Zadružna Zveza—with classic red, blue, and white colors (for the Slovenian flag). Next is the noisy, pink, zigzagged **Cooperative Bank.** The bank was designed by Ivan Vurnik, an ambitious Slovenian architect who wanted to invent a distinctive national style after World War I, when the Habsburg Empire broke up and Central and East-

ern Europe's nations were proudly emerging for the first time.

• *Head back to Prešeren Square, then cross the Triple Bridge. The TI is straight ahead, and on your left is the first colonnade of Ljubljana's market.*

RIVERSIDE MARKET AREA
The east side of the river is the city's most colorful and historic quarter, packed with Old World ambience.

▲▲Riverside Market (Tržnice)
In Ljubljana's thriving Old Town market, big-city Slovenes enjoy buying direct from the producer. The market, worth an amble any time, is best on summer Fridays for its "Open Kitchen" street-food festival (see "Eating in Ljubljana," later); and on Saturday mornings any time of year, when the townspeople take their time wandering the stalls. Prices go down as the day gets late and as the week goes on. In this tiny capital of a tiny country, you may even see the president searching for the perfect melon.

The market area is slated for a future "modernization," so it may be torn up (or reorganized) when you visit.

The riverside **colonnade,** which echoes the long-gone medieval city wall, was designed by Jože Plečnik. This first stretch—nearest the Triple Bridge—is good for souvenirs: woodcarvings, replica painted frontboards from beehives, honey products (including honey brandy), and lots of colorful candles.

Farther in, the market is almost all local, and the colonnade is populated by butchers, bakers, fishermen, and lazy cafés. Peek down at the actual river and see how the architect wanted the town and river to connect. The lower arcade hosts a robust, stinky fish market *(ribarnica)*—to take a whiff, head down the spiral stairs at the end of the souvenir stalls.

• *Across from these stairs, you reach the...*

Small Market Square (Pogačarjev Trg)

This square hosts the lively **Open Kitchen** street-food festival each Friday from spring through fall. The rest of the time, it simply serves as overflow for the main market square, which we'll see soon.

On your right, at the corner of the market square, notice the 10-foot-tall concrete **cone.** Plečnik wanted to make Ljubljana the "Athens of the North" and imagined a huge cone-shaped national acropolis—a complex for government, museums, and culture. This ambitious plan didn't make it off the drawing board, but part of Plečnik's Greek idea came true: this marketplace, based on an ancient Greek agora. Plečnik's cone still captures the Slovenes' imaginations...and adorns Slovenia's €0.10 coin.

At the top of this square, the tall domes mark the 18th-century **cathedral,** which stands on the site of a 13th-century Romanesque church. (We'll visit the cathedral from the other side later on this walk.)

The building at the end of the small market square is the seminary palace, with the **market hall** *(pokrita tržnica)* in its basement. Just left of the central door, Tus Boutique sells products created or curated by Ana Roš—celebrity chef at the world-renowned Hiša Franko restaurant high in the Julian Alps (described on page 846).

Go through the central door of the seminary to enter the market hall, with vendors selling cheeses, meats, baked goods, dried fruits, nuts, and other goodies (Mon-Fri 7:00-16:00, Sat until 14:00, closed Sun). This place is worth a graze—walk all the way through. Most merchants are happy to give you a free sample (point to what you want, and say *probat, prosim*—"a taste, please").

Leaving the market hall at the opposite end, look to your right to see the little **scales** in the wooden kiosks marked *Kontrolna Tehtnica*—allowing buyers to immediately check whether the producer cheated them (not a common problem, but just in case). The Habsburg days left locals with the old German saying, "Trust is good; control is better." Nearby, look for the innovative "Nonstop

Mlekomat" stand, a vending machine that lets you buy a plastic bottle and fill it with a liter of raw, unskimmed, farm-fresh milk for €1.

• *From here, you're looking out over the...*

Main Market Square (Vodnikov Trg)

The square is packed with produce and clothing stands. (The colorful flower market hides behind the market hall.) Now's a good

time to do a little browsing. The vendors in the row nearest the colonnade sell fruit from all over, but the ones located deeper in the market sell only locally grown produce. Tell the vendor what you want—it's considered rude for customers to touch the fruits and vegetables before they've paid for them. Over time, shoppers develop friendships with their favorite producers. On busy days, you'll see a long line at one stand, while the other merchants stand bored. Your choice is simple: Get in line, or eat subpar produce.

• *Along the river at the bottom of the main market square is the...*

Butchers' Bridge

Jože Plečnik designed a huge roofed bridge to be built here, but—like so many of his designs—the plans were scuttled. Decades later, Mayor Zoran Janković finally constructed this modern version of the bridge. While it looks nothing like Plečnik's original plans, the bridge kept the old name and has been embraced by the community (there's a handy public WC down below on the lower level). Almost as soon as it was built, the bridge's railings were covered with padlocks—part of the Europe-wide craze for young couples to commemorate their love. The bridge's sculptures—a mournful Adam and Eve being evicted from the Garden of Eden, and weird little lizards breaking out of their eggs along the railing—are by local artist Jakov Brdar, who enjoys hanging out here.

• *From the bridge, follow the colonnade the rest of the way to its end. It terminates at the...*

▲Dragon Bridge (Zmajski Most)

The dragon has been the symbol of Ljubljana for centuries, ever since Jason (of Argonauts and Golden Fleece fame) supposedly slew one in a nearby swamp. This is one of the few notable bits of Ljubljana architecture *not* by Plečnik (but by Jurij Zaninović, a fellow student of Vienna architect Otto Wagner). While the dragon is the star of this very photogenic Art Nouveau bridge, the bridge

itself was officially dedicated to the 40th anniversary of Habsburg emperor Franz Josef's reign (see the dates on the side: 1848-1888). Tapping into the emp's vanity got new projects funded—vital when the city later rebuilt after the 1895 earthquake.

• *Turn around and continue browsing your way through the main market square, heading toward its top end. Directly across the street from the top of the square, look for the* **funicular** *that trundles tourists up to* **Ljubljana Castle.** *You could zip up there now (see "More Sights in Ljubljana," later)—or hold off on your visit and stick with me.*

Facing the funicular, turn right and walk with the market on your right, passing the big statue of Slovene poet Valentin Vodnik and heading for the big dome. We're entering...

LJUBLJANA'S OLD TOWN

The historic center of Ljubljana stretches along one long street that curls around the base of its castle-topped hill, beginning near the market.

• *The first part is called...*

Cyril and Methodius Square (Ciril-Metodov Trg)

Named for Byzantine missionaries who introduced Christianity to the Slavs (and invented the forerunner of the Cyrillic alphabet), this misnamed "square" is really just the first stretch of Ljubljana's Old Town drag. In the early 19th century, Ljubljana was little more than this solitary main street (plus a small "New Town" across the river). Cyril and Methodius Square is great for a browse, with fun window shopping. As you pass bollards that rise up from the street to block cars, you enter the mostly traffic-free cobbled zone.

• *The big, yellow building on the right is Ljubljana's...*

▲Cathedral (Stolnica)

Ljubljana's cathedral is dedicated to St. Nicholas, protector against floods and patron saint of the fishermen and boatmen who have long come to sell their catch at the market. While the interior is worth a peek, the intricately sculpted **bronze doors**—created for Pope John Paul II's visit here in 1996—are even more interesting.

Take a close look at the door about two-thirds of the way down the building, with images of the six 20th-century bishops of Ljubljana. (If you're heading inside the cathedral, go through this door.) Another even more impressive bronze door is around the end of the building (hook right). You'll find it under the high arch (both described next).

Cost and Hours: €2, generally daily 11:00-18:00 but opens Tue at 14:00 and Sun at 13:30, on weekends closes for an hour around 15:30.

Visiting the Cathedral: Enter through the side door. In this Italian Baroque space, the transept is surrounded by sculp-

tures of four bishops of Roman Ljubljana (when it was called Emona, or Aemon). Left of the main altar, notice the distinctive chair. This was designed by the very religious Jože Plečnik, whose brother was a priest here. Look up over the nave to enjoy the recently restored, gorgeous ceiling fresco. You'll exit through the main door.

Bronze Main Door: Take a close look at this remarkable door. Buried deep in the fecund soil of the nation's ancient and pagan history, the linden tree of life sprouts with the story of the Slovenes. The ceramic pots represent the original Roman settlement here. Just to the left, above the tree, are the Byzantine missionaries Cyril and Methodius, who came here to convert the Slavs to Christianity in the ninth century. Just above, Crusaders and Ottomans do battle. Near the top, see the Slovenes going into the cave—entering the dark 20th century (World War I, World War II, and communism). At the top is Pope John Paul II (the first Slavic pontiff, who also helped inspire the fall of communism). Beneath him are two men who are on track to becoming Slovenia's first saints; the one on the right is the Venerable Frederic Baraga, a 19th-century bishop who became a missionary in Michigan and codified Chippewa grammar (notice the Native American relief on the book he's holding). In the upper-right corner is a sun, which has been shining since Slovenia gained its independence in 1991.

• *Carry on past the cathedral on Cyril and Methodius Square. Soon you'll run into the giant fountain that marks Ljubljana's...*

▲Town Square (Mestni Trg)

The **Fountain of Three Carniolan Rivers** is inspired in style and theme by Rome's many fountains. The figures with vases represent this region's three main rivers: Ljubljanica, Sava, and Krka. This is one of many works in town by Francesco Robba, an Italian who came to Ljubljana for a job, fell in love with a Slovene, and stayed here the rest of his life—decorating the city's churches with beautiful Baroque altars. (This is a replica; Robba's original fountain is at the National Gallery.)

From the fountain, look down the wide gap between the buildings (and beyond the Triple Bridge) to see the giant pink church: We've done a near-loop, and you're just a minute's walk (across the bridge) from Prešeren Square. We'll do another loop now, in the opposite direction.

Just beyond the fountain on the left is the **Town Hall** (Rotovž), highlighted by its clock tower and pillared loggia. Step inside the Renaissance courtyard to see paintings, artifacts, and (high on one wall of the atrium) a map of late 17th-century Ljubljana. Studying this map, notice how the river, hill, and wall worked together to fortify the town. Courtyards like this (but humbler) are hidden throughout the city. As rent in these old places is cheap, many such courtyards host funky, characteristic little businesses.

Back out on the square, turn with the Town Hall on your left. We'll continue down the Old Town's main drag, connecting to two other "squares"—Stari Trg (Old Square) and Gornji Trg (Upper Square)—which have long since grown together into one big, atmospheric promenade lined with quaint boutiques, great restaurants, and cafés. As you walk, keep your eyes open for Ljubljana's mascot dragon—it's everywhere.

• *Begin heading down the...*

▲Old Town Shopping Zone

Even for nonshoppers, this strip is a delight to browse, offering an ethnographic and culinary introduction to Slovenia. Several shops along this strip specialize in typical Slovenian products.

A block past the Town Hall on the left, at Mestni Trg 7 (yellow sign), **Honey House** sells products harvested by beekeeper Luka. For tips on browsing your honey options, see page 810. Next door, at #8, **Piranske Soline** sells products from the giant salt pans that sit just south of Piran on Slovenia's tiny coastline (www.soline. si). And across the street, at #19, the recommended **Güjžina** specializes in the cuisine of Prekmurje in northeastern Slovenia, with strong Hungarian influences...and a vegan twist.

Farther along, on the right (at #17), **Galerija Idrijske Čipke** shows off handmade lace from the town of Idrija (www.idrija-lace. com). Next door, **Dobrote Dolenjske** sells a variety of flavored schnapps and gins, plus some handicrafts from the southeast Dolenje region...not to mention *medvedova salama*, bear salami (www. dobrote-dolenjske.si). Across the street, at #10, notice the long passage that leads to one of Ljubljana's characteristic courtyards.

Continue along the street (which here changes names from Mestni Trg to Stari Trg), passing more fun shops. On the left, at Stari Trg 3, **Cha** tea shop sells over 100 varieties of tea, plus porcelain teapots and cups from all over. A few steps down on the left at #5, **Cafetino** serves more than 20 types of coffee—from espresso to Turkish-style—and has beans to take home.

Now you'll wade through a stretch of enticing restaurants with wonderful outdoor tables (for my recommendations here, see the Old Town listings in "Eating in Ljubljana," later). Notice Julija and Romeo, facing each other wistfully across the street.

Just after the little "restaurant row," on the right, at #10, **Le Potica** sells (pricey) miniature versions of Slovenia's traditional Bundt-style cake, *potica* (POH-teet-sah). From here, you'll pass several more shops made-to-order for window shopping, including funky boutiques and rare-book and antique shops. **Romantika**, with Ljubljana's best gelato, has a branch on the left at #15. If you smell something heavenly, watch for the recommended **Osem**, which bakes up fresh bread daily (on the left, at #17). Just past that, at #19, is the recommended restaurant **Altrokè**, with cuisine from Istria, in southern Slovenia.

The cobbled charm culminates at the square called **Gornji Trg**. Look uphill and notice the village charms of some of the oldest buildings in town: four medieval houses with rooflines slanted at the ends, different from the others on this street.

• *Just past the square's Hercules Fountain, turn right (on Stiška Ulica) through the gap in the buildings to the...*

▲▲Ljubljanica Riverbank

Now let's loop back on ourselves, yet again. Turn right and stroll for a couple of minutes along this beautiful promenade—worth ▲▲▲ on a sunny day, when the café tables are full. This part of the embankment is sleepy; farther along it's a convivial people zone, packed with Slovenes out enjoying their capital.

Halfway to the first bridge—just after the first bunch of café tables—pause at the little notch and look down at the river and its **embankments.** Notice in particular the angled embankments across the river with seating carved out. These embankments were designed by (who else?) the great architect Jože Plečnik, who walked along this river every day on his way to the office.

• *While you could follow this promenade all the way back to the Triple Bridge and Prešeren Square—just a few minutes away—we're only going as far as the first bridge, with the tall pillars (Cobblers' Bridge). We'll cross the river here to explore some of Ljubljana's architectural mas-*

terpieces. And that means we're entering the world of Jože Plečnik. Walk halfway across the bridge and pause for a moment.

JOŽE PLEČNIK'S LJUBLJANA

Jože Plečnik is to Ljubljana what Antoni Gaudí is to Barcelona: a homegrown, amazingly prolific genius who reshaped his town with a unique and beautiful vision. And Plečnik's mark on Ljubljana, much like Gaudí's on Barcelona, has a way of turning people who couldn't care less about architecture into fans. There's plenty to see. In addition to the Triple Bridge, the riverside market and embankments, and the sights we're about to see, Plečnik designed the embankments along the Gradaščica River in the Trnovo neighborhood; the rebuilt Roman wall along Mirje street, south of the center; the Church of St. Francis, with its classicist bell tower; St. Michael's Church on the Marsh; Orel Stadium; Žale Cemetery; and many more buildings throughout Slovenia.

▲Cobblers' Bridge (Čevljarski Most)

Named for the cobblers (shoemakers) who set up shop along the river in olden times, the bridge encapsulates Plečnik's style per-

haps better than any other structure: simple, clean lines adorned with classical columns. Ideal for people-watching (with the castle hovering scenically overhead—look behind you), this is one of Ljubljana's most appealing spots.

• *Cross Cobblers' Bridge, turn left, and walk one short block to the big fountain, which marks the bottom of a broad plaza called* **Novi Trg**. *Turn right and head to the top of Novi Trg, where you'll run into a red-brick building embedded with gray granite blocks in an irregular checkerboard pattern. This is the...*

▲▲National and University Library (Narodna in Univerzitetna Knjižnica, or NUK)

Widely regarded as Plečnik's masterpiece, this building is a bit

underwhelming...until an understanding of its symbolism brings it to life. Aside from being a great work of architecture, the building also houses the most important library in Slovenia, with more than two million books (about one per Slovene). The library is supposed to receive a copy of each new book printed in the country. In a freaky bit of bad luck, this was the only building in town damaged in World War II, when a plane crashed into it. But the people didn't want to see their books go up in flames—so hundreds of locals formed a human chain, risking life and limb to save the books from the burning building.

On the surface, the red-and-gray color scheme of the **exterior** evokes the red soil and chunks of granite of the Karst region, south of Ljubljana. But on a deeper level, the library's design conveys the theme of overcoming obstacles to attain knowledge. In the facade, the blocks of irregular size and shape represent a complex numerological pattern that suggests barriers on the path to enlightenment. The sculpture on the river side (to the left) is Moses—known for leading his people through 40 years of hardship to the Promised Land. On the right side of the building, find the horse-head door-

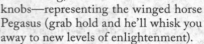

knobs—representing the winged horse Pegasus (grab hold and he'll whisk you away to new levels of enlightenment).

If you go inside, you'll notice the main **staircase** is dark and gloomy—modeled after an Egyptian tomb. But at the top, through the door marked *Velika Čitalnica*, is the bright, airy main reading room: the ultimate goal, a place of learning. The top-floor windows are shaped roughly like open books. Sadly, most of the time you can't actually enter the reading room; if it's closed, you can look at postcards in the shop, and imagine young Ljubljanans hunched studiously over their books, surrounded by Plečnik's bookshelves, railings, and high windows.

Cost and Hours: The library is free to enter and usually open Mon-Fri 10:00-18:00, Sat 14:30-18:00, closed Sun except in sum-

mer. The quiet main reading room is open to visitors (for €5) only during very brief periods: Most of the year, you can enter on Saturday afternoons (14:30-18:00), but hours are longer during the student break in the summer (mid-July-mid-Aug Mon-Sat 10:00-18:00, Sun 11:00-19:00).

• *Back outside, head back to the corner where we got our first look at the library. As you face the building from the top of Novi Trg, turn left and head one block down Gosposka street. On your left, you'll run into the...*

▲City Museum of Ljubljana
(Mestni Muzej Ljubljana)

Though not a Plečnik sight, this thoughtfully presented, kid-friendly museum, located in the Auersperg Palace, offers a high-tech, in-depth look at the story of this city using a wide range of well-described artifacts (all in English). In the **cellar** are Roman ruins (including remains of the original Roman road and sewer system, found right here) and layers of medieval artifacts. A model of the modern city—sitting upon footprints of the Roman (red) and medieval (blue) settlements—illustrates Ljubljana's many layers of history.

Upstairs, the excellent **permanent exhibit** traces the history of this crossroads city, starting with the museum's prized possession, the world's oldest wooden wheel on an axle, dating from around 3200 BC and discovered in the Ljubljana marshlands. In the contemporary section, you'll see an actual Fiat Zastava 750 car, the classic "Fičko" car that everyone owned—or wanted to own—in communist Yugoslavia (sort of a proto-Yugo).

Cost and Hours: €6, more for temporary exhibits, Tue-Sun 10:00-18:00, closed Mon, Gosposka 15, +386 1 241 2510, www.mgml.si.

Nearby: Your ticket includes admission to two archaeological sites nearby (May-Oct only)—pick up a map at the front desk.

• *With the museum at your back, you're facing yet another town square. On the left side of the square, just past the big, boxy, orange building, step through the gate into the courtyard of the ...*

Križanke Theater

The Teutonic Knights of the Cross established this monastery around 1230, and it was rebuilt in Baroque style in 1715. In 1945—after the Socialist Federal Republic of Yugoslavia came to power—the monastery complex was nationalized and closed. In 1952, city leaders decided to repurpose the space as an outdoor venue for the Ljubljana Summer Theatre. (It's still used for this purpose; the box office is on this courtyard.) Near the end of his life, Jože Plečnik drew up the designs for the theater, which turned out to be his last major work.

Plečnik modified the existing structure with new features, as well as elements recycled from other projects. For example, just inside the courtyard, on the left, the two saints on pillars were originally part of a local school building. On these pillars, notice the hammer, sickle, and star motif—unusual in the works of Plečnik but reflecting the time in which he did this project. On the right, look for the grapevine running along the side of the courtyard. Plečnik loved to incorporate grapevines (a subtle symbol for Christianity) into his works—even ones like this, commissioned by atheistic authorities. Sgraffito (etched plaster) decorations extend along the left side of the courtyard, incorporating Slovenian folk motifs, Ljubljana dragons, and the red, white, and blue color scheme of the Yugoslav flag.

• *Exiting the Križanke, turn left and head a few more steps up to the top of the square, marked by the obelisk. This is...*

French Revolution Square (Trg Francoske Revolucije)

Plečnik designed the obelisk in the middle of the square to com-memorate Napoleon's short-lived decision to make Ljubljana the capital of his Illyrian Provinces. It's rare to find anything honoring Napoleon outside Paris, but he was good to Ljubljana. Under his rule, Slovenian culture flourished, the Slovene language became widely recognized and respected for the first time, schools were es-tablished, and roads and infrastructure were improved. The monu-ment contains ashes of the unknown French soldiers who died in 1813, when the region went from French to Austrian control.

Detour to Jože Plečnik House: There's one more major Plečnik sight, and it's a big one: the house he lived in, now a mu-seum. It's about a 10-minute walk away, and described later, under "More Sights in Ljubljana." If you're on a Plečnik roll, you can bail out of this walk and head there now (for location, see the "Lju-bljana" map, earlier): From the obelisk, turn left and walk down Emonska toward the twin-spired church. You'll pass (on the left) the delightful Krakovo district—a patch of green countryside in downtown Ljubljana. Many of the veggies you see in the river-side market come from these carefully tended gardens. When you reach the Gradaščica stream, head over the bridge (also designed by Plečnik) and go around the left side of the church to find the house.

• *To finish our walk and head back toward where we started, turn right at the obelisk (heading the way Napoleon is looking), and continue along the back of the library. After one block, turn right down Turjaška and continue straight down Novi Trg to the river. Turn left, pass the Cob-blers' Bridge, and keep going (with the river on your right) for one more minute. When you reach the big staircase on your left (with the Gustav Mahler statue on the far side), head up it. From the top of the stairs, bear right into the vast expanse of...*

CONGRESS SQUARE (KONGRESNI TRG)

This grassy, tree-lined square hosts big events, from political rallies to music performances to celebrations. It's ringed by some of Lju-bljana's most important buildings: the university headquarters, the Baroque Ursuline Church of the Holy Trinity, a classical mansion called the Kazina, and the Philharmonic Hall.

The greenbelt at the heart of the square, called Park Zvezda ("Star Park") for its radiating paths, is fronted by several inviting cafés and restaurants; the recommended **Zvezda Kavarna,** near the lower corner, is a top spot for its local cakes and ice cream.

Halfway up the square, in the middle of the grassy section, the giant **anchor** celebrates the day in 1954 when Slovenia took possession of its tiny coastline, between Koper and Piran.

Just beyond that, notice the giant open space with two giant slabs, three trees, and six towering Slovenian flags. This is the **Monument to the Victims of All Wars,** erected in 2016, honoring the many lives lost to pointless conflict. The words along the base of the step are from 20th-century poet Oton Župančič: "One homeland is given to each one of us, and one life, and one death."

At the top end of the square, by the entry to a pedestrian underpass, a Roman sarcophagus sits under a gilded statue of a **Roman citizen**—a replica of a Roman tomb sculpture from 1,700 years ago, when this town was called Emona. The busy street above you has been the site of the main trading route through town since ancient Roman times.

• *Our walk ends where Ljubljana began. A variety of museums lie just west of Slovenska Cesta (the big street at the end of this square), leading eventually to Tivoli Park. To visit these now, you can carry on under this underpass, pop out the other side, and turn to page 754.*

Otherwise, head back toward the river to the bottom of Congress Square, turn left, and in about one minute you'll be on Prešeren Square, where we began. Or, you could head to the water and nurse a coffee along Ljubljana's idyllic riverfront promenade.

More Sights in Ljubljana

Ljubljana is bursting with well-presented, we-try-harder museums celebrating Slovenian history and culture. These include the Slovenian History Exhibition at the castle, the City Museum of Ljubljana (described in my "Ljubljana Walk"), and the Contemporary History Museum in Tivoli Park. As these are similar and largely overlapping, if you get museumed out easily, just pick the one that's handiest to your sightseeing plan.

▲Ljubljana Castle (Ljubljanski Grad)

The castle above town offers enjoyable views over Ljubljana's rooftops, the surrounding countryside, and the Alps on the horizon. There has probably been a settlement on this site since prehistoric times, though the first true fortress here was Roman. The 12th-century version was gradually added on to over the centuries, until it fell into disrepair in the 17th century. Today's castle—rebuilt in the 1940s and renovated in the 1970s—is a hollow-feeling replica, lacking any sense of real history. However, in recent years they've filled this shell with some worthwhile attractions and respectable

LJUBLJANA

restaurants. The castle is a popular venue for the Ljubljana Festival, with concerts throughout the summer (+386 1 306 4293, www.ljubljanafestival.si).

Cost and Hours: The grounds are free to visit and open daily June-Sept 9:00-22:00, April-May and Oct until 20:00, shorter hours Nov-March. A ticket for the exhibits inside is €12, or €16 with the round-trip funicular. The exhibits close earlier: June-Sept at 20:00, April-May and Oct at 19:00, even earlier Nov-March.

Information: +386 1 232 9994, www.ljubljanskigrad.si.

Tours and Other Activities: For a few euros more you can rent an audioguide or take part in a variety of tours and themed activities, including a "Time Machine" guided tour (daily June-Sept, weekends only Oct-May), an "Escape Castle" game (where you solve a series of puzzles around the castle grounds), and even Friday-night jazz concerts. Options change frequently; get details on the castle website or when buying tickets.

Getting to the Castle: A slick **funicular** whisks visitors to the top in a jiff (€3.30 one-way, €6 round-trip, included in combo-ticket described earlier; runs every 10 minutes during castle open hours, 1-minute ride; catch it at Krekov Trg, near the main market square). At the top, you'll find free WCs and a few easy flights of stairs up into the heart of the castle complex (or take the elevator). There are also two handy **trails** from town up to the castle. The steeper-but-faster route begins near the Dragon Bridge: Find Študentovska lane, facing the statue of Valentin Vodnik in the market. This lane dead-ends at a gravel path, which you'll follow up to a fork. Turn left to zigzag up the steepest and fastest route, which deposits you just below the castle wall; from here, turn left again and curl around the wall to reach the main drawbridge. Slower but a bit less steep is from a street called Reber, just off Stari Trg, a few blocks south of the Town Hall: Walk up to the top of Reber, and, at the dead end, turn right and start climbing up the stairs. From here on out, keep bearing left, then go right when you're just under the castle (follow *Grad* signs).

Visiting the Castle: The castle's information office, where you can pick up your audioguide or meet a tour, is near the main gate (from the funicular, follow the yellow *i* sign up the stairs). In the main castle courtyard, the sights cluster in two areas. The best sights are near the base of the tallest tower: The entrance to the history exhibit is to the left; the "Virtual Castle" film, chapel, penitentiary, and tower climb are to the right. To the right of that is the rounded Erasmus Tower, with the Museum of Puppetry. The upper floors of the castle complex house two wedding halls—Ljubljana's most popular places to get married (free for locals).

The **Slovenian History Exhibition** offers a concise but engaging overview of this little country's story. As you enter, ask to borrow the free audioguide, then head downstairs and work your way up. Dark display cases light up when you approach, revealing artifacts, video clips, and touchscreens with more information. A unique feature of the museum is that you're invited to touch replicas of important historic items (in many cases, the originals are in other Ljubljana museums). The top floor (go up the glassed-in staircase) is the most interesting—covering the tumultuous 20th century. You'll learn about topics ranging from the battlefields of World War I, to the creation of Yugoslavia, to the fascist occupation and harrowing Italian-run concentration camps of World War II, to the cult of personality around Partisan-war-hero-turned-Yugoslav-president Tito, to Slovenia's bid for independence.

Entering the door to the right of the tower, you'll first find the small **penitentiary exhibit,** recalling the post-Napoleonic era, when the castle was converted to a prison. It saw the most action during World War I, when it housed political prisoners (including the beloved Slovenian writer Ivan Cankar) and POWs. Modest exhibits inside actual former cells describe the history and list the names of past inmates.

If you head downstairs from the entrance, you'll find a Gothic **chapel** with Baroque paintings of St. George (Ljubljana's patron saint, the dragon-slayer) and coats of arms of the various aristocratic families that have called this castle home.

Heading up the stairs, you'll find the informative, entertaining, and nicely animated **"Virtual Castle" film,** in which Ljubljana's mascot dragon describes this hill's layers of history (12 minutes, plays on the half-hour; often in English, but otherwise borrow English headset).

Finally, climb the 92 spiral steps up to the **castle tower,** with one of the best views in town.

Don't miss the oddly fascinating **Museum of Puppetry** (ride up the elevator to the left as you face the round Erasmus Tower). This traces the history of puppetry as an art form, which flourished in the Modernist milieu of early 20th-century Ljubljana.

The castle also often has **temporary exhibits**—look for signs or ask at the information desk.

Eating: You can combine your visit to the castle with a meal at the recommended **$$$ Gostilna na Gradu,** with the best traditional Slovenian food in town, or the top-end **$$$$ Strelec** (both described later, under "Eating in Ljubljana"). **$ Gradska Kavana**

LJUBLJANA

("Castle Café") serves only drinks and cakes, and **$ Gradska Vinoteka** ("Castle Winery") is a wine bar operated by Strelec.

▲▲Jože Plečnik House (Plečnikova Zbirka)

One of Ljubljana's most interesting sights is the house of the architect who redesigned much of the city. Today, the house is decorated exactly as it was the day Plečnik died, containing much of his equipment, models, and plans. It can be toured only with a guide, whose enthusiasm brings the place to life. Still furnished with unique, Plečnik-designed furniture, one-of-a-kind inventions, and favorite souvenirs from his travels, the house paints an unusually intimate portrait of an artist. It's a ▲▲▲ pilgrimage for those who get caught up in Ljubljana's idiosyncratic sense of style.

Cost and Hours: €8 for the worthwhile tour, €5 for just the modest museum and gardens; Tue-Sun 10:00-18:00—last tour departs at 17:00, closed Mon, 45-minute English tours begin at the top of each hour; Karunova 4, +386 1 280 1604, www.mgml.si.

Getting Tickets: Tours are limited to seven people and can sell out, especially on summer weekends. Consider calling ahead or emailing plecnik@mgml.si to save a space. Otherwise, it's smart to show up 15-20 minutes early at busy times.

Getting There: It's directly behind the twin steeples of the Trnovo Church, south of the town center. The 15-minute stroll from the center—the same one Plečnik took to work each day—is nearly as enjoyable as the house itself. You can either walk south along the river, then turn right onto Gradaška and stroll along the stream to the church, or, from French Revolution Square, head south on Emonska. If taking Emonska, you'll pass through the garden district of Krakovo, where pea patches and characteristic Old World buildings gracefully cohabitate.

Background: Ljubljana's favorite son lived here from 1921 until his death, in 1957. He added on to an existing house, building a circular bedroom for himself and filling the place with bric-a-brac he designed, as well as artifacts, photos, and gifts from around the world that inspired him as he shaped Ljubljana. Living a simple, almost monastic lifestyle, Plečnik knew what he liked, and these tastes are mirrored in his home.

Visiting the House: While waiting for your tour to begin, explore the modest but engaging **museum,** offering biographical details about Plečnik along with his personal effects (such as notebooks, tools, and eyeglasses). Look for the small model of Ljubljana

LJUBLJANA

Jože Plečnik (1872-1957)

No other single architect has shaped one city as Jože Plečnik (YOH-zheh PLAYCH-neek) shaped Ljubljana. From libraries, cemeteries, and stadiums to riverside embankments and market halls, Plečnik left his mark everywhere.

Plečnik was born in Ljubljana to a cabinet maker. He dabbled as a self-trained architect, catching the eye of the great Secessionist architect Otto Wagner, who invited him to study in Vienna. Plečnik's first commissions, around the turn of the 20th century in Vienna, were pretty standard, Art Nouveau. Then Tomáš Masaryk, president of the new nation of Czechoslovakia, decided that Prague Castle could use a new look by a Slavic architect. In 1921, Masaryk chose Jože Plečnik, who sprinkled the castle grounds with his distinctive touches. By now, Plečnik had perfected his simple, eye-pleasing style, which mixes modern and classical influences with ample columns and pyramids—at once austere and playful.

By the time Plečnik finished in Prague, he had made a name for himself. His prime years were spent creating for the Kingdom of Yugoslavia (before the ideology-driven era of Tito). Plečnik returned home to Ljubljana and set to work redesigning the city, both as an architect and as an urban planner. He lived in a humble house (now a recommended museum) behind the Trnovo Church. On his daily walk to work, he pondered ways to make the city even more livable. As you wander through town, notice how thoughtfully he  incorporated people, nature, Slovenian heritage, town vistas, and symbolism into his works—it's feng shui on a grand urban scale.

For all of Plečnik's ideas that became reality, even more did not. After World War II, the very religious Plečnik fell out of favor with the communist government. (It's fun to imagine how this city might look if Plečnik had always gotten his way.) After his death, in 1957, Plečnik was all but forgotten by Slovenes and scholars alike.

But a 1986 exposition about Plečnik at Paris' Pompidou Center jump-started interest in the architect. Within a few years, Plečnik was back in vogue. Today, scholars laud him as a genius who was ahead of his time...while locals and tourists enjoy the elegant simplicity of his works.

that locates the many structures he designed all around the city. You'll also see descriptions and photos of his greatest works, and large wooden models of two of his biggest "unrealized plans" that never made it off the drawing board: the cone-shaped "Cathedral of Freedom" and the roofed Butchers' Bridge at the market. One room features his redesign of Prague Castle, including a small model of his gardens and walkways. You can try sitting on chairs that Plečnik designed while you watch a video loop of short films about the architect.

The **tour** takes you through the actual rooms where Plečnik lived: kitchen, circular bedroom, sitting room, studio, and greenhouse. As you tour the place, appreciate the subtle details. Notice how reverently your guide (like other Slovenes) speaks of this man. Contrast the humbleness of Plečnik's home with the dynamic impact he had on the cityscape of Ljubljana and the cultural heritage of Slovenia. Wandering Plečnik's hallways, it's hard not to be tickled by his sheer creativity and by the unique world he forged for himself. As a visitor to his home, you're in good company. He invited only his closest friends here—except during World War II, when Ljubljana was occupied by Nazis and the university was closed, and Plečnik allowed his students to work with him here.

THE MUSEUM ZONE AND TIVOLI PARK

The west side of the river—beyond Prešeren Square and Congress Square—is the heart of modern Ljubljana, and home to several prominent squares and fine museums. I've listed these sights roughly in order from Congress Square and linked them with walking directions. For locations and to trace this route, see the "Ljubljana" map, earlier.

• *The easiest way to get to this side of town is through the underpass (beneath Slovenska Cesta) at the top of Congress Square. Emerging on the other side of the underpass, walk straight through the gap in the Maxi shopping center into the...*

▲Square of the Republic (Trg Republike)

This unusual plaza is ringed by an odd collection of buildings. While hardly quaint, the Square of the Republic gives you a good taste of a modern corner of Ljubljana. And it's historic—this is where Slovenia declared its independence in 1991.

The **twin office towers** (with the world's biggest digital watch, flashing the date, time, and temperature) were designed

by Plečnik's protégé, Edvard Ravnikar. As harrowing as these structures seem, imagine if the builders had followed the original plans—the towers would be twice as tall as they are now and connected by a bridge, representing the gateway to Ljubljana. These buildings were originally designed as the Slovenian parliament, but they were scaled back when Tito didn't approve (it would have made Slovenia's parliament bigger than the Yugoslav parliament in Belgrade).

Instead, the **Slovenian Parliament** is across the square, in the low-profile office building with the sculpted entryway. The carvings are in the Socialist Realist style, celebrating the noble Slovenian people conforming to communist ideals for the good of the entire society.

Completing the square are a huge conference center (Cankarjev Dom, the white building behind the skyscrapers), a shopping mall, and some public art.

• *Just a block north, across the street and through the grassy park (Trg Narodni Herojev), you'll find the...*

Slovenian National Museum (Narodni Muzej Slovenije) and Slovenian Museum of Natural History (Prirodoslovni Muzej Slovenije)

These two museums share a single historic building facing a park behind the Parliament. They're both skippable but worth considering if you have a special interest or if it's a rainy day.

Cost and Hours: €8 for National Museum, €4 for Natural History Museum, or €10 for both, some English descriptions, both open daily 10:00-18:00, Prešernova 20, +386 1 241 4400, www.nms.si and www.pms-lj.si.

Visiting the Museums: The **National Museum** focuses on archaeological finds (their Metelkova branch—described later—features applied arts). On the ground floor are temporary exhibits and a lapidarium with carved-stone Roman monuments and exhibits on Egyptian mummies. Upstairs and to the right are more exhibits of the National Museum, with archaeological findings, including the museum's two prized possessions: a fragment of a 45,000-year-old Neanderthal flute fashioned from a cave bear's femur—supposedly the world's oldest musical instrument; and the "figural situla," a beautifully decorated hammered-bronze bucket from the fifth century BC. Embossed with scenes of everyday Iron Age life, this object has been a gold mine of information for archaeologists.

Upstairs and to the left is the **Natural History** exhibit, featuring the flora and fauna of Slovenia. You'll see partial skeletons of a mammoth and a cave bear; plenty of stuffed reptiles, fish, and birds; and an exhibit on "human fish" (*Proteus anguinus*—long,

LJUBLJANA

skinny, pale-pink, sightless salamanders unique to caves in this part of Europe).

At the far end of the building is a glassed-in annex displaying Roman stone monuments (free).

• *Turning left around the museum building and walking one block, you'll see the* **US Embassy.** *This pretty yellow chalet (with brown trim and a red roof, at Prešernova Cesta 31) wins my vote for quaintest embassy building in the world. (Resist the urge to snap a photo...those guards are all business.) Just up Prešernova Cesta from the embassy (to the right) are two decent art museums.*

Museum of Modern Art (Moderna Galerija Ljubljana)

This museum has a permanent collection of modern and contemporary Slovenian artists, as well as temporary exhibits by both homegrown and international artists. To explore the "Continuities and Ruptures" permanent collection (aptly named for a place with such a fractured, up-and-down history), borrow the English floor plan and take a chronological spin through the 20th century. Unusual for a "modern" art museum is the room with Partisan art, with stiff, improvised, communist-style posters from the days when Tito and his crew were just a ragtag militia movement.

Cost and Hours: €5, ask about combo-ticket with contemporary branch at Metelkova—see page 761; Tue-Sun 10:00-18:00, July-Aug Thu until 20:00, closed Mon year-round; Cankarjeva 15, +386 1 241 6800, www.mg-lj.si.

▲National Gallery (Narodna Galerija)

This solid museum presents a good, chronological exhibit of works by Slovenian and European artists, as well as temporary exhibits. Although Slovenia doesn't have a particularly renowned artistic tradition, this well-presented collection nicely paints a picture of the nation's story and culture.

Cost and Hours: €8, more for special exhibits, permanent collection free first Sun of the month; open Tue-Sun 10:00-18:00, Thu until 20:00, closed Mon; two entrances: one at Cankarjeva 20 facing the National Museum, and another at the big glass box between two older buildings at Prešernova 24; +386 1 241 5418, www.ng-slo.si.

Visiting the Museum: Enter through the main (historic) building. Downstairs is a skippable collection of medieval church art; upstairs are works from the 17th through 19th century. Spend some time with Marko Pernhart's Romantic views of the Slovenian countryside, including stunning panoramas of the Julian Alps (ringing the top of the stairwell).

Then you'll cross the modern skybridge (peeking down to see the original Fountain of Three Carniolan Rivers, from the Old Town's central square) to the 19th and 20th centuries. Find and savor the evocative portraits—bursting with personality—by Ivana Kobilca (1861-1926), a Slovenian painter working on the cusp of Impressionism. Art lovers enjoy her serene and lifelike *Summer* (1889-1890), in which a young woman (Kobilca's self-portrait) plays with kids and flowers. Also look for pointillist works by Ivan Grohar (1867-1911), who painted Slovenian landscapes with a dash of Van Gogh and a dab of Seurat. Look for Grohar's painting *The Sower,* which is noteworthy because it appears on Slovenia's €0.05 coins. On your way out, stop by the small room near the Cankarjeva entrance that displays small, faded, abstracted works by another Slovenian artist, Zoran Mušič (1909-2005).

• *By the busy road near the art museums, look for the distinctive Neo-Byzantine design (tall domes with narrow slits) of the...*

▲▲Serbian Orthodox Church of Sts. Cyril and Methodius

Ljubljana's most striking church interior isn't Catholic, but Orthodox. This church was built in 1936, soon after the Slovenes joined

a political union with the Serbs. Wealthy Slovenia attracted its poorer neighbors from the south—so it built this church for that community. Since 1991, the Serb population has continued to grow, as people from the struggling corners of the former Yugoslavia flock to prosperous Slovenia. Its gorgeous interior—which feels closer to Moscow than to Rome—offers visitors a taste of this important faith.

Cost and Hours: Free, daily 8:00-19:00; divine liturgy Sun at 8:30, other days services at 8:30 and 18:00; Prešernova 35, www.spc-ljubljana.si.

Visiting the Church: Step inside for the best glimpse of the Orthodox faith this side of Sarajevo. The church is colorfully decorated without a hint of the 21st century, mirroring a very conservative religion. Much of the church's art consists of copies of famous frescoes that decorate medieval Serbian Orthodox monasteries throughout the Balkans. On the balcony (at the back of the nave), you'll see Cyrillic script that explains the history of the church. Notice that there are no pews, because worshippers stand throughout the service. On the left, find the little room with tubs of water, where the faithful light tall, skinny candles (purchased at the little window in the back corner). At the front of the church, the painted wooden screen, or iconostasis, is believed to separate our material

LJUBLJANA

world from the spiritual realm behind it. Ponder the fact that several centuries ago, before the Catholic Church began to adapt to a changing world, all Christians worshipped this way. For more on the Orthodox faith, see the sidebar on page 1025.

• *On the other side of the busy street is...*

Tivoli Park (Park Tivoli)

This huge park, just west of the center, is where Slovenes relax on summer weekends. The easiest access is through the underpass from Cankarjeva Cesta (between the Serbian Orthodox Church and the Museum of Modern Art). As you emerge, the Neoclassical pillars leading down the promenade make it clear that this part of the park was designed by Jože Plečnik. Along this "main boulevard" of the park, various changing photographic exhibitions are displayed.

• *Aside from taking a leisurely stroll, the best thing to do in the park is visit the...*

▲Contemporary History Museum (Muzej Novejše Zgodovine)

In a Baroque mansion (Cekinov Grad) in Tivoli Park, a well-done exhibit called "Slovenians in the 20th Century" traces the country's most eventful hundred years—from World War I, through the Yugoslav period, to independence in 1991 and EU membership today. Out front is a yellow Zastava, a make of car that was ubiquitous during the Yugoslav years. Inside, the ground floor displays temporary exhibits, and upstairs you'll find several rooms using models, dioramas, light-and-sound effects, and English explanations to creatively tell the story of one of Europe's youngest nations. While it's a little difficult to fully appreciate, the creativity and the spunky spirit of the place are truly enjoyable.

Cost and Hours: €5, permanent exhibit free first Sun of the month; Tue-Sun 10:00-18:00, closed Mon; in Tivoli Park at Celovška Cesta 23, +386 1 300 9610, www.muzej-nz.si.

Getting There: The museum is a 20-minute walk from the center, best combined with a wander through Tivoli Park. The fastest approach: As you emerge from the Cankarjeva Cesta underpass into the park, climb up the stairs, then turn right and go straight ahead for five minutes. Continue up the ramp, turn left after the tennis courts, and look for the big pink-and-white mansion on the hill.

Visiting the Museum: The exhibit begins at the dawn of the 20th century, during Slovenia's waning days as part of the Austro-Hungarian Empire. Spiral stairs lead up to more exhibits about

World War I. Back on the main floor, you'll walk through a simulated trench from the Soča Front, then learn about the creation of the post-World War I Kingdom of Serbs, Croats, and Slovenes (or, as this exhibit pointedly puts it, "Kingdom of Slovenes, Croats, and Serbs"). During this time, some of what had historically been Slovenian became part of Italy.

Your footfalls echo loudly as you enter the room describing Slovenia's WWII experience. You'll learn how, during that war, Slovenia was divided between neighboring fascist powers Germany, Italy, and Hungary. Each one tried (but failed) to exert linguistic and cultural control over the people, hoping to eradicate the Slovenian national identity. Video screens show subtitled interviews with people who lived through those war years.

Passing through the ballroom, you reach the "Slovenia 1946-1960" exhibit, outlining both the good (modernization) and the bad (prison camps and secret police) of the early Tito years. Despite his ruthless early rule, Tito remains popular here; under his stern bust, page through the photo album of Tito's visits to Slovenia. Find the display of the country's former currencies. Examine the Yugoslav dinar and notice that the figureheads on that communist currency were generic, idealized workers, farmers, and other members of the proletariat...except for a few notable individuals (including Tito). Meanwhile, Slovenia's short-lived post-Yugoslav currency, the *tolar* (1991-2006, R.I.P.), featured artists and scientists rather than heads of state and generals.

The most evocative room (1991-2008) has artifacts from the Slovenes' brave declaration of independence from a hostile Yugoslavia in 1991. The well-organized Slovenes had only to weather a 10-day skirmish to gain their freedom. It's chilling to think that, at one point, bombers were en route to level this gorgeous city. The planes were called back at the last minute by a Yugoslav People's Army officer with allegiances to Slovenia.

Nearby: As you exit, the giant, modern, blocky, light-blue building across the busy road is the **Pivovarna Union**—the brewery for Ljubljana's favorite industrial-produced beer, with a brewpub and the option of a brewery tour (www.union-experience.si).
• *On your way back to the center, you could stop by...*

▲The Skyscraper (Nebotičnik)
This 1933 building was the first skyscraper in Slovenia, for a time the tallest building in Central Europe, and one of the earliest European buildings clearly influenced by American architecture. Art Deco inside and out, it's a thrill for architecture fans and anyone who enjoys a great view—the top floor, which hosts a restaurant, café, and observation deck, offers the best panorama of Ljubljana's skyline. Zip up in the elevator to floor #12, with a **$ café** where you

can enjoy a drink or a light meal with unobstructed views over the city and castle. (There's wonderful outdoor seating. In bad weather, head up the spiral stairs to the glassed-in terrace.)

Cost and Hours: Free to ride the elevator up for a peek—but you should buy at least a drink if you want to stick around; terrace and café open daily 9:00-late; 2 blocks from Prešeren Square at Štefanova 1, +386 40 601 787, www.neboticnik.si.

METELKOVA

Three museums face each other on a slick modern plaza next to the park called Tabor, about a 15-minute walk northeast of Prešeren Square in the dull but up-and-coming district of Metelkova. Nearby, you can explore the funky squatters' colony of Metelkova City (with Ljubljana's famous prison-turned-youth hostel). For locations, see the "Ljubljana" map, earlier.

▲▲Slovenian Ethnographic Museum (Slovenski Etnografski Muzej)

Housed in a state-of-the-art facility, this delightful museum is Ljubljana's most underrated attraction. With both permanent and temporary exhibits, the museum strives to explain what it is to be Slovene, with well-presented and well-described cultural artifacts from around the country. If you've caught the Slovenian folk-culture itch, this is the place to scratch it.

Cost and Hours: €6, free first Sun of month; open Tue-Sun 10:00-18:00, Thu until 20:00, closed Mon; great café, Metelkova 2, +386 1 300 8745, www.etno-muzej.si.

Visiting the Museum: The ground and first floors have good temporary exhibits; two permanent exhibits are upstairs.

The best exhibit, filling the third floor, is called **"Between Nature and Culture."** As you exit the elevator, turn left and find the shrunken head, which comes with a refreshingly frank exhibit that acknowledges the shortsighted tendency for museum curators—including at this museum—to emphasize things that are foreign or different. Continue through "Reflections of Distant Worlds" (non-European cultures) to reach the core of the collection, which focuses on Slovenia. A good but slow-moving film visits the country's four major regions. Another exhibit ponders how people half a world away—in Slovenia and in North America—simultaneously invented a similar solution (snowshoes) for a common problem. One display deconstructs Slovenian clichés (including this country's odd fascination with its traditional hayracks). The arrangement of the collection emphasizes the evolution of an increasingly complicated civilization, from basic farming tools to ceramics to modern technology. You'll see exhibits on traditional Slovenian beekeeping, blacksmithing, weaving, shoemaking, costumes and customs, pottery, furniture, and religious objects. The children's "Ethnoalphabet" area features an A-to-Ž array of engaging, hands-on activities.

The other permanent exhibit, **Plečnik's Lectarija,** shows off fixtures and fittings from an arts-and-crafts shop on Congress Square that was designed by Slovenia's great architect. It's a rare opportunity to poke around inside a (re-created) Plečnik interior. The exhibit also examines how Plečnik was inspired by traditional Slovenian crafts—and specifically by a nearby shop, selling candles and honey products, that the architect used to patronize.

Slovenian National Museum-Metelkova (Narodni Muzej Slovenije)

Next door to the Ethnographic Museum is this facility, where items (mostly applied arts) from the Slovenian National Museum that were formerly tucked away in storage are now displayed on two floors. The very pretty historical bric-a-brac is neatly presented without much context—it's just an excuse to get a bunch of interesting stuff out into public view. Each room has a different collection: furniture, pottery and ceramics, church vestments, weapons and armor, and more. The painting gallery is nicely organized by century and style. The museum also features temporary exhibits. Everything's labeled in English.

Cost and Hours: €8; Tue-Sun 10:00-18:00, Thu until 20:00, closed Mon; Maistrova 1, +386 1 230 7032, www.nms.si.

Museum of Contemporary Art-Metelkova (Muzej Sodobne Umetnosti Metelkova, MSUM)

This cutting-edge branch of the Museum of Modern Art showcases changing exhibitions of present-day, mostly Slovenian and Central European artists. The modern space is at once sleek and playful, making this museum worth a visit for art lovers who appreciate works from the 1960s to the present.

Cost and Hours: €5, ask about combo-ticket with Museum of Modern Art; Tue-Sun 10:00-18:00, July-Aug Thu until 20:00, closed Mon year-round; Maistrova 3, +386 1 241 6825, www.mg-lj.si.

Metelkova City (Metelkova Mesto)

The heart of Slovenia's counterculture, this former military installation is now a funky, graffiti-slathered squatter's colony, billed as an "autonomous cultural center." Built by the Habsburgs in the 1880s, the complex—with barracks, warehouses, and a prison—was used by a laundry list of later occupiers, from Italian fascists to Nazis to the Yugoslav People's Army. After Yugoslavia pulled its troops out of Slovenia (following the Ten-Day War), the cluster of buildings sat derelict and abandoned. In 1993, transient artists moved

LJUBLJANA

in and set up galleries, theaters, bars, and nightclubs. Though controversial at first, Meltelkova City has gradually become accepted by most Ljubljanans, and the city (which owns the property) not only tolerates but also actively encourages this hotbed of youthful artistic expression. While edgy, this place is fascinating to explore and a great spot to ogle street art—it's sleepy by day and lively by night (www.metelkovamesto.org).

Anchoring the area is **Hostel Celica,** one of Europe's most notable youth hostels, which fills a former prison building. Twenty artists were invited to decorate cells that have been turned into accommodations, and the ground floor features vibrant public spaces, a good and affordable restaurant (a nice place for a lunch or a light dinner), and a shoes-off "Oriental café." You can drop by to see the building anytime, and ask to borrow a flashlight to explore the dank and gloomy basement solitary confinement cells, with a small but interesting exhibition on the history of the building (and the various prisoners who have called it home—including Janez Janša, who did time here during communism and later became Slovenia's prime minister...twice). But if you visit, try to go at 13:00 for a free guided tour of the complex (tours run daily; you can try calling to arrange a tour at other times, +386 1 230 9700, www.hostelcelica.com).

Shopping in Ljubljana

Ljubljana, with its easygoing ambience and countless boutiques, is made-to-order for whiling away an afternoon shopping. It's also a fun place to stock up on souvenirs. Popular items include wood carvings and models (especially of the characteristic hayracks that dot the countryside), different flavors of schnapps (the kind with a whole Williams pear inside—cultivated to actually grow right into the bottle—is a particularly fun gift), honey mead brandy (*medica*— sweet and smooth), bars of soap wrapped in wool (good for exfoliating), and those adorable painted panels from beehives (described on page 810). Rounding out the list of traditional Slovenian items are wrought-iron products from Kropa, crystal from Rogaska, lace from Idrija, and salt from Piran. The following neighborhoods are ideal places to browse.

AT CIRIL-METODOV TRG
AND NEAR THE MARKET

The most atmospheric trinket-shopping is in the first stretch of the **market colonnade,** along the riverfront next to the Triple Bridge. See the "Ljubljana Hotels and Restaurants" map for locations.

Trgovina Ika, a small artisan boutique with its own hip and idiosyncratic sense of style, is a delightful place to browse for truly authentic Slovenian stuff that goes beyond souvenirs (variable hours, usually Mon-Fri 9:00-19:30, Sat until 18:00, closed Sun, Ciril-Metodov Trg 13, +386 1 123 21743).

If you're looking for more traditional souvenirs that are serious handicrafts rather than trinkets, drop by the **Rustika** gallery, just over the Triple Bridge (on the castle side). In addition to beehive panels, they also have lace, painted chests and boxes, and other tasteful, local mementos (daily 10:00-19:00, Stritarjeva 9, +386 31 459 509). A bigger but more downscale souvenir shop is **Dom Trgovina,** on the main market square (Mon-Sat 9:00-21:00, Sun 10:00-20:30, Ciril-Metodov Trg 5).

Kraševka sells high-quality artisanal products (mostly edible) from the Karst region, and also acts as a sort of information office for that area (Mon-Fri 9:00-18:00, Sat until 15:00, closed Sun, Vodnikov Trg 4, +386 1 232 1445).

IN THE OLD TOWN

Ljubljana's main Old Town street—which changes names from Mestni Trg to Stari Trg, then Gornji Trg—is also lined with several characteristic shops, selling a few of the unique gift items produced in this proud little country. Unless otherwise noted, all of these shops are open long hours on weekdays (often until 20:00); most close a bit earlier on Saturdays (around 17:00), and close in the early afternoon on Sundays (usually by 13:00 or 14:00).

This area is covered in my "Ljubljana Walk," earlier; see the "Ljubljana Center" map for locations. Make it a point to seek out these goodies on Mestni Trg: honey (**Honey House,** at #7), sea salt from Slovenia's tiny coastline (**Piranske Soline,** at #8), handmade lace from Idrija (**Galerija Idrijske Čipke,** at #17), and brandies and handicrafts from the Dolenje region (**Dobrote Dolenjske,** also at #17).

Chocolate Shops: Three tempting, high-end (yet still affordable) *čokoladnice* are within about a five-minute walk of each other, along Ljubljana's Old Town main drag. **Čokoladnica Cukrček** is the grande dame of this scene, best known for its foil-wrapped "Prešeren Balls" chocolates—a clever and civic-minded take on Salzburg's "Mozart Balls," replacing the composer with Slovenia's greatest poet (Ciril-Metodov Trg 19, www.cukrcek.si). **La Chocolate** is slightly less expensive and feels a bit more modern (Mestni Trg 8, www.lachocolate.si). And **Čokoladnica Ljubljana** attempts to compete with dragon-themed chocolates (Mestni Trg 11, www.cokoladnica-lj.si).

Sleeping in Ljubljana

Ljubljana has good accommodations in all price ranges. I've focused my listings in or within easy walking distance of the city center. To get the best value, book ahead and book directly with the hotel. The most expensive hotels raise their prices even more during conventions (Sept-Oct, and sometimes also June).

$$$$ Heritage Hotel, filling a 400-year-old building facing the Cobblers' Bridge—near, but not too near, the liveliest stretch of the embankment—is a tempting splurge. Its 20 rooms are modern and stylish but retain a respect for tradition; some even come with heavy old beams (air-con, elevator, Čevljarska 2, +386 1 421 1400, www.hotelheritage.si, welcome@hotelheritage.si).

$$$$ Lesar Hotel Angel, on a cobbled square in the Old Town, feels plush and high-end. Its 14 rooms have crisp white decor, and the private garden is inviting (air-con, lots of stairs with no elevator, Gornji Trg 7, +386 1 425 5089, www.angelhotel.si, info@angelhotel.si).

$$$ Vander Urbani Resort is a novel concept: Nestled central as can be just off the riverfront embankment, it really does feel like an intensely hip resort in the city center—right down to the minuscule rooftop swimming pool and sundeck. The hotel prides itself on the cutting-edge urban design of its 20 rooms—with lots of plain concrete—and tries to use Slovenian and organic products wherever possible (air-con, elevator, café, restaurant, champagne bar, Krojaška Ulica 6, +386 1 200 9000, www.vanderhotel.com, info@vanderhotel.com).

$$$ Cubo Hotel is a jolt of trendy minimalism on Ljubljana's hotel scene. Its 26 large rooms are the best place in town for sleek, urban elegance. Ask for a room on the quiet courtyard rather than facing the busy street (air-con, elevator, valet parking, Slovenska Cesta 15, +386 1 425 6000, www.hotelcubo.com, reception@hotelcubo.com).

$$ Hotel Mrak has 34 small but well-equipped rooms in a pleasant neighborhood near French Revolution Square. This trusty place—recently updated, with stylish business-class rooms—is my sentimental favorite in Ljubljana (RS%, air-con, elevator, breakfast terrace under "the oldest vine in Slovenia," pay parking, Rimska 4, +386 1 421 9650, www.hotelmrak.si, info@hotelmrak.si, Kuharič family).

$$ Meščanka ("City Woman") rents seven cozy, well-equipped rooms and apartments in a fantastic location right along the bustling riverfront promenade. The decor is mod, funky, and colorful, and the good windows work hard to provide silence (breakfast extra at next-door restaurant, air-con, self check-in,

Sleep Code

Hotels are categorized according to the average price of a standard double room with breakfast in high season. 1 euro (€) = about $1.10.

$$$$	**Splurge:** Most rooms over €200
$$$	**Pricier:** €150-200
$$	**Moderate:** €100-150
$	**Budget:** €50-100
¢	**Backpacker:** Under €50
RS%	**Rick Steves discount**

Unless otherwise noted, credit cards are accepted, and hotel staff speak basic English. Comparison-shop by checking prices at several hotels (on each hotel's own website, on a booking site, or by email). For the best deal, *book directly with the hotel*. Ask for a discount if paying in cash; if the listing includes **RS%**, request a Rick Steves discount.

Ključavničarska 4, +386 51 880 044, www.mescanka.si, info@mescanka.si, Julija).

$$ Slamič B&B has 17 modern rooms with hardwood floors, tasteful decor, and absentee management. It's over an appealing upscale café in a nondescript but central neighborhood (air-con, pay parking, reception open daily 7:30-23:00, Kersnikova 1, +386 1 433 8233, www.slamic.si, info@slamic.si).

$$ Adora Hotel, tucked behind a church at the edge of the cobbled Old Town zone, has 10 rooms with a restrained rustic style (air-con, elevator, free loaner bikes, pay parking, Rožna Ulica 7, +386 82 057 240, www.adorahotel.si, info@adorahotel.si).

$$ Art Hotel is a good value tucked down a courtyard a 10-minute walk from the heart of town, in a busy student zone. Its 10 straightforward rooms are an afterthought to the youthful, artsy café (air-con, elevator, Soteska 8, +386 1 252 6800, https://art.worhot.com, arthotel@mihovec.si).

$ Barbo Palace, in an excellent location a few steps from Congress Square and the river, is the best bet in town for a touch of history at a good price. Its 12 apartments and four rooms—all refurbished and very spacious—fill an antique building around a classic Old World atrium courtyard (no breakfast but kitchenettes in the apartments, air-con, elevator, reception open 8:00-20:00—call ahead if arriving later, Gosposka 1, +386 70 322 822, www.barbopalace.si, info@barbopalace.si).

$ Penzion Pod Lipo has 10 rooms above a restaurant about a 12-minute walk from Prešeren Square. While the rooms are dated and simple, the place is affordable and thoughtfully run by jolly Marjan (breakfast extra, family room, sometimes unstaffed—let

Ljubljana Hotels & Restaurants

To Contemporary History Museum

Tivoli Park

To Pivovarna Union Brewery

7

GOSPOSVETSKA

KERSNIKOVA ULICA

SLOVENSKA CESTA

CIGALETOVA

CESTA

SERBIAN ORTHODOX CHURCH

NATIONAL GALLERY

Ajdovščina Park

Miklošičev Park

DALMATINOVA ULICA

ŠTEFANOVA ULICA

TIVOLSKA

CANKARJEVA CESTA

39

THE SKYSCRAPER

19 **16**

GRAND HOTEL UNION

NAZORJEVA ULICA

ČOPOVA ULICA

MODERN ART MUSEUM

NATIONAL THEATER

US EMBASSY

TOMSIČEVA ULICA

SLOVENIAN NATIONAL MUSEUM & NATURAL HISTORY MUSEUM

POST

FRANCISCAN CHURCH

Trg Narodni Herojev

Prešeren Square

ŠUBIČEVA ULICA

PARLIAMENT

UNDER-PASS

MEM. TO THE VICTIMS OF ALL WARS

30

TRIPLE BRIDGE

i

36

Ribji Square

14

Square of the Republic

P

Congress Square

WOLFOVA

BR. BRIDGE

River

3

6

OLD

ERJAVČEVA CESTA

CESTA

ULICA

ULICA

22

32

MESTNI TRG

PREŠERNOVA

TWIN OFFICE TOWERS

CESTA

4

10

20

COBBLERS BRIDGE

13

GREGORČIČEVA

IGRIŠKA ULICA

9

VEGOVA

UNIVERSITY

Novi Trg

NATIONAL & UNIVERSITY LIBRARY

FOUNTAIN

STARI TRG

39

RIMSKA CESTA

11

SLOVENSKA CESTA

21

French Revolution Square

28

REBER

15

LEVITŠKOV TRG

5

BREG

Ljubljanica

AŠKERČEVA CESTA

N.U.K. II P

KRIŽANKE THEATER

GOSPOSKA

CITY MUSEUM

ROMAN CITY WALL

ZOISOVA CESTA

ST. JAMES BRIDGE

MIRJE

EMONSKA CESTA

Krakovo Gardens

BARJANSKA CESTA

Krakovo Gardens

KRAKOVO

REČNA UL.

FOOTBRIDGE

GRADAŠKA ULICA

PLEČNIK HOUSE

EIPPROVA ULICA

Accommodations
1. Heritage Hotel
2. Lesar Hotel Angel
3. Vander Urbani Resort
4. Cubo Hotel
5. Hotel Mrak
6. Meščanka Rooms
7. Slamič B&B
8. Adora Hotel
9. Art Hotel
10. Barbo Palace
11. Penzion Pod Lipo
12. Hostel Celica

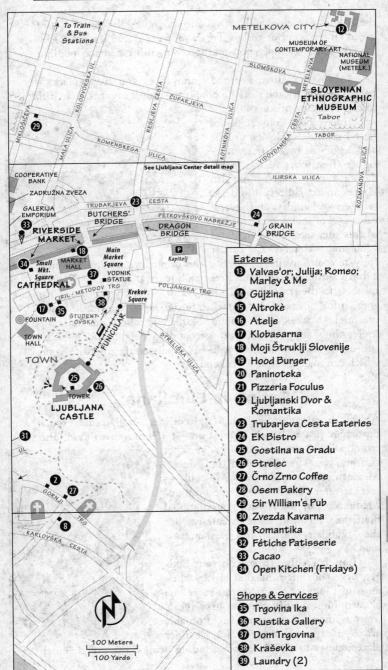

Eateries

13 Valvas'or; Julija; Romeo; Marley & Me
14 Güjžina
15 Altrokè
16 Atelje
17 Klobasarna
18 Moji Štruklji Slovenije
19 Hood Burger
20 Paninoteka
21 Pizzeria Foculus
22 Ljubljanski Dvor & Romantika
23 Trubarjeva Cesta Eateries
24 EK Bistro
25 Gostilna na Gradu
26 Strelec
27 Črno Zrno Coffee
28 Osem Bakery
29 Sir William's Pub
30 Zvezda Kavarna
31 Romantika
32 Fétiche Patisserie
33 Cacao
34 Open Kitchen (Fridays)

Shops & Services

35 Trgovina Ika
36 Rustika Gallery
37 Dom Trgovina
38 Kraševka
39 Laundry (2)

them know when you'll arrive, air-con, guest kitchen, putting green on terrace, Borstnikov Trg 3, +386 1 251 1683, mobile +386 31 809 893, www.penzion-podlipo.com, info@penzion-podlipo.com).

¢ **Hostel Celica,** a proud, innovative, and lively place, is owned by the city and run by a nonprofit student organization. This former military prison's 20 cells *(celica)* have been converted into hostel rooms—each one unique and decorated by a different designer (free tours of the hostel daily at 13:00). The building also houses an art gallery, info desk, self-service laundry, and several eateries. For more on the history of this site, see "More Sights in Ljubljana: Metelkova," earlier

(private rooms available, offers active excursions around Slovenia, a dull 15-minute walk from Prešeren Square at Metelkova 8, eight minutes to the train station, +386 1 230 9700, www.hostelcelica.com, info@hostelcelica.com). The hostel hosts live-music events one night a week until around 24:00, but otherwise maintains "quiet time" after 23:00. The surrounding neighborhood—a bit run-down and remote, but safe—is a happening nightlife zone, which can make for noisy weekends.

Eating in Ljubljana

At this crossroads of cultures (and cuisines), Italian and French flavors are just as "local" as meat-and-starch Slovenian food. This cosmopolitan city also dabbles in other cuisines; you'll find Thai, Indian, Chinese, Mexican, and much more. Most places seem to offer a similar menu of Slovenian/Mediterranean fare with international flourishes. To locate these restaurants, see the "Ljubljana Hotels and Restaurants" map.

Lunch Deals: To stretch your budget, have your main meal at lunch, when most of Ljubljana's top eateries serve one or two high-quality three-course meals (starter, main, dessert) at an affordable price—usually around €15 (or, at finer places, closer to €20-25), not including drinks. I've noted "lunch special" where applicable. Many places offer these deals only on weekdays.

Traditional Slovenian Food: Because Slovenes head into the countryside when they want traditional fare, Ljubljana isn't the best place to find authentic Slovenian grub. But if you'd like to try some, your best budget bets are **Klobasarna** or **Moji Štruklji Slovenije;** for a more formal sit-down meal, head for **Gostilna na Gradu** at the castle. Other places feature "regional" cuisines, such as Pannonian, from northeast Slovenia **(Güjžina),** or Istrian, from the Adriatic coast **(Altrokè).** For a night of traditional food and culture (on the corny side), check out the **Slovenian Evening** dinner and folklore show, held at one of two restaurants near the Triple Bridge (around €60/person, for details and to book see www. slovenian-evening.com).

"Open Kitchen" Street-Food Festival: On Fridays from spring through fall, Ljubljana has one of the most appealing street-food markets anywhere: the Open Kitchen (Odprta Kuhna), which fills the first market square below the cathedral (across the Triple Bridge from Prešeren Square) with stalls featuring delicious creations by Slovenian chefs. Most places have big plates for around €6-8; you'll run out of stomach space well before you run out of money (festival runs mid-March-late Oct Fri 10:00-21:00; can be cancelled when it rains; at Pogačarjev Trg, www.odprtakuhna.si).

IN THE CITY CENTER
Sit-Down Meals in the Old Town

The main drag through the Old Town (which starts at the Town Hall and changes names as it goes: Mestni Trg, then Stari Trg, then Gornji Trg) is lined with inviting eateries. Several popular options cluster in one particularly atmospheric stretch; all except Romeo offer a similar menu of Mediterranean-Slovenian cuisine and wonderful outdoor seating: **$$$$ Valvas'or,** the upscale option, has a dressy dining room and a posh gold color scheme (weekday lunch special, closed Sun, Stari Trg 7, +386 1 425 0455). **$$$ Julija** features homey country-Slovenian decor inside (lunch specials, daily, Stari Trg 9, +386 1 425 6463). **$ Romeo,** across the street, is a lowbrow bar serving so-so "global fusion" food, from Mexican to crêpes...but the name sure is clever (get it? "Romeo and Julija"). And **$$ Marley & Me** comes with a warm welcome from Matej (weekday lunch specials, daily, Stari Trg 9, +386 8 380 6610). Additional options are just a few steps away.

$$ Güjžina features food and wine from the Hungarian-influenced region of Slovenia called Prekmurje, done with a twist—it's all vegan. This is an odd match for such a meat-heavy cuisine, and some dishes are more successful than others. But it's satisfying to dig into a small kettle of rich, flavorful *bograč*—a spicy, goulash-

---

Restaurant Code

Eateries in this book are categorized according to the average
cost of a typical main course. Drinks, desserts, and splurge
items can raise the price considerably. 1 euro (€) = about $1.10.

$$$$	**Splurge:** Most main courses over €20
$$$	**Pricier:** €15-20
$$	**Moderate:** €10-15
$	**Budget:** Under €10

In Slovenia, a takeout spot is **$**, a basic sit-down eatery is **$$**,
a casual but more upscale restaurant is **$$$**, and a swanky
splurge is **$$$$**.

---

like stew—and the roasted dumplings called *dödöle*. This is also a
great place to taste some of Prekmurje's underrated wines and to
sample *gibanica* poppy-seed layer cake—originating in Prekmurje
and beloved throughout Slovenia (long hours daily, Mestni Trg 19,
+386 83 806 446).

$$$$ Altrokè highlights cuisine from Istria—the region
shared by southern Slovenia and northern Croatia. That means
Adriatic seafood, *pršut* (prosciutto), and lots of truffles, served in
a cozy stone-walled dining room right along the Old Town's main
drag (daily, Stari Trg 19, +386 82 055 282).

Top-End Splurge Nearby: Just a short walk away from this
zone, across the Triple Bridge, **$$$$ Atelje** is a notch above. Chef
Jorg Zupan has earned a Michelin star for his "simple, but refined"
cuisine, and designs a seasonal menu that mixes Slovenian and in-
ternational ingredients and influences. Atelje fills a beautiful retro
space next to Grand Hotel Union, just a block off Prešeren Square,
with a few inviting al fresco tables out front. They have only fixed-
price *menu*s: dinner is seven courses for over €100; lunch is a more
budget-friendly three courses for €35. Either way, book well ahead
(closed Sun, Nazorjeva 2, +386 1 308 1907, www.restavracijaatelje.
com).

Fast and Cheap

$ Klobasarna is a budget foodie option specializing in *kranjska
klobasa*—traditional Carniolan sausage, from the Slovenian up-
lands. The menu is simple—one wiener or two, extra for seasonal
soup—and delicious. The soups are hearty and filling, often either
jota (turnip stew) or *ričet* (barley stew). They also serve the Slovenian
dumplings called *štruklji* (daily, Sun lunch only, Ciril-Metodov Trg
15, +386 51 605 017).

$ Moji Štruklji Slovenije ("My Slovenian Dumplings"), in
the market colonnade, is a handy spot to sample the traditional

Slovenian rolled dumplings called *štruklji*. They have over 20 varieties, both sweet and savory, which are fun to peruse in the display case. The interior seating is tight, so grab an outdoor table tucked under the colonnade. They also sell hearty Slovenian stews and soups (Mon-Sat 7:00-20:00, Fri until 22:00, Sun 10:00-18:00, shorter hours Nov-March, Adamič-Lundrovo Nabrežje 1, +386 59 042 190).

$ Hood Burger, part of a locally beloved chain, is Slovenia's answer to In-N-Out. The owners pride themselves on using locally sourced ingredients ("100 percent Slovenian beef!") and cultivate a personal relationship with their producers. The result is tasty, authentic burgers (daily, handiest location is just off Prešeren Square at Nazorjeva 4).

$ Paninoteka, with wonderful outdoor seating overlooking Cobblers' Bridge and nice indoor seating, has affordable, tasty sandwiches; their full menu is good but more expensive (daily, Jurčičev Trg 3, +386 40 349 329).

Pizzerias: $$ Pizzeria Foculus, tucked in a boring alleyway a few short blocks up from the river, has a loyal local following, a happening atmosphere, an inviting interior, a few outdoor tables, and some of Ljubljana's favorite pizza (over 50 types, daily, just off French Revolution Square across the street from Plečnik's National and University Library at Gregorčičeva 3, +386 1 251 5643).

$$ Ljubljanski Dvor enjoys the most convenient and scenic location of any pizzeria in town. On a sunny summer day, the outdoor riverside terrace is unbeatable; I'd skip the dull interior and their pricier pasta restaurant around the corner (daily, 50 yards from Cobblers' Bridge at Dvorni Trg 1, +386 1 251 6555). Ljubljanski Dvor also has a handy **$ takeout window** around back on Congress Square. Enjoy a cheap slice at one of their outdoor tables facing the square, or get it to go and munch it along the river.

Funky Student Zone on Trubarjeva Cesta: Here you'll find a variety of cheap global fare, from falafel to Asian noodles to pizza by the slice, mixed in among home decor galleries, vape shops, and erotic boutiques. A few blocks east, detour a short block to the riverfront to find **$$ EK Bistro,** a brunch/lunch spot with a big foodie reputation (daily, Petkovškovo Nabrežje 65, +386 51 624 061).

AT THE CASTLE

Ljubljana's castle complex has some basic eateries, and two high-end splurges—one traditional, the other a bit snobby and modern. For either of these, reserve ahead before making the trip.

$$$ Gostilna na Gradu offers Slovenian cuisine in the castle courtyard high above town—if you don't mind going up to the castle to get it (the handy funicular costs €6 round-trip). It serves up a seasonal menu of traditional flavors with modern flair at fairly high prices. Choose between the dull vaulted interior, the glassed-in arcade, or an outdoor table (Mon-Sat 12:00-22:00—last seating at 20:00, Sun 12:00-17:00—last seating at 15:00, Grajska Planota 1, +386 820 51931, www.jezersek.si).

$$$$ Strelec (STREH-lets) is a heavily themed splurge run by chef Igor Jagodic. The elaborately described menu items are based on real historical recipes. It's pretentious, but it's earned a Michelin star and is worth booking ahead for foodies (Mon-Fri dinner only, Sat lunch and dinner, closed Sun, +386 31 687 648, www.kaval-group.si).

DRINKS AND TREATS

Riverfront Cafés: Enjoying a coffee, beer, or ice-cream cone along the breezy Ljubljanica River embankment (between the Triple and Cobblers' bridges) is Ljubljana's single best experience—worth ▲▲▲. Tables spill onto the street, and some of the best-dressed, best-looking students on the planet happily fill them day and night. (A common question from first-time visitors to Ljubljana: "Doesn't

anybody here have a job?") This is some of the top people-watching in Europe. When ordering, the easiest choice is a *bela kava* (white coffee)—a caffe latte. For location, see the "Ljubljana Center" map, earlier.

Quality Coffee: While the riverfront strip has good coffee and amazing ambience, coffee fanatics may want something more serious. **Črno Zrno,** tucked on historic Gornji Trg at the end of the Old Town drag, is owned by Alexander Nino, a coffee snob who sources beans from his native Colombia and serves a wide variety of coffee drinks in a tiny, colorfully tiled, hole-in-the-wall interior. If you take milk or sugar with your coffee, be prepared to defend your request (daily, Gornji Trg 17, +386 31 446 398).

Bakery: $ Osem ("Eight"), along the Old Town's main drag, is a simple space that bakes breads from scratch each morning. You'll smell it before you see it (daily, Sat until 13:00, closed Sun, Stari Trg 17, +386 40 562 699).

Microbrews: Sir William's Pub is where beer aficionados go to get a taste of Slovenia's burgeoning craft-beer scene. It has a few outdoor tables and a classic British pub interior, and a thoughtfully curated menu of both domestic and international microbrews on tap and by the bottle (no food, long hours Mon-Fri, Sat-Sun from 17:00, Tavčarjeva Ulica 8A, +386 59 944 825).

Cakes: Zvezda Kavarna, a trendy, central place at the bottom of Congress Square, is a local favorite for cakes, pastries, and ice cream. A nostalgic specialty here—once popular in communist times and recently reintroduced to great acclaim—is the *emona kocka* (Emona cube), a layer cake with nuts, cake, and chocolate (long hours daily, Sun until 20:00, Kongresni Trg 3, +386 1 421 9090). Their **deli,** just around the corner toward Prešeren Square, has takeaway coffee and smoothies, a wide variety of cakes to go, and some of the most decadent ice cream in town (same hours).

Ice Cream: Ljubljana is known for its Italian gelato-style ice cream. **Romantika,** just up the steps from the river, is the foodies' choice, with creative and delicious artisanal flavors (just uphill from Ljubljanksi Dvor pizzeria at Dvorni Trg 1; a second branch is just across the river in the Old Town, at Stari Trg 15). **Fétiche Patisserie,** along the riverfront café embankment, is another good choice, with unusual, pungent, Asian-themed flavors. Other favorites include **Cacao,** across the river from the market (and just up the river from Prešeren Square), which also has wonderful embankment seating; and **Zvezda's** deli.

Ljubljana Connections

As Slovenia's transportation hub, Ljubljana is well connected to both domestic and international destinations. When checking schedules, be aware of city name variations: In Slovene, Vienna is "Dunaj," Budapest is "Budimpešta," and Venice is "Benétke."

Local Alternative: When considering bus and train connections, don't overlook the very handy **GoOpti** shared transfer service, which is often more convenient, faster, and not much more expensive. Locals swear by this service for airport transfers and reaching otherwise tricky-to-connect places like Venice and Istria; it can even be handy for getting to Zagreb, if the train schedule doesn't suit your plans (for details, see "By Shared Shuttle Service," later).

BY TRAIN

From Ljubljana by Train to: Lesce-Bled (roughly hourly, 40-60 minutes—but bus is better because it goes right to Bled town center), **Postojna** (nearly hourly, 1 hour), **Divača** (close to Škocjan Caves— free shuttle bus meets some connections, nearly hourly, 2 hours), **Sežana** (close to Lipica, nearly hourly, 2 hours), **Piran** (direct bus is better—see later; otherwise allow 4 hours, train to Koper, 2/day, 2.5 hours; then bus to Piran, 7/day, 30 minutes), **Maribor** (hourly, 2-3 hours, most direct, some with a transfer in Zidani Most), **Ptuj** (2/day direct, 2.5 hours, nearly hourly with transfer in Pragersko or Maribor), **Zagreb** (3/day direct, 2.5 hours), **Rijeka** (2/day direct, 3 hours), **Pula** (1/day with change at Divaca, likely in summer only,

4 hours), **Split** (2/day, including 1 night train, 9 hours on the train, plus layover time in Zagreb), **Vienna** (that's **Dunaj** in Slovene, 1/day direct, 6 hours; otherwise 4/day with transfer in Villach or Maribor, 6 hours), **Budapest** (that's **Budimpešta** in Slovene; 1/day direct, 8.5 hours, other connections possible with 1-2 changes but complicated, no convenient night train), **Venice** (called **Benétke** in Slovene; fastest by bus or GoOpti—see later; otherwise 2/day with transfer in Trieste, 5 hours), **Salzburg** (1/day direct, 4.5 hours; an additional 2/day possible with transfer in Villach), **Munich** (2/day direct, 6.5 hours, including 1 night train; also possible 2/day with transfer in Villach). If heading to **Italy**, you can ride the train to **Trieste** (2/day, 2.5 hours) and connect to high-speed Italian trains from there. Train info: www.slo-zeleznice.si.

BY BUS

The bus station is a low-profile building in front of the train station. Most buses depart from the numbered stalls in the middle of the street. For any of these buses, you can book online or buy tickets at the bus station ticket windows or at the automated e-kart kiosk (pay with credit card or cash)—not from the driver. For bus information, pick up one of the blue phones inside the station to be connected to a helpful English-speaking operator. Most timetables can be found at www.ap-ljubljana.si or https://getbybus.com. Buses operated by Flixbus have their own schedules and departure point, described later; tickets are only sold on their website (www.flixbus. com).

From Ljubljana to Popular Side Trips: Bled (Mon-Sat hourly—usually at the top of each hour, fewer on Sun, 1.5 hours), **Postojna Caves** (3/day, 1 hour; or ride an hourly bus to Postojna town and walk or taxi from there), **Divača** (close to **Škocjan Caves,** about every 2-3 hours, 1.5 hours), **Piran** (5/day Mon-Fri, 2/day Sat, 4/day Sun, 2.5 hours, more with change in Portorož).

Into the Julian Alps: Direct buses run from Ljubljana to the towns of **Bovec** and **Kobarid** via the valley town of Idrija (Mon-Fri 2/day, likely at 11:15 and 18:00; Sat-Sun only at 18:00; about 3 hours to Kobarid, 4 hours to Bovec). You can ask if there are direct buses that take the super-scenic route over the **Vršič Pass** (which take longer but add breathtaking views)—they run irregularly. To take this route, it's more likely you'll have to first head to the town of Kranjska Gora—in the valley just below Vršič—and change buses there (only possible in summer—otherwise the pass may be closed due to weather).

To Croatia: Slovenia is not well connected with Croatia's Istria, though Flixbus usually provides connections (typically 1-2/day, stopping at **Rovinj** and/or **Pula,** about 4-5 hours). Other bus companies also connect to the transit hubs of **Zagreb** (8-10/day, fewer on weekends, 2.5 hours) and **Rijeka** (2/day, fewer off-season, 2.5 hours).

International Destinations on Flixbus: In addition to the Rovinj and Pula connections I've noted, Flixbus offers frequent, direct, long-distance buses to cities including **Zagreb** (2.5 hours), **Rijeka** (2.5 hours), **Venice** (4 hours), **Vienna** (5.5 hours), **Munich** (5.5 hours), and **Budapest** (6.5 hours)—often faster and cheaper than by train. These buses depart from platform/*peron* 29/30; check schedules and buy tickets at www.flixbus.com.

BY SHARED SHUTTLE SERVICE

If bus and train schedules don't quite serve your needs, **GoOpti**—a company with an innovative business model for shared minibus transfers—can be a convenient and inexpensive alternative. Slovenes love it. First, go to www.goopti.com and select your destination, date, and preferred arrival or departure time, and book a slot. Twenty-four hours before your trip, you'll receive an update with the specific pickup time, based on the needs of other passengers. Prices can flex dramatically, but it's quite affordable (for example, an advance nonrefundable purchase from Ljubljana could be €15 to Piran, or €25 to Venice or Zagreb). They also offer airport transfers to or from downtown Ljubljana for €10-12. For a few euros extra, they can pick you up at your hotel rather than the train or bus station; to lock in a specific time, you can pay even more for a "VIP" transfer. Reserve in advance for this popular service, which can be fully booked a day (or longer) ahead.

GoOpti reaches destinations throughout Slovenia (including Ljubljana, the airport, Lake Bled, towns in the Karst such as Postojna and Sežana, and Piran and other Slovenian coastal destinations), but it's also handy for farther-flung international destinations—such as Venice or its airport, Trieste, various Austrian cities (Vienna, Salzburg, Klagenfurt, etc.), and Croatian cities such as Zagreb, Rovinj, and Pula.

BY PLANE

Slovenia's only **airport** (code: LJU) is 14 miles north of Ljubljana, about halfway to Bled. Confusingly, the airport goes by three names: Ljubljana Airport (the international version), Brnik (for the town that it's near), and Jože Pučnik Airport (a local politician). The airport is small and manageable. If you're on an early-morning flight, don't bother showing up before 5:00, when the airport opens. Airport info: +386 4 206 1000, www.lju-airport.si.

Getting to Downtown Ljubljana: Exiting the baggage-claim area, you'll see desks lined up offering €10-12/person shared **shuttle** rides into Ljubljana that take about 30 minutes. Well-established outfits include GoOpti (www.goopti.com—just described),

Nomago (www.nomago.eu), and Markun (www.markun-shuttle.com). While it's better to book these ahead, they often have space for those who just show up. Most drop you at the bus/train station area, though you may be able to pay about €5 extra for door-to-door service. These companies also go from downtown *to* the airport; book online in advance.

Otherwise, you could take **public bus** #28 (labeled *Ljubljana-Brnik,* to the right as you exit the airport; Mon-Fri 2/hour until 20:00—faster departures at :30 past the hour, otherwise 45 minutes, about €5-6 depending on route; 7/day Sat-Sun). Most expensive is a **taxi;** the fair rate is around €40, but the rip-off cabbies who wait at the airport charge much more. It's best to call for a taxi (or ask the info desk to call one for you).

To Lake Bled: Several Bled-based companies offer handy shared shuttle services for connecting to the airport. For tips on going from the airport directly to Lake Bled, see "Lake Bled Connections" in the next chapter.

Airport Alternatives: Ljubljana's airport—the only one in the country—charges high taxes and fees, and has limited connections to some European destinations. To save money (or to avoid a layover), many Slovenes fly in and out of relatively nearby airports in neighboring countries: **Zagreb** (2-hour drive from Ljubljana), **Venice** (3-hour drive from Ljubljana), **Trieste** (2-hour drive from Ljubljana), and **Klagenfurt/Kärnten** (especially for those going to Lake Bled, from which it's a 2-hour drive). To get between these airports and your Slovenian destination, GoOpti, described earlier, is typically cheaper than a taxi and more convenient than a bus or train connection.

LAKE BLED

Lake Bled—Slovenia's leading mountain resort—comes complete with a sweeping alpine panorama, a fairy-tale island, a cliff-hanging medieval castle, a lazy lakeside promenade, and the country's most sought-after desserts. And the charms of its glorious mountain scenery and traditional folk life only crescendo as you explore the surrounding areas. Taken together, there are few more enjoyable places to be on vacation.

Since the Habsburg days, Lake Bled (locals pronounce it like "blade") has been *the* place where Slovenes wow visiting diplomats. In the late 19th century, local aristocrats surrounded the humble lakefront village with classy villas. Tito also had one of his vacation homes here (today's Hotel Vila Bled), where he entertained illustrious guests.

Lake Bled has plenty of ways to idle away an afternoon. While the lake's main town, also called Bled, is more functional than quaint, it offers postcard views of the lake and handy access to the region. Hike up to Bled Castle for intoxicating vistas. Ride a traditional *pletna* boat out to the island, climb up to the church, ring the bell, and make a wish. Wander or bike the dreamy path around the lake. Sit on a dock, dip your feet in the water, and watch the lake's resident swans. Then dive into some of Bled's famous cakes while you take in the view of Triglav, Slovenia's favorite mountain. Bled quiets down at night—there's no nightlife beyond a handful of pubs—giving hikers and other holidaymakers a chance to recharge.

Bled is also a great jumping-off point for a car trip through the Julian Alps (see next chapter), and a wide variety of other worthwhile side trips begin right at its doorstep. These include the less-developed lake named Bohinj, even deeper in the mountains;

a spectacular hike in the nearby mountain gorge of Vintgar; and the pleasant Old Town of Radovljica, with its charming pedestrian zone and fascinating little beekeeping museum.

PLANNING YOUR TIME

Bled and its neighboring mountains deserve at least two days. With one day, spend it in and around Bled (or spend a quick morning in Bled and an afternoon day-tripping). With a second day and a car, drive through the Julian Alps using the self-guided tour in the next chapter. The circular route takes you up and over the stunning Vršič Pass, then down the scenic and historic Soča River Valley. Without a car, skip the second day, or spend it doing nearby day trips: Bus or bike to Radovljica and its bee museum, hike Vintgar Gorge, or visit Lake Bohinj (all described under "Near Lake Bled," at the end of this chapter).

Be prepared for heavy crowds in July and August, and on weekends in spring and fall (when the lake is popular with Slovenian day-trippers). The road into Bled town can get seriously backed up: The drive in from the highway, which normally takes 10 minutes, can take 40 minutes or more—and parking is scarce. Do your best to arrive early or late, and book ahead for Vintgar Gorge, which can sell out.

Orientation to Lake Bled

The town of Bled is on the east end of 1.5-mile-long Lake Bled. The lakefront is lined with soothing parks and boxy resort hotels. A 3.5-mile path meanders around the lake. As no motorized boats are allowed, Lake Bled is particularly peaceful.

The tourist center of Bled has two parts, which melt into each other: a simple village and a cluster of giant hotels. The main thoroughfare, called **Ljubljanska Cesta,** leads out of Bled town toward Ljubljana and most other destinations. Just up from the lakefront is the modern **commercial center** (Trgovski Center Bled), with a supermarket, ATM, shops, and a smattering of lively cafés. Nicknamed "Gaddafi," the commercial center was designed for a city in Libya, but the deal fell through—so the practical Slovenes built it here instead.

Bled's Old Town, under the castle, has a web of tight streets and big-but-humble old houses surrounding the pointy spire of

Lake Bled

St. Martin's Church. In this area, you'll find the bus station, some good restaurants, a few hostels, and more locals than tourists.

The mountains poking above the ridge at the far end of the lake are the Julian Alps, crowned by the three peaks of Mount Triglav. The big mountain behind the town of Bled is Stol ("Chair"), part of the Karavanke range that defines the Austrian border.

TOURIST INFORMATION

Bled's most central TI is in the long, lakefront casino building across the street from the big, white Hotel Park (as you face the lake, the TI is hiding around the front at the far left end, overlooking the lake). Pick up the map with the lake on one side and the whole region on the other and the free, up-to-date Bled information booklet. Get advice on hikes and day trips, and if you're doing any serious hiking, spring for a good regional map. They also rent bikes (mid-April-mid-Oct Mon-Sat 9:00-18:00, Sun until 17:00 plus July-Aug Mon-Sat 8:00-20:00; off-season Mon-Sat 9:00-17:00, Sun until 16:00; Cesta Svobode 10, +386 4 574 1122, www.bled.si).

The TI's other branch—handy for drivers, on the main road out of town—conveniently shares an office with the **Triglav Na-**

tional Park Information Center, which offers advice for those heading into the mountains. The center, with free parking, is called "Triglavska Roža" (bike rentals, maps and guidebooks for sale; daily 8:00-18:00, off-season until 16:00; Ljubljanska Cesta 27, +386 4 578 0205, www.tnp.si).

ARRIVAL IN BLED

By Train: Two train stations have the name "Bled." The **Bled Jezero** (Bled Lake) station is across the lake from Bled town and is used only by infrequent, slow, tourist-oriented trains into the mountains. You're much more likely to use the **Lesce-Bled** station, about 2.5 miles from Bled in the village of Lesce (pronounced lest-SEH). The Lesce-Bled station is on the main line toward Austria and has far better connections to Ljubljana and international destinations. When buying a train ticket or checking schedules, request "Lesce-Bled" rather than just "Bled."

From the **Lesce-Bled station,** you can take the bus into Bled town (2-3/hour, 10 minutes, catch it across the street from the train station), or pay about €15 for a taxi. If taking the train out of Lesce-Bled, buy tickets online, at this station, or on the train—tickets are not sold in Bled town.

By Bus: Bled's main bus station is a steep five-minute hike up from the lake in the Old Town; to reach the lake, walk straight down Cesta Svobode—the downhill street behind the station. Note that many buses also stop on the way into town, along Ljubljanska Cesta, which is handier for walking to many of my recommended accommodations (for details, see "Sleeping in Bled," later)—be sure to ask your driver.

By Car: Coming from Ljubljana, you'll wind your way into Bled on Ljubljanska Cesta, which rumbles through the middle of town before swinging left at the lake. Parking can be challenging. Local accommodations have a line on free parking nearby—ask when you book. If you're here for a quick visit, you can try to find a spot in the short-term parking lot just above the commercial center (free for 1 hour, €2/2 hours, 2-hour limit). If that lot is full—as it often is—there are several small lots tucked behind the big hotels in the wooded zone between the commercial center and the bus station—carefully check signs to understand the time limits (typically €2/hour, 2-4-hour limit).

The best option is often the lot by the ice rink, Sports Hall Bled, which often has spaces when others are full; nearby, there's a privately run lot just above and across the street from the Town Hall (on Prešernova Cesta). For longer-term parking, you'll find cheaper lots with no time limits on Seliška street, which curves just above town (€1/hour)—look for the lot at the kindergarten *(vrtec),* across from the big Spar and Mercator supermarkets; or for one called "Seliška 2," which is a bit closer to the Old Town.

For more driving tips, see "Route Tips for Drivers" under "Lake Bled Connections," later.

By Plane: For details on getting from Ljubljana's airport to Bled, see "Lake Bled Connections," later.

HELPFUL HINTS

Laundry: Call **Anže Štalc** to arrange drop-off, then pick up your clean and folded clothes 24 hours later (same-day express service available, +386 41 575 522). The **Speed Queen** self-service launderette, near the top of town, is surprisingly luxe, with massaging recliners (daily 6:00-21:00, Prešernova Cesta 50, +386 41 366 323).

Car Rental: The Julian Alps are ideal by car. Several companies have branches in Bled, including **Europcar** (+386 31 382 055), **Budget** (+386 41 578 0320), and **Hertz** (+386 4 201 6999).

Massage and Spa Treatments: If you're here to relax, consider a visit to the **Essense** wellness center at the recommended Alp Penzion. This modern, classy facility—hiding in the country-side about a 20-minute walk or 5-minute taxi ride above the lake—offers a wide range of spa treatments, including pedicures and Thai massage (arrange in advance, Cankarjeva Cesta 20A, +386 40 996 666, www.essense.si). You'll also find wellness centers with massage, saunas, and whirlpools at a few of the big hotels (all open to nonguests). The biggest is the **Živa** spa at the Rikli Balance Hotel, with a swimming pool, lakeview hot tubs, and massages; Hotel Park's **Thai Center** spa also offers good massages (info for both at www.sava-hotels-resorts.com). There are also spas at **Hotel Astoria,** the **Bled Rose Hotel,** and for guests only at the **Grand Hotel Toplice** and **Hotel Lovec.**

GETTING AROUND LAKE BLED (LITERALLY)

By Bike: You can rent a mountain bike at several points around town, including the TI (€5/hour, €13/3 hours, €17/half-day, €20/day). While walking around the lake is slo-mo bliss, biking it lets you fast-forward between the views of your choice. If you go clockwise, you'll use the busy lakefront road for the first stretch, but after the village of Mlino, traffic thins out. The best views are from the lakefront gravel path; pedestrians have priority, but courteous cyclists are welcome. (The paved road is higher up, with not-as-good views.)

Biking is also a great way to reach Vintgar Gorge—about three mostly level miles one-way, perfect for combining a coun-tryside pedal with a walk immersed in nature. The separated bike

LAKE BLED

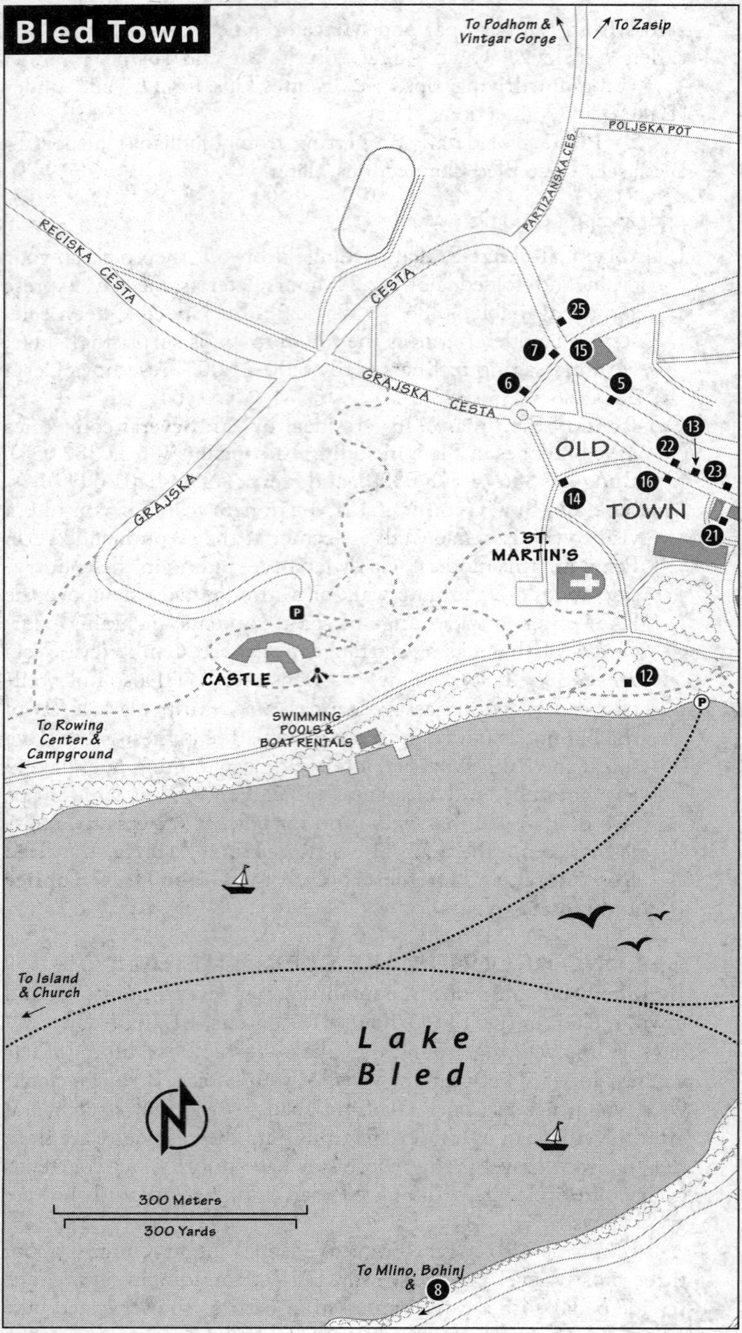

Bled Town

To Podhom &
Vintgar Gorge

To Zasip

POLJSKA POT

REČIŠKA CESTA

CESTA

PARTIZANSKA CES.

25

7 15

GRAJSKA CESTA

6

5

13

OLD

22

GRAJSKA

16

23

14

TOWN

21

ST.
MARTIN'S

P

CASTLE

12

P

To Rowing
Center &
Campground

SWIMMING
POOLS &
BOAT RENTALS

To Island
& Church

Lake
Bled

N

300 Meters

300 Yards

To Mlino, Bohinj
&

8

LAKE BLED

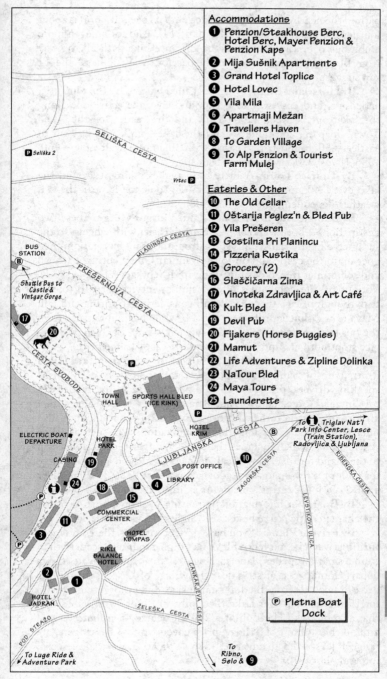

Accommodations

1. Penzion/Steakhouse Berc, Hotel Berc, Mayer Penzion & Penzion Kaps
2. Mija Sušnik Apartments
3. Grand Hotel Toplice
4. Hotel Lovec
5. Vila Mila
6. Apartmaji Mežan
7. Travellers Haven
8. To Garden Village
9. To Alp Penzion & Tourist Farm Mulej

Eateries & Other

10. The Old Cellar
11. Oštarija Peglez'n & Bled Pub
12. Vila Prešeren
13. Gostilna Pri Planincu
14. Pizzeria Rustika
15. Grocery (2)
16. Slaščičarna Zima
17. Vinoteka Zdravljica & Art Café
18. Kult Bled
19. Devil Pub
20. Fijakers (Horse Buggies)
21. Mamut
22. Life Adventures & Zipline Dolinka
23. NaTour Bled
24. Maya Tours
25. Launderette

SELIŠKA CESTA

P Seliška 2

Vrtec P

BUS STATION

Shuttle Bus to Castle & Vintgar Gorge

PREŠERNOVA CESTA

MLADINSKA CESTA

CESTA SVOBODE

ELECTRIC BOAT DEPARTURE

TOWN HALL

SPORTS HALL BLED (ICE RINK)

CASINO

HOTEL PARK

HOTEL KRIM

To Triglav Nat'l Park Info Center, Lesce (Train Station), Radovljica & Ljubljana

LJUBLJANSKA CESTA

POST OFFICE

LIBRARY

ZAGORŠKA CESTA

RIBENSKA CESTA

LEVSTIKOVA ULICA

COMMERCIAL CENTER

HOTEL KOMPAS

RIKLI BALANCE HOTEL

CANKARJEVA CESTA

HOTEL JADRAN

POD STRAŽO

ŽELEŠKA CESTA

To Luge Ride & Adventure Park

To Ribno, Selo & ⑨

P **Pletna Boat Dock**

LAKE BLED

path to the nearby town of Radovljica (and its bee museum) is about four level miles one-way (get details at TI). And for an even more ambitious trip, ask about the long-distance bike path all the way from Bled to Kranjska Gora, at the base of the Vršič Pass. The TI can suggest other ideas.

By Horse and Buggy: Buggies called *fijaker*s are the romantic, expensive, and easy way to get around the lake. Hire one along the lakefront between Hotel Park and the castle (see the "Bled Town" map for location; around the lake—€50, one-way up to castle—€50, round-trip to castle with 30-minute wait time—€60, +386 41 710 970, www.fijaker-bled.si).

By Tourist Train: A little train makes a circuit around the lake every 40 minutes in summer (€5, look for it near the TI, weather-dependent, +386 51 337 478).

By Shuttle Bus to the Castle and Vintgar Gorge: These two destinations—both walkable—are much easier with wheels. In the summer, a handy shuttle bus starts from the main bus station, then goes up to the castle and on to the Vintgar Gorge entrance (cheap and sometimes free; 6/day mid-June–mid-Sept, get schedule at TI). Various private companies offer a similar service for €10 round-trip; though pricey, these are worth considering in spring and fall: Maya runs a shuttle from near the TI, while Mamut departs from the bus station (for details, check at each office). Each shuttle service stops both at Vintgar Gorge and the castle (same price).

By Taxi: Your hotel can call a taxi for you. Or contact **Bled Tours,** run by Sandi, Anže, Cvetka, and their team of English-speaking drivers (prices for up to 3 people: €12 to the castle, €18 to Vintgar Gorge, €60 to Ljubljana airport, €140 to Klagenfurt airport in Austria, other airport transfers on request). They also offer self-guided excursions that include admission, such as "Bled All-in-One," which includes the castle, Vintgar Gorge, and a trip to the island for €100 (or you can do Bled Castle and Vintgar Gorge for €50, or a few hours in Radovljica for €35; +386 31 205 611 or +386 31 321 122, https://bledtours.si, info@bledtours.si).

By Boat: For information on renting your own boat or riding the characteristic *pletna* boats, see "Sights at Lake Bled," later.

By Private Plane: If you have perfect weather, there's no more thrilling way to experience Slovenia's high-mountain scenery than from a small propeller plane soaring over the peaks. Private flights depart from a grass airstrip near the village of Lesce, a 10-minute drive or taxi ride from Bled. It's expensive...but unforgettable (€100 for 15-minute hop over Lake Bled only, €210 for 30-minute flight that also buzzes Lake Bohinj, €280 for deluxe 45-minute version around the summit of Triglav, price covers up to 3 passengers, arrange at least a day in advance, +386 41 959 035, www.alc-lesce.si, info@alc-lesce.si).

Tours at Lake Bled

Local Guides

Tina Hiti and **Sašo Golub,** an energetic couple, are excellent guides who enjoy sharing the town and region they love with American visitors (€90 for 2-hour walking tour of Bled, arrange several days in advance, www.pg-slovenia.com, info@pg-slovenia.com, Tina +386 40 166 554, Sašo +386 40 524 774). Tina and Sašo are especially handy for side-tripping into the countryside if you don't want to drive yourself. Their most popular trip is a day in the Julian Alps (€280 round-trip from Bled, €50 extra to pick up or drop off in Ljubljana, extra charge for 5 or more people, €10/person extra for picnic lunch). They also offer food tours, airport transfers, and trips in the Slovenian countryside to research your roots. As Tina and Sašo both lead tours for me in Europe, they may send you off with a well-trained substitute—sometimes Tina's father, **Gorazd,** a former Yugoslav Olympian in ice hockey who brings the older generation's perspective to the trip; or perhaps **Petra, Nina, Grega,** or the other **Grega.**

Excursions

To hit several far-flung day-trip destinations in one go, consider a package tour from Bled. Destinations range from Ljubljana and the Karst region to the Austrian Lakes to Venice. For example, an all-day Julian Alps trip to the Vršič Pass and Soča Valley runs about €90 per person (sold by various agencies around town—ask the TI). Note that two people can rent a car for the day for less than the cost of a tour and do it at their own pace using the self-guided driving tour in the next chapter.

Adventure Trips

One popular choice is an all-day white-water rafting trip on the Soča River (around €145/person including transportation from Lake Bled, or closer to €55 if you meet them there). Other options include canyoning, river tubing, mountain biking, paragliding, and rock climbing.

Three companies have offices near Bled's bus station: **Mamut** (+386 40 121 900, www.slovenija.eu.com), **Life Adventures** (+386 40 508 853, www.lifeadventures.si), and **NaTour Bled** (+386 70 644 621, www.natour-bled.si). **Maya Tours** is near the TI, in the lakefront casino building (+386 4 020 3405, www.bledtransfers.si). Note that these companies tend to attract a young, sometimes rowdy crowd that enjoys lubricating their adventures with alcohol. Another option, **Zipline Dolinka,** offers a 2.5-hour zipline course (with seven runs) that zigzags over an alpine river near Bled (+386 31 845 900, www.zipline-dolinka.si).

Sights at Lake Bled

Bled doesn't have many sights, but there are plenty of rewarding and pleasant activities.

▲▲▲Walk Around the Lake

Strolling the 3.5-mile lake perimeter is enjoyable, peaceful, and scenic. At a leisurely pace, it takes about an hour and a half...not counting stops to snap photos of the ever-changing view. For the more adventurous, hiking paths lead up into the hills surrounding the lake (ask TI for details and maps).

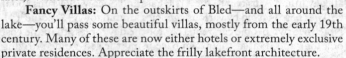

I've listed a few things to tune in to as you stroll, starting in the town of Bled and going clockwise (with the lake on your right; see the "Lake Bled" map earlier in this chapter)—but you could just as easily do it in reverse. Just hold the book upside-down.

Straža and Luge Ride: Just after the big, lakeside Grand Hotel Toplice, on the inland side of the lake, is the hill called Straža. Above you (but not visible from here) is the thrilling luge ride and other adventure park activities (described later). Watch for the trail up from the lake.

Fancy Villas: On the outskirts of Bled—and all around the lake—you'll pass some beautiful villas, mostly from the early 19th century. Many of these are now either hotels or extremely exclusive private residences. Appreciate the frilly lakefront architecture.

Mlino: This village—the only real settlement of any size on the lake beyond Bled town—is where the *pletna* boats originated; many of the families who run trips out to Bled's island still live here. The town also has a couple of good restaurants (the only sit-down options you'll see for a while) and a handy Mercator grocery store, if you'd like to stock up on snacks or drinks.

Tito's Vila Bled: As the path passes below a wooded cliff, a grand staircase leads up to a giant hilltop mansion. This was a residence of Marshal Tito, where the dictator entertained international big shots, from Indira Gandhi to Nikita Khrushchev to Kim Il-Sung to Raúl Castro. Today, it's the fancy Hotel Bled (still relatively affordable if you can find a deal online). The hotel's café terrace is typically open only for guests; higher on the hill is **Café Belvedere**—where you can enjoy beautiful views of Lake Bled along with a coffee and *kremšnita* cake, either inside or out on the terrace (cakes and drinks only, daily 10:00-18:00, until 20:00 in summer, closed Oct-April, walk up from Vila Bled). On the lakeside path, you'll walk under this building—it's the giant box on tall stilts.

LAKE BLED

Grand Views: The stretch between Vila Bled and Velika Zaka has perhaps the very best views on the entire lake, closer to the island than at any other point. As you walk, the island and castle shift positions, lining up in a series of beautiful compositions. *Pletna* boats trundle back and forth, adding to the lovely scenery.

Lakefront Boardwalk: Where the road pulls away from the lake a bit, don't miss the pleasant boardwalk (accessed by stairs) that runs right along the lake—offering great views to the island.

Velika Zaka/Campground: This area—at the farthest point on the lake from town—is where rowing competitions begin (or end). It has some humble eateries, a campground, and some wooden piers popular with swimmers. This is a good place to rent a boat to row out to the island. Hikes into the hills above leave from here, too.

Rowing Center: Approaching the northwest corner of the lake, be sure to detour through the gate to the water to appreciate Lake Bled's proud tradition of rowing. Bled has hosted multiple European and world championships. Town officials even lengthened the lake a bit (creating the divot we just passed in Velika Zaka) so it would perfectly fit standard two-kilometer laps, with 100 meters more for the turn. Lake Bled has produced many Olympic medalists—they've won gold in Sydney, silver in Athens, and bronze in London. You'll likely see crews practicing out on the water and young rowers jogging around the lake.

Swimming Pool, Under the Castle, and Back to Town: The final stretch into Bled town is (slightly) less scenic but still an enjoyable stroll. If you're planning to hike up to the castle, watch for trails leading up through the woods on your left (or you can wait until you're back in town and head up more steeply from there). Just below the castle is the town's swimming pool, popular on hot summer days.

Coming into town, you'll walk below the pointy spire of St. Martin's Church, then pass the recommended Vila Prešeren restaurant, with its dreamy lakefront terrace. The inviting shoreline park between here and the big hotels is a fun place to relax and linger; near the far end, 100 yards or so before the casino/TI building, look for the relief map of the entire lake and surrounding hills.

If you haven't made it out to the island yet, there's a handy *pletna* departure point just under the TI (described next).

▲▲The Island (Blejski Otok)

Bled's little island—capped by a super-cute church—nudges the lake's quaintness level over the top. It has no official name; locals call it simply "The Island" (*Otok*). While it's pretty to look at from afar, it's also fun to visit.

The island has long been a sacred site with a romantic twist.

On summer Saturdays, a steady procession of brides and grooms, cheered on by their entourages, heads for the island. Ninety-nine steps lead from the island's dock up to the Church of the Assumption on top. It's tradition for the groom to carry—or *try* to carry—his bride up all of these steps. About four out of five are successful (proving themselves "fit for marriage"). During the communist era, the church was closed and weddings were outlawed here. But the tradition reemerged—illegally—even before the regime ended, with a clandestine ceremony in 1989.

Cost and Hours: Free to visit island; church—€12, ticket includes tower climb, May-Sept daily 9:00-19:00, April and Oct until 18:00, Nov-March until 16:00.

Getting There: The most romantic route to the island is a cruise on one of the distinctive *pletna* boats (€15/person round-trip, trip takes 20-25 minutes each way, includes 30-minute stay on the island—allow about 1.5 hours for the full experience; might have to wait for more passengers to fill the boat; boats generally run from dawn, last boat leaves one hour before church closes; replaced by enclosed electric boats in winter—unless the lake freezes, in which case you can rent ice skates; +386 31 316 575). Look for *pletna* boats at various spots around the lake. If you're in town, the handiest options are directly below the TI, or in front of Grand Hotel Toplice. Note that *pletna* boatmen stick close to the 30-minute waiting time on the island—which can go very fast. Another option—cheaper but far less romantic—is to take an **electric boat** (€12 round-trip, departs about hourly from the lakefront below the TI). You could also **rent your own boat** or **SUP** (stand-up paddleboard) and row to the island (see "Boating" listing, later).

Visiting the Island: At the top of the stairs, the **Potičnica café** sells *potica,* the Slovenian nut-roll cake that's traditional at Christmastime but delicious any day of the year. The attached **souvenir shop** is the best in Bled, well stocked with a variety of high-quality Slovenian gifts, trinkets, and keepsakes. Upstairs in the same building is an easy-to-miss **art gallery,** which displays changing exhibits.

The island's main attraction is the **church.** An eighth-century Slavic pagan temple dedicated to the goddess of love and fertility once stood here; the current Baroque version (with Venetian flair—the bell tower is separate from the main church) is the fifth to occupy this spot. Go inside and find the rope for the church bell, hanging in the middle of the aisle just before the altar. A local superstition claims that if you can get this bell to ring three times with one big pull of the rope, your dreams will come true.

Your ticket also includes the **bell tower.** At 91 steps, it's a shorter climb than the one up from the boat dock. Up top, you'll find a restored pendulum mechanism from 1890 and sweeping lake views that are marred by a mesh covering that makes it impossible to snap a clear picture.

To descend by a different route, walk down the trail behind the church (around the right side), then follow the path around the island's perimeter back to where your *pletna* boat awaits.

▲▲Bled Castle (Blejski Grad)

Bled's cliff-hanging castle, dating in one form or another from 1,000 years ago, was the seat of the Austrian bishops of Brixen, who controlled Bled in the Middle  Ages. Today, it's a fine tourist attraction with a little history and lots of big views. The various sights at the castle— a history museum, a frescoed chapel, an old-fashioned printing press, and a wine cellar—are more cute than interesting, but the real reason to come up here is to bask in the sweeping panoramas over Lake Bled and the surrounding mountainscapes.

Cost and Hours: €15; daily 8:00-20:00, Nov-March until 18:00, printing press and wine cellar close one hour earlier; +386 4 572 9782, www.blejski-grad.si.

Getting There: To really earn those views, you can **hike** up the steep hill (about 20 minutes if you're in decent shape). The handiest trails are behind big St. Martin's Church: Walk past the front door of the church with the lake at your back, and look left after the first set of houses for the *Grad* signs marking the steepest route (follow the wooden stakes all the way up the steep switchback steps); or, for a longer but less steep route, continue past the church on the same street about five minutes, bearing uphill (left) at the fork, and find the *Blejski Grad - Castle - 10 Min* sign just after the Penzion Bledec hostel on the left. Once you're on this second trail, don't take the sharp-left uphill turn at the fork toward the shed (instead, continue straight up, around the back of the hill).

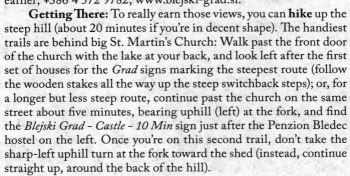

LAKE BLED

Pletna Boats

The *pletna* is an important symbol of Lake Bled. In addition to providing a pleasant way to reach the island, these boats carry on a tradition dating back for generations. In the 17th century, Habsburg empress Maria Theresa granted the villagers from Mlino—the little town along the lakefront just beyond Bled—special permission to ferry visitors to the island. (This provided a much-needed source of income for Mlino residents, who had very limit  ed access to farmland.) They built their *pletna*s by hand, using a special design passed down from father to son for centuries—like the equally iconic gondolas of Venice. Eventually, this imperial decree and family tradition evolved into a modern union of *pletna* oarsmen, which continues to this day.

Today, *pletna* boats are still hand-built according to that same centuries-old design. There's no keel, so the skilled oars

men work hard to steer the flat-bottomed boat with each stroke—boats piloted by an inexperienced oarsman can slide around on very windy days. There are 21 official *pletna*s on Lake Bled, all belonging to the same union. The gondoliers dump all their earnings into one fund, give a cut to the tourist board, and divide the rest evenly amongst themselves. Occasionally a new family tries to break into the cartel, underselling his competitors with a "black market" boat that looks the same as the official ones. While some see this as a violation of a centuries-old tradition, others view it as good old capitalism. Either way, competition is fierce.

If you'd rather skip the hike, you have several options. If you have a **car,** simply drive up (€3/hour for parking). Otherwise, consider a **shuttle bus** (either the official TI bus or a private shuttle; see "Getting Around Lake Bled," earlier). A **taxi** runs about €12. Or—if you're wealthy and romantic—consider a **horse and buggy** (€50, €10 extra for driver to wait 30 minutes and bring you back down). Note: These options take you only to the parking lot, from which it's still a steep and slippery-when-wet five-minute hike up to the castle.

Eating: The **$$$$ restaurant** at the castle is pricey, but worth the splurge for the views and excellent, rotating menu featuring regional cuisine (à la carte for lunch; fixed-price multicourse dinners). Come for dinner while it's still light out and savor the setting. Call far ahead to book a view table—they fill up quickly. If you have a reservation to dine here, it's free to enter the castle grounds, but you'll still pay for parking (daily in summer, shorter hours off-season, +386 4 620 3444, www.jezersek.si). Paupers can grab a basic sandwich at the simple **$ café** by the round tower or bring their own **picnic** to munch along the wall with million-dollar views over Lake Bled.

Summer Performances: In July and August, the castle hosts a weekly, kid-pleasing, knights'-tournament-themed show called "Sir Lambergar's Adventure" (likely Tue at 17:00, 30 minutes; details on castle website).

Visiting the Castle: After buying your ticket, go through the gate and huff the rest of the way up to the outer courtyard. We'll tour the castle clockwise, starting from here. The castle is continually being spruced up, so some details may be different than described.

Turning left at the entrance, you'll pass WCs, then the door to Mojster Janez's working replica of a **printing press** *(grajska tiskarna/manufaktura)* from Gutenberg's time. You can buy your own custom-made souvenir certificate using this very old technology. While this may seem like a gimmick, there's actually some history here. The printing press was a critical tool in the evolution of Slovenia's culture. Look above the press for a life-size mannequin of Primož Trubar (1508-1586), a Slovenian cross between Martin Luther and Johannes Gutenberg. In Trubar's time, Slovene was considered a crude peasants' language—not just unworthy, but illegal to print. So this Reformer went to Germany and, in 1550—using presses like this one—wrote and printed the first two books in the Slovene language: *Abecedarium* (an alphabet primer to teach Slovenes how to read) and *Catechismus* (a simplified version of the New Testament). Trubar smuggled his printed books back to Slovenia and, en route to Ljubljana, was briefly given refuge in this castle. (Trubar is still much-revered today, appearing on the Slovenian €1 coin.) Up the stairs is an exhibition in English about early printing methods and their importance in the Protestant Reformation, whose goal was to get the Word of God more easily into the hands of everyday people. You'll also see one of those first Trubar books—notice it was printed in Tübingen, Germany, an early enclave of the Reformation.

Just past the printing press is the castle's oldest tower, from the 11th century, which is filled with a **"Beehouse"** selling various honey products and other souvenirs under a hive-like dome. Nearby is a **café terrace** with grand views offering reasonably priced drinks and cakes.

Begin climbing the stairs up to grander and grander **views** over the lake. Reaching the terrace at the very top, you'll find the best vistas, the restaurant, a tiny **chapel** with 3-D frescoes that make it seem much bigger than it is (next to the museum entrance), a small shop, and the well-presented castle **museum,** which strains to make the story of Bled, the castle, and the surrounding region of Carniola interesting.

When you're done up here, head down the semicircular staircase between the museum and restaurant (passing WCs). Come back down into the lower courtyard and turn left down the ramp to find the **wine cellar,** where you can bottle and cork your own souvenir bottle of wine.

Before leaving the castle, climb the stairs (just past the wine cellar) up to the wooden **defensive gallery** for the best views in town of the mountains east of Bled. The biggest one is called Stol (Chair). In the foreground, you can see the steeple marking the town of Podhom; just to the left, the folds in the hills hide the dramatic Vintgar Gorge (described later).

Boating

You'll find **rental rowboats** at various points around the lake (€25/1.5 hours). Look for them at Pension Pletna in the lakeside village of Mlino (a scenic 15-minute walk around the lake from Bled), at the swimming pool under the castle (the closest but priciest option), under Grand Hotel Toplice, and in the modern building just before the campground on the far end of the lake. You can also rent **stand-up paddleboards** (SUPs) in Mlino or at various points around the lake, including by the boathouse at the far end (€10-12/hour).

Swimming

Lake Bled has several suitable spots for a swim. The swimming-pool complex under the castle uses lake water and routinely earns the "blue flag," meaning the water is top-quality. There's also a waterslide and an inviting cluster of sunning beds (€9 to swim all day, less for afternoon only, daily 9:00-19:00, until 20:00 at busy times, closed late Sept-mid-June and in bad weather, +386 4 578 0528). Lake Bled's main beach is

at the campground at the far end of the lake, though you can also swim near the village of Mlino.

▲Luge Ride (Poletno Sankanje)

Bled's "summer toboggan" luge ride, atop Mount Straža overlooking the lake, allows you to scream down a steep, curvy metal rail track on a little plastic sled. A chairlift takes you to the top of the track, where you'll sit on your sled, take a deep breath, and remind yourself: Pull back on the stick to slow down, push forward on the stick to go faster. You'll drop 480 feet in altitude on the 570-yard-long track, speeding up to about 25 miles per hour as you race toward the lake.

Cost and Hours: €10/ride, cheaper for multiple rides, weather-dependent—if it rains, you can't go. In summer, it's open daily (July-Aug 10:00-19:00, June and early Sept 11:00-18:00); in shoulder season it opens only on good-weather weekends (mid-Sept-mid-Oct and mid-April-May 11:00-17:00). It's closed mid-Oct-mid-April (+386 4 578 0534, www.straza-bled.si).

Getting There: The base of the chairlift is on the hillside just south of town; to get there, head up to the neighborhood just above Grand Hotel Toplice, and follow *Straža* signs with the lake on your right (by car or by foot).

Nearby: Near the base of the chairlift are other attractions, including an airbag jump and a tubing hill. Up near the top of the chairlift is Adventure Park (Pustolovski Park): a series of five high-ropes courses designed for everyone age five and up (€22 for adults, €18 for kids 7-14, €10 for kids under 7, similar hours to luge ride, last entry 2 hours before closing, +386 31 761 661, www.pustolovski-park-bled.si).

▲Kralov Med Beehive Demonstration

Tucked in Selo village, a long walk or short drive from Bled, this fascinating countryside sight is worth ▲▲▲ (or zzz) for fans of

the apicultural arts. Local beekeepers Blaž and Danijela Ambrožič have built an apiary (freestanding house of beehives) and teach visitors all about this very Slovenian form of agriculture. First you'll see the painted panels, with bees buzzing in and  out. Their prized possession is a gigantic Winnie-the-Pooh-style hive that they transplanted from a tree trunk. They'll demonstrate how you can hold your hand within inches of the buzzing hive without getting stung, thanks to the peaceful nature of the indig-

LAKE BLED

enous Carniolan bee. Inside, you can watch through a big (and safe) window as they pull out the honeycomb frames from the hive and work with the bees. You'll see the centrifuge-like device they use to safely extract honey from the comb. In another hut is an "apitherapy" room, where a specially designed bunk lets you watch and listen to the mesmerizing bees without any danger of being stung. You can also sample (and buy) different types of honey and pollen, along with other bee-related gifts. Outside is a perennial garden that demonstrates when various plants blossom, providing much-needed pollen for the bees.

Cost and Hours: €8/person and up, call or email a few days ahead to arrange a time and establish the price, demonstrations usually last an hour plus and may run for just two people, apiary and parking are next to the house at Selo pri Bledu 42—once parked there, call Danijela at +386 41 227 407 or Blaž at +386 41 657 120 and they'll come meet you, www.kralov-med.si, ambrozicdanijela@gmail.com.

Getting There: Blaž's beehives are in the village of Selo, a five-minute drive or taxi ride or a 30-minute walk from Bled town. Head out of town along the lake (past Grand Hotel Toplice), then turn left (inland) at the Mercator grocery store in the village of Mlino. In the next village, Selo, look for the two colorful beehive apiaries below the main road, just above the recommended Tourist Farm Mulej.

Dornk Excursion Farm

This offbeat but endearing sight, in the village of Mlino (conveniently close to the beehive demonstration listed above), is hard to explain: It's a country pub with homemade beer and schnapps; it's also a folk museum/ethnography collection; but really it's just a chance to hang out with some nice local people and see some interesting things. Monika and her family live in a typical old farmhouse with a giant barn next door. She spends the winter distilling her own schnapps and brewing six different types of beer. Then, through the summer season, she invites travelers to come for a drink (admission free but tips appreciated; typically open daily May-mid-Oct 12:00-18:00 or later; Mlinska Cesta 28, +386 40 652 527, www.dornk-bled.com).

While you're there, they'll invite you into the family home, which feels like a folk museum ("last renovated in 1774")—especially the "black kitchen," so named because the wood fire fills the top of the room with smoke (to flavor and preserve meat hanging from two giant beams) before it exits on the far side. The walls are charred with centuries' worth of carbon; it smells like a smokehouse. They'll also show you the "white kitchen"—the newer (but still traditional) space where they do most of their cooking today.

If you're interested and it's not too busy, they'll take you across to the barn and show you two huge rooms packed to the gills with the family's collections—especially remarkable embroideries created by Monika's mother Simona, plus dozens of different Nativity scenes and all manner of other bric-a-brac. Upstairs are old farm tools ("of interest only to farmers, not city slickers," Monika explains). So, feel free to swing by. Order a beer, schnapps, or homemade juice. If you'd like a bite to eat, get the "farmer's snack"—a plate of locally produced cold cuts and cheeses. (The "shepherd's snack" is just the cheeses.) Sometimes they have desserts, too.

Like I said: All of this is a little hard to explain. But if it sounds like something you might like...then you'd probably like it.

Nightlife in Bled

Bled is quiet after hours. However, the town does have a few fun bars that are lively with a young crowd (all open nightly until late). Since many young people in Bled are students at the local tourism school, they're likely to speak English...and eager to practice with a native speaker. Try a Smile, a Corona-type Slovenian lager. *Šnops* (schnapps) is a local specialty—popular flavors are plum *(slivovka)*, honey *(medica)*, blueberry *(borovničevec)*, and pear *(hruškovec)*.

Kick things off with the fun-loving local gang at **Gostilna Pri Planincu** near the bus station (described later, under "Eating in Bled"). Then head down Cesta Svobode toward the lake. On the left, you'll come to **Art Café**, with a trendy ambience, then the mellow **Vinoteka Zdravljica,** with Slovenian wines by the glass for €3-5. Around the lake just below the commercial center, **Bled Pub** (a.k.a. The Cocktail Bar or Troha, for the family that owns it) is a trendy late-night spot where bartenders sling a dizzying array of mixed drinks to an appreciative, youthful crowd (between the commercial center and the lake, above the recommended Oštarija Peglez'n restaurant). If you're still standing, several other bars and cafés percolate in the commercial center, including **Kult Bled,** facing the main road at the base of the round tower. Slathered with iconic film images and neon colors, it attracts a thirtysomething crowd and occasionally hosts live music. **Devil** is open even later (on the lower level of Hotel Park, facing the lake); a nightclub/disco is at the other end of the same complex.

LAKE BLED

Sleeping in Bled

Places here book up early, so reserve well ahead.

PENSIONS ABOVE THE LAKE

These friendly, cozy, characteristic accommodations are Bled's best values. But it's important to **book direct**—you'll typically save around 15-20 percent compared to booking through a third-party website. These places are perched on a hilltop a 5-to-10-minute climb up from the lake (easier than it sounds). There are two ways to get here from the town center: Walk around the lake to Grand Hotel Toplice, then cross the street and go up the stairs around the right side of the Hotel Jadran. Or, from the main road into town (Ljubljanska Cesta), take the small service road just above the commercial center (in front of Hotel Lovec), and loop up around the big Kompas and Rikli Balance hotels. If arriving by bus, ask nicely if your driver will let you disembark along Ljubljanska Cesta (just above the traffic light) to avoid the long walk from the bus station. From this bus stop, you can walk down Ljubljanska Cesta and take the road just above the post office, which leads up to this area.

$$$ Penzion Berc (pronounced "berts") is the priciest option in this area, with 11 sharp, comfortable, woody rooms—all with balconies—filling a tidy chalet. It's well run by Miha, who charges more because he includes thoughtful touches like free loaner electric bikes and minifridges stocked with free drinks. He also runs the recommended Steakhouse Berc and arranges excursions (air-con, Želeška Cesta 15, +386 4 574 1838, www.penzion-berc.si, info@penzion-berc.si).

$$ Hotel Berc, across the street and run by Miha's brother, Luka, has 17 nearly-as-nice rooms with balconies, loaner bikes, and lower rates (cash only, air-con, Pod Stražo 13, +386 4 576 5658, www.berc-sp.si, hotel@berc-sp.si).

$$ Mayer Penzion, next door and thoughtfully run by the Trseglav family (relatives of the Berc brothers), comes with 13 rooms (air-con in some rooms, family rooms, elevator, Želeška Cesta 7, +386 4 576 5740, www. mayer-sp.si, penzion@mayer-sp. si).

$$ Penzion Kaps, conscientiously run by Peter (whose father, Anton, is a great craftsman) and Darija, has 13 comfortable rooms with balconies, modern bathrooms, minifridges, and classic old wood carvings. The inviting breakfast room in the basement clusters around a giant ceramic stove (cash only, family rooms, air-con, laundry service, Želeška Cesta 22, +386 41 618 513, www.penzion-kaps.si, info@penzion-kaps.si).

$ Friendly **Mija Sušnik** rents out two comfortable two-bedroom apartments. Modern, tidy, and equipped with kitchens, these are a good budget choice for families (cash only, no breakfast, laundry service, free parking, Želeška Cesta 3, +386 4 574 1731, mobile +386 40 872 278, susnik@bled-holiday.com). It's just toward the lake from the bigger pensions, with a big crucifix out front. Her sister Ivanka also rents apartments, but they're farther from the lake.

ON OR NEAR THE LAKE

You'll pay a premium to be closer to the lake—but it's hard to argue with the convenience.

$$$$ **Grand Hotel Toplice** (TOHP-leet-seh) is the grande dame of Bled, with 87 high-ceilinged rooms, parquet floors, a genteel lakeview café/lounge, posh decor, all the amenities, and a long list of high-profile guests—from Madeleine Albright to Jordan's King Hussein to Slovene-by-marriage Donald Trump. This place is a bit faded these days, but it's still a classic. Rooms in the back are cheaper but have no lake views and overlook a noisy street—get one as high up as possible (air-con, elevator, free parking, Cesta Svobode 12, +386 4 579 1000, www.hotel-toplice.com, ghtoplice@hotelibled.com). The hotel's name—*toplice*—means "spa"; guests are free to use the hotel's swanky, natural-spring-fed indoor swimming pool (a chilly 72 degrees Fahrenheit).

$$$ **Hotel Lovec** (LOH-vets) sits in a convenient (but not quite lakefront) location along the main road just above the commercial center. Nicely appointed inside and out, and run by a helpful staff (including Tomaž, who enjoys offering guests free tours, lectures, and other activities), it's professional yet welcoming. Its 61 well-designed rooms come with all the comforts, an excellent breakfast, and a respected restaurant (family rooms, air-con, elevator, free parking, Ljubljanska Cesta 6, +386 4 620 4100, www.lovechotel.com, reservations@kompas-lovec.com).

NEAR THE OLD TOWN

$$ **Vila Mila** rents seven one-bedroom apartments in a handsome, beautifully renovated house at the top of the Old Town. It comes with a pleasant terraced garden and an eco-friendly focus (air-con, handy parking garage, Grajska Cesta 20, +386 51 501 909, www.vilamila.si).

$$ **Apartmaji Mežan,** run by welcoming Janez and Saša, has four family-friendly apartments in a modern home buried in the middle of town, just uphill from the church. As it's next to an old barn, it's technically a tourist farm (cash only, no breakfast, Rikli-

LAKE BLED

jeva 6, +386 41 210 290, www.apartmaji-mezan.si, sasa.mezan@gmail.com).

¢ **Travellers Haven** is a low-key hostel run by Colleen. The beds fill eight rooms in a nicely renovated hundred-year-old villa in the Old Town. The hangout areas are inviting, though the tight bathrooms offer little privacy and there are no lockers (Riklijeva Cesta 1, +386 41 396 545, thbled1@gmail.com).

OUTSIDE TOWN

The following listings are a bit farther out: Alp Penzion is a 20-minute walk from the lakefront but still doable for nondrivers, while the tourist farm and "glampground" are best for drivers. See the "Lake Bled" map for locations.

$$$$ Garden Village, alternately billed as a "glampground" and a "green resort," combines the closeness to nature of camping with the amenities of a hip resort. From the main lodge, restaurant, and rustic pond/pool, the complex tumbles down a ravine toward a gushing river, connected by slippery plank walks. You can stay in a tree house, a glamping tent, a simpler pier tent on stilts over the river, or an apartment in the main building. All of these include breakfast, Wi-Fi, and other amenities, but additional charges for cleaning and shorter stays can add up (on the road toward Lake Bohinj, turn off on the left just before Vila Bled, Cesta Gorenjskega odreda 16, +386 8 389 9220, www.gardenvillagebled.com, reservations@gardenvillagebled.com).

$$ Alp Penzion makes the most of a peaceful countryside setting amid hayfields, within a 20-minute, partly uphill walk of the lake (better for drivers or for those who don't mind the walk). With 12 rooms (some with balconies) and a hangout garden, this kid-friendly place is enthusiastically family run (air-con, free loaner bikes, Cankarjeva Cesta 20A, +386 41 350 558, www.alp-penzion.com, bled@alp-penzion.com). Next door is the relaxing Essense spa (described earlier, under "Helpful Hints").

$$ Tourist Farm Mulej, possible for hardy walkers but much better for drivers, is a new but traditional farmhouse in a tranquil valley about a half-mile from the lake (1.5 miles from Bled town). Damjana and Jože, who run this working farm (with 140 milk cows...and their smells), also rent out eight modern rooms and two apartments—all with balconies—and serve breakfasts made with food they produce (RS%, cash only, family rooms, air-con, Selo pri Bledu 42a, +386 4 574 4617 or +386 4 022 4888, www.mulej-bled.si, info.mulej@gmail.com). The farmhouse is in the village of Selo—drive along the lakeside road south from Bled, then turn off in Mlino toward Selo and look for the signs (to the right) once in the village. They also offer 10 apartments in a townhouse dating from 1662, in the center of the village.

Eating in Bled

With a finite number of restaurants, places can fill up at dinner-time—it's best to book ahead. In addition to the places recommended here, consider the high-quality (and expensive) restaurant up at the castle, described earlier.

$$$$ The Old Cellar, a short walk up from the lakefront hotel zone, feels nicely rustic yet sophisticated, but not pretentious. The service is sharp, the seating (in a series of traditional rooms, or outside) is appealing, and the food is a satisfying combination of traditional Slovenian ingredients and modern technique—such as the "porcini cappuccino," a delicious mushroom soup topped with a flavorful foam (Mon-Thu dinner only, Fri-Sun lunch and dinner, up a gravel road from busy Ljubljanska Cesta, Zagoriška 12, +386 40 412 556, www.oldcellarbled.com).

$$$$ Steakhouse Berc—just up the hill from the lakefront, at the recommended Penzion Berc—is a dreamy splurge restaurant. You'll dine at white-tablecloth tables positioned just so on the lush lawn, or in the country-cozy interior. The menu of well-executed international dishes with a Slovenian spin will satisfy steak lovers, though the prices can add up (Mon-Sat dinner only, likely closed Sun, Želeška Cesta 15, +386 4 574 1838, www.penzion-berc.si).

$$$ Oštarija Peglez'n (The Old Iron), conveniently located on the main road between the commercial center and the lake, cooks up tasty Slovenian and Mediterranean meals, with an emphasis on fish and fun family-style shareable skillets. Choose between the delightful Slovenian cottage interior or the shady streetside terrace (daily, Cesta Svobode 19A, +386 4 574 4218).

$$$ Vila Prešeren is a handy lakeside choice featuring international cuisine (as well as some traditional Slovenian dishes) at tables on a giant terrace reaching down to the lakefront. I'd come here only in good weather, when you can linger on the terrace over a meal, a drink, or a classic Lake Bled dessert; otherwise, skip it (long hours daily, Veslaška Promenada 14, +386 4 575 2510, https://vilapreseren.com).

$$$ Gostilna Pri Planincu (By the Mountaineers) is a homey, informal bar coated with license plates and packed with fun-loving, sometimes rowdy locals. A big, dull dining area sprawls behind the small, local-feeling pub, and there's outdoor seating out front and on the side patio. The menu features huge portions of stick-to-your-ribs Slovenian pub grub, plus Balkan grilled-meat specialties. Service is playfully opinionated and not always efficient—don't come here if you're in a rush (daily, Grajska Cesta 8, +386 4 574 1613, www.pri-planincu.com). Upstairs is a timbered **$$ pizzeria** dishing up wood-fired pies. The cartoon mural along the outside of the restaurant shows different types of mountaineers (from

Bled Desserts

While you're in Bled, be sure to enjoy the town's specialty, a cream cake called ***kremna rezina*** (KRAYM-nah ray-ZEE-nah; often referred to by its German-derived name, ***kremšnita,*** KRAYM-shnee-tah). It's a layer of cream and a thick layer of vanilla custard artfully sandwiched between sheets of delicate, crispy crust. Heavenly. Slovenes travel from all over the country to sample this famous dessert. You may also see some newfangled strawberry and chocolate *kremšnita* variations, but purists swear by the original.

Slightly less renowned—but just as tasty—is ***grmada*** (gur-MAH-dah, "bonfire"). This dessert was developed by Hotel Jelovica as a way to get rid of their day-old leftovers. They take yesterday's cake; add rum, milk, custard, and raisins; and top it off with whipped cream and chocolate syrup.

There's also *prekmurska gibanica*—or just ***gibanica*** (gee-bah-NEET-sah) for short. Originating in the Hungarian corner of the country, *gibanica* is an earthy pastry filled with poppy seeds, walnuts, apples, and cheese, and drizzled with rum.

Yet another dessert is the very traditional ***potica*** (poh-TEET-sah), a walnut roll that's usually eaten at Christmastime. While it's rare to find this in bakeries, the café on the island in the lake sells several varieties.

Desserts are typically enjoyed with a lake-and-mountains view—the best spots are the terrace at Vila Prešeren, the Panorama restaurant by Grand Hotel Toplice, and the terrace across from Hotel Park (figure around €5 for cake and coffee at any of these places). For a more local place—but lacking a lakeview setting—consider the recommended Slaščičarna Zima (only slightly cheaper).

left to right): thief, normal, mooch ("gopher"), climber, and naked (...well, almost).

$$ Pizzeria Rustika, a cozy and convivial spot tucked deep in the Old Town, offers good wood-fired pizzas and salads. Its upstairs terrace is relaxing on a balmy evening (daily, Riklijeva Cesta 13, +386 4 576 8900).

Supermarket: The **$ Mercator** grocery store, in the commercial center, has the makings for a bang-up picnic. They sell €3 sandwiches to go or will make you one to order (point to what you want). This is a great option for hikers and budget travelers (Mon-Fri 8:00-19:00, Sat until 18:00, closed Sun). There's another location closer to the Old Town and castle (Mon-Sat 7:00-21:00, closed Sun), and a much larger one on busy Seliška road just outside the town center.

Dessert: While tourists generally gulp down their cream cakes on a hotel restaurant's lakefront terrace, residents favor the desserts at **Slaščičarna Zima** (a.k.a. the Brown Bear, for the bear on the sign). It's nicely untouristy and has a small outdoor terrace, but lacks the views and atmosphere of the lakeside spots (daily 8:00-21:00, near bus station at Grajska Cesta 3, +386 4 574 1616).

Lake Bled Connections

The most convenient train connections to Bled use the Lesce-Bled station, about 2.5 miles away (see "Arrival in Bled," earlier). Remember, when buying a train ticket to Lake Bled, make it clear that you want to go to the **Lesce-Bled station** (not the Bled Jezero station, which is poorly connected to the main line).

Note that if you're going to **Ljubljana,** it's better to take the bus (which leaves from Bled town itself) rather than the train (which leaves from the Lesce-Bled train station).

If traveling by **bus,** confirm times at the TI, on schedules posted at the Bled bus station, or online. Most buses are operated by Arriva (https://arriva.si, schedules but no tickets online). You can book tickets online at www.ap-ljubljana.si, but you'll have to print them; otherwise, you can buy them on the bus. For buses operated by Flixbus, you can only buy tickets online, then show your QR code when you board (no ticket office, no on-bus purchase).

From Lesce-Bled by Train to: Ljubljana (roughly hourly, 40-60 minutes), **Salzburg** (1/day direct, 4 hours; 2/day with a change in Villach, Austria), **Munich** (1/day direct, 6 hours; 2/day with a change in Villach, Austria), **Vienna** (that's **Dunaj** in Slovene, 3/day, 5.5-6 hours, transfer in Villach), **Venice** (only 1/day convenient option with transfer in Villach, 6 hours; consider a GoOpti minibus—see next listing), **Zagreb** (3/day direct, 3-3.5 hours).

By Bus to: Ljubljana (Mon-Sat 1-2/hour—usually at :30 and sometimes :00 past the hour, fewer on Sun, 1.25 hours), **Radovljica** (2-3/hour, fewer Sat-Sun, 15 minutes), **Lesce-Bled train station** (2-3/hour, fewer Sat-Sun, 10 minutes), **Lake Bohinj** (hourly at :20 past the hour, 40 minutes to Bohinj Jezero stop, 50 minutes to Bohinj Vogel or Bohinj Zlatorog stop), **Vintgar Gorge** (direct tourist bus runs 6/day mid-June-Aug, private shuttle buses at other times; also possible to take a public bus to Podhom or Spodnje Gorje and walk 15 minutes; for details, see "Vintgar Gorge," later).

By Shared Minivan Shuttle: GoOpti can also be an efficient and affordable way to link Lake Bled to various destinations near and far, including the airport. When figuring out a long journey, be sure to compare GoOpti to your other options (www.goopti.com).

By Plane: Ljubljana Airport (code: LJU) is between Lake Bled and Ljubljana, about a 45-minute drive from Bled. To connect Bled and the airport, the best compromise of cost and speed is to book a shared minivan transfer with **GoOpti,** which usually runs around €15 (see "Ljubljana Connections" at the end of the previous chapter). Other Bled-based shuttle buses make the trip for around €20; to see what best matches your schedule, check with **Mamut** (www.slovenija.eu.com) or **Maya** (www.bledtransfers.si). Because these run somewhat irregularly, it's always best to book ahead. A taxi costs around €50-60 (set price up front—since it's outside town, they don't use the meter; I'd book ahead with **Bled Tours** for a similar price—see page 784).

Route Tips for Drivers: Bled is less than an hour north of Ljubljana on the slick A-2 expressway. The exit is marked for *Lesce,* but you'll also see signs for *Bled,* which will lead you directly to the lake (where the road becomes Ljubljanska Cesta). At the main roundabout, soon after exiting the expressway, a towering metal obelisk honors Slavko Avsenik, the oompah bandleader from nearby Begunje who became an international sensation. At the base of that steel stiletto is Avsenik's name, a giant accordion, and an umbrella (part of the local folk costume in this rainy climate).

To reach **Radovljica** (bee museum) or **Lesce** (train station), drive out of Bled on Ljubljanska Cesta toward the expressway. Watch for the turnoff to *Lesce* on the right. They're on the same road: Lesce first (to reach train station, divert right when entering town), then Radovljica. (Signs to *Radovljica* will divert you out to the main road that parallels the expressway, then back down into Radovljica; instead, follow signs to *Lesce* and drive through that town for the more direct route.) Also along this road, between Lesce and Radovljica, is the well-marked turnoff to the road to **Kropa** (with its Iron Forging Museum).

Near Lake Bled

The countryside around Bled offers several day trips that can be done easily without a car (bus connection information is described in each section). The three trips listed here are more convenient than can't-miss, but each is worthwhile on a longer visit, and all give you a good taste of the Julian Alps. For a self-guided driving tour through the Julian Alps, see the next chapter.

Vintgar Gorge

For those seeking a spectacular walk, Vintgar (VEENT-gar), worth ▲▲, is one of my favorite low-impact hikes in Slovenia or Croatia. Just north of Bled, the River Radovna has carved this mile-long, picturesque gorge into the mountainside. Boardwalks and bridges put you right in the middle of the magic in this "poor man's Plitvice." Shaded and relatively cool, this is a refreshing place for a walk on a hot day (and extra cold on a cool day—bundle up).

The gorge—easily reachable from Bled by bus or foot—works well for those who are itching for a hike but don't have a car. From the entrance, allow about two hours for a round-trip hike, including time for photos (and there will be photos).

Cost and Hours: €10 to enter gorge; open daily in summer 8:00-18:00, longer hours July-Aug, shorter hours in shoulder season, may be closed off-season, confirm hours online; +386 4 572 5266, https://vintgar.si.

Crowd-Beating Tips: Vintgar Gorge can be crowded and can sell out, especially in summer and on good-weather weekends in spring and fall. Buying tickets online in advance is required at certain times (typically before 13:00) and a good idea anytime. Early risers can arrive near opening to avoid the worst of the crowds, which peak late morning; otherwise, aim for later in the day. Online booking is preferred, but it's possible to prebuy tickets in person at the Mamut tour agency near Bled's bus station.

Getting to Vintgar Gorge: The gorge is 2.5 miles north of Bled. To reach the gorge entrance, you can drive (10 minutes), walk (about an hour one-way), pedal a rental bike (about 30 minutes,

Near Lake Bled

To Planica,
Predel Pass
& Tarviso, Italy

Kranjska Gora

202

206

Mojstrana

Vršič
Pass

206

**Mount
Triglav**

To
Bovec &
Kobarid

J U L I A N

A L P S

S L O V

Mostnica R.

Savica
Waterfall

**Lake
Bohinj**

633

Ukanc

ST. JOHN
THE BAPTIST

TRAIN
STN.

Bohinj
Ukanc (B)

(B) Bohinj
Vogel

ZLATOROG
STATUE

**Ribčev
Laz** (B)

**Bohinjska
Bistrica**

WWI
CEMETERY

P

Polje

(CABLE CAR)

MERJASEC

Vogel Mountain

(CHAIRLIFT)

**Orlove
Glave**

Podbrdo

Car Train to
Most na Soči

LAKE BLED

AUSTRIA

(TUNNEL)

To Villach and
Klagenfurt Airport

KARAVANKE MTNS.

A2

Jesenice

▲ Stol Mtn.

Radovna

Radovna R.

Radovna R.

Vintgar
Gorge

ST.
CATH.

Radovna R.

Zirovnica

P

Podhom

Zasip

209

Spodnje Gorje

Begunje

Krnica

Lake
Bled

BLED JEZERO
STATION

LESCE-BLED
STATION

Bled
Town

Lesce

Mošnje

Mlino

A2

Selo

Radovljica

To
Airport &
Ljubljana

See Lake Bled
& Bled Town
detail maps

E N I A

ℹ & APICULTURAL
MUSEUM

Sava River

209

To
Ljubljana

IRON FORGING
MUSEUM

Kropa

Sava Bohinjka R.

J E L O V I C A
P L A T E A U

JAMNIK CHURCH /
VIEWPOINT

909

Jamnik

N

635

Dražgoše

5 Kilometers

5 Miles

Železniki

403

To
To Škofja Loka
& Ljubljana

403

LAKE BLED

easiest with an electric bike), take a shuttle bus (about 10 minutes), or take a public bus (15-minute ride plus 15-minute walk).

Drivers follow signs to *Podhom*, then *Vintgar* (see walking/cycling instructions, next), and pay €5 to park near the gorge entrance.

Walkers and **cyclists** leave Bled on the road between the castle and St. Martin's Church and take the uphill (left) road at the fork. Just after the little yellow chapel, turn right on the road with the big tree, then immediately left at the Mercator grocery store. When the road swings left, continue straight onto Partizanska (marked for *Podhom* and *Zasip;* ignore the bus sign for *Vintgar* pointing left). At the fork just after the little bridge, go left for Podhom, then simply follow signs for *Vintgar.*

The easiest option for a quick visit is to take a **shuttle bus** to the gorge entrance. In the peak of summer (generally mid-June–Aug), the TI runs a cheap, sometimes free, shuttle bus to the gorge. At other times, you can pay €10 round-trip for a bus operated by a private agency. Mamut lets you book the shuttle bus and the gorge entry time slot at the same time (book at www.vintgarshuttle.com or at their office near Bled's bus station); with other companies (including Maya, near the TI), you'll book the gorge entrance separately. These round-trip shuttles conveniently retrieve you where you exit the gorge via the green trail, near the Church of St. Catherine, and return you to Bled about 2.5 hours after you leave town. Just be very clear on the location and departure time for your return shuttle.

Finally, hourly **public bus** connections can get you close (none Sat-Sun, 15-minute trip): Take the bus either to Podhom or Spodnje Gorje (take bus in direction of Krnica); from either of these bus stops, it's a 15-minute walk to the gorge (follow signs for *Vintgar*).

Gorge Hike: Visiting Vintgar is a one-way, approximately two-hour loop: You'll hike to the end of the gorge on boardwalks, then take your pick of routes to huff up through the woods out of the gorge and return to the starting point (or meet your shuttle home).

From the ticket booth, the boardwalk trail (sometimes a bit slippery) crisscrosses over the most dramatic and narrow stretch; you'll tiptoe over several waterfalls and marvel at the clarity of the water. Then the gorge—and the trail—flattens out and passes under a high stone footbridge and over a scenic dam. Finally, at the end of the gorge, you'll reach a footbridge over a plunging waterfall (next to a snack stand and WCs). For more views, continue on five minutes downhill (following *Pod Slap* signs), then circle over the river again to reach a knoll where you can peer up at the waterfall and bridge you just crossed.

Returning to the Entrance: At the end of Vintgar Gorge, you have a few options for completing the loop and returning to the entrance.

The **green trail** takes you up to the right, to the Church of St. Catherine (Sv. Katarina). Behind the snack stand deep in the gorge, find the trail marked *Pod Katarina*. You'll go uphill for 25 strenuous minutes before cresting the hill and enjoying beautiful views over Bled town and the region. There's a handy bar next to the church for refreshments. If you booked a round-trip shuttle, you'll generally meet it near the church (or down in the village of Zasip)—confirm specifics before you head out.

Alternatively, from St. Catherine's, you can follow signs back to the main entrance and parking lot in about 30 minutes. Another option from St. Catherine is to continue straight down the road about 10 minutes to the typical, narrow old village of Zasip. In Zasip, you can catch a public bus back to Bled (Mon-Fri hourly, none Sat-Sun, 15 minutes; look for the bus stop near Gostilna Kurej). Otherwise, it's about a 30-minute walk from Zasip back to Lake Bled.

The **red trail,** steeper but more direct, gets you back to the entrance in about 45 minutes. At the end of the gorge, head left and follow signs about 20 minutes up to the cemetery in Blejska Dobrava. From there, you'll walk through the village to find the forest path that leads you back to the entrance.

Radovljica

The town of Radovljica (rah-DOH-vleet-sah, "Radol'ca" for short), perched on a plateau above the Sava River, has the quaint Old Town that Bled lacks. And, refreshingly, it also lacks the worst of Bled's summer crowds. The traffic-free core of the town, once hemmed in by a stout wall (still faintly visible in some areas), is jammed with historic buildings that surround the long,  skinny main square called Linhartov Trg. While you can see the entirety of Radovljica's Old Town in just a few minutes, it's a pleasant place to linger: Go for a stroll, nurse a coffee, or enjoy a meal. Beyond its tidy charm, the main reason to visit Radovljica is to tour its small but fascinating beekeeping museum. Skip the town on Mondays, when the museum is closed; many shops—another big draw here—are closed on Sundays.

Tourist Information: The enthusiastic TI loves to help visitors appreciate the town (daily 9:00-19:00, shorter hours late Oct-early May, Linhartov Trg 1, +386 4 531 5112, www.radolca.si).

GETTING TO RADOVLJICA

Buses to Radovljica generally leave Bled at least every half-hour (fewer on weekends, buy ticket from driver, 15-minute trip). Once in Radovljica, to reach the town center and the bee museum from the bus station, leave the station going straight ahead, cross the bus parking lot and the next street, then turn left down the far street (following brown sign for *Staro Mesto*). In five minutes, you'll reach the start of the pedestrianized Linhartov Trg (with the TI on the right and the start of my Old Town Stroll).

Drivers leave Bled on Ljubljanska Cesta and follow the directions under "Route Tips for Drivers" under "Lake Bled Connections," earlier. The road dead-ends at Radovljica's pedestrian zone, where you'll find a parking lot (on the right; usually free for 3 hours, check signs carefully), the entrance to the Old Town, and the TI. There's also a nice viewpoint at the end of the parking lot.

A handy **bike** path scenically and peacefully connects Bled with Radovljica (about 4 miles, get details at TI).

Sights in Radovljica

▲Old Town Stroll

Radovljica's Old Town is easy and fun to explore. Begin on the big roundabout just before the entrance of town. Over your left shoulder, **Radolška Čokolada** makes their own chocolates (you can see their production facility inside the shop) and sells both bars and pralines with some interesting flavors (closed Mon, tastings and chocolate-making classes by arrangement, Gorenjska Cesta 4, +386 91 687 518).

Across the square, on the left as you enter the Old Town, **Vinoteka Sodček** is a wine bar and shop that offers a handy opportunity to purchase and learn about Slovenian wines. Their €20 tasting includes wines, cheese, and *pršut* (prosciutto)—call ahead to arrange (closed Sun, Linhartov Trg 8, +386 4 531 5071, Aleš).

Now head up the main street, passing the **TI** on your right. A bit beyond that, you'll see **Radovljica Manufaktura,** which sells rustic pottery inspired by local designs (closed Sun; there's another branch farther along on the left).

Soon after, the street opens up into **Linhartov Trg,** a charming square fronted by historic buildings. This end of the square has several tempting cafés and eateries (see "Eating in Radovljica," later). If you just want to sip a coffee in the sun, **Vidičeva Hiša** café, on the left, serves great ice cream and cakes.

LAKE BLED

Farther along, on the right, you'll see a monument with a student holding a big medallion image of **Josipina Hočevar,** a Radovljica native who later helped fund the town's water system (see the old well nearby), as well as a school and many important buildings in Krško, near Zagreb. Next to that is the **Šivičeva Hiša,** an atmospheric late-Gothic house with a gallery that's open to the public (closed Sun-Mon). If you go a block down any street to the right, you'll come to a good valley **viewpoint** emphasizing Radovljica's dramatic position on a long promontory (the best view is at the far end of the main square).

Dominating the main part of the square is the big, yellow **town "castle"** (actually a mansion); upstairs you'll find the **Apicultural Museum** (described next), the Linhart Museum, and the Baroque Hall.

Beyond the mansion (and connected to it by a gallery) is **St. Peter's Church;** to its right is its rectory, where you can dip into the pretty courtyard.

Circle all the way around the church, then go through the gate to the edge of the ravine. Burrowed into the hillside is a **WWII-era bunker** left behind by

the Nazis. Peeking into the window of the bunker, you'll see it's been turned into a chapel dedicated to Edith Stein, a 20th-century Polish Jew who became a Carmelite nun but was arrested by the Nazis and executed at Auschwitz. She was later sainted by Pope John Paul II (notice the menorah and Star of David inside the chapel, on the right). Though she has no official ties to Radovljica, locals are inspired by Edith's example.

▲▲Apicultural Museum (Čebelarski Muzej)

This museum celebrates Slovenia's long and very proud beekeeping heritage. The earnest exhibits about the history and science of beekeeping are oddly fascinating. The highlight is the extensive collection of colorfully painted frontboard panels from beehives—one of Slovenia's most cherished folk arts. Replicas of these panels are sold in souvenir shops nationwide, but these are the real deal. Everything is well described in English.

Cost and Hours: €8; Tue-Sun 10:00-18:00, closed Mon; upstairs at Linhartov Trg 1, handy free WCs downstairs, +386 4 532 0520, www.mro.si.

Visiting the Museum: The first room, **Cultural Heritage,** introduces the big players: the local Carniolan bee; beekeeper ex-

Slovenian Beekeeping

Slovenian farmer Anton Janša (1734-1773) is considered the father of modern beekeeping. Habsburg empress Maria Theresa brought him to Vienna to become Europe's first official teacher of this art. Even today, beekeeping is considered a crucial part of Slovenian culture. The area around Lake Bled (Carniola) has about 6,000 inhabitants, including 65 beekeepers who manage 5,000 hives—the most bees per capita of any place in Europe.

Slovenian hives always face southeast, to enjoy sun in the morning and shade in the afternoon. Each individual hive is painted in bright colors, often depicting creative folk scenes, which help both the bees and the beekeepers distinguish the hives. Replicas of those characteristic beehive panels are available at shops in Bled and Ljubljana and make for appealing souvenirs.

The taste of honey can differ tremendously from hive to hive and is determined by the specific flowers and blossoms from which a hive's bees gathered pollen. In general, honeys made from mixed flowers and linden blossoms have the sweetest, mildest flavor; those made from chestnut or pine trees can have a bitter aftertaste.

Besides honey, beekeepers also make money by raising new queen bees. Each hive has one, and they can't be bred—one of the larvae is simply fed special "royal jelly" that encourages her to become a leader. In the springtime, when bees are born, the beekeeper keeps a close eye on the hive to figure out whether there are any potential queens. If he finds one, he'll move the old queen—who brings half the hive with her—to a new home (before she can find one on her own).

Slovenes still reserve an importance and affection for bees that's rare in modern times. For example, the Slovene language has different words for "to give birth" and "to die": one they use exclusively for humans and bees, and a different one for all other animals. If a beekeeper dies, it's believed that the new beekeeper must formally "introduce" themselves to the hive by going there and explaining to the bees what has happened; otherwise, the bees become confused and agitated, and often die themselves.

To learn more about Slovenian beekeeping, visit the insightful Apicultural Museum in Radovljica. For an even more vivid, practical experience, call Blaž at Kralov Med, near Bled, for a demonstration (see "Sights at Lake Bled," earlier). At either place, you'll get a sense for just how proud Slovenes are of their bees.

traordinaire Anton Janša, who first developed the art and science of apiculture; and, of course, the boxlike, stacking wooden beehives (called *kranjič*) that are unique to this region. You'll learn about the various members of the bee colony and see a unique bear-shaped hive.

Next, **Life of the Carniolan Bee** explains the science, anatomy, and activities of our protagonist—including how members of the hive communicate with one another. There's also an actual beehive, with bees that come and go through a hole in the nearby window (summer only).

Bees and People illustrates how Slovenian beekeepers have cleverly harnessed the skills of their buzzy minions. You'll see different hives, from hollowed-out trunks to baskets to various other vessels more smartly engineered for the task at hand.

Across the room, survey the many tools used by beekeepers. When a new queen bee is born, the old queen takes half the hive's bees to a new location. In the past, experienced beekeepers used the long, skinny instrument (a beehive stethoscope) to figure out when the swarm was working up a steady buzz, indicating they were ready to fly the coop. Then, once the bees had moved to a nearby tree, the beekeeper used the big spoons to retrieve the queen—surrounded by an angry ball of her subjects—from her new home before she could get settled in. (Notice the teensy little cage for the queen, which looks like it belongs in a dollhouse.) The beekeeper transferred the furious gang into a man-made hive designed for easier, more sanitary collection of honey. You'll see scrapers and knives used to shape the honeycomb, as well as tools used to create smoke, which makes bees less aggressive. Even today, some of Slovenia's old-fashioned beekeepers simply light up a cigarette and blow smoke on any bees that get ornery.

You'll also see a variety of presses used to squeeze every last drop of honey out of the comb. Look for the wooden rack, which was worn like a backpack (see the illustration): Dedicated beekeepers would trudge uphill with their hives to help the bees reach higher and higher blossoms as the summer wore on. The centerpiece of this room is a mockup of a beekeeper's shed, where many of these items come together.

The fourth room features the museum's highlight: whimsically painted **beehive frontboards** (called *panjske končnice*). Beekeepers, believing these paintings would help the bees find their way home, developed a tradition of decorating their hives with religious, historical, and satirical folk themes. It was also a

creative way to mark their own hives. The oldest panel dates from 1758, but the practice really took off in the 19th century.

The most interesting panels capture Slovenian village life. The case marked "Craftsmen and Motifs for Everyday Life" reveals some old stereotypes: Tailors, thought to be slow and deliberate, are shown in one panel being chased by snails and in another by goats. And some stereotypes are with us still—look for the two farmers fighting over a cow, while a lawyer milks the cow. Among the "Hunting Motifs," you'll see a fox shaving a hunter, evoking an old Slovenian saying about "shaving the fool." And the scene with the hunter's funeral shows all the animals happy...except his dog.

Perhaps most memorable are panels in the case labeled "Men and Women," which blur the line between humorous and misogynistic: Look for the devil sharpening a woman's tongue on a wheel, the mill where old women are put in and young women are pulled out, or the man carrying a cross—and his wife—on his back. Equal-opportunity offenders, beekeepers also painted scenes of drunk men being yanked out of bars and away from card games by their wives. In another, a wife catches her husband with his mistress.

Next up is the **Room of Slovenian Beekeeping,** which reverently traces the evolution of apiculture since the groundbreaking work of Anton Janša—you'll see diagrams of his many inventions, and copies of some of his books.

The **Path of the Carniolan Bee** shows how this local insect—favored by beekeepers for its relatively mellow personality and fast growth in springtime—has been exported throughout the world, thanks to its adaptability to new climates. You'll meet some of the bee merchants who helped spread the species.

Finally, **Crafts and Beekeeping** is a roundup of the many products—beyond just honey—that are derived from the hard work of bees, including pollen (considered by Slovenes and others to be the perfect all-purpose health aid), beeswax, honey bread, candles, and so on.

Eating in Radovljica

Several Radovljica restaurants near the bee museum have view terraces overlooking the surrounding mountains and valleys.

$$$$ Hiša Linhart is the town's big splurge and only destination restaurant—and worth booking ahead. Chef Uroš Štefelin, who grew up in the area, uses local ingredients and modern techniques to create delicious multicourse meals that highlight the very best of contemporary Slovenian cooking. The few tables out front are filled with locals drinking coffee and beer; the beautifully restored interior, classy yet comfortable, attracts foodies who've done their homework. While it's quite pricey at dinner, they make a point of offering more affordable lunches—partly to also serve the local community (closed Mon, may close Sun, Linhartov Trg 17, +386 8 384 3470, www.hisalinhart.si). They also rent eight hotel rooms upstairs, run a cooking school, and host a farmers market on the first Saturday of each month on the square out front.

$$ Lectar offers hearty, very traditional Slovenian fare in a rural-feeling setting with a user-friendly menu. Their several heavily decorated rooms are often filled with tour groups, but in good weather, don't miss the terrace out back (daily, family-friendly, Linhartov Trg 2, +386 4 537 4800). The restaurant is known for its heart-shaped gingerbread cookies (called *lect*), inscribed with messages of love. In the cellar, you can take a free look at their workshop and a collection of these cookies...some for sale, of course.

$$$ Gostilna Avguštin, across the street, has a simpler atmosphere and a more ambitious menu, which includes some pricey splurges. The food and service are uneven, but it works in a pinch, and their terrace in back enjoys an even better view than Lectar's (daily, Linhartov Trg 15, +386 4 531 4163).

Lake Bohinj

The pristine alpine Lake Bohinj (BOH-heen), 16 miles southwest of Bled, enjoys a quieter scene and (in clear weather) even better vistas of Triglav and the surrounding mountains. This is a real back-to-nature experience, with just a smattering of hotels and campgrounds, rather than the well-oiled resort machine of Bled. While spectacular in clear, sunny weather, it's disappointing

in the clouds (and, because of its position deep in the mountains, it can be socked in here even when it's clear in Bled—locals claim Bohinj is the rainiest place in Slovenia). But if the weather is great and you're finding Bled too touristy, go to Bohinj.

GETTING TO LAKE BOHINJ

From Bled, hourly **buses** depart at :20 past each hour for Bohinj, stopping at three destinations: Bohinj Jezero (the village of Ribčev Laz, 40 minutes), then Bohinj Pod Voglom (a 10-minute walk below the base of the Vogel Mountain cable car, 50 minutes), and finally a few hundred yards more to Bohinj Ukanc (the charming village area of Ukanc, with the under-construction Hotel Zlatorog and the start of a one-hour hike to the Savica Waterfall trailhead). In summer (July-Aug), one daily bus continues all the way to the Savica Waterfall trailhead. Off-season, there are fewer buses—confirm times before you depart.

By **car,** Bohinj is about 30 minutes from Bled (depending on traffic). Drivers leave Bled going south along the lakefront road, Cesta Svobode; in the village of Mlino, you'll peel off from the lake and follow signs to *Boh Bistrica.* You'll pass through a *soteska* (canyon) just wide enough for a river, a road, and a rail line; this railroad was built more than 120 years ago by the Austro-Hungarian Empire to connect their bustling port of Trieste (now in Italy, just over the Slovenian border) with Vienna. Once in the town of Bohinjska Bistrica, turn right, following *Boh Jezero* signs. The road takes you to the village of Ribčev Laz and along the lakefront road with all the attractions. From the lake, you can follow this road all the way to the Vogel cable-car parking lot; at the Vogel turnoff, you can continue straight ahead to reach the Savica Waterfall trailhead, or turn right and cross the bridge to curl around the far end of the lake and see the pristine river that feeds the lake (which flows out of the pool at the base of the Savica Waterfall).

Sights at Lake Bohinj

A visit to Bohinj has three main options: a village (offering boat trips on the lake and a picturesque church), a cable car (and nearby cemetery), and a waterfall hike. I've listed them as you'll reach them along the main road from Bled, which runs along the south side of the lake. The lake's website is helpful: www.bohinj.si.

Ribčev Laz Village

Coming from Bled, your first views of Bohinj will be from the village called **Ribčev Laz** (loosely translated as "Good Fishin' Hole") at the southeast corner of the lake. Here you'll find a TI, a handful of hotels and ice-cream stands, and the Bohinj Jezero bus stop.

As you approach town, get oriented: The main road passes a big complex (on the left) with the TI, a Mercator supermarket, and a post office. Across the street, capping a little hill, look for the beloved statue of the four Bohinj-area mountaineers who first summited Mount Triglav on August 26, 1778.

Just beyond, where the road hits the lake, just to the right (over the stone bridge) is the village's lakefront church, **St. John the Baptist.** The church is not open to visitors, but it's still picturesque when viewed from the lakeshore—and views from the stone bridge, overlooking the lake, are grand.

But most traffic swings left at the lake and follows its south shore to reach Bohinj's most popular activities. First, you'll pass a dock where you can catch an electric **tourist boat** to make a silent circuit around the lake (one-hour round-trip-€12, 30-minute one-way trip to the far end of the lake-€9, 5/day April-Oct). The boat stop at the far end of the lake is a 10-minute walk from the Vogel cable car (described next). Across from the Ribčev Laz dock, under the trees, is a fun concrete 3-D model of Triglav.

Just past the boat dock, perched on a mini-mountain along the lakeshore, is a statue of **Zlatorog,** the Golden Horn—a mythical chamois-like creature native to the Julian Alps. From there, the road follows the lakeshore to the next several sights (listed in order).

▲Vogel Mountain Cable Car

For a mountain perch without the sweat, take the cable car up to the top of Vogel Mountain (5,036 feet), offering impressive panoramic views of Mount Triglav and the Julian Alps. On a clear day, this is the best mountain panorama you can get without wings (the light is best in the morning).

Cost and Hours: €28 round-trip, daily 8:00-18:00, runs every 30 minutes in summer and continuously in winter, closed Nov, www.vogel.si.

Getting There: To reach the cable-car station, drivers follow brown signs to *Vogel* (to the left off the main lakefront road); by bus, get off at the Bohinj Pod Voglom stop (request this stop from driver) and hike about 10 minutes up the steep road on the left (away from the lake).

Visiting the Summit: After you arrive at the top, savor the views from the metal platform where you exit the cable car...just don't look down. Walking up through the cable-car station (past the Viharnik snack bar, with basic food and far-from-basic views), you'll pop out at the summit, a ski-in-winter, hike-in-summer area with a pasture filled with grazing cows and smaller chairlifts to various recreation areas.

The first chairlift is designed for skiers and doesn't run in summer, but if you hike down into the little valley, you can take the

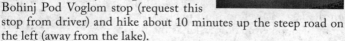

LAKE BLED

second chairlift up the adjacent summit (Orlove Glave) for views into another valley on the other side. Then, from Orlove Glave, you can hike or ride the chairlift back to where you started. With plenty of time and very strong knees, you could even hike from Orlove Glave all the way back down to Lake Bohinj.

World War I Cemetery

Back down below the cable car, on the main road just beyond the Bohinj Pod Voglom bus stop, look for the metal gate on the left (marked *1915-1917*) that leads to the final resting place for some WWI Soča Front soldiers (see sidebar on page 841). No fighting occurred here (it was mostly on the other side of these mountains); injured soldiers were brought to a nearby hospital, and those who didn't recover ended up here. Notice that many of the names are not Slovenian but Hungarian, Polish, Czech, and so on—a reminder that the entire multiethnic Austro-Hungarian Empire was involved in the fighting. If you're walking down from the cable-car station, the cemetery makes for a poignant detour on your way to the main road (look for it through the trees).

Savica Waterfall (Slap Savica)

Up the valley beyond the end of the lake is Bohinj's final treat, a waterfall called Slap Savica (sah-VEET-sah). Hardy hikers enjoy

following the moderate-to-strenuous uphill trail (including 553 stairs) to see the cascade, which dumps into a remarkably pure pool of aquamarine snowmelt.

Cost and Hours: €4 in summer, €3 in shoulder season; open daily from 8:00 until dusk, closed off-season; allow up to 1.5 hours for the round-trip hike.

Getting There: Drivers follow the lakefront road to where it ends, right at the trailhead (€4 parking). Without a car, getting to the trailhead is a hassle. Boats on the lake, as well as most public buses from Bled, take you only as far as the Bohinj Ukanc stop—still a one-hour hike from the trailhead. However, in summer (July-Aug), one bus a day goes from Bled all the way to the Savica trailhead (likely departing Bled at 10:00, returning at 12:20). Otherwise, you can change to a local bus in the Bohinj area to reach the falls.

THE JULIAN ALPS

Vršič Pass • Soča River Valley • Bovec • Kobarid

The countryside around Lake Bled is plenty beautiful. But to max out your Slovenian mountain experience, head for the cut-glass peaks of the Julian Alps. The northwestern corner of Slovenia—within yodeling distance of Austria and Italy—is where mountain culture has a Slavic accent.

The Slovenian mountainsides are laced with hiking paths, blanketed in deep forests, gurgling with intensely colorful rivers, and speckled with ski resorts and vacation chalets. And in the center of it all is Mount Triglav—ol' "Three Heads"—Slovenia's national symbol and, at 9,396 feet, its tallest mountain.

The single best day in the Julian Alps is spent driving up and over the 50 hairpin turns of breathtaking Vršič Pass (vur-SHEECH) and back down via the Soča (SOH-chah) River Valley, lined with offbeat nooks and Hemingway-haunted crannies. As you curl between the peaks, you'll enjoy stunning high-mountain scenery, whitewater rivers with superb fishing, rustic rest stops, thought-provoking WWI sights, and charming hamlets.

A pair of Soča Valley towns watches over the region. Centrally situated Bovec is all about good times (it's the whitewater-adventure sports hub), while Kobarid has Old World charm and attends to more serious matters (WWI history). Bovec and Kobarid are pleasant, functional, and convenient home bases for lingering in this gloriously beautiful region. I've also recommended a handful of countryside hotels and tourist farms.

PLANNING YOUR TIME

Most visitors do this area as a satisfying surgical strike on a full-day side trip from Lake Bled or Ljubljana. But there's plenty here to make it worth slowing down and spending a night (or even longer). If you'd like to take advantage of the Soča Valley's hiking trails, evocative WWI historical sites, and many adventure sports (especially river rafting on the Soča), and have some flexibility for the ever-changing weather, give yourself multiple nights.

Crowd Challenges: In the summer (July-Aug), this area can be very crowded with Slovenian vacationers. On peak-season weekends, some of the Vršič Pass parking lots (such as next to the Russian Chapel or at the summit) fill up, making it impossible to pull over and look around. The best advice is to avoid doing this trip in high summer, especially on weekends; if you have no choice, anticipate crowds, allow yourself a little extra time, and pack along some patience.

GETTING AROUND THE JULIAN ALPS

The Julian Alps are best by **car.** Consider renting a car here, if only for the day, to achieve maximum mountain thrills. I've included a self-guided drive that incorporates the best of the Julian Alps: Vršič Pass (usually open May-Oct) and the Soča Valley.

If you're without your own wheels, hiring a **local guide with a car** can be a great value, maximizing not only what you see but also what you learn. Or you can choose a cheaper but less personalized day-trip **excursion** from Bled. (See "Tours at Lake Bled," in the previous chapter.)

In the summer, a **public bus** more or less follows my driving-tour route over the Vršič Pass. These buses usually depart from Kranjska Gora, at the base of the pass, and reach Bovec in about two hours (and Kobarid about an hour later; 4-6/hour in summer). Be aware that most direct connections from Ljubljana to Bovec, Kobarid, and other Soča Valley towns skip Vršič Pass and instead take a lower-altitude, less thrilling route to the south, via Idrija (1-2/day, about 4 hours total). If you have your heart set on experiencing the Vršič Pass, do your homework to find a route that includes that road (likely via Kranjska Gora; current schedules are at www.ap-ljubljana.si or https://getbybus.com).

Julian Alps Drive

VRŠIČ PASS LOOP

This all-day, self-guided drive—rated ▲▲▲—takes you over the highest mountain pass in Slovenia, with stunning scenery and a few quirky sights along the way. From waterfalls to hiking trails,

WWI history to queasy suspension bridges, this trip has something for everyone.

Most of the Julian Alps are encompassed by Triglav National Park (Triglavski Narodni Park). This drive starts and ends in either Bled or Ljubljana, going over the Vršič Pass and through the Soča River Valley. While it's not for stick-shift novices, all but the most timid drivers will agree that the scenery is worth the many hairpin turns. Frequent pullouts offer plenty of opportunities to relax, stretch your legs, and enjoy the vistas.

Planning Your Drive: This drive can be done in a day (about 5 hours of driving), but consider spending the night along the way for a more leisurely pace. You can return to your starting point, or do this trip one-way as a very scenic detour between Bled and Ljubljana. These rough estimates do not include stops: Bled to the top of Vršič Pass—1 hour (30 minutes more from Ljubljana; add about 30 minutes round-trip for Planica ski-jump detour), Vršič Pass to Trenta (start of Soča Valley)—30 minutes, Trenta to Bovec—30 minutes, Bovec to Kobarid—30 minutes, Kobarid to Ljubljana or Bled—2 hours.

The best sources of information are the Bled TI (see the Lake Bled chapter), the Triglav National Park Information Center in Trenta, and the TIs in Bovec and Kobarid (described later in this chapter). Local TIs hand out good, free maps covering this area, and sell more detailed ones. If the pass is closed—or so clogged with traffic that you want to avoid it—you can still access the Soča Valley by looping around through Italy and taking the **Predel Pass**—a route nearly as scenic as this main option. Just reverse the Predel Pass route described on page 831.

From Bled or Ljubljana to Vršič Pass

From Bled or Ljubljana, take the A-2 expressway north, enjoying views of Mount Triglav on the left as you drive. About 10 minutes past Bled, you'll approach the industrial city of **Jesenice,** whose iron- and steelworks once filled this valley with multicolored smoke. (It was nicknamed the "Detroit of Yugosla-

Slovenia's Julian Alps

via.") Many of these old factories closed in the 1980s, and the air is much cleaner now.

Just after the giant smokestack with the billboards, the little gaggle of colorful houses on the right (just next to the freeway) is **Kurja Vas** ("Chicken Village"). This unassuming place is locally famous for producing hockey players: 18 of the 20 players on the 1971 Yugoslav hockey team—which went to the World Championships—were from this tiny hamlet.

As you zip past Jesenice, keep your eye out for the **exit** marked *Jesenice-zahod, Trbiž/Tarvisio, Kr. Gora,* and *Hrušica* (it's after the

Accommodations & Eateries

1 Pristava Lepena Resort
2 Holiday House Natura
3 Tourist Farm Pri Plajerju
4 Restavracija Mangrt
5 Tourist Farm Kranjc
6 Nebesa Chalets
7 Hiša Franko Restaurant

gas station, just before the tunnel to Austria). When you exit, turn left toward *Kranjska Gora* and *Trbiž/Tarvisio* (yellow sign).

Just after the exit, the big turquoise building surrounded by tall lights was the former border station (the overpass you'll go under leads into Austria). Locals have fond memories of visiting Austria during the Yugoslav days, when they smuggled back forbidden Western goods. Some items weren't available at home (VCRs, Coca-Cola, designer clothes); other goods were simply better in Austria (chocolate, coffee, dishwasher soap).

Just after the exit, you'll cross the Sava River. The main river of the former Yugoslavia, this 600-mile-long waterway begins in these mountains, flows past Ljubljana and Zagreb, defines the Croatian-Bosnian border, and finally joins the Danube in Belgrade. According to some geologists, the Balkans begin on the south bank of the Sava.

Slovenes brag that their country—"with 56 percent of the land covered in forest"—is Europe's second-greenest. As you drive toward Kranjska Gora, take in all this greenery...and the characteristic Slovenian hayracks (recognized as part of the national heritage and now preserved). The **Vrata Valley** (on the left) is a popular starting point for climbing Mount Triglav. Paralleling the road on the left is a "rails-to-trails" bike path—converted from an old railway bed—that loops from here through Italy and Austria, allowing bikers to connect three countries in one day.

About two miles from the highway turnoff, at the intersection in **Dovje,** watch on the right for the statue of Jakob Aljaž, who actually bought Triglav—back when such a thing was possible (he's pointing at his purchase). About five miles later, in **Gozd Martuljek,** you'll cross a bridge and enjoy a great head-on view of Špik Mountain.

From here, it's about three miles to **Kranjska Gora,** a leading winter resort particularly popular with Croatian skiers. As every Slovene and Croatian wants a ski bungalow here, this area has some of the highest property values in the country.

Entering Kranjska Gora, you'll see a turnoff to the left marked for *Bovec* and *Vršič*, which leads cars up to the pass. But winter sports fanatics (or anyone, on a clear day) may first want to take a 30-minute **detour** to see the biggest ski jump in the world, a few miles ahead at **Planica:** Stay straight through Kranjska Gora, then turn left at signs for *Planica*. You'll drive in along a row of eight dizzyingly high ski jumps to the modern, wood-clad Nor-

dic Center (pay parking), with 360-degree views of alpine scenery. Today's competitors routinely set new world records (currently 832 feet) on the outrageously steep ski-flying jump directly across from the Nordic Center. Thrill seekers who'd like to get a small taste of that experience can invest €29 (or €49 for a tandem run) in the adrenaline-pumping zipline that runs parallel to the jump. For something lower-impact, explore the Nordic Center, which has an info desk, WCs in the basement, a café with a sunny terrace, a small alpine-sports museum (overpriced and skippable for non-enthusiasts), and a wind-tunnel skydiving simulator (free entry to Nordic Center, daily July-Sept 9:00-18:00, March-June and Oct until 17:00, winter until 16:00, www.nc-planica.si). In the lower stairwell, peek through the window into the parking garage—where, in summer, artificial snow is pumped in for cross-country ski practice.

Before leaving Planica, ponder this: From this spot, you're a few minutes' walk from both Italy and Austria.

Back in Kranjska Gora, follow the signs for *Vršič*. You'll pass (on the right) a lovely alpine lake called **Jasna,** created by damming the runoff-fed Pišnica streams that flow down the mountain toward the Sava. This is a popular place for fly-fishing and swimming (look for the tall, wooden diving structure). On the lakeshore, watch for the bronze Golden Horn statue (similar to one at Lake Bohnj)—a popular photo op. The touristy restaurants and cafés here are some of the last you'll see for a while.

Before long, you'll officially enter **Triglav National Park** and come to the first of this road's 50 hairpin turns (24 up, then 26 down)—each one numbered and labeled with the altitude in meters. Notice that the turns are cobbled to provide better traction. If the drive seems daunting, remember that 50-seat tour buses routinely conquer this pass...if they can do it, so can you. Better yet, imagine—and watch for—the bicyclists who regularly pedal to the top. The best can do it in less than 30 minutes—faster than driving.

After switchback #8, with the cute waterfall, park your car on the right and hike up the stairs on the left to the little **Russian Orthodox chapel.** This road was built during World War I by at least 10,000 Russian POWs of the Austro-Hungarian Empire to supply the Soča Front. The POWs lived and worked in terrible conditions, and several hundred died of illness and exposure. On March 8, 1916, an avalanche thundered down the mountains, killing hundreds more workers. This chapel was built where the final casualty was found. Take a minute to

pay your respects to those who built the road you're enjoying today.

Back on the road, continue up, up, up the switchbacks. As you smell the clutch burn, be glad it's a rental. After #16, keep an eye out (on the left) for **Tonkina Koča**—one of many mountain huts situated partway up the road, where hikers can pause for a break, a rustic meal, or even an overnight (its deck is a nice place to nurse a drink; open mid-June–mid-Sept, +386 41 396 645).

Just beyond, after #17, look up as high as you can on the cliff

JULIAN ALPS

Mount Triglav

Mount Triglav ("Three Heads") stands watch over the Julian Alps, and all of Slovenia. Slovenes say that its three peaks are the guardians of the water, air, and earth. This mountain defines Slovenes, even adorning the nation's flag: You'll often see the national seal, with three peaks (the two squiggly lines under it represent the Adriatic). Or take a look at Slovenia's €0.50 coin.

From the town of Bled, you'll see Triglav peeking up over the ridge on a clear day. (You'll get an even better view from nearby Lake Bohinj.)

It's said that you're not a true Slovene until you've climbed Triglav. One native took these words very seriously and climbed the mountain 853 times...in one year. Climbing to the summit—at 9,396 feet—is an attainable goal for any hiker in good shape. If you're here for a while and want to become an honorary Slovene, befriend a local and ask if he or she will take you to the top. Or join a tour; several local companies specialize in summiting visitors.

If mountain climbing isn't your style, relax at an outdoor café with a piece of cream cake and a view of Triglav. It won't make you a Slovene...but it's close enough on a quick visit.

face to see sunlight streaming through a **"window"** in the rock. This natural formation, a popular destination for intrepid hikers, is big enough for the Statue of Liberty to crawl through.

After #22, at the pullout for Erjavčeva Koča restaurant, you may see tour-bus groups making a fuss about the mountain vista. They're looking for a ghostly face in the cliff wall, supposedly belonging to the mythical figure **Ajda.** This village girl was cursed by the townspeople after correctly predicting the death of the Zlatorog (Golden Horn), a magical, beloved, chamois-like animal. Her tiny image is just above the tree line, a little to the right—try to get someone to point her out to you (you can see her best if you stand at the signpost near the road). The picnic tables here are one of the best places along this drive for a do-it-yourself feast.

After #24, you reach the **summit** (5,285 feet). Consider

Hemingway in the Julian Alps

It was against the scenic backdrop of the Slovenian Alps that a young man from Oak Park, Illinois, first came to Europe—the continent with which he would forever be identified. After graduating from high school in 1917 and working briefly as a newspaper reporter, young Ernest Hemingway wanted to join the war effort in Europe. Bad vision kept him out of the army, but he craved combat experience—so he joined the Red Cross Ambulance Corps instead.

After a short detour through Paris, Hemingway was sent to the Italian Front. On his first day, he was given the job of retrieving human remains—gruesomely disfigured body parts—after the explosion of a munitions factory. Later he came to the Lower Piave Valley, not far from the Soča Front. In July 1918, his ambulance was hit by a mortar shell. Despite his injuries, he saved an Italian soldier who was also wounded. According to legend, Hemingway packed his own wound with cigarette butts to stop the flow of blood.

Sent to Milan to recuperate, Hemingway fell in love with a nurse, but she later left him for an Italian military officer. A decade later, Hemingway wrote about Kobarid (using its Italian name, Caporetto), the war, and his case of youthful heartbreak in *A Farewell to Arms*.

getting out of the car to enjoy the views. Hike up to the Tičarjev Dom hut for a snack or drink on the grand view terrace. On the right, a long gravel chute gives hikers a thrilling glissade. (From the pullout just beyond #26, it's easy to view hikers "skiing" down.) If you have time and energy to burn, consider hiking from the summit about 20 minutes uphill to the Poštarski Dom ("Postman's Lodge," with good food). Along the way, you'll see the ruins of a cable-car line, which ran supplies between here and the valley floor during World War I.

As you begin the descent, keep an eye out for old WWI debris. A lonely guard tunnel stands after #28, followed by a tunnel marked *1916* (on the left) that was part of the road's original path. A bit later, watch for the turnoff at the right, at a little gravel parking lot with a picnic table (labeled *Viewpoint Šupca*). From the platform viewpoint, you can see mountain valleys formed in two different ways: To the left, the jagged V-shaped Soča Valley, carved by a raging river; and on the right, the gentle U-shaped Trenta Valley, gouged by a glacier.

Continuing down, you'll see abandoned checkpoints from when this was the border between Italy and the Austro-Hungarian Empire. At #48 is a statue of **Julius Kugy,** an Italian botanist who explored the alpine flora of this region.

At #49, the road to the right (marked *Izvir Soče*) leads to the **source of the Soča River.** If you feel like stretching your legs, drive about five minutes down this road to a restaurant parking lot. From here, you can take a challenging 20-minute uphill hike (which includes some stretches where you'll cling to guide wires) to the Soča source. This is also the starting point for the well-explained, 12-mile Soča Trail (Soška Pot), which leads all the way to the town of Bovec.

Nearing the end of the switchbacks, follow signs for *Bovec*. Crossing the Soča River, you begin the second half of this trip.

From Vršič Pass to Soča River Valley

During World War I, the terrain between here and the Adriatic made up the Soča (Isonzo) Front. As you follow the Soča River south, down what's nicknamed the "Valley of the Cemeteries," the scenic mountainsides tell the tale of this terrible warfare. Imagine a young Ernest Hemingway driving his ambulance through these same hills (see sidebar).

But it's not all so gloomy. There are plenty of other diversions—interesting villages and churches, waterfalls and suspension bridges, and more. Perhaps most impressive is the remarkable clarity and milky-blue color of the Soča itself, which Slovenes proudly call their "emerald river."

After switchback #49, you'll cross a bridge, then pass a church and a botanical garden of alpine plants (Alpinum Juliana, summer only).

At long last—well after you think you're done with the pass—you finally reach the last Vršič switchback (#50), which sends you into the village of **Trenta.** As you get to the cluster of buildings in Trenta's "downtown," look on the left for the **Triglav National Park Information Center,** which also serves as a regional TI (May-Oct daily 10:00-18:00, closed Nov-April, +386 5 388 9330, www.tnp.si). The €6 museum here provides

a look (with English explanations) at the park's flora, fauna, traditional culture, and mountaineering history. An AV show celebrates the region's forests, and a poetic 15-minute slideshow explains the wonders and fragility of the park (included in museum entry, ask for English version as you enter).

After Trenta, you'll pass through a tunnel; then, on the left, look for a classic **suspension footbridge.** Pull over to walk out for a bounce, enjoying the river's crystal-clear water and the spectacular mountain panorama. Or you can take your pick among many such bridges for the next several miles; the best is coming up soon (I'll point it out).

About five miles beyond Trenta, in the town of Soča, is the **Church of St. Joseph** (with reddish-brown steeple, tucked behind the big tree on the right). During World War II, an artist hiding out in the mountains filled this church with patriotic symbolism. The interior is bathed in Yugoslav red, white, and blue—a brave statement made when such nationalistic sentiments were dangerous. On the ceiling is St. Michael (clad in Yugoslav colors) with Yugoslavia's three WWII enemies at his feet: the eagle (Germany), the wolf (Italy), and the serpent (Japan). The tops of the walls along the nave are lined with Slavic saints. Finally, look carefully at the Stations of the Cross and find the faces of hated Yugoslav enemies: a lederhosen-clad Hitler (pulling a rope to lift up the cross; fourth from altar on left) and Mussolini (seated, as Herod; first from altar on right).

Behind the church, above the lovingly tended town graveyard, the stylized cross on the hill marks a **WWI cemetery**—the

final resting place of some 1,400 Austro-Hungarian soldiers who were killed in action. Notice one small corner of the main cemetery (just before the WWI section) that's marked with a red star and labeled *Padli Borci Nov* (Our Fallen Fighters). These are the graves of local Partisans who—two generations later—fought alongside Tito to force out the Nazis (notice the death dates: 1943, 1944, 1945).

For another good example of how the Soča River cuts like God's band saw into the land, stop about two minutes past the church at the small gravel lot (on the left) marked *Velika Korita Soče* **(Grand Canyon of Soča).** While the entire Soča Valley is dramatic, this half-mile stretch, 30 to 50 feet deep, is considered the most impressive. Venture out onto the **suspension bridge** over the gorge. If the water's high, notice the many side streams pouring into the churning river in a series of mini-waterfalls. For more views, cross over the bridge and hike down along the treacherously uneven and narrow rocky path downstream to another bridge.

Just beyond the suspension bridge is the turnoff (on the left) to the Lepena Valley, home of the recommended Pristava Lepena ranch, with accommodations, a restaurant, and Lipizzaner horses (see "Sleeping in Bovec," later). If you head up this valley, you'll find a big gravel pullout on the right (marked *Velika Korita*) that lets you cross another springy bridge over a particularly wide stretch of the river. This is a popular place for those who enjoy hiking up alongside the "Grand Canyon" we passed earlier (about 5 miles round-trip, uneven terrain).

A few miles after the Lepena Valley turnoff, watch on the left for the large **barn** (marked *Žičnica Golobar*). Pull over here if you'd like a close look at one of the stations for a primitive, industrial cable-car line, which was used mostly for logging.

Soon you'll exit the national park, pass a WWI graveyard (on the left), and come to a fork in the road. The main route leads

to the left, through Bovec. But first, take a two-mile **detour** to the right (marked *Trbiž/Tarvisio* and *Predel/Kluže*), where the WWI **Kluže Fortress** keeps a close watch over the narrowest part of a valley leading to Italy (free to enter main courtyard, €3 for exhibit about local history and nature; June-Sept daily 9:00-17:00, may be open later in July-Aug, likely closed Oct-May). In the 15th century, the Italians had a fort here to defend against the Ottomans. Five hundred years later, during World War I, Austrians used it to keep Italians out of their territory. Notice the ladder rungs fixed to the cliff face across the road from the fort, allowing soldiers to get up to the mountaintop quickly.

Back on the main road, immediately after the Kluže turnoff, watch for the gravel pullout on the left (look for the green sign with old photos). To see some original **WWI-era fortifications,** pull over here and hike on the gravel path 10 minutes through the woods to reach the Ravelnik Outdoor Museum. Here you can see trenches dug into the dirt and rocks, abandoned pillboxes, rusty sheds, and other features of an evocative wartime landscape. Though not entirely typical of Soča Front embattlements—which were mostly high on the mountaintops—Ravelnik offers a more accessible taste of those times. (For a more authentic, mountaintop outdoor museum, drive 30 minutes beyond Kobarid and up to Kolovrat—described on page 843.)

Continue following the main road to **Bovec,** which saw some of the most vicious fighting of the Soča Front. The town was hit hard by earthquakes in 1994, 1998, and 2004, but today it's been rebuilt and is the adventure-sports capital of the Soča River Valley, famous for its whitewater activities. For good lunch stops in Bovec, turn right at the roundabout as you first reach the town; you'll pass Martinov Hram's inviting restaurant terrace on the right, and soon after, the outdoor tables for Thirsty River brewery, with tempting food stands nearby (for details, see "Eating in Bovec," later). But if you're not eating or spending the night in Bovec, you could skip the town entirely (continue along the main road to bypass the town center).

About three miles past Bovec, as you cross the bridge (with the yellow *Boka* sign), look high up on the rock wall in the gorge to your right to spot the **Boka waterfall,** which carves a deep gutter into the cliff as it tumbles into the valley. (Can't find it? Keep an eye on the left side of the cliff, tucked back in a nook.) Hardy hikers can climb up for a better view of this fall—the trailhead is just after the bridge on the right—but it's a strenuous hike.

Head south along the spectacularly turquoise river. When you pass the intersection at the humble village of Žaga, you're just four miles from Italy. Continuing south, you'll pass a pullout (just before Srpenica) that is a popular put-in point for kayaking trips along the river.

After Srpenica, you'll pass the huge **TKK** factory complex, which produces a wide range of chemicals.

Carry on a few more miles. Soon you'll see signs for **Kobarid,** home to a sleepy main square and some fascinating WWI sights. Don't blink or you'll miss the Kobarid turnoff on the right (just before the big tower advertising the local creamery). Exit here, and you'll drive into town past the highly recommended **Kobarid Museum,** which tells the tale of the WWI-era Soča Front. Farther along, you'll reach the tidy main square, a good place to park—pay at the meter or on your phone—and then explore town or walk back to the museum. Driving up to the Italian mausoleum that hovers over the town is a must. (These sights are described later, under "Sights in Kobarid.")

Leaving Kobarid, continue south along the Soča to **Tolmin.** (For a steep, scenic detour to some poignant WWI sites, you can turn off in Idrsko to reach the Kolovrat Outdoor Museum—described on page 843.) Notice the architecture transitioning from a woodsy Austrian vibe to more stony Italian (this area was historically Italian).

Before you reach Tolmin, decide on your preferred route back to civilization...

From the Soča River Valley to Ljubljana

There are two ways to complete a loop trip back to Ljubljana through more varied scenery. The first route is faster and more scenic; the second route is longer and a bit smoother. Either option brings you back to the A-1 expressway south of Ljubljana, and will get you to the city in about two hours. To reach Bled, follow either route, then carry on northward for another hour. (For more direct routes to Bled, see the next section.)

Idrija Route: This ruggedly scenic approach takes you along ever-narrower valleys and through the charming town of Idrija. Begin by driving through Tolmin on the main road, following the Soča River to Most na Soči. Enjoy the valley scenery as you twist through the hills, following the Idrijca River. About 40 minutes after Most na Soči, you'll reach the outer limits of the town of **Idrija** (EE-dree-yah), well known among Slovenes for its tourable mercury mine (www.muzej-idrija-cerkno.si), delicate lace *(čipko)*, and tasty *žlikrofi* (filled dumplings, like ravioli). Idrija (pop. 6,000) feels like a once-gloomy post-industrial city that's enjoying renewed life (www.visit-idrija.si). If you're ready for a bite, several restaurants in town offer a chance to sample *žlikrofi;* I ate well at **$ Gostilna Mlinar,** a guesthouse high above town (try their sampler plate of three types of *žlikrofi;* closed Mon-Wed; turn left at the bridge just before you enter Idrija, then twist up the narrow road, watching for the guesthouse on the right at the very top of town, +386 5 377 6316). From Idrija, it's another 30 minutes to the expressway (at Logatec); from there, you can head north to Ljubljana in less than 30 minutes.

Nova Gorica Route: This route, which swings to the southwest, starts at the roundabout before you reach Tolmin (head to the right, toward *Nova Gorica*). Along this road, you'll pass a hydroelectric dam and go under a 1906 rail viaduct that once connected this area to the port of Trieste. In the charming town of **Kanal,** you'll cross over the Soča on a picturesque bridge. Farther along, the striking **Solkan Bridge** (another link in the Trieste rail line) is the longest single-span stone arch bridge in the world.

About 40 minutes from the Tolmin area, you arrive in **Nova Gorica.** This fairly dull city is divided in half by the Italian border (the Italian side is called "Gorizia"). Because Italians aren't allowed to gamble in their hometowns, Nova Gorica is packed with casinos—including Europe's biggest. Rocks spell out the words *NAŠ TITO* ("Our Tito") on a hillside above town—a strange relic of an earlier age. From Nova Gorica, you can hop on the H-4 expressway, which links easily to the main A-1 expressway (from here, it's about an hour to Ljubljana, and 30 minutes farther to Bled). The road from Nova Gorica to Ljubljana takes you through the heart of the Karst region—famous for its wineries and caves.

From the Soča River Valley to Bled

Car Train Option: The fastest route from Tolmin to Bled is to load your car onto a "Car Train" (Autovlak, a.k.a. "Motorail") that cuts directly through the mountains. The train departs from Most na Soči (just south of Tolmin, along the Idrija route just described) and arrives at Bohinjska Bistrica, near Lake Bohinj, about 45 minutes later (€14/car; departs 4/day, including handy afternoon departures at 14:45 year-round and 18:43 in high season; confirm schedule at the Bled TI before making the trip, www.slo-zeleznice.si). Reservations are not necessary, but plan to arrive at the train station about 30 minutes before the scheduled departure to allow time to load the car. Note: The train can be quite jerky and bumpy, and you're required to stay inside your car the entire time. If you're claustrophobic, prone to motion sickness, or both, consider giving this train a miss. For others, it's a hoot.

To get to the car train, drive through Tolmin to Most na Soči. About a mile past Most na Soči, watch on the right for the big bridge over the river, marked for *Čepovan* and *železniška postaja* (train station). Cross the bridge and turn right to find the train station; once there, go around the far-left side of the long station building and drive up the ramp to wait your turn to load. After the train takes off, you'll cross a scenic viaduct, then twist through the mountains, going through multiple tunnels, including a final 10-minute passage from Podbrdo beneath the mountains to Bohinjska Bistrica, where you'll unload your car. From there, it's less than a half-hour drive back to Bled, or a 10-minute drive (in the opposite direction) to Lake Bohinj.

Through Italy via Predel Pass: Although this route requires some backtracking, it also includes a fun detour through Italy—and some different scenery. From Kobarid, drive back the way you came (through Bovec), then turn off for the Kluže Fortress, marked for *Predel* and *Italy*. In a few miles, after passing the fort, the road curves up through two small villages (first Log pod Mangartom—with a recommended restaurant—then Strmec na Predelu). Continue past the ruined fortress and cross the Italian border (there's generally no need to stop). Then curl down a few hairpin turns past the end of tranquil, scenic Lake Predel, and continue straight through the industrial city of Cave del Predil (overhead are the five rounded peaks of the Cinque Punte formation) and along the valley road, following signs for *Slovenia*. Approaching Tarvisio, turn right (continuing to follow signs for *Kranjska Gora* and Slovenia); from here, it's about a half-hour (10 miles) back across the Slovenian border to Kranjska Gora. This is where you first began your ascent of the Vršič Pass—just retrace your steps back to Bled.

Other Driving Routes: The fastest route (about 2 hours) essentially follows the car-train route, but goes over rather than through the mountains. This route is partially on a twisty, rough, poor-quality road (go through Tolmin, turn off just after the train station at Bača pri Modreju to Podbrdo, then from Petrovo Brdo take a very curvy road through the mountains into Bohinjska Bistrica and on to Bled). For timid drivers, start out on the Idrija route toward Ljubljana (described earlier), but turn off in Straža (before Idrija—watch for turnoff to *Cerkno*) toward Gorenja Vas, Skofja Loka, and Kranj, then continue on to Bled.

Bovec

The biggest town in the area, with about 1,600 people, Bovec (BOH-vets) has a happening main square and all the tourist amenities. It's best known as a hub for whitewater adventure sports. While not exactly quaint, Bovec is pleasant enough to qualify as a good lunch stop or overnight home base. Functional and handy, it's a nice jolt of civilization wedged between the skyscraping alpine cliffs.

Orientation to Bovec

TOURIST INFORMATION
The helpful TI is just a few steps off the main square (July-Aug daily 8:30-19:00; Sept daily 9:00-17:00; June and Oct Mon-Fri 8:30-16:00, Sat-Sun 9:00-13:00; shorter hours off-season; Trg Golobarskih Žrtev 8, +386 5 302 9647, www.soca-valley.com).

ARRIVAL IN BOVEC
The main road skirts Bovec, but you can turn off (watch for signs on the right) to go through the heart of town, then rejoin the main road farther along. The turnoff road goes right past the main square, Trg Golobarskih Žrtev, with the TI, various tour companies, and eateries.

Parking is tight in high season (May-Sept). Your best bet is to drive into town, and then, when you reach the main square, make a sharp right turn uphill, then turn right again just before the church (following the *P 80 m* sign). This leads you to a big gravel parking lot a five-minute walk downhill to town. To park a bit closer, try the big parking lot behind the Mercator supermarket (on the left just before the main square). Both lots may charge to park in high season—check signs carefully.

Activities near Bovec

As the de facto capital of Slovenia's "Adrenaline Valley," Bovec offers many opportunities to enjoy the nature all around it. For great mountain views of the surrounding terrain, simply hike five minutes up (or drive) to the church at the top of town.

Adventure Sports

An ever-changing roster of local adventure-travel companies run a variety of tours that will get you out on the rushing, crystal-clear waters of the Soča River. The Bovec TI is a good source of information. Well-established tour outfits include Bovec Šport Centar (www.bovec-sc.si) and Soča Rafting (www.socarafting.si), but it's also a good idea to consult recent online reviews. Most of these activities come with some degree of risk; use common sense and investigate the company's safety record.

The main options are rafting, kayaking, and hydrospeeding (a masochistic variation on boogie boarding—lying face-down on a short surfboard and shooting headfirst toward the rapids). The official season is March 15 until October 31, but from an adrenaline perspective, these activities are best in spring—when the water is highest. The river is tamer in summer; by fall, water levels are very low.

When conditions are ideal, most **rafting** companies put in near the Boka waterfall (just downriver from Bovec) and pick up at the village of Trnovo ob Soči. (When water levels are low, companies put in near Sprenica instead.) Most rafting trips last about 2.5-3 hours, with about 1.5 hours actually on the river and extra time to swim.

Kayaking is available at various points along the river, with a dramatic range in level of difficulty; the TI's free river map outlines your options and notes areas that are unsafe. To get a glimpse of kayakers, hang out at Napoleon Bridge, just outside Kobarid.

The most popular place for **canyoning**—a risky activity that involves wading and rappelling in rushing rivers, always with a guide—is in Canyon Sušec, about halfway between Bovec and Kobarid.

The Soča River is also popular for fishing, predominantly for the endemic marble trout. Only **fly fishing** is allowed; some areas are catch-and-release, and all areas require a permit.

Other popular activities include skydiving and paragliding, biking (including electric mountain bikes), ziplines (there's a course above Bovec and another high in the Učja Valley), and even—*gasp!*—golf (Bovec has a 9-hole course, www.golfbovec.si).

Sightseeing Flights and Skydiving

Bovec's little airport is used mainly for skydiving flights (see www. skydivebovec.com). But **Janez Let** runs scenic sightseeing flights (+386 41 262 726, www.janezlet.si).

Kanin Cable Car

A cable car slo-o-owly trundles visitors 7,200 feet above sea level to near the summit of Mount Kanin, which overlooks Bovec and a scenic swath of the Soča Valley. On a clear day, you can see all the way to the Adriatic. Up top, you can walk around an irregular limestone landscape (but watch your step—there are some extremely deep hidden crevasses) and pay extra to try out a fixed-anchor (a.k.a. *via ferrata*) climbing course.

Cost and Hours: €25 round-trip, 35 minutes each way, hours sporadic and weather-dependent but typically June-mid-Sept daily 8:00-16:00, Sat-Sun only in shoulder season, bottom station is just outside Bovec near the road to Kobarid, www.kanin.si.

Sleeping in Bovec

Dobra Vila and Hotel Sanje ob Soči are situated near the turnoff from the main road into central Bovec (about a 10-minute walk into town). Martinov Hram and Stari Kovač are closer to the main square, in the town center.

$$$ Dobra Vila, run with class by Juri, has 11 boldly stylish yet classic rooms, a large back terrace, and a garden sauna. You'll stay in a gorgeously restored former telephone office that feels like a sophisticated whisper of ages past (air-con, Mala vas 112, +386 5 389 6400, www.dobra-vila-bovec.si, welcome@dobra-vila-bovec.si).

$$ Hotel Sanje ob Soči means "Dreams by the Soča"—which describes both what you'll do here and the vision that entrepreneurial owners Boštjan and Valentina have for their sleek, modern, spa-like lodgings. The 10 rooms and nine apartments fill a pine-clad, Scandinavian-feeling shell on the edge of Bovec. The rooms—all with terraces, and each one named for the mountain that dominates its view—are fairly simple and Ikea-furnished (breakfast extra, air-con, children's play area, Mala vas 105a, +386 5 389 6000, mobile +386 31 331 690, www.sanjeobsoci.com, info@ sanjeobsoci.com).

$ Martinov Hram has 12 nice, modern rooms over a popular restaurant a few steps from Bovec's main square. While the rooms are an afterthought to the busy restaurant (reception at the bar), they're comfortable (rooms on sunny side have air-con, Trg Golo-barskih Žrtev 27, +386 5 388 6214, www.martinov-hram.si, sara.berginc@gmail.com).

$ Stari Kovač B&B is your basic budget option, with eight apartments in an old-feeling guesthouse with woody charm, a steep block downhill from the main square (breakfast extra, cash only, Rupa 3, +386 5 388 6699, mobile +386 41 646 427, www.starikovac.com, info@starikovac.com).

NEAR BOVEC

$$$ Pristava Lepena is a relaxing oasis hiding out in the Lepena Valley just north of Bovec. This place is its own little village, with a series of rustic-looking but comfy cabins, a restaurant, an exercise room, a kids' play area, an outdoor swimming pool, a sauna/whirlpool, and resident Lipizzaner horses and mountain goats, plus a children's farm with chickens and rabbits. The 16 cozy rooms have wood-burning stoves and all the amenities (closed mid-Oct-March except around Christmas and New Year, multinight stays preferred, lunch and dinner extra; just south of the village of Soča, exit the main road at the sign for *Lepena,* then follow signs to Lepena 2; +386 5 388 9900, mobile +386 41 671 981, www.pristava-lepena.com, info@pristavalepena.com).

$$$ Holiday House Natura, run by sweet Jelena, is a rustic yet comfortable five-person home with a kitchen, dining terrace, and two bedrooms perched on a ridge just outside of Bovec, with a small farm just outside your front door and sweeping views over the valley. This is an ideal spot to escape into nature while still being just a short drive from town (Ravni Laz 6, +386 41 832 774, www.bovechouse.com, bovecavantura@gmail.com). They also have an apartment in Bovec.

$$ Tourist Farm Pri Plajerju is on a picturesque plateau at the edge of Trenta (at the bottom of the Vršič Pass road). Run by the Pretner family (gregarious Marko is a park ranger, shy Stanka is "the boss"), this organic farm raises sheep and rents five apartments in three buildings separate from the main house. There are also "hikers' rooms" where you sleep on hay mattresses and share a bathroom with other close-to-nature guests. The location, deeper in the mountains, makes it a bit less convenient for side-tripping—it's 30 minutes to Bovec and an hour to Kobarid (breakfast and dinner extra; watch for signs to the left after coming over the pass and going through Trenta, Trenta 16a; +386 5 388 9209, mobile +386 41 600 590, www.eko-plajer.com, info@eko-plajer.com).

Eating in Bovec

In addition to the predictable fare, Bovec specializes in mountain food, including trout, lamb, foraged wild mushrooms, and the stick-to-your-ribs melty cheese fritter called *frika*. The local dessert is *bovški krafi*—dumplings stuffed with local-grown dried and chopped-up miniature pears (Martinov Hram is a good place to try this dish).

$$$ Martinov Hram, run by the Berginc family (sisters Sara and Suzi), has an inviting outdoor terrace under a grape trellis. Inside, the nicely traditional decor pairs well with regional specialties and homemade bread (closed Mon; on the main road through Bovec, just before the main square on the right at Trg Golobarskih Žrtev 27; +386 5 388 6214).

Brewpub and Alpine Street Food: $ Thirsty River is an inviting microbrew tasting room with a wonderful location right on Bovec's main square. The basic interior is rustic and cozy, but in good weather, the outdoor tables will kill your momentum (as will the excellent beers; long hours daily). In summer, a row of little **wooden sheds** is set up along the road nearby, serving up appealing street food. The best of these is **$ Bovec Kitch'n** (Bovška Kuhn'ca), where Bojan and daughter Anja serve up delicious, filling portions of hearty mountain foods, with lots of mushrooms and melted cheese, plus local trout and lamb (roughly May-Sept daily 16:00-20:00, closed off-season, +386 41 695 744). When closed, the sign reads *Sem šel po gobe* ("I went mushroom hunting").

NEAR BOVEC

$$$$ Restavracija Mangrt is well worth the scenic 15-minute drive from Bovec. It fills a cozy traditional inn with chef Tomaž Sovdat's delicious modern food, driven by local ingredients and culinary traditions, but with modern flourishes. The service is also excellent. Book ahead (you can do it online) before making the drive (Thu-Fri 18:00-22:00, Sat-Sun 12:00-15:00 & 18:00-22:00, closed Mon-Wed, Log pod Mangartom 57, +386 41 219 332, www.restavracijamangrt.si). To get here, from the intersection just east of Bovec, follow the valley past the Kluže Fortress to the idyllic mountain town of Log pod Mangartom. The restaurant is right along the main road in the heart of the village.

$$$$ Pristava Lepena—a recommended hotel listed earlier—is also open to nonguests for meals in their big, rustic dining room. Although pricey, a meal here comes with a beautiful 15-minute drive and a peek at the lovely Lepena Valley (daily 12:00-22:00).

Bovec Connections

From Bovec by Bus to: Kobarid (6/day Mon-Fri, 2-3/day Sat-Sun, 30 minutes), **Ljubljana** (see "Getting Around the Julian Alps," earlier, for connections via the Vršič Pass and Kranjska Gora, or via Idrija).

Kobarid

Kobarid (KOH-bah-reed) feels older, a bit smaller (pop. 1,090), and a bit more appealing than its big

brother Bovec. This humble settlement was immortalized by Ernest Hemingway, who drove an ambulance in these mountains during World War I. He described Kobarid as "a little white town with a campanile in a valley. It was a clean little town and there was a fine fountain in the square." Sounds about right. Even though Kobarid loves to tout its Hemingway connection, historians believe that Papa did not actually visit Kobarid until he came back after the war to research his book.

Aside from its brush with literary greatness, Kobarid is known as a hub of information about the Soča Front (with an excellent WWI museum, a hilltop Italian mausoleum, and walks that connect to surrounding sites). You won't find the fountain Hemingway wrote about—it's since been covered up by houses. You will find a modern statue of Simon Gregorčič (overlooking the main intersection), the beloved Slovenian priest-poet who came from and wrote about the Soča Valley.

Orientation to Kobarid

The main road, Gregorčičeva, cuts right through the heart of little Kobarid, bisecting its main square (Trg Svobode).

TOURIST INFORMATION

The TI has good information on the entire area (July-Aug daily 9:00-19:00; June and Sept Mon-Fri 9:00-17:00, Sat 9:00-16:00, Sun 9:00-13:00; off-season shorter hours and closed Sat and/or Sun; on the main square at Trg Svobode 16—follow the white

JULIAN ALPS

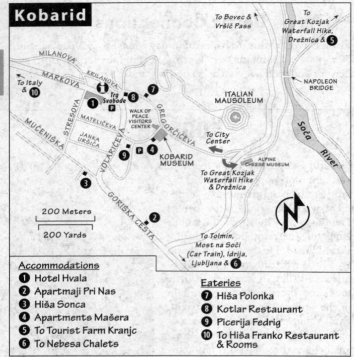

Kobarid

To Bovec &
Vršič Pass

To
Great Kozjak
Waterfall Hike,
Drežnica & **5**

MILANOVA

MARKOVA

KRILANOVA

To Italy
& **10**

NAPOLEON
BRIDGE

STREGOVA

MATELIČEVA

1
Trg
Svobode **8**

1

7

GREGORČIČEVA

ITALIAN
MAUSOLEUM

Soča River

MUČENIŠKA

JANKA
URŠIĆA

VOLARIČEVA

WALK OF
PEACE
VISITORS
CENTER

To City
Center

9

**KOBARID
MUSEUM**

ALPINE
CHEESE MUSEUM

To Great Kozjak
Waterfall Hike
& Drežnica

3

GORIŠKA CESTA

200 Meters

200 Yards

2

To Tolmin,
Most na Soči
(Car Train), Idrija,
Ljubljana & **6**

N

Accommodations
- **1** Hotel Hvala
- **2** Apartmaji Pri Nas
- **3** Hiša Sonca
- **4** Apartments Mašera
- **5** To Tourist Farm Kranjc
- **6** To Nebesa Chalets

Eateries
- **7** Hiša Polonka
- **8** Kotlar Restaurant
- **9** Picerija Fedrig
- **10** To Hiša Franko Restaurant
  & Rooms

footprints behind the statue of Gregorčič, +386 5 380 0490, www.
soca-valley.com).

ARRIVAL IN KOBARID

Driving into town from Bovec, watch carefully on the right for the
poorly marked first turnoff into Kobarid (if you miss the turnoff,
just carry on a bit longer, then turn right later to reach the main
square). Turning into town, you could make a sharp left to reach
the cheese factory (marked by the big modern tower) and Great
Kozjak Waterfall trail, or continue straight ahead to pass the Kobarid Museum, then the main square. You'll find pay parking on
the main square, from which it's an easy five-minute stroll back to
the museum (pay by phone at the meter). Another parking lot is
behind the museum, next to a playing field.

Sights in Kobarid

▲▲Kobarid Museum (Kobariški Muzej)

This old-school but world-class museum—worth ▲▲▲ for history buffs—offers a haunting look at the tragedy of the Soča Front.
The tasteful exhibits, with good English descriptions and a pacifist

tone, take an even-handed approach to the fighting—without getting hung up on identifying the "good guys" and the "bad guys." The museum's focus is not on the guns and heroes but on the big picture of the front and the stories of the common people who fought and died here.

Cost and Hours: €8, daily 9:00-18:00, July-Aug until 20:00, Oct-March 10:00-17:00, Gregorčičeva 10, +386 5 389 0000, www.kobariski-muzej.si.

Tours: History buffs can call ahead to arrange a private tour of the collection or the sights outside. You can also arrange a guide through the Walk of Peace Visitors Center, listed later.

Visiting the Museum: The entry is lined with hastily made cement and barbed-wire gravestones, flags representing all the nationalities involved in the fighting, and pictures of soldiers and nurses from diverse backgrounds who were brought together at the Soča Front. The rooms in this front part of the museum typically show good temporary exhibits about the war.

Buy your ticket and ask to watch the English version of the 20-minute film on the history of the Soča Front (informative but dry, focused on military history).

The first floor up is divided into several rooms, which you'll tour counterclockwise. The White Room—filled with rusty crampons, wire-cutters, pickaxes, and shovels—explains wintertime conditions at the front. What looks like a bear trap was actually used to trap enemy soldiers. The Room of the Rear shows the day-to-day activities away from the front line, from supplying troops to more mundane activities (milking cows, washing clothes, getting a shave, lifting weights, playing with a dog). Peruse the case of personal effects that troops carried to the front line. The somber and heartbreaking Black Room commemorates the more than one million casualties of the Soča Front. Horrific images of war injuries juxtaposed with medals earned prompts the question, was it worth it? Nearby is a display case of artificial limbs. The little altar was purchased by schoolchildren, who sent it to the front to offer the troops some solace. The door—etched with personal messages from troops—was relocated here from a military prison near Kobarid.

Through the door marked *The Krn Range Room* (also on the first floor up), pass the small model of the mountaintop war zone and find your way to the Kobarid Rooms, which trace the history of this region from antiquity to today. High on the wall, look for the timelines explaining the area's turbulent past. In the second room, a timeline shows wave after wave of invaders (including Ottomans, Habsburgs, and Napoleon). In the next room, above a display case with military uniforms, another timeline shows the many flags that flew over Kobarid's main square during the 20th century alone.

On the top floor, you'll see a giant model of the surrounding mountains, painstakingly tracing the successful Austrian-German *Blitzkrieg* attack during the Battle of Kobarid. Crawl into the small cave and press the button to hear a patriotic song about a soldier, who reads a letter he's written to his family.

▲▲Italian Mausoleum (Kostnica)

The 55 miles between Kobarid and the Adriatic are dotted with more than 75 cemeteries, reminders of the countless casualties on

the Soča Front. One of the most dramatic is this mausoleum, overlooking Kobarid. The access road, across Kobarid's main square from the side of the church, is marked by stone gate towers with the word *Kostnica*—one tower is topped with a cross and the other with a star for the Italian army.

Take the road up Gradič Hill—passing Stations of the Cross—to the mausoleum. Built in 1938 (when this was still part of Italy) around the existing Church of St. Anthony, this octagonal pyramid holds the remains of 7,014 Italian soldiers. The stark, cold Neoclassical architecture is pure Mussolini. Names are listed alphabetically, along with mass graves for more than 1,700 unknown soldiers *(militi ignoti)*.

Walk behind the church and enjoy the **view.** Scan the WWI battlements high on the mountain's rock face. Incredibly, troops fought on these treacherous ridges; civilians in the valleys only heard the distant battles. Looking up and down the valley, notice the "signal churches" evenly spaced on hilltops, each barely within view of the next—an ancient method for quickly spreading messages or warnings across long distances.

If the **church** is open, go inside and look above the door to see a brave soldier standing over the body of a fallen comrade, fending off enemies with nothing but rocks.

When Mussolini came to dedicate the mausoleum, local revolutionaries plotted an assassination attempt that they believed couldn't fail. A young man planned to suicide-bomb Mussolini as the leader came back into town from this hilltop. But as Mus-

JULIAN ALPS

The Soča (Isonzo) Front

The valley in Slovenia's northwest corner—called Soča in Slovene and Isonzo in Italian—saw some of World War I's fiercest fighting. In a series of 12 battles involving 22 different nationalities along a 60-mile-long front, 300,000 soldiers died, 700,000 were wounded, and 100,000 were declared MIA. In addition, tens of thousands of civilians died. A young Ernest Hemingway, who drove an ambulance for the Italian army in nearby fighting, would later write the novel *A Farewell to Arms* about the battles here.

On April 26, 1915, Italy joined the Allies. A month later, it declared war on the Austro-Hungarian Empire (which includ-

ed Slovenia). Italy unexpectedly invaded the Soča Valley, quickly taking the tiny town of Kobarid. For the next 29 months, Italy launched 10 more offensives against the Austro-Hungarian army, which was encamped on higher ground on the mountaintops. None of the Italian offensives was successful, even though the Italians outnumbered their opponents three to one. This was unimaginably difficult warfare—Italy had to attack uphill, waging war high in the mountains, in the harshest of conditions. The fighting coincided with the most brutal winter in a century. Some 60,000 soldiers were killed by avalanches.

Why would people fight so fiercely over such inhospitable terrain? At the time, Slovenia was the natural route from Italy to the Austro-Hungarian capitals at Vienna and Budapest. The Italians believed that if they could hold this valley and push over the mountains, Vienna—and victory—would be theirs.

On October 24, 1917, Austria-Hungary and Germany launched a counterattack that sent 600,000 soldiers down into the town of Kobarid. This crucial twelfth battle of the Soča Front, better known as the Battle of Kobarid, caught the Italian forces off guard. Within three days, the Italians were forced to retreat. The Austrians called their victory the "Miracle at Kobarid." But Italy felt differently. The Italians see the battle of Caporetto (the Italian name for Kobarid) as their Alamo. To this day, when an Italian finds himself in a mess, he might say, "At least it's not a Caporetto."

A year later, Italy came back—this time with the aid of British, French, and US forces—and easily retook this area. On November 4, 1918, Austria-Hungary conceded defeat. After more than a million casualties, the fighting at Soča was finally over.

JULIAN ALPS

solini's car drove past, the would-be assassin looked at his fellow townspeople around him, realized the innocent blood he would also spill, and had a last-minute change of heart. Mussolini's trip was uneventful, and fascism continued to thrive in Italy.

Near the mausoleum, you'll see a small, skippable **museum** displaying items from WWI that have been discovered in the area.

Alpine Cheese Museum

This humble exhibit, at the big Planika ("Edelweiss") dairy at the edge of town, examines the history of cheesemaking in this area since ancient times. It's part of a larger facility that also includes a supermarket (stocked with ample local dairy products) and a very local-feeling café. The museum is inside the big barn across the parking lot.

Cost and Hours: €5, Mon-Sat 10:00-12:00 & 15:00-17:00, closed Sun and Oct-April, Gregorčičeva 32, +386 5 384 1013, www.mlekarna-planika.si. To get here, turn right into Kobarid, then take the sharp left that leads you down beneath the underpass to the cheese factory (marked by the tall modern tower).

▲Great Kozjak Waterfall (Veliki Kozjak) Hike

For a rewarding, fairly easy hike, consider trekking to the Great Kozjak Waterfall—a dramatic cascade that plunges 50 feet through

a narrow cavern into a beautiful pool. It's just over a mile each way from the parking lot; allow 1.5 hours total to linger and explore. Far from undiscovered, Great Kozjak can be crowded during peak season—in summer, time your visit early or late.

Cost and Hours: €4, daily 8:00-20:00.

Getting There: The waterfall is across the river from Kobarid's town center. While it's easier and more rewarding to start at the official trailhead parking lot, you can walk all the way there from Kobarid (adds about 20 minutes each way). On foot or by car, follow brown signs for *Slap Kozjak* under the main road, over the Napoleon Bridge, and then left at the fork. After Kamp Koren, watch on the left for the turnoff to the big waterfall parking lot (payment required). You'll carry on along the gravel road by foot the rest of the way.

Hiking to the Waterfall: Leaving the parking lot, the gravel road passes colorful beehives and cheese stands before a steep descent toward the Soča. The riverbank is a popular swimming, sunbathing, and picnic area. You'll pass a fun, bouncy suspension bridge, then reach the stone bridge over the "Little Kozjak." From here, follow the Kozjak stream uphill to the payment hut (signs for

Slap Kozjak/Waterfall), noticing the clarity of the water. Hiking upon rocks, over little bridges, and up stone steps, you'll hear the big waterfall before you see it. The footing can be wet and slippery in some points, with a cable in the rock wall you can grab for stability. But that powerful cascade is a satisfying payoff for the effort. You'll head back out the way you came in.

WWI Sights near Kobarid

Several outdoor museums in the area let you get close to the places where the fighting actually occurred. Some are reachable by car, while others require a challenging mountain hike.

▲Walk of Peace (Pot Miru)

This walking route—which extends more than 140 miles from these mountains all the way to the Adriatic—is designed to link museums, cemeteries, churches, and other sites related to the warfare of the Soča Front. But it also introduces visitors to all aspects of the region's culture and natural sites. To learn more about shorter hikes along its route, and the many outdoor museums and cemeteries in this region, visit the **Walk of Peace Foundation Visitors Center,** across the street from the Kobarid Museum. They hand out good, free maps and booklets, and sell a fine guidebook to WWI sights in the area. Tour their engaging, state-of-the-art exhibition, with additional temporary exhibits upstairs (free, July-Aug Mon-Fri 9:00-19:00, Sat-Sun 10:00-13:00 & 14:00-19:00, shorter hours spring and fall, closed Nov-March—but you can try knocking on weekdays, Gregorčičeva 8, +386 5 389 0167, www.potmiru.si). They can arrange **guides** to join you for part of the walk. Contact them at least one day ahead to check their schedule and/or arrange a tour.

Kobarid Historical Walk

This shorter walk to WWI sights around Kobarid is well explained by the free brochure available at the TI, museum, and visitors center (3 miles, mostly uphill, allow 3-5 hours; or you can just do a shorter, easier stretch along the river, 1-2 hours).

▲Kolovrat Outdoor Museum

For drivers (especially those headed to points south) who want a vivid, high-altitude look at what life was like along the Soča Front, this is perhaps the area's best outdoor museum (worth the detour and ▲▲ for anyone interested in the Soča Front). It's located high on a ridge—straddling Slovenia and Italy—about 30 minutes from Kobarid, manageable on the way to the Karst, Goriška Brda, Venice, or Croatia.

This area—an Italian-built mountaintop fortification—is free and always open. The gentle pasture sprawling away from the park-

JULIAN ALPS

ing area is scattered with half-ruined concrete bunkers; if you walk through this area and keep going, you'll be in Italy in five minutes. Most interesting is the hilltop above, where trenches carved into the rock have been excavated and restored. Peer out through strategically placed viewpoint slits and imagine the impossibly difficult life of the soldiers stationed along the Soča Front.

Getting There: Leave Kobarid on the main road toward Tolmin. Just a mile out of town, in the village of Idrsko, turn right

toward *Livek* and twist up, up, up the hillside. At the far end of the village of Livek, watch for brown *Kolovrat* signs to the left. Following this road, you'll drive along a mountain spine for about five miles, watching for the small parking area and information boards for Kolovrat. When you're ready to leave the museum, carry on along the same road, then turn left at the fork to wind back down into Tolmin.

Sleeping in Kobarid

My first listing is right on the main square. The others hide on side streets about a block off the main road through town.

$$ Hotel Hvala is the only real hotel in town. Run by the Hvala family, its 32 contemporary rooms are faded but central; the cheaper "mansard" rooms are on the top floor. The mural on the wall in the elevator shaft tells the story of the Soča Valley as you go up toward the top floor (some rooms with air-con, elevator, Trg Svobode 1, +386 5 389 9300, www.hotelhvala.si, info@hotelhvala.si).

$ Apartmaji Pri Nas ("Our Place") has six stylish apartments in a pleasant suburban home along the main road that skirts the town center. They also have two little modern freestanding cabins (no breakfast but kitchens in each unit, air-con, Goriška Cesta 5, +386 31 377 585, www.pri-nas.si, prinas.kobarid@gmail.com).

$ Hiša Sonca ("House of the Sun"), in a cheery, yellow house along the main road, has two comfortable, air-conditioned rooms (sharing a well-equipped kitchen, a "salt spa" with infrared sauna, and lots of stairs) and one big apartment that sleeps up to seven. My favorite place in Kobarid, it's well run by Natalija, who has another apartment in her home a block closer to the town center (breakfast extra, cash only, laundry service, 2 blocks from main square at Mučeniška 1, +386 31 664 253, www.apartmakobarid. com, hisasonca@gmail.com).

$ Apartments Mašera has six spacious rooms, plus four apartments (all with kitchens and a balcony or terrace) in a big, sprawling building tucked behind the Kobarid Museum (breakfast extra, air-con, Gregorčičeva 10, +386 5 389 1210, www.apartments-masera-si.book.direct, apamasera@gmail.com, Martin and Petra).

IN THE MOUNTAINS HIGH ABOVE KOBARID

Rustic Village Farm Stay: One of my favorite Soča Valley accommodations hides in a tiny village a twisty 10-minute drive up from Kobarid's main square. **$ Tourist Farm Kranjc** is a remote but scenic working sheep farm with eight comfortable rooms, organic meals prepared with homegrown produce, and a huge view terrace. This farm—which feels traditional, but has modern style (including a wellness/spa/sauna area)—is a bit less convenient to the sights, but it's ideal if you want to huddle high in the mountains (dinner extra, air-con, also ask about their "glamping" cots with private bathroom, Koseč 7, +386 5 384 8562, +386 41 946 088, www.turizem-kranjc.si, info@turizem-kranjc.si, Urška and the Kranjc family). It's in the village of Koseč. From Kobarid, leave town by crossing the Napoleon Bridge (toward Kamp Koren and Great Kozjak Waterfall). Just after that bridge, turn left and twist up to Drežnica, where you'll turn right to reach Koseč. Upon entering the village, look for signs directing you up the steep road to the left.

Eating in and near Kobarid

While Kobarid has a handful of good eateries, foodies make a pilgrimage for Hiša Franko—just outside town.

$$ Hiša Polonka ("Blue House"), a side project of the people who run the esteemed Hiša Franko (see next), is my favorite stop in town. Conveniently located on the road between Kobarid's main square and the museum, this is *the* place for well-prepared traditional, local fare (including microbrews) at reasonable prices. The vibe is pubby and casual; the service is relaxed (Thu-Fri 17:00-22:00, Sat-Sun from 12:00, closed Mon-Wed, Gregorčičeva 1, +386 5 995 8194).

$$$ Kotlar Restaurant, on the main square, has a classy interior that sprawls around the prow of a faux sailboat. The emphasis is on seafood and locally sourced meats. It's a handy, central place for a meal when other options are closed (daily 12:00-23:00, Trg Svobode 11, +386 5 389 1110, www.kotlarkobarid.com).

$ Picerija Fedrig serves up basic but good pizzas (flexible hours but usually Mon-Tue 17:00-21:30, Wed-Sun from 12:00, shorter hours and closed Mon-Tue off-season, Volaričeva 11, +386 5 389 0115).

JULIAN ALPS

MICHELIN-STARRED FINE DINING NEAR KOBARID

$$$$ Hiša Franko, a five-minute drive outside of Kobarid, is becoming internationally known as Slovenia's top restaurant. Chef Ana Roš (profiled on *Chef's Table* and named World's Best Female Chef 2017) has a deep respect for locally sourced ingredients and Slovenian alpine culinary tradition. But she's also experimental, injecting international touches into her cooking. Sommelier Valter Kramar elegantly pairs Slovenian wines with each course. You'll want to book far ahead for modern Slovenian cuisine at its very best (fixed-price meals only, Thu-Sun 12:00-16:00 & 19:00-23:00, closed Mon-Wed, Staro Selo 1, they also rent rooms, +386 5 389 4120, www.hisafranko.com, info@hisafranko.com). To reach Hiša Franko, leave Kobarid following signs for *Italija* and *Robič*, and look for the restaurant's sign on the right.

Kobarid Connections

From Kobarid by Bus to: Bovec (6/day Mon-Fri, 2-3/day Sat-Sun, 30 minutes), **Ljubljana** (see "Getting Around the Julian Alps," earlier, for connecting to Ljubljana via the Vršič Pass and Kranjska Gora, or faster via Idrija).

AUSTRIA

Österreich

VIENNA

Wien

Vienna is the capital of Austria, the cradle of classical music, the home of the rich Habsburg heritage, and one of the world's most livable cities. Many buildings still reflect the elegance of the 18th and 19th centuries, when Vienna was at the forefront of the arts and sciences. The city center is skyscraper-free, pedestrian friendly, dotted with quiet parks, and traversed by electric trams. Within just a few steps, you can nibble a decadent slice of Sacher torte over coffee with new friends, watch trained stallions prance, and ogle the crown jewels of the Habsburg empire.

For much of its 2,500-year history, Vienna (*Wien* in German—pronounced "veen") was on the frontier of "civilized" Europe. Located on the south bank of the Danube, it was threatened by Germanic tribes (in Roman times), marauding Magyars (today's Hungarians, 10th century), Mongol raiders (13th century), Ottomans (the sieges of 1529 and 1683), and the USSR (during the Cold War, it was surrounded on three sides by the Iron Curtain).

The Habsburgs—who ruled for seven centuries, until 1918—transformed Vienna into the capital of a sprawling empire with some 50 million subjects...the majority of whom didn't even speak German. The Habsburgs built their empire by making love, not war. Empress Maria Theresa, who ruled in the late 1700s, was famous both for her astute leadership and for cleverly marrying

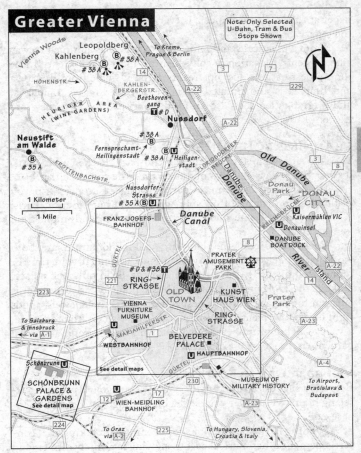

Greater Vienna

Note: Only Selected U-Bahn, Tram & Bus Stops Shown

Vienna Woods

Leopoldberg

Kahlenberg
B # 38 A
38 A
HÖHENSTR.

KAHLEN-BERGERSTR.

HEURIGER AREA (WINE GARDENS)

To Krems, Prague & Berlin

Beethoven-gang
T # D

Nussdorf

Neustift am Walde
B
35 A
KROTTENBACHSTR.

Fernsprechamt-Heiligenstadt
38 A
B
B U
38 A Heiligen-stadt

Nussdorfer-Strasse
35 A B U

1 Kilometer

1 Mile

FRANZ-JOSEFS-BAHNHOF

Danube Canal

GÜRTEL

D & #38
T
RING-STRASSE

OLD TOWN

VIENNA FURNITURE MUSEUM

U
MARIAHILFERSTR.
1

WESTBAHNHOF

To Salzburg & Innsbruck
← via A-1

Schönbrunn U

SCHÖNBRUNN PALACE & GARDENS
See detail map

224

See detail maps

GÜRTEL

U
12
17
WIEN-MEIDLING BAHNHOF

To Graz via A-2
225

PRATER AMUSEMENT PARK

KUNST HAUS WIEN

RING-STRASSE

BELVEDERE PALACE

U HAUPTBAHNHOF

230
← MUSEUM OF MILITARY HISTORY

A-23

To Hungary, Slovenia, Croatia & Italy

Old Danube

3

8

Donau Park "DONAU CITY"

U Kaisermühlen VIC

U Donauinsel

■ DANUBE BOAT DOCK

8

Danube

FLORIDSDORFER BRÜCKE

Danube River Island

REICHSBRÜCKE

Prater Park

A-22

14

A-23

A-4

To Airport, Bratislava & Budapest

many of her 16 children (including Marie Antoinette) into royal families around Europe.

Vienna reached its zenith in the 19th century, when it was on par with London and Paris in size and importance. This cultural powerhouse was home to groundbreaking composers (Beethoven, Mozart, Brahms, Strauss, Haydn), scientists (Freud, Doppler), architects (Wagner, Loos), and painters (Klimt, Schiele, Kokoschka). By the turn of the 20th century, Vienna sat on the cusp between stuffy Old World monarchism and "subversive" modern trends.

After the turmoil of two world wars and the loss of Austria's empire, Vienna has settled down into a laid-back, pleasant place where culture is still king. It's a city of top-notch museums, big and small. Compared with most modern European urban centers, the pace of life is slow. People nurse coffee and pastries over the daily paper at cafés. Classical music is everywhere, and the waltz is still the rage.

From a practical standpoint, Vienna serves as a prime gateway city. Its central location is convenient to most major Central European destinations. Just upstream on the Danube from Budapest and Bratislava, and situated farther east than Prague, Ljubljana, and Zagreb, Vienna is also an ideal launchpad for a journey into Eastern Europe.

PLANNING YOUR TIME

For a big city, Vienna is pleasant and laid-back. Packed with sights, it's worth two days and two nights on even the speediest trip.

If you're visiting Vienna as part of a longer European trip, you could sleep on the train on your way in and out—Berlin, Paris, Kraków, Venice, Rome, and Frankfurt are each a handy night-train journey away.

Palace Choices: The Hofburg and Schönbrunn are both world-class palaces, but seeing both is redundant if your time or money is limited. If you're rushed and can fit in only one palace, make it the Hofburg. It comes with the popular Sisi Museum, is adjacent to perhaps Europe's best collection of crown jewels, and is right in the town center, making for an easy visit. With more time, a visit to Schönbrunn—set outside town amid a grand and regal garden—is also a great experience.

Vienna in One to Four Days

Below is a suggested itinerary for how to spend your daytime sightseeing hours. Whenever you need a break, linger in a classic Viennese café.

Evenings: The best options for evenings are taking in a concert, opera, or other musical event; enjoying a leisurely dinner (and people-watching) in the stately old town; heading out to the *Heuriger* wine pubs in the foothills of the Vienna Woods; or touring the Haus der Musik interactive music museum (open nightly until 22:00). Plan your evenings based on the schedule of musical events. If you've downloaded my audio tours (see page 26), both the Vienna City Walk and Ringstrasse Tram Tour work wonderfully in the evening.

Day 1

9:00   Circle the Ringstrasse by tram (following my self-guided tram tour).

10:30   Drop by the TI for planning and ticket needs.

11:00   Tour the Vienna State Opera (schedule varies, check online).

14:00   Follow my Vienna City Walk, including visits to the

Austria Almanac

Official Name: Republik Österreich ("Eastern Realm"), or simply Österreich.

Size: With 32,400 square miles, Austria is similar in size to South Carolina. Of Austria's 8.9 million people, 91 percent are ethnic Austrians; 4 percent are from the former Yugoslavia. Three out of four Austrians are Catholic; about one in 20 is Muslim.

Geography: The northeast is flat and well populated; the less-populated southwest is mountainous, with the Alps rising up to the 12,450-foot Grossglockner peak. The 1,770-mile-long Danube River meanders west to east through the upper part of the country, passing through Vienna.

Latitude and Longitude: 47°N and 13°E. The latitude is the same as that of Minnesota or Washington state.

Major Cities: One in five Austrians lives in the capital of Vienna (1.8 million in the city; 2.9 million in the greater metropolitan area). Other cities include Graz (population 300,000), Linz (206,000), and Salzburg (152,000).

Economy: Austria's gross domestic product is $477 billion (similar to that of Massachusetts). Its per-capita GDP of $53,300 is among Europe's highest. One of its biggest moneymakers is tourism. Austria produces wood, paper products (nearly half the land is forested)...and Red Bull Energy Drink.

Government: Austria's official head of state is the federal president, elected directly by the people. The president then appoints the chancellor—traditionally the leader of the largest party in the National Council—who is the official head of government. Parliament is split into the National Council and the Federal Council. Austria is the only EU nation with a minimum voting age of 16.

Flag: Three horizontal bands of red, white, and red.

Cuisine: Austrian treats include Wiener schnitzel (breaded veal cutlet), *Knödel* (dumplings), *Apfelstrudel* (apple strudel), *Kaiserschmarrn* (fluffy pieces of caramelized crêpe served with fruit or nuts), and fancy desserts like the Sacher torte, Vienna's famous chocolate cake.

Language: Austria's official language is German. It's customary to greet people in the breakfast room and those you pass on the streets or meet in shops. The Austrian version of "Hi" is a cheerful *"Grüss Gott."* You'll get the correct pronunciation after the first volley—listen and copy.

Gemütlichkeit: Austria is mellow and relaxed compared to Deutschland. *Gemütlichkeit* is the word most often used to describe this special Austrian cozy-and-easy approach to life. On the other hand, Austria feels relatively stiff and formal compared to most of Central Europe (except maybe Hungary).

VIENNA

Kaisergruft and St. Stephen's Cathedral (nave closes at 16:30, or 17:30 July-Aug).

18:00 Dinner and romantic stroll in the old center.

Day 2

9:00 Browse the colorful Naschmarkt.

11:00 Tour the Kunsthistorisches Museum.

14:00 Tour the Hofburg Palace Imperial Apartments and Treasury.

Evening See options earlier.

Day 3

8:00 Tour Schönbrunn Palace to enjoy the imperial apartments and grounds (reserve in advance).

14:00 Visit Belvedere Palace, with its fine Viennese art and great city views.

Evening See options earlier.

Day 4

Depending on your interests, enjoy the engaging Karlsplatz sights (Karlskirche, the Secession) or the Natural History Museum. Do some shopping along Mariahilfer Strasse. Or rent a bike and head out to the modern Donau City "downtown" sector, Danube Island (for fun people-watching), and Prater Park (with its amusement park).

Orientation to Vienna

Vienna sits between the Vienna Woods (Wienerwald) and the Danube River (Donau). The Alps, which arc across Europe from Marseille, end at Vienna's wooded hills, providing a popular playground for walking and sipping new wine. This greenery's momentum carries on into the city. More than half of Vienna is parkland, filled with ponds, gardens, trees, and statue-maker memories of Austria's glory days.

Think of the city map as a target with concentric circles: The bull's-eye is St. Stephen's Cathedral, the towering spired church south of the Danube. Surrounding that is the old town, bound tightly by the circular road known as the Ringstrasse, marking what used to be the city wall. The Gürtel, a broader, later ring road, contains the rest of downtown. Outside the Gürtel lies the uninteresting sprawl of modern Vienna.

Much of Vienna's sightseeing—and most of my recommended restaurants—are located in the old town, inside the Ringstrasse. Walking across this circular area takes about 30 minutes. St. Stephen's Cathedral sits in the center, at the intersection of the two main (pedestrian-only) streets: Kärntner Strasse and the Graben.

Several sights sit along, or just beyond, the Ringstrasse: To the southwest are the Hofburg and related Habsburg sights, as well as the Kunsthistorisches Museum; to the south is a cluster of intriguing sights near Karlsplatz; to the southeast is Belvedere Palace. A branch of the Danube River borders the Ring to the north. As a tourist, concern yourself only with this compact old center. When you do, sprawling Vienna becomes easily manageable.

TOURIST INFORMATION

Vienna's main TI is a block behind the Vienna State Opera at Albertinaplatz (daily 9:00-18:00, includes theater box office, +43 1 24 553, www.vienna.info). It's a rare example of a TI in Europe that is really a service (possible because tourists pay for it with a hotel tax). There's also a TI at the airport (daily 9:00-18:00).

You'll get the same price here for theater tickets as you would at the venues or from the goofy salespeople on the street—the advantage here is that they have all the options, you can review them with a knowledgeable salesperson, and you can study the various venues. They also sell ferry tickets (to Bratislava, Slovakia) and intercity bus tickets.

Look for two good brochures: *Walks in Vienna* (with a schedule of walking tours—see "Tours in Vienna," later) and *Route* (a helpful guide with seven self-guided city walks). The quarterly program *Spot* lists cultural highlights in town (including concerts).

ARRIVAL IN VIENNA

For a rundown on Vienna's various train stations and its airport, see "Vienna Connections," at the end of this chapter.

HELPFUL HINTS

Book Ahead: It's wise to book your Schönbrunn Palace visit and reserved seats for the Vienna Boys' Choir online in advance. Otherwise, a fancy dinner or any tours you hope to take are all you should be concerned with in advance.

Music Sightseeing Priorities: Be wary of Vienna's various music sights. Many "homes of composers" are disappointing. My advice to music lovers is to take in a concert, tour the Vienna State Opera or snare cheap standing-room tickets to see a performance there, enjoy the Haus der Musik, or scour the wonderful Collection of Historic Musical Instruments in the Neue Burg (New Wing) of the Hofburg (included in your World Museum Vienna ticket). If in town on a Sunday, don't miss

VIENNA

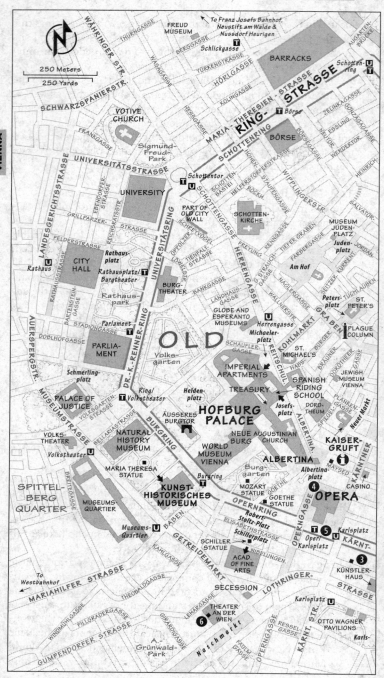

VIENNA

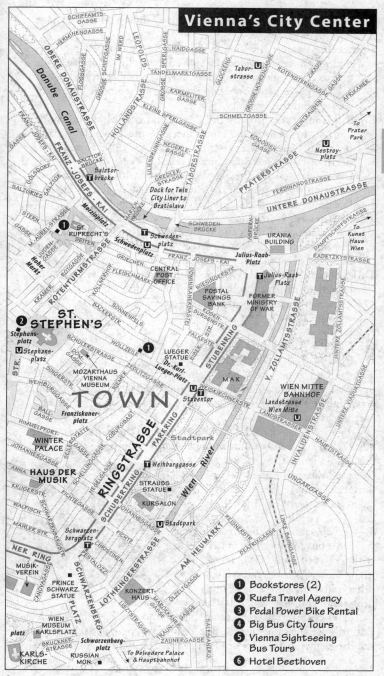

Vienna's City Center

1 Bookstores (2)
2 Ruefa Travel Agency
3 Pedal Power Bike Rental
4 Big Bus City Tours
5 Vienna Sightseeing Bus Tours
6 Hotel Beethoven

the glorious music at the Augustinian Church Mass (see page 887).

Sightseeing Passes: The Vienna Pass is pricey and only a good option for those who value the convenience of the hop-on, hop-off bus (generally not necessary in this walkable city). The Sisi Ticket makes sense for those wanting to see both Habsburg palaces and the Treasury.

English Bookstore: Stop by the woody and cool **Shakespeare & Co.,** in the historic and atmospheric Ruprechtsviertel district near the Danube Canal (Mon-Sat 9:00-21:00, closed Sun, north of Hoher Markt at Sterngasse 2, +43 1 535 5053, www.shakespeare.co.at). The biggest bookstore with a good English selection is **Morawa** (near the cathedral at Wollzeile 11). For locations, see the "Vienna's City Center" map.

Travel Agency: Conveniently located on Stephansplatz, **Ruefa** sells tickets for flights and trains (Mon-Fri 9:00-18:30, closed Sat-Sun, Stephansplatz 10—see "Vienna's City Center" map on page 854, +43 1 513 4524, Sandra speaks English).

Toll Sticker: If you're driving on highways in Austria, you're required to display a toll sticker. Your rental car may already come with the necessary sticker—ask. For details, see "Tolls" on page 1114.

GETTING AROUND VIENNA
By Public Transportation

Take full advantage of Vienna's efficient transit system, operated by **Wiener Linien,** which includes trams, buses, the U-Bahn (subway), and the S-Bahn (faster suburban trains). It's fast, clean, and easy to navigate.

I generally stick to the tram to zip around the Ring (trams #1, #2, #71, #D, and #O) and take the U-Bahn to outlying sights, hotels, and Vienna's train stations (see the "Vienna's Public Transportation" map). There are five color-coded U-Bahn lines: U-1 red, U-2 purple, U-3 orange, U-4 green, and U-6 brown. If you see a bus number that starts with *N* (such as #N38), it's a night bus, which operates after other public transit stops running. Transit info: +43 1 790 9100, www.wienerlinien.at.

Tickets and Passes: Trams, buses, and the U-Bahn and S-Bahn all use the same tickets. Except on days spent entirely within the Ring, buying a single- or multiday pass is usually a good investment (and pays off if you take at least four trips). Many people find that once they have a pass, they end up using the system more.

Buy tickets from vending machines (easy and in English), ticket offices in stations, or at some tobacco shops. Not all trams have ticket machines, so it's best to purchase tickets ahead of time. You cannot purchase tickets on buses.

You have lots of choices:

- Single tickets (€2.40, €2.60 on tram, good for one journey with necessary transfers)
- 24-hour transit pass (€8)
- 48-hour transit pass (€14.10)
- 72-hour transit pass (€17.10)
- There's also a 7-day transit pass (*Wochenkarte*, €17.10) and a 8-day "Climate Ticket" (*Acht-Tage-Klimakarte*, €40.80, can be shared).

Transit Tips: To get your bearings on buses, trams, the U-Bahn, and the S-Bahn, know the end-of-the-line stop in the direction you're heading. For example, if you're in the city center at Stephansplatz and you want to take the U-Bahn to the main train station (Hauptbahnhof), you'd take U-1 going in the direction "Oberlaa."

Stamp your ticket at the barriers in U-Bahn and S-Bahn stations, and in the machines on trams and buses (stamp multiple-use passes only the first time you board). When purchasing tickets from vending machines, you can choose to have them validated before being printed. There are no formal checks, but you may see random stops; cheaters pay a stiff fine (about €115), plus the cost of the ticket.

On some trams, stop announcements are voice-only and easy to miss—carry a map and stay alert. Rookies miss stops because they fail to open the door. Push buttons, pull latches—do whatever it takes.

Before you exit a U-Bahn station, study the wall-mounted street map and choose the most efficient exit.

Cute little electric buses wind through the tangled old center (from Schottentor to Stubentor). Bus #1A is best for a joyride—hop on and see where it takes you.

By Taxi or Uber

Though the city has a great public transit system and most of your time will be spent in the essentially traffic-free old town, you may need the occasional taxi. You can try waving one down, but locals either go to a taxi stand (there's generally one nearby) or call one. All Uber drivers in Vienna are also taxis—so, while Uber works here just like back home, it's essentially a taxi call service. Uber

VIENNA

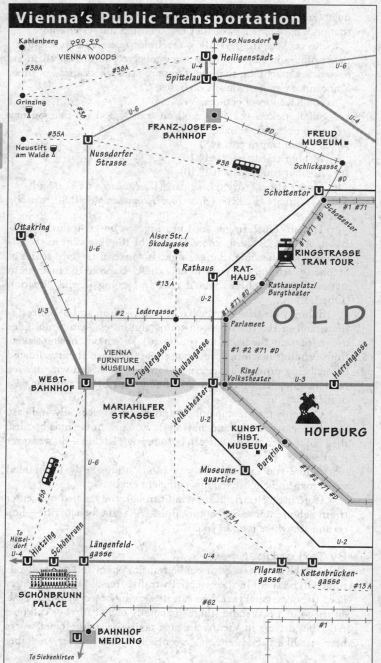

Vienna's Public Transportation

VIENNA

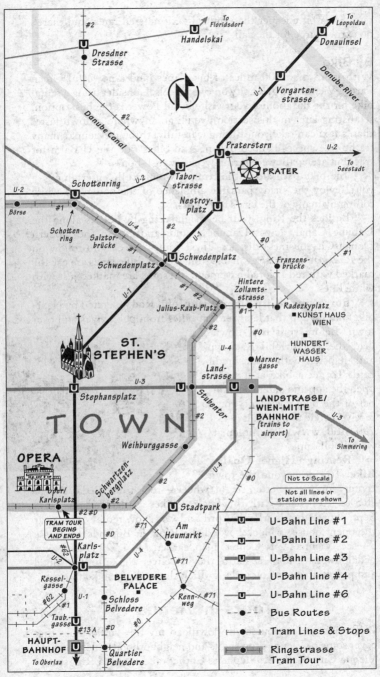

VIENNA

rates are a bit cheaper than official taxi metered rates, and there's no extra charge for the call.

By Bike

With more than 600 miles of bike lanes (and a powerful Green Party), Vienna is a great city on two wheels. Consider using a rental bike for the duration of your visit (Pedal Power is the best option, see listing later in this section); you'll go anywhere in town faster than a taxi can take you. Biking (carefully) through Vienna's many traffic-free spaces is no problem. And bikes ride the U-Bahn for free (but aren't allowed during weekday rush hours).

The bike path along the Ring is wonderfully entertaining—you'll enjoy the shady parklike ambience of the boulevard while rolling by many of the city's top sights.

Besides the Ring, your best sightseeing by bike is along the Danube Canal, across Danube Island, and out to the modern Donau City business district. These routes are easy to follow on the *Radkarte* bike map available from the TI. Bike lanes are usually marked with red-colored pavement, but some are marked just with white lines.

Borrowing a City Bike: WienMobil Rad (operated by Nextbike) has an app that lets you rent bikes from public racks all over town. Before your trip, download the WienMobil Rad app and register with your credit card. To get a bike at a stand, open the app and enter the number of the bike you want; you'll receive a code to unlock it (+43 1 790 9100, www.wienerlinien.at/ wienmobil-app).

Renting a Higher-Quality Bike: To ride beyond the town center—or for a better set of wheels—rent from **Pedal Power** (RS%—10 percent with this book, e-bikes available, daily May-Sept, shorter hours March-April and Oct-Nov, rental office near the opera house, a block beyond the Ring, at Bösendorferstrasse 5—see "Vienna's City Center" map, earlier, +43 1 729 7234, www. pedalpower.at). For €17 extra, they'll deliver a bike to your hotel and pick it up when you're done. They also organize bike tours.

Tours in Vienna

♪ To sightsee on your own, download my free audio tours that cover some of Vienna's top sights and neighborhoods, including my Vienna City Walk, St. Stephen's Cathedral Tour, and Ringstrasse

Tram Tour. The city walk and tram tour start at the opera house and work nicely in the evening as well as during the day. The cathedral tour can be spliced into the city walk for efficiency.

ON FOOT
TI's "Walks in Vienna" Program

The TI's *Walks in Vienna* brochure lists more than a dozen walks—many given in English, all for €20. Their basic 1.5-hour "Vienna at First Glance" introductory walk is usually offered daily in English throughout the summer (leaves from in front of the TI, reservations smart, +43 664 260 4388, www.wienguide.at).

Good Vienna Tours

This company (one of several offering such walks) runs a "pay what you like" 2.5-hour, English-only walk through the city center. While my Vienna City Walk is much more succinct, this can be an entertaining ramble with a local telling stories of the city. (Unlike other countries offering "free" walks, Austria requires that such guides be trained and licensed.) Just show up (pay what you think it's worth at the end—no coins, paper only, daily departures at 10:00 and 14:00, also at 17:00 July-Aug, maximum 35 people, meet at fountain at tip of Albertina across from TI, +43 664 554 4315, www.goodviennatours.eu).

Food Tours

There are many good food tours capitalizing on the rich culinary heritage of Vienna and its "CCC" (Coffee, Cake, and Chocolate) culture. **GTOUR** (Genuss-Touren Food Tours) leads an array of small-group tours (4-8 people) in English, but their Naschmarkt tour is the best seller (€50/person, RS%—10 percent discount, use code "RSbook"; 2.5 hours, 10 stops). Tours depart most mornings at 9:00. They also do a popular coffeehouse tour, stopping to enjoy coffee and pastries at three coffeehouses (€55/person, 3 hours, +43 699 1234 7000, www.gtour.at).

ON WHEELS
Hop-On, Hop-Off Bus Tours

Two companies (Big Bus—red, Vienna Sightseeing—yellow) offer a complicated and busy program of hop-on, hop-off bus tours—but I don't recommend them. Both offer 24-, 48-, and 72-hour tickets, including a circular bus route (with departures every 20 minutes) and options to add river cruises and walking tours. Prices start at around €32 for 24 hours. You'll see booths at major stops (including the opera house for Vienna Sightseeing and Albertinaplatz for Big Bus) with flyers and staff that lay out all the options. While the ride can be scenic, gets you from sight to sight conveniently, and offers a stress-free overview, the recorded narration is almost worthless and cluttered with instructions, warnings, and cross-promotions.

Ringstrasse Tram Tour

One of Europe's great streets, the Ringstrasse is lined with many of the city's top sights. Take a tram ride around the Ring with my free audio tour (see page 26), which gives you a fun orientation and a ridiculously quick glimpse of some major sights as you glide by. No one tram makes the entire loop around the Ring, but you can see it all by transferring from tram #2 to tram #1 at the Schwedenplatz stop. You can use a single transit ticket (€2.40) to cover the whole route, including the transfer (though you can't interrupt your trip, except to transfer). However, with a transit pass, you're free to hop on and off as you like. For more on riding Vienna's trams, see "Getting Around Vienna," earlier.

Pedal Power

English tours cover the central district in three hours and run daily at 10:00 from May to September (€37/person, RS%—10 percent with this book, includes bike, €20 extra to keep bike for the day). They also rent bikes *sans* tour (for contact info, see listing under "Getting Around Vienna—By Bike," earlier).

Horse-and-Buggy Tour

These traditional 19th-century horse-and-buggies, called *Fiaker*, take rich romantics on clip-clop tours lasting 20 minutes (Old Town—€55), 40 minutes (Old Town and the Ring—€95), or one hour (all of the above, but more thorough—€120). Before the advent of cars, one-horse versions of these served as Vienna's taxis. You can share the ride and cost with up to four people (some may allow five).

LOCAL GUIDES

Vienna becomes particularly vivid and meaningful with the help of a private guide. I've enjoyed working with these guides; any of them can set you up with another good guide if they are already booked.

Quality Conventional Guides: Lisa Zeiler is a good storyteller with years of guiding experience (€160/2 hours, +43 699 1203 7550, lisa.zeiler@gmx.at). **Adrienn Bartek-Rhomberg** offers themed walks in the city as well as Schönbrunn Palace tours (€200/3 hours, €370/full day on foot, €360 "Panorama City Tour"—a 4-hour minibus and walking tour for up to six people,

+43 650 826 6965, www.experience-vienna.at, office@experience-vienna.at).

Philosopher Guides: Wolfgang Höfler, a generalist with a knack for having psychoanalytical fun with history, enjoys the big changes of the 19th and 20th centuries. He'll take you around on foot or by bike (€180/2 hours, €50 for each additional hour, bike tours—€180/3 hours, +43 676 304 4940, www.vienna-aktivtours.com, hofwolf@gmail.com). **Gerhard Strassgschwandtner,** who runs the Third Man Museum (see page 918), is passionate about history in all its marvelous complexity (€160/2 hours, +43 676 475 7818, www.special-vienna.com, gerhard@special-vienna.com).

Vienna City Walk

This self-guided walk connects the top three sights in Vienna's old center: the Vienna State Opera, St. Stephen's Cathedral, and Hofburg Palace. These and many of the other sights you'll see along this walk are covered in more detail later in this chapter (see "Sights in Vienna," later).

Allow one hour for the walk itself, more time if you plan to stop at any major sights along the way. This walk works just as well in the evening as it does during the day, as long as you don't plan on touring some of the sights you'll pass.

Tours: ∩ Download my free Vienna City Walk audio tour. For efficiency, splice my St. Stephen's Cathedral audio tour into this walk.

• *Begin at the square outside Vienna's landmark opera house, home of the Vienna State Opera. (The entrance faces the Ringstrasse; we're starting at the busy pedestrian square that's to the right of the entrance as you're facing it.)*

❶ Opera House

If Vienna is the world capital of classical music, this building is its throne room, one of the planet's premier houses of music. It's

typical of Vienna's 19th-century buildings in that it features a revival style—Neo-Renaissance—with arched windows, half-columns, and the sloping, copper mansard roof typical of French Renaissance *châteaux.*

Since the structure was built in 1869, almost all of the opera world's luminaries have passed through here. Its

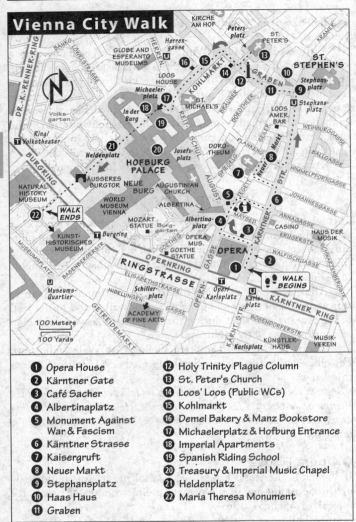

Vienna City Walk

1. Opera House
2. Kärntner Gate
3. Café Sacher
4. Albertinaplatz
5. Monument Against War & Fascism
6. Kärntner Strasse
7. Kaisergruft
8. Neuer Markt
9. Stephansplatz
10. Haas Haus
11. Graben
12. Holy Trinity Plague Column
13. St. Peter's Church
14. Loos' Loos (Public WCs)
15. Kohlmarkt
16. Demel Bakery & Manz Bookstore
17. Michaelerplatz & Hofburg Entrance
18. Imperial Apartments
19. Spanish Riding School
20. Treasury & Imperial Music Chapel
21. Heldenplatz
22. Maria Theresa Monument

former musical directors include Gustav Mahler, Herbert von Karajan, and Richard Strauss. Luciano Pavarotti, Maria Callas, Placido Domingo, and many other greats have sung from its stage.

In the pavement along the side of the opera house (and all along Kärntner Strasse, the bustling shopping street we'll visit shortly), you'll find plaques forming a Hollywood-style walk of fame. These represent the stars of classical music—famous composers, singers, musicians, and conductors. Look up at the building. During opera season, you'll notice the giant outdoor screen that shows some live performances (as noted in the posted schedules and on the screen itself).

If you're a fan, take a guided tour of the opera. Or consider an evening performance (standing-room tickets are surprisingly cheap; see "Entertainment in Vienna," later). Regular tickets are sold at the opera's box office on Kärntner Strasse. For information about other entertainment options during your visit, check in at the Wien Ticket kiosk in the booth on this square.

The opera house marks a busy intersection in Vienna, where Kärntner Strasse meets the Ring. The Karlsplatz U-Bahn station in front of the opera is an underground shopping mall with fast food, newsstands, and lots of pickpockets.

• *With your back to the Ringstrasse and the opera house on your left, face the busy pedestrian boulevard that leads into the center of town.*

❷ Kärntner Gate

Even though the center of town sits on an irregular medieval street plan, you'll notice the parallel rows of more modern, uniform buildings in front of you. These were built where the city wall once stood. The opera's lower stage is where the old moat used to be—outside the walls. This was a main gate, through which a road led to the Kärnten (Carinthia) region of southern Austria.

Notice the pedestrian signals and how they feature both gay and straight couples. Vienna's Green Party is part of the city's current ruling coalition, and they like to remind the world that, while Austria's national government is more conservative (reflecting the fears and concerns of rural and small-town voters), Vienna celebrates diversity.

• *Walk behind the opera and across the street toward the dark-red awning to find the famous...*

❸ Café Sacher

This is the home of the world's classiest chocolate cake, the Sacher torte: two layers of cake separated by apricot jam and covered in dark-chocolate icing, usually served with whipped cream. It was invented in a fit of improvisation in 1832 by Franz Sacher, dessert chef to Prince Metternich (the mastermind diplomat who redrew the map of post-Napoleonic Europe). The cake became world famous when the inventor's son served it next door at his hotel (you may have noticed the fancy

door attendants). Look through the windows for a peek at 19th-century elegance. Many locals complain that the cakes here have gone downhill, and some tourists are surprised by how dry they are—you really need that dollop of *Schlagobers*.

For a more genuine serving of 19th-century Viennese elegance, have your coffee and cake at the recommended **Gerstner Café** (facing the opera, back on Kärntner Strasse at #51). Enter under the green awnings, climb to the third level, and spend a little time back in the 1860s.

• *Continue past Hotel Sacher. On a corner (to the right) at the end of the street, the Vienna TI has a handy ticket desk for concerts. And dead ahead is a small, triangular, cobbled square adorned with memorial sculptures.*

❹ Albertinaplatz

Overlooking the square, the tan-and-white Neoclassical building marks the tip of the Hofburg Palace—the sprawling complex of

buildings that was long the seat of Habsburg power (we'll end this walk at the palace's center). The balustraded terrace up top was originally part of Vienna's defensive rampart. Later, it was the balcony of Empress Maria Theresa's daughter Maria Christina, who lived at this end of the palace. Today, her home houses the **Albertina Museum,** topped by a sleek, controversial titanium canopy (called the "diving board" by critics). The museum's plush, 19th-century state rooms are the only Neoclassical (post-Rococo) palace rooms anywhere in the Habsburg realm.

High above (just left of the "diving board"), a statue of **Archduke Albrecht** looks down on the city. A symbol of Habsburg oppression, he brutally suppressed popular uprisings in Vienna and Italy in the mid-1800s.

At street level is a grand **fountain of Danubius,** the Danube River god, flanked by six little gods. Each represents a major tributary that feeds the Danube as it flows through Austria.

The **hot dog stand** to the left of Danubius is known for its quality local sausages. This is the operagoers' hangout...they gather here in their fine ballgowns and tuxedos enjoying some of the best of Vienna's beloved wurst. By the way, this is the only sausage stand in town that sells champagne by the glass. And that bunny on the rooftop? It's a reminder that the famous Albrecht Dürer watercolor *Hare* is in the adjacent Albertina Museum.

Albertinaplatz itself is filled with sculptures that make up the powerful, thought-provoking ❺ **Monument Against War and**

Fascism, which commemorates the dark years when Austria came under Nazi rule (1938-1945). Viewing this monument gains even more emotional impact when you realize what happened on this spot: During a WWII bombing attack, several hundred people were buried alive when the cellar they were using as shelter was demolished.

Austria was led into World War II by Germany, which annexed the country in 1938 with disturbingly little resistance, saying Austrians were wannabe Germans anyway. But Austrians are not Germans (this makes for an interesting topic of conversation with Austrians you may meet). They're proud to tell you that Austria was founded in the 10th century, whereas Germany wasn't born until 1870. For seven years just before and during World War II (1938-1945), there was no Austria. In 1955, after 10 years of joint occupation by the victorious Allies, Austria regained total independence on the condition that it would be forever neutral (and never join NATO or the Warsaw Pact). To this day, Austria is outside of NATO (and Germany).

Behind the monument is **Café Tirolerhof,** a classic Viennese café. Refreshingly air-conditioned, it's full of things that time has passed by: chandeliers, marble tables, upholstered booths, formally dressed servers, and newspapers.

• *From the café, turn right on Führichsgasse. Walk one block until you hit...*

❻ Kärntner Strasse

This grand, traffic-free street is the people-watching delight of this in-love-with-life city. Today's Kärntner Strasse (KAYRNT-

ner SHTRAH-seh) is mostly a crass commercial pedestrian mall—its famed elegant shops long gone. But locals know it's the same road Crusaders marched down as they headed off from St. Stephen's Cathedral for the Holy Land in the 12th century. Today, it's full of shoppers.

Where Führichsgasse meets Kärntner Strasse, note the old Grundemann Esterházy Palace—now a **Casino** (across the street and to your right, at #41)—once elegant, now tacky, it exemplifies the worst of the

street's evolution. Turn left to head up Kärntner Strasse, going away from the opera house. As you walk, be sure to look up, above the modern storefronts, for glimpses of the street's former glory.

Local shops can't compete with international chains, considering the high rent here. But one venerable shop that has survived is near the end of the block, on the left at #26: **J & L Lobmeyr Crystal** ("Founded in 1823") still has its impressive brown storefront with gold trim, statues, and the Habsburg double eagle. In the market for some $400 napkin rings? Lobmeyr's your place. Inside, breathe in the classic Old World ambience as you peruse the wares and visit the glass museum (free entry; ground floor—glasses and chandeliers, first floor—silver and Murano glass, second floor—museum; closed Sun).

• *At the end of the block, turn left on Marco d'Aviano Gasse (passing the fragrant flower stall) to make a short detour to the square called Neuer Markt. Straight ahead is an orange-ish church with a triangular roof and cross, the Capuchin Church. In its basement is the…*

❼ Kaisergruft

Under the church sits the Imperial Crypt, filled with what's left of Austria's emperors, empresses, and other Habsburg royalty. For centuries, Vienna was the heart of a vast empire ruled by the Habsburg family, and here is where they lie buried in their fancy pewter coffins. You'll find all the Habsburg greats, including Maria Theresa, her son Josef II (Mozart's patron), Franz Josef, and Empress Sisi. Before moving on, consider paying your respects here.

• *Stretching north from the Kaisergruft is the square called…*

❽ Neuer Markt

Survey the architecture lining this square—a good mix, from 1700s to post World War II. You can tell which buildings replaced bombed-out ones. This square was once congested with parked cars, but a new-in-2022 underground garage turned Neuer Markt into the people-friendly space it is today.

A block farther down, in the center of Neuer Markt, is the **four rivers fountain** showing Lady Providence surrounded by figures symbolizing the rivers that flow into the Danube. The sexy statues offended Empress Maria Theresa, who actually organized "Chastity Commissions" to defend her capital city's moral standards.

VIENNA

• *Return to Kärntner Strasse, where you'll turn left. Continuing down Kärntner Strasse, you'll find lots of shops filled with merchandise to entice tourists. Pass the U-Bahn station (which has WCs) where the street spills into Vienna's main square...*

❾ Stephansplatz

The cathedral's frilly spire looms overhead, worshippers and tourists pour inside the church, and shoppers buzz around the outside. You're at the center of Vienna.

The Gothic **St. Stephen's Cathedral** (c. 1300-1450) is known for its 450-foot south tower; its colorful, patterned roof; and its place in Viennese history. When it was built, it was a huge church for what was then a small town, and it helped put the fledgling city on the map. At this point, you may want to take a break from this walk to tour the church (for details, see page 892 or 🎧 download my audio tour).

Where Kärntner Strasse hits Stephansplatz, the grand, soot-covered building with red columns is the **Equitable Building** (filled with lawyers, bankers, and insurance brokers). It's a fine example of Neoclassicism from the turn of the 20th century—look up and imagine how slick Vienna must have felt in 1900.

Facing St. Stephen's is the sleek concrete-and-glass ❿ **Haas Haus,** a postmodern building by noted Austrian architect Hans Hollein (finished in 1990). The curved facade is supposed to echo the Roman fortress of Vindobona (its ruins were found near here). Although the Viennese initially protested having this stark modern tower right next to their beloved cathedral, since then, it's become a fixture of Vienna's main square. Notice how the smooth, rounded glass reflects St. Stephen's pointy architecture, providing a great photo opportunity—especially at twilight.

• *Exit the square with your back to the cathedral. Walk past the Haas Haus and bear right down the street called the...*

⓫ Graben

This was once a *Graben,* or ditch—originally the moat for the Roman military camp. Back during Vienna's 19th-century heyday, more than 200,000 people were packed into the city's inner center (inside the Ringstrasse), walking on dirt streets. Today this area houses 20,000. The Graben was a busy street with three lanes of traffic until the 1970s, when the city inaugurated its new subway system and the street was turned into one of Europe's first pedestrian-only zones. Take a moment to enjoy a slow 360-degree spin tour. Absorb the scene—you're standing in an area surrounded by history, postwar rebuilding, grand architecture, fine cafés, and people enjoying life...for me, quintessential Europe.

Stroll down the Graben. Eventually you reach Dorotheer-gasse, on your left, which leads (after two more long blocks) to the **Dorotheum** auction house. Consider poking your nose in here later for some fancy window shopping. Also along this street are two recommended eateries: the sandwich shop Trześniewski—one of my favorite places for lunch—and the classic Café Hawelka.

In the middle of the Graben pedestrian zone is the extrava-gantly blobby ⓬ **Holy Trinity plague column** *(Pestsäule)*. The 60-foot pillar of clouds sprouts angels and cherubs, with the wonderfully gilded Father, Son, and Holy Ghost at the top (all protect-ed by an anti-pigeon net).

In 1679, Vienna was hit by a massive epidemic of bubonic plague. Around 75,000 Viennese died—about a third of the city. Emperor Leopold I dropped to his knees (something emperors never did in public) and begged God to save the city. (Find Leopold about a quarter of the way up the monument, just above the brown banner. Hint: The typical inbreeding of royal fami-lies left him with a gaping underbite.) His prayer was heard by Lady Faith (the statue below Leopold, carry-ing a cross). With the help of a heartless little cupid, she tosses an old naked woman—symbolizing the plague—into the abyss and saves the city. In gratitude, Leopold vowed to erect this monu-ment, which became a model for cities throughout the empire that were ravaged by the same plague. (The three golden banners repre-sent the core of that empire: Austria, Hungary, and Bohemia.)

• *Thirty yards past the plague monu-ment, look down the short street to the right, which frames a Baroque church with a stately green dome.*

⓭ St. Peter's Church

Leopold I ordered this church to be built as a thank-you for surviving the 1679 plague. The church stands on the site of a much older church that may have been Vienna's first (or second) Christian church. Inside, St.

Peter's shows Vienna at its Baroque best. Note that the church offers free organ concerts (daily at 15:00, advertised at the entry).
• *Continue west on the Graben, where you'll immediately find some stairs leading underground to...*

⓮ Loos' Loos

In about 1900, a local chemical maker needed a publicity stunt to prove that his chemicals really got things clean. He purchased two wine cellars under the Graben and had them turned into classy WCs in the Modernist style (designed by Adolf Loos, a turn-of-the-20th-century architect), complete with chandeliers and finely crafted mahogany. While the chandeliers are gone, the restrooms remain a relatively appealing place to do your business. (In the men's room, the urinals survive but are enjoying a peaceful retirement behind protective glass.) Locals and tourists happily pay €0.50 for a quick visit.
• *The Graben dead-ends at the aristocratic supermarket Julius Meinl am Graben. From here, you could turn right into Vienna's "golden corner," with the city's finest shops. But we'll turn left. In the distance is the big green-and-gold dome of the Hofburg, where we'll head soon. The street leading up to the Hofburg is...*

⓯ Kohlmarkt

This is Vienna's most elegant and unaffordable shopping street, lined with Cartier, Armani, Gucci, Tiffany, and the emperor's palace at the end. Strolling Kohlmarkt, daydream about ⓰ **Demel,** the ultimate Viennese chocolate shop (#14, daily 9:00-19:00). While people line up to enjoy their famous café, there's no wait to walk through the café to the shop in back, where you'll find a room filled with Art Nouveau boxes of Empress Sisi's choco-dreams come true: *Kandierte Veilchen* (candied violet petals), *Katzenzungen* (cats' tongues), and so on. The cakes here are moist (compared with the dry Sacher tortes). Shops like this boast "K.u.K."—signifying that during the Habsburgs' heyday, it was patronized by the *König und Kaiser* (king and emperor—same guy).

Next to Demel, the **Manz Bookstore** has a Loos-designed facade.
• *Kohlmarkt ends at the square called...*

VIENNA

⑰ Michaelerplatz

This square is dominated by the **Hofburg Palace.** Study the grand Neo-Baroque facade, dating from about 1900. The four heroic giants illustrate Hercules wrestling with his great challenges (Emperor Franz Josef, who commissioned the gate, felt he could relate). The facade's Hercules statues remind mere mortals to stay in their place.

In the center of this square, a scant bit of **Roman Vienna** lies exposed just beneath street level.

Michaelerplatz Spin Tour: Do a slow, clockwise pan to get your bearings, starting (over your left shoulder as you face the Hofburg) with **St. Michael's Church**, which offers fascinating tours of its crypt. To the right of that is the fancy **Loden-Plankl shop,** with traditional Austrian formalwear, including dirndls. Farther to the right, across Augustinerstrasse, is the wing of the palace that houses the **Spanish Riding School** and its famous white Lipizzaner stallions. Farther down this street lies **Josefsplatz,** with the **Augustinian Church,** and the Dorotheum auction house. At the end of the street are Albertinaplatz and the opera house (where we started this walk).

Continue your spin: Two buildings over from the Hofburg (to the right), the **Loos House** has a facade featuring a perfectly geometrical grid of square columns and windows. Compared to the Neo-Baroque facade of the Hofburg, the stern Modernism of the Loos House appears to be from an entirely different age. And yet, both of these were built in the same generation, roughly around 1900. In many ways, this jarring juxtaposition exemplifies the architectural turmoil of the turn of the 20th century and represents the passing of the torch from Europe's age of divine monarchs to the modern era.

• *Let's take a look at where Austria's glorious history began—at the...*

Hofburg Imperial Palace

This is the complex of palaces where the Habsburg emperors lived out their lives (except in summer, when they resided at Schönbrunn Palace). Enter the Hofburg through the gate, where you immediately find yourself beneath a big rotunda (the netting is there to keep birds from perching). The doorway on the right is the entrance to the ⑱ **Imperial Apartments,** where the Habsburg emperors once lived in chandeliered elegance. Today, you can tour its lavish rooms, as

well as a museum about Empress Sisi, and a porcelain and silver collection. To the left is the ticket office for the ⓲ **Spanish Riding School.**

Continuing on, you emerge from the rotunda into the main courtyard of the Hofburg, called **In der Burg.** The Caesar-like statue is of Habsburg emperor Franz II (1768-1835), grandson of Maria Theresa, grandfather of Franz Josef, and father-in-law of Napoleon. Behind him is a tower with three kinds of clocks (the yellow disc shows the phase of the moon tonight). To the right of Franz are the Imperial Apartments, and to the left are the offices of Austria's mostly ceremonial president (the more powerful chancellor lives in a building just behind this courtyard).

Franz Josef faces the oldest part of the palace. The colorful red, black, and gold gateway (behind you), which used to have a drawbridge, leads over the moat and into the 13th-century Swiss Court (Schweizerhof), named for the Swiss mercenary guards once stationed there. Study the gate. Imagine the drawbridge and the chain. Notice the Habsburg coat of arms with the imperial eagle above and the Renaissance painting on the ceiling of the passageway.

As you enter the Gothic courtyard, you're passing into the historic core of the palace, the site of the first fortress, and, historically, the place of last refuge. Here you'll find the ⓴ **Treasury** (Schatzkammer) and the **Imperial Music Chapel** (Hofmusikkapelle), where the Boys' Choir sings Mass. Ever since Joseph Haydn and Franz Schubert were choirboys here, visitors have gathered like groupies on Sundays to hear the famed choir sing.

Returning to the bigger In der Burg courtyard, face Franz and turn left, passing through the **tunnel,** with a few tourist shops and restaurants, to spill out into spacious ⓴ **Heldenplatz** (Heroes' Square). On the left is the impressive curved facade of the **World Museum Vienna** (formerly the New Palace). This vast wing was built in the early 1900s to be the new Habsburg living quarters and was meant to have a matching building facing it. But in 1914, the heir to the throne, Archduke Franz Ferdinand—while waiting politely for his long-lived uncle, Emperor Franz Josef, to die—was assassinated in Sarajevo. The archduke's death sparked World War I and the eventual end of eight centuries of Habsburg rule.

Heldenplatz Spin Tour: Make a slow 360-degree turn and imagine this huge square filled with people.

In 1938, 300,000 Viennese gathered here, entirely filling vast Heroes' Square, to welcome Adolf Hitler and celebrate their annexation with Germany—the *Anschluss.* The Nazi tyrant stood on the balcony of the then New Palace and declared, "Before the face of German history, I declare my former homeland now a part of the

VIENNA

Vienna at a Glance

▲▲▲**Hofburg Imperial Apartments** Lavish main residence of the Habsburgs. **Hours:** Daily 9:00-17:30, July-Aug until 18:00. See page 879.

▲▲▲**Hofburg Treasury** The Habsburgs' collection of jewels, crowns, and other valuables—the best on the Continent. **Hours:** Wed-Mon 9:00-17:30, closed Tue. See page 883.

▲▲▲**St. Stephen's Cathedral** Enormous, historic Gothic cathedral in the center of Vienna. **Hours:** Foyer and north aisle—daily 6:00-22:00; main nave—Mon-Sat 9:00-11:30 & 13:00-16:30, Sun 13:00-16:30, July-Aug until 17:30. See page 892.

▲▲▲**Vienna State Opera** Dazzling, world-famous opera house. **Hours:** By guided tour only; schedule varies, but more tours generally in the afternoon and in July-Aug. See page 895.

▲▲▲**Kunsthistorisches Museum** World-class exhibit of the Habsburgs' art collection, including works by Raphael, Titian, Caravaggio, Rembrandt, and Bruegel. **Hours:** Daily 10:00-18:00, Thu until 21:00, closed Mon Sept-May. See page 898.

▲▲▲**Schönbrunn Palace** Spectacular summer residence of the Habsburgs, rivaling the grandeur of Versailles. **Hours:** Daily 9:00-17:00, July-Aug until 17:30. See page 909.

▲▲**World Museum Vienna** Several collections, including armor, musical instruments, and ethnographic treasures in the elegant halls of a Habsburg palace. **Hours:** Thu-Mon 10:00-18:00, Tue until 21:00, closed Wed. See page 885.

▲▲**Albertina Museum** Habsburg residence with state apartments, world-class collection of graphic arts and modernist classics, and first-rate special exhibits. **Hours:** Daily 10:00-18:00, Wed and Fri until 21:00. See page 888.

▲▲**Kaisergruft** Crypt for the Habsburg royalty. **Hours:** Daily 10:00-18:00. See page 889.

▲▲**Haus der Musik** Modern museum with interactive exhibits on Vienna's favorite pastime. **Hours:** Daily 10:00-22:00. See page 895.

▲▲**Natural History Museum** Big, beautiful catalog of the natural world, featuring the ancient *Venus of Willendorf.* **Hours:** Thu-Mon 9:00-18:30, Wed until 21:00, closed Tue. See page 901.

▲▲**Belvedere Palace** Elegant palace of Prince Eugene of Savoy, with a collection of 19th- and 20th-century Austrian art (including Klimt). **Hours:** Daily 10:00-18:00. See page 905.

▲**Spanish Riding School** Prancing white Lipizzaner stallions. **Hours:** Performances nearly year-round (except Jan and mid-June-mid-Aug), usually Sat-Sun at 11:00, plus morning exercises generally Tue-Fri 10:00-11:00 (except July-mid-Aug). See page 886.

▲**St. Michael's Church Crypt** Final resting place of about 100 wealthy 18th-century Viennese. **Hours:** By tour only (usually in German), Fri-Sat, schedule varies. See page 891.

▲**St. Peter's Church** Beautiful Baroque church in the old center. **Hours:** Mon-Fri 8:00-19:00, Sat-Sun from 9:00. See page 896.

▲**Karlskirche** Baroque church offering the unique chance to ride an elevator up into the dome. **Hours:** Mon-Sat 9:00-18:00, Sun 11:00-19:00. See page 903.

▲**Academy of Fine Arts Painting Gallery** Small but exciting rotating art exhibits spanning centuries. **Hours:** Tue-Sun 10:00-18:00, closed Mon. See page 903.

▲**The Secession** Art Nouveau exterior and Klimt paintings in situ. **Hours:** Tue-Sun 10:00-18:00, closed Mon. See page 903.

▲**Naschmarkt** Sprawling, lively outdoor market. **Hours:** Mon-Fri 6:00-19:30, Sat until 18:00, closed Sun, closes earlier in winter. See page 904.

▲**Kunst Haus Wien** Modern art museum dedicated to zany local artist Hundertwasser. **Hours:** Daily 10:00-18:00. See page 907.

VIENNA

Third Reich. One of the pearls of the Third Reich will be Vienna." He never said "Austria," a word that was now forbidden.

When pondering why the Austrians—eyes teary with joy and vigorously waving their Nazi flags—so willingly accepted Hitler's rule, it's important to remember that Austria was already a fascist nation. Austrian chancellor Engelbert Dollfuss, though pro-Catholic, pro-Habsburg, and anti-Hitler, was a dictator who silenced any left-wing opposition. Also, memories of the grand Habsburg Empire were still fresh in the collective psyche. The once vast and mighty empire of 50 million at its 19th-century peak came out of World War I a tiny landlocked land of six million that now suffered terrible unemployment. The opportunistic Hitler promised jobs along with a return to greatness—and the Austrian people gobbled it up.

• *Walk on through the Greek-columned passageway (the **Äusseres Burgtor**), cross the Ringstrasse, and stand between the giant Kunsthistorisches and Natural History Museums, built in the 1880s to house the private art and scientific collections of the empire and to celebrate its culture and power. A huge statue of the powerful Empress Maria Theresa stands in the center of it all.*

㉒ Maria Theresa Monument

Vienna's biggest monument shows the empress (the empire's only female ruler) holding a scroll from her father granting the right of a woman to inherit his throne. The statues and reliefs surrounding her speak volumes about her reign: Her four top generals sit on horseback while her four top advisers stand. Behind them, reliefs celebrate cultural leaders of her day, including little Wolfie Mozart with mentor "Papa" Joseph Haydn (with his hand on Mozart's shoulder, facing the Natural History Museum). The moral of this propaganda: that a strong military and a wise ruler are prerequisites for a thriving culture—attributes that characterized the 40-year rule of the woman who was perhaps Austria's greatest monarch.

• *Our walk is finished. You're in the heart of Viennese sightseeing. Surrounding this square are some of the city's top museums. And the Hofburg Palace itself contains many of Vienna's best sights and museums. From the opera to the Hofburg, from chocolate to churches, from St. Stephen's to Sacher tortes—Vienna waits for you.*

Sights in Vienna

Vienna has a dizzying number of sights and museums, which cover the city's rich culture and vivid history through everything from paintings to music to furniture to prancing horses. Just perusing the list on your TI-issued Vienna city map can be overwhelming. To get you started, I've selected the sights that are most essential, rewarding, and user-friendly, and arranged them by neighborhood for handy sightseeing.

SIGHTSEEING PASSES AND COMBO-TICKETS

Avid sightseers should consider a pass or combo-ticket, but do the math first. Add up the cost of all the sights you think you'll see, then consider whether you'd like to use the hop-on, hop-off bus to get around (included with the Vienna Pass). If you prefer to walk or take public transportation, you may be better off with one or more of the combo-tickets described below. Note that those under 19 get in free to state-run museums and sights.

Passes: The **Vienna Card** and the **Vienna Pass** are likely not worthwhile for most travelers (especially for youth and seniors over 65, who get a discount anyway). The Vienna Pass includes entry to the city's top 70 sights and unlimited access to Vienna Sightseeing's hop-on, hop-off tour buses (€85/1 day, €119/2 days, €149/3 days; purchase at TIs and several other locations around town—check at www.viennapass.com). It also lets you skip lines at some sights, but not at the Schönbrunn Palace where lines are the most frustrating.

Combo-Tickets: The €40 **Sisi Ticket** covers the Hofburg Imperial Apartments (with its Sisi Museum and Silver Collection— must see both on the same day), Schönbrunn Palace's Grand Tour, and the Vienna Furniture Museum. At Schönbrunn, the ticket lets you enter the palace immediately, without a reserved entry time. Buy your Sisi Ticket in advance online (www.schoenbrunn.at or www.sisimuseum-hofburg.at) or at the Vienna Furniture Museum, where lines are shorter.

If you're seeing the **Hofburg Treasury** (royal regalia and crown jewels) and the **Kunsthistorisches** (world-class art collection), the €24 combo-ticket saves you money.

The **Haus der Musik** (mod museum with interactive exhibits) has a combo deal with **Mozarthaus Vienna** (exhibits and artifacts about the great composer) for €20—saving a few euros for music lovers (though the Mozarthaus will likely disappoint all but the most die-hard Mozart fans).

HOFBURG PALACE SIGHTS

The imposing Imperial Palace, with 640 years of architecture, art, and history, demands your attention. This first Habsburg residence grew with the family empire from the 13th century until 1913, when the last "new wing" opened. The winter residence of the Habsburg rulers until 1918, the Hofburg is still home to the Austrian president's office, 5,000 government workers, and several important museums.

Don't get confused by the Hofburg's myriad courtyards and many museums. Focus on three sights: the Imperial Apartments,

VIENNA

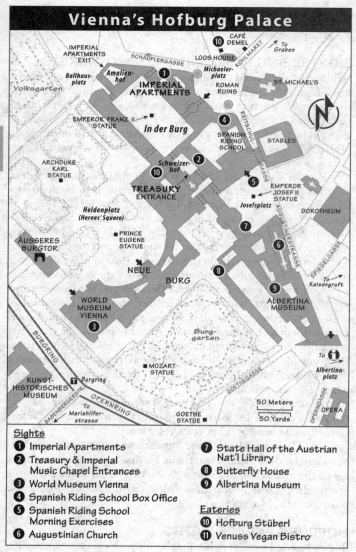

Vienna's Hofburg Palace

Sights

① Imperial Apartments

② Treasury & Imperial
Music Chapel Entrances

③ World Museum Vienna

④ Spanish Riding School Box Office

⑤ Spanish Riding School
Morning Exercises

⑥ Augustinian Church

⑦ State Hall of the Austrian
Nat'l Library

⑧ Butterfly House

⑨ Albertina Museum

Eateries

⑩ Hofburg Stüberl

⑪ Venuss Vegan Bistro

the Treasury, and the museums in the Neue Burg (New Wing).
With more time, consider the Hofburg's many other sights, covering various facets of the imperial lifestyle.

Eating at the Hofburg: Down the tunnel between the In der
Burg courtyard and Heldenplatz is the tiny but handy **$ Hofburg
Stüberl** sandwich bar—ideal for a cool, quiet sit and a drink or
snack (open daily). The recommended **$$ Venuss Vegan Bistro** is

a vegan-gelical place that almost makes you a believer (closed Sun, half a block off Michaelerplatz at Herrengasse 6).

Hofburg Palace
▲▲▲Hofburg Imperial Apartments (Kaiserappartements)

These lavish, Versailles-type, "wish-I-were-God" royal rooms are the downtown version of the suburban Schönbrunn Palace. Palace visits are a one-way romp through three sections: a porcelain and silver collection, a museum dedicated to the enigmatic and troubled Empress Sisi, and the luxurious apartments themselves.

The Imperial Apartments are a mix of Old World luxury and modern 19th-century conveniences. Here, Emperor Franz Josef I lived and worked along with his wife Elisabeth, known as Sisi. The Sisi Museum traces the development of her legend, analyzing her fabulous but tragic life as a 19th-century Princess Diana. You'll read bits of her poetic writing, see exact copies of her now-lost jewelry, and learn about her escapes, dieting mania, and chocolate bills.

Cost and Hours: €16, includes well-done audioguide, covered by Sisi Ticket; daily 9:00-17:30, July-Aug until 18:00, last entry one hour before closing; €4 guided English tours daily at 14:00; enter from under rotunda just off Michaelerplatz, through Michaelertor gate; +43 1 533 7570, www.sisimuseum-hofburg.at.

Overview: Your ticket grants you admission to three exhibits, which you'll visit on a one-way route. The first floor holds a collection of precious porcelain and silver knickknacks (Silberkammer). You then go upstairs to the Sisi Museum, which has displays about her life. This leads into the 20 or so rooms of the Imperial Apartments (Kaiserappartements), starting in Franz Josef's rooms, then heading into the dozen rooms where his wife Sisi lived.

If you listen to the entire audioguide, allow 40 minutes for the porcelain and silver collection, 30 minutes for the Sisi Museum, and 40 minutes for the apartments.

Visiting the Imperial Apartments: Your visit (and the excellent audioguide) starts on the ground floor.

Imperial Porcelain and Silver Collection: Browse the collection to gawk at the opulence and to take in some colorful Habsburg trivia. (Who'da thunk that the court had an official way to fold a napkin—and that the technique remains a closely guarded secret?) Still, I wouldn't bog down here; as there's much more to see upstairs.

Once you're through all those rooms of dishes, climb the stairs—the same staircase used by the emperors and empresses who lived here. At the top is a timeline of Sisi's life. Swipe your ticket to pass through the turnstile, consider the rare WC ("Go when you can, not when you have to"), and enter the room with the model of

VIENNA

the Hofburg. Circle to the far side to find where you're standing right now, near the Hofburg's largest dome. That dome tops the entrance to the Hofburg from Michaelerplatz.

A world within a world, the Hofburg was a kind of forbidden city accessible only to the ruling elite until 1891. Stand at the center and imagine the unfinished bit filled in, and ponder the imperial greatness of the palace complex. To the left of the dome (as you face the facade) is the steeple of the Augustinian Church. It was there, in 1854, that Franz Josef married 16-year-old Elisabeth of Bavaria and their story began.

Sisi Museum: Empress Elisabeth (1837-1898)—a.k.a. "Sisi" (SEE-see)—was Franz Josef's mysterious, beautiful, and narcissistic wife. This museum traces her fabulous but tragic life.

The exhibit starts with Sisi's sad end, showing her **death mask,** photos of her **funeral procession** (by the Hercules statues facing Michaelerplatz), and an **engraving** of a grieving Franz Josef. It was at her death that the obscure, private empress' legend began to grow.

Sisi was nearly 5'8" (a head taller than her husband), had a 20-inch waist (she wore very tight corsets), and weighed only about 100 pounds. (Her waistline eventually grew...to 21 inches. That was at age 50, after giving birth to four children.) A statue, a copy of one of 30 statues that were erected in her honor in European cities, shows her holding one of her trademark fans. It doesn't show off her magnificent hair, however, which reached down as far as her ankles in her youth.

Imperial Apartments: These were the private apartments and public meeting rooms for the emperor and empress. Franz Josef's apartments illustrate the lifestyle of the last legendary Habsburg. In these rooms, he met with advisers and welcomed foreign dignitaries; hosted lavish, white-gloved balls and stuffy formal dinners; and raised his children. He slept (alone) on his austere bed while his beloved wife Sisi retreated to her own rooms. He suffered through the execution of his brother, the suicide of his son and heir, the murder of his wife, and the assassination of his nephew, Archduke Ferdinand, which sparked World War I and spelled the end of the Habsburg monarchy.

Among the rooms you'll see is the **audience chamber** where Franz Josef received commoners from around the empire. Imagine you've traveled for days to have your say before the emperor. You're wearing your new fancy suit—Franz Josef required that men coming before him wear a tailcoat, and women a black gown with a train. He'd stand at the **lectern** (far left) as the visiting commoners had their say (but for no more than two-and-a-half minutes). On the lectern is a partial **list** of 56 appointments he had on Janu-

Sisi (1837-1898)

Empress Elisabeth—Franz Josef's beautiful wife—was the 19th-century equivalent of Princess Diana. Born on Christmas Eve and known as "Sisi" since childhood, she became an instant celebrity when she married Franz Josef at 16.

The daughter of a Bavarian duke, Sisi enjoyed an idyllic girlhood riding horses in the forests near Munich. But after

marrying, she became obsessed with preserving her reputation as a beautiful empress, maintaining her Barbie-doll figure (her goal: to stay under 110 pounds), and tending to her fairy-tale, ankle-length hair. In the 1860s, she was considered one of the most beautiful women in the world. But, despite severe dieting and fanatical exercise, age—not to mention the near impossibility of adhering to such demanding standards of feminine beauty—took their toll. After turning 30, she refused to allow photographs or portraits, and was generally seen in public with a delicate fan covering her face (and bad teeth).

Complex and influential, Sisi was adored by Franz Josef, whom she respected. Although Franz Josef was supposed to have married Sisi's sister Helene (in an arranged diplomatic marriage), he fell in love with Sisi instead. It was one of the Habsburgs' few marriages for love.

Sisi had a special affinity for Hungary. She enthusiastically studied and spoke Hungarian, and her personal mission and political cause was promoting Hungary's bid for autonomy within the empire—which her husband accommodated in 1867 by dividing his empire into the "Dual Monarchy" of the Austro-Hungarian Empire. Her personal tragedy was the death of her son Rudolf, the crown prince, in an apparent suicide (an incident often dramatized as the "Mayerling Affair," named after the royal hunting lodge where it happened). Disliking Vienna and the confines of the court and eager for time out of the spotlight, Sisi traveled more and more frequently. (She spent so much time in Budapest, and with Hungarian statesman Count Andrássy, that many believe her third daughter to be the count's.)

As the years passed, the restless Sisi and her hardworking husband became estranged. In 1898, while visiting Geneva, Switzerland, she was murdered by an Italian anarchist. Sisi's beauty, bittersweet life, and tragic death helped create her larger-than-life legacy. However, her importance is often inflated by melodramatic accounts of her life. The Sisi Museum (here in the Hofburg) seeks to tell a more accurate story.

Emperor Franz Josef (1830-1916)

Franz Josef I—who ruled for 68 years (1848-1916)—was the embodiment of the Habsburg Empire as it finished its six-century-long ride. Born in 1830, Franz Josef had a stern upbringing that instilled in him a powerful sense of duty and—like so many men of power—a love of all things military.

His uncle, Ferdinand I, suffered from profound epilepsy, which prevented him from being an effective ruler. As the revolutions of 1848 rattled royal families throughout Europe, the Habsburgs forced Ferdinand to abdicate and put 18-year-old Franz Josef on the throne. He spent the first part of his long reign understandably paranoid, as social discontent continued to simmer.

Franz Josef was very conservative. But worse, he wrongly believed that he was a talented military tactician, leading Austria into catastrophic battles against Italy (which was fighting for its unification and independence) in the 1860s.

Wearing his uniform to the end, Franz Josef never saw what a dinosaur his monarchy was becoming. He had no interest in democracy and pointedly never set foot in Austria's parliament building. His passion for low-grade paperwork earned him the nickname "Joe Bureaucrat." Mired in these petty details, he missed the big picture. In 1914, he helped start a Great War that ultimately ended the age of monarchs. The year 1918 marked the end of Europe's big royal families: Hohenzollerns (Prussia), Romanovs (Russia), and Habsburgs (Austria).

ary 3, 1910 (three columns: family name, meeting topic, and *Anmerkung*—the emperor's "action log").

Franz Josef's **study** evokes how seriously the emperor took his responsibilities as the top official of a vast empire. Famously energetic, Franz Josef lived a spartan life dedicated to duty; in his **bedroom,** notice his no-frills **iron bed.** He typically rose before dawn and started his day in prayer, kneeling at the **prayer stool** against the far wall. While he had a typical emperor's share of mistresses, his dresser was always well stocked with **photos** of Sisi.

Sisi's bedroom was refurbished in the Neo-Rococo style in 1854. The room always had lots of fresh flowers. Sisi not only slept here but also lived here—the bed was rolled in and out daily—until her death in 1898. The **desk** is where she sat and wrote her letters and sad poems. In her **dressing/exercise room,** servants worked three hours a day on Sisi's famous hair, while she passed the time reading and learning Hungarian. She'd exercise on the **wooden structure** and on the **rings** suspended from the doorway to the left. Afterward, she'd get a massage on the red-covered **bed.**

In the **small salon,** notice the portrait of **Crown Prince Rudolf,** Franz Josef's and Sisi's only son. On the morning of January 30, 1889, the 30-year-old Rudolf and a beautiful baroness were found shot dead in an apparent murder-suicide in his hunting lodge in Mayerling. The scandal shocked the empire and tainted the Habsburgs; Sisi retreated further into her fantasy world, and Franz Josef carried on stoically with a broken heart.

The tour ends in the **dining room.** It's dinnertime, and Franz Josef has called his extended family together. The settings are modest...just silver. Gold was saved for formal state dinners. Next to each name card was a menu listing the chef responsible for each dish. (Talk about pressure.) Franz Josef enforced strict protocol at mealtime: No one could speak without being spoken to by the emperor, and no one could eat after he was done. While the rest of Europe was growing democracy and expanding personal freedoms, the Habsburgs preserved their ossified worldview to the bitter end.

In 1918, World War I ended, Austria was created as a modern nation-state, the Habsburgs were tossed out...and Hofburg Palace was destined to become the museum you've just toured.

▲▲▲Hofburg Treasury (Kaiserliche Schatzkammer Wien)

One of the world's most stunning collections of royal regalia, the Hofburg Treasury shows off sparkling crowns, jewels, gowns, and assorted Habsburg bling in 21 darkened rooms. The treasures, well explained by an audioguide, include the crown of the Holy Roman Emperor, Charlemagne's saber, a unicorn horn, and more precious gems than you can shake a scepter at.

Cost and Hours: €14, €24 combo-ticket with Kunsthistorisches; Wed-Mon 9:00-17:30, closed Tue; audioguide-€5 or €7/2 people; from the Hofburg's central courtyard pass through the black, red, and gold gate, then follow *Schatzkammer* signs to the Schweizerhof; +43 1 525 240, www.kaiserliche-schatzkammer.at.

Visiting the Treasury: The Habsburgs saw themselves as the successors to the ancient Roman emperors, and they wanted crowns and royal regalia to match the pomp of the ancients. They used these precious objects for coronation ceremonies, official ribbon-cutting events, and their own personal pleasure. You'll see the prestigious crowns and accoutrements of the rulers of the Holy Roman Empire (a medieval alliance of Germanic kingdoms so named because it wanted to be considered the continuation of the Roman Empire). Here's a rundown of the highlights (the audioguide is much more complete).

Room 2: The personal **crown of Rudolf II** (1602) occupies the center of the room along with its accompanying scepter and orb; a bust of Rudolf II (1552-1612) sits nearby. The crown's design symbolically merges a bishop's miter ("Holy"), the arch across the top of a Roman emperor's helmet ("Roman"), and the typical medieval king's crown ("Emperor").

Two centuries later (1806), this crown and scepter became the official regalia of Austria's rulers, as seen in the large **portrait of Franz I** (the open-legged guy behind you). Napoleon Bonaparte had just conquered Austria and dissolved the Holy Roman Empire. Franz (r. 1792-1835) was allowed to remain in power, but he had to downgrade his title from "Franz II, Holy Roman Emperor" to "Franz I, Emperor of Austria."

Rooms 3 and 4: These rooms contain some of the **coronation vestments and regalia** needed for the new Austrian (not Holy Roman) Emperor. There was a different one for each of the emperor's subsidiary titles—for example, King of Hungary or King of Lombardy. So many crowns and kingdoms in the Habsburgs' vast empire!

Room 5: Ponder the **Cradle of the King of Rome,** once occupied by Napoleon's son, who was born in 1811 and made King of Rome. While pledging allegiance to democracy, Napoleon in fact crowned himself Emperor of France and hobnobbed with Europe's royalty. When his wife Josephine could not bear him a male heir, Napoleon divorced her and married into the Habsburg family.

Room 6: For Divine Right kings, even child-rearing was a sacred ritual that needed elaborate regalia for public ceremonies. The 23-pound **gold basin and pitcher** were used to baptize noble children, who were dressed in the **baptismal dresses** displayed nearby.

Room 7: These **jewels** are the true "treasures," a cabinet of wonders used by Habsburgs to impress their relatives (or to hock when funds got low).

Religious Rooms: Several rooms display **religious objects**—crucifixes, chalices, mini-altarpieces, reliquaries, and bishops' vestments. Like the medieval kings who preceded them, Habsburg rulers mixed the institutions of church and state, so these precious religious accoutrements were also part of their display of secular power.

Regalia of the Holy Roman Empire: The next few rooms contain some of the oldest and most venerated objects in the Treasury—the robes, crowns, and sacred objects of the Holy Roman Emperor.

The big red-silk and gold-thread **coronation mantle,** nearly 900 years old, was worn by Holy Roman Emperors when they received their crown. The collection's highlight is the 10th-century **crown of the Holy Roman Emperor.** It was probably made for Otto I (c. 960), the first king to call himself Holy Roman Emperor. The Imperial Crown swirls with

symbolism "proving" that the emperor was both holy and Roman: The cross on top says the HRE ruled as Christ's representative on earth, and the jeweled arch over the top is reminiscent of the parade helmet of ancient Romans.

Nearby is the 11th-century **Imperial Cross** that preceded the emperor in ceremonies. Encrusted with jewels, it had a hollow compartment (its core is wood) that carried substantial chunks thought to be from *the* cross on which Jesus was crucified and *the* Holy Lance used to pierce his side (both pieces are displayed in the same glass case).

Another case has additional objects used in the coronation ceremony: The **orb** (orbs were modeled on late-Roman ceremonial objects, then topped with the cross) and **scepter** (the one with the oak leaves), along with the sword, were carried ahead of the emperor in the procession. In earlier times, these objects were thought to have belonged to Charlemagne himself, the greatest ruler of medieval Europe, but in fact they're mostly from 300 to 400 years later (c. 1200).

Now picture all this regalia used together. The **Josef II painting** shows the coronation of Maria Theresa's son as Holy Roman Emperor in 1764. Set in a church in Frankfurt (filled with the bigwigs—literally—of the day), Josef is wearing the same crown and royal garb that you've just seen.

More Hofburg Sights
▲▲World Museum Vienna (Weltmuseum Wien)

The World Museum Vienna houses several museums: They're all part of one grand building and covered by one ticket. The World Museum is technically only the mezzanine level, which houses an expansive ethnology collection. The same ticket also grants you access to the Imperial Armory (with a killer collection of medieval weapons) and the impressive Collection of Historic Musical Instruments. An added bonus of the World Museum is a chance to wander among the royal Habsburg halls, stairways, and painted ceilings virtually alone.

Cost and Hours: €16; Thu-Mon 10:00-18:00, Tue until 21:00, closed Wed; +43 1 534 30 5052, www.weltmuseumwien.at. While there are short English descriptions throughout, investing in the €5 audioguide triples the value of your visit.

▲Spanish Riding School (Spanische Hofreitschule)

This stately 300-year-old Baroque hall at the Hofburg Palace is the home of the renowned Lipizzaner stallions. The magnificent building was an impressive expanse in its day. Built without central pillars, it offers clear views of the prancing horses under lavish chandeliers, with a grand painting of Emperor Charles VI on horseback at the head of the hall.

Lipizzaner stallions are known for their noble gait and Baroque profile. These regal horses have changed shape with the tenor of the times: They were bred strong and stout during wars, and frilly and slender in more cultured eras. But they're always born black, fade to gray, and turn a distinctive white in adulthood.

Seeing the Horses and Buying Tickets: The school offers three ways to see the horses—performances, morning exercises, and guided tours of the stables (check the events list on the school's **website** at www.srs.at). You can purchase tickets online or at the **box office** (opens at 9:00, located inside the Hofburg—go through the main Hofburg entryway from Michaelerplatz, then turn left into the first passage, +43 1 533 9031). Photos are not allowed at any events, nor are children under age 3.

To **see the horses for free,** just walk by the stables at any time of day when the horses are in town. From the covered passageway across from Josefsplatz, there's a big window from where you can usually see the horses poking their heads out of their stalls.

Performances: The Lipizzaner stallions put on great 80-minute performances featuring choreographed moves to jaunty recorded Viennese classical music. The pricey seats book up months in advance, but standing room is usually available the same day. With just a few rows of seats and close-up standing-room spots, there's not a bad view in the house (seats about €50-160, standing room about €25, prices vary depending on the show; Feb-mid-June and mid-Aug-Dec usually Sat-Sun at 11:00, no shows Jan and mid-June-mid-Aug).

Morning Exercises: For a less expensive, more casual experience, morning exercises with music take place on weekday mornings in the same hall and are open to the public. Don't have high expectations, as the horses often do little more than trot and warm up. Tourists line up early at Josefsplatz (the large courtyard between Michaelerplatz and Albertinaplatz). Tuesdays are busiest

(€15, family discounts; tickets may be available at the door in high season, but best to buy in advance online or at the box office; can also buy at visitors center on Michaelerplatz; generally Tue-Fri 10:00-11:00, no exercises July-mid-Aug).

Guided Tours: One-hour guided tours in English are given almost every afternoon year-round. You'll see the Winter Riding School with its grand Baroque architecture, the Summer Riding School in a shady courtyard, and the stables (€19; tours usually daily at 13:00, 14:00, 15:00, and 16:00; reserve ahead by emailing office@srs.at or calling the box office).

▲Augustinian Church (Augustinerkirche)

Built into the Hofburg, this is the Gothic and Neo-Gothic church where the Habsburgs got married. Today, the royal hearts are in the church vault.

Cost and Hours: Church—free, open long hours daily; vault—€3, viewable by German tour only after Sunday Mass at about 12:45; at Augustinerstrasse 3, facing Josefsplatz.

Visiting the Church: Process up the main aisle as if you're a bride or groom. In the front (above the altar on the right), notice the windows from which royals witnessed the Mass in private. Look back at what's considered the finest pipe organ in Vienna (you'll often hear someone practicing).

From the front, circle back to the right, walking up the aisle along the right wall to see three sights. A wooden door leads to a crypt with the hearts of 54 Habsburg nobles in urns. Next is a chapel dedicated to Charles I, the last Habsburg emperor (r. 1916-1918). Pushed by present-day Habsburg royalists who worship here, Charles is beatified and on a path to sainthood. Finally, don't miss the exquisite, pyramid-shaped memorial (by the Italian sculptor Antonio Canova) to Maria Theresa's favorite daughter, Maria Christina.

The church's 11:00 Sunday Mass is a hit with music lovers. It's both a Mass and a concert, often with an orchestra accompanying the choir (acoustics are best in front). Pay by contributing to the offering plate or buying their music afterward. Check posters by the entry or www.hochamt.at to see what's on—typically you'll hear one of Mozart's or Haydn's many short Masses.

State Hall (Prunksaal) of the Austrian National Library

The National Library's State Hall (Prunksaal) is a postcard-perfect Baroque library (entered from Josefsplatz, next to the Augustinian Church). In this former imperial library, with a statue of Charles VI in the center, you'll find yourself whispering. The setting takes you back to 1730 and gives you the sense that, in imperial times, knowledge of the world was for the elite—and with that knowledge, the elite had power. The glorious paintings (with impressive

3-D) celebrate high culture and the library's patron, Charles VI. More than 200,000 old books line the walls, but patrons go elsewhere to read them—the hall is just for show these days. Special exhibits fill glass cases down the nave-like main aisle with literary treasures, all well described in English.

Cost and Hours: €10; Tue-Sun 10:00-18:00, may be open until 21:00 on Thu, closed Mon; +43 1 53 410, www.onb.ac.at.

Butterfly House (Schmetterlinghaus) in the Palace Garden (Burggarten)

The Burggarten greenbelt, once the backyard of the Hofburg and now a people's park, welcomes visitors to loiter on the grass. The iron-and-glass pavilion (c. 1910 with playful Art Nouveau touches) now houses the recommended **Palmenhaus** and a small, fluttery butterfly exhibit. Watching the 400 free-flying butterflies is trippy.

Cost and Hours: €7; Mon-Fri 10:00-16:45, Sat-Sun until 18:15, daily until 15:45 in off-season; +43 1 533 8570, www. schmetterlinghaus.at.

▲▲Albertina Museum

This impressive museum has three highlights: the imposing state rooms of the former palace, noteworthy collections of classic modernist paintings and European graphic arts (sketches, etching, watercolors—especially Dürer), and excellent temporary exhibits.

The building, at the southern tip of the Hofburg complex (near the opera), was the residence of Maria Theresa's favorite daughter, Maria Christina, who was allowed to marry for love rather than political strategy. Her many sisters were jealous. (Marie-Antoinette had to marry the French king...and lost her head over it.) Maria Christina's husband, Albert of Saxony, was a great collector of original drawings and prints, which he amassed to cover all the important art movements from the late Middle Ages until the early 19th century (including prized works by Dürer, Rembrandt, and Rubens). As it's Albert and Christina's gallery, it's charmingly called the "Alber-tina."

Cost and Hours: €17.90; daily 10:00-18:00, Wed and Fri until 21:00; overlooking Albertinaplatz across from the TI and opera, +43 1 534 830, www.albertina.at.

Visiting the Museum: After the turnstile, you'll pass some temporary exhibits. Climbing the stairs, you reach the main attractions (clearly labeled)—the state rooms *(Prunkräume)* on your left on level 1, and the Batliner Collection on your right on level 2. Excellent special exhibitions (generally featuring modern art and included in your ticket) are shown on level 2 and in the basement galleries.

State Rooms (*Prunkräume*, level 1): Wander freely under chandeliers and across parquet floors through a handful of rooms of 18th-century imperial splendor, unconstrained by velvet ropes. The exhibit spaces (never crowded, well described in English, and air-conditioned) are nearly as impressive as those at Schönbrunn Palace. Many rooms are often closed for special functions, but even a few rooms give a good look at imperial Classicism—this is the only post-Rococo palace in the Habsburg realm.

Batliner Collection (level 2): This manageable collection sweeps you quickly through modern art history, featuring minor works by major artists (such as Monet, Renoir, Munch, Picasso, Degas, and Matisse, among others). Though the collection is permanent, what's on display rotates through about 100 works selected from the 300 in the archives.

Church Crypts near the Hofburg

Two churches near the Hofburg offer starkly different looks at dearly departed Viennese: the Habsburg coffins in the Kaisergruft and the commoners' graves in St. Michael's Church.

▲▲Kaisergruft (Imperial Crypt)

Visiting the imperial remains of the Habsburg family is not as easy as you might imagine. As bodies needed to lie in state to prove to nobility that they were actually dead (in an age of "seeing is believing"), the newly dead were gutted like a fish, with all the quick-to-go-bad parts removed (hearts and innards). These original organ donors left their bodies—about 150 in all—in the unassuming Kaisergruft, their hearts in the Augustinian Church (viewable Sun after Mass), and their entrails in the crypt below St. Stephen's Cathedral.

Cost and Hours: €8, daily 10:00-18:00, free map includes Habsburg family tree and a chart locating each coffin, crypt is in the Capuchin Church at Tegetthoffstrasse 2 at Neuer Markt; +43 1 512 685 388.

Visiting the Kaisergruft: Descend into a crypt full of gray metal tombs. Start up the path, through tombs ranging from simple caskets to increasingly big monuments with elaborate metalwork ornamentation. You soon reach the massive pewter tomb of **Maria Theresa** under the dome, enjoying natural light. The only female Habsburg monarch, she had to be granted special dispensation to rule. Her 40-year reign was enlightened and progressive. She and her husband, **Franz I,** recline Etruscan-style atop their

VIENNA

Empress Maria Theresa (1717-1780) and Her Son, Emperor Josef II (1741-1790)

Maria Theresa was the only woman to officially rule the Habsburg Empire in that family's 640-year reign. She was a strong and effective empress (r. 1740-1780), but Austrians are also quick to remember Maria Theresa as the mother of 16 children (10 survived into adulthood). Ponder the fact that the most powerful woman in Europe either was pregnant or had a newborn for most of her reign. Maria Theresa ruled after the Austrian defeat of the Ottomans, when Europe recognized Austria as a great power. (Her rival, the Prussian king, said, "When at last the Habsburgs get a great man, it's a woman.")

Maria Theresa's reign marked the end of the feudal system and the beginning of the era of the grand state. The first of the modern rulers of the Age of Enlightenment, she was a great social reformer. During her reign, she avoided wars and expanded her empire by skillfully marrying her children into the right families. For instance, after daughter Marie-Antoinette's marriage into the French Bourbon family (to Louis XVI), a country that had been an enemy became an ally. (Unfortunately for Marie-Antoinette, Maria Theresa's timing was off.)

To stay in power during an era of revolution, Maria Theresa had to be in tune with her age. She taxed the Church and the nobility, provided six years of obligatory education to all children, and granted free health care to all in her realm. Maria Theresa also welcomed the boy genius Mozart into her court.

The empress' legacy lived on in her son, Josef II, who ruled as emperor for a decade (1780-1790). He was an even more avid reformer, building on his mother's accomplishments. An enlightened monarch, Josef mothballed the too-extravagant Schönbrunn Palace, secularized the monasteries, established religious tolerance within his realm, freed the serfs, made possible the founding of Austria's first general hospital, and promoted relatively enlightened treatment of the mentally ill. Josef was a model of practicality (for example, he banned slow-to-decompose coffins and allowed no more than six candles at funerals)—and very unpopular with other royals. But his policies succeeded in preempting the revolutionary anger of the age, largely enabling Austria to avoid the anti-monarchist turmoil that shook so much of the rest of Europe.

fancy coffin, gazing into each other's eyes as a cherub crowns them with glory. At the four corners of the tomb are the Habsburgs' four crowns: the Holy Roman Empire, Hungary, Bohemia, and Lombardy. At his parents' feet lies **Josef II,** the patron of Mozart and Beethoven. Compare the Rococo splendor of Maria Theresa's tomb with the simple coffin of Josef, who was known for his down-to-earth ruling style during the Age of Enlightenment.

Head on through the next room—created in 1960—featuring Napoleon's wife, Marie Louise, and a plaque to Franz Ferdinand (assassinated in 1914 in Sarajevo). Then head down three steps to a room illustrating the Habsburgs' fading 19th-century glory. There's the appropriately austere military tomb of the long-reigning **Franz Josef** (ruled 1848 to 1916, see sidebar on page 882). Alongside is his wife, **Elisabeth**—a.k.a. Sisi (see

page 881)—who always wins the "Most Flowers" award. Their son was Crown Prince **Rudolf.** Rudolf and his teenage mistress supposedly committed suicide together in 1889 at Mayerling hunting lodge...or was it murder?

In the final room (with humbler copper tombs), you reach the final Habsburgs. **Karl I** (see his bust, not a tomb), the last of the Habsburg rulers, was deposed in 1918 and died in exile. His sons Crown Prince **Otto** and Archduke **Karl Ludwig** are entombed near their mother, **Zita.**

▲St. Michael's Church Crypt (Michaelerkirche)

St. Michael's Church, which faces the Hofburg on Michaelerplatz, offers a striking contrast to the imperial crypt. Tours take visitors underground to see a typical church crypt, filled with the rotting wooden coffins of well-to-do commoners.

Cost and Hours: €8 for 45-minute tour (crypt only accessible by tour), tours run Fri-Sat only, check website to confirm schedule and language—tours may be in German only, wait at church entrance at the sign advertising the tour and pay the guide directly, +43 650 533 8003, www.michaelerkirche.at.

Visiting the Crypt: Climbing below the church, you'll see about a hundred 18th-century coffins and stand on three feet of debris, surrounded by niches filled with stacked lumber from decayed coffins and countless bones. You'll meet 18th-century mummies in their original clothes—one wearing lederhosen and a wig;

VIENNA

VIENNA

another clutching a cross and wearing high heels painted with flowers. You'll learn about death in those times, including how the wealthy—not wanting to end up in standard shallow graves—instead paid to be laid to rest below the church, and how, in 1783, Emperor Josef II ended the practice of cemetery burials in cities but allowed the rich to become the stinking rich in crypts under churches.

MORE SIGHTS WITHIN THE RING
▲▲▲St. Stephen's Cathedral (Stephansdom)

This massive Gothic church with the skyscraping spire sits at the center of Vienna. Its highlights are the impressive exterior, the view from the top of the south tower, a carved pulpit, and a handful of quirky sights associated with Mozart and the Habsburg rulers.

Cost and Hours: Church foyer and north aisle—free, daily 6:00-22:00; main nave—€6, includes audioguide, Mon-Sat 9:00-11:30 & 13:00-16:30, Sun 13:00-16:30, July-Aug until 17:30; south and north towers and catacombs have varying costs and hours—see below; English Mass each Sat at 19:00, +43 1 515 523 054, www.stephanskirche.at.

Tours: Entry fee includes audioguide. ∩ Or download my free St. Stephen's Cathedral audio tour.

Catacombs: The catacombs are open to the public only by guided tour (€6, daily 10:00-11:30 & 13:30-16:30, tours generally depart on the half-hour and are in German and English together). Just be at the stairs in the left/north transept to meet the guide—you'll pay at the end. You'll see a crypt for bishops and archbishops, and Crock-Pots of Habsburg guts filling dusty shelves.

Towers: The iconic **south tower** rewards a tough climb up a claustrophobic, 343-step staircase with dizzying views through windows near the top. You can reach it via the entrance outside the church, around the right as you face the west facade (€5.50, daily 9:00-17:30).

The shorter **north tower** holds the famous "Pummerin" bell, and you ascend via elevator (no stairs). While not as high as the south tower, the views are still great (€6, daily 9:00-20:30, entrance inside the church on the left/north side of the nave; you can access this elevator without buying a ticket for the main nave).

⊘ Self-Guided Tour: As you face the church's main entry, go to the right across the little square. From here, you can absorb the sheer magnitude of this massive church, with its skyscraping spire.

Exterior: The church we see today is the third one on this spot. A tall, black, glassy info post describes the Virgil Chapel that stood here 800 years ago. Its dank shell survives today below your feet, viewable from the nearby U-Bahn station. Today's church dates mainly from 1300 to 1450, when builders expanded on an earlier structure and added two huge towers at the end of each transept.

The impressive 450-foot **south tower**—capped with a golden orb and cross—took 65 years to build and was finished in 1433. The tower is a rarity among medieval churches in that it was completed before the Gothic style—and the age of faith—petered out.

The cathedral was heavily damaged at the end of World War II. The original timbered Gothic roof burned, the cathedral's huge bell crashed to the ground, and the fire raged for two days. Civic pride prompted a financial outpouring, and the roof was rebuilt to its original splendor by 1952—doubly impressive considering the bombed-out state of the impoverished country at that time.

Main Entrance: The Romanesque-style main entrance includes bits of the oldest part of the church (which stood here in the 1200s). Right behind you is the site of Vindobona, a Roman garrison town. Before the Romans converted to Christianity, there was a pagan temple here, and this entrance pays homage to that ancient heritage. Roman-era statues are embedded inside the facade, and the two **octagonal towers** flanking the main doorway are dubbed the "heathen towers" because they're built with a few recycled Roman stones (flipped over to hide the pagan inscriptions and expose the smooth sides).

• *Enter the church.*

Cathedral Interior: The immense nave is more than a football field long and nine stories tall. It's lined with clusters of slender pillars that soar upward to support the ribbed crisscross arches of the ceiling. Stylistically, the nave is Gothic with a Baroque overlay.

Over the main doorway is the choir loft, with the 12,000-pipe **organ,** a 1960 replacement for the famous one destroyed during World War II. Along the left wall is the **gift shop.** Step in to marvel at the 14th-century statuary decorating its wall—some of the finest carvings in the church.

To the left of the gift shop is the gated entrance to the **Chapel of Prince Eugene of Savoy.** Prince Eugene (1663-1736), a seminary student from France, arrived in Vienna in 1683 as the city was about to be overrun by the Ottoman Turks. He volunteered for the army and helped save the city, launching a brilliant career as a military man for the Habsburgs. When he died, the grateful Austrians buried him here, under this chapel, marked by a tomb hatch in the floor.

• *Nearby is the entrance to the* **main nave.** *Buy a ticket and start down the nave toward the altar. At the second pillar on the left is the...*

Pulpit: The Gothic sandstone pulpit (c. 1500) is a masterpiece carved from three separate blocks (see if you can find the seams).

A spiral stairway winds up to the lectern, surrounded and supported by the four "Latin Church Fathers," who translated the Bible into Latin in the fourth century (making it more widely accessible to the faithful) and whose writings influenced early Catholic dogma. Each has a very different and very human facial expression (from back to front): Ambrose (daydreamer), Jerome (skeptic), Gregory (explainer), and Augustine (listener).

Find the guy peeking out from under the stairs. This may be a rare **self-portrait of the sculptor** (in medieval times, art was done for the glory of God, and artists worked anonymously). He leans out from a window, sculptor's compass in hand, to observe the world and his work.

• *Continue up the nave. Halfway up turn right and enter the south transept. Go all the way to the doors, then look left to find the...*

Mozart Plaque: Wolfgang Amadeus Mozart (1756-1791) spent most of his brief adult life in Vienna. He attended Mass and was married in St. Stephen's, and two of his children were baptized here. Mozart lived at the heart of Viennese society—among musicians, actors, and aristocrats. After his early success, Mozart fell on hard times. When he died at 35, his remains were dumped into a mass grave outside town. But he was honored with a funeral service here in St. Stephen's.

• *Now head to the chapel at the front-right corner of the church.*

Tomb of Frederick III: This imposing, red-marble tomb is like a big king-size-bed coffin with an effigy of Frederick lying on top (not visible—but there's a photo of the effigy on the left). The top of the tomb is decorated with his coats of arms, representing the many territories he ruled over. Frederick III (1415-1493) is considered the "father" of Vienna for turning the small village into a royal city with a cosmopolitan feel.

• *Walk to the middle of the church.*

High Altar: The tall, ornate, black marble altarpiece (1641, by Tobias and Johann Pock) is topped with a statue of Mary that barely fits under the towering vaults of the ceiling. It frames a large painting of the stoning of St. Stephen, painted on copper. Stephen (at the bottom), having refused to stop professing his faith, is pelted with rocks by angry pagans. As he kneels, ready to die, he gazes up to see a vision of Christ, the cross, and the angels of heaven.

▲▲▲Vienna State Opera (Wiener Staatsoper)

The opera house, facing the Ring and near the TI, is a central point for any visitor. Vienna remains one of the world's great cities for classical music, and this building still belts out some of the finest opera, both classic and cutting-edge. While the critical reception of the building 130 years ago led the architect to commit suicide, and though it's been rebuilt since its destruction by WWII bombs, it's still a sumptuous place. The interior has a chandeliered lobby and carpeted staircases perfect for making the scene. The theater itself features five wraparound balconies, gold-and-red decor, and a bracelet-like chandelier. The only way to see the opera house interior (be-

sides attending a performance) is with a guided 40-minute tour.

Cost and Hours: €13, tour schedule varies depending on rehearsals and performances—generally more tours in the afternoon and in July-Aug (when there are no performances), fewer tours Sept-June; reserve your spot online or risk it and show up at the tour entrance 30 minutes in advance; current month's tour schedule posted online, at the tour entrance (on Operngasse), and at the box office (on Kärntner Strasse); +43 1 514 444 2250, www.wiener-staatsoper.at/en/staatsoper/guided-tours.

▲▲Haus der Musik

Vienna's "House of Music" is a fun and interactive experience that celebrates this hometown forte. The museum, spread over several floors and well described in English, is unique for its effective use of touchscreen computers and headphones to explore the physics of sound. One floor is dedicated to the heavyweight Viennese composers (Mozart, Beethoven, and company) who virtually created classical music as we know it. Really experiencing the place takes time. It's open late and is so interactive, relaxing, and fun that it can be considered an activity more than a sight—an evening of joy for music lovers.

Cost and Hours: €16, half-price after 20:00, €20 combo-ticket with Mozarthaus, daily 10:00-22:00, two blocks from the opera house at Seilerstätte 30, +43 1 513 4850, www.hausdermusik.com.

VIENNA

Visiting the Museum: It's a one-way system; just follow the arrows on the floor. Scan the museum's posted QR code for additional information to enhance your visit. The **first floor** highlights the Vienna Philharmonic Orchestra, known the world over for their New Year's Eve concerts. (In a mini concert hall, a one-hour video—on a loop—lets you enjoy the event.) See Toscanini's baton, Mahler's cap, and well-used scores. Throw the dice to randomly "compose" a piece of music. The **second floor** explores the physics of sound. Enjoy the dark space and stop to notice isolated sounds of things you encounter every day. At the "instrumentarium," four giant instruments, including a drum, demonstrate the principles of sound generation. Through these interactive exhibits, you'll explore the nature of sound and music; I could actually hear what I thought only a piano tuner could discern. You can twist, dissect, and bend sounds to make your own musical language, merging your voice with a duck's quack or a city's traffic roar. The **third floor** celebrates the famous hometown boys—Haydn, Mozart, Beethoven, Schubert, Strauss (father and son), Mahler, Schönberg, Webern, and Berg. Before leaving, head to the **top floor** and pick up a virtual baton to conduct the Vienna Philharmonic.

▲Dorotheum Auction House (Palais Dorotheum)

For an aristocrat's flea market, drop by Austria's answer to Sotheby's. The ground floor has shops, an info desk with a schedule of upcoming auctions (Sept-June only), and a few auction items. Some pieces are available for immediate sale (marked *VKP,* for *Verkaufpreis*—"sales price"), while others are up for auction (marked *DIFF. RUF*).

The first floor (above the mezzanine) has antique furniture and fancy knick-knacks; the second floor has a showy antique gallery with fixed prices. Wandering through here, you feel like you're touring a museum with exhibits you can buy.

Cost and Hours: Free, Mon-Fri 10:00-18:00, Sat 9:00-17:00, closed Sun, classy little café on second floor, between the Graben pedestrian street and Hofburg at Dorotheergasse 17, +43 1 515 60, www.dorotheum.com.

▲St. Peter's Church (Peterskirche)

Baroque Vienna is at its best in this architectural gem, tucked away a few steps from the Graben. Admire the rose-and-gold, oval-shaped Baroque interior, topped with a ceiling fresco of Mary kneeling to be crowned by Jesus and the Father, while the dove of the Holy Spirit floats way up in the lantern. The church's sumptuous elements—especially the organ, altar painting, pulpit, and coat of arms (in the base of the dome) of church founder Leopold I—make St. Peter's one of the city's most beautiful and ornate churches.

Cost and Hours: Free, Mon-Fri 8:00-19:00, Sat-Sun from 9:00, free organ concerts daily at 15:00, just off the Graben between the Plague Monument and Kohlmarkt, +43 1 533 6433, www.peterskirche.at.

Mozarthaus Vienna Museum

In September 1784, 27-year-old Wolfgang Amadeus Mozart moved into this spacious apartment with his wife, Constanze, and their week-old son Karl. For the next three years, this was the epicenter of Viennese high life. It was here that Mozart wrote *Marriage of Figaro* and *Don Giovanni* and established himself as the toast of Vienna. Today, the actual apartments are pretty boring (mostly bare rooms), but the museum does flesh out Mozart's Vienna years with paintings, videos, and a few period pieces.

Cost and Hours: €12, includes audioguide, €20 combo-ticket with Haus der Musik; Tue-Sun 10:00-18:00, closed Mon; a block behind the cathedral, go through arcade at #5a and walk 50 yards to Domgasse 5, +43 1 512 1791, www.mozarthausvienna.at.

Jewish Museum Vienna (Jüdisches Museum Wien)

The museum operates two buildings a 10-minute walk apart. The main museum is on Dorotheergasse (near the Hofburg), and a smaller, more archaeological exhibit is at Judenplatz, which is also the site of a Holocaust memorial (near Am Hof).

The **Jewish Museum Dorotheergasse** (near the Hofburg) fills a four-story downtown building with exhibits, a bookstore, and a small, reasonably priced café serving Middle Eastern fare. The main part of the exhibit is on the second floor, covering the history of Vienna's Jews up to World War II; a ground-floor exhibit carries the story forward to the present day.

The smaller, less interesting **Museum Judenplatz** (near Am Hof) was built around the scant remains of the medieval synagogue that served Vienna's 1,500 Jewish residents up until their massacre in 1420. Its main exhibit is an underground hall where you see the synagogue's foundations. The classy square above the ruins, called Judenplatz, is now dominated by a blocky **memorial** to the 65,000 Viennese Jews killed by the Nazis.

Cost and Hours: €12 ticket includes both museums; Dorotheergasse location, at #11—Sun-Fri 10:00-18:00, closed Sat, multimedia guide-€3; Judenplatz location, at #8—Sun-Thu 10:00-18:00, Fri until 17:00, closed Sat; +43 1 535 0431, www.jmw.at.

MUSEUM DISTRICT

In the 19th century, the Habsburgs planned to link their palace and museum buildings with a series of arches across the Ringstrasse. Although that dream was never fully realized, the awe-inspiring museums still face off across Maria-Theresien-Platz, with a monument to Maria Theresa at its center.

▲▲▲Kunsthistorisches Museum

The Kunsthistorwhateveritis Museum—let's just say "Kunst" (koonst)—houses the family collection of Austria's luxury-loving

Habsburg rulers. Their joie de vivre is reflected in this collection—some of the most beautiful, sexy, and fun art from two centuries (c. 1450-1650). At their peak of power in the 1500s, the Habsburgs ruled Austria, Germany, northern Italy, the Netherlands, and Spain—and you'll see a wide variety of art from all these places and beyond.

While there's little Viennese art here, you will find world-class European masterpieces galore (including canvases by Raphael, Caravaggio, Velázquez, Rubens, Vermeer, Rembrandt, and a particularly exquisite roomful of Bruegels), all well displayed on one glorious floor, plus a fine display of Egyptian, classical, and applied arts.

Cost and Hours: €18, €24 combo-ticket with Hofburg Treasury; daily 10:00-18:00, Thu until 21:00, closed Mon Sept-May; audioguide-€6 or €8/2 people; on the Ringstrasse at Maria-Theresien-Platz, U: Volkstheater/Museumsplatz, +43 1 525 240, www.khm.at.

Visiting the Museum: Of its many exhibits, we'll tour only the Picture Gallery (Gemäldegalerie) on the first floor. Italian-Spanish-French art is on one half of the floor, and Northern European art is on the other. The museum constantly moves around paintings, so be flexible, pick up the current floor plan in the lobby, and use it to locate the highlights from this tour.

Canaletto, Habsburg Palaces: In Saal VII, you'll see glimpses of Baroque art showcasing over-the-top emotions and pudgy, winged babies (the surefire mark of Baroque). Find paintings by **Canaletto** of the former Habsburg palaces—Schönbrunn and Belvedere—one of which also shows the Viennese skyline in the distance.

Caravaggio, *Madonna of the Rosary* and *David with the Head of Goliath:* Caravaggio's *Madonna of the Rosary* (the biggest canvas in the room) may be titled for the Virgin, but the star of the

canvas is the plump young Jesus. He casually balances on his mother's knee, one hand rubbing his plump tummy. St. Dominic, to the left of the mother and child, distributes rosaries to an imploring crowd (notice their dirty feet—typical of Caravaggio's honest realism).

VIENNA

In *David with the Head of Goliath*, Caravaggio turns a familiar Bible story into a third-degree interrogation as David shoves the dripping head of the slain giant right in our noses. This David is not a heroic Renaissance Man like Michelangelo's famous statue, but a homeless teen that Caravaggio paid to portray God's servant. And the severed head of Goliath is none other than Caravaggio himself, an in-your-face self-portrait.

Velázquez, Habsburg Family Portraits: When the Habsburgs ruled both Austria and Spain, cousins kept in touch through portraits of themselves and their kids. Diego Velázquez was the greatest of Spain's "photojournalist" painters—heavily influenced by Caravaggio's realism, capturing his subjects without passing judgment, flattering, or glorifying them.

For example, watch little Margarita Habsburg grow up in three different portraits on the same wall, from age two to age nine. Margarita was destined from birth to marry her Austrian cousin, the future Emperor Leopold I. Pictures like these, sent from Spain every few years, let her pen pal/fiancé get to know her.

Arcimboldo, Portraits of the Seasons: These four cleverly deceptive portraits by the Habsburg court painter, Giuseppe Arcimboldo, depict the four seasons (and elements) as people. For example, take *Summer*—a.k.a. "Fruit Face." With a pickle nose, pear chin, and corn-husk ears, this guy literally is what he eats. Its grotesque weirdness makes it typical of Mannerist art.

Titian, *Ecce Homo*: In the long career of Titian the Venetian (it rhymes), he painted portraits, Christian Madonnas, and sexy Venuses with equal ease. In the large canvas *Ecce Homo*, a crowd mills about, when suddenly there's a commotion. They nudge each other and start to point. Follow their gaze diagonally up the stairs to a battered figure entering

way up in the corner. "Ecce Homo!" says Pilate. "Behold the man." And he presents Jesus to the mob.

Raphael, *Madonna of the Meadow:* Young Raphael epitomized the spirit of the High Renaissance, combining symmetry, grace, beauty, and emotion. This Madonna is a mountain of motherly love—Mary's head is the summit and her flowing robe is the base—enfolding Baby Jesus and John the Baptist. The geometric perfection, serene landscape, and Mary's adoring face make this a masterpiece of sheer grace—but then you get punched by an ironic fist: The cross the little tykes play with foreshadows their gruesome deaths.

Titian, *Danae:* Titian's *Danae* features a luscious nude reclining in bed, as she's about to be seduced. Zeus, the king of the gods, descends as a shower of gold to consort with her—you can almost see the human form of Zeus within the cloud. Danae is enraptured, opening her legs to receive him, while her servant tries to catch the heavenly spurt with a golden dish. How could ultra-conservative Catholic emperors have tolerated such a downright pagan and erotic painting? Apparently, without a problem.

Correggio and Parmigianino: Explore the smaller side rooms, which display excellent small canvases. Look for Correggio's *Jupiter and Io,* showing Zeus seducing another female, this time disguised as a cloud. Parmigianino's *Self-Portrait in a Convex Mirror* depicts the artist gazing into a convex mirror and perfectly reproducing the curved reflection on a convex piece of wood. Amazing.

Exit this wing of the museum via Saal I. Next we'll explore the other half of this floor, dedicated to Northern European art.

Peter Paul Rubens: In Rubens' *Self-Portrait* (likely Room 20) admire the darling of Catholic-dominated Flanders (northern Belgium) in his prime: famous, wealthy, well traveled, the friend of kings and princes, an artist, diplomat, man about town, and—obviously—confident. Rubens' work runs the gamut, from realistic portraits to lounging nudes, from Greek myths to altarpieces, from pious devotion to violent sex. But can we be sure it's Baroque? Ah yes, I'm sure you'll find a pudgy, winged baby somewhere, hovering in the heavens.

Jan Vermeer: In his small canvases, the Dutch painter Jan Vermeer quiets the world down to where we can hear our own heartbeat, letting us appreciate the beauty in common things. The curtain opens and we see *The Art of Painting,* a behind-the-scenes look at Vermeer at work. He's painting a model dressed in blue, starting with her laurel-leaf headdress. The studio is its own dollhouse world framed by a chair in the foreground and the wall in back. Then Vermeer fills this space with the few gems he wants us to focus on—the chandelier, the map, the painter's costume. Everything is lit by a crystal-clear light, letting us see these everyday items with fresh eyes.

Rembrandt van Rijn: Rembrandt became wealthy by painting portraits of Holland's upwardly mobile businessmen, but his greatest subject was himself. In his *Large Self-Portrait* we see the hands-on-hips, defiant, open-stance determination of a man who will do what he wants, and if people don't like it, tough. In typical Rembrandt style, most of the canvas is a dark, smudgy brown, with only the side of his face glowing from the darkness. (Remember Caravaggio? Rembrandt did.)

Pieter Bruegel the Elder: The undisputed master of the slice-of-life village scene was Pieter Bruegel the Elder (c. 1525-1569)—think of him as the Norman Rockwell of the 16th century. He celebrated the peasants' simple life, but he also skewered their weaknesses—not to single them out as hicks, but as universal examples of human folly. About a quarter of all known Bruegel paintings are gathered in this exciting room.

The Peasant Wedding, Bruegel's most famous work, is less about the wedding than the food. It's a farmers' feeding frenzy, as the barnful of wedding guests scramble to get their share of free eats. Everyone's going at it, including a kid in an oversized red cap who cleans the bowl with his fingers. In the middle of it all, look who's been completely forgotten—the demure bride sitting in front of the blue-green cloth.

▲▲Natural History Museum (Naturhistorisches Museum)

The twin building facing the Kunsthistorisches Museum still serves the exact purpose for which it was built: to show off the Habsburgs' vast collection of plant, animal, and mineral specimens and artifacts. It's grown to become an exceptionally well-organized and enjoyable catalogue of the natural world, with 20 million objects, including moon rocks, dinosaur stuff, and the fist-sized *Venus of Willendorf* (at 25,000 years old, the world's oldest sex symbol). Even though the museum has kept its old-school charm, nearly everything on display is presented and described well enough to engage any visitor, from kids to scientifically inclined grown-ups.

Cost and Hours: €14; Thu-Mon

9:00-18:30, Wed until 21:00, closed Tue; €6 audioguide ("Top 100") isn't necessary but can help you hit the highlights; on the Ringstrasse at Maria-Theresien-Platz, U: Volkstheater/Museumsplatz, +43 1 521 770, www.nhm-wien.ac.at.

MuseumsQuartier

The vast grounds of the former imperial stables now corral a cutting-edge cultural center for contemporary arts and design. Among several impressive museums, the best are the Leopold Museum, specializing in 20th-century Austrian modernists (Egon Schiele, Gustav Klimt, and Oskar Kokoschka, among others) and the Museum of Modern Art, Austria's leading gallery for international modern and contemporary art. For many, the MuseumsQuartier is most enjoyable as a spot to gather in the evening for a light, fun meal; cocktails; and people-watching.

Cost and Hours: Leopold Museum—€15, Wed-Mon 10:00-18:00, some Thu until 21:00, closed Tue except in summer, audioguide-€4 or €7/2 people, +43 1 525 700, www.leopoldmuseum.org; Museum of Modern Art—€14, Tue-Sun 10:00-18:00, closed Mon, good multimedia guide-€4, +43 1 52 5000, www.mumok.at. The main entrance/visitors center is at Museumsplatz 1 (ask about combo-tickets if visiting more than just the Leopold and Modern Art museums). U: Volkstheater/Museumsplatz, +43 1 523 5881, www.mqw.at.

KARLSPLATZ AND NEARBY

These sights cluster around Karlsplatz, just southeast of the Ringstrasse. If you're walking from central Vienna, use the U-Bahn station entrance at the opera house and follow the passageways to avoid crossing busy boulevards.

Karlsplatz

This picnic-friendly square, with its Henry Moore sculpture in the pond, faces the imposing facade of Vienna's Technical University. The massive, domed Karlskirche and its twin spiral columns dominate the square. The small green, white, and gold pavilions that line the street across the square from the church are from the late-19th-century municipal train system *(Stadtbahn)*. With curvy iron frames, decorative marble slabs, and painted gold trim, these are pioneering works in the Jugendstil style, designed by the Modernist architect **Otto Wagner,** who influenced Klimt and the Secessionists. One of the pavilions has a sweet little exhibit on Wagner that illustrates the Art Nouveau lifestyle around 1900 (€5, Tue-Sun 10:00-18:00, closed Mon and Nov-March, near the Ringstrasse, +43 1 5058 7478 5180, www.wienmuseum.at).

VIENNA

▲Karlskirche (St. Charles Church)

This "votive church" was proposed by Emperor Charles VI and dedicated to his patron saint, St. Charles Borromeo, in 1713 when an epidemic spared Vienna. The church offers some over-the-top Baroque designs, with a unique combination of columns (showing scenes from Borromeo's life, à la Trajan's Column in Rome), a classic pediment, an elliptical dome, and a terrific close-up look at its frescoes, thanks to a construction elevator that's open to the public. The dome's colorful 13,500-square-foot fresco—painted in the 1730s by Johann Michael Rottmayr—shows Signor Borromeo (in red-and-white bishop's robes) gazing up into heaven, spreading his arms wide, and pleading with Christ to spare Vienna from the plague. Skip the dome if you're even slightly afraid of heights.

Cost and Hours: €8, Mon-Sat 9:00-18:00, Sun 11:00-19:00, dome elevator runs until 17:30, pick up the free info booklet, www.karlskirche.at. There are often classical music concerts performed here on period instruments (usually Thu-Sat, www.concert-vienna.info).

▲Academy of Fine Arts Painting Gallery (Akademie der Bildenden Künste Gemäldegalerie)

Vienna's art academy has a small but impressive collection of paintings to inspire and instruct its students. The gallery rotates temporary exhibits—everything from the masters to modern art—to illustrate contemporary themes. The highlights—the *Last Judgment* triptych by the master of medieval surrealism, Hieronymus Bosch, and works by Guardi, Titian, Rubens, and Van Dyck—are generally featured in the rotating themed exhibits.

Cost and Hours: €9, Tue-Sun 10:00-18:00, closed Mon, three blocks from the opera house at Schillerplatz 3, +43 1 588 162 201, www.kunstsammlungenakademie.at. There's a fine and cheap cafeteria on the ground floor with hot lunches on weekdays.

▲The Secession

This little building was created by the Vienna Secession movement, a group of nonconformist artists led by Gustav Klimt, Otto Wagner, and friends. (For more on the art movement, see the sidebar.)

Having turned their backs on the stuffy official art academy, the Secessionists used the building to display their radical art. The stylized trees carved into the exterior walls and the building's bushy "golden cabbage" rooftop are symbolic of a cycle of renewal. Today, the Secession continues to showcase contemporary cutting-edge art, and it preserves Gustav Klimt's famous *Beethoven Frieze*. A masterpiece of Viennese Art Nouveau, this 105-foot-long fresco was the multimedia centerpiece of a 1902 exhibition honoring Ludwig van Beethoven.

Cost and Hours: €9.50 includes special exhibits, Tue-Sun 10:00-18:00, closed Mon, audioguide-€3, Friedrichstrasse 12, +43 1 587 5307, www.secession.at.

▲Naschmarkt

In 1898, the city decided to cover up its Vienna River. The long, wide square they created was filled with a lively produce market that still bustles most days. The stalls of the Naschmarkt (roughly meaning "Nibble Market") stretch along Wienzeile street, just a short stroll south of the opera house. This is where top chefs like to get their ingredients. And it's long been known as *the* place to get exotic faraway foods. In fact, locals say, "From here start the Balkans."

Hours and Location: Mon-Fri 6:00-19:30, Sat until 18:00, closed Sun, closes earlier in winter; restaurants open until 23:00. The market stretches southwest from the opera to Kettenbrückengasse, between Linke Wienzeile and Rechte Wienzeile. I like to ride the U-Bahn to Kettenbrückengasse, then walk the length of the market back to the opera. Picnickers can grab their grub in the market and head over to Karlsplatz or the Burggarten.

Visiting the Naschmarkt: This "Belly of Vienna" has two parallel lanes. The right lane consists of market stalls, while the left lane is mostly eateries. In recent years, many stalls have been taken over by hip bars and eateries, bringing a youthful vibe and fun new flavors to the market scene. Food stalls make it clear that the Eastern European influences of the Habsburg times remain today. Wander through spices, exotic fruits, olives, cheeses, baklava, and more. From here, the market progresses from cheaper sausage stands and Turkish *döner kebab* stalls

to trendier (and more expensive) eateries and upscale stalls. You'll pass Zur Eisernen Zeit—the oldest *Beisl* (bistro) in the market. At the gourmet vinegar stall, you can sample the vinegar the way you would perfume—with a drop on your wrist (see photo).

Each Saturday, the Naschmarkt is infested with a huge flea

market that stretches southwest of the Kettenbrückengasse U-Bahn station (Sat 6:30-14:00).

▲Wien Museum Karlsplatz

This underappreciated city history museum walks you through the story of Vienna with well-presented artifacts and good English descriptions. While closed for a major renovation, the museum is slated to reopen in its refreshed quarters in 2024 (Karlsplatz 8, +43 1 505 8747, www.wienmuseum.at).

VIENNA

SIGHTS BEYOND THE RING

The following sights are located outside the Ringstrasse but inside the Gürtel, or outer ring road (see the "Greater Vienna" map on page 849).

South of the Ring

▲▲Belvedere Palace (Schloss Belvedere)

This is the elegant palace of Prince Eugene of Savoy (1663-1736), the still much-appreciated conqueror of the Ottomans. Today, you can tour Eugene's lavish palace, see sweeping views of the gardens and the Vienna skyline, and enjoy world-class art starring Gustav Klimt, French Impressionism, and a grab bag of other 19th- and early 20th-century artists. While Vienna's other art collections show off works by masters from around Europe, this has the city's best collection of homegrown artists.

The palace complex includes the Upper Palace (world-class art collection), smaller Lower Palace (historical rooms and temporary exhibits), the Belvedere 21 (modern pavilion mostly filled with contemporary art), and pleasantly beautiful Baroque-style gardens (free and fun to explore). For most visitors, only the Upper Palace is worth the entrance fee.

Cost and Hours: €18 for Upper Belvedere Palace only, €26 for Upper and Lower Palaces (and special exhibits), gardens—free; daily 10:00-18:00, grounds open until dusk; audioguide-€5; good English descriptions; entrance at Prinz-Eugen-Strasse 27, +43 1 795 570, www.belvedere.at.

Eating at the Belvedere: There's a charming little sit-down café on the ground floor of the Upper Palace; in summer you can dine outdoors in the garden.

Getting There: The palace is a 20-minute walk south of the Ring. To get there from the center, catch tram #D at the opera house (direction: Absberggasse). Get off at the Schloss Belvedere stop (just below the Upper Palace gate), cross the street, walk uphill one block, go through the gate (on left), and look immediately to the right for the small building with the ticket office.

Visiting the Upper Palace: The two grand buildings of the Belvedere Palace are separated by a fine garden that slopes down from the Upper to Lower Palace. For our purposes, the Upper Palace is what matters. Be aware that exhibits change frequently, so some of the things I mention here may not be on display during your visit. There are two grand floors, set around impressive middle halls, plus a third floor worth a peek. Throughout, look for small illustrations that show the rooms as they looked in Eugene's day.

From the entrance, climb the staircase to the first floor and enter a grand red-and-gold, chandeliered **Marble Hall.** This was Prince Eugene's party room.

Belvedere means "beautiful view," and the view from the Marble Hall is the most iconic of the city (it's notably captured in Canaletto's painting displayed at the Kunsthistorisches Museum). Look over the Baroque gardens, the Lower Palace, and the city.

Then head to the **East Wing.** Sumptuous paintings by **Gustav Klimt** and his contemporaries (including Monet) fill the rooms in the East Wing. To Klimt, all art was erotic art. He painted during the turn of the 20th century, when Vienna was a splendid laboratory of hedonism. Even fully clothed, his women have a bewitching eroticism in a world full of pollen and pistils.

At the far end of the East Wing you'll find what is perhaps Klimt's best-known painting, *The Kiss,* where two lovers are wrapped up in the colorful gold-and-jeweled cloak of bliss. Klimt's woman is no longer dominating, but submissive, abandoning herself to her man in a fertile field and a vast universe. In a glow emanating from a radiance of desire, the body she presses against is a self-portrait of the artist himself. While Klimt's works are seductive and other-worldly, **Egon Schiele**'s tend to be darker and more introspective. One of Schiele's most recognizable works, *The Embrace,* shows a couple engaged in an erotically  charged, rippling moment of passion. Striking a darker tone is *The Family.* This melancholy painting from 1918 is Schiele's last major painting—he and his pregnant wife died in the influenza epidemic that swept through Europe after World War I.

The **rest of the Upper Palace** collection goes through the whole range of 19th- and 20th-century art: Historicism, Romanticism, Impressionism, Realism, tired tourism, Expressionism, Art Nouveau, and early Modernism. In the West Wing of the first floor is the Belvedere's collection of Austrian Baroque art, including a fascinating corner room of grotesquely grimacing heads by **Franz Xaver Messerschmidt** (1736-1783), a quirky 18th-century Habsburg court sculptor who left the imperial life to follow his own, somewhat deranged muse. After his promising career was cut short by mental illness, Messerschmidt relocated to Bratislava and spent the rest of his days sculpting a series of eerily lifelike "character heads" *(Kopfstücke)* whose unusual faces are contorted by extreme emotions.

▲Kunst Haus Wien and Museum Hundertwasserhaus

This "make yourself at home" museum and nearby apartment com-

plex are a hit with lovers of modern art, mixing the work and philosophy of local painter/environmentalist Friedensreich Hundertwasser (1928-2000), a.k.a. "100H$_2$O."

The museum provides by far the best look at Hundertwasser, but for an actual lived-in apartment complex by the green master, walk 10 minutes to the one-with-nature Hundertwasserhaus (at Löwengasse and Kegelgasse). This complex of 50 apartments, subsidized by the government to provide affordable housing, was built in the 1980s as a breath of architectural fresh air in a city of boring, blocky apartment complexes. While not open to visitors, it's worth seeing for its fun and colorful patchwork exterior.

Cost and Hours: €11 for museum, €12 combo-ticket includes special exhibitions, open daily 10:00-18:00, audioguide-€3, +43 1 712 0491, www.kunsthauswien.com.

Getting There: It's located at Untere Weissgerberstrasse 13, near the Radetzkyplatz stop on trams #O and #1 (signs point the way). Take the U-Bahn to Landstrasse and either walk 10 minutes downhill (north) along Untere Viaduktgasse (a block east of the station), or transfer to tram #O (direction: Praterstern) and ride three stops to Radetzkyplatz.

▲Prater Park (Wiener Prater)

Since the 1780s, when the reformist Emperor Josef II gave his hunting grounds to the people of Vienna as a public park, this place has been Vienna's playground. For the tourist, the "Prater" is the sugary-smelling, tired, and sprawling amusement park *(Wurstel-prater)*. For locals, the "Prater" is the vast, adjacent green park with its three-mile-long, tree-lined main boulevard (Hauptallee). The park still tempts visitors with its huge 220-foot-tall, famous, and lazy Ferris wheel *(Riesenrad)*, fun roller coasters, bumper cars, Lilliputian railroad, and endless eateries. Especially if you're traveling with kids, this is a fun place to share the evening with thousands of Viennese and tourists.

Cost and Hours: Park is free and always open; amusement park—rides cost €2-8 and run May-Oct roughly 10:00-22:00 but often later in good weather in summer, fewer rides open in off-season; U: Praterstern, www.prater.at.

North of the Ring
Sigmund Freud Museum
Freud enthusiasts (and detractors) enjoy seeing the apartment and home office of the man who fundamentally changed our understanding of the human psyche. Dr. Sigmund Freud (1856-1939), a graduate of Vienna University, established his practice here in 1891. For the next 47 years, he received troubled patients who hoped to find peace by telling him their dreams, life traumas, and secret urges. It was here that he wrote his influential works, including the landmark *Interpretation of Dreams* (1899). The museum is narrowly focused on Freud's life. If you're looking for a critical appraisal of whether he was a cocaine-addicted charlatan or a sincere doctor groping toward an understanding of human nature, you won't find it here.

Cost and Hours: €14, Wed-Mon 10:00-18:00, closed Tue, tiny bookshop, half-block from the Schlickgasse stop on tram #D, Berggasse 19, +43 1 319 1596, www.freud-museum.at.

West of the Ring
▲Mariahilfer Strasse Stroll
While there are more stately and elegant streets in the central district, the best opportunity to simply feel the pulse of workaday Viennese life is a little farther out, along Mariahilfer Strasse. The street is mostly pedestrian-only and is fast becoming an attraction in itself. An easy plan is to ride the U-3 to the Zieglergasse stop, then stroll and browse your way downhill to the MuseumsQuartier U-Bahn station. For a map of this area, see page 924.

If you're interested in how Austria handles its people's appetite for marijuana, seek out this interesting shop: Bushplanet Headshop (Mon-Fri 10:00-19:00, Sat until 18:00, closed Sun, Esterhazygasse 32, near the Neubaugasse U-Bahn stop,www.bushplanet.at). For a fine and free city view (along with reasonable eating), escalate to the top floor of the honeycombed Gerngross shopping center and find the Brandauer restaurant (at Mariahilfer Strasse #42).

SIGHTS ON VIENNA'S OUTSKIRTS
▲▲▲Schönbrunn Palace (Schloss Schönbrunn)

The Habsburgs' former summer residence, just a 10-minute subway ride from downtown Vienna, is second only to Versailles among Europe's grand palaces.

Originally built in the 16th century as a small hunting lodge near a beautiful spring *(schön-brunn)*, the residence grew over the next 300 years into the palace you see today. The highlight of the vast complex's many sights is a tour of the Imperial Apartments where the Habsburg nobles lived (including Maria Theresa and her 16 children, and Franz Josef and Sisi). You can also stroll the palace gardens, visit the world's oldest zoo, and view royal transport from the 19th century at the Imperial Carriage Museum.

Cost: Visits to the palace are by timed-entry tour (book in advance). There are two tour options for the Imperial Apartments (both come with audioguides). The best is the 40-room **Grand Tour**, which includes both the rooms of Franz Josef and Sisi, as well as the more impressive Rococo rooms of Maria Theresa (€26, 50 minutes, covered by Sisi Ticket). The **Imperial Tour** covers only the less interesting first 22 rooms (€22, 35 minutes).

If venturing beyond the apartments, consider the **Classic Pass** combo-ticket, which includes the Grand Tour, as well as the Gloriette viewing terrace, maze, orangery, and privy garden (€31, available April-Oct only).

Hours: Imperial Apartments open daily 9:00-17:00, July-Aug until 17:30; gardens generally open 6:30-20:00 but varies with season. The palace is busiest from 9:00 to 12:00, and crowds start to subside after 14:00.

Information: +43 1 811 130, www.schoenbrunn.at.

Advance Tickets Recommended: In summer and on good-weather weekends, book your entry time in advance online. Otherwise, you'll likely have to stand in line at the ticket desk, and then you'll probably have to wait again for your assigned entry time—which could be hours later. Those with a Sisi Ticket can enter without a reserved entry time (buy your Sisi Ticket online or at the Vienna Furniture Museum—see page 877 for details).

If you don't have a reservation, come early or late in the day.

VIENNA

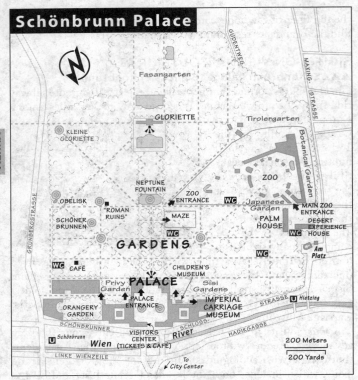

You can save some time in line by using one of the ticket machines. If you have extra time before your entry time, spend it exploring the gardens or Imperial Carriage Museum.

Getting There: Schönbrunn is an easy 10-minute subway ride from downtown Vienna. Take U-4 (which conveniently leaves from Karlsplatz) to Schönbrunn (direction: Hütteldorf) and follow signs for *Schloss Schönbrunn*. Exit bearing right, then cross the busy road and continue to the right to the far, far end of the long yellow building. There you'll find the visitors center, where tickets are sold.

Planning Your Time: Allow at least three hours (including transit time) for your excursion to Schönbrunn Palace. The palace itself is sprawling and can be mobbed. After viewing the Imperial Apartments, wander the gardens (most of which are free). With more time and energy, pick and choose among the other sightseeing options and buy tickets as you go.

▲▲▲Imperial Apartments

In the 1500s, the Habsburgs built a small hunting lodge near a beautiful spring *(schön-brunn)*, and for the next three centuries, they made it their summer getaway from stuffy Vienna. The palace's exterior (late 1600s) is Baroque, but the interior was finished under Maria Theresa (mid-1700s) in let-them-eat-cake Rococo.

Visiting the Apartments: Your tour of the apartments, accompanied by an audioguide, follows a clearly signed one-way route. Think of the following minitour as a series of breadcrumbs, leading you along while the audioguide fills in the details.

Begin in the **guards' room,** where jauntily dressed mannequins of Franz Josef's bodyguards introduce you to his luxurious world. Continue through the Billiard Room to the **Walnut Room.** Wow. Rococo-style wood paneling and gilding decorate this room where Franz Josef—a hard-working modern monarch—received official visitors. Nearby is the **study**—Franz Josef (see his mustachioed portrait) worked at this desk, sometimes joined by his beautiful, brown-haired wife Sisi (see her portrait). In the **bedchamber,** a praying stool, iron bed, and little toilet all attest to Franz Josef's spartan lifestyle (though the paintings here remind us of the grand scale of his palace).

Empress Sisi's Study and Dressing Room: See her portrait in a black dress, as well as a reconstruction of the spiral staircase that once led down to her apartments. The long-haired mannequin and makeup jars in the dressing room indicate how obsessive Sisi was about her looks.

Franz Josef's and Sisi's Bedroom: The huge wood-carved double bed suggests marital bliss, but the bed is not authentic—and as for the bliss, history suggests otherwise.

Follow along to the **dining room.** The whole family ate here at the huge table; today it's set with dinnerware owned by Maria Theresa and Sisi. Next is the **children's room,** with portraits of Maria Theresa (on the easel) and some of her 11 (similar-looking) daughters.

Hall of Mirrors: In this room, six-year-old Mozart performed for Maria Theresa and her family (1762). He amazed them by playing without being able to see the keys, he jumped playfully into the empress' lap, and he even asked six-year-old Marie-Antoinette to marry him.

Great Gallery: Imagine the parties they had here: waltzers spinning across the floor, lit by chandeliers reflecting off the mirrors, beneath stunning ceiling frescoes—and outside, views of the gardens and the Gloriette monument (described later). When WWII bombs rained on Vienna, the palace was largely spared. It took only one direct hit—crashing through this ballroom—but thankfully, that bomb was a dud.

More Fancy Rooms: It was in the **Blue Chinese Salon,** in 1918, that the last Habsburg emperor Karl I made the decision to relinquish power, marking the end of more than six centuries of

Habsburg rule. Up next, the black-lacquer **Vieux-Laque Room** was remodeled by Maria Theresa as a memorial to her beloved husband, who died unexpectedly. Continue to the **Napoleon Room.** When Napoleon conquered Austria, he took over Schönbrunn and made this his bedroom. He dumped Josephine and took a Habsburg princess as his bride, and they had a son (cutely pictured holding a wreath of flowers).

Rich Bedchamber: This darkened room has what may have been Maria Theresa's wedding bed, where she and her husband Franz produced 16 children. Then comes their **study,** with a fitting end to this palace tour—a painting showing the happy couple who left their mark all over Schönbrunn.

▲▲Palace Gardens

The large, manicured grounds fill the palace's backyard, dominated by a hill-topping monument called the Gloriette. Unlike the gardens of Versailles, meant to shut out the real world, Schönbrunn's park was opened to the public in 1779 while the monarchy was in full swing. Today, it's a delightful, sprawling place to wander— especially on a sunny day. You can spend hours here, enjoying the views and the people-watching. And most of the park is free,  as it has been for centuries (open daily sunrise to dusk, entrance on either side of the palace).

If the weather is good, huff up the zigzag path above the Neptune Fountain to the **Gloriette,** a purely decorative monument celebrating an obscure Austrian military victory. To gain access to the view terraces, you can pay for a pricey drink in the café or shell out for an admission ticket (€4.50)—but views are about as good from the lawn just in front of the monument.

Getting Around the Gardens: A tourist train makes the rounds all day, connecting Schönbrunn's many attractions (€8, 2/hour in peak season, none Nov-mid-March, one-hour circuit).

Schönbrunn Zoo (Tiergarten Schönbrunn)

The world's oldest zoo, next door to the palace grounds, was built in 1752 by Maria Theresa's husband for the entertainment and education of the court. He later opened it up to the public—provided they wore proper attire. Today, it's a modern A (anteater) to Z (zebra) menagerie that's especially appealing to families.

Cost and Hours: Adults-€24, kids-€14, daily 9:00-18:30, closes earlier off-season, www.zoovienna.at.

▲Imperial Carriage Museum (Kaiserliche Wagenburg)

The Schönbrunn coach museum is a 19th-century traffic jam of 50 impressive royal carriages and sleighs. It's overpriced (but worth it if you have extra time before your palace reservation). Highlights include silly sedan chairs, the death-black hearse carriage (used for Franz Josef in 1916, and most recently for Empress Zita in 1989), and an extravagantly gilded imperial carriage pulled by eight Cinderella horses.

Cost and Hours: €12, daily 9:00-17:00, shorter hours off-season, audioguide-€2, 200 yards from palace, walk through right arch as you face palace, +43 1 525 242 500, www.kaiserliche-wagenburg.at.

Entertainment in Vienna

Vienna—the birthplace of what we call classical music—still thrives as Europe's music capital. On any given evening, you'll have your choice of opera, Strauss waltzes, Mozart chamber concerts, and lighthearted musicals. The Vienna Boys' Choir lives up to its worldwide reputation.

Besides music, you can spend an evening enjoying art, watching a classic film, or sipping Viennese wine in a village wine garden. Be sure to save some energy for Vienna after dark.

MUSIC

In Vienna, it's music *con brio* from September through June, reaching a symphonic climax during the Vienna Festival each May and June. Sadly, in summer (generally July and August), the Boys' Choir, opera, and many other serious music companies are—like you—on vacation. But it's OK: Vienna hums year-round with live classical music, and tickets to touristy, crowd-pleasing shows are always available.

For music lovers, Vienna is also an opportunity to make pilgrimages to the homes (now mostly small museums) of their favorite composers. If you're a fan of Schubert, Brahms, Haydn, Beethoven, or Mozart, there's a sight for you. But I find these homes inconveniently located and generally underwhelming. The centrally located Haus der Musik (see listing under "Sights in Vienna," earlier) is my favorite setting for celebrating the great musicians and composers who called Vienna home.

Venues: Vienna remains the music capital of Europe, with 10,000 seats in various venues around town mostly booked with classical performances. The best-known entertainment venues are the Staatsoper (State Opera House), the Volksoper (for musicals and operettas), the Theater an der Wien (opera and other performances), the Wiener Musikverein (home of the Vienna Philharmonic

Orchestra), and the Wiener Konzerthaus (various events). Schedules for these venues are listed in the *Spot* arts brochure (available at
TI). You can also check event listings at www.viennaconcerts.com.

Buying Tickets: Most tickets run from €45 to €60 (plus a
stiff booking fee when purchased in advance by phone or online,
or through a box office like the one at the TI). A few venues charge
as little as €30; look around if you're not set on any particular concert. While it's easy to book tickets online long in advance, spontaneity is also workable, as there are invariably people selling their
extra tickets at face value or less outside the door before concert
time. If you call a concert hall directly, they can advise you on the
availability of (cheaper) tickets at the door. Vienna takes care of
its starving artists (and tourists) by offering cheap standing-room
tickets to top-notch music and opera (generally an hour before each
performance).

Vienna Boys' Choir (Wiener Sängerknaben)

The boys sing (from a high balcony, heard but not seen) at the 9:15
Sunday Mass from mid-September through June in the Hofburg's
Imperial Music Chapel (Hofmusikkapelle). The entrance is at
Schweizerhof; you can get there from In der Burg square or go
through the tunnel from Josefsplatz.

Choir Tickets: Reserved seats must be booked in advance (€12-43; reserve online or by sending an email to office@
hofmusikkapelle.gv.at; call +43 1 533 9927 for information only—
they can't book tickets at this number; www.hofmusikkapelle.
gv.at).

Standing-Room Access: Much easier, standing room inside
is free and open to the first 60 who line up. Even better, rather than
line up early, you can simply swing by and stand in the narthex just
outside, where you can hear the boys and see the Mass on a TV
monitor.

Friday Option: The Boys' Choir also performs at the **MuTh**
concert hall on some Fridays at 17:00 during peak season (€39-62,
Am Augartenspitz 1 in Augarten park, U: Taborstrasse, +43 1 347
8080, www.muth.at, tickets@muth.at).

Rick's Crude Tip: They're talented kids, but, for my taste, not
worth all the commotion. Remember, many churches have great
music during Sunday Mass. Just 200 yards from the Hofburg's
Boys' Choir chapel, the Augustinian Church has a glorious 11:00
service each Sunday (which generally features its wonderful organ,
a choir, and a small orchestra; see listing on page 887), and St.
Stephen's Cathedral has one of the largest pipe organs in Europe.

Opera

Vienna State Opera (Wiener Staatsoper)

The Vienna State Opera puts on 300 performances a year (in July and August the singers are on summer break). Since there are different operas nearly nightly, you'll see big trucks out back and constant action backstage—all the sets need to be switched each day. The excellent "electronic libretto" translation screens help make the experience worthwhile for opera newbies. Dress is casual—but do your best.

Opera Tickets: Main-floor seats go for €79-240; bargain hunters get limited-view seats for €16-30. Those under 27 can buy a youth ticket to very good seats for €20. You can book tickets online (www.wiener-staatsoper.at) or in person at the opera's box office on Kärntner Strasse (Mon-Sat 10:00-18:00 or until one hour before each performance, Sun until 13:00). Note that premier performances are generally jam-packed.

Standing-Room Tickets: Unless a top tenor is in town, it's easy to get one of 460 standing-room tickets (*Stehplätze*, €15 up top or €18 downstairs, one ticket/person). While the front doors open one hour before the show starts, a side door (middle of building, on the Operngasse side) opens 90 minutes before curtain time, giving those in the know an early grab at standing-room tickets. Just walk straight in, then head right until you see the ticket booth marked *Stehplätze*. Spaces are numbered—show up early and try for the "Parterre" section, where you'll end up dead-center at stage level, directly under the Emperor's Box. Otherwise, you can choose between the third floor *(Balkon)*, or the fourth floor *(Galerie)*.

Rick's Crude Tip: For me, three hours is a lot of opera. But just to see and hear Vienna's opera in action for an hour or so is a treat. And if you go, you'll get the added entertainment of seeing Vienna all dressed up. I'd buy a standing-room ticket and plan to watch the first part of the show. Before cutting out, have a glass of champagne at the opera's most glamorous bar (on the first floor, center front).

"Live Opera on the Square": Demonstrating its commitment to bringing opera to the masses, each spring and fall the Vienna State Opera projects several performances live on a huge screen on its building, puts out chairs for the public to enjoy...and it's all free. (These showings are noted as *Oper Live am Platz* in the official opera schedule and are posted all around the opera building. They are also listed in the *Spot* brochure and at www.wiener-staatsoper.at.)

Vienna Volksoper

For less-serious operettas and musicals, try Vienna's other opera house, located along the Gürtel, west of the city center (see *Spot* brochure or ask at TI for schedule, Währinger Strasse 78, +43 1 5144 43670, www.volksoper.at).

Theater an der Wien

Considered the oldest theater in Vienna, this venue was designed in 1801 for Mozart operas—intimate, with just a thousand seats. It treats Vienna's music lovers to a different opera every month (except summer), most with a contemporary setting and modern interpretation (facing the Naschmarkt at Linke Wienzeile 6, +43 1 58 885, www.theater-wien.at).

Touristy Mozart and Strauss Concerts

Powdered-wig, costumed orchestra performances of the greatest hits of Mozart and Strauss are given almost nightly in grand traditional settings. These are casual, easygoing concerts with lots of tour groups attending. While there's not a Viennese person in the audience, the tourists generally enjoy the evening.

Mozarthaus Concert Venue

Of the many fine venues in Vienna, the Sala Terrena at Mozarthaus might be my favorite. Intimate chamber-music concerts with musicians in historic costume take place in a small room richly decorated in Venetian Renaissance style (€42-69; Wed, Fri, and Sun at 19:30, Sat at 18:00; near St. Stephen's Cathedral at Singerstrasse 7, +43 1 911 9077, www.mozarthaus.at). Don't confuse this with the Mozarthaus Vienna Museum on Domgasse, which also holds concerts.

Strauss and Mozart Concerts in the Kursalon

For years Strauss and Mozart concerts have been held in the Kursalon, the hall where the "Waltz King" himself directed wildly popular concerts 100 years ago (€63-105, concerts generally nightly at 20:30, Johannesgasse 33 at corner of Parkring, tram #2: Weihburggasse or U: Stadtpark, +43 1 512 5790 to check on availability—generally no problem to reserve—or buy online at www.soundofvienna.at). Shows last two hours and are a mix of ballet, waltzes, and a 15-piece orchestra. It's touristy, but the performance is playful, visually fun, good quality for most, and with a tried-and-tested, crowd-pleasing format.

EVENING SCENE

Vienna is a great place to just be out and about on a balmy evening. While tourists are attracted to the historic central district and its charming, floodlit corners, locals go elsewhere. Depending on your mood and taste, you can join them. Survey and then enjoy lively scenes with bars, cafés, trendy restaurants, and theaters in these areas: **Donaukanal** (the Danube Canal, especially popular in the summer for its imported beaches), **Naschmarkt** (after the produce stalls close up, the bars and eateries bring new life to the place through the evening), **MuseumsQuartier** (surrounded by far-out museums, a young scene of bars with local students filling the courtyard), and **City Hall** (on the parklike Rathausplatz, where in summer free concerts and a food circus of eateries attract huge local crowds—described next).

Open-Air Music-Film Series and Food Circus

A convivial, free-to-everyone people scene erupts each evening in summer (July-Aug) on Rathausplatz, the welcoming park in front of City Hall (right on the Ringstrasse). Thousands of people keep a food circus of simple stalls busy. There's not a plastic cup anywhere, just real plates and glasses—Vienna wants the quality of eating to be as high as the music that's about to begin. And most stalls are outposts of local  restaurants—including some of Vienna's most esteemed—making this a fun and easy way to sample some of the city's most interesting options. About 2,000 spots on comfy benches face a 60-foot-wide screen up against the City Hall's Neo-Gothic facade. When darkness falls, an announcer explains the program, and then the music starts. The program is different every night, so check the website—it's mostly films of opera and classical concerts, but with some jazz and R&B too (www.filmfestival-rathausplatz.at, programs generally last about 2 hours, starting when it's dark—between 21:30 in July and 20:30 in Aug).

Balls and Waltzing

Renowned for its ball scene, Vienna boasts hundreds of balls each year, where the classic dance is the waltz. The height of ball season falls generally between December and February, when Viennese and visitors of all ages dress up and swirl to music ranging from waltzes to jazz to contemporary beats. Balls are put on by the Vienna Philharmonic, Vienna Boys' Choir, Vienna State Opera, and others (search for events at www.events.wien.info). The glamorous **Hofburg Silvesterball** traditionally takes place on New Year's Eve at the Hofburg Palace, featuring big-name orchestras, bands, and opera singers; a sumptuous dinner; and a champagne toast (www.hofburgsilvesterball.com).

English Cinema

Several great theaters offer three or four screens of English movies nightly (€8-11). **Burg Kino,** a block from the opera house, facing the Ring, plays contemporary movies plus the classic *The Third Man* (see next listing, Opernring 19, +43 1 587 8406, www.burgkino.at). **English Cinema Haydn** is near my recommended hotels on Mariahilfer Strasse (Mariahilfer Strasse 57—see the map on page 924, +43 1 587 2262, www.haydnkino.at), and **Artis International Cinema** is right in the town center a few minutes from the cathedral (Schultergasse 5, +43 1 535 6570, www.cineplexx.at/center/artis-international).

The Third Man at Burg Kino

This European noir thriller released in 1949 takes place in post-WWII Vienna—which was then a city divided, like Berlin, among the four victorious Allies. Starring Orson Welles, it's a tale of intrigue in a city afraid of falling under Soviet rule (€9-10, in English; about 2-3 showings weekly—check schedule at www.burgkino.at).

Third Man fans will love the quirky ▲**Third Man Museum** (Dritte Mann Museum), a lovingly curated collection of artifacts about the film, its popularity around the world, and postwar Vienna (€10, RS%—€2 discount with this book, Sat only 14:00-18:00, also guided tours at other times by appointment, tour lasts 80 minutes; U: Kettenbrückengasse, a long block south of the Naschmarkt at Pressgasse 25, +43 676 47 57 818, www.3mpc.net).

Sleeping in Vienna

Accommodations in Vienna are plentiful and relatively affordable compared to other European cities. Expect to pay more for rooms within the Ring. For less expensive accommodations, look at my recommendations around Mariahilfer Strasse. Expect rates to spike for conventions and to drop in low season (usually Nov and Jan-March).

Many of the hotels I've listed here share buildings with other businesses or residences, which can mean lots of stairs or (hopefully) an elevator. Viennese elevators and stairwells can be confusing: In most of Europe, 0 is the ground floor, and 1 is the first floor up (our "second floor"). But in Vienna, thanks to a Habsburg-legacy quirk, older buildings have at least one extra "mezzanine" floor (labeled on elevators as P, H, M, and/or A) between the ground floor and the "first" floor, so floor 1 can actually be what we'd call the second, third, or even fourth floor.

WITHIN THE RING

You'll pay extra to sleep in the atmospheric old center, but if you can afford it, staying here gives you the classiest Vienna experience and enables you to walk to most sights. You won't need a car (and it's difficult and expensive to park one here), but if you are coming with one, plan ahead and ask your hotel where to park.

$$$$ Hotel am Stephansplatz is a four-star business hotel with 53 rooms. It's plush but not over-the-top, and reasonably priced for its sleek comfort and central location facing the cathedral. Every detail is modern and quality, and breakfast is superb, with an up-close view of the city waking up around the cathedral (air-con, elevator, gym and sauna, Stephansplatz 9, U: Stephansplatz, +43 1 534 050, https://hotelamstephansplatz.at, welcome@hotelamstephansplatz.at).

$$$$ Pension Nossek offers 32 rooms on the second floor of a city-center building, with a great location on the pedestrian-only Graben. The rooms are modern and well appointed, while the hallways feel a bit tattered (air-con, elevator, Graben 17, U: Stephansplatz, +43 1 5337 0410, www.pension-nossek.at, reservation@pension-nossek.at).

$$$ Aviano Boutique Hotel is a friendly, family-run place and the best value among my pricier listings. It has 17 rooms, all comfortable and some beautiful, with flowery carpets and other Baroque frills. It's on the third and fourth floors of a typical city-center building but feels peaceful (breakfast extra, fans—and ask for a cooler room facing the courtyard in summer, elevator, between Neuer Markt and Kärntner Strasse at Marco d'Avianogasse 1, U: Karl-

Sleep Code

Hotels in this book are categorized according to the average price of a standard double room with breakfast in high season. 1 euro (€) = about $1.10.

$$$$	**Splurge:** Most rooms over €200
$$$	**Pricier:** €150-200
$$	**Moderate:** €100-150
$	**Budget:** €50-100
¢	**Backpacker:** Under €50
RS%	**Rick Steves discount**

Unless otherwise noted, credit cards are accepted, hotel staff speak basic English, and free Wi-Fi is available. Comparison-shop by checking prices at several hotels (on each hotel's own website, on a booking site, or by email). For the best deal, *book directly with the hotel*. Ask for a discount if paying in cash; if the listing includes **RS%**, request a Rick Steves discount.

splatz or Stephansplatz, +43 1 512 8330, www.avianoboutiquehotel. com, office@avianoboutiquehotel.com, Frau Kavka).

$$$ Hotel Pertschy, circling an old courtyard, is big and elegantly creaky. Its 55 huge rooms have chandeliers and nice Baroque touches, but the hallways are threadbare. Ask for a quieter room away from the noise of horse-and-buggy tours (family rooms, fans, elevator, Habsburgergasse 5, U: Stephansplatz, +43 1 534 490, www.pertschy.com, info@pertschy.com).

$$$ Hotel zur Wiener Staatsoper is quiet, with a more traditional elegance than many of my other listings. Its 14 large rooms come with high ceilings, chandeliers, and fancy carpets on parquet floors (air-con, elevator, a block from the opera house at Krugerstrasse 11; U: Karlsplatz, +43 1 513 1274, www.hotel-staatsoper.at, info@hotel-staatsoper.at, manager Ursula).

$$$ Pension A und A, with nine rooms, feels like you are in an upscale youth hostel with white minimalist hallways and contemporary style in the rooms (air-con, Habsburgergasse 3, U: Stephansplatz, +43 1 890 5128, www.aundapension.com, office@ aunda.at).

$$$ Hotel Das Tigra occupies a 17th-century building with 78 classic rooms and modern touches. The smart decor tells the story of Mozart, who reportedly stayed here for several weeks as a boy when the hotel was still a private home (air-con, Tiefer Graben 14, U: Herrengasse, +43 1 533 96410, www.hotel-tigra.at, info@ hotel-tigra.at).

$$ Motel One Staatsoper, part of a German chain of "budget design hotels," features sleek, smallish, modern rooms outfitted with quality materials but no frills, a 24-hour reception, and

VIENNA

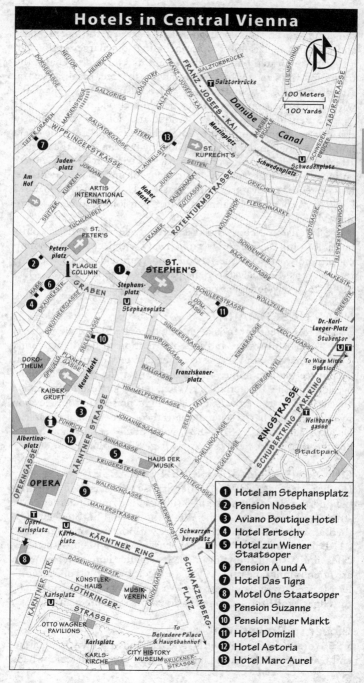

Hotels in Central Vienna

1. Hotel am Stephansplatz
2. Pension Nossek
3. Aviano Boutique Hotel
4. Hotel Pertschy
5. Hotel zur Wiener Staatsoper
6. Pension A und A
7. Hotel Das Tigra
8. Motel One Staatsoper
9. Pension Suzanne
10. Pension Neuer Markt
11. Hotel Domizil
12. Hotel Astoria
13. Hotel Marc Aurel

funky lounge spaces; it's perfect for budget travelers looking for something nicer. This location—right between the opera house and Karlsplatz—has 400 rooms, including some larger options, in a smartly renovated building that's kept its Old World charm (no triples but you can slip in a child under 6 for free, breakfast extra, air-con, elevator, Elisabethstrasse 5, U: Karlsplatz, +43 1 585 0505, www.motel-one.com, wien-staatsoper@motel-one.com).

$$ Pension Suzanne, as Baroque and doily as you'll find in this price range, is wonderfully located a few yards from the opera house. It's small and without a real lobby but run with the class of a bigger hotel. The 26 rooms are packed with properly Viennese antique furnishings (spacious apartment for up to 6 also available, fans on request, elevator, Walfischgasse 4, U: Karlsplatz, +43 1 513 2507, www.pension-suzanne.at, info@pension-suzanne.at, manager Michael).

$$ Pension Neuer Markt is perfectly central, with 35 comfy but faded pink rooms, and worn hallways with a cruise-ship ambience (in hot weather request a quiet courtyard-side room when you reserve, fans, tiny elevator, Seilergasse 9, U: Stephansplatz, +43 1 512 2316, www.hotelpension.at, neuermarkt@hotelpension.at).

NEAR NASCHMARKT

$$$$ Hotel Beethoven is a smartly decorated boutique property with 47 colorful rooms and lots of attention to detail. Its comfy communal spaces and access to coffee and tea throughout the day keep it feeling like home. The location, near the Naschmarkt and overlooking the Theater an der Wien, puts you close to the action but away from the crowds and late-night noise (air-con, elevator, swanky cocktail bar, weekend classical concerts, Papagenogasse 6, U: Karlsplatz, +43 1 587 44820, www.hotel-beethoven.at, info@hotelbeethoven.at). See the map on page 855 for location.

ON OR NEAR MARIAHILFER STRASSE

Lively, pedestrianized Mariahilfer Strasse connects the Westbahnhof and the city center. The U-3 subway line runs underneath the street on its way between the Westbahnhof and St. Stephen's Cathedral, and most of these listings are within a five-minute walk of a U-Bahn stop. This vibrant, inexpensive area is filled with stores, cafés, and a small shopping mall. Its smaller hotels and pensions are often immigrant-run. As you'd expect, the far end of Mariahilfer Strasse (around and past the Westbahnhof) is rougher around the edges, while the section near downtown is more gentrified.

Closer to Downtown

$$$ Hotel Kugel is run with style by hands-on owners Johannes and Christina Roller. Its 25 unique rooms, most with canopy beds, are a good value and decorated with a feminine touch. The junior suites offer a modern alternative (wonderful breakfast, fans, some tram noise, Siebensterngasse 43, at corner with Neubaugasse, U: Neubaugasse, +43 1 523 3355, www.hotelkugel.at, office@hotelkugel.at).

$$$ Hotel Gilbert, near the MuseumsQuartier, offers a modern break from crusty old Vienna. Its 57 rooms and cozy bohemian-inspired lounge spaces attract a young, environmentally conscious clientele (air-con, Breite Gasse 9, U: Volkstheater, +43 1 523 1345, www.hotel-gilbert.at, welcome@hotel-gilbert.at).

$$ NH Collection Wien Zentrum, part of a Spanish chain, is a stern, stylish-but-passionless business hotel on Mariahilfer Strasse. It rents 73 rooms, including a few "suites" that are ideal for families (breakfast extra, air-con, elevator, Mariahilfer Strasse 78, U: Zieglergasse, +43 1 524 5600, www.nh-hotels.com, nhcollectionwienzentrum@nh-hotels.com).

$$ Hotel Pension Corvinus is proudly run by a hardworking Hungarian family: parents Miklós and Judith and sons Anthony and Zoltán. Its 15 comfortable rooms, although in a nondescript building, are surprisingly bright and spacious with nice extra touches (discount if you pay cash, ask about family rooms and apartments with kitchens, espresso machine in rooms, air-con, elevator, Mariahilfer Strasse 57, U: Neubaugasse, +43 1 587 7239, www.corvinus.at, hotel@corvinus.at).

$ K&T Boardinghouse rents five modern, spacious rooms on the first floor of a quiet building a block off Mariahilfer Strasse (cash only but reserve with credit card or PayPal, 2-night minimum, no breakfast, pay air-con, Chwallagasse 2, U: Neubaugasse, +43 676 553 6063, www.ktboardinghouse.at, k.t@chello.at, Tina). From Mariahilfer Strasse, turn left at Café Ritter and walk down Schadekgasse one short block; tiny Chwallagasse is the first right.

Near the Westbahnhof

$$ Motel One Westbahnhof, a more affordable outpost of the chain described earlier, under "Within the Ring," has 441 rooms, lots of modern flair, and a vibrant lobby with plenty of inviting spaces to unwind (no triples but you can slip in a child under 6 for free, breakfast extra, air-con, attached to the Westbahnhof at Europaplatz 3, +43 1 359 350, www.motel-one.com, wein-westbahnhof@motel-one.com).

$$ Hotel Ibis Wien Mariahilf, an impersonal high-rise hotel with American charm, is ideal for anyone tired of quaint old Europe. Its 341 cookie-cutter rooms are bright, comfortable, and modern, with all the conveniences (breakfast extra, air-con, elevator, exit Westbahnhof to the right and walk 400 yards, Mariahilfer

VIENNA

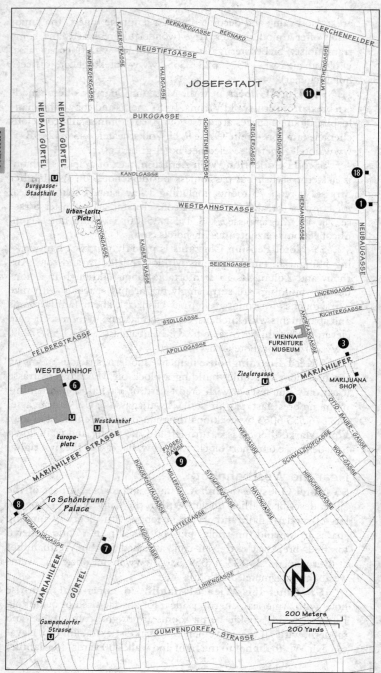

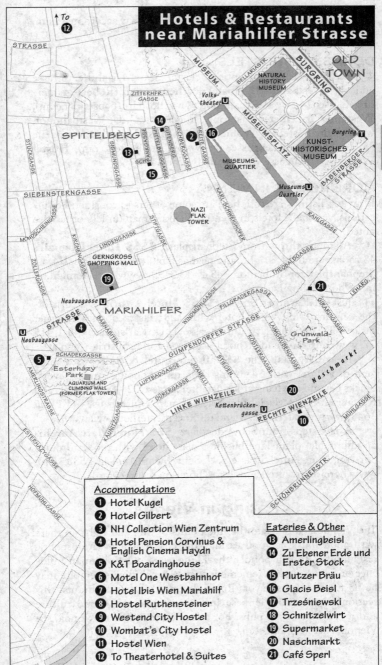

Hotels & Restaurants near Mariahilfer Strasse

VIENNA

Accommodations
1. Hotel Kugel
2. Hotel Gilbert
3. NH Collection Wien Zentrum
4. Hotel Pension Corvinus & English Cinema Haydn
5. K&T Boardinghouse
6. Motel One Westbahnhof
7. Hotel Ibis Wien Mariahilf
8. Hostel Ruthensteiner
9. Westend City Hostel
10. Wombat's City Hostel
11. Hostel Wien
12. To Theaterhotel & Suites

Eateries & Other
13. Amerlingbeisl
14. Zu Ebener Erde und Erster Stock
15. Plutzer Bräu
16. Glacis Beisl
17. Trześniewski
18. Schnitzelwirt
19. Supermarket
20. Naschmarkt
21. Café Sperl

Map labels: STRASSE, To 12, MUSEUM, BELLARIASTR., Natural History Museum, BURGRING, OLD TOWN, ZITTERHFR.-GASSE, Volks-theater U, MUSEUMSPLATZ, Burgring T, Kunst-Historisches Museum, BABENBERGER-STRASSE, SPITTELBERG, GUTENBERG, KIRCHBERGGASSE, BREITE GASSE, STUCKGASSE, SIGMUNDSGASSE, SPITTELBERGGASSE, SCH., MUSEUMS-QUARTIER, Museums-Quartier U, SIEBENSTERNGASSE, KARL-SCHWEIGHOFER, RAHLGASSE, MONDSCHEINGASSE, KIRCHENGASSE, LINDENGASSE, STIFTGASSE, NAZI FLAK TOWER, THEOBALDGASSE, ZOLLERGASSE, GERNGROSS SHOPPING MALL, 19, Neubaugasse U, MARIAHILFER, WINDMÜHLGASSE, FILLGRADERGASSE, LANGGRUBENGASSE, GIRARDIGASSE, 21, LEHARG., U Neubaugasse, STRASSE, 4, BARNABITEN, GUMPENDORFER STRASSE, KÖSTLERGASSE, A. Grünwald-Park, 5, SCHADEKGASSE, Esterházy Park, AQUARIUM AND CLIMBING WALL (FORMER FLAK TOWER), LUFTBADGASSE, JOANELLI, STIEGEN, Naschmarkt, AMERLINGSTRASSE, KAUNITZGASSE, DÜRERGASSE, LINKE WIENZEILE, Kettenbrücken-gasse, 20, RECHTE WIENZEILE, 10, MÜHLGASSE, ESTERHÁZYGASSE, HOFMÜHLGASSE, SCHÖNBRUNNERSTR.

Gürtel 22, U: Westbahnhof, +43 1 59 998, www.accorhotels.com, h0796@accor.com).

DORMS AND HOSTELS

¢ These budget-minded options cluster near Mariahilfer Strasse and the Westbahnhof: **Hostel Ruthensteiner** (Robert-Hamerling-Gasse 24, U: Westbahnhof, www.hostelruthensteiner.com), **Westend City Hostel** (cash only, Fügergasse 3, U: Westbahnhof, www.viennahostel.at), **Wombat's City Hostel** (Rechte Wienzeile 35, U: Kettenbrückengasse, www.wombats-hostels.com), **Hostel Wien** (Myrthengasse 7, www.1070vienna.at).

MORE HOTELS IN VIENNA

If my top listings are full, here are some others to consider. For locations, see the "Hotels in Central Vienna" map (unless otherwise noted).

A stone's throw from Stephansplatz, **$$$$ Hotel Domizil**'s 43 rooms are light, bright, and neat as a pin (Schulerstrasse 14, U: Stephansplatz or Stubentor, +43 1 513 3199, www.hoteldomizil.at, info@hoteldomizil.at).

Just off Kärntner Strasse, **$$$$ Hotel Astoria** is a turn-of-the-century Old World hotel with 128 classy rooms (Kärntner Strasse 32, entrance at Führichgasse 1, U: Karlsplatz, +43 1 515 77, www.austria-trend.at/hotel-astoria, astoria@austria-trend.at).

Near City Hall, the **$$$ Theaterhotel & Suites** is a shiny gem of a hotel with 54 rooms on a fun shopping street (several blocks beyond the Ring at Josefstädter Strasse 22—see "Hotels and Restaurants near Mariahilfer Strasse" map, U: Rathaus, +43 1 405 3648, www.theaterhotel-wien.at, info@theaterhotel-wien.at).

A few steps from Schwedenplatz, **$$$ Hotel Marc Aurel** is an affordable, plain-Jane business-class hotel with modern rooms (air-con, Marc Aurel Strasse 8, U: Schwedenplatz, +43 1 533 3640, www.hotel-marcaurel.com, info@hotel-marcaurel.com).

Eating in Vienna

The Viennese appreciate the fine points of life, and right up there with good music is good eating. The city has many atmospheric restaurants. As you ponder the Hungarian and Bohemian influence on many menus, remember that Vienna's diverse empire may be no more, but its flavors linger. In addition to restaurants, this section covers two Viennese institutions: the city's café culture and its *Heuriger* wine pubs. For a fun foodie guide to Vienna, see ViennaWuerstelstand.com.

Restaurant Code

Eateries in this book are categorized according to the average cost of a typical main course. Drinks, desserts, and splurge items can raise the price considerably. 1 euro (€) = about $1.10.

$$$$	**Splurge:** Most main courses over €20
$$$	**Pricier:** €15-20
$$	**Moderate:** €10-15
$	**Budget:** Under €10

In Austria, a wurst stand or other takeout spot is **$**, a beer hall, *Biergarten,* or basic sit-down eatery is **$$**, a casual but more upscale restaurant is **$$$**, and a swanky splurge is **$$$$**.

EATING TIPS

Austrian Specialties: Traditional Austrian dishes tend to be meat-heavy (although fish is very popular and generally good in this landlocked country). The classic Austrian dish is Wiener schnitzel (a veal cutlet that's been pounded flat, breaded, and fried). Pork schnitzel, which is cheaper, is also common. Austrian *Gulasch,* a meat stew, is a favorite comfort food. Sausage *(Wurst)* is also a staple.

Best of the Wurst: Sausage *(Wurst)* is a staple here. Most restaurants offer it (often as the cheapest thing on the menu), but it's more commonly eaten at a takeout stand *(Würstelstand).*

Sausages can be boiled or grilled. The generic term *Bratwurst* simply means "grilled sausage." *Brühwurst* is boiled. Generally, the darker the weenie, the spicier.

At sausage stands, wurst usually comes in or with a roll *(Semmel).* You might be given the choice of a slice of bread *(Brot),* a pretzel *(Breze),* or, in restaurants, potato salad. Sauces and sides include *Senf* (mustard; ask for *süss*—sweet, or *scharf*—spicy), ketchup or curry-ketchup *(Currysauce),* *Kraut* (sauerkraut), and sometimes horseradish (called *Kren* in Austria and southern Germany).

Local Specialty: *Tafelspitz,* a favorite of Emperor Franz Josef, is boiled beef served in a vegetable soup with bone marrow. The waitstaff will delicately put the beef on your plate, leaving you with the vegetable soup broth to enjoy. Fish out the bone marrow and eat it with toasted dark bread. Then tackle the boiled beef with crème spinach and apple horseradish sauce. The *Tafelspitz* is big and typically shared.

Viennese Drinks: *Gemischter Satz* is a wine that's uniquely Viennese. A blend of grapes grown and harvested together in the same vineyard, it was long considered a cheap table wine. Now it's more respected and worth trying. For a nonalcoholic and refreshing local drink, I like *Apfelsaft gespritzt* (called *Apfelschorle* in Germany), which is apple juice mixed with soda. For a refreshing light-beer drink, go for *Radler* (half beer, half lemonade).

FINE DINING IN THE CENTER

The heart of the city offers plenty of options for a relaxing and expensive dining experience; here are some of my favorites. Reservations are always wise in the evening.

$$$$ Labstelle is my choice for a romantic meal in the town center. With a Bib Gourmand Michelin rating, the chef offers a no-schnitzel menu with a nose-to-tail and farm-to-table ethic. The enticing menu changes seasonally, meets special dietary needs, and celebrates modern Austrian cuisine—always beautifully presented (lunch specials, closed Sun, Lugeck 6, +43 1 236 2122, https://labstelle.at).

$$$ Magazin serves all the meaty classics to a smart local clientele in a romantic setting. The proudly Austrian menu is inviting, the wine list is good, and the atmosphere makes you want to sip schnapps (daily, Riemergasse 14, +43 1 512 7787, https://magazin-riemergasse14.at).

$$$ Artner Restaurant am Franziskanerplatz is a classy place that's a favorite of Austrian politicians. Diners enjoy the cozy interior as well as the outside seating on a quaint square. They offer an inviting modern international menu with nicely presented dishes, including gourmet hamburgers and great steaks (lunch specials, closed Sun, Franziskanerplatz 5, +43 1 503 5034, www.artner.co.at).

$$$ Die Feinkosterei Schwarz-Hirsch offers a small-is-beautiful menu of only Austrian food and wine in a romantic interior. With fine little plates priced at €8-12 each, it's a fun way to experience top-quality traditional dishes family-style. Three plates per person makes a filling meal...eat your way through the menu (daily, inside and outside seating faces the Holocaust memorial at Judenplatz 7, +43 1 396 1421, www.feinkosterei.wien).

$$ Zum Schwarzen Kameel Bistro ("The Black Camel") has a posh, gourmet Viennese **$$$$** restaurant in the back with a thriving and more casual wine bar fronting the street. The delightfully Art Nouveau wine bar, filled with a professional local crowd enjoying small plates from the fancy restaurant kitchen, is *the* place for horseradish and thin-sliced ham (*Beinschinken mit Kren; Achtung*—the horseradish is *hot*). Eat well by ordering high on the menu; eat cheaply by sticking with the tiny open-face finger sandwiches (€2 each, self-serve from counter, with a diet-busting selection of little pastries to assemble, too). Stand, grab a stool, find a table on the street, or sit anywhere you can (prices are the same)—it's customary to share tables (daily, Bognergasse 5, +43 1 533 8125, https://schwarzeskameel.at).

$$$ Zum Weissen Rauchfangkehrer ("The White Chimney Sweep"), with a cozy woody interior and live piano nightly, is popular for its rustic-if-kitschy elegance, traditional cuisine, and enthusiasm for schnapps (daily, near the cathedral at Weihburggasse 4, +43 1 512 3471, www.weisser-rauchfangkehrer.at).

$$$$ Palmenhaus overlooks the Hofburg Palace Garden. Tucked away in a green and peaceful corner two blocks behind the opera house, this is a world apart. If you want to eat modern Austrian/Mediterranean cuisine surrounded by palm trees, this is the place. It's an elegant, dressy, and expensive place at night, but there are moderately priced daily specials for lunch—and since it's at the edge of a park, it's great for families (12:00-15:00). They specialize in fresh fish with generous vegetables (daily, extensive wine list, always a good vegetarian option, indoors in greenhouse or outdoors, Burggarten 1, +43 1 533 1033, www.palmenhaus.at).

CASUAL EATERIES AND TRADITIONAL STANDBYS
Near St. Stephen's Cathedral

These eateries are within about a five-minute walk of the cathedral (U: Stephansplatz).

$$ Kaffee Alt-Wien has a sprawling conviviality that draws you in past several fun spaces as you choose where you'll eat...and then makes you want to just hang out. There's a happy university vibe with artsy posters and a friendly energy. Its small menu is bar food: goulash, schnitzel, beer, and wine (daily, Bäckerstrasse 9, +43 1 512 5222).

$$ Gigerl Stadtheuriger offers a near-*Heuriger* wine-cellar experience without leaving the city center. Sit and order from the menu (*Gulasch*, schnitzel, and so on) or go to the self-service counter and point to what looks good. As in other *Heurigen,* food is designed to go well with the wine. It's sold by the piece or weight; 100 grams *(10 dag)* is about a quarter-pound (cheese and cold meats cost about €5 per 100 grams, salads are about €2 per 100 grams; price sheet posted on wall to right of buffet line). They also have entrées, spinach strudel, quiche, *Apfelstrudel,* and, of course, casks of new and local wines. Servers take your wine order (closed Sun, indoor/outdoor seating, behind cathedral, a block off Kärntner Strasse, just off Rauhensteingasse on Blumenstock, +43 1 513 4431).

$ Trześniewski is an institution—justly famous for its elegant open-face finger sandwiches and small beers. Three different sandwiches and a *kleines Bier (Pfiff)* make a fun, fast, light, and inexpensive lunch. Point to whichever delights look tasty (or grab the English translation sheet and take time to study your 22 sandwich options). The classic favorites are *Geflügelleber* (chicken liver), *Matjes mit Zwiebel* (herring with onions), and *Speck mit Ei* (bacon

VIENNA

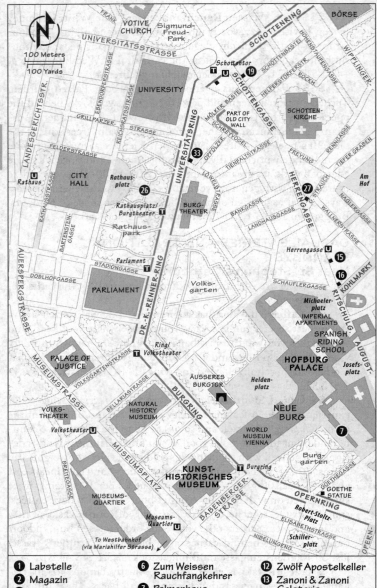

1 Labstelle
2 Magazin
3 Artner Restaurant am Franziskanerplatz
4 Die Feinkosterei Schwarz-Hirsch
5 Zum Schwarzen Kameel Bistro
6 Zum Weissen Rauchfangkehrer
7 Palmenhaus
8 Kaffee Alt-Wien
9 Gigerl Stadtheuriger
10 Trześniewski
11 Reinthaler's Beisl & Café Hawelka
12 Zwölf Apostelkeller
13 Zanoni & Zanoni Gelateria
14 Eis Greissler
15 Venuss Vegan Bistro
16 Billa Supermarket on Michaelerplatz
17 Restaurant Ofenloch

VIENNA

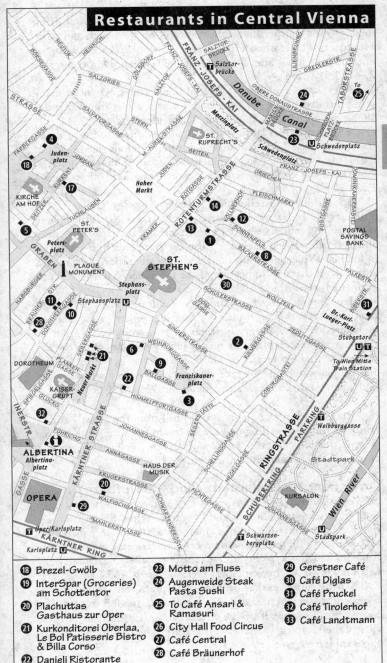

Restaurants in Central Vienna

18 Brezel-Gwölb

19 InterSpar (Groceries) am Schottentor

20 Plachuttas Gasthaus zur Oper

21 Kurkonditorei Oberlaa, Le Bol Patisserie Bistro & Billa Corso

22 Danieli Ristorante

23 Motto am Fluss

24 Augenweide Steak Pasta Sushi

25 To Café Ansari & Ramasuri

26 City Hall Food Circus

27 Café Central

28 Café Bräunerhof

29 Gerstner Café

30 Café Diglas

31 Café Pruckel

32 Café Tirolerhof

33 Café Landtmann

and eggs). Pay for your sandwiches and a drink. Take your drink
tokens to the staffperson on the right. Sit on the bench and scoot
over to a tiny table when a spot opens up (Mon-Fri early-19:30, Sat
until 18:00, closed Sun, 50 yards off the Graben; Dorotheergasse
2, +43 1 512 3291).

They have a branch at Mariahilfer Strasse 95 (near many
recommended hotels—see the map on page 924, Mon-Fri early-
19:00, Sat until 18:00, closed Sun, U: Zieglergasse).

$$ Reinthaler's Beisl is another time warp that serves simple,
traditional fare all day. Its fun, classic interior winds way back, and
it also has a few tables on the quiet street (daily, Dorotheergasse 4,
a block off the Graben—across the street from Trześniewski, +43
1 513 1249).

$$ Zwölf Apostelkeller ("Twelve Apostles Cellar") is a
500-year-old cellar where tourists enjoy a boisterous atmosphere
with strolling musicians under massive medieval arches. The cheap
and accessible menu includes Austrian standards and plenty of
light bites. Wine glasses are a quarter-liter rather than the standard
eighth...and that's an indication of the fun diners have here (daily,
Sonnenfelsgasse 3, +43 1 512 6777).

Ice Cream: *Gelateria* **Zanoni & Zanoni,** run by an Italian
family for several generations, is a fun, high-energy spot mobbed
by happy Viennese hungry for their €3 two-scoop cones from an
extravagant ice-cream lover's menu. Just two blocks from the cathedral, with a big terrace of tables, it's a classic scene for licking
and people-watching—or take it to go and grab a spot under the
Gutenberg statue a block away (daily until late, Lugeck 7, +43 1
512 7979).

Eis Greissler, just 50 yards downhill from the crowds at Zanoni, is a tiny shop selling organic ice cream from a farm in Lower
Austria. It's back to tasty basics with flavors like goat cheese and
cinnamon carrot cake (Rotenturmstrasse 14).

On or near Michaelerplatz (and the Hofburg)

$$ Venuss Vegan Bistro is owned by a vegan-gelical with a mis-
sion: to raise appreciation of good vegan cooking. Select from ei-
ther a cold or hot buffet to fill a small, medium, or large plate (€5,
€10, or €13) in this bright, modern cafeteria. It's easy to over-order:
A medium plate was plenty for me (fine outside seating, closed Sun,
half a block off Michaelerplatz at Herrengasse 6, +43 1 890 8309).

$ Billa Supermarket on Michaelerplatz sells top-end gro-
ceries and has a practical deli where you can assemble a salad or a
cooked meal, pay for it by the weight, and eat it on tables with a
view of the Hofburg (Mon-Sat early-20:00, closed Sun, Schaufler-
gasse at Herrengasse).

Near Am Hof Square

The streets around the square called Am Hof (U: Herrengasse) hide atmospheric medieval lanes with both indoor and outdoor eating action.

$$$ Restaurant Ofenloch serves good, traditional Viennese cuisine with formal service, both indoors and out. This delightfully intimate 300-year-old eatery has a refined yet relaxed ambience (closed Sun, Kurrentgasse 8, +43 1 533 8844).

$$ Brezel-Gwölb, a Tolkienesque nook with tight indoor tables and outdoor dining on a quiet little square, serves simple Viennese classics in an unforgettable atmosphere. With its dark and candlelit interior and secretive-feeling outdoor seating, it's ideal for a romantic late-night glass of wine (three-course weekday lunch specials—including vegetarian option, open daily; leave Am Hof on Drahtgasse, then take first left to Ledererhof 9; +43 1 533 8811).

Toward the University: $ InterSpar (Groceries) am Schottentor is a supermarket in a very fancy shell—a former Rothschild bank building from 1912 (following a global trend of banks vacating fancy downtown digs for more practical locations). They have a great deli section with hot and cold meals that are cheap and to go (Mon-Sat early-20:00, closed Sun, at Schottentor tram stop, picnic in the park across the Ring, near the Votive Church).

Near the Opera

These eateries are within a five-minute walk of the opera house (U: Karlsplatz).

$$$ Plachuttas Gasthaus zur Oper, a proudly Austrian place a block from the opera, has a contemporary, classy interior and inviting seating on the street. It's big, high-energy, and specializes in the local classics like *Tafelspitz* (boiled beef) and Wiener schnitzel—they actually hand out a little souvenir recipe titled "the art of the perfect Wiener schnitzel" (daily, Walfischgasse 5, +43 1 512 2251).

$$ Kurkonditorei Oberlaa serves light meals, daily specials, salads, and vegetarian dishes along with high-end pastries. It may not have the royal and plush fame of Demel (the sweet shop noted on my "Vienna City Walk"), but this is a top choice among Viennese connoisseurs serious about the quality of their pastries. With outdoor seating on Neuer Markt, it's particularly nice on a summer day. Upstairs has more temptations and good seating (great selection of cakes, daily early-20:00, Neuer Markt 16, +43 1 5132 9360).

$$ Le Bol Patisserie Bistro (next to Oberlaa) is a modern place with an old-school French vibe, serving fine salads, baguette sandwiches, and fresh croissants. You can sit on a small terrace or inside the cozy bistro, and the staff speaks to you in French (long hours daily, Neuer Markt 14, +43 699 1030 1899).

$$$ Danieli Ristorante is your best classy Italian value in the Old Town. White-tablecloth dressy but not stuffy, it has reasonable prices. Dine in their elegant, air-conditioned back room or on the street (thin and crispy pizza, daily, 30 yards off Kärntner Strasse opposite Neuer Markt at Himmelpfortgasse 3, +43 1 513 7913).

Supermarket: A top-end version of the Billa supermarket chain, **Billa Corso** has three floors of food and sells hot, ready-made meals (by weight). They also have a great deli selection of salads, soups, and picnic items (daily early-20:00, Neuer Markt 17, on the corner where Seilergasse hits Neuer Markt, +43 1 961 2133).

On or over the Danube Canal

Convenient to the cathedral and on the Ringstrasse tram route are Schwedenplatz and the Danube Canal. My first recommendation overlooks the canal, and the second is immediately across it. The last two are neighborhood favorites, a couple of blocks farther away on a charming street well beyond the tourists.

$$ Motto am Fluss feels a bit like a cruise ship moored high above the Danube Canal. While there's a fancier restaurant inside the modern cabin, you can enjoy open-air café dining on the deck with a simple menu of burgers, pasta, salad, and daily specials (long hours daily, breakfast until 11:45 on weekdays and 16:00 on weekends; reservations smart, Franz-Josefs-Kai 2, +43 1 252 5511, www.mottoamfluss.at).

$$$$ Augenweide Steak Pasta Sushi is a long, skinny, street-level place facing the Danube Canal. With a name that means "Eye Candy," it opened in 2022 and was an instant hit with locals for its youthful, creative energy and three diverse yet enticing kitchens (gourmet burgers, closed Sun, Obere Donaustrasse 97, +43 1 366 0202, https://augenweide.wien).

$$$ Café Ansari is an upscale, family-run place with a fun mix of Georgian/Arabic/Mediterranean cuisine, mellow jazz, and a modern art interior. With lots of thoughtful touches and peaceful seating outside, you're in for a memorable meal here (closed Sun, Praterstrasse 15, +43 1 276 5102, http://cafeansari.at).

$$ Ramasuri is a mod and youthful place with a playful menu and hip, fun service that didn't get the "be a grumpy waiter in Vienna" memo. It has casual and comfy seating inside and out (long hours daily, Praterstrasse 19, +43 676 466 8060, http://ramasuri.at).

City Hall Food Circus

During the summer, scores of outdoor food stands and picnic tables are set up in the park in front of the City Hall (Rathausplatz). The great thing here is the energy of the crowd and a feeling that you're truly eating as the Viennese do...not schnitzel and quaint traditions, but trendy "world food" with young people out having fun (July-Aug daily from 11:00 until late, U: Rathaus).

Spittelberg

This charming cobbled grid of traffic-free lanes is a favorite dining neighborhood for the Viennese. It's handy, set between the MuseumsQuartier and Mariahilfer Strasse (U: Volkstheater). Tables tumble down sidewalks and into breezy courtyards; the charming buildings here date mostly from the early 1800s, before the Mariahilfer Strasse neighborhood was built. It's only worth a special trip on a balmy summer evening, as it's dead in bad weather. Stroll Spittelberggasse, Schrankgasse, and Gutenberggasse, then pick your favorite. Don't miss the vine-strewn wine garden at Schrankgasse 1. To locate these restaurants, see the map on page 924.

$$ Amerlingbeisl is a charming, local place with a casual atmosphere both on the cobbled street and in its vine-covered courtyard. It's a great value, serving a mix of traditional Austrian and international dishes (check the board with daily specials—some vegetarian, open daily, shorter hours in winter, Stiftgasse 8, +43 1 526 1660).

$$$ Zu Ebener Erde und Erster Stock (loosely translated as "Downstairs, Upstairs") is a popular little restaurant with a mostly traditional Austrian menu that includes their signature *Tafelspitz* (boiled beef). Filling a cute 1750 building, it's true to its name, with two dining rooms: a casual and woody downstairs (traditionally for the poor) and a fancy upstairs (where the wealthy convened). There are also a few al fresco tables along the quiet side street (seasonal specials, closed Sat-Sun, Burggasse 13, +43 1 523 6254, www.zu-ebener-erde-und-erster-stock.at).

$$$ Plutzer Bräu, next door to Amerlingbeisl, is a big, sprawling, impersonal brewpub serving forgettable pub grub: ribs, burgers, traditional dishes, and Czech beer (Mon-Fri from 15:00, Sat-Sun from 11:30, Schrankgasse 4, +43 1 526 1215).

$$ Glacis Beisl, at the top edge of the MuseumsQuartier just before Spittelberg, is popular with locals. A gravelly wine garden tucked next to a city fortification, its outdoor tables and breezy ambience are particularly appealing on a balmy evening  (weekday lunch specials, open daily, Breitegasse 4, +43 1 526 5660, www.glacisbeisl.at).

Mariahilfer Strasse and the Naschmarkt

Mariahilfer Strasse is filled with reasonable cafés serving all types of cuisine. For locations, see the map on page 924.

$$ Trześniewski's sandwich bar is *the* place for a quick yet traditional bite. Consider the branch at Mariahilfer Strasse 95 (see the Trześniewski listing earlier in this chapter for ordering tips), or its imitators (one is at #91).

$ Schnitzelwirt is an old classic with a 1950s patina and a mixed local and tourist clientele. In this working-class place, no one finishes their schnitzel (notice the self-serve butcher paper and plastic bags for leftovers). Walking to the back, you pass the kitchen piled high with breaded cutlets waiting for the deep fryer. The schnitzels are served with a starch or salad; if you order the smallest portion, you may want to add a side dish (closed Sun, Neubaugasse 52, U: Neubaugasse, +43 1 523 3771).

Supermarket: Look for the big **Billa Plus** in the basement of the Gerngross shopping mall at Mariahilfer Strasse 42 (Mon-Fri until 20:00, Sat until 18:00, closed Sun, U: Neubaugasse).

Naschmarkt: For a picnic or a trendy dinner, try the Naschmarkt, Vienna's sprawling produce market. This thriving Old World scene comes with plenty of fresh produce, cheap local-style eateries, cafés, kebab and sausage stands, and the best-value sushi in town (market open Mon-Fri 6:00-19:30, Sat until 18:00, closed Sun, closes earlier in winter; restaurants open later; U: Karlsplatz, follow *Karlsplatz* signs out of the station). Pic-  nickers can buy supplies at the market and eat on nearby Karlsplatz (plenty of chairs facing the Karlskirche) or pop into the nearby Burggarten, behind the famous Mozart statue.

In recent years, the Naschmarkt has become fashionable for dinner (or cocktails), with an amazing variety of local and international eateries to choose from. The best plan: Stroll through the entire market to survey the options, and then pick the place that appeals. For more on the Naschmarkt, see page 904.

VIENNA'S CAFÉ CULTURE

Vienna is known for its classic cafés—perfect places to sip some coffee, nibble a pastry, and read a newspaper. You can typically order light lunches as well. A café is also a great place to try one of Vienna's famous desserts, as the city is the birthplace of the Sacher torte and a bevy of other cakes and pastry treats. It's standard practice for your coffee to be served on a little silver tray, with a glass of tap water and perhaps a piece of chocolate on the side.

Coffee-Ordering Lingo: As in Italy and France, coffee drinks in Austria are espresso-based. *Kaffee* means coffee and *Milch* is milk; *Obers* is cream, while *Schlagobers* is whipped cream. Here are some Austrian coffee terms: Use them elsewhere, and you'll probably get a funny look (some are unique just to Vienna).

Schwarzer or **Mokka:** Straight, black espresso; order it *kleiner* (small) or *grosser* (big)

Verlängerter ("lengthened"): Espresso with water, like an Americano

Brauner: With a little milk

Schale Gold ("golden cup"): With a little cream (Vienna)

Mélange: Like a cappuccino

Franziskaner: A *Mélange* with whipped cream rather than foamed milk, often topped with chocolate flakes

Kapuziner: Strong coffee with a dollop of sweetened cream

Verkehrt ("inverted") or **Milchkaffee:** Two-thirds milk and one-third coffee (Vienna)

Einspänner ("buggy"): With lots and lots of whipped cream, served in a glass with a handle (It was the drink of horse-and-buggy drivers, who only had one hand free.)

Fiaker ("horse-and-buggy driver"): Black, served with a *sliwowitz* (plum schnapps) or rum (Vienna)

(Wiener) Eiskaffee: Coffee with ice cream

Maria Theresia: Coffee with orange liqueur

Cafés in the Old Center

These are some of my favorite **$** Viennese cafés located inside the Ring (see the "Restaurants in Central Vienna" map, earlier).

Café Central is overrun with tourists. Still, it remains a classic place: lavish under Neo-Gothic columns, celebrated by 19th-century Austrian writers, and featuring live piano entertainment—schmaltzy tunes on a fine, Vienna-made Bösendorfer each evening from 17:00 to 22:00 (Mon-Sat early-22:00, Sun from 10:00, corner of Herrengasse and Strauchgasse, U: Herrengasse, +43 1 533 3764).

Café Bräunerhof, between the Hofburg and the Graben, offers traditional ambience with few tourists and live music on weekends (Sat-Sun 15:00-18:00), along with cheap lunches on weekdays

(Mon-Fri early-19:00, Sat-Sun until 18:00, no hot food after 15:00, Stallburggasse 2, U: Stephansplatz, +43 1 512 3893).

Café Hawelka has a dark, "brooding Trotsky" atmosphere, paintings by struggling artists who couldn't pay for coffee, a saloon-wood flavor, chalkboard menu (no hot food), smokey velvet couches, an international selection of newspapers, and a phone that rings for regulars (long hours daily, just off the Graben at Dorotheergasse 6, U: Stephansplatz, +43 1 512 8230).

Gerstner Café, facing the opera house in a grand 1860s Ringstrasse building, maintains a royal elegance. Climb to the third level to be immersed in the over-the-top world of Vienna's 19th-century elites. It's a nice alternative to the touristy and overpriced Café Sacher for your Sacher torte (small sandwiches and pastries, fancy café lunch menu, closed Sun, Kärntner Strasse 51, +43 1 526 1361).

Other Classics in the Old Center: All of these places are open long hours daily: **Café Diglas** (good lunches, piano nightly, two blocks behind St. Stephen's Cathedral at Wollzeile 10), **Café Pruckel** (across from Stadtpark at Stubenring 24), **Café Tirolerhof** (two blocks from the opera house, behind the TI on Tegetthoffstrasse, at Führichgasse 8), and **Café Landtmann** (directly across from the City Hall on the Ringstrasse at Universitätsring 4). The Landtmann is unique, as it's the only grand café built along the Ring with all the other grand buildings.

Near the Naschmarkt

Café Sperl dates from 1880 and is still furnished identically to the day it opened—from the coat tree to the chairs (long hours Mon-Sat, Sun until 20:00, closed in July-Aug, near the Naschmarkt at Gumpendorfer Strasse 11—see the map on page 924, U: MuseumsQuartier, +43 1 586 4158).

WEIN IN WIEN: VIENNA'S WINE GARDENS

The *Heuriger* (HOY-rih-gur) is unique to Vienna, dating back to the 1780s, when Emperor Josef II decreed that vintners needed no special license to serve their own wines and juices to the public in their own homes. Many families grabbed this opportunity and opened *Heurigen* (HOY-rih-gehn)—wine-garden restaurants.

A tradition was born. Today, *Heurigen* are licensed but do their best to maintain the old-village atmosphere, serving each fall's vintage until November

11 of the following year, when a new vintage year begins. To go with your wine, a *Heuriger* serves a variety of prepared foods that you choose from a deli counter. This is the most intimidating part of the *Heuriger* experience for tourists, but it's easily conquered. Some *Heurigen* compromise by offering a regular menu that you can order from. At many establishments, strolling musicians entertain—and ask for tips.

Ordering at the Counter: Think of a full-service deli counter at an American supermarket with a seating section nearby. Choose from the array of prepared items and hot dishes, pay at the buffet counter, and find a table. Then order (and pay for) your wine or other drinks from the waiter who will appear at your table.

Food is generally sold by weight, often in *"10 dag"* units (that's 100 grams, or about a quarter-pound). The buffet has several sections: The core of your meal is a warm dish, generally meat (such as ham, roast beef, roast chicken, roulade, or meatloaf) carved off a big hunk. There are also warm sides *(Beilagen)*, such as casseroles and sauerkraut, and a wide variety of cold salads and spreads. Rounding out the menu are bread and cheese (they'll slice it off for you).

Neustift am Walde

This district is easy to reach by public transit and you'll actually see the vineyards.

Getting There: Take the U-6 subway to Nussdorfer Strasse, then ride bus #35A (direction: Salmannsdorf, roughly 18 minutes, leaves from stop across the street from north side of the U-Bahn station). For Weinhof Zimmerman, get off at the Agnesgasse stop; for the other two, use the Neustift am Walde stop.

$$ Weinhof Zimmermann, a 10-minute uphill walk from the bus stop, is my favorite. It's a sprawling farmhouse where the green tables on patios echo the terraced fields all around. The idyllic setting comes with rabbits in petting cages, great food, fine hillside vistas, and a coziness unmatched by the other *Heurigen* mentioned here (opens at 15:00 Tue-Sat, 12:00 on Sun, closed Mon, +43 1 440 1207). From the Agnesgasse stop, hike a block uphill and turn left on Mitterwurzergasse to #20.

$$ Das Schreiberhaus Heurigen-Restaurant is a popular, family-owned place right at the bus stop. Its creaky, old-time dining rooms are papered with celebrity photos. There are 600 spaces inside and another 600 outside, music nightly after 19:00 unless it's slow, and a cobbled backyard that climbs in steps up to the vineyards. Alone among my listings, this place sometimes offers a cheap all-you-can-eat lunch buffet on weekdays (Thu-Fri from 17:00, Sat-Sun from 12:00, sometimes open Mon-Wed, Rathstrasse 54, +43 1 440 3844).

$$ Fuhrgassl Huber can accommodate 1,000 people inside and just as many outside. You can lose yourself in its sprawling backyard, with vineyards streaking up the hill from terraced tables. Musicians stroll most nights after 19:00 (opens at 14:00 Mon-Sat, 12:00 on Sun, a few steps past Das Schreiberhaus at Neustift am Walde 68, +43 1 440 1405, family Huber).

Nussdorf

This untouristy district, characteristic and popular with the Viennese, feels very real, with a working-class vibe, streets lined with local shops, and characteristic *Heurigen* that feel a little bit rougher around the edges.

Getting There: Take tram #D from the Ringstrasse (get on near opera, Hofburg/Kunsthistorisches Museum, or City Hall) to its endpoint, the Beethovengang stop (despite what it says on the front of the tram, the Nussdorf stop isn't the end—stay on for one more stop). Exit the tram, cross the tracks, go uphill 40 yards, and look for Schübel-Auer and Kierlinger on your right. Mayer am Pfarrplatz is a 10-minute walk from the tram stop.

Getting Home: Trams run less frequently in the evening, so be prepared to wait or ask one of the waitstaff to call a taxi.

$ Schübel-Auer Heuriger is my favorite here, with a peaceful leafy garden and a rustic interior. The buffet is big and user-friendly—most dishes are labeled and the patient staff speak English (opens at 16:00 Tue-Sat, 12:00 on Sun, closed Mon and generally Sun-Wed off-season, Kahlenberger Strasse 22, +43 1 370 2222).

$ Heuriger Kierlinger, next door, is also good, with a particularly rollicking, woody room around its buffet and a courtyard shaded with chestnut trees (opens at 15:30, closed most of August and periodically in off-season, Kahlenberger Strasse 20, +43 1 370 2264).

$$$ Mayer am Pfarrplatz is a bustling place with plenty of seating—choose from the indoor restaurant filled with photos of famous guests or the elegant ivy-covered outdoor spaces that tempt you to stay a while (seasonal menu, opens at 12:00, Pfarrplatz 2, +43 1 370 1287).

Vienna Connections

BY TRAIN

Vienna has an impressive Hauptbahnhof (main train station) from which most—but not all—trains depart. Be sure to confirm which station your train uses. From Vienna's two biggest stations (Hauptbahnhof and Westbahnhof), the handiest connection to the center is the U-Bahn (subway). For some stations, there's also a handy tram connection. (See the "Vienna's Public Transportation" map in the "Orientation to Vienna" section.)

For schedules, check Germany's excellent all-Europe timetable at www.bahn.com, and consider downloading the user-friendly DB Navigator app. The Austrian federal railway's timetable at www.oebb.at includes prices, but it doesn't always remind you about discounts or special passes.

Wien Hauptbahnhof

Vienna's huge central station (just a few U-Bahn stops south of downtown) has 12 pass-through tracks, shopping, and all the services you may need—including baggage lockers, a *Reisezentrum* (where you can ask travel-related questions; long hours daily), food court (some outlets open very late), restaurants (including an outpost of the recommended Oberlaa pastry shop), ATMs, grocery stores (some open daily until late), drugstores, bookstores, mobile-phone shops, a car-rental desk (Europcar), a bike-rental shop, and a post office. Many shops are open late and (unlike in the city center) some are open on Sunday.

Getting to the City Center: To reach the center, including all my recommended hotels there, ride the U-1 (subway) for two to four stops (direction: Leopoldau) to Karlsplatz, Stephansplatz, or Schwedenplatz—from the main hall follow the red *U1* signs; ticket machines are near the escalators. You can also take tram #D (which runs along the Ring) from outside the main entrance. To reach Mariahilfer Strasse, ride U-1 three stops to Stephansplatz, then change to U-3 (direction: Ottaring), or hop on bus #13A. Tram #O runs from the station to Landstrasse and the Wien-Mitte station (for airport trains).

When timing any train trip out of Vienna, keep in mind that the U-Bahn stop is a bit of a walk from the main train platforms—allow at least 10 minutes to get from the U-Bahn stop to your train.

Westbahnhof

This station (at the west end of Mariahilfer Strasse, on the U-3 and U-6 lines) has a bright, user-friendly mall of services, shops, and eateries (including the recommended Trześniewski—near track 9—with cheap and elegant finger sandwiches). You'll find a ticket office (daily 6:00-20:00), travel agencies, grocery stores, ATMs, a post office, and baggage lockers (on the ground floor by the WC).

The private **Westbahn** train (www.westbahn.at), which connects Vienna and Salzburg, leaves from here and offers an alternative to the state-run ÖBB trains. For purchase on short notice, Westbahn's regular fares are half those of ÖBB, with the option to buy your ticket on board.

Getting to the City Center: For the center, follow orange signs to the U-3 (direction: Simmering). If your hotel is along Mariahilfer Strasse, your stop is on this line, but it may be simpler to walk.

Franz-Josefs-Bahnhof

This small station in the northern part of the city serves **Krems** and other points on the **north bank of the Danube.** Connections from **Český Krumlov** in the Czech Republic sometimes arrive here, too.

Getting to the City Center: There's no U-Bahn stop at the station, but convenient tram #D connects it to the city center. Also note that trains coming into town from this direction stop at the Spittelau station (on the U-4 and U-6 lines), one stop before they end at the Franz-Josefs-Bahnhof; consider hopping off your train at Spittelau for a handy connection to other points in Vienna. (Similarly, if you're headed out of town and you're not near the tram #D route, take the U-Bahn to Spittelau and catch your train there.)

Wien-Mitte Bahnhof

This smaller station, just east of the Ring, is the terminus for the CAT and S-Bahn (suburban trains) to the airport and sits below a busy shopping mall. Be aware that its U-Bahn (subway) station is called "Landstrasse." From here, take the U-3 to hotels near Stephansplatz or Mariahilfer Strasse, and the U-4 to hotels that are closer to the airport. It's also connected directly to the Hauptbahnhof by tram #O.

Train Connections

Before leaving your hotel, confirm which station your train leaves from.

From Vienna by Train to: Bratislava (2/hour, 1 hour, alternating between Bratislava's main station and Petržalka station, or try going by bus or boat; described in the Bratislava chapter), **Salzburg** (3/hour, 2.5-3 hours), **Hallstatt** (at least hourly, 4 hours, most change in Attnang-Puchheim), **Budapest** (nearly hourly, 2.5 hours; can be cheaper by bus: hourly, 3 hours, www.flixbus.com), **Prague** (7/day direct, 4 hours; more with change; night train, 6 hours), **Český Krumlov** (5/day with 2 changes, 5 hours), **Munich** (7/day direct, 4 hours; otherwise about hourly, 4.5 hours, transfer in Salzburg), **Zürich** (5/day direct, 8 hours; nearly hourly with 1-2 changes, 9 hours; night train, 9 hours), **Ljubljana** (1/day direct, 6 hours; 4/day with change in Villach, 6.5 hours), **Zagreb** (4/day, 7-9 hours, 1 direct, others with 1-3 changes), **Kraków** (3/day, 6-7 hours with 1-2 changes; night train, 8 hours), **Warsaw** (3/day, including 2 direct, 7 hours; night train, 8 hours), **Rome** (4/day, 12.5 hours, 1-3 changes; night train, 14 hours), **Venice** (2/day direct, 8 hours; 3/day with changes, 8-10 hours; night train, 11 hours), **Frankfurt** (5/day direct, 6.5 hours; night train, 9 hours).

BY BUS

The main bus station is located just east of the Ring at the U-3 Erdberg stop. **Flixbus** offers dirt-cheap rates to **Salzburg, Budapest, Prague, Bratislava,** and points beyond (www.flixbus.com).

BY PLANE
Vienna International Airport

The airport, 12 miles from the center, is easy to reach from downtown (code: VIE, www.viennaairport.com). The arrivals hall has an array of services: TI, shops, ATMs, eateries, and a handy supermarket. Ramps lead down to the lower-level train station.

Getting Between the Airport and Central Vienna

By Train: Trains connect the airport with the Wien-Mitte Bahnhof, on the east side of the Ring (described earlier). Choose between two ways of getting to Wien-Mitte: the regular S-7 S-Bahn train (€4.30, 24 minutes) and the express CAT train (€12, 16 minutes). Both run twice an hour on the same tracks. The airport tries to steer tourists into taking the CAT train, but it's hard to justify spending almost €8 to save eight minutes of time. I'd take the S-7, unless the CAT is departing first and you're in a big hurry. Trains from downtown start running about 5:00, while the last train from the airport leaves about 23:30.

To take the **S-Bahn,** from the arrivals hall, go down either of the big ramps, follow the red *ÖBB* signs, then buy a regular two-zone public transport ticket from the multilingual red ticket machines. It's easiest to just type in your final destination and let the machine do the work. The €4.30 price includes any transfers to other trams, city buses, and S- and U-Bahn lines (see www.wienerlinien.at). Be aware that the Wien-Mitte Bahnhof U-Bahn station is called "Landstrasse." ÖBB Railjet trains also run from the airport to Vienna's Hauptbahnhof (to connect to U-1) and to Wien Meidling (to connect to U-6).

If you'll be using public transportation in Vienna a lot, consider buying a transit pass from the machines instead of a single ticket (see "Getting Around Vienna," near the beginning of this chapter). As these passes are only valid in Vienna's central zone, you'll need to also buy a €2.40 single ticket to cover the stretch between the airport and the limits of the inner zone.

To take the fast **CAT** (which stands for "City Airport Train"), follow the green signage down the ramp to your right as you come out into the arrivals hall and buy a ticket from the green machines (one-way-€12, or €14.40 to also cover the connecting link from

Wien-Mitte to your final destination by public transit; round-trip ticket valid 30 days-€21, 4 tickets-€42; usually departs both airport and downtown around :08 and :38 past the hour, www.cityairporttrain.com).

By Bus: Convenient express airport buses go to various points in Vienna, including Morzinplatz/Schwedenplatz U-Bahn station (for city-center hotels, 20 minutes) and Westbahnhof (for Maria-hilfer Strasse hotels, 45 minutes). Double check your destination as you board (€9, round-trip-€15, 1/hour, buy ticket from driver, +43 51 717 for info, www.viennaairportlines.at).

By Taxi: The 30-minute ride into town costs a fixed €36 from the several companies with desks in the arrivals hall. You can also take a taxi from the taxi rank outside; you'll pay the metered rate (plus a trivial baggage surcharge), which should come out about the same. Save by riding the cheap train/bus downtown, then taking a taxi to your destination. An Uber ride to the airport is around €30.

Connecting the Airport and Other Cities

Direct buses serve **Bratislava** and its airport (1-2/hour, 1 hour, buses leave from platforms 7, 8, and 9; two companies: **Flixbus,** www.flixbus.com, and **Slovak Lines/Postbus,** www.slovaklines.sk), **Budapest** (almost hourly, 3 hours, www.flixbus.com), **Prague** (4/day, 7 hours, www.studentagency.eu, also stops in **Brno**).

Bratislava Airport

The airport in nearby Bratislava, Slovakia—a hub for some low-cost flights—is an hour away from Vienna (see the Bratislava chapter).

German Survival Phrases

In the phonetics, ī sounds like the long i in "light," and bolded syllables are stressed.

Good day.	Grüss Gott.	**grews** gote
Do you speak English?	Sprechen Sie Englisch?	**shprehkh**-ehn zee **ehng**-lish
Yes. / No.	Ja. / Nein.	yah / nīn
I (don't) understand.	Ich verstehe (nicht).	ikh fehr-**shtay**-heh (nikht)
Please.	Bitte.	**bit**-teh
Thank you.	Danke.	**dahng**-keh
I'm sorry.	Es tut mir leid.	ehs toot meer līt
Excuse me.	Entschuldigung.	ehnt-**shool**-dig-oong
No problem.	Kein Problem.	kīn proh-**blaym**
(Very) good.	(Sehr) gut.	(zehr) goot
Goodbye.	Auf Wiedersehen.	owf **vee**-der-zayn
one / two	eins / zwei	īns / tsvī
three / four	drei / vier	drī / feer
five / six	fünf / sechs	fewnf / zehkhs
seven / eight	sieben / acht	**zee**-behn / ahkht
nine / ten	neun / zehn	noyn / tsayn
How much is it?	Wieviel kostet das?	**vee**-feel **kohs**-teht dahs
Write it?	Schreiben?	**shrī**-behn
Is it free?	Ist es umsonst?	ist ehs oom-**zohnst**
Included?	Inklusive?	in-kloo-**zee**-veh
Where can I buy / find...?	Wo kann ich kaufen / finden...?	voh kahn ikh **kow**-fehn / **fin**-dehn
I'd like / We'd like...	Ich hätte gern / Wir hätten gern...	ikh **heh**-teh gehrn / veer **heh**-tehn gehrn
...a room.	...ein Zimmer.	īn **tsim**-mer
...a ticket to ____.	...eine Fahrkarte nach ____.	ī-neh **far**-kar-teh nahkh ____
Is it possible?	Ist es möglich?	ist ehs **mur**-glikh
Where is...?	Wo ist...?	voh ist
...the train station	...der Bahnhof	dehr **bahn**-hohf
...the bus station	...der Busbahnhof	dehr **boos**-bahn-hohf
...the tourist information office	...das Touristeninformationsbüro	dahs too-**ris**-tehn-in-for-maht-see-**ohns**-bew-**roh**
...the toilet	...die Toilette	dee toh-**leh**-teh
men / women	Herren / Damen	**hehr**-rehn / **dah**-mehn
left / right	links / rechts	links / rehkhts
straight	geradeaus	geh-**rah**-deh-**ows**
What time does this open / close?	Um wieviel Uhr wird hier geöffnet / geschlossen?	oom **vee**-feel oor veerd heer geh-**urf**-neht / geh-**shloh**-sehn
At what time?	Um wieviel Uhr?	oom **vee**-feel oor
Just a moment.	Moment.	moh-**mehnt**
now / soon / later	jetzt / bald / später	yehtst / bahld / **shpay**-ter
today / tomorrow	heute / morgen	**hoy**-teh / **mor**-gehn

In a German/Austrian Restaurant

I'd like / We'd like...	Ich hätte gern / Wir hätten gern...
	ikh **heh**-teh gehrn / veer **heh**-tehn gehrn
...a reservation for...	...eine Reservierung für... ī-neh reh-zer-**feer**-oong fewr
...a table for one / two.	...einen Tisch für eine Person / zwei Personen.
	ī-nehn tish fewr ī-neh pehr-**zohn** / tsvī pehr-**zoh**-nehn
...the menu (in English), please.	...die Speisekarte (auf Englisch), bitte.
	dee **shpī**-zeh-kar-teh (owf **ehng**-lish) **bit**-teh
nonsmoking	Nichtraucher **nikht**-rowkh-er
Is this seat free?	Ist hier frei? ist heer frī
service (not) included	Trinkgeld (nicht) inklusive
	trink-gehlt (nikht) in-kloo-**zee**-veh
cover charge	Eintritt **īn**-trit
to go	zum Mitnehmen tsoom **mit**-nay-mehn
with / without	mit / ohne mit / **oh**-neh
and / or	und / oder oont / **oh**-der
menu (of the day)	(Tages-) Karte (**tah**-gehs-) **kar**-teh
set meal for tourists	Touristenmenü too-**ris**-tehn-meh-new
specialty of the house	Spezialität des Hauses
	shpayt-see-ah-lee-**tayt** dehs **how**-zehs
breakfast / lunch / dinner	Frühstück / Mittagessen / Abendessen
	frew-shtuhk / **mit**-ah-geh-sehn / **ah**-behn-deh-sehn
appetizers	Vorspeise **for**-shpī-zeh
bread / cheese	Brot / Käse broht / **kay**-zeh
sandwich	Sandwich **zahnd**-vich
soup / salad	Suppe / Salat **zup**-peh / zah-**laht**
meat / poultry	Fleisch / Geflügel flīsh / geh-**flew**-gehl
fish / seafood	Fisch / Meeresfrüchte fish / **mee**-rehs-**froysh**-teh
fruit / vegetables	Obst / Gemüse ohpst / geh-**mew**-zeh
dessert	Nachspeise **nahkh**-shpī-zeh
tap water	Leitungswasser **lī**-toongs-vah-ser
mineral water	Mineralwasser meen-eh-**rahl**-vah-ser
milk	Milch milsh
(orange) juice	(Orangen-) Saft (oh-**rahn**-zhehn-) zahft
coffee / tea	Kaffee / Tee kah-**fay** / tay
wine	Wei vīn
red / white	rot / weiß roht / vīs
glass / bottle	Glas / Flasche glahs / **flah**-sheh
beer	Bier beer
Cheers!	Prost! prohst
More. / Another.	Mehr. / Noch eins. mehr / nohkh īns
The same.	Das gleiche. dahs **glīkh**-eh
The bill, please.	Rechnung, bitte. **rehkh**-noong **bit**-teh
tip	Trinkgeld **trink**-gehlt
Delicious!	Lecker! **lehk**-er

For more user-friendly German phrases, check out *Rick Steves German Phrase Book*.

SLOVAKIA

Slovensko

BRATISLAVA

The Slovak capital, Bratislava, is an unexpected charmer. Its old town bursts with colorfully restored facades, lively outdoor cafés, and swanky boutiques. The ramshackle industrial quarter to the east is rapidly being redeveloped into a forest of skyscrapers. The hilltop castle gleams from a recent facelift. And even the glum communist-era suburb of Petržalka has undergone a Technicolor makeover. Bratislava and Vienna have forged a new twin-city alliance for trade and commerce, making this truly the nexus of Central Europe.

It's easy to get the feeling that workaday Bratislavans—who strike some visitors as gruff—are being pulled to the cutting edge of the 21st century kicking and screaming. But many Slovaks embrace the changes and fancy themselves as the yang to Vienna's yin: If Vienna is a staid, elderly aristocrat sipping coffee, then Bratislava is a vivacious, young professional jet-setting around Europe. Bratislava at night is a lively place; thanks in part to tens of thousands of university students, its youthful center thrives.

Bratislava's location on the Danube (and the tourist circuit) makes it a convenient "on the way" destination between Budapest and Vienna. I admit that Bratislava used to leave me cold, but changes over the last 15 to 20 years have transformed it into a delightful destination. And its energy is inspiring.

PLANNING YOUR TIME

A few hours are enough to get the gist of Bratislava but may leave you wishing you had more time to explore this off-the-beaten-path European capital. Head straight to the old town and follow my self-guided walk, finishing with one or more of the city's fine viewpoints: Ascend to the "UFO" observation deck atop the funky bridge, ride the elevator up to the Sky Bar for a peek (and maybe a drink), or hike up to the castle for the views. With more time, stroll along the Danube riverbank to the thriving, modern Eurovea development. If you spend the evening in Bratislava, you'll find it lively with students, busy cafés, and nightlife.

Note that many museums and galleries are closed on Monday (except for Bratislava Castle, which is closed on Tuesday).

Day-Tripping Tip: Bratislava can be done as a long side trip from Budapest (or a short one from Vienna), but it's most convenient as a stopover to break up the journey between Budapest and Vienna. Pay careful attention to train schedules, as connections alternate between Bratislava's two train stations: Hlavná Stanica (serving all trains to/from Prague and Budapest and half of all trains to/from Vienna) and Petržalka (remaining trains to/from Vienna). If checking your bag at the station, be sure that your return or onward connection will depart from there.

Orientation to Bratislava

With 475,000 residents, Bratislava is Slovakia's capital and biggest city. It has a compact, colorful old town *(staré mesto)*, with the castle on the hill above. Most of the old town is traffic-free. This small area is surrounded by a vast construction zone, rotting residential districts desperately in need of beautification, and a sprawling communist-built suburb that is seeing new life (Petržalka, across the river).

TOURIST INFORMATION

The helpful TI is at Klobučnícka 2, on Primate's Square behind the Old Town Hall (daily 9:00-18:00, Nov-April until 17:00, +421 2 16186, www.visitbratislava.com). In summer, a branch opens at the main train station (Hlavná Stanica; daily 9:30-17:00).

Bratislava City Card: The TI sells this card (€20/1 day, €25/2 days), which includes free transit and free or discounted admission to local sights. It's worthwhile only if you're doing the included old town walking tour (€15 without the card—see "Tours in Bratislava," later). A cheaper option covers sights only, no public transit.

ARRIVAL IN BRATISLAVA

For information on Bratislava's trains, buses, riverboats, and airport, see "Bratislava Connections" at the end of this chapter.

HELPFUL HINTS

Taxis: Taxis come in handy here but are poorly regulated—drivers can charge whatever they want. Any ride in the city center

Welcome to Slovakia

Sitting quietly in the very center of Central Europe, wedged between bigger and stronger nations (Hungary, Austria, the Czech Republic, and Poland), Slovakia was brutally disfigured by the communists, then overshadowed by the Czechs. But in recent years, this fledgling republic has found its wings. Locals brag that the region around Bratislava has the hottest economy and highest income per capita of any region in the former communist region of Europe.

Early economic reforms caused two very different Slovakias to emerge: the modern, industrialized, flat, affluent west, centered on the capital of Bratislava; and the poorer, mountainous, "backward" east, with high unemployment and traditional lifestyles. Thanks to loads of money from the EU, that's old news, and the east now looks better than the west.

Slovakia spent most of its history as someone else's backyard. For centuries it was ruled from Budapest and known as "Upper Hungary." At other times it was an important chunk of the Habsburg Empire, ruled from neighboring Vienna. But many visitors think first of another era: the 75 years that Slovakia was joined with the Czech Republic as the country of "Czechoslovakia," a satellite of Soviet Russia. From its start following World War I, this union of Czechs and Slovaks was troubled; some Slo-

should be around €5. Cabbies waiting at the train station and tourist spots (such as the castle), however, often quote an inflated, flat price—usually €10-15. To improve your odds, call a taxi rather than hailing one on the street (or ask a hotelier or restaurant staffer to call one for you), or use a taxi with a logo and telephone number prominently on the door, and insist that they use the meter. Locals use ride-sharing apps like HOPIN or Bolt for the best rates.

Supermarket: Centrally located, **Billa** is big and handy. Find it across from the Philharmonic, on Mostová street (Mon-Sat 7:00-21:00, Sun from 8:00).

Local Guidebook: For in-depth suggestions on Bratislava sightseeing, dining, and more, look for the eye-pleasing *Bratislava Active* guidebook (around €12, sold at every postcard rack).

Toll Sticker: Slovakia requires cars on its expressways to display a toll sticker. If your car doesn't have one, buy one at some border crossings or at a gas station when you cross the border.

---

vaks chafed at being ruled from Prague, while many Czechs resented the financial burden of their poorer neighbors to the east.

After the Czech Republic threw off communism in 1989's peaceful Velvet Revolution, its separate peoples began to think of the future. The Slovaks wanted to rename the country Czecho-Slovakia (with that all-important hyphen signifying an equal partnership) and give themselves more autonomy. The Czechs balked, relations deteriorated, and Slovak nationalist candidate Vladimír Mečiar fared surprisingly well in the 1992 elections. Taking it as a sign that the two groups wanted to part ways, politicians pushed through (in just three months) the peaceful separation of the now-independent Czech and Slovak Republics. The "Velvet Divorce" became official on January 1, 1993.

At first the Slovaks struggled. Communist rule had been particularly unkind to them, and their economy was in shambles. Visionary leaders set forth bold solutions, including a flat tax (19 percent), followed by EU membership in 2004 and adoption of the euro currency in 2009. Before long, major international corporations noticed the same thing the Soviets had: This is a great place to build stuff, thanks to its strategic location (300 million consumers live within a day's drive), low labor costs, and well-trained workforce. Today, multiple foreign automakers have plants here (Slovakia produces one million cars a year), and with its rapid technological development, Slovakia is gaining a reputation as the Silicon Valley of Central Europe.

Bratislava's success story is impressive. The capital region enjoys almost full employment and is poised to lead Slovakia into a bright future.

You don't need one if you'll be dipping into the country on minor roads—only for major highways. For details, see "Tolls" on page 1114.

Tours in Bratislava

Walking Tours

The TI offers a one-hour **old town walking tour** in English every day at 14:00 (€15, free with Bratislava City Card, must book at least 2 hours in advance). For €36, two people can book a private 1.25-hour tour with the same guides at whatever time is convenient. The TI can arrange this for you with a few hours' notice (see "Tourist Information," earlier). This can be a great way to become friends with the city.

BRATISLAVA

Local Guide

MS Agency, run by **Martin Sloboda,** offers quality guides (€160/3 hours, €190/4 hours, +421 905 627 265, www. bratislava-guide.sk, sloboda@ msagency.sk). Martin, a can-do entrepreneur and tireless Bratislava booster (and author of the great *Bratislava Active*

guidebook described earlier), helped me put this chapter together. He's part of the ambitious young generation that came of age as communism fell—and whose energy and leadership are reshaping the city.

Bratislava Old Town Walk

This self-guided orientation walk circles delightfully traffic-free old Bratislava (figure 1.5 hours, not including sightseeing stops).

• *Start on the bridge about 50 yards uphill from the green copper spire of the watchtower, St. Michael's Gate (it looks like a church spire, at the top of the old town)—with the tram tracks of the ring road just beyond.*

❶ St. Michael's Bridge

You're standing below a watchtower marking St. Michael's Gate (Michalská Brána), part of the town's medieval wall. It's capped with the Archangel Michael busy killing a dragon.

The Hungarian king gave Pressburg (as Bratislava was called back then) city status in 1291. This meant the city had permission to fortify, offer protection, and tax trade. Bratislava was at the crossroads of two medieval trade routes (the north-south "Amber Route" from the Baltics to the Mediterranean, and the east-west "Oriental Route" along the Danube). You're standing over the former dry moat, now a garden of the city library and an outdoor concert venue.

Before heading in to the old town, look away from the tower. Notice the once-sleek Art Deco building on the right. Now a bar, when it was built in 1929 it was a supermodern department store designed to show off Bata shoes (a Czechoslovakian company that was once the largest shoe company in the world).

• *Stroll over the bridge and enter the old center. You're outside the wall, walking through a barbican—shaped like an "L" for better defense. Pause just after passing under the gate.*

Slovakia Almanac

Official Name: Slovenská Republika, though locals call it Slovensko. The nation is the eastern half of the former Czechoslovakia (split peaceably in 1993).

Population: 5.5 million people. The majority are native Slovaks who are Roman Catholic and speak Slovak. But one in ten has Hungarian roots ("stranded" here when Hungary lost this land after WWI), and many—likely between 2 and 8 percent—are Roma.

Latitude and Longitude: 48°N and 19°E (similar latitude to Paris or Vancouver, BC).

Area: 19,000 square miles (the size of Massachusetts and New Hampshire put together).

Geography: The northeastern half of Slovakia features the beautiful rolling hills and spiky, jagged peaks of the Carpathian Mountains. The southwestern half is quite flat—a continuation of the Great Hungarian Plain.

Biggest Cities: Only two cities have more than 100,000 inhabitants: Bratislava in the west (the capital, 475,000) and Košice in the east (240,000).

Economy: The gross domestic product is about $116 billion, and the GDP per capita is about $21,000.

Currency: Slovakia uses the euro (€1 = about $1.10).

Government: Slovakia's mostly figurehead president heads a government that isn't dominated by any single political party. Slovakia also has a 150-seat National Council (like a parliament), the leader of which is the prime minister.

Flag: Horizontal bands of white, blue, and red with a shield bearing a "patriarchal cross" (with two crossbars instead of one) atop three humps. The three humps represent three historic mountain ranges of Slovakia: Mátra (now in northern Hungary, near Eger), Fatra, and Tatra. The double-barred cross represents St. Stephen (István) of Hungary, commemorating the many centuries that Slovakia was part of Hungary.

Language: The official language is Slovak, which is closely related to Czech and Polish—although many Bratislavans also speak English. The local word used informally for both "hi" and "bye" is easy to remember: *ahoj* (pronounced "AH-hoy," like a pirate). "Please" is *prosím* (PROH-seem), "thank you" is *ďakujem* (DYAH-koo-yehm), "good" is *dobrý* (DOH-bree), and "Cheers!" is *Na zdravie!* (nah ZDRAH-vyeh).

BRATISLAVA

Bratislava

Accommodations

1. Marrol's Boutique Hotel
2. Roset Hotel & Residence
3. Radisson Blu Carlton Hotel
4. To Loft Hotel & Wilson Palace
5. Beigli Hotel & Garden
6. Garni Hotel Virgo

Eateries & Other

7. Bratislavská Flagship Restaurant & Pivovar
8. Výčap u Ernőho
9. Foodstock
10. Mecheche Snack Bar
11. Urban House
12. Carnevalle, Zylinder & Café Verne
13. Sky Bar Restaurant
14. Konditorei Kormuth
15. Kaffee Mayer & Café Mondieu
16. Čajovňa V Podzemí
17. Supermarket

ULICA PALISÁDY
STEJNOVA
PANENSKÁ
LYCEJNÁ
KOZIA ULICA
KONVENTNÁ
RODYJAYOR
ZOCHOVA
STAROMESTSKÁ
ŽUPNÉ NÁM.
SVORADOVA
ST. STEPHEN
Zochova #95
ZAMOCKA ULICA
BAŠTOVÁ
Fashion Courtyard
KLARISKÁ
KAPITULSKÁ
KRÁTKA
STRELECKÁ
ŽIDOVSKÁ
TOWN WALL
PREPOŠTSKÁ
OLD
VENTÚRSKA
SUMMER RIDING SCHOOL
CASTLE
ENTRY
KNIGHTS HALL
PARLIAMENT
VODNÝ
TREASURE ROOM
TICKETS
STAROMESTSKÁ
OLD FOUNTAIN
SVÄTOPLUK STATUE
ST. MARTIN'S CATHEDRAL
ZÁM. SCHODY
LUCULUS GELATO
SCHODY PRI STAREJ VODÁRNI
HOLOCAUST MEMORIAL
HANS CHRISTIAN ANDERSEN STATUE
NÁBR. ARMÁDNEHO GENERÁLA L. SVOBODU
Most SNP (Bus stop under bridge)
RÁZUSOVO NÁBR.
To Vienna
TWIN CITY BOAT DOCK
SNP BRIDGE
100 Meters
100 Yards
To Petržalka
"UFO" OBSERVATION DECK

BRATISLAVA

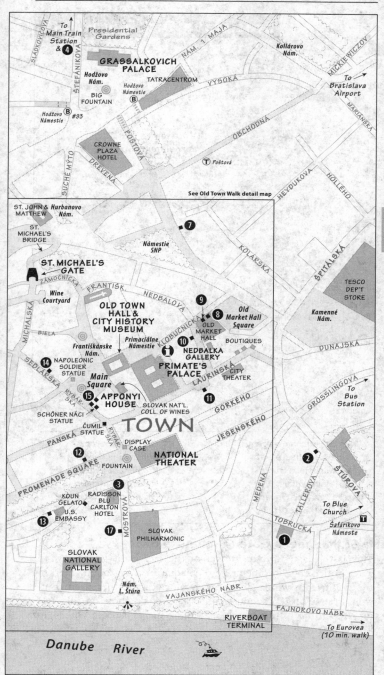

To Main Train Station & 4

Presidential Gardens

SLADKOVIČOVA

ŠTEFÁNIKOVA

NÁM. 1 MAJA

Kollárovo Nám.

MICKIEWICZOV

GRASSALKOVICH PALACE

Hodžovo Nám.

TATRACENTRUM

VYSOKÁ

To Bratislava Airport

Hodžovo Námestie

B

BIG FOUNTAIN

Hodžovo Námestie B

#93

OBCHODNÁ

MARIÁNSKA

POŠTOVÁ

SUCHÉ MÝTO

DREVENÁ

CROWNE PLAZA HOTEL

T Poštová

HEYDUKOVA

HOLLÉHO

See Old Town Walk detail map

ST. JOHN & MATTHEW

Hurbanovo Nám.

Námestie SNP

ŠPITÁLSKA

ST. MICHAEL'S BRIDGE

KOLÁRSKA

TESCO DEP'T STORE

ST. MICHAEL'S GATE

ZÁMOČNÍCKA

FRANTIŠK.

NEDBALOVA

9

Wine Courtyard

8

Old Market Hall Square

Kamenné Nám.

MICHALSKA

OLD TOWN HALL & CITY HISTORY MUSEUM

KLOBUČNÍCKA

OLD MARKET HALL

DUNAJSKÁ

BIELA

Františkánske Nám.

Primaciálne Námestie

i

10

NEDBALKA GALLERY

BOUTIQUES

SEDLÁRSKA

14

NAPOLEONIC SOLDIER STATUE

PRIMATE'S PALACE

LAURINSKÁ

CITY THEATER

Main Square

15

APPONYI HOUSE

GÖRKÉHO

GRÖSSLINGOVA

RYBÁR. SKA

SCHÖNER NÁCI STATUE

ČUMIL STATUE

SLOVAK NAT'L. COLL. OF WINES

11

To Bus Station

PANSKÁ

RYBÁRSKA

TOWN

DISPLAY CASE

JESENSKÉHO

2

KOUN GELATO

FOUNTAIN

12

PROMENADE SQUARE

NATIONAL THEATER

MEDENA

TALLEROVA

ŠTÚROVA

To Blue Church

13

U.S. EMBASSY

3

RADISSON BLU CARLTON HOTEL

MOSTOVÁ

TOBRUCKÁ

Šafárikovo Námestie

T

SLOVAK NATIONAL GALLERY

17

Slovak Philharmonic

1

Nám. L. Štúra

VAJANSKÉHO NÁBR.

FAJNOROVO NÁBR.

RIVERBOAT TERMINAL

To Eurovea (10 min. walk)

Danube   River

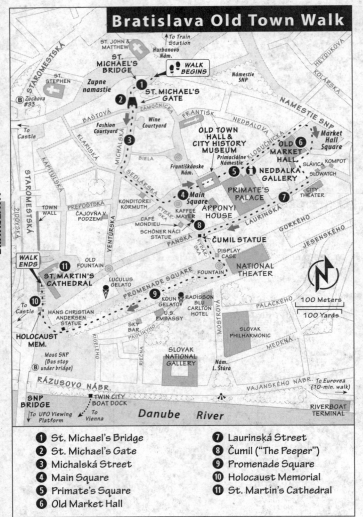

Bratislava Old Town Walk

1 St. Michael's Bridge
2 St. Michael's Gate
3 Michalská Street
4 Main Square
5 Primate's Square
6 Old Market Hall
7 Laurinská Street
8 Čumil ("The Peeper")
9 Promenade Square
10 Holocaust Memorial
11 St. Martin's Cathedral

❷ St. Michael's Gate (Michalská Brána)

This is the last surviving tower of the city wall. Just below the gate, notice the "kilometer zero" plaque in the ground, marking the point from which distances in Slovakia are measured. But I wouldn't trust the distances...unless we're somehow on the equator. According to this, the North and South Poles are both 4,667 kilometers away.

• *Before you stretches...*

➌ Michalská Street

Pretty as it is now, Bratislava's old center was a decrepit ghost town during the communist era. The communist regime believed that Bratislavans of the future would live in large, efficient apartment buildings. They saw the old town as a useless relic of the bad old days of poor plumbing, cramped living spaces, social injustice, and German domination—a view that left no room to respect, or maintain, the town's physical heritage.

For example, notice the uniform cobbles underfoot. In the 1950s, the communists sold Bratislava's original medieval cobbles to cute German towns that were rebuilding themselves in a way that preserved their elegant Old World character. Locals avoided this stripped-down, desolate corner of the city, preferring to spend time in the Petržalka suburb across the river.

With the fall of communism in 1989, the new government began sorting out who had the rights to the old town's buildings and returning them to their original owners. During this time, little repair or development took place (since there was no point investing in a building until ownership was clearly established). By 1998, most of the property issues were resolved. The city made the old town traffic-free, spruced up the public buildings, and encouraged private owners to restore their buildings as well.

Two decades later, the result is this delightful street, lined with inviting cafés and restaurants. Poke around to experience Bratislava's charm, and notice that many of the people surrounding you are likely locals enjoying their newfound prosperity. This is a contrast to many European capitals like Prague, where locals avoid the tourist-filled old town center. Thanks to the Slovaks, who don't like to brag, Bratislava has managed to keep a low profile.

Courtyards and passageways—most of them open to the public—burrow through the city's buildings. Half a block down on the left, the courtyard at #12 was once home to vintners; their former cellars are now coffee shops, massage parlors, crafts boutiques, and cigar shops. More dead-end passages with characteristic shops are across the street, at #7 and #5.

• *Two blocks down from St. Michael's Gate, where the street changes to Ventúrska (at the signpost and big rock in the street), turn left along Sedlárska street.*

Peek into **Konditorei Kormuth** *(a few doors down on the right, at #8) and enjoy the elaborate window display. Mr. Kormüth dedicated* *many years and lots of money to creating a 17th-century setting for his café, with original furnishings and the history of the city beautifully painted on the walls. For roughly €10, you can enjoy a coffee and slice of cake made from old recipes from the Austro-Hungarian Empire and served on historical china in this unforgettable setting.*

Farther on, you reach the historic...

❹ Main Square (Hlavné Námestie)

This modest square, the centerpiece of Bratislava's old town, feels too petite for a national capital. Its style is a mishmash—every building around it seems to date from a different architectural period.

The **fountain,** the most beautiful and historic in town, is a history lesson just waiting to happen. It celebrates the 1563 coronation of Maximillian II— the first Habsburg emperor to also be crowned "King of Hungary." Back then, Slovakia was part of Hungary, which was ruled from Austria. (Got that?) As a mark of respect to the locals, Austrian emperors were crowned a second time, as Hungarian kings. (The German phrase for this arrangement—*König und Kaiser,* "king and emperor," often abbreviated *"K+K"*—remains a mark of quality to this day.) I suppose if your choice as a Hungarian was to be ruled by the Ottomans or by an Austrian Habsburg, the answer was easy.

This arrangement also helps explain why Vienna and Bratislava—the present-day capitals of Austria and Slovakia—are the closest of any two capitals in Europe (you can actually see the lights of one from the other). This closeness wasn't an accident—it was for security. Long before "Slovakia" existed, Bratislava (then called Pozsony) was the capital of "rump" Hungary—what was left of Hungary after most of its territory, including the capital, Buda, was conquered by the Ottomans. Bratislava was as far from the Ottoman Turks as possible while still being in Hungary and very well fortified. The castle crowning the hill high above the old town was the royal residence and protector of the crown jewels during this time. (For more on the complicated tricultural mix of the city— Austrian/German, Hungarian, and Slavic/Slovak—see the "City of Three Cultures" sidebar, later.)

Standing in the middle of the main square, do a quick clockwise spin tour. (You'll need to circle around the fountain to see everything.) Begin with the bold yellow tower of the **Old Town Hall** (Stará Radnica), which dominates the square. It's Gothic at the core but with a Baroque facade. Near the bottom of the tower,

BRATISLAVA

to the left of the pointed window, find the Napoleonic cannonball embedded in the facade. It recalls Napoleon's two sieges of Bratislava (the 1809 siege was 42 days long), which caused massive suffering—even worse than during World War II (the French consumed all the wine). This is just one of several cannonballs around town.

Down the street to the right of the Old Town Hall is the **Apponyi House,** the mansion of an 18th-century aristocrat that also holds the Slovak National Collection of Wine (described later, under "Sights in Bratislava").

Turn farther right and note the venerable cafés. The classic choice is **Kaffee Mayer,** with dark awnings and outdoor seating facing the fountain. They've been selling coffee and cakes to a genteel clientele since 1873. You can enjoy your pick-me-up in the swanky old interior or out on the square.

At the corner in front of Kaffee Mayer (you may have to walk closer to see it) is a beloved statue. The jovial chap doffing his top hat is **Schöner Náci,** who lived in Bratislava until the 1960s. This eccentric old man, a poor carpet cleaner, would dress up in his one black suit and top hat and go strolling through the city, offering gifts to the women he fancied. (He'd often whisper *"schön"*—German for "pretty," which is how he got his nickname.) Schöner Náci now gets to spend eternity greeting visitors outside his favorite café.

Across the street, the Art Nouveau **Café Mondieu** is known for its 1904 Klimt-style mosaics. The building was once a bank. These days the barista stands where a different kind of bean counter once did.

Now walk toward the Old Town Hall. In December, the square transforms into the city's popular and atmospheric Christmas market. Step through the passageway leading to the Old Town Hall's gorgeously restored courtyard, with its Renaissance arcades. (The entrance to the excellent **City History Museum**—described later—is inside the courtyard.)

• *Continue all the way through the courtyard into...*

❺ Primate's Square (Primaciálne Námestie)

The pink mansion on the right is the **Primate's Palace**—the new town hall in the old archbishop's residence—with a fine interior decorated with English tapestries (described later). At the far end of this square is the **TI.**

Continue straight ahead (with the TI on your right) down the street called Klobučnícka—**"Hatters Street."** In the Middle Ages, craftsmen gathered according to their trade, and streets were named for the craft found there. If you needed a hat, you knew where to find one.

BRATISLAVA

• *Continue two blocks straight ahead to a square on your right, fronted by a fine two-story Neoclassical market hall.*

❻ Old Market Hall (Stará Tržnica)

Built in 1910, today this busy community center hosts concerts and a Saturday market. The market hall square is a lively gathering place, too; see details on its monthly food-truck festivals under "Eating in Bratislava," later.

On the right side of the square is a stark 12-story building—the tallest in town before WWII. If it looks barren, that was the point. It's from the Bauhaus school—all the rage among German architects between the world wars. The battle cry for these harbingers of modernity: "Form follows function," "less is more," and "luxury does not require ornamentation." Today, its ground floor is home to a dingy bingo parlor (visitors welcome).

The bombs of World War II mostly spared the old town but pulverized a nearby oil refinery and dynamite plant—targeted by Allies because they were a key part of the occupying Nazi war economy. But a few bombs went awry and hit the area just uphill from here, which accounts for all the post-1945 buildings. The concrete jungle beyond the tram tracks is modernist architecture of the 1960s communist era.

• *Find a door just to the left of the Old Market Hall facade marked* Centrál Pasáž *(press buzzer if closed). It leads you through a 1920s Art Deco shopping gallery (cutting-edge a century ago) to a busy pedestrian boulevard.*

❼ Laurinská Street—Bratislava's Fashion Drag

This street is lined with fun-to-browse boutiques. In the little nook where the street bends (just to the left) are three popular, very Slovak shops: **Slowatch** (upstairs in the Buffet store), with casual clothes and bags; **Slávica,** a high-end design shop with jewelry and accessories; and **Kompot,** selling a fun variety of unique, Slovak-themed T-shirts. This is a good spot to browse for a quality, non-kitschy souvenir.

Across from where you entered the street is the chillingly blocky facade of the communist-era **City Theater** (Mestské Divadlo). On the upper floor are Socialist Realist stained-glass windows—hard to see during the day, but illuminated at night, like a communist night light. We'll see the much fancier National Theater in a moment.

Turn right on Laurinská and notice the Bratislava city seal hanging above you (a three-towered castle with a gate half-open). Stroll like a local for three long blocks, people-watching and window-shopping at more high-end shops.

• *Look out, or you might stumble over a bronze fellow peeking out of a manhole.*

❽ Čumil ("The Peeper")

Čumil was the first—and is still the favorite—of the many whimsical statues that dot Bratislava's old town (such as Schöner Náci,

whom we met earlier). Most date from the late 1990s, when city leaders wanted to entice locals back into the newly prettied-up and fun-loving center. There's no story behind this one; the artist simply wanted to create a playful icon and let the townspeople make up their own tales. Čumil has survived being driven over

by a truck—twice—and he's still grinning.

• *Turn left at the man in the manhole and follow Rybárska to reach the long, skinny square called...*

❾ Promenade Square (Hviezdoslavovo Námestie)

At the near end of this square is Bratislava's impressive opera house, the silver-topped **Slovak National Theater** (Slovenské Národné

Divadlo). When the theater opened in the 1880s, half the shows were in German and half in Hungarian. Today, the official language is Slovak. Across the way, the opulent, beige Neo-Baroque building is home to the Slovak Philharmonic (Slovenská Filharmónia).

Right in front of the opera house, look down into the round, glass **display case** to see the foundation of the one-time Fishermen's Gate into the city. Water surrounds the base of the gate: This entire square was once a tributary of the Danube, and the Radisson Blu Carlton Hotel (long the VIP hotel in town) across the way was once a series of inns on different islands. The buildings along the old town side of the square mark where the city wall once stood. Now the square is a lively zone on balmy evenings, with several good restaurants offering al fresco tables jammed with happy diners.

Turn right and stroll down the long square. Underfoot is a gigantic, cobbled version of Bratislava's city seal. After passing a

BRATISLAVA

City of Three Cultures: Pressburg, Pozsony, Bratislava

Historically more of an Austrian and Hungarian city than a Slovak one, Bratislava has always been a Central European melting pot.

Over the years, notable visitors from Hans Christian Andersen to Casanova have sung the praises of this bustling burg on the Danube.

For most of its history, Bratislava was part of the Austrian Empire and known as Pressburg, with a primarily German-speaking population. (Only the surrounding rural areas were Slovak.) The Hungarians used Pozsony (as they called it) as their capital during the 150 years that Buda and Pest were occupied by Ottoman invaders.

By its turn-of-the-20th-century glory days, the city was a rich intersection of cultures—about 40 percent German, 40 percent Hungarian, and 20 percent Slovak. Shop clerks greeted customers in all three languages. It was said that the mornings belonged to the Slovaks (farmers who came into the city to sell their wares at market), the afternoons to the Hungarians (diplomats and office workers filling the cafés), and the evenings to the Austrians (wine producers who ran convivial neighborhood wine pubs where all three groups would gather). In those wine pubs, the vintner would listen to which language his customers used, then bring them a glass with the serving size expected in their home country: 0.3 liters for Hungarians, 0.25 liters for Austrians, and 0.2 liters for Slovaks (a distinction that still exists today). Jews (one-tenth of the population) and Roma (then called Gypsies) rounded out the city's ethnic brew.

statue of the square's namesake (Pavol Országh Hviezdoslav, a beloved Slovak poet), look for an ugly fence and barriers on the left. As usual, the US Embassy is the most heavily fortified building in the capital.

Just past the embassy is the low-profile entrance to the **Sky Bar,** an affordable rooftop restaurant with excellent views (ride the elevator to the seventh floor). The glass-roofed pavilion in the center of the square is a popular venue for summer concerts. Behind it, on the old-town side of the square, is **Luculus,** where people are likely lined up outside for ice cream. (For ice cream without a lineup, you can backtrack to **Koun Gelato**—just before the US Embassy and immediately to the right of the Carlton Hotel.) On

When the new nation of Czechoslovakia was formed from the rubble of World War I, the city shed its German and Hungarian names and took the newly created Slavic name of Bratislava. The Slovak population was on the rise, but the city remained tricultural.

World War II changed all of that. With the dissolution of Czechoslovakia, Slovakia became an "independent" country under the thumb of the Nazis—who all but wiped out the Jewish population. At the end of the war, Czechoslovakia reunited under the USSR and expelled the city's ethnic Germans and Hungarians in retribution for the misdeeds of Hitler and Horthy (Hungary's wartime leader).

Bratislava's urban heritage suffered terribly under the communists. The historic city's multilayered charm and delicate cultural fabric were ripped apart, then shrouded in gray. The communists were prouder of their ultramodern SNP Bridge than of the city's historic Jewish quarter—which they razed to make way for the bridge. Now the bridge and its highway slice through the center of the old town, and heavy traffic rattles the stained-glass windows of St. Martin's Cathedral. The city's Germanic heritage was also deliberately obscured.

But Bratislava's most recent chapter is one of great success. Since the fall of communism, the city has gone from gloomy victim to thriving economic center and social hub. With a healthy free market economy, it now has the chance to re-create itself as Slovakia's national capital. And its advantageous position on the Danube, a short commute from Vienna, is prompting its redevelopment as one of Europe's up-and-coming cities. Once again, the streets of Bratislava are filled with German- and Hungarian-speakers...tourists and business travelers from nearby Vienna and Budapest.

BRATISLAVA

the right near the end of the park, a statue of **Hans Christian Andersen** is a reminder that the Danish storyteller enjoyed his visit to Bratislava, too.

• *Reaching the end of the square, you run into the barrier for a busy highway. Turn right and walk one block to find the big, black marble slab facing a modern monument.*

❿ Holocaust Memorial

This was the site of Bratislava's original synagogue. You can see an etching of the building in the big slab. At the base of the memorial sculpture, look for the word "Remember" carved into the granite in Hebrew and Slovak, commemorating the 70,000 Slovak Jews who were murdered during the Holocaust (out of a total population of 90,000 Slovak Jews). The fact that the town's main synagogue and main church (described next) were located side by side illustrates the tolerance that characterized Bratislava before Hitler. Ponder the modern statue: the open doors of an evacuated home with shadows of people who once lived there, all crowned with bullet holes and the Star of David. It evokes the fate of the tens of thousands of Slovak Jews who died in the Holocaust.

Hike up the stairs to the adjacent church. At the top of the stairs, pause to appreciate the view. Looking toward the river, you can't miss the huge **SNP Bridge** (Most SNP), the communists' pride and joy. The "SNP" is shorthand for the 1944 Slovak National Uprising against the Nazis, a common focus of communist remembrance. As with most Soviet-era landmarks in former communist countries, locals aren't crazy about this structure—not only for the questionable Starship *Enterprise* design, but also because of the oppressive regime it represented. However, the restaurant and observation deck up top have been renovated into a posh eatery called (appropriately enough) "UFO." You can visit it for the views, a drink, or a full meal. (For details, see the listing, later.)

The bridge was a groundbreaking design in 1972, but the freeway that runs across it messed up the city. If the highway thundering a few feet in front of this historic church's door were any closer, the off-ramp would go through the nave. In the next decade, the plan is to move the highway into a tunnel that will emerge at the bridge—returning peace to this corner of Bratislava.

• *Now turn your attention to the church towering overhead.*

⓫ St. Martin's Cathedral (Dóm Sv. Martina)

Nineteen Hungarian kings and queens were crowned in this church—more than anywhere else in Hungary. A replica of the Hungarian crown still tops the steeple. There's relatively little to see inside the cathedral, but if it's open, duck in (Mon-Sat 9:00-11:30 & 13:00-18:00, Sun 13:45-16:30). In the fairly gloomy interior you'll find some fine carved-wood altarpieces (a Slovak specialty).

Just beyond the church is a stretch of the 15th-century **town wall.** The church was actually built into the wall, which explains its unusual north-side entry. In fact, look up to notice the fortified watchtower built into the corner of the church just above you.

• *Our walk is over. From here you could either hike up to the* **castle** *(backtracking to the Holocaust Memorial, take the*

underpass beneath the high-way, go up the stairs on the right marked by the Hrad/ Castle *sign, then turn left up the stepped lane marked* Zámocké Schody), *hike over the SNP Bridge (pedestrian walkway on lower level) to ride the elevator up the* **UFO viewing platform**, *or head for the river and stroll downstream to the thriving and futuristic new Bratislava—***Eurovea** *(all of these are described under "Sights in Bratislava," later).*

Or you could carry on as described next to end up back where you started...

Back to St. Michael's Gate

Continue the rest of the way around the church and take the grand stony staircase back down to busy Panská street. Turn left and follow Panská to the corner with Ventúrska. The **old fountain** here marks the actual cross point of the two great medieval trade routes (north-south from the Baltics to the Mediterranean, and east-west along the Danube). Head left, uphill (or north toward the Baltics, if you're an amber merchant) toward St. Michael's Gate.

Over the next few blocks, you may see the names of great **composers** on plaques marking historical buildings. Franz Liszt performed in Bratislava at age nine for local aristocrats and was discovered and sent to Vienna. Beethoven composed his *Moonlight Sonata* here. Mozart performed here at age six. Haydn conducted the orchestra here, and in the 20th century Béla Bartók called Bratislava home.

If you feel like a cup of tea along the way—or you're nervous about a nuclear attack—climb through the thick iron door at #9 on the left (a long block after the fountain) and down into **Čajovňa V Podzemí** ("The Underground Tea Room," Mon-Fri 11:00-22:00, Sat-Sun from 14:00), which fills an old bomb shelter with pillows, incense, and herby frills. A couple more blocks takes you back to where you started this walk.

Sights in Bratislava

Although Bratislava's museums are underwhelming—and you could easily have a great day here without visiting any—a few right in the old town are worth considering.

ON OR NEAR THE OLD TOWN'S MAIN SQUARE
▲Primate's Palace (Primaciálny Palác)

This tastefully restored French-Neoclassical mansion (formerly the residence of the archbishop, or "primate") dates from 1781. The re-ligious counterpart of the castle, it filled in for Esztergom—the Hungarian religious capital—after that city was taken by the Ottomans in 1543. Even after the Ottoman defeat in the 1680s, this remained the winter residence of Hungary's arch-bishops. In the courtyard gur-gles a fountain with St. George slaying a three-headed dragon; the exhibits are upstairs.

Cost and Hours: €3, Tue-Sun 10:00-17:00, closed Mon, Pri-maciálne Námestie 2, +421 2 5935 6394, www.visitbratislava.com.

Visiting the Museum: The palace, which now serves as the town hall, offers one fine floor of exhibits. Follow signs up the grand staircase to the ticket counter, then proceed up one more flight to the entrance lobby. From here, the Hall of Mirrors is on your left, straight ahead leads you to a series of state apartments decorated with precious tapestries (on the right), and at the far end is a long picture gallery leading to the chapel.

Portraits hang in the lobby of the German-speaking royals who ruled Hungary, which ruled the Slovaks, who lived in this part of the vast Habsburg empire...history here is like a set of Russian stacking dolls. You'll see not one but two portraits of Habsburg empress Maria Theresa—young and old—as well as her father, Charles VI; and her son, Josef II. While Hungary was under Ot-toman occupation, these Habsburg emperors came to Bratislava to also be crowned "kings of Hungary."

Hall of Mirrors: This is perhaps the most historic room in the city. In 1805, the "Peace of Pressburg" treaty was signed here, sort-ing out logistics after Napoleon beat the Austrians and Russians at the Battle of Austerlitz. This victory marked the peak of Napoleon's power. Today, the hall is used for concerts, city council meetings, and other important events. On the wall in the antechamber is a list of Bratislava's mayors since the 1280s.

State Rooms and Tapestries: This series of large public rooms, originally designed to impress, is now an art gallery. Distributed through several of these rooms is the museum's pride, and for many its highlight: a series of six English tapestries illustrating the ancient Greek myth of the tragic love between Hero and Leander.

The tapestries were woven in England by Flemish weavers for the court of King Charles I (in the 1630s). They were kept in London's Hampton Court Palace until Charles was deposed and beheaded in 1649. Cromwell sold them to France to help fund his civil war, but after 1650, they disappeared...for centuries. In 1903, restorers broke through a false wall in this mansion and discovered the six tapestries, neatly folded and perfectly preserved. Nobody knows how they got here (perhaps they were squirreled away during the Napoleonic invasion, and whoever hid them didn't survive). The archbishop—who had just sold the palace to the city—cried foul and tried to claim the tapestries (valued at triple the sales price of the entire palace), but the city said, "A deal's a deal."

Picture Gallery and Chapel: After traipsing through the grand rooms, go to the end of the main corridor and turn left down the hallway. This leads through the smaller rooms of the archbishop's private quarters, which are now a picture gallery decorated with minor Dutch, Flemish, German, and Italian paintings. At the end of this hall, a bay window looks down into the archbishop's private chapel. When the archbishop became too ill to walk down to Mass, this window was built so he could take part in the service in his pajamas.

▲City History Museum (Mestské Múzeum)

Delving thoughtfully into Bratislava's past, this museum is rich in artifacts and well described in English and by the included audioguide. The core of the museum offers a sprawling, chronological look at local history through the 1920s, on two floors. The first floor features ecclesiastical art, including wood-carved statues. Upstairs, you'll have a chance to climb up into the Old Town Hall's tower, offering so-so views over the square, cathedral, and castle. Then you'll see more exhibits in rooms once used by the town council—courthouse, council hall, chapel, and so on. This is a fascinating look at Habsburg rule and slice-of-life Bratislava in the early 20th century. Look for the model of "Pressburg" during the age of Maria Theresa. Farther along, trilingual street signs are a reminder that, historically, this was a city of three cultures and three languages (Slovak, German, Hungarian). The finale is down in the cellar: a graphic torture exhibit in the "law and order" zone, with replicas of torture equipment from the 16th through 18th century. At the far end of the exhibit, crouch down the passage to see three dreary and depressing cells...enough to make anybody behave.

Cost and Hours: €7, includes excellent audioguide, €8 com-

BRATISLAVA

bo-ticket with Apponyi House; open Tue-Sun 10:00-18:00, closed Mon; in the Old Town Hall—enter through courtyard, +421 2 259 100 812, https://muzeumbratislava.sk.

Apponyi House (Apponyiho Palác)

This nicely restored mansion of a Hungarian aristocrat is meaningless without the included audioguide (dull but informative). The museum has two parts. The cellar and ground floor feature an interesting exhibit on the vineyards of the nearby "Small Carpathian" hills, with historic presses and barrels and a replica of an old-time wine-pub table. (If this exhibit interests you, consider a stop at the Slovak National Collection of Wine, also at Apponyi House and listed next.) Upstairs are two floors of urban apartments from old Bratislava, called the Museum of Period Rooms. The first floor up shows off the 18th-century Rococo-style rooms of the nobility—fine but not ostentatious, with ceramic stoves. The second floor up (with lower ceilings and simpler decor) illustrates 19th-century bourgeois/middle-class lifestyles, including period clothing and some Empire-style furniture.

Cost and Hours: €5, includes audioguide, €8 combo-ticket with City History Museum; Tue-Sun 10:00-18:00, closed Mon; Radničná 1, +421 2 5910 0856, https://muzeumbratislava.sk.

Slovak National Collection of Wine

Run by the union of Slovak vintners, this room at the Apponyi House showcases the region's wines, 80 percent of which are white. Filling a 16th-century brick-vaulted wine cellar, it features 100 Slovak wines that are open and eager to be tasted. Pick up the degustation list and track down what you like. An English-speaking sommelier is at your service.

Cost and Hours: Small tastings with explanations are an option, but for €30 you can taste up to 72 wines in 100 minutes...do this at the end of your sightseeing day (Tue-Fri 10:00-19:00, Sat from 11:00, closed Sun-Mon, Radničná 1, +421 2 4552 9967, www.salonvin.sk).

▲Nedbalka Gallery of Slovak Modern Art

This sleek, modern gallery is owned by a local tech millionaire and run as a private nonprofit. Ride the elevator to the top floor and work chronologically through the permanent collection of 20th-century Slovak art on four delightful floors. The ground floor is dedicated to temporary exhibits. You'll notice glass is big in Slovakia (Chihuly is a Czech name, and Dale is well known and celebrated here). Admission includes a tablet multimedia guide and a nice coffee in the café.

Cost and Hours: €5, Tue-Sun 13:00-19:00, closed Mon, next to the Old Market Hall at Nedbalova 17, +421 2 2076 6031, www.nedbalka.sk.

BEYOND THE OLD TOWN
Bratislava Castle and Museum (Bratislavský Hrad a Múzeum)

The imposing Bratislava Castle, crowning Bratislava's hill, is the city's most prominent landmark. Big and iconic as it is, it's frankly

dull up close—and the exhibits inside, although expanding, are not too exciting. Still, it's almost obligatory to head up here simply for the grand views over Bratislava and the Danube... though, if the weather's bad, you'd be forgiven for skipping it.

Cost and Hours: Castle grounds—free, museum—€12; Wed-Mon 10:00-18:00, Nov-March 9:00-17:00, closed Tue year-round, last entry one hour before closing; +421 2 2048 3104, www.snm.sk.

Getting There: For the best walking route to the castle, see the end of the "Bratislava Old Town Walk," earlier in this chapter.

Background: When Habsburg empress Maria Theresa took a liking to Bratislava in the 18th century, she transformed the castle from a military fortress to a royal residence suitable for holding court. She added a summer riding school (the U-shaped complex next to the castle), an enclosed winter riding school out back, and lots more. Maria Theresa's favorite daughter, Maria Christina, lived

here with her husband, Albert, when they were newlyweds. Locals nicknamed the place "little Schönbrunn," in reference to the Habsburgs' summer palace on the outskirts of Vienna.

The palace became a fortress-garrison during the Napoleonic Wars, then burned to the ground in an 1811 fire started by careless soldiers, and was left as a ruin for 150 years. An extensive rebuild, based on the original plans discovered in the Habsburg archives in 2008, has breathed new life into the castle (which is surrounded by a delightful public park).

Visiting the Castle: The best part of a visit here is the **grand view balcony** in front, overlooking the Danube, the Petržalka suburb across the river (marked by the SNP Bridge—described next), and—just below and upstream—the nondescript, boxy, white office building that houses the Slovak parliament. The castle is surrounded by gardens that are enjoyable on a nice day.

The dynamic statue in front of the castle's main entrance—with a knight waving his sword, rearing up on horseback—honors **Svätopluk** (846–894), the warrior-king who ruled over Great Moravia. His reign was the Slovaks' historical high-water mark, when its territory included parts of the present-day Czech Republic, Austria, Germany, Poland, Bulgaria, Romania, Serbia, Croatia, and Slovenia. Unfortunately, this dominance was short-lived; in the early 10th century, soon after Svätopluk's death, his kingdom was invaded by Magyars and folded into what became the Kingdom of Hungary—which Slovak lands would remain a part of for a thousand years. "Slovakia" has existed as a sovereign nation only since 1993; before that, you have to go all the way back to Svätopluk.

The castle **interior** features some interactive exhibits and an opportunity to climb its tallest tower. Inside, you'll pass through a modest exhibit about the restoration of the castle, then make your way up the grand, red-carpeted staircase to several floors of exhibits. On the third floor is a café (tucked amid a fun exhibit of nostalgic advertisements) and the "History of Slovakia" exhibit, which begins with the prehistoric Celts, tracks the arrival of the Slavs, and ends with the fall of Great Moravia after Svätopluk's time. Also on this floor, you can climb 87 steep, vertigo-inducing stairs to the top of the Crown Tower—the tallest part of the castle—for views over the city and the Danube basin (though the views from up top are not that much better than from down below).

▲▲SNP Bridge and UFO

Bratislava's flying-saucer-capped bridge, completed in 1972 in heavy-handed communist style, has been reclaimed by capital-

ists. The saucer-shaped structure called the UFO (at the Petržalka end of the bridge) is now a spruced-up café/restaurant and observation deck, allowing sweeping 360-degree views of Bratislava from about 300 feet above the Danube.

Cost and Hours: €9.90, for €3 more you can return for the view after dark, elevator free if you have a meal reservation or order food at the pricey restaurant; elevator open daily 10:00-23:00, restaurant opens at 12:00; +421 2 6252 0300, www.u-f-o.sk.

Getting There: Walk across the bridge from the old town (walkways cross the bridge on a level below the road; the elevator entrance is a few steps down from the downstream-side walkway).

Visiting the UFO: The **"elevator"** that takes you up is actually a funicular—you may notice you're moving at an angle. At the top, walk up the stairs to the observation deck, passing photos of the bridge's construction.

Begin by viewing the **castle** and **old town.** The area to the right of the old town, between and beyond the skyscrapers, is a massive construction zone where the new Bratislava is taking shape.

The huge TV tower caps a forested hill beyond the old town. Below and to the left of it, the pointy monument is **Slavín,** where more than 6,800 Soviet soldiers who fought to liberate Bratislava from the Nazis are buried. Under communist rule, a nearby church was forced to take down its steeple so as not to draw attention away from the huge Soviet soldier on top of the monument.

Now turn 180 degrees and cross the platform to face **Petržalka,** a planned communist suburb that sprouted here in the 1970s. The site was once occupied by a village, and the various districts of modern Petržalka still carry their original names (which now seem ironic): "Meadows" *(Háje),* "Woods" *(Lúky),* and "Courtyards" *(Dvory).* The ambitious communist planners envisioned a city laced with Venetian-style canals to help drain the marshy land, but the plans were abandoned after the harsh crackdown on the 1968 Prague Spring uprising. Without the incentives of private ownership, all they succeeded in creating was a grim, decaying sea of miserable concrete apartment *paneláky* ("panel buildings," so-called because they're made of huge prefab panels).

Today, one in six Bratislavans lives in Petržalka, and things are looking better. Like Dorothy opening the door to Oz, the formerly drab buildings have been splashed with bright new colors, and the interiors have been modernized. Far from being a slum, Petržalka is now a popular neighborhood for Bratislavan yuppies who can't yet afford to build their dream houses.

Petržalka is also a big suburban-style shopping zone (note the supermall down below). But there's still some history here. The **park** called Sad Janka Kráľa (originally, in German, Aupark)—just downriver from the bridge—was technically the first public park in Europe in the 1770s and is still a popular place for locals to relax and court.

BRATISLAVA

Scanning the **horizon** beyond Petržalka, two things stick out: on the left, the old communist oil refinery (which has been fully updated and is now state of the art); and on the right, a forest of modern windmills. These are just over the border, in Austria...and Bratislava is sure to grow in that direction quickly. Austria is about three miles that way, and Hungary is about six miles farther to the left.

Before you leave, consider a drink at the café. If nothing else, be sure to use the memorable WCs.

Blue Church of St. Elisabeth (Kostol Svätej Alžbety)

Just east of the old town—through a nicely manicured new park— is a lovely little neighborhood of cheery, colorful Art Nouveau buildings. The main landmark here is the gentle-blue, fancifully decorated Church of St. Elisabeth—also called simply the "Little Blue Church." It's straight out of a fairy tale, with rounded edges, pretty flourishes, and vivid colors. Designed by the great Hungarian Secessionist architect Ödön Lechner and completed in 1913, it's worth the short walk from the old town for architecture fans. While the public open hours are limited, you can often peek through the glass doors to see the similarly soft and pretty interior (Bezručova 2).

▲Eurovea and the New Bratislava

Just downstream from the old town is the modern Eurovea com-

plex, with four layers, each a quarter-mile long: a riverside park, luxury condos, a thriving modern shopping mall, and an office park. While it's essentially a big riverfront shopping mall, those looking for a peek at the "new Bratislava" find it worth the lovely, short riverfront stroll from the old town...which is also a chance to check out all the moored riverboats.

Eurovea's central public space is a fountain- and statue-filled people zone between the Danube and Bratislava's new National Theater. Directly in front of the theater, the pavement is pulled back to show original Roman paving stones that were excavated here (a reminder of the city's long history as a trade crossroads). At the river end of the square, under the lion-topped pillar, a statue features General Milan Rastislav Štefánik, who represented Slovakia in a 1918 meeting in Pittsburgh and signed the "Pittsburgh Agreement"—creating the combined state of Česko-Slovensko. He's holding a bronze copy of the document as he looks out at the Danube.

The riverfront strip of Eurovea is the embryo of a huge vision for a new Bratislava. Dozens of skyscrapers are being built at once, as the city's old industrial zone (destroyed in World War II and now destined to be the city's future tech-industry home) is one big construction site.

Exploring the old town gives you a taste of where this country has been. But wandering this riverside park, enjoying a drink in one of its chic outdoor lounges, and then browsing the thriving mall, you'll enjoy a glimpse of where Slovakia is heading.

Sleeping in Bratislava

For locations, see the "Bratislava" map, earlier. Bratislava's hotels are similar in price range to Vienna (see page 954).

$$ Marrol's Boutique Hotel, on a quiet urban street, is the town's most enticing option. Although the immediate neighborhood isn't interesting, it's just a five-minute walk from the old town, the public spaces are plush and luxurious, and its 54 rooms are tastefully appointed Old World country-style (air-con, elevator, gorgeous lounge and nice garden terrace, Tobrucká 4, +421 2 5778 4600, www.hotelmarrols.sk, rec@hotelmarrols.sk).

$$ Roset Hotel & Residence, facing the ring road's tram tracks at the eastern edge of the old town (with some street noise), feels classy and upmarket. Its 26 rooms are spacious and plush (air-con, elevator, Štúrova 10, +421 917 373 209, www.rosethotel.sk, reservations@rosethotel.sk).

$$ Radisson Blu Carlton Hotel has been hosting VIPs for decades, with 170 rooms and all the big corporate trappings and expected services. It's perfectly located, facing the National Theater and Promenade Square (air-con, elevator, Hviezdoslavovo Námestie 3, +421 2 5939 0000, www.radissonblu.com/hotel-bratislava, reservation.bratislava@radissonblu.com).

$$ Loft Hotel is an appealing midrange choice, tucked along

BRATISLAVA

the highway between the main train station and the old town (ask for a quieter back room facing the garden). It's professional, stylish, and trendy—with comfy leather couches in the lobby, an on-site brewpub, and a staff that prides itself on its service. Of the 121 rooms, the "standard" rooms are fine; consider paying a bit more for a cushier, retro-industrial "premiere" room (air-con, elevator, coffee machine in rooms, Štefánikova 4, +421 2 5751 1000, www.lofthotel.sk, reservation@lofthotel.sk). They also have 10 more expensive, high-end rooms and apartments in the attached **Wilson Palace**, in the original building facing the main road.

$$ Beigli Hotel & Garden is a tight little hotel with a peaceful back garden tucked just inside St. Michael's Gate in the old town. The 14 rooms are modern and comfortable, and the location—on a picturesque lane—is ideal. Locals love this spot for celebrating a special occasion (air-con, elevator, Baštová 4, +421 910 749 242, www.hotelbeigli.sk, office@hotelbeigli.sk).

$$ Garni Hotel Virgo, on a quiet residential street an eight-minute walk from the old town, rents 12 boutique-ish rooms (breakfast extra, reserve ahead for parking, Panenská 14, reception located at Panenská 5, +421 948 350 878, info@apartvirgo.sk). They also have some apartments in a nearby hotel.

Eating in Bratislava

Slovak cooking involves some Hungarian and Austrian influences, but it's closer to Czech cuisine—lots of starches and gravy, and plenty of pork, cabbage, pota-toes, and dumplings. Keep an eye out for Slovakia's intensely filling national dish, *bryndzové halušky* (small potato dumplings with sheep's cheese and bits of bacon). For a fun drink and snack that locals love, try a Vinea grape soda and a sweet, crescent-shaped *Pressburger* bagel in any bar or café.

Like the Czechs, the Slovaks produce excellent beer (*pivo*, PEE-voh). The dominant brand is Zlatý Bažant ("Golden Pheasant"). Bratislava's beer halls are good places to sample Slovak beers—whether macrobrews or microbrews—and to get a hearty, affordable meal of stick-to-your-ribs pub grub. The Bratislava region also produces wines, similar to the ones that Vienna is known for. But, as nearly all is consumed locally, most outsiders don't think of Slovakia as wine country.

Bratislava is packed with inviting new eateries. In addition to heavy Slovak staples, you'll find trendy new bars and bistros and a smattering of non-European offerings. The best plan may be to stroll the old town and keep your eyes open for the setting and cuisine that appeals to you most. Or consider the areas listed next. All are within a short walk and offer a better, more interesting dining experience than the grotesquely touristy eateries that line Michalská street and other busy streets in the old town. For locations, see the "Bratislava" map, earlier.

Traditional Beer Hall on Námestie SNP

A couple of blocks north of the old town (and named for the Slovak National Uprising), the right side of this square is dominated by the following operation:

$$ **Bratislavská Flagship Restaurant** is a sprawling complex of eateries. The main location (door on the right) is the Bratislavská Reštaurácia. Walk through a maze of old-timey rooms, then up a flight of stairs to a huge dining hall that smells hoppy and feels happy (with the waitstaff sporting "Bar-tislava" and "Bra-tislava" T-shirts). The menu features classic Slovak dishes, and the portions are hearty and cheap. For a more intimate setting, the door to the left leads to the tight, woody Kláštorný Pivovar ("Monastery Brewery"), with a cozier ambience and the same menu. They also have tables outside on the square (daily, Námestie SNP 8, +421 917 927 673).

Near the Old Market Hall

While there's often nothing actually inside the Old Market Hall (which fills a city block at the eastern edge of the old town, a five-minute walk from the main square), it's surrounded by intriguing and trendy options. Once a month, the square in front features a "Street Food Park" with a wide variety of food trucks (worth planning around—check schedule at www.staratrznica.sk). At other times, walk around the block to survey your options (listed in order, from the front door).

$ **Výčap u Ernőho** is a popular, no-frills beer hall with a row of taps up front featuring a changing selection of quality beers. If you'd like to enjoy Slovak beers with local hipsters instead of the sloppy beer-hall tourist crowd, do it here (no food, Sun-Fri 16:00-24:00, Sat from 12:00, Námestie SNP 25, +421 948 360 153).

$ **Foodstock** is an enticing, hip, and healthy vegetarian place that advertises "good mood food." It got its start as a food truck and now serves up a brief menu of delicious Asian-inspired dishes (including their popular gyoza) and all-you-can-drink homemade iced teas in a patchouli-scented space (daily, Klobučnícka 6, +421 905 456 654).

$$ **Mecheche Snack Bar** serves tiny, fancy sandwiches as

if channeling a Barcelona tapas bar (Tue-Sat 17:00-24:00, closed Sun-Mon, Nedbalova 12, +421 948 853 444).

$$ Urban House, behind the Old Market Hall on fashionable Laurinská street, is California-trendy with a sprawling, industrial-mod, woody-bookstore ambience; great outdoor tables; and an appealing menu. The food (burgers, pizza, and so on) is nothing special, but the scene is fun (long hours daily, Laurinská 14, +421 911 755 205).

Restaurants on Promenade Square (Hviezdoslavovo Námestie)

This square is lined with restaurants, nearly all with open-feeling interior seating and mellow tables out on the square under the trees—ideal for enjoying the promenade of strollers. There's no traffic, just the sound of fountains and the breeze. A strip of three places, side by side, makes for easy comparison-shopping; for a view, head up to Sky Bar.

$$$ Carnevalle is a hit for its steak. Their greeting? "Nice to meat you!" Their indoors feels outdoors—a spacious, glassed-in dining hall—and their tables on the square are inviting. The tasty dishes are nicely presented by a professional waitstaff (daily until late, at #20, +421 903 123 164).

$$$ Zylinder ("Top Hat") re-creates a circa-1900 atmosphere to serve classy bourgeoise cuisine that leans closer to Austrian than traditional Slovak—think sausages and schnitzels (long hours daily, at #19, +421 903 123 134).

$ Café Verne, university-owned and unburdened by the high rent of its neighbors, feels like the dive bar of the strip—with mismatched antique tables spilling out onto the cobbles. It has a cozy, lowbrow, and mellow student vibe with stick-to-your-rib plates (pasta, goulash, salads) and drinks. You get what you pay for, but the price is right (long hours daily, at #18, +421 2 5443 0514).

Rooftop View: $$$$ Sky Bar Restaurant, just past the fenced-in US Embassy, features a Thai-meets-Mediterranean menu on its seventh-floor open-roof terrace. It's a pretentious place, with local big shots dropping by and stuffy service. But the food's good, and so are the views. It's smart to reserve a view table in advance to dine here—or just drop by for a pricey vodka cocktail (Tue-Sat 17:00-24:00, closed Sun-Mon, Hviezdoslavovo Námestie 7, +421 948 109 400, www.skybar.sk).

Eurovea

This modern development facing the Danube River (a short walk downstream from the old town) has huge outdoor terraces rollicking with happy eaters. A variety of upscale and high-energy **$$-$$$ restaurants** lines the swanky riverfront residential and shopping-mall complex. Options include international—French, Italian, Brazilian—as well as branches of the Czech beer-hall chain **Kolkovna** and the British pan-Asian restaurant **Wagamama**. Or head to the **$ food court** in the shopping mall, where you'll eat cheap. While the restaurants here are nothing special, it's a fun excuse for a stroll along the Danube promenade, and to get a peek at the emerging "new Bratislava" zone beyond the old-town cobbles.

Bratislava Connections

BY TRAIN

Bratislava has two major train stations: the main station, walkable to some accommodations and the old town (Hlavná Stanica, abbreviated "Bratislava hl. st." on schedules); and Petržalka station, in a suburb across the river and linked to town by bus. When checking schedules, pay attention to which station your train uses. Frequent bus #93 connects the two stations in about 10 minutes. For public transit info and maps, see http://imhd.sk.

Hlavná Stanica (Main Train Station)

This decrepit station is about a half-mile north of the old town. A left-luggage desk is to your right as you exit the tracks (*úschovňa batožín;* confirm open hours for pickup). There are also a few lockers along track 1; more are to the left from the main hall (after the vending machines and through the door). The station also has a TI window, and there's an ATM in the main hall. A nicer, more modern waiting area is down the hallway to the left (with the tracks at your back).

Getting Downtown: It's a short bus ride or a boring 15-minute walk to the town center. (**Taxis** stand by, but with rip-off prices—they'll try to charge €15 rather than the legitimate €5 drop charge for the short ride. You can try insisting on the meter, but since they're basically unregulated, it likely won't help.)

Bus #93 leaves every five minutes from the right-hand curb 50 yards in front of the station; it stops at Grassalkovich Palace, Zochova (nearest the old town), and Most SNP (the bus station under the SNP Bridge, by the river). Buy a 30-minute *základný lístok/basic* ticket from the machine for €0.90 and stamp it as you get on the bus.

To **walk** downtown, exit out the station's front door and follow the covered walkway past the bus stops. After the road bends right, take the pedestrian overpass, then head straight downhill on the busy main drag, Štefánikova. You'll pass the presidential gardens, then Grassalkovich Palace, Slovakia's "White House." The old town—marked by the green steeple of St. Michael's Gate (the start of my self-guided walk)—is a long block ahead of you.

Petržalka Train Station (ŽST Petržalka)

The main hall has an ATM and luggage lockers (by the door to the tracks).

Getting Downtown: Two different buses head to the old town from opposite sides of the station. For either bus, buy a 15-minute *základný lístok/basic* ticket from the machine for €0.90 and stamp it as you board. The stop closest to the old town is Zochova. **Bus #80** stops closest to the station but makes more stops on the way to town: From the main hall, turn right to find the stop (direction: Kollárovo nám). **Bus #93** is more direct but a longer walk from the station: Take the long tunnel under the tracks, exit on the other side, and follow the crosswalk straight across the busy highway to find the stop (direction: Hlavná Stanica).

Train Connections

From Bratislava by Train to: Budapest (6/day direct, 2.5 hours, most from main station), **Vienna** (2/hour, 1 hour; half from main station usually leaving hourly at :38, half from Petržalka usually leaving hourly at :15), **Sopron** (nearly hourly direct from Petržalka, 2.5 hours on RegionalExpress/REX), **Prague** (7/day direct, 4.5 hours, from main station). To reach other Hungarian destinations (including **Eger** and **Pécs**), it's generally easiest to change in Budapest.

BY BUS

Two companies run handy buses that connect Bratislava, Vienna, and the airports in each city for about €10: Flixbus (www.flixbus.com) and Slovak Lines/Postbus (+421 2 5542 2734, www.slovaklines.sk). You can book ahead online, or (if arriving at the airport) just take whichever connection is leaving first.

BY BOAT

Riverboats run on the Danube several times a day, connecting Bratislava to Vienna. Conveniently, these boats dock right in front of Bratislava's old town. While they are more expensive, less frequent, and slower than the train, some travelers enjoy getting out on the Danube. (Sail with your passport, as you'll be crossing a border.)

The fast **Twin City Liner** runs modern catamarans between Vienna's Schwedenplatz (where Vienna's town center hits the canal) and a dock at the edge of Bratislava's old town, along Fajnorovo Nábrežie (€31-36 each way, 3 or more/day, early April-Oct only, 1.5 hours; reservations smart, +43 1 904 8880, www.twincityliner.com).

BY PLANE

While Bratislava has a small airport (used mostly by discount airlines), the Vienna Airport is so close it's considered the local airport.

Bratislava Airport (Letisko Bratislava)

This airport (code: BTS, www.bts.aero) is six miles northeast of downtown Bratislava. Budget airline Ryanair has many flights here. Some airlines market it as "Vienna-Bratislava," thanks to its proximity to both capitals. It's compact and manageable, with all the usual amenities.

From the Airport to Downtown Bratislava: The airport has easy **public bus** connections to Bratislava's main train station (Hlavná Stanica, 1-hour ticket-€1.30, bus #61, 3-4/hour, 30 minutes). A **taxi** from the airport into central Bratislava should cost about €20.

To Budapest: Take the bus or taxi to Bratislava's main train station, then hop a train to Budapest.

To Vienna: You can take **Flixbus** (www.flixbus.com) or **Slovak Lines/Postbus** (www.slovaklines.sk) to the Erdberg stop on Vienna's U-3 subway line or the Hauptbahnhof (roughly €10, runs every 1-2 hours, 1.5 hours). A **taxi** from Bratislava Airport directly to Vienna costs €60-90 (depending on whether you use a cheaper Slovak or more expensive Austrian cab).

Vienna International Airport

This airport, 12 miles from downtown Vienna and 30 miles from downtown Bratislava, is well connected to both capitals (code: VIE, www.viennaairport.com). If you're heading straight to Bratislava, there's no need to go into Vienna from here. The easiest option is to take the Flixbus or Slovak Lines/Postbus bus described earlier. Check schedules on the airport website (under "Arrival & Parking") or ask the airport TI which bus is leaving first, then head straight out the door and hop on. After about 45 minutes, the bus stops in downtown Bratislava, then heads to the Bratislava airport.

BRATISLAVA

MORE CENTRAL & EASTERN EUROPE

MORE CENTRAL & EASTERN EUROPE

The preceding chapters cover what I consider to be, for most travelers, the core of Central Europe. But several neighboring lands—some of them on the cusp of "Central" and "Eastern" Europe—are also worth considering for a visit.

The next five chapters offer a brief, practical introduction to countries that lie just beyond the core of this book. Because this is designed to get you started—with candid advice about where to go and what you might do in each place—I've included only the most basic advice for logistics such as transportation, accommodations, and restaurants. These chapters are intended only as a first step—not the final word. In each one, I offer a quick overview, a rundown of practical country facts, some itinerary-planning advice, a few tips on the local cuisine and language, and a concise rundown of the best destinations (focusing on the attractions that are most deserving of your valuable time).

In the following pages, you'll find an overview of these destinations:

Croatia: Central Europe's Riviera is a natural add-on for travelers going to Slovenia—it's just down the road. For a quick taste of Croatia, you can dip into the northern Istrian Peninsula (which borders Slovenia) and enjoy one of Croatia's top seaside towns, Rovinj. Those taking the train between Budapest and Ljubljana will pass through Croatia's underrated capital, Zagreb, which is worth at least a few hours' exploration (or even a night or two). And if you have plenty of time, you can head south—via the waterfall wonderland of Plitvice Lakes National Park—to the Dalmatian Coast: Dubrovnik, Split, and the islands of Hvar and Korčula.

Bosnia-Herzegovina: Croatia wraps around this inviting country, with a dramatic landscape and a vibrant culture. I've focused on two top destinations: The small city of Mostar is an easy side trip from Croatia's Dalmatian Coast and offers an accessible and intriguing first look at Bosnia. With more time, it's rewarding to venture farther to the even more engaging capital, Sarajevo.

Montenegro: Just south of Croatia, Montenegro's glorious Bay of Kotor—with stunning scenery and characteristic seaside towns—is an easy side trip for those based in Dubrovnik. With more time, you could head up into the hills to see the historic capital, Cetinje.

Bulgaria: A cultural detour that's well worth taking, Bulgaria involves a long overland journey (through the rugged Balkan Peninsula) or a quick flight from the core Central European countries. From the mellow and user-friendly capital, Sofia, you can head for the fun and fascinating second city, Plovdiv; the dramatically set historic capital, Veliko Tarnovo; and a variety of countryside sights: remote and majestic Rila Monastery, the ancient artifacts and fragrant rose fields of the Thracian Plain, and mountain-capping monuments such as the bizarre communist-era conference hall called Buzludzha.

Romania: Romania is a big, crazy, fascinating, time-consuming destination—but for many, it's worth the effort. Romania borders Hungary, and parts are accessible on a long train ride or drive from Budapest. But given the long distances, it may be easier to fly into Bucharest (the capital) and continue from there. Bucharest deserves a quick look, but the main concentration of famous sights is a few hours north, in Transylvania. Choose a home-base town or two (the best options are Brașov—near castles, Sighișoara—near fortified churches, and Sibiu—best all-around town)...and then explore. If you're captivated by traditional folk life, you could take the long drive even farther north, to the rustic corner called Maramureș. With even more time, consider swinging through the northeastern region of Bucovina, famous for its vividly painted monasteries.

Additional Information: For some of these countries—Croatia, Bosnia-Herzegovina, and Montenegro—you can find complete coverage in my guidebook *Rick Steves Croatia & Slovenia*. For the others—Bulgaria and Romania—there are plenty of guidebooks and online resources available to fill in the gaps and advance your planning. Also, in Bulgaria and Romania, local guides are particularly affordable and worth hiring to make your trip-planning easier—I've recommended my favorites in each country.

CROATIA

Hrvatska

Sunny beaches, succulent seafood, and a taste of *la dolce vita*...in Central Europe?

With thousands of miles of inviting seafront, Croatia's coastline is Central Europe's Riviera. Holidaymakers love its pebbly beaches, predictably balmy summer weather, and dramatic mountains. Croatia is also historic. From ruined Roman arenas and Byzantine mosaics to Venetian bell towers, Habsburg villas, and even communist concrete, past rulers have left their mark. And for thoughtful travelers, a trip to Croatia comes with an opportunity to better understand Europe's most violent conflict since World War II: the breakup of Yugoslavia. All in all, Croatia offers something to everyone—there's good reason that it's one of Europe's hottest emerging destinations.

Where to Go: Croatia has more than 3,600 miles of coastline and more than a thousand islands. To be selective, zoom in on these three areas:

The **Dalmatian Coast,** a dramatic limestone coastline, features a bustling big city with the best ancient ruins in the country (Split), several alluring islands (most notably Korčula and Hvar), and Croatia's showcase city: romantic, walled Dubrovnik.

Istria, a wedge-shaped peninsula in northern Croatia, has rolling hills, wineries, truffles, charming hill towns, ancient ruins (in Pula), and the finest coastal town between Venice and Dubrovnik: Rovinj.

The **Croatian interior** boasts the country's surprisingly ap-

pealing capital, Zagreb, which lies near Hungary and Austria. And two hours south, deep in the countryside, is one of Europe's top natural wonders, Plitvice Lakes National Park.

For a quick visit of just a few days, focus on either the Dalmatian Coast (and possibly add in some Bosnia and Montenegro—covered in the next two chapters) or the sights in the north (Istria and the interior). With a week or more, you can hit the highlights of all three regions.

Seasonality: Croatia is the most seasonal destination in this book. July and August are the peak of peak—everything is jammed up with European vacationers, and prices are high. Late May, June, September, and early October are the best times to visit...it's cooler (but still warm) and less crowded. Off-season (after about mid-October, or before early May), while big cities like Dubrovnik and Split remain open for business, smaller towns close up tight.

Accommodations: Especially in the coastal towns, hotels tend to be big, overpriced resorts. Instead, carefully consider private accommodations: a *soba* (room) or *apartman* (apartment). These offer double the cultural intimacy for a fraction the price of

Croatia Practicalities

Currency: Croatia uses the euro: €1 = $1.10.

Geography and People: The country is 22,000 square miles, similar to West Virginia. Of the 4.5 million people, 90 percent are ethnic Croats (Catholic) and 4.5 percent are Serbs (Orthodox). Its biggest cities are the capital, Zagreb (pop. 790,000), and Split (pop. 178,000). The country's GDP is $95 billion ($24,700 GDP per capita).

Snapshot History: After losing their independence to Hungary in 1102, the Croats watched as most of their coastline became Venetian and their interior was conquered by Ottomans. Croatia was "rescued" by the Habsburgs, but after World War I it became part of Yugoslavia—a decision many Croats regretted until they finally gained independence in 1991 through a bitter war with their Serb neighbors. Today, Croatia is proudly independent.

Famous Croatians: Roman Emperor Diocletian, explorer Marco Polo, Nikola Tesla (a Croatia-born Serb), and several Croatian-Americans, including Roger Maris, John Malkovich, John Kasich, and Dennis Kucinich.

Consular Services in Zagreb: The US Embassy is at Ulica Thomasa Jeffersona 2 (+385 1 661 2300, https://hr.usembassy.gov). The Canadian Embassy is at Prilaz Đure Deželića 4 (+385 1 488 1200, www.croatia.gc.ca).

Tourist Information: https://croatia.hr

a big hotel—and many are quite comfortable and hotelesque, with modern amenities and all of the independence you like. For the best prices, book directly (I've listed contact information for my favorites).

Getting Around: Croatia's trains are of limited usefulness, but their bus network is strong (for schedules, see www.getbybus.com or www.autobusni-kolodvor.com). Coastal destinations (including the islands) are well connected by bus and by ferry—either big, lumbering car ferries (mostly operated by Jadrolinija, www.jadrolinija.hr) or speedy catamarans (handy ones on the Dalmatian Coast include www.jadrolinija.hr, www.krilo.hr, and www.tp-line.hr). Croatia is also easy for drivers, with excellent roads, including a slick network of expressways (with tolls).

Croatian Cuisine: Like Italian fare, Croatian cooking includes lots of pasta, pizza, seafood, and *pršut* (prosciutto). Fill the tank at a pizzeria, but every so often splurge on a seafood feast. Try octopus salad or "black risotto" (a rice dish with cuttlefish simmered in its own ink). Ice-cream stands are abundant. In the interior, meat is popular (especially prepared with a *peka*—simmered for hours under a metal baking lid covered in hot coals). While the cuisine scene in most of the famous coastal destinations is un-inspired, Istria—with its proximity to Italy and its own abundant truffles—is a step above. Croatia also produces excellent wines (*bijelo* is white, *crno* is red).

Croatian Language: Most Croatians speak excellent English, so the language barrier is minimal. But just in case, here are a few helpful Croatian phrases: "Hello" is *Dobar dan* (formal) or *Bok* (informal), "Please" is *Molim,* "Thank you" is *Hvala,* and "Goodbye" is *Do viđenija.*

Top Croatian Destinations

The following sections are designed to get you started planning a trip to Croatia. For in-depth coverage—including self-guided walks and museum tours, detailed hotel and restaurant listings, and lots of practical advice—consider my *Rick Steves Croatia & Slovenia* guidebook.

THE DALMATIAN COAST

Of Croatia's long coastline, the southern third—stretching 200 miles from Zadar to Dubrovnik—contains many of the country's most popular destinations.

▲▲▲Dubrovnik

Dubrovnik is a living fairy tale that shouldn't be missed. It feels like a small town today, but 500 years ago, Dubrovnik was an in-

dependent city-state and major maritime power, with the third-biggest navy in the Mediterranean. Still jutting confidently into the sea and ringed by thick medieval walls, Dubrovnik deserves its nickname: the Pearl of the Adriatic. Within the ramparts, the traffic-free Old Town is a fun jumble of steep alleys, low-impact museums, al fresco cafés, and kid-friendly squares. For tourist information, see www.tzdubrovnik.hr.

Visiting Dubrovnik: Though it's a sprawling city of 50,000 people, most visitors focus on its compact Old Town. Simply strolling the ▲▲▲ **Stradun** (main drag) is a highlight. Several churches, museums, and other attractions hide within the City Walls. All of them are skippable, but it's worth dipping into the fine ▲ **cathedral** (with its quirky treasury collection), the restful cloisters of the

CROATIA

▲ **Franciscan and Dominican monasteries** (each with a modest museum), and the ▲ **Rector's Palace** (the historical residence of the rulers of this independent city-state). The Old Town also has a historical synagogue, a finely decorated Serbian Orthodox church and icon collection, good ethnographic and maritime museums, an aquarium, and a poignant exhibition of wartime photography.

Dubrovnik's single-best attraction is strolling the scenic mile-and-a-quarter around the top of the remarkably well-preserved ▲▲▲ **City Walls.** As you meander along this lofty perch—with a sea of orange roofs on one side and the azure sea on the other—you'll get your bearings, peer into secluded gardens, and snap pictures like mad of the ever-changing views. Walk the walls early or late—the ticket line gets long with cruise-ship passengers at midday.

For an even higher viewpoint, ride the ▲▲▲ **cable car** from just above the City Walls up to the summit of Mount Srđ. There you'll enjoy sweeping views down over the red rooftops of Dubrovnik and out to offshore islands that recede into the sunset (www.dubrovnikcablecar.com).

The city can get very crowded midday, so it can be nice to escape to a nearby **beach** (several scenic spots line the road outside the Ploče Gate, southeast of the Old Town). Or head to the **Old Port**—at the mouth of the Old Town—where local captains offer sightseeing cruises. Popular destinations include little Lokrum Island (just offshore, great hiking and uncrowded beaches) and the Elaphite Islands (a trio of larger islands, each with small villages and beaches).

Sleeping in Dubrovnik: $$ Dubrovnik Gardens is located in a private little garden inside the Old Town (Roberto, www.dubrovnikgardens.com). For private rooms on a sleepy, skinny, stepped lane inside the Old Town, try **$ Villa Ragusa** (run by Pero, www.villaragusadubrovnik.com) or **$ Apartments Paviša** (run by a different Pero, pero.pavisa@gmail.com); if they're full, their neighbors often have rooms. Other good rooms around town include **$$$ Van Bloemen Apartments** (Marc, www.vanbloemen.com), **$$$ Jadranka Benussi** (www.dubrovnik-benussi.com), and the simple but cheery **$ Plaza Apartments** (Lidija, lidydu@yahoo.com).

Eating in Dubrovnik: Avoid the overpriced tourist traps on the main drag and on the glitzy "restaurant row," Prijeko street. One exception is **Nishta,** a well-run vegetarian eatery with an eclectic international menu (on Prijeko street, www.nishtarestaurant.com). For traditional Dalmatian food done well, try **Kopun,** on a gravelly square facing a church (Poljana Ruđera Boškovića 7, www.restaurantkopun.com). **Azur** has Mediterranean food with an Asian twist (buried in back lanes at the top of town, www.azurvision.com), and **Lady Pi-Pi** has rustic traditional food cooked on an open grill (+385 20 321 154). To sample local wines, don't miss **D'Vino Wine Bar** (Palmotićeva 4a, www.dvino.net). And for the most scenic setting in town, get a drink at one of two bars called **Cold Drinks "Buža"**—that means "hole in the wall"—which is literally what you'll have to climb through to reach these delightful perches, clinging like barnacles to the seaward side of the City Walls (ask locals for help to find the entrances).

Private Drivers: Many travelers splurge on hiring their own private driver for side trips to destinations described in the next two chapters: Bosnia's Mostar and Montenegro's Bay of Kotor (figure around €300 for a full-day trip). Good options include **Pepo Klaić** (www.dubrovnikshoretrip.com), **Robi Anđušić** (www.dubrovniktravelexperience.com), and **Petar Vlašić** (www.dubrovnikrivieratours.com).

▲▲Split

Split (pronounced as it's spelled) is Croatia's second city. If you've been hopping along the coast, landing in urban Split feels like a return to civilization. While most Dalmatian coastal towns seem made for tourists, Split is real and vibrant—a shipbuilding city with ugly sprawl surrounding an atmospheric Old Town, which teems with Croatians living life to the fullest. As this is a

transportation hub for the coast, you'll likely pass through at some point. It's well worth spending a night (or more) to fully experience this underrated city. For tourist information, see www.visitsplit.com.

Though Split throbs to a modern, youthful beat, its history goes way back—all the way to the Roman Empire. And today, Split has some of the best Roman ruins this side of Italy. In the fourth century AD, the Roman Emperor Diocletian (245-313) wanted to retire in his native Dalmatia, so he built a huge palace here. Eventually, the palace was abandoned. Then locals, fleeing seventh-century Slavic invaders, moved in and made themselves at home, and a medieval town sprouted from the rubble of the old palace.

This—combined with Venetian influence starting in the 15th century—has left Split a fascinating study in the layers of history.

Visiting Split: The city's top experience is exploring the ruins of ▲▲▲ **Diocletian's Palace,** which are integrated into the townscape of the Old Town. The Old Town's streets were literally the hallways of the palaces; you can see where later settlers grafted windows and doors onto the original structure. And those windows and doors are still in use today.

Begin by exploring **Diocletian's Cellars,** the cavelike foundation that Roman engineers built to support the massive palace. Then

head up to the **Peristyle**—once the palace's grand entryway, it's now the Old Town's main square. Café cushions line the steps (buy a drink if you want to rest on one), and up the stairs is a majestic entry vestibule where a cappella singers perform traditional Dalmatian *klapa* music.

Towering over the Peristyle is the **Cathedral of St. Domnius,** which began life as Diocletian's mausoleum. Inside, you can see what was supposed to be the final resting place of the emperor, who was notorious for torturing Christians. In a bit of poetic justice, today his mausoleum is a cathedral honoring those martyrs... and Diocletian is nowhere to be found.

Another wonderful experience is sauntering along Split's main pedestrian promenade, called **the Riva.** Filling the broad strip between the Old Town (Diocletian's Palace) and the busy modern port, it's the perfect place to people-watch, lick an ice-cream cone, or nurse a coffee. Best around sunset—when it seems the whole town is out strolling—this mellow scene also sprawls up Marmontova street from the harbor.

Most of Split's museums (covering city history, archaeology, ethnography, and an old synagogue) are skippable. But one is a must: the ▲▲ **Meštrović Gallery,** displaying the works of local sculptor Ivan Meštrović (1883-1962). After a successful career in interwar Yugoslavia, Meštrović built a mansion and studio overlooking the Adriatic Sea on the outskirts of Split. Today that mansion—an easy bus or taxi ride from the Old Town—displays his expressive sculptures, which were greatly admired by his contemporary, Auguste Rodin. Meštrović's works still grace parks and squares all over Croatia (and in Chicago, where the artist fled after World War II).

Split is also a great city for relaxing. It has several distinctive and inviting squares; a green park peninsula, called **Marjan,** with hiking trails and beaches; and a lively, user-friendly nightlife scene.

Sleeping in Split: Just outside of the Old Town are some small, well-run guesthouses, including **$$ Villa Ana** (www.villaana-split.hr); and bigger hotels, such as **$$$ Hotel Luxe** (www.hotelluxesplit.com). Within the Old Town—which can be noisy at night, especially on weekends—you can splurge at **$$$$ Marmont Hotel** (www.marmonthotel.com) or the cozy luxury B&B called **$$$$ Palača Judita** (www.juditapalace.com), or sleep more affordably at **$ Kaleta Apartments** (www.kaletaapartments.com) or **$$ Sobe "Base"** (www.base-rooms.com).

Eating in Split: You'll eat well inside the Old Town at the hole-in-the-wall **Villa Spiza** (Petra Kružića 3), the high-end bistro **Bokeria** (Domaldova 8), or the back-streets **Ćiri Biri Bela** (Plinarska 6). More options are just a short walk west of the Old Town, in the Varoš neighborhood: cozy **Konoba Fetivi** (Tomića Stine 4) or the bustling **Šperun Restaurant** (Šperun 3).

▲▲Dalmatian Islands: Korčula and Hvar

Croatia is famous for its islands, and some of the most popular are in Dalmatia. Many travelers argue that *their* favorite island is the very best island, but I'll let you in on a little secret: They're all equally good. While each has its claim to fame, the Croatian islands are essentially variations on a theme: a warm stone Old Town with a Venetian bell tower, a tidy boat-speckled harbor, ample seafood restaurants, a few refurbished resort hotels on the edge of town, and *sobe* and *apartman* signs by every other doorbell. My two favorites are relatively well connected to each other and to the mainland: ritzy Hvar and mellow, dramatically situated Korčula.

Hvar: Hvar's hip cachet, upscale-ritzy "Croatian Riviera" buzz, and easy proximity to Split (one hour by express catamaran) have quickly turned this tidy Dalmatian fishing village into one of the most popular destinations in Croatia (www.visithvar.hr). With a charming old town, a ruined fortress overhead,

CROATIA

luxury yachts bobbing in the harbor, and arguably the best nightlife in Croatia, Hvar is an enjoyable place to be on vacation. You can tour its churches, or visit the Benedictine convent where nuns make delicate lace from natural plant fibers. Or, to get out of town, enjoy one of the island's beaches, go for a hike, or take a boat ride to the offshore Pakleni Islands.

Good rooms in and near Hvar town include **$ Apartments Nona** (ivanka.hvar@gmail.com) and **$$ Ivana and Paško Ukić** (ivanaukic@net.hr)—both buried in the steep lanes above the town center. Just a 10-minute walk west of the Old Town is **$ Apartments Mare** (Marica and Gianni, www.apartments-mare-hvar.com). For a centrally located splurge hotel, try **$$$$ Villa Nora** (www.villanora.eu) or **$$$ Hotel Park** (www.hotelparkhvar.com).

For meals, consider **Konoba Menego,** serving Croatian classics tapas-style (in the steep lanes above the main square, www.menego.hr); **Alviž,** with simple but delicious meals near the bus station (Hanibala Lucića 1); **Dalmatino,** with high-end cooking at reasonable prices just off the main square (Sveti Marak 1, www.dalmatino-hvar.com); or **Fig,** a hip place with a varied menu (www.figrestaurants.com).

Korčula: The island town of Korčula (KOHR-choo-lah)—a bit closer to Dubrovnik, with workable connections—boasts an atmospheric Old Town, a smattering of little museums, and a dramatic, fjord-like mountain backdrop. Humbler and sleepier than its glitzy big sister Hvar, Korčula has an appealing backwater charm (www.visitkorcula.eu). The peninsular Old Town pokes out into the Adriatic, with a fish-skeleton street plan, a variety of museums (including the supposed former home of Marco Polo, whom Korčulans claim was born here), and a variety of pizza, pasta, and seafood restaurants. Twice weekly in summer, Lazy Korčula snaps to life when locals perform a medieval folk dance called the *Moreška*.

My favorite private rooms are **$$ M&J Central Suites** (mjcentralsuites@yahoo.com) and **$ Royal Apartments** (Zvonko and Marija, www.korcularoyalapartments.com). The best hotel option is **$$$$ Hotel Korsal** (www.hotel-korsal.com).

Several great restaurants—including **Aterina**—are on the square called Trg Korčulanskih Klesara i Kipara. For a scenic setting, browse the eateries along the seawall, from the basic **Pizzeria Tedeschi** to Asian-fusion **Silk** to the splurgy **LD Restaurant** and **Filippi**.

ISTRIA

Idyllic Istria, the wedge-shaped peninsula at Croatia's northwest corner, reveals itself to you gradually and seductively: Pungent truffles, Roman ruins, striking hill towns, quaint coastal villages, carefully cultivated food and wine, and breezy Italian culture all compete for your attention. The highlight is the gorgeous seaside town of Rovinj, but with more time (and a car), Istria has much to offer. Everything mentioned here is within a one-hour drive of Rovinj.

▲▲▲Rovinj

Among Croatian coastal towns, Rovinj (roh-VEEN) is particularly romantic (www.rovinj-tourism.com). Its streets are delightfully twisty, its ancient houses are characteristically crumbling, and its harbor—lively with real-life fishermen—is as salty as they come. Like a little Venice on a hill, Rovinj is the atmospheric setting of your Croatian seaside dreams.

Visiting Rovinj: Rovinj's main attraction is simply its gorgeous ▲▲▲ **Old Town**—rising dramatically from the Adriatic as though being pulled up to heaven by its grand bell tower. Enjoy stunning views from the town parking lot, then walk into town, pausing at the lively open-air market. Once inside the Old Town, you're swallowed up by a creaky and colorful townscape.

Narrow, stepped lanes climb up the hill to the ▲ **Church of St. Euphemia,** where you can learn about the local patron saint and climb rickety stairs up to the top of the bell tower. Rovinj has a few low-impact museums, including the ▲ **House of the Batana Boat,** celebrating a unique local fishing boat and the culture that goes along with it (www.batana.org). Rovinj has some rocky beaches, with sandy ones a short bike or boat ride away.

Sleeping in Rovinj: This town is a delightful home base for exploring Istria. The Old Town holds several appealing private rooms and guesthouses, including **$$ Villa Markiz** (Milica and Andrej, stylish apartments, www.markizrovinj.com), **$$ Casa Garzotto** (with rustic rooms and apartments scattered around the Old Town, www.casa-garzotto.com), and **$ Hey Rovinj** (fresh, creative, and youthful, at the top of town, www.heyrovinj.com). Higher-end options in the Old Town include **$$$$ The Melegran** (www.melegran.com) and **$$$$ Hotel Spirito Santo** (www.hotel-spiritosanto.com).

CROATIA

Eating in Rovinj: Restaurants line up along Rovinj's "restaurant row" facing the harbor; good options include classy **Scuba,** rustic **Veli Jože,** romantic **Santa Croce,** and—at the end of the strip—the scenic splurge **La Puntuleina.** In the evening, a few places along this strip have romantic cocktails overlooking a flood-lit sea. In the mainland part of town, you'll find good food and good value at **Bookeria** (with a literary theme and Croatian/international dishes, Trg Pignaton) and **Maestral** (affordable seafood and pizzas with views across Rovinj's harbor, Obala V. Nazora).

▲▲Istrian Hill Towns

Istria's interior is dotted with sleepy, picturesque hill towns, speckled with wineries and olive-oil farms, embedded with precious truffles, and grooved by meandering rural roads. Spend a half-day (or more) joyriding from town to town, stopping at some countryside wineries and making time for a truffle feast.

Visiting the Istrian Hill Towns: The most appealing hill town is **Motovun,** overlooking vineyards and truffle-filled oak forests. Hike up its shop-lined main street to the cute little square with a pretty church, the big Hotel Kaštel, and views over the countryside. Behind the hotel is a sweet little museum of town history. Motovun is also a foodie destination, with a pair of excellent restaurants for an Istrian meal: the trendy but unpretentious **Mondo Konoba** (just below the Old Town's lower gate), and the more traditional **Konoba pod Voltom** (inside the Old Town's upper gate).

Other fine hill towns include **Grožnjan** (a time warp on a bluff—flatter and easier to drive to than Motovun), **Buje** (more workaday), and **Završje** (almost deserted and very atmospheric). Most towns have a restaurant specializing in truffle dishes, but Istria's gastronomic epicenter is **Livade,** in the valley below Motovun. This is home to the local Zigante truffle company, with a big shop and upscale restaurant.

Wine lovers enjoy stopping for tastings at countryside wineries, which are scattered across the region. Near Momjan (northwest of Motovun), good choices are the traditional **Kabola** (www.kabola.hr) and the sophisticated **Kozlović** (www.kozlovic.hr).

▲Pula

At Istria's southern tip, Pula is a big, industrial port city. But its urban core holds priceless ancient Roman ruins that rival Split's. Park near the remarkably well-preserved amphitheater, which is worth touring. Then walk into the town center. On the main square (formerly the ancient forum) is a largely intact ancient temple; a Roman floor mosaic hides behind some nearby shops.

CROATIA'S INTERIOR

Most travelers to Croatia focus exclusively on the coast. That's a shame, because they miss the country's interior—with two of its best destinations: the capital city and a stunning natural wonder.

▲▲Zagreb

You can't get a complete picture of modern Croatia without a visit here—away from the touristy resorts, in the lively and livable city

that is home to one in every six Croatians. In Zagreb, you'll find historic neighborhoods, a thriving café culture, my favorite urban people-watching in Croatia, an Old World streetscape, and virtually no tourists. The city is also the country's best destination for museum-going and has Croatia's best foodie scene (both in short supply along the coast).

Visiting Zagreb: Zagreb's main square, **Jelačić Square** (Trg bana Jelačića) is a hive of activity. Shoppers, commuters, and trams zip in and out of the square. The surrounding downtown zone is a delight to explore, with galleries, boutiques, and gourmet coffee shops.

Near Jelačić Square, a short funicular climbs up to Zagreb's old town, called Gradec. Its centerpiece is St. Mark's Square, where governmental buildings (including the parliament and president's residence) face the colorfully tiled roof of the Church of St. Mark.

Two of Croatia's top museums are within a block of St. Mark's Square. The small but riveting **▲▲▲ Croatian Museum of Naive Art** displays lovingly detailed works by self-taught peasant artists—dating from the early 20th century, when art-world insiders sought to prove that artistic ability was an inborn

talent (www.hmnu.hr). And nearby, the innovative ▲▲ **Museum of Broken Relationships** collects true stories of failed couples from around the world, tells their story in their own words, and displays the tale alongside an actual item that embodies the relationship (https://brokenships.com). The Gradec area also has a fine city history museum and an atelier and collection of works of the great Croatian sculptor, Ivan Meštrović.

The adjacent, formerly walled district of Kaptol is home to Zagreb's ▲▲ **cathedral**—containing various monuments celebrating the city's tumultuous history and Croatia's proud Catholic heritage.

Between Gradec and Kaptol is Zagreb's colorful (and largely untouristy) indoor-outdoor public **market,** a fun place to browse for a picnic. Nearby is the trendy café street called **Tkalčićeva,** with lots of lively al fresco eateries and the best people-watching in town.

Sleeping in Zagreb: Good, central choices include the simple and affordable **$$ Hotel Park 45** (www.hotelpark45.hr), the cozy-yet-modern **$$ Jägerhorn Hotel** (www.hotel-jagerhorn.hr), or the fancier **$$$ Amadria Park Hotel Capital** (www.amadriapark. com). Smaller B&B-type options include **$ Sobe Zagreb 17** (www. sobezagreb17.com) or **$ 4 City Windows** (www.4citywindows. com).

Eating in Zagreb: It's fun to browse the restaurants along the bustling, traffic-free Tkalčićeva street, including the big, sloppy **Pivnica Mali Medo** (a Czech-style beer hall, at #36) or **La Štruk,** specializing in the local ravioli, *štrukli* (Skalinska 5). For foodie places in the downtown zone around Jelačić Square, check out **Ficlek** (Pod Zidom 5), **Bistro Beštija** (Masarykova 11), **Theatrium by Filho** (Teslina 7), or **Lari & Penati** (Petrinjska 42A).

▲▲▲Plitvice Lakes National Park

Plitvice (PLEET-veet-seh) is one of Europe's most spectacular natural wonders. Imagine Niagara Falls diced and sprinkled over a heavily forested Grand Canyon. There's nothing like this lush valley of 16 terraced lakes, separated by natural travertine dams and laced together by waterfalls, boat rides, and miles of pleasant plank walks (www.np-plitvicka-jezera.hr).

Visiting Plitvice: Deep in the countryside about two hours south of Zagreb (roughly on the way to Split), Plitvice is worth a little extra effort to reach. It's easiest for drivers, but many public buses from Zagreb or Split also stop here (bus stop along main road—ask locals or the driver to be clear on where to get off or on, best connections are provided by the summer-only Prijevoz Knežević express bus and/or Flixbus).

Once at the park, you can see the highlights in just a few hours' walk. It's easy (on well-tended paths and boardwalks) but can get

crowded—in busy times, get an early start. (It works well to arrive in the evening, sleep near the park, hit the trails first thing the next morning, then move on to your next destination after lunch.) The lakes are divided into two sections,
upper and lower. I prefer to buy my park ticket at Entrance 1 and do the Lower Lakes first. You'll hike steeply down to the trail, then walk gradually uphill—past glorious cascades and pools of strangely colorful water—to the largest lake. From there, an electric boat shuttles you silently across to the Upper Lakes, which is yet another wonderland of boardwalks, waterfalls, and tranquil ponds. From the far end, you can ride a shuttle bus back to your starting point.

Sleeping and Eating at Plitvice: Most visitors stay at the national park lodges, which are functional but comfortable and come with industrial-strength dining rooms. The best choices are **$$$ Hotel Plitvice** and **$$ Hotel Jezero** (www.np-plitvicka-jezera.hr). For a more personal experience, drivers should stay at a family-run inn outside the park. My favorite, just a couple of minutes south of Plitvice, is the friendly **$$ Plitvice Mirić Inn** (www.plitvice-croatia.com). Others cluster near the road about 10 minutes' drive north of Plitvice, including the big, roadside **$$$$ Hotel Degenija** (www.hotel-degenija.com; also has restaurant—ideal for dinner). For lunch near the trails, a few humble eateries—ranging from basic grocery stores selling sandwiches to sit-down places—cluster near the park entrances and near the boat dock at the top of the Lower Lakes. Since the food at the park eateries is nothing special, consider packing a picnic instead.

CROATIA

BOSNIA-HERZEGOVINA

Bosna i Hercegovina

In the 1990s, Bosnia-Herzegovina became synonymous with war, sectarian violence, and genocide. That's a shame, because for so much of its history this remarkable land has represented exactly the opposite. While skittish travelers may never experience it for themselves, Bosnia-Herzegovina boasts a unique mix of cultures and faiths, kind and welcoming people who pride themselves on their hospitality... and some of the most captivating sightseeing in southeastern Europe. A visit here offers a fas-

cinating opportunity to sample the cultures of three major faiths within a relatively small area: In the same day, you can inhale incense in a mystical-feeling Serbian Orthodox church, hear the subtle clicking of rosary beads in a Roman Catholic cathedral, and listen to the Muslim call to prayer echo across a skyline of prickly minarets.

Where to Go: The highlights of Bosnia are just a short drive from Croatia's Dalmatian Coast. Many side-trip from Dubrovnik or Split to **Mostar,** which is the country's most accessible and tourist-friendly town. But for a more authentic and complete Bosnian experience, it's worth going a few hours farther to reach **Sarajevo**—the gorgeously set capital, with its fascinating history (both old and recent), excellent sightseeing, and lively contemporary life. Three or four days is enough time to visit both great cities, with quick stops in some other towns and attractions in between, giving you an insightful first look at Bosnia.

Getting Around: Trains are slow and old (www.zfbh.ba); lo-

Bosnia-Herzegovina

100 Kilometers
100 Miles

CROATIA

SERBIA

Bihać
Novi Grad
Banja Luka
Doboj
Brčko
Bijelina
Bosna R.
Zvornik
Zavidovići

BOSNIA-HERZEGOVINA

Drvar
Jajce
Travnik
Zenica
Srebrenica
Vrbas R.
Bugojno
Visoko
Sarajevo
Višegrad
Ivan Planina
Goražde
Livno
Jablanica
Konjic
Foča
Drina R.
Široki Brijeg
Neretva R.
Mostar
Blagaj
Međugorje
Počitelj
Bileća
Trebinje
MONTE-NEGRO
Adriatic Sea
Dubrovnik
Podgorica

DINARIC ALPS

Republika Srpska
Muslim-Croat Federation

cals prefer to go by bus (https://getbybus.com usually catches most of your options). Bosnia is also a fine country for driving: The roads are good (though there are few freeways), and traffic is light. Given the mountainous terrain, affordable flights can save time; for example, Croatia Airlines flies affordably and frequently between Sarajevo and Zagreb (www.croatiaairlines.com).

Bosnian Cuisine: The local food resembles what you may think of as "Greek" or "Turkish" food—with lots of tomatoes, peppers, soft cheeses, and grilled meats. The top street food is *burek*—a savory phyllo-dough pastry filled with meat, cheese, or spinach. Another Bosnian classic is *ćevapčići* (or *ćevapi*), a mix of minced meat (usually lamb and beef) formed into a sausage-link shape, then grilled. It's served with other grilled meats, chopped raw onions, a soft and spreadable cheese called *kajmak*, the pita-like *lepinje* bread, and the powerful red pepper

BOSNIA-HERZEGOVINA

and eggplant spread called *ajvar*. Bosnian desserts are gooey with honey: baklava or the shredded-wheat-style *kadaif*. And Bosnian coffee *(bosanska kafa)*—a hearty unfiltered brew simmered in a copper kettle and served in a little ceramic cup—is as much a slow-down-and-smell-the-tulips social ritual as it is a drink.

Bosnian Language: English is widely spoken, especially in tourist areas. Bosnian is very close to Croatian (in fact, until a generation ago they were considered one language); key phrases include these pleasantries: "Hello" is *Dobar dan* (formal) or *Zdravo* (informal), "Please" is *Molim,* "Thank you" is *Hvala,* and "Goodbye" is *Do viđenija.* Bosniaks and Croats use basically the same Roman alphabet we do, while Serbs use the Cyrillic alphabet. You'll see both alphabets on currency, official documents, and road signs, but the Roman alphabet predominates in the destinations covered here.

Top Bosnian Destinations

The following sections are designed to get you started planning a trip to Bosnia. For in-depth coverage—including self-guided walks and museum tours, detailed hotel and restaurant listings, and lots of practical advice—pick up my *Rick Steves Croatia & Slovenia* guidebook.

▲▲▲Sarajevo

Though once torn by the wars of the 1990s, the Bosnian capital of Sarajevo—picturesequely situated in a mountain valley blanketed with cute Monopoly houses—is a comfortable and safe place to visit (www.sarajevo-tourism. com). It's a city of powerful experiences: Step into historic houses of worship from each of this region's four major faiths— Muslim, Catholic, Orthodox Christian, and Jewish—and notice the similarities. Visit the  street corner where World War I began. Climb up into the hills to the Olympic stadium that commanded the world's attention in 1984, or ascend even higher for sweeping views over the capital. Make friends with a gregarious Sarajevan—it's easy to do—and ask about the best way to prepare and drink Bosnian coffee. Ponder the scars of war, hunch over to squeeze through the tunnel that was the besieged Sarajevans' one lifeline to the world, and listen to a local relate personal stories from the harrowing time of the siege. Shop your way through the copper-laden canyons of the Turkish-style bazaar, bartering down the price of a hand-hammered Bos-

Bosnia Practicalities

Money: The official currency is the convertible mark (*konvertibilna marka*, abbreviated KM locally, BAM internationally). 1 KM = about €0.50 or $0.50.

Geography and People: Bosnia and Herzegovina are two distinct regions that share the same mountainous country (19,741 square miles—about the size of West Virginia). Bosnia constitutes the majority of the country (in the north, with a continental climate), while Herzegovina is the southern tip (about a fifth of the total area, with a hotter Mediterranean climate). The country is home to about 3.9 million people.

The capital, Sarajevo, has an estimated 346,000 people; Mostar is Herzegovina's biggest city (with approximately 105,000 people) and unofficial capital. Someone who lives in Bosnia-Herzegovina, regardless of ethnicity, is called a "Bosnian." A southern Slav who practices Islam is called a "Bosniak." Today, about half of all Bosnians are Bosniaks, about a third are Orthodox Serbs, and 15 percent are Catholic Croats. The country's economy has struggled since the war—the per-capita GDP is around $12,800.

Snapshot History: Bosnia's history was dominated first by the Illyrians, then by the Romans, and eventually by the Slavs. In the late 15th century, the Ottoman Empire began a 400-year domination of the country. Many of the Ottomans' subjects converted to Islam, and their descendants remain Muslims today. Bosnia-Herzegovina became part of the Austro-Hungarian Empire in 1878, then Yugoslavia after World War I. During World War II, Bosnia was the cradle of Tito's Partisan Army and the birthplace of a new Yugoslavia.

When that country broke apart, Bosnia declared independence in the spring of 1992. The bloody war that ensued came to an end in 1995 with the Dayton Peace Accords, which gerrymandered the nation into two major, semi-autonomous zones: the Federation of Bosnia and Herzegovina (shared by Bosniaks and Croats, roughly in the western and central parts of the country) and the Republika Srpska (dominated by Serbs, generally to the north and east).

Consular Services in Sarajevo: The US Embassy is at Ulica Robert C. Frasure 1 (+387 33 704 000, http://ba.usembassy.gov). The nearest Canadian Embassy is in Budapest, Hungary (see page 1074).

Helpful Tourism Website: www.tourismbih.com

BOSNIA-HERZEGOVINA

nian coffee set. Relax in a hidden caravansary, take a slow drag on a *šiša* (water pipe spewing sweet plumes of fruity smoke), and sample some honey-dripping pastry treats. Go ahead—it's OK to enjoy Sarajevo.

Visiting Sarajevo: Sarajevo is brought to life with the help of a good local guide; **Amir Telibečirović** is excellent and affordable (teleamir@gmail.com).

Begin in the Ottoman-flavored Old Town, called the **Baščaršija**—with cobbles, bazaars, minarets, and hardworking coppersmiths. In this area, ogle Sarajevo's iconic fountain (called Sebilj), do some window-shopping, and consider dropping into the good ▲ **City History Museum,** filling a former covered market. After hours, don't miss the atmospheric courtyard called Trgovke—filled with gregarious locals, thumping Balkan music, and the sweet smoke of water pipes.

A few blocks to the west begins a totally different-feeling part of town, with Habsburg-style architecture from the late 19th and

early 20th centuries (the short-lived period when Bosnia was part of Austria-Hungary). The main drag, **Ferhadija,** feels worlds—rather than steps—away from the Baščaršija. During this Habsburg era, Sarajevo was the site of one of the most famous and important events in modern history: the assassination of the Habsburg heir, Franz Ferdinand, in 1914. You can see the riverside corner where the archduke and his wife were shot, visit the adjacent museum, or walk five minutes along the river to see the finest piece of architecture from this period, the Neo-Moorish City Hall, which Franz Ferdinand visited on that fateful day.

In this central zone of Sarajevo, various historic houses of worship sit a few steps apart. Stop in at Sarajevo's big, showpiece ▲▲ **Gazi Husrev-Bey Mosque** and associated buildings; the atmospheric ▲ **Old Serbian Orthodox Church,** with a museum of icons; the Neo-Gothic **Catholic Cathedral;** and the city's ▲▲ **Old Synagogue and Bosnian Jewish Museum.** (For more Jewish heritage, the sometimes-closed National Museum displays the priceless Jewish prayer book called the Sarajevo Haggadah.)

Sarajevo offers many powerful lessons in the grotesque genocide of the Yugoslav

Wars. In the early 1990s, this multiethnic city—surrounded by the snipers of Bosnian Serb leaders Radovan Karadžić and Ratko Mladić—withstood the longest siege in modern military history (more than 1,300 days). Many locals are willing to share their harrowing stories from that time—being relentlessly shelled and shot at, day in and day out, for three and a half years. All around the city, watch for blast craters in the pavement that have been filled with red resin; these memorials, called "Sarajevo roses," have been preserved to commemorate that difficult time.

For sites relating to the siege, visit the still-busy **Markale Market,** the site of a notorious bombing that killed dozens of innocent shoppers. The emotionally wrenching **Memorial to the Children of Sarajevo** pays respects to the more than 1,600 children who were among the estimated 10,000 Sarajevans killed during the siege. (The outstanding ▲▲ **War Childhood Museum** features

items and stories from local children.) A few blocks away, walk through the skyscraper zone called Marijin Dvor, which was then known as **"Sniper Alley"**—where gunmen on the hillsides above would rain bullets down on civilians trying to live their lives in peace. And in the town center, the ▲▲ **Srebrenica Exhibition** collects photography and video testimony about the brutal ethnic cleansing campaign that systematically murdered at least 8,000 residents of a small Bosnian town.

Perhaps the most powerful sight relating to the Siege of Sarajevo is the ▲▲ **Sarajevo War Tunnel Museum,** where you can walk through a short stretch of the claustrophobic supply tunnel that ran a half-mile underneath the airport runway during the siege. This was the only safe way for besieged Sarajevans to escape to the outside world and bring home supplies to their loved ones (a taxi ride from downtown, www.tunelspasa.ba).

Sleeping in Sarajevo: Friendly, well-run guesthouses in or near the Old Town include **$ Halvat Guest House** (www.halvat.com.ba) and **$ Hotel Old Town** (www.hoteloldtown.ba). **$$ Isa Begov Hamam Hotel** fills part of an Ottoman-style bathhouse (www.isabegovhotel.com). For a big, international-style hotel a long walk or short drive from the Old Town, try **$$$ Swissôtel Sarajevo** (www.swissotel.com).

Eating in Sarajevo: There are plenty of options for traditional Bosnian fare in the Old Town. My favorite *burek*s (savory phyllo pastry) are at **Buregdžinica Sač** (just off the main square, in the alley called Bravadžiluk Mali). Good choices for *ćevapčići* are **Mrkva** (Bravadžiluk 15) and **Petica** (Oprkanj 2). In the modern part of town, the more cosmopolitan **Žara Iz Duvara** (Dženetića Čik) and **Mala Kuhinja** (Tina Ujevića 13) serve a mix of international and Bosnian fare. And for a scenic meal—with sweeping views over Sarajevo's valley—head up into the hills to the pricier (but still affordable) **Kibe Mahala** (Vrbanjuša 164, easiest to reach by taxi, www.kibemahala.ba).

▲▲Mostar

For those side-tripping into Bosnia from the Dalmatian Coast, Mostar is ideal: It's a convenient and very accessible microcosm of traditional Bosnian culture.

Mostar straddles the banks of the gorgeous Neretva River, with tributaries and waterfalls that carve their way through the rocky landscape. The sightseeing—mosques, old Turkish-style houses, and the city's spine-tingling Old Bridge—is engaging. And for those interested in recent history, the locals—who saw their city torn apart by the Yugoslav Wars of the 1990s, and have worked hard to rebuild—are often eager to share their stories. If you're curious about Bosnia and only have a day to spend here, Mostar is the place.

Visiting Mostar: Almost everything of interest is within about a 15-minute walk in the town center. A local guide helps bring both the history and the powerful recent stories to life. I recommend **Alma Elezović** (aelezovic@gmail.com); her husband, Ermin, can be hired to drive you around Bosnia, or even to pick you up in Croatia.

The city's centerpiece and icon is its **Old Bridge,** commissioned in 1557 by the Ottoman Sultan Süleyman the Magnificent. Dramatically arched and flanked by two boxy towers, the bridge is stirring. In 1993, as the various factions of the city fought amongst themselves, Serb artillery on the mountaintop above fired on the Bosniak-held bridge. It was destroyed and fell into the river. In 2004, the bridge was rebuilt and remains a

symbol of reconciliation. And today, as they have for generations, local young men hustle for tips from tourists before they swan-dive from the bridge 75 feet down into the icy-cold Neretva below.

The area around the bridge has a few small historical and photo exhibitions about the war, and a cobbled bazaar (called Coppersmiths' Street) where locals sell trinkets to tourists.

As it continues to repair itself, Mostar still has poignant reminders of the war, such as a few bombed-out husks of buildings, tucked between rebuilt ones. And scattered around Mostar are "new" cemeteries—former parks now filled with turban-shaped headstones, each one marked *1993* or *1994*. When the Serb forces laid siege to the Muslims in Mostar's Old Town, bodies had to be buried in small parks in the city center, in the dark of night, for fear of snipers. Today, the city remains effectively divided, between the Muslim community (around the Old Bridge, where most tourists go) and the Croat community (the modern sprawl to the west).

For those interested in Islam, Mostar offers the opportunity to visit various mosques. ▲ **Koski Mehmet-Pasha Mosque,** over-looking the Old Bridge, is the most representative and welcomes tourists. And you can step into a historical ▲ **Ottoman-style house** to see how Mostarians lived under the rule of the sultans and pashas (the Bišćević House or the Muslibegović House—both just above

the river not far from the bridge—are equally good). Across the river is the towering concrete steeple of the **Church of Sts. Peter and Paul**—built after the war by local Croats, seemingly to one-up the minarets all over town.

Sleeping in Mostar: Guesthouses here are a great value. I like the **$$ Muslibegović House** (a historical monument that also welcomes guests into its traditional rooms with modern comforts, www.muslibegovichouse.com), **$ Shangri La Mansion** (on the hill above the Old Bridge, www.shangrila.com.ba), **$ Villa Anri** (modern comfort near the Old Bridge, villa.anri@gmail.com), and **$ Hotel Kriva Ćuprija** (lots of rooms tucked deep in the river valley near the Old Bridge—plus more in a modern annex, www.hotel-mostar.ba).

Eating in Mostar: It seems all Mostar restaurants have the same tourist-oriented menu of Bosnian classics: grilled-meat *ćevapčići*, flaky *burek* pastries, and so on. Most visitors prioritize the view over the food, settling in at one of the places clinging to the lush cliffs overlooking the river, with stunning views of the Old

Bridge. For slightly better food (but less exciting views), **Restoran Hindin Han** has somewhat more refined food and a nice setting on a smaller canyon (Jusovina 10), and **Irma-Tima,** on the main drag near the Old Bridge, has great grilled meats (Onešćukova).

▲Sights near Mostar

Drivers exploring the area near Mostar can choose from several tempting stopovers.

Just outside of Mostar, the historical capital of **Blagaj** has an old dervish monastery *(tekija)* that sits at the bottom of a dramatic cliff face, where the Buna River bubbles up from underground.

On the main road between Mostar and the Dalmatian Coast, it's hard to resist stopping at **Počitelj**—dramatically set on chalky mountains, with a ruined castle and a proud mosque and minaret.

Also between Mostar and the coast—on a less-traveled route—is a powerful site of pilgrimage for Catholics: **Međugorje,** where six local teens claimed to have seen miraculous visions of the Virgin Mary in 1981. While there's little to see beyond a modern church, believers (and the curious) find something spiritually powerful here.

MONTENEGRO

Crna Gora

Small and rugged, Montenegro gets overlooked. It's tucked in a rocky and complicated part of the world between Croatia, Serbia, and Albania. And yet, it's a temptingly short drive from the region's top destination, Dubrovnik. Today's Montenegro is a strange mix of big-money international investment (Russian-owned luxury resort hotels, the exclusive Porto Montenegro yacht harbor) and local poverty (which is evident as you pass

through ragtag cities and humble towns). But nothing can mar Montenegro's natural beauty: Devote a day (or more) to making this easy side trip, and you'll discover a land of stunning mountains, bays, and forests.

Where to Go: Most people see Montenegro as a quick side trip from Dubrovnik—which, for those on a tight timeframe, is a smart plan. The main highlight is the **Bay of Kotor,** with scenery that only improves on Croatia's Dalmatian Coast; some fine seaside towns (including tiny Perast and atmospheric Kotor); and the chance to ride out to a church-topped island in the middle of the bay, wrapped in 360 degrees of stunning scenery. With more time, beach bums can head for the **Budva Riviera,** celebrity seekers can daydream about past glories at the striking hotel-peninsula of **Sveti Stefan,** and romantics can corkscrew up into the mountains to sample the Balkans' best smoked ham at **Njeguši** and visit the country's remote original capital at **Cetinje.**

Getting Around: Most visitors drive in for the day from

Montenegro Practicalities

Money: Though it's not a member of the European Union, Montenegro uses the euro: €1 = about $1.10.

Geography and People: Montenegro (5,415 square miles, slightly smaller than Connecticut) is home to about 605,000 people. Of these, the vast majority are Eastern Orthodox Christians (45 percent Montenegrins, 29 percent Serbs), with minority groups of Muslims (including Bosniaks and Albanians, about 11 percent total) and Catholics (1 percent). The country is characterized by a rocky terrain that rises straight up from the Adriatic and almost immediately becomes a steep mountain range. Montenegro has 182 miles of coastline, about a third of which constitutes the Bay of Kotor. The only real city is the capital, Podgorica (177,000 people). Montenegro is a relatively poor country (per capita GDP is $20,600).

Snapshot History: Named "Black Mountain" for the thickly forested hills that sailors saw when approaching, Montenegro was first inhabited by the ancient Illyrians (the mysterious distant ancestors of today's Albanians), who were later conquered by the Romans. Slavic migrants established a sovereign state here in the 10th century, and in the 14th century, the area flourished under the powerful Serbian emperor Dušan the Mighty. But with the rising threat of the Ottomans, the Montenegrin coastline became part of the Republic of Venice for about 450 years (15th-19th century). In the 20th century, Montenegro joined Yugoslavia (and was often overshadowed by its "big brother," Serbia)—until it declared independence from Serbia, peacefully, in a landmark vote on June 3, 2006.

Consular Services in Podgorica: The US Embassy is at Džona Džeksona 2 (+382 20 410 500, https://me.usembassy.gov); Canadians use the embassy in Belgrade, Serbia (+381 11 306 3000, www.international.gc.ca/country-pays/serbia-serbie).

Tourist Information: www.montenegro.travel

Dubrovnik, either on their own, with a Dubrovnik-based private driver (see page 989), or with a package tour. Montenegro is also relatively well served by buses (see www.getbybus.com). It's also a popular and easy cruise port—ships put in right across the street from Kotor's Old Town.

Montenegrin Cuisine: Along the Bay of Kotor, the cuisine is similar to Croatia's—that means seafood, pasta, and pizza. *Njeguški pršut* is the rich, salty, smoky prosciutto from the village of Njeguši (described later) that goes well with the local cow's cheese—smoked, of course. Montenegro also produces some surprisingly good wines (Plantaže Podgorica is the biggest company): A good red is the dry, medium-bodied *vranac* (related to zinfandel), and for white, you'll see the dry, fruity *krstač* (similar to Riesling).

Montenegrin Language: Montenegrin is closely related to both Croatian and Bosnian. "Hello" is *Dobar dan* (formal) or *Zdravo* (informal), "Please" is *Molim*, "Thank you" is *Hvala*, and "Goodbye" is *Do viđenija*. You'll see both the Roman and Cyrillic alphabet used, more or less equally; for a crash course in Cyrillic, see page 1018.

Top Montenegrin Destinations

The following sections are designed to get you started planning a trip to Montenegro. For in-depth coverage—including a self-guided driving tour, detailed hotel and restaurant listings, and lots of practical advice—pick up my *Rick Steves Croatia & Slovenia* guidebook.

▲▲Bay of Kotor Driving Loop
For a look at the untamed Adriatic, take a spin on the winding road around Montenegro's steep and secluded Bay of Kotor. The area's

main town, also called Kotor, has been protected from centuries of would-be invaders by its position at the deepest point of the fjord—and by its imposing town wall, which scrambles in a zigzag line up the mountain behind it. Wander the enjoyably seedy streets of Kotor, drop into some Orthodox churches, and sip a coffee at an al fresco café.

Visiting the Bay of Kotor: Most people do a loop around the Bay of Kotor in one day from Dubrovnik. Here's the basic plan:

From Dubrovnik, head south on the main coastal road (signs to *Ćilipi*), past Cavtat and the airport; in about 40 minutes, you'll reach the **border** at Debeli Brijeg (where you'll need to show your passport and your rental car's proof-of-insurance "green card"). To avoid lines at the border, get an early start—on busy summer weekends, consider leaving Dubrovnik by 7:30 to beat the tour buses. (There's also a less crowded alternate border crossing called Konfin—ask locals for directions.)

Once across the border, you'll head through the big, dreary city of **Herceg Novi,** then curve around the headland at the **Verige Strait**—the quarter-mile-wide entrance to the huge, fjord-like bay (underlining Kotor's strategic importance). From here, you'll curl along the bay's waters—through crescendoing scenery and tiny towns—until you reach the village of ▲ **Perast.** Park, stretch your legs, and explore this tiny, well-preserved town (with a big waterfront main square and a half-built cathedral).

From Perast, pay a few euros per person to be shuttled out across the bay for a closer look at a pair of islands: **St. George** (Sv. Đorđe) and ▲▲ **Our Lady of the Rocks** (Gospa od Škrpjela). It's said that two local fishermen saw a light emanating from a reef deep below the surface near the isle of St. George. Discovering an icon of Mary, they were

inspired to build a second island on that holy spot. So, for two centuries, locals dropped rocks and even sank old ships there—eventually creating the island of Our Lady of the Rocks. You can stroll the island and dip into the church, filled with votives honoring the miraculous icon that was found here.

Back in Perast, get back on the road and carry on around the bay about another 30 minutes until you reach the town of **Kotor;**

with more time, you can continue farther to the **Budva Riviera,** or head up into the mountains and **Cetinje** (all described later).

To return to Dubrovnik, just head back the way you came. Or, for a shortcut (and to see different scenery), you can continue around the bay past Kotor, then continue all the way around to Lepetani, where a frequent and easy ferry *(trajekt)* travels a few minutes across the bay to Kamenari—near Herceg Novi and a short drive from the Croatian border.

▲▲Kotor

Butted up against a steep cliff, cradled by a calm sea, naturally sheltered by its deep-in-the-fjord position, and watched over by an imposing network of fortifications, the town of Kotor is as impressive as it is well protected. Though it has enjoyed a long and illustrious history, today's Kotor is a time-capsule retreat for travelers seeking an unspoiled Adriatic town (www.kotor.travel). For a good local guide, contact **Stefan Đukanović** (www.miroandsons.com, djukan@t-com.me).

Visiting Kotor: You can see the entire compact Old Town in a short stroll. Pass through the Main Town Gate (with a TI kiosk) and into the **Square of Arms,** fronted by a grand old palace and the town's bell tower. From here, get lost in the twisty lanes.

Make your way to the ▲ **Cathedral of St. Tryphon,** with its mismatched towers, fine interior, and quirky treasury collection (featuring an icon that, like Montenegro itself, seems to merge Eastern and Western Christian traditions). Just off the cathedral square, you can dip into the **Maritime Museum of Montenegro,** with modest exhibits on the bay's history and seafaring traditions.

A few lanes over, ▲ **St. Luke's Square** has two Eastern Orthodox Churches—one big, one little. Either offers a fascinating look at the Eastern Orthodox faith (see page 1025).

Kotor's main attraction—for those who are fit enough to tackle it—is climbing the ▲▲ **city walls** that zigzag up the sheer cliff face behind town. (If there's a more elaborate city wall in Europe, I haven't seen it.) This involves climbing 1,355 steps (an elevation gain of more than 700 feet)—don't overestimate your endurance or underestimate the heat. Find the ticket desk and trailhead at the back-left corner of the Old Town (near St. Mary's Church, through the alley with the two arches over it). Then get climbing, following a clockwise route that ascends to the Church of Our Lady of Health (the halfway mark), then all the way up to the Fortress of St. John. Allow at least an hour and a half round-trip, wear good shoes (uneven and rocky footing), and bring plenty of water and sun protection.

Sleeping in Kotor: I'd rather bunk in Dubrovnik—Kotor is pricey and can be noisy after dark. But if you need a bed, consider the stony-chic **$$$ Hotel Villa Duomo** (www.villaduomo. com), the businesslike and super-central **$$$ Hotel Vardar** (www. hotelvardar.com), or the affordable **$ D&Sons Apartments** (www. dandsons.com).

Eating in Kotor: Cesarica offers unpretentious seafood in a casual, stony interior buried deep in the Old Town (Stari Grad 375). Just around the harbor, you'll find the simple and rustic **Tanjga** barbecue place, with huge portions of grilled meat; and the more refined **Restaurant Galion,** for seafood overlooking the boats (Šuranj bb).

Budva Riviera

A 15-mile stretch of coarse-sand and fine-pebble beaches runs along the coastline about 30 minutes south of Kotor. This "Budva Riviera" is unappealingly built up with a mix of cheap and luxury resort hotels. But the seafront is inviting, and the main town, **Budva,** has a charming Old Town crammed with souvenir shops and holidaymaking Serbs and Russians. Two churches (Catholic and Orthodox) face each other near the town's imposing (but empty) citadel.

The main draw along the Budva Riviera is the famous hotel island of ▲ **Sveti Stefan**—which hovers like a mirage just offshore, about a 20-minute drive south of Budva. Once an actual, living town (connected to the mainland only by a narrow, natural causeway), Sveti Stefan was converted into a luxury hotel in the 1950s. Its promise of privacy attracted celebrities, rock stars, royalty, and dignitaries—from Sophia Loren to Kirk Douglas

to Sly Stallone. More recently, it was again renovated into a super-exclusive, €1,000-plus-a-night resort. Only paying guests (no exceptions) can actually enter the island, but anyone is free to gaze over it from the road above, or to rent a pricey chair on the beaches that flank its causeway (there are a few free beach areas—ask the guard for pointers).

Montenegrin Interior

While the coastline gets all the buzz, the true heart of Montenegro beats behind the sheer wall of mountains rising up from that seafront. From near Kotor, an almost comically twisty road spirals up, up, up to the village of **Njeguši**—famous among Montenegrins for two reasons: as the hometown of the House of Petrović-Njegoš, the dynasty that ruled Montenegro for much of its history (1696-1918); and as the birthplace of Montenegrins' favorite food, the smoke-cured ham called *Njeguški pršut* (sold by various restaurants in town).

From here, the road winds across a startlingly desolate landscape to **Cetinje**—the now-humble historic capital of Montenegro.

Stuck in an economic rut, Cetinje tickles romantic historians but has few tangible sights. On its main square is a collection of small museums, and nearby—marking the birthplace of the town—is the local monastery, dedicated to a charismatic local priest who famously carried a cross in one hand and a sword in the other, established the first set of laws among Montenegrins, and inspired his people to defend Christian Montenegro against the Muslim Ottomans.

Even higher up from Cetinje, a winding road heads up to the mountaintop monument called **Lovćen,** which is capped by an elaborate mausoleum—designed by the great 20th-century Croatian sculptor Ivan Meštrović and devoted to King Petar II Petrović-Njegoš. From here, you can ogle the grandiose statues of a long-forgotten dynasty and, in the turn of a head, see a significant percentage of Montenegro.

BULGARIA

България / Bălgariya

Endearing, surprising Bulgaria is a rewarding and often over-looked destination. With a prime location at the intersection of civilizations—going all the way back to antiquity—it has an un-usually rich cultural heritage.
Despite (or perhaps because of) the country's tumultuous history, the Bulgarian people are sweet and soulful—eager to share their homeland's many underappreciated gems. Travelers who venture here enjoy thriving cities, remarkable ancient sites, a flavorful cuisine, a ruggedly beautiful landscape, and powerful memories. If more travelers realized how impressive (and how affordable) Bulgaria is, it'd be jammed. But they don't...so it isn't. You'll feel like you're in on the region's best-kept secret.

Where to Go: I've arranged this chapter's destinations in a counterclockwise loop that focuses on the highlights. On a short visit, the culturally rich "second city" of **Plovdiv** is the most rewarding choice. With more time, the church-and-museum-packed modern capital of **Sofia** and the historic capital of **Veliko Tarnovo**—with its dramatic setting and chatty craftspeople—each deserve a day. With even more time, make a pilgrimage to the stunningly set **Rila Monastery** (worth the effort) and linger a bit at the **Thracian Plain** (ancient tombs) and **Shipka Pass** (modern monuments)—both between Plovdiv and Veliko Tarnovo. If you have time to spare and want to hit the beach, consider adding the **Black Sea Coast**.

Getting Around: Trains (www.bdz.bg/en) and **buses** (www.

bgrazpisanie.com) connect the country well—if slowly—and make sense for those linking up the cities. But if you want to explore the countryside, **driving** here is relatively easy (outside of congested Sofia). Major roads are in good repair (though back roads can be somewhat deteriorated), traffic is fairly light, and drivers are generally courteous. To use expressways, you'll need a toll sticker (most cars rented here come with one).

Bulgarian Cuisine: Bulgaria boasts one of the tastiest and most interesting cuisines of Central Europe. Similar to Greek or

Turkish food, Bulgarian cooking includes plenty of red peppers and tomatoes, hearty grilled meats, crumbly cheeses, and lots of herbs and spices. (The pungent, powdered savory spice mix called *chubritsa*—used in just about everything—is a great culinary souvenir. The bright-red, tomatoes-peppers-and-eggplant

condiment *lyutenitsa* also packs a punch.) When in Bulgaria, I begin each meal with a *shopska* salad: chopped tomatoes, cucumbers, onions, parsley, and sometimes red peppers, all with a generous topping of feta-like cheese called *sirene*. Yogurt *(kiselo mlyako)* is big in Bulgaria. One of the tastiest ways to try it is in the refreshing cucumber-and-yogurt cold soup *tarator*—sprinkled with nuts, dill, and olive oil. For the main dish, you'll see lots of grilled meats; staples include *kyufte* (meatballs) and *kebapche* (kebabs). Another beloved dish is *sarmia*—stuffed grape or cabbage leaves. And the

Bulgaria Practicalities

Money: The currency is the Bulgarian lev/лев (plural leva/лева), which is divided into 100 stotinki/стотинки. $1 = about 1.75 leva.

Geography and People: Bulgaria is 43,000 square miles, roughly the size of Tennessee, with just over 7 million people. About 85 percent are ethnic Bulgarians, with large minorities of Muslims (9 percent, mostly of Turkish ancestry) and Roma (about 5 percent). It's fairly mountainous and bounded by the Danube to the north and the Black Sea to the east. Most people live in cities in the central plain, including the capital, Sofia (pop. 1.2 million), Plovdiv (340,000), and Varna (335,000). Bulgaria is one of the EU's poorest countries (per capita GDP: $24,400).

Snapshot History: At the intersection of the Greek, Turkish, and Slavic worlds, Bulgaria has quite a history. The Thracians had a robust culture here during antiquity. After the fall of Rome, the Slavs (sixth century) and Bulgars (seventh century) created the First Bulgarian Kingdom (9th-10th century)—which reached its peak during the reign of Simeon the Great (r. 893-927). After a period of decline, the Asen dynasty oversaw a medieval golden age (12th-14th century), when the Second Bulgarian Kingdom stretched from the Black Sea to the Adriatic. Then the Ottomans invaded, absorbing Bulgaria into their empire for 482 years. In 1877-1878, a Bulgarian-Russian army secured independence, giving rise to modern Bulgaria...and a series of devastating Balkan Wars with neighbors, which led to defeat in World War I. Since then, Bulgaria has taken a more peaceful tack, becoming part of the Soviet Bloc (1945-1989), and is now a modern, capitalistic, and democratic member of the EU.

Famous Bulgarians: Spartacus (leader of a slave revolt) was born in ancient Thrace. Cyril and Methodius—the missionary brothers who invented the Cyrillic alphabet and introduced Christianity to the Slavs in the ninth century—were born in Thessaloniki (then part of Bulgaria). In modern times, famous Bulgarians include opera singer Boris Christoff, "monument-wrapping" artist Christo, and actress Nina Dobrev.

Consular Services in Sofia: The US Embassy is at Ulitsa Kozyak 16 (+359 2937 5100, http://bg.usembassy.gov). Canadians use the embassy in Bucharest, Romania (see page 1038).

Tourist Information: www.bulgariatravel.org

main Bulgarian street food is *banitsa*—a savory, cheesy phyllo-dough pastry (like a *burek* or a Greek *kopeta*) that's also popular at breakfast. And for dessert, Bulgarian sweets resemble Turkish ones: phyllo- and honey-based (baklava, *kadaif*) and halva (with sesame or sunflower-seed tahini). Bulgaria produces some decent wines that are worth trying...but not writing home about.

Bulgarian Language: Bulgarian is a Slavic language, closely related to Russian, Croatian, Bosnian, and Serbian. Bulgaria officially uses the Cyrillic alphabet—intimidating at first, but easy to sound out, once you've done a little studying (see the sidebar). Many Bulgarians—particularly those in the tourist trade—speak some English. In this chapter, I've listed both the Cyrillic and Roman spellings for key place names. Some key phrases: "Hello" is *Zdravejte*/Здравейте (formal) or just *Zdravei*/Здравей (informal), "Please" is *Molya te*/Моля те, "Thank you" is *Blagodarya*/Благодаря, and "Goodbye" is *Dovizhdane*/Довиждане.

Local Guide: In Bulgaria, hiring your own guide is a great investment. Stefan Bozadzhiev and the gang at **Lyuba Tours** offer everything from architectural walks of Sofia to fully guided, in-depth private tours around Bulgaria (www.lyubatours.com). Thanks to Stefan and Lyuba Tours for their help with the information in this chapter.

Top Bulgarian Destinations

The following sections are designed to get you started planning a trip to Bulgaria.

▲▲Sofia (София)

Bulgaria's capital, Sofia (locals say SOHF-yuh, not soh-FEE-ya) is delightfully livable, with an airy street plan, fine architecture, lush parks, snow-capped mountains on the horizon, and a relaxed pace of life (www.visitsofia.bg).

Visiting Sofia: Most of the sights mentioned here are in the easily walkable town center; a slick two-line Metro system and extensive tram network make longer jumps easy.

Sofia's ▲▲▲ **Alexander Nevsky Cathedral** is one of the largest Orthodox churches in Christendom—and the only national church I can think of that's named for an important saint of a different country: Russia. (The Bulgarians feel a Slavic kinship with Russia, who helped liberate them from nearly five centuries of Ottoman rule. The church is dedicated to Russian soldiers lost in that fight.) Built at about the same time as the Eiffel Tower, it's newer than it looks—with a steel frame clad in limestone veneer and invisible buttresses that hold up its cascading gold and copper domes. The church is a pan-national creation, designed by Rus-

Learning the Cyrillic Alphabet

If you're going to Bulgaria—even if just on a short visit—you'll have a much richer, smoother experience if you take the time to learn the Cyrillic alphabet. Once you know the basics, you can (slowly) sound out signs, and some of those very long, confusing words will become familiar.

The table shows the Cyrillic alphabet (both capital and lowercase), and in the second column, the Roman equivalent. Notice that the letters fall—very roughly—into four categories: Some letters are basically the same sound as in English, such as A, E, K, M, O, and T. Others are easy if you know the Greek alphabet: Г—gamma (g), Д—delta (d), П—pi (p), and Ф—phi (f). Some are unique to Cyrillic; most of these are "fricative" sounds, like ts, sh, ch, sht, or kh (Ж, З, Ц, Ч, Ш, Щ, Х). And the fourth category seems designed to trip you up: "false friends" that have a different sound than the Roman letter they resemble, such as В, С, Н, Р, Х, and У. It can be helpful to remember that the "backward" Roman consonants are actually vowels (И, Й, Я).

Cyrillic	Roman	Cyrillic	Roman
Аа	a	Пп	p
Бб	b	Рр	r
Вв	v	Сс	s
Гг	g	Тт	t
Дд	d	Уу	u
Ее	e	Фф	f
Жж	zh	Хх	kh
Зз	z	Цц	ts
Ии	i	Чч	ch
Йй	y	Шш	sh
Кк	k	Щщ	sht
Лл	l	Ъъ	uh
Мм	m	ьь	y
Нн	n	Юю	yu
Оо	o	Яя	ya

sian architects and decorated with Venetian mosaics, Slovenian oak doors, and Bohemian crystal chandeliers.

Inside, you're immersed in a rich aroma of incense and beeswax candle smoke. Shoulder-level candelabras represent prayers for the living; knee-level ones are for the deceased (buy candles in the entryway). Every available surface is slathered with gold-mosaic icons—depicting 247 saints and 25 scenes from the life of Jesus. In front of the marble iconostasis are two marble thrones: One for the czar, and the other for the patriarch (head of the Bulgarian Orthodox Church). Per tradition, the czar's throne is bigger—demonstrating the Orthodox belief that a divinely ordained monarch has supremacy over the head of the church (the opposite of Catholic tradition). And yet, the czar's throne faces the pulpit, where an eagle (symbol of the Church) hovers in judgment over a lion (symbol of the czar)—a none-too-subtle reminder that the final reckoning comes later. On the smaller iconostasis to the left of the main altar, a cheeky Czech artist infused his saints with personality rare in Orthodox church art. Mary looks like a real mom, tenderly kissing the arm of her Baby Jesus—who's not a serene cherub, but a fidgety toddler.

Across the street is Sofia's most historic church, and its namesake: the ▲ **Church of Sveta Sofia** ("Holy Wisdom"), with an austere brick basilica floor plan. The core of the church was built by the Byzantine emperor Justinian in the sixth century. Underfoot sprawl lovingly excavated mosaic floors (now a museum). Outside, the **Tomb of the Unknown Soldier** is guarded by a stone lion—the national symbol—who looks not proud or fierce, but sad...suggesting the Bulgarians' generally pacifistic attitude after a grueling 20th century.

From this area, enjoy the parks, squares, and streets of Sofia's mellow downtown. Sofia even has an actual **yellow brick road.** When Austria's emperor Franz Josef visited Sofia in 1907, he had to trudge through muddy streets. When he was invited back, he donated these bricks—made from a vivid-yellow limestone—to pave Sofia's streets.

A few blocks to the west (just follow the yellow brick road), you'll run into **Independence Square** (Ploshtad Nezavisimost)—

ringed by an ensemble of severe communist-style governmental buildings called the Largo. The former Communist Party House—with its bold spire—faces a 65-foot-tall pillar that was once occupied by Vladimir Lenin. Today, that pillar is topped by a statue of **Sveta Sofia** (Holy Wisdom). Near the pillar, head down into the Metro underpass to see Roman ruins dating back two millennia. Archaeologists are constantly finding, excavating, and displaying fragments of the Roman town of "Serdica"—a reminder that an ancient world sprawls beneath the feet of modern commuters.

Just to the right of the former communist HQ is a little square fronted by the president's residence (featuring an extremely modest changing of the guard out front) and—housed in a huge former mosque—the ▲ **National Archaeological Museum,** with an exquisite collection of golden jewelry from ancient Thrace (www. naim.bg).

One block north of the Sveta Sofia monument is the **central market hall,** a great place to pick up a snack or some picnic fixings. Tucked just behind the market is Europe's third-largest **synagogue,** designed by an Austrian architect in the early 20th century (www.sofiasynagogue. com). Bulgaria was one of the only countries in Nazi territory that refused to turn its Jewish population over to Hitler. All 49,000 Bulgarian Jews survived the Holocaust.

Across the busy street from the market is the elegant, early-20th-century **Central Mineral Baths** complex, now renovated and gleaming (and home to the city history museum). Sofia prides itself on its natural springs, which attracted the first settlers here in ancient times. Poke through the park on the left (near the tram stop) to find a bunch of perpetually flowing public taps, where locals fill up big jugs of warm, mineral-tasting, supposedly very healthy spring water.

From this area, the pedestrianized, shop-and-restaurant-lined **Vitosha Boulevard** runs to the south. This lively people zone is where the people of Sofia promenade, nurse a coffee, and catch up with friends. It leads to the communist-era **National Palace of Culture** and a surrounding park—with Sofians enjoying their city while ignoring the boldly socialist-style architecture.

Those interested in the communist period can track down some other intriguing artifacts. Just to the northeast, in Knyazheska Park, stands the **Monument of the Soviet Army,** honoring the Soviets who helped liberate Bulgaria in World War II. One panel on the side of the main plinth is regularly (and creatively) defaced with pointed political graffiti.

To see more statues that once intimidated the cityscape, head about three miles southeast of the center to the ▲ **Museum of Socialist Art.** You'll see—preaching their message to each other in an empty field—the Lenin that once topped the pillar in the center of town; Georgi Dimitrov, the "Bulgarian Lenin"; the red star that capped the Communist Party HQ; and several stoic soldiers and workers.

Two more important sights are in the Boyana district, in the foothills of Mount Vitosha, about five miles southwest of the center. The humble brick ▲▲ **Boyana Church** contains a treasure trove of stunning 13th-century frescoes, combining a strong Orthodox faith with very early-Renaissance Western European styles (think Giotto). The Boyana frescoes are unique in their early use of basic perspective, fluid motion, natural rather than stiff poses, subjects with real human emotions and personalities, and the skillful use of bold colors to suggest three dimensions—you can practically see bodies moving around under the subjects' clothes (www.boyanachurch.org). Nearby, housed in a particularly boxy old communist-era palace, is the ▲ **National Historical Museum,** with a fine collection of fragments from the full span of Bulgarian history (www.historymuseum.org).

Sleeping in Sofia: Two good options in the walkable town center are the professional, upscale **$$ Crystal Palace Boutique Hotel** (www.crystalpalace-sofia.com) and the simpler **$ Arte Hotel** (www.artehotelbg.com).

Eating in Sofia: It's easy to simply stroll Vitosha Boulevard, which is lined with tempting options. Along here I've eaten well at **Shtastliveca** (Щастливеца, long menu of traditional Bulgarian dishes in a kitschy mod-traditional setting, at #27, www.shtastliveca.com). A pocket of fun, trendier eateries is just west of Vistosha near Karnigradska and Solunska streets. And for a youthful, fast-changing foodie scene, explore the streets just east of the City Garden (behind the National Theatre). In this area, **Raketa Rakia Bar** is a trendy, communist-kitsch-themed nightspot with Bulgarian cuisine and more than 100 types of *rakia* (Balkan firewater; at Yanko Sakazov 17).

▲▲▲Rila Monastery (Rilski Manastir/Рилски Манастир)

Bulgaria's spiritual heart and soul reside about 80 miles south of the capital, deep in the Rila (REE-lah) Mountains. Here you'll find Rila Monastery—a fortress on the outside, spiritual sanctuary inside. The monastery was founded in the 930s by Bulgaria's patron saint, St. John of Rila (or Ivan Rilski, as Bulgarians call him), who came here seeking a hermetic way of life.

During the Dark Ages, monks at Rila kept the faint embers of

Bulgarian Orthodox thought glowing. Later, during a period of Ottoman occupation—when conversion to Islam was strongly encouraged—remote monasteries like Rila became lifeboats for the Bulgarian faith, language, literature, and cultural artifacts. Today, Rila is a place of pilgrimage for Bulgarians, who consider it their faith's single most important site. And tourists are amazed by its pristine setting (tucked between mountains and forests), the reverent spirituality that fills its stony courtyard, and the vivid art that decorates its church.

Visiting Rila Monastery: The monastery is best for drivers, who can reach it in about two hours from Sofia (mostly on the slick A-3 expressway). It's also possible to reach by public bus, or—better—on a dedicated shuttle bus (also stops at Boyana Church—described earlier, reserve ahead, www.rilamonasterybus.com).

Stepping from the parking lot through the hulking outer wall, you emerge into a serene courtyard facing a red-and-white-striped church and a mountain backdrop. The stout **Hrelyo Tower** is the oldest part of the complex, from the 1330s; this was the place of last refuge in case of attack.

The complex's centerpiece church was built in the 1830s, after a fire. The walls and ceilings of its **porch** are slathered with

sumptuous, colorful frescoes— all crammed with details and symbolism. You'll see biblical stories, angels, devils, saints, and sinners. One elaborate scene shows the 40 days of trials your soul goes through after death, as a guardian angel accompanies the soul—represented by a small child—through a gauntlet of temptations.

The **church interior** is gloomy and atmospheric—air heavy with candle soot and incense. Next to each important icon hangs a small towel, used to wipe off smeared lipstick from reverent kisses. The right transept holds the heart of Czar Boris III, who capably led his country through World War II. Boris preserved Bulgarian sovereignty by politically allying with Nazi Germany. And yet, the czar defied orders to send Bulgaria's Jewish population to concentration camps and refused to formally declare war on Bulgaria's biggest historic ally, the Soviet Union. Because Hitler needed access to Bulgaria's Black Sea ports—and lacked the resources to invade—he put up with it...until the summer of 1943, when Boris died mysteriously after a private audience with Hitler in Berlin. Many suspect a slow-acting poison, and Boris remains revered by the Bulgarian people.

Behind the church, find the **museum** holding treasures that devoted Bulgarians have donated or created to honor their most hallowed site. The highlight is the Rafail Cross, with 23 panels (each smaller than a deck of cards) depicting 36 Bible scenes populated by 650 toothpick-sized figures, all on a cross about the size of a hubcap. The monk who carved it over the course of 12 years literally went blind in the process—yet another remarkable act of devotion in this place that specializes in it.

Sleeping and Eating at Rila Monastery: While Rila is an active monastery (with resident monks), some of the **$ cells** have been converted into rustic accommodations for pilgrims and tourists (www.rilamonastery.info). Eateries cluster outside the north entrance to the monastery (opposite the parking lot), and additional hotels and restaurants line the road between the monastery and the expressway.

▲▲▲Plovdiv (Пловдив)

If you visit only one city in Bulgaria, make it Plovdiv (PLOHV-div). The country's "second city," Plovdiv has it all: excellent sightseeing, a charming Old Town, and a bustling New Town (www.visitplovdiv.com). It's fascinating to explore and easy to enjoy. And people have enjoyed it for a very long time: Plovdiv claims to be one of the oldest continually inhabited cities in the world. The ancient Greeks dubbed it Philippopolis (for the father of Alexander the Great), and the Romans called it Trimontium (for the "three hills" it was built upon). Today you'll see a ruined acropolis, a well-preserved ancient theater, gorgeous 19th-century homes filled with the art of local painters, Bulgaria's most thriving pedestrian boulevard, and a hipster zone with creative restaurants and even more creative graffiti.

Visiting Plovdiv: Plovdiv has two parallel worlds, just steps apart and equally worth exploring: The Old Town (draped over a hill) and the New Town (filling the flat valley below). The city is compact—you can easily see everything on foot.

The **Old Town** blankets the slopes of some of the many hills that make up Plovdiv. Its rustic streets—with ankle-wrecking riverstone cobbles—are lined with dozens of homes in the eye-pleasing **Bulgarian National Revival style.** In the mid-19th century, when the ruling Ottoman Empire was in decline, the Bulgarians sought to celebrate their

culture with this unique style: wooden-beam construction with upper floors that bulge outward, tastefully painted in vivid colors.

Today, many of these buildings house museums, including the ▲ **Hindliyan House**—dating from 1840 and decorated to the taste of its merchant owner. It still feels lived in, with opulent sitting rooms, a starburst-painted ceiling, a Turkish-style *hamam*, a rose-water fountain, and "souvenir" wall paintings showing off some of the merchant's far-flung business travels, from Stockholm to Venice.

Another house contains an art gallery celebrating a little-known but supremely talented Bulgarian painter. ▲▲▲ **Zlatyu Boyadzhiev** (1903-1976) was already a well-established artist when, in 1951, he suffered a stroke that rendered his right hand useless. Boldly embarking on a second act, Boyadzhiev's left hand began painting scenes that looked nothing like the ones his right hand had produced. Over the next 25 years, he reveled in bright colors with a childlike exuberance, slapping thick, Van Gogh-like brushstrokes onto the canvas. Boyadzhiev's best works feature timeless slices of peasant life: People praying not in temples but under trees. Locals

sitting around a public fountain sipping glasses of wine. Peasant women clustered around a fire, knitting as they eke out warmth. A fattened pig being slaughtered for Christmas; above the victim, each weathered face could tell a story.

Boyadzhiev also had a subversive streak. In *Public Prayer,* scrawny villagers come together to pray for good fortune; everyone is skinny...except the fat priest. In *The Orphanage,* a motley collection of disabled beggars (and their disabled pets) huddle behind their larger-than-life chieftain. Boyadzhiev was also captivated by the Karakachani, a nomadic tribe that herded their woolly sheep throughout the Balkans until the communists ended their way of life in the 1950s. Boyadzhiev worked under the communist regime but managed to buck the predominant Socialist Realism style. Because he glorified peasant life without threatening any of the communists' sacred cows, Boyadzhiev was allowed to carry on. This makes Boyadzhiev the rare artist who thrived under communism... and also had real talent.

The Old Town hillside also has some ancient sites. Up at the very top of town, the scant remains of the **acropolis** offer grand views over the modern skyline. And partway down the hill is a remarkably intact ▲▲ **ancient theater.** This 5,000-seat the-

BULGARIA

Eastern Orthodox Church

Bulgaria is one of many Central/Eastern European countries that is predominantly Eastern Orthodox Christian. (Others include entire nations—Russia, Serbia, and Greece—or a significant percentage of the population, as in Bosnia, Montenegro, and Slovenia.)

As you explore an Orthodox church, keep in mind that these churches carry on the earliest traditions of the Christian faith. Orthodox and Catholic Christianity came from the same roots, so the oldest surviving early Christian churches (such as the stave churches of Norway) have many of the same features as today's Orthodox churches.

Notice that there are no pews. Worshippers stand through the service, as a sign of respect (though some older parishioners sit on the seats along the walls). Women stand on the left side, men on the right (equal distance from the altar—to represent that all are equal before God). The Orthodox Church uses essentially the same Bible as Catholics, but it's written in the Cyrillic alphabet, which you'll see displayed around any Orthodox church. Following Old Testament Judeo-Christian tradition, the Bible is kept on the altar behind the iconostasis, the big screen in the middle of the room covered with curtains and icons (golden paintings of saints), which separates the material world from the spiritual one. At certain times during the service, the curtains or doors are opened so the congregation can see the Holy Book.

Unlike the decorations in many Catholic churches, Orthodox icons are not intended to be lifelike. Packed with intricate symbolism, and cast against a shimmering golden background, they're meant to remind viewers of the metaphysical nature of Jesus and the saints rather than of their physical form, which is considered irrelevant. You'll almost never see a statue, which is thought to overemphasize the physical world...and, to Orthodox people, feels a little too close to violating the commandment, "Thou shalt not worship graven images." Orthodox services generally involve chanting (a dialogue that goes back and forth between the priest and the congregation), and the church is filled with the evocative aroma of incense.

The incense, chanting, icons, and standing up are all intended to heighten the experience of worship. While many Catholic and Protestant services tend to be more of a theoretical and rote consideration of religious issues (come on—don't tell me you've never dozed through the sermon), Orthodox services are about creating a religious experience. Each of these elements does its part to help the worshipper transcend the physical world and join in communion with the spiritual one.

ater—built by Emperor Trajan—wasn't discovered until the 1960s. Now excavated, the theater's wall is mostly intact, the stony seats are still etched with their original numbers, and the acoustics remain perfect. Plays are performed here regularly.

Just below the theater, an underpass below the busy main thoroughfare leads to the **New Town**. The twisty streets straight ahead constitute the district called **Kapana** ("The Mousetrap"). Not long ago, this was a dreary, deserted, and dangerous quarter. But an initiative to pedestrianize and cobble the streets has turned the area into a hipster paradise. The streets are lined with bars, cafés, and creative galleries (look for PLOVEdiv, with prints that put a whimsical pop-culture spin on old communist icons). This zone also has more than its share of creative, government-subsidized graffiti. Local authorities figure that street artists will tag buildings anyway—so they might as well focus all that creativity and pay them to do it.

A couple of blocks south, you'll pop out at the ▲ **Dzhumaya Mosque.** Dating from the 1360s, this mosque is one of the few that remain of the dozens that filled the streets of Plovdiv during Ottoman times. Renovated in 2006, today the evocative mosque is an active house of worship serving Plovdiv's substantial Muslim population. Outside of prayer times, visitors are invited to step inside.

Directly in front of the mosque, they've excavated the seats at the end of a long and skinny ▲▲ **stadium** built in the first century

AD. You can walk down to see the seats, or just enjoy a drink at the café. On some evenings, outdoor movies and other events fill this space.

From here, the ancient racecourse runs (unseen) beneath Plovdiv's **main walking street** (officially named Knyaz Alexander I Street). Lined with cafés and busy shoppers, this drag is a delightful place to simply stroll. Partway down, at the grand staircase, look for the big blocky footprint in the middle of the street—marking what was the far end of the stadium. Those stairs lead up behind the burgundy-colored National Theatre; along its back wall is more city-sponsored graffiti (facing a rocky cliff with graffiti of Bulgarian VIPs).

Back on the main drag, continue heading south, past the American fast-food chain Макдоналдс. Soon after, the street opens up into an inviting fountain square. Just beyond is the giant, blocky, communist-era post office, anchoring the vast Central Square (Ploshtad Tsentralen)—which still has intimidating echoes of communist times, from the elite communist-era Hotel Trimontium (now a more run-of-the-mill Ramada) to the conceptual sculpture-fountain. Sprawling on your right is the gorgeous Tsar Simeon Garden, a well-used public park with footpaths, fountains, playgrounds, and the people of Plovdiv enjoying their city.

Sleeping in Plovdiv: In the Old Town, **$ Hebros Hotel** fills a cozy old Bulgarian National Revival mansion with characteristic rooms and a great restaurant (www.hebros-hotel.com). The smaller **$ Family Hotel at Renaissance Square,** between the Old and New Towns, is also a good choice (www.atrenaissancesq.com). At the other end of town, **$$ Hotel Trimontium**—once the top-of-the-top communist-era hotel—is now a comfortable Ramada with easy access to the New Town's main drag (www.wyndhamhotels.com).

Eating in Plovdiv: The Kapana ("Mousetrap") district has several trendy bars and cafes, and the excellent **Pavaj** (Паваж) restaurant, which updates Bulgarian classics and international dishes with a hipster/foodie aesthetic (Zlatarska 7). The recommended **Hotel Hebros** has a restaurant with an upscale (but still affordable) vibe and well-executed, upscale Bulgarian dishes served in a classy dining room or on a leafy patio (www.hebros-hotel.com). On or near the New Town's main walking drag, consider the tacky but popular **Happy** chain (basically the Applebees of Bulgaria, Vasil Levski 2, www.happy.bg), the more upscale-feeling **Hemingway** (Gurko 10, www.hemingway.bg), or the kitschy-touristy-traditional **Dayana** (Даяна, most central branch at Knyaz Al. Dondukov-Korsakov 4, www.dayanabg.com).

Nearby: About a half-hour south of Plovdiv, in the Rhodope Mountain foothills, is **Bachkovo Monastery** (Бачковски манастир). It plays second fiddle to Rila—with a less romantic location and less dramatic frescoes—but for those based in Plovdiv, it's far easier to reach. Come here for an accessible look at a soulful Bulgarian Orthodox monastery. The

BULGARIA

two-story ossuary has some particularly fine frescoes from the 11th through 14th centuries.

▲Thracian Plain (Тракийска Низина)

Defined by Bulgaria's two major mountain ranges, the Thracian Plain was a busy funnel of trade throughout ancient times. This was the home of the Thracians (see the sidebar), who left behind tombs filled with ancient treasure.

Kazanlak (Казанлък, KAH-zahn-luk), with around 50,000 people, is the main town of the Thracian Plain. The workaday town—with a broad main square and a low-rise, communist-concrete aesthetic—is mainly of interest for sights relating to the Thracian tombs (www.muzei-kazanlak.org).

In the town of Kazanlak itself, the **Kazanlak replica tomb** demonstrates how even in the afterlife, the deceased would be

surrounded by colorful slices of Thracian life. You'll squeeze through a narrow passage, then crouch under a dome painted with vivid scenes: the eternal banquet of the Thracian who's buried here, flanked by servants, musicians, and horses.

Three more interesting tombs are within about a 10-minute drive of Kazanlak. At **Shushmanets** (Шушманец, SHOOSH-mah-nets), you can see how a single, stout column supported a heavy load. You'll also see a block with a well-worn hole, illustrating how the double stone doors could swing open and closed on a pivot. Nearby, **Ostrusha** (Оструша, OS-troo-sha) began as a temple. The entire block-like structure was carved out of one gigantic chunk of rock. That's 60 tons—triple the size of the blocks used for the Egyptian pyramids—transported here from the mountains 12 miles away. And then they had to carve it without cracking it. On the ceiling inside survives a fresco of a ghostly, enigmatic face—showing how

Thracians were usually depicted as redheads. And **Kosmatka** (Косматка, kos-MAT-kah)— the tomb of Seuthes III—lets you peek into a multichambered tomb similar to the Kazanlak replica.

For a look at some of the breathtaking items found inside those tombs, back in Kazanlak, visit the ▲ **Iskra-Kazanlak**

The Thracians and Their Tombs

Four centuries before Christ—when Socrates and Plato were doing their thing in Athens (about 300 miles to the south)—today's Bulgaria was known as Thrace, with a sophisticated civilization all its own. Famous Thracian figures include Spartacus (the charismatic leader of a Roman slave rebellion), Orpheus (a mythical musician and poet, likely based on an actual Thracian prince), and several emperors (including Justinian the Great). Thracians traded with other civilizations near and far. They had a reputation as redheads and fearsome fighters. And they had a remarkable skill for crafting jewelry as exquisite as anything you'll see today.

Thracians buried their royalty in distinctive, igloo-shaped tombs that were covered in earth. Dozens of these tombs (called *tumuli*) are scattered across the Thracian Plain, along with hundreds of decoy mounds designed to fool grave robbers. Buried deep under those piles of earth, the tombs were impressive feats of fourth-century-BC engineering. The dead were buried with troves of golden treasure, now displayed in museums throughout Bulgaria (including the museum in Kazanlak and Sofia's National Archaeological Museum and National Historical Museum).

Fans of ancient sites enjoy visiting a few of the tombs near Kazanlak, the region's main town (described in this chapter). True aficionados make a pilgrimage to the even bigger and more impressively decorated tomb at Sveshtari, in northeastern Bulgaria (about 4 hours from Kazanlak, or 2.5 hours from Veliko Tarnovo). Either way, you'll be impressed by the sophisticated engineering and delicate artistry of people who lived two and a half millennia ago.

Historical Museum. The museum includes a room of Thracian artifacts: an intimidating helmet, with an attachable wreath of gilded leaves; a double-handled golden wine cup, or kylix; a solid-gold clamshell case; and some finely detailed jewelry. Red-and-black Greek vases were likely obtained in exchange for Thracian copper ore and gold.

Kazanlak is also the capital of Bulgaria's **rose-oil** industry. (This area is known as the "Valley of the Roses.") Each May and June, hardworking laborers rise early to pick the delicate roses that have bloomed overnight, then take them to a distillery where they can be converted to fragrant oil. (It looks—and smells—like they're making very rosy moonshine.) Shops around town—and all over Bulgaria—sell the final product. It all culminates in Kazanlak's Rose Festival, usually in early June.

Sleeping in Kazanlak: The accommodations here are nothing

BULGARIA

special; **$ Hotel Palas** is central, just a short walk from the main square (www.hotel-palas.com).

▲▲Balkan Mountains and Shipka Pass

Between the Thracian Plain and Veliko Tarnovo run the Balkan Mountains (which gave their name to this entire peninsula). Crossing over this range, you'll pass several worthwhile sights. For a visual orientation, scan the mountainous horizon from the valley near Kazanlak and try to pick out three big landmarks: the flying-saucer shaped Buzludzha monument, the blocky Shipka Pass monument, and—down below that—the glimmering golden domes of Shipka Church.

▲▲ **Buzludzha** (Бузлуджа, BOOZ-lood-zhah)—an abandoned monument to the Bulgarian Communist Party—is easily

worth ▲▲▲ for those captivated by Bulgaria's communist heritage. This gigantic conference hall was built in the 1980s, in the waning days of communist rule. With the end of the Cold War and the arrival of capitalism, Buzludzha was abandoned. Today, you can drive up, up, up into the mountains and stand before this decaying souvenir of a failed system. The lyrics of the international communist anthem are literally falling off the walls. And the Coke-aping "Enjoy Communism" graffiti makes it clear who won the Cold War.

The structure is officially closed, and recently there's been talk of renovating it, at long last. It may be possible to find a way inside the structure (this is—I cannot stress enough—at your own risk). The interior is an eerie, crumbling world of vandalized propaganda, muddy asbestos, a roof that's barely held up by its hammer and sickle, and disintegrating mosaics—once so proud, and now just a humble artifact of a fallen empire. The monument is a twisty, 20-minute (each way) drive from the valley. To find the road up, look for the turnoff along the main road between Kazanlak and Shipka, marked by the stoic communist-era statue standing by a pillar.

The sumptuous ▲▲ **Shipka Church** sits on a hillside above the simple town of Shipka. The church—completed in 1902 by some of the leading Russian architects of the day—is exuberant "Muscovite-style"...over-the-top Baroque-meets-Byzantine. It's dedicated to the Russian and Bulgarian troops (now buried in the crypt) who fought fiercely to defeat the Ottomans in 1877 (see next). Stepping inside, you enter a world of glittering icons, a rich haze of incense, and hundreds of tall, skinny candles. The 175-foot-tall steeple, flanked by bulbous golden onion domes that shimmer in the sunshine, holds a giant bell cast from discarded artillery cartridges after the battle.

Higher up on the road to Veliko Tarnovo, you'll pass a turnoff for **Shipka Pass** (Shipchenski Prohod/Шипченски Проход). It's worth a quick detour to the monument marking the summit. A long staircase leads up to the boxy tower that honors the pivotal 1877 battle—fought right here—in which elite Russian forces came to help homegrown Bulgarian troops put an end to the nearly five centuries of Ottoman rule. This was a key turning point in Bulgarian history and led directly to the creation of a modern, fully independent Bulgarian state. It also gave Bulgarians a soft spot for their big ally, Russia (unlike in most of Eastern Europe, where Russia is seen as an unwanted bully). This is partly why, a century later, Bulgaria was the most docile of the Soviet satellite states.

Descending from Shipka Pass on the north (Veliko Tarnovo) slope, you'll coast into the town of Palauzovo. Here you can turn off for a 30-minute drive to ▲ **Tryavna** (Трявна, tree-AHV-nah), a touristy village with an abundance of traditional Bulgarian National Revival-style homes. Stout stone foundations support whitewashed walls and heavy slate roofs, and each door seems to lead to a souvenir shop. While you can also see a version of this style in Plovdiv and in Veliko Tarnovo, Tryavna is a pleasant stretch-your-legs small-town option. From here, you can simply continue north (via Tsareva Livada) to rejoin the main Veliko Tarnovo road.

If you skip the Tryavna turnoff, you'll pass through the big, gritty city of **Gabrovo** (Габрово). Filling an isolated valley with heavy industry, Gabrovo is the butt of many jokes for its people's thrifty ways. But these days, Gabrovo has the last laugh as the home of a museum called the House of Humor and Satire (you'll pass right by it on the main road, www.humorhouse.bg).

▲▲Veliko Tarnovo (Велико Търново)

One of Europe's most dramatically set cities, Veliko Tarnovo (VEH-lee-koh TAR-noh-voh) bunny-hops through a misty gorge at a sharp bend of the Yantra River. The town's hillsides are blanketed with both traditional homes and dreary concrete housing blocks. In this town that's more vertical than horizontal, going for a walk around the block feels like climbing a ladder. Tarnovo was the capital of the Second Bulgarian Kingdom, which was the medieval high-water mark of Bulgarian civilization. Today, with 70,000 inhabitants, and a prestigious university with around 18,000 students, it's called *Veliko* (Great) Tarnovo to honor its illustrious past. Aside from its stunning setting and rich history, Veliko Tarnovo offers the chance to meet some crafts-

people, scramble around a ruined castle, and side-trip to several worthwhile sights (www.velikoturnovo.info).

Visiting Veliko Tarnovo: Perched on the rim of a gorge, Veliko Tarnovo is shaped like a natural amphitheater. And center stage—dominating a little peninsula

defined by the tight river bend—is a giant sword thrusting skyward, ringed by fearsome horseback warriors. This monument commemorates the **Asen clan,** who ruled over the Second Bulgarian Kingdom (13th-14th century). According to legend, these brothers planted their sword on this spot and said, "Here shall be Bulgaria." While Bulgarian history can be obscure to outsiders, the Second Bulgarian Kingdom really was a big deal—an era when the Asen dynasty dominated the Balkan Peninsula from Ukraine to Greece. Their decline ushered in the Ottoman rule that would dominate Bulgarian history for nearly five centuries. You can circle all the way around town to find the bridge that goes out to the monument (and the art gallery just behind it); the best views from afar are along the charming, cobbled Gurko Street (near Hotel Gurko).

Veliko Tarnovo's town center lines up along **Stambolov Street,** which follows the curve of the river a few very steep blocks uphill. Branching off from this main drag is the town's most appealing lane, Rakovski Street—which I think of as ▲▲ **"Craftspeople Street."** Along this cobbled street are several talented artisans who enjoy inviting visitors to watch them create traditional crafts. Do some window-shopping, and

drop in on any shop that grabs your attention: Silversmith Todor Kushlev creates intricate filigree jewelry by hand—or, in the case of his blowtorch—by mouth. Nina and her son create pottery with patterns dating back centuries. Miglena operates an old-fashioned loom. Rumi carves wooden items. Rashko painstakingly paints icons. And Greti carefully pours a thin stream of dough onto a spinning griddle to create delicate shredded wheat-like strands for the honey-soaked treat *kadaif*. (She doesn't sell the *kadaif*, mind you—just the strands. B.Y.O. honey.)

Farther south, Stambolov Street passes above what many consider to be the first parliament of Bulgaria—today the **Revival and Assembly Museum.** With the 1877-1878 expulsion of the Ottoman Empire (with Russian help), Bulgaria was free to create a modern nation. The National Assembly convened right here for the first time in 1879 and ratified a constitution. Today, you can see the original assembly hall and peruse a fine museum with vivid photographs documenting the Bulgarian National Revival movement and the creation of the modern Bulgarian state (www. museumvt.com). The building itself was designed by Kolyu Ficheto (1800-1881)—Bulgaria's leading 19th-century architect—who is honored by a statue out front. On a little crest just above, the striking, green-domed **Cathedral of the Nativity of the Virgin** (Rozhdestvo Bogorodichno, also designed by Ficheto) has a terrace with a great view over the gorge and castle.

Just over the ridge, the ruins of ▲ **Tsarevets Fortress** mark the site of the heavily fortified Asen headquarters. While little survives, tourists enjoy nocking imaginary arrows from the bastions, taking in the views, and tiptoeing up to the so-called "Execution Rock"—where no ax or gallows were needed...just a firm shove into a deep gorge. The (reconstructed) church at the summit has unusual modern decorations. These were commissioned by Lyudmila Zhivkova (1942-1981)—the communist-era President of Art and Culture (and daughter of the Bulgarian dictator)—who, after surviving a car wreck and getting into yoga, used her influence to try to merge communist ideology with counterculture art and New Age philosophy. (She was being groomed as her father's heir apparent, and it would have been fascinating to see what direction she'd have steered the country...if she hadn't died—mysteriously, some say—of a brain tumor at age 38.) An elevator zips sightseers up to the steeple's crenelated top for the best high-altitude views in town.

Sleeping and Eating in Veliko Tarnovo: Friendly **$ Hotel Gurko** enjoys an atmospheric Old Town setting. They also have a decent restaurant, but I prefer to hike (essentially straight uphill) to **Shtastliveca** (Щастливеца); reserve a table on the little cliff-hanging terrace with breathtaking canyon views (Stambolov 79, www.shtastliveca.com).

▲Arbanasi (Арбанаси)

The village of Arbanasi (ahr-bah-NAH-see), which overlooks Veliko Tarnovo from an adjacent ridge (about a 15-minute drive away), is a handy side trip. The main attraction here is the **▲▲ Church of the Nativity,** with magnificent frescoes in a dark, claustrophobic, wonderfully historic-feeling space. Typical of modest 16th- and 17th-century Orthodox church architecture (under Ottoman rule), it feels like a hay barn

inside. The L-shaped gallery curves into the nave—and all of it is covered in still-vivid frescoes. Nearby, the **Konstantsalieva House** re-creates life here during Ottoman times. Also in Arbanasi, perched overlooking Veliko Tarnovo, is the **Arbanasi Palace Hotel**—the former residence of communist dictator Todor Zhivkov, who ruled Bulgaria for 35 years (the longest of any socialist dictator in Europe). While definitely faded, the hotel still enjoys the same grand views over Veliko Tarnovo that lured Zhivkov here—and you can sleep in his presidential suite.

Black Sea Coast (Chernomorie/Черноморие)

With more time, consider venturing to the eastern edge of Bulgaria: the Black Sea Coast, a popular budget beach destination for in-the-know Brits and Europeans. While I'm more drawn to Bulgaria's cultural treasures (and beaches are better in Croatia or Greece), the Black Sea Coast has its fans and helps round out your Bulgaria experience.

The main coastal city is **Varna** (Варна, VAR-nah). Varna has a skyscraper core; long, sandy, resort-lined beaches; the lush and sprawling Primorski ("Seaside") Park; ancient ruins, including a second-century Roman bathhouse; beautiful churches; and the excellent Varna Archaeological Museum, displaying the oldest jewelry in the world (from the fifth millennium BC), discovered in a local necropolis (visit.varna.bg).

The small-town alternative is **Nesebar** (Несебър, neh-SAY-bar), connected to the rest of Bulgaria by a narrow isthmus watched over by an iconic windmill (www.visitnessebar.org). This little town has an unusually rich cultural heritage, with artifacts from ancient Greek, Roman, Byzantine, Ottoman, and Bulgarian National Revival times. Nesebar is known for its many fine, partly ruined, striped-brick, Byzantine-style churches. It's also an enjoyable place to simply let your pulse slow, hit the beach, go for a boat ride, and get to know some real, working fishermen. And, for a little more activity, Nesebar adjoins the hard-partying, aptly-named **Sunny Beach** (Slanchev Bryag/Слънчев бряг) resort—as popular now as when it was purpose-built in communist times.

ROMANIA

România

Still haunted by legends of Vlad the Impaler and Nicolae Ceaușescu, Romania is complex—with an epic history, a multifaceted ethnic mix, and an unusually rich cultural heritage. It may not be the easiest place to travel, but for adventurous souls, it's exceptionally rewarding. It's a land that layers gritty cities, charming cobbled towns, glorious castles, ragtag countryside, cut-glass peaks, playing chicken with horse carts, and connecting with kindhearted people living in a crazy world...sometimes all in the same day. Love it or hate it (and often both at once), Romania provides a powerful and memorable travel experience.

Where to Go: Romania is a vast and varied country. To focus your visit, break it into four chunks: Wallachia (Bucharest), Transylvania (cute towns and castles),

Maramureș (traditional folk life), and Bucovina (painted monasteries).

Wallachia consists of Romania's flatlands, wrapped around the Carpathian Mountains and stretching from Transylvania to the Danube (and Bulgaria). From a traveler's perspective, the only city here worth visiting is **Bucharest**. The exquisite **Peleș Castle** is also (just barely) in Wallachia but feels closer to Transylvania.

Transylvania is Romania's heartland and where most visitors focus their time. You could spend many days here, sampling great cities, evocative castles and fortified churches, and a mountainous landscape. For home-base towns, big but charming **Brașov** works

well for venturing into the mountains and touring castles (including **Bran**, **Râşnov**, and **Peleş**). Little, well-preserved **Sighişoara** is the most charming town and handy for touring fortified churches (such as the ones in **Biertan** and **Viscri**). **Sibiu** is Romania's most livable city, with a thriving historical core; it's relatively close to the dramatic **Corvin Castle**. And sprawling **Cluj-Napoca**, Transylvania's biggest city and de facto capital, has bustling squares, inviting parks, and busy nightlife.

Maramureş—in the far-north of the country, squeezed just inside the Ukrainian border—is time-consuming to reach. But it's definitely worth the effort for those interested in **traditional lifestyles** (and the gorgeous **Merry Cemetery**). Make a home base in the countryside near **Sighetu Marmaţiei** and explore.

Bucovina, another traditional region to the east of Transylvania, is famous for its glorious **painted monasteries** (mostly near the town of Gura Humorului).

When planning your itinerary, don't underestimate the long distances (or the slow traffic). To avoid spending all of your time on the road, be selective. With just a few days, focus on Transylvania, dividing your time between two home-base towns (Braşov and Sighişoara are handiest). With more time, add Maramureş and/or Bucharest. Bucovina's painted monasteries are beautiful, but the region has little else to see, and it's a time-consuming detour—include Bucovina only if you have ample time. For an even longer visit, the Dobrogea region (with the lush Danube Delta and the city of Constanţa)—not covered in this book—is the most logical add-on.

Getting Around: Bucharest and other big cities are relatively

ROMANIA

Romania Practicalities

Money: Romanians use the leu ("lion"): $1 = about 4.50 lei. One leu is broken down into 100 bani.

Geography and People: Romania is 92,000 square miles, about the size of Oregon. Of its 22 million people, the majority consider themselves ethnic Romanians (83 percent), with large minorities of Hungarians (just over 6 percent) and Roma (3-4 percent); many Romanians are a mix of these, along with strong German and Russian/Ukrainian influences.

The Carpathian Mountains take a big bite out of the middle of Romania, defining its biggest and most famous region, Transylvania (and several cultural fault lines). The capital and biggest city is Bucharest (pop. 2 million); other large cities (around 300,000 each) are Cluj-Napoca, Iaşi, Timişoara, and Braşov. Although a member of the EU since 2007, Romania struggles economically (per capita GDP: $30,800).

Snapshot History: Romania's pagan Dacian tribes were taken over by Roman Empire soldiers. Though most returned to Rome, they left behind their DNA and language (which evolved into Romanian). In the late ninth century came the Hungarians, who would rule the core of the region (Transylvania) for nearly a millennium. In the 12th century, seeking help to settle and defend the land, the ruling Hungarian dukes invited German (or "Saxon") merchants to establish towns and villages, and trade here.

Meanwhile, powerful eastern neighbors—Russia and the Ottoman Empire—frequently invaded and occupied other parts of the Romanian lands. In the late 19th century, Romania finally threw off its foreign rulers and imported royalty from Germany (King Carol I) to help lead them into the modern age.

After World War II, Romania became part of the communist bloc and had one of the worst communist periods in Europe (under megalomaniacal strongman Nicolae Ceauşescu). In 1989, Ceauşescu was executed, and Romania began a new chapter: capitalistic, democratic, and fully independent.

Famous Romanians: Gymnast Nadia Comăneci (and coaches Béla and Márta Károlyi, of Hungarian ancestry), author Elie Wiesel (born to a Jewish family in Maramureş), composer George Enescu, and public radio commentator Andrei Codrescu.

Consular Services in Bucharest: The US Embassy is at Bulevardul Dr. Liviu Librescu 4 (+40 21 200 3300); the Canadian Embassy is at StradaTuberozelor 1 (+40 21 307 5000).

Tourist Information: www.romaniatourism.com

well connected by the slow **train** network (www.cfrcalatori.ro) or by **bus** (www.autogari.ro). But visitors wanting to scour the countryside—which is Romania's most appealing draw—are better off **driving.** Roads are in decent condition, but progress is slow; there are virtually no expressways, country roads are generally two-lane, and city bypasses are rare—you'll usually have to drive right through the town center. On the other hand, drivers get a front-row seat for Romania's weird and wonderful ways—it's fascinating to just watch life unfold.

Romanian Cuisine: Romanian cooking is heavy peasant fare. Meals begin with a wooden platter of rustic mountain cheeses, greasy pork (including *jumări*—little strips of pork fat), and raw onions. Next is a simple but tasty soup *(supă)*; a variety of "sour soups" called *ciorbă*, made with a base of fermented bran, are available (and typically delicious). Then comes the main course: pork, chicken, or fish. One popular protein is *mici* (MEE-chee)—minced-meat grilled sausages (like *ćevapčići* in the former Yugoslavia). Polenta *(mămăligă)*—often drizzled with sour cream—is the standard side, and *sarmale* (cabbage roll) is the national dish. A filling dessert is *papanași*—baseball-sized fried doughnuts smothered in jam and sour cream. Romanian wines and beers are nothing special, but try the fruity, 100-proof Romanian moonshine, *palinka* (a.k.a. *țuică*)... carefully. They say that when you drink *palinka,* "Your brain is OK, but your body is not OK."

Romanian Language: Romanian is a Romance language. If you speak French, Spanish, or Italian, you'll find that you may understand Romanian...a little. For example, "Good evening" is *Bună seara.* The character *ș* sounds like "sh," and *ț* is "ts." Some key survival phrases: "Hello" is *Bună ziua* (formal) or *Alo* (informal), "Please" is *Vă rog,* "Thank you" is *Mulțumesc* (or simply *Mersi*), and "Goodbye" is *La revedere.*

Local Guides: Hiring your own guide here is an exceptional investment. Prices are affordable, the guides I've recommended are top-notch, and Romania is much easier to take with a little local help. I've personally worked with each of the following guides and highly recommend their services. While I've listed each one's area of specialty, most of them work throughout the country—consider hiring one to be with you for several stops (or even your entire trip): **Daniel Gheorghiță** at Covinnus Travel (throughout Romania, www.covinnus.com, office@covinnus.com), **Dan Nica** (Bucharest and beyond, www.tourguidesromania.com, dsnica@gmail.com), **Ana Adamoae** (Bucharest and Transylvania, www.guidedtoursbucharest.wordpress.com, aadamoae@gmail.com), **Ciprian "Chip" Slemco** at Hello Bucovina (Bucovina and throughout Romania—and beyond, www.hellobucovina.com, contact@hellobucovina.com),

ROMANIA

and **Teo Ivanciuc** (just Maramureş, www.maramurestour.com, teofilivanciuc@yahoo.com).

Top Romanian Destinations

WALLACHIA
▲Bucharest (Bucureşti)

Romania's capital, Bucharest—with about two million people—is a muscular and gritty tangle of buildings. It can be hard to like at

first glance, but with a thoughtful look, it reveals its charms. Between the dreary apartment blocks hides an impressive architectural heritage. Once called the "Little Paris of the East," Bucharest flourished in the late 19th century, when independent Romania was born. Later, it was brutally disfigured by the communist dictator Ceauşescu, who left behind a starkly Socialist-style residential zone and the city's main landmark (the Palace of the Parliament). But today's Bucharest is working hard to move forward. In recent years, they've rejuvenated the once-derelict Old Town—transforming it into one of the liveliest nightlife zones in the region. Taken together, Bucharest is a fascinating place to grapple with for a day or two.

Visiting Bucharest: For a glimpse at Bucharest's genteel past, go for a stroll along ▲▲ **Victory Avenue** (Calea Victoriei)—with

grand belle époque architecture that has recently been scrubbed of its communist-era grime. Pause by the horseback statue of King Carol I (1839-1914), across the street from the Royal Palace. In the 1860s, Romania became a modern state for the first time. With no royal family to call their own, the Romanians went shop-

ping for a king who could connect their country to the European mainstream. They found one in Germany, where a prince looking for a throne agreed to become King Carol I of Romania. King Carol embraced his new homeland: He learned the language and adopted the culture while bringing Western reforms and securing true independence for Romania. Under King Carol, Bucharest blossomed. He imported French architects to give Bucharest the romantic allure visitors still enjoy along Victory Avenue. Just up the street is the **Athenaeum** concert hall, one of the finest examples of Bucharest's golden age of architecture.

Nearby, **Revolution Square** (Piața Revoluției) is marked by a stark monument honoring the more than 1,000 Romanians who died to bring freedom to their country in 1989. It stands in front of the former Communist Party Headquarters, where dictator Nicolae Ceaușescu would deliver speeches from the little balcony. On December 21, 1989—as revolution swept Romania—Ceaușescu had to abandon his podium midspeech when the crowd turned on him. (For the rest of the story, see the sidebar.)

Just a few blocks south sits Bucharest's ▲▲ **Old Town.** From communist times through the early 2000s, this area was deserted, dilapidated, and dangerous. But now it's being systematically rejuvenated. Grand, glittering belle époque buildings (including several bank headquarters) have been scrubbed and polished. Formerly abandoned shopping galleries are newly inviting. Historical monuments—like the delightful Hanul Manuc, an early-19th-century caravansary—have been painstakingly restored. And an al fresco dining and drinking scene enlivens the traffic-free streets. The lanes of the Old Town are a revelation after dark (especially on weekends), when the entire neighborhood feels like one big, sprawling cocktail party.

Also scattered around the Old Town are a few modest but colorfully decorated Romanian Orthodox churches. Observing passersby in front of any church, you'll notice that—while religion was discouraged in communist times—these days, faith is an increasingly important part of everyday life. One of the best examples is the tiny ▲ **Biserica Stavropoleos convent,** unas-

sumingly tucked between trendy restaurants and ritzy offices. Still tended by cloaked nuns, it feels like a transplanted time warp. A colorful *Last Judgment* painting fills the entranceway, and the little garden courtyard offers visitors a peaceful respite from the busy city.

Thriving as it is today, Bucharest's Old Town was lucky to survive the communist period. In the early 1980s, after an inspiring visit to North Korea, Nicolae Ceaușescu ripped out 80 percent of the historical center—30,000 houses, schools, and churches—to create the **Civic Center** (Centrul Civic) district, with wide boulevards, stone-faced apartment blocks, gurgling fountains, and a Pyongyang aesthetic. (Urban planners managed to save a few

Nicolae Ceaușescu (1918-1989)

From uneducated peasant roots, Nicolae Ceaușescu (chow-SHESS-koo) rose through the communist ranks to take power in 1965. During his 24 years in power, Ceaușescu's brittle mental health and ballooning ego made him arguably Europe's most damaging communist dictator aside from Joseph Stalin. Early on, his aggressive deals with foreign leaders mortgaged Romania's future. (He turned his back on the Warsaw Pact and favored partnering with nonaligned countries in Asia and Africa—which made him paranoid about the likelihood of a Soviet invasion.) And later, Ceaușescu grew obsessed with paying off the country's debt just as he was becoming addicted to grandiose projects without budgets.

In the 1970s and 1980s, Ceaușescu erected massive factories and refineries, dammed the Danube, rerouted rivers for irrigation, and built an impossibly twisty road over the country's steepest mountains (see page 1046). And in his capital, Ceaușescu razed 80 percent of the historical quarter to build a new "Civic Center" district, capped by a palace fit for a megalomaniac.

Meanwhile, Ceaușescu exported vital resources even as his own people were starving. Expired frozen fish was all you could buy in grocery stores, and many Romanians resorted to subsistence farming and raised their own pigs to survive the harsh winters. As a cost-saving measure, power was routinely cut off at night, and hot and cold water were intermittent. To stem a dwindling population, Ceaușescu outlawed abortion and divorce, and extended elite status to mothers of multiple children. (Tens of thousands of unwanted children were later abandoned, creating a surge in US adoptions of Romanian orphans during the 1990s.) Ceaușescu also employed ruthless Stalinesque tactics to keep dissent at a minimum—through his huge, KGB-style secret-police force, the Securitate.

All of this created a powerful anti-Ceaușescu sentiment. In the late fall of 1989, with winds of change sweeping across the Eastern Bloc, revolution reached Romania. As Ceaușescu delivered a speech, furious protesters filled the square. Ceaușescu ordered the police to open fire, while he fled to a dramatic rooftop helicopter rescue. But Ceaușescu and his wife were soon arrested, given a brief televised trial, and shot on Christmas Day 1989. To reassure the Romanians that their hated ruler was gone for good, the Ceaușescus' bodies were shown on national television. In all of Eastern Europe, Romania was the only country where the transition from communism to democracy came with a violent revolution—and the only one that ended in an execution.

Even now, Romanians are scarred from the Ceaușescu years. His legacy—economical, psychological, and physical—looms large. Looking back on Ceaușescu's excesses, Romanians say, "We can't even paint everything Ceaușescu built."

churches by secretly relocating them inside city blocks, where you can still find them today.) This area, just across the neglected little river from the Old Town, is worth a stroll to better understand the scale of Ceaușescu's ambition, not to mention his ego.

In the core of the Civic Center, rows of fountains lead from Unity Square (Piața Unirii) to the massive ▲▲▲ **Palace of Parlia-**

ment—the largest build-ing in Europe (four mil-lion square feet, with more than a thousand rooms). Ceaușescu built this mon-strosity as a symbol of his power. Today it houses the Romanian parliament, three skippable museums, and an international con-ference center—and is still about 70 percent vacant space.

Guided tours lead gawking visitors around its cavernous, empty, and dimly lit halls (if they turned on all the lights, the palace would consume as much electricity as a small city). On the one-hour tour (bring your passport, www.cic.cdep.ro/en), visitors see the grand entry hall; the theater, with its gargantuan five-ton crystal chandelier; and the ballroom, big enough to host a football match and with a glass ceiling that, it's rumored, could slide open to allow a helicopter to land. You'll also step out onto the balcony that Ceaușescu designed specifically for delivering speeches, while looking down a boulevard grand enough to echo his self-impor-tance. (To be sure it met his expectations, builders erected full-scale cardboard models of facades along the entire street for his personal sign-off.)

Throughout the tour, ogle the details: The wall-to-wall car-pets had to be delivered in pieces and sewn together on-site. The

curtains are stitched with silver-and-gold threads. Garage-sized "pocket doors" slide up into mar-ble frames. Huge as the building is above ground, it's built into the top of a hill—so there's even more of it below ground. Most of the structure is steel and concrete, wrapped in a marble veneer—more than 10 mil-lion square feet of it. The building sinks a quarter-inch each year under its own sheer weight. They say underground tunnels go all

ROMANIA

the way to the airport—an emergency escape route for the paranoid Ceaușescu.

The dictator threw resources at his pet project like a crazed pharaoh. For six years, 700 architects and 20,000 laborers worked on it 24/7. Hundreds of workers died. Total cost: around three billion dollars. And even then, a third of the interior was never completed. Ceaușescu was executed halfway through its construction, and overnight, the "Presidential Palace" became the "Palace of the People"—and those people were stuck with it. Nobody could possibly afford to buy the building, and finishing it was cheaper than tearing it down. When it finally opened in 1994, the Romanian people—whose food had been rationed for years to help pay for the palace—were both wonderstruck and repulsed when they wandered its opulent halls.

Next door, others are carrying on Ceaușescu's legacy of outsize projects. Just to the southwest, work crews are erecting the world's largest Orthodox church: The **Romanian People's Salvation Cathedral,** with a capacity of 6,000 worshippers, was consecrated in 2018 (though it's still not complete).

While Bucharest has plenty of fine museums, on a short visit I find it more interesting to simply explore the zones described above and tour the parliament. But to dig deeper into the story of Romania, consider the **National Museum of Romanian History** (in the Old Town, www.mnir.ro) and the **National Museum of the Romanian Peasant** (folk-life artifacts on Victory Square/Piața Victoriei, www.muzeultaranuluiroman.ro; this is redundant if you're heading to Maramureș).

Sleeping in Bucharest: The small, welcoming **$ Rembrandt Hotel** is well located at the edge of the bustling Old Town dining and nightlife zone (www.rembrandt.ro). Also central is the more upscale, suite-oriented **$$ Hotel Cișmigiu** (www.hotelcismigiu.ro).

Eating in Bucharest: The Old Town has ample dining options; for a memorable meal of Romanian classics, consider the upmarket-beer-hall vibe of **Caru' cu Bere** (www.carucubere.ro) or the atmospheric caravansary setting of **Hanul' lui Manuc** (www.hanulluimanuc.ro).

▲▲▲Peleș Castle

Peleș (PEH-lesh) Castle, on a wooded hillside above the lovely mountain resort town of Sinaia, is Romania's answer to Bavaria's Neuschwanstein: a fanciful, over-the-top, Romantic interpretation of a Gothic hunting palace, prickly with spires but far too pretty to repel an actual siege. Designed to impress, Peleș ranks among Europe's best Romantic Age palaces.

Background: Peleș was built in the 1880s by King Carol I, who had moved here from Germany. Carol was desperate to keep up with his rivals back home (such as "Mad" King Ludwig of Bavaria). And so, in a mountainous and forested landscape that reminded him of Germany, Carol imported German architects to create the ultimate palace. Here at Peleş, King Carol and Queen Elizabeth felt free from the stifling climate of German royalty: They slept together in the same bed, dressed in Romanian peasant costume, and decorated the place with Transylvanian folk themes. But Carol didn't abandon his German efficiency. Audiences took place standing at his upright desk and lasted about five minutes. His queen, Elizabeth (look for her portrait in traditional Romanian costume), used her Germanic know-how to both celebrate and elevate her adopted culture. Inspired by Transylvanian fairy tales, Elizabeth even wrote some of her own. It's no wonder that many contemporary Romanians still have great affection for their onetime-imported royalty.

Visiting Peleş Castle: You can get inside only with a guided tour (www.peles.ro). The interior is a rich world of sumptuous detail: cozy wood-paneled elegance, glittering Bohemian crystal chandeliers, whimsical paintings, colorful stoves, gilded stucco, Meissen porcelain, secret passages, and elaborate knickknacks (watch for the teak elephant table—a gift from the maharajah of India). Tours begin in the Hall of Honor—with

its red carpets, grand staircase, venerable portraits, and inlaid-wood pictures of German castles (suggesting the king's sense of one-upmanship). One particularly grandiose apartment—built for Emperor Franz Josef, who never actually slept here—has leather-tooled walls and a cozy breakfast room in the turret. In the Music Room, Queen Elizabeth hosted concerts and literary gatherings—and had scenes from her fairy tales painted on the walls. Meanwhile, the king's impressive armory collection (Europe's largest at the time) was designed both to intimidate and to stoke conversation. The private music halls and theaters were the site of many exclusive performances. And the library shows off the royal couple's passion for education. But remember: This was a Romantic Age, faux-medieval castle, built in the 1880s, so it also had all the modern conveniences: bathrooms with running water, forced-air heating, elevators, a central vacuum cleaner system, and even its own power plant.

If one castle isn't enough, you can also visit a second palace nearby, built by the next king (Carol's nephew)—a half-timbered mini-Peleş called **Pelişor Castle.**

▲▲Transfăgărăşan Road

The most challenging road connecting Bucharest to Transylvania—and, quite possibly, between any two points in Europe—is the Transfăgărăşan (trans-fah-gah-rah-SHAHN) Road. It twists and turns and bends back on itself several times as it crosses the cut-glass peaks of the Făgăraş Mountains, summiting at 6,670 feet.

This improbable road is another artifact of Nicolae Ceauşescu's rule. Following the 1968 Soviet invasion of Czechoslovakia to put down the Prague Spring uprising, a paranoid Ceauşescu wanted an escape route from Romania's flat capital to its easier-to-defend mountains. According to the story, Ceauşescu simply put his finger on a map and said, "Build it here." And they did. After incalculable costs and 40 workers' lives lost, Ceauşescu's dream was complete.

Today, the 56-mile-long Transfăgărăşan Road has little practical value, but it's a popular scenic drive for tourists...as long as you're very comfortable with mountain driving. (Note that the road is only open when all snow has melted—typically late June through late October.) Consider the Transfăgărăşan as a time-consuming but super-scenic alternate route for connecting Transylvania (it's off E-68, between Braşov and Sibiu) to Bucharest (via Piteşti, where you can hop on the freeway).

At the southern (Bucharest) end of the pass, you'll pass **Poenari Castle.** Unlike the "Dracula Castle" at Bran (described later), Poenari has a real connection to Vlad Ţepeş, who actually spent time here. (It's quite different than Bran, with a less striking interior; unless you have time and calories to burn, it's not worth the 1,400 stairs to reach the entrance.)

TRANSYLVANIA
▲Braşov

Braşov (BRAH-shohv), about a three-hour drive north of Bucharest, is scenically tucked against Carpathian foothills. Braşov was one of the original seven towns founded by

Transylvanian History

Transylvania's castle-capped hills and fortress-like churches are a testament to a hard-fought past. With a stout tower standing guard over every village, it's clear this region has been a crossroads of history.

From the late ninth century until the end of World War I, Transylvania was part of Hungary. The Hungarian dukes who ruled this remote region called it Erdély (which, like "transsylvania," means "beyond the forest"). Seeking help to settle the rugged land and to defend it against potential invasions from Tatars and Ottomans, the Hungarians invited merchants from today's Luxembourg, Belgium, and northwestern Germany to establish towns and trade here. Those settlers—called "Saxons"—founded seven fortified towns, including Brașov, Sighișoara, and Sibiu. (The German name for Transylvania is Siebenbürgen—"Seven Towns.") Meanwhile, German settlers in the countryside, who were outside of town walls and vulnerable to attack, beefed up their churches.

And so, for much of its history, Transylvania was divided along these societal strata: Hungarian rulers, German merchants, and Romanian peasants. But in modern times, things began to change. During a late 19th-century wave of emigration, many Saxons relocated to Germany. Then Hungary came up on the losing side of World War I, making Transylvania part of Romania. In the waning days of World War II, many Saxons fled the advancing Soviet Army, and under communism, the Romanian government literally sold its few remaining Saxons back to Germany.

And then there are the Roma (whom Romanians—eager to avoid any "Roma" vs. "Romanian" confusion—usually call Gypsies; see page 208). Today, Romania has one of Europe's largest Roma populations: officially 620,000 people, but—considering the difficulty of conducting a census of people who live off the grid—likely far more. The classic Roma stereotype is of desperately poor people living in shacks on the edge of town. You'll see plenty of that in Romania, but that's only part of the story. Most Roma live side by side with their Romanian neighbors, more or less integrated into mainstream society.

In today's Transylvania, the German minority is less than 1 percent. The Hungarian minority (about 6 percent of the population)—called Székelys—are scattered around Romania but are concentrated in Hungarian-speaking enclaves in the central part of the country (east of Târgu Mureș). Travelers who can recognize each language are aware they're in a Balkan melting pot. Today, most Transylvanian towns are home to a mix of Romanians, Roma, Hungarians, and sometimes a few Germans—fitting for a region with such a rich and complex history.

Saxon settlers (see the sidebar). It thrived then. It thrived during the Ceauşescu years, when it was aggressively developed into an industrial powerhouse. And it thrives today, with a rejuvenated old-town center that's a popular springboard for the mountains: hiking in the summer, skiing in the winter, and castle-hopping anytime. Enjoyable but low-impact on its own, Braşov is an ideal home base for a Transylvanian "castle day"—with a car and an early start, you can easily side-trip to Peleş, Bran, and Râşnov in a single day.

Visiting Braşov: While Braşov's main appeal is its convenient location, its gorgeous main square and pedestrianized core are a big bonus. The town is a fine mix of tourism and real, contemporary Romanian life. Its main square, **Piaţa Sfatului**—and the lively walking streets that flow away from it—are a delightful people zone.

Braşov's centerpiece is the **Black Church** (Biserica Neagră). The biggest Gothic church between Vienna and Istanbul, it got its nickname when it was charred by a 1689 fire. Inside, each bank of pews is lovingly decorated with the seal of the guild that financed it—suggesting the importance of trades and crafts in medieval Transylvania. The goldsmiths and other wealthy guilds sat near the front; poorer guilds, like the tailors and weavers, had the cheap seats in back. The mid-nave pews are reversible—with backs that can be flipped to face either the pulpit or the grand pipe organ. And the most extensive Turkish-carpet collection outside of Turkey fills the nave. These were donated by European traders, pilgrims, and crusaders who passed through this crossroads town on their way home from the Holy Land.

For a low-impact hike, head north across the little river and walk a few minutes up into the hills, where you can visit the **Black Tower** and the **White Tower**—part of the stout network of fortifications that protected the city in its medieval heyday. From the White Tower, you enjoy sweeping views over the tidy town center, the cable car that trundles to the adjacent mountaintop, and the big, white, Hollywood-like letters that spell out B-R-A-Ş-O-V.

Beyond the delightful urban core, Braşov features row after row of uniform concrete apartment blocks. But, revealing the city's relative affluence, many are now refurbished and colorfully repainted. The sprawl is for good reason: Soon after the Iron Curtain slammed shut, Braşov was rechristened Oraşul Stalin—"Stalintown." Ceauşescu built an extensive network of auto and armaments factories here, imported and retrained peasants

from the wilds of Moldavia to staff them, and erected forests of concrete apartment blocks to house them. (For a time, Brașov was Romania's second-biggest city.) Trees with white bark were strategically planted on the hillside above to spell out the name S-T-A-L-I-N. And newlyweds felt compelled to have their picture taken with a big statue of "Father" Stalin in the park.

Sleeping in Brașov: Several cozy guesthouses are in the town center, including **$ Hotel Bella Muzica** (www.bellamuzica.ro) and the simpler **$ Casa Albert** (www.casa-albert.ro). For a glitzy option near the train station (in the modern sprawl—a long walk or short drive from the Old Town), **$$ Hotel Kronwell** is a big, slick design hotel with all the comforts (www.kronwell.com).

Eating in Brașov: You'll find plenty of options in the pedestrianized town center. **La Ceaun** ("The Cauldron") is good for traditional Romanian fare (www.laceaun.com), while the Italian-oriented **Prato** feels dressier but is still affordable (www.prato.ro). Both have appealing outdoor tables.

▲▲Castles near Brașov

You can link up all three of these castles in one busy day from Brașov. Or consider stopping off at Peleș on your way between Bucharest and Brașov, letting you linger and enjoy some time in Brașov itself.

The single best castle in the area (technically in Wallachia, just over the hills from Brașov) is **▲▲▲ Peleș Castle,** described earlier.

The mega-touristy **▲▲ Bran Castle** perches evocatively on a bluff overlooking a busy valley road (www.bran-castle.com). De-

spite the tacky vampire-themed kitsch that clutters up the pathway, Bran has virtually no real connection to Dracula or to Vlad the Impaler...but it sure is striking. Fanciful legends aside, Bran is a good example of an authentic medieval fortress, dating from the 14th century. In the 1920s, Romania's royal family converted Bran into a rustic country retreat. And that, rather than vampires, is what you'll learn about in the whitewashed interior. As you follow the one-way route through the castle, exhibits introduce you to Romania's King Ferdinand I (the nephew of King Carol I) and his wife, Princess Marie (the granddaughter of Britain's Queen Victoria). Bran is also simply a fun kid-in-the-castle experience: Exploring the MC Escher floor plan, you'll discover a humble armory, a secret passage, and a fairy-tale courtyard.

Dracula: Behind the Cape

Transylvania's tourist industry loves to milk its connection to Dracula. In reality, Dracula was the invention of a British novelist who never set foot in Transylvania, but was inspired, in part, by a real historical figure called Vlad the Impaler. Confused? To help you sort out fact from legend, here are the basics:

Vlad III (1431-1477) was a 15th-century prince of Wallachia who was taken captive by his Ottoman rivals. Some say he rotted in a prison, while others believe he apprenticed at the sultan's court in Constantinople. Either way, after six years the authorities believed him "rehabilitated" and returned him to his homeland—with the expectation that he would serve as their obedient puppet ruler of Wallachia.

Instead, Vlad quickly turned on his former captors and joined the Hungarian fight to push back the Ottoman advance into Europe. According to later (and likely exaggerated) accounts, Vlad's methods for dealing with his enemies were brutal: Slowly and sadistically, he'd drive stakes into the bodies of his victims as they screamed in agony. Then he'd display their mutilated corpses along busy roads as a warning to would-be foes. Vlad dispatched tens of thousands of victims this way, earning him a vivid nickname: Vlad Țepeș—"the Impaler." He was also known by another name: Dracula, stemming from his father's membership in the chivalric "Order of the Dragon" (Dracul in Romanian).

While feared by the Transylvanian nobles, Vlad the Impaler was beloved by the peasants, who cheered his heroic defense of their homeland. And after his death, his legend only grew in a Europe terrified of the ever-looming threat of Ottoman invasion.

By the late 1800s, the English novelist Bram Stoker (1847-1912)—like many before and after him—found his imagination captivated by the sadism of Vlad the Impaler. Stoker was also inspired by completely separate Transylvanian folk tales of the undead. Stoker merged the two storylines and, in 1897, published the Victorian Gothic novel Dracula. Stoker never traveled to Romania to research his book; the vampire called Dracula, and his evocative Transylvanian settings, all came purely from Stoker's imagination.

All of this means that—from a sightseer's perspective—there are no actual sights in Romania relating to "Dracula," and only tenuous ties to Vlad the Impaler. Vlad may have lived for a brief time in Sighișoara. But it's likely that he never even set foot in the most famous "Dracula" sight, Bran Castle (at most, he spent a night or two there). Of course, the locals will never set you straight...all that Dracula lore is just too lucrative.

▲ **Râşnov Castle** (RUZH-nohv) is your ru-ined-fortress-on-a-moun-taintop experience. From the humble village of Râşnov (with its own Hol-lywood-like sign on the hills), you'll curl around the back of the hill, park,

buy your ticket, then hike or ride a shuttle bus to the castle on top. Once inside the stout walls, a few houses and turrets still stand, which—along with the foundations of others—give you a sense of the safety these castles provided during difficult times. Râşnov also enjoys grand views down over the valley.

▲▲Sighişoara

Sighişoara (sih-gih-SHO-rah, pop. 28,000) is Romania's show-piece jewel-box town—the Transylvanian version of Rothenburg ob der Tauber or Český Krumlov. Sighişoara is the best-preserved of the original seven Saxon towns—it feels like a time warp. Sleep here if cuddly cobbles are your goal. Sighişoara is also a good home base for seeing the forti-fied churches, or as a stopover between Braşov and Maramureş.

Visiting Sighişoara: The en-tire fortified hilltop of Sighişoara—perched on a little plateau halfway up a wooded hill—forms the town's mighty **Citadel.** (Many tourists who come to Sighişoara ask, "So where's the castle?" They don't realize they're already in it.) This walled area was both a home to craftsmen and a place of last refuge in case of invasions or raids—which were frequent. Nine of Sighişoara's 15 pointy-topped watchtowers still survive—each one named for the guild that de-fended it.

Sighişoara's icon is its **Clock Tower**—marked with symbols that proudly trumpet its special privileges. Inside, visitors spiral up and up on creaky wooden stairs, and peek out over the shoulders of the figures that change with the day of the week. At each landing are modest exhibits: a model of the town at its peak, and a display of the products of each of the main guilds that put this place on the map.

For a Dracula photo op, you'll find a statue of **Vlad Ţepeş** (who may have lived here briefly) on the square called Piaţa Muzeului, just above the Monastery Church; nearby, a garden terrace features views over the rooftops of Sighișoara's workaday modern town.

From Sighișoara's town center, a covered staircase—called the **"Stairs of the Students"**—leads 175 steps up to the hilltop. After every sixth step is a landing—a reminder to rest on the seventh day.

At the top, a school, a church, and a cemetery honor those original Saxon pioneers. German names fill the graveyard. And inside the **church** is a collection of artifacts from smaller German churches around the region—most now all but abandoned. You can see how, when austere Lutheranism reached Transylvania, frugal village churches kept their old Catholic altars but removed the showiest statues. Dowry chests were found squirrelled away in the attic of a village church, untouched for centuries. The tomb of a furrier recalls a time when it was cheaper to wear heavy cloaks on Sunday morning than to heat this huge space.

Sleeping in Sighișoara: Several quaint hotels and pensions line the cobbled streets of the Citadel. The biggest outfit is **$ Hotel Sighișoara** and its annex, the upscale **$$ Fronius Residence** (www.sighisoarahotels.ro). Or try the simpler **$ Pension am Schneiderturm.**

Eating in Sighișoara: In this touristy town, don't go looking for a memorable meal—just pick the setting you enjoy best. I've eaten well at **Casa cu Cerb** (www.casacucerb.ro) and at the recommended **Hotel Sighișoara.**

▲▲Fortified Saxon Churches

Some of Romania's best castles aren't castles at all—they're churches. While big towns like Sighișoara and Brașov were well protected, smaller Saxon settlements were vulnerable—especially after a devastating Tatar invasion in the 13th century. So what did the industrious settlers do? They fortified their churches.

Dozens of fortified German churches—mostly built in the 13th and 14th centuries—are scattered across Transylvania. From the outside, they look like medieval fortresses: beefy bastions, stout lookout towers, narrow slits for raining arrows on enemies, distinctly Transylvanian trapezoidal turrets (to shed the heavy snowfall), and wraparound defensive galleries. While most Germans have long since left Romania, their heritage lives on here: The signs, the services, and the hymnals in the pews are all still in German. And periodically, some of these churches hold Lutheran services.

Visiting Fortified Churches: As you explore Transylvania—especially the area between Braşov and Sighişoara—you'll drive past several of these fortified churches (a particularly fine example is in Saschiz). But a few are worth going a bit out of your way to see.

Close to Braşov, **Prejmer** (PREHZH-mehr) has a particularly well-preserved, half-timbered-and-whitewashed courtyard, showing how townspeople could flock into the protection of the church in times of crisis. Each cell was reserved for one family—notice that each rustic door is labeled. You can even see the little one-room "schoolhouse" tucked into the wall. (Nearby, **Hărman** has another well-preserved example.)

Between Sighişoara and Sibiu, **Biertan** (BEER-tahn) has one of the newest fortified churches (early 16th century)—illus-

trating the architecture style at its most evolved. Looking out from the top, you can see the surviving three concentric walls (of the original five) that protect the church. But stepping inside, you could be in any village church in medieval Germany. The original 16th-century stone pulpit still stands. And, like the Black Church in Braşov, each bank of pews is marked with the seal of a local guild. On the door to the left of the altar, the locksmiths' guild showed off with an elaborate locking mechanism. In the church courtyard is a "divorce chamber," where a quarrelling couple would be forced to share one bed, one pot, and one plate—for however long it took to resolve their differences. (From 1500 to 1800, only one divorce was recorded.)

The whitewashed and ramshackle church of **Viscri** (VEE-scree, from the German Weiss Kirch—white church), hidden

deep in the hills between Braşov and Sighişoara, is one of the oldest (c. 1100). Most of the pews don't have backs. That's because of the starched dresses and long headdresses of traditional village women, who wanted to avoid creases. The pews with backs were for the only families who were from elsewhere: the preacher's and the teacher's. The very humble dirt-street town of Viscri—where locals selling colorful woolens to tourists seems to be the only

ROMANIA

economy—is fun to explore. One of the houses belongs to (believe it or not) King Charles, who loves the anonymity this off-the-grid corner of Europe provides. Locals claim that then-Prince Charles and Prince Harry retreated here to hide from the press in the days following the 2011 royal wedding of William and Kate.

▲▲Sibiu

Charming Sibiu (SEE-bee-yoo) may be Romania's most livable city. Sibiu began life as Hermannstadt, the biggest and most im-

portant of the original seven Saxon towns. And today, while only about one in a hundred residents has German ancestry, Sibiu's tidy townscape still feels very Germanic. (In 2000, Sibiu elected Klaus Iohannis to be the first German mayor in Romania since World War II; beloved and hugely successful locally, he went on to be elected Romania's president in 2014.) While not quite as practical a home base as Brașov or Sighișoara (it's farther from Transylvania's main sights), Sibiu is more appealing in its own right. It's just the right size to be interesting yet still manageable (pop. 150,000), and the creaky, cobbled, atmospheric, and mostly traffic-free city center is a delightful place to simply hang out.

Visiting Sibiu: The atmospheric Upper Town core consists of three interlocking squares, each with a different personality: The aptly named **Grand Square** (Piața Mare) dominates an inviting and wide-open expanse fronted by stately municipal buildings (climb the Council Tower for sweeping views over town). **Small Square** (Piață Mică) is quaint, lined with al fresco cafés and a double-decker street plan that offers fine views from the "Liar's Bridge." And **Huet Square** (Piața Huet) is dominated by the gigantic German Protestant church—a reminder of Sibiu's strong Saxon pedigree.

From Grand Square, a pedestrian street called **Strada Nicolae Bălcescu** bursts with life as it proceeds several blocks south through the city center. Where the traffic-free zone ends, turn left and follow Strada Cetății along a tranquil park that delineates the former moat—passing three stout fortified brick **towers** that stand as bold reminders of Sibiu's militaristic past.

Beyond simply strolling its tidy core, Sibiu has some low-impact sightseeing options. Its giant, Neo-Byzantine-style ▲ **Holy Trinity Cathedral** is one of the country's most impressive Romanian Orthodox churches. The ▲ **Brukenthal Museum** collects a wealth of both Romanian and European artwork (www.brukenthalmuseum.ro). And ASTRA, a Romanian literature and culture society, operates several museums of its own, including one of the country's best ▲ **open-air folk museums** on the outskirts of town (www.muzeulastra.ro).

▲▲Corvin Castle (Castelul Corvinilor; a.k.a. Hunyadi/ Hunedoara Castle)

Corvin Castle may be the most visually striking reminder that Transylvania was part of Hungary for most of its history. This is the home castle of János Hunyadi, the hero of the 15th-century fight against the Ottomans, and his son, Mátyás Corvinus, who became the only Hungarian king in more than 600 years of foreign rule (see page 627). With a certain "Hogwarts Gothic" quality, Corvin is also one of the most picturesque castles in a country where picturesque castles are a forté. When Budapest was building a faux-"Transylvanian" castle in their City Park in 1896, they modeled it after this one (see page 620). The evocative but mostly-empty castle sits unceremoniously along a gritty road on the outskirts of Hunedoara—about a 1.5-hour drive west of Sibiu (www.castelulcorvinilor.ro). While striking, it's worth the long detour only if you're a connoisseur of Transylvanian castles, Hungarian history, or both (or if you're driving from central Transylvania to Timișoara or Hungary).

Nearby: The area around Hunedoara has one of Romania's highest concentrations of **"Gypsy palaces"**: over-the-top-ostentatious mansions built just outside city limits by powerful members of the Roma community. Strik-ing and controversial (and rumored to be funded through illegal activity), these are worth a fascinat-ing drive-by to appreci-ate one more facet of the  Romanian Roma experience. Be discreet about stopping or taking photos—the people living here often don't appreciate unwanted attention. Several "Gypsy palaces" line up along road 687, at the south end of Hunedoara, on the way to Călan (beginning just east of Corvin Castle).

Cluj-Napoca

Cluj-Napoca—or simply Cluj (kloozh) for short—is Transylvania's de facto capital and a major center of culture, universities, and business. While the compact historical core has its charm, the busy sprawl of Cluj feels like an urban jungle—making it challenging to appreciate on a quick visit. For that reason, Cluj ranks lower on my

ROMANIA

list of "must-visit" Transylvanian cities. But if you go, you'll find a congested historic core that's worth a stroll.

Visiting Cluj: The city's landmarks reflect its multiethnic heritage—like Transylvania itself, it's a mix of Romanian, Hungarian, and German. Towering high above Unity Square (Piaţa Unirii) is the Gothic steeple of ▲ **St. Michael's Church,** built by Hungarian Catholics in the 15th century. Nearby stands a bulky statue of the Hungarian king **Mátyás Corvinus**—honoring Cluj's substantial Hungarian-speaking minority (about

15 percent of the population). But just a couple of blocks to the east—as if to one-up the Hungarians—stands the skinny, slotted dome of the ▲ **Dormition of the Theotokos Romanian Ortho-dox Cathedral,** and out front, a statue of Avram Iancu, a proud Romanian who fought *against* Hungarian influence in Transylvania. Just to the northwest, between the Old Town and the river, is Cluj's lively and inviting **Central Park,** with beautifully restored pavilions and the city's cutting-edge soccer stadium. After hours, youthful Cluj is busy with nightlife. The university zone to the west—called Haşdeu—is edgy. Mellower and more inviting is the **Museum Square** (Piaţa Muzeului) pedestrian zone, tucked in the heart of the Old Town.

MARAMUREŞ

Maramureş (mah-rah-MOO-rehsh) is Europe's most traditional corner. Here you'll find time-warp locals farming fields, getting around by horse cart, and living agrarian—almost biblical—life-styles, seemingly oblivious to the modern world just over the hills. This is the place in Romania to savor being far off the beaten track: Slow down, go for a lazy drive, pull over at anything that catches your eye, and marvel at the simplicity of it all. While it

takes some effort to reach, Maramureş is well worth the effort for those who want to see a real, living open-air folk museum.

Orientation: To the north of sprawling Transylvania, the tourist's Maramureş is small: a skinny sliver of land between the Gutâi Mountains and the Ukrainian border. From Transylvania, it's a long drive up to the main city of Maramureş—dreary Baia

Mare, with Europe's third-tallest smokestack looming overhead—and even then, you're still more than an hour away, over a twisty mountain pass. The best corner of Maramureş clusters around the town of Sighetu Marmaţiei.

Local Guide: Particularly here in Maramureş, a good local guide is an essential investment to get the most of out of your time (and to make it worth the long drive here). Knowledgeable **Teo Ivanciuc** excels at putting you in touch with traditional lifestyles and giving them meaning (see page 1040 for contact info).

Sleeping in Maramureş: Expect rustic but cozy accommodations. While Sighetu Marmaţiei has some big hotels, for the full Maramureş experience, stay in the countryside. Local guide **$ Teo Ivanciuc,** listed above, rents rooms (www.amizadil.com)—or can refer you to other locals who do. For a bigger but still-traditional option, try **$ Hotel Grădina Morii,** on the outskirts of Sighetu Marmaţiei (www.hotelgradinamorii.ro).

Sighetu Marmaţiei

With close to 40,000 inhabitants, "Sighet" (SEE-geht, as locals call it) is the area's main town. Many locals don't even call it Sighet—they just call it "the town." With a scruffy main square (which hosts a daily farmers market) and dreary apartment blocks, Sighet is not particularly attractive—but you can't avoid passing through several times on your visit to Maramureş.

Sighet was the birthplace of the Holocaust survivor, author, and Nobel Peace Prize laureate **Elie Wiesel** (whose novel *Night* is a definitive work of Holocaust literature). His birthplace—near a synagogue that the Nazis burned down in 1944 (now rebuilt)—is today a modest museum, with informational signs and a few artifacts. Wiesel lived in Sighet until he was taken away to Auschwitz at age 16.

Thanks to its remote location—closer to Budapest than to Bucharest—communist-era Sighet became a sort of "Siberia of Romania." It was the site of the Securitate's main prison, where dissenters, intellectuals, clergy, journalists, and political opponents of the regime were sent to rot, far from mainstream society. Many died. Today, the prison houses the ▲▲ **Memorial for the Victims of Communism,** with a modern, powerful, well-presented exhibit detailing the communist period in Romania (www.memorialsighet.ro).

Sighet also has a good **Village Museum** (with wooden houses) and an **Ethnographic Museum,** but you don't really need them—Maramureş itself is the best sight.

▲▲▲Maramureş Joyriding

Maramureş is a rolling, pastoral landscape speckled with haystacks. Go for an aimless drive and just take it all in. Thanks to its rug-

ROMANIA

ged landscape and great distance from Bucharest, Maramureș avoided communist farm collectivization—so people still tend their small family plots by hand. Horse carts outnumber cars. Men in overalls and funny little straw hats pile hay onto their wooden wagons. Women wear big, puffy skirts just above the knee, babushkas on their heads, and baskets laden with heavy goods on their backs. While not ignorant of the modern world, Maramureș feels like Europe's Amish Country, where centuries-old ways endure. It's not for the benefit of tourists—it's just their way of life.

Locals are very open and welcoming to curious travelers. This is an ideal place to be an amateur anthropologist...simply observe the way people live. (While you can do this on your own, it's easier and more rewarding with a local guide.)

Wander through any village and peek into family compounds. Each one is marked with a huge, ceremonial wooden gateway—

just big enough for a hay-loaded horse cart to trot through. (These gateways show off the Romanian knack for flaunting whatever wealth you have... even if it's not much. Another status symbol is hanging colorful pots from tree branches.) The gates are carved with a whole iconography of local symbols: starburst (pagan sun worship), wolf teeth (protection), bull horns (masculinity), leaves (nature), and—most importantly—the "rope of life" motif, a helix-like design suggesting the continuity of life from generation to generation. Inside each courtyard, you'll usually see—in addition to the main house—a humble barn with a paddock, a garden patch, and an old-fashioned, hand-pulled well.

You'll be surprised how often you'll be invited inside. Many Maramureș residents are eager to show curious visitors their humble homes. Every house has a "show room," where people collect their nicest belongings: colorful piles of blankets, pillows, and so on (often from the dowry of the woman of the house). This room is reserved exclusively for guests, while the family spends most of their time in much humbler surroundings.

It's fine to simply wander around the area and see what you may stumble upon, but here are some areas you could focus on:

The little **Cosău River Valley**—especially the stretch between Călinești and Budești (each with a wooden church)—is a picturesque throwback. The rushing river powers all manner of medieval industry. You'll see carpet laundries, where wooden canals channel water into a naturally powered spin cycle. People use the flowing water to operate brandy stills, making their own plum firewater *(horinca)*. Grist mills grind grains into both polenta and animal feed. And tucked deep inside family compounds, people spin wool into yarn and use creaky old looms to weave it into a loose fabric. That fabric is then taken to a fulling mill, where water-powered wooden hammers pound and pound and pound, mashing it into a dense, heavy material that's used in the traditional winter costume.

For a scenic drive, take the **high road** between Călinești and Văleni, offering high-altitude views over the rolling farm fields of Maramureș—and, if you're lucky, hardworking farmers making haystacks.

From Văleni, you can coast down into **Bârsana,** which has the busy wood workshop of Toader Bârsan. Out in the courtyard, young lumberjacks artfully carve new wooden gates that look old. Toader himself sits on the stoop, hand-carving trinkets and wearing his distinctive little Maramureș straw hat. He loves to explain how he once met Hillary Clinton. (The wooden Bârsana monastery complex—described later—is at the edge of this town.)

Horse Market: Ocna Șugatag, a larger, functional town sitting on a plateau, is fairly dull—except on Thursday mornings, when the weekly livestock market makes it feel like a 17th-century car show. The people-watching is marvelous.

▲▲▲Merry Cemetery (Cimitirul Vesel)

A 30-minute drive west of Sighet is one of Romania's top cultural treasures: the Merry Cemetery. In 1935, woodcarver Stan Ioan Pătraș—inspired by a long-forgotten local tradition for colorful grave markers—began filling the Săpânța village cemetery with a forest of technicolor memorials. Today there are more than 1,300—each one with a pointy roof to protect from the rain, a paint-

ing of the departed doing something they loved (or in the moment of death), and a whimsical poem. It's all painted a cheery blue to match the heavens where the souls are headed. The Merry Cemetery is a poignant celebration of each individual's life, a chronicle of village history, and an irreverent raspberry in the face of death.

Although the cemetery is dubbed "merry," many of the poems are downright morose. Tales of young lives cut short by tragic accidents, warriors mowed down in the prime of life, or people who simply never found happiness are a reminder that death, and life, are sometimes nothing to be cheerful about.

Even if you can't read the poems, the images speak volumes: Weaver. Loved bikes. Television repairman. Soldier. Hit by a car. Struck by lightning. Nagging mother-in-law.

Tucked behind the church, you can find the grave of the artist who started it all, Stan Ioan Pătraș, who died in 1977. His apprentices carry on the work today.

Nearby: Across the highway (and a half-mile back toward Sighet), **Săpânța Peri Monastery Church** towers 250 feet tall. Completed in 2003, the church demonstrates that in Maramureș, wood remains as popular as it ever was. Inside, the technical mastery of Maramureș woodworkers is on display: chunky but precisely cut dovetailing keeps massive walls firmly in place, and the artistic shinglework cascades tidily from peak to eaves.

▲▲Wooden Churches

In Maramureș, surrounded by thickly forested mountains, wood is king. And some of the finest wooden churches in Europe are right here. These centuries-old structures resemble Norwegian stave churches but with less flair. They are graceful wooden pagodas with eye-pleasing lines angling up to the heavens. Inside, faded "wood frescoes" look like silly-puttied Sunday comics pages, stretched out and plastered against the wall—illustrating a medieval interpretation of Christianity. Dozens of these churches are scattered around the region, but most are generally closed to the public (local guides can usually get the key). Some of the churches are modern, including the **Săpânța Peri** monastery church (near the Merry Cemetery, described earlier) and a striking ensemble of wooden ecclesiastical buildings at the **Bârsana** monastery complex (about a 30-minute drive southeast of Sighet).

ROMANIA

BUCOVINA

Within the large, eastern Romanian region of Moldavia sits the smaller sub-region called Bucovina (BOO-koh-vee-nah)—known

for its traditional folk life, rolling Carpathian foot-hills, and, most of all, glorious painted mon-asteries. Unfortunately, Bucovina presents a time-consuming detour for travelers connecting the core of Transylvania with the folk-culture treasures

of Maramureș. If you're very tight on time, Bucovina is skippable, as there's relatively little to see in this region beyond the monaster-ies. But if you can make the time, the monasteries are worth the trip.

Local Tours: If you make a special trip to Bucovina, invest in a tour to connect the painted monasteries (and other cultural sights) and bring them to life. **Hello Bucovina,** well run by Cipri-an "Chip" Slemco, offers a range of well-designed tours, from a quick spin to the monasteries to multiday routes connecting Bu-covina, the rest of Moldavia, and neighboring countries (www.hellobucovina.com).

▲▲Painted Monasteries of Bucovina

Remote and feisty Bucovina sits on the cusp of cultures. It's just outside the Carpathian Mountains, squeezed between two would-

be oppressors: The Hun-garians of Transylvania to the west, and the Ot-tomans to the east. So maybe it's no surprise that this stubbornly traditional region chose to cling fast to its faith in the rough-and-tumble 15th and 16th centuries, erecting dozens

of fortified and vividly decorated monasteries. And today, many of the churches still survive—their outside walls slathered in colorful Byzantine-style fresco murals of saints and Bible stories.

Background: The tradition of painted monasteries began during the reign of Prince Stephen the Great of Moldavia (1433-1504)—a contemporary of Vlad the Impaler of Wallachia, King Mátyás Corvinus of Hungary, and Sultan Mehmet the Con-queror of the Ottoman Empire. It was a frightening time, as big egos struggled for control of the Romanian lands—but Stephen the Great stubbornly asserted his Romanian Orthodox faith. According to legend, to celebrate his many military victories, Stephen would climb a mountain, shoot arrows into the rolling hills, and build a monastery where each arrow fell. Stephen's son, Petru Rareș (1487-1546), was inspired by Renaissance frescoes on a visit to Florence and decided to decorate the monasteries with a similar technique. Their Moldavian subjects were very poor, very religious, and eager to do God's work for low wages. And most people were illiterate, making the vivid illustrations a powerful educational tool. Of the dozens of monasteries built by Stephen the Great, nine still survive.

While each church has its own unique flourishes, all of them are wrapped in glorious, exceptionally well-preserved frescoes. You'll see row after row of saintly icons, local religious figures, ancient philosophers, Bible stories, lush visions of heaven, terrifying depictions of hell, and epic historical scenes. Each church has its own distinctive coloring (for example, "Voroneț blue").

Each church has a giant *Last Judgment* **mural** on its western wall. These are packed with symbolism that's worth disentangling. (While this works best at Voroneț, the basic composition is standard across churches.) Striping the mural are five horizontal tiers (top to bottom):

1. At the top sits God, flanked by 12 signs of the zodiac—merging Christian and pagan beliefs, driving home the eternal nature of God, and evoking the 12 Apostles.

2. Floating in a celestial bubble is Jesus—in his "furious vengeance" mode. He's flanked by Mary, John the Baptist, and pews with 12 seated Apostles (with other saintly figures in the cheap seats behind them). From Jesus flows a river of flames that spreads out toward the lower-right corner...and the open mouth of a hideous, multiheaded Beelzebub.

3. A dove (the Holy Spirit) sits on the Throne of Judgment, flanked by Adam and Eve—who committed the original sin, and are now eyewitnesses to how it all turns out. To the right—cut off from the holiness by Jesus' river of flames—are condemned pagans (depicted as the Moldavians' historical enemies: Jews, Ottomans, Tatars, and Armenians). At the front of this pack, Moses gestures frantically with the Ten Commandments, hoping for some last-minute conversions. Meanwhile, to the left of the river of flames

stand smug clumps of righteous believers: prophets, bishops, theologians, and so on.

4. Below the Holy Spirit, the hand of God holds the scales of judgment. Drama ensues, as angels and devils pile good and bad deeds on the scale in a struggle for the man's soul. On the right, hideous beasts prowl a barren landscape where souls emerge from tombs—hoping to be rescued by the angels. Below them, a female figure lovingly cradles a ship—representing salvation even for those lost at sea. Meanwhile, on the left end of this tier is a saintly legion, halos aglow.

5. Finally, along the bottom level, we see (from left to right) the saved, kicking back in the garden of paradise (look for Mary, the archangels Gabriel and Michael, Abraham, Isaac, Jacob, the face of Moses' burning bush, and the cross-toting thief who repented as he was crucified next to Jesus); the righteous waiting to enter heaven, led by St. Peter—about to use his key to open that golden door; and King David playing a traditional Moldavian instrument (one of many subtle references to local culture) in a mountainous terrain, flanked by the deaths of a righteous man (saved by angels) and a sinner (skewered by devils).

Elsewhere on the church, you'll typically see a *Tree of Jesse*, tracing Jesus' family tree from Mary all the way back to Jesse and King David. Another standard Orthodox theme is the *Deesis*, with Christ Pantocrator ("Ruler of All") enthroned in heaven and surrounded by saints. And many churches illustrate the Christian defense of Constantinople (today's Istanbul) during the Persian siege of 626. The "Persians" are dressed in Turkish clothes...a

not-so-subtle reminder that these monasteries were built as bastions of Christendom against the rising tide of Islam.

You'll also see lots of unofficial decoration. Bucovina's painted monasteries were a popular destination in the Romantic Age of the late 19th century, when Bucovina was part of the Habsburg Empire. Mostly German-speaking tourists scratched their own initials into the colorful plaster—century-old-graffiti that's still readable.

Assuming there are

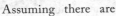

no services going on, you can enter the church itself. People enter at the porch—traditionally, the unbaptized could go no farther. Inside, each church is divided into three sections, representing the holy trinity. First comes the pro-nous (pro-nave—sometimes outside on smaller churches), where regular people worshipped. Then comes the nous (nave), with benches for VIPs and a fresco of the donor who built the church. Finally, there's the altar area, with the iconostasis. Each section is richly decorated with golden icons and colorful frescoes.

You may see a priest or nun walking around the courtyard, knocking on a piece of wood with a mallet. This means it's time for worship—and for tourists to leave the church interior.

Visiting the Painted Monasteries: The best painted monasteries are near the town of Gura Humorului (pop. 12,000). On a quick, targeted visit, you can simply visit Voroneţ (the best one overall) and Humor—each about a 10-minute drive from Gura Humorului (in opposite directions). With more time, do a loop through the hills north of Gura Humorului to also see Moldoviţa and Suceviţa. I've listed these in the order of an all-day loop.

Voroneţ Monastery (voh-roh-NETS, from 1487) is the most striking and most famous—sometimes called the "Sistine Chapel of the East." Its vivid frescoes—

with their distinctive "Voroneţ blue" hue—are sumptuous and richly detailed. Voroneţ also has the finest *Last Judgment* fresco. You could stare at it for hours, picking out details (see "Background," earlier). If you see only one painted monastery, make it this one.

Moldoviţa Monastery (MOHL-doh-veet-sah, from 1532) is less crowded, filling a serene courtyard, and has art nearly as impressive as Voroneţ's. Moldoviţa has a particularly evocative fresco showing the siege of Constantinople, a fine *Tree of Jesse* mural, and the most evident examples of "graffiti" scratched into the plaster by 19th-century tourists (especially under the porch).

Between Moldoviţa and Suceviţa, you'll twist up and over a dramatic mountain pass with great views.

Suceviţa Monastery (SOO-cheh-veet-sah) was the final painted monastery built (1581), with the best-preserved fortifications and the biggest, richest interior. Even more than the others, from the outside it feels more like a fortress than a monastery. The frescoes include a particularly exquisite *Ladder to Paradise* (or *Jacob's Ladder*): The angled ladder (where each rung represents a holy virtue required to reach heaven) slices the composition in half, with a heavenly host of angels at the top and, below, grotesque beasts torturing sinners who missed a rung. If you're in shape, hike up the steep hill behind for a fine view down over the monastery, the valley, and the wooded hills.

Just west of Sucevița, and on the way to Humor, you'll pass through the workaday town of Marginea—famous for its many black pottery workshops.

Humor Monastery (a.k.a. Humorului, hoo-moo-ROO-lee, from 1530) is sleepier and lower impact, with a lone fortified tower that stands taller than the church itself. Its *Last Judgment* fresco curls up under the roofline of the porch, protected from the elements.

Sleeping near the Painted Monasteries: The handiest home base is the functional crossroads town of Gura Humorului, which has several big hotels and smaller guesthouses. To sleep in the countryside, try **$ Casa Bunicilor,** a rustic but comfortable retreat a few minutes' drive out of town, near the Humor Monastery (www.casabunicilor.com).

Nearby: Suceava (soo-cheh-AH-vah, pop. 90,000), Bucovina's largest city, is about 25 miles to the east. It's workable as a home base, but its sparse sights (an empty-feeling old fortress and a mediocre open-air folk museum) and its distance from the monasteries make it less appealing than Gura Humorului.

UNDERSTANDING YUGOSLAVIA

If you're struggling to understand the complicated breakup of Yugoslavia, read this admittedly oversimplified, as-impartial-as-possible history to get you started. (For a more complete version, see www.ricksteves.com/yugo.)

The Balkan Peninsula—between the Adriatic and the Black Sea, basically running from Hungary to Greece—has always been a crossroads of cultures, divided by a series of cultural, ethnic, and religious fault lines. The most important religious influences were **Western Christianity** (i.e., Roman Catholicism, introduced by Charlemagne and later championed by the Austrian Habsburgs), **Eastern Orthodox Christianity** (from the Byzantine Empire), and **Islam** (from the Ottomans).

Two major historical factors made the Balkans what they are today: The first was the **split of the Roman Empire** in the fourth century AD, dividing the Balkans down the middle into Roman Catholic (west) and Byzantine Orthodox (east)—roughly along today's Bosnian-Serbian border. The second was the **invasion of the Ottomans** (from today's Turkey) in the 14th century, which kicked off five centuries of Islamic influence in Bosnia-Herzegovina and Serbia, further dividing the Balkans into Christian (north) and Muslim (south).

Because of these and other events, several distinct ethnic identities emerged. The major ethnicities of Yugoslavia are all considered "South Slavs." They're all descended from the same ancestors and speak closely-related languages, but are distinguished by their religious practices. Roman Catholic **Croats** and **Slovenes** are found mostly west of the Dinaric Mountains (Croats along the Adriatic coast and Slovenes farther north, in the Alps); Orthodox Christian **Serbs** live mostly east of the Dinaric range; and Muslim **Bosniaks** (whose ancestors converted to Islam under the

UNDERSTANDING YUGOSLAVIA

Yugoslav Succession

Legend:
- —— Former Yugoslavia Border
- —— Current Borders
- ·········· Province within Serbia
- SLOVENE Language
- "Serbian Krajina" (Serb-controlled Croatia 1991-1995)
- Republika Srpska (Serb territory in Bosnia-Herz.)

Ottomans) live mostly in the Dinaric Mountains. The region also has several smaller ethnic groups: the Slavic **Montenegrins** and **Macedonians,** plus **Hungarians** (concentrated in the north) and **Albanians** (concentrated in Kosovo and the south). The groups overlapped a lot—which is exactly why the breakup of Yugoslavia was so contentious.

The lands of Yugoslavia were shuttled between various kingdoms and empires for much of their history, but by the late 19th century, most of the area was part of the Austro-Hungarian Empire. When that empire split apart at the end of World War I, the various mostly-Slavic groups in the region formed a new country: Yugoslavia ("Land of the South Slavs"). The union was almost immediately contentious, as various groups—especially Serbs and Croats—struggled to take control. By the dawn of World War II, it was already clear that Yugoslavia was a troubled proposition.

The seeds of the 1990s interethnic conflict were planted in World War II. Yugoslavia was invaded by Nazi Germany, then chopped up into puppet states for the Axis Powers. Some groups

UNDERSTANDING YUGOSLAVIA

Tito (1892-1980)

The Republic of Yugoslavia was the vision of a single man, who made it reality. Josip Broz—better known as Marshal Tito—presided over the most peaceful and prosperous era in this region's long and troubled history. Three decades after his death, Tito is beloved by many of his former subjects...and yet, he was a communist dictator who dealt brutally with his political enemies. This love-him-and-hate-him autocrat is one of the most complex figures in the history of this very complicated land.

Josip Broz was born in 1892 to a Slovenian mother and a Croatian father in the northern part of today's Croatia (then part of the Austro-Hungarian Empire). After growing up in the rural countryside, he was trained as a metalworker. He was drafted into the Austro-Hungarian army, went to fight on the Eastern Front during World War I, and was captured and sent to Russia as a prisoner of war. Freed by Bolsheviks, Broz fell in with the Communist Revolution...and never looked back.

At war's end, Broz returned home to the newly independent Yugoslavia, where he worked alongside the Soviets to build a national Communist Party. As a clandestine communist operative, he adopted the code name he kept for the rest of his life: Tito. Some believe this was a Spanish name he picked up while participating in that country's civil war, while others half-joke that the name came from Tito's authoritarian style: *"Ti, to!"* means "You, do this!" But one thing's clear: In this land where a person's name instantly identifies his ethnicity, "Tito" is ethnically neutral.

When the Nazis occupied Yugoslavia, Tito raised and commanded a homegrown, communist Partisan Army. Through guerilla tactics, Tito's clever maneuvering, and sheer determination, the Partisans liberated their country. And because they did so mostly without support from the USSR, Yugoslavia was able to set its own postwar course.

The war hero Tito quickly became the "president for life" of postwar Yugoslavia. But even as he introduced communism to his country, he retained some elements of a free-market economy—firmly declining to become a satellite of Moscow. He also pioneered the worldwide Non-Aligned Movement, joining with nations in Africa, the Middle East, Asia, and Latin America in refusing to ally with the US or USSR. Stubborn but suitably cautious, Tito expertly walked a tightrope between East and West.

There was a dark side to Tito. In the early years of his regime, Tito resorted to brutal, Stalin-esque tactics to assert his control. Immediately following World War II, the Partisan Army massacred tens of thousands of soldiers who had supported the Nazis. Then Tito systematically arrested, tried, tortured, or executed those who did not accept his new regime. Survivors whose lives were ruined during this reign of terror will never forgive Tito for what he did.

But once he gained full control, Tito moved away from strong-arm tactics and into a warm-and-fuzzy era of Yugoslav brotherhood. Tito believed that the disparate peoples of Yugoslavia could live in harmony. For example, every Yugoslav male had to serve in the People's Army, and Tito made sure that each unit was a microcosm of the complete Yugoslavia—with equal representation from each ethnic group. Yugoslavs from diverse backgrounds were required to work together and socialize—as a result, they became friends. He also worked toward economic diversification: Yugoslav tanks, some of the best in the world, were made of parts assembled in five different republics.

Tito's reign is a case study in the power of the cult of personality. Rocks on hillsides throughout Yugoslavia were rearranged to spell "TITO," and his portrait hung over every family's dinner table. Each of the six republics renamed one of its cities for their dictator. The main street and square in virtually every town were renamed for Tito. Each year, young people would embark on a months-long, Olympics-style relay, from each corner of Yugoslavia, to present a ceremonial baton to Tito on his official birthday (May 25). Tito also had vacation villas in all of Yugoslavia's most beautiful areas, including Lake Bled, the Brijuni Islands, and the Montenegrin coast. People sang patriotic anthems to their Druža (Comrade) Tito: "Comrade Tito, we pledge an oath to you."

Tito died in 1980 in a Slovenian hospital. His body went on a grand tour of the Yugoslav capitals: Ljubljana, Zagreb, Sarajevo, and Belgrade, where he was buried before hundreds of thousands of mourners, including more heads of state than at any other funeral in history. At his request, his tomb was placed in the greenhouse where he enjoyed spending time.

The genuine outpouring of grief at Tito's death might seem unusual for a man who was, on paper, an authoritarian communist dictator. But even today, many former Yugoslavs—especially Slovenes and Bosniaks—believe that his iron-fisted government was a necessary evil that kept the country strong and united. The eventual balance Tito struck between communism and capitalism, and between the competing interests of his ethnically diverse nation, led to this region's most stable and prosperous era. In a recent poll in Slovenia, Tito had a higher approval rating than any present-day politician, and 80 percent of Slovenes said they had a positive impression of him.

And yet, the Yugoslavs' respect for their former leader was not enough to keep them together. Tito's death began a long, slow chain reaction that led to the end of Yugoslavia. As the decades pass, the old joke seems more and more appropriate: Yugoslavia had eight distinct peoples in six republics, with five languages, three religions (Orthodox Christian, Catholic, and Muslim), and two alphabets (Roman and Cyrillic), but only one Yugoslav—Tito.

took advantage of changing circumstances in wartime Yugoslavia to exact revenge on their former compatriots. In occupied Croatia, the puppet Ustaše government imprisoned and executed large numbers of Serbs. In the eastern mountains, a Serbian royalist paramilitary group called the Četniks were every bit as brutal against Croats and Bosniaks. A third group—the homegrown Partisan Army—fought against Nazis, Ustaše, and Četniks to secure freedom for Yugoslavia. Unlike the other "Eastern European" countries, Yugoslavia was not liberated by the Soviet Union. This unique status allowed it to determine its own path after the war.

After the short but rocky Yugoslav union between the World Wars, it seemed that no one could hold the southern Slavs together in a single nation. But one man could, and did: Partisan war hero Josip Broz, who is better known by his code name, Tito. With a Slovene for a mother, a Croat for a father, a Serb for a wife, and a home in Belgrade, Tito was a true Yugoslav. Tito had a compelling vision that this fractured union of the South Slavs could function (see the sidebar).

Tito's new incarnation of Yugoslavia aimed for a more equitable division of powers. It was made up of six republics, each dominated by one ethnic group: **Croatia, Slovenia, Serbia, Bosnia-Herzegovina, Montenegro,** and **Macedonia.** Within Serbia, Tito set up two autonomous provinces, each one an enclave for an ethnicity that was a minority in greater Yugoslavia: Albanians in **Kosovo** (to the south) and Hungarians in **Vojvodina** (to the north). By allowing these two provinces some degree of independence, Tito hoped they would balance the political clout of Serbia, preventing a single republic from dominating the union.

While each republic had a measure of self-rule, the union was carefully overseen by President-for-Life Tito. Tito respected—and even celebrated—the diversity of his union, but he placed Yugoslav unity above all. He said that the borders between the republics should be "like white lines in a marble column."

Tito's Yugoslavia was communist, but it wasn't Soviet communism. He refused to formally join either the Warsaw Pact or NATO, and ingeniously played the East and the West against each other. Economically, Tito's vision was for a "third way," somewhere between communism and capitalism. While large industries were collectivized, small businesses were also permitted. Though Yugoslavs could not become really rich, through hard work it was possible to attain modest wealth to buy a snazzy car, a vacation home, Western imports, and other niceties. Yugoslavia was also the most free and open of the communist states. Tourists (from both East and West) flocked here for vacation, and Yugoslavs could travel to far more places abroad than could residents of the Eastern Bloc.

Tito died in 1980, and before long, the fragile union he had held together started to unravel. The breakup began in the late 1980s in the autonomous province of Kosovo, with squabbles between the Serb minority and the ethnic-Albanian majority. Serbian politician Slobodan Milošević traveled to Kosovo to rouse his Serb comrades, which alarmed some of the other republics. When Milošević-led Serbia annexed Kosovo soon after, and negotiations among the Yugoslav republics broke down, Croatia and Slovenia decided it was time to declare independence (both on June 25, 1991). Small, relatively homogenous Slovenia weathered a brief 10-day skirmish (see page 715), while Croatia—which had a large Serb minority—was pulled into a gruesome war lasting several years. Bosnia-Herzegovina declared its independence a few months later. But, because that republic was by far Yugoslavia's most ethnically diverse (with large populations of Muslim Bosniaks, Serbs, and Croats), its separation was hotly contested—plunging Bosnia into a horrifying four years of guerrilla warfare, medieval-style sieges, systematic rape, and ethnic cleansing.

Peace accords in 1995 brought an end to most of the hostilities throughout Yugoslavia, establishing the borders of Croatia and Bosnia that still exist today. Over the next several years, Slobodan Milošević and others accused of war crimes were arrested and tried by an international tribunal at The Hague, Netherlands (though Milošević died behind bars before a verdict was handed down). Later, additional parts of the former Yugoslavia split off, leaving behind seven independent nations where once was one: Croatia, Slovenia, Bosnia-Herzegovina, Montenegro, Serbia, Macedonia, and Kosovo.

Peace has reigned in these countries for more than two decades. The physical scars of war have mostly been repaired. And, considering that hospitality has been a forte of this region since long before the age of Yugoslavia, outside visitors feel welcome and safe—and are impressed at the candor of the people they meet, who are often willing to share their own wartime experiences. But, understandably, the psychological scars will take the longest to heal. Tensions still persist between formerly warring groups.

Thoughtful visitors to the former Yugoslavia grapple with trying to understand what happened here just a generation ago. Many find it hard to get an impartial take on the current situation, or even on historical "facts." A very wise Bosniak once told me, "Listen to all three sides—Muslim, Serb, and Croat. Then decide for yourself what you think." A Serb told me a similar local saying: "You have to look at the apple from all sides."

PRACTICALITIES

Travel Tips 1072
Money 1078
Sightseeing.................... 1085
Sleeping 1090
Eating........................ 1097
Staying Connected 1102
Transportation 1104
Resources from Rick Steves 1115

This chapter covers the practical skills of European travel: how to get tourist information, pay for things, sightsee efficiently, find good-value accommodations, eat affordably but well, use technology wisely, and get between destinations smoothly. For more information on these topics, see RickSteves.com/travel-tips.

Travel Tips

Travel Advisories: Before traveling, check updated health and safety conditions, including restrictions for your destination, at Travel.State.gov (US State Department travel pages) and CDC.gov (Centers for Disease Control and Prevention). The US embassy websites for each country are good sources of information (see later).

While most countries no longer require proof of Covid-19 vaccination for entry, some sights or tours may still have vaccination requirements (check websites). Even if it's not required for your itinerary, it's smart to pack a copy of your vaccine record and/or store a photo of your Covid-19 vaccine card on your phone.

ETIAS Registration: The European Union may soon require

US and Canadian citizens to register online with the European Travel Information and Authorization System (ETIAS) before entering Schengen Zone countries (quick and easy process). For the latest, check https://travel-europe.europa.eu/etias_en.

Tourist Information: National tourist offices are a wealth of information (see websites below).

In Central Europe, a good first stop in every town is generally the tourist information office (abbreviated **TI** in this book). You'll find local TIs are usually well organized and always have an English-speaking staff. While many TIs in Central Europe are still primarily government run—and therefore have the sole priority of helping you have a better trip—others are in cahoots with local, private tour operators, which tends to color their advice. I find TIs a great place to flip through brochures, pick up a free map, and ask basic questions. But I supplement what I learn there with advice from my hotel, other local contacts, and online sources. TIs also offer information on public transit (including bus and train schedules), walking tours, special events, and nightlife.

Czech Tourist Office: VisitCzechRepublic.com

Polish Tourist Office: Poland.travel

Hungarian Tourist Office: VisitHungary.com

Slovenian Tourist Office: Slovenia.info

Austrian Tourist Office: Austria.info

Slovakian Tourist Office: Slovakia.travel

Emergency and Medical Help: In all of the countries in this book, dial 112 for any emergency service—ambulance, police, or fire (operators typically speak English). If you get sick, do as the locals do and go to a pharmacist for advice. Or ask at your hotel for help—they'll know the nearest medical and emergency services.

Theft or Loss: To replace a passport, you'll need to go in person to the appropriate embassy or consulate (see next). If your credit and debit cards disappear, cancel and replace them (see "Damage Control for Lost Cards" on page 1082). File a police report, either on the spot or within a day or two; you'll need it to submit an insurance claim for lost or stolen items, and it can help with replacing your passport or credit and debit cards. For help with a lost phone, see "Damage Control for Lost Phones" on page 1103. For more information, see RickSteves.com/help.

US Embassies and Consulates: For additional information, visit the US State Department's website, Travel.State.gov. At any of these, it's advisable to call ahead to ensure they're open, and some may require an appointment.

Austria—Boltzmanngasse 16, Vienna, +43 1 313 390; consular services at Parkring 12a, Vienna; At.USEmbassy.gov.

Czech Republic—Tržiště 15, Prague, +420 257 022 000, Cz.USEmbassy.gov.

PRACTICALITIES

Hungary—Szabadság Tér 12, Budapest, +36 1 475 4400, Hu.USEmbassy.gov.

Poland—Aleje Ujazdowskie 29, Warsaw, +48 22 504 2000, Pl.USEmbassy.gov; also a US Consulate in Kraków at Ulica Stolarska 9, +48 12 424 5100, Pl.USEmbassy.gov/embassy-consulate/krakow.

Slovakia—Hviezdoslavovo Námestie 4, Bratislava, +421 2 5443 3338, Sk.USEmbassy.gov.

Slovenia—Prešernova 31, Ljubljana, +386 1 200 5500, Si.USEmbassy.gov.

Canadian Embassies and Consulates: For after-hours emergencies, Canadian citizens can call collect to the Foreign Services Office in Ottawa at +1 613 996 8885.

Austria—Laurenzerberg 2, Vienna, +43 1 531 383 000, Austria.gc.ca.

Czech Republic—Ve Struhách 95/2, Prague, +420 272 101 800, CzechRepublic.gc.ca.

Hungary—Ganz Utca 12, Budapest, +36 1 392 3360, Hungary.gc.ca; also provides services for Bosnia-Herzegovina and Slovenia.

Poland—Ulica Jana Matejki 1, Warsaw, Poland.gc.ca.

Slovakia—Mostová 2, Bratislava, +421 2 5920 4031, SlovakRepublic.gc.ca.

Slovenia (consulate office)—Linhartova Cesta 49a, Ljubljana; +386 1 252 4444, Slovenia.gc.ca; some services provided through Canadian Embassy in Budapest, Hungary (listed above).

Borders: All of the core countries in this book have officially joined the open-borders Schengen Agreement. That means that there are no border checks between any of these countries, or between them and Western European countries such as Germany, Austria, and Italy. You'll usually zip through the border without stopping, though in a few cases, you may need to stop briefly to flash a passport.

Non-Schengen countries (including Bosnia-Herzegovina, Montenegro, Bulgaria, and Romania) still have traditional border checkpoints—you'll have to stop upon entering or exiting these countries. But whether traveling by car, train, or bus, you'll find that border crossings are generally a nonevent: Flash your passport, maybe wait a few minutes, and move on. Drivers may be asked to show proof of car insurance ("green card"), so be sure you have this when you pick up your rental car.

Time Zones: Most of the countries listed in this book are generally six/nine hours ahead of the East/West Coasts of the US. (Bulgaria and Romania are one hour ahead of the rest of these countries—that's seven/ten hours ahead of the East/West Coasts.) The exceptions are the beginning and end of Daylight Saving

---

Travel Insurance

Travel insurance can minimize the considerable financial risks of traveling: accidents, illness, missed flights, canceled tours, lost baggage, theft, terrorism, travel-company bankruptcies, natural disasters, emergency evacuation, and getting your body home in case you die. The decision to buy travel insurance (and how much) depends on your situation. First look into what coverage you already have; many premium credit cards include a generous degree of coverage, and other expenses may be covered through your health insurance, or homeowners or rental insurance. Then consider how likely it is that you'll need to change or cancel (for example, if you or a loved one is in frail health), how much of your prepaid trip costs are nonrefundable, and your risk tolerance.

It costs money to buy away the financial risk of travel. Compare that cost to the likelihood you'll need it and whether you're the gambling type. The way I see it, if insurance costs 10 percent of your total trip cost, but chances are slim that you'll need it, statistically, you're better off going without. But emotionally, it still might be a good investment. You can compare insurance policies and costs at InsureMyTrip.com.

PRACTICALITIES

Time: Europe "springs forward" the last Sunday in March (two weeks after most of North America), and "falls back" the last Sunday in October (one week before North America). For a handy time converter, use the world clock app on your phone or download one (see www.timeanddate.com).

Weekends: Saturdays are virtually weekdays, but with earlier closing hours and no rush hour (though transportation connections can be less frequent than on weekdays). Sundays have the same pros and cons as they do for travelers in the US (special events, limited hours, banks and many shops generally closed, limited public-transportation options, no rush hour).

Watt's Up? Europe's electrical system is 220 volts, instead of North America's 110 volts. Most electronics (laptops, phones, cameras) and appliances (hair dryers, CPAP machines) convert automatically, so you won't need a converter, but you will need an adapter plug with two round prongs, sold inexpensively at travel stores in the US.

Rip up this book! Turn chapters into mini guidebooks: Break the book's spine and use a utility knife to slice apart chapters, keeping gummy edges intact. Reinforce the chapter spines with clear wide tape, use a heavy-duty stapler, or make or buy a cheap cover (see the Travel Store at RickSteves.com), swapping out chapters as you travel.

Discounts: Discounts for sights are generally not listed in this

PRACTICALITIES

LGBTQ+ Travel in Central Europe

LGBTQ+ travelers may wonder whether they should travel in Central Europe—and specifically in countries (such as Hungary and Poland) that have been in the news for their anti-LGBTQ+ policies. Here are some factors to consider.

First, all countries in Central Europe are not alike. ILGA, a gay rights advocacy NGO, ranks European countries on how LGBTQ+-friendly they are (www.ilga-europe.org). **Slovenia** and **Austria** are in the middle of the pack; the **Czech Republic** and **Slovakia** still have antiquated policies but are working toward greater acceptance. Broadly speaking, these are progressive societies where LGBTQ+ rights are trending toward parity with much of the US and Western Europe. Poland and Hungary rank near the bottom on a European scale, for different reasons. (Equaldex.com is another useful resource offering country-by-country policy and public-opinion insights.)

Poland is devoutly Catholic, and religion is often entangled with politics and policy—which causes it to skew more conservative than the European norm. This makes Poland a challenging place to be gay or trans. Large cities—especially certain neighborhoods—can be more hospitable, offering venues where anyone can live more openly. But in broader society, LGBTQ+ people are largely invisible, and public displays of affection are rare; "don't ask, don't tell" is the status quo.

Poland has no legal recognition of same-sex partnerships, and the constitution defines marriage as between a man and a woman. The ruling Law and Justice party (PiS) has often blocked pro-LGBTQ+ legislation. In 2019, after Warsaw's mayor signed a declaration of LGBTQ+ rights, PiS officials in several conservative areas declared "LGBT-free zones"—a political stunt that LGBTQ+ Poles and their allies found threatening and discriminatory.

But there are some signs of progress. Warsaw has hosted an "Equality Parade" each summer since 2001. Robert Biedroń, a popular and well-respected Polish politician, is openly gay and in a same-sex marriage (conducted abroad). And other contemporary Poles—writers, artists, and people of culture—are vocal in sharing their experiences of being LGBTQ+ in Poland.

Hungary has also become known for its anti-LGBTQ+ politics. In 2020, Prime Minister Viktor Orbán's government withdrew legal recognition of transgender people. In 2021, Orbán's party enacted a law "taking more severe action against pedophile offenders"—offensively conflating LGBTQ+ people with pedophiles.

In a broader application of Florida's "Don't Say Gay" bill, the Hungarian law bans public expression of non-heteronormative content in schools, or in any media aimed at people under 18, ostensibly for the "protection of children." These policies have sparked outrage and condemnation from many European countries, as well as the European Commission and the United States. US ambassador David Pressman, himself in a same-sex marriage, reports that many of his Hungarian counterparts have become overly preoccupied with this new anti-LGBTQ+ agenda.

And what about the Hungarian on the street? Especially in cosmopolitan Budapest, you'll find a greater acceptance of LGBTQ+ people. Unlike Poland, Hungary recognizes legal same-sex partnerships—though not marriages. But more conservative Hungarians—especially outside of urban centers—have been stoked by Orbán's anti-LGBTQ+ talking points and may express more disapproval, even hostility, toward what they consider a threat to their "Christian traditions."

In both Poland and Hungary, you'll encounter a wide diversity of beliefs and attitudes. Just as in some parts of the US, even as the political pendulum has swung against LGBTQ+ rights, there are still many locals who find that trend abhorrent. Ultimately, two questions face LGBTQ+ travelers who are considering a trip to Poland or Hungary: Is it safe to visit? And *should* you visit a place that doesn't respect who you are?

On the first question, LGBTQ+ travelers have told me that—especially if they can pass as straight and cisgender—they have felt largely safe visiting these places. Big, progressive cities (like Budapest or Warsaw), and especially certain neighborhoods, may not feel different from other parts of Europe or the US. But in smaller towns and more conservative areas, public displays of affection between LGBTQ+ people could attract unwanted attention, occasional insensitive remarks, and potentially (though rarely) threats or violence. In these places, keeping a low profile is—unfortunately—probably the most prudent approach.

As for the second question: That's a decision for each traveler—whether LGBTQ+ or an ally—to decide personally. If you simply can't stomach the idea of traveling to a place that doesn't honor LGBTQ+ rights, I certainly wouldn't blame you for going elsewhere.

That said, some travelers see value in the transformative potential of people-to-people interactions. When you travel, you meet new friends from every walk of life and exchange perspectives. When we get to know each other, it becomes more difficult to dehumanize and demonize one another. And you can travel intentionally, spending money in a way that supports local LGBTQ+ people and their allies.

PRACTICALITIES

book. However, seniors (age 65 and over), youths under 18, and students and teachers with proper identification cards (obtain from www.isic.org) can get discounts at many sights—always ask. Some discounts are available only to European citizens.

Online Translation Tip: The Google Translate app converts spoken or typed English into most European languages (and vice versa) and can also translate text it "reads" with your phone's camera. Google's Chrome browser instantly translates websites; Translate.google.com and DeepL.com are also handy.

Going Green: There's plenty you can do to reduce your environmental footprint when traveling. When practical, take a train instead of a flight within Europe, and use public transportation within cities. In hotels, use the "Do Not Disturb" sign to avoid daily linen and towel changes (or hang up your towels to signal you'll reuse them). Bring a reusable shopping tote and refillable water bottle (Europe's tap water is safe to drink). Skip printed materials that you don't plan to keep—get your info online instead. To find out how Rick Steves' Europe is offsetting carbon emissions with a self-imposed carbon tax, see RickSteves.com/about-us/climate-smart.

Money

Here's my basic strategy for using money wisely in Europe. I pack the following and keep it all safe in my money belt.

Credit Card: You'll use your credit card for purchases both big (hotels, advance tickets) and small (little shops, food stands). Some European businesses have gone cashless, making a card your only payment option. A "tap-to-pay" or "contactless" card is widely accepted and simple to use.

Debit Card: Use this at ATMs to withdraw a small amount of local cash. Wait until you arrive to get local currency (European airports have plenty of ATMs); if you buy foreign currency before your trip, you'll pay bad stateside exchange rates. While many transactions are by card these days, cash can help you out of a jam if your card randomly doesn't work and can be useful to pay for things like tips and local guides.

Backup Card: Some travelers carry a third card (debit or credit; ideally from a different bank) in case one gets lost or simply doesn't work.

Stash of Cash: I carry $100-200 in US dollars as a cash backup, which comes in handy in an emergency (for example, if your debit card gets eaten by the machine).

EXCHANGE RATES

Most of the countries in this book still use their traditional currencies. Only the ones listed below use the euro—and the others are
unlikely to adopt it anytime soon. But even in countries that don't
officially use the euro, many businesses (especially hotels) quote
prices in euros anyway.

Here are the rough exchange rates for each country. I've also
suggested a strategy for roughly converting prices into US dollars.
Note that in some cases, I've favored easier-to-remember equations
even if they offer less-precise conversions. For a more precise conversion, use the online tool at Oanda.com.

1 euro (€) = about $1.10 (used in Slovenia, Austria, Slovakia,
and Croatia, and unofficially elsewhere). To convert prices in euros
to dollars, add about 10 percent: €20 = about $22, €50 = about $55.
Like the dollar, one euro (€) is broken into 100 cents. Coins range
from €0.01 to €2, and bills from €5 to €200.

20 Czech crowns (*koruna*, Kč) = about $1. To roughly convert
prices in crowns to dollars, divide by 2 and drop the last digit. So
that tasty lunch for 160 Kč is about $8.

4 Polish złoty (zł, or PLN) = about $1. To calculate prices in
dollars, divide by four: 80 zł = about $20.

350 Hungarian forints (Ft, or HUF) = about $1. To very
roughly figure dollars, divide by three and drop the last two digits:
1,000 Ft = about $3.

So, that 20 zł Polish woodcarving is about $5, the 5,000 Ft
Hungarian dinner is about $16, and the 2,000 Kč taxi ride through
Prague is...uh-oh.

BEFORE YOU GO

Know your cards. For credit cards, Visa and Mastercard are universal, while American Express and Discover are less common. US
debit cards with a Visa or Mastercard logo will work in any European ATM.

Go "contactless." Contactless pay options are now standard in
much of Europe. Check to see if you already have—or can get—a
tap-to-pay version of your credit card (look on the card for the
tap-to-pay symbol—four curvy lines) and consider setting up your
smartphone for contactless payment (see next section for details).
Both options are more secure than a physical credit card: Instead of
recording your credit-card number, a one-time encrypted "token"
enables the purchase and expires shortly afterward.

Know your PIN. Make sure you know the numeric four-digit
PIN for each of your cards, both debit and credit. Request it if you
don't have one, as it may be required for some purchases. Allow
time to receive the information by mail—it's not always possible to
obtain your PIN online or by phone.

Report your travel dates. Some banks want to know that you'll be using your debit and credit cards overseas, specifically when and where you're headed. Depending on your bank, you can do this either online or over the phone.

Adjust your ATM withdrawal limit. Find out how much you can withdraw daily and ask for a higher daily limit if you want to get more cash at once. Note that European ATMs will withdraw funds only from checking accounts, not savings accounts.

Find out about fees. For any purchase or withdrawal made with a card, you may be charged a currency conversion fee (1-3 percent) and/or a Visa or Mastercard international transaction fee (less than 1 percent). Shop around; you can compare credit cards on Bankrate.com. Some cards offer lower international fees than others—and some don't charge any at all. If you're getting a bad deal, consider getting a new card. Most credit unions and some airline loyalty cards have low or no international transaction fees.

IN EUROPE
Using Credit Cards and Payment Apps
Tap-to-Pay or Contactless Cards: These cards have the usual chip and/or magnetic stripe, but with the addition of a contactless symbol. Simply tap your card against a contactless reader to complete a transaction—no PIN or signature required (except in some cases as a security measure for larger purchases). This is by far the easiest way to pay and is available in much of Europe.

Payment Apps: Just like at home, you can pay with your smartphone or smartwatch by linking a credit card to an app such as Apple Pay or Google Pay. To pay, hold your phone near a contactless reader; you may need to verify the transaction with a face scan, fingerprint scan, or passcode. If you've arrived in Europe without a tap-to-pay card, you can easily set up your phone to work in this way.

Will My US Card Work? Usually, yes. On rare occasions, you may run into a situation where your card doesn't work. This is most likely at self-service payment machines (such as transit-ticket kiosks, tollbooths, or fuel pumps). Usually a tap-to-pay card does the trick in these situations. If not, look for a cashier who can process your payment manually, or use cash. Drivers should be prepared to move on to the next gas station if necessary. (In some countries, gas stations sell prepaid gas cards, which you can purchase with any US card). When approaching a toll plaza or ferry ticket line, use the "cash" lane.

Always Choose to Pay in the Local Currency: When making a credit-card transaction, the payment terminal will often ask whether you want to pay in US dollars or in the local currency.

Always refuse the conversion and choose the local currency. While this "service"—called Dynamic Currency Conversion (DCC)—offers the illusion of convenience, it comes with a poor exchange rate and/or higher fees, and you'll wind up losing money.

Using Cash

Cash Machines: European cash machines work just like they do at home—except they spit out local currency instead of dollars. In Europe, the universal term for an ATM is "bankomat."

There are two broad categories of cash machines. The best choice are ones operated by a bank, which offer local cash calculated at the day's standard bank-to-bank rate. Look for a cash machine marked with a bank logo, and ideally use one just outside a brick-and-mortar bank (in the rare event that you have any issues).

The other type are cash machines run by exchange or money-transfer companies, which have unfavorable rates, higher fees, or both. These can be marked Euronet, Travelex, Your Cash, and Cashzone—and often they're simply marked generically, as "bankomat" or "ATM," with no other identification. Avoid these unless you enjoy paying too much for your local cash.

Unfortunately, these rip-off exchange ATMs are often the only option at airports and train stations. On arrival, consider finding a cashless way to get downtown, then find a real bank near your hotel to withdraw local currency.

If your debit card doesn't work, try a lower amount—your request may have exceeded your withdrawal limit or the ATM's limit. If you still have a problem, try a different ATM or come back later.

Remember: If the ATM offers to let you convert your withdrawal to US dollars, choose the local currency for the best rates.

Exchanging Cash: Minimize exchanging money in Europe; it's expensive (you'll generally lose 5 to 10 percent). But because the countries in this region have different currencies, you may wind up with leftover cash. Coins can't be exchanged once you leave the country, so spend them before you cross the border. Bills are easy to convert to your next country's currency at exchange booths, but remember that regular banks have the best rates for the conversion.

Security Tips

Pickpockets target tourists. Keep your backup cash, credit cards, and passport secure in your money belt, and carry only a day's spending money and one card in your front pocket or wallet.

Before inserting your card into an ATM, inspect the front of the machine. If anything looks crooked, loose, or damaged, it could be a sign of a card-skimming device. When entering your PIN, carefully block other people's view of the keypad.

Avoid using a debit card for purchases. Because a debit card pulls funds directly from your bank account, potential charges incurred by a thief will stay on your account while your bank investigates.

To access your accounts online while traveling, be sure to use a secure connection (see the "Tips on Internet Security" sidebar, later).

Damage Control for Lost Cards

If you lose your credit or debit card, report the loss immediately to your bank (using a secure app) or the following global customer-assistance centers. With a mobile phone, call these 24-hour US numbers: Visa (+1 303 967 1096), Mastercard (+1 636 722 7111), and American Express (+1 336 393 1111).

You'll need to provide the primary cardholder's identification-verification details (such as birth date, mother's maiden name, or Social Security number). You can generally receive a temporary card within two or three business days in Europe (see RickSteves.com/help for more).

If you report your loss within two days, you typically won't be responsible for unauthorized transactions on your account, although many banks charge a liability fee.

TIPPING

Tipping in Europe isn't as automatic and generous as it is in the US. For special service, tips are appreciated, but not expected. As in the US, the proper amount depends on your resources, tipping philosophy, and the circumstances, but some general guidelines apply.

Restaurants: At sit-down eateries, tip a small amount by rounding up the bill 5-10 percent. In a few cities (like Prague and Budapest), a service charge may be automatically added to your bill; look for this carefully to avoid double-tipping. If paying with a credit card, be prepared to tip separately with cash or coins; credit card receipts don't have a tip line. For details on tipping in restaurants, see page 1099.

Taxis: For a typical ride, round up your fare a bit (for instance, if the fare is €42, pay €45). If the cabbie hauls your bags and zips you to the airport to help you catch your flight, you might want to toss in a little more.

Services: For local guides, private drivers, or others who spend several hours with you and significantly improve the quality of your trip, a healthy tip (of around 10 percent) is not extravagant. In general, if someone in the tourism or service industry does a good job for you, a small tip (the equivalent of a euro or two) is appropriate... but not required. If you're not sure whether (or how much) to tip, ask a local for advice.

Central Europe and the European Union (EU)

The European Union (EU) began as a political and economic alliance of mostly Western European nations, with Germany, France, and Italy at the helm. But since 2004, 11 formerly communist Central European countries—including most of the ones in this book—have joined the EU, shifting the geographical and political center of Europe from Brussels to Prague. This enlargement of the EU—creating what's been termed a "New Europe"—has been a fitful process.

Some Central Europeans, concerned that EU bureaucracy could threaten their prized traditions, are "Euroskeptics." Upon joining the EU, one Polish farmer grumbled that he had to get "passports" for each of his cows. And many are simply exhausted after generations of shifting borders. A wise Czech grandmother pointed out that in her lifetime, her hometown had been ruled from Vienna (Habsburgs), Berlin (Nazis), and Moscow (communists). She said, "Now that we're finally ruled from Prague, why would we want to turn our power over to Brussels?"

Long-standing EU members also had their doubts. Wealthy nations had already spent vast fortunes to improve the economies of poorer members (such as Portugal, Greece, and Ireland), and were reluctant to take on more "charity cases." And some Westerners fretted about the influx of cheap labor endangering local employment opportunities.

Two decades on, however, the advantages of EU enlargement are evident. New expressways, airports, train stations, and museums throughout Central Europe were subsidized by EU funds. Countries that have adopted the euro currency (including Slovenia, Slovakia, and Croatia) match up well economically with their fellow EU members. And, just as intended, Western European companies have enjoyed easier access to affordable resources and labor.

More recently, with the rising tide of nativism and illiberalism on the eastern fringes of Europe—Putin in Russia, Erdoğan in Turkey, Orbán in Hungary—the EU provides a powerful counterbalance. The EU offers both a carrot and a stick in advocating for democracy and open society.

The importance of the EU was highlighted again in 2022, when Russia invaded Ukraine. While some feared that the fighting could spill over into neighboring countries such as Poland or Hungary, people living in those places were greatly reassured by their membership in the EU (and in NATO).

In a sense, a generation of EU membership has created a new "Iron Curtain" through the middle of Europe. That line now runs between Central European members of the EU—such as the Czech Republic, Poland, Hungary, and Slovenia—and lands farther east, such as Ukraine, that are not EU members. At least...not yet.

PRACTICALITIES

VAT Rates

To be eligible to get a VAT refund, you usually need to spend the listed minimum at a single store.

Country of Purchase	VAT Standard Rate*	Minimum in Local Currency	Approx. Minimum in US $
Austria	20%	€75.01	$82
Czech Republic	21%	2,001 Kč	$100
Hungary	27%	54,001 Ft	$155
Poland	23%	200 zł	$50
Slovakia	20%	€175.01	$192
Slovenia	22%	€50.01	$55

*VAT rates fluctuate based on many factors, including what kind of item you are buying. Your refund will likely be less than the rate listed above, especially if it's subject to processing fees.

GETTING A VAT REFUND

Wrapped into the purchase price of your Central European souvenirs is a value-added tax (VAT) that varies per country—see the sidebar for specific rates. You're entitled to get most of that tax back if you make a purchase of more than a set amount at a store that participates in the VAT refund scheme. Typically, you must ring up the minimum at a single retailer—you can't add up your purchases from various shops to reach the required amount. (If the store ships the goods to your US home, VAT is not assessed on your purchase.)

Getting your refund is straightforward...and worthwhile if you spend a significant amount.

At the Merchant: Have the merchant completely fill out the refund document (they'll ask for your passport; a photo of your passport usually works). Keep track of the paperwork and your original sales receipt. Note that you're not supposed to use your purchased goods before you leave Europe.

At the Border or Airport: Process your VAT document with the customs agent who deals with VAT refunds at your last stop in the country in which you made your purchase (or, if you bought it in the European Union, at your last stop in the EU; allow plenty of extra time to deal with this process and have your purchased items easily accessible for inspection). At some airports, you'll go to a customs office to get your documents stamped and then to a separate VAT refund service (such as Global Blue or Planet) to process the refund. Elsewhere, a single VAT desk handles the whole thing, or you may be able to do it at a self-validation kiosk. (Note that re-fund services typically extract a 4 percent fee, but you're paying for the convenience of receiving your money in cash immediately or as a credit to your card.) Otherwise, you'll need to mail the stamped refund documents to the address given by the merchant.

CUSTOMS FOR AMERICAN SHOPPERS

You can take home $800 worth of items per person duty-free, once every 31 days. Many processed and packaged foods are allowed, in-cluding cheeses, dried herbs, jams, baked goods, candy, chocolate, oil, vinegar, condiments, and honey. Fresh fruits and vegetables and most meats are not allowed, with exceptions for some canned items. As for alcohol, you can bring in one liter duty-free (it can be packed securely in your checked luggage, along with any other liquid-containing items).

To bring alcohol (or liquid-packed foods) in your carry-on bag on your flight home, buy it at a duty-free shop at the airport. You'll increase your odds of getting it onto a connecting flight if it's pack-aged in a "STEB"—a secure, tamper-evident bag. But stay away from liquids in opaque, ceramic, or metallic containers, which usu-ally cannot be successfully screened (STEB or no STEB).

For details on allowable goods, customs rules, and duty rates, visit Help.cbp.gov.

Sightseeing

Central Europe offers high-quality, affordable sightseeing. Galler-ies proudly show off local artists that you may not be familiar with: Prague's Alphonse Mucha, Poland's Stanisław Wyspiański, Hun-gary's Tivadar Csontváry Kosztka, Croatia's Ivan Meštrović, and Bulgaria's Zlatyu Boyadzhiev are just some of the names that will have you wondering why your art history classes left out this part of Europe. Another Central European specialty is historical muse-ums; often newly opened, these generally do a thoughtful and stir-ring job of telling the story of a particular time and place: Warsaw's Museum of the History of Polish Jews, Budapest's House of Terror, Gdańsk's European Solidarity Center, and so on. And sumptuous interiors—like Budapest's Parliament or Opera House, or War-saw's Royal Palace—evoke the grandeur of an illustrious history.

Sightseeing can be hard work. Use these tips to make your visits to Central Europe's finest sights meaningful, fun, efficient, and painless.

MAPS AND NAVIGATION TOOLS

Your best navigation tool is on your phone. **Google Maps** (and similar mapping apps) offer turn-by-turn directions for walking and driving, as well as detailed public transit instructions in most big cities. Simply plug in a destination and instantly get detailed directions for reaching it on foot or by subway, bus, or tram—including where to catch it, how long it takes, where to get off, and how far you'll walk at the other end.

To conserve data, most mapping apps let you download maps in advance (do this when you're on strong Wi-Fi). However, offline maps may not include every feature (most in-city public transit navigation doesn't work offline). For more on how to get online with your phone during your trip, see page 1102.

For offline navigation, the maps in this book are concise and simple, designed to help you locate recommended destinations, sights, hotels, and restaurants. In Europe, simple paper maps are generally free at TIs and hotels; maps with more detail are sold at newsstands and bookstores.

PLAN AHEAD

Set up an itinerary that allows you to fit in all your must-see sights. For a one-stop look at opening hours, see this book's "At a Glance" sidebars for major cities (Prague, Kraków, Warsaw, Budapest, Ljubljana, and Vienna).

Don't put off visiting a must-see sight—you never know when a place will close unexpectedly for a holiday, strike, or restoration. Opening days and hours can fluctuate; confirm the latest with the TI or at the sight's official website (listed throughout this book).

Many museums are closed or have reduced hours at least a few days a year, especially on holidays such as Christmas, New Year's, and Labor Day (May 1). A list of holidays is in the appendix; check for possible closures during your trip. In summer, some sights may stay open late. Off-season hours may be shorter.

Going at the right time helps avoid crowds. This book offers tips on the best times to see specific sights. Try visiting popular sights very early or very late. Evening visits (when possible) are usually more peaceful, with fewer crowds. Late morning is usually the worst time to visit a popular sight.

If you plan to hire a local guide, reserve ahead by email. Popular guides can get booked up.

Study up. To get the most out of the sight descriptions in this book, read them before you visit. Note: To avoid redundancy, many cultural or historical details are explained for one sight in this book and not repeated for another; to get the full picture, read the entire chapter for each destination you'll visit.

RESERVATIONS AND ADVANCE TICKETS

Many popular sights come with long ticket-buying lines. Visitors who buy tickets online in advance (or who have a museum pass covering key sights) can skip the line and waltz right in. Advance tickets are generally timed-entry, meaning you're guaranteed admission on a certain date and time.

For some sights, buying ahead is **required** (tickets aren't sold at the sight and it's the only way to get in). At other sights, buying ahead is **recommended** to skip the line and save time. And for many sights, advance tickets are **available** but unnecessary: At these uncrowded sights you can simply arrive, buy a ticket, and go in.

Don't confuse the reservation options: available, recommended, and required. Use my advice in this book as a guide. Note any must-see sights that sell out long in advance and be prepared to buy tickets early. If you do your research, you'll know the smart strategy.

Given how precious your vacation time is, I'd book in advance both where it's required (as soon as your dates are firm) and where it will save time in a long line (in some cases, you can do this even on the day you plan to visit). You'll definitely want to book well in advance for Auschwitz-Birkenau, the Oskar Schindler Factory Museum in Kraków, and the Hungarian Parliament in Budapest. In Vienna, reserve a day or two ahead for Schönbrunn Palace.

You'll generally be emailed a digital ticket with a code that you'll store on your phone to scan at the entrance (if you prefer, you can print it out). At the sight, look for the ticket-holders line rather than the ticket-buying line; you may still have to wait in a security line.

Sightseeing Passes: Some cities offer sightseeing passes that include free or discounted admission to several sights. Do the math to determine if a sightseeing pass makes sense for your visit. Even with a sightseeing pass, you'll often still need to make reservations for the most popular sights.

AT SIGHTS

Here's what you can typically expect:

Entering: You may not be allowed to enter if you arrive too close to closing time. And guards start ushering people out well before the actual closing time, so don't save the best for last.

Some sights have a security check. Allow extra time for these lines. Many sights require you to check day packs and coats. (If you'd rather not check your day pack, try carrying it tucked under your arm as you enter.)

Photography: If the museum's photo policy isn't clearly posted, ask a guard. Generally, taking photos without a flash or tripod is allowed. Some sights ban selfie sticks; others ban photos altogether.

Audioguides and Apps: I've produced free, downloadable

Researching Your Roots in Central Europe

For the millions of North Americans who have Polish, Czech, Hungarian, Slovenian, or other Central European roots, walking in the footsteps of your ancestors can be an unforgettable experience. One of this book's co-authors has done just that, and managed to reconnect with living relatives in rural Polish villages outside Kraków. While not everyone gets that lucky, here are some pointers to increase your odds of success:

Do your homework. Don't just head to Europe with a faint recollection of an ancestral village name and expect to stumble into a long-lost relation. Dig through documents, family bibles, old photos, and other heirlooms to track down any details.

Gather key information. Most helpful are the name of the **city, town, or village;** full **first and last names** of ancestors (be aware the spelling, or even the entire name, may have changed upon emigration); and any **dates** you can find for birth, baptism, marriage, emigration, or death.

Check online resources. Start with the free, comprehensive FamilySearch.org (operated by the LDS Church). Ancestry.com is popular but pricey; try it for free at a library before investing in a subscription. Also check US government resources such as Archives.gov and EllisIsland.org. Find out if there are any local genealogical societies in your community. Facebook groups can also be helpful.

Understand the history and geography. Most locations in Central Europe have not been part of the same country throughout history. You may have been told that your ancestors were born in Hungary, only to discover that your ancestral village is now in Romania or Slovakia. You may think you're Czech but find out your ancestors spoke German—or vice versa. Emigration records often noted "Austrian" as a catchall that could include Poles, Hungarians, Slovaks, Croats, or Jews.

This is why it's critical to pinpoint the location of your ancestral village, town, or city—realizing that it may have a different name today (for instance, "Breslau" became "Wrocław" after World War II). Then, read up on that town to understand the political and linguistic reality when your ancestors lived there.

Here's a case study: During the Partitions (1795-1918), the territory of Poland was divided among three neighboring powers. The German, Russian, and Austrian sectors managed their recordkeeping differently. In the Austrian and German zones, most records are in Latin, following a standardized column format. The Russian zone can be trickier; records are often flowery narrative passages, and can be handwritten in Cyrillic.

Track down the appropriate church to look for records or gravestones. Even if you find it, it may just be a starting point. Many churches were supposed to send vital records to the state archives during the 1950s; it varies whether these records can still be found at the church, elsewhere, or not at all. Also be aware that in many European cemeteries, graves are not owned in perpetuity; after a family stops paying for the plot, it may be dug up and reused by a new leaseholder.

Consider enlisting professional assistance. Some travelers enjoy the experience of doing their own homework; others are more results-focused and happy to pay a professional. Genealogy research organizations on both sides of the Atlantic can help; I recommend some in this book. For example, Prague-based Tom and Marie Zahn have been helping my readers track their Czech roots for decades (www.pathfinders.cz). Getting outside help is especially worthwhile for those with Jewish roots, whose records and cemeteries are more likely to have been wiped out during the Holocaust. A good general site is JewishGen.org. For those with Hungarian Jewish ancestry, check out Milev.hu; for Polish Jews, try JRI-Poland.org.

Hire a local guide/driver/translator. Especially if your ancestors came from a small town rather than a city, hiring someone who can drive you straight there saves time and frustration. With sufficient planning, your guide may be able to contact local authorities and have other leads lined up. Most important, if you do track down living relatives, you can't assume they speak English. I can't overstate the importance of having a friendly and fluent local helper to provide an introduction, to ease the shock of being visited by a long-lost cousin from America, and to translate the conversation. Local guides or drivers listed throughout this book are often happy to help with this task.

Prepare for surprises...and, maybe, disappointment. There's no guarantee that your search will turn up any conclusive connections. If you have some luck, you may find yourself on a pensive stroll through a gloomy cemetery, past moss-covered headstones bearing your family name. But consider the possibility that you'll meet some distant relatives. Brainstorm portable, replaceable items you might bring along that could be meaningful (perhaps copies of family photos they may not have seen).

Regardless of how "successful" your search turns out to be, simply carrying out that search—and setting foot in the place where generations of your ancestors spent their lives—can be an incredibly powerful experience. Good luck!

audio tours for my Prague City Walk, Vienna City Walk, Vienna's St. Stephen's Cathedral, and Vienna's Ringstrasse Tram Tour; look for the 🎧 in this book. For more on my audio tours, see page 26.

Some sights offer audioguides with dull recorded descriptions in English. Often you'll use free Wi-Fi to download the tour to your mobile device on the spot; less frequently, you'll borrow or rent a device preloaded with the audio content at the museum. Bring your own plug-in earbuds to enjoy better sound (with a splitter, two can often share one rented device).

Expect Changes: Artwork can be on tour, on loan, out sick, or shifted at the whim of the curator. Pick up a floor plan as you enter and ask museum staff if you can't find a particular item.

Services: Important sights usually have a reasonably priced on-site café or cafeteria (handy and air-conditioned places to rejuvenate during a long visit). The WCs at sights are free and generally clean.

Before Leaving: At the gift shop, scan the postcard rack or thumb through a guidebook to be sure you haven't overlooked something that you'd like to see. Every sight or museum offers more than what is covered in this book. Use the information I provide as an introduction—not the final word.

Sleeping

Extensive and opinionated listings of good-value rooms are a major feature of this book's Sleeping sections. Rather than list accommodations scattered throughout a town, I choose hotels in my favorite neighborhoods that are convenient to your sightseeing.

My recommendations run the gamut, from dorm beds to luxurious rooms with all the comforts. I like places that are clean, central, relatively quiet at night, reasonably priced, friendly, small enough to have a hands-on owner or manager, and run with a respect for local traditions. I'm more impressed by a handy location and fun-loving philosophy than oversized TVs and a fancy gym. Most of my recommendations fall short of perfection. But if I can find a place with most of these features, it's a keeper.

Book your accommodations as soon as your itinerary is set, especially if you want to stay at one of my top listings or if you'll be traveling during busy times. For certain popular destinations, I've also noted times of year when accommodations are likely to book up fast. Also see the appendix for a list of major holidays and festivals in Central Europe.

Some people make reservations a few days ahead as they travel. This approach fosters spontaneity, and booking sites make it easy to find available rooms, but—especially during busy times—you run the risk of settling for lesser-value accommodations.

Sleep Code

Hotels in this book are categorized according to the average price of a standard double room with breakfast in high season.

	Slovenia, Austria	Czech Republic	Poland	Hungary
$$$$ **Splurge**	over €200	over 4,700 Kč	over 900 zł	over 80,000 Ft
$$$ **Pricier**	€150-200	3,500-4,700 Kč	700-900 zł	60,000-80,000 Ft
$$ **Moderate**	€100-150	2,300-3,500 Kč	500-700 zł	40,000-60,000 Ft
$ **Budget**	€50-100	1,200-2,300 Kč	250-500 zł	20,000-40,000 Ft
¢ **Backpacker**	under €50	under 1,200 Kč	under 250 zł	under 20,000 Ft

Unless otherwise noted, credit cards are accepted and hotel staff speak basic English. Comparison-shop by checking prices at several hotels (on each hotel's own website, on a booking site, or by email). For the best deal, *book directly with the hotel.* Ask for a discount if paying in cash; if the listing includes **RS%,** request a Rick Steves discount.

PRACTICALITIES

RATES AND DEALS

I've categorized my recommended accommodations based on price, indicated with a dollar-sign rating (see sidebar). Room prices can fluctuate significantly with demand and amenities (size, views, and so on), but relative price categories remain constant. City taxes, which can vary from place to place, are generally insignificant (a few dollars per person, per night).

Some accommodations quote their rates in euros, while others use the local currency.

Booking Direct: Once your dates are set, compare prices at several hotels. You can do this by checking hotel websites and booking sites such as Hotels.com or Booking.com. After you've zeroed in on your choice, book directly with the hotel itself by phone, by email, or on the hotel's website. This increases the chances that the hotelier will be able to accommodate special needs or requests (such as shifting your reservation). When you book direct, the owner avoids the commission paid to booking sites—in exchange, ask if they can give you a discount, a nicer room, or a free breakfast (if it's not already included).

Getting a Discount: Some hotels extend a discount to those who pay cash or stay longer than three nights. And some accommodations offer a special discount for Rick Steves readers, indi-

PRACTICALITIES

Using Online Services to Your Advantage

From booking services to user reviews, online businesses play a big role in planning a trip. Take advantage of their pluses—and be wise to their downsides.

Booking Sites

Booking websites such as Booking.com and Hotels.com offer one-stop shopping for hotels. While convenient for travelers, they're both a blessing and a curse for small, independent, family-run hotels. Without a presence on these sites, small hotels become almost invisible. But to be listed, a hotel must pay a sizable commission...and promise that its own website won't undercut the price on the booking-service site.

Here's the work-around: Use the big sites to research what's out there, then book directly with the hotel. The price will likely be the same as via a booking site, but your money goes to the hotel, not agency commissions. As a savvy consumer, remember: When you book with an online service, you're adding a middleman who takes a cut. To support small, family-run hotels, book direct.

Short-Term Rental Sites

Rental juggernaut Airbnb and other short-term rental sites allow travelers to rent rooms and apartments, often providing more value, space, and amenities than a cookie-cutter hotel. Airbnb fans appreciate feeling part of a neighborhood and getting into a daily routine as "temporary Europeans." Some places are run by thoughtful hosts, allowing you to get to know a local and keep your money in the community; but beware: Others are impersonally managed by large, absentee agencies.

Critics of Airbnb see it as a threat to "traditional Europe." Landlords can make more money renting to short-stay travelers, driving rents up—and local residents out. Traditional businesses

cated in this guidebook by the abbreviation **"RS%."** Discounts vary: Ask for details when you reserve. Generally, to qualify for this discount, you must book direct (not through a booking site), mention this book when you reserve, show this book upon arrival, and sometimes pay cash or stay a certain number of nights. In some cases, you may need to enter a discount code (which I've provided in the listing) in the booking form on the hotel's website. Rick Steves discounts apply to readers with either print or digital books. Understandably, discounts do not apply to promotional rates.

TYPES OF ACCOMMODATIONS
Hotels

In Central Europe, you can choose from a delightful variety of stylish and charming hotels and guesthouses. And rates are rea-

PRACTICALITIES

are replaced by ones that cater to tourists. And the character and charm that made those neighborhoods desirable to tourists in the first place goes too. Some cities have cracked down, requiring owners to obtain a license and to occupy rental properties part of the year (and staging disruptive "inspections" that inconvenience guests).

As a lover of Europe, I share the worry of those who see residents nudged aside by tourists. But as an advocate for travelers, I appreciate the value Airbnb can provide in offering the chance to stay in a local building or neighborhood with potentially fewer tourists.

User Reviews

User-generated review sites and apps such as Yelp and TripAdvisor can give you a consensus of opinions about everything from hotels and restaurants to sights and nightlife. If you scan reviews of a restaurant or hotel and see several complaints about noise or a rotten location, you've gained insight that can help in your decision-making.

As a guidebook writer, my sense is that there is a big difference between the uncurated information on a review site and the vetted listings in a guidebook. A user review is based on the limited experience of one person, who stayed at just one hotel in a given city and ate at a few restaurants there. A guidebook is the work of a trained researcher who forms a well-developed basis for comparison by visiting many restaurants and hotels year after year.

Both types of information have their place, and in many ways, they're complementary. If something is well reviewed in a guidebook and also gets good online reviews, it's likely a winner.

sonable; you can find a central, straightforward-but-comfortable double for $100 just about anywhere. Plan on spending $100-150 per double in big cities, and $70-100 in smaller towns. You can uncover some bargains, but I think it's worth paying  a little more for comfort and a good location.

Some hotels can add an extra bed (for a small charge) to turn a double into a triple; some offer larger rooms for four or more people (I call these "family rooms" in the listings). In general, a triple room is cheaper than the cost of a double and a single. Three or four people can economize by requesting one big room.

Arrival and Check-In: Hotels and B&Bs are sometimes located on the higher floors of a multipurpose building with a secured door. In that case, look for your hotel's name on the buttons by the main entrance. When you ring the bell, you'll be buzzed in.

Hotel elevators are common, though small, and some older buildings still lack them. If stairs are unavoidable, you can ask the front desk for help carrying your bags up.

Most European countries require hotels to collect your name, nationality, and passport number. At check-in, the receptionist might ask for your passport and may keep it for several hours. If you're not comfortable leaving your passport at the desk, bring a copy to give them instead.

If you're arriving in the morning, your room probably won't be ready. Check your bag safely at the hotel and dive right into sightseeing.

In Your Room: Most hotel rooms have a TV and free Wi-Fi, which can vary in strength and quality. Simpler places rarely have a room phone.

Breakfast and Meals: Breakfast, almost always served buffet-style, usually includes rolls, cold cuts, cheese, cereal, yogurt, fruit, coffee, milk, and juice; many places also provide eggs, either hard-boiled or scrambled.

Checking Out: While it's customary to pay for your room upon departure, it can be a good idea to settle your bill the day before, when you're not in a hurry and while the manager's in.

Hotelier Help: Hoteliers can be a good source of advice. Most know their city well and can assist you with everything from public transit and airport connections to finding a good restaurant, the nearest launderette, or a late-night pharmacy.

Hotel Hassles: Even at the best places, mechanical breakdowns occur: Sinks leak, hot water turns cold, toilets may gurgle or smell, the Wi-Fi goes out, or the air-conditioning dies when you need it most. Report your concerns clearly and calmly at the front desk.

If you find that night noise is a problem (if, for instance, your room is over a nightclub or facing a busy street), ask for a quieter room in the back or on an upper floor. To guard against theft in your room, keep valuables out of sight. Some rooms come with a safe, and other hotels have safes at the front desk. I rarely bother to use one and in a lifetime of travel, I've never had anything stolen from my room.

For more complicated problems, don't expect instant results. Above all, keep a positive attitude. Remember, you're on vacation.

PRACTICALITIES

If your hotel is a disappointment, spend more time out enjoying the place you came to see.

Rooms in Private Homes

Private accommodations offer travelers a characteristic and money-saving alternative for a fraction of the price of a hotel. Rooms in private homes are called *sobe* in Slovenia and Croatia; the German word *Zimmer* works there, too, and throughout Central Europe. These places are inexpensive, at least as comfortable as a cheap hotel, and a good way to get some local insight. The boss changes the sheets, so people staying several nights are most desirable—and those who stay fewer than three nights are often charged extra. While you can't expect your host to also be your tour guide, some are interested in getting to know the travelers who pass through their home.

Short-Term Rentals

A short-term rental—whether an apartment, a house, or a room in a private residence—is a popular alternative, especially if you plan to settle in one location for several nights. For stays longer than a few days, you can usually find a rental that's comparable to—and cheaper than—a hotel room with similar amenities. Plus, you'll get a behind-the-scenes peek into how locals live.

Many places require a minimum stay and have strict cancellation policies. And you're generally on your own: There's no reception desk, breakfast, or daily cleaning service.

Finding Accommodations: Websites such as Airbnb, FlipKey, Booking.com, and VRBO let you browse a wide range of properties. Alternatively, rental agencies such as Interhomeusa.com and Rentavilla.com can provide a more personalized service (their curated listings are also more expensive).

Before you commit, be clear on the location. I like to virtually "explore" the neighborhood using Google Street View. Also consider the proximity to public transportation and how well connected the property is with the rest of the city. Ask about amenities (elevator, air-con, laundry, Wi-Fi, parking, etc.). Reviews from previous guests can help identify trouble spots.

Think about the kind of experience you want: Just a key and an affordable bed...or a chance to get to know a local? Some hosts offer self check-in and minimal contact; others enjoy interacting with you. Read the description and reviews to help shape your decision.

Confirming and Paying: Many places require payment in full before your trip, usually through the listing site. Be wary of owners who want to take your transaction offline; this gives you no recourse if things go awry. Never agree to wire money (a key indicator of a fraudulent transaction).

PRACTICALITIES

PRACTICALITIES

Making Hotel Reservations

Given the erratic accommodations values in Central Europe (and the quality of the places I've found for this book), I recommend that you reserve your rooms as soon as you've pinned down your travel dates. For busy national holidays, it's wise to reserve far in advance (see the appendix).

Requesting a Reservation: For family-run hotels, it's generally best to book your room directly via email or phone. For business-class and chain hotels, or if you'd rather book online, reserve directly through the hotel's official website (not a booking website). Here's what the hotelier wants to know:

- Type(s) of rooms you want and number of guests
- Number of nights you'll stay
- Arrival and departure dates, written European-style as day/month (18/06 or 18 June)
- Special requests (en suite bathroom, cheapest room, twin beds vs. double bed, quiet room)
- Applicable discounts (such as a Rick Steves discount, cash discount, or promotional rate)

Confirming a Reservation: Most places will request a credit-card number to hold your room. If the hotel's website doesn't have a secure form where you can enter the number directly, share this info via a phone call.

Canceling a Reservation: If you must cancel, it's courteous—and smart—to do so with as much notice as possible, especially for

Apartments or Houses: If you're staying in one place for several nights, it's worth considering an apartment or rental house. These can be especially cost-effective for groups and families. European apartments, like hotel rooms, tend to be small by US standards. But they often come with laundry facilities and small, equipped kitchens, making it easier and cheaper to dine in.

Other Options: Swapping homes with a local works for people with an appealing place to offer (don't assume where you live is not interesting to Europeans). Good places to start are HomeExchange.com and LoveHomeSwap.com.

Hostels

A hostel provides cheap beds in dorms where you sleep alongside strangers for usually under $20-30 per night. Travelers of any age are welcome if they don't mind dorm-style accommodations and meeting other travelers. Most hostels offer kitchen facilities, guest computers, Wi-Fi, and a self-service laundry. Hostels almost always provide bedding, but the towel's up to you (though you can usually rent one). Family and private rooms are often available.

From:	rick@ricksteves.com
Sent:	Today
To:	info@hotelcentral.com
Subject:	Reservation request for 19-22 July

Dear Hotel Central,

I would like to stay at your hotel. Please let me know if you have a room available and the price for:
- 2 people
- Double bed and en suite bathroom in a quiet room
- Arriving 19 July, departing 22 July (3 nights)

Thank you!
Rick Steves

smaller family-run places. Cancellation policies can be strict; read the fine print before you book. Many discount deals require pre-payment and can be expensive to change or cancel.

Reconfirming a Reservation: Always call or email to reconfirm your reservation a few days in advance. For B&Bs or very small hotels, I call again on my arrival day to tell my host what time to expect me (especially important if arriving after 17:00).

Phoning: For tips on calling hotels overseas, see page 1104.

Independent hostels tend to be easygoing, colorful, and informal (no membership required; www.hostelworld.com). You may pay slightly less by booking directly with the hostel. **Official hostels** are part of Hostelling International (HI) and share a booking site (www.hihostels.com). HI hostels typically require that you be a member or else pay a bit more per night.

Eating

Central Europe offers good food for relatively little money—especially if you steer clear of the easy-to-avoid tourist-trap restaurants. This is affordable sightseeing for your palate.

Slavic cuisine has a reputation for being heavy and hearty, with lots of pork, potatoes, and cabbage. And, to be fair, some of that reputation is well earned. But the food here is also delicious, and there's a lot more diversity from country to country than you might expect. For example, Hungarian cuisine is rich and spicy (think paprika), while Slovenia has a knack for Mediterranean cooking (seafood, pastas), and Polish food is more "northern" (with lots of

dill, berries, and cream). Tune in to the regional and national spe-
cialties and customs (see each country's introduction in this book
for details).

For a change of pace, seek out vegetarian, Italian, Middle
Eastern, Indian, sushi, and other global places, which are especially
good in big cities such as Prague,
Budapest, Kraków, Warsaw, and
Ljubljana (I've listed a few tasty
options).

For listings in this guidebook, I look for restaurants that
are convenient to your hotel and
sightseeing. When restaurant
hunting, choose a spot filled
with locals, not the place with
the big neon signs boasting,
"We Speak English." Venturing even a block or two off the main
drag leads to higher-quality food for a better price.

Locals eat better at lower-rent locales. Most restaurants tack a
menu on their door for browsers and have an English menu inside.
If the place isn't full, you can usually just seat yourself (get a server's
attention to be sure your preferred table is OK)—the American-
style host, with a carefully managed waiting list, isn't common
here. Once seated, feel free to take your time. In fact, it might be
difficult to dine in a hurry. Only a rude server will rush you. Good
service is relaxed (slow to an American).

When you're in the mood for something halfway between a
restaurant and a picnic meal, look for takeout food stands, bakeries
(with sandwiches and savory pastries to go), shops selling pizza by
the slice, or simple little eateries offering fast and easy sit-down
restaurant food. In Poland, don't miss the enticingly cheap "milk
bar" cafeterias (see page 230). Many grocery stores sell sandwiches,
and others might be willing to make one for you from what's in the
deli case.

The Czech Republic is beer country, with Europe's best and
cheapest brew. Poland also has fine beer, but the national drink
is *wódka*. Hungary and Slovenia are known for their wines. Each
country has its own distinctive liqueur, but they all have some variation on *slivovice* (SLEE-voh-veet-seh)—a plum brandy so highly
valued that it's the de facto currency of the Carpathian Mountains
(used for bartering with farmers and other mountain folk). Menus
list drink size by the tenth of a liter, or deciliter (dl). Nondrink-
ers will find all the standard types of Coke and Pepsi, along with
some fun-to-sample local alternatives (such as Slovenia's Cockta,
described on page 718).

Restaurant Price Code

Eateries in this book are categorized according to the average cost of a typical main course. Drinks, desserts, and splurge items can raise the price considerably.

	Slovenia, Austria	Czech Republic	Poland	Hungary
$$$$ **Splurge**	over €20	over 475 Kč	over 90 zł	over 8,000 Ft
$$$ **Pricier**	€15-20	350-475 Kč	70-90 zł	6,000-8,000 Ft
$$ **Moderate**	€10-15	200-350 Kč	50-70 zł	4,000-6,000 Ft
$ **Budget**	Under €10	Under 200 Kč	Under 50 zł	Under 4,000 Ft

In Central Europe, a milk bar or takeout spot is **$,** a basic sit-down eatery is **$$,** a casual but more upscale restaurant is **$$$,** and a swanky splurge is **$$$$.**

TIPPING

Tip only at restaurants that have table service. If you order your food at a counter, don't tip.

At restaurants that have a waitstaff, round up the bill 5-10 percent after a good meal. My rule of thumb is to estimate about 10 percent, then round slightly to reach a convenient total (for a 370 Kč meal, I pay 400 Kč—an 8 percent tip). Anywhere in Central Europe, a tip of over 10 percent is overly generous, verging on extravagant.

At most restaurants in Budapest, and at tourist-oriented ones in Prague, a service fee of around 10-12 percent is automatically added to the bill. Check your bill carefully; if this appears, then there's no need to tip any extra. If you're not sure whether your bill includes the tip, just ask.

RESTAURANT PRICING AND HOURS

I've categorized my recommended eateries based on the average price of a typical main course, indicated with a dollar-sign rating (see sidebar). Obviously, expensive specialties, fine wine, appetizers, and dessert can significantly increase your final bill.

The categories also indicate the personality of a place: **Budget** eateries include street food, takeaway, order-at-the-counter shops, basic cafeterias, and bakeries selling sandwiches. **Moderate** eateries are nice (but not fancy) sit-down restaurants, ideal for a pleas-

Hurdling the Language Barrier

Many visitors are pleasantly surprised to find that the language barrier in Central Europe is minimal. Frankly, I find it easier to communicate in Hungary or Slovenia than in France or Spain. Why? Because these countries are small and not politically powerful, and their residents realize it's unreasonable to expect visitors to learn Hungarian or Slovene. It's essential to find a common language with the rest of the world—so they learn English early and well. (I've had surprisingly eloquent conversations with Slovenian grade-schoolers.)

Central Europeans, realizing that their language challenges outsiders, often invent easier nicknames for themselves—Šárka goes by "Sara," György introduces himself as "George," Andrzej becomes "Andrew," and Jaroslav tells you, "Call me Jerry." They're trying to meet you in the middle. Show your appreciation and make things easier on them by reading the following pointers.

Languages of Central Europe

The people in most of this book's destinations speak **Slavic** languages. These are closely related and, to varying degrees, mutually intelligible. A Czech and a Slovene can understand each other about as well as a Spaniard and an Italian. (Spellings change—for example, Czech *hrad,* or "castle," becomes Slovene *grad.*)

Slavic languages have simple vocabularies but are highly inflected (as in Latin, meaning is conveyed by changing the ends of words). Slavic words are notorious for their long strings of consonants, and pronunciation can be tricky for outsiders. In fact, when the Christian missionaries Cyril and Methodius came to these lands a millennium ago, they invented a whole new alphabet to represent these strange Slavic sounds. A modified version of that alphabet—called Cyrillic—is still used today in eastern Slavic countries. Of the places mentioned in this book, Cyrillic is common only in Bulgaria, and in some parts of Bosnia and Montenegro. (For a Cyrillic primer, see page 1018.)

Fortunately, nearly all the destinations covered in this book use the same Roman alphabet we do. However, they do add various diacritics—little markings below and above letters—to represent a wider range of sounds (for example, č, ą, ó, đ, ł). While these may look intimidating, they're logical and easy to memorize. For example, while we add an *h* after a *c* to make the *ch* sound, the Czechs and Slovenes simply top it with a "little roof": č.

Hungarian is another story altogether—it's completely unrelated to Slavic languages, or to almost any other European language. (For more on the Magyar tongue, see the end of the Hungary chapter.) And **Romanian** is a Romance language, distantly related to Italian and French.

German is spoken in Vienna, and can be a useful second language throughout Central Europe, especially if you're interacting with somebody over about age 50. (While few people under communism learned English, German rivaled Russian as a popular second language.) A few words of **Italian** can be handy in Slovenia and Croatia.

Communication Tips

Even without a common language, it's relatively easy to get your point across with a combination of gestures, shared words, and writing things down. For instance, to buy a train ticket at a small-town station, just write the name of where you're going and the time you want to travel.

There are certain universal English words that all Central Europeans know: hello, please, thank you, super, pardon, stop, menu, problem, and no problem. Another handy word is *servus* (SEHR-voos)—the old-fashioned greeting from the Habsburg days.

Download and use the free Google Translate app. If you're puzzling over a sign in a shop window, aim your phone's camera at it for an instant translation. Or if you're trying to get a point across to a new friend, you can speak into your phone in English,

and it'll spit out a translation—either in a clear robot voice, or in easy-to-read text.

Looking at some of the intimidatingly long words and strange letters in these countries, it's easy to throw up your arms in defeat. But unlike English, Central European languages are entirely phonetic—you can always sound out words with confidence, once you learn a few basic rules. In each of this book's country introductions, you'll find a list of unique letters and letter combinations, which provide the building blocks for sounding out words. This book also provides Survival Phrases for each language. Equipped with these tools, do your best to get an ear for the language and try it out. You may be surprised how quickly you get comfortable.

Regardless of how much (or how little) of the local language you speak, don't be afraid to interact with locals. Often a simple smile is the only icebreaker you need. And knowing even a word or two of their language—which is more than most visitors bother with—will further endear you to anyone you meet. Give it your best shot, and the natives will appreciate your efforts.

ant meal with good-quality food. Most of my listings fall in this category—great for a taste of the local cuisine at a reasonable price.

Pricier eateries are a notch up, with more attention paid to the setting, presentation, and (often inventive) cuisine. **Splurge** eateries are dress-up-for-a-special-occasion swanky—typically with an elegant setting, polished service, and pricey and refined cuisine.

Most of my restaurant listings are open daily for lunch and dinner; I've noted exceptions.

Staying Connected

A mobile device is an indispensable tool for efficient travel. Fortunately, staying connected in Europe gets less complicated (and less expensive) each year. You can use your devices much like you do at home, by either getting an international plan or connecting to free Wi-Fi whenever possible. Another option is to buy a European SIM card for your mobile phone. More details are at RickSteves. com/phoning.

USING YOUR PHONE IN EUROPE
Here are some budget tips and options.

Sign up for an international plan. To stay connected at a lower cost, sign up for an international service plan through your carrier. Most providers offer a simple bundle that includes calling, messaging, and data. Your normal plan may already include international coverage (for example, T-Mobile's covers unlimited text and low-speed data, plus reasonable per-minute voice calls).

Use free Wi-Fi whenever possible. Unless you have an unlimited-data plan, save most of your online tasks for Wi-Fi. Most accommodations in Europe offer free Wi-Fi. Many cafés (including Starbucks and McDonald's) offer hotspots for customers; ask for the password when you buy something. You may also find Wi-Fi at TIs, city squares, major museums, public transit hubs, airports, and aboard trains and buses.

Minimize the use of your cellular network. The best way to make sure you're not accidentally burning through data is to put your device in "airplane" mode (which also disables phone calls and texts) and connect to Wi-Fi as needed. Turn on your cellular network (or turn off airplane mode) only when you can't find Wi-Fi.

Save large-data tasks for Wi-Fi. If your included data is slow or metered, wait until you're on Wi-Fi to Skype or FaceTime, download apps, stream videos, or do other megabyte-greedy tasks. Using a navigation app such as Google Maps over a cellular network can require lots of data, so download maps when you're on Wi-Fi, then use the app offline.

Limit automatic updates. By default, your device constantly

Tips on Internet Security

Make sure that your device is running the latest versions of its operating system, security software, and apps. Next, ensure that your device and apps are password-protected (enable facial recognition where possible). On the road, use only secure, password-protected Wi-Fi. Ask the hotel or café staff for the specific name of their network, and make sure you log on to that exact one.

If you must access your financial info online, use a banking app rather than accessing your account via a browser, and use a cellular connection, not Wi-Fi. If you're very concerned, consider subscribing to a VPN (virtual private network).

PRACTICALITIES

checks for a data connection and updates app content. Check your device's settings menu for ways to turn this off.

Use Wi-Fi calling and messaging apps. Skype, FaceTime, and Google Meet are great for making free or low-cost calls or sending texts over Wi-Fi worldwide. WhatsApp is especially popular with Europeans and is often the easiest way to communicate with guides, drivers, or other local contacts.

Buy a European SIM card. If you anticipate making a lot of local calls, need a local phone number, or your provider's international-data rates are expensive, consider getting a European SIM card to replace the one in your (unlocked) device. SIM cards are sold at department-store electronics counters and some newsstands (you may need to show your passport), and vending machines. If you need help setting it up, buy one at a mobile-phone shop. Some newer devices may also allow you to download an eSIM from an international provider.

There are generally no roaming charges when using a European SIM card in other EU countries, but confirm when you buy.

Damage Control for Lost Phones: Losing your phone can be a significant inconvenience. Before you leave home, make sure your device is set up for automatic cloud backups, and enable the "find my phone" feature (make sure you have access to it from another device, like your travel partner's phone or a laptop). Familiarize yourself with your phone's "lost and lock" mode, which you should enable from another device if it goes missing. Report the loss to your mobile carrier; if your phone remains lost, use the "wipe" feature to erase its data.

MAIL

For details on sending packages to your own home or to others, visit Cbp.gov, then select "Travel" and "Know Before You Go." The Central European postal services work fine, but for quick transat-

PRACTICALITIES

How to Dial

Here's how to dial from anywhere in the US or Europe, using the phone numbers of recommended hotels in Prague, Czech Republic (221 771 011); Budapest, Hungary (1 269 0222); and Vienna, Austria (01 534 050) as examples. If a number starts with 0, drop it when dialing from country to country.

From a US Mobile Phone

Phone numbers in this book are presented exactly as you would dial them from a US mobile phone, from any location. For international access, press and hold 0 (zero) to get a + sign, then dial the country code (see the chart) and phone number.

▸ To call the Prague hotel, dial +420 221 771 011.
▸ To call the Budapest hotel, dial +36 1 269 0222.
▸ To call the Vienna hotel, dial +43 1 534 050.

From a US Landline

Replace + with 011 (US/Canada access code), then dial the country code and phone number.

▸ To call the Prague hotel from your home landline, dial 011 420 221 771 011.
▸ To call the Budapest hotel, dial 011 36 1 269 0222.
▸ To call Vienna hotel, dial 011 43 1 534 050.

Country Codes	
Czech Republic	420
Poland	48
Hungary	36
Slovenia	386
Austria	43
Slovakia	421
Croatia	385
Bosnia-Herzeg.	387
Montenegro	382
Bulgaria	359
Romania	40

lantic delivery (in either direction), consider services such as DHL (www.dhl.com).

Transportation

In Central Europe, I travel mostly by public transportation. For long distances between big cities (such as Prague to Kraków, Warsaw to Budapest, or Vienna to Ljubljana), I prefer to take a cheap flight or a night train. For shorter distances (like Gdańsk to Warsaw or Budapest to Bratislava), I take a daytime train or bus. In areas with lots of exciting day-trip possibilities, such as the Czech countryside (castles) or Slovenia's Julian Alps (mountain scenery), I rent a car for a day or two. Or you can hire a local driver to take you around—freeing you up to enjoy the scenery...and the company (in this book, I recommend several drivers and tour guides with cars).

From a European Landline
To call from country to country, replace + with 00 (Europe access code), then dial the country code and phone number.
► To call the Prague hotel from a Hungarian landline, dial 00 420 221 771 011.
► To call the Budapest hotel from an Austrian landline, dial 00 36 1 269 0222.
► To call the Vienna hotel from a Croatian landline, dial 00 43 1 534 050.
► To call my US office from a Czech landline, dial 00 1 425 771 8303.

To call within a country, drop the country code and dial the phone number. Phone numbers in Austria, Slovakia, Croatia, Bosnia-Herzegovina, Montenegro, Bulgaria, and Romania require an initial 0 when dialing domestically. Polish and Czech numbers do not. In Hungary, if you are dialing from a landline, you must first dial 06 when calling to a different city or to a mobile phone.
► To call the Prague hotel from a Czech landline, dial 221 771 011.
► To call the Budapest hotel from a Hungarian landline, dial 06 1 269 0222.
► To call the Vienna hotel from an Austrian phone, dial 01 534 050.

More Dialing Tips
Local Numbers: European phone numbers and area codes can vary in length and spacing, even within the same country. Mobile phones use separate prefixes.

Toll and Toll-Free Calls: It's generally not possible to dial European toll or toll-free numbers from a US mobile or landline (although you can sometimes get through using Skype). Look for a direct-dial number instead.

Calling the US from a US Mobile Phone, While Abroad: Dial +1, area code, and number.

More Phoning Help: See HowToCallAbroad.com.

If you're tackling an ambitious itinerary spanning several countries, think carefully before renting a car for your entire trip. Distances are long, driving and parking in big cities is stressful, and the international drop-off fees can be prohibitively expensive (details later).

When deciding between flights, car rental, and train or bus trips, be aware of the potential downside of each option: A car is an expensive headache in any major city; with trains and buses you're at the mercy of a timetable; flying entails a trek to and from a usually distant airport and leaves a larger carbon footprint.

For more detailed information on transportation throughout Europe, see RickSteves.com/transportation.

TRAINS
Trains are generally punctual and cover cities well, but frustrating schedules make a few out-of-the-way destinations difficult—or

impossible—to reach (usually the bus will get you there instead; see "Buses," later).

Schedules: Pick up train schedules from stations as you go, or print them out from an online source. To study ahead on the web, check Bahn.com, Germany's excellent all-Europe timetable. Individual countries also have their own train timetable websites:

- **Czech Republic:** https://idos.idnes.cz
- **Poland:** www.intercity.pl
- **Hungary:** www.mavcsoport.hu
- **Slovenia:** https://potniski.sz.si
- **Austria:** www.oebb.at
- **Slovakia:** www.zssk.sk

Tickets: You can usually buy tickets in advance online and receive your electronic ticket via email to show on your phone. Otherwise, buy tickets at the train station. Try using the ticket machines, which typically have English instructions and take American credit cards.

Some tickets may not be available through the machines, in which case you'll buy tickets from a staffed ticket window. In many big-city train stations, it can be tricky to find the correct line (you'll see separate ticket windows for domestic trips, international journeys, immediate departures, and other concerns). Before getting in line, confirm with fellow travelers that you've chosen the right one. Many ticket sellers speak limited English—be prepared to write out your destination and time.

While most short-haul journeys do not require a reservation, you are required to reserve for some high-speed trains (including premium trains in Poland, such as the Warsaw-Kraków express). Schedules will indicate when a seat assignment is required on EuroCity or InterCity long-distance trains (particularly in Hungary). It's also smart to reserve a sleeping berth if you're taking a night train.

Night Trains: To cover the long distances between the major destinations in this book, consider using night trains. Each night on the train saves a day for sightseeing. However, Central European night trains aren't as new, plush, or comfy as those in Western Europe (such as Austria's slick Nightjet). Expect a bumpy, noisy ride and basic WCs. In general, if a higher degree of comfort is important to you, look for an affordable flight (see "Flights," later), hire a driver to take you door-to-door (perhaps with some sightseeing stops en route), or take a day train. Thefts on night trains can occur, so lock the door of your compartment and secure your belongings (to make it difficult—or at least noisy—for thieves to rip you off). When sleeping on a night train, I wear my money belt.

Rail Passes: Since point-to-point train tickets are cheap

Public Transportation in Central Europe

throughout Central Europe, a rail pass isn't likely to save you much money.

Each country except Slovakia, Bosnia, and Montenegro has its own individual Eurail pass, valid only within that country. The more expensive Eurail Global Pass covers most of Europe, including all the countries in this book, but is priced on the assumption that you'll use it to cover long trips or travel in more expensive Western countries.

For more detailed advice on figuring out the smartest rail pass options for your train trip, and for point-to-point ticket-cost maps, visit RickSteves.com/rail.

BUSES

Increasingly, private bus companies are offering stiff competition to the established rail lines, with cheaper and sometimes faster connections between major cities, especially on international routes. The dominant outfit in Central Europe is the German-owned Flixbus (www.flixbus.com), which offers easy online booking and generally comfortable buses with air-conditioning and Wi-Fi. Other companies seem to come and go regularly, so search online to find the latest options (GetByBus.com is a good place to start).

There are areas within Central Europe where buses are simply better than trains. For example, in Slovenia, Ljubljana and Lake Bled are connected by both train and bus—but the bus station is right in the town center of Bled, while the train station is a few miles away. And a few destinations are accessible only by bus. When in doubt, ask at the local TI for advice.

TAXIS AND RIDE-BOOKING SERVICES

In Central Europe, legitimate taxis are an excellent value. In many cities, two people can travel short distances by cab for little more than the cost of bus or subway tickets. However, corruption is rampant and difficult to tame. Be sure you're using a well-established local company. In countries where taxis are well regulated, it's easy to spot legit cabs (for example, in Budapest they have yellow license plates). In other countries, taxis can charge whatever they want— and hopping in the first one you see in front of a train station or major sight and paying what's on the meter is a great way to get overcharged. Locals always call for a cab from a reputable company (I've listed phone numbers throughout this book)—and get a fair fare. You can ask your hotel, the restaurant where you're dining, or even TIs inside train stations to call you a legitimate taxi.

To avoid the risk of getting ripped off, I typically use **ride-booking apps.** In the Czech Republic, Poland, Slovenia, and many other places, Uber works just like back home. In other places, where Uber may not operate, you can still use apps to order a taxi;

for example, in Hungary, you can order a taxi using the Bolt app. (Free Now is another taxi-hailing app that works in much of Europe.) Whether Uber or a competitor, these apps are a convenient alternative to calling a dispatcher or finding a taxi stand; prices are fixed up front, so you can't be overcharged, and you can pay with a credit card (through the app). Figure out which apps work in the country you're visiting, and if necessary, set them up on your phone.

RENTING A CAR

It's cheaper to arrange most car rentals from the US, so research and compare rates before you go. Most of the major US rental agencies (including Avis, Budget, Enterprise, Hertz, and Thrifty) have offices throughout Europe. Also consider the two major Europe-based agencies, Europcar and Sixt. Consolidators such as Auto Europe (www.autoeurope.com—or the sometimes cheaper www.autoeurope.eu) compare rates at several companies to get you the best deal.

Wherever you book, always read the fine print. Check for add-on charges—such as one-way drop-off fees, airport surcharges, or mandatory insurance policies—that aren't included in the "total price."

Rental Costs and Considerations

If you book well in advance, expect to pay roughly $350-500 for a one-week rental for a basic compact car. Allow extra for supplemental insurance, fuel, tolls, and parking. To save money on fuel, request a diesel car.

Manual vs. Automatic: Cars with manual transmission are more common in Europe and generally cheaper than automatic. If you need an automatic, it's wise to book well in advance. When selecting a car, don't be tempted by a larger model, as it won't be as maneuverable on narrow, winding roads or when squeezing into tight parking lots.

Age Restrictions: Some rental companies impose minimum and maximum age limits. Young drivers (25 and under) and seniors (69 and up) should check the rental policies and rules section of car rental websites.

Choosing Pickup/Drop-off Locations: Always check the hours of the locations you choose: Many rental offices close from midday Saturday until Monday morning and, in smaller towns, at lunchtime. When selecting an office, confirm the location on a map. A downtown site might seem more convenient than the airport but could actually be in the suburbs or buried deep in big-city streets. Pedestrianized and one-way streets can make navigation tricky when returning a car at a big-city office or urban train station. Wherever you select, get precise details on the location and allow ample time to find it.

Have the Right License: If you're renting a car in Central Europe, bring your driver's license. In Austria, Bulgaria, the Czech Republic, Hungary, Poland, Romania, Slovenia, or Slovakia, you're also technically required to have an International Driving Permit—an official translation of your license (sold at AAA offices for about $20 plus the cost of two passport-type photos; see www.aaa.com). How this is enforced varies; I've never needed one.

Crossing Borders in a Rental Car: It's typically not a problem to cross borders between Schengen countries—but if venturing beyond this open-borders area (for example, into Bosnia-Herzegovina), there may be restrictions.

Always tell your car-rental company exactly which countries you'll be entering. Some companies levy extra insurance fees for trips taken in certain countries with certain cars (such as BMWs, Mercedes, and convertibles). Double-check with your rental agent that you have all the documentation you need before you drive off; at border checkpoints, it's likely you'll be asked to present proof of insurance (called a "green card"). Note that picking up a car in one country and dropping it off in another can be quite expensive—see "International Drop-Off Fees," below.

Picking Up Your Car: Before driving off in your rental car, check it thoroughly and make sure any damage is noted on your rental agreement. Rental agencies in Europe tend to charge for even minor damage, so be sure to mark everything. Find out how your car's gearshift, lights, turn signals, wipers, GPS, and fuel cap function, and know what kind of fuel the car takes (diesel is common in Europe). When you return the car, make sure the agent verifies its condition with you.

International Drop-Off Fees

If you're planning a multicountry itinerary by car, be aware of often-astronomical international drop-off fees. There's typically no extra charge for picking up and dropping off a car at different locations within the same country—but you'll pay through the nose to drop off across the border. (For example, you can generally pick up a car in Kraków, drive it six hours to Gdańsk, and turn it in there for no charge—but if you drive the same car from Vienna just an hour to Bratislava and drop it off, it can cost you hundreds of extra dollars.)

For some itineraries, you may just have to live with the extra expense. But in most cases, you can plan your itinerary smartly to avoid it. Some people plan a circular itinerary (for example, Prague-Kraków-Budapest-Bratislava-Vienna-Prague) to ensure they can drop the car off where they picked it up. Others connect the longer distances on their itinerary with trains or flights, then rent a car

Driving in Central Europe

N · Not to Scale

GERMANY

To Gdańsk

Toruń · 110m · 2h

Warsaw

135m · 3h

180m · 3h

Berlin

190m · 3.5h

Poznań

120m 2.25h

POLAND

265m · 4.5h

140m · 2.5h

210m · 3.5h

185m · 3.5h

390m · 7h

Dresden

Częstochowa · 90m · 2h

65m 1.75h

65m 1.5h

Terezín · 40m · 1h

290m · 5.5h · Auschwitz

40m · 1.25h

Kraków

Prague · 25k · .75h

40m · 1.25h

CZECH REPUBLIC

80m · 2.75h · 100m

Karlštejn Castle

Kutná Hora

Zakopane

45m 1.5h

100m · 2.25h

130m · 2h

175m · 3.5h

Poprad

210m · 3.5h

200m · 4h

SLOVAKIA

Český Krumlov

135m · 3.25h

Brno

200m · 3.5h

115m · 3.5h

240m · 4h

80m 2h

80m 1.5h

240m · 5.5h

140m · 2.5h

Vienna · 40m · 1h

Bratislava

Eger

Munich

200m · 3.5h

125m · 2h

80m · 2h

90m 1.5h

Salzburg

235m · 4h

150m · 2.5h

Budapest

To Maramureș 270m · 6h

AUSTRIA

240m 4h →

290m · 5h

145m · 2.5h

To Cluj-Napoca 280m · 6.5h

520m · 10h

150m · 2.5h

Pécs

HUNGARY

To Bucharest

Bled

30m 1h

60m 1.5h

Ljubljana

SLOVENIA

290m · 3.5h

SERBIA

75m 2h

140m · 2h

Zagreb

ITALY

100m · 4h

260m · 4h

CROATIA

Trieste

100m · 1.75h

90m · 2h

260m · 6h

50m · 1.5h

Rovinj

Rijeka

85m · 2h

Venice

30m · .75h

55m 1.5h

240m · 3.5h

BOSNIA-HERZEGOVINA

Pula

Plitvice

Sarajevo

To Sofia 380m · 9h

85m 1.75h

90m 2.5h

Adriatic Sea

Zadar · 100m · 2h

Mostar

110m · 2.5h

105m · 2.5h

65m 2h

Ston

35m 1h

MONT.

Split

35m · 1h

60m 2h

Korčula

Dubrovnik

Kotor

Note: Your times may vary based on traffic, construction, and road conditions.

m = miles
h = hours

PRACTICALITIES

strategically for a day or two in places where it's warranted (such as the Czech or Slovenian countryside). This is a particularly smart plan when visiting big cities, where a car is an expensive and worthless burden (i.e., fighting urban traffic and paying for pricey secure parking).

Car Insurance Options

When you rent a car in Europe, the price typically includes liability insurance, which covers harm to other cars or motorists—but not the rental car itself. To limit your financial risk in case of damage to the rental, choose one of these options: Buy a Collision Damage Waiver (CDW; also called "loss damage waiver" or LDW by some firms) with a low or zero deductible from the car-rental company (roughly 30-40 percent extra), get coverage through your credit card (essentially "free," but more complicated if you need to use it), or get collision insurance as part of a larger travel-insurance policy.

Basic **CDW** costs $15-30 a day and typically comes with a $1,000-2,000 deductible, reducing but not eliminating your financial responsibility. When you reserve or pick up the car, you'll be offered the chance to "buy down" the deductible to zero (for an additional $10-30/day; this is sometimes called "super CDW" or "zero-deductible coverage").

If you opt for **credit-card coverage,** you must decline all coverage offered by the car-rental company—which means they can place a hold on your card to cover the deductible. In case of damage, it can be time-consuming to resolve the charges. Before relying on this option, quiz your card company about how it works. If you're already purchasing a **travel-insurance policy** for your trip, adding collision coverage can be an economical choice. Both of these options are typically valid everywhere in Europe except the Republic of Ireland and Italy.

For more on car-rental insurance, see RickSteves.com/cdw.

Navigation Options

If you'll be navigating using your phone, remember to bring a car charger. Most rental cars are equipped with a USB port so you can run your phone's GPS through the dashboard display, but it can also be smart to bring a device mount.

Your Mobile Phone: The mapping app on your phone works fine for navigating Europe's roads. To save on data, most apps allow you to download maps for offline use (do this before you need them, when you have a strong Wi-Fi signal). Some apps—including Google Maps—provide offline route directions, but you'll need data access for current traffic. For more on using a mapping app, see "Using Your Phone in Europe," earlier.

GPS Devices: Most cars come with a dedicated GPS unit,

though it's sometimes an add-on cost (about $15-20/day). The unit may come loaded only with maps for its home country; if you need additional maps, ask. Make sure you know how to use the device—and that the language is set to English—before you drive off.

Paper Maps and Atlases: Even when navigating primarily with GPS, I always have a paper map, ideally a big, detailed regional road map. It's invaluable for getting the big picture, understanding alternate routes, and filling in if my phone runs out of juice. The free maps you get from your car-rental company usually don't have enough detail. It's smart to buy a better map before you go, or pick one up at a local gas station, bookshop, newsstand, or tourist shop.

Driving

Road Rules: Be aware of typical European road rules; for example, many countries—including most of the ones in this book—require headlights to be on at all times, and nearly all forbid handheld mobile-phone use. In Europe, you're not allowed to turn right on a red light unless a sign or signal specifically authorizes it, and on expressways it's illegal to pass drivers on the right. Ask your car-rental company about these rules, or check the "International Travel" section at Travel.state.gov (enter a country in the "Learn About Your Destination" box, then click on "Travel and Transportation").

Fuel: Gas is expensive—often about $6-8 per gallon. Diesel cars are more common in Europe than back home, so be sure you know what type of fuel your car takes before you fill up. Some pumps are color coded: Unleaded pumps are green and labeled "E," while diesel pumps (often yellow or black) are labeled "B."

AND LEARN THESE ROAD SIGNS

Speed Limit (km/hr)	Yield	No Passing	End of No Passing Zone
One Way	Intersection	Main Road	Expressway
Danger	No Entry	Cars Prohibited	All Vehicles Prohibited
No Through Road	Restrictions No Longer Apply	Yield to Oncoming Traffic	No Stopping
Parking	No Parking	Customs or Toll Road	Peace

Road Conditions: Central Europe is nearing the end of an impressive binge of superhighway construction. It's not unusual to discover that a much faster road has been built between major destinations since your five-year-old map was published. (This is another good reason to travel with the most up-to-date maps possible, and study them before each drive.) Over the last several years, superhighways have opened between Dresden and Prague (A-17) and between Warsaw and Berlin (A-2).

Occasionally, backcountry roads are the only option. These can be bumpy and slow, but they're almost always paved (or, at least, they once were). In Poland, where the network of new expressways isn't yet complete, locals travel long distances on two-lane country roads. Since each lane is about a lane and a half wide, passing is commonplace. Slower drivers should keep to the far right of their lane to allow faster cars to zip past them. Especially in Croatia and Slovenia, keep a close eye out for bikers—you'll see scads of them on mountain roads, struggling to earn a thrilling downhill run.

Tolls: In many countries, driving on highways requires a toll sticker. These include the **Czech Republic** (*dálniční známka*, 310 Kč/10 days, 440 Kč/1 month, https://edalnice.cz), **Slovakia** (*úhrada*, €12/10 days, €17/1 month, https://eznamka.sk), **Hungary** (*autópálya matrica*, 5,500 Ft/10 days, 8,900 Ft/1 month, https://nemzetiutdij.hu), **Slovenia** (*vinjeta*, €15/week, €30/month, www.dars.si), and **Austria** (*Vignette*, €9.90/10 days, €29/2 months, www.asfinag.at). Fines for not having a toll sticker can be stiff.

Your rental car probably already comes with a toll sticker (ask at the rental agency). If it doesn't—or if you're crossing into a different country from where you rented the car—you have to get a sticker. The best way to do that is by going to one of the websites listed above to register your rental car for an electronic sticker. You'll need the license plate number and possibly the VIN number.

If you don't get an electronic sticker, you'll need to buy a physical sticker to affix to the windshield. Look for a large gas station near the border. At the border itself, you may find machines or sales points for buying one. However, be warned that some unscrupulous private agencies at certain borders try to sell stickers at a markup. The safest bet is to buy it online or ensure that you're using an official sales outlet. (If the price they charge is much higher than the ones listed above, be suspicious.)

Poland and **Croatia** have a different system: You'll take a toll ticket as you enter the expressway, then pay when you get off based on how far you've traveled.

Parking: Parking is a costly headache in big cities. You'll pay about $15-30 a day to park safely. Rental-car theft can be a problem in cities (especially Prague), so ask at your hotel for advice.

FLIGHTS

To compare flights, begin with an online travel search engine: Google Flights is comprehensive and easy to use, and Skyscanner includes many inexpensive flights within Europe. To avoid unpleasant surprises, before you book be sure to read the small print about refunds, changes, and the costs for "extras" such as reserving a seat, checking a bag, or printing a boarding pass.

Flights to Europe: Start looking for international flights about four to six months before your trip, especially for peak-season travel. Depending on your itinerary, it can be efficient and no more expensive to fly into one city and out of another.

Flights Within Europe: Flying between European cities is surprisingly affordable. Before buying a long-distance train or bus ticket, check the cost of a flight on one of Europe's airlines, whether a major carrier or a no-frills outfit. Two well-established budget airlines are based in Central Europe: **Wizz Air** (https://wizzair.com, with a hub in Budapest) and **Smart Wings** (www.smartwings.com, based in Prague). Well-known cheapo airlines that fly to Central European destinations include EasyJet, RyanAir, and **Norwegian**. Be aware that flying with a discount airline can have drawbacks, such as minimal customer service and time-consuming treks to secondary airports.

Many national carriers also charge reasonable fares for short-distance trips. For example, check out Poland's LOT Airlines (www.lot.com). On recent trips, I've flown affordably on LOT between Kraków and Ljubljana, and between Kraków and Budapest, avoiding lengthy overland journeys.

Flying to the US and Canada: Because security is extra tight for flights to the US, be sure to give yourself plenty of time at the airport (see www.tsa.gov for the latest rules).

Resources from Rick Steves

Begin Your Trip at RickSteves.com

My mobile-friendly **website** is *the* place to explore Europe in preparation for your trip. You'll find thousands of fun articles, beautiful photos, videos, and radio interviews; a wealth of money-saving tips for planning your dream trip; travel news dispatches; a video library of travel talks; our latest guidebook updates (RickSteves. com/update); and the free Rick Steves Audio Europe app. You can also follow me on Facebook, Instagram, and Twitter.

Our **Travel Forum** is a well-groomed collection of message boards where our travel-savvy community answers questions and shares their personal travel experiences—and our well-traveled staff chimes in when they can be helpful (RickSteves.com/forums).

Our **online Travel Store** offers bags and accessories that I've designed to help you travel smarter and lighter. These include my popular carry-on bags (which I live out of four months a year), money belts, totes, toiletries kits, adapters, guidebooks, and planning maps (RickSteves.com/shop).

Our website can also help you find the perfect **rail pass** for your itinerary and your budget, with easy, one-stop shopping for rail passes, seat reservations, and point-to-point tickets (RickSteves. com/rail).

Rick Steves' Tours, Guidebooks, TV Shows, and More

Small-Group Tours: Want to travel with greater efficiency and less stress? We offer more than 40 itineraries reaching the best destinations in this book...and beyond. Each year about 30,000 travelers join us on about 1,000 Rick Steves bus tours. You'll enjoy great guides and a fun bunch of travel partners (with small groups of 24 to 28 travelers). You'll find European adventures to fit every vacation length. For all the details, and to book a tour, visit RickSteves. com/tours or call us at +1 425 771 8303.

Books: This book is just one of many books in my series on European travel, which includes country and city guidebooks, Snapshots (excerpted chapters from bigger guides), Pocket Guides (full-color little books on big cities), "Best Of" guidebooks (condensed, full-color country guides), and my budget-travel skills handbook, *Rick Steves Europe Through the Back Door.* A complete list of my titles—including phrase books, cruising guides, and travelogues on European art, history, and culture—appears near the end of this book.

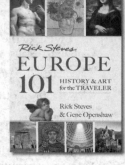

TV Shows and Video Library: My public television series, *Rick Steves' Europe,* covers Europe from top to bottom with over 100 half-hour episodes—and we're working on new shows every year. Watch full episodes for free (RickSteves.com/tv). My free online video library, Rick Steves Classroom Europe, offers a searchable database of short video clips on European history, culture, and geography (Classroom. RickSteves.com).

Monday Night Travel Talks: To raise your travel I.Q., join our virtual travel party every Monday, featuring Rick Steves guides discussing European destinations, art, culture, food, travel tips, and more. Join the live events or check out the video recordings (RickSteves.com/mnt).

Audio Tours on My Free App: I've produced 60 free, self-guided audio tours of the top sights in Europe. For those tours and other audio content, get my free **Rick Steves Audio Europe app,** an extensive online library organized by destination. For more on my app, visit RickSteves.com/audioeurope.

Radio: My weekly public radio show, *Travel with Rick Steves,* features interviews with travel experts from around the world. It airs on 400 public radio stations across the US. An archive of programs is available at RickSteves.com/radio.

Podcasts: You can enjoy my travel content via several free podcasts. The podcast version of my radio show brings you a weekly, hour-long travel conversation. My other podcasts include a selection of video clips from my public television show, and video recordings of my travel classes (RickSteves.com/podcasts).

PRACTICALITIES

APPENDIX

Holidays & Festivals 1119
Books & Films 1122
Conversions & Climate 1127
Packing Checklist 1130
Pronouncing Central European
  Place Names .1131

Holidays and Festivals

This list includes selected festivals in this region, plus national holidays observed throughout Central Europe. Many sights and banks close on national holidays—keep this in mind when planning your itinerary. Catholic holidays are celebrated in Poland, Slovakia, and Slovenia (and to a lesser extent in Hungary and the Czech Republic). Before planning a trip around a festival, verify the dates with the festival website, the tourist office, or my "Upcoming Holidays and Festivals" web page at RickSteves.com/europe/festivals.

Jan 1	New Year's Day
Jan 6	Epiphany, Catholic countries
Jan 19	Anniversary of Jan Palach's death, Prague (flowers in Wenceslas Square)
Feb 8	National Day of Culture, Slovenia (celebrates Slovenian culture and national poet France Prešeren)
March	One World International Human Rights Film Festival, Prague (www.oneworld.cz)
March-April	Ramadan (Muslim holy month): March 10-April 9, 2024; Feb 28-March 29, 2025

APPENDIX

March 15	National Day, Hungary (celebrates 1848 Revolution)
Late March	Ski Jumping World Cup Finals, Planica, Slovenia (3 days, www.planica.si)
March/April	Easter weekend (Good Friday-Easter Monday): March 29-April 1, 2024; April 18-21, 2025
April	Budapest Spring Festival (2 weeks; opera, ballet, classical music; https://budapestitavaszifesztival.hu)
April 27	National Resistance Day, Slovenia
April 30	Witches' Night, Czech Republic (similar to Halloween, with bonfires)
May	Ascension (Catholic countries): May 9, 2024; May 29, 2025
Early May	Prague International Marathon (www.runczech.com)
May 1	Labor Day
May 3	Constitution Day, Poland (celebrates Europe's first constitution)
May 8	Liberation Day, Czech Republic and Slovakia
May/June	Pentecost and Whitmonday (Catholic countries): May 19-20, 2024; June 8-9, 2025
May/June	Vienna Festival of Arts and Music (www.festwochen.at)
May/June	Corpus Christi (Catholic countries): May 30, 2024; June 19, 2025
Mid-May-early June	"Prague Spring" Music Festival (https://festival.cz)
Late May-mid-June	Jewish Art Days, Budapest (2 weeks, www.zsidomuveszetinapok.hu)
June	Five-Petalled Rose Celebration, Český Krumlov, Czech Republic (medieval festival and knights' tournament, www.ckrumlov.info)
June/July	Prague Proms, Prague (music festival, www.pragueproms.cz)
June 25	National Day, Slovenia
Late June	Wianki Midsummer Festival, Kraków, Poland (wreaths on rafts in Vistula River, fireworks, music)
Late June	Jewish Culture Festival, Kraków, Poland (www.jewishfestival.pl)
Late June	Midsummer Eve celebrations, Austria

July 5	Sts. Cyril and Methodius Day, Czech Republic and Slovakia
July 6	Jan Hus Day, Czech Republic
Early July–Sept	Ljubljana Festival, Slovenia (https://ljubljanafestival.si)
Mid-July–mid-Aug	International Music Festival, Český Krumlov, Czech Republic (www.festivalkrumlov.cz)
Late July	Formula 1 races, Budapest (www.formula1.com)
Late July–mid-Aug	St. Dominic's Fair, Gdańsk, Poland (3 weeks of market stalls, music, and general revelry)
Aug	Sziget Festival, Budapest (rock and pop music, https://szigetfestival.com)
Aug 15	Assumption of Mary (Catholic countries)
Aug 20	St. István's Day, Hungary (also known as Constitution Day; fireworks, celebrations)
Aug 29	National Uprising Day, Slovakia (commemorates uprising against Nazis)
Sept	Dvořák's Prague Music Festival, Prague (www.dvorakovapraha.cz)
Sept 1	Constitution Day, Slovakia
Sept 28	St. Wenceslas Day, Czech Republic (celebrates national patron saint and Czech statehood)
Sept/Oct	Jewish High Holy Days (Rosh Hashanah: Oct 2-4, 2024, Sept 22-24, 2025; Yom Kippur: Oct 11-12, 2024, Oct 1-2, 2025; Jewish sights may close)
Oct 23	Republic Day, Hungary (remembrances of 1956 Uprising)
Oct 26	National Day, Austria
Oct 28	Independence Day, Czech Republic
Oct 31	Reformation Day, Slovenia
Nov 1	All Saints' Day/Remembrance Day, Catholic countries (religious festival, some closures)
Nov 11	Independence Day, Poland; St. Martin's Day, Austria and Slovenia (official first day of wine season)
Nov 17	Velvet Revolution Anniversary, Czech Republic and Slovakia
Dec 5	St. Nicholas Eve, Prague (St. Nick gives gifts to children in town square)
Dec 24-25	Christmas Eve and Christmas Day
Dec 26	Boxing Day/St. Stephen's Day; Independence and Unity Day, Slovenia
Dec 31	St. Sylvester's Day, Prague and Vienna (fireworks)

APPENDIX

Books and Films

To learn about Central Europe past and present, check out a few of these books or films.

Nonfiction

Lonnie Johnson's *Central Europe: Enemies, Neighbors, Friends* is the best historical overview of the countries in this book. Timothy Garton Ash has written several good "eyewitness account" books analyzing the fall of communism in Europe, including *History of the Present* and *The Magic Lantern*. Michael Meyer's *The Year That Changed the World* intimately chronicles the exciting events of 1989, culminating in the fall of the Berlin Wall. Anne Applebaum's *Iron Curtain: The Crushing of Eastern Europe 1944-1956* is a readable account of how the Soviets exerted their influence on the nations they had just liberated from the Nazis; her *Gulag: A History* delves into one particularly odious mechanism they used to intimidate their subjects. Tina Rosenberg's dense but thought-provoking *The Haunted Land* asks how those who actively supported communism should be treated in the postcommunist age. And Benjamin Curtis' *The Habsburgs: The History of a Dynasty* is an illuminating portrait of the Austrian imperial family that shaped so much of Central European history.

Patrick Leigh Fermor's *Between the Woods and the Water* is the vivid memoir of a young man who traveled by foot and on horseback across the Balkan Peninsula (including Hungary) in 1933. Rebecca West's classic, bricklike *Black Lamb and Grey Falcon* is the definitive travelogue of the Yugoslav lands (written during a journey between the two world wars).

James Michener's *The Bridge at Andau* tells the story of the 1956 Uprising in Budapest, and the Hungarians who fled following its crushing defeat.

For a more recent take, Croatian journalist Slavenka Drakulić has written a quartet of insightful essay collections from a woman's perspective: *Café Europa: Life After Communism*, *The Balkan Express*, *How We Survived Communism and Even Laughed*, and *A Guided Tour Through the Museum of Communism*. Drakulić's *They Would Never Hurt a Fly* profiles Yugoslav war criminals.

Dominika Dery's memoir, *The Twelve Little Cakes*, traces her experience growing up in communist Czechoslovakia in the 1970s.

For a thorough explanation of how and why Yugoslavia broke apart, read *Yugoslavia: Death of a Nation* (by Laura Silber and Allan Little).

For information on Central European Roma (Gypsies), consider the textbook-style *We Are the Romani People* by Ian Hancock, and the more literary *Bury Me Standing* by Isabel Fonseca.

Fiction

The most prominent works of Central European fiction have come from the Czechs. These include *I Served the King of England* (Bohumil Hrabal), *The Unbearable Lightness of Being* (Milan Kundera), and *The Good Soldier Švejk* (Jaroslav Hašek). Czech existentialist writer Franz Kafka wrote many well-known novels, including *The Trial* and *The Metamorphosis*. Bruce Chatwin's *Utz* is set in communist Prague.

James Michener's *Poland* is a hefty look into the history of the Poles. *Zlateh the Goat* (Isaac Bashevis Singer) includes seven folktales of Jewish Central and Eastern Europe. Joseph Roth's *The Radetzky March* details the decline of an aristocratic Slovenian family in the Austro-Hungarian Empire.

Imre Kertész, a Hungarian Jewish Auschwitz survivor who won the Nobel Prize for Literature in 2002, is best known for his semiautobiographical novel *Fatelessness (Sorstalanság)*, which chronicles the experience of a young concentration-camp prisoner. Márai Sándor's reflective *Embers* paints a rich picture of cobblestoned, gaslit Vienna just before the empire's glory began to fade.

Arthur Phillips' confusingly titled 2002 novel *Prague* tells the story of American expats negotiating young-adult life in postcommunist Budapest, where they often feel one-upped by their compatriots doing the same in the Czech capital (hence the title).

Films

Each of these countries has produced fine films. Below are a few highlights.

Czech Republic

The Czech film industry is one of the strongest in Central Europe; even under communism, its films were seen and honored worldwide. Before he directed *One Flew Over the Cuckoo's Nest* and *Amadeus,* Miloš Forman directed *Loves of a Blonde* (1965), about the relationship between a rural Czech woman and a jazz pianist from Prague; and *The Firemen's Ball* (1967), a satirical look at small-town Czechoslovakia under communism. Another Czech New Wave film, *Intimate Lighting* (1965), finds two musicians reuniting in the 1960s.

In *Alice* (1988), Czech artist Jan Švankmajer adapts Lewis Carroll's *Alice's Adventures in Wonderland* in stop-motion animation combined with live action. The comedy *Czech Dream* (2004) features two film students who document the opening of a fake hypermarket in a hilarious, disturbing commentary on consumerism.

Two films directed by Jiří Menzel cover everyday life during World War II. The Oscar-winning *Closely Watched Trains* (1966) follows a young Czech man working at a German-occupied train station. *I Served the King of England* (2006), an adaptation of Bohumil Hrabal's novel, finds a man reminiscing about his past as an ambitious waiter who suffers the consequences of World War II.

Other great Czech films about World War II include *Divided We Fall* (2000), where a Czech couple hides a Jewish friend during Nazi occupation; *Protektor* (2009), whose main character must reconcile his job at a Nazi-propaganda radio station and his relationship with his Jewish wife; and *All My Loved Ones* (1999), the story of a Jewish family whose son is sent to England in the "Kindertransports" organized by Nicholas Winton (the British humanitarian who saved almost 700 Czech Jewish children).

Recent Czech films also cover life under communism and the Velvet Revolution. *The Elementary School* (1991), set in the late 1940s, looks at a rowdy classroom in suburban Prague that faces reform under the strict guidance of a war-hero teacher. The mystery *In the Shadow* (2012) tracks a burglary in 1950s Czechoslovakia that sets off a political investigation of Jewish immigrants. *Larks on a String* (1990) covers bourgeois Czechs who are forced into communist labor camps and struggle to maintain their humanity. The TV miniseries *Burning Bush* (2013) details the communist occupation of Czechoslovakia and the Prague Spring, focusing on Jan Palach, the Czech student who set himself on fire and died in protest against the Soviet occupation. In the Oscar-winning *Kolya* (1996), a concert cellist in Soviet-controlled Czechoslovakia must care for an abandoned Russian boy just before the Velvet Revolution breaks out.

The Czechs also have a wonderful animation tradition that successfully competes with Walt Disney in Central Europe and China. The most popular character is Krtek (or Krteček, "Little Mole"), who gets in and out of trouble. You'll see plush black-and-white Krtek figures everywhere. Křemílek and Vochomůrka are brothers who live in the woods, Maxipes Fík is a clever dog, and the duo Pat and Mat are builders who can't seem to get anything right.

Poland

Several Polish films have won Oscars and major awards at Cannes. In *Katyń* (2007), acclaimed, Oscar-winning director Andrzej Wajda re-creates the Soviet Army's massacre of around 22,000 Polish officers, enlisted men, and civilians during World War II. Some of Wajda's earlier works include *Ashes and Diamonds* (1958), *The Promised Land* (1979), and the two-part series *Man of Marble* (1977) and *Man of Iron* (1981).

Polish filmmaker Krzysztof Kieslowski made several masterpieces, including *The Decalogue* (1989), consisting of 10 short films inspired by the Ten Commandments. Kieslowski also filmed the multilingual Three Colors Trilogy: *Red* (1994), *White* (1994), and *Blue* (1993).

Among other recent films, one Polish favorite is *Karol: A Man Who Became Pope* (2005), a Polish-Italian biopic made in English about the humble beginnings of St. John Paul II. Another fascinating religious tale is *Ida* (2014), the story of a young novitiate nun in 1960s Poland, who—just before taking her vows—discovers a terrible family secret.

A trip to the poignant Holocaust sites of Poland—Auschwitz, Kazimierz (in Kraków), and Warsaw's former ghetto area—is made immeasurably richer if you watch *Schindler's List* and *The Pianist* before you go (see "Hollywood Meets Central Europe," later).

Hungary

The surreal dark comedy *Kontroll* (2003) is about ticket inspectors on the Budapest Metró whose lives are turned upside down by a serial killer lurking in the shadows. *Fateless,* the 2005 adaptation of Imre Kertész's Nobel Prize-winning novel about a young man in a concentration camp, was scripted by Kertész himself. *The Witness* (a.k.a. *Without a Trace,* 1969), a cult classic about a simple man who mysteriously wins the favor of communist bigwigs, is a biting satire of the darkest days of Soviet rule. *Time Stands Still* (1981), a hit at the 1982 Cannes Film Festival, tells the story of young Hungarians in the 1960s. *Children of Glory* (2006) dramatizes the true story of the Hungarian water polo team that defiantly trounced the Soviets at the Olympics just after the 1956 Uprising.

Slovenia (and Other Former Yugoslav Countries)

To grasp the wars that shook this region in the early 1990s, there's no better film than the Slovene-produced *No Man's Land,* which won the 2002 Oscar for Best Foreign Film. Angelina Jolie wrote and directed (but did not appear in) 2011's wrenching, difficult-to-watch *In the Land of Blood and Honey,* a love story set against the grotesque backdrop of the war in Bosnia.

On a lighter note, a classic from Tito-era Yugoslavia, *The Battle of Neretva* (1969), imported Hollywood talent in the form of Yul Brynner and Orson Welles to tell the story of a pivotal and inspiring battle in the fight against the Nazis. More recent Croatian films worth watching include *Border Post* (2006), about various Yugoslav soldiers working together just before the war broke out; and *When Father Was Away on Business* (1985), about a prisoner on the Tito-era gulag island of Goli Otok, near Rab. Other local movies include *Armin* (2007), *How the War Started on My Island* (1996), *Underground* (1995), and *Tito and Me* (1992).

Documentaries

Documentaries about this region are also worth looking for. The BBC produced a remarkable, definitive six-hour documentary series called *The Death of Yugoslavia,* featuring interviews with all of the key players (it's difficult to find on DVD, but try searching for "Death of Yugoslavia" on YouTube; the book *Yugoslavia: Death of a Nation,* noted earlier, was a companion piece to this film). The BBC also produced a harrowing documentary about the infamous Bosnian massacre, *Srebrenica: A Cry from the Grave* (also available on YouTube). The 1998 Oscar-winning documentary *The Last Days* recounts the fate of Jews when the Nazis took over Hungary in 1944.

Hollywood Meets Central Europe

Several award-winning films have covered key moments in Central European history. *Schindler's List* (1993), Steven Spielberg's Best Picture winner, tells the story of a compassionate German businessman in Kraków who saved his Jewish workers during the Holocaust. Roman Polanski's *The Pianist* (2002) is a biopic about the struggle for survival of Władysław Szpilman (played by Adrien Brody, in an Oscar-winning role), a Jewish concert pianist in Holocaust-era Warsaw.

The Unbearable Lightness of Being (1988), starring a young Daniel Day-Lewis, adapts the Milan Kundera novel about a love triangle set against the backdrop of the Prague Spring uprising. And *Sunshine* (1999, starring Ralph Fiennes, directed by István Szabó) somewhat melodramatically traces three generations of an aristocratic Jewish family in Budapest, from the golden age, through the Holocaust, to the Cold War.

Two acclaimed German movies offer excellent insight into the surreal and paranoid days of the Soviet Bloc. The Oscar-winning *Lives of Others* (2006) chronicles the constant surveillance that the communist regime employed to keep potential dissidents in line. For a funny and nostalgic look at postcommunist Europe's fitful transition to capitalism, *Good Bye Lenin!* (2003) can't be beat. Another insightful look at this period of communist paranoia is Steven Spielberg's 2015 *Bridge of Spies,* which follows Tom Hanks into 1960s Berlin—just as the Berlin Wall is going up—to walk the diplomatic tightrope of a prisoner swap with the Soviets.

Central European filmmakers have always been very active in Hollywood. "Crossover" directors—who started out making films in their own countries and then turned out English-language Oscar winners—include Michael Curtiz (from Hungary; *Casablanca, White Christmas*), Miloš Forman (from Czechoslovakia; *One Flew Over the Cuckoo's Nest, Amadeus*), and Roman Polanski (from Poland; *Chinatown, The Pianist*). Other great Central European filmmakers include Steven Spielberg's favorite cinematographer, Janusz

Kamiński, from Poland (*Schindler's List, Saving Private Ryan, Lincoln,* and most other Spielberg films).

You may recognize Central Europe backdrops in many blockbuster Hollywood movies—particularly Prague, whose low costs and well-trained filmmaking workforce appeal to studios. In many cases, Prague stands in for another European city. Films shot at least partly in Prague include everything from *Amadeus* to *Mission: Impossible,* from *The Chronicles of Narnia* to *Wanted,* from *The Bourne Identity* to the *Hostel* films, and from *Hannibal* to *Shanghai Knights.* Elsewhere in the Czech Republic, they've filmed the James Bond reboot *Casino Royale* and *The Illusionist.* Many American studios have taken advantage of Hungary's low prices to film would-be blockbusters in Budapest, including *Spy, A Good Day to Die Hard,* and *Mission: Impossible—Ghost Protocol.* More often, Budapest stands in for other cities—for example, as Buenos Aires in the 1996 film *Evita,* and as various European locales in Stephen Spielberg's 2005 film *Munich.*

Conversions and Climate

Numbers and Stumblers

- Europeans write a few of their numbers differently than we do. 1 = 1, 4 = 4, 7 = 7.
- In Europe, dates appear as day/month, so Christmas is 25/12. In Hungary, dates appear as year/month/day, so Christmas 2025 is 2025/12/25 (or dots can be used instead: 2025.12.25).
- Commas are decimal points and decimals are commas. A dollar and a half is $1,50, one thousand is 1.000, and there are 5.280 feet in a mile.
- Hungarians usually list their surname first (for example, Bartók Béla instead of Béla Bartók).
- When counting with fingers, start with your thumb. If you hold up your first finger to request one item, you'll probably get two.
- What Americans call the second floor of a building is the first floor in Europe.
- On escalators and moving sidewalks, Europeans keep the left "lane" open for passing. Keep to the right.

Metric Conversions

A **kilogram** equals 1,000 grams (about 2.2 pounds). One hundred **grams** (a common unit at markets) is about a quarter-pound. One **liter** is about a quart, or almost four to a gallon.

A **kilometer** is six-tenths of a mile. To convert kilometers to miles, cut the kilometers in half and add back 10 percent of the original (120 km: 60 + 12 = 72 miles). One **meter** is 39 inches—just over a yard.

1 foot = 0.3 meter	1 square yard = 0.8 square meter
1 yard = 0.9 meter	1 square mile = 2.6 square kilometers
1 mile = 1.6 kilometers	1 ounce = 28 grams
1 centimeter = 0.4 inch	1 quart = 0.95 liter
1 meter = 39.4 inches	1 kilogram = 2.2 pounds
1 kilometer = 0.62 mile	32°F = 0°C

Clothing Sizes

When shopping for clothing, use these US-to-European comparisons as general guidelines (but note that no conversion is perfect).

Women: For pants and dresses, add 30-32 (US 10 = European 40-42). For blouses and sweaters, add 8 for most of Europe (US 32 = European 40). For shoes, add 30-31 (US 7 = European 37/38).

Men: For shirts, multiply by 2 and add about 8 (US 15 = European 38). For jackets and suits, add 10. For shoes, add 32-34.

Children: Clothing is sized by height—in centimeters (2.5 cm = 1 inch), so a US size 8 roughly equates to 132-140. For shoes up to size 13, add 16-18; and for sizes 1 and up, add 30-32.

Central Europe's Climate

First line is the average daily high; second line, average daily low; third line, average days with some rain. For more detailed weather statistics for destinations in this book (as well as the rest of the world), check Wunderground.com.

J	F	M	A	M	J	J	A	S	O	N	D

AUSTRIA • Vienna

34°	38°	47°	58°	67°	73°	76°	75°	68°	56°	45°	37°
25°	28°	30°	42°	50°	56°	60°	59°	53°	44°	37°	30°
15	14	13	13	13	14	13	13	10	13	14	15

CZECH REPUBLIC • Prague

31°	34°	44°	54°	64°	70°	73°	72°	65°	53°	42°	34°
23°	24°	30°	38°	46°	52°	55°	55°	49°	41°	33°	27°
13	11	10	11	13	12	13	12	10	13	12	13

HUNGARY • Budapest

34°	39°	50°	62°	71°	78°	82°	81°	74°	61°	47°	39°
25°	28°	35°	44°	52°	58°	62°	60°	53°	44°	38°	30°
13	12	11	11	13	13	10	9	7	10	14	13

J	F	M	A	M	J	J	A	S	O	N	D

POLAND • Kraków

32°	34°	45°	55°	67°	72°	76°	73°	66°	56°	44°	37°
22°	22°	30°	38°	48°	54°	58°	56°	49°	42°	33°	28°
16	15	12	15	12	15	16	15	12	14	15	16

SLOVENIA • Ljubljana

36°	41°	50°	60°	68°	75°	80°	78°	71°	59°	47°	39°
25°	25°	32°	40°	48°	54°	57°	57°	51°	43°	36°	30°
7	7	7	9	10	9	6	6	6	7	9	9

Fahrenheit and Celsius Conversion

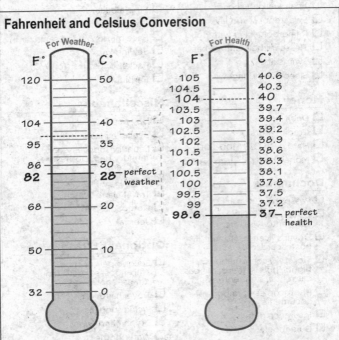

Europe takes its temperature using the Celsius scale, while we opt for Fahrenheit. For a rough conversion from Celsius to Fahrenheit, double the number and add 30. For weather, remember that 28°C is 82°F—perfect. For health, 37°C is just right. At a launderette, 30°C is cold, 40°C is warm (usually the default setting), 60°C is hot, and 95°C is boiling. Your air-conditioner should be set at about 20°C.

APPENDIX

Packing Checklist

Whether you're traveling for five days or five weeks, you won't need more than this. Pack light to enjoy the sweet freedom of true mobility.

Clothing

- ☐ 5 shirts: long- & short-sleeve
- ☐ 2 pairs pants (or skirts/capris)
- ☐ 1 pair shorts
- ☐ 5 pairs underwear & socks
- ☐ 1 pair walking shoes
- ☐ Sweater or warm layer
- ☐ Rainproof jacket with hood
- ☐ Tie, scarf, belt, and/or hat
- ☐ Swimsuit
- ☐ Sleepwear/loungewear

Money

- ☐ Debit card(s)
- ☐ Credit card(s)
- ☐ Hard cash (US $100-200)
- ☐ Money belt

Documents

- ☐ Passport
- ☐ Other required ID: Vaccine card, entry visa, etc.
- ☐ Driver's license, student ID, hostel card, etc.
- ☐ Tickets & confirmations: flights, hotels, trains, rail pass, car rental, sight entries
- ☐ Photocopies of important documents
- ☐ Insurance details
- ☐ Guidebooks & maps

Electronics

- ☐ Mobile phone
- ☐ Camera & related gear
- ☐ Tablet/ebook reader/laptop
- ☐ Headphones/earbuds
- ☐ Chargers & batteries
- ☐ Phone car charger & mount (or GPS device)
- ☐ Plug adapters

Toiletries

- ☐ Basics: soap, shampoo, toothbrush, toothpaste, floss, deodorant, sunscreen, brush/comb, etc.
- ☐ Medicines & vitamins
- ☐ First-aid kit
- ☐ Glasses/contacts/sunglasses
- ☐ Face masks & hand sanitizer
- ☐ Sewing kit
- ☐ Packet of tissues (for WC)
- ☐ Earplugs

Miscellaneous

- ☐ Day pack
- ☐ Sealable plastic baggies
- ☐ Laundry supplies: soap, laundry bag, clothesline, spot remover
- ☐ Small umbrella
- ☐ Travel alarm/watch
- ☐ Notepad & pen
- ☐ Journal

Optional Extras

- ☐ Second pair of shoes (flip-flops, sandals, tennis shoes, boots)
- ☐ Travel hairdryer
- ☐ Picnic supplies
- ☐ Disinfecting wipes
- ☐ Water bottle
- ☐ Fold-up tote bag
- ☐ Small flashlight
- ☐ Mini binoculars
- ☐ Small towel or washcloth
- ☐ Inflatable pillow/neck rest
- ☐ Tiny lock
- ☐ Address list (to mail postcards)
- ☐ Extra passport photos

APPENDIX

Pronouncing Central European Place Names

Remember that in all of these languages, j is pronounced as "y" and c is pronounced "ts." Diacritical markings over most consonants (such as č, š, ś, or ž) have the same effect as putting an h after it in English; for example, č is "ch," š or ś is "sh," ž is "zh."

Name	Pronounced
Auschwitz (Concentration Camp, Poland)	OWSH-vits
Birkenau (Concentration Camp, Poland)	BEER-keh-now
Bled (Slovenia)	bled (as it's spelled); locals say "blayd"
Bohinj (Slovenia)	BOH-heen
Bovec (Slovenia)	BOH-vets
Bratislava (Slovakia)	brah-tee-SLAH-vah
Budapest (Hungary)	BOO-dah-pest in English, BOO-daw-pesht in Hungarian
Český Krumlov (Czech Republic)	CHESS-key KROOM-lohv
Eger (Hungary)	EH-gehr
Gdańsk (Poland)	guh-DAYNSK
Gdynia (Poland)	guh-DIN-yah
Kazimierz (Poland)	kah-ZHEE-mezh
Kobarid (Slovenia)	KOH-bah-reed
Konopiště (Castle, Czech Republic)	KOH-noh-peesh-tyeh
Kraków (Poland)	KRACK-cow in English, KROCK-oof in Polish
Kutná Hora (Czech Republic)	KOOT-nah HO-rah
Ljubljana (Slovenia)	lyoob-lyee-AH-nah
Oświęcim (Poland)	ohsh-VEENCH-im
Praha (Czech name for Prague, Czech Republic)	PRAH-hah
Radovljica (Slovenia)	rah-DOH-vleet-suh
Soča (River Valley, Slovenia)	SOH-chah
Sopot (Poland)	SOH-poht
Terezín (Concentration Camp, Czech Republic)	TEH-reh-zeen
Vintgar (Gorge, Slovenia)	VEENT-gar
Vršič (Pass, Slovenia)	vur-SHEECH
Warszawa (Polish name for Warsaw, Poland)	vah-SHAH-vah
Wieliczka (Salt Mine, Poland)	veel-EECH-kah
Wien (German name for Vienna, Austria)	veen

APPENDIX

INDEX

A

A. Blikle (Warsaw): 390, 436–437
Academy of Fine Arts Painting Gallery (Vienna): 875, 903
Academy of Music, former (Budapest): 616, 647
Accommodation: See Sleeping; and specific destinations
Acropolis (Plovdiv): 1024, 1026
Adventure Park (Bled): 793
Airbnb: 24, 1092–1093, 1095
Airlines (airfares): 23, 1115
Airports: Bratislava, 944, 979; Budapest, 572–573; Gdańsk, 447; Kraków, 246–248; Ljubljana, 775–776, 802; Prague, 158–159; Vienna, 943–944, 979; Warsaw, 381–382
Ajda: 824
Aladár Bitskey Swimming Pool (Eger): 697
Albertina Museum (Vienna): 866, 874, 888–889
Albertinaplatz (Vienna): 866–867
Alexander Nevsky Cathedral (Sofia): 1017–1019
Almanac: Austria, 851; Bosnia-Herzegovina, 1001; Bulgaria, 1016; Croatia, 986; Czech Republic, 32; Hungary, 542; Montenegro, 1008; Poland, 219; Romania, 1038; Slovakia, 953; Slovenia, 714–715
Alpine Cheese Museum (Kobarid): 842
Alps, the: See Julian Alps
Amber: about, 471; exhibits, 448, 466, 470–472, 518; shopping for, 331, 334, 494
Amber Museum (Gdańsk): 448, 466, 470–472
Am Hof Square (Vienna): 897; eating, 933
Amphitheater (Pula): 994–995
Ancestors, researching: 1088–1089
Andersen, Hans Christian: 963
Andrássy út (Budapest): 565, 598–599, 610–616; cafés, 675; eating, 665–666; maps, 611, 655;

self-guided walk, 610–616; sleeping, 653–656
Apartment rentals: 24, 1092–1093, 1095–1096
Apicultural Museum (Radovljica): 809–812
Applied Arts Museum (Budapest): 622
Apponyi House (Bratislava): 959, 968
Apps: 26, 1102–1103; Budapest, 567, 581; Czech Republic, 56; language translation, 28; maps and navigation, 1085–1086, 1112–1113; messaging, 1103; payment, 26, 1080; ride sharing, 1108–1109; sightseeing, 1087, 1090; user reviews, 1093
Aqua Eger: 697–702
Aquariums: 508, 988
Aquincum (Budapest): 682–683
Arbanasi: 1034
Arbanasi Palace Hotel: 1034
"Arbeit Macht Frei" Gate (Auschwitz): 360
Archbishop's Palace (Eger), 690; (Kraków), 267–268; (Prague), 120
Archdiocesan Museum (Kraków): 273, 297–298
Armory (Gdańsk), 452, 463; (Kraków), 283; (Malbork Castle), 518–519
Artěl (Prague): 125, 126
Art Gallery of the Central Bohemian Region (Kutná Hora): 166
Art Nouveau: Bratislava, 959, 972; Budapest, 599, 616; Kraków, 258–259, 263, 268–269, 292; Ljubljana, 725, 735, 753; Prague, 70, 76, 77–78, 89, 95, 98–99, 105, 125, 126; Vienna, 871, 902, 903–904, 907
Art of the Orient (Kraków): 283
Artus Court (Gdańsk): 448, 458, 470; (Toruń), 529
Astronomical Clock (Gdańsk), 462; (Prague), 72–73
Astronomical Museum (Eger): 696
Athenaeum (Bucharest): 1040–1041

ATMs: 26, 1078–1082. *See also
    specific destinations*
Auction house, in Vienna: 870, 896
Audio Europe, Rick Steves: 26, 1117
Augustinian Church (Vienna): 887
Auschwitz-Birkenau: 12–13,
    356–374; guided tours, 254–255;
    maps, 357, 362, 370; orientation,
    357–359; reservations, 25, 358;
    self-guided tour, 359–373; tours,
    361, 374; transportation, 357, 374
Austria: 848–944; almanac, 851;
    climate, 1128; cuisine, 927–928;
    embassies, 1073; language, 851;
    tourist office, 1073. *See also*
    Vienna
Austrian National Library (Vienna):
    887–888

B

Bachkovo Monastery: 1027–1028
Balkan Mountains: 1030–1031
Balkan Peninsula: *See* Yugoslavia,
    understanding
Bálna Budapest: 605, 651
Banks (banking): alerting to travel,
    26. *See also* Money
Barber's Bridge (Český Krumlov):
    197
Barbican (Kraków), 255–256; (War-
    saw), 401
Bar mleczny: See Milk bars, in Poland
Baroque Library (Eger): 696
Baroque Theater (Český Krumlov):
    199, 201–202
Bârsana: 1059
Baščaršija (Sarajevo): 1002
Bata'a (Prague): 126
Batana boats, in Rovinj: 993
Baths: Budapest, 633–645; Eger,
    697–699; Egerszálok, 699–702;
    Sofia, 1020
Batliner Collection (Vienna): 889
Batthyány tér (Budapest): 566, 672
Bay of Kotor: 1007, 1009–1011
Beaches: Black Sea Coast, 1034–
    1035; Bled Lake, 792–793; Du-
    brovnik, 988; Hel Peninsula, 511;
    Hvar, 992; Korčula, 992; Rovinj,
    993; Sopot, 507; Split, 991
Bear Pits (Český Krumlov): 198
Beekeeping, in Slovenia: 712, 743,
    760–761, 793–794, 809–812
Beer: 1098; Czech Republic, 44,

45, 123, 147, 151–152, 205–206;
    Hungary, 557, 648–651, 706;
    Poland, 349, 353, 398, 536; Slova-
    kia, 974, 975; Slovenia, 718–719,
    759, 772
Belváros (Budapest): *See* Pest
    Downtown
Belvedere Palace (Vienna): 875,
    905–907
Beneš, Edvard: 37, 202–203
Berlin Wall (Gdańsk): 467
Biertan Church: 1053
Biking: Bled, 781–782, 784; Buda-
    pest, 575, 600; Český Krumlov,
    194; Kraków, 250, 254; Ljubljana,
    731; Prague, 57; Vienna, 860, 862
Birkenau: *See* Auschwitz-Birkenau
Biserica Stavropoleos Convent
    (Bucharest): 1041
Bishop Erazm Ciołek Palace
    (Kraków): 272–273, 294
Black Church (Brașov): 1048
Black Light Theater (Prague):
    127–128
Black Madonna House (Prague): 76
Black Madonna of Czestochowa:
    257–258, 400, 465–466
Black Sea Coast: 1034–1035
Black Tower (Brașov): 1048
Blagaj: 1006
Bled: 778–802; eating, 799–801;
    helpful hints, 781; map, 782–783;
    nightlife, 795; sights/activities,
    786–795; sleeping, 796–798; tour-
    ist information, 779–780; tours,
    785; transportation, 780–781,
    784, 801–802
Bled, Lake: 14, 777–778, 786–789,
    792–793; boating, 787, 788, 790,
    792; guided tours, 785; maps, 779,
    804–805; swimming, 792–793
Bled Adventure Park: 793
Bled Car Train: 830–831
Bled Castle: 789–792
Bled Island: 787–789
Blejska Grad: 789–792
Blejski Otok: 787–789
Blue Church of St. Elisabeth
    (Bratislava): 972
Boat travel and cruises: map, 1107;
    Bled Lake, 787, 788, 790, 792;
    Bohinj Lake, 815; Bratislava, 978;
    Budapest, 582, 603–604; Croatia,
    986; Danube River, 582, 603–

604, 978; Gdańsk, 503; Gdynia, 503, 510; Hel Peninsula, 503, 511; Ljubljana, 732; Vltava River, 206–207; Westerplatte, 503

Bohemia: 31, 33; map, 31. *See also* Český Krumlov; Prague

Bohinj, Lake: 813–816

Boka waterfall: 829

Bone Church (Kutná Hora): 169–171

Books, recommended: 1122–1123

Border crossings: 1074, 1110; and VAT, 1084–1085

Bosch, Hieronymus: 903

Bosnia-Herzegovina: 17, 982–983, 998–1006; almanac, 1001; cuisine, 999–1000; currency, 1001; history, 1001; map, 999; top destinations, 1000–1006; tourist office, 1073; transportation, 998–999

Bosnian convertible marks: 1001

Bosnian Jewish Museum (Sarajevo): 1002

Bosnian language: 1000

Bovec: 828–829, 832–837; eating, 828–829, 836; sights/activities, 828–829, 833–834; sleeping, 834–835; tourist information, 832; transportation, 832, 837

Bovec Airport: 834

Boyadzhiev, Zlatyu: 1024

Boyana Church (Sofia): 1021

Bożego Ciała street (Kraków): 306–307

Boznańska, Olga: 263, 413

Bran Castle: 1049

Brașov: 1036–1037, 1046, 1048–1049; castles near, 1049, 1051; eating, 1049; sleeping, 1049

Bratislava: 17, 948–979; eating, 974–977; helpful hints, 949–951; history of, 962–963; maps, 954–956; planning tips, 948–949; self-guided walk, 952–965; sights/activities, 952–973; sleeping, 973–974; tourist information, 949; tours, 951–952; transportation, 977–979

Bratislava Airport: 944, 979

Bratislava Castle and Museum: 969–970

Bratislava City Card: 949

Bratislava City History Museum: 959, 967–968

Bratislava City Theater: 960

Bratislava Main Square: 958–959, 966–967

Bratislava Old Market Hall: 960, 975–976

Bratislava Old Town Hall: 958–959

Bratislava Promenade Square: 961–963; eating, 976

Bratislavská (Bratislava): 975

"Broadway Quarter" (Budapest): 612–613

Broz, Josip: *See* Tito

Brukenthal Museum (Sibiu): 1054–1055

Bucharest: 1036, 1040–1044; eating, 1044; sleeping, 1044

Bucovina: 1037, 1061–1065

Buda (Budapest): 565–567, 622–634; at a glance, 587; baths, 640–645; cafés, 675; eating, 671–672; maps, 623, 660; sights, 622–634; sleeping, 657, 661

Buda Hills (Budapest): 632

Budapest: 14, 563–677; at a glance, 586–587; arrival in, 567–573; baths, 633–645; best views, 576; cafés, 673–674; eating, 662–675; entertainment, 645–648; excursion areas, 678–684; helpful hints, 573–576; history of, 568; layout of, 564–567; neighborhoods, 564–567; nightlife, 648–651; planning tips, 563–564; rip-offs, 573–574; shopping, 651–653; sights/activities, 583–645; sleeping, 653–661; tourist information, 567; tours, 581–583; transportation, 567–573, 576–581, 675–677. *See also specific neighborhoods*

Budapest Card: 567, 577

Budapest City Park: 586, 620; map, 618–619

Budapest Great Synagogue: 586, 606–609

Budapest History Museum: 626, 628

Budapest Liszt Ferenc Airport: 572–573

Budapest Museum of Ethnography: 617–618

Budapest Museum of Fine Arts: 617

Budapest Retro Experience: 599

Budapest Spring Festival: 1120

Budapest Uprising (1956): *See* Hungarian Uprising

Budgeting: 23–24
Budva Riviera: 1007, 1012–1013
Buje: 994
Bulgaria: 17, 983, 1014–1035; alma-nac, 1016; cuisine, 1015–1016; currency, 1016; history, 1016; map, 1015; top destinations, 1017–1035; tours, 1017; transpor-tation, 1014–1015
Bulgarian language: 1017
Bull's Blood (wine): 558, 685, 702, 703
Buna River: 1006
Burggarten (Vienna): 888
Burg Kino (Vienna): 918
Buses (bus travel): 1108; best three-week trip, 20–21; map, 1107; Auschwitz, 374; Bled, 780, 801; Bohinj Lake, 813–814; Bosnia-Herzegovina, 998–999; Bratislava, 978; Budapest, 580, 582, 676; Bulgaria, 1014–1015; Český Krumlov, 192, 214; Eger, 687, 706–707; Gdańsk, 447; Ju-lian Alps, 818; Kraków, 245–246, 249, 355; Ljubljana, 727, 730–731, 774–775; Prague, 58–61, 158; Romania, 1039; Toruń, 527, 537; Vienna, 856–857, 858–859, 861–862, 943; Warsaw, 382, 386, 442
Bush, George H. W.: 597
Butchers' Bridge (Ljubljana): 740
Butterfly House (Vienna): 888
Buzludzha: 1030–1031

C
Cabs: 1108–1109; tipping, 1082. See also specific destinations
Café Mondieu (Bratislava): 959
Café Sacher (Vienna): 865–866
Café Tirolerhof (Vienna): 867, 938
Camera obscura: 696–697
Canadian embassies and consulates: 1074
Canaletto: 391, 393, 405, 898
Canyoning: 832
Caravaggio: 898–899
Car insurance: 1112
Car rentals: 23, 1109–1112. See also specific destinations
Car travel (driving): 1113–1115; dis-tance and time, 1111; navigation options, 1112–1113; road signs,

1113; Bay of Kotor, 1009–1010; Bled, 780–781, 802, 830–831; Bohinj Lake, 814; Bosnia-Herzegovina, 999; Budapest, 573, 677; Bulgaria, 1015; Český Krumlov, 192; Eger, 687; Julian Alps, 818–832; Konopiště Castle, 186; Kraków, 246; Ljubljana, 727; Montenegro, 1007–1008; Romania, 1039
Casinos: 830, 867
Castle Gardens (Český Krumlov): 203
Castle Hill (Budapest): 565–566, 622–632; cafés, 632, 675; eating, 671–672; map, 623
Castle Quarter (Prague): 51–52, 105–124; at a glance, 65; eating, 147–148; maps, 106–107, 134–135
Castle Square (Prague): 119–120
Castle Square (Warsaw): 387, 397–399, 402–403
Cathedral of the Nativity of the Virgin (Veliko Tarnovo): 1033
Cathedral of Two Saint Johns (Toruń): 530–531
Cavtat: 1010
Ceaușescu, Nicolae: 1036, 1038, 1041, 1042, 1043–1044, 1046, 1048
Celetná street (Prague): 58, 76, 124
Cell (mobile) phones: 26, 1102–1103. See also Apps
"Central Europe": use of term, 7–8
Central Mineral Baths (Sofia): 1020
Central Park (Cluj): 1056
Ceremonial Hall (Prague): 87
Černín Palace (Prague): 123–124
České Budějovice: 213–214
Český Krumlov: 12, 190–214; eating, 212–213; helpful hints, 192, 194; history of, 202–203; layout of, 191–192; map, 193; planning tips, 191; self-guided walk, 195–199; sights/activities, 194–209; sleeping, 209–211; tour-ist information, 192; tours, 194; transportation, 192, 213–214
Český Krumlov Castle: 197–203
Český Krumlov Main Square: 196–197
Český Krumlov Museum of Re-gional History: 195–196, 205
Český Krumlov Synagogue: 204

Cetinje: 1011, 1013

Chain Bridge (Budapest): 564, 599–600

Changing of the Guard: Budapest, 628; Prague, 110–111; Warsaw, 395

Charles Bridge (Prague): 52, 57, 64, 82–83; map, 68–69

Charles IV Square (Prague): 80–81

Charles University (Prague): 76–77

Chełmoński, Józef: 286, 287, 412

Chocolate: 233, 390, 436–437, 763, 808, 871

Chopin, Fryderyk: 391, 397, 413–414, 428–429, 530; birth house (Zelazowa Wola), 414; concerts, 414, 428, 430–431; Museum (Warsaw), 413–414, 431

Chopin International Airport (Warsaw): 381

Christ Bearing the Cross statue (Warsaw): 392

Christmas markets: 19, 959

Church of the Assumption (Lake Bled): 788

Church of the Nativity (Arbanasi): 1034

Church of the Nuns of the Visitation (Warsaw): 392–393

Cimrman, Jára: 31, 40

Citadella (Budapest): 633

City Museum of Ljubljana: 733, 747

Civic Center (Bucharest): 1041, 1043

Classroom Europe, Rick Steves: 26, 1116–1117

Climate: 1128–1129

Cloth Hall (Kraków): 252, 264–265, 284–288, 331

Clothing sizes: 1128

Cluj-Napoca: 1055–1056

Cobblers' Bridge (Ljubljana): 725, 745

Coffee, Viennese: 936–937

Cold War Museum (Prague): 64–65, 94–95

Cold War Museum (Warsaw): 400

Collegium Maius (Kraków): 266–267, 296–297

Comăneci, Nadia: 1038

Communism: 1068–1071; Bulgaria, 1019–1021, 1024, 1030, 1034; Czech Republic, 37–38, 92–96, 98, 101–102, 104; Hungary,

550–552, 568, 677–682; Poland, 225–227, 328–330, 386, 388–389; Romania, 1041, 1042, 1057; Slovakia, 950–951, 970–972

Communism Museum (Prague): 65, 98

Concentration camps: Auschwitz-Birkenau, 356–374; Terezín, 175–185

Congress Square (Ljubljana): 748–749

Consulates: 1073–1074

Contemporary History Museum (Ljubljana): 733, 758–759

Cooperative Bank (Ljubljana): 738

Copernicus, Nicolaus: 123, 222, 266, 327, 390–391, 416, 529–530; House (Toruń), 534–535

Copernicus Science Center (Warsaw): 387, 414–415

Čopova (Ljubljana): 735

Coppersmiths' Street (Mostar): 1005

Corvin Castle: 1055

Cosău River Valley: 1059

Costs of trip: 23–24

Costume jewelry and beads, shopping for: 125–126

Court Theater (Budapest): 628

Covid-19 pandemic: 231; entry requirements, 1072

Cracow: See Kraków

"Craftspeople Street" (Veliko Tarnovo): 1032–1033

Crane (Gdańsk): 459, 473

Credit cards: 26, 1078–1082, 1112

Croatia: 17, 982, 984–997; accommodations, overview, 985–986; almanac, 986; cuisine, 986–987; history, 986; map, 985; overview, 984–987; top destinations, 987–997; tourist office, 1073

Croatian kunas: 986, 1001

Croatian language: 987

Croatian Museum of Naive Art (Zagreb): 995–996

Croatian Parliament (Zagreb): 995

Croatian wines: 989, 994

Crooked House (Sopot): 506

Crown Treasury (Kraków): 283

Cruises: See Boat travel and cruises

Cuisine: See Eating; and specific destinations

Čumil (Bratislava): 961

Curie, Marie: 402; Museum (Warsaw), 387, 401, 408
Currency and exchange: 1078–1080; Bosnia-Herzegovina, 1001; Bulgaria, 1016; Croatia, 986; Czech Republic, 32, 1079; Hungary, 542, 574, 1079; Montenegro, 1008; Poland, 219, 1079; Romania, 1038; Slovakia, 953; Slovenia, 714
Customs regulations: 1085
Cyril and Methodius Square (Ljubljana): 741
Cyrillic alphabet: 1000, 1009, 1017, 1018, 1100–1101
Czartoryski Museum (Kraków): 252, 258, 288–292
Czech crowns: 32, 1079
Czech dumplings *(knedlíky):* 42, 149
Czech language: 44, 46–48; restaurant phrases, 48; survival phrases, 47
Czech Museum of Silver (Kutná Hora): 166, 169, 173–174
Czech Philharmonic (Prague): 128
Czech puppets: 125, 205
Czech Republic: 30–214; at a glance, 12; almanac, 32; climate, 1128; cuisine, 41–43, 139–140; currency, 32, 1079; embassies, 1073; helpful hints, 33; history, 33–39, 202–203; map, 31; movies, 1123–1124; overview, 30–46; today, 39, 41; tourist office, 1073. *See also* Český Krumlov; Prague
Czech State Opera (Prague): 129

D

Dalmatian Coast: 984, 987–992
Dalmatian Islands: 991–992
Danube Bend: 683–684
Danube Canal (Vienna): 917; eating, 934
Danube Promenade (Budapest): 603–604
Danube River: Bratislava, 948, 978; Budapest, 563, 564–565, 582, 599–601, 603–604, 683; cruises, 582, 603–604, 978; Vienna, 852
Da Vinci, Leonardo: 290–291
Deák Ferenc utca (Budapest): 602
Deák ter (Budapest): 610
Debit cards: 26, 1078–1082
De Gaulle, Charles: 388, 395

Déli/Southern Station (Budapest): 572
Demel (Vienna): 871
Demjén Thermal Baths (Egerszálok): 700–702
Dining: *See* Eating; *and specific destinations*
Dinosaurs: 605–606, 755–756, 901–902
Diocletian: 986, 989–990
Discounts: *See* Money-saving tips
Dísz tér (Budapest): 628
Divine Mercy Sanctuary (Kraków): 318–320
Dlouhá street (Prague): 126, 144
Dobó, István: 691–692
Dobó Square (Eger): 691–693
Dobó utca (Budapest): 693
Dobrá Čajovna (Český Krumlov), 213; (Kutná Hora), 174; (Prague), 154
Dominican Church (Kraków): 271–272, 297
Dominican Monastery (Dubrovnik): 988
Donaukanal (Vienna): 917
Dornk Excursion Farm: 794–795
Dorotheum (Vienna): 870, 896
Dracula: 1046, 1049, 1050, 1051–1052
Dragon Bridge (Ljubljana): 740–741
Driving: *See* Car travel
Dubček, Alexander: 37, 93, 95
Dubrovnik: 987–989; eating, 988–989; sleeping, 988
Dubrovnik Cathedral: 987–988
Dubrovnik City Walls: 988
Dürer, Albrecht: 617, 866, 888
Dzhumaya Mosque (Plovdiv): 1026

E

Easter: 1120; in Poland, 220
"Eastern Europe": use of term, 7
Eastern Orthodox Church: overview, 1025
Eating: 1097–1102; Austria, 851, 927–928; Bosnia-Herzegovina, 999–1000; budgeting, 23; Bulgaria, 1015–1016; Croatia, 986–987; Czech Republic, 41–43, 139–140; Hungary, 554–557; money-saving tips, 24; Montenegro, 1008; Poland, 231–235; restaurant pricing and hours, 1099, 1102; Romania,

1039; Slovakia, 974–975; Slovenia, 717–720, 769, 800. *See also specific destinations*

Economy: Austria, 851; Czech Republic, 32; Hungary, 542; Poland, 219, 231; Slovakia, 953; Slovenia, 713

Eger: 14, 685–707; baths, 697–699; eating, 705–706; helpful hints, 688; map, 686; planning tips, 686–687; self-guided walk, 688–693; sights/activities, 688–693; sleeping, 703–704; tourist information, 687; transportation, 687, 706–707

Eger Castle: 693–695
Eger Cathedral: 689–690
Eger Lyceum: 688–689, 695–697
Eger Market Hall: 688
Eger Minaret: 692
Egerszalók: 703; baths, 699–702, 707; wineries, 703
Eger Thermal Bath: 698
Eger Town Hall: 691
Eger Turkish Bath: 698–699
Eger wine: 558, 685, 687, 693, 699, 702, 703, 706
Elaphite Islands: 988
Electricity: 1075
Elektrownia Powiśle (Warsaw): 415, 437, 439–440
Elisabeth, Empress: *See* Sisi, Empress
Elisabeth Bridge (Budapest): 564–565
Embassies: 1073–1074
Emergencies: 1073. *See also specific destinations*
Emigration Museum (Gdynia): 508–511
Entertainment: budgeting, 23. *See also* Music; *and specific destinations*
Environmental footprint (going green): 1078
Equitable Building (Vienna): 869
Estates Theater (Prague): 76, 129
Esztergom Basilica: 683–684
Eszterházy tér (Eger): 688–689
ETIAS (European Travel Information and Authorization System): 25, 1072–1073
Euphemia, Saint: 993
Euro currency: 713, 953, 1008, 1079

European Solidarity Center (Gdańsk): 448, 480–485, 502
European Union (EU): 1083; Bulgaria, 1016; Czech Republic, 39; Hungary, 552–553; Montenegro, 1008; Poland, 227–228; Slovenia, 710–711, 716
Eurovea (Bratislava): 965, 972–973; eating, 976–977
Events: *See* Festivals
Exchange rates: *See* Currency and exchange

F

Fahrenheit, Daniel: 455, 458
Fairy Tale House (Český Krumlov): 205
Falk, Peter: 601
Falk Miksa utca (Budapest): 592, 601, 651
"Fashion Street" (Budapest): 602
Ferhadija (Sarajevo): 1002
Festivals: 1119–1121; Český Krumlov, 192, 194, 1119, 1120; Vienna, 917–918, 1120
Films, recommended: 1123–1127
Fishermen's Bastion (Budapest): 632
Fishmarket Square (Gdańsk): 473
Flag: Austria, 851; Czech Republic, 32; Hungary, 542; Poland, 219; Slovakia, 953; Slovenia, 713
Florian Gate (Kraków): 257–258
Floriańska street (Kraków): 258–259
Foksal street (Warsaw): 390, 436
Fontanna Cosmopolis (Toruń): 535
Food. *See also* Eating; *and specific destinations*
Food tours: Bled, 785; Kraków, 254; Vienna, 861; Warsaw, 383, 386
Fortified Saxon churches, in Romania: 1052–1054
Forum (Gdańsk): 452, 494
Forum Przestrzenie (Kraków): 340
Fountain of Three Carniolian Rivers (Ljubljana): 742–743
Franciscan Garden (Prague): 97
Franciscan Monastery (Dubrovnik): 988
Frank, Anne: 364
Franz Ferdinand, Archduke of Austria: 184, 185–189, 873, 880, 891, 1002
Franz Josef, Emperor: 187, 547, 575, 610, 612, 630, 683, 725, 741, 876,

927, 1019, 1045; biographical sketch, 882; Hofburg (Vienna), 872–873, 879–883; Schönbrunn (Vienna), 909–912
Franz-Josefs-Bahnhof (Vienna): 942
Franz Liszt Academy of Music (Budapest): 613, 647
Franz Liszt Museum (Budapest): 616
Franz Liszt Square (Budapest): 613, 648–649
French Revolution Square (Ljubljana): 748
Freud, Sigmund: 88; Museum (Vienna), 908
Freud (Sigmund) Museum (Vienna): 908
Fruit Market (Prague): 76
Fryderyk Chopin International Airport (Warsaw): 381
Füzesabony: 706

G
Gabrovo: 1031
Galerija Emporium (Ljubljana): 735
Galicia Jewish Museum (Kraków): 309
Gallery of Masterpieces (Warsaw): 406
Gallery of 19th-Century Polish Art (Kraków): 252, 265, 284–288
Garnets, shopping for: 125
GASK (Kutná Hora): 166
Gazi Husrev-Bey Mosque (Sarajevo): 1002
Gdańsk: 13, 443–503; at a glance, 448; eating, 499–502; entertainment, 494–495; excursion areas, 503–511; history of, 454–455, 476–477, 479; layout of, 445–446; maps, 450–451, 496–497, 504; planning tips, 443–445; self-guided walks, 449–467; shopping, 494; sights/activities, 449–494; sleeping, 495–499; tourist information, 446; tours, 447, 449; transportation, 446–447, 502–503
Gdańsk, Historical Zone of the Free City of: 458, 472
Gdańsk Archaeological Museum: 459, 472
Gdańsk Armory: 452, 463
Gdańsk Main Town: *See* Main Town

Gdańsk Main Town Hall: 448, 457, 468–470
Gdańsk Market Hall: 464
Gdańsk National Maritime Museum: 472–473
Gdańsk Old Town Hall: 467
Gdańsk Shakespeare Theater: 473
Gdańsk Shipyard: 445, 448, 467, 474–480
Gdańsk Tourist Card: 446
Gdynia: 503, 507–5511
Gellért Baths (Budapest): 587, 633–634, 640–643; map, 642
Gellért Hill (Budapest): 566, 633–634
Genealogical research: 1088–1089
Geography: Austria, 851; Bosnia-Herzegovina, 1001; Bulgaria, 1016; Croatia, 986; Czech Republic, 32; Hungary, 542; Montenegro, 1008; Poland, 219; Romania, 1038; Slovakia, 953; Slovenia, 713
Georgian cuisine: 234
Gerbeaud (Budapest): 602
German language: 851, 1101; restaurant phrases, 946; survival phrases, 945
Ghetto Heroes Square (Kraków), 311; (Warsaw), 417–418
Gingerbread: 530, 532, 534, 813
Gingerbread Museum (Toruń): 534
Gloriette (Vienna): 912
Gödöllő Royal Palace (Budapest): 683
Golden Gate (Gdańsk), 452–453; (Prague), 116
Golden Lane (Prague): 118
GoOpti (Slovenia): 773–776, 801–802
Goose That Laid the Golden Egg (Toruń): 532
Gornji trg (Ljubljana): 744, 769
Government: Austria, 851; Czech Republic, 32, 39, 41; Hungary, 542, 553–554; Poland, 219, 228–229; Slovakia, 953; Slovenia, 713, 716–717. *See also* Parliament
Gozsdu Udvar (Budapest): 609, 650, 665
Graben (Vienna): 869–870
Gradec (Zagreb): 995
Granary Island (Gdańsk): 459, 498–499
Grand Canyon of Soča: 827

Grand Hotel Sopot: 507
Grand Hotel Union (Ljubljana): 735, 738
Great Boulevard (Budapest): 565; cafés, 674
Great Kozjak Waterfall: 842–843
Great Market Hall (Budapest): 586, 604–605, 651, 670–671
Great Mill (Gdańsk): 466
Great Synagogue (Budapest): 586, 606–609
Green Gate (Gdańsk): 458
Gresham Palace (Budapest): 599
Grodzka street (Kraków): 269–272; milk bars, 350–351
Grožnjan: 994
Grunwald Monument (Kraków): 257
Guidebooks, Rick Steves: 1116; updates, 27, 1116
Gura Humorului: sleeping, 1065
Gutenberg Printing House Museum (Kutná Hora): 166
Gypsies: See Roma

H
Haas Haus (Vienna): 869
Habsburg Empire: overview, 7–8, 35–36, 122, 546–548, 714–715, 848–849, 986. See also specific rulers and sights
Hajós utca (Budapest): 653
Hala Koszyki (Warsaw): 438
Halik, Tony: 535
"Hatters Street" (Bratislava): 959
Hauptmann House (Ljubljana): 735
Haus der Musik (Vienna): 874, 877, 895–896, 913
Havel, Václav: 30–31, 38, 39, 95, 96, 122, 485
Havelská Market (Prague): 64, 79, 124, 139–140
Havlíček Square (Kutná Hora): 168–169
Haydn, Joseph: 873, 876, 896, 965
Heldenplatz (Vienna): 873, 876
Hel Peninsula: 503, 511
Hemingway, Ernest: 715, 825, 826, 837, 841
Herceg Novi: 1010
Heroes' Square (Budapest): 586, 616–617; map, 618–619
Heurigen, in Vienna: 938–940
Heweliusz Park (Gdańsk): 466

Heydrich, Reinhard: 36
High Synagogue (Kraków): 310
Hiking: Bled, 786, 789–790; Budapest, 622, 624; Český Krumlov, 206; Kobarid, 843; Kotor, 1011–1012; Kozjak Waterfall, 842–843; Motovun, 994; Mount Triglav, 822, 824–825; Plitvice Lakes, 996–997; Savica Waterfall, 816; Sirens' Valley, 702–703; Split, 991; Vintgar Gorge, 803, 806; Vogel Mountain, 815–816
Hill of the Cross (Český Krumlov): 206
Hindliyan House (Plovdiv): 1024
Hiša Franko (Kobarid): 846
Historical Zone of the Free City of Gdańsk: 458, 472
History: understanding Yugoslavia, 1066–1071. See also Communism; Habsburg Empire; World War I; World War II; and specific destinations
Hockey: 785, 820
Hofburg Palace (Vienna): 872–873, 874, 877–889; eating, 878–879, 929; Imperial Apartments, 872–873, 874, 879–883; map, 878; Treasury, 873, 874, 883–885; World Museum Vienna, 873, 874, 885–886
Holešovice Train Station (Prague): 157–158
Holidays: 1119–1121
Hollein, Hans: 869
Holocaust Memorial (Bratislava): 963–964
Holocaust Memorial Center (Budapest): 586, 621–622
Holocaust Monument (Budapest): 593
Holy Cross Chapel (Kraków): 277–278
Holy Cross Chapel (Prague): 110
Holy Cross Church (Warsaw): 391–392
Holy House (Prague): 124
Holy Trinity Cathedral (Sibiu): 1054
Holy Trinity Church (Kraków): 297
Holy Trinity Plague Column (Vienna): 870
Horní Bridge (Český Krumlov): 195
Horní Street (Český Krumlov): 195–196

Horseback riding: 732

Horse market, in Ocna Şugatag: 1059

Horses, Lipizzaner stallions, in Vienna: 875, 886–887

Hospital in the Rock and Nuclear Bunker (Budapest): 587, 632

Hostel Celica (Ljubljana): 730, 762, 768

Hostels: overview, 1096–1097. *See also specific destinations*

Hotels: overview, 1092–1095; rates and deals, 23–24, 1091–1092; reservations, 1096–1097. *See also specific destinations*

Hotel Bristol (Warsaw): 393, 433–434

Hotel Růže (Český Krumlov): 196

Hotel u Prince (Prague): 57, 145

Hot springs: *See* Baths

House by the Bell (Prague): 72

House of Music Hungary (Budapest): 586, 618–619, 647

House of Terror (Budapest): 586, 613–616

House of the Batana Boat (Rovinj): 993

House of the Black Madonna (Prague): 76

Hradčany (Prague): *See* Castle Quarter

Hrádek Castle (Kutná Hora): 173–174

Huet Square (Sibiu): 1054

Humor Monastery: 1065

Hundertwasserhaus (Vienna): 907

Hunedoara Castle: 1055

Hungária Koncert (Budapest): 648

Hungarian Agriculture Museum (Budapest): 620

Hungarian forints: 542, 574, 1079

Hungarian Jewish Museum (Budapest): 608

Hungarian language: 559–562, 1100–1101; restaurant phrases, 562; survival phrases, 561

Hungarian National Gallery (Budapest): 587, 626

Hungarian National Museum (Budapest): 587, 605–606

Hungarian Parliament (Budapest): 575, 583, 586, 588–589; tickets, 25, 588

Hungarian State Opera House (Budapest): 586, 610, 612, 646–647

Hungarian Uprising (1956): 551, 568, 590–591, 592–593, 682; monuments, in Budapest, 575, 592–593, 615–616

Hungary: 540–707; at a glance, 14; almanac, 542; climate, 1128; cuisine, 554–557; currency, 542, 574, 1079; embassies, 1074; helpful hints, 542–543; history, 543–552; LGBTQ+ travel, 1076–1077; map, 541; movies, 1125; overview, 540–562; today, 552–554; tourist office, 1073. *See also* Budapest; Eger

Hunger Wall (Prague): 104

Hunyadi, János: 545, 627, 1055

Hus, Jan: 31, 34–35, 40, 67–68, 77, 112, 122, 170, 1121; biographical sketch, 71; Memorial (Prague), 67–68

Hvar Island: 991–992

Hviezdoslavovo Námestie (Bratislava): 961–963; eating, 976

I

Idrija: 830

Image Theater (Prague): 127–128

Imperial Apartments (Hofburg; Vienna): 872–873, 874, 879–883

Imperial Apartments (Schönbrunn Palace; Vienna): 909–913

Imperial Carriage Museum (Vienna): 913

Imperial Crypt (Vienna): 868, 874, 889, 891

Imperial Furniture Collection (Vienna): 875, 909–910

Imperial Music Chapel (Vienna): 873, 914

Independence Square (Sofia): 1019

In der Burg (Vienna): 873

Infant of Prague: 104

Information: 1073. *See also specific destinations*

Internet security: 1103

Isaac Synagogue (Kraków): 306, 340, 352

Iskra-Kazanlak Historical Museum (Kazanlak): 1029–1030

Istria: 984, 993–995; transportation, 774–775. *See also* Rovinj

Istrian hill towns: 994

István (Stephen), Saint: 544, 598, 631–632, 633, 683–684, 691, 693–694, 1121
Italian Court (Kutná Hora): 169
Italian Mausoleum (Kobarid): 840, 842
Italy: Predel Pass, 831
Itineraries: designing your own, 18–19, 22; top destinations, 12–17. *See also specific destinations*

J
Jadrolinija: 986
Jadwiga, Saint: 221–222, 277, 521
Jagiellonian University (Kraków): 266–267, 296–297
Jalta Hotel (Prague): 94–95
J & L Lobmeyr Crystal (Vienna): 868
Jan Hus Memorial (Prague): 67–68
Janković, Zoran: 716, 725, 740
Jankowski, Henryk: 465–466
Jasna: 823
Jászai Mari Tér (Budapest): 601
Jelačić Square (Zagreb): 995
Jerusalem Avenue (Warsaw): 386, 388
Jesenice: 819–820
Jewish Cemeteries (Kraków): 253, 301–302, 303, 309–310
Jewish Community Center (Kraków): 310
Jewish Ghetto (Warsaw): 416–424
Jewish Local History Collection of Elisabethtown (Budapest): 610
Jewish (Judenplatz) Memorial (Vienna): 897
Jewish Museums (Budapest), 608; (Kraków), 309; (Prague), 83–88; (Sarajevo), 1002; (Vienna), 897; (Warsaw), 418, 420–423
Jewish Quarter (Budapest): 583, 605–610; eating, 662–665. *See also* Seventh Disrict
Jewish Quarter (Kraków): *See* Kazimierz
Jewish Quarter (Prague): 51, 64, 83–89; eating, 145; guided tours, 66; map, 84; shopping, 125
John of Nepomuk, Saint: 82–83, 115, 197
John Paul II, Pope (Karol Wojtyła): 240, 241, 247, 266–268, 317–324, 391–392, 393–394, 475, 478, 484,

631, 742, 809, 1125; Archdiocesan Museum (Kraków), 273, 297–298; biographical sketch, 270–271; Chapel (Kraków), 277; Family Home Museum (Wadowice), 322–324; Great Sanctuary (Kraków), 320–321; Wawel Cathedral Museum (Kraków), 278–279
John Paul II Great Sanctuary (Kraków): 320–321
John Paul II Kraków-Balice Airport: 246–248
Jósef, Attila: 593
Josefov (Prague): *See* Jewish Quarter
Josefsplatz (Vienna): 872, 886
Joyce, James: 144
Józefa street (Kraków): 307, 334, 340
Jože Plečnik House (Ljubljana): 733, 748, 752–754
Judah Square (Kraków): 308, 351–352
Julian Alps: 14, 817–846; map, 820–821; planning tips, 817–818; self-guided driving tour, 818–832; tours, 784, 818; transportation, 818. *See also* Bled

K
Kaffee Mayer (Bratislava): 959
Kafka, Franz: 88, 94, 1123
Kaiserappartements (Vienna): 872–873, 874, 879–883
Kaisergruft (Vienna): 868, 874, 889, 891
Kaiserliche Schatzkammer Wien (Vienna): 873, 874, 883–885
Kampa Island (Prague): 101–102
Kanonicza street (Kraków): 272–273
Kapana (Plovdiv): 1026
Karlova street (Prague): 58, 80, 124–125
Karlskirche (Vienna): 875, 903
Karlsplatz (Vienna): 902
Kärntner Gate (Vienna): 865
Kärntner Strasse (Vienna): 853, 867–868
Karski, Jan: 302–303, 417–418
Kazanlak: 1028–1029; sleeping, 1029–1030
Kazimierz (Kraków): 240–241, 298–310; eating, 351–354; maps, 301, 338, 352; nightlife, 337–340,

354; shopping, 334; sights,
298–310; sleeping, 346
Kazimierz (the Great): 221, 246,
261, 264, 275, 277, 279, 300
Kazimierz Market Square (Kraków):
307–308
Kazimierz Monument (Kraków):
300
Keleti/Eastern Station (Budapest):
569
Kinský Palace (Prague): 70
Király utca (Budapest): 652–653
Klagenfurt Airport: 776
Klášterní Pivovar (Prague): 123, 147
Klausen Synagogue (Prague): 87
Klauzál Market (Budapest): 665
Klementinum (Prague): 80
Klet' Mountain: 195
Klezmer music, in Kraków: 303,
304, 337–340
Klimt, Gustav: 902–906
Kluže Fortress: 828
Knin Cable Car (Bovec): 834
Kobarid: 829, 837–846; eating, 845–
846; map, 838; sights/activities,
829, 838–844; sleeping, 844–845;
tourist information, 837–838
Kobarid Museum: 829, 838–840
Kohlmarkt (Vienna): 871
Kolbe, Saint Maksymilian: 268, 365,
366–367, 689
Kolodko Minis: 596
Kolovrat Outdoor Museum (Ko-
barid): 843–844
Konopiště Castle: 185–189
Konstantsalieva House (Arbanasi):
1034
Korčula: 992
Korczak, Janusz: 419, 422
Kościuszko, Tadeusz: 223, 274, 278,
285–286, 331, 405
Kościuszko Mound (Kraków):
330–331
Koski Mehmet-Pasha Mosque
(Mostar): 1005
Kosmatka: 1028–1029
Kossuth, Lajos: 592
Kossuth tér (Budapest): 589,
592–593
Kostnice v Sedlci (Kutná Hora):
169–171
Kotor: 1010–1012; eating, 1012;
sleeping, 1012
Kotor City Walls: 1011–1012

Kozjak Waterfall: 842–843
Krakovo (Ljubljana): 726, 748
Kraków: 12, 239–355; at a glance,
252–253; eating, 346–354;
entertainment, 335–340; helpful
hints, 248–249; history, 246–247;
layout of, 240–241; maps,
242–243, 301, 332–333, 338,
344–345, 352; neighborhoods,
240–241; planning tips, 239–240;
self-guided walk, 255–273;
shopping, 331–335; sights/activi-
ties, 255–331; sleeping, 341–346;
tourist information, 241, 244;
tours, 250–255; transportation,
244–248, 249–250, 355
Kraków City Walls: 255–256
Kraków Cloth Hall: 252, 264–265,
284–288, 331
Kraków Ethnographic Museum:
307–308
Kraków Main Market Square: 252,
262, 264; eating, 346–347; enter-
tainment, 335
Krakowskie Przedmieście (Warsaw):
390–397
Kraków Tourist Card: 241
Kraków Town Hall Tower: 265–266
Kralov Med Beehive Demonstration
(Selo): 793–794
Kranjc Tourist Farm: 845
Kranjska Gora: 822
Križanke Theater (Ljubljana):
747–748
Křížový Vrch: 206
Krumlov Castle (Český Krumlov):
197–203
Krzysztofory Palace (Kraków): 296
Kubicki Arcades (Warsaw):
406–407
Kucinich, Dennis: 986
Kugy, Julius: 825
Kukliński, Ryszard: 400
Kunst Haus Wien Museum (Vi-
enna): 875, 907
Kunsthistorisches Museum (Vi-
enna): 874, 898–901
Kupa Synagogue (Kraków): 310
Kurja Vas: 820
Kursalon (Vienna): 916–917
Kürtőskalács: 673
Kutná Hora: 161–175; eating, 174–
175; map, 164–165; self-guided
walk, 165–169; sights/activities,

165–174; sleeping, 174–175; tourist information, 163; transportation, 163, 164, 175

L
Lady with an Ermine (da Vinci): 290–291
Lake Bled region: 777–802; map, 779. *See also* Bled
Lángos: 605, 669, 670, 672–673
Language: 28; Austria, 851; Bosnia, 1000; Croatia, 987; Czech Republic, 44, 46–48; restaurant phrases, 48; survival phrases, 47; German restaurant phrases, 946; German survival phrases, 945; Hungary, 559–562, 1100–1101; restaurant phrases, 562; survival phrases, 561; Montenegro, 1009; online translation tip, 1078; place names pronunciation, 1131; Poland, 235–238; restaurant phrases, 238; survival phrases, 237; Romania, 1039; Slovakia, 953; Slovenia, 720–722; restaurant phrases, 722; survival phrases, 721
Language barrier: 445, 1100–1101
Laurinská Street (Bratislava): 960
Łazienki Park (1944): 387, 428–429, 430
Legenda Cruises (Budapest): 582, 603–604
Lennon Wall (Prague): 103–104
Leopold Museum (Vienna): 902
Leopold Town (Budapest): 565, 583, 588–601; maps, 584–585, 667; sights, 583, 588–601; sleeping, 657
Lepena Valley: 827–828
Lesce: 773, 780, 801
Lesser Town (Prague): 52, 100–105; at a glance, 65; eating, 145–147; maps, 102–103, 134–135; nightlife, 129–130; sights, 100–105; sleeping, 132–133, 138
Lesser Town Square (Prague): 100–101
LGBTQ+ travel: 1076–1077
Liberation Monuments (Budapest): 633, 680
Liberty Bridge (Budapest): 565, 575
Libeskind, Daniel: 416
Linhartov Trg (Radovljica): 808

Lipizzaner stallions, in Vienna: 875, 886–887
Liszt, Franz: 613; Museum (Budapest), 616
Liszt Ferenc Airport (Budapest): 572–573
Little Dobó Square (Eger): 693
Little Princess, The (Budapest): 603
Little Quarter (Prague): *See* Lesser Town
Livade: 994
Ljubljana: 14, 723–776; at a glance, 733; best views, 730; eating, 768–773; helpful hints, 730; history of, 724–725; layout of, 725–726; maps, 728–729, 736–737, 766–767; planning tips, 724–725; self-guided walk, 732–749; shopping, 743–744, 762–763; sights/activities, 732–762; sleeping, 764–768; tourist information, 726; tours, 731–732; transportation, 726–727, 730–731, 773–776
Ljubljana Airport: 775–776, 802
Ljubljana Castle: 733, 741, 749–752; eating, 751–752, 771–772
Ljubljana Cathedral: 733, 741–742
Ljubljana City Museum: 733, 747
Ljubljana Contemporary History Museum: 733, 758–759
Ljubljana Main Market Square: 740
Ljubljana Riverside Market: 733, 738–739
Ljubljana Skyscraper: 731, 759–760
Ljubljana Small Market Square: 739–740
Ljubljana Tourist Card: 726
Ljubljana Town Hall: 743
Ljubljana Town Square: 742–743
Ljubljana US Embassy: 756
Ljubljanica River: 725–726, 734, 744; cafés, 772; cruises, 732
Lobkowicz Palace (Prague): 65, 119
Lobmeyr Crystal (Vienna): 868
Log pod Mangartom: eating, 836
Long Market (Gdańsk): 457–458
Loos, Adolf: 871; House (Vienna), 872
Lord's Ark Church (Kraków): 330
Loreta Church (Prague): 65, 108–109, 124
Loreta Square (Prague): 123–124
Loreto Chapel (Budapest): 630–631
Lost Wawel (Kraków): 283

Lovćen: 1013
Luge, at Lake Bled: 793
Lyceum (Eger): 688–689, 695–697

M
McDonald's (Budapest): 602
Magic Praha (Prague): 58
Magic Tower (Eger): 696–697
Mail: 1103–1104
Main Market Square (Kraków): 252, 262, 264; eating, 346–347; entertainment, 335
Main Market Square (Ljubljana): 740
Main Town (Gdańsk): 445, 449–463, 467–473; eating, 499–502; map, 450–451; sights, 467–473; sleeping, 495–498
Main Town Hall (Gdańsk): 448, 457, 468–470
Maisel Synagogue (Prague): 85
Maksymilian Kolbe, Saint: 268, 365, 366–367, 689
Malá Strana (Prague): *See* Lesser Town
Malbork Castle: 513–525; map, 516
Malczewski, Jacek: 263, 288, 412, 413
Maps: *See* Map Index
Maramureş: 1037, 1056–1059, 1060
Marco Polo: 986, 992
Margaret Bridge (Budapest): 564
Margaret Island (Budapest): 587, 600–601
Mariacka street (Gdańsk): 460, 494
Mariahilfer Strasse (Vienna): 908–909; eating, 936; map, 924–925; sleeping, 922
Maria Theresa, Empress: 101, 104, 111, 175, 589, 688, 790, 810, 848–849, 866, 868–869, 873, 889–891, 909–912, 969; biographical sketch, 889, 890; Monument (Vienna), 876
Maritime Museum of Montenegro (Kotor): 1011
Marjan (Split): 991
Markale Market (Sarajevo): 1003
Markets: Bratislava, 959; Budapest, 586, 604–605, 649, 651, 665, 670–671; Český Krumlov, 194; Christmas, 19, 959; Eger, 688; Gdańsk, 464; Kraków, 257, 264–265, 306, 339–340; Kutná

Hora, 167; Ljubljana, 730, 733, 738–739, 739, 762; Prague, 64, 76, 79, 124, 139–140; Sarajevo, 1003; Sofia, 1020; Vienna, 875, 904–905; Warsaw, 438; Zagreb, 996
Martinický Palace (Prague): 120
Mary Magdalene Square (Kraków): 272
Masaryk, Tomáš Garrigue: 36, 120, 122, 168–169, 753
Matejko, Jan: 256, 260, 285–286, 406, 409–411; biographical sketch, 410
Matthias Church (Budapest): 587, 629–631
Mátyás (Matthias) Corvinus: 545–546, 617, 625, 627, 1055, 1056; biographical sketch, 627
Medical emergencies: 1073. *See also specific destinations*
Medieval Art Museum (Prague): 64, 90
Međugorje: 1006
Mehoffer, Józef: 263, 269, 292, 412–413
Meiselsa street (Kraków): 306–307
Melantrichova street (Prague): 58, 79
Memento Park (Budapest): 587, 677–682; map, 678
Memling, Hans: 444, 491–492
Memorial for the Victims of Communism (Sighet): 1057
Memorial Garden (Budapest): 608
Memorial to the Children of Sarajevo: 1003
Memorial to the Victims of 1969 (Prague): 94
Merry Cemetery: 1059–1060
Meštrović, Ivan: 996, 1013; Gallery (Split), 990–991
Metelkova (Ljubljana): 726, 760–762
Metric conversions: 1127–1128
Metro: Budapest, 576–579; Prague, 58–59, 61–62; Vienna, 856–857, 858–859; Warsaw, 383
Michaelerkirche (Vienna): 875, 891–892
Michaelerplatz (Vienna): 872; eating, 932
Michalská street (Bratislava): 957–958
Michalská street (Prague): 124

Mickiewicz, Adam: 223, 247, 262, 264, 276, 396, 416

Miklošičeva cesta (Ljubljana): 735, 738

Milk bars, in Poland: 230, 272, 349–351, 390, 500

Millennium City Center (Budapest): 648

Millennium Monument (Budapest): 575, 617

Ministry of Agriculture (Budapest): 592

Minorite Church (Eger): 691

Mitoraj, Igor: 265–266

Mlino: 786, 790, 793, 794–795

Młoda Polska: 258–259, 263, 268, 288, 412–413

Mobile phones: 26, 1102–1103. *See also* Apps

MOCAK (Kraków): 317

Modlin Airport (Warsaw): 381–382

Mokotowska street (Warsaw): 430, 439

Moldoviţa Monastery: 1064

Money: 26, 1078–1085; average daily expenses, 23; budgeting, 23–24. *See also* Currency and exchange

Money-saving tips (discounts): 23–24, 1075, 1078; eating, 24; sleeping, 23–24, 1091–1092. *See also specific destinations*

Monte Cassino Heroes Street (Sopot): 506

Montenegrin language: 1009

Montenegro: 983, 1007–1013; almanac, 1008; cuisine, 1008; currency, 1008; history, 1008; map, 1009; top destinations, 1009–1013; transportation, 1007–1008

Montenegro Maritime Museum (Kotor): 1011

Monument Against War and Fascism (Vienna): 866–867

Monument of the Fallen Shipyard Workers (Gdańsk): 474–477

Monument of the Soviet Army (Sofia): 1020

Monument to the Hungarian Victims of the Nazis (Budapest): 597

Monument to the Victims of All Wars (Ljubljana): 749

Monument to Victims of Communism (Prague): 104

Moser (Prague): 125

Mostar: 998, 1004–1006; eating, 1005–1006; sleeping, 1005

Mostar Old Bridge: 1004–1005

Most SNP (Bratislava): 964, 970–972

Motława River: 458–459, 501–502

Motovun: 994

Mount Straža: 793

Mount Triglav: 822, 824–825

Movies, recommended: 1123–1127

Mozart, Wolfgang Amadeus: 76, 129, 890, 896, 965; concerts, 128, 916–917; House (Vienna), 877, 897, 916

Mozarthaus Vienna Museum: 877, 897, 916

Mucha, Alphonse: 36, 78, 112, 114; Museum (Prague), 65, 97–98

Műcsarnok (Budapest): 617

Municipal House (Prague): 64, 77–78, 98–99; eating, 149–150

Museum Kampa (Prague): 101–102

Museum of Broken Relationships (Zagreb): 996

Museum of Communism (Prague): 65, 98

Museum of Contemporary Art in Kraków: 317

Museum of Contemporary Art-Metelkova (Ljubljana): 761

Museum of Ethnography (Budapest): 617–618

Museum of Fine Arts (Budapest): 617

Museum of Gdańsk: 467–470, 467–473

Museum of Hungarian Agriculture (Budapest): 620

Museum of Kraków: 241, 244, 248

Museum of Medieval Art (Prague): 64, 90

Museum of Modern Art (Bratislava), 968–969; (Ljubljana), 756; (Vienna), 902

Museum of Municipal Engineering (Kraków): 308

Museum of Puppetry (Ljubljana): 751

Museum of Regional History (Český Krumlov): 195–196, 205

Museum of Socialist Art (Sofia): 1020–1021

Museum of the History of Polish Jews (Warsaw): 387, 418, 420–423

Museum of the History of Toruń: 533

Museum of the Second World War (Gdańsk): 448, 485–491

Museum of Toruń Gingerbread: 534

Museum of Warsaw: 387, 407–408

MuseumsQuartier (Vienna): 902, 917

Music: Budapest, 586, 618–619, 646–648; Eger, 688; Gdańsk, 494; Kraków, 335–340; Prague, 128–130; Vienna, 853, 856, 873, 913–917, 913–918; Haus der Musik, 874, 877, 895–896, 913; Warsaw, 430–431. *See also* Opera; *and specific composers*

Muzeum Fryderyka Chopina (Warsaw): 413–414, 431

Muzeum Powstania Warszawskiego (Warsaw): 387, 425, 427–428

Mysia 3 (Warsaw): 430

N

Náci, Schöner: 959, 961

Nagy, Imre: 551–552, 553, 591, 594–595, 601, 616; biographical sketch, 594

Nagymező utca (Budapest): 612

Náměstí Svornosti (Český Krumlov): 191, 196–197

Na Příkopě (Prague): 58, 78–79, 98, 124; sights, 98–99

Národní třída (Prague): 96, 124–125; eating, 150

Naschmarkt (Vienna): 875, 904–905, 917; eating, 936; sleeping near, 922

National and University Library (Ljubljana): 733, 745–746

National Archaeological Museum (Sofia): 1020

National Dance Theater (Budapest): 648

National Gallery (Budapest), 587, 626; (Ljubljana), 756–757

National Library (Vienna): 887–888

National Maritime Museum (Gdańsk): 472–473

National Museum (Budapest), 587,

605–606; (Gdańsk), 491–492; (Kraków), 284–294; (Ljubljana), 755–756; (Prague), 57, 94; (Warsaw), 387, 409–413

National Museum of Romanian History (Bucharest): 1044

National Museum of the Romanian Peasant (Bucharest): 1044

National Palace of Culture (Sofia): 1020

National Theater (Bratislava), 961; (Prague), 129

Nativity of the Virgin Cathedral (Veliko Tarnovo): 1033

Na Valech Gardens (Prague): 119

Nedbalka Gallery of Slovak Modern Art (Bratislava): 968–969

Nerudova street (Prague): 101

Nesebar: 1034–1035

Neuer Markt (Vienna): 868–869

Neustift am Walde: 939–940

"New Europe" and the EU: 1083

New Jewish Cemetery (Kraków): 253, 303, 309–310

New Palace Museums (Vienna): *See* World Museum Vienna

New Town (Plovdiv): 1026

New Town (Prague): 51, 90–99; at a glance, 64–65; cafés, 153–154; eating, 148–150; maps, 92, 136–137; nightlife, 129; sights, 90–99; sleeping, 138

New Town (Warsaw): 377, 401–402; map, 378; nightlife, 431

New Town Market Square (Toruń): 532

New Town Square (Warsaw): 401

New York Café (Budapest): 613, 674

Njeguši: 1013

Nordic Center (Planica): 822–823

Nova Gorica: 830

Nové Mesto (Prague): *See* New Town

Nowa Huta (Kraków): 328–330

Nowogrodzka street (Warsaw): 435

Nowy Świat Street (Warsaw): 386, 388, 389–390; eating, 436

Nussdorf: 940

Nyugati/Western Station (Budapest): 569, 572

O

Óbuda (Budapest): 564, 622, 682–683

Ocna Şugatag: 1059
Oktogon (Budapest): 613
Old Bridge (Mostar): 1004–1005
Old Jewish Cemetery (Kraków): 253, 301–302
Old Jewish Cemetery (Prague): 86
Old Market (Kraków): 257
Old-New Synagogue (Prague): 88
Old Port (Dubrovnik): 988
Old Royal Palace (Prague): 117
Old Serbian Orthodox Church (Sarajevo): 1002
Old Synagogue (Kraków): 304
Old Town (Bratislava): 949, 952–969; eating, 975–976; map, 956; self-guided walk, 952–965
Old Town (Bucharest): 1041
Old Town (Český Krumlov): 191–192, 194–199; eating, 212–213; map, 193; sleeping, 209–210
Old Town (Dubrovnik): 988
Old Town (Gdańsk): 445, 463–467; map, 450–451
Old Town (Kraków): 240, 273–298; eating, 346–351; entertainment, 335–337; maps, 242–243, 332–333, 344–345; shopping, 331, 334–335; sights, 273–298; sleeping, 341–343
Old Town (Ljubljana): 741–745; eating, 769–771; shopping, 763; sleeping, 764–765, 768
Old Town (Plovdiv): 1024, 1026
Old Town (Prague): 51, 67–90; at a glance, 64; cafés, 152–153; eating, 141–145; guided tours, 63; maps, 68–69, 84, 132, 142; nightlife, 129; self-guided walk, 66–83; sights, 83–88; sleeping, 130–132
Old Town (Rovinj): 993
Old Town (Sarajevo): 1002
Old Town (Warsaw): 377, 403–408; eating, 440–441; map, 384–385; nightlife, 431; self-guided walk, 397–401; sleeping, 433–434
Old Town Hall (Prague): 72–73
Old Town Market Square (Toruń): 528–530
Old Town Market Square (Warsaw): 387, 400–401
Old Town Square (Prague): 57, 64, 67–73; eating, 145; map, 70
Oliwa Cathedral (Gdańsk): 493

Open Kitchen (Ljubljana): 730, 739, 769
Opera: Budapest, 586, 610, 612, 646–647; Prague, 129; Vienna, 863–865, 874, 895, 915–916
Orbán, Viktor: 41, 229, 552–554, 568, 589, 597, 628, 1076–1077
Ordynacka street (Warsaw): 390
Organic architecture, of Hungary: 701
Orthodox Synagogue (Budapest): 609
Ostrogski Castle (Warsaw): 413–414
Ostrusha: 1028
Oświęcim: 356, 374
Otok Island: 787–789
Our Lady of the Rocks: 1010
Our Lady Victorious Church (Prague): 104

P
Packing tips and checklist: 26, 1130
Painted Monasteries of Bucovina: 1061–1065
Palace of Culture and Science (Warsaw): 379, 415–416
Palace on the Water (Warsaw): 429
Palach, Jan: 93, 94, 1119, 1124
Palacký Square (Kutná Hora): 168
Palm Tree Circle (Warsaw): 379, 386, 388–389, 409, 432; eating, 435–436
Paprika: 555, 556, 604, 652
Párisi Nagy Áruház (Budapest): 612–613
Pařížská street (Prague): 126
Park Zvezda (Ljubljana): 748–749
Parliament: Croatian (Zagreb), 995; Hungarian (Budapest), 575, 583, 586, 588–589; Romanian (Bucharest), 1043–1044; Slovenian (Ljubljana), 755
Passports: 25, 1073–1074, 1081
Path of Remembrance (Warsaw): 423
Peleş Castle: 1036, 1044–1046, 1049
Pelişor Castle: 1046
Perast: 1010
Pest (Budapest): 565, 583–622; at a glance, 586–587; baths, 637–640; cafés, 673–675; eating, 662–671; maps, 584–585, 611, 618, 658–659; sights, 583–622; sleeping, 653–657. See also Budapest

Pest Downtown (Town Center; Budapest): 565, 601–604; cafés, 674–675; eating, 669–671; maps, 584–585, 658–659; sights, 601–604; sleeping, 656–657

Pesti Vigadó (Budapest): 647

Peterskirche (Vienna): 870–871, 875, 896–897

Petřín Hill (Prague): 65, 104–105

Petržalka (Bratislava): 970–972

Pharmacy Under the Eagle (Kraków): 253, 311–312

Phones: *See* Telephones

Pianist, The (movie): 419, 422, 423, 424, 1126

Pienkowska, Alina: 479

Piłsudski Square (Warsaw): 393–395

Pinkas Synagogue (Prague): 85, 128

Pivovar Český Krumlov Brewery: 205–206

Pivovarna Union (Ljubljana): 759

Place names, pronunciation: 1131

Plac Mariacki (Kraków): 331, 334

Plac Nowy (Kraków): 306, 338–339, 353

Plac Rapackiego (Toruń): 527

Plac Szczepański (Kraków): 294, 348

Plac Wolnica (Kraków): 307–308

Plac Zbawiciela (Warsaw): 430, 431; eating, 438–439

Plague Column (Prague), 120; (Vienna), 870

Planetariums: 415, 529

Planica: 822–823, 1120

Planty (Kraków): 256, 267

Plečnik, Jože: 117, 119, 723, 725, 726, 733, 734–735, 738–742, 745–748, 758, 761; biographical sketch, 753; House (Ljubljana), 733, 748, 752, 754

Plešivecká (Český Krumlov): 211, 213

Pletna boats: 777, 786, 788, 790, 792

Plitvice Lakes National Park: 996–997

Plovdiv: 1023–1028; eating, 1027; sleeping, 1027

Počitelj: 1006

Podgórze (Kraków): 310–317

Poenari Castle: 1046

"Polack jokes": 223–224

Poland: 216–537; at a glance, 12–13; almanac, 219; climate, 1129; cuisine, 231–235; currency, 219, 1079; embassies, 1074; helpful hints, 218, 220; history, 220–229, 261; LGBTQ+ travel, 1076–1077; map, 217; movies, 1124–1125; overview, 216–236; today, 227–231; tourist office, 1073. *See also specific destinations*

Polanski, Roman: 1126

Polish History Museum (Warsaw): 408

Polish language: 235–238; restaurant phrases, 238; survival phrases, 237

Polish National Railways: 218, 220

Polish Vodka Museum (Warsaw): 429–430

Polish zloty: 219, 1079

Pomerania: 13, 512–537

Popiełuszko, Jerzy: 466

Popper Synagogue (Kraków): 303

Post offices: 1103–1104. *See also specific destinations*

Powder Bridge (Prague): 110–111

Powder Tower (Prague): 77

Powiśle (Warsaw): 415, 437, 439–440

Poznańska street (Warsaw): 439

Praga (Warsaw): 429–430

Prague: 12, 49–160; at a glance, 64–65; best views, 57, 140; cafés, 152–154; eating, 139–154; entertainment, 127–130; excursion areas, 161–189; helpful hints, 53, 56–58; layout of, 51–52; neighborhoods, 51–52; planning tips, 49–50; rip-offs, 53; self-guided walk, 66–83; shopping, 124–127; sights/activities, 67–124; sleeping, 130–139; teahouses, 154; tourist information, 52–53; tours, 63–66; transportation, 53, 58–62, 155–160. *See also specific neighborhoods*

Prague Castle: 52, 81, 105–120; map, 106–107; orientation, 65, 109–110; planning tips, 107–109; self-guided tour, 110–120; transportation, 105–107

Prague CoolPass: 53

Prague Old Town Hall: 72–73

Prague Proms: 1120

Prague Spring: 37, 93, 95, 474, 482, 971, 1120

Prague Symphony Orchestra: 128
Prater Park (Vienna): 907–908
Predel Pass: 831
Prejmer Church: 1053
Prešeren, France: 715, 726, 732, 734
Prešeren Square (Ljubljana): 732, 734–735
Primate's Palace (Bratislava): 959, 966–967
Prison Tower (Gdańsk): 452
Private rooms: overview, 1095. *See also specific destinations*
Professors' Garden (Kraków): 267
Promenade Square (Bratislava): 961–963
Pršut: 717, 986, 1008, 1013
Pula: 994–995
Pula Amphitheater: 994–995
Puppet Museum (Český Krumlov): 205
Puppets: 125, 205, 751

R
Ráday utca (Budapest): 649
Radovljica: 807–813
Radziwiłł Palace (Warsaw): 396
Rafting: Soča River, 785, 833; Vltava River, 206–207
Rail passes: 33, 1106, 1108, 1116
Rail travel: *See* Train travel
Rákóczi, Ferenc: 547, 592
Ramparts Garden (Prague): 119
Raphael: 292, 900
Râşnov Castle: 1051
Reading, recommended: 1122–1123
Reagan, Ronald: 329, 595, 597
Rector's Palace (Dubrovnik): 988
Red Hall (Gdańsk): 469
Rembrandt van Rijn: 290, 406, 888, 901
Remu'h Synagogue (Kraków): 302
Rental properties: 24, 1092–1093, 1095–1096
Republic Square (Prague): 140
Resources from Rick Steves: 1115–1117
Restaurants: *See* Eating; *and specific destinations*
Revival and Assembly Museum (Veliko Tarnovo): 1033
Revolution Square (Bucharest): 1041
Rhodope Mountain: 1027–1028
Ribčev Laz Village: 814–815
Rila Monastery: 1021–1023

Ringstrasse (Vienna): 852–853, 862
Riva (Split): 990
Roma (Gypsies): 208; Bulgaria, 1016; Czech Republic, 208, 212; Poland, 365, 368; Romania, 1038, 1047, 1055; Slovakia, 953, 962
Roman Acropolis (Plovdiv): 1024, 1026
Roman Amphitheater (Pula): 994–995
Romania: 17, 983, 1036–1065; almanac, 1038; cuisine, 1039; currency, 1038; history, 1038, 1047; map, 1037; top destinations, 1040–1065; tour guides, 1039–1040; tours, 1039; transportation, 1037–1038
Romanian language: 1039
Romanian leu: 1038
Romanian Parliament (Bucharest): 1043–1044
Romanian People's Salvation Cathedral (Bucharest): 1044
Roman sites (ancient Romans): 568, 634, 747, 749, 872, 893, 989–990, 994–995, 1001, 1008, 1019, 1023, 1024, 1026, 1066
Roman Stadium (Plovdiv): 1026
Rose Celebration (Český Krumlov): 192, 1120
Rose oil, in Bulgaria: 1029
Round Tower (Český Krumlov): 198, 200–201
Rovinj: 993–994
Royal Castle (Warsaw): 387, 398, 403–407
Royal Palace (Budapest): 625–626
Royal Private Apartments (Kraków): 283
Royal State Rooms (Kraków): 282–283
Royal Summer Palace (Prague): 106
Royal Way (Gdańsk), 448, 453, 456–457; (Kraków), 255–273; (Prague), 52; (Warsaw), 377, 386–397
Rubens, Peter Paul: 900
Rubik, Ernő: 541
Rubinstein, Helena: 303, 346
Rudas Baths (Budapest): 587, 634, 643–645
Ruin pubs, in Budapest: 649–650
Rumbach Street Synagogue (Budapest): 609–610, 648

Rustika (Ljubljana): 763
Ruszwurm (Budapest): 632, 671
Rynek Underground Museum
  (Kraków): 253, 262, 294–296

S
Sacher torte: 851, 865–866, 938
St. Adalbert Church (Kraków): 264
St. Agnes Convent (Prague): 90
St. Andrea: 703
St. Andrew's Church (Kraków): 272
St. Anne's Church (Warsaw):
  396–397, 431
St. Barbara's Cathedral (Kutná
  Hora): 171–172
St. Barbara's Cathedral and Park
  (Kutná Hora): 165–166
St. Bridget's Church (Gdańsk): 448,
  465–466
St. Catherine's Church (Gdańsk):
  464–465
St. Charles Church (Vienna): 875,
  903
St. Dominic's Fair (Gdańsk): 444,
  1121
St. Domnius Cathedral (Split): 990
St. Elizabeth's Church (Bratislava):
  972
St. Euphemia Church (Rovinj): 993
St. Francis Basilica (Kraków): 252,
  268–269
St. George Basilica (Prague): 118
St. George Island: 1010
St. István's Basilica (Budapest): 587,
  598, 648; concerts, 648; eating
  near, 666, 668–669
St. James Church (Prague): 75–76
St. John's Street (Warsaw): 399
St. John the Baptist Cathedral
  (Warsaw): 399–400, 431
St. Joseph Church (Soča): 827
St. Luke's Square (Kotor): 1011
St. Martin's Cathedral (Bratislava):
  964
St. Martin's Church (Warsaw):
  398–399
St. Mary's Basilica (Kutná Hora):
  171
St. Mary's Church (Gdańsk): 448,
  460–463
St. Mary's Church (Kraków): 252,
  259–262
St. Mary's Church (Lbubljana): 735

St. Mary's Church (Malbork Castle):
  524–525
St. Michael's Bridge (Bratislava):
  952
St. Michael's Church (Cluj): 1056
St. Michael's Church (Vienna): 875,
  891–892
St. Michael's Gate (Bratislava): 956,
  965
St. Nicholas Church (Gdańsk): 464
St. Nicholas Church (Prague): 70,
  100–101
St. Peter's Church (Vienna):
  870–871, 875, 896–897
Sts. Cyril and Methodius Serbian
  Orthodox Church (Ljubljana):
  733, 757–758
Saints Peter and Paul Church
  (Kraków): 272, 335–336
Sts. Peter and Paul Franciscan
  Church (Mostar): 1005
St. Stephen's Cathedral (Vienna):
  869, 874, 892–895; eating near,
  929, 932
St. Tryphon Cathedral (Kotor): 1011
St. Vitus Cathedral (Prague): 65,
  111–116; map, 113
St. Vitus Church (Český Krumlov):
  196
St. Vitus Treasury (Prague): 110
Sala BHP (Gdańsk): 485
Salt Hill Thermal Spa (Egerszálok):
  700
Salt mines: 324–328
Sandomierska Tower (Kraków):
  281–282
Sándor Palace (Budapest): 628
Săpânţa Peri Monastery Church:
  1060
Sarajevo: 998, 1000–1004; eating,
  1003–1004; sleeping, 1003
Sarajevo City History Museum:
  1002
Sarajevo Old Synagogue: 1002
Sarajevo War Tunnel Museum: 1003
Savica Waterfall: 816
Saxon churches, in Romania:
  1052–1054
Saxon Garden (Warsaw): 394
Schiele, Egon: 906
Schindler's Factory Museum
  (Kraków): 253, 312–317
Schindler's List (movie): 300, 307,

310–311, 314–317, 369, 1125, 1126

Schloss Belvedere (Vienna): 875, 905–907

Schönbrunn Palace (Vienna): 25, 874, 909–913; map, 910

Schönbrunn Zoo (Vienna): 912

Schwarzenberg Palace (Prague): 120

Seasons: 19

Secession, the (Vienna): 875, 903–904

Sedlec Bone Church (Kutná Hora): 169–171

Seidel Photo Studio Museum (Český Krumlov): 204

Serbian Orthodox Church of Sts. Cyril and Methodius (Ljubljana): 733, 757–758

Seventh District (Budapest): 648; eating, 662–665; maps, 585, 664; ruin pubs, 649–650; shopping, 652–653; sleeping, 654, 656

Shakespeare & Co. (Vienna): 856

Shakespeare and Sons (Prague): 56, 126

Shakespeare Theater (Gdańsk): 473

Shipka Church: 1030–1031

Shipka Pass: 1031

Shopping: budgeting, 23; clothing sizes, 1128; VAT refunds, 1084–1085. See also Markets; and specific destinations

Shushmanets: 1028

Sibiu: 1054–1055

Sighetu Marmației: 1057

Sighișoara: 1037, 1051–1052

Sightseeing: best three-week trip, 20–21; general tips, 1086, 1087, 1090; maps and navigation tools, 1085–1086; reservations and advance tickets, 25, 1086–1087; top destinations, 12–17. See also specific sights and destinations

Sigmund Freud Museum (Vienna): 908

SIM cards: 1103

Sirens' Valley: 702–703

Sisi (Elisabeth), Empress: 575, 631, 683; biographical sketch, 881; Hofburg (Vienna), 872–873, 877–883; Imperial Crypt (Vienna), 868, 891; Museum (Vienna), 880; Schönbrunn (Vienna), 909–912

Ski jumping: 822, 1120

Skłodowska, Maria: See Curie, Marie

Sky Bar (Bratislava): 962, 976

Skydiving: 732, 833–834

Skyscraper, the (Ljubljana): 731, 759–760

Sleep code: 1091

Sleeping: 1090–1097; booking sites, 1092; budgeting, 23; rates and deals, 23–24, 1091–1092; reservations, 23–24, 25, 1096–1097; types of accommodations, 1092–1097; user reviews, 1093. See also specific destinations

Slovakia: 948–979; almanac, 953; cuisine, 974–975; currency, 953; embassies, 1074; history, 950–951; tourist office, 1073. See also Bratislava

Slovak language: 953

Slovak National Collection of Wine (Bratislava): 968

Slovak Philharmonic (Bratislava): 961

Slovenia: 710–846; at a glance, 14; almanac, 713; climate, 1129; cuisine, 717–720, 769, 800; currency, 713; embassies, 1074; helpful hints, 712, 714; history, 714–716, 714–717, 724–725, 841; map, 711; movies, 1125; overview, 710–722; today, 716–717; tourist office, 1073. See also Julian Alps; Kobarid; Lake Bled region; Ljubljana

Slovenian Ethnographic Museum (Ljubljana): 733, 760–761

Slovenian History Exhibition (Ljubljana): 751

Slovenian language: 720–722; restaurant phrases, 722; survival phrases, 721

Slovenian Museum of Natural History (Ljubljana): 755–756

Slovenian National Gallery (Ljubljana): 756–757

Slovenian National Museum (Ljubljana): 755–756

Slovenian National Museum-Metelkova (Ljubljana): 761

Slovenian Parliament (Ljubljana): 755

Slovenian wines: 719, 792, 808

Small Boulevard (Budapest): 565, 605–610

Small Market Square (Ljubljana): 739–740

Smartphones: 26, 1102–1103. *See also* Apps

"Sniper Alley" (Sarajevo): 1003

SNP Bridge (Bratislava): 964, 970–972

Soča (Isonzo) Front: 715, 826, 828–829, 841

Soča River: 817, 826, 827, 833; fishing, 833; rafting, 785, 833

Soča River Valley: 826–829

Soccer: 398, 1056

Sofia: 1017–1021; eating, 1021; sleeping, 1021

Sofia National Archaeological Museum: 1020

Sofia National Historical Museum: 1021

Sofia Synagogue: 1020

Solidarity Center (Gdańsk): 448, 467, 480–485, 502

Solidarity movement: 221, 227, 448, 455, 467, 474–485

Solidarity Square (Gdańsk): 467, 474–477

Sopot: 505–507

Sopot Molo (Pier): 505–507

Sopron: 676, 978

Soros, George: 541, 607

Spanish Riding School (Vienna): 873, 875, 886–887

Spanish Synagogue (Prague): 87–88

Spartacus: 1016, 1029

Spas: *See* Baths

Special events: *See* Festivals

Spittelberg (Vienna): 935

Split: 989–991; eating, 991; sleeping, 991

Square of the Republic (Ljubljana): 754–755

Srebrenica Exhibition (Sarajevo): 1003

Śródmieście (Warsaw): 379, 433, 438–439

Staatsoper (Vienna): 863–865, 874, 895, 915–916; eating near, 933–934

Stained-Glass Workshop and Museum (Kraków): 253, 298

Stambolov street (Veliko Tarnovo): 1032

Stanisław Wyspiański Museum (Kraków): 252, 292–294

Staré Mesto (Prague): *See* Old Town

Stare Miasto (Kraków): *See* Old Town

Stari Most (Mostar): 1004–1005

State Hall (Vienna): 887–888

State Opera (Prague): 129

State Opera (Vienna): *See* Vienna State Opera

Statue Park (Budapest): 587, 677–682; map, 678

Štefánik, Milan Rastislav: 973

Stephansdom (Vienna): 869, 874, 892–895; eating near, 929, 932

Stephansplatz (Vienna): 869

Stephen, Saint: *See* István, Saint

Sternberg Palace (Prague): 120

Stolarska street (Kraków): 337, 348–349

Stone Fountain (Kutná Hora): 167

Stone House (Kutná Hora): 167

Story of Prague Casle Exhibit: 117–118

Stoss, Veit: 260

Strada Nicolae Bālcescu (Sibiu): 1054

Stradun (Dubrovnik): 987–988

Strahov Monastery and Library (Prague): 57, 65, 108–109, 121, 123

Strauss, Richard: 896, 916–917

Straw Tower (Gdańsk): 452

Straža: 786

Subway: *See* Metro

Suceava: 1065

Sucevița Monastery: 1064–1065

Summer terraces (*teto*), in Budapest: 650–651

Sunny Beach: 1035

Supreme Court (Budapest): 592

Sveta Sofia Church (Sofia): 1019

Sveti Stefan: 1007, 1012–1013

Swimming: *See* Beaches

Synagogues: overview, 305. *See also specific synagogues*

Szabadság tér (Budapest): 595, 597

Széchenyi Baths (Budapest): 586, 621, 637–640; map, 639

Széchenyi utca (Eger): 690–691, 706

Szentendre: 683

Szentháromság tér (Budapest): 629

Szołayski House (Kraków): 294

T

Tadeusz Sendzimir Steelworks (Kraków): 330

Tárnok utca (Budapest): 628

Taxes: VAT refunds, 1084–1085

Taxis: 1108–1109; tipping, 1082. *See also specific destinations*

Telephones: 1102–1103; how to dial, 1104–1105

Tempel Synagogue (Kraków): 310

Temperatures, average monthly: 1128–1129

Terezín Children's Art Exhibit (Prague): 86

Terezín Memorial: 175–185; map, 178–179; self-guided tour, 178–185

Terror Háza (Budapest): 586, 613–616

Terror Museum (Budapest): 586, 613–616

Tesla, Nikoka: 986

Teutonic Knights: 221–222, 257, 277, 286, 410–411, 454, 461, 512–525, 747–748; biographical sketch, 521

Theater an der Wien (Vienna): 916

Theft alerts: 27, 1073, 1081–1082, 1106; Budapest, 573–574; Prague, 53, 56

Theotokos Romanian Orthodox Cathedral (Cluj): 1056

Thermal baths: *See* Baths

Third Man, The (movie): 918

Third Man Museum (Vienna): 918

Thracian Plain: 1028–1030

Time Tunnel (Eger): 689

Time zones: 1074–1075

Tipping: 1082, 1099

Tito (Josip Broz): 715, 751, 755, 759, 786, 827, 1070–1071, 1125; biographical sketch, 1068–1069; Vila Bled, 786

Tivoli Park (Ljubljana): 758

Tokaji Aszú: 558

Toll stickers: 33, 543, 714, 856, 950–951, 1114

Tolmin: 829

Tomb of the Unknown Soldier (Sofia): 1019

Tomb of the Unknown Soldier (Warsaw): 394–395

Tonkina Koča: 823

Torture Chamber (Gdańsk): 452

Toruń: 526–537; eating, 536–537; map, 528–529; self-guided walk, 527–533; sights/activities, 527–535; sleeping, 535–536; transportation, 527, 537

Toruń Castle: 532–533

Toruń City History Museums: 533

Toruń Fortress Museum: 535

Toruń New Town Market Square: 532

Toruń Old Town Hall: 528–529, 533

Toruń Old Town Market Square: 528–530

Toskánský Palace (Prague): 120

Tour guides: 26, 27. *See also specific destinations*

Tourist information: 1073. *See also specific destinations*

Tours: Rick Steves, 1116. *See also specific destinations*

Train travel: 1105–1108; best three-week trip, 20–21; map, 1107; night trains, 1106; Bled, 780, 801; Bratislava, 977–978; Budapest, 567, 569, 572, 579, 675–676; Bulgaria, 1014–1015; Český Krumlov, 192, 214; Croatia, 986; Eger, 687, 706; Gdańsk, 446–447, 502–503; Konopiště Castle, 186; Kraków, 244–245, 355; Kutná Hora, 163, 175; Ljubljana, 726–727, 773–774; Poland, 218, 220; Prague, 155–158; Romania, 1039; Toruń, 527, 537; Vienna, 940–943; Warsaw, 379–381, 441–442

Trajan: 1026

Transfăgărășan Road: 1046

Transportation: 1104–1115; best three-week trip, 20–21; budgeting, 23; map, 1107. *See also* Airports; Boat travel and cruises; Buses; Car travel; Train travel; *and specific destinations*

Transylvania: 1036–1037, 1046–1056; history, 1047

Travel advisories: 1072

Travel documents: 25

Travelers Museum (Toruń): 535

Travel insurance: 26, 1075, 1112

Travel smarts: 27–28

Travel tips: 1072–1075, 1078

Treasury (Vienna): 873, 874, 883–885

Treaty of Trianon: 548–549, 614
Tree of Life (Budapest): 608
Trenta: 826; sleeping, 835
Tri-City: 503–511; map, 504. *See also* Gdańsk
Triglav National Park: 819, 822, 823, 826; Information Center, 779–780, 819, 826
Trip costs: 23–24
Triple Bridge (Ljubljana): 725, 734, 738
Tryavna: 1031
Tsarevets Fortress (Veliko Tarnovo): 1033
Turkish Bath (Eger): 698–699
Turul Bird (Budapest): 625
Two Saint Johns Cathedral (Toruń): 530–531
Tycho Brahe: 35, 74, 77
Týn Church (Prague): 72, 74–75

U

Uber: 1108–1109. *See also specific destinations*
UFO at New Bridge (Bratislava): 964, 965, 970–972
Ukraine: cuisine, 234; Russian invasion, 229, 231
Ulica Chmielna (Warsaw): 390
Ulica Długa (Gdańsk): 448, 453, 456–457, 494
Ulica Józefa (Kraków): 307, 334, 340
Ulica Mariacka (Gdańsk): 460, 494
Ulica Mokotowska (Warsaw): 430, 439
Ulica Piwna (Gdańsk): 463
Ulica Piwna (Warsaw): 398
Ulica św. Wawrzyńca (Kraków): 308
Ulica Szeroka (Kraków): 299–300, 302–304, 309
Ulica Szeroka (Toruń): 531–532
Üllői út (Budapest): 621–622
Umschlagplatz (Warsaw): 423
Ungelt Courtyard (Prague): 75, 124
Unicum: 557, 652
Uphagen House (Gdańsk): 448, 456, 468
Upland Gate (Gdańsk): 449
Upper Castle (Český Krumlov): 201

V

Váci utca (Budapest): 602–603, 651; eating, 669–671; sleeping, 656

Václav Havel Airport (Prague): 158–159
Vajdahunyad Castle (Budapest): 586, 620
Varga, Imre: 608, 680–681, 682
Varna: 1034
Varso Tower (Warsaw): 416
Vasa Chapel (Kraków): 277
Vasarely, Victor: 682
VAT refunds: 1084–1085
Velika Zaka: 787
Veliko Tarnovo: 1031–1034
Velvet Revolution of 1989: 38, 40, 77, 95, 96, 97, 594, 951, 1121
Venus of Willendorf: 901
Verige Strait: 1010
Vermeer, Jan: 900–901
Vértanúk Tere (Budapest): 594–595
Via Musica (Prague): 72, 74, 127
Victory Avenue (Bucharest): 1040
Vienna: 17, 848–944; at a glance, 874–875; cafés, 936–938; eating, 926–940; entertainment, 913–918; helpful hints, 853, 856; history of, 848–850; layout of, 852–853; maps, 849, 854–855, 864, 921, 924–925, 930–931; nightlife, 917–918; planning tips, 850, 852; self-guided walk, 863–876; sights/activities, 863–913; sleeping, 919–926; tourist information, 853; tours, 860–863; transportation, 856–860, 940–944; wine gardens, 938–940
Vienna Boys' Choir: 873, 914
Vienna Card: 877
Vienna City Hall: 917–918, 934–935
Vienna Festival: 913, 1120
Vienna International Airport: 943–944, 979
Vienna Natural History Museum: 875, 901–902
Vienna Pass: 856, 877
Vienna Philharmonic Orchestra: 896
Vienna Secession: 875, 903–904
Vienna State Opera: 863–865, 874, 895, 915–916; eating near, 933–934
Vienna Volksoper: 916
Vienna Woods: 852
Vietnamese Market (Kutná Hora): 167

INDEX

Vila Bled: 786
Villa Richter (Prague): 57, 140, 147
Vinohrady (Prague): 57, 151
Vintgar Gorge: 803–807
Viscri Church: 1053–1054
Visegrád: 683
Visitor information: 1073. *See also specific destinations*
Vistula River: 240, 281, 377, 431
Vitosha Boulevard (Sofia): 1020
Vitus, Saint: 115, 196
Víziváros (Budapest): 566, 657, 661; sleeping, 661
Vltava River: 51–52, 81–82, 190, 191, 195–196; canoeing and rafting, 206–207
Vodka Museum (Warsaw): 429–430
Vogel Mountain Cable Car: 815–816
Voroneț Monastery: 1064
Vörösmarty tér (Budapest): 601–602
Vrata Valley: 822
Vršič Pass: 818–826

W

Wadowice: 270, 321–324
Wagenburg Carriage Museum (Vienna): 913
Wagner, Otto: 609–610, 740, 753, 902, 903–904
Walentynowicz, Anna: 479
Wałęsa, Lech: 221, 227, 271, 328, 455, 459, 465, 467, 474, 478, 479, 481, 483–485; biographical sketch, 476–477
Walk of Peace (Kobarid): 843
Wallachia: 1036, 1040–1046
Wallenberg, Raoul: 608–609
Warsaw: 13, 375–442; at a glance, 387; eating, 434–441; entertainment, 430–431; layout of, 377, 379; maps, 378, 384–385; planning tips, 377; self-guided walk, 386–403; shopping, 430; sights/activities, 386–430; sleeping, 431–434; tourist information, 379; tours, 383, 386; transportation, 379–383, 441–442
Warsaw Castle Square: 387, 397–399, 402–403
Warsaw Ghetto Uprising (1943): 376, 417–418, 419
Warsaw Museum: 387, 407–408
Warsaw Old Town Market Square: 387, 400–401
Warsaw Royal Castle: 387, 398, 403–407
Warsaw University: 392
Warsaw Uprising (1944): 376, 399, 424–428; Monument, 424–425; Museum, 387, 425, 427–428
Washington, George: 619
Wawel Castle (Kraków): 252, 279–284
Wawel Castle Museums (Kraków): 282–284
Wawel Cathedral (Kraków): 252, 274–279
Wawel Hill (Kraków): 240, 273
Weather: 19, 27–28, 1128–1129
Wenceslas, Saint: 90–91, 115–116, 1121
Wenceslas Chapel (Prague): 115–116
Wenceslas Square (Prague): 64, 79, 90–97; cafés, 153; shopping, 126
Westbahnhof (Vienna): 941–942
Westerplatte (Gdańsk): 493–494, 503
White Tower (Brașov): 1048
Wieliczka Salt Mine: 324–328; guided tours, 254–255
Wien: *See* Vienna
Wiener Staatsoper: 863–865, 874, 895, 915–916
Wien Hauptbahnhof (Vienna): 941
Wien Museum Karlsplatz (Vienna): 875, 905
Wiesel, Elie: 1038, 1057
Wine: Croatia, 994; Hungary, 558, 651, 668, 685, 687, 693, 699, 702, 703; Slovakia, 968; Slovenia, 719, 792, 808
Wine gardens, in Vienna: 938–940
Winter Hall (Gdańsk): 469
Winter Synagogue (Prague): 88
Wojtyła, Karol: *See* John Paul II, Pope
World Museum Vienna: 873, 874, 885–886
World War I: 8, 36, 759; Austria, 848; Bosnia-Herzegovina, 1001; Bulgaria, 1016; Czech Republic, 202; Hungary, 548–549, 568; Poland, 224; Slovenia, 715, 816, 823, 827, 828, 837, 840–844; Soča (Isonzo) Front, 715, 827, 828–829, 841
World War II: 8, 1067, 1070; Austria, 848, 866–867, 873, 876;

Bulgaria, 1020; Czech Republic, 36–37, 175–185, 202–203; Hungary, 550, 613–616, 632; Poland, 217, 224–225, 247, 304, 306, 312–317, 363, 376, 398, 424–428, 455, 485–491, 493–494; Slovakia, 963–964; Slovenia, 715, 759, 809; Warsaw, 387, 416–424. *See also* Concentration camps
World War II Museum (Gdańsk): 448, 485–491
Wurst, in Vienna: 927
Wyspiański, Stanisław: 260–261, 263, 268–269, 298, 413; Museum (Kraków), 252, 292–294
Wyspiański Pavilion (Kraków): 241, 269–270
Wyszyński, Stefan: 392–393, 399, 465

Y
Yugoslavia, understanding: 1066–1071

Z
Zadružna Zveza (Ljubljana): 738
Žaga: 829
Zagreb: 995–996; eating, 996; sleeping, 996
Zagreb Cathedral: 996
Završje: 994
Zelazowa Wola: 414
Zhivkov, Todor: 1034
Zhivkova, Lyudmila: 1033
Ziplines: 785, 822
Žižkov TV tower (Prague): 57, 150–151
Zlatá Koruna Abbey: 207, 209
Złota 44 (Warsaw): 416
Złote Tarasy Shopping Mall (Warsaw): 416
Zoo, in Vienna: 912

MAP INDEX

Color Maps
Central Europe's Top Destinations: 11
Central Europe's Best Three-Week Trip by Public Transportation: 21

Back Matter
Central & Eastern Europe
Czech Republic
Hungary
Poland
Slovenia
Warsaw
Prague
Budapest
Kraków's Old Town
Vienna

Czech Republic
Czech Republic: 31

Prague
Prague Overview: 52
Greater Prague: 54–55
Prague Public Transportation: 60–61
Old Town & Charles Bridge Walk: 68–69
Old Town Square: 70
Prague's Jewish Quarter: 84
Prague's New Town: 92
Prague's Lesser Town: 102–103
Prague Castle Overview: 106–107
Prague Castle Detail : 108–109
St. Vitus Cathedral: 113
Hotels in Prague's Old Town: 132
Restaurants & Hotels in the Lesser Town & Castle Quarter: 134–135
Hotels & Restaurants in the New Town & Nearby: 136–137
Restaurants in Prague's Old Town: 142

Near Prague
Day Trips: 162
Kutná Hora: 164–165
Terezín: 178–179

Český Krumlov
Český Krumlov: 193

Poland
Poland: 217

Kraków
Kraków's Old Town: 242–243
Kazimierz Walk: 301
Kraków's Old Town Shopping & Entertainment: 332–333
Kazimierz Entertainment & Nightlife: 338
Kraków's Old Town Hotels & Restaurants: 344–345
Kazimierz Hotels & Restaurants: 352

Auschwitz-Birkenau
Greater Auschwitz: 357
Auschwitz I: 362
Auschwitz II – Birkenau: 370

Warsaw
Warsaw Overview: 378
Central Warsaw: 384–385

Gdańsk & The Tri-City
Gdańsk Walk: 450–451
Gdańsk Hotels & Restaurants: 496–497
Gdańsk Day Trips: 504

Pomerania
Malbork Castle: 516
Toruń: 528

Hungary
Hungary: 541
Pre-Trianon Hungary: 549

Budapest
Budapest Neighborhoods: 566
Budapest Overview: 570–571
Budapest Transit: 578
Pest: 584–585
Andrássy Út Walk: 611
Heroes' Square & City Park: 618–619

Buda: 623
Széchenyi Baths: 639
Gellért Baths: 642
Andrássy Út Hotels & Restaurants: 655
Downtown Pest Hotels & Restaurants: 658–659
Buda Hotels & Restaurants: 660
The Seventh District: 664
Leopold Town Hotels & Restaurants: 667
Memento Park: 678

Eger
Eger: 686

Slovenia
Slovenia: 711

Ljubljana
Ljubljana: 728–729
Ljubljana Center: 736–737
Ljubljana Hotels & Restaurants: 766–767

Lake Bled
Lake Bled: 779
Bled Town: 782–783
Near Lake Bled: 804–805

The Julian Alps
Slovenia's Julian Alps: 820–821
Kobarid: 838

Vienna
Greater Vienna: 849
Vienna's City Center: 854–855

Vienna's Public Transportation: 858–859
Vienna City Walk: 864
Vienna's Hofburg Palace: 878
Schönbrunn Palace: 910
Hotels in Central Vienna: 921
Hotels & Restaurants near Mariahilfer Strasse: 924–925
Restaurants in Central Vienna: 930–931

Bratislava
Bratislava: 954–955
Bratislava Old Town Walk: 956

Croatia
Croatia: 985

Bosnia-Herzegovina
Bosnia-Herzegovina: 999

Montenegro
Montenegro: 1009

Bulgaria
Bulgaria: 1015

Romania
Romania: 1037

Understanding Yugoslavia
Yugoslav Succession: 1067

Practicalities
Public Transportation in Central Europe: 1107
Driving in Central Europe: 1111

MAP INDEX

Our website enhances this book and turns

Explore Europe

At ricksteves.com you can browse through thousands of articles, videos, photos and radio interviews, plus find a wealth of money-saving travel tips for planning your dream trip. And with our mobile-friendly website, you can easily access all this great travel information anywhere you go.

TV Shows

Preview the places you'll visit by watching entire half-hour episodes of *Rick Steves' Europe* (choose from all 100 shows) on-demand, for free.

kstev...n

your travel dreams into affordable reality

Radio Interviews

Enjoy ready access to Rick's vast library of radio interviews covering travel tips and cultural insights that relate specifically to your Europe travel plans.

Travel Forums

Learn, ask, share! Our online community of savvy travelers is a great resource for first-time travelers to Europe, as well as seasoned pros.

Travel News

Subscribe to our free Travel News e-newsletter, and get monthly updates from Rick on what's happening in Europe.

Classroom Europe®

Check out our free resource for educators with 500 short video clips from the *Rick Steves' Europe* TV show.

Audio Europe™

Rick's Free Travel App

Get your FREE **Rick Steves Audio Europe**™ app to enjoy…

- Dozens of self-guided tours of Europe's top museums, sights and historic walks
- Hundreds of tracks filled with cultural insights and sightseeing tips from Rick's radio interviews
- All organized into handy geographic playlists
- For Apple and Android

With Rick whispering in your ear, Europe gets even better.

Find out more at ricksteves.com

Gear up for your next adventure at ricksteves.com

Light Luggage

Pack light and right with Rick Steves' affordable, custom-designed rolling carry-on bags, backpacks, day packs and shoulder bags.

Accessories

From packing cubes to moneybelts and beyond, Rick has personally selected the travel goodies that will help your trip go smoother.

Shop at ricksteves.com

Save time and energy

This guidebook is your independent-travel toolkit. But for all it delivers, it's still up to you to devote the time and energy it takes to manage the preparation and logistics that are essential for a happy trip. If that's a hassle, there's a solution.

Rick Steves Tours

A Rick Steves tour takes you to Europe's most interesting places with great

with minimum stress

guides and small groups. We follow Rick's favorite itineraries, ride in comfy buses, stay in family-run hotels, and bring you intimately close to the Europe you've traveled so far to see. Most importantly, we take away the logistical headaches so you can focus on the fun.

Join the fun

This year we'll take thousands of free-spirited travelers—nearly half of them repeat customers—along with us on 50 different itineraries, from Athens to Istanbul. Is a Rick Steves tour the right fit for your travel dreams?

Find out at ricksteves.com, where you can also check seat availability and sign up. Europe is best experienced with happy travel partners. We hope you can join us.

See our itineraries at ricksteves.com

BEST OF GUIDES

Full-color guides in an easy-to-scan format. Focused on top sights and experiences in the most popular European destinations

Best of England
Best of Europe
Best of France
Best of Germany
Best of Ireland
Best of Italy
Best of Scotland
Best of Spain

COMPREHENSIVE GUIDES

City, country, and regional guides printed on Bible-thin paper. Packed with detailed coverage for a multi-week trip exploring iconic sights and venturing off the beaten path

Amsterdam & the Netherlands
Barcelona
Belgium: Bruges, Brussels,
  Antwerp & Ghent
Berlin
Budapest
Central Europe
Croatia & Slovenia
England
Florence & Tuscany
France
Germany
Great Britain
Greece: Athens & the Peloponnese
Iceland
Ireland
Istanbul
Italy
London
Paris
Portugal
Prague & the Czech Republic
Provence & the French Riviera
Rome
Scandinavia
Scotland
Sicily
Spain
Switzerland
Venice
Vienna, Salzburg & Tirol

HE BEST OF ROME

e, Italy's capital, is studded with
n remnants and floodlit-fountain
s. From the Vatican to the Colos-
with crazy traffic in between, Rome
derful, huge, and exhausting. The
, the heat, and the weighty history

of the Eternal City where Caesars walked
can make tourists wilt. Recharge by taking siestas, gelato breaks, and after-dark
walks, strolling from one atmospheric
square to another in the refreshing evening air.

*Pantheon—which
 dome until the
 2,000 years old
 ier 1,500).*

*Athens in the Vat-
 s the humanistic*

*diators fought
 ther, entertaining*

ome ristorante.

POCKET GUIDES
Compact color guides for shorter trips

Amsterdam
Athens
Barcelona
Florence
Italy's Cinque Terre
London
Munich & Salzburg

Paris
Prague
Rome
Venice
Vienna

SNAPSHOT GUIDES
Focused single-destination coverage

Basque Country: Spain & France
Copenhagen & the Best of Denmark
Dublin
Dubrovnik
Edinburgh
Hill Towns of Central Italy
Krakow, Warsaw & Gdansk
Lisbon
Loire Valley
Madrid & Toledo
Milan & the Italian Lakes District
Naples & the Amalfi Coast
Nice & the French Riviera
Normandy
Northern Ireland
Norway
Reykjavík
Rothenburg & the Rhine
Sevilla, Granada & Southern Spain
St. Petersburg, Helsinki & Tallinn
Stockholm

CRUISE PORTS GUIDES
Reference for cruise ports of call

Mediterranean Cruise Ports
Scandinavian & Northern European
 Cruise Ports

Complete your library with...

TRAVEL SKILLS & CULTURE
*Study up on travel skills and gain
insight on history and culture*

Europe 101
Europe Through the Back Door
Europe's Top 100 Masterpieces
European Christmas
European Easter
European Festivals
For the Love of Europe
Italy for Food Lovers
Travel as a Political Act

PHRASE BOOKS & DICTIONARIES
French
French, Italian & German
German
Italian
Portuguese
Spanish

PLANNING MAPS
Britain, Ireland & London
Europe
France & Paris
Germany, Austria & Switzerland
Iceland
Ireland
Italy
Scotland
Spain & Portugal

Credits

RESEARCHER

For help with this edition, Rick and Cameron relied on...

Cary Walker

Cary discovered international travel during college and has been feeding her wanderlust ever since. A former teacher, she believes that Europe is the best classroom for those who travel with an open mind. When not researching guidebooks or leading Rick Steves' Europe tours, she resides in Dallas, with her husband Brian and three well-traveled stepsons.

CONTRIBUTORS
Gene Openshaw

Gene has co-authored more than a dozen books with Rick, specializing in Europe's art, history, and culture. In particular, their *Europe 101: History and Art for the Traveler* and *Europe's Top 100 Masterpieces* have helped bring European art to life. Gene also writes for Rick's television shows, produces the audio tours, and is a regular guest on Rick's radio show. For public TV, Gene has co-authored two television specials with Rick: *Fascism in Europe* and the ambitious six-hour series *Art of Europe*. Outside of the travel world, Gene has composed an opera called *Matter,* a violin sonata, and dozens of songs. Gene lives near Seattle, where he roots for the Mariners in good times and bad. Check out his latest book on art, travel, and love: *Michelangelo at Midlife.*

Honza Vihan

Honza, who co-authors *Rick Steves Prague & the Czech Republic,* grew up roaming the Czech countryside in search of the Wild West. Once the borders opened in 1989, he set off for South Dakota. His journey took him to China, Honduras, and India, where he contributed to several travel guides. Based in Prague, Honza raises three teenage kids, coaches hockey, and teaches Buddhism.

ACKNOWLEDGMENTS

The authors would like to acknowledge our friends and colleagues for their invaluable insights. Thanks to Ian Watson, Dave Hoerlein, Rick Garman, Trevor Holmes, and Ben Curtis; *děkuji* to Honza Vihan (Czech Republic); *dziękuję* to Katarzyna Derlicka, Agnieszka Syroka, Tomasz Klimek, and Andrzej Durman (Poland); *köszönjük szépen* to Péter Pölczman, Andrea Makkay, Elemér Boreczky, George Farkas, Etelka Parine Berecz, Eszter Bokros, and István Koteczki (Hungary); *hvala lepa* to Marijan Krišković, Tina Hiti, Sašo Golub, Amir Telibečirović, Bojan Kočar, Barbara Jakopič, and Gorazd Hiti (Slovenia, Croatia, and Bosnia); *d'akujeme* to Susana Minich (Slovakia); Благодаря ти много to Lyuba Boyanin and Stefan Bozadzhiev (Bulgaria); and *mulţumim mult* to Daniel Gheorghiţă, Dan Nica, Ana Adamoae, Ciprian Slemco, and Teo Ivanciuc (Romania).

Thank you to Risa Laib for her 25-plus years of dedication to the Rick Steves guidebook series.

PHOTO CREDITS

Avalon Travel
Hachette Book Group
1700 Fourth Street
Berkeley, CA 94710

Printed in Canada by Friesens.
11th Edition. First printing January 2024.

ISBN 978-1-64171-557-7

For the latest on Rick's talks, guidebooks, tours, public television series, and public radio show, contact Rick Steves' Europe, 130 Fourth Avenue North, Edmonds, WA 98020, +1 425 771 8303, RickSteves.com, rick@ricksteves.com.

Rick Steves' Europe
Managing Editor: Jennifer Madison Davis
Editorial Group Manager: Cathy Lu
Editors: Glenn Eriksen, Julie Fanselow, Suzanne Kotz, Rosie Leutzinger, Matthew Lombardi, Teresa Nemeth, Jessica Shaw, Carrie Shepherd, Chelsea Wing
Researcher: Cary Walker
Contributors: Gene Openshaw, Honza Vihan
Creative Director: Sandra Hundacker
Maps & Graphics: Orin Dubrow, David C. Hoerlein, Lauren Mills, Mary Rostad

Avalon Travel
Senior Editor & Series Manager: Madhu Prasher
Associate Managing Editors: Jamie Andrade, Sierra Machado
Copy Editor: Maggie Ryan
Proofreader: Elizabeth Jang
Indexer: Stephen Callahan
Production: Jane Musser, Lisi Baldwin, Ravina Schneider
Cover Design: Kimberly Glyder Design
Maps & Graphics: Kat Bennett

Central & Eastern Europe

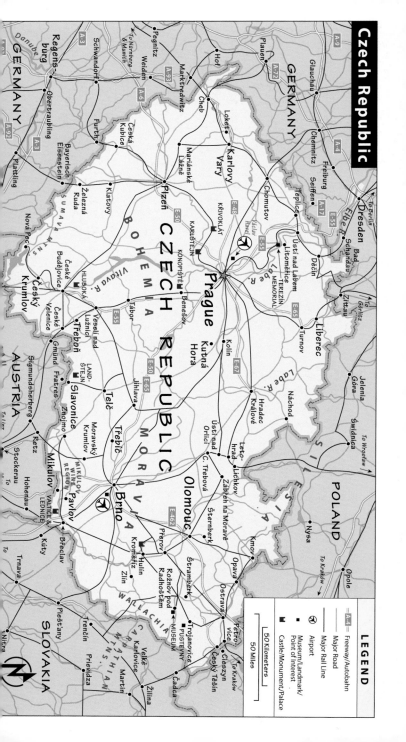

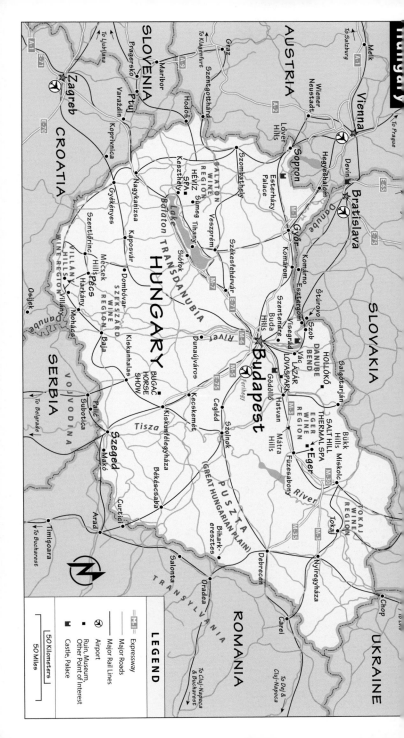

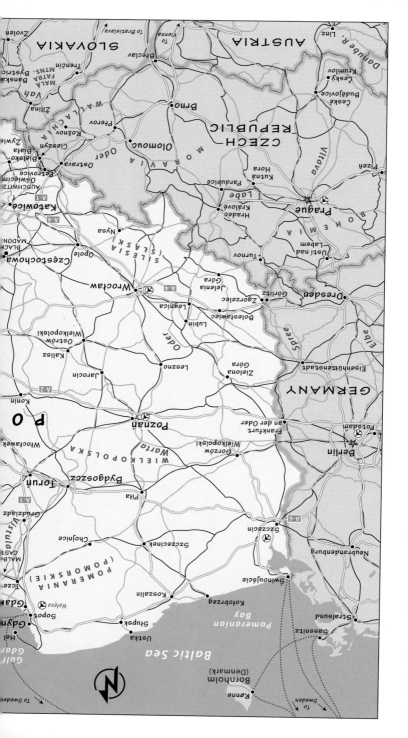

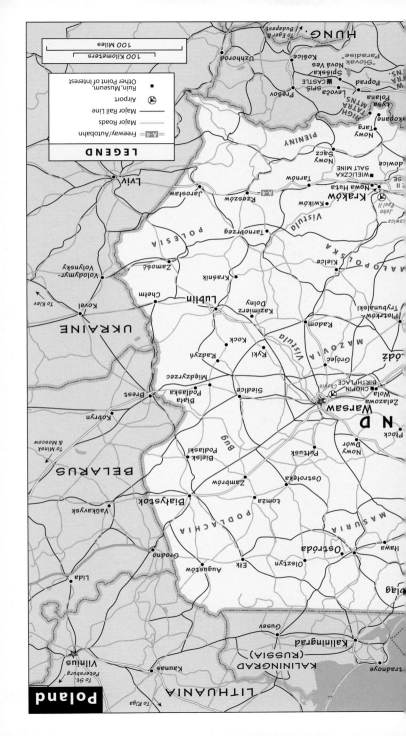

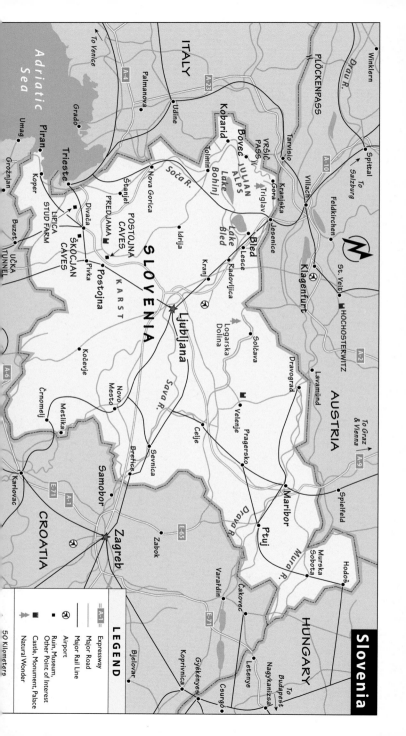

Slovenia

LEGEND

==A-1== Expressway

Major Road

Major Rail Line

✈ Airport

■ Ruin, Museum, Other Point of Interest

■ Castle, Monument, Palace

⬥ Natural Wonder

50 Kilometers

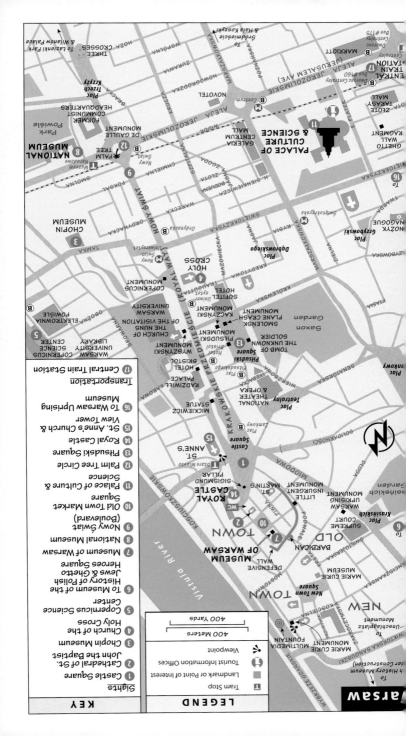

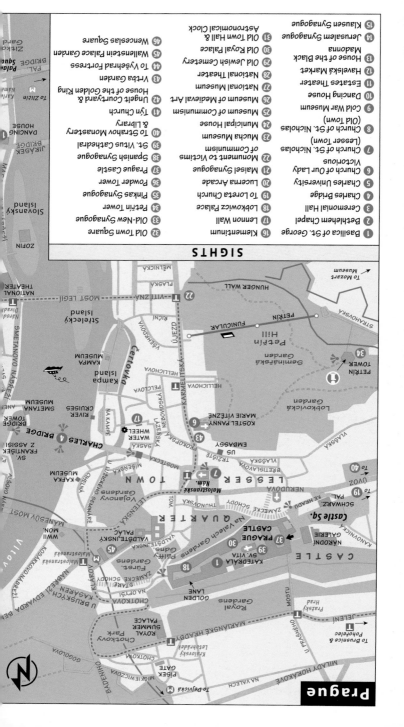

Prague

SIGHTS

1. Basilica of St. George
2. Bethlehem Chapel
3. Ceremonial Hall
4. Charles Bridge
5. Charles University
6. Church of Our Lady Victorious
7. Church of St. Nicholas (Lesser Town)
8. Church of St. Nicholas (Old Town)
9. Cold War Museum
10. Dancing House
11. Estates Theater
12. Havelská Market
13. House of the Black Madonna
14. Jerusalem Synagogue
15. Klausen Synagogue
16. Klementinum
17. Lennon Wall
18. Lobkowicz Palace
19. To Loreta Church
20. Lucerna Arcade
21. Maisel Synagogue
22. Monument to Victims of Communism
23. Mucha Museum
24. Municipal House
25. Museum of Communism
26. Museum of Medieval Art
27. National Museum
28. National Theater
29. Old Jewish Cemetery
30. Old Royal Palace
31. Old Town Hall & Astronomical Clock
32. Old Town Square
33. Old-New Synagogue
34. Petřín Tower
35. Pinkas Synagogue
36. Powder Tower
37. Prague Castle
38. Spanish Synagogue
39. St. Vitus Cathedral
40. To Strahov Monastery & Library
41. Týn Church
42. Ungelt Courtyard & House of the Golden Ring
43. Vrtba Garden
44. To Vyšehrad Fortress
45. Wallenstein Palace Garden
46. Wenceslas Square

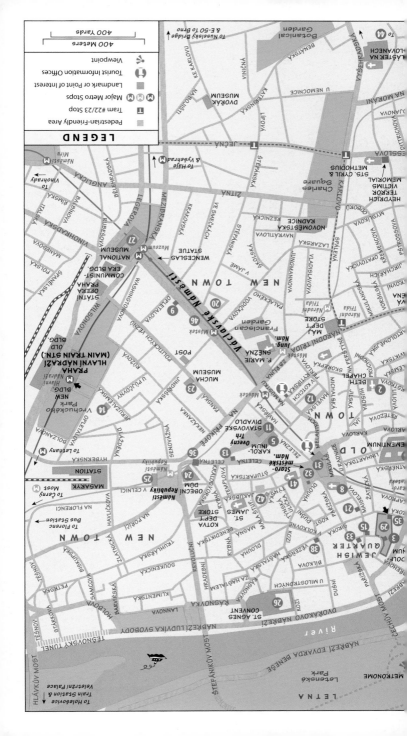

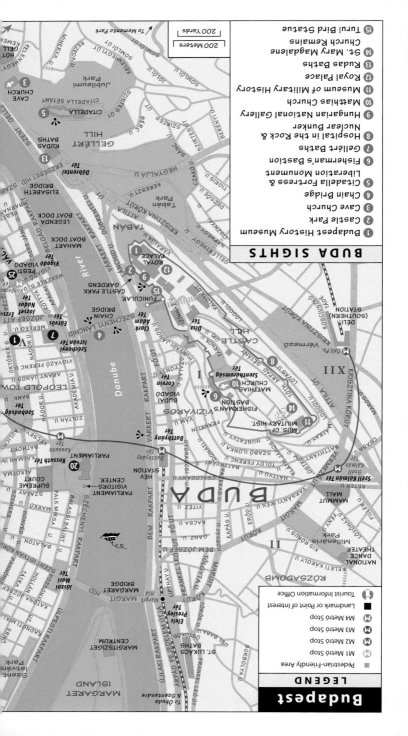

Budapest

BUDA SIGHTS

1. Budapest History Museum
2. Castle Park
3. Cave Church
4. Chain Bridge
5. Citadella Fortress & Liberation Monument
6. Fisherman's Bastion
7. Gellért Baths
8. Hospital in the Rock & Nuclear Bunker
9. Hungarian National Gallery
10. Matthias Church
11. Museum of Military History
12. Royal Palace
13. Rudas Baths
14. St. Mary Magdalene Church Remains
15. Turul Bird Statue

LEGEND

- Pedestrian-Friendly Area
- Ⓜ M1 Metro Stop
- Ⓜ M2 Metro Stop
- Ⓜ M3 Metro Stop
- Ⓜ M4 Metro Stop
- ■ Landmark or Point of Interest
- ❶ Tourist Information Office

200 Meters

200 Yards

BUDA

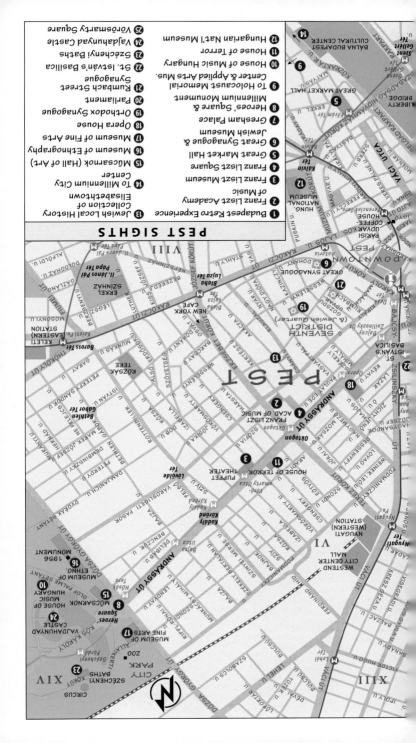

PEST SIGHTS

1. Budapest Retro Experience
2. Franz Liszt Academy of Music
3. Franz Liszt Museum
4. Franz Liszt Square
5. Great Market Hall
6. Great Synagogue & Jewish Museum
7. Gresham Palace
8. Heroes' Square & Millennium Monument
9. To Holocaust Memorial Center & Applied Arts Mus.
10. House of Music Hungary
11. House of Terror
12. Hungarian Nat'l Museum
13. Jewish Local History Collection of Elisabethtown
14. To Millennium City Center
15. Műcsarnok (Hall of Art)
16. Museum of Ethnography
17. Museum of Fine Arts
18. Opera House
19. Orthodox Synagogue
20. Parliament
21. Rumbach Street Synagogue
22. St. István's Basilica
23. Széchenyi Baths
24. Vajdahunyad Castle
25. Vörösmarty Square

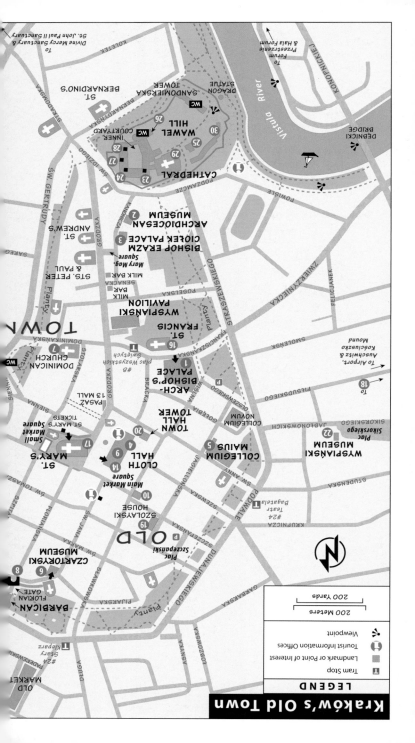

Kraków's Old Town

LEGEND

🚊 Tram Stop

◼ Landmark or Point of Interest

🛈 Tourist Information Offices

📷 Viewpoint

200 Meters	
200 Yards	

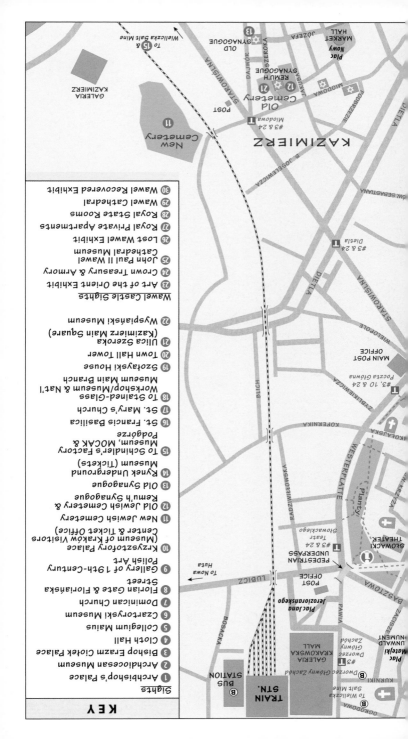

KEY

Sights

1. Archbishop's Palace
2. Archdiocesan Museum
3. Bishop Erazm Ciołek Palace
4. Cloth Hall
5. Collegium Maius
6. Czartoryski Museum
7. Dominican Church
8. Florian Gate & Floriańska Street
9. Gallery of 19th-Century Polish Art
10. Krzysztofory Palace (Museum of Kraków Visitors Center & Ticket Office)
11. New Jewish Cemetery
12. Old Jewish Cemetery & Remu'h Synagogue
13. Old Synagogue
14. Rynek Underground Museum (Tickets)
15. To Schindler's Factory Museum, MOCAK & Podgórze
16. St. Francis Basilica
17. St. Mary's Church
18. To Stained-Glass Workshop/Museum & Nat'l Museum Main Branch
19. Szołayski House
20. Town Hall Tower
21. Ulica Szeroka (Kazimierz Main Square)
22. Wyspiański Museum

Wawel Castle Sights

23. Art of the Orient Exhibit
24. Crown Treasury & Armory
25. John Paul II Wawel Cathedral Museum
26. Lost Wawel Exhibit
27. Royal Private Apartments
28. Royal State Rooms
29. Wawel Cathedral
30. Wawel Recovered Exhibit

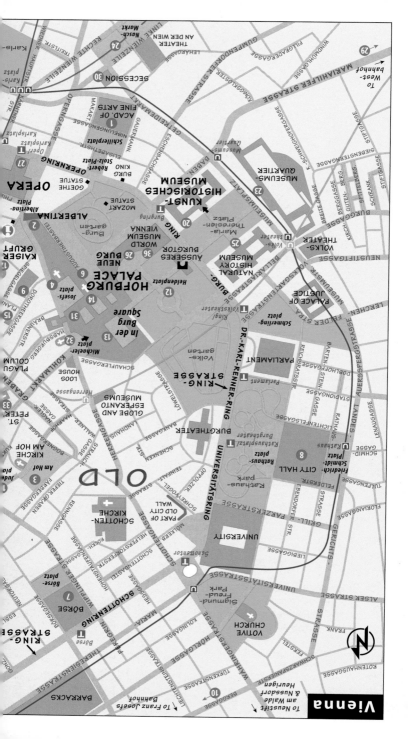

Vienna